Instructor's Resource Manual to Accompany

LISTEN

Instructor's Resource Manual to Accompany

LISTEN

SIXTH EDITION

Joseph Kerman ◆ Gary Tomlinson

Mark Harbold

Elmhurst College

Bedford / St. Martin's

Boston ◆ New York

Manufactured in the United States of America.

1   0   9   8   7
f   e   d   c   b   a

For information, write: Bedford/St. Martin's, 75 Arlington Street, Boston, MA 02116
(617-399-4000)

ISBN-10: 0-312-45893-2
ISBN-13: 978-0-312-45893-5

Acknowledgments

Arnold Schoenberg, excerpts from *Pierrot lunaire.* Used by permission
of Belmont Music Publishers, Pacific Palisades, CA 90272.

Preface

This edition of the *Instructor's Resource Manual to Accompany* LISTEN, Sixth Edition, retains the most useful features of previous editions. Reflecting significant changes in Kerman and Tomlinson's new edition, the most substantial changes here concern works that are new to *Listen,* such as Wagner's *The Valkyrie,* Prokofiev's *Alexander Nevsky,* and Adams's *El Niño.* As in previous editions, whether you need complete lesson plans or just a few short listening ideas to demonstrate sonata form, you can easily find what you need in this manual.

Highlights of this new edition include lecture suggestions for every chapter and every listening example in the new textbook; updated lists of multimedia resources; a revised appendix on pedagogical uses of technology and online teaching tools; an index with thousands of useful musical examples from the *Listen* recordings for all important terms in the textbook; and annotated reading lists for instructors who need to bone up on music history, world music, and related topics.

❧ How to Use This Manual

This manual contains resources for first-time teaching associates as well as for professors who have taught for many years. Beginning instructors may appreciate the teaching objectives, detailed lesson plans, and lecture suggestions for every chapter in the textbook. Experienced professionals may make more use of the chapter outlines, creative teaching ideas, and lists of additional recordings and multimedia resources.

This manual is designed so that you can quickly find what you are looking for. The manual begins with a detailed table of contents. If you want ideas for class discussion of topics in Chapter 9, turn to the table of contents, find Chapter 9, and look under *Additional Teaching Suggestions*—Class Discussion Ideas to find the relevant page number. If you would like to use a DVD opera recording in Chapter 17 but don't know what's available, turn to the table of contents, find Chapter 17, and look under *Multimedia Resources*—Video Recordings.

The following resource materials are provided for each textbook chapter. The descriptions that follow offer a sense of the range of resources available in this manual.

Chapter Outline

A list of headings in the textbook chapter, with page numbers.

Important Terms

A list of all terms that Kerman and Tomlinson highlight in boldface, along with other terms that students need to understand.

Teaching Objectives

Lists of both the overall objectives and the listening objectives for each chapter—the primary goals one hopes to accomplish in class.

Lecture Suggestions

Detailed lesson plans and suggested lecture materials that follow the order of the textbook chapter, designed primarily for beginning teachers. This section further provides analytical diagrams with timings (and measure numbers for some longer works) for recorded examples from the *Listen* textbook that have no Listening Charts.

For instructors who are unfamiliar with the non-Western examples included in the Global Perspectives segments, this section provides several pages of historical, cultural, and other background information before proceeding on to specific lecture suggestions for each work.

Additional Teaching Suggestions

◆ **Lecture-Demonstration Ideas**   Creative ideas for class presentations that expand on or go beyond the textbook chapter.

◆ **Class Discussion Ideas**   Questions you can use to generate class discussion.

◆ **Listening Ideas**   Creative suggestions for listening exercises that expand on or go beyond the listening materials provided with the textbook chapter.

◆ **Further Listening Examples**   Teaching suggestions for in-class listening exercises that present works related to the chapter but not included in the *Listen* recordings.

Multimedia Resources

◆ **Further Listening Charts and Texts**   A list of Appendix I Listening Charts for important works appropriate to the chapter but not included in the recordings; also, a list of texts and translations provided in Appendix II for vocal works appropriate to the chapter but not included in the recordings (or for which the textbook does not provide a complete translation).

◆ **Sound Recordings**   An annotated discography of recommended CD recordings appropriate to the chapter.

◆ **Video Recordings**   An annotated listing of recommended DVD and videotape recordings appropriate to the chapter.

◆ **Software**   An annotated listing of recommended software and CD-ROM packages that can be used for classroom demonstrations or homework assignments.

Additional materials can be found in the appendices at the end of the manual:

Appendix I

A collection of Listening Charts for alternative works not included in the *Listen* recordings. These can be used instead of or in addition to the listening examples in the textbook.

Appendix II

A collection of texts and translations for works in the Further Listening Examples sections of this manual, as well as for some listening examples in the textbook for which complete text and translation are not provided.

Appendix III

Thousands of musical examples from the *Listen* recordings keyed to an alphabetical list of important terms from the textbook. This can be an invaluable tool for anyone who needs to quickly find musical examples to demonstrate important concepts from the textbook.

Appendix IV

Practical suggestions for instructors who want to use computer technology in their classroom, especially geared toward neophytes. This appendix contains useful ideas concerning teaching strategies, the use of the Internet and online course-management systems, and some thoughts about hardware and software issues.

Appendix V

A bibliography for instructors who want to do additional research to prepare for their music appreciation course. Resources are listed for all major composers and Global Perspectives examples in the *Listen* textbook. In addition to an extensive listing of sources for information on world music and American music, the appendix includes reference books; general histories; period histories; dictionaries; and books on special topics such as women in music, musical genres, form and analysis, opera, popular music, jazz, and acoustics. The final section lists primary sources that can be used to "personalize" student encounters with important composers and cultures—sources that allow composers, musicians, and eyewitnesses to speak for themselves through interviews, memoirs, letters, quotations, diaries, lectures, writings, historical documents, photographs, and the like.

❦ Acknowledgments

As always, I am grateful for the friendly and able assistance of the staff at the Elmhurst College Library. I would especially like to acknowledge the contributions of Kathy Willis, head of circulation as well as interlibrary loan, and Elaine Fetyko Page, head of technical services.

Virginia Dixon deserves much of the credit for this book's existence. Without my wife's unfailing support and encouragement, this book would have taken much longer than it did! I cannot thank her enough.

Thanks are long overdue to Dr. Seppo Saari, Finnish musician, scholar, and educator, for his invaluable assistance helping me find information on Kaija Saariaho for both the fifth and sixth editions.

I must again express my gratitude to the authors of the new *Listen* textbook. Joe Kerman and Gary Tomlinson approach their tasks with the utmost integrity, sincerity, and high-mindedness. It has been a pleasure to work with them.

Finally, I want to thank the folks at Bedford/St. Martin's for allowing me to participate in this project. Developmental Editor Carrie Thompson has been prompt and professional in handling my frequent questions and suggestions and always cordial and congenial in keeping me on track—many thanks! Editor David Mogolov has provided welcome encouragement, and he continues to be a good sounding board for new ideas. I am also grateful to Editor in Chief Karen Henry, who stays on top of so many things behind the scenes and keeps everyone and everything running smoothly. Thanks to all of you for making this project so enjoyable. It has been a pleasure to work with you.

Mark Harbold
Elmhurst College
June 2007

Contents

Instructor's Resource Manual to Accompany

LISTEN

CHAPTER 1

Music, Sound, and Time

Chapter Outline

Boldface indicates works in the recording set.

Important Terms

vibrations	dynamics	*piano*	*più forte*	*decrescendo*	partials
pitch	amplitude	*mezzo*	*meno forte*	*diminuendo*	overtones
frequency	decibels	*pianissimo*	*subito*	tone color	duration
scales	*forte*	*fortissimo*	*crescendo*	timbre	rhythm

Teaching Objectives

❦ Overall Objectives

Students must understand the following concepts in order to listen more effectively:

1. Listening is the primary tool for understanding and enjoying music. Repeated listening to a single piece enables one to hear more and more, enhancing understanding and enjoyment.

2. Concepts and terms aid the process of learning to listen attentively; they increase awareness as they pinpoint specific elements of the aural experience. These elements need to be pointed out at first.

3. A musical experience is the cumulative result of several factors: elements of music working together (rhythm, pitch, dynamics, tone color, and so on); the effect

of these sounds and associated words and images on the listener; and the listener's interpretation of this effect based on past experiences and understanding.

This chapter will help students acquire familiarity with:

1. Fundamental properties of sounds: especially frequency, amplitude, overtones, and duration.

2. Musical concepts and vocabulary associated with these fundamental properties: especially pitch, dynamics, tone color, and rhythm.

❧ Listening Objectives

After completing this chapter, students should be able to:

1. Distinguish between definite and indefinite pitch and between high and low pitches.

2. Distinguish various degrees of loudness and identify *crescendo* and *decrescendo*.

3. Identify the sounds of different voices and instrument families.

4. Listen more attentively for basic elements of music.

Lecture Suggestions

❧ To the Instructor

There are many ways to cover the fundamentals of music. I believe it is crucial to provide as many listening examples as you can throughout this unit. Here are some reasons why.

1. Listening is important. The *Listen* textbook dedicates itself to the proposition that listening is a significant, meaningful activity—thus the book's title! You can't learn to drive a car, ride a bicycle, dance the tango, or listen to a symphony simply by reading a book. The book may help, but you must learn by doing.

2. Guided practice is important. Imagine a self-taught piano student taking his first lesson—the teacher shakes her head, knowing how much work it will take to help the student unlearn years of bad habits. Practice makes permanent, and bad practice makes a mess. The acquisition of listening skills also requires practice, and most students in your class don't know how to practice. They need your help, especially at the beginning of the term. Frequent guided, in-class listening experiences allow students to make sense of their perceptions, to check their understanding against yours, and to make adjustments where necessary. Good listening habits can deepen their appreciation and increase their independence as listeners.

3. Repeated exposure to the same pieces is important. Two significant factors exert the greatest influence on one's appreciation of a particular musical style, any style. The first factor is the influence of a close friend, respected mentor, or significant other who likes that music; the second is *repeated* listening. You can't do much about the first factor, but you can do a great deal to help your students listen to the same pieces repeatedly. You can make assignments that

require intensive listening, but I also recommend playing pieces in class on different occasions spread over the term. Introduce as many pieces as you can in Unit I ("Hi, how are you?"), work through the pieces in detail as they appear in Units II through V ("Hi, we have to talk"), and play older pieces again when they offer interesting comparisons with newer works ("Hi, remember me?").

Most of the ideas found in this manual stem from these principles. Throughout Unit I you will find lists of listening excerpts that can illuminate and enliven your class presentations. Of course, the discussion component in each listening exercise is an essential part of the learning process. Work to create an affirming, nonjudgmental manner in your classroom; when students feel intimidated, the whole process short-circuits. You must encourage students to share their perceptions, and when they are way off target you must learn to gently guide them toward another understanding. Approach their ideas with humility—important truths are often buried in student ideas that sound "wrong" at first hearing.

This edition of *Listen* offers a resource that you and your students will find extremely helpful—the *Listen* Companion DVD. Packaged with every copy of the textbook, this disc provides musical examples designed to help students zero in on the elements of music covered in Unit I. These supplemental examples allow students to practice listening skills independent of the classroom setting, but don't let this lull you into thinking that you can spend less time on fundamentals—remember the preceding item 2! Think of it this way: The *Listen* DVD provides tools that allow your students to study more effectively. Better preparation means higher quality classroom discussion. But you must take time to introduce these tools and to take your students on a "walking tour," that is, to show them how to use the *Listen* DVD.

So where are the Interactive Listening Charts for the Sixth Edition? You can now find them online—in both Mac and Windows versions!—at bedfordstmartins.com/listen. Suggestions for introducing the Interactive Listening Charts are included in the section on Wagner's Prelude to *The Valkyrie*. The *Listen* Web site also includes the Instruments of the Orchestra demo and Interactive Tutorials to help students practice listening for fundamental elements.

The following sections of this chapter offer a collection of teaching suggestions and musical examples from the *Listen* recordings that may prove helpful. Sprinkled throughout are also listening examples from the *Listen* DVD and some thoughts on how to use it well.

One last note: The first unit of this manual models the concept of repeated listening (described in item 3) in two ways. First, it suggests listening examples from many of the pieces found in Chapters 5 through 23, a good way to introduce this literature early in the course. Second, it frequently refers to the major work in this unit, Britten's *Young Person's Guide to the Orchestra* (Listening Chart 2). Discussed in Chapter 4, the Britten *Guide* serves as an example of musical form, but you will surely use it in Chapter 3 to introduce orchestral instruments, and its frequent changes of mood and character make it an ideal source of illustrations for almost every element of music covered in Unit I. If this focus sounds appealing, watch for the Britten examples in the lists that follow.

❼ Introduction to Listening

On the first day of class, choose four excerpts that differ dramatically from one another—for instance, "Ya Sin" (Qur'anic recitation); Mozart's Piano Concerto in A, I; Stravinsky's *The Rite of Spring* ("The Game of Abduction"); and Solomon Linda's "Anoku Gonda." Ask students to write answers to the following questions as they listen; then play about forty seconds' worth of each excerpt.

1. What mood does each piece create?

2. What makes these pieces different from each other?

On the board, make one column for each excerpt. Ask students to discuss their written comments. As they do, write their key points in the appropriate columns on the board. The lists on the board will usually include a mixture of descriptive adjectives and terms referring to elements of music. Use class discussion to draw out the following points:

1. Distinguish between compositional means and effect as you review terms on the board. "Means" are the ways musical elements are used; "effect" is the mood that is created.

2. Note the many terms on the board that refer to elements of music, and name those elements. Some elements that may come up follow:

    1. pitch   8. melody (phrases, etc.)
    2. dynamics   9. texture
    3. tone color   10. consonance/dissonance
    4. scales   11. mode
    5. rhythm   12. modulation
    6. meter   13. instruments and their families
    7. tempo   14. form

It is not crucial to list every element—it is enough to make students aware that these elements exist and that you will study these concepts in more detail in the remainder of Unit I. Point out that it is impossible to discuss music without talking about the elements of music, whether or not the "correct" words are used.

3. Note the descriptive adjectives on the board. Although students will use different words, the words they choose usually belong to the same family, all pointing to the same mood or feeling. This offers a springboard for a discussion of musical meaning.

4. Encourage students to think in terms of means and effect when they encounter any piece of music. When the "mood" (effect) of a piece is identified first, the probability is high that students will more quickly determine the most significant uses of elements (means) in the music.

5. Encourage discussion of the different cultures, functions, historical periods, and styles represented by these four excerpts. Regardless of the setting, music is a vital part of human experience.

6. Ask how this listening experience felt compared with their usual listening experiences. Many will find that active listening is hard work.

WAGNER Prelude to *The Valkyrie*

Listening Charts are a significant feature of the *Listen* textbook. When used with understanding, they enable students to work through a large quantity of music independently. The Interactive Listening Charts available online should make it even easier for students to reconcile the chart and its printed words with the sounds they hear. For technology-savvy students, these interactive charts provide an attractive alternative to the printed ones in the textbook. Though they are dwindling in number, the technophobes in your class may panic if you *begin* with the interactive charts. First use examples from the textbook. When students are comfortable with the printed Listening Charts, you can introduce the interactive versions.

As you introduce features of the charts, start with the textbook introduction titled "To the Student." This section provides a Listening Chart excerpt that has been annotated to show students how to take advantage of its amenities. Talk through the important features with your class: the composer and title, where to find the recording in the *Listen* anthology, the total time, timings within the piece (which can be followed with a CD timer or digital stopwatch), the outline of main events and sections, the descriptive comments for each section, and main themes in musical notation. Suggest ways of using the charts to maximize familiarity with the music (browsing through the chart to get a sense of overall shape before listening, using timings to identify main themes before listening straight through, and so on). Finally, ask your students to compare the annotated chart in the introduction with Listening Chart 1 in the textbook's "Prelude" on page 5. If you have time, play through excerpts from Wagner's Prelude to model effective uses of these guides for your class.

Now introduce the Interactive Listening Charts. One of the most valuable tools provided with the *Listen* textbook, this package allows users to listen straight through, jump around, and repeat sections as often as necessary. For the sake of your technophobes, start at the beginning and take a step-by-step approach. Take your students to the *Listen* Web site. Show them how to select and download the right version for their computer (Mac or Windows). Then start it up and show how to navigate to the correct chart. Once you get there, demonstrate the features of the chart, especially the ability to jump to any section at will. Make the point that the print and interactive versions of the Listening Charts provide the same layout and content, guiding listeners to significant musical features in every passage. Students should feel free to choose whichever version best suits their needs. You might also think of ways to use these effectively in your teaching!

The primary purpose of this introduction is to acquaint students with the use of Listening Charts. It is not necessary to work through the musical details of the Wagner Prelude at this point. In fact, the textbook's "Prelude" was written to encourage a one-on-one encounter between the student and the music. Your students need to get comfortable with the idea of making time to listen attentively, and this first section of the textbook provides a relatively painless initial experience. Make this the first take-home assignment, to read the "Prelude" and listen to Wagner's Prelude. At the next class meeting, take time to "decompress." Find out how it went, what problems (and successes) students encountered, and what questions came up. The follow-up session also offers a good opportunity to specifically deal with musical issues surrounding Wagner's Prelude.

↱ Sound Vibrations

This lecture-demonstration summarizes many of the features the authors outline in Chapter 1. A description (with any available visual aids) of how sounds are produced by vibrating objects, how they travel to the ear, and how they are perceived by the human ear, can be very helpful. Use A440 on the piano as a starting point, and make these observations:

1. The piano string vibrates back and forth 440 times each second.

2. The vibrating string pushes the air molecules around it back and forth 440 times a second. They jostle each other at the same frequency, creating sound waves.

3. These sound waves radiate outwards, like waves in a pond, at a speed of about 1,000 feet (about 305 meters) per second.

4. The ear, constructed like a satellite dish, intercepts these vibrating air molecules.

5. The vibrating air molecules set the eardrum in motion at the same rate of vibration. This vibration, in turn, finds its way to the corresponding auditory nerve in the cochlea, which sends an electrical impulse that is perceived by the brain of the listener as A440.

6. The sound-processing ability of the human ear is quite extraordinary. Even complex sound patterns such as noise, environmental sound, orchestral music, and so on are received by the ear as composite sound shapes that the brain interprets and translates into their individual sounds.

7. As you play A440, note the power of even this single sound to change the entire atmosphere of the classroom!

Even if you only have a piano, an effective acoustics demonstration is possible. Changes in frequency and amplitude are easy to illustrate and understand. The relation between frequency and pitch can be demonstrated by playing a variety of tones at the keyboard and explaining that the higher pitches are created by faster vibration. The relation between amplitude and dynamics can be demonstrated by striking pitches loudly and softly, pointing out that the more forceful the vibration, the more air is displaced, and the louder the sound is.

It is more difficult to explain overtones and their effect on wave shape and tone color, since overtones cannot normally be heard. Nonetheless, the phenomenon of resonance makes it possible to do just that on the piano. Resonance works for any two objects that vibrate at the same frequency: If the first object is set into vibration and the second is nearby, the second object will vibrate sympathetically with the first. If the two objects do not naturally vibrate at the same frequency, the second object will not vibrate sympathetically with the first. This can be demonstrated with two tuning forks, at the piano — and even when singing in the shower (the shower walls vibrate in sympathy with your voice at certain pitches!).

You can isolate overtones one at a time using this technique: Hold down low C (great C) silently on the piano to lift the damper. If you strike any key that belongs to the overtone series for low C (c, g, c^1, e^1, g^1, b-flat^1, c^2, etc.), the vibration of the higher string will set the low C string into vibration at the frequency of the higher string. When you release the upper key, the low C string will continue to vibrate at the higher frequency of the other vibrating string. If you strike a few higher notes that do not belong to the overtone series of low C, the lower string will not vibrate at those frequencies. Several conclusions can be drawn:

1. Only the higher vibrations (overtones) that are part of the normal vibration of the low C string can vibrate sympathetically with the higher strings. This demonstration offers proof that these higher pitches are part of the sound we hear when the low C string is struck normally.

2. Note that all overtones are much softer than the fundamental tone. This helps explain why we do not notice them when hearing the low C played normally.

3. Note that the higher overtones are generally softer than the lower ones. Point out that the relative strength of each overtone is one factor that gives the piano its distinctive tone color. Other instruments may create these same overtones as components in their sounds, but the relative strengths of different overtones on the clarinet will be different from those on the piano or the sitar or the violin. Overtones are one key to tone color.

Another factor affecting tone color can be demonstrated at the piano. Every instrument's tone color is affected by a noise component related to the sound-producing mechanism. On the piano the noise component is the "thwack" created when the hammer strikes the strings. This can be heard most easily by playing c^5 loudly, especially if you reach inside the piano and manually damp the c^5 strings (highest note on the piano). Once students hear the "thwack" isolated, they can begin to hear it on lower notes as well. Other noises include the scraping of the bow on bowed stringed instruments, tonguing effects or the sound of air blowing through the tubes of woodwinds, and the buzzing lips of trumpet players.

You might also call attention to attack and decay characteristics for the sound of the piano. Students will hear a sharp attack and a rapid initial decay to a long sustain at a lower dynamic level. When other instruments are introduced later, point out how their sound characteristics differ.

Pitch (Frequency)

If you did not use the preceding acoustics demonstration to introduce frequency, begin by pointing out the relationship between frequency and pitch. Using the Schubert "Unfinished" Symphony example from the *Listen* DVD, work through Listening Exercise 1 on textbook page 9, looking specifically at pitch for now. If you have not yet introduced the Listening Exercises and Listening Charts, take time to talk through these features and show your class how to use them. Of course, one example is not enough to help your students identify features of pitch with confidence. Choose further examples from the *Listen* recordings, such as the following, that allow students to really *hear* the differences between definite and indefinite pitch, high and low pitch, and male and female voice types. (Start each selection at the beginning unless otherwise indicated.) For more suggestions, see the Index of Terms and Musical Examples (Appendix III).

Definite pitch	Josquin, "Mille regrets"
	LeBrun, Sonata in F, Rondeau
	I Lotring, *Bopong* (definite—but not equal-tempered!)
	Britten, *The Young Person's Guide to the Orchestra* (DVD—track 20)
Indefinite pitch	Japanese kabuki play, *Dojoji* (0:09–0:52)
	Varèse, *Poème électronique* (0:00–0:29)
	Drums of Benin, "Ako"
	Britten, *The Young Person's Guide to the Orchestra* (DVD—percussion theme, track 20, 1:19–1:36)
High pitch	Handel, *Messiah*, "Glory to God" (1:19–1:31, 1:41–1:53)
	Japanese *gagaku* orchestra, *Etenraku* (0:00–0:50)
	Ligeti, *Lux aeterna* (track 12, 1:39–2:28)
	Britten, *The Young Person's Guide to the Orchestra* (DVD—Variation 1, track 21, 0:00–0:36; Variation 5, track 22, 0:00–0:33; Variation 11, track 23, 0:51–1:22)
Low pitch	Berlioz, *Fantastic* Symphony, V (track 4, 0:00–0:21)
	Wagner, Prelude to *The Valkyrie* (beginning)
	Adams, *El Niño*, "Pues mi Dios ha nacido a penar" (beginning)
	Britten, *The Young Person's Guide to the Orchestra* (DVD—Variation 8, track 22, 2:52–3:48; Variation 12, track 23, 1:22–2:32)

High and low pitch	Handel, *Messiah*, "Glory to God" (1:19–2:01)
	Beethoven, Quartet in F, Op. 135, II (at 1:35)
	Berlioz, *Fantastic* Symphony, V (track 2, 0:00–0:50)
	Prokofiev, *Alexander Nevsky*, "The Battle on the Ice," first excerpt
Female voices	Hildegard, "Columba aspexit"
	Ligeti, *Lux aeterna* (track 12, 0:00–2:27)
	Saariaho, *From the Grammar of Dreams*
Male voices	Pérotin, "Alleluia. Diffusa est gratia"
	Adams, *El Niño*, "When Herod Heard"
	Linda, "Anoku Gonda"
Soprano voice	Purcell, *Dido and Aeneas*, "When I am laid in earth" (at 0:57)
	Verdi, *Aida*, Act IV, Scene ii (Tomb scene)—Arioso II (track 11, 0:00–1:07)
	Saariaho, *From the Grammar of Dreams*
Alto (mezzo-soprano) voice	Handel, *Julius Caesar*, "La giustizia"
	Adams, *El Niño*, "Pues mi Dios ha nacido a penar"
	Gershwin, "Who Cares?" (DVD)
Tenor voice	Bernart, "La dousa votz"
	Verdi, *Aida*, Act IV, Scene ii (Tomb scene)—Radames
	Bernstein, *West Side Story*, "Cool" (0:00–1:00)
Bass (baritone) voice	Mozart, *Don Giovanni*, Act I, "Ho capito"
	Schubert, "Erlkönig"
	Adams, *El Niño*, "When Herod Heard"

૧ Dynamics (Amplitude)

If you did not use the acoustics demonstration (at the beginning of these Lecture Suggestions) to introduce loudness, begin by pointing out the relation between loudness (amplitude) and dynamics. Note that musicians measure loudness on a relative scale, not as precisely as they do pitch. The dynamic markings listed on textbook page 8 occur on a continuous spectrum between soft and loud. Now is a good time to revisit Listening Exercise 1 from textbook page 9. Use the same "Unfinished" Symphony example (from the *Listen* DVD) that you used to look at pitch, but this time focus on Schubert's use of dynamics. As usual, further examples of *forte, piano, crescendo,* and *decrescendo* are highly recommended. See the Index of Terms and Musical Examples (Appendix III) for suggestions beyond those listed here:

Forte	Beethoven, Symphony No. 5, IV (track 18, 0:00–0:32)
	Stravinsky, *The Rite of Spring*, Part 1 (track 24, 2:04–2:23; track 27, 0:52–1:33)
	Prokofiev, *Alexander Nevsky*, "The Battle on the Ice," first excerpt (5:14–end), second excerpt (0:00–0:20, 0:38–0:57)

	Britten, *The Young Person's Guide to the Orchestra* (DVD—Theme, track 20, 0:00–0:19, 1:36–1:55, and track 25, 1:54–end; Variation 5, track 19, 0:00–0:33)
Piano	Schubert, Moment Musical No. 2 in A-flat (0:00–0:53)
	Debussy, Three Nocturnes, *Clouds* (track 15, 0:00–0:34; track 20, 0:54–end)
	Prokofiev, *Alexander Nevsky,* "The Battle on the Ice," first excerpt (beginning)
	Britten, *The Young Person's Guide to the Orchestra* (DVD—Theme for Woodwind choir (track 20, 0:23–0:39); Variation 1, track 21, 0:00–0:15; Variation 6, track 22, 0:33–1:53)
Crescendo	I Lotring, *Bopong* (3:40–4:04)
	Beethoven, Symphony No. 5, III–IV (track 17, 2:52–track 18, 0:34)
	Wagner, Prelude to *The Valkyrie* (1:24–2:10)
	Britten, *The Young Person's Guide to the Orchestra* (DVD—Theme for Brass choir, track 20, 0:45–1:00; Fugue, track 25)
Decrescendo	Handel, *Messiah,* "Glory to God" (2:51–end)
	Beethoven, Symphony No. 5 in C Minor, III (track 17, 1:02–1:36)
	Bernstein, *West Side Story,* "Cool" (3:27–end)
	Britten, *The Young Person's Guide to the Orchestra* (DVD—Transition, track 20, 0:19–0:23)
Crescendo and decrescendo	I Lotring, *Bopong*
	Berlioz, *Fantastic* Symphony, V (track 2, 0:00–1:40; track 2, 1:40–track 3, 1:37)
	Reich, *Music for 18 Musicians,* Introduction

♪ Tone Color: Overtones

Instrument Families

If you did not use the acoustics demonstration (at the beginning of these Lecture Suggestions) to introduce overtones, begin by describing the relation between overtones and tone color. Specific instruments are covered later, in the textbook's Interlude B, but now is a good time to introduce the primary families of instruments: strings, woodwinds, brass, percussion, keyboards, plucked strings, and human voices. The main emphasis should be placed on awareness that different instruments and families sound different. Point out that changes in tone color can be obvious (instruments from different families) or more subtle (high and low instruments from the same family or high and low pitches on the same instrument). Play a few high and low pitches on the piano to make your point. The authors include a Listening Exercise on textbook page 9, but it is good to choose further examples that demonstrate each of the seven main families. See the Index of Terms and Musical Examples (Appendix III) for suggestions beyond the following:

Bowed strings	Bach, Orchestral Suite No. 3 in D, Air
	Mahler, Symphony No. 1, III (track 10)
	Schubert, String Quartet in A Minor (DVD)
	Britten, *The Young Person's Guide to the Orchestra* (DVD—Theme for String choir, track 20, 1:04–1:19; Variations 5–8, track 22, 0:00–3:48)

Woodwinds	Japanese *gagaku* orchestra, *Etenraku*—*hichiriki, ryuteki, sho*
	Tchaikovsky, *Romeo and Juliet* (track 19, 0:00–0:32)
	Stravinsky, *The Rite of Spring,* Part I—Introduction (track 21, 0:00–track 22, 0:40)
	Britten, *The Young Person's Guide to the Orchestra* (DVD—Theme for Woodwind choir, track 20, 0:23–0:39; Variations 1–4, track 21)
Brass	Gabrieli, "O magnum mysterium"
	Wagner, Prelude to *The Valkyrie* (1:37–2:27)
	Musorgsky, *Pictures at an Exhibition,* "Promenade" (0:00–0:34)
	Britten, *The Young Person's Guide to the Orchestra* (DVD—Theme for Brass choir, track 20, 0:45–1:00; Variations 9–12, track 23)
Percussion	I Lotring, *Bopong*
	Stravinsky, *The Rite of Spring,* Part I—"The Game of Abduction" (track 25)
	Bartók, Music for Strings, Percussion, and Celesta, II (track 4)
	Britten, *The Young Person's Guide to the Orchestra* (DVD—percussion theme, track 20, 1:19–1:36; Variation 13, track 24)
Keyboard	Frescobaldi, Suite—organ
	Chopin, Nocturne in F-sharp, Op. 15, No. 2—piano
	Joplin, "Maple Leaf Rag"—piano (DVD)
Plucked strings	Anonymous, "Kemp's Jig"—lute
	Foday Musa Suso, "Laminba"—kora
	Davis, *Bitches Brew*—electric guitar
	Britten, *The Young Person's Guide to the Orchestra*— harp (DVD—Variation 9, track 22, 3:48–4:45)
Human voice	Weelkes, "As Vesta Was from Latmos Hill Descending"— madrigal group: mixed solo voices
	Pygmy polyphony, "Elephant-Hunt Song"—mixed solo voices
	Adams, *El Niño,* "Woe unto Them That Call Evil Good"— mixed chorus

Within certain instrumental families, instruments are grouped, like the human voice, in soprano, alto, tenor, and bass registers, in order that a large range can be covered by like-sounding instruments. For example, the strings (violin, viola, cello, and bass viol), the double reeds (oboe, English horn, bassoon, and contrabassoon), and the saxophones follow the SATB model.

Chamber Music and Orchestral Music

So far we have dealt with the tone colors of different families, but instruments and voices are most often used in groups, called ensembles. The number and types of instruments and voices used in an ensemble contribute to the overall tone color of the music. Some ensembles use the colors of only one family; many others combine two or more families. Some are large ensembles, like orchestras, choirs, or bands, which have 40 to 120 performers or more; others are small, as we find in chamber music. Chamber music usually has one instrument per part. The most familiar chamber genre is the string quartet (two violins, viola, and cello). Trios, quintets, sextets, and so on combine strings, winds, and keyboard in various ways. Solo works have been written for almost every instrument, with or without keyboard accompaniment.

Orchestral music is more diverse than one might think, given the growth of the orchestra from the Baroque period to the twentieth century. Choose some musical examples that permit comparison of chamber music and orchestral music, and choose others that trace the growth of the orchestra, such as those listed here. Ask students to identify instrumental families in each excerpt. See Appendix III for more examples.

Chamber	Josquin, "Mille regrets" (vocal chamber music)
	LeBrun, Sonata in F, Rondeau
	Reich, *Music for 18 Musicians*
Orchestra	Baroque—Vivaldi, Violin Concerto in G, *La stravaganza*
	Classical—Haydn, Symphony No. 95
	Romantic—Wagner, Prelude to *The Valkyrie*
	Twentieth Century—Britten, *The Young Person's Guide to the Orchestra* (DVD)
	Twenty-First Century—Adams, *El Niño*
	Japanese *gagaku* orchestra—*Etenraku*
	Balinese *gamelan pelegongan*—I Lotring, *Bopong*

♩ Duration

Of the four main concepts introduced in this chapter, duration is probably the simplest to understand and hear. This one is also somewhat unusual. The first three—pitch, dynamics, and tone color—stem from the acoustic properties of sounds themselves: frequency, amplitude, and overtones. Duration, however, pertains only to the distance in time between a sound's beginning and its end. As John Cage pointed out, duration (or rhythm) is the only musical element that applies equally to sounds and silence. Choose examples from the recorded anthology that allow students to hear the differences between long and short durations. Of course, most music mixes a variety of durations together. (Where timings are not provided in the lists that follow, the beginning of each selection is appropriate.) See Appendix III for more suggested examples.

Long durations	Japanese *gagaku* orchestra, *Etenraku*
	Josquin, "Mille regrets"
	Copland, *Appalachian Spring*, Section 1
	Britten, *The Young Person's Guide to the Orchestra* (DVD—Variation 2, track 21, 0:36–1:42; Variation 10, track 23, 0:00–0:51)
Short durations	Bach, *Brandenburg* Concerto No. 5, I
	Copland, *Appalachian Spring*, Section 2
	Reich, *Music for 18 Musicians*
	Britten, *The Young Person's Guide to the Orchestra* (DVD—Variation 11, track 23, 0:51–1:22; Variation 13, track 24)

Long and short   Wagner, Prelude to *The Valkyrie*—simultaneous (0:59–2:08)

Linda, "Anoku Gonda"—successive

Britten, *The Young Person's Guide to the Orchestra*—simultaneous (DVD—Variation 6, track 22, 0:33–1:53)

Additional Teaching Suggestions

❼ Lecture-Demonstration Ideas

1. On the first day of class, ask students to describe their musical background. Engage them in a discussion about the types of music they enjoy—what they expect from it, how they listen to it, what concerts they've been to, and what those concerts were like. With any luck, your students will enjoy a variety of different styles. This discussion can break the ice and establish the importance of music in their lives.

2. *What does music express?* Prepare a presentation on music as a language. If you have background in language theory, explain and explore the differences between connotative (music) and denotative (spoken) languages. In grossly simplified terms, our words *represent* things objectively, while music *evokes* or *suggests* things in a more subjective manner. It helps to point out connotative elements in verbal language and denotative elements in music; these are not rigid categories, after all. Students accept course materials more readily when they have a sense of what music "means."

3. Bring a synthesizer, an oscilloscope (many physics or nursing departments have one available), and a microphone to class. The oscilloscope makes it possible for the class to see sound waves as the sounds are produced. The synthesizer makes it possible to produce a wide variety of sound waves quickly and easily. The microphone (with proper amplification) makes it possible for students and instructor to create many different sounds, vocal or instrumental, on the spur of the moment. As the class experiments with a variety of different sounds, students can instantly see and hear the effect of changes in frequency, timbre, and volume.

4. Play with sounds in class. If your classroom is not equipped with a computer, take your students to a computer lab. Software packages such as Propellerhead's *Reason* (studio workstation) or Arturia's *Moog Modular V* (softsynth) include waveform generators that allow you to create waveforms and change their shape and overtone content at will. For an easy-to-use version of software, try Scott Lipscomb's cross-platform *Waveform Program*, available as a free download at lipscomb.umn.edu/stuff.htm. These are wonderful tools for demonstrating the relation between overtones, wave shape, and tone color, and they can also serve as springboards for a discussion of musical elements (see the next section, Multimedia Resources).

5. Bring simple household objects to class to demonstrate the principles of sound production for different families of instruments. For the flute family, bring a pop bottle or a cider jug; for reeds, bring a thin yardstick (hold one end flat on a desk or table with the other end hanging over the edge; bend the edge end up as far as you can, and let go while pulling the other end across the table); for brass, bring a length of garden hose or a paper-towel tube; for

strings, bring a rubber band. Experiment with the length or volume of the air column or with the tension of the string.

6. Interlude B in Chapter 3 of the textbook takes a typical Western approach, categorizing instruments in families according to how sound is produced. Many instruments from around the world don't fit nicely into this scheme, so prepare your students now to think differently. To keep this exercise simple, stick with percussion instruments. Why not classify percussion instruments according to the material they are made of? Refer students to textbook pages 42 and 44, and ask them what these instruments are made of. Some are made of metal, some of wood, and some use a skin or membrane. Write these terms on the board, and ask students to link each instrument listed with the appropriate material. Be sure to play examples from the *Listen* set, and ask the class if they hear the sound of metal, wood, or membranes. The following pieces work especially well: I Lotring's *Bopong;* the Japanese *gagaku* orchestra playing *Etenraku;* the excerpt from the Beijing opera, *The Prince Who Changed into a Cat* (0:00–0:24); Gershwin's Piano Prelude No. 1; and the example of the drums of Benin, "Ako." The listening part is easy enough to get students interested and get them thinking as well.

♪ Class Discussion Ideas

1. *How do you listen to music?* A short presentation on Copland's three planes of listening—sensuous, expressive, and sheerly musical—serves well as a prelude to discussion.[1] Ask students which plane represents their usual mode of listening. Don't make value judgments; all three planes are important. This discussion introduces the idea that we listen in more than one way and that this course will explore different modes of listening.

2. *Which elements of music are most important to you?* or *What do you listen for in music?* These are wide-open questions with no right or wrong answers, but they can engage students where they are and open up a surprising variety of important musical issues.

3. *What do you like best about music?* A good beat? Beauty? A soothing escape? This is another broad question designed to engage students and stress the important role of music in human experience.

4. Ask the class to name any sounds they can think of—the more unusual the better. Then analyze these sounds using the tools covered in this chapter. Ask students to identify characteristic features of each sound named—its pitch, loudness, color, and duration. This exercise can help students gain skill in describing individual sounds, musical or otherwise.

5. *What sounds are appropriate for music?* A few students may insist that it's not music unless real musical instruments are used or unless it has a real melody (what about rap or percussion music?), but most are open to many possibilities—perhaps they have heard the sound of a toilet flushing on an underground rock album, unusual sampled sounds on a techno-pop album, or environmental sounds on a New Age album. Further resources that can stimulate

---

[1]Aaron Copland, *What to Listen for in Music,* rev. ed. New York: New American Library, 1957, pp. 18–23.

class discussion include John Cage's "Credo: The Future of Music," reprinted in his book *Silence,*[2] recordings of *musique concrète* (LeCaine's *Dripsody*), Varèse's *Poème électronique,* or the example of the drums of Benin, "Ako," from the *Listen* set.

❡ Listening Ideas

1. Show your students slides of paintings, and ask them to decide which one best captures the mood of Wagner's Prelude to *The Valkyrie.* Ask the class to study the paintings while listening to the music. In the discussion that follows, have them compare elements of the paintings with elements of the music. Colors can be compared with musical timbre, brush strokes and surface texture with musical articulation, sight lines and focal points with melody, perspective and foreground/background with musical texture, and composition and relationships between parts with musical form. This can help stimulate thinking about elements of music.

2. Ask students to bring recordings of music they like. (Agree on the selections beforehand if you want to avoid duplication.) Use these recordings for class listening and discussion just as you used Wagner's Prelude and other examples in the Lecture Suggestions. The sooner you establish that listening skills are appropriate tools for any kind of music, the better.

3. To give students more practice identifying musical means and effect, use the suggestions for Tchaikovsky's *Nutcracker* Suite in the next subsection, Further Listening Examples.

4. Compare classically trained singers with early blues singers; consider especially their differing uses of pitch and timbre. Classical examples are plentiful in the *Listen* recordings—"Là ci darem la mano" from Mozart's *Don Giovanni,* Schubert's "Erlkönig," R. Schumann's "Im wunderschönen Monat Mai," or the Tomb Scene from Verdi's *Aida* will do. Sippie Wallace's performance of the "If You Ever Been Down" Blues from the *Listen* set or any recordings by Bessie Smith or Robert Johnson provide good examples of early blues singers. In the discussion that follows, draw attention to the greater variety of vocal colors and the pitch bending of the blues style. You can also call attention to the freedom of expression permitted the blues artist versus the classical artist's desire to realize the composer's intentions as faithfully as possible.

5. Bring a recording of Penderecki's *Threnody for the Victims of Hiroshima* to class. Traditional concepts of melody, harmony, texture, or tonality (introduced in Chapter 3) contribute little to an understanding of this work. *Threnody* relies on concepts introduced in this chapter—high and low pitch clusters, sounds of indefinite pitch, varied dynamics, and unusual tone colors (fifty-two bowed stringed instruments are the only sound sources!)—to create a dramatic, unnerving soundscape.

6. Play a recording of Étude No. 7 from Elliott Carter's *Eight Etudes and a Fantasy for Woodwind Quartet* (1950). The pitch information in this work is minimal—all four instruments play g^1 (the G above middle C). This work relies on dynamics and patterns of tone color changes for its shape. Challenge

---

[2]John Cage, *Silence: Lectures and Writings by John Cage.* Middletown, CT: Wesleyan University Press, 1961, pp. 3–6.

students to describe the overall shape of this work and to name the elements that create that shape.

7. Play a recording of Schoenberg's Five Orchestral Pieces, Op. 16, III, for the class. This famous movement exemplifies Schoenberg's use of *Klangfarbenmelodie*, or tone-color melody. The gradually changing pitches in Schoenberg's harmonies are far less important than his constantly changing instrumentation. Schoenberg achieves a climax in this work by increasing the rate of instrumental change, not through *crescendo*. Students will have a difficult time picking out specific instruments in this work; Schoenberg deliberately created a brief overlap between the end of one chord and the beginning of the next to mask each new entrance. Nonetheless, repeated listening to specific passages will sensitize students to the constantly changing colors in this work.

8. The authors refer to the human voice as "the first, most beautiful, and most widely used of all the sources of music." Your students can probably already tell the difference between classical, pop, and blues vocal styles. Take time to show them other possible ways of using the human voice. Sample some of the following examples from the *Listen* set: the Qur'anic chant "Ya Sin"; the Hawai'ian chant *mele pule*; the Japanese kabuki play, *Dojoji* (0:54–1:54); the excerpt from the Beijing opera, *The Prince Who Changed into a Cat* (0:40–end); Schoenberg's "The Moonfleck," from *Pierrot lunaire*; Saariaho's *From the Grammar of Dreams*; the Meeting Scene from Bernstein's *West Side Story*; and Gershwin's "Who Cares?" (from the *Listen* DVD). Ask your students which they like best.

♪ Further Listening Examples

TCHAIKOVSKY *Nutcracker* Suite, Op. 71a

The *Listen* DVD includes the "Dance of the Sugar-Plum Fairy" in Chapter 4 as an example of form, but this and the other short dances that make up the *Nutcracker* Suite are ideal for observing and examining the musical elements discussed in this chapter—and are utterly charming as well. Photocopy the Listening Chart in Appendix I as a transparency or as handouts for the class. Display the Listening Chart, and then play the music, pointing out each section as it goes by. (See Appendix I for this and other Listening Charts.)

These short "characteristic" dances, so distinctive in color and mood, provide especially good examples of the concepts discussed in this chapter—pitch, dynamics, tone color, and duration. As you play each dance, ask your students to identify the musical elements that give it the character indicated by its title. For example, to what degree is the "Russian Dance" really Russian sounding (it is quite evocative of a Cossack-type dance), and what musical elements contribute to create this particularly "Russian" sound? The following brief sketches of each dance are meant to facilitate a discussion of musical "character."

"Overture Miniature." *The Nutcracker* is a fairy tale for children. The brief overture perfectly evokes the light, simple, and lyric mood that pervades the entire ballet.

"March." Invigorating, this rhythmic movement features particularly the winds and brass.

"Dance of the Sugar-Plum Fairy." This whimsical, weightless, slightly mysterious dance features the bell-like celesta and pizzicato strings.

"Russian Dance." Short motives, sharp accents, and syncopation characterize this vigorous Cossack dance.

" Arabian Dance." Quiet and mysterious, this dance features a melismatic, vaguely Middle Eastern melody and ostinato accompaniment.

"Chinese Dance." Pizzicato strings, glockenspiel, extremely high wind melodies, and trills combine to create an exotic musical mood. Note the pedal/ostinato that, as in the "Arabian Dance," creates a certain non-Western-sounding musical underpinning.

"Dance of the Pan-Pipes." The fluty main tune perfectly evokes the sound of children's reed pipes.

"Waltz of the Flowers." Three different themes represent various sorts of flowers. This bright, brilliant music reflects the multihued flowers it describes.

Multimedia Resources

⁊ Further Listening Charts and Texts

Tchaikovsky, *Nutcracker* Suite, Op. 71a (see Appendix I). This listening chart can be used with the exercise described in Further Listening Examples.

⁊ Sound Recordings

Carter, *The Best of the New York Woodwind Quintet,* Vol. 1. New York Woodwind Quintet. Boston Skyline 137 (CD). Contains Carter's *Eight Etudes and a Fantasy* along with works by Barber, Nielsen, and others. Try this recording if you use Listening Idea 6.

Johnson, Robert. *The Complete Recordings.* Columbia Legacy C2K 64916 (CD). Classic 1936–37 recordings by the influential Delta blues singer. Try this recording if you use Listening Idea 4.

LeCaine, *Hugh LeCaine.* EMF Media EM115 (CD). Various electronic works by this twentieth-century composer, including his humorous *musique concrète* classic, *Dripsody.* Try this recording if you use Class Discussion Idea 5. Available at www.cdemusic.org.

Penderecki, *Matrix 5—Anaklasis—Threnody.* Polish Radio National Symphony Orchestra and London Symphony Orchestra. EMI Classics CDM 5 65077 2 (CD). Collection of significant Penderecki orchestral works from 1959 to 1974, including the famous *Threnody for the Victims of Hiroshima;* conducted by the composer. Use this recording of *Threnody* if you try Listening Idea 5.

Schoenberg, *Serenade/Five Pieces for Orchestra.* BBC Symphony Orchestra. Sony Classical 48463 (CD). Fine performances of Schoenberg's Five Orchestral Pieces, Op. 16, *Serenade,* and *Ode to Napoleon;* conducted by Boulez. Try this recording if you use Listening Idea 7.

Smith, Bessie. *Bessie Smith—The Collection.* Columbia Legacy CK 44441 (CD). Sixteen classic recordings by the "Empress of the Blues" from 1923 to 1933. Try this recording if you use Listening Idea 4.

Tchaikovsky, *Ballet Suites*. Berlin Philharmonic. Deutsche Grammophon 449 726-2 (CD). Superb performances of suites from *The Nutcracker, Swan Lake,* and *Sleeping Beauty;* conducted by Rostropovich. Try this recording if you use Listening Idea 3 or the Further Listening Examples suggestions for this work.

⑦ Video Recordings

The Essence of an Instrument. Science and Music Series. www.films.com (DVD and VHS, color, 26 minutes). Study of instruments from the perspective of acoustic requirements for production of sound. Covers pitch production, amplification, sound quality, and problems of sound synthesis.

Music: Emotion and Feeling in Sound. www.insight-media.com (VHS, color, 30 minutes). Poet Maya Angelou narrates this study of the elements of music. It moves from electronic representation of sound waves to concepts of timbre, consonance, and dynamics. Performances of works by Beethoven, Mahler, and Ashworth demonstrate the interplay of elements in real music.

The Physics of Music. www.insight-media.com (VHS, color, 22 minutes). Video looks at the relationships between waveforms and pitch, frequency, loudness, tone color, timbre, scales, and octaves.

Tchaikovsky, *Nutcracker.* Kultur Video (DVD and VHS, color, 100 minutes). Re-release of this 1968 recording of the Royal Ballet at Covent Garden features the incomparable Rudolf Nureyev and Merle Park. Useful if you use the exercise in Further Listening Examples.

Tchaikovsky, *Nutcracker.* Kultur Video (DVD and VHS, color, 105 minutes). Re-release of this 1978 recording features the renowned Bolshoi Ballet with dancers Yekaterina Maximova and Vladimir Vasiliev. Useful if you use suggestions for this work in Further Listening Examples.

What Is Music? Science and Music Series. www.films.com (DVD and VHS, color, 26 minutes). Examines sound waves, the nature of "musical" sounds, and the role of culture in musical perception.

⑦ Software

Amadeus II. www.hairersoft.com (Macintosh). Inexpensive shareware package for sound recording and editing. The oscilloscope feature does spectral analysis in real time—in other words, you can play or sing any sound and instantly see what the sound wave looks like! This is a wonderful tool for your lecture on acoustics. Use this as an in-class substitute for Lecture-Demonstration Idea 4.

The Art of Listening to Music. www.insight-media.com (CD-ROM—Macintosh or Windows). Exploring a wide variety of music and sounds, this package provides examples of melody, harmony, timbre, and rhythm. A useful introduction to listening.

Making More Music. New York: Voyager/Learn Technologies Interactive (CD-ROM—Macintosh or Windows). A more "adult" version of *Making Music,* this easy-to-use yet surprisingly sophisticated composing software is fun to play with. Best of all for your students, no musical experience is required! Try this package if you use Lecture-Demonstration Idea 4. Available at www .cdemusic.org.

Moog Modular V. www.arturia.com (Macintosh or Windows). One of many softsynths (software synthesizers) available today, this one emulates the original Moog modular synthesizer on your computer screen. The beauty of these early synthesizers? You could always follow the patch cords and see exactly how each sound was routed and controlled. You can create various waveforms for demonstration in class. Try a softsynth if you use Lecture-Demonstration Idea 4—but only if you have experience with sound synthesis.

Music Conservatory. Voyetra Turtle Beach (CD-ROM—Windows). Inexpensive all-in-one guide to the world of music, this package provides an overview of music history, composers, instruments, and music theory. Geared toward nonmusicians.

Music Is Physics. www.insight-media.com (CD-ROM—Macintosh or Windows). This package looks at acoustics, sound waves, and the human ear. It also introduces music notation and musical instruments.

Reason. www.propellerheads.se (Macintosh or Windows). This amazing "studio-in-a-box" provides software equivalents for all of the modules you would normally find in a music production studio: synthesizers, drum machine, effects, processors, mixing board, and so on. Try this if you use Lecture-Demonstration Idea 4.

Sibelius Instruments. www.sibelius.com (Macintosh or Windows). Part of the Sibelius educational suite, this interactive encyclopedia of instruments can be very useful in demonstrating features and sounds of individual instruments as well as various musical ensembles, such as the Late Romantic orchestra. Try this if you use Lecture-Demonstration Idea 4.

Stravinsky: The Rite of Spring. Voyager CD Companion Series. New York: Voyager, 1990 (CD-ROM—Macintosh). This serves as just one example of many CD-ROM packages designed to introduce listeners to important works. Voyager invented the "multimedia guide to great music on CD-ROM" genre— this was one of their first releases. Now legacy (outdated) software, the Voyager packages do not run on Macintosh's current System X. Still, similar products can still be found, and many include a hypertext introduction to the elements of music geared toward nonmusicians.

CHAPTER 2

Rhythm and Pitch

Chapter Outline

Boldface indicates works in the recording set.

Important Terms

rhythm	duple meter	*adagio*	pitch	whole step	*staccato*
beat	triple meter	*andante*	scale	playing in tune	triplet
accent	compound meter	*moderato*	interval	notes	time signatures
sforzando	quintuple meter	*allegretto*	octave	rests	staff
meter	nonmetrical	*allegro*	diatonic scale	dotted notes/rests	ledger lines
measure	syncopation	*presto*	chromatic scale	dotted rhythms	clefs
bar	tempo	*accelerando*	flat	ties	naturals
bar lines	metronome marks	*ritardando*	sharp	slurs	key signatures
simple meter	tempo indications	fermata	half step	*legato*	scores

Teaching Objectives

❧ Overall Objectives

This chapter will help students acquire familiarity with:

1. Fundamental elements of music related to time and pitch: rhythm, meter, tempo, pitch, and scales.

2. Musical concepts and vocabulary associated with these elements of music.

3. *(optional)* Principles of music notation, providing awareness of the complexity of detail needed to notate musical ideas.

4. *(optional)* The function of various markings in a musical score.

❧ Listening Objectives

After completing this chapter, students should be able to listen for and identify:

1. Metrical and nonmetrical music.

2. Duple, triple, and compound meters.

3. Changes in tempo, pitch, and scales.

Lecture Suggestions

Music may be the "universal language," but many of the concepts described in this chapter correspond to Western modes of thinking about music. Given that *Listen* focuses primarily on Western music, students need to understand its basic principles. The Global Perspectives recordings, however, provide constant reminders that the Western approach is not the only one—far from it. These excerpts from around the world can help you broaden and clarify your students' understanding of concepts introduced in the textbook. For that reason, the suggested listening examples are peppered with excerpts from the Global Perspectives curriculum. Continuing the focus from Chapter 1, you will also find examples from the *Listen* DVD, especially from Britten's *Young Person's Guide to the Orchestra.*

Again, there are many ways to cover basic elements of music. It is important to provide as many listening examples as you can for each element. You are encouraged to seek out your own creative approaches to this material. The following is a collection of suggestions and musical examples that may prove helpful.

❧ Rhythm

Rhythm is one of the most fascinating, puzzling aspects of music. We experience time in a thousand ways—under different circumstances, five minutes can seem like an eternity or fly by in an instant. Music expresses the many ways we experience time through rhythm, the time element in music. I define *rhythm* as the relation between sounds in time. These time relations create countless patterns that can be classified in various ways.

Different cultures perceive musical time differently. Balinese musicians start with a long time span that is divided and subdivided at many levels. Indian musicians start with shorter time spans divided into specific, often irregular groupings called *tala*. Other traditions let the rhythms of the spoken word define the experience of time. In most cultures, fundamental distinctions can be drawn between metrical and nonmetrical music, whether or not the cultures share a Western understanding of meter. Start by playing two excerpts of approximately equal length (play just less than a minute of each)—one metrical, the other nonmetrical. The following examples work well along with the *Listen* DVD excerpts on textbook page 15; choose one from each category or see Appendix III for more suggestions.

Metrical	Haydn, Symphony No. 95, III (track 30, 0:00–0:50)
	Prokofiev, *Alexander Nevsky*, "The Battle on the Ice," first excerpt (1:44); second excerpt
	Adams, *El Niño*, "When Herod Heard" and "Woe unto Them That Call Evil Good"
Nonmetrical	Japanese *gagaku* orchestra, *Etenraku* (0:00–0:50)
	Debussy, *Clouds* (track 20, 0:00–0:54)
	Prokofiev, *Alexander Nevsky*, "The Battle on the Ice," first excerpt (0:00–1:43)

Ask students to write their reactions as they listen, answering these questions:

1. How is my experience of time different as I listen to each excerpt?

2. What makes the passage of time feel different in each excerpt?

3. Which excerpt feels longer?

It is fun to ask which excerpt was longer, especially if both are nearly the same length. Some will choose the metrical example because they heard many sound events in a regularly marked musical space; others will choose the nonmetrical excerpt because the suspension of "normal" musical time (lack of a beat) allows them to experience each moment more intensely. Either way, this reinforces the idea that humans do not sense time in an accurate, chronological manner. After you listen, ask students to share their reactions, and draw out as many rhythmic concepts (beat, accent, articulation, and so on) as you can from the comments they make, especially the concept of the beat (a regular, recurring pulse). Most music familiar to your students relies on a clearly audible beat. Point out that some musical works or styles do not rely on a beat; these are referred to as nonmetrical. (Actually, *nonmetrical* can refer to several different situations: to works with an audible beat but no regular, repeating pattern of stressed and unstressed beats; to works with no beat; and even to works where a conductor keeps a strict beat, but the beat is not audible—the beat serving as a point of reference around which random events can be synchronized.) After you have explained the concept of the beat, double-check their understanding by clapping three different patterns—a repeated short-short-long pattern, a random pattern, and a steady beat. Ask which pattern was a beat pattern.

To introduce concepts of accent and meter, play three short excerpts for purposes of comparison. Choose one that presents a beat without accents, one that presents a beat with irregular accents, and one that presents a regular metric pattern. Possibilities include:

Pulse— *no accents*	Verdi, *Aida,* Act IV, Scene ii (Tomb scene)—Part 3 (track 9, 2:41–3:16)
	Navajo song, "K'adnikini'ya'"
	Reich, *Music for 18 Musicians,* Introduction
Irregular accents	Beethoven, Quartet in F, Op. 135, II (0:00–0:33)
	Stravinsky, *The Rite of Spring,* Part I—"Dance of the Adolescents" (track 23)
	Reich, *Music for 18 Musicians,* Section I
Regular accents	LeBrun, Sonata in F, Rondeau
	Mozart, *Don Giovanni,* "Là ci darem la mano" (0:00–0:40)
	Prokofiev, *Alexander Nevsky,* "The Battle on the Ice," second excerpt

Ask students to clap or tap along with the music (or even teach them basic conducting patterns) while listening for regular, recurring patterns of two or three beats. When the excerpts are done, have students compare their reactions to the three excerpts. Point out that metric accents are not necessarily loud; accent is often created by a sudden louder dynamic, but it can also be created by longer duration, orchestration, or pitch patterns that emphasize a particular note (repeated note, highest note, lowest note, unexpected note). To prove your point, play a repeating "oom-pah-pah" pattern at the piano—but accent the wrong beat. Even when one of the "pahs" is accented, students still hear the "oom" as the downbeat.

Once students become accustomed to the idea of listening for recurring metric patterns, let them practice distinguishing between duple and triple meter. Start by marching with a verbal "*left*-right-*left*-right" pattern (duple meter); then play a simple "oom-pah-pah" pattern on the piano (triple meter). Then supplement the excerpts from Listening Exercise 2 (textbook page 15) with some of these recorded examples—in random order (start at the beginning unless otherwise indicated). See Appendix III for more possibilities.

Duple	Anonymous, "Kemp's Jig"
	Handel, *Messiah,* Hallelujah Chorus
	Mozart, Piano Concerto in A, K. 488, I
	I Lotring, *Bopong*
	Britten, *The Young Person's Guide to the Orchestra* (DVD—Variation 1, track 21, 0:00–0:36; Variation 11, track 23, 0:51–1:22; Variation 12, track 23, 1:22–2:32; Fugue, track 25, 0:00–1:54)
Triple	Anonymous, Galliard, "Daphne"
	Vivaldi, Violin Concerto in G, *La stravaganza,* II
	Beethoven, Symphony No. 5 in C Minor, III
	Wagner, Prelude to *The Valkyrie*
	Britten, *The Young Person's Guide to the Orchestra* (DVD—Theme, track 20, 0:00–0:19; Variation 3, track 21, 1:42–2:21; Variation 5, track 22, 0:00–0:33; Variation 7, track 22, 1:53–2:52; Variation 13, track 24)

In the discussion that follows each excerpt, ask students to identify instruments and musical patterns that maintained the beat, as well as techniques used to emphasize the downbeat—perhaps a particular instrument plays only on the downbeat, or the downbeat is louder, and so on. Don't hesitate to play an example more than once. If students do not get the correct answer, ask them to count along with you. Be patient; some students will feel their way in slowly.

Compound meter is more difficult to perceive. Play a few examples so that the class senses the fast triple division of the beat. In fact, some will understand it best as a triple meter that goes so fast that you can't clap on every beat. Possible examples follow:

> Frescobaldi, Suite: Corrente
>
> Haydn, Symphony No. 95, II
>
> Schubert, "Erlkönig"
>
> Schubert, Moment Musical No. 2 in A-flat
>
> Beethoven, Piano Concerto No. 5, "Emperor," III (DVD)

At first it is enough if students can consistently identify duple and triple meter. Compound meter is most useful in alerting students to the presence of different rhythmic levels. Beats can be divided to create a faster subpulse. Beats can also be grouped together to form measures. By extension, measures can be grouped to form phrases, phrases to form periods, periods to form larger sections, and so on, until you get to the duration of the entire piece. We perceive musical relationships on many different rhythmic levels.

Perception of meter is only the first step in comprehending rhythmic relationships. Some more complex effects (*rubato*, jazz syncopation, metrical modulation, and so on) will be studied later on, but syncopation is first mentioned here. Syncopation is created by placing an accent where it is not expected, an accent that works against the normal metric accent. Metric accents must be clear for syncopation to be perceived; if no downbeat is expected, we can talk about random accents, but not syncopation. Play several examples. Ask students to clap, tap, or conduct the beat to feel the effect of the syncopation. You can stamp or clap with the syncopated notes to emphasize the contrast between students' beat and the syncopation. Use some of these excerpts to supplement the examples in Listening Exercises 2 and 3 on textbook pages 15 and 16.

Syncopation	I Lotring, *Bopong* (4:03–end)
	Beethoven, Quartet in F, Op. 135, II (0:00–0:33)
	Tchaikovsky, *Romeo and Juliet* (track 26, 0:35–51)
	Gershwin, Piano Prelude No. 1

♪ Tempo

Once the concept of beat is clear, tempo is easily explained. Refer students to the list of tempo indications on textbook page 15. Play examples such as those here so that students can hear the effect of different tempi. See Appendix III for more possibilities.

Slow	Japanese *gagaku* orchestra, *Etenraku*
	Schubert, Moment Musical No. 2 in A-flat
	Copland, *Appalachian Spring*, Section 1
	Britten, *The Young Person's Guide to the Orchestra* (DVD—Variation 2, track 21, 0:36–1:42; Variation 7, track 22, 1:53–2:52; Variation 10, track 23, 0:00–0:51)

Moderate	Mozart, Piano Concerto in A, K. 488, I
	Mahler, Symphony No. 1, III
	Copland, *Appalachian Spring,* Section 5
	Britten, *The Young Person's Guide to the Orchestra* (DVD—Theme, track 20; Variation 13, track 24)
Fast	Beethoven, Symphony No. 5 in C Minor, III—Trio (track 17); IV—Coda (track 19, 3:55–end)
	Copland, *Appalachian Spring,* Section 2
	Drums of Benin, "Ako"
	Britten, *The Young Person's Guide to the Orchestra* (DVD—Variation 1, track 21, 0:00–0:36; Variation 5, track 22, 0:00–0:33; Variation 11, track 23, 0:51–1:22; Fugue, track 25)

Note that some works, such as Beethoven's Symphony No. 5: IV and Linda's "Anoku Gonda," change tempo at various points.

More complex effects, such as *accelerando* and *ritardando*, result from changes in tempo. The following examples can be used; see Appendix III for more suggestions.

Accelerando	Japanese *gagaku* orchestra, *Etenraku* (extremely gradual)
	Beethoven, Symphony No. 5 in C Minor, IV—Coda (track 19, 3:43–3:55)
	Prokofiev, *Alexander Nevsky,* "The Battle on the Ice," first excerpt (1:44–2:00, 3:42–4:06)
Ritardando	R. Schumann, *Dichterliebe,* "Die alten, bösen Lieder" (1:17–1:48)
	Wagner, Prelude to *The Valkyrie* (3:02–3:30)
	Prokofiev, *Alexander Nevsky,* "The Battle on the Ice," second excerpt (2:41–2:58)

❦ Pitch

If you have not already done so, use the Lecture Suggestions on pitch in Chapter 1 of this manual to introduce concepts of definite and indefinite pitch, high and low pitch, and male and female voice types.

Introduce students to specific pitches on the keyboard. Use the keyboard diagram on textbook page 18, or draw a two-octave keyboard on the board. Point out the pattern of black keys on the keyboard (alternating groups of two and three). Show students how to find an anchor pitch (C or A works well) in relation to the pattern of black keys. Then show them how to find other pitches (the other white keys) from their anchor pitch. Finally, introduce sharps and flats. By the time you finish, students should be able to find the keys that correspond to each letter name, with or without sharps and flats.

Once students know letter names at the keyboard, it is much easier to explain the octave. To demonstrate the phenomenon of the octave, play several versions of the same tune ("Yankee Doodle," for instance). First play the melody alone; then play it in parallel octaves. Follow this with versions in parallel 5ths, 2nds, 7ths, or any interval you like. Ask students to describe the effect of each version. Point out that men and women singing a tune together normally sing an octave apart.

ꝑ Scales

Introduce half steps and whole steps by using the keyboard diagrams on textbook page 18 (or draw a two-octave keyboard on the board). When you explain half steps as the distance between adjacent notes on the keyboard, make sure students understand why E and F are adjacent, but F and G are not.

In the Western tradition, a scale is a collection (palette) of pitches that composers draw from to create musical structures. Have students count out the number of half steps between scale steps in both the chromatic and diatonic scales.

chromatic scale:	C	C#	D	D#	E	F	F#	G	G#	A	A#	B	C		
no. of half steps:		1	1	1	1	1	1	1	1	1	1	1		=	12
major scale:	C		D		E	F		G		A		B	C		
no. of half steps:		2		2		1	2		2		2	1		=	12

Point out that the chromatic scale is symmetrical, but the diatonic scale is not. (This is important in the next chapter.) Play both scales at the keyboard. Then play a few simple melodies based on the major scale ("Yankee Doodle," "My Country, 'Tis of Thee," "Row, Row, Row Your Boat," and so on), and identify scale steps by number or solfège syllable. Finish with a few excerpts such as these based on diatonic, chromatic, and non-Western scales. See Appendix III for more possibilities.

Chromatic	Purcell, *Dido and Aeneas,* "When I am laid in earth" (first six notes at 0:57)
	Chopin, Nocturne in F-sharp, Op. 15, No. 2 (0:33–0:47, 0:57–1:11, 2:19–2:28)
	Berlioz, *Fantastic* Symphony, V (track 6, 0:55–1:32)
	Ligeti, *Lux aeterna*
Diatonic	Bernart, "La dousa votz"
	Bach, *Brandenburg* Concerto No. 5, I—ritornello (track 1, 0:00–0:19)
	Berlioz, *Fantastic* Symphony, V (track 5, 0:00–0:27)
	Beijing opera, *The Prince Who Changed into a Cat* (0:24–end)
Non-Western	Qur'anic Chant, "Ya Sin"
	Foday Musa Suso, Gambian song
	I Lotring, *Bopong*

(The Berlioz excerpts compare diatonic and chromatic versions of the same theme!)

If students have a keyboard (or a diagram of a keyboard) handy, you can train them to build major scales on any pitch. Knowledge of notation is unnecessary—they just need to remember two things:

ꝑ the pattern of whole and half steps in the major scale

ꝑ to use each letter name (except the tonic) only *once* in a diatonic scale

ꝑ Interlude A: Musical Notation

The point made by the authors in the first paragraph on textbook page 21 merits careful attention. The symbols covered in Interlude A properly belong to the Western tradition. Many traditions use no notation whatsoever; musical knowledge and repertoire are passed from master to pupil via oral tradition. Other traditions have devised their own symbols and notational conventions. Yet others have adopted Western notation out of convenience, due to missionization, and so on. This is not to say that Western notation is "best" or that other traditions are less "advanced" than our own—they are simply different. In fact, Western notation's limitations become all too clear when we use its symbols in an attempt to represent the music of India, Bali, or other traditions. The complex rhythms, unequal temperaments, and unusual tone qualities associated with many world musics simply cannot be represented in Western notation. In many cases, the attempt to do so only clouds our understanding of indigenous concepts. For instance, much Balinese music *could* be notated in 4/4 meter, but that would not help us understand the large-scale temporal units (up to a minute long) that lie at the heart of the Balinese understanding of rhythm.

One purpose of the authors' second paragraph and accompanying graphs (textbook page 21) is to get students used to the idea that the elements studied in Chapters 1 and 2 must be combined in various ways to create structures that give music meaning. Melody, of course, relies on the elements of time and pitch, texture relies on the combination of melody with other melodies or musical figures, and so on. Now that we have dissected music to find its basic elements, we must reassemble these elements in Chapters 3 and 4 in ways that give music meaning and "life."

As for the rest of this interlude, nonmusicians cannot be expected to know all of the details it provides. The authors include this material in one section so that it can be referred to when needed. I find it most useful to work from the score page on textbook page 24. (Photocopy a transparency, or scan it for display if you like.) It is much easier to understand notes, rests, dots, ties, measures, bar lines, time signatures, staves, ledger lines, clefs, and key signatures in context. This exercise also provides insight into the world of the performing musician—students can see what the performer must know and do to play the music.

Work through the labeled items on this score page one at a time, explain each in as much detail as necessary, and play different lines and a recording of the page. Take time with pitch notation, meter and key signatures, the relationships of rests and note values within each bar, the synchronization of parts in the score, and the arrangement of instruments by family. Students generally find the visual relationship between clef symbols (treble, bass, movable C) and corresponding pitch names (G, F, C) interesting, and the mnemonics for remembering pitch locations (*All Cows Eat Grass* or F-A-C-E) can be entertaining. Emphasize the complex set of symbols needed to notate the many elements of simple musical sounds: pitch, dynamics, tone color, scale, rhythm, and tempo.

Additional Teaching Suggestions

¶ Lecture-Demonstration Ideas

1. Take your class to a piano lab (if available). A keyboard lab can become an invaluable tool as you introduce concepts of pitch, scale, rhythm, and notation. Use simple exercises in finding pitches, counting half and whole steps, playing chromatic and major scales, reading simple pitch patterns in basic

hand position, and reading melodies that use simple rhythms. Keep it simple, take one step at a time, and let students have fun. For some, this will be their first music-making experience. Time at the keyboard will significantly increase understanding of concepts in this unit, and you can build on what they learn in the lab when you return to the classroom. Some practical concerns: Two students per instrument works just fine at this level. Teachers with more students than lab seats can try a rotation schedule—while part of the class uses the lab, the rest can work on carefully planned small group activities. If you can make it work, it's worth the effort.

2. Bring several examples of music notation to class. Provocative examples include early plainchant notation (without staff!), traditional plainchant notation (four-line staff and neumes), pictorial scores by Baude Cordier ("Belle bonne"), a lead sheet from a jazz "fake" book, non-Western notations, and contemporary scores by Krzysztof Penderecki or George Crumb. If you have recordings for each score, so much the better. Good sources for scores and recordings are standard music history textbooks (illustrations and color plates) and the anthologies of scores and recordings that accompany them (e.g., Burkholder's *History of Western Music*, 7th ed., New York: W.W. Norton, 2006). This exercise works well either as an introduction to music notation or as a supplement to the textbook's introduction to notation in Interlude A.

3. Introduce your class to other concepts of the scale. The modern Western scale is simply a palette of available pitches a composer can use in any way, but older traditions viewed scales in a more prescriptive manner. Start with excerpts from Leeman Perkins's article on church modes from the Middle Ages and Renaissance.[1] In early times the Western scale was understood as a set of melodic figures defined by such features as its final, dominant, range, register, and so on. For an even more inclusive understanding of scale, read excerpts from page 38 of Amnon Shiloah's article on Arabic scales.[2] Shiloah lists particularly fascinating correspondences between modes and everything from signs of the zodiac to odors to alphabetical letters. For further comparison, you could add the Baroque "doctrine of affections" to the discussion, whereby specific keys were associated with certain attributes. These ideas continued to hold sway in Beethoven's symphonies, where E-flat major and F major retain their traditional association with "heroic" and "pastoral" qualities, respectively.

4. *What is the relationship between the musical work and the musical performance?* Display a score page so that students can see it clearly. (Digitized Scores for classroom display are available in the instructor resources on the *Listen* Web site.) Ask them how they like this music! Apologize profusely for "forgetting" they don't read music. Then play a few lines at a keyboard to help them out, and when that doesn't work so well, play a recording. Of course, the point is not their opinion of the music; this demonstration serves rather to highlight the importance of the score. For students who don't read music, the score can seem meaningless, just as an American novel would seem meaningless to someone who doesn't read English. But for someone who reads scores, the musical work can exist *independent* of its performance, just as a novel pos-

---

[1]Leeman L. Perkins, "Mode and Structure in the Masses of Josquin." *Journal of the American Musicological Society,* 26, 2 (1973), pp. 189–239.

[2]Amnon Shiloah, "The Arabic Concept of Mode." *Journal of the American Musicological Society* (1981), p. 38.

sesses meaning even when you don't read it out loud—through an internal reading (or internal performance). This concept lies at the heart of the relationship between the work and the performance in the Western classical tradition. *Can you think of any music with a different relationship between the work and the score?* Use this follow-up question to draw out examples that don't fit the Western classical tradition. Many exist, including blues works and others where no notation exists—where the work cannot exist independent of its performance (except perhaps in memory or a recording). To further discussion, bring both a lead sheet and two different recordings of the same tune— an old "standard" works best. Recordings of "standard" pop tunes by jazz and popular artists are plentiful, and someone in your department surely owns a "fake" or a "real" book of music. Display the lead sheet for your students. Compared to the score you displayed earlier, it looks incomplete—just a tune and some chord symbols. At the keyboard, play the tune, and, if you can, sound out some of the chords as well. Then play the two recordings back to back, and ask students to compare them. They are the same tune, maybe the same chords, but the accompaniments differ. The rhythm section, ubiquitous in popular music and jazz, operates according to its own mix of oral and written traditions, and two performances of the same work played by the same rhythm section can differ dramatically. The lead sheet guides both performances, but it is no score in the classical sense. Understanding the range of possible relationships between the work and its performance in our Western traditions helps prepare students to understand a similar range of musical relationships around the world.

❼ Class Discussion Ideas

1. *How do we experience time?* Ask students to list (on paper) real-life experiences when they felt these emotions: excitement, boredom, peacefulness, and terror. As students describe their experiences, ask them how quickly (or slowly) time passed in each situation. You should get a wide range of different experiences of time. Of course, humans possess no built-in chronometer. The same five-minute span can seem like an eternity or fly past in an instant, depending on the nature of the experience. Point out that music, as an art that exists in time, can express the many different ways humans experience time in their lives.

2. As an introduction to music notation (before they read Interlude A), assign students the task of writing a very short musical composition (six to eight notes are enough). Ask them to imagine the pitches (and sing them or use a keyboard to find them, if necessary), how loud or soft, how long or short the notes are, the type of instrument, how fast or slow, and so on. Then ask them to write down their composition *without* using conventional musical notation; they must invent their own notation. When they come back to class, engage them in a discussion about the problems they encountered as they attempted to notate different elements of the music.

3. As a small group alternative to Class Discussion Idea 2, divide your class into five groups, one for each element—pitch, dynamics, tone color, rhythm, and tempo. Play the first eight measures of the first movement of Beethoven's Symphony No. 5, and ask each group to invent notation for their own element. Play the Beethoven piece as many times as needed while each group notates its own element. The pitch group may need the most help; sit down with

them at the keyboard, and show them the notes of the melody. When they have finished, ask each group to present its notation and report on the problems they encountered.

4. *Is music notation important? Why, or why not?* Our "literate" Western tradition relies on notation in many ways, but many cultures never developed even a rudimentary notation system. Clearly the music didn't disappear just because no one wrote it down. These questions can take you into a discussion of the strengths and weaknesses of "written" and "oral" traditions, good preparation for the Global Perspectives and jazz examples you will cover later in the course.

♪ Listening Ideas

1. Listen to musical examples based on asymmetric meters— 5/4, 7/8, or 3+3+2/8, for instance. Possible examples include the 5/4 waltz movement from Tchaikovsky's Symphony No. 6, "America" (in 3+3+2+2+2/8) from Bernstein's *West Side Story* (the musical from Chapter 23), the Bulgarian rhythms from Bartók's Music for Strings, Percussion, and Celesta: IV, the Navajo song "K'adnikini'ya'" (4+7 at the beginning—count the irregular phrase lengths against the steady drumbeat), or the Beatles' "All You Need Is Love" (some measures in 7/4). Count along with each of these examples so that students become accustomed to the skewed regularity and vitality of these examples. See Sound Recordings in the next section for suggested CDs.

2. Listen to music created with equal-tempered scales that divide the octave into thirteen or more equal pitches. Easley Blackwood has written many such works, including a series of études, each based on a different equal-tempered scale. Or try one of Charles Ives's *Three Quarter-Tone Pieces*. These ear-bending works present intriguing possibilities couched in surprisingly accessible musical idioms. See Sound Recordings for suggested CDs.

3. Listen to music created with microtonal scales based on pure intonation (*not* equal-tempered). Harry Partch, one of the best-known advocates of pure intonation, writes of the "lie" of equal temperament in his book *Genesis of a Music*. This book also provides valuable background material on his tuning system and the instruments he built to make his music possible. Many of his works have been recorded. Columbia Records once released several albums of Partch's music, but Partch is currently best represented on the CRI (Composers' Recordings) and Innova (American Composers Forum) labels. Representative works include *Daphne of the Dunes*, *The Bewitched*, *Castor & Pollux*, and *The Delusion of the Fury*. Also of interest are the speech-based works for which he developed a precise microtonal notation system, including *U.S. Highball* and *Barstow: Eight Hitchhiker Inscriptions from a Highway Railing at Barstow, California*. See Multimedia Resources for audio and video recordings.

4. Listen to Global Perspectives examples based on scales that don't fit Western diatonic or chromatic patterns. The following examples work especially well: the Qur'anic chant "Ya Sin," Foday Musa Suso's "Laminba" song, I Lotring's *Bopong*, and the Navajo song "K'adnikini'ya'." In "Ya Sin" we find microtonal inflections; "Laminba" and *Bopong* rely on seven- and five-note scales in non-Western temperaments; and the Navajo song uses only a four-note scale. Play along at the piano to demonstrate how Western equal temperament is often out of tune with scales from other cultures.

Multimedia Resources

❼ Sound Recordings

Bartók, *Concerto for Orchestra—Music for Percussion, Strings, and Celesta*. Chicago Symphony Orchestra. RCA Victor 61504 (CD). Vividly atmospheric, superbly recorded performances of Bartók's music; conducted by Reiner. Try this recording if you use Listening Idea 1.

Beatles, *Magical Mystery Tour*. EMI CDP 7 48062 2 (CD). Includes "All You Need Is Love" and other great Beatles songs. Try this recording if you use Listening Idea 1.

Bernstein, *West Side Story*. Original Broadway Cast Recording. Columbia Legacy SK 60724 (CD). First recording of Bernstein's classic musical; includes "America." Try this recording if you use Listening Idea 1.

Blackwood, *Microtonal Compositions by Easley Blackwood*. Easley Blackwood. Cedille CDR 90000 018 (CD). This CD contains Blackwood's *Twelve Microtonal Etudes for Electronic Music Media*, Op. 28; *Fanfare in 19-note Equal Tuning*, Op. 28a; and *Suite for Guitar in 15-note Equal Tuning*, Op. 33. Try this recording if you use Listening Idea 2.

Ives, *A Continuum Portrait*, Vol. 3. Continuum. Naxos 8559194 (CD). This CD contains Ives's *Three Quarter-Tone Pieces, Five Take-offs, Hallowe'en,* and *Sunrise*. Try this recording if you use Listening Idea 2.

Partch, *Enclosure 6: The Delusion of the Fury*. Innova NV136 (CD). Perhaps Partch's masterpiece, this musical-theatrical work captures the "corporeal" qualities the composer sought. Try this recording if you use Listening Idea 3. Available from www.cdemusic.org.

Partch, *The Harry Partch Collection*, Vol. 2. Gate 5 Ensemble. New World Records 80622 (CD). Collection of instrumental and vocal works in Partch's distinctive microtonal idiom; conducted by the composer. Includes *San Francisco, And on the Seventh Day Petals Fell in Petaluma, The Letter, U.S. Highball,* and *Barstow: Eight Hitchhiker Inscriptions from a Highway Railing at Barstow, California*. Try this recording if you use Listening Idea 3. Available from www.cdemusic.org.

Tchaikovsky, *Symphony No. 6*. Leningrad Philharmonic. Erato 2292-45756-2 AW (CD). Passionate, definitive performance of Tchaikovsky's final symphony; conducted by Mravinsky. Try this recording if you use Listening Idea 1.

❼ Video Recordings

Equal Temperament. Howard Goodall's Big Bangs: Turning Points in Music History Series. www.films.com (DVD or VHS, color, 51 minutes). A fascinating look at the evolution of pitch relationships and temperament.

Following a Score. Understanding Music Series. www.films.com (DVD or VHS, color, 25 minutes). George Fenton and Judith Weir narrate this guided tour through the scores of string quartets by Haydn and Borodin. The video helps students who can't read music learn to identify interesting features in the score.

Notation: The Thin Red Line. Howard Goodall's Big Bangs: Turning Points in Music History Series. www.films.com (DVD or VHS, color, 51 minutes). Entertaining look at the development of music notation.

Partch, *Enclosure 4: Delusion of the Fury*. St. Paul, Minn.: American Composers Forum—Innova 404 (VHS, color, 105 minutes). Madeline Tourtelot's film of Partch's major work for the theater; musical direction by Danlee Mitchell. Also includes a half-hour television special on Partch with excerpts from *Daphne of the Dunes* and *And on the Seventh Day Petals Fell in Petaluma*. Try this video if you use Listening Idea 3. Available at www.cdemusic.org.

The Physics of Music. www.insight-media.com (DVD or VHS, color, 22 minutes). This video explores the nature of musical sounds, looking at frequency (pitch), amplitude (dynamics), and timbre (color) in relation to waveforms.

Rhythm. Exploring the World of Music Series. www.learner.org (VHS, color, 30 minutes). Annenberg/CPB video explores this fundamental element with examples from the United States, Japan, West Africa, and India.

Scales, Synthesizers and Samplers. Science and Music Series. www.films.com (DVD or VHS, color, 26 minutes). Looks at origin of scales in the context of a study of harpsichord, piano, and synthesizer. Emphasis on the relationship between science and music.

Taking Note. Understanding Music Series. www.films.com (DVD or VHS, color, 25 minutes). George Fenton and Judith Weir narrate this look at the history and practice of music notation. Excerpts from a Corelli solo sonata bring out the relationship between notation and improvisation.

20th Century Music for Two Pianos. Joseph and Anthony Paratore. Geneon Entertainment 10524 (DVD). This disc contains works and arrangements for two pianos by Stravinsky, Gershwin, and Ives. Try this recording of Ives's *Three Quarter-Tone Pieces* if you use Listening Idea 2.

♪ Software

Elements of Music. www.ecsmedia.com (CD-ROM—Macintosh or Windows). Entry-level program uses random drills to teach elements of music through the keyboard and music notation.

Explorations: A New Approach to Music Fundamentals, 2nd ed. Boston: McGraw-Hill, 1998. Macintosh software and textbook by Timothy Kolosick provide instruction in writing (notation), reading, and hearing elements of music: pitch, scales, and rhythm. A tone-color dialog box allows you to create your own timbres by experimenting with the number and strength of individual overtones. This package has limited applications in an appreciation class but makes a wonderful resource for students who want to go beyond what the course offers.

Keyboard Note Drill. www.ecsmedia.com (CD-ROM—Macintosh or Windows). This and several other programs from ecsmedia teach elementary keyboard skills. Exercises on the keys of the keyboard, note names, and half and whole steps. Useful if you try Lecture-Demonstration Idea 1.

Music for Musicians and Singers—on CD-ROM. www.films.com (Windows). Tutorials on pitch, note values, scales, chords, tempo, and so on. Useful for musicians or novices.

The Music Kit, 4th ed. CAI version. New York: W.W. Norton, 2001 (Macintosh or Windows). Tom Manoff's software, workbook, and scorebook provide instruction in writing (notation) and reading elements of music: pitch and scales. Aural feedback is provided for many exercises, and sight-singing exercises are new to this edition. This package is most useful for your students who want to learn some music theory on their own.

Sibelius Auralia. www.sibelius.com (Macintosh or Windows). Part of the Sibelius educational suite, this package focuses on the development of aural skills. The sections on interval and scale identification are useful for this chapter, but even more intriguing are the drills where you sing into a microphone and the computer evaluates your intonation, pitch accuracy, and so on.

CHAPTER 3

The Structures of Music

Chapter Outline

Boldface indicates works in the recording set.

Important Terms

melody	consonance	non-imitative polyphony	woodwind instruments
tune	dissonance	tonality	single reed
phrases	resolution	tonal music	double reed
balance	resolved	tonic	brass instruments
parallelism	texture	modality	overblowing
contrast	monophony	modes	percussion instruments
sequence	monophonic texture	major mode	pitched percussion instruments
climax	heterophony	minor mode	unpitched percussion instruments
cadence	homophony	chromatic scale	orchestra
form	homophonic texture	keys	orchestral seating plan
motive	polyphony	modulation	choirs (sections)
theme	polyphonic texture	stringed instruments	keyboard instruments
accompaniments	counterpoint	instrument families	action
chords	contrapuntal writing	sound box	stops
harmonized	imitation	bow	plucked stringed instruments
harmony	imitative polyphony	pizzicato	

(Instructors may add individual instruments from Interlude B.)

Teaching Objectives

❦ Overall Objectives

This chapter will help students acquire familiarity with these basic structures of music:

1. *Melody*—its constituent parts, internal relationships, and uses.

2. *Harmony*—chords, their relationships to each other and to melody, and their varying degrees of tension and resolution.

3. *Texture*—monophony, heterophony, homophony, polyphony, and related concepts.

4. *Tonality and modality*—the concept of tonality and the major and minor scales that support it.

5. *(optional)* Western musical instruments and the modern Western orchestra.

❦ Listening Objectives

After completing this chapter, students should be able to:

1. Listen for phrase relationships and motives within a melody and describe the character of a melody.

2. Develop sensitivity to degrees of tension and resolution created by harmony.

3. Distinguish between monophonic, heterophonic, homophonic, and polyphonic textures and recognize imitation.

4. Listen more attentively for tonal centers and major and minor mode, as well as distinguish between final and weak cadences.

5. *(optional)* Identify instrument families and listen more carefully for the sound of specific instruments.

Lecture Suggestions

♪ Melody

The concept of melody is virtually universal. Begin with a few general comments about the nature of melody, a structure that combines pitch and rhythm, and its traditional role as the primary bearer of musical meaning. Include the authors' definition: a coherent succession of pitches. The textbook introduces other terms that relate to melody, though some of them describe Global Perspectives examples less well than they do Western music. Nonetheless, it remains important to include world music excerpts to help students clarify and deepen their understanding of Western concepts. Wherever possible, Global Perspectives examples from the *Listen* recordings and the *Listen* DVD are listed in this chapter.

Make sure students understand the following terms before you proceed any further.

Tune—a simple, easily singable melody that is coherent and complete

Phrase—a section of a melody or a tune, often two, four, or eight measures long

Cadence—a stopping or pausing place at the end of a phrase, section, or complete work

Motive—a short fragment of melody or rhythm used to construct a long section or work

Theme—the basic subject matter of a piece of music; can be a phrase, motive, or tune

These terms can be introduced in lecture format or phenomenologically—as you play through and identify the features of a specific piece of music. Use simple melodies as examples. "The Star-Spangled Banner" follows up on the textbook's discussion of tunes, but folk songs such as "On Top of Old Smoky" work equally well.

The authors provide a masterly contextual discussion of the preceding terms (as well as parallelism, contrast, sequence, and climax) in their Listening Exercise on Gershwin's "Who Cares?" on textbook page 27. Follow this with similar in-class discussion of other melodies. Comparison of several examples helps heighten awareness of aspects of melody. As students listen to different excerpts, ask them to write notes on the elements they perceive (review Chapters 1 and 2) and on the character of each melody. You can use any of the following excerpts. See Appendix III for more possibilities.

Melody	Hildegard, "Columba aspexit," or Anonymous, "In paradisum"
	Beethoven, Symphony No. 5 in C Minor, I (track 5)
	Tchaikovsky, *Romeo and Juliet* (track 27, 0:56–2:01)
	Britten, *The Young Person's Guide to the Orchestra* (DVD—Theme, track 20, 0:00–0:19)

Ask students to describe what they heard; then list the different elements and melodic characteristics they mention on the board. Pay special attention to comments that relate to concepts in the textbook's discussion of melody: tune, phrase, balance between phrases, parallelism and contrast, sequence, climax, cadence, and motive. Other questions can generate further discussion: Which melodies best fit the definition of *tune*? Which contain examples of motive? Which contain examples of sequence? In which excerpt are phrases most clearly defined?

Play as many tunes as possible so that your class gets plenty of practice recognizing phrase relationships. At first, have students listen for phrase beginnings and endings. Once they can find these with confidence, ask them to listen for parallelism and contrast, and teach them to use letters of the alphabet to represent these relationships (**a** for phrase 1 and phrases that parallel phrase 1, and **b**, etc., for contrasting phrases). For tunes you plan to spend time with, have students count measures (that is, downbeats—*1*-2-3-4, *2*-2-3-4, *3*-2-3-4, and so on) as they listen to compare phrase lengths. This is also a good place to compare the strengths of different cadences. The following examples are among the clearest tunes in the recorded anthology. Compare these with the tune in Listening Exercise 4.

Tunes	Anonymous, "Kemp's Jig"
	Mozart, *Don Giovanni,* "Là ci darem la mano" (0:00–0:40)
	Mahler, Symphony No. 1, III (track 7, 0:00–0:33)
	Copland, *Appalachian Spring,* Section 5 (0:00–0:36)
	Joplin, "Maple Leaf Rag" (DVD—2:34–end)

This work sharpens memory skills that students will need later to perceive large-scale relationships and musical forms. The time you take here is time well spent.

⁊ Harmony

Harmony, more than any of the other concepts covered in this chapter, belongs primarily to the Western musical tradition. As the Global Perspectives examples make clear, much of the world's music uses monophonic or heterophonic textures. Other traditions employ polyphonic textures, but without concern for the triadic sonorities so typical of Western harmony. In many cases, the very presence of triadic harmonies in music from other lands points to Western influence, as in "Anoku Gonda" and South Africa's *isicathamiya* tradition. Thus, the following section focuses mostly on Western concepts, though Global Perspectives excerpts are suggested where they can illuminate the concept at hand.

Harmony refers to vertical, or simultaneous, relationships between pitches in a musical work. You can easily train students to understand and create the most essential chord in Western harmony—a basic triad. If you taught students to build major scales in Chapter 2, so much the better, but even a passing familiarity with the major scale in *solfège* will suffice. Tell students that triads form the basis for harmony in most Western music—in fact, in most music they know. Draw a keyboard diagram on the board. Using notes of the C major scale, explain that they can build triads by taking any note of the major scale and adding every other scale tone until they have three notes. For instance, if you start with *do*, you will omit *re*, include *mi*, omit *fa*, and include *sol—do-mi-sol* gives you a triad built on scale step one. If you start on scale step two, you end up with *re-fa-la*; scale step three yields *mi-sol-ti*; and so on. Point out these relationships on the board diagram, and use a keyboard instrument to demonstrate the derivation of these triads from the scale.

Next, take a single triad—C major, for instance—and play several different versions of that triad at the keyboard to show students how composers use triads to create chords. Play some versions with E or G in the bass to demonstrate the concept of chord inversion. Play some versions with just three notes and some with as many notes as your fingers can grab to demonstrate the concept of pitch doubling. Play versions in different registers on the keyboard to demonstrate harmony's coloristic possibilities. Finally, play arpeggiated and oom-pah-pah versions to demonstrate how our ears can create harmonic meaning from non-simultaneous pitch information. Make the point that any combination of the pitches C, E, and G can be heard as a C major chord.

Once students become aware that you can build triads on any step of the scale, introduce them to the relative stability and instability of different scale tones—concepts that affect our sense of tonality (see Tonality and Modality later in this chapter). Almost all students know the major scale in *solfège* (thanks to *The Sound of Music*). Remind them of the scale, and point out that the major scale is an *asymmetric* collection of pitches that reinforce *do* as tonic. Play and/or sing the scale up as far as *ti* and stop. Ask them how they feel. Let them hear the entire scale again, this time ending on *do*. Ask them how they feel now. *Ti* is the most unstable scale tone, and it helps to establish *do* as the most stable scale tone. Just as *do* is the most stable note of the scale, the triad built on *do* is the most stable triad. Just as *ti* is the most unstable note of the scale, the chord built on *ti* is the most unstable triad—and the chord built on *sol*, which contains *ti* (*sol-ti-re*), shares much of *ti*'s instability. Play simple major-key chord progressions to demonstrate these concepts—progressions that start on tonic, move to dominant or leading tone triads, and resolve to tonic. For instance:

$$\text{I–IV–vii}^{\circ 6}\text{–I} \quad \text{or} \quad \text{I–ii}^{6}\text{–V–I} \quad \text{or} \quad \text{I–vi–IV–V–I}$$

Help students to understand that the same principles of tension and release that color melodic motion affect chord progression. Tension and release can be further heightened by adding notes that do not belong to the basic chord, notes that create a sense of dissonance—of not belonging.

Consonance and Dissonance

Two important concepts associated with Western harmony (and texture as well) are consonance and dissonance. Dissonant sounds create tension, a need to resolve; consonant sounds seem at rest, resolving previous tensions. These concepts depend on context, of course. Play a few examples at the keyboard. The famous chord from Schoenberg's *Farben* (Five Pieces for Orchestra, Op. 16, III)—c, g♯, b, e¹, a¹—might sound dissonant in a progression containing diatonic triads, but it would sound consonant after a few tone clusters made of half steps. The following excerpts contain examples of consonance, dissonance, and resolution. See Appendix III for more examples.

Consonance	Palestrina, *Pope Marcellus* Mass, "Qui tollis" from the *Gloria*
	Chopin, Nocturne in F-sharp, Op. 15, No. 2 (0:00–0:26)
	Copland, *Appalachian Spring*, Section 5 (0:00–0:36)

Dissonance	Japanese *kabuki* play, *Dojoji* (*noh* flute passages)
	Bach, Orchestral Suite No. 3 in D, Air (2:51–3:10)
	Stravinsky, *The Rite of Spring*, Part I—"Dance of the Adolescents" (track 23, 0:00–0:33)
	Britten, *The Young Person's Guide to the Orchestra* (DVD—Variation 10, track 23, 0:00–0:51)
Resolution	Bach, *Brandenburg* Concerto No. 5, I (track 2, 1:29–end)
	Beethoven, Symphony No. 5 in C Minor, II (track 14, 1:02–1:41)
	Chopin, Nocturne in F-sharp, Op. 15, No. 2 (1:27–2:28)

❦ Texture

Melody looks at horizontal successions of pitches—musical lines. Texture looks at the vertical, simultaneous relationships. We are forced to consider not only a melody but all other lines and figures that accompany or exist alongside a melody. As with melody, texture is a universal phenomenon. Different cultures may understand relationships within a texture differently, but the terms introduced here provide useful frames of reference for the discussion of texture. Between Western and Global Perspectives examples, each texture type is well represented in the *Listen* anthology.

To get students used to listening past the melody, it helps to start with a theme and variations movement based on a familiar melody. The more familiar the tune, the easier it is to ignore the melody and focus on the background. The Listening Exercise 5 excerpt from Beethoven's Symphony No. 9 (textbook page 31) provides an ideal example for use as an assignment or in class. Many of your students will immediately recognize the tune, whether or not they know it as the "Ode to Joy" theme. Take the theme and its variations one at a time. For each variation, ask students to identify the instrument or instruments playing the melody and to describe everything happening "behind" the melody. Use the authors' discussion as a frame of reference, but go into more detail as you parse the texture with your class.

Follow Beethoven's Ninth with another example. The tune of Copland's *Appalachian Spring*, Section 5, is especially familiar. Just as before, play the theme and the variations one at a time, and ask students to identify who plays the melody and what's going on "behind" the melody. Here are some examples of what to look for in the first few variations:

Theme—In the statement of the theme (0:00–0:36), the melody is played by solo clarinet, while flute, piccolo, and harp play long tones on offbeats as accompaniment.

Variation 1—In Variation 1, muted trumpets and, later, horns, flute, and piccolo play long, off-beat tones behind an oboe melody.

Variation 2—The beginning of Variation 2 is more dramatic: String pizzicato, horns, and glockenspiel mix with staccato woodwinds, harp, and piano in jaunty repeating patterns that create an active wall of sound to accompany the melody, played by trombone and violas. The second phrase of Variation 2 states the theme in imitation, first by trombone and violas, then by horns and violins, and finally by cellos and basses in a simplified version.

In the discussion that follows, compile a list of student observations on the board. At the end, point out the importance of texture in establishing the change of mood from one variation to the next. After all, it was not the melody that changed—it was the texture!

Use as many examples as possible as you introduce each texture described by the textbook. In addition to Beethoven's Ninth, the authors give one example of imitative polyphony in the Listening Exercise 5 on textbook page 31, but students need more excerpts to practice listening for texture. When introducing texture, I find it helpful to pose three questions that students can use methodically to determine the texture of the music, now and throughout the course.

1. How many "lines" can you hear?

These "lines" can be melodies or accompanimental figures or chords—whatever they are, it is important to identify all distinct elements in the texture. If the answer to this question is "one," the texture is monophonic—you're done. If the answer is two or more, proceed to question 2. Of course, there is a third option. In some textures two or more instruments may play the same basic notes, but one is more active than the others, adding ornaments or playing more elaborate figures. In that case the texture is heterophonic—you're done.

2. a. Is the foreground/background relationship consistent, or

   b. Are all lines equally interesting?

If one melody stands in the foreground and the other lines support that one melody (as if in the "background"), the texture is homophonic. If the lines are all equally interesting (equally melodic), the texture is polyphonic. In both cases, proceed to question 3.

3. How similar or different are the "lines" when compared with each other?

Both homophonic and polyphonic textures divide into two subcategories. Homophonic textures will be either homorhythmic (chordal) or melody-and-accompaniment textures. Polyphonic textures either use imitation or they do not. This third question helps students to pinpoint the subcategories they have chosen as either homophonic or polyphonic.

For homophonic textures, ask students to define question 3's "similarity" in terms of rhythm. That is, if none of the "lines" demonstrate rhythmic independence from the main melody, the texture is homorhythmic. In contrast, if the melody and other "lines" are rhythmically distinct, the texture is melody and accompaniment.

For polyphonic textures, students can look at melodic contour as well as rhythm when they assess similarity. Where students find little or no similarity between "lines," the texture is non-imitative polyphony. However, where "lines" are clearly identical (or nearly so) in contour and rhythm, the texture can be classified as imitative polyphony. Of course, when imitation is present, the similar "lines" will follow each other successively.

Armed with these questions, your students are ready to play "Name That Texture." The process of wrestling with these questions as they apply these terms to musical examples can be fruitful if you can help them learn from the "wrong" answers. Remember that students perceive the same music you perceive—their perceptions are not wrong, though they can misinterpret one of their perceptions. Ask many questions to clarify what they hear so that you can help them reinterpret. Students will be much more comfortable with melody than with texture, and you want them to have a good experience learning to identify texture.

A particularly good example that combines three different textures (and suggests that texture can change often within a piece of music) is "Glory to God" from Handel's *Messiah*. Write the three main phrases of text—"Glory to God," "and peace on earth," and "good will"—on the board. Ask students to identify the choral textures (ignore instruments for now) associated with each phrase: homophony (homorhythmic) for "Glory to God," monophony for "and peace on earth," and polyphony (imitative) for "good will." This initial example provides immediate comparisons and prepares for further exercises.

Here are possible examples of different textures to supplement the Listening Exercise 5 excerpts. They can be used sequentially or in random order. See Appendix III for more possibilities.

Monophony   Hildegard, "Columba aspexit"

                         Qur'anic recitation, "Ya Sin"

                         Musorgsky, *Pictures at an Exhibition*, "Promenade" (0:00–0:08, 0:17–0:22, 0:26–0:31)

Heterophony   Japanese *gagaku* orchestra, *Etenraku*

                         Japanese kabuki play, *Dojoji* (Parts 2, 3, and 5)

                         Beijing opera, *The Prince Who Changed into a Cat* (0:24–end)

Before you proceed with homophony, explain melody-and-accompaniment and homorhythmic (chordal or chorale-style) textures. Melody-and-accompaniment textures are easiest to identify; homorhythmic textures can be confused with non-imitative polyphony. Point out that even though the bass line or inner voices often have melodic interest, they do not exhibit the rhythmic independence of most polyphonic textures. All voices follow the rhythm of the soprano melody.

Homophony   Inca processional music, "Hanaq pachap kusikuynin"

                         Mozart, Symphony No. 40 in G Minor, K. 550, I (track 16, 0:00–0:24)

                         Chopin, Nocturne in F-sharp, Op. 15, No. 2 (0:00–0:57)

                         Ellington, "Conga Brava" (0:00–0:44)

                         Britten, *The Young Person's Guide to the Orchestra* (DVD—Theme, track 20; Variation 5, track 19, 0:00–0:33)

As you play the following polyphonic excerpts, give special attention to the concept of imitation. A familiar round like "Frère Jacques" helps to convey the concept quickly. Some students will confuse imitation with homophonic texture at first, since their attention is naturally drawn to the familiar melody as it appears in each new voice—the other voices seem to fade into the background. Point out that in homophonic textures the foreground melody generally remains in a single voice, while in imitation the "foreground" melody jumps from one voice to another.

Imitative   Josquin, *Pange lingua* Mass, Kyrie
polyphony   Frescobaldi, Suite: Canzona

                         Berlioz, *Fantastic* Symphony, V—"Witches' Round Dance" (track 5, 0:00–0:27)

                         Bernstein, *West Side Story*, "Cool"—Fugue (1:11–2:25)

                         Britten, *The Young Person's Guide to the Orchestra* (DVD—Fugue, track 25, 0:00–1:54)

Non-imitative polyphony	Pérotin, "Alleluia. Diffusa est gratia" (0:36–2:36)
	Pygmy polyphony, "Elephant-Hunt Song"
	Bach, Cantata No. 4, "Christ lag in Todesbanden," Stanza 3
	Wagner, Prelude to *The Valkyrie* (1:37–2:09, 3:16–4:00)
	Britten, *The Young Person's Guide to the Orchestra* (DVD—Variation 2, track 21, 0:52–1:42; Theme climax, track 25, 1:54–end)

♪ Tonality and Modality

The concept of tonality is also nearly universal. Many world musics do not create the strong harmonic pull toward the tonic so characteristic of Western music (from the "common-practice" era, at least), and musicians from other nations may understand the tonic somewhat differently than Westerners do, but the concept of a tonal center remains a relatively standard feature everywhere. No music from any non-Western tradition corresponds to the notion of atonality practiced by Schoenberg or other Western avant-garde composers of the twentieth century.

Tonality

Introduce tonality by playing two examples, one tonal, the other atonal, such as the following. See Appendix III for additional examples.

Tonal	Bach, *Brandenburg* Concerto No. 5, I—ritornello (track 1, 0:00–0:19)
	LeBrun, Sonata in F, Rondeau
	Beethoven, Symphony No. 5 in C Minor, IV—Theme 1 (track 18, 0:00–0:33)
	Beijing opera, *The Prince Who Changed into a Cat* (0:24–end)
	Reich, *Music for 18 Musicians*
Atonal	Schoenberg, *Pierrot lunaire*, "The Moonfleck"
	Webern, *Five Orchestral Pieces*, Op. 10, No. 4
	Ligeti, *Lux aeterna* (track 12, 0:00–0:39)
	Varèse, *Poème électronique*
	Saariaho, *From the Grammar of Dreams*, I

Ask students to identify the character of each excerpt and to describe what makes these examples different from one another other. They will sense the uneasy, unresolved tension of the atonal example, but this discussion will raise some questions that cannot be easily answered without further explanation. The authors define *tonality* as the "centrality of one note." Put in another way, the tonal center is a musical center of gravity. But how does one hear that center?

Just as you did for the harmony exercise (earlier in this chapter), play an ascending major scale, but stop on *ti*. Follow this with several short melodic ideas, each one ending on a different note of the scale. Ask students which fragments sound most final. They soon start to sense the tension when melodies fail to end on *do* as well as a sense of resolution and completion when melodies return to *do*. For the sake of contrast, play a symmetrical scale, such as a whole-tone scale. It quickly becomes evident that a tonal center is much harder to find when all intervals are the same—in fact, the whole-tone scale sounds much less stable than the major scale.

This is a good time to introduce an exercise in cadences, while students are listening for *do*. The authors speak of the shades of finality that are possible in cadences (see textbook page 26). They also mention final cadences when they offer pointers about hearing major and minor mode, but they do not discuss the differences between *authentic* and *half* cadences—you can either introduce these terms or speak in terms of final-sounding cadences and weak or incomplete cadences. One technique students can use to identify cadences in any excerpt is to hum *do* continuously. Help them to find *do*. When an incomplete cadence comes, *do* will not fit into the chord; when a final cadence comes, *do* will fit. As students listen to an excerpt, you can play *do* periodically at the piano to reinforce the tonic (or even to substitute for humming). Once a phrase is finished, you can play both *do* and the cadence chord for closer comparison. The Navajo song "K'adnikini'ya'" provides an excellent introduction from a purely melodic standpoint. Every phrase except the final one ends on scale step two—all cadences are half cadences except the final one!

Select a variety of musical examples that present authentic and half cadences, such as these. For more suggestions, see Appendix III.

Half cadence	Vivaldi, Violin Concerto in G, *La stravaganza,* II (0:00–0:19)
	Mozart, Piano Concerto in A, K. 488, I (track 37, 0:00–0:15, 0:56–1:11)
	Schubert, String Quartet in A Minor (DVD—0:00–0:20, 0:21–0:45, 1:39–1:55, 1:56–2:05)
	Britten, *The Young Person's Guide to the Orchestra* (DVD—Theme, track 20, 0:00–0:04)
Authentic cadence	Anonymous, "Kemp's Jig" (0:00–0:04, 0:09–0:19)
	Haydn, Symphony No. 95, II (track 25, 0:00–0:26); III (track 30, 0:00–0:09); IV (track 33, 0:00–0:36)
	R. Schumann, *Carnaval,* "Eusebius" (0:00–0:11)
	Schubert, String Quartet in A Minor (DVD—0:47–1:05, 1:04–1:27, 2:06–2:15)
Half and authentic cadences	Handel, *Julius Caesar,* "La giustizia" (0:00–0:15, 1:10–1:46)
	Haydn, Symphony No. 95, II (Theme, track 25)
	Mozart, *Don Giovanni,* "Là ci darem la mano" (0:00–0:17)
	Britten, *The Young Person's Guide to the Orchestra* (DVD—Theme, track 20, 0:00–0:18)

Modality: Major and Minor/Hearing the Major and Minor Modes

Although tonality is a nearly universal phenomenon, the concept of major and minor modes remains a more specifically Western conceit. In fact, musicians from many other nations must wonder why Westerners limit themselves to only two scales! Indian music makes use of at least one hundred scales, with hundreds more theoretically possible. India may be an extreme example, but most traditions that approach melody with the same sophistication the West devotes to harmony commonly use a great variety of scales. Nonetheless, the majority of your students will find two scales enough of a challenge for now.

Listening Exercise 6 on textbook page 36 provides an excellent major/minor example: Schubert's String Quartet in A Minor. The Schubert tune will not be familiar to most students, so save it for later. Introduce your students to the differences between major and minor mode by playing familiar tunes in both the right and the wrong modes. For an intriguing example, try Mahler's Symphony No. 1 from the *Listen* recordings. The Mahler offers a minor mode version of the familiar tune "Frère Jacques." Many students know the tune already, which makes this an ideal in-class exercise. For the benefit of those who don't, take time to teach "Frère Jacques"; unless they really struggle, make them sing it as a round. Then play an excerpt from Mahler's Symphony No. 1, and ask students to compare the round they sang with Mahler's minor-mode version. Follow up with other familiar tunes, playing examples such as "Happy Birthday" or "Twinkle, Twinkle Little Star." Once you finish the tune in major mode, play it again in the parallel minor (same tonic). Ask students to describe the difference in character. If you wish, try the same exercise with a minor mode tune transposed to major, perhaps "Joshua Fit the Battle of Jericho," "We Three Kings," or "Greensleeves." Students will use a variety of adjectives to describe the difference.

A direct comparison of parallel major and minor scales is now in order. Students know the pattern of whole and half steps in the major scale from Chapter 2. Have them help you construct a major scale (on any pitch). Introduce the pattern of whole and half steps for the minor scale and have students help you construct a minor scale on the same pitch as the major scale. Call attention to the differences as you compare steps 3, 6, and 7 in both scales. These notes are all lower in the minor scale, which will account for the darker, less bright quality students may have described previously. Emphasize scale step 3, the note that gives the most characteristic minor or major sound. Refer students to the examples of final cadences in major and minor keys on textbook page 34, and play or sing through these examples.

Conclude this exercise with as many musical excerpts as time permits. This is a good time to work through the Schubert example from Listening Exercise 6 on textbook page 36. Follow that with as many of the following possibilities as you can—preferably in random order. Some of these excerpts come from traditions that do not define scales as "major" or "minor"; they are included to indicate points of similarity between Western and non-Western traditions. If students have trouble with an example, play it at the keyboard in the parallel minor or major mode. Students will hear mode more easily when direct comparison can be made, but push them to identify mode without comparison as much as possible.

Major mode	Navajo song, "K'adnikini'ya'"
	Beethoven, Quartet in F, Op. 135, II (0:00–0:33)
	Copland, *Appalachian Spring*, Section 5 (0:00–0:36)
	Joplin, "Maple Leaf Rag" (DVD)
	Britten, *The Young Person's Guide to the Orchestra* (DVD—Theme for Woodwind choir, track 20, 0:23–0:39; Theme for Brass choir, track 20, 0:45–1:00)
Minor mode	Purcell, *Dido and Aeneas*, "When I am laid in earth" (at 0:57)
	Mozart, Symphony No. 40 in G Minor, K. 550, I (track 16, 0:00–0:24)
	Schubert, "Erlkönig" (0:00–0:54)
	Mahler, Symphony No. 1, III (track 7, 0:00–0:33)
	Britten, *The Young Person's Guide to the Orchestra* (DVD—Theme, track 20, 0:00–0:19)

Major/minor   Frescobaldi, Suite: Passacaglia (1:11–end)

Vivaldi, Violin Concerto in G, *La stravaganza*, II—Variation 6 and Theme (2:03–end)

Haydn, Symphony No. 95, II (Variations 2–3, tracks 27–28); III (Minuet a'–Trio, track 30, 1:39–track 31, 0:26); IV (2nd Rondo–Episode 2, track 35)

Beethoven, Symphony No. 5 in C Minor, III (track 16, 0:00–track 17, 0:32)

Schubert, String Quartet in A Minor (DVD—0:00–1:05)

Modulation

As practiced by Western composers of the "common-practice" era, modulation is a uniquely Western phenomenon. (Since Western composers limit themselves to only two scales, they should be permitted to create variety somehow—it only seems fair.) Some non-Western traditions allow for comparable changes of scale, but most other cultures stay with the same scale throughout a piece. For the first time in this chapter, you will find no Global Perspectives examples in the list of suggestions.

Once students can find tonal centers securely, try a few examples that modulate. In most of the preceding examples, the mode changed, but *do* did not. You must explain that in a modulation, the tonal center will change when the music begins to use notes of a different scale—a new *do* will occur. Alert them to the disorientation they will perceive when the modulation takes place. Start with the Beethoven "Emperor" Concerto excerpt in Listening Exercise 6 on textbook page 36; then follow up with some of these examples.

Modulation   Bach, Orchestral Suite No. 3 in D, "Gavotte" (0:00–0:14)

Mozart, Symphony No. 40 in G Minor, K. 550, I (track 16, 0:00–track 17, 0:11)

Beethoven, Symphony No. 5 in C Minor, II (track 14, 1:02–1:41) and IV (track 18, 0:00–1:11)

Prokofiev, *Alexander Nevsky*, "The Battle on the Ice," second excerpt (0:00–1:07)

Britten, *The Young Person's Guide to the Orchestra* (DVD—Themes for Full Orchestra and Woodwind choir, track 20, 0:00–0:39)

♩ Interlude B: Musical Instruments

Instrument families were introduced in the Lecture Suggestions for Chapter 1 of this manual. Now it is time to move from general to specific. How much detail should you go into? That is up to you and the interest of your class. Nonetheless, it is crucial that students learn to recognize the sound of each instrument. Live demonstration works far better than straight lecture. If possible, invite guest artists to your class for show-and-tell. If not, do it yourself. No matter what your level of expertise, bring any instruments you can make a sound on to class and have fun with them. You can also ask students who play to bring their instruments along. As an alternative, use video recordings of orchestral concerts. Anything that helps students link the image of an instrument with its sound enhances the learning experience. The video excerpt from *The Rite of Spring* on the *Listen* DVD is a helpful example. In addition, make sure to investigate the Instruments of the Orchestra resource on the *Listen* Web site. At the very least, you will want to encourage your students to use this on their own, but you may find it a useful classroom tool as well.

The *Listen* DVD recording of Britten's *The Young Person's Guide to the Orchestra* makes a wonderful resource for this introduction. Included in Chapter 4 as an example of form, this work begs to be used as part of your Chapter 3 presentation. At the very least, use the themes for full orchestra and various instrumental choirs from the work's beginning as well as selected variations that illustrate the sounds of the main instrument families (strings, flutes, single reeds, double reeds, etc.). Don't forget to use Listening Chart 2 as part of your in-class presentation. Of course, you probably don't have time to use the complete work both here *and* in Chapter 4, so now is the time to decide where it fits best into your schedule. Here in Chapter 3 it makes a terrific introduction to individual instruments, but in Chapter 4 it provides a wonderful review of the entire first unit, including instrumental timbres.

How much more of the Britten you use now *also* depends on how you plan to cover specific instruments during the term. Of course, you can always take one or two class hours in the first unit, describe how sounds are produced on each instrument, and play all of the Britten plus short excerpts from the *Listen* anthology (see Appendix III). Still, no rule says you must introduce all instruments here at the beginning of the term. You may want to try a second approach that spreads detailed discussions of specific instruments over the entire term. Violins can be discussed when we first hear them in works by Monteverdi and Purcell in the Early Baroque chapter (7); the piano in the Other Classical Genres chapter (13; Mozart, Piano Concerto in A, K. 488, I); tuba in the Early Romantics chapter (16; Berlioz, *Fantastic* Symphony, V); and so on. The second approach offers a welcome change of pace when class meetings run two hours or more, as is often the case for summer courses, courses that meet once a week, or concentrated courses that last only three or four weeks.

Whichever approach you use, emphasize the concepts underlying sound production on each instrument and let them listen (and watch)! For strings and brass, explain how sounds are produced and modified on at least one instrument in each family; concepts remain the same for other members of the family. For woodwinds, explain how sounds are produced and modified in the flute, single-reed, and double-reed families. For percussion instruments, take your class to the rehearsal room where percussion instruments are kept at your school, if possible; be sure to demonstrate (or have a percussionist demonstrate) different sticks and mallets as well as the instruments themselves.

You may notice that Interlude B does not list or describe instruments from the Global Perspectives curriculum. The authors of the textbook mention these instruments only to recommend that you take the second approach previously suggested. If that was your preference anyway, you're covered. However, if you opt for the first approach suggested, you will most likely want to introduce Western and non-Western instruments side by side. Since the textbook doesn't identify any Global Perspectives instruments in Unit I, I have provided here a more-or-less complete list of the non-Western instruments heard in the *Listen* recordings. It roughly follows Geneviève Dournon's adaptation of the standard Hornbostel-Sachs instrument classification system.[1] Use this list to find recordings of non-Western instruments for comparison with Western ones. To find listening examples for Western instruments, consult Appendix III, an

---

[1]Geneviève Dournon, "Organology," from Helen Myers, ed., *Ethnomusicology: An Introduction* (The Norton/Grove Handbooks in Music). New York: W. W. Norton, 1992, pp. 245–300.

alphabetical index that contains most instruments from Interlude B with a list of recorded *Listen* examples for every entry. Between Appendix III and the following list, you can find listening examples for any instruments featured in the *Listen* set. See Multimedia Resources at the end of the chapter for useful audio and video recordings and CD-ROM packages to supplement your presentation.

Idiophones

Concussion	*pan* (wooden clapper)—Beijing opera, *The Prince Who Changed into a Cat*
	po (brass cymbals)—Beijing opera, *The Prince Who Changed into a Cat*
	two sticks—Pygmy polyphony, "Elephant-Hunt Song"
Struck, solid body (metallophones)	*gangsa jongkok* (5 keys)—I Lotring, *Bopong*
	single-octave *gendèr* (5 keys)—I Lotring, *Bopong*
	gendèr barangan (13 keys)—I Lotring, *Bopong*
	gendèr gedé (13 keys)—I Lotring, *Bopong*
Struck, hollow body	*hsiao-lo* (small brass gong)—Beijing opera, The Prince Who Changed into a Cat
	kelenang (small bronze gong)—I Lotring, *Bopong*
	kemong (small bronze gong)—I Lotring, *Bopong*
	kempur (small bronze gong)—I Lotring, *Bopong*
	ta-lo (large brass gong)—Beijing opera, *The Prince Who Changed into a Cat*

Membranophones

Percussion (struck)	*bata* (two-headed conical drums)—Drums of Benin, "Ako"
	drum (small two-headed drum)—Navajo song, "K'adnikini'ya'"
	kakko (small two-headed drum)—Japanese *gagaku* orchestra, *Etenraku*
	kendang (two-headed drum)—I Lotring, *Bopong*
	kotsuzumi (hourglass tension drum)—Japanese kabuki play, *Dojoji*
	otsuzumi (hourglass tension drum)—Japanese kabuki play, *Dojoji*
	taiko (shallow two-headed drum)—Japanese kabuki play, *Dojoji*
	tsuridaiko (large two-headed drum)—Japanese *gagaku* orchestra, *Etenraku*

Chordophones

Zithers	*gakuso* (13 strings)—Japanese *gagaku* orchestra, *Etenraku*
Lutes	*biwa* (4 strings)—Japanese *gagaku* orchestra, *Etenraku*
	shamisen (3 strings)—Japanese kabuki play, *Dojoji*
Harp lutes	*kora* (21 strings)—Foday Musa Suso, "Laminba"
	yueqin (4 strings)—Beijing opera, *The Prince Who Changed into a Cat*
Fiddles	*erhu* (2 strings)—Beijing opera, *The Prince Who Changed into a Cat*
	jinghu (2 strings)—Beijing opera, *The Prince Who Changed into a Cat*

Aerophones

Flutes, end blown	*suling gambuh* (6-hole bamboo flute)—I Lotring, *Bopong*
Flutes, side blown	*noh* (7-hole bamboo flute)—Japanese kabuki play, *Dojoji*
	ryuteki (7-hole bamboo flute)—Japanese *gagaku* orchestra, *Etenraku*
Reeds, free	*sho* (17-pipe mouth organ)—Japanese *gagaku* orchestra, *Etenraku*
Reeds, double	*hichiriki* (9-hole bamboo oboe)—Japanese *gagaku* orchestra, *Etenraku*

Additional Teaching Suggestions

✻ Lecture-Demonstration Ideas

1. Return to the keyboard lab for work on major and minor scales and melodic cadences. Five minutes at the keyboard comparing scale step 3 in parallel major and minor scales will be more useful than an hour-long lecture. For work on cadences, play a few short phrases in the same key, each ending on different scale steps. Ask students to compare these and determine which one sounds most final.

2. Bring a harpsichord to class (or vice versa). Discuss the differences between construction of the harpsichord and of the piano. Point out the limitations of the harpsichord with respect to dynamics.

3. Invite performing musicians to demonstrate their instruments for the class. Have your guests come all at once, or spread them out over the term. In addition to helping students understand the mechanism and sound of an instrument, this experience provides an opportunity to learn about the life and interests of a musician.

4. Help your students learn to listen for other features of melody. Select examples that consider a melody's range (wide or narrow?), contour (arch shaped or other?), motion (smooth or disjunct?), phrase lengths (regular or irregular?), phrase relationships (repetition, contrast, motives, and so on), and continuity (clear cadences or continuous motion?). This exercise can increase sensitivity to many important aspects of melody.

5. For an outside assignment, have students construct simple musical instruments using only objects they can find at home. If you wish, limit the amount they can spend (or discourage spending money altogether). Be sure to establish some guidelines; for instance, instruments should produce more than one pitch, they should be durable enough to last through an extended performance, and students should be able to play their own instruments. Once the instruments are finished, you can use them in many ways. In class, have each student play and describe the construction of his or her instrument; then ask the class to determine which family it belongs to (use families from Interlude B or the Hornbostel-Sachs classification system, described in Listening Idea 6).

Or divide the class into group, and have them compose ensemble pieces for their instruments (no notation required). When each group performs its piece for the rest of the class, ask the students to identify features of its melody, harmony, texture, and tonality (if present). For helpful resources, consult Sound Recordings in the next section or a recent book by Bart Hopkin, *Making Simple Musical Instruments: A Melodious Collection of Strings, Winds, Drums and More* (Lark Publishing, n.d.).

6. If your department has a computer lab equipped with either *GarageBand* (Macintosh) or *Acid* (Windows), let your students experiment for themselves with the different structures you introduce in Chapter 3, including melody, harmony, texture, and instrumental colors. These loop (ostinato)-based programs make it super easy (and a lot of fun) to create short compositions without much training. All you need is a ten-minute tutorial, and they'll be off and running!

℣ Class Discussion Ideas

1. *Which melodies do you like best*? After playing a number of melodies, ask students to pick out the tunes they liked and to explain what elements they liked best. This forces students to define their preferences and think critically about them.

2. *Which is most important in establishing the mood of a piece of music: melody, harmony, texture, or key and mode?* Prepare one or two pieces that you can play in several versions so that you can demonstrate the effect of melody or accompaniment alone and of changes in melody, texture, or key and mode.

℣ Listening Ideas

1. Invite students to bring recordings of their favorite tunes to class. In most cases, these tunes will work well as vehicles to reinforce new terminology and concepts related to melody, harmony, texture, and tonality. This exercise again makes the point that concepts from *Listen* apply to all styles of music, not just to the "classical" or "world music" examples from the textbook.

2. To review elements of music, prepare a series of short musical excerpts, divide the class into competing teams, and play a listening game. Here are two possibilities: (1) devise an "Elements of Music Olympics" with six listening events; or (2) use a Trivial Pursuit board and redesignate the categories to match the authors' six elements of music. Students compete by hearing and identifying different aspects of melody, dynamics, texture, tone color (including instruments), scales (tonality/harmony), and rhythm. Offer prizes for the winners if you like.

3. As an assignment, have students listen to a piece of music they really like—any piece at all. They should prepare a short verbal report that describes the elements of music they hear in this piece and bring the recording to class. Spend time in class listening to the music and sharing the reports. This works well as an individual assignment or as a group project—in fact, with fewer of them, group presentations take less time.

4. Arrange with your school's band or orchestra department to allow students to attend a band or orchestra rehearsal. The main purpose is to make them listen to sounds of different instruments, but they will learn a great deal about music making in large ensembles as they follow the rehearsal. Encourage them to satisfy their curiosity by asking questions of musicians and the conductor after the rehearsal or during breaks. Have students write a one-page report describing their experience and the instruments they heard.

5. Use recordings and other multimedia resources to explore the sounds of instruments with your students. Some CD-ROM packages (see Software), suggestions in Further Listening Examples for Ravel's *Boléro*, and Garrison Keillor's lighthearted *Young Lutheran's Guide to the Orchestra* (see Sound Recordings) all provide good exposure to Western orchestral instruments. Be sure to check Video Recordings for video resources on instruments.

6. Introduce your students to the Hornbostel-Sachs instrument classification system.[2] The families described in Interlude B of the textbook work well enough for Western instruments, but the Hornbostel-Sachs successfully accommodates most instruments from around the world. Once students have a sense of the main categories, play examples and ask students to classify them. Use Appendix III and the list of Global Perspectives instruments that ends Interlude B above to help you find examples from the *Listen* recordings. This exercise helps students hear the differences between various materials and sound-production techniques, precisely the tools they need to distinguish the sounds of different instruments. See Sound Recordings for useful CDs from outside sources, especially *Instruments de Musique du Monde*.

♪ Further Listening Examples

RAVEL *Boléro*

If you have time to move beyond simply introducing instruments and their sounds, consider using Maurice Ravel's *Boléro* (c. 15 minutes) to present the concepts of orchestration, the art and craft of combining instruments effectively, and the use of instrumental weight in the orchestral ensemble. The shape of this work is one long *crescendo*, and Ravel demonstrates a shrewd grasp of the loudness and weight of each instrument as he gradually builds intensity. In fact, Ravel's *crescendo* is created more by changes in orchestration than by changes in dynamics. You can copy the following chart onto the board for use as a reference while the music plays.

A^1	flute
A^2	clarinet
B^1	bassoon
B^2	E-flat clarinet
A^3	oboe d'amore
A^4	flute and muted trumpet

---

[2]If you are unfamiliar with this system, consult "Instruments, classification of," an article in the *New Grove Dictionary of Music and Musicians* (by Klaus Wachsmann et al.). The authors outline the system, and the appendix supplies Erich Hornbostel's and Curt Sachs's own introduction as well.

B^3	tenor saxophone
B^4	sopranino saxophone
A^5	piccolos, French horn, and celesta
A^6	oboe, oboe d'amore, English horn, and clarinets
B^5	trombone
B^6	piccolo, flutes, oboes, English horn, clarinets, tenor saxophone
A^7	piccolo, flutes, oboes, clarinets, violin 1
A^8	piccolo, flutes, oboes, English horn, clarinets, tenor saxophone, violins 1 and 2
B^7	piccolo, flutes, oboes, English horn, trumpet, violins 1 and 2
B^8	piccolo, flutes, oboes, English horn, clarinets, trombone, sopranino saxophone, violins 1 and 2, violas, cellos
A^9	piccolo, flutes, 4 trumpets, sopranino saxophone, tenor saxophone, violin 1
B^9	piccolo, flutes, 4 trumpets, trombone, sopranino saxophone, tenor saxophone, violin 1
Coda	*tutti*

Multimedia Resources

♪ Sound Recordings

Gravikords, Whirlies & Pyrophones: Experimental Musical Instruments. Ellipsis Arts (Book/CD). This unusual recording features works for newly created musical instruments. Excerpts range from Harry Partch to Clara Rockmore to Robert Moog. This makes an interesting supplement to Lecture-Demonstration Idea 5.

Instruments de Musique du Monde [Musical Instruments of the World]. Le Chant du Monde LDX 274 675 (CD). Single-disc collection of thirty-six instruments from around the world, including chordophones, membranophones, aerophones, and idiophones. No excerpt is shorter than 1:25. The excellent accompanying 120-page booklet contains eighty-eight photographs and detailed notes in English and French. Highly recommended if you use Listening Idea 6. Available at www.worldmusicstore.com.

Keillor, *Lake Wobegon Loyalty Days.* Garrison Keillor and the Minnesota Orchestra. Virgin Classics 07777 59583-2 (CD). This recording contains Keillor's *The Young Lutheran's Guide to the Orchestra.* The music isn't much to rave about, but Keillor's comments are lots of fun. Keillor fans should consider using this recording as part of an introduction to instruments of the orchestra. Try this recording if you use Listening Idea 5.

Let's Make Music: An Interactive Musical Trip around the World. Hal Leonard 815057 (Book/CD). Designed for K–6, this book/CD set is full of multicultural songs and activities. Of particular interest here, it provides instructions for creating musical instruments, including a Nigerian *shekere*, Mexican *maracas*, an Indian wood scraper, a Sioux frame drum, and so on, from recycled materials. If you use Lecture-Demonstration Idea 5, try this resource for some ideas.

Ravel, *Boléro*. Orchestre symphonique de Montréal. Decca 289 460 214-2 (CD). Brilliant recordings of works by Ravel in an inexpensive Double Decca release; conducted by Dutoit. Try this recording if you use suggestions for Ravel's *Boléro* in Further Listening Examples.

♪ Video Recordings

Bernstein in Paris—The Ravel Concerts. Kultur (DVD, color). This excellent video includes performances of several famous Ravel works by the National Orchestra of France; conducted by Leonard Bernstein. Try this recording if you use suggestions for *Bolero* in Further Listening Examples.

The Boléro. www.pyramidmedia.com (DVD or VHS, color, 26 minutes). Academy Award–winning video follows Zubin Mehta and the Los Angeles Philharmonic through rehearsals and a performance of Ravel's *Boléro*. Useful if you try suggestions for this work in Further Listening Examples.

Delaware Music Series (NEH Videodisc Project). Newark, Del.: Office of Computer-Based Instruction, University of Delaware (DVD, color). This invaluable video series contains demonstrations of both modern and eighteenth-century orchestral and keyboard instruments. It also includes video recordings of standard repertory. A superb resource for lecture-demonstrations on instruments and sound production.

The History of Musical Instruments Series. www.films.com. *The Clarinet, The Saxophone, The Harp, The Trumpet, Percussion Instruments, The Flute, The Piano, The Oboe, The Violin, The Guitar, Bass Instruments, The Synthesizer, The Organ* (DVD or VHS, color, 28 minutes each). This thirteen-part series introduces various instruments and their origins, history, and construction.

Keyboard Instruments. www.insight-media.com (VHS, color, 37 minutes). An introduction to primary keyboard instruments and the composers and music associated with them. Covers the psaltery, dulcimer, harpsichord, clavichord, piano, and electronic keyboards.

Melody. www.learner.org (VHS, color, 30 minutes). Annenberg/CPB video explores this fundamental element with examples from the Western classical tradition, Arabic *maqam* tradition, and Indian *raga*.

Music. www.films.com (DVD or VHS, color, 23 minutes). New video looks at the nature of and interactions between instruments, performers, music itself, and the perceptions of the listener. Especially interesting insights into human perception as well as the relation between musical instruments and musical style.

Orchestra! Series. www.films.com. *Introduction to the Orchestra, Upper Strings, Woodwinds, Lower Strings, Brass, Percussion, Piano, The Art of Conducting, The Maestro* (DVD or VHS, 28 minutes each). In this nine-part series, host Dudley Moore and conductor Sir Georg Solti look at each section of the orchestra while they work through orchestral literature in chronological sequence.

The Quiver of Life. The Music of Man Series. Home Vision (VHS, color, 60 minutes). Host Yehudi Menuhin examines the human impulse to make music from prehistoric times to ancient Greece and in cultures around the world. An introduction to music and instruments of the world with an impassioned argument for the importance of music in human experience.

Science and Music Series. www.films.com (DVD or VHS, color). This intriguing series investigates the relation between science and music. Especially useful for Chapter 3 are *The Essence of an Instrument* (60 minutes); *Science, Strings and Symphonies* (26 minutes); *Technology, Trumpets and Tunes* (26 minutes); and *Scales, Synthesizers and Samplers* (26 minutes).

Timbre: The Color of Music. www.learner.org (DVD or VHS, color, 30 minutes). Annenberg/CPB video explores tone color with examples from the United States, Japan, India, Indonesia, and West Africa.

Understanding Music Series. www.films.com (DVD or VHS, color, 25 minutes each). George Fenton and Judith Weir narrate this look at topics ranging from scales and modulation to harmonization, notation, and orchestration to the art of the composer and chamber musician. Especially useful for Chapter 3 are *A Change of Key, Composing,* and *Ensembles in Performance.*

❦ Software

GarageBand www.apple.com (Macintosh) or *Acid* www.acidplanet.com (Windows). These programs make it really easy (and a lot of fun) to create compositions by dragging ready-made loops (ostinatos) onto a sequencer-like screen. Some loops are MIDI-based, while others use digital audio samples. Users can add or subtract instruments freely and even edit the ostinatos to create more interesting patterns. Try this if you use Lecture-Demonstration Idea 6.

Instruments of the Symphony Orchestra. www.mccormicksnet.com (CD-ROM—Macintosh or Windows). Multimedia guide introduces Western instruments one at a time with demonstrations.

Musical Instruments of the Symphony Orchestra. Future Vision (CD-ROM—Windows). Inexpensive guide to orchestral instruments of music. Geared toward nonmusicians. Available at www.cdaccess.com.

Sibelius Compass. www.sibelius.com (Macintosh or Windows). Part of the Sibelius educational suite, this package provides tools for beginning composers. The "Theory and Practice" module helps users learn about basic materials of composition. Reminiscent of Subotnick's *Making Music* series, the "Tracker" module includes an intuitive sequencer interface that makes it easy to cut and paste basic materials to create melodies, inversions, canons, ostinatos, different textures, and so on. Try this if you use Lecture-Demonstration Idea 4.

Sibelius Instruments. www.sibelius.com (Macintosh or Windows). Part of the Sibelius educational suite, this interactive encyclopedia of instruments can be very useful in demonstrating features and sounds of individual instruments as well as various musical ensembles, such as the Late Romantic orchestra. Try this if you use Lecture-Demonstration Idea 4.

CHAPTER 4

Musical Form
and Musical Style

Chapter Outline

Boldface indicates works in the recording set.

Important Terms

form	repetition	transition	fugue
memory	contrast	genre	**ABA′** form
outer form	return	style	
inner form	variation	lifestyle	
nesting	introduction	variation form	

Teaching Objectives

⁊ Overall Objectives

This chapter will help students acquire familiarity with:

1. Elements of form (dynamics, tone color, rhythm, melody, harmony, texture, and tonality) and the principles of repetition, contrast, return, and variation that guide their use.

2. The role of memory and anticipation in the perception of musical form.

3. The concepts of "outer form," "inner form," and genre.

4. Musical style and its relation to lifestyle and culture.

❼ Listening Objectives

After completing this chapter, students should be able to listen for:

1. Repetition, contrast, return, and variation.

2. Distinctive elements in musical styles.

Lecture Suggestions

Many concepts introduced in the previous two chapters come out of Western musical traditions. This chapter also introduces some specifically Western constructs, notably its forms and genres, but that is not the main focus here. Instead, this chapter deals with concepts that apply to any music—repetition, contrast, return, and variation. No matter what form, no matter what genre, style, or culture, these phenomena provide the information needed to talk about any type of musical structure.

This chapter could serve equally well as the first chapter of Unit II; it introduces significant concepts that are fleshed out in Units II through V. At the same time, the fundamental concepts of form and style require perception of the elements and structures introduced in Chapters 1 through 3. The experience of listening for form and style can help students summarize previously acquired skills within a meaningful context. As with any chapter in this textbook, understanding results from careful listening. Several listening examples follow that help prepare students to listen for repetition, contrast, and variation as well as for distinctive elements in different musical styles.

❼ Form in Music

The Role of Memory

Form cannot be heard independently. Our sense of form emerges from our perception of a combination of other musical elements and structures. As a result, form is not as easy to hear as the concepts in previous chapters. Two items are needed for successful perception of musical form. First, to perceive the significant changes that define sections in music, students must possess conscious awareness of the elements and structures of music. Second, to perceive relationships between these sections, students must cultivate a memory for musical ideas. The textbook does not emphasize the role of memory as strongly as it might, but students need to understand the importance of a sharpened memory for musical ideas.

Students can develop memory by listening for sections and their relationships. Start with four examples that demonstrate, respectively, the principles of repetition, contrast, variation, and contrast and return. Discuss the differences between these four principles, and show students how to diagram each one. Repetition (**a a**) and contrast (**a b**) are straightforward enough, but take time to clarify variation and return. Variation (**a a′**), or varied repetition, combines both repetition and contrast—simultaneously! The variation must resemble the theme closely enough to be recognized as the theme, but something must also be changed, or varied. Return (**a b a**) is repetition *after* contrast. Ordinary repetition can never be return since the music never went anywhere else. A simple analogy—when you go walking, you can't return home (**a**) without going away (**b**) first. If you just walk around the house, you can't return home.

After playing and talking through one example of each, play other excerpts in random order. Ask students to describe what they have heard and to identify which principle is at work. The following lists offer many possible excerpts. You will not have time for all of them, so feel free to pick and choose. It is a good idea to begin with shorter excerpts and gradually move to longer ones. You can work on one list at a time or mix up your examples by skipping from list to list. These preliminary exercises provide excellent preparation for the works in Listening Exercise 7 on textbook page 50.

Repetition	Frescobaldi, Suite: Balletto (0:00–0:16); Corrente (0:00–0:20)
	Mozart, *Don Giovanni,* "Là ci darem la mano" (0:00–0:40)
	R. Schumann, *Dichterliebe,* Op. 48, "Im wunderschönen Monat Mai" (0:15–1:32)
	Ellington, *Conga Brava* (0:00–0:44)
Contrast	Mozart, Symphony No. 40 in G Minor, K. 550, I (track 16)
	Wagner, Prelude to *The Valkyrie* (1:24–2:33)
	Bernstein, *West Side Story,* "Cha-Cha" and Meeting scene (track 27)
	Joplin, "Maple Leaf Rag" (DVD—0:00–1:06)
Variation	Anonymous, Galliard, "Daphne"
	Chopin, Nocturne in F-sharp, Op. 15, No. 2 (0:00–0:57)
	Parker and Davis, *Out of Nowhere* (0:00–1:34)
	Beethoven, Symphony No. 9, IV (DVD—0:00–1:35)
Contrast and return	Bach, *Brandenburg* Concerto No. 5, I (track 1, 0:00–0:50)
	LeBrun, Sonata in F, Rondeau (0:00–0:50, 0:50–1:42, or entire movement)
	R. Schumann, *Carnaval,* Op. 9, "Eusebius" (0:00–0:52)
	Prokofiev, *Alexander Nevsky,* "The Battle on the Ice," second excerpt (0:00–1:07)

Once students have built some skill at identifying repetition, contrast, variation, and contrast and return, turn to Listening Exercise 7 on textbook page 50. You can either work through these two pieces in class or assign them for out-of-class listening. Either way, take some class time to process these works by Schubert and Tchaikovsky. Perhaps the most important point to make concerns the use of varied repetition in these pieces. No rule that says composers must repeat themselves literally in any situation involving repetition or return. In fact, as small as it may seem, this issue begs one of the most crucial questions composers face when they write music. Composers must constantly hold two fundamental yet contradictory principles in tension, rather like the Chinese concept of *yin* and *yang*. These twin laws of musical structure are *unity* and *variety*. A work must hang together, or cohere. Everything must sound as if it belongs. To help guarantee this unity, composers use repetition and return. Yet a work must be interesting, must grab the listener's attention. Music can never succumb to the cardinal sin in any work of art—boredom! To ensure variety, composers use contrast and variation. Make sure students understand that although both are necessary, unity and variety pull in opposite directions. Balancing the two is difficult. Too much unity leads to boredom, too much variety to disintegration and incomprehensibility. No matter what form you choose—sonata, rondo, passacaglia, or binary—each in its own way balances the concerns of unity and variety. These principles form the foundation of *any* musical form.

Back to the issue of varied repetition—on the face of it, this device allows composers to honor both unity and variety simultaneously, but that hardly explains the prevalence of this practice. Varied repetition appears so frequently that it has risen nearly to the level of a musical law, and not just for composers! Even performers learn that making music means you never sing or play a phrase the same way twice, even when observing the composer's repeat signs. Varied repetition (or return) also makes important demands on the listening experience. It is not enough to simply *notice* that a repetition or return is different. The fact of its difference forces us to ask how it is changed—and why. In some cases the variation may be subtle or purely decorative, but in other cases it can force a complete re-evaluation of the *meaning* of a passage (as in the transformation of the "Love Theme" that ends Tchaikovsky's *Romeo and Juliet*). In this sense, varied repetition becomes a significant *expressive* tool, not just a formal device—thus its appeal to composers. And since a musical idea can be varied in countless ways, this humble technique points us toward the infinite expressive possibilities of the musical art.

Inner and Outer Form

Kerman and Tomlinson present this concept nicely with examples drawn from poetry and architecture. You can use short examples for a class demonstration. Any two examples based on the same musical form ("outer form") will work. Explain to the class the principles of the outer form for the specific form you selected. Ask the students to note similarities and differences between the examples as they listen. In the discussion that follows, make a list of similarities and differences noted by the students. Point out that many of the similarities relate to the outer form, whereas the differences are all part of the inner form—the features that give each work its distinctive character and moods. Possible listening excerpts include:

Variation forms   Vivaldi, Violin Concerto in G, *La stravaganza,* II (0:00–1:42)

Haydn, Symphony No. 95, II

Copland, *Appalachian Spring,* Section 5 (0:00–1:42)

Ritornello/Rondo   Bach, *Brandenburg* Concerto No. 5 (track 1, 0:00–track 2, 0:05)

Haydn, Symphony No. 95, IV (track 33, 0:00–track 35, 0:28)

Musorgsky, *Pictures at an Exhibition,* "The Great Gate at Kiev" (0:00–2:13)

Genre

A sharp distinction between form and genre is helpful from the start. Form is the internal structure of a work or movement. *Genre* refers to general categories determined by text, style, function, and performing forces, categories that include symphony, opera, string quartet, Mass, oratorio, concerto, and so on. Various forms and genres are listed on textbook pages 50 and 51; ask students to identify and describe the ones they have heard of. They may not know many, but they can often describe something of the function or performing forces nonetheless.

Begin the following exercise by listing several genres—symphony, opera, solo song, and chant will do. You can use listening examples to generate further discussion of function and performing forces in different genres (style will be covered in the next section). Ask students to write answers to these questions as they listen:

1. What is the function of this music? (public or private entertainment? worship? patriotic? commercial?)

2. What are the performing forces?

As the discussion unfolds, take every appropriate opportunity to sharpen the distinction between form and genre. Some Global Perspectives examples are included in the following list of possible listening examples. Of course, not all of them precisely match the expectations we have for the Western version of each genre, but the overriding similarities suggest that at least some genres possess universal significance.

Symphony	Haydn, Symphony No. 95, I
	Beethoven, Symphony No. 5 in C Minor, Op. 67, I
Opera	Verdi, *Aida,* "Tomb Scene," Act IV, scene ii
	Wagner, *The Valkyrie*
	Beijing opera, *The Prince Who Changed into a Cat*
Solo song	Foday Musa Suso, "Laminba"
	Schubert, "Erlkönig"
Chant	Introit, "In paradisum"
	Qur'anic chant, "Ya Sin"

♪ Musical Style

The *combination* of distinctive, characteristic uses of musical elements and structures constitutes musical style. One can speak of the style of a given composer (I Lotring or Beethoven), of a "school" of musicians with similar esthetic aims (the Second Viennese School or bebop), or of an entire culture, past (Renaissance or Romantic) or present (United States or Japan). Some musicologists have even attempted to define style features for an entire continent, such as Africa.

Students are most familiar with contemporary Western popular styles, as a general rule. You can use this to your advantage. Assign groups of students to bring recordings of two pieces in contrasting styles to class. As part of their preparation, ask them to list distinctive features of each piece. The list should include as many of the elements and structures from Chapters 1 through 3 (pitch, dynamics, tone color, scales, rhythm, tempo, melody, texture, and key and mode) as your students can hear. In class, play and discuss as many pieces as time permits. If different groups bring examples of the same style, so much the better. Students need to listen to a broad sampling of works in a single style to begin to recognize the distinctive and characteristic features in that style. Make the point that one must examine *every* musical element and structure to develop a sense of what *combination* is characteristic and distinctive in any musical style.

If you prefer to have greater control over listening examples used in class, select several examples in two contrasting styles. You can compare the styles of two composers, two schools, or two cultures. Work through the same process—examine each element and structure in each work to determine the characteristics of each style. Possible examples include:

Composers

| *I Lotring* | *Bopong* |
| *Beethoven* | Symphony No. 5 in C Minor, Op. 67 |

Schools

Second Viennese School Schoenberg, *Pierrot lunaire*
Berg, *Wozzeck*

Bebop   Parker and Davis, "Out of Nowhere"

Historical Cultures

Renaissance   Josquin, *Pange lingua* Mass
Josquin, "Mille regrets"
Weelkes, "As Vesta Was from Latmos Hill Descending"
Anonymous, Galliard, "Daphne"

Romantic   R. Schumann, *Dichterliebe* songs
Chopin, Nocturne in F-sharp, Op. 15, No. 2
Berlioz, *Fantastic* Symphony
Wagner, *The Valkyrie*
Tchaikovsky, *Romeo and Juliet*

"Modern" Cultures

United States   Copland, *Appalachian Spring*
Adams, *El Niño*
Bernstein, *West Side Story*

Japan   Japanese *gagaku* orchestra, *Etenraku*
Japanese kabuki play, *Dojoji*

Continents

Africa   Pygmy polyphony, "Elephant-Hunt Song"
Drums of Benin, "Ako"
Linda, "Anoku Gonda"

Asia   Japanese *gagaku* orchestra, *Etenraku*
I Lotring, *Bopong*
Beijing opera, *The Prince Who Changed into a Cat*

The authors' discussion of lifestyle can be incorporated into this class exercise by asking students to describe the lifestyle they associate with each of the musical examples heard in class, whether brought by students or provided by the instructor.

BRITTEN *The Young Person's Guide to the Orchestra*

The obvious place to cover this work was in Chapter 3, but the fact that Kerman and Tomlinson include it here makes an important point. This *Guide* is *not* a one-dimensional work whose value rests solely in its ability to introduce instruments. Like all of Britten's music, it is a carefully crafted, uniquely shaped work that provides a completely satisfying musical experience independent of any didactic purpose. By placing this work in Chapter 4, the authors call attention to its musical form as encapsulated in Britten's own subtitle—"Variations and Fugue on a Theme of Purcell." Here it can also serve as a capstone experience, a summation of all musical elements (not just instruments) covered in this and previous chapters. If you used the Britten excerpts from the Lecture Suggestions for this unit, you and your students already know how richly varied the sections of this work can be.

If you used this work in its entirety to introduce instruments in Chapter 3, you can abbreviate your coverage here. Play some excerpts from the initial theme section and the variations, and follow that with the entire fugue. If you saved the complete Britten for this moment, now is the time to play it through from beginning to end! Display (Interactive) Listening Chart 2, and point out each section as it goes by. If you wish, you can also put the following chart on the board.

Introduction	Woodwinds	Brass	Strings	Percussion
tutti	flutes & piccolo	French horns	violins	timpani
woodwinds	oboes	trumpets	violas	bass drum & cymbal
brass	clarinets	trombone & tuba	cellos	tambourine
strings	bassoons		bass viols	triangle
percussion			harp	snare drum
tutti				chinese block
				xylophone & castanets
				gong
				whip (ensemble)

After all instruments are heard, fugue entrances reintroduce the instruments in the same order, starting with the flutes.

Whether you play excerpts or the entire piece, make the following points in your class discussion of this work.

1. The work consists of three main sections that can be easily distinguished: the theme, a set of thirteen variations, and the closing fugue.

2. The first section introduces the theme played by the full orchestra and by each large group: woodwinds, brass, strings, and percussion. Take a quick look at the motives that make up the theme: the initial rising arpeggio, the ascending/descending scales in m. 2, and the extended arpeggio sequence that ends the theme. Taken by themselves, these theme statements themselves serve as a set of rather traditional variations on the theme, and it is easy to follow the main melody all the way through this section. Referring to various elements of music, point out similarities and differences between these six theme statements. Especially interesting is the percussion theme (track 20, 1:19–1:36). The authors suggest that Britten "cheated" here, but it is fascinating to discover how many ideas from the initial theme find their way into the percussion theme statement. Unity is the underlying principle here.

3. The second section provides a series of thirteen rather unconventional variations. Students who want to find complete statements of the theme here will be disappointed. Instead, Britten bases each variation on a few motives extracted from the theme, particularly the ascending arpeggio from m. 1 and the ascending/descending scale pattern from m. 2. If you wish, point out these motives in a few variations. Nonetheless, the overall emphasis in this section is on contrasts, and often fantastical contrasts at that. Successive variations exhibit often striking differences in mood and character. A discussion of these differences provides another good opportunity to review the elements of music. Variety is the underlying principle here.

4. The third section's fugue zips along at breakneck tempo. You will cover fugue in more detail later, but for now point out that a fugue is based on a single melodic idea that gets passed from instrument to instrument in a busy imitative polyphonic texture. The subject for this fugue derives from the extended sequence pattern that concludes the theme, appropriate for the ending section. This flurry of activity works effectively to bring the piece to an exciting conclusion. Unity is the principle underlying this section's melodic construction, but variety controls its changing contexts.

5. The overall shape moves from the relative stability and unity of the theme statements to the constant uncertainty and variety of the variations. In the final section we want a return to stability, and while the fugue provides excitement and a reliably consistent melody, its very busy-ness works against a feeling of stability. And so Britten satisfies that need by bringing back the complete theme one last time in a grand, majestic, supremely satisfying climax to this long work—a fitting expression of the importance of unity.

Compared to many works we will study in subsequent chapters, the form of Britten's *Young Person's Guide* is unique; it doesn't fit easily into any one particular structural mold. We hear features of variation form, fugal form, and, with the move from stability to instability and back, even ternary form. This is not a sign of weakness but rather points to the flexibility and creativity required of any good composer. But regardless of the form, Britten cannot escape wrestling with the principles of unity and variety. The success or failure of any musical work depends on the composer's ability to creatively navigate between these two extremes. In the chapters that follow, we will find frequent opportunities to test this out.

Additional Teaching Suggestions

♩ Lecture-Demonstration Ideas

1. Introduce students to the six Western style periods covered by the textbook: Middle Ages, Renaissance, Baroque, Classical, Romantic, and the twentieth century. A broad preview of coming attractions can help at this point, both to pique your class's interest and to offer a sense of perspective—an outline to be fleshed out later. You can engage students in a discussion of the vastly different lifestyles associated with each of these eras in history, especially if you refer to recent or classic movies that depict these periods: *Tristan and Isolde* for the Middle Ages, *Farinelli* for the Baroque era, *Amadeus* for the Classical period, *Immortal Beloved* or *Impromptu* for early Romanticism, and *Moulin Rouge* for early twentieth century, for instance.

2. Bring a slide show to class to generate discussion about historical style periods. Your art department can often supply pictures, or check Multimedia Resources at the end of each chapter of this manual for video recordings or CD-ROM packages geared toward the history of art. Students respond positively to images of medieval castles and cathedrals, Renaissance paintings and churches from Venice or Rome, Baroque church organs, the splendor of Versailles, and so on. Many pictures will also permit discussion of inner versus outer form or of the lifestyle of specific periods.

3. Invite a composer to visit your class with his or her own scores and recordings. Composers like to discuss their own "style"—the characteristic ways they use form and the other elements and structures of music. This offers a unique means of reviewing Unit I, and, as you prepare for Unit II, meeting a live composer allows students to view dead composers as real people, too. So that students can understand music history as a living tradition, ask your guest to identify past composers or styles that influenced his or her style. Keep the atmosphere informal, come with lots of questions, and encourage students to ask questions at any time.

4. To prime your students for upcoming Global Perspectives segments, bring a slide show to class to generate discussion about world music—you can call it "Around the World in 100 Days" (or however long your term is). You might be surprised at the number of places you can find pictures at your school. Your library and the departments of art, geography, anthropology, and foreign languages can often offer resources. You can also check Multimedia Resources at the end of each chapter of this manual for video recordings or CD-ROM packages geared toward music of the world. Students respond positively to images of Japan, Bali, India, South Africa, Peru, and so on. Add an extra dimension by playing music from the countries whose images you display.

5. Work through a complete piece with your students to demonstrate the interaction between repetition, contrast, return, and variation in context. The minuet from Mozart's *Eine kleine Nachtmusik* works especially well. Starting with just the first phrase, play through the minuet additively, including a new phrase or two each time. Label the phrases on the board (**a**, **b**, **c**, and so on) as students identify them. Students will find this piece easy to master because its phrases and sections are short, simple, and fairly regular. It also provides good practice diagraming formal relationships.

	MINUET **A** |: a :||: b a′ :|	TRIO **B** |: c :||: d c :|	MINUET **A** a b a′
Length in measures:	8 4 4	8 4 8	8 4 4

At the end, note that the principles of repetition, contrast, and return can be found within each section (**a a b′ b a′**—note also the presence of variation in the minuet's **a′**). Further, the principles of contrast and return define the overall structure of this movement (**A B A**).

❦ Class Discussion Ideas

1. Encourage students to discuss the organizational basis of other arts and disciplines, such as poetry, painting, literature, and architecture. Draw as many parallels as you can to musical form. For example, a textbook is divided into

units (movements?), chapters (large sections), paragraphs (themes and transitions), and sentences (phrases). You might group students according to their majors and assign each group to brainstorm about principles of organization in their own discipline.

2. *Why bother with forms and rigid structures—don't they interfere with the composer's creative freedom?* As the discussion evolves, help students to understand that most forms are not rigid structures—they simply define specific ways of presenting musical materials. Further, even if they do not use specific forms, composers are preoccupied with form. To the extent that composers are concerned about unity and variety, the order of events, or the overall expressive shape of a composition, they are concerned about form.

3. *What words can I use to refer to a musical composition?* Students tend to use words such as *song* and *movement* indiscriminately. Suggest some alternatives: musical *work*, musical *composition*, *piece* of music, and so on. They will learn specific uses for *song* and *movement* later.

4. *How can I understand a lifestyle different from my own?* Ask your students to take three minutes and write about a friend, relative, or acquaintance who comes from a culture different from their own. Ask them to describe any difficulties they had with understanding each other and how they resolved them. Next, divide the class into small groups so that each student can tell his or her story. Ask the groups to look for common themes. Afterward, ask each group to report on two or three common themes from their discussion. For many of your students, music history and modern "classical" music represent foreign cultures—some of them will have an easier time with Global Perspectives! This exercise can start students thinking about the challenges in their upcoming encounters with the "voice of the other."

♪ Listening Ideas

1. Play familiar examples from any of the six Western style periods covered by the textbook: Middle Ages, Renaissance, Baroque, Classical, Romantic, and the twentieth century. This works well as a follow-up to Lecture-Demonstration Idea 1. Choose examples that your students may have heard (from television, movies, and so on), and ask them to guess which style period the music belongs to. It doesn't matter if their answers are right or wrong; try to draw out the reasons for their answers. What did they hear that led them to associate the music with the lifestyle of the Renaissance or the twentieth century? Refer to Sound Recordings for suggested recordings. Possible examples include:

Middle Ages	Anonymous, "In paradisum"
	Pérotin, "Alleluia. Diffusa est gratia"
Renaissance	Palestrina, *Pope Marcellus* Mass
	Weelkes, "As Vesta Was from Latmos Hill Descending"
Baroque	Bach, Toccata and Fugue in D Minor
	Handel, *Messiah*, Hallelujah Chorus
Classical	Mozart, *Eine kleine Nachtmusik*, I
	Beethoven, Symphony No. 5, I

Romantic	Puccini, *La Bohème*
	Tchaikovsky, *1812 Overture*
Twentieth century	Barber, Adagio for Strings
	Stravinsky, *The Rite of Spring*, "Dance of the Adolescents"

2. Create your own listening charts for one or more musical forms! With some knowledge of multimedia tools, such as *Flash* (Windows or Macintosh), *iMovie* (Windows or Macintosh), or *TimeSketch Editor* (Windows or Macintosh), you can create a chart for any musical form you like with any CD or MP3 recordings you have available. Better yet, try Scott Lipscomb's BubbleMachine (www.lipscomb.umn.edu/stuff.htm)—it's easy to use, and it's free! By using identical listening charts for all examples of any given form, students can quickly grasp the outer form. As students compare one work with another, they can readily hear the inner form of each one. If you want ready-made packages, read about the *Anatomy of Music* CD-ROM or the TimeSketch Series under the Software heading. See Appendix IV for more information about computer technology and teaching strategies.

3. Play versions of the same tune performed in different styles. When the tune is the same in each version, students are forced to focus on other elements to draw their conclusions. Refer to Sound Recordings for suggested recordings. Possible examples include:

Passion Chorale

Baroque	Bach, *Christmas Oratorio*, "Wie soll ich dich empfangen" and "Nun seid Ihr wohl gerochen"
	Bach, *St. Matthew Passion*, four chorale settings of Passion Chorale
	Bach, Chorale Prelude, "Herzlich tut mich verlangen"
Twentieth century	Paul Simon, "American Tune"

My Favorite Things

Musical	Rodgers and Hammerstein, "My Favorite Things" from *The Sound of Music*
Jazz	John Coltrane Quartet, *My Favorite Things*

4. Play "Where in the world am I?" with your class. Play examples from non-Western musical styles that students are likely to recognize. Ask them which country each excerpt comes from, and have them guess the function of the music (public or private entertainment? worship? patriotic? commercial?). It doesn't matter if their answers are right or wrong; try to draw out the reasons for their answers. What did they hear that led them to associate the music with one culture or another? Your students may surprise you, though—it is amazing how sounds immediately create a sense of location! Possible examples include:

Middle East	Qur'anic chant, "Ya Sin"
Japan	Japanese kabuki play, *Dojoji*
Bali	I Lotring, *Bopong*
India	Rag *Mauj-Khammaj* (from *Listen*, Fifth Edition)
China	Beijing opera, *The Prince Who Changed into a Cat*

Peru	Simon and Garfunkel, "El Condor Pasa (If I Could)" (from *Bridge over Troubled Water*)
Native America	"K'adnikini'ya'"
Benin	Drums of Benin, "Ako"
South Africa	Linda, "Anoku Gonda," or Ladysmith Black Mambazo and Paul Simon, "Homeless" (from *Graceland*)

Multimedia Resources

♪ Sound Recordings

Bach, *Christmas Oratorio*. English Baroque Soloists and Monteverdi Choir. Deutsche Grammophon Archiv 423-232-2 (CD). A superb performance on period instruments that captures the exhilaration of this festive work; conducted by Gardiner. Outstanding vocal soloists include Anne Sofie von Otter and Anthony Rolfe-Johnson. Try this recording of "Wie soll ich dich empfangen" and "Nun seid Ihr wohl gerochen" if you use Listening Idea 3.

Bach: Complete Toccatas and Fugues. David Schrader. Cedille Records CDR 90000 006 (CD). The first recording to feature all of Bach's toccatas and fugues on one CD; performed on a Jaeckel organ. Try this recording if you use Listening Idea 1. Available from www.cedillerecords.org.

Bach, *Great Organ Works*. Peter Hurford. London 443485-2 (CD). Impressive collection of famous pieces includes Toccata and Fugue in D Minor (BWV 565) and Passacaglia and Fugue in C Minor (BWV 582). Use this recording of the Toccata and Fugue in D Minor or "Herzlich tut mich verlangen" (based on the Passion Chorale) if you try Listening Ideas 1 or 3.

Bach, *St. Matthew Passion*. Bach Collegium Japan. Bis 1000/2 (CD). One of the best period performances available; conducted by Masaaki Suzuki. Suzuki studied with Ton Koopman and in several respects surpasses his teacher's work, especially in sheer beauty of sound. Contains four chorale harmonizations based on the Passion Chorale. Try this recording if you use Listening Idea 3.

Barber, *Adagio for Strings*. Academy of St. Martin in the Fields. Argo 417 818-2 (CD). Deeply felt performance of Barber's best-known work; conducted by Marriner. Also includes works by Ives, Cowell, and Copland. Try this recording if you use Listening Idea 1.

Coltrane, *My Favorite Things*. Atlantic 1361-2 (CD). Includes several of Coltrane's most attractive mode-based improvisations. If you try Listening Idea 3, use this jazz version of the Rodgers and Hammerstein tune "My Favorite Things."

Mozart, *Eine kleine Nachtmusik [The Great Serenades]*. Academy of St. Martin in the Fields. Philips 464 022-2 (CD). Fine performances of Mozart serenades on modern instruments; conducted by Neville Marriner. Includes *Eine kleine Nachtmusik*, K. 525. Try this recording if you use Lecture-Demonstration Idea 5 or Listening Idea 1.

Puccini, *La Bohème*. Philharmonia Orchestra. EMI 5 56120 2 (Enhanced CD). Marvelous recent recording of this Puccini masterwork. Soloists include

Roberto Alagna, Leontina Vaduva, Thomas Hampson, Ruth Ann Swenson, Samuel Ramey, and Simon Keenlyside; conducted by Pappano. Try this recording if you use Listening Idea 1.

Simon, Paul. *Graceland*. Warner Brothers 46430 (Enhanced CD). Landmark 1986 album features collaborations with many South African musicians, including Joseph Shabalala and Ladysmith Black Mambazo. Use this recording if you try Listening Idea 4.

Simon, Paul. *There Goes Rhymin' Simon*. Warner Brothers WB 25589 (CD). Contains "American Tune." Use this contemporary chorale harmonization based on the Passion Chorale if you try Listening Idea 3.

Simon and Garfunkel, *Bridge over Troubled Water*. Columbia Legacy 66004 (CD). Contains "El Condor Pasa (If I Could)." Use this recording if you try Listening Idea 4.

The Sound of Music: 40th Anniversary Special Edition. RCA Victor 8287672556 (CD). Soundtrack recording of the classic Rodgers and Hammerstein musical features Julie Andrews singing "My Favorite Things." Use this recording if you try Listening Idea 3.

Tchaikovsky, *1812 Overture [Tchaikovsky Festival]*. Royal Philharmonic Orchestra. Naxos 8.550500 (CD). A gem from the Naxos catalog. Excellent performances of orchestral showpieces by Tchaikovsky; conducted by Adrian Leaper. Try this recording if you use Listening Idea 1.

Video Recordings

Music and Culture. www.insight-media.com (VHS, color, 40 minutes). This package covers both the four-group instrument classification system used by ethnomusicologists and the cultural uses of instruments in Polynesia, Africa, and Native America. Provides some insights into the relation between lifestyle and musical style.

Music Is Style. www.insight-media.com (DVD or VHS, color, 29 minutes). Murry Sidlin and the National Symphony show how music reflects its era of creation. Special emphasis on Baroque, Classical, Romantic, and twentieth-century styles.

The Nature of Music. Kultur 0074 (VHS, color, 120 minutes). Jeremy Marre's film examines music in many world cultures, including Bali, Brazil, and Arabia. Special emphasis given to interactions between nature, society, and music. Available at www.worldmusicstore.com.

Theory and Practice. Understanding Music Series. www.films.com (DVD or VHS, color, 25 minutes). George Fenton and Judith Weir narrate this look at the relation between theory and composition and between skill and inspiration. Examples are taken from the working manuscripts of composers from two different historical cultures—Handel and Beethoven.

Vibrations and Pagan Rites. Music in Time Series. www.films.com (DVD or VHS, color, 60 minutes). James Galway describes the development of Western music. Looks at music of each style period the authors describe as they demonstrate the "ageless . . . human impulse to make music." Makes the point that knowledge of music history is necessary for appreciation of music. Serves best as an introduction to a historical survey.

¶ Software

Anatomy of Music. tinoteca.com (CD-ROM—Windows). This simple CD-ROM package effectively demonstrates the authors' discussion of outer versus inner form. For each of the forms it covers (including sonata and minuet forms), the author provides several musical examples. Identical listening charts for each example of a form clarify the features of the outer form; multiple examples of each form help students to appreciate inner form.

Beethoven's 5th Symphony. Future Vision (CD-ROM—Macintosh or Windows). A multimedia guide to Beethoven's famous symphony. Features detailed analysis, video clips, primary source readings, and a biography. Try this package if you use Listening Idea 1 above. Available at www.cdaccess.com.

The History of Music. www.mccormicksnet.com (CD-ROM—Macintosh or Windows). The two-disc set covers instruments, styles, and composers from the Middle Ages to the present day.

Making More Music. New York: Voyager/Learn Technologies Interactive (CD-ROM—Macintosh or Windows). A more "adult" version of *Making Music*, this easy-to-use yet surprisingly sophisticated composing software is fun to play with. Best of all for your students, no musical experience is required! Morton Subotnick designed it from the ground up as a tool to encourage musical imagination. Available at www.cdemusic.org.

Music Conservatory. Voyetra Turtle Beach (CD-ROM—Windows). Inexpensive all-in-one guide to the world of music, this package provides an overview of music history, composers, instruments, and music theory. Geared toward nonmusicians. Available at www.cdaccess.com.

Music Terminology. www.ecsmedia.com (CD-ROM—Macintosh or Windows). This simple package can be used as a review of terms studied in Unit I. It includes a glossary of terms and several types of tests and quizzes.

TimeSketch Editor or *TimeSketch Editor Pro.* www.ecsmedia.com (CD-ROM—Macintosh or Windows). Easy-to-use tool allows you to create your own interactive listening charts using audio CD, MP3, MIDI, AIF, or WAV files. The Pro version lets you upload charts to the Internet. Useful for your own presentations or for student assignments on form. Try this package if you use Listening Idea 2.

TimeSketch Series. www.ecsmedia.com (CD-ROM—Macintosh or Windows). Ready-made interactive listening charts provide a wonderful resource as you explore musical form in class. Charts are available for major works by Bach (Toccata and Fugue in D Minor), Beethoven (Symphony No. 5), Berlioz (*Fantastic* Symphony), Brahms, Musorgsky (*Pictures at an Exhibition*), Mozart (Symphony No. 40), Miles Davis, and others. Try this series if you use Listening Idea 1.

CHAPTER 5

The Middle Ages

Chapter Outline

Boldface indicates works in the recording set.

Important Terms

jongleurs	medieval modes	recitation	Preface	sequence	troubadours
plainchant	vihuela	reciting tone	antiphon	drone	trouvères

Minnesingers	estampies	*ars antiqua*	Qur'anic recitation	*mele hula*
alba	organum	*ars nova*	*azan*	*ho'zho'ni* songs
pastourelle	melismas	isorhythm	*muezzin*	vocables
strophic form	motet	hocket	*mele pule*	Enemy Way ceremony

Teaching Objectives

❧ Overall Objectives

This chapter will help students acquire familiarity with:

1. Principal styles of the Middle Ages as reflections of the lifestyle of church or court:

    a. plainchant

    b. secular songs and dances, especially the music of the troubadours

    c. Notre Dame organum

    d. *ars nova* motets

2. The evolution of polyphony and rhythmic notation in the Middle Ages as found in:

    a. the development of organum   c. the *ars nova*

    b. Notre Dame organum   d. motets of Machaut

3. Chant as a universal phenomenon associated with religious ritual, especially:

    a. Gregorian plainchant   c. Hawai'ian *mele pule*

    b. Qur'anic recitation   d. Navajo *ho'zho'ni* songs

❧ Listening Objectives

After completing this chapter, students should be able to:

1. Hear how elements and structures of music were typically used in the Middle Ages.

2. Identify and follow principal types of music written in the Middle Ages: plainchant, troubadour songs, Notre Dame organum, and *ars nova* motets.

3. Hear similarities and differences between different types of chant: Gregorian plainchant, Qur'anic recitation, Hawai'ian *mele pule*, and Navajo *ho'zho'ni* songs.

Lecture Suggestions

Long ago and far away . . . in many ways this describes the twin thrusts of this chapter as well as the unit that follows. Both the music of the Middle Ages and the examples in Global Perspectives may seem historically, culturally, and aurally distant to modern listeners. There are exceptions, of course. Thanks to the phenomenal success of Angel's series of *Chant* recordings by the Benedictine

monks of Santo Domingo de Silos, many students can boast a passing familiarity with plainchant. And world music has infiltrated the music world to
such an extent that virtually all students have encountered it—whether they
realize it or not. Even so, it is safe to assume that most of the music in this
chapter will be completely foreign to their ears. How exciting! Seize the opportunity to make this music come to life for your students. As much as possible, immerse your class in the sounds and sights of the Middle Ages and the
Islamic, Hawai'ian, and Navajo cultures represented in Global Perspectives.
Whether long ago or far away, a clear understanding of unfamiliar cultures
and lifestyles will help your students make sense of various musical styles.

Time is an issue. Throughout the course you must make decisions about
where to spend class time; no class can cover it all. This manual provides suggestions for most major topics in the *Listen* textbook with the understanding
that individual instructors must pick and choose. Many instructors cover Unit II
quickly; some omit this unit entirely. I recommend at least brief coverage of this
material; music of the Middle Ages has influenced music from the Renaissance
to the present day, including the examples by Reich in Chapter 22.

❦ Why Global Perspectives?

The challenges identified above—unfamiliarity and lack of time—can appear
even more daunting for instructors with no experience in non-Western music.
In fact, it is altogether too easy to find excuses to omit the Global Perspectives
segments; that would be a shame, for this material offers substantial rewards.
If you find the prospect of teaching world music examples at all intimidating
or cumbersome, consider the following:

1. You don't have to be an expert. Remember, the main focus of this textbook
is listening, and you can do that! Start from the listening angle, and add to
your knowledge of other cultures and styles as you go along.

2. Begin gradually. You don't have to use every Global Perspectives example
the first time. Start with the ones that you feel most comfortable with or that
make particularly interesting connections with Western music. Then build up
your repertory gradually.

3. The *Listen* format makes it easier. By weaving a Global Perspectives segment into many chapters, the textbook begs a comparative approach. It provides a ready-made context for understanding and drawing connections
between cultures. Best of all, you don't have to teach world music as a stand-
alone unit.

4. Resources are easy to find. This manual provides detailed background material on each culture covered in the textbook as well as references to many outside sources. Given the recent groundswell of interest in world music, both in
popular music and the scholarly arena, resources have never been easier to find.

Once you overcome your reasons not to use the Global Perspectives curriculum, it is helpful to think on the positive side. Why *should* you use Global
Perspectives? What are the "substantial rewards" promised above?

First, a world music perspective can help clarify our understanding of
Western music. Until we step outside our own tradition or culture, we fail to
see and correctly interpret some of its salient features because we are simply too
close to it; we lack perspective. To determine if a feature of Western music has
universal human significance or is unique to our culture, we must step outside

of the Western tradition. Such a perspective further provides a context for framing and answering the most difficult "how" and "why" questions our students ask.

Second, an approach that encourages students to look for connections between Western music and other musics of the world can stimulate greater intellectual curiosity. It also acknowledges what was true all along—Western music did not develop in a vacuum. In fact, the history of music is filled with examples of cross-fertilization between cultures, and turn-of-the-century "exoticism" proves not so unusual after all.

Third, students can learn to listen for elements of music more easily. Teachers often forget just how difficult it is for nonmusicians to perceive and explain complex musical phenomena. Separating out one element from another can be especially tricky. The answer is guided practice with more examples and more varied examples, especially examples that differ from the formats and formulas of Western traditions. One or two examples from beyond Europe may provide just the clarification a student needs to sharpen an understanding of texture or melody.

Fourth, the students who populate our classrooms are no longer exclusively nineteen-year-old kids of European descent who have never been outside of Kansas. For many of them, Western music is a foreign tradition, and a course in Western music is a course in ethnomusicology. The Global Perspectives curriculum offers a profound way to honor the traditions your students represent. By the way, don't hesitate to draw on student experiences of other world cultures; many of your students bring an expertise that can enrich the classroom experience in powerful ways.

One last note—use video recordings whenever possible as you present Global Perspectives materials. In the Western tradition, musicians have been trained to focus on the purely musical aspects of any composition they encounter. This reflects the sharp distinctions our culture makes between music and literature, theater, or art. In many cultures, however, these become false distinctions, especially where the music is but one element in a ritual or ceremony that melds several significant modes of human expression. The *Listen* recordings provide one point of entry into other cultures, but to rely exclusively on sound recordings is to run the danger of suggesting that all music can be fully understood through listening alone. Video recordings come closer to conveying the fullness and richness of the many forms of cultural expression in which music participates. To help get you started, each chapter recommends some video materials (see Video Recordings under Multimedia Resources at the end of each chapter). And remember, when introducing new cultures, one picture is worth a thousand notes.

The Middle Ages—A Brief Description

The Middle Ages span the years from 476 C.E., the fall of the Roman Empire, to around 1400 (or 1450, three years shy of the fall of the Byzantine Empire to the Ottoman armies of Sultan Mehmed II). Ask students to recall anything they know about the period, whether from prior study or from movies about Robin Hood, King Arthur, or the Crusades. List important points on the board. Make sure the following items are mentioned:

1. Europe was periodically under invasion (Goths, Huns, Vikings, Mongols, Moors, etc.).

2. European access to international commerce and communication dropped off.

3. As commerce suffered, the European economy shifted to feudalism.

4. Mass migrations resulted from invasions, famine, and plagues.

5. The average person lived under primitive, often brutal conditions.

6. Much of the education and technology of Greco-Roman civilization was lost in the West.

Before you move to musical examples, offer these comprehensive observations about the Middle Ages:

1. There was a slow but sure movement away from the absolute authority of the church in all matters.

2. The evolution of polyphony and music notation represent quantum leaps in the development of music.

✎ Music and the Church: Plainchant

The Roman Catholic Church was the primary patron of art and education and the single greatest preserver of Western civilization during the Middle Ages. The music of the church supported the functions of worship and contemplation. The same impulse that led the church to standardize liturgy and education led the church to standardize music through the development of music notation. By the year 1000, church musicians had tackled and solved the incredible problem of how to notate pitches, an accomplishment on a par with the invention of the alphabet.

PLAINCHANT **Preface for Mass on Whit Sunday, "Vere dignum"**

PLAINCHANT **Gregorian antiphon, "In paradisum"**

First play the antiphon, "In paradisum." Have students choose adjectives that describe the mood created by the music. Then ask them to reconcile the harsh realities of the Middle Ages (from the foregoing discussion) with the spirit of this music. This should prove a difficult task, but it highlights the relationship between church and culture in the Middle Ages. The world was regarded as a dangerous place filled with temptations, sinfulness, demons, and death. The church dominated medieval culture, yet it also stood as a place apart and was looked on as the only stronghold against barbarism, ignorance, and sin— against all that was worldly. This opposition is the key to understanding plainchant, a music that avoids fleeting worldly pleasures in order to point toward eternal truth and salvation.

Play the antiphon again. This time ask students to look for characteristic uses of musical elements and structures. Put a checklist of elements and structures on the board and be sure to cover each in the discussion that follows. (You may wish to refer to this list when discussing works in later chapters.) The list should include:

pitch	scales	melody	key and mode
dynamics	rhythm	harmony	form
tone color	tempo	texture	

As you work through the list, the class will notice the smooth contour and legato character of the melodic line; the moderate dynamic level; the use of male voices without accompaniment; the easy, solemn pacing; and the almost-but-not-quite repetition of melodic motives. Most striking, however, is the lack of meter; strong cadences; or clear, symmetrical phrase relationships. These features create chant's characteristic floating, otherworldly quality—passionate yet serene. Next, have students create a list of features associated with a "tune" (Chapter 3). As you compare the two lists, point out that the features we find pleasurable in a tune are precisely the features that are avoided in chant. Plainchant creates a world apart, one that avoids any association with secular songs or dance music.

Now ask the class to listen for similarities and differences as you play the preface, "Vere dignum," sung on a reciting tone. The most obvious difference is the simplification of the melody's contours; now it sounds like a series of recited tones connected by short melodic motives. Notice also a greater rhythmic freedom that includes frequent ornamentation, the use of solo voice, the somewhat nasal tone quality, and the repetition of the melody at "Domine sancte Pater" and each subsequent phrase beginning. Compared with the more songlike antiphon, this chant feels closer to a stylized form of speech.

Once students have a clear sense of the contrasts between plainsong and recitation, take time to place these two works in their liturgical context. As with any other type of chant, the music finds its fullest meaning within its context and purpose in worship. (This perspective is particularly important for those who present the chant examples in Global Perspectives, below.) "In paradisum" comes from the Requiem Mass, the standard funeral service of the Roman Catholic Church. Positioned at the very end of the Mass, this burial antiphon accompanied the procession from the church to the graveyard, an image vividly painted by the authors. The Preface, on the other hand, is a fixed feature of the everyday Roman Catholic Mass; as such, it will be familiar to any students who are Catholic (or Episcopalian). Part of the Liturgy of the Eucharist (see p. 109 of this manual for a complete order of worship for the Mass), the Preface marks the Elevation of the Host, the moment where the priest presents the bread and wine. It also immediately precedes the Sanctus ("Holy, holy, holy Lord"), one of the most awe-filled moments of the entire Mass. Both *Listen* examples would have been familiar to contemporary listeners.

HILDEGARD OF BINGEN Plainchant sequence, "Columba aspexit"

Begin by playing the music. At first hearing, "Columba aspexit" sounds quite similar to the antiphon "In paradisum." As one listens repeatedly, however, one begins to sense the many arresting differences between the two. Once again, ask the class to use the checklist of musical elements and structures as they listen and compare these two works. Obvious differences include the use of women's voices, the accompanying drone, and the regular alternation between soloist and choir. Less obvious, but equally significant, is the unusually wide range of the melody, occasionally soaring into very high registers to intensify the melody's expressiveness. Of course, Hildegard's significance extends well beyond what we can hear in the music itself. Point out that, in spite of the preponderance of all-male chant recordings, music making was a significant part of daily life for women in convents across Europe. Further, in an era when composers remained deliberately anonymous, Hildegard, a woman, stands out as one of the earliest composers whose names we know. Fortunately, Hildegard was also an abbess, a mystic seer, and a prolific author. Much of her work survives to the present day, providing a remarkably full picture of her life and thought—we know more about Hildegard than about several major Renaissance composers who lived three centuries later.

Play the music one last time to focus on the structure of the sequence—statement of **A** by soprano, repetition by chorus, statement of **B** by the soprano, repetition by the chorus, and so on. This repetition can be difficult to hear at first, due to the irregularity of phrase lengths and the lack of any phrase-to-phrase repetition, but awareness of the alternation between soloist and chorus can help students hear this large-scale repetition more clearly. The "outer form"—called the sequence—was one of the standard musical-poetic forms in liturgical music of the Middle Ages, but Hildegard's fills that form with a deeply spiritual music whose inner form impresses the listener with its simultaneous serenity and ecstasy.

Sacred Chant

Even though the textbook places the Global Perspectives material at the end of Chapter 5, this is the best place to cover Qur'anic recitation, Hawai'ian *mele pule*, and Navajo *ho'zho'ni* songs, immediately following your comparison of "In paradisum" and "Columba aspexit." See the lecture suggestions following the Machaut motet for background and ideas in presenting this material.

7 Music at Court

BERNART DE VENTADORN Troubadour song, "La dousa votz"

To heighten the contrast between plainchant and "tunes," play this song immediately after you have finished with Hildegard's sequence. Here the beat and meter are clear and repetition is easily perceived. Whereas plainchant belongs to another world, this song is down-to-earth and accessible. Work through the checklist of musical elements and structures again as a technique to identify differences in musical style. The following are characteristic features of many secular songs from the late Middle Ages.

1. The poet expresses the joys and sorrows of earthly love.

2. The form of each stanza is **a a′ b.**

3. Medieval modes are used (Mixolydian mode here—the same as "In paradisum" and Hildegard's sequence).

Stress once again the importance of rhythm. Ask the class what this song expresses about life in the Middle Ages. This is the music that relates most closely to the chivalric codes of behavior that many students know from movies. Two final points: (1) troubadour songs constitute the first large body of notated music not related to the church, which suggests movement away from the authority of the church; (2) the scores for these songs contain only a single melody line, a fact that highlights the role of well-educated guesses in early music performance. (See Listening Idea 7 below.)

❦ The Evolution of Polyphony

The development of notated polyphony marks the single most decisive turning point in the music of the Middle Ages, perhaps in the history of Western music. It signals a shift to music that is composed, notated, and polyphonic. This represents a radical change from oral, improvisational traditions based on one primary melody—traditions that still characterize most non-Western music. The Western classical music tradition is the result of this fundamental change.

Organum, the first important genre of notated polyphonic music, starts with a preexisting chant melody and adds one or more melodies in counterpoint with the first. Kerman and Tomlinson describe several stages in its development. Watching the added melody become more distinct and independent is like looking at photographs that show the growth of a fetus in the womb. We observe the birth of a wholly new tradition in Western music.

PÉROTIN **Organum, "Alleluia. Diffusa est gratia"**

An independent added melody created problems in coordinating two or more voices, problems that were solved by the development of rhythmic notation. The Notre Dame school invented one of the earliest recognizable systems of rhythmic notation, based on a set of six simple rhythmic patterns that were repeated again and again. The notation permits precise coordination of two or more melodies but imposes severe restrictions on freedom of rhythmic expression. Play the organal portion, which starts at 0:37 on the recording, and ask students to listen to the top voice and tap or clap the beat. They may not grasp it immediately, especially since the eighth note comes on the beat in this 6/8 pattern (see textbook page 69), but as the pattern becomes more regular (and given a little help) they can begin to feel the pulse.

Now play the entire excerpt. Ask students to use the checklist of elements and structures to describe features of the two different styles they hear—plainchant and organum. As part of the discussion that follows, place organum in its proper context. Organum serves roughly the same role as the ornate adornment of initial letters in medieval illuminations (the authors provide an example on textbook page 59), in which most letters are plain but some are oversized and embellished. Music used in worship was still primarily plainchant; organum was used to highlight words or phrases at key points in the service. Explain that the full text is a song of praise for the birth of the Virgin Mary, who, as mother of Jesus, enjoyed special reverence in the devotions, liturgy, and celebrations of Roman Catholics for much of the Middle Ages and beyond. Point out that Alleluias were reserved for specific seasons and celebrations in the church year and that even the plainchant versions of Alleluias were among the most beautiful and ornate chant melodies written. Alleluias are still a special part of the Catholic liturgy today.

Play the music again so that students can listen for the chant melody on which the organum is based—the slowly changing drone at the bottom of the organal texture. They will notice that the lowest voice sometimes moves almost as quickly as the two upper voices, but most of the time it sustains very long notes, serving as a stable foundation for the voices that arch above it. The role of the Notre Dame composer was to add new melodies over a preexisting melody (and Pérotin never identified himself as the composer of this music—a scribe we call Anonymous 4 tipped us off). Ask students how this compares with their idea of what composers do.

This music represents the final stage in the development of organum. The next steps in the evolution of polyphony and a more sophisticated rhythmic notation took place in the motet.

❦ Later Medieval Polyphony

In the late Middle Ages, the impulses toward greater melodic independence and more advanced rhythmic notation went hand in hand. The motet developed an extreme independence not only between its melodies and its rhythms, but in its texts as well—each voice might have its own words! On the rhythmic front, Philippe de Vitry (the first composer whose birthday we know—Halloween, 1291) developed a notation system sophisticated enough to remain in use for more than two centuries. His system, outlined in a treatise titled *Ars nova,* permitted notation of rhythms so complicated that some cannot be written easily in modern notation. The triumph of the Middle Ages is that it not only discovered radically new ways of thinking about music, but also developed and refined new techniques of composition and notation to a remarkably sophisticated level.

MACHAUT Motet, "Quant en moi"

Play the piece. This music is difficult to follow. Play it again and use the checklist of elements and structures to generate discussion.

Pitch—intervals and chord types are unfamiliar

Dynamics—moderate level throughout

Tone color—soprano, tenor, and viol used throughout

Scale—not clearly recognizable

Rhythm—quirky, but much more varied than in Notre Dame organum

Tempo—moderately fast

Melody—there are resting points between phrases, but voices do not rest together, and cadences are not familiar

Texture—nonimitative polyphony

Mode and key—some major and minor chords, but scale not clear, tonal center not clear

This exercise reveals some of the difficulties in following this music. The following exercise highlights another difficulty. Ask a student to read Stanza 1 of the soprano's poem from textbook page 71. While the student reads, you should read the tenor's poem as indicated below. Make sure you articulate the hocket as clearly as you can ("Fearing—To hope—Feigning—to have").

SOPRANO'S POEM	TENOR'S POEM
When I was first visited by	Thanks
Love, he so very sweetly	to
Enamored my heart;	love
A glance is what he gave me as a gift,	and
And along with amorous sentiments	consummate
He presented me with this delightful idea:	beauty
	Fearing,
To hope	Feigning
to have	
Grace, and no rejections,	Are what
But never in my whole life	consume me
Was boldness a gift he meant for me.	entirely.

Ask students how well they were able to follow the two poems. Taken by themselves, text and music present the difficulty of two separate levels of meaning, but two texts stretch our ability to perceive the whole. Take time to point out the clever wordplay in the hocket—the two texts are not treated independently at this point, and each amplifies the meaning of the other. Listen to the first stanza on the recording, especially to follow the text and listen for the hocket (see Listening Idea 8 below).

Rhythm is perhaps the most important element. Dynamics and tone color do not play a significant role. Given unfamiliar uses of pitch, scale, melody, and key, students will perceive rhythm as the element that defines phrase endings (cessation of rhythmic activity) and clarifies the independence of the voices. Further, Machaut uses rhythm to provide the underlying structure for the motet in a technique known as isorhythm. Each voice has its own long, repeating rhythmic patterns. These patterns are difficult to hear in the soprano and tenor parts, but a shorter, clearer pattern is used in the bottom voice, played by the viol. Students can follow it if you count it out for them. The pattern of durations (in beats) is:

9	9	3	6	9	9	9
		(rest)				(rest)

Write these numbers on the board. Play the motet and count aloud the durations for each note the viol plays while pointing to the appropriate number on the board. (After six repetitions, the viol part plays the pattern six more times at triple tempo.) After a few times through, the beginning of the pattern is easy to spot since it follows a long rest. Point out that only rhythms repeat; the pitch patterns change constantly.

Play the motet one last time. Ask students if the music makes any more sense the last time through than the first. Point out that this music was regarded as an extremely intellectual (as well as musical) exercise, unlike troubadour songs or plainchant. It reflects the hierarchical medieval understanding of music (based on Boethius), which placed music of the spheres (and the mental discipline required to understand the proportions and workings of the cosmos) at the top, while relegating performed music and actual sounds to the lowest position. Although it cannot be proved, Machaut's mathematical proportions almost suggest an attempt to reproduce the music of the spheres.

See Further Listening Examples below for more examples of plainchant, another troubadour song, an estampie, and another example of organum (by Léonin).

♩ Global Perspectives 1: Sacred Chant

The perfect place to incorporate these materials is alongside your discussion of Gregorian chant—the Roman Catholic version of sacred chant. Of course, chant is a near-universal phenomenon associated with religious ritual and ceremony in cultures around the globe. In many ancient, primitive cultures, music was thought to possess sacred, even magical, power. As the centuries have passed, music has retained a strong association with religious practices. In fact, almost every culture possesses a long-standing tradition of religious music, and many employ styles of singing and music making that set this music apart from secular styles, just as we discovered with plainchant.

Islamic Culture

There are perhaps no cultures more misunderstood and maligned by many Americans than those associated with "Islam." Adversarial encounters with Islam are woven into Western history and consciousness. The story of Europe in the Middle Ages documents Christendom's constant fear of Islamic invasion, as well as the crusades that were mounted to retake the holy city of Jerusalem from the "heathen horde." United States history also records conflicts with Islamic peoples, as when the Marines fought "our country's battles" on "the shores of Tripoli." The Iraq War is the culmination of some twenty years of tension between the United States and Iraq, Iran, and Libya. These two decades have witnessed the "Desert Storm" conflict; terrorist attacks mounted by Muslim extremists against cruise ships, military vessels, and U.S. embassies in Africa and the Middle East; the horrifying spectacle of the September 11, 2001, attacks; and the subsequent invasions of Afghanistan and Iraq.

Can you cover this musical example without veering into discussion of the events that have dominated the world stage in the recent past? You can, but why pass up a golden opportunity to help students better understand the diversity and complexity of Islamic cultures? This may still be a sore topic for some students, and great sensitivity will be required of you. After all, centuries of fear, suspicion, and hostility have crystallized in the "war on terrorism." And yet, most Americans harbor a fascination with Islam. Even though they know very little of Islamic religion, history, or culture, the deep schism between Iraq's Sunni and Shi'ite Muslims has made them aware of contradictions and divisions within Islam. The nightly news and a host of special television reports speak directly to this new and genuine curiosity, and with it has emerged a profound "teachable moment." Now, more than ever, it is crucial to talk about Islam and seek a deeper understanding.

There is no one right way to handle this discussion (though there are several wrong ways). You have several things in your favor, however. This chapter's focus on chant and its universality makes a deep impression on most students, coming for some as a revelation. In addition, the intensity of Qur'anic recitation, especially by comparison with the other Chapter 5 chant examples, conveys a sense of the deep spiritual passion of Islam. The notes below on Islam's contributions to Western culture can also help; these historical facts are not well known to many U.S. citizens. In any event, you must draw on your own skills and experience and find a strategy with which you feel comfortable. Make sure you know where you want the discussion to go, and devise (in advance) several questions to help guide the conversation. If you encounter students who are bitter or hostile, you might ask: *Is it fair to judge an entire religion based on the actions of extremists*? (Can one judge Christianity on the basis of the Ku Klux Klan or those who murder abortion clinic doctors or nurses?)

This would be an excellent opportunity to invite an expert into your class. Even if you are Muslim yourself, a member of your school's religion faculty or a representative from a local mosque (see Lecture-Demonstration Idea 5 below) could provide invaluable insights and perspective for your students. (It is likely that some of your students will be Muslims, but don't put them on the spot unless you've first sounded them out outside of class!) Further resources include the teaching suggestions below and several books under the Qur'anic Recitation heading in Appendix V. As is typical of this manual's coverage of each Global Perspectives module, the notes below provide not only teaching suggestions for the music but also an overview of the history and culture of the society that created the music. The overview is primarily designed as background material to assist you in your class preparation, but feel free to use any of this material as part of your lecture.

Let's start with a bit of history. Islam began in 610 C.E. when Muhammad (c. 571–632 C.E.), a native of Mecca, saw the angel Gabriel (the same one who appeared to the Virgin Mary) in a vision. In a subsequent series of visitations that spanned twenty years, Gabriel gave to Muhammad the contents of the

Qur'an, the holy book of Islam. As he shared what he had learned, he quickly gathered followers, but he also made enemies and was forced to flee with his followers to Medina in 622. This event, the hegira, marks the beginning of the Islamic calendar. Muhammad found a receptive audience for his message in Medina, and in 630 he returned to Mecca at the head of an army to forcibly take control. Through a combination of shrewd political maneuvers and military force, Islam had taken control of the western half of modern Saudi Arabia by the time Muhammad left this earth in 632. Over the next century, Islam spread dramatically to encompass a region including Arabia, the Middle East (Jerusalem fell in 638), Persia, northern Africa, and Spain. Muslim armies threatened the heart of Christendom until they were finally turned back in the West by the Franks at Poitiers (732) and in the east by Byzantine forces at Constantinople (677 and 717). The Mediterranean was no longer the Romans' *mare nostrum* (our sea). Now it was the Islamic empire that dominated major trade routes on land and sea, and the Islamic nations flourished economically and culturally. The next several centuries saw major advances in Islamic scholarship, science, and arts. In fact, the West owes several great debts to Islamic culture. Paper, a Chinese invention, came to Europe by way of Islamic countries, which quickly developed bookmaking and calligraphy to a high artistic level. Islamic scholars, heirs to the same Greek culture revered in Europe, preserved many ancient Greek writings that never would have come to the attention of Western European scholars but for the careful stewardship of their Islamic counterparts. And we should all thank Allah that Arabic numerals—with their concept of a zero—replaced the old Roman numerals.[1]

Some background on the Qur'an is also important to our discussion. Even a brief perusal of the Qur'an reveals the presence of many names familiar to readers of the Torah or the Bible: Noah, Abraham, Moses, King David, and even Jesus and his mother, Mary. One quickly realizes that Islam shares precisely the same roots, stories, and traditions as Judaism and Christianity, and all three faiths share essential beliefs as well—belief in one God and belief in divine revelation, among others. Nonetheless, the nature and function of the Qur'an remains quite different from that of Jewish or Christian Scripture. This is perhaps the biggest stumbling block for products of Western culture—the Qur'an is not conceived of as a "book" to be studied and analyzed; it is, rather, a set of divinely inspired words to be recited as an act of worship. Muhammad himself was instructed in proper recitation by the angel Gabriel, and he had to rehearse passages until the angel was satisfied that Muhammad had the correct meaning.[2] The tradition of the Qur'an remains an oral tradition, and when it was finally written down after Muhammad left the earth, it was not for the purpose of study and dissemination but to preserve the text from possible corruption.

Qur'anic Recitation

The very presence of recitation, which sounds to us like music, brings up one of the most curious contradictions in Islam. The great debate over the role of music in worship has raged on since the departure of Muhammad, whose own thoughts on the subject created just enough ambiguity to fuel continuous disagreements. Muhammad, in spite of many comments on music's power to mislead the faithful, is said to have enjoyed recitation (for which he found

---

[1]Just try adding or subtracting without a zero! It's easy to demonstrate this for musicians because our traditional system of measuring intervals has no zero. We start with one—the unison. We know that stacking two thirds gives us a fifth, but that's like saying that 3 + 3 = 5!

[2]Arabic is a tricky language, and proper accentuation is crucial to the meaning of the phrase.

precedent in King David's psalm singing) and even some other forms of music making. Still, there is no question that music was forbidden as a religious practice by the major schools of Islamic thought that developed after Muhammad. Allowances were made in most traditions for the use of recitation, call to prayer, and limited hymn singing, but a special vocabulary was developed for these genres to make it clear that this was not music, certainly not in the secular sense. Practitioners today still guard carefully against the intrusion of elements that might make these genres sound too much like music. The harshness of the restrictions against music has varied across the Arab world. Shi'ite Muslims allow no music apart from recitation and other religious uses and feel great ambivalence about even listening to secular music, while others, notably the Sufi orders, have allowed and even encouraged musical expression and dance as part of worship. Sufi orders had an especially strong influence in Turkey, where our *Listen* recording was made and where the secular modes (*maqamat*) probably first made their way into Qur'anic recitation. In addition, Turkey is one of the few places where traditional Sufi dervish dancing is still reenacted annually, and it remains open to a greater variety of music making than many other Islamic countries.

Qur'anic recitation as practiced today probably differs significantly from the recitation sanctioned by Muhammad. There is great variety from region to region in the Islamic world. Some modern styles of recitation remain simple, straightforward, and diatonic, including a modern style developed for average Muslims (*murattal*), one that helps them reap the benefits and blessings of recitation in private devotion without rigorous training. Other styles—full of complex ornaments and melismas—demand a virtuoso approach which makes judicious use of some significant changes in Arabic secular music of the past millennium, such as the understanding of musical modes (*maqamat*) shaped between the thirteenth and seventeenth centuries. What remains important in all styles of recitation is a complex set of principles (*tajwid*) that guides proper declamation and sound of the words. *Tajwid* deals with the rhythm, duration of syllables, correct pronunciation, articulation, emphasis, requirement that each phrase fit into a single breath, and so on. Not surprisingly, it takes years of study to memorize the Qur'an and master *tajwid*.

One of the most striking aspects of Qur'anic recitation is the role of improvisation in its melodic construction. Reciters do not use the same melody each time they recite a given chapter or verse of the Qur'an. In fact, they are forbidden to do so, for melodic repetition would draw attention away from the words. In addition, fixed melodies are typical of "music," and "music," as we have seen, is not permitted in Islamic worship. Instead, reciters choose modes (*maqamat*) and improvise melodic figures that seem best suited to express the text's meaning.

In traditional Arabic thought, the concept of *maqam* is much broader than the Western notion of scale. Like medieval European modes, *maqamat* incorporate the concepts of range, register, melodic flow, and initial, final, and prominent notes, but each *maqam* was also thought to correspond to "planets, signs of the zodiac, seasons, day and night, hours, elements, humours, temperaments, virtues, classes of men, colors, odors, raw materials, alphabetical letters, and poetry and poetical meters."[3] Further, each person was said to have a *maqam* that best suited his personality. Although most modern reciters no longer hold to these old correspondences, there is still a sense that certain

[3]Amnon Shiloah, "The Arabic Concept of Mode." *Journal of the American Musicological Society* (1981), p. 38.

maqamat are best suited to certain emotions, and skilled reciters modulate from *maqam* to *maqam* both for a change of mood and expression and to communicate more directly with as many audience members as they can. Although there are 12 basic *maqamat,* at least 347 are theoretically possible through the process of combination, giving the reciter many expressive options. Another difference between Arabic modes and Western scales is the temperament. The octave divides into twenty-four parts, though not into equal-tempered quarter tones. Rather, semitones come in two sizes, 90 and 114 cents (equal-tempered semitones are 100 cents wide), and the resulting whole steps can be any of three different sizes, 180, 204, or 228 cents. Augmented seconds, long associated with music of the Middle East, figure prominently in many of the scales used, and they also come in different sizes.

The prevalence of many of today's virtuoso styles can be traced back to Cairo and Istanbul, two important centers for the study and practice of recitation. It takes true mastery to reconcile the demands of *tajwid* with the endless possibilities of melodic figure and *maqam*, to communicate effectively and expressively with an audience, and to avoid crossing into the domain of "music." Such ability requires rigorous training, but virtuoso practitioners are highly prized and well rewarded in the Islamic world. The most significant school of recitation is located in Cairo, and the Egyptian style dominates much of the Islamic world, especially now that recordings and radio broadcasts of recitation have become commonplace. Of course, given the nature of this oral tradition, virtuoso recitation is a performance art, and most reciters appreciate the encouragement and approval of the audience, many of whom are true aficionados.

Ya Sin, Surah XXXVI   The recitation found in the *Listen* recordings comes from Surah (chapter) 36 of the Qur'an. It is customary to recite an entire chapter; however, since it takes about twenty minutes to recite all eighty-three verses of Surah 36, the *Listen* recording provides only the first two minutes of the chapter (the first ten verses). It is best to present this example immediately after you cover Gregorian chant, since these two types share so many features. As the textbook points out, both are monophonic, nonmetric vocal music. If you wish, begin with a brief introduction based on some of the background material above. (A complete English translation with Romanized transliteration of the Arabic text for our excerpt can be found in Appendix II—this makes it much easier to follow the words.)

Then ask students to listen for the same elements and structures they tried to find in Gregorian chant. Once again, put the checklist of musical elements and structures on the board (see discussion of "In paradisum" above). In the discussion that follows, draw out the following features. The pitch level starts out low, gradually rising to higher and higher notes. The tone color, that of a solo voice, often has a nasal quality, dwelling on consonants like *m* or *n*. This is not typical of the Arabic language in general, but it is one of the stylized requirements of *tajwid*. The guttural sounds, on the other hand, stem from the language. The scale sounds much like a minor scale, but with occasional chromatic alterations (raised scale degrees three or six). As in Gregorian chant, the rhythm is nonmetric, yet the rhythm feels much freer and less predictable than the flowing steadiness of the chant rhythms. The rhythm in this example feels much closer to speech rhythm than does that in "In paradisum." The melody seems to happen in fits and starts, with irregular phrases ornamented by trills, shakes, and other melodic figures. The textbook describes how the melody circles around the dominant, much like the reciting tones found in the **B** section of our Gregorian introit. The texture is monophonic, but unlike the choral sound of plainchant, this example features the solo voice typical of recitation. Given the improvised nature of the melody and the requirement that recitation avoid melodic repetition, the form is free. In fact, recitation has resisted notation precisely because the melodies are freshly improvised with each performance. Notating recitation would be like notating a jazz solo—interesting for study purposes, but not something to perform again note-for-note.

The textbook also discusses the Islamic call to prayer, the *azan* (*adhan*), which offers another style of Islamic chant—one that permits some internal repetition. See Listening Ideas below if you would like to include a call to prayer in your presentation.

Hawai'i

The Hawai'ian Islands belong to the East Polynesian region of the Pacific and were probably settled around 650 C.E. by Polynesians from the Marquesas Islands. Contact with the West began with the arrival of Captain James Cook in 1778. Initially, contact with outsiders had very little influence on native Hawai'ian culture, but the arrival of Christian missionaries from New England in 1820 immediately produced substantial, perhaps irreversible, changes. Within five years, Christianity essentially replaced traditional Hawai'ian religion, and the missionaries' emphasis on hymn singing and musical training brought the islanders face-to-face with Western musical traditions, which they adopted with zeal. By the 1870s, when Hawai'ian traditional music seemed in danger of disappearing, it underwent a significant revival, but new genres that mixed Hawai'ian and Western elements continued to emerge and grow in popularity. Contacts with the United States continued to increase. In 1893 a group of American businessmen overthrew the Hawai'ian constitutional monarchy, established c. 1819, and created their own republic. Annexed by the United States in 1898, Hawai'i became the fiftieth state in 1959. Hawai'ian fervor to assimilate American influences again placed traditional music in danger of extinction, and scholars and musicians began yet another revival in the 1970s.

Given the ease with which Hawai'ians have assimilated outside influences over the past two centuries, it is difficult to reconstruct traditional, precontact Hawai'ian music. In 1981 Elizabeth Tatar observed noticeable differences between contemporary performances of traditional music and recordings made in the 1920s and 1930s in the areas of the Hawai'ian chain least affected by Western influences. She also discovered that many terms used in turn-of-the-century publications to describe traditional musical styles and categories had fallen out of use in modern Hawai'i.[4] Thankfully, Tatar is only one of many recent figures working to recover, reconstruct, and revive old Hawai'ian traditions.

Traditional Hawai'ian Music   The vast majority of traditional Hawai'ian music is song (*mele*)—that is, poetic texts performed by voice with or without instruments. Songs are distinguished from one another on the basis of their intended mode of performance, their poetic type, and the vocal style used. These distinctions are not related hierarchically but can overlap each other in numerous combinations, though the choice of vocal style is usually determined by both the mode of performance and the poetic type.

1. The two performance modes are distinguished by the presence or absence of dance. *Mele hula* refers to songs accompanied by dance, and *mele oli* to songs not intended for performance with dance. The chief musical difference

---

[4]Elizabeth Tatar, "Toward a Description of Precontact Music in Hawai'i." *Ethnomusicology* (1981), p. 483.

lies in their treatment of meter. *Mele hula* is metric for the purpose of coordination with the dance; *mele oli* is nonmetric, relying more on speech rhythms. It is possible to perform *mele hula* without the accompaniment of dance, but *mele oli* cannot be performed with dance.

2. Many traditional poetic types exist, distinguished from each other on the basis of their social function. Ranging from most sacred to most secular, some of the major categories include prayers to gods (*mele pule*); genealogical chants (*mele ku'auhau* and *mele ko'ihonua*); chants that honor people, including name chants (*mele inoa*), genital chants (*mele ma'i*), and songs of lamentation (*mele kanikau*); and love songs (*mele ho'oipoipo*).

3. Six vocal styles are used in traditional Hawai'ian music. The first five are used in *mele oli*, whereas the sixth is associated with *mele hula*. Each one is also associated with one or more specific poetic types. As a group, they range on a spectrum from spoken chant of indeterminate pitch to a style based on long, sustained, highly ornamented pitches.

    a. *Kepakepa* employs rapid, speechlike delivery of long phrases and is commonly used for long prayers and genealogies.

    b. *Kawele* uses a more sustained, higher, more definitely pitched delivery of shorter phrases and is also used for prayers and genealogies.

    c. *Olioli*, delivered on a sustained pitch with vibrato, is appropriate to all poetic types except laments and dirges.

    d. *Ho'aeae*, which makes use of long sustained pitches with elaborate vibrato patterns, is most often found in love songs.

    e. *Ho'ouweuwe*, distinguished by long, sustained wails with voice breaks, is used exclusively in laments and dirges.

    f. *'Ai ha'a*, associated with *mele hula*, employs low, growl-like patterns in a specific meter.

In addition, many types of vocal ornaments are applied by the singers, each ornament associated with one or more vocal styles. The textbook identifies *i'i*, a pronounced vibrato used especially in the last four vocal styles listed. Other ornaments include glides, loud attacks, growls, clucking, and glottal stops.

Mele pule   The recorded example actually includes two short prayers—"Aia no ke akua la i uka" and "Ike ia Kaukini e lawai'a manu." Translations for these *mele* can be difficult to find, but knowing the words really helps students understand what this is about. Only the first line was readily available for the first song—*The god is at work in the hills* (from Nathaniel B. Emerson's *Pele and Hiiaka—A Hawaiian Myth*). An invocation to the Pele, the fire goddess, this is a genuine example of *mele pule*. A more complete translation is available for the second *mele*, however (see Appendix II). As it turns out, "Ike ia Kaukini e lawai'a manu" (*You will recognize Kaukini, the bird catcher*) is not *mele pule* at all, but an example of *mele inoa*, a name chant. It commemorates the faithfulness and gruesome fate of Kaukini, the royal bird catcher. The king's favorite delicacy was the *Puoali'i* bird, but once when Kaukini could not find one, two unscrupulous courtiers served the king a different bird, neither tasty nor fresh. Passing it off as *Puoali'i*, the two told the angry king it had been supplied by the bird catcher. Unaware of their duplicity, the king had the innocent Kaukini roasted on a spit! As with the Qur'anic recitation, it is most effective to introduce this material side by side with plainchant. *Mele pule* provides yet another example of sacred chant, and one that shares many similarities with

Christian and Islamic chant. Feel free to introduce this chant with some of the background material given above.

As with the previous examples, use the list of musical elements and structures to help guide student listening. Play the recorded example and solicit student observations afterward. In the discussion that follows, bring out the following points. This example uses only one primary pitch, barely touching on one other secondary pitch. How can music with such a minimal melody maintain interest? The tone color, as in Islamic recitation, is that of a solo voice, though this time a woman's voice is featured. Further, the tones produced by the chanter are not quite spoken word or song but a kind of heightened speech, heightened further by the vocal ornaments used in this recording. These ornaments include the vibrato mentioned in the textbook (*i'i*) as well as glottal stops. In fact, these ornaments constitute the chief expressive devices in this music. As in the forms of chant heard earlier, the rhythm is nonmetric, though the *mele pule* comes closer to natural speech in its vocal quality and rhythm than does Islamic or Catholic chant. The final two features, monophonic texture and free form—or at least a form that follows the poetic structure—again point to the essential similarities between the religious chant of all three cultures.

If you have time, play the clip of Maori chant from *The Whale Rider* (about 4 or 5 minutes into the movie). One of the elders sings a lament over the body of a mother who has died in childbirth. While the language is different, and while recorded Hawai'ian songs of lamentation (*mele kanikau*) sound rather different than either *mele pule* or this Maori chant, you and your students will be struck by the extraordinary similarity between this lament and the two short *Listen* examples. Despite the thousands of miles that separate New Zealand and Hawai'i, both cultures derive from the East Polynesian subgroup (the myth of the "whale rider" points to the long sea voyages undertaken by the Polynesians). This clip makes that shared cultural identity as plain as day.

Native American Song

Native American song presents a large and diverse body of music. It includes songs of the ancient Aztecs and Inca, and its origins predate the beginnings of recorded history in the Americas. Making our task more difficult, these varied traditions have undergone significant change, especially since the arrival of European conquerors, missionaries, and settlers several hundred years ago. In North America, the movement of settlers farther and farther west forced many Native Americans into smaller and smaller territories, and many tribes were uprooted and transplanted to reservations far from their original lands. A little over a hundred years ago, fearing these ancient traditions might die out forever, dedicated ethnomusicologists and anthropologists began to record and document the music and culture of many tribes. The efforts of Washington Matthews, Alice Cunningham Fletcher, James Mooney, Frances Densmore, Natalie Curtis, and others in North America thus paralleled the work of Kodály and Bartók in eastern Europe.

Fortunately, many Native American musical styles have maintained their vitality in spite of the encroachment of Western civilization, though not quite in the form one might have anticipated. Banding together for mutual support and encouragement, the once-individual styles of many tribes, especially in the Great Plains, have gradually merged into a more generalized pan-Indian style, noted by researchers as early as the 1930s. Other tribes—such as the Navajo, who were able to keep their land and maintain a large population—have preserved their traditions more or less unchanged. The song below, "K'adnikini'ya'," reflects the enormous stability of the unique Navajo traditions.

Native American song reflects the diversity of life's activities. Some songs are as old as the Native American cultures themselves; others come in dreams. Many are associated with hunting or planting, with spinning or grinding corn, with love or war, or with dances of all kinds. Many of them bear comparison with the chant we study in this chapter, especially for their association with sacred, magical, or healing rituals. Life-cycle rituals in particular are universally celebrated by Native Americans, as they are anywhere in the world. Special rituals mark one's birth, naming, puberty, marriage, name change (when an adult accomplishes something so significant that the old name no longer fits), healing from disease, and death. These are defining moments in a human life, full of mystery, magic, and power; music, dance, and word fuse at such moments to raise them above everyday experience and to invoke divine assistance and blessing. In all cases, songs have power—power to elevate a moment or experience; power to strengthen, heal, and restore; and power to invoke spirits beyond ourselves.

The best place to cover this material is right alongside your discussion of Gregorian chant, Qur'anic recitation, and Hawai'ian *mele pule*. All of these examples share several interesting features, although the Navajo example is unusual in its steady rhythmic pulse. The following materials provide background information on the history, culture, and music of the Navajo as well as specific lecture suggestions for "K'adnikini'ya'." For a contrasting example of Native American song, see the Plains style Grass Dance song in Further Listening Examples below.

Navajo Song

Except for their traumatic removal to Fort Sumner between 1864 and 1868, the Navajo have had the great good fortune to remain on their own land throughout the history of the United States. Their reservation, which encompasses much of northeastern Arizona, remains one of the largest in the nation. This relative stability has permitted the Navajo to preserve many of their traditions to a degree that is impossible for many other tribes. In fact, Navajo rituals would likely have perished without this stability. Navajo ceremonies rank among the most elaborate in all of Native America; some run for as long as nine days, with carefully prescribed songs, dances, and other ritual activities that must be performed in the proper order.

Most Native American traditions employ song as part of sacred ritual, but they also make use of a wide variety of songs for other purposes. In the Navajo tradition, virtually all songs are associated with ritual or ceremony. All music is sacred to the Navajo because all music possesses power—power to summon deities, power to protect, and power to restore strength and health. Gary Witherspoon offers the following description of this ritual power. "The language of Navajo ritual is performative, not descriptive. Ritual language does not describe how things are; it determines how they will be. Ritual language is not impotent; it is powerful. It commands, compels, organizes, transforms, and restores. It disperses evil, reverses disorder, neutralizes pain, overcomes fear, eliminates illness, relieves anxiety, and restores order, health, and well-being."[5] David McAllester, in his landmark study of Enemy Way music, likens Navajo songs to high-voltage electrical wires.[6] If you have the appropriate

[5]Gary Witherspoon, *Language and Art in the Navajo Universe*. Ann Arbor: University of Michigan Press, 1977, p. 34.

[6]David P. McAllester, *Enemy Way Music*. Papers of the Peabody Museum of American Archaeology and Ethnology, Harvard University 41, 3 (1954).

training and preparation, you can handle electrical wires safely; without such training, you stay away. The Navajo treat songs in much the same manner, but not all songs possess the same potency. The most powerful songs are sung only by ceremonial experts of the tribe; laypeople will never sing these songs—they are too dangerous. At the opposite end of the spectrum are much less potent songs that can be sung by anyone, either as part of a specific ceremony or at any time for more general recreation. The largest body of Navajo songs falling into the latter category are associated with the Enemy Way ceremony.

The Enemy Way (or Squaw Dance) is a three-day healing ceremony that protects and frees the "patient" (the ritual recipient) from the ghosts of outsiders with whom the patient once had contact. Such ceremonies were especially common in the years after World War II when Navajo war veterans returned home experiencing the aftereffects of combat.[7] Once a member of the tribe determines that the ceremony is needed, participants are gathered and a ritual practitioner comes in to make preparations, which often include chanting, singing, and dancing. David McAllester provides the following summary of the Enemy Way.[8]

> First Day . . .The "rattle" stick is decorated and carried by the patient and a large following to the camp of the stick receiver.
>
> First Night . . . First night of public singing and a few hours of dancing take place at the camp of the stick receiver.
>
> Second Day . . . Party from patient's camp sings outside stick receiver's hogan and receives presents. . . . Party from patient's camp returns home. . . . The stick receiver's camp is moved to within a few miles of the patient's camp.
>
> Second Night . . . Second night of public singing and a few hours of dancing take place at the new camp of the stick receiver's party.
>
> Third Day . . . Stick receiver's party moves to the patient's camp, and a sham battle takes place, after which the stick receiver's camp is set up next to the patient's camp. . . . Party from stick receiver's camp sings outside patient's hogan and receives presents. . . . Blackening of patient, performance of Enemy Way rites, and shooting of scalp take place.
>
> Third Night . . . Circle dance, walking songs, serenade, and third night of public singing with a few hours of dancing take place. . . . At dawn a brief ceremony concludes the Enemy Way. This may include the singing of Blessing Way songs.

One can quickly see from the outline the significance of the role of the ritual practitioner. The chants and songs, the ritual actions and their sequence, every detail must be committed to memory—an incredible, even daunting, feat of memorization. And the practitioners must know what they are doing; any mistake lessens the efficacy of the ceremony. But even the ceremonial experts can't memorize every ritual; most do well to memorize three or so. Like medical doctors, they specialize in one set of rituals or another; and like doctors, the services they render are highly prized and generously rewarded. The practitioner expects to be paid, and the recipients of his services expect to pay, and

---

[7]As many of your students learned in the recent movie *Windtalkers*, Navajo soldiers played a significant role in U.S. military operations in the Pacific theater of World War II. In the attempt to create a secret code that the Japanese could not crack, someone remembered the complexity of the Navajo language. The communications corps brought in Navajo soldiers who shared top-secret messages in a code based on their native tongue. The Japanese never deciphered the complexities of Navajo speech, and these Native American soldiers did their new country a great service.

[8]McAllester, *Enemy Way Music*, p. 8.

no one seems to resent the situation. Most Navajo believe that failure to pay would compromise the effectiveness of the ritual. Any who wish to become practitioners must also pay the expert in order to watch and learn the ritual for themselves. This system of apprenticeship is part of the system by which students learn to handle these "high-voltage" songs.

"K'adnikini'ya'"   "K'adnikini'ya'" is a ceremonial song used to end the last night of the Enemy Way. As the authors point out, the song was composed during the period of captivity at Fort Sumner, and the translation of the title, "I'm leaving," may reflect on their time of exile. The only other word with a translatable meaning, "ho'zho'ni," which means "beautiful" or "holy," is a sacred word that appears in many Navajo ritual songs. The other "words" of the song are vocables. The other vocables are used in typical fashion, inserted before, after, or in the middle of translatable words of the text, or as an invocation on the tonic pitch that begins each phrase (the **a** motive in the chart below).

Little is known about the origin of Navajo vocables; however, two theories have been advanced. In the most commonly held view, vocables were originally real words with specific meanings, but their meanings were lost or forgotten over time. The opposite view, advanced by McAllester in his *Enemy Way Music*, suggests that older songs used only vocables, and that the proportion of "real" words has increased in recent times. It has also been suggested that vocables were the original language of Navajo songs, a kind of sacred, powerful language whose full meaning was unknowable for humans.

Just as we will see in our look at Aztec vocables in Chapter 6 of this manual, Navajo vocables cannot be described as meaningless, and they most certainly cannot be changed from one performance to the next. They are fixed, not arbitrary, and they contribute in specific ways to the meaning of a song. Charlotte Frisbie finds several categories of vocables in Navajo practice.[9]

Onomatopoetic words, or sound symbols—these represent the characteristic sounds of specific deities, animals, or activities.

Archaic words—for some the meaning is still known; others have been forgotten.

Foreign words—generally from other Native American languages (this appears to be the case for the "hé-yuh-eh, yáng-a-ang-a" vocables that begin each section).

Poetic or musical embellishment—inserted before, after, or in the middle of words, these vocables elaborate, punctuate, or otherwise emphasize translatable words in the text, for either poetic or musical reasons (the Aztec vocables fall into this last category).

In fact, the song title's first syllable—"k'ad," meaning "now"—represents yet another type of vocable. This syllable, although a translatable word, is frequently used at the beginning of ceremonial song texts or phrases, more or less independent of its original meaning.

When you present this song to your class, begin with some background information. At the very least, describe the significance and power of Navajo songs and briefly outline the Enemy Way ceremony. If you have time, give your class the lowdown on vocables; otherwise, a working definition will suffice.

---

[9]Charlotte J. Frisbie, "Vocables in Navajo Ceremonial Music." *Ethnomusicology* (September 1980), pp. 347–92.

Make sure students have read textbook page 75 and refer them to the *Listen* chart on that page. Display the checklist of musical elements and structures, play the song for your class, and again solicit their reactions. A comparative approach can be useful this time, especially since it calls attention to the diversity of Native American song styles. In the discussion that follows, draw out the following points.

Melody—again, based on simple patterns of repetition and contrast. Melodic shape is quite different, however; each phrase starts and ends low with an upward arch in the middle. Phrases are again irregular in length, but consistent when repeated. Phrase relationships can be mapped as follows.

Sections:	**A**	**A repeated**	**B**	**A returns**	
Phrases:	**a a b b′**	**a b b′**	**a c**	**a b b′**	**a′**
Beats:	4 4 7 7	4 7 7	4 7	4 7 7	6

Note the consistent use of the **a** phrase as an invocation at the beginning of each section. Further, each section ends with exactly the same three-beat motive; the concluding three-beat pattern that distinguishes the **b′** phrase from the **b** phrase shows up again at the end of the **c** phrase.

Harmony—none, monophonic texture. Melody uses four notes of a pentatonic scale.

Rhythm—steady, unchanging drum beat supports the melody.

Dynamics—moderate, relaxed dynamics throughout. No significant variety.

Texture—monophonic texture, again a single melody over a simple drum beat.

Color—much more relaxed sound, yet with a slight nasal coloration and a bit of vibrato. Solo voice with a steady tone throughout. Only a single drummer.

Form—irregular. Easier to describe than to label, it includes an **A** refrain and its repetition, seven repetitions of a **B** section (like an ostinato), and the return of **A**.

Text—Two translatable words; the rest are vocables.

Comparison of the Navajo song with previous examples of chant reveals some features that are similar, especially its dynamics, texture, and vocal color, yet it exhibits some surprising differences as well. The most striking differences appear in its melody, rhythm, form, and text. Unlike the other chant examples, this *ho'zho'ni* song uses a drum that establishes a regular pulse. It also uses repetition, almost ostinato-like in the **B** section, that gives this song an easily recognizable shape and form. This same quality carries over into the melody's construction, which consists of short motives frequently repeated. This melody is certainly more varied than the Hawai'ian *mele pule*, but more regular and less complex than Gregorian chant ("In paradisum") or Qur'anic recitation, and far less virtuosic than the latter. Finally, this song's ritual power does not derive from words that have a precise, translatable meaning, as would be the case in recitation of the Qur'an or the Bible. The song's words, vocables, and ritual context all combine to give this song its power.

This comparison also provides an excellent example of oral as opposed to written traditions. All of these chant traditions began as oral traditions, words and melodies passed from teacher to pupil, from one generation to the next, without any reference to a written text. Western music evolved into a written tradition during the Middle Ages, and Islamic scholars (themselves part of a long-standing written tradition) wrote out the Qur'an to preserve it from corruption. However, many other traditions, including Hawai'ian and Navajo cultures, have remained oral traditions. Of course, oral traditions require phenomenal feats of memorization, and for this reason those of us who grew up in written traditions tend to be suspicious of oral cultures. We never had to memorize so much material and we cannot imagine how anyone could, so we assume it cannot be done, or at least that it cannot be done reliably. And our assumptions are false. Research has demonstrated that oral cultures transmit cultural artifacts from one generation to the next with a remarkably high degree of accuracy.

When changes occur in an oral tradition, the cause is generally a collision of cultures, not faulty memory. As an example, many younger Navajo have discovered the intertribal powwow, and they enjoy the more exciting, "fancy" singing of the Plains style (see Further Listening Examples below). When they try to bring that high-pitched singing style into Navajo rituals, however, they quickly tire and drop out. In the Plains style, drum groups rarely sing longer than half an hour at a time, but Navajo rituals often last all night long. Once the younger Navajo drop out, the singers who carry the songs throughout the night are the older men (middle-aged and above), the ones who use a more relaxed vocal style. The melodic construction of this *ho'zho'ni* song actually helps ritual practitioners who must learn it. At first glance, it might appear that this song's irregular form would make memorization difficult. As we saw earlier, however, this melody employs a high degree of repetition, with many short melodic formulas used to begin and end sections. These formulas go a long way toward helping ritualists memorize such a large body of songs.

To sum up, Navajo songs possess magical and spiritual power. Their use is reserved for those who are trained to handle them properly. As a result, recreational singing plays only a minor role in Navajo traditions, some of the primary exceptions being the sway songs, dance songs, gift songs, and circle dance songs associated with the Enemy Way. Singing is not "for fun"; a song is considered a good song if it fulfills its ritual purpose properly. Due to this spiritually utilitarian view, the Navajo have a difficult time even understanding questions about the esthetic value of different melodies, just as we struggle to grasp the spiritual power of such simple songs. Native Americans represent "the other" in our midst. Will we learn to hear them before they become too much like us?

Additional Teaching Suggestions

⁊ Lecture-Demonstration Ideas

1. Invite a Catholic priest to class. Ask him to talk about monastic life, the Mass, and the Offices. Not all priests are experts on medieval liturgy, but most are familiar with monastic disciplines. Their presence alone embodies centuries of tradition, and they offer a unique perspective on materials from Chapter 5. Older priests will remember the pre–Vatican II Latin liturgy.

2. Invite a singer who specializes in early music or a vocal early music group to class. Some groups specialize in plainchant; others perform medieval liturgical drama now and then. A workshop setting that includes performance and discussion of the music works best.

3. Invite a musician member of the Society for Creative Anachronism to class. A society member assumes a fictitious identity as a personage from medieval or Renaissance times. A combination of research and imagination is used to flesh out as specifically as possible the career, social standing, personality, and lifestyle of the alter ego. Depending on the member's "identity," you might learn about the lifestyle of a nun, a troubadour, or a wandering jongleur. Sometimes offbeat (like many musicians!), members offer unusual insights.

4. Create a slide show of artworks and architecture from the Middle Ages. Play music of the Middle Ages while students study the images on the screen.

5. Invite a representative from a local mosque to speak to your class. Since so many American students know so little about Islamic faith and culture, this can be a real learning experience. Ask your guest to talk about Muhammad, the history of Islam, important Muslim beliefs, and the Islamic view of music. Especially pertinent would be a discussion of the Qur'an, Qur'anic recitation, and the meaning of Surah 36—the one recited in the *Listen* recordings.

6. To bring these cultures to life for your students, create a "travelogue" of Islamic countries, Hawai'i, or the Navajo Nation. Show slides that depict important cities, places of worship, artworks, architecture, and music making. Play appropriate music while students study the images on the screen.

7. Invite Native American musicians to class. Many drum groups include at least one respected member devoted to keeping old traditions alive who is willing to share those traditions with any who will listen. Your guests can often sing, play, or even dance, but even more important are the insights they can offer into the beliefs and traditions that underlie the music. Make sure your students prepare questions in advance.

8. Take your class to an intertribal powwow (see Further Listening Examples below). No longer restricted to large, flat expanses of the Plains states, these Native American celebrations now occur year-round in all parts of North America. During the winter months, they move into gymnasiums and field houses, and intertribal clubs sponsor these events in urban areas throughout the United States. Let your students experience Native American songs and dances firsthand.

❡ Class Discussion Ideas

1. *What connections can you make between the musical style of plainchant and the monastic lifestyle?* Monks led simple, regulated lives, and devoted much time to prayer and worship. How does the music reflect this?

2. Hildegard of Bingen was a remarkable woman with diverse talents as poet, abbess, theologian, and composer. Carol Neuls-Bates's *Women in Music* (New York: Harper & Row, 1982, pp. 17–20) includes a letter from Hildegard that reveals her tenacity, sly wit, and approach to reasoned argumentation. Read the letter (or make it assigned reading) and ask students to analyze her arguments. This provides fascinating insights into the medieval mind. Further readings from Barbara Lachman's marvelous historical novel *The Journal of Hildegard of Bingen* (New York: Bell Tower, 1993) can help flesh out Hildegard's life, visions, and thought as well as the ordered lifestyle of the sisters at the Rupertsberg Abbey.

3. Give your students a different perspective on the use of modes in the Middle Ages and the Renaissance. Early notions of modal usage prove much more specific and restrictive than our modern notion of how to compose in a given key. Share excerpts from Leeman Perkins's article[10] on early modal practice that show how a mode was defined by such features as its final, dominant, range, register, and melodic figures. This understanding of mode comes much closer to the traditional Arabic concept of mode than to modern Western understanding of scale (see Class Discussion Idea 4 below for further possibilities for comparison).

4. Introduce your class to the Arabic concept of mode. Amnon Shiloah's article on Arabic concepts of mode[11] provides particularly fascinating correspondences between modes and everything from signs of the zodiac to odors to alphabetical letters. Ask students to compare this with what they know of Western scales, or to relate this to their own life experience in some way. For further comparison, you could add the Baroque "doctrine of affections" to the discussion, according to which specific keys were associated with certain attributes. These ideas continued to hold sway in Beethoven's symphonies, where E-flat major and F major retain their traditional association with "heroic" and "pastoral" qualities, respectively.

5. *Why is sacred chant so prevalent around the world?* For many students, the universality of chant is one of the most eye-opening features of this chapter. This and the following provide some open-ended questions to prod discussion of issues that are bound to come up. Why not just read sacred scriptures? Why use a different style of singing? Does chant really add something to the experience of sacred scriptures and prayer?

6. *What experiences have you had since 9/11/01 that have changed your perception of Islamic cultures?* Students have been touched in surprising ways by personal encounters, college-sponsored speakers or events, or even television specials concerning Islam. Tapping into this wealth of personal experience can lead to fascinating classroom discussion.

7. Use slides or images of Native Americans to trigger discussion of the history of Native America. Many students already know a great deal about one or more tribes, and they know at least something about the treatment of Indians by the U.S. government, if only by way of movies like *Dances with Wolves* or *The Last of the Mohicans*. Your school's library contains many books with relevant photographs and other useful images. If you wish, supplement your images with quotations from Native Americans about their history, culture, and beliefs. *Black Elk Speaks* is especially useful for this purpose.[12] As a preparation for the Global Perspectives materials above, this discussion can help students understand what they know and, more important, what they don't know about Native Americans. You can help them see past the distortions presented by history and the media.

---

[10]Leeman L. Perkins, "Mode and Structure in the Masses of Josquin." *Journal of the American Musicological Society* 26, 2 (1973), pp. 189–239.

[11]Shiloah, "Arabic Concept of Mode," p. 38.

[12]Black Elk and John G. Neihardt, *Black Elk Speaks: Being the Life Story of a Holy Man of the Oglala Sioux*. Lincoln: University of Nebraska Press, 1979.

✎ Listening Ideas

1. Find scores for as many Middle Ages listening examples as possible—not modern transcriptions or arrangements but facsimiles or versions that come as close as possible to the original notation. Discussion of the often puzzling relationship between the notation and the recorded performances reveals how few elements were specified in medieval notation, raises the issue of rhythmic notation, and asks how we know when instruments are appropriate. If you cannot find scores for the Kerman and Tomlinson selections, you can easily find scores and recordings for similar works.

2. Bring plainchant (and organum) to life by placing the music in its original context. Take the class to a chapel for an informal service of matins or vespers, or hold one in your classroom. Ask the class to imagine themselves as monks and nuns, and do all you can to create the atmosphere of the monastery. Find recordings and consult the *Liber usualis* for readings and other elements of the liturgy. Call a Catholic priest if you need help.

3. Find recorded examples in each of the medieval modes: Dorian, Phrygian, Lydian, and Mixolydian. Play these for your class, and ask students to describe the mood or effect of each piece. Can they hear a difference in mood? (A Lydian mode plainchant example is not readily available in *Listen* materials; if you can find one, great—if not, three are enough.) See Sound Recordings below for any chants not included in *Listen*.

Dorian   "Ave maris stella" or "Vere dignum"

Phrygian   Anonymous, "Pange lingua"

Mixolydian   Anonymous, "In paradisum," or Hildegard, "Columba aspexit"

4. Play examples of early organum. *Listen* describes stages in the development of organum on textbook page 67. Recordings can easily be found in anthologies that accompany standard music history texts, such as Burkholder's *History of Western Music*, 7th ed. (W. W. Norton, 2006). The recorded examples are short, and they clarify the *Listen* discussion nicely. If you have time, this exercise is well worth the trouble. This step-by-step approach also offers insight into the problems polyphony posed for music notation.

5. Play chant recordings that challenge the traditional Solesmes approach. Several recent recordings, notably by the Ensemble Organum ("Vere dignum" is one example), contain efforts to re-create the sounds of various traditions of Catholic chant from the Middle Ages. Especially pertinent is "Alleluia. Dominus regnavit" from *Chants de l'église de Rome: Vêpres du jour de Pâques* (see Sound Recordings below), a recording that re-creates the sound of the early Roman chant that influenced Charlemagne so powerfully. This style from the early Middle Ages reflects a time when the division between the Western (Roman) and Eastern (Byzantine) halves of Christendom was less distinct, and the Eastern qualities of this performance beg comparison with Qur'anic recitation. An added bonus: This Alleluia also includes examples of early melismatic organum.

6. Play further examples of Qur'anic recitation and a call to prayer for purposes of comparison. *The Music of Islam*, Volume Ten: *Qur'an Recitation, Istanbul, Turkey* (see Sound Recordings below) contains the complete recording of Surah 36, the one included in the textbook. This CD also includes a call to

prayer and examples of different styles of recitation, ranging from very simple (Furqan, Surah 25) to extremely ornate and melismatic (Fatiha, Surah 1).

7. Play examples of "troubadour" music from other cultures. The Sudanese minstrel song from Global Perspectives 3 (*Listen*, Chapter 7) reflects the ancient bardic tradition; more contemporary examples can be found in the music of early blues singers like Robert Johnson (see Sound Recordings below). In each of these, the focus is on the solo singer, accompanied simply by a plucked stringed instrument. Or, if you wish, find examples of your own from contemporary popular music.

8. For an unusual example of a hocketlike technique, play the Sudanese waza trumpet example from *Listen: Brief Fourth Edition*. Since each instrument in the waza ensemble can produce only one pitch, the very act of producing a melody requires a hocketlike alternation between instruments, just as one would find in a handbell choir, with a wind chime, or in *The Sound of Music,* when the von Trapp children each take a different solfège syllable. Renaissance and Baroque catches, some of them bawdy, rely on hocket to produce surprise meanings when performed as a round. Any of these examples can serve to make hocket seem less "intellectual" and more expressive.

9. Play more examples of Native American music to offer your students a greater sense of its diversity. Sound Recordings, below, lists several useful CDs. *Powwow Songs: Music of the Plains Indians* offers examples for comparison with the Grass Dance song in Further Listening Examples below; *Gathering of Nations Pow Wow 2000* provides music from an intertribal powwow; and *Navajo Songs from Canyon de Chelly* contains other songs from the Navajo tradition. For some variety, *Dancing Buffalo* includes flute songs and hymns from the southern Plains, and *Songs of Earth, Water, Fire and Sky* samples music from many Native American traditions not discussed in the textbook.

10. Listen to songs by two American composers who answered Dvořák's challenge (see textbook page 395) to use indigenous music as the basis for art music. Arthur Farwell and Charles Cadman both wrote songs, piano works, and even an opera based on Native American melodies and themes. Of course you will want to compare their songs with the genuine article as discussed in the Global Perspectives section of this chapter. *An Old Song Resung* includes song cycles by both composers (see Sound Recordings below).

11. In a presentation at a recent conference,[13] ethnomusicologist Dale A. Olsen suggested using recent Native American popular songs, in styles ranging from country to rap, as a means of introducing concepts important in the study of traditional Native American musics. Once students grasp these concepts in familiar contexts, the transition to less familiar musics becomes easier. These pop songs also provide wonderful examples of the transculturation (cross-fertilization between two cultures) that makes this music a living tradition. See Sound Recordings below for suggested examples by Julian B, John Trudell, XIT, Cherokee Rose, and Ulali.

---

[13]Dale A. Olsen, "Teaching Native American Music from Pop to Traditional: The Importance of Song Texts," a paper in the symposium "Alternative and Creative Instructional Approaches to Teaching Native American Music Cultures," Meeting of the College Music Society, Kansas City, MO, September 26, 2002.

⁊ Further Listening Examples

Plainchant

Several examples of plainchant allow students to sample the variety of moods and melodic types available. See Appendix II for texts and translations, Sound Recordings below for suggested recordings, and Video Recordings below for an unusual recording of "Dies Irae."

GREGORIAN HYMN "Ave maris stella"

This lovely hymn was sung on all feasts honoring the Blessed Virgin Mary. It employs the Dorian mode, strophic form, and neumatic text setting (a few notes for each syllable). Kerman and Tomlinson discuss Dufay's setting of this hymn in Chapter 6.

GREGORIAN INTROIT "Requiem aeternam"

This introit was sung at the beginning of the Requiem Mass, the traditional Catholic funeral service. It employs the Mixolydian mode, response-verse-response form, and melismatic text setting (many notes for each syllable).

SEQUENCE "Dies irae"

This chant was sung as part of the traditional Requiem Mass. It may be the most famous plainchant in music history, used by Hector Berlioz in his *Fantastic* Symphony, by Franz Liszt in his *Totentanz*, and by George Crumb in *Black Angels*. Thomas of Celano's poem describes the terrible rigors and anguish of Judgment Day. It employs the Dorian mode, strophic form, and syllabic text setting (one note per syllable). If you wish, play Berlioz's version of this tune for contrast: Berlioz, *Fantastic* Symphony, V (track 4).

GREGORIAN HYMN "Pange lingua"

This lovely hymn was sung on Corpus Christi, a feast celebrating the Holy Eucharist, and on Good Friday. It employs the Phrygian mode, strophic form, and mostly syllabic text setting. *Listen* discusses the Josquin Mass based on this hymn in Chapter 6.

Troubadour Song

BEATRITZ, COMTESSA DE DIA "A chantar"

Possibly the only surviving song by a trobairitz (female troubadour), it is based on a poem that exists in two slightly different versions. This song exhibits Dorian mode and an **a a b** (or **a b a b c d b** if you go phrase by phrase) form for each stanza. The text deals with the dark side of courtly love: deceit and betrayal. See *Bella Domna* in Sound Recordings for suggested performances; texts, translations, and a score can be found in the score anthologies that accompany Burkholder's *History of Western Music* (New York: W. W. Norton, 2006).

Estampie

La tierche estampie roial

This typical instrumental estampie is characterized by lively rhythms in compound duple meter. The instrumentation on this recording features two vielles (forerunner of the violin), harp, recorders, and a tabor (drum). Point out that just as with the troubadour songs, the notation provides only a melody line for this dance. Although dance was an important activity in the Middle Ages, very little dance music from the time survives, as most dance musicians were uneducated due to their low social standing.

Notre Dame Organum

LÉONIN **Organum on the plainchant "Alleluia. Viderunt omnes"**

This organum for Christmas Day was likely composed by Léonin, one of Pérotin's predecessors at Notre Dame. Only two voices are used, and it lacks the rhythmic vitality of Pérotin's work, but it is similar in concept and construction. Use the same techniques here that you used with the Pérotin above. See Burkholder in the Sound Recordings for performances, and Appendix II for text and translation.

PÉROTIN **Organum quadruplum on the plainchant gradual "Viderunt omnes"**

This organum for Christmas Day was probably composed by Pérotin. He wrote only two examples of organum quadruplum, and they are the earliest surviving examples of four-voice polyphony in music history. This music is especially remarkable for its rich texture, rhythmic vitality, and motivic interplay. Use the same techniques here that you used with the Pérotin above. See Sound Recordings for performances, and Appendix II for text and translation.

Plains Style and the Intertribal Powwow

Use this material if you would like to expose your students to a second example of native American song. This Plains style Grass Dance song appeared in *Listen: Brief Fourth Edition*. You can use the recordings that accompanied that edition or see the *Powwow Songs: Music of the Plains Indians* CD in Sound Recordings below. Just as with any Global Experiences module, this material includes both background material and teaching suggestions on the music itself.

The proliferation of the intertribal powwow has proved to be one of the most fascinating phenomena in Native American music of the twentieth century. Perhaps the most notable feature of these powwows has been the emergence of a pan-Indian style, as described by James Howard (to whom I am indebted for much of the information below).[14] These phenomena were observed as early as the 1930s and noticed again in the 1950s, but intertribal powwows have grown exponentially since the 1980s. Powwows have recently come to look much the same whether they are held in California, Oklahoma, North

---

[14]James H. Howard, "Pan-Indianism in Native American Music and Dance." *Ethnomusicology* (January 1983), pp. 71–82.

Dakota, Massachusetts, or Florida. Even more curious, no matter which tribe hosts the powwow, the most common dances belong to the traditions of the Plains tribes.

The home of the pan-Indian movement has been traced to Oklahoma, formerly known as "Indian Territory." In the 1830s and 1840s, the U.S. government removed tribes to this territory from the settled regions of the country, including eastern, southern, and midwestern states and territories. With so many new tribes clustered together with the original residents of the southern Plains, it is no surprise that cross-fertilization occurred. At first, individual tribes stuck mostly to their own traditions, but governmental bans on indigenous religious practices and the gradual death of the last generations who remembered life before the reservations meant the loss of many songs, dances, and rituals. This loss, coupled with the Depression, which affected all of the United States, made the period from the 1920s to the 1940s a low point in Native American history. But from the 1950s on, many Native Americans worked to honor and preserve their way of life. The intertribal powwow slowly gained momentum in the Plains, generally favoring the popular Grass Dance and other songs and dances of the Plains area.

In the northern Plains, the American Indian Movement occupation of Wounded Knee in 1973 gave intertribalism a big boost, calling attention as it did to Native American rights, contributions, and traditions. Their theme song was a new song composed in the Grass Dance style, and music of the Plains again became associated with universal Native American concerns. From this point on, the intertribal powwow began to spread across the United States and Canada.

Outside of the Plains region, the music and dance of pan-Indianism was most readily taken up by smaller tribes whose traditions were lost in the first half of the twentieth century. For them, the intertribal powwows provided a genuine Native American tradition to adopt as their own, not to mention the support and encouragement of other tribes. Larger, more stable tribes have been slower to adopt pan-Indianism—and for a variety of reasons. As we will see below, the Navajo managed to maintain their own sacred ritual traditions throughout the twentieth century, but younger Navajo have been attracted in increasing numbers by the more dramatic, more secular music of intertribal powwows. Even in Oklahoma, not all tribes were quick to jump on the bandwagon. The Seminole and other members of the "Five Civilized Tribes" have long shunned practices of the "coarse, uncivilized" Plains tribes, but again younger members find the powwows attractive. In most cases where tribes have maintained their own traditions, intertribal powwows have come to be regarded as a significant addition to, not a substitution for, their own practices. Regardless of background, all participants value the sense of larger community provided by the intertribal powwows.

Although northern and southern Plains practices differ somewhat, a typical intertribal powwow today includes several common features. The setting is a large, open space; it could be a field, a stadium, or a field house. Large drums are positioned around the perimeter of the central dancing area. Drum groups from various tribes are present, along with many others who attend to dance, observe, or otherwise join in the festivities. Over the course of a few days, drum groups take turns performing songs for different kinds of dances. Each drum group consists of about six men and women seated around the drum they all beat as they sing their songs. Dancers move in a large circle in the central dancing area. Some dancers use simple shuffling steps; others dress in traditional bonnets and tunics and employ the much more elaborate gestures and movements of "fancy" dancing. Popular dances include gourd dances, round dances, and war dances such as the Grass Dance. A special dance often honors the war veterans in attendance—warriors still command respect. Adjacent to the dancing area are concessions that sell fried bread, CDs, T-shirts, Native American clothing and crafts, and so on. Clearly the social aspect of these gatherings has far superseded their original ceremonial nature.

The songs that accompany the dances are surprisingly similar, given the variety of tribes often represented. This again points to the pan-Indian nature of these gatherings, and the musical style reflects the influence of Plains styles more than anything else. Most of the songs use a simple stanzaic structure (strophic form), with stanzas repeated as many times as the performers feel necessary. Each stanza typically starts at a high pitch, and subsequent phrases drop lower and lower. The melody itself is constructed from the notes of a pentatonic scale. Singers favor a tense, harsh, often nasal vocal quality, and they tend to pulse rhythmically on sustained notes. A call-and-response format is typical; a lead singer starts each stanza and is soon joined by the other singers in the drum group. The singers also beat the drum around which they seat themselves for performance. Their steady, unison drum beat sets the tempo, marks important divisions with louder drum beats, and occasionally accelerates the tempo, especially toward the end of a song.

Plains Style Grass Dance Song

The Omaha Grass Dance, one of the most significant genres at today's intertribal powwows, probably emerged in the 1840s. According to Orin T. Hatton,[15] the Omaha tribe had moved from the eastern woodlands to modern-day Nebraska sometime in the eighteenth century. In this new setting, the shamanistic Pawnee Iruska traditions blended with elements of an old Omaha men's society, Poo-ge-thun. This new synthesis was given full expression in a new Omaha warrior-dance society, the Hethushka Society, a group that sought to honor historic acts of exceptional bravery and to encourage the same in their own day. The Grass Dance grew out of this tradition, though its music clearly reflects the Pawnee Iruska influence. By the late 1850s, the Grass Dance had spread to the Yankton Sioux; and in 1860, it made its way to the Teton Sioux. Over the next twenty years, it spread quickly to most other northern Plains tribes. Its popularity likely stemmed from two factors: The song, with its emphasis on bravery, came on the scene at a time when many Plains tribes were at war with the U.S. government, and its music and dance were much more exciting than most other indigenous dance songs of the Plains. The popularity of the Grass Dance helped to ensure its survival through the lean years between the world wars, and it has reemerged as one of the most popular pan-Indian dances associated with today's intertribal powwows.

When you present this song to your class, start with some of the background material presented above. Many of your students possess at least passing familiarity with the recent powwow phenomenon described above. Use that familiarity to your advantage and start by describing a typical intertribal powwow. Follow that with a brief summary of the Grass Dance's history; then move to the music itself. Display the list of musical elements and structures, play the song for your class, and solicit their reactions. Use the discussion that follows to make the following points.

---

[15]Orin T. Hatton, "In the Tradition: Grass Dance Musical Style and Female Powwow Singers." *Ethnomusicology* (spring/summer 1986), pp. 197–222.

Melody—based on a simple pattern of repetition and contrast. The first phrase starts high; the **b** and **c** phrases get progressively lower. Phrases are irregular in length but consistent from stanza to stanza. They can be mapped as follows.

Phrase:	a	a	b	c	b	c
Beats:	11 or 12	18	18	20	18	(16—interrupted by next stanza)

Harmony—none, monophonic texture. Scale type is pentatonic.

Rhythm—steady drum beat supports the melody, with gradual accelerando starting in the third stanza. Melody notes carefully avoid exact synchronization of drum beats.

Dynamics—singers on the loud side throughout. Drum at more moderate level, with special hard beats to articulate important points of demarcation. A crescendo accompanies the accelerando beginning in the third stanza. Note the five hard beats that end the coda—a typical concluding pattern.

Texture—monophonic texture, a single melody over a simple drum pattern.

Color—tense, harsh, nasal sound quality. Pulsing quality on sustained notes. Solo voice at beginning of each stanza, with other voices joining in on the repetition of the first phrase. Hoots and hollers accompany entrance of other voices.

Form—strophic form, a single stanza repeated four times with a brief coda at the end. Plains songs typically repeat the last phrase or two of the stanza as a coda.

Text—consists of vocables, various syllables whose meanings we do not know for certain.

Finally, draw attention to several features associated with good singing and drumming in the Plains style. Good singers are prized for their vocal timbre (somewhat different in different regions) as well as the high range, clarity, loudness, and endurance of their voices. Good singers have also both memorized a large repertory of songs and mastered the art of singing between the drum beats. Since the singers also play the drums, the skills associated with good drumming are similar to those for singers. Drummers must also master the drum strokes and precise synchronization that contribute to a full drum sound. In addition, they must be able to keep tempo, synchronize with other players in accelerando passages, and learn the accented beat patterns used for special articulation. Some writers have commented on the "simplicity" of the Plains style, but skill and practice are required to perform this music well.

Comparison of Plains and Navajo songs (see "K'adnikini'ya'" in Lecture Suggestions on page 86) reveals that many features are surprisingly similar, including melodic structure, scale type, steady drum beats, texture, and text. Differences can be found in their melodic contour and their rhythmic and dynamic variety, but the most striking differences relate to their use of tone color and form.

One other primary difference is not a purely musical one; rather, it reflects the current uses of these two songs. As mentioned earlier, Navajo songs possess magical and spiritual power. Their use is reserved for those who are trained to handle them properly. The Grass Dance song reflects a different cultural setting altogether. It once belonged to dance ceremonies designed to instill courage and encourage bravery, but in the modern intertribal powwow it has become more of a social phenomenon. The dance brings people of many tribes together in a social and recreational context, and the songs can be sung anywhere, anytime, and in any context. If these songs possess any power today, it can be found in the very act of participation in this old tradition. Participants find power in this act of self-definition, both as individuals reclaiming their roots and as a community that knows the power of Native American unity. This power is easier for most Americans to understand than the power of Navajo song, and it may reflect the greater degree to which the intertribal powwow has assimilated mainstream American values.

Multimedia Resources

♩ Further Listening Charts and Texts

See Appendix II for texts and translations if you use these works from Further Listening Examples above:

> Gregorian hymn, "Ave maris stella"
>
> Gregorian introit, "Requiem aeternam"
>
> Sequence, "Dies irae"
>
> Gregorian hymn, "Pange lingua"
>
> Léonin, organum on the plainchant "Alleluia. Viderunt omnes"
>
> Pérotin, organum quadruplum on the plainchant gradual "Viderunt omnes"

♩ Sound Recordings

Bella Domna—The Medieval Woman: Lover, Poet, Patroness and Saint. Mara Kiek and Sinfonye. Hyperion CDA66382 (CD). Excellent recording of medieval works revolving around women, including estampies and songs by Beatritz, Comtessa de Dia, Richart de Fournival, and others. Use this recording if you try suggestions for "A chantar" or the estampie in Further Listening Examples above.

Burkholder, *History of Western Music*, 7th ed. New York: W. W. Norton, 2006. The CDs that accompany this standard music-history textbook contain recordings of several works suggested in Further Listening Examples above: Beatritz's "A chantar" and both Léonin's and Pérotin's versions of "Alleluia. Viderunt omnes." Standard music-history textbooks like this one now also provide interactive listening charts for their anthologies; check with a musicologist in your department to see what's available.

Chant. Choir of the Benedictine Monastery of Santo Domingo de Silos. EMI Classics CDZ 62735 (CD). One of the best-selling classical discs of 1994, with sequels that took us to the millennium—and it's the same plainchant we all studied as undergraduates! Serves well to expose students to the melodic variety and range of expression found in plainchant.

Chants de l'église de Rome: Vêpres du jour de Pâques [Chants of the Roman Church: Easter Day Vespers]. Ensemble Organum. Harmonia Mundi HMC 901604 (CD). Attempt to re-create the sound of early Roman plainchant from the sixth to the thirteenth century. Performances include early examples of melismatic organum and reflect Eastern influences from the Byzantine half of

Christendom. Wonderful corrective to the soothing but historically questionable Solesmes style, which has dominated so many chant recordings.

Cherokee Rose, *To All the Wild Horses*. Clearlight Music (CD). Collection of original songs by Cherokee Rose, a self-described "black Irish Indian." Cherokee Rose is also a reference to the white wild rose that grows along the Trail of Tears. This album incorporates many traditional Native American elements into a style that ranges from folk to soft rock. Try this recording if you use Listening Idea 11 above.

A Dance in the Garden of Mirth. The Dufay Collective. Chandos Records CHAN 9320 (CD). This virtuoso early music ensemble provides a rich sampling of instrumental music from the late Middle Ages. If you use suggestions in Further Listening Examples above for "La tierce estampie roial" or want other examples of the estampie for your class, get this recording.

Dancing Buffalo: Dances and Flute Songs from the Southern Plains. Cornel Pewewardy and the Alliance West Singers. Music of the World CDT-130 (CD). Collection of dances, hymns, and flute songs of the Kiowa and Comanche peoples. Detailed liner notes. Try this recording for further examples of Plains style music or if you use Listening Idea 9 above.

An English Ladymass: Medieval Chant and Polyphony. Anonymous 4. Harmonia Mundi HMU 907080 (CD). One of several outstanding CDs by this women's quartet, it contains a mixture of English medieval plainchant, motets, and the like. Not only do these performances remind us that music making was not purely a male activity in the Middle Ages, but they also rank among the finest recordings of this literature. Other recent Anonymous 4 CDs include *La bele Marie: Songs to the Virgin from 13th Century France* and *The Second Circle: Love Songs of Francesco Landini*. Try this recording if you use suggestions for "Ave maris stella" in Further Listening Examples above. (Dufay's polyphonic setting of this hymn is described in Chapter 6 of the textbook.)

Gathering of Nations Pow Wow 2000: Millennium Celebration, Vols. 1 and 2. Various drum groups. Sound of America Recordings SOAR-205-CD and SOAR-209-CD (CD). Live recordings of one of the largest powwows of recent times. Various Plains tribes are represented, but the music represents the pan-Indian style that has developed in the past century. Good follow-up to the Plains style example in Further Listening Examples above. Try this recording if you use Listening Idea 9 above.

Hawai'ian Drum Dance Chants: Sounds of Power in Time. Smithsonian Folkways SFW40015 (CD). Recordings by Hawai'ian traditional musicians, some from the 1980s, some transfers from valuable cylinder recordings dating back to 1933. This CD contains the *mele pule* chants found in the *Listen* set. Includes some chant in *mele oli* style (without dance), but focuses primarily on *mele hula*—metric chant with dance. Provides a good overview of Hawai'ian traditional music, with excellent liner notes by Elizabeth Tatar.

Hildegard, *Canticles of Ecstasy*. Sequentia. Deutsche Harmonia Mundi 05472 77320 2 (CD). The music of Hildegard has enjoyed a recording boom in recent years. Sequentia, an ensemble of women's voices that specializes in Hildegard's music, has recently rerecorded her *Ordo virtutum*, one of the earliest liturgical dramas. This recording contains a selection of chants inspired by Hildegard's mystic visions.

Hildegard, *A Feather on the Breath of God*. Gothic Voices. Hyperion CDA66039 (CD). This recording won a Gramophone Record Award when it was released in 1983. It remains one of the most beautiful recordings of Hildegard's music, performed by male as well as female voices. It includes "Columba aspexit," the plainchant sequence discussed in *Listen*.

Johnson, Robert. *Robert Johnson: The Complete Recordings*. Columbia/ Legacy C2K 64916 (CD). Complete recordings of perhaps the most famous early blues master. Johnson represents an even older tradition, that of the self-accompanied troubadour. Use this recording if you try Listening Idea 7 above.

Josquin, *Missa Pange lingua; Missa La sol fa re mi*. Tallis Scholars. Gimell CDGIM 009 (CD). Contains two Renaissance Masses by Josquin and the plainchant hymn "Pange lingua." The textbook covers the Pange lingua Mass in Chapter 6. Try this recording if you use suggestions for this hymn in Further Listening above.

Julian B. *Once Upon a Genocide*. Sound of America Records: Warrior 605 (CD). Outspoken, often angry rap-inspired songs about Native American concerns by Julian B. Try "The Spirit of Crazy Horse" from this recording if you use Listening Idea 11 above.

The Mirror of Narcissus. Gothic Voices. Hyperion CDA66087 (CD). Beautifully sung performances of ballades, virelais, motets, and a rondeau by Machaut, directed by Christopher Page. All parts are sung here (unlike the Machaut motet in the *Listen* set), reflecting recent scholarly notions concerning performance practice in the Middle Ages. Try this recording if you want to explore other music by Machaut.

The Music of Islam, Volume Ten: *Qur'an Recitation, Istanbul, Turkey*. Celestial Harmonies 13150-2 (CD). Contains a complete recording of "Ya Sin," Surah 36, the example described in the textbook. Also contains a call to prayer and many complete chapters from the Qur'an, ranging in length from 0:43 to 20:22. Performances by expert practitioners trained in the renowned Istanbul school. To find this CD, visit www.worldmusicstore.com.

Na Leo Hawai'i Kahiko: The Master Chanters of Hawai'i—Songs of Old Hawai'i. Mountain Apple Company MACD 2043 (CD). A collection of rare historical recordings from the archives of the Bernice Pauahi Bishop Museum's Department of Anthropology. This highly recommended CD provides the truest picture available of traditional Hawai'ian song and chant. You can get this and other rare Hawai'ian recordings directly from the museum—go to www.bishopmuseum.org/store.html, click on the *Shop Pacifica* link, and choose *Music, Video & Computer*.

Navajo Songs from Canyon de Chelly. New World Records 80406-2 (CD). The *Listen* recording of "K'adnikini'ya'" was taken from this CD in the excellent New World Records catalog. Helpful liner notes. Strongly recommended for further examples of Navajo song. Try this recording if you use Listening Idea 9 above.

New World Records (701 Seventh Ave., New York, N.Y. 10036). This record label was created at the time of the U.S. bicentennial to record hitherto unavailable works by American composers and performing musicians. Recordings document many important types of American music, past and present. Most relevant to this chapter are the many recordings of Native American music. New World recordings are a treasure trove of Americana—often hard to find, but worth the effort.

Officium. Jan Garbarek and the Hilliard Ensemble. ECM Records New Series 1525 (CD). This unusual recording consists of Jan Garbarek's saxophone improvisations over a mix of plainchant and liturgical polyphony by medieval and Renaissance composers such as Pérotin, Dufay, Morales, and de la Rue.

An Old Song Resung. William Parker and William Huckaby. New World Records NW 80463-2 (CD). Collection of songs by Arthur Farwell, Charles Cadman, Charles Tomlinson Griffes, and Charles Ives. Most interesting for this chapter are Farwell's Indian Songs and Cadman's American Indian Songs. Try this recording if you use Listening Idea 10 above.

Palestrina, *Missa pro defunctis; Motets.* Chanticleer. Teldec Das Alte Werk 4509-94561-2 (CD). Contains gorgeous performances of Palestrina's polyphony, but use this CD if you try suggestions for the Gregorian introit "Requiem aeternam" in Further Listening Examples above.

Palestrina, *Missa Viri Galilaei.* La Chapelle Royale/Ensemble Organum. Harmonia Mundi France HMC 1951388 (CD). A complete performance by Ensemble Organum of the Preface "Vere dignum" covered in the textbook, followed by Palestrina's Renaissance Mass of the same name. Plainchant performances of the movements of the Proper are interspersed among Palestrina's polyphonic settings of the Ordinary, and the Preface provides an example of Catholic recitation, especially useful for comparison with the Islamic, Hawai'ian, and Navajo examples. Interestingly, Palestrina's Mass makes no reference to the Gregorian introit ("Viri Galilaei"); it is, rather, a parody Mass based on Palestrina's motet of the same name. The introit melody is included on this recording only because it is the introit proper to the Feast of the Ascension, for which Palestrina composed this Mass.

Paris 1200: Pérotin and Léonin, Chant and Polyphony from 12th Century France. Lionheart. Nimbus NI 5547 (CD). Recent recording of chant and organum from the Notre Dame school, including a complete performance of "Alleluia. Diffusa est gratia" from the *Listen* set. A good choice if you want to explore other works of Léonin and Pérotin, though the track list fails to indicate which works are ascribed to which composer (not that we know for certain!).

Pérotin. The Hilliard Ensemble. ECM Records 837751 (CD). The preeminent early music ensemble performs several of Pérotin's most famous organa in up to four voices. A wonderful recording if you want to explore other works of the Notre Dame school. Highly recommended if you use the four-voice "Viderunt omnes" in Further Listening Examples above.

Powwow Songs: Music of the Plains Indians. ARC Music 1653 (CD). Excellent collection contains two groups of songs: one from the southern Plains, the other northern. Originally released as New World Records 80343-2. Useful liner notes. Strongly recommended for further examples of Plains style, or if you use Listening Idea 9 or the Grass Dance song in Further Listening Examples above.

Songs of Earth, Water, Fire and Sky: Music of the American Indian. New World Records NW 80246-2 (CD). Another excellent recording from the New World Records catalog, this sampler of Native American music includes examples from around the country. Includes dances from the San Juan, Seneca, Arapaho, Plains (southern and northern), Creek, Yurok, Navajo, and Cherokee traditions. Excellent liner notes. Try this recording if you use Listening Idea 9 above.

Trudell, John. *AKA Grafitti Man.* Rykodisc RCD 10223 (CD). This album by musician/activist John Trudell earned Bob Dylan's admiration. It consists mostly of thoughtful, provocative spoken poetry accompanied by a rock band.

"Bombs over Baghdad" was written in response to the Gulf War but works just as well in 2007. Try this recording if you use Listening Idea 11 above.

Ulali. *Mahk Jchi.* Original Vision Records (CD). A First Nations women's *a cappella* trio with an exciting, distinctive sound. Although the members are Tuscarora, Mayan, Apache, and Yaqui, they draw on many Native American traditions. Accompanied only by indigenous percussion instruments, their singing is clearly influenced by traditional styles, with perhaps the occasional pop inflection. Try the title track if you use Listening Idea 11 above.

XIT. *Silent Warrior.* Sound of America Records SOAR 102 (CD). One of the early Native American rock bands, XIT makes use of both rock and indigenous instruments with occasional backup strings. For a time they were regarded as ambassadors for the American Indian Movement, and Native American pride is a prominent theme. Try "We Live" from this recording if you use Listening Idea 11 above.

♪ Video Recordings

Chants Encounter. www.insight-media.com (DVD or VHS, 28 minutes). A look at a wide variety of chant traditions, including Greek, Chinese, Hopi, Mayan, Tibetan, and Catholic. Useful supplement to your study of chant.

[Dies Irae] *Delaware Music Series* (NEH Videodisc Project). Newark, Del.: Office of Computer-Based Instruction, University of Delaware (DVD). Performance by students at Catholic University; conducted by Robert Shafer. The DVD contains a video performance with stereo sound.

Discovering American Indian Music. www.insight-media.com (DVD or VHS, 24 minutes). Looks at various Native American traditions. Most interesting for this chapter is a Navajo corn-grinding song.

Early Musical Instruments Series. www.films.com (DVD or VHS, color, 30 minutes each): *Reed Instruments, Flutes and Whistles, Plucked Instruments, Bowed Instruments, Keyboard and Percussion,* and *Brass Instruments.* David Munrow narrates this series that shows what the instruments look like, how they sound, and how they are played. Performances by Christopher Hogwood and other members of the Early Music Consort of London. Useful if you have a strong interest in the subject and plan to spend some time with the Middle Ages.

Ecstatic Circle. Audio Forum/Video Forum (DVD or VHS, color). A look at the tradition of Islamic dervish dancing, with footage from modern reenactments.

The First Secular Music. Music in Time Series. www.films.com (DVD or VHS, color, 60 minutes). James Galway covers each major topic from *Listen,* Chapter 5. Examples include Gregorian, Hebrew, and Greek chants; Minnesinger song; organum by Léonin and Pérotin; an estampie; secular works by Machaut and Landini; and sacred polyphony by Machaut, Dunstable, and Dufay.

The Flowering of Harmony. The Music of Man Series. Home Vision (VHS, color, 60 minutes). Yehudi Menuhin traces the development of music from ancient traditions of northern India and Crete through Gregorian chant, organum, estampies, troubadour song, and Machaut to the Renaissance music of Dufay, Palestrina, Gabrieli, and others. Traces the evolution of music notation in rare manuscripts from the Bodleian Library. Concentrates mostly on medieval music, for which it provides a good overview. Spotty coverage of the Renaissance. References to other world cultures help place Western music in context.

Hawaiian Rainbow. WinStar Home Entertainment (DVD or VHS, color, 85 minutes). Fascinating documentary looks at the entire range of Hawai'ian music through performances, performer interviews, and scholarly commentary by Ricardo Trimillos and George Kanahele. Examples cover chant, hula, various song traditions, and music for ukelele, slack-key guitar, and steel guitar. Recommended for a broad overview.

Hildegard von Bingen in Portrait—Ordo virtutum. BBC Opus Arte (DVD, color, 70 minutes). Performance by Vox Animae of this early morality play—in Latin with English subtitles. The bonus disc contains lots of useful goodies, including Hildegard's artwork and interviews with experts such as theologian Matthew Fox. A wonderful supplement to your look at Hildegard's sequence.

The History of Music, Part 1. www.insight-media.com (VHS, color, 89 minutes). The section on the Middle Ages covers plainchant, polyphony, the motet, and the music of Machaut and Landini.

JVC Video Anthology of World Music and Dance. Tapes 16 through 18 from this excellent video series offer music from the Middle East and Islamic Africa. Of particular interest are examples 16-1 and 16-10, a Turkish *azan* and dervish dancing, respectively. Tape 30 provides extensive examples of music and dance from the Polynesian island group—nothing specifically from Hawai'i, but some examples offer interesting comparisons. Highly recommended for your presentation of Global Perspectives materials for this chapter.

JVC Video Anthology of World Music and Dance. Tape 27 from this excellent video series offers music of Native Americans. This tape contains extensive examples of music and dance from the Nez Percé tribe of the plateau region, useful for comparison with Navajo and Plains style songs. Highly recommended for your presentation of Global Perspectives materials for this chapter.

Kumu Hula: Keepers of a Culture. WinStar Home Entertainment (DVD or VHS, color, 85 minutes). Fascinating documentary looks at ancient dance and musical traditions of Hawai'i via interviews with hula masters and performances by them and their students. Primary focus on traditional, not modern, hula.

Medieval Art and Music. www.insight-media.com (DVD or VHS, color, 35 minutes). This still-image video provides a concise, visually appealing introduction to important artistic and musical trends in the Middle Ages.

Music in the Twelfth Century (VHS, color, 55 minutes). Covers major musical developments in the twelfth century, including notation, theater, and polyphony. Members of the Folger Consort perform plainchant, crusade songs, and polyphonic works by Léonin and Pérotin.

Notation: The Thin Red Line. Howard Goodall's Big Bangs: Turning Points in Music History Series. www.films.com (DVD or VHS, color, 51 minutes). Entertaining look at one of the major discoveries of the Middle Ages—the development of music notation.

Sacred Sounds: Music of the World, Songs of the Soul. www.films.com (DVD or VHS, color, 58 minutes). Documentary takes us to the Festival of World Sacred Music in Morocco. Includes examples from Christian, Islamic, and Jewish traditions. Valuable supplement to your study of chant.

Thy Kiss of a Divine Nature—The Contemporary Pérotin. Hilliard Ensemble (DVD, color, 95 minutes). Beautiful performances of many of Pérotin's major works, interleaved with interviews with the musicians, director, and so on. Bonus discs provide documentary materials with input from renowned scholars.

Includes a performance of the Pérotin organum from the *Listen* set as well as the four-voice organum in Further Listening Examples above. Highly recommended.

Vibrations and Pagan Rites. Music in Time Series. www.films.com (DVD or VHS, color, 60 minutes). James Galway describes the development of Western music. Looks at music of each style period the authors describe, as they demonstrate the "ageless . . . human impulse to make music." Makes the point that knowledge of music history is necessary for appreciation of music. Serves best as an introduction to a historical survey.

Voices from Heaven: The Religious Music of Europe in the Middle Ages. www.films.com (DVD or VHS, color, 57 minutes). Performances from Paris, Moscow, Vienna, and Assisi provide examples from Catholic, Orthodox, and Jewish traditions. Useful supplement to your study of chant.

Wisconsin Powwow and Naamikaaged: Dancer for the People. Smithsonian/Folkways SFW48004 (VHS, color, two tapes). These two videos examine the Ojibwe peoples of northern Wisconsin. The first takes us to an Ojibwe powwow; the second follows a young Ojibwe dancer and singer as he prepares for a powwow.

♪ Software

The History of Music, Part 1. www.mccormicksnet.com (CD-ROM—Windows or Macintosh). The section on the Middle Ages covers plainchant, polyphony, the motet, and the music of Machaut and Landini.

History Through Art: The Middle Ages. Zane Publishing (CD-ROM—Windows or Macintosh). The Middle Ages volume of this inexpensive CD-ROM series contains several hundred full-screen images, including illuminated manuscripts, medieval painting and triptychs, and many fine examples of period architecture. Quality of screen images is variable, but it's hard to argue with the price. Available from www.cdaccess.com.

The Norton Masterworks CD-ROM. New York: W. W. Norton (CD-ROM—Macintosh). Authors Daniel Jacobson and Timothy Koozin provide a clever multimedia introduction to twelve important works, including the medieval organum "Haec dies." Features animated, guided listening resources as well as information on the composers, eras, genres, and the works themselves.

CHAPTER 6

The Renaissance

Chapter Outline

Boldface indicates works in the recording set.

Important Terms

Renaissance	Mass	declamation	pavan	colonialism
paraphrase	block chord	word painting	galliard	Aztecs
hymn	*a cappella*	motet	jig	Inca
chansons	point of imitation	madrigal	stylization	processional music

Teaching Objectives

❧ Overall Objectives

This chapter will help students acquire familiarity with:

1. Principal genres of the Renaissance as reflections of a more humanist attitude that takes pleasure in the sounds and expressive possibilities of music:

- a. Mass
- b. motet
- c. chanson
- d. madrigal
- e. dances

2. The lives and music of Guillaume Dufay, Josquin Desprez, Giovanni Pierluigi da Palestrina, and Thomas Weelkes.

3. Renaissance Europe's unstoppable urge to explore, conquer, colonize, and convert "primitive" cultures in far corners of the world, and especially the impact of that urge on Aztec and Incan music and culture.

4. The meeting of Spanish and Andean cultures in Peru, and its impact on music.

❧ Listening Objectives

After completing this chapter, students should be able to:

1. Hear how elements and structures of music are typically used in "High Renaissance" style.

2. Identify and follow genres of Renaissance music, especially the harmonized hymn, Mass, chanson, madrigal, and dance music.

3. Listen for and identify expressive techniques of Renaissance music, especially declamation and word painting.

4. Hear significant features of processional music from the Andes.

Lecture Suggestions

The Renaissance is often called the "Age of Exploration." As musicians, we can think of this in terms of the new sounds and harmonies explored by Renaissance composers, but the phrase refers to the many explorers sent out by European nations in search of wealth and territory. It sounds quite romantic when you imagine the travel, adventure, and discovery, but when you ponder the cost to peoples and nations already living in the "New World," you quickly realize that colonialism is another word for European imperialism. This chapter looks at both musical and territorial exploration. It begins with an overview of important developments in European music and continues with a look at Spanish colonialism in Aztec and Inca nations. Two fascinating trends emerge in the "New World": (1) the use of European art music as a tool for Spanish missionaries, and (2) the syncretic fusion of elements from Spanish and indigenous cultures.

7 New Attitudes

A slow decline in the church's influence continued throughout the Renaissance, setting off a period of exploration and questioning in almost all activities. The recovery of ancient Greek and Roman ("pagan") philosophical writings and artworks provided new models and inspiration for thinkers and artists. The Renaissance placed new trust in sensory experience as a reliable guide to understanding the world. Observation became the basis for modern scientific method, and the pleasurable aspects of sensory experience became important guidelines in the arts. The following movements and trends played a powerful role.

Humanism—The dominant intellectual movement of the Renaissance, humanism focused on human life, experiences, and accomplishments, replacing the medieval focus on religious doctrine and the afterlife.

Exploration—This Age of Exploration saw voyages of discovery and conquest by Columbus, Magellan, and many others.

Classicism—The "rediscovery" of the language, literature, philosophy, art, and architecture of ancient Greece and Rome fascinated people of the Renaissance.

Reformation—The power of the Catholic Church was profoundly shaken by Protestant reformers. Key figures were Martin Luther, Jean Calvin, and King Henry VIII. The Counter-Reformation was the church's response.

Education—The rise of secular power meant the rise of education outside the church. Aristocrats and the upper middle class hired scholars to educate their children.

The printing press—Johann Gutenberg invented movable type around 1450. The effect of this invention on literacy and education is incalculable. The subsequent development of movable type for printing music (c. 1500) revolutionized the music business.

Art—Inspired by Greek and Roman art, Renaissance artists depicted the world around them with new clarity and perspective. They took pleasure in accurate depiction of the human body, something that had not been valued in the Middle Ages. This golden age of art and architecture boasts the creations of artists such as Brunelleschi, Botticelli, Titian, Donatello, Raphael, Michelangelo, and Leonardo da Vinci.

Music—The discoveries of Pythagoras were reexamined and expanded for the first time in centuries. The Greek philosophers and their ideas about music and expression were taken to heart by some late Renaissance composers.

What does this mean for Renaissance music? Renaissance composers explored music's pleasurable, expressive qualities, as opposed to the intellectual, mannered qualities prized by *ars nova* composers. At this point, stop to compare these two examples.

Machaut, "Quant en moi"

Palestrina, *Pope Marcellus* Mass, "Qui tollis"

Ask students to pinpoint the elements and structures of music that sound more pleasurable or expressive in the music of Palestrina. In the discussion that follows, guide the students toward the following observations about the Palestrina.

Dynamics—Different weights are created as voices drop out and come back in. The variety is enjoyable.

Tone color—The music is vocal in conception and uses the voices without accompaniment—*a cappella*. Six-voice texture creates a richness that three parts cannot match.

Scales, key, and mode—Similar scales are used in both works, but Palestrina uses the notes in ways that draw our ears to pitch centers. The stability and sense of direction are satisfying.

Rhythm and tempo—Based on Philippe de Vitry's system, the rhythmic notation is similar for both works, but Palestrina prefers simpler rhythms that follow the natural declamation of the words more closely.

Pitch and melody—Melodic lines feel more singable and provide satisfying melodic shapes and contours.

Texture—The mixture of homophonic and polyphonic textures ensures variety. Prominent use of homophony ensures that words will be heard clearly.

Harmony—Renaissance composers became acutely aware of the harmonic interaction of polyphonic lines, and they favored the harmonies they considered most pleasurable. They developed guidelines to control carefully the use of consonant and dissonant intervals, guidelines that remained in effect for centuries. Although it is difficult for students to hear the "perfect beauty" medieval listeners prized in Machaut's music, Palestrina's work remains recognizably beautiful today.

The Palestrina Mass, on all counts, sounds more expressive and more pleasurable than the motet by the more intellectually oriented Machaut. This work belongs to the late Renaissance. Now let us back up and see what happened between Machaut and Palestrina.

DUFAY Harmonized hymn, "Ave maris stella"

Play the music for the class and ask students to describe what they hear. Dufay's harmonized hymn is a superb example of the new, simpler, consonant *a cappella* Renaissance sound. The contrast between the late medieval style and Dufay's music is striking. The Dufay is simpler, smoother, and more gracious and accessible than the cerebral, complex Machaut motet. At the same time, the Dufay lacks the richness and variety of the Palestrina Mass. Nonetheless, both Renaissance works demonstrate warm, pleasant, homogeneous sonorities.

Point out specific features of Dufay's hymn: strophic form and paraphrase technique. Any student who has ever sung hymns in a worship service has had experience with (but rarely knowledge of) strophic form. Before you delve into paraphrase technique, familiarize students with the hymn tune "Ave maris stella" by playing it several times. Once they know the tune, the paraphrase technique can be readily heard if you either play notes of the chant on the keyboard while playing the recording of the harmonized version (to provide a live demonstration of the notated example on textbook page 78) or play individual phrases of the chant version and the harmonized version back to back. (For the complete text and translation for this hymn, see Appendix II.)

The Mass

The most significant, substantial genre of the Renaissance was the Mass. It was the ultimate statement of a composer's artistic prowess, just as the symphony was to composers after Beethoven. The great composers of the Renaissance—Dufay, Josquin, and Palestrina—were great masters of the Mass.

Early on, Renaissance composers faced the daunting problem of achieving coherence in the music of the Mass. Most of the Mass was sung—in plainchant, just as in the Middle Ages—so Renaissance composers did not feel obliged to provide new polyphonic music for the entire Mass. Instead, they focused on certain portions of the worship service. The chart below lists the traditional order of events in the Mass during the Renaissance. Write it on the board or photocopy and project a transparency. It is not important for students to memorize the chart; it is simply a useful tool in pointing out that (1) polyphonic portions of the Mass were not performed consecutively but were separated by other events; and (2) the composed portions were based on Mass texts that remained the same throughout the year.[1] Compositions that could be used for every Mass appealed to Renaissance composers who, like modern composers, wanted frequent performances of their music.

In the chart, *Ordinary* refers to texts that remain the same every time Mass is said; *Proper* refers to texts that change every time Mass is said in order to reflect different events in the church year, such as Christmas, Easter, and feast days. The third column indicates the portions of the Mass that were usually composed (polyphonic), those that used traditional plainsong, and those that were recited (or intoned) on a single pitch.

Latin texts and English translations for the Ordinary portions of the Mass can be found in *The New Harvard Dictionary of Music* (ed. Don Randel) or the score anthologies that accompany Burkholder's *History of Western Music* (W. W. Norton).

Liturgy of the Word

Introit	Proper	plainsong
Kyrie	Ordinary	polyphonic
Gloria	Ordinary	polyphonic
Collect	Proper	recited
Epistle	Proper	recited
Gradual	Proper	plainsong
Alleluia or Tract	Proper	plainsong
Sequence	Proper	plainsong
Gospel	Proper	recited
Homily (Sermon)	(optional)	spoken
Credo	Ordinary	polyphonic

Liturgy of the Eucharist

Offertory	Proper	plainsong
Secret	Proper	recited
Preface	Proper	recited
Sanctus	Ordinary	polyphonic
Canon	Ordinary	recited
Pater noster	Ordinary	recited
Agnus Dei	Ordinary	polyphonic
Communion	Proper	plainsong
Postcommunion Prayer	Proper	recited
Ite, missa est	Ordinary	recited
Response	Ordinary	recited

---

[1]Pérotin and other composers of the Notre Dame school, on the other hand, composed polyphony only for the most important holy days and feasts of the church year.

Now the problem comes into focus: How can a composer write music for the Kyrie, Gloria, Credo, Sanctus, and Agnus Dei so that they do not feel like five different, separate pieces? The solution adopted by many Renaissance composers was to use the same melody as the basis for each polyphonic section of the Mass. They frequently borrowed plainchant melodies for this purpose, but composers often used secular tunes as well. The melody would be paraphrased and used in a variety of ways, according to tradition and the composer's creativity.

ANONYMOUS "Pange lingua"

JOSQUIN *Pange lingua* Mass

Josquin's *Pange lingua* Mass provides a good example of a procedure used by many composers to unify the Mass. This work is based on a plainchant hymn, "Pange lingua." Play the plainchant melody. The class will note that its mood and character are similar to what they heard in plainchant melodies from Chapter 5. Point out that this melody would be as familiar and beloved to the monks, priests, and clerics (or nuns) who sang it as many patriotic tunes or seasonal songs are to us today ("America" or "Jingle Bells," for example). Next, play just the first phrase, "Pange lingua gloriosi," often enough that students recognize it. Now play the recording of the first phrase of Josquin's Kyrie. Flip back and forth between first phrases of chant and Kyrie until students make the connection. Then play the first phrase of the "Qui tollis" (from the Gloria), a paraphrased version of the first six notes of the chant, and point out that Josquin uses the "Pange lingua" melody in every section of the Mass. Ask students to study the chart and imagine the effect created within the worship service when each polyphonic section is based on this same tune. Not only are the five sections of Josquin's Mass tightly organized, but the whole worship service is bound together and unified by the chant melody. The five polyphonic movements provided recurring points of familiarity that turned the whole of the Mass into a profound artistic experience.

The High Renaissance Style

The textbook introduces several features of High Renaissance style and places the most emphasis on that style's characteristic mixture of imitation and homophony.

Dynamics—relatively constant

Tone color—a cappella sound (voices unaccompanied) was the ideal

Scale, key, and mode—medieval modes

Rhythm and tempo—rhythm fluid, no sharp accents, meter often obscured, tempo relatively constant

Pitch and melody—medium register, never very high or very low, smooth motion with ups and downs carefully balanced

Texture—mixture of imitative polyphony and homophony

Harmony—consonant chords with mild, carefully controlled dissonances

Play Kyrie I of Josquin's *Pange lingua* Mass again. Ask students to compare what they hear with the list of characteristics above and to identify the texture. In the discussion that follows, point out that this section uses four-voice imitative polyphony based on the first phrase of the "Pange lingua" chant melody. Identify it as a point of imitation. The Christe and Kyrie II are also points of imitation; the Christe is based on the third phrase of the "Pange lingua" melody, "Sanguinisque pretiosi" (if you wish, you can take a minute to play recordings and compare the "Sanguinisque" phrase of the chant with the beginning of the Christe). Conclude by playing the entire Kyrie.

Ask students if any features on the list were not evident in the Josquin. They should notice there is no real homophony in the Kyrie. Play the "Qui tollis" section of the Gloria while students follow the words in the *Listen* Guide on textbook page 84. Ask them to listen for alternation between imitative polyphony and homophony (indicated by lower- and uppercase type). In the discussion that follows, ask students to describe the differences between the two textures. Josquin favors polyphony and uses many patterns of imitation, but he reserves homophony for words or phrases he wants to emphasize. "Have mercy upon us," "Hear our prayer," and "You alone are the most high, Jesus Christ" stand out because all voices speak these words simultaneously. The mixture of these two textures becomes a powerful expressive tool that allows Josquin to set off and emphasize particularly meaningful phrases; Josquin's use of homophony is analogous to the halo in Renaissance painting.

7 Music as Expression

Declamation and word painting are two devices identified by Kerman and Tomlinson as evidence of new sensitivity to the text. Declamation figures prominently in the homophonic passages of the Josquin Mass (described above) and the Palestrina Mass (described below), and word painting will be discussed in the next section along with Weelkes's madrigal, but there was also a middle stage between declamation and word painting—emotional expression. Good declamation simply guarantees that the words will speak naturally, and later text painting often seems superficial, but Josquin was one of the first composers to consistently capture and express the *feelings* evoked by the words. This kind of expression was not considered appropriate for the Mass, however, where the words were always the same and where the weight of tradition was sometimes stifling. It is in Josquin's sacred motets and particularly in his secular chansons that this new expressiveness emerges with full force.

JOSQUIN Chanson, "Mille regrets"

One of Josquin's most outstanding chansons, "Mille regrets" beautifully expresses the melancholy feeling that became his trademark. With the Mass movements above, you can focus on clear-cut examples of imitative polyphony and strict homophony, but Josquin handles his textures with far greater subtlety here. In many homophonic passages, he has voices weaving in and out and entering earlier or later than the others, and in the one true example of imitation in four voices (at "Qu'on me verra"), the entrances are only one beat apart; by the time students hear the full phrase in one voice, the other four have already entered. Rather than focus on textures that may prove difficult to hear, use declamation and emotional expression as points of entry for this music.

Start with the words. Kerman and Tomlinson refer to these as a "string of clichés," but the emotional meaning is spelled out in no uncertain terms. Without playing the music, ask students what kind of music would fit these words. Should it be fast or slow? major or minor? consonant or dissonant? and so on. Which words and phrases seem to call for special treatment? And what exactly does the final sentence mean? Now play the chanson and ask students to compare Josquin's setting with their expectations. Of course it *is* slow and minorish and somewhat dissonant, but note also how clearly the words are declaimed in spite of the varied textures. Next, take time to zero in on some specific passages and expressive techniques, especially the use of repetition to intensify the expression.

"De vous abandonner" and "Et d'élonger"—Note the similarity between these two phrases—almost a repetition—followed immediately by a real repetition of "Et d'élonger." But also note that no two statements are alike. Clearly these two differ in text and rhythm, but there are also subtle differences in texture. The tenor answers the upper two voices one beat later in "de vous abandonner," while the two "Et d'élonger" statements are more homorhythmic, but also notice how the tenor takes over the bass line in the second "Et d'élonger."

"Votre face amoureuse"—Here the repetition becomes quasi-imitative as lower voices answer the upper voices. Note the darker sound of the second statement.

"J'ai si grand deuil"—The authors refer to this as a particularly effective homophonic moment. It stands out not only because of its unanimous statement of such crucial lyrics ("I feel such great sorrow") but also because it is the first time in the piece that all four voices sing together. With voices weaving in and out, Josquin gives us a different combination of voices every few measures, and he can save the full ensemble for special moments such as this. (This handling of texture is one of the most striking differences between Josquin and Machaut.)

"Et peine douloureuse"—Similar to "votre face amoureuse," this lovely bit of paired imitation has the lower voices again answer the upper ones. Note how Josquin emphasizes the word "peine" (pain), both with rhythmic elongation and the expressive use of the half-step interval in the lower voice. This chanson is written in Phrygian mode, close to a natural minor scale but with a half step between the first two scale steps. Here Josquin uses scale steps 1 and 2 very effectively in the lower voice of each pair.

"Qu'on me verra"—In the only full-fledged point of imitation in the piece, Josquin seems to suggest the *many* people who will observe his sorrow and pain.

"Bref mes jours déffiner"—Note once again the intensification Josquin achieves through repetition. We hear this phrase three times at the very end, and this time all four voices sing the words in rhythmic unison. The first two statements give us literal repetition for the first time in the piece, while the third sets up the plagal cadence that ends the piece. Point out how this cadence feels less complete than the more usual authentic cadence, as if to suggest that the poet's pain (unlike his life?) will not end any time soon.

Finally, draw attention to the prominent role played by the top voice. The *superius* sings almost continuously (it only drops out twice), and since it is frequently placed high above the *altus* (unusually so!), it dominates the texture. As a result, the texture often sounds like melody and accompaniment even though it is a four-voice polyphonic work. Many polyphonic works can be confusing—we are never sure who we should listen to at any given moment. Josquin removes that distraction here; we are free to focus on his beautiful, bittersweet expression of the words. This music points us (and Renaissance music as a whole) in new directions. Let us see how Palestrina and Weelkes make use of Josquin's innovations.

ʸ Late Renaissance Music

PALESTRINA *Pope Marcellus* Mass

Play the "Qui tollis" from Josquin's *Pange lingua* Mass again and follow it with the "Qui tollis" from Palestrina's late Renaissance *Pope Marcellus* Mass. Ask the class to describe how they differ. The differences show how the High Renaissance *a cappella* style changed after Josquin.

1. The Palestrina "Qui tollis" is much more homophonic than the Josquin.

2. Palestrina used a much larger and richer choir than Josquin—six voice parts to Josquin's four.

3. Palestrina's declamation is much clearer than Josquin's.

4. The Palestrina shows the change from the rather stern liturgical polyphony of Josquin to the rich, sonorous, more sensuous-sounding music of the late sixteenth century.

In the discussion that follows, you can call attention to Palestrina's role in the Counter-Reformation (see Listening Idea 3 below). Even later generations regarded Palestrina's music as the most perfect, polished expression of the High Renaissance *a cappella* style. Be sure to reinforce the importance of clear declamation. Palestrina often uses chordal homophony to achieve clear declamation. Students can hear the clarity, but a quick comparison of the Josquin and Palestrina texts (textbook pages 84 and 88) can really drive the point home. On these pages, the textbook highlights homophonic phrases with capital letters. Students can see at a glance that Palestrina's "Qui tollis" is almost entirely homophonic, compared with only a few phrases in Josquin's. In the recorded Palestrina performance, the Tallis Scholars go beyond mere polish or clarity with a spirited response to the text. They echo the reflective, penitent quality of the "Qui tollis" section, and they provide vigorous affirmation in the closing section, "Quoniam tu solus sanctus." In Palestrina's Gloria, we can see that the text expression Josquin used in his secular chansons is now an expected feature of sacred music—even the Mass.

WEELKES Madrigal, "As Vesta Was from Latmos Hill Descending"

The madrigal is the most important of several secular genres to emerge during the Renaissance. If the Mass itself had become more expressive by the end of the Renaissance, then it was only natural for secular music to move even further in that direction. The "expressive" side of Renaissance music is most fully realized in the madrigal. By use of clear declamation and word painting, Renaissance madrigal composers provided musical illustration of the words. Here at the end of the Renaissance, text expression was taken for granted—and in a more extreme form than we saw with Josquin. In fact, text painting took text expression to the next level, providing musical ideas that *vividly* conveyed specific words and images in the text.

Ask students to look at the text of Weelkes's "As Vesta Was from Latmos Hill Descending" on page 90 of the textbook. As a prelude to listening, read the text with the students and emphasize highlighted words and the musical devices that illustrate them. On a keyboard, play some high notes and descending or ascending scales to demonstrate these devices. The chart makes it easy to hear the devices that are used, but it does not specifically describe the role of texture. Ask students to listen for texture (imitation or homophony) at each highlighted word or phrase. Play the music. In the discussion that follows, ask students to describe how the use of imitation or homophony enhanced the word painting, especially at the phrases "running down," "two by two, then three by three," "together," and "Long live fair Oriana!" At the end, imitation conveys spontaneous, irregular cheering wonderfully well, just as homophony captures the sense of "together" after the paired and trebled imitation of that phrase's beginning.

❼ Instrumental Music: Early Developments

During the Renaissance, instrumental music never approached the primary position held by vocal music, but it did assume increasing importance as time went on. Instrumental music approached equality with vocal music in the Baroque period (and finally achieved it in the Classical era). Some instructors prefer to cover this material later, along with Baroque instrumental music. There are, however, advantages to the textbook's order of presentation. First, instrumental music in the proper context offers a balanced picture of Renaissance musical life. Second, a quick look at this music at the end of this chapter provides a nice transition to Baroque music. Whatever your preference, make the following points:

1. Renaissance dance music was primarily instrumental.

2. Social dance and dance music became increasingly popular during the Renaissance.

3. Toward the end of the Renaissance, certain composers began to write stylized dances that were not intended for dancing.

4. These stylized dances were sometimes arrangements of popular dances and were often more complex than earlier Renaissance dance pieces.

ANONYMOUS **Galliard, "Daphne"**

The galliard, a leaping dance in compound meter, became extremely popular in the late Renaissance. Like many Renaissance dances, its rhythmic pattern and tempo were dictated by the dance steps themselves. You can see the galliard's basic rhythmic pattern (with its emphasis on the fourth note) and the dance steps in this chart.

kick – kick – kick – jump – and – land
left   right left   right   —   left (reversed the second time)

A quick comparison of this pattern with the notated version of the tune on textbook page 91 reveals that this galliard employs the typical compound meter but never states the rhythmic pattern precisely; this points to the stylization the authors describe on textbook page 91. A less obvious feature of stylization is the slow tempo of this performance—a tempo that would leave a leaping dancer hanging in the air longer than gravity permits.

With these warnings in mind, ask students to listen for elements and structures of music in this piece, then play it for them. After the class has listed and discussed characteristic features of the music, ask them which elements of "High Renaissance" style can be found in this music. This dance piece differs in many respects from that style: violin family instruments are used in place of voices, beat is emphasized, meter is clear, rhythmic patterns repeat, a single primary melody contains clear cadences and repeated phrases, and the texture is primarily homophonic. Whereas sacred music often avoided association with everyday human life and experience, dance music was allied with bodily movement from its beginning.

This work also reveals several early solutions of problems that Baroque instrumental composers would wrestle with throughout the next era. With instrumental music, composers could not rely on the meaning and structure that the text provides in vocal music. Composers were forced to find purely musical techniques to create variety and coherence. Study *Listen*'s analysis of the form of this galliard's tune with your students (**a a b b c c**—on textbook page 91). Play the first complete statement of the tune (0:00–1:35) and point out how the composer achieves coherence through the repetition of sections and variety through the use of three contrasting sections. Within the tune itself, the composer relies on the principles of repetition and contrast. Then play the entire dance (two complete statements of the tune) and ask students to compare both versions of the tune. To help students hear the differences more clearly, prepare ahead so that you can play **a** from the first half and **a** from the second half side by side. As the authors point out, the lead violin ornaments the melody the second time through. In your discussion of the second statement, point out the contrast in the melody line and the simultaneous repetition in the supporting voices. The structure of the entire work relies on the principle of variation, with its simultaneous use of both repetition and contrast.

ANONYMOUS "Kemp's Jig"

After you play this for the class, point out similarities and differences between the two dances. The jig is even livelier than a typical galliard. This version features recorder, lute, and viola da gamba, but in other respects this music is similar to the galliard "Daphne." Even its form demonstrates the same principles of repetition, contrast, and variation as the galliard. This tuneful jig comes closer to true Renaissance popular music than any other example in the *Listen* anthology. As such, it offers less of the stylization that we heard in the galliard. The authors cite the irregular cadences of the **b** section as evidence of sophistication. Note that they label the fifth measure of **b** as a cadence—and at the same time it sounds like the beginning of the final four measure group. This elision, at once an ending and a beginning, provides further evidence of this little jig's sophistication.

ϓ Global Perspectives 2: Music and Early European Colonialism

Colonialism seems "long ago and far away," yet as recently as the nineteenth and twentieth centuries it was still in full swing. In 1884 the European nations gathered to establish ground rules in the "scramble for Africa." As leaders of the civilized world, it was their "duty" to protect and educate other cultures less "civilized" than their own. It was equally their duty to protect and extend the economic interests of European businesses. And it wasn't just Africa; any "unclaimed" (by other European nations, that is) areas of the world were up for grabs. By the beginning of World War I, most of the third world was under direct European control. Bali, for instance, did not become a Dutch colony until the first decade of the 1900s, and only later in that century did many African nations see independence from their European colonizers. The situation was quite different in Central and South America, however. European colonialism had begun much earlier in these regions, and by the end of the nineteenth century, nearly all of South America had thrown off Spanish and Portuguese domination, thanks to the revolutions begun by Simón Bolívar.

Latin America provided one of the first testing grounds for European colonialism. This chapter's Global Perspectives segment examines the impact of the Spanish conquest on both Aztec and Incan cultures. The notes below will begin with a look at Aztec culture and music at the time of the conquest, followed by a study of the effect of transculturation—or the cross-fertilization between cultures—in the case of the Spanish and the Inca.

Cultural Conquest and Music

With its emphasis on exploration, this Global Perspectives segment offers a good opportunity to lay the groundwork for further study of music beyond Europe. The material on sacred chant provided an initial encounter but one whose context was similar enough to that of Western chant to partially obscure the "voice of the other." Subsequent examples, however, will bring us face to face with difference.

The following exercise can help prepare your students to deal with difference. First set the scene. Ask the students to pretend they are explorers of the 1500s who have discovered a faraway land. They have just arrived in a village to meet the inhabitants of this strange land. They hear the sound of music and, drawn to it, they witness something they have never before seen or heard. Without giving the class further information, play at least five minutes from any video you like that depicts music making (without narration) from a non-Western culture, the less familiar the better.[2] Then ask them to answer these questions about their experience:

❧ How do you describe what happened?

❧ How do you explain what happened?

❧ How does it compare with music making you've experienced?

❧ What more do you need to know to interpret what happened?

One of music's most striking and powerful features is its uncanny ability to instantly conjure up a sense of time, place, and occasion. The discussion that follows will naturally raise such issues as social function and meaning, and will provide an excellent opportunity to gently question the unexamined assumptions many students make concerning written versus oral traditions, "civilized" versus "primitive," Western versus non-Western instruments and singing styles, and so on. The last question, "What more do you need to know . . . ?" can help students understand what is truly required to make an informed judgment. It points to knowledge as an antidote to prejudging, and it allows you to weave their ideas into an introduction to the concerns and methods of ethnomusicological study. To bone up a bit on ethnomusicology, consult the *New Grove Dictionary* article on ethnomusicology or one of the many excellent books available on the subject (see Appendix V). The chapter headings in Helen Myers's *Ethnomusicology: An Introduction* (New York: W. W. Norton, 1992) give a good

---

[2]The JVC Video Anthology is an excellent resource. For other possibilities, see Video Recordings below or in any other chapters containing a Global Perspectives module (Chapters 5, 7, 13, 18, and 23).

sense of the range of issues the ethnomusicologist must confront: "Fieldwork," "Field Technology," "Ethnography of Music," "Transcription," "Notation," "Analysis of Musical Style," "Historical Ethnomusicology," "Iconography," "Organology," "The Biology of Music-Making," "Dance," "Ethical Issues," "Gender and Music," and so on.

This exercise can be crucial in making students aware of attitudes necessary for meaningful exploration of world music. These include an openness to the new and unfamiliar, a willingness to suspend judgment pending further information, and a genuine curiosity to understand other peoples and cultures. Let students know up front that they don't have to "like" everything you play for them (and they won't). It is much more important to understand what to listen for, how the music is made, the music's purpose and function, and the features that give it meaning in its culture. Through a deepened understanding of another culture, students can come to appreciate their own traditions more keenly.

For a follow-up exercise that allows students to examine biases found in European chronicles of Aztec religious ceremonies, try Class Discussion Idea 5 below.

Music of the Aztecs

The textbook briefly mentions some of the fascinating eyewitness accounts of Aztec rituals; the following paragraphs offer background on the history and music of the Aztecs, the Spanish conquest, and the absorption of some native Mexicans into the European musical establishment, especially in Mexico's churches and cathedrals. You can use this material in several ways in the classroom or simply to assist in your own preparation. If you want specific ideas for classroom presentations, follow the links to Additional Teaching Suggestions that are sprinkled throughout this section.

The Aztecs first moved into central Mexico around 1200 and established a permanent settlement, Tenochtitlán, in 1325. Over the next two centuries, Aztec power and influence grew enormously through a series of alliances. By the time of Moctezuma II (r. 1502–1520), the Aztec Empire numbered ten million citizens and extended throughout central Mexico from the Pacific to the Gulf Coast. Along the way, the Aztecs appropriated some of the trappings and lore of the previous dominant culture of the region, the Toltecs, including the story of one of their rulers, Quetzalcóatl, whose refusal to allow human sacrifice offended the gods. When forced to flee, he vowed to return someday.

Aztec society was organized in a hierarchy of classes, ranging from the royal family down to the working class—usually conquered peoples. Near the top was a professional caste responsible for music at all Aztec religious rituals and ceremonies. Like a guild, this caste provided years of rigorous training for its members, and masters spent much time in rehearsal—a necessity, since caste members were busy providing music (all memorized) for public ceremonies in a 260-day liturgical calendar, and any public mistakes led to the offender's immediate execution.

Ritual observances were devoted to many different Aztec deities, both male and female. Spanish chroniclers report the details of many of these ceremonies, which often involved human sacrifice and ritual cannibalism. They also record accounts of ritual dance so elaborate and so perfectly synchronized that the Spaniards were awestruck. Cortés even took a group of them back to Europe, where they danced for Spain's King Charles V and the pope. The textbook provides excerpts from some of these firsthand accounts; see Class Discussion Idea 5 or Appendix V for modern translations of extended eyewitness accounts of Aztec rituals.

Music was so thoroughly integrated into religious observance that the Náhua language contains no separate word for music. The language does include words for musical activities, however, such as singing, blowing through a wind instrument, striking a drum, making sounds with feet, and dancing. Singing and dancing were evidently a significant part of religious ritual, though much attention has been placed on Aztec instruments, examples of which still survive today.

Aerophones and percussion were the primary Aztec instruments. Different types of flutes and trumpets figured prominently in certain rituals. The two most important percussion instruments were the *huéhuetl* and the *teponaztli*. The *huéhuetl* was a membranophone made from a large log. Elaborately carved, it stood on one end with a membrane stretched over the top end. The *teponaztli* was an idiophone. A large, hollowed log was placed on its side, and a large H-shaped hole was carved out to create two wooden tongues, which were tuned to two different pitches. In addition to its role as a musical instrument, this slit drum sometimes served as a ritual vessel into which sacrificial human blood was poured. In fact, both the *huéhuetl* and the *teponaztli* were so strongly associated with religious ritual that the drums themselves became objects of worship, regarded as gods forced into exile. Both drums are still used in native Mexican folk music today, a reminder of their significance many centuries ago. (See Lecture-Demonstration Idea 5 below for a more creative presentation on Aztec culture and music.)

Everything changed with the arrival of Cortés and his *conquistadors* in 1519. Cortés took his time learning the political lay of the land and developing alliances, especially with the peoples of Tlaxcallan, probably the chief source of Aztec sacrificial victims. Moctezuma II was lulled into indecision, fearing that Cortés might be Quetzalcóatl returned from the east. In the end, European diseases such as smallpox did more damage than Cortés's armies, and by 1521 Mexica, the Aztec empire, had become New Spain. Once under Spanish control, it took only two years for Spanish missionaries to arrive. The missionaries, just as Cortés before them, took time to learn local customs. They built churches on the sites of Aztec temples and emphasized church holidays that corresponded to high holy days in the Aztec calendar. To a limited extent, they sometimes allowed native Mexican music and dancing as part of Catholic worship.

After the conquest, it did not take long for Aztec musicians, who had formerly held such privileged positions, to be trained to occupy similar positions singing European music in the new Catholic churches. Even after the church hierarchy issued edicts requiring a uniformly high skill level of all choristers (designed to discourage Indian musicians), a remarkably high number of Aztecs demonstrated sufficient proficiency to stay on. Indians made significant contributions as singers, organists, instrument makers, composers, and music copyists. As a result, Mexican churches soon became renowned throughout the "New World" for the excellence of their music. Manuel de Zumaya (c. 1678–1756), composer at Mexico City Cathedral, was probably the first Mexican-born composer to master the techniques of European Renaissance polyphony. In 1715 Zumaya became the first Mexican-born *maestro de capilla*. Zumaya also composed the first opera produced in North America (the second in the New World), *La Parténope*. His opera has not survived, but his church music demonstrates his command of Renaissance and Baroque European compositional techniques (see Listening Idea 5 below).

Zumaya was also the first composer to write music inspired by the story of the Virgin of Guadalupe. In 1531 an Indian neophyte named Juan Diego claimed he had been visited by the Virgin Mary on Mount Tepeyac (near

Mexico City). Eventually Bishop Juan de Zumárraga became convinced of the authenticity of the visitation, but native Mexicans needed no convincing. Such a vision would have inspired awe and devotion anywhere in Christendom, but this Virgin had Indian features, and she appeared to an Indian, not a European. For the first time, Christianity took on an Indian face. The Basilica of Our Lady of Guadalupe, which houses Juan Diego's cloak in its reliquary, still draws pilgrims to Mexico City. Religious festivities surrounding the Virgin of Guadalupe remain among the most popular in Aztec regions of modern Mexico, and many composers since Zumaya have written music for the Virgin's feast day (see Listening Idea 6 below).

What has become of Aztec music and culture? The Náhua language is still spoken by about a million Mexicans. Many ancient instruments continue to be used in Mexican folk traditions. It is safe to assume that features of Aztec musical style live on in contemporary folk music, though it is difficult to say with certainty just what those features might be. The Aztecs did not provide us with any examples of music notation that would allow us to re-create the sounds and melodies of their music. In the article "Ideologies of Aztec Song" (*Journal of the American Musicological Society* [1995], pp. 343–79), Gary Tomlinson surmises that a song glyph in the Codex Borbonicus may have served as a kind of musical representation, one in which the painted images parallel the rich experience of the sung ritual. But even the glyphs were most likely not intended to guide performers. And so we are left with riddles and mysteries about a culture so close and yet so far away. The Aztecs provide a tantalizing object lesson in the difficulties of listening for the "voice of the other."

Music of the Inca

The fate of the Incas paralleled that of the Aztecs in striking ways. Spanish conquerors toppled a mighty empire, European diseases devastated the native population, the riches of the new colony were exported back to Spain to bolster the European economy, and priests and missionaries arrived to convert the "heathens." But somewhere along the way, New Spain failed to replicate the old Spain completely. The meeting of these two cultures resulted in unanticipated changes on both sides. This syncretism resulted in new traditions that borrowed from both sides of the cultural divide.

The next few pages provide two kinds of background material: (1) a general look at Peruvian history and culture before the conquest, and (2) a more specific look at interactions between Spanish and Peruvian cultures during the colonial period. This section concludes with teaching suggestions for "Hanaq pachap kusikuynin."

Peru before the Spanish Conquest Incan civilization developed late in Peruvian history. The earliest surviving structures built in the territories bounded by modern-day Peru are ceremonial mounds at Aspero dating back to 2600 B.C.E. Most early residents lived along the desert coast, but soon communities sprang up along the river valleys and in the high mountain regions of Peru. During the Initial Period (1800–800 B.C.E.) the coast dwellers built elaborate irrigation systems that enabled them to create new farmland. The Chavín people developed distinctive, influential artistic and architectural styles during the Early Horizon period (800–200 B.C.E.), and a more complex society began to emerge around Lake Titicaca. Around 100 B.C.E. the first South American state was established along the Moche River, and Nazca culture dominated the southern coastal regions. The Moche state reached its peak between 200 and 400 C.E.; at the same time the Tiahuanaco state around Lake Titicaca was beginning a period of expansion. The cities of Tiahuanaco and Huari had both established substantial empires by 600 C.E. Following their collapse c. 1000 C.E., the influence of the Chimú people began to spread. By 1200 the Chimú dominated the coastal regions.

At about the same time, Manco Capac founded a new state at Cuzco—the Inca state. For two hundred years the Inca state expanded little beyond the Cuzco valley, but during the fifteenth century it grew by leaps and bounds. Under the leadership of Pachacutec (r. 1438–1471) and his son Tupac Yupanqui (r. 1471–1493), the Inca Empire became the largest ever in the precontact Americas, with a population of more than twelve million. On a modern-day map of South America, you can see the extent of the empire by following the mountains and the coast from Quito, Ecuador, south beyond Santiago, Chile, a distance of more than 2,500 miles. A rigid hierarchy extended from the emperor down to overseers responsible for groups of ten families each; this elaborate but efficient administrative system kept things running smoothly. A standing army stood ready to answer threats to the empire, and a system of paved roads second only to that of the ancient Romans (in preindustrial times) made it possible for them to respond quickly. Men could be drafted as needed for various purposes, whether to serve in the army or to build roads, terraces for agriculture, or fortresses. Machu Picchu, the most famous Inca site today, may have been built in this manner as a religious center and/or frontier outpost.

On the musical front, Incan culture stood head and shoulders above all other indigenous American musics in both the variety and sophistication of its musical instruments. Even the colloquialisms of the Quechua language abounded with references to musical instruments, unlike most other Native American languages. Percussion instruments and trumpets were highly prized, but most ubiquitous (and sophisticated) of all were the flutes and raftpipes (*antaras*) that still characterize indigenous Andean music. Archeological evidence demonstrates the variety of instruments and their construction, but we must rely on eyewitness reports of the Spaniards who first came to this land for an understanding of contexts in which music was used, among them Poma de Ayala (c. 1615) and Pablo Joseph de Arriaga (1621).[3] All evidence suggests that music served many significant roles in everyday life and ritual, serving as well to establish the authority of the Inca (emperor) and Colla (empress). Ironically, the very first Spanish-Incan encounter involved music. In 1526, Spanish ships intercepted an Incan seagoing vessel loaded with riches. The native sailors were traveling north to purchase large shells used to create the most prestigious and highly prized of all Incan instruments, conch-shell trumpets.

The Meeting of Cultures in Peru   In the early sixteenth century, a smallpox epidemic (brought by the Spanish) worked its way down the Pacific coast from Panama. One of its victims was the Inca emperor Huayna Capac, and his death in 1525 spawned a civil war between his two sons, Atahuallpa and Huáscar. Atahuallpa finally won in 1532, but the empire was so weakened by its internal struggles that Francisco Pizarro and his Spanish invaders experienced no significant difficulties in their 1533 conquest. In a daring raid,

---

[3]For further information and fascinating eyewitness accounts of the Peruvian musical scene during the period from 1500 to 1795, see the writings of Robert Murrell Stevenson, especially *Music in Aztec and Inca Territory* (Berkeley: University of California Press, 1968) and *The Music of Peru: Aboriginal and Viceroyal Epochs* (Washington, D.C.: Pan American Union, 1960). The former contains a full seventy pages of eyewitness accounts.

Pizarro's men kidnapped Atahuallpa, who was eventually executed. The Inca power structure, so dependent on a strong central leader, proved helpless to resist once he was removed. The Spaniards established a puppet emperor, but when he led a revolt against them, they put their own men in charge, establishing a new government along the lines of the old one. Once in charge, the Spanish used the Incas as cheap labor, forcing many of them to work in the mines. When they began to run out of Incas, they imported Africans to dig out their silver. The Spanish wanted silver and gold to send back home, and a mine at Potosi, south of Lake Titicaca, became the largest silver-producing mine in the world. In order to facilitate commerce and transportation of goods, they also established the city of Ciudad de los Reyes (Lima), which quickly became one of the major cities of New Spain.

The social system that developed was rigidly stratified. At the top were the wealthy European-born Spaniards who held the most significant posts in the government and the church. The second level down consisted of creoles. Curiously, the creoles were equally full-blooded Spaniards—but they happened to be born in the New World, and that counted against them. The mestizo group, those with mixed Spanish and Indian blood, populated the third level. At the bottom level were the Africans and the native Indians. Not surprisingly, this structure changed little once independence was achieved in the nineteenth century—the creoles moved into the top level, but no significant changes occurred below that.

Just as in Mexico, missionaries and priests quickly followed the Spanish armies into the new colonies. Churches, cathedrals, and seminaries were built, and musicians from Europe came to provide the same Renaissance polyphonic music they knew from their experiences in Spanish cathedrals. Even the earliest European observers noted the musical abilities of the Incans, in one instance reporting on a flute ensemble that quickly and easily learned to perform European polyphonic songs. Further, many Spanish instruments—guitars, vihuelas, shawms, and the like—were quickly taken up and reproduced by indigenous musicians. The *charango,* a guitarlike instrument often constructed from an armadillo shell, was adopted in many regions. (This native version of the guitar has become so much a part of the Peruvian musical fabric that most folk musicians now believe the instrument to be indigenous to Peru.)

The Spaniards soon decided to train native musicians, who proved remarkably fast learners. Trained musicians had enjoyed high status in Incan society, and these gifted students eagerly sought similar positions in the social order of New Spain. Of course, in any given church the *maestro de capilla* and perhaps one or two assistants were European, but in order to re-create the splendors of Spanish Renaissance polyphony, the majority of performers had to be native Incan musicians. And with such fine local talent available, the major cathedrals in Cuzco and Lima and even in smaller local churches quickly developed the practice of singing (rather than saying) Mass using at least a basic plainchant repertory and often the elaborate polyphony typical of European cathedrals. Of course, much of the music performed came from Europe. For instance, a collection of Masses by the great Spanish composer Morales was evidently used in the late sixteenth century at the cathedral in Cuzco, the Incan capital. Cuzco and Lima quickly became two of the most important musical centers in all of New Spain, capable of performing the most sophisticated music in the most recent European styles. Eventually this even included opera. Tomás de Torrejón y Velasco, *maestro de capilla* at the Lima Cathedral from 1676 to 1728, wrote the first opera to be produced in the New World, his *La púrpura de la rosa* of 1701.

Inca Processional Music   While the major cathedrals pursued European styles and frowned on native musical practices, the churches established by the missionaries followed an entirely different approach. The missionaries believed that conversion to Christianity would occur more swiftly if native Incas were permitted to bring their own music and dance into the worship experience. The missionaries also discovered that music was their most powerful tool in converting the Incas, and in some cases they even set Indian melodies in a European polyphonic manner for use in worship. This syncretic approach, practiced by Catholic missionaries throughout the New World, ultimately proved extremely successful, and it helped to guarantee the ongoing vitality of indigenous music in the colonies. It is striking testimony to the prevalence of this practice that the first polyphonic work published in the New World, "Hanaq pachap kusikuynin," was a European-style liturgical setting of a text in the Quechua language. This work provides a wonderful example of such cross-fertilization.

Right off the bat, impress upon your class the historical importance of this work. This is the very first polyphonic (melody and harmony) work published *anywhere* in North or South America. As such, it is part of the musical heritage of every American student. That the words employ the Quechua tongue is all the more remarkable given the clear European bias of the Spanish conquerors, yet this speaks powerfully of the cultural blending encouraged by the Catholic missionaries. As you continue your introduction to this work, feel free to use any of the materials above.

As you turn to the music itself, it works best to present this work right alongside the Dufay hymn and the Palestrina Mass. With the Dufay it shares the strophic form typical of most hymns; with the Palestrina, the simple block chords that help make the words clearly audible, as recommended by the Council of Trent.

Start by playing just the first stanza (the first 36 seconds). Establish some basic features of this work. The minor scale gives it a seriousness that is warmed by occasional moves to the relative major. The melodic lines (except for the bass) move primarily by step, giving this music the same smoothness heard in European polyphony. Still, the melody contains enough leaps to provide a bit of drama, and the eighth-note pairs on beat 2 that begin phrases 3, 4, and 5 also keep us guessing.

Next, get to know the basic structure of each stanza. Note the clear beginnings and cadences that mark each of the six phrases as well as the lack of repetition within the stanza. In spite of the through-composed nature of the stanza, the music divides into fairly regular phrases, as the chart below demonstrates.

Phrases:	a	b	c	d	e	f
Length:	3 m.	3 m.	4 m.	3 m.	3 m.	4 m.

In fact, the grouping suggests two groups of three phrases, with the longest phrase concluding each group. The two four-measure phrases are further set apart by the suspensions that appear in their third measures, dissonances enhanced in the third phrase by the Phrygian inflection in the bass.

Once the basic features of this work are well understood, take time to compare this music with Dufay's hymn "Ave maris stella" and with the "Qui tollis" from Palestrina's *Pope Marcellus* Mass. This need not take long; the main goal is to verify similarities between "Hanaq pachap kusikuynin" and its European counterparts. Differences are few. The Andean processional actually sounds warmer than the Dufay hymn, which is not surprising, since it was influenced by late, not early, Renaissance style. And it will not sound as polished as the Palestrina, due partly to the performance on the recorded set and partly to the composer. After all, Palestrina was one of the greatest masters of the late Renaissance, and few composers could withstand such a comparison. Nonetheless, lack of polish does not diminish the expressive qualities of this Andean work, and if eyewitness accounts can be believed, perhaps the Incan singers sang with greater skill than those heard on this recording!

Conclude with a consideration of the text. After all, the Quechua words make this work truly distinctive. Some students may notice that the preponderance of hard consonants subtly undermines the smooth flow typical of European models. Make sure that students understand the worship context for which this work was intended. In his 1631 publication of this work, Juan Pérez Bocanegra indicates that it was "composed to be sung in processions as they [Incan parishioners] enter their churches on Lady-Days."[4] Processions had been an important part of special celebrations in Incan culture, and it is likely that traditional clothing and instruments were permitted as part of these Christian processions. This importation of an indigenous practice into the celebration of important Christian feast days provides a textbook example of the syncretic practices of Catholic missionaries in New Spain.

Additional Teaching Suggestions

⁊ Lecture-Demonstration Ideas

1. Invite an early music vocal group to class. Most groups keep Renaissance works in their repertory, especially madrigals and chansons, and sometimes motets and Mass movements. The musicians can even demonstrate characteristic features of Renaissance style, such as imitation, homophony, declamation, and word painting. A workshop setting that includes performance and discussion of the music works best. And if they can sing and help you pick apart one of the *Listen* works by Josquin, Palestrina, or Weelkes, so much the better!

2. Bring pictures of Renaissance paintings, sculpture, and architecture to class. The art department at your school may have a collection of slides you can borrow, or you can use commercial CD-ROM and video packages (see Multimedia Resources below). Point out the use of perspective and color as well as the realistic portrayal of the human figure. Any of these images can enhance your introduction to the Renaissance. For instance, pictures of the Sistine Chapel and St. Peter's Basilica (in Vatican City) make a wonderful backdrop for Palestrina's Mass.

3. Invite instrumentalists who specialize in early music to class. A recorder soloist, lutenist, or a consort of any size can provide fascinating insights into Renaissance music and the problems of performing this music today. There is no substitute for direct contact with the instruments and their sounds. If live musicians are not available, you can at least bring pictures of Renaissance instruments to class. Jeremy Montagu's *The World of Medieval and Renaissance Musical Instruments* (Woodstock, N.Y.: Overlook Press, 1976) offers a wealth of illustrations—color and black-and-white photographs of early instruments, paintings, woodcuts, illuminations, and other artwork depicting early instruments and performers.

---

[4]Stevenson's *The Music of Peru,* p. 47. Pp. 47–50 contain a facsimile reproduction of the four voice parts from the original publication along with a modern transcription in score.

4. Invite a dancer who knows Renaissance dances to class, or check out a copy of *Arbeau's Orchesography* (New York: Dover, 1967) and teach yourself some Renaissance dances (most are not difficult). Demonstrate a pavan, a jig, a galliard, and so on. Relationships between dance steps and musical tempo can be explored. These dances can come to life as students make connections with their own social dancing experiences.

5. Create a slide show for your study of Aztec and Peruvian cultures. Many departments at your school are likely to have images you can borrow, including art, foreign languages, geography, or anthropology. Pictures of artwork, architecture, musical instruments, Aztec ruins, Mexican cities and countryside, Machu Picchu and other Incan ruins, the cities of Lima and Cuzco, Lake Titicaca, and the Andes mountains can help bring this material to life.

6. Introduce your class to eyewitness accounts of Peruvian music from the sixteenth and seventeenth centuries. The entire concluding chapter of Robert Stevenson's *Music in Aztec and Inca Territory* (Berkeley: University of California Press, 1968) is devoted to such accounts. These examples point to the syncretism the authors describe in this chapter's Global Perspectives materials, and they demonstrate the relative stability of indigenous Peruvian musical traditions.

⁊ Class Discussion Ideas

1. *What would life be like without radio, TV, or any form of recorded music?* This wide-open question works well at the beginning of the chapter, especially with a follow-up question: *Where would you have to go to hear music in the Renaissance?* Students begin to see that music serves many of the same functions in Renaissance times and modern times—liturgical and ceremonial support, private and public entertainment, dance, and so on. The concept of music's social function also provides an important point of contact with the Global Perspectives material. Your students may grasp this more readily than musicians trained by generations of traditional musicologists (who often ignored such questions), but understanding a music's social function is no less important in the study of Western music than in any other world music.

2. Compare medieval and Renaissance art as a means of uncovering characteristics of the Renaissance worldview. Use illustrations in the textbook, slides from the art department, books from the library, or some of the multimedia resources below. Compare the use of perspective and color as well as the representation of the human figure. Ask the class how these works differ in their portrayal of human experience. Which seems more realistic, more true to life? Why?

3. Compare modern musical concepts (*Listen*, Chapters 1–4) with Renaissance understanding. In the 1500s, Tinctoris wrote his *Dictionary of Musical Terms* (a modern edition is available—New York: Da Capo Press, 1978). Read (or prepare a handout of) definitions of terms from Tinctoris. Compare these definitions with Kerman and Tomlinson's definitions of the same terms. Tinctoris includes terms such as *harmony* (*armonia*), *color, consonance, counterpoint, Mass, mode, melody, music, musician,* and *octave.* This permits review of Unit I as well.

4. *Were Renaissance composers anything like musicians today?* Start by reading excerpts from the letter by one of Ercole d'Este's ambassadors quoted in the

Josquin article in the *New Grove Dictionary of Music and Musicians*. The letter reads like a scouting report for a major-league sports franchise. The writer compares Josquin's irregular work habits and high-priced contract with Isaac's eager-to-please temperament and more modest salary demands. Josquin was the juicier plum, and Ercole paid his price. Ask students to compare this story with other stories they have heard about musicians and contract negotiations.

5. *How did explorers respond to unfamiliar cultures?* Share such accounts with your students and ask them to look for biases in these Spanish critiques of Aztec culture. Translations of these writings can be found in Frank Llewellyn Harrison's *Time, Place and Music* (Amsterdam: Frits Knuf, 1973) and Robert Stevenson's *Music in Aztec and Inca Territory* (Berkeley: University of California Press, 1968). To sharpen your own sense of the role of cultural bias in the encounter with the "other," refer to Gary Tomlinson's article on Aztec song.[5]

6. *What matters most in a good musical performance?* The *sikuri* ensemble song "Manuelita" (see Further Listening Examples below) raises important questions about the relationship between actual and "ideal" performances of the same music. Start by asking students what they value most in a good musical performance. Answers may vary widely. Bring up examples of performances that may be less than ideal: karaoke singing; congregational singing of hymns in church; sing-along numbers at rock, folk, or pop music concerts; elementary or middle school band and orchestra concerts; carol sings; *Messiah* sing-alongs; or renditions of "Happy Birthday" or even "Louie, Louie" by the Kingsmen. What is the value of these less-than-ideal performances?

♪ Listening Ideas

1. Compare medieval and Renaissance motets. Machaut's "Quant en moi" and Josquin's "Absalon, fili mi" (see Further Listening Examples below) serve well to engage the class in comparison of medieval and Renaissance styles and to introduce the Renaissance motet. These two pose striking contrasts in language, subject matter, and use of musical elements and structures. Josquin's darkly expressive motet also contains examples of typical dovetailed (overlapping) points of imitation.

2. Play early, middle, and late Renaissance secular works to illustrate the evolution of expressiveness in secular vocal music. Dufay's "Hélas mon dueil," Josquin's "Mille regrets" or "Scaramella va alla guerra" (see Further Listening Examples below), and Weelkes's "As Vesta Was from Latmos Hill Descending" serve well. Josquin's sense of declamation and expression (mid-Renaissance) allows his words to speak more naturally than Dufay's (early Renaissance). Weelkes (late Renaissance) goes even further in the use of note patterns and textures to illustrate the text—word painting.

---

[5]Gary Tomlinson, "Ideologies of Aztec Song." *Journal of the American Musicological Society* (1995), pp. 343–79. Tomlinson describes how Western scholars looking at other cultures are hampered by Western understandings of the relationship between spoken and written language, and between speech and music, poetry, or metaphor, in part because of our phonetic, alphabetic approach to written language. While Tomlinson's article is probably not appropriate for introductory-level music appreciation students, it can help your teaching by making you more sensitive to the biases of Western observers who, failing to find the hallmarks of Western civilization in Aztec culture, attributed a lack of sophistication to the Aztecs rather than to their own powers of observation.

3. Let students judge for themselves whether Palestrina's music satisfies the Council of Trent's canon on music to be used in the Mass: "The whole plan of singing in musical modes should be constituted not to give empty pleasure to the ear, but in such a way that the words be clearly understood by all, and thus the hearts of the listeners be drawn to desire of heavenly harmonies, in the contemplation of the joys of the blessed" (from Grout and Palisca's *History of Western Music*, 5th ed., p. 250). Play the Kyrie from Josquin's *Pange lingua* Mass (pre–Council of Trent) and the "Qui tollis" from Palestrina's *Pope Marcellus* Mass (during Council of Trent). Ask students which piece best meets the requirement that "the words be clearly understood by all."

4. Play Renaissance Masses that use devices other than a plainchant cantus firmus to achieve unity. Ockeghem's Missa *Mi-Mi* (see Sound Recordings below) provides a good example of a motto (head-motive) Mass, in which each movement begins with the same motive—the bass's descending fifth in this case. Palestrina's Missa *Viri Galilaei* is a parody Mass, a work that borrows two or more voices from a preexisting polyphonic work, in this case one of Palestrina's own motets. The recording led by Philippe Herreweghe (see Sound Recordings below) includes performances of Palestrina's complete Mass as well as the motet, facilitating easy comparison between the two. It is especially interesting to demonstrate how Palestrina adapts the top two voices of the motet for use at the beginning of each Mass movement.

5. Although no examples of authentic Aztec music survive today, you can introduce your class to music that reflects the blending of Spanish and Mexican or Peruvian cultures. An excellent example can be found in the music of Manuel de Zumaya, who became the first native Mexican *maestro de capilla* in 1715 at the Mexico City Cathedral. Chanticleer's *Mexican Baroque* CD (see Sound Recordings below) contains a Zumaya motet, "Hieremiae Prophetae Lamentationes," that demonstrates his mastery of Renaissance polyphonic writing. Play it for your class alongside examples by Josquin or Palestrina. Your students won't hear much difference in terms of stylistic features, so thoroughly did Zumaya absorb European musical style. For a contrasting example that demonstrates the clear influence of indigenous traditions, try the Harp Consort's *Missa Mexicana* CD (see Sound Recordings below). The featured composer is Juan Gutiérrez de Padilla, *maestro de capilla* in the town of Puebla de los Angeles starting in 1629. This recording features Gutiérrez de Padilla's Missa *Ego flos campi* and surrounds it with *xácaras* and other works that demonstrate the indigenous dances and rhythms that influenced this Mass. Padilla's music still reflects European influences but is often imbued with vivacious dance rhythms. *Nueva España* and *Spain in the New World* in Sound Recordings below provide further useful examples.

6. Introduce your students to another Indian-European connection. The story of the Virgin of Guadalupe (described under Music of the Aztecs above) inspired many new compositions in the centuries after her appearance to an Indian neophyte. The first such work was composed by native Mexican Manuel de Zumaya, and many other composers soon followed suit. One such work is a set of vespers for the Virgin of Guadalupe written by Ignacio Jerúsalem, an Italian composer who served as *maestro de capilla* at Mexico City Cathedral from 1749 to 1769. Jerúsalem's work, coupled with works by Zumaya and recorded by Chanticleer (see Sound Recordings below), is typical of the music of late Baroque and early Classical European composers.

7. Introduce your students to music of Morales and Victoria, Spanish composers whose music was likely performed by Incan musicians at the cathedrals

in Cuzco and Lima. By 1553, European publications of Masses and motets by Morales had reached New Spain, and Victoria's works were being sold in Lima by 1598. Morales's "Emendemus in melius" and Victoria's "O vos omnes" and "O magnum mysterium" serve as good examples for comparison with "Hanaq pachap kusikuynin."

8. Compare "Manuelita" (see Further Listening Examples below) with performances by the ensemble that inspired the Centro Social Conima. *Mountain Music of Peru*, Volume II (see Sound Recordings below), the CD from which "Manuelita" was taken, also contains examples performed by Qhantati Ururi, a *sikuri* ensemble from the Conimo district. Most similar to "Manuelita" is "Social Dance," another work from the *lento sikuri* genre; "Easter Music" provides a contrasting work in a faster tempo from the *sikuri ligeros* genre.

♪ Further Listening Examples

DUFAY Harmonized hymn, "Veni Creator Spiritus"

Use this for another example of Dufay's paraphrase technique. See Sound Recordings below for a performance, and Appendix II for text and translation.

DUFAY "Hélas mon dueil"

JOSQUIN "Petite Camusette"

Prior to the madrigal, the chanson was the principal genre of secular vocal music. These two examples can be used to demonstrate the evolution of secular music earlier in the Renaissance. Dufay's three-voice chanson introduces only a touch of imitation, while Josquin's six voices imitate each other constantly. See Sound Recordings below for suggested CDs, and Appendix II for texts and translations.

JOSQUIN "Scaramella va alla guerra"

This Italian secular song's lilt and homophonic texture move away from the learned polyphony of Josquin's "Petite Camusette." See Sound Recordings below for a performance, and Appendix II for text and translation.

GREGORIAN HYMN "Pange lingua"

The recordings for this edition of the textbook contain only the first phrase of this plainchant, just before the Kyrie from Josquin's *Pange lingua* Mass. Since Josquin refers to subsequent phrases of the chant melody in the Kyrie and other movements of the Mass, it helps to play a more complete recording of this lovely melody for your students. See Sound Recordings for more information on recordings, and Appendix II for text and translation of the first verse.

JOSQUIN *Ave maris stella* Mass, Kyrie and Agnus Dei

This works especially well since students were introduced to Dufay's harmonization of the "Ave maris stella" plainchant earlier in this chapter. This work, probably from Josquin's middle period, is a tenor Mass. As was the custom in many early Renaissance Masses, a paraphrased version of the chant melody serves as the tenor line, though Josquin uses motives from "Ave maris stella" in other voices throughout the Mass. In contrast, Josquin's *Pange lingua* Mass does not always use the borrowed melody in the tenor line—the chant melody pervades all four voices. Both Masses exhibit characteristics of High Renaissance style. The Kyrie text is the same as for the *Pange lingua* Mass; see textbook page 83. See Appendix II for text and translation for the Agnus Dei, and Sound Recordings below for performances.

JOSQUIN "Absalon, fili mi"

The textbook mentions the Renaissance motet on page 88, but provides no recorded examples. This dark, expressive motet contains examples of typical dovetailed (overlapping) points of imitation, in contrast with the full cadences in the Kyrie from Josquin's *Pange lingua* Mass. To capture the mood of King David's lament for his dead son, Absalom, Josquin wrote this motet for an unusual combination of four low male voices. See Sound Recordings below for a performance, and Appendix II for text and translation.

BYRD "Sing joyfully unto God"

To sample another motet and demonstrate the impact of the Reformation on music, try this English anthem by late Renaissance English composer William Byrd. All of the typical features of High Renaissance sacred music can be found here, along with some vivid text painting (especially at "Blow the trumpet"). The English text makes it easy for students to follow along. See Sound Recordings below for a performance, and Appendix II for the text.

ARCADELT "Il bianco e dolce cigno"

GESUALDO "Moro, lasso"

GIBBONS "The silver Swanne"

The madrigal originated in Italy, as the authors point out. Arcadelt's Italian madrigal, with its subtle melancholy (and subtle innuendo in the "mille morte" of the last line), provides an example of the music that intrigued Elizabethan composers; Gibbons's English work picks up on Arcadelt's swan-song theme, but this time to extract a moral lesson. The Gesualdo madrigal, on the other hand, demonstrates the extreme, jarring text expression practiced by some late Renaissance practitioners of the Italian madrigal. See Sound Recordings below for performances and Appendix II for texts and translations.

ANONYMOUS Pavan and Galliard, "Celeste Giglio"

CAROUBEL Pavana de Spaigne

HOLBORNE Noel's Galliard

The *Listen* recordings provide a galliard, but not the pavan that was so often coupled with it. The *Terpsichore: Tanzmusik der Renaissance und des Frühbarock* CD (see Sound Recordings below) contains all three of these examples. Either pavan permits students to hear the duple meter and processional character typical of that dance, and the galliards offer a clearer example of that dance's characteristic "kick-kick-kick-jump—and land" rhythm (though the Holborne is a bit slow for the required leaping steps).

A PERUVIAN RAFTPIPE ORCHESTRA "**Manuelita**"

Both historically and culturally, this example provides a wonderful follow-up to your coverage of "Hanaq pachap kusikuynin" above. A contemporary example, "Manuelita" nonetheless reflects an indigenous tradition whose roots extend back at least as far as the Nazca period, well before the Inca or the Spanish conquest. Nowadays, this attractive music enjoys a degree of popularity that can probably be traced back to the 1960s when Simon and Garfunkel used both an Andean folk tune and Andean raftpipes in "El Condor Pasa (If I Could)." Judging by the frequent appearance of Andean musicians at civic festivals and art fairs across the United States, this music's popularity continues today.

Lecture Suggestions above provided a brief history of Peru before the Spanish conquest and a look at the interaction between Spanish and Peruvian cultures during the colonial period. The next few pages provide two kinds of background material: a summary of Peruvian history since independence and a specific look at the Aymara communities near Lake Titicaca, whose musical practices are reflected in "Manuelita." These pages take a close look at the customs of the mountain district of Conimo and follow those customs to the coastal city of Lima, where many Conimo natives have resettled during the past fifty years. This section concludes with teaching suggestions for "Manuelita." Recordings can be found in either the recorded set for *Listen: Brief Fourth Edition* or the Smithsonian/Folkways *Mountain Music of Peru*, Volume II (see Sound Recordings below).

Independence and Change

A Peruvian-led revolt in the late eighteenth century failed, but Argentine revolutionary forces under General José de San Martin took Lima and proclaimed Peru's independence in 1821. The armies of Simón Bolívar, the "liberator of South America," finally ousted the last Spanish forces from Peru in 1824. The Spanish were not ready to relinquish their colonies just yet, however, and they mounted a counterinvasion in 1866. Finally the Spanish government gave up, recognizing Peru's independence in a treaty signed in 1879.

Except for a brief period when Peru became part of Bolivia, Peru has essentially governed its own affairs since the 1820s. Government has alternated between civilian-led regimes and military rule. In 1980 a military junta stepped down, acceding power to a newly elected civilian government. Sorely tested between 1981 and 1992 by insurrections led by Maoist revolutionaries calling themselves the Shining Path (*Sendero Luminoso*), the government somehow managed to maintain control. Many of the guerrillas were arrested or killed in the early 1990s; since then, the organization has been unable to mount any significant opposition.

Aymara Music and Social Structure in the Conimo District

Most of *altiplano* Peru is populated by Quechua-speaking peoples, but at the country's southern tip is a region of Aymara speakers that extends through Bolivia into northern Chile; the Aymara speakers number about two million overall. Most of the Peruvian Aymara live in the Puno province, an area around the northern end of Lake Titicaca. All along the mountain chain, indigenous Peruvian musics have flourished for centuries, even during the years of Spanish occupation. Eyewitness accounts dating from the sixteenth century already pointed to the variety of musical types and styles in the mountain regions. One account from the Conimo district described forty different styles of music and dance at a single fiesta. The diversity of folk styles continues to be more extreme in the Puno province than elsewhere in Peru.

The contexts for music making clearly reflect a Spanish Catholic influence. Spanish missionaries worked hard to root out indigenous religious practices, but they gave special emphasis to the feast days that matched important celebrations in the Inca religious-agricultural calendar. To this day, many of those same religious holidays are celebrated with elaborate three- to five-day fiestas involving dance and music of the region. Some festivals, like the Quechua Santiago (Saint James) fiesta celebrated in the Junin province, have Catholic roots, but current Santiagos bear little relation to the Catholic feast day, focusing instead on cattle-marking ceremonies that have overtones of birth and fertility rituals. Of course, Carnival remains one of the most popular and widespread festivals in Peru, as it is throughout the Catholic world. A striking feature of most Peruvian fiestas is the musical competition between instrumental ensembles from each nearby community.

Many instruments used in the highlands reflect Spanish roots. Some are clearly European, such as the violin, trumpet, saxophone, and clarinet. Others reflect a blend of indigenous and Spanish traditions, including the charango and other stringed instruments. Nonetheless, the ubiquitous flute family instruments are purely Peruvian. The Aymara use several types of flutes, including two varieties of end-blown duct flute, the *pinkillu* and the *tarka*, but the Andean instruments best known to outsiders are the panpipes—or raftpipes, to use the proper term. The most common Aymara panpipe is the *siku*, and no fiesta can go by without performances by *sikuri* ensembles. Most recorded Aymara music is instrumental, and most musical instruments are played only by men. Aymara women dance and sing at fiestas, and they preserve a repertory of folk songs for various purposes.

Strange as it may sound, the Aymara *siku* cannot be played as a solo instrument. These panpipes are constructed in pairs; one instrument, the *ira* (leader), provides every other scale tone; its mate, the *arka* (follower), provides the notes in between. Thus, players must perform in pairs, using a hocketlike alternation to produce a complete melody. Ideally, the two must "play as one," leaving no gaps between one note and the next. This paired performance practice indicates that the panpipes were designed with ensemble playing in mind, and a typical ensemble involves eight pairs of differently sized instruments. The different sizes permit doubling at the octave, fourth, or fifth, though a more recent innovation (from the 1920s) permits doubling at the third as well, requiring an additional two pairs of instruments. In festival performance situations, up to fifty musicians may play at once, resulting in extensive doubling of like instruments. Players deliberately play a bit sharp or flat to create a shimmering "wide" unison, a special tone quality associated with *sikuri* ensembles.

This ensemble music faithfully reflects social values and structures in the Conimo district, as Thomas Turino points out.[6] Conflict-resolution skills are virtually nonexistent in Aymara communities. Instead, emphasis is placed on cooperation for the good of the group. Leadership roles are shared, passed from person to person regardless of qualifications or skills. In this context, group identity takes on heightened significance, as if to make up for the devaluation of individual identity. The strength of this group identity becomes especially evident in the contests between *sikuri* ensembles of different communities. Each ensemble has its own traditions and works hard to create a

---

[6]Thomas Turino, "The Coherence of Social Style and Musical Creation Among the Aymara in Southern Peru." *Ethnomusicology* 33, 1 (winter 1989), pp. 1–30.

unique musical style distinct from those of neighboring communities. True to their nonconfrontational manner, the judging of these contests occurs informally; no official decisions are handed down, since that would bring shame and embarrassment on those who lost. At many fiestas, several groups may declare themselves the best-of-the-fest, and everyone goes home happy.

North Americans often define themselves by their jobs. To perform in a *sikuri* ensemble provides Aymara communities with a similar kind of self-definition. Music making is not a matter of individual expression for the Aymara (they don't even rehearse alone); it remains a social activity with deep roots in a community's identity. Thus, in the operation of a *sikuri* ensemble we can see in microcosm the operation of Aymara society in general. *Sikuri* performances occur at fiestas as often as once a month. In the weeks preceding the fiesta, the ensemble leader solicits the participation of other master musicians in the community. The leader cannot appear to be forceful or coercive—a leader who pushes too hard doesn't remain leader for long. Once the leader secures sufficient participation to guarantee a performance, a rehearsal is scheduled for the night before the fiesta. At the rehearsal, the ensemble must create two or three new compositions that they hope will win them the praise of the ensembles they compete against. (Unlike other folk music traditions that preserve a body of ancient tunes, the Aymara prize ever-new melodies composed according to traditional principles.) The compositional process is a group effort. Individuals will try out ideas on their instruments. No one ever criticizes another person's ideas directly; if others like an idea, they begin to play along with it, perhaps adding new embellishments or melodic twists (subject to group approval); if they dislike an idea, they ignore it and the composer tries out other ideas instead. When the entire group begins to play along with a phrase they all like, that phrase becomes part of the composition. Sometimes a member will bring in a newly composed tune. This tune is subject to the same process, however, and the group often adds or changes ideas until everyone is satisfied. In either case, a new composition is announced as the creation of the group as a whole. This process of consensus precisely mirrors other social interactions in Aymara communities.

Whereas a core of perhaps a dozen musicians participates in the compositional process, up to fifty community musicians may participate in the fiesta performances. Since the unrehearsed musicians must learn the new compositions by ear during the performance itself, the tunes generally include frequent motivic repetition and certain stock melodic formulas known to all. The additional instruments may not be in tune with the core ensemble, and they may not play all the right notes, but they almost invariably provide additional sound and energy. Interestingly, no one ever criticizes the extras. Skilled musicians may talk about how a good performance should go, but no one seems to mind the discrepancy between ideal and actual performances.

Centro Social Conima and the Aymara in Lima

In the face of so many pressures for change, whether from other districts, the Peruvian government, or the pervasive influence of popular musics from the United States, *sikuri* ensemble music (along with other indigenous musics) has become a powerful means of maintaining community identity. Since the 1950s, many residents of the poor mountain regions of Peru have moved to the major cities, especially Lima, looking for work and better opportunities. For the Aymara, leaving the communities that gave them a sense of identity has proved especially traumatic, and most of them have banded together with others from their home districts to re-create communities that echo the ones they knew back home. The Centro Social Conima in Lima, formed by former residents of the Conimo district, is one such club. The club provides a network for mutual support, and members regularly gather to celebrate the same fiestas that were so important back in the mountains—using the same instruments, and playing, dancing, and singing in the same manner. The club makes some concessions; *sikuri* ensemble music dominates urban fiestas, since these ensembles have proved more acceptable and popular in Lima than music for *pinkillus* or *tarkas*. Still, such clubs provide a profoundly meaningful opportunity for the transplanted Aymara to be who they are, wherever they find themselves.

"Manuelita"

Our recording of "Manuelita" features the *sikuri* ensemble of the Centro Social Conima described above. They model their performances after a specific *sikuri* ensemble from the Conimo district, the Qhantati Ururi. To guarantee authenticity, the Lima Conimeños work from recordings of this group from the highlands. They use the same instruments as their *altiplano* counterparts, an ensemble of raftpipes played in pairs accompanied by a drum. (The Andean street musicians heard in many cities of the United States often mix raftpipes with a variety of plucked string instruments, but this practice does not follow the authentic Peruvian folk tradition.) This recording captures a rehearsal that took place in the home of one of the members. The ensemble includes twenty *siku* players and three *bombos* (drums).

Begin your presentation with some background material. Feel free to use any of the information provided above, but make sure you include at least some ideas from the section titled "Aymara Music and Social Structure in the Conimo District." Especially important are the paragraphs describing the relationships of instruments within the ensemble, the compositional process, and performance practices at the major fiestas. Let them know that this melody belongs to the *lento sikuri* genre. As the Spanish word *lento* suggests, the tempo is generally slow, at least in comparison with faster *sikuri* genres. Also typical of the genre is a somewhat melancholy quality.

Once students understand the context, display the list of musical elements and structures and play the music (don't refer them to the Additional Listening Chart from Appendix I yet). Afterward, ask students to describe what they heard. Perhaps the most striking feature of this music is the physical sound of the instruments. Breathy, yet full, the timbre possesses a shimmering quality, the result of multiple doublings that are slightly out of tune. Additional fullness and a sense of harmony are provided by extensive doubling of the melody in thirds, fifths, and octaves, a sound typical of many Conimeño ensembles. Unlike most Western harmony, these chords result from persistent parallel motion (similar to sounds heard in Debussy; see Chapter 20). The parallel motion makes the question of texture tricky—is it a single melody doubled in strict parallel motion (expanded monophonic), or is it melody-and-accompaniment texture? Point out the use of minor mode—even sixteenth-century observers commented on a pervasive "sadness" in Andean folk music. The dynamics remain loud (for flutes) throughout, though the sound becomes slightly softer when the melody dips into a lower register. Note the use of duple meter and the feeling that the pipes and the drums are not always quite synchronized.

Some students will notice a lot of repetition. Take the opportunity to note that the structure of "Manuelita" is absolutely typical of *sikuri* ensemble music, following the usual **a a b b c c** form. You may notice that the **c** phrase is quite similar to the **a** phrase; this results from the characteristic repetition of motives in each phrase of the melody and from the Conimo tendency to make contrasts subtle. In fact, all three phrases end in the same manner. Remember that repetition is an advantage in this music, since most *sikuri* ensemble performers must learn the melody by ear during the premiere performance. Show students how this works by displaying a diagram of the melody's motivic structure. Assuming each measure to be a motive, the diagram should look like this:

Phrase 1 (**a**)	Phrase 2 (**b**)	Phrase 3 (**c**)
v w x y z	**t u x y z**	**w x y z**

With the help of this diagram, students can easily see the important relationships within this melody. Note that the last three measures (**x y z**) of each phrase are identical, and that the third phrase is the same as the first, but without its opening **v** motive (thus **c**). The only true contrast comes with the **t** and **u** motives in the first two measures of the second phrase. To make this clear to your students, play through the first minute of "Manuelita," up to the beginning of the second stanza, and point to each motive as it goes by.

Now display the Additional Listening Chart from Appendix I. Here students can see why the drums and raftpipes sound out-of-synch; the consistent use of syncopation means that the melody often falls just before or after the drum, which always comes on the beat. Play the entire piece one final time and draw attention to several items related to Conimeño performance practices. In addition to frequent repetition of motives within the melody, the stanza itself repeats again and again—three times in our recording. Remind students that the repetition enables performers to learn the melody quickly, and point out that fiesta performances may repeat a melody for up to forty minutes. Finally, note the frequent raggedness of this performance; the players don't always attack their notes simultaneously. This may only be a rehearsal, but make students aware that a fiesta performance might be even worse, since it would involve many performers who never attended the rehearsal!

As the notes above suggest, the Aymara do not regard these imperfections as a serious problem. Participation is so crucial to individual and community identity that the gap between the "ideal" and the actual performance must be accepted. Again we must appreciate the difficulty of truly understanding the "voice of the other." A story from the lore surrounding Charles Ives can put this concept in perspective. When Ives was a church organist, a member of the congregation approached him about the "problem" of old man S., who sang congregational hymns with great fervor but was always far off-key and much too loud. Ives responded indignantly, telling the church member that old man S. had more music in his little finger than the rest of the congregation combined. Skilled Aymara musicians can readily identify the features of a "perfect" performance, but they also know that the significance of music in their culture goes far beyond merely esthetic considerations.

Multimedia Resources

♪ Further Listening Charts and Texts

See Appendix I for a listening chart if you use these works from Further Listening Examples above:

A Peruvian Raftpipe Orchestra: Centro Social Conima, "Manuelita"

See Appendix II for texts and translations if you use these works from Further Listening Examples above:

Dufay, "Veni Creator Spiritus"

Dufay, "Hélas mon dueil"

Josquin, "Petite Camusette"

Josquin, "Scaramella va alla guerra"

Anonymous, "Pange lingua"

Josquin, *Ave maris stella* Mass, Kyrie and Agnus Dei

Josquin, "Absalon, fili mi"

Arcadelt, "Il bianco e dolce cigno"

Gesualdo, "Moro, lasso"

Gibbons, "The silver Swanne"

♩ Sound Recordings

Byrd, *The Great Service*. Tallis Scholars. Gimell 454 911-2 (CD). Wonderful performances of Byrd's music for Anglican worship, reflecting the concerns of the English Reformation. Use this recording if you try suggestions for Byrd's "Sing joyfully unto God" in Further Listening Examples above.

Dufay, *Chansons*. Bernhard Landauer & Ensemble Unicorn. Naxos 8.553458 (CD). Decent recordings of seventeen Dufay chansons, and it's hard to beat the price. Try this recording if you use Listening Idea 2 or the Further Listening Examples suggestion above for Dufay's "Hélas mon dueil."

Dufay, *Hymns*. Schola Hungarica. Hungaroton HCD 12951 (CD). Performances of fifteen hymn settings by Dufay as well as the plainchant melodies on which they were based, as found in the Cambrai Antiphonal. Use this recording for a complete performance of the "Ave maris stella" setting in the textbook or if you try the Further Listening Examples suggestion above for Dufay's "Veni Creator Spiritus" setting.

English and Italian Renaissance Madrigals. The Hilliard Ensemble. Virgin Veritas 7243 5 61671 2 4 (CD). Wonderful performances of Italian and English madrigals by one of the finest early music ensembles. Weelkes is well represented on the English disc, which also includes music of Morley, Wilbye, Bennet, Gibbons, Tomkins, Ward, and Vautor. The Italian disc contains madrigals by Arcadelt, Verdelot, da Rore, Willaert, Marenzio, and di Lasso. Try this recording if you use suggestions for Gibbons's "The silver Swanne" or Arcadelt's "Il bianco e dolce cigno" in Further Listening Examples above.

An English Ladymass: Medieval Chant and Polyphony. Anonymous 4. Harmonia Mundi HMU 907080 (CD). One of several outstanding CDs by this women's quartet, it contains a mixture of English medieval plainchant, motets, and the like. Try this recording if you want to compare the original plainchant hymn, "Ave maris stella," with Dufay's polyphonic setting.

Gesualdo, *O Dolorosa Gioia*. Concerto Italiano. Opus 111 (CD). Superb recording of late Renaissance madrigals by Gesualdo, Luzzaschi, and others. Use this recording if you try suggestions for the *Moro, lasso* Mass in Further Listening Examples above.

Josquin, Missa "Ave maris stella"; Vergil Motetten. Dufay Ensemble. Ars Musici AM 1278-2 (CD). Fine recording of Josquin Mass and motets. Use this recording if you try suggestions for the *Ave maris stella* Mass in Further Listening Examples above.

Josquin, *Missa Pange lingua; Missa La sol fa re mi*. The Tallis Scholars. Gimell Records CDGIM 009 (CD). Peter Phillips leads this prominent early music ensemble in performances of two complete Josquin masses, including the *Pange lingua* Mass, described in the textbook, and the complete plainchant melody on which the Mass is based. Use this recording to supplement your presentation of the *Pange lingua* Mass.

Josquin, *Motets et Chansons*. The Hilliard Ensemble. Virgin 61302 (CD). One of the loveliest performances of Josquin's vocal music available on CD, it includes a mixture of motets and secular works. "Ave Maria . . . virgo serena" (a 4), "El grillo," and the *Listen* chanson "Mille regrets" are outstanding. Use this recording if you try Listening Ideas 1 and 2 or the suggestions for Josquin's "Absalon, fili mi," "Petite Camusette," or "Scaramella va alla guerra" in Further Listening Examples above.

"The King's Delight," *17 C. Ballads for Voice and Violin Band*. The King's Noyse. Harmonia Mundi HMU 907101 (CD). Delightful performances of late Renaissance and early Baroque songs, dances, and instrumental music. Performed by an ensemble of violin family instruments with soprano Ellen Hargis and the eminent lutenist Paul O'Dette. Contains a complete performance of the galliard "Daphne."

Madrigal History Tour. King's Singers. EMI CDM 7 69837 2 (CD). Famed vocal ensemble performs Renaissance secular vocal music from the major western European nations. Includes recordings of works suggested in Further Listening Examples above: Arcadelt's "Il bianco e dolce cigno" and Gibbons's "The silver Swanne."

Matins for the Virgin of Guadalupe. Chanticleer. Teldec 3984-21829-2 (CD). Music written for the feast day of the Virgin of Guadalupe. Recording features music written in Baroque and early Classical styles by two composers associated with Mexico City Cathedral, Ignacio de Jerúsalem and Manuel de Zumaya. Use this recording if you try Listening Idea 6 above.

Mexican Baroque. Chanticleer. Teldec Das Alte Werk 4509-96353-2 (CD). Music written for Mexico City Cathedral by two composers who served as *maestro de capilla* there, Ignacio de Jerúsalem and Manuel de Zumaya; Zumaya was the first Mexican-born composer to serve in that post. This fascinating music demonstrates clear European influence; its styles range from late Renaissance polyphony to early Classical homophony. Use this recording if you try Listening Idea 5 above.

Missa Mexicana. The Harp Consort, Andrew Lawrence-King, dir. Harmonia Mundi France HMU 907293 (CD). Excellent new recording contains Missa *Ego flos campi*, written for the church at Puebla de los Angeles by its *maestro de capilla*, Juan de Padilla, surrounded here by *xácaras* and other works that demonstrate indigenous dances and rhythms that influenced the composer. Much of this fascinating music demonstrates clear European influence, but the vivacious Mexican dance rhythms give it a unique flavor, and the African-influenced "Cumbées" by de Murcia even includes "blue" notes. It also contains a sensual Peruvian song filled with double entendres, "Marizápalos bajo una tarde." Use this recording if you try Listening Idea 5 above.

Mountain Music of Peru, Volume I. Smithsonian Folkways SFW40020 (CD). Excellent collection of Peruvian folk and popular music with extensive examples from the Quechua-speaking community of Q'eros. No liner notes. Use this recording for further examples of Andean music.

Mountain Music of Peru, Volume II. Smithsonian Folkways SFW40406 (CD). Excellent collection of Peruvian folk music from both Quechua- and Aymara-speaking regions of the Andes. Excellent, comprehensive liner notes. Use this recording if you try Listening Idea 8 or suggestions for "Manuelita" in Further Listening Examples above.

Nueva España. Boston Camerata, Joel Cohen, dir. Erato 2292-45977-2 (CD). Wonderful recording conveys the richness of musical life in Mexico and Peru shortly after the conquest. Works range from liturgical to dance music, and even include examples in Náhuatl and Quechua, among them two versions of "Hanaq pachap kusikuynin"—one a lovely *a cappella* version, the other with instruments. Try this recording for alternative performances of this piece or if you use Listening Idea 5 above.

Ockeghem, *Missa Mi-Mi*. The Clerks' Group. ASV Gaudeamus CD GAU 139 (CD). Beautiful singing in performances of the Mass and motets by Ockeghem, Obrecht, Busnois, and Isaac; directed by Edward Wickham. Try this recording if you use Listening Idea 4 above.

Officium. Jan Garbarek and the Hilliard Ensemble. ECM Records New Series 1525 (CD). This unusual recording consists of Jan Garbarek's saxophone improvisations over a mix of plainchant and liturgical polyphony by medieval and Renaissance composers such as Pérotin, Dufay, Morales, and de la Rue. Try this recording for an unusual version of the Dufay work discussed in the textbook, "Ave maris stella."

Palestrina, *Missa Viri Galilaei*. La Chapelle Royale/Ensemble Organum. Harmonia Mundi HMC 901388 (CD). A complete performance by Ensemble Organum of the introit "Viri Galilaei," covered in the textbook, followed by Palestrina's parody Mass of the same name. Like many recent recordings that place Renaissance polyphonic Masses in their liturgical context, this one intersperses plainchant performances of the movements of the Proper among Palestrina's polyphonic settings of the Ordinary, re-creating a late sixteenth-century Mass for the Feast of the Ascension. Unlike the Josquin tenor Mass covered in this chapter, Palestrina's is a parody Mass based on his own motet of the same name (not on the plainchant introit). Use this recording if you try Listening Idea 4.

Silk Road Journeys. Yo-Yo Ma & the Silk Road Ensemble. Sony Classical SK 89782 (CD). In some ways the ultimate "crossover" album, this recording blends traditional and modern, folk and classical, East and West. The musicians, their instruments, and the songs come from India, Iran, the United States, Mongolia, and China. Of particular interest in Chapter 6 is a dance from the Italian Renaissance, Filippo Azzaiolo's "Chi passa per'sta strada," performed on violins, cello, bass, *pipas*, *erhu*, *sheng*, *tabla*, and other percussion. The sound of the non-Western instruments comes surprisingly close to that of early Western instruments, and the musicians improvise a series of variations that foreshadows the Baroque variation forms discussed in Chapter 7. Best of all, this performance fully captures the freewheeling spirit that must have typified Renaissance dance music at any but the highest social levels. Highly recommended as a supplement to your coverage of Renaissance dances.

Spain in the New World. Hesperus. Koch International Classics 3-7451 2H1 (CD). Recording conveys the richness of musical life in New Spain with examples from Spain, Mexico, Peru, Bolivia, Colombia, and Guatemala shortly after the conquest. Works range from liturgical to dance music. Try this recording if you use Listening Idea 5 above.

Terpsichore: Tanzmusik der Renaissance und des Frühbarock. Konrad Ragossnig and the Ulsamer Collegium. Deutsche Grammophon Archiv 415 294-2 (CD). Delightful collection of Renaissance and early Baroque dances. Try this recording if you use suggestions in Further Listening Examples above for the set of dances that begins with "Celeste Giglio."

The Tallis Scholars Live in Rome. The Tallis Scholars. Gimell Records CDGIM 994 (CD). Peter Phillips leads this prominent early music ensemble in gorgeous performances recorded live at Palestrina's church, Santa Maria Maggiore, on the four hundredth anniversary of the composer's death. The disc includes several Palestrina motets, the complete *Pope Marcellus* Mass, and Allegri's "Miserere," the work the young Mozart took down in dictation during a visit to Rome.

Torrejón y Velasco, *La púrpura de la rosa*. The Harp Consort. Deutsche Harmonia Mundi 05472 77355 2 (CD). Exciting new recording of the first opera composed *and* performed in the New World—in Lima, Peru, 1701. This music often draws on South American dance rhythms accompanied by a Spanish continuo-band. Features soloists Judith Malafronte and Ellen Hargis; conducted by Andrew Lawrence-King. Try this recording as a supplement to your coverage of Global Perspectives materials above.

♩ Video Recordings

Early Instruments. www.insight-media.com (DVD or VHS, color, 2 discs or tapes, 19 minutes each). Videos introduce important instruments, including recorder, crumhorn, lute, rebec, viol, portative organ, shawm, sackbut, and cornett.

Early Musical Instruments Series. www.films.com (DVD or VHS, color, 30 minutes each): Reed Instruments, Flutes and Whistles, Plucked Instruments, Bowed Instruments, Keyboard and Percussion, and Brass Instruments. David Munrow narrates this series that shows what the instruments look like, how they sound, and how they are played. Performances by Christopher Hogwood and other members of the Early Music Consort of London. Useful if you have a strong interest in the subject and plan to spend some time with the Renaissance.

Echoes of Jacobean England. *Echoes of the Past* Series. www.films.com (DVD or VHS, color, 39 minutes). A look at England during the reign of King James. A good supplement to the study of the English madrigal, it looks at music of Campion, Dowland, and others.

1492: A Portrait in Music. Norman: University of Oklahoma Center for Music Television (VHS, color, 60 minutes). The Waverly Consort performs early Renaissance music in this picture of life in 1492, seen through the eyes of Christopher Columbus. Performances were filmed at historic sites in Granada, Córdoba, Salamanca, Seville, and Barcelona. Can serve as a fascinating prelude to study of the Aztec conquest.

The Golden Age. Music in Time Series. www.films.com (DVD or VHS, color, 60 minutes). James Galway covers the Elizabethan period in England and contemporary developments in Italy and France. The first half works well for this chapter: It includes madrigals and songs by Morley, Marenzio, Weelkes ("As Vesta Was from Latmos Hill Descending"), Dowland, and Gibbons; dances and other instrumental works by Holborn, Dowland, and Bull; and a motet by Byrd. The second half fits Chapter 7: It includes music by Caccini, Monteverdi, Marini, Lully, and Purcell. Helpful if you plan to cover Chapters 6 and 7 quickly.

The History of Music, Part 1. www.insight-media.com (VHS, color, 89 minutes). The section on the Renaissance covers polyphony and music of Dufay, Ockeghem, and Josquin.

JVC/Smithsonian Folkways Video Anthology of Music and Dance of the Americas. This excellent six-volume set includes extensive examples of Peruvian music in Volumes 5 and 6. Highly recommended for your presentation of Global Perspectives materials for this chapter.

JVC Video Anthology of World Music and Dance. Tape 28 from this excellent video series offers music from Latin America. Of particular interest are examples 28-10 through 28-13, folk songs from Bolivia. The Aymara peoples are even more populous in Bolivia than in Peru, and these songs offer interesting comparisons with the *sikuri* ensemble music in Further Listening Examples above.

Music of Mexico and South America. www.insight-media.com (VHS, color, 60 minutes). A broad overview of Latin American music and traditions. Special consideration given to the mingling of indigenous and Western cultures.

The Music of the Devil, the Bear, and the Condor. Cinema Guild 103 (VHS, 52 minutes). This film looks at the music festivals and ceremonies of the Aymara peoples of southeastern Peru. Fascinating connections with Global Perspectives materials for this chapter.

Old Masters. Culture Fix Series. www.films.com (DVD or VHS, color, 29 minutes). Looks at the techniques and artists of the Renaissance and Baroque, including Leonardo, Michelangelo, and Rembrandt. Useful supplement to your study of Renaissance music.

Qeros: The Shape of Survival. Mystic Fire Video 76281 (VHS, 53 minutes). Ethnologist John Cohen's film on the music and rituals of the Quechua-speaking Qeros people of the Peruvian Andes.

The Renaissance. Music in Time Series. www.films.com (DVD or VHS, color, 60 minutes). James Galway examines the role of the church and of French and Burgundian patrons in the development of Renaissance style. Includes chansons by Dufay, Binchois, Josquin, Claudin, and Lassus; Masses by Ockeghem and Palestrina; motets by Taverner, Palestrina, Victoria, and Giovanni Gabrieli; and instrumental works by Andrea Gabrieli and Milán.

Renaissance Art and Music. www.insight-media.com (DVD or VHS, color, 54 minutes). This still-image video provides a concise, visually appealing introduction to important artistic and musical trends in the Renaissance. Contains artwork of Donatello, Giotto, Fra Angelico, Raphael, Michelangelo, Leonardo, Titian, Dürer, and El Greco; music by Dufay, Josquin, Lasso, and Palestrina.

Rome: Out of the Darkness. Man and Music Series. www.films.com (DVD or VHS, color, 53 minutes). Renaissance music in Rome with some performances in the Sistine Chapel. Includes motets by Dufay and Lassus, Masses by Josquin and Palestrina (*Pope Marcellus* Mass), and madrigals by Marenzio.

The Tallis Scholars: Live in Rome. Gimell GIMDN 904 (DVD, color, 82 minutes). Peter Phillips leads the renowned Tallis Scholars in gorgeous performances recorded live at Palestrina's church, Santa Maria Maggiore, on the four hundredth anniversary of the composer's death. The building's breathtaking architecture and warm resonance make this video a treat for both the eye and the ear. The performance includes several Palestrina motets, the complete *Pope Marcellus* Mass (excerpts described in *Listen*), and Allegri's "Miserere," the work the young Mozart took down in dictation during a visit to Rome. Highly recommended.

♪ Software

The History of Music, Part 1. www.mccormicksnet.com (CD-ROM—Windows/Macintosh). CD-ROM version of the video listed above. The section on the Renaissance covers Renaissance polyphony and the music of Dufay, Ockeghem, and Josquin.

History Through Art: Renaissance. Zane Publishing (CD-ROM—Windows or Macintosh). The Renaissance volume of this inexpensive CD-ROM series contains several hundred full-screen images, including artworks by Leonardo, Michelangelo, Raphael, and others. Quality of screen images is variable, but its price is very low. Available from www.cdaccess.com.

The Norton Masterworks CD-ROM. New York: W. W. Norton (CD-ROM—Macintosh). Authors Daniel Jacobson and Timothy Koozin provide a clever multimedia introduction to twelve important works, including Josquin's motet "Ave Maria." Features animated, guided listening resources as well as information on the composers, eras, genres, and the works themselves.

CHAPTER 7

The Early Baroque Period

Chapter Outline

Boldface indicates works in the recording set.

Important Terms

Baroque	aria	variations	passacaglia	interlocking ostinatos
basso continuo	arioso	registrations	chromaticism	hocket
ground bass	chorus	toccatas	ostinato	hunting song
basso ostinato	dance	canzonas	minstrel	
functional harmony	suites	movements	*jangar*	
opera	virtuosity	balletto	lyre	
recitative	fugue	corrente	pygmy polyphony	

Teaching Objectives

ʔ Overall Objectives

This chapter will help students acquire familiarity with:

1. Early Baroque genres as expressions of emotionality, exaggeration, extravagance, and control:

    a. Venetian motet

    b. opera

    c. trio sonata

2. The lives and music of Giovanni Gabrieli, Claudio Monteverdi, Henry Purcell, and Girolamo Frescobaldi.

3. The role of the solo singer, instrumental ensembles, and ostinato patterns in music of Europe and the Gambia.

4. The Mbuti tribe and their polyphonic songs as unique expressions of ostinato form.

ʔ Listening Objectives

After completing this chapter, students should be able to:

1. Hear and identify how elements and structures of music are typically used in the early Baroque style.

2. Identify and follow the genres of early Baroque music, especially the Venetian motet, opera, and trio sonata.

3. Hear and identify expressive techniques of early Baroque music.

4. Hear important features of Gambian minstrel song and recognize these connections between early Baroque and Gambian musics:

    a. the importance of the solo singer

    b. repeating patterns (ostinato and ground bass)

5. Hear interlocking ostinatos and other important features of Mbuti songs.

Lecture Suggestions

Chapter 7 completes Kerman and Tomlinson's survey of early music and also provides an ideal introduction to Baroque music, covered in Unit III. The textbook's discussion of the Baroque dualism of freedom of expression (emotionality, exaggeration, and extravagance) versus clarity and control (expressed in more systematic use of form) is invaluable. This dualism, the Baroque genius for theatricality, the rise of instrumental music, and the increasing influence of dance all provide natural and easily perceived distinctions between the Renaissance and Baroque periods.

    A detailed examination of the technical aspects of Baroque music is not necessary at this point. The authors use Chapter 7 to introduce elements of

Baroque music—specifically rhythm and meter, basso continuo, and functional harmony—but they cover this same material in greater depth in Chapter 8. This leaves the instructor free to focus on contrasts between Renaissance and Baroque music and on the primary trends that shaped early Baroque style. These motifs stand out even more clearly when set against the Global Perspectives materials on Gambian and Mbuti music, a rich counterpoint with many shared themes.

❦ From Renaissance to Baroque

The two columns below identify important differences between Renaissance and Baroque music. You can put them on the board and refer to them when you play musical examples from Chapter 7.

Renaissance Music	Baroque Music
voice the ideal; instruments inferior	instrumental music equally important
voices used in ensembles	solo voice most important
a cappella	voices accompanied by instruments (basso continuo)
natural, simple musical ideas	artifice and virtuosity
irregular, floating rhythms	clear, dancelike rhythms
modal harmony	functional harmony
music for church and chamber	music for *theater*, church, and chamber
text declamation and word painting	music expresses emotions

GIOVANNI GABRIELI Motet, "O magnum mysterium"

Saint Mark's Cathedral in Venice saw the development of an entirely new musical esthetic, one that celebrated magnificence and pomp rather than the Renaissance ideals of balance and order. The cathedral's two widely spaced choir lofts were exploited by many late Renaissance composers who wrote brilliant echo effects into their music. Giovanni Gabrieli replaced Renaissance imitative polyphony with imitation between two or more choirs of voices and instruments. Kerman and Tomlinson rightly make the point that although these effects provide early examples of stereophonic sound, modern stereo equipment cannot yet capture the full effect of this polychoral music.

Play the motet and ask students to compare what they hear with items on the list above. Gabrieli's music reflects many aspects of the transition from Renaissance to Baroque. It demonstrates Renaissance characteristics such as voices organized into ensembles, text declamation, and word painting. Baroque characteristics include equal treatment of voices and instruments as well as clear, dancelike rhythms, especially in the triple-meter sections. Unique to Venice is the interplay between different choirs of voices and instruments (which can be heard on a stereo sound system). This work deploys two choirs (seven different vocal and instrumental parts in each) with organ accompaniment.

Gabrieli follows Renaissance formal procedure in introducing new melodic materials for each new phrase of text. Play the music again while students listen for these changing patterns—the hushed awe of "O magnum mysterium," the more intimate warmth of "et admirabile sacramentum," the mild dissonance of "iacentem in presepio" (to emphasize the incongruence of God incarnate lying in a hay holder), and the celebration of the alleluias. These diverse, extravagantly sonorous elements are held together by calculated contrasts that build momentum, by similarities between the beginning and the end, and by alleluia repetitions that intensify the climax.

⁊ Style Features of Early Baroque Music

The Baroque period was characterized by scientific inquiry and observation and by a celebration of order, logic, and human control of the environment. Alongside the expression of emotions ("Dido's Lament") and extravagance (Gabrieli's "O magnum mysterium"), Baroque music reflected the period's fascination with control, regularity, and logic. This brief discussion of elements of Baroque musical style will plant ideas that can be built on when these elements are explored in detail in Unit III.

Play the aria from Monteverdi's *Coronation of Poppea* to illustrate clearly the key elements of Baroque style. Ask the class to compare what they hear with the list of contrasts between Renaissance and Baroque styles above. In the discussion that follows, draw out the following points:

Rhythm and meter—Melodic rhythm and meter became more systematic and precise during the Baroque. The beat and meter are clear and vivaciously dancelike in many of Monteverdi's passages.

Major and minor modes—The major and minor scales and systems of temperament that make modulation to any key possible were products of the systematic scientific thought of the Baroque. The Monteverdi piece makes use of the major scale, with its inevitable pull toward the tonic.

Functional harmony—The leading tone in both major and minor scales creates their strong pull toward the tonic. The systematized science of harmonic function, in which each chord plays a specific role in relation to a tonic chord (the result of tendencies in the motion of each voice to or from the tonic), developed during the Baroque. Of course, once you strengthen the tonic, modulation acquires greater dramatic power. Note how Monteverdi uses different tonalities expressively: the initial minor key that supports Poppea's uncertainty, the stronger major key affirmations at "No, no, non temo," and the completely unambiguous major key ending starting at "Per me guerreggia."

Basso continuo—The basso continuo is a uniquely Baroque invention in which a group of instruments plays not only the bass line but also the accompanimental harmonies of a piece of music. The continuous articulation of harmonies by the continuo gives Baroque music a sense of foundation, control, and harmonic clarity even in the most complex polyphonic passages. The continuo can be heard most readily in passages for solo instruments, as in this aria, but it supports music for full orchestra as well.

Instrumental music—Perhaps the most extraordinary musical development of the Baroque was the growth of purely instrumental music. That people would be willing to listen to music without voices meant that such abstract, absolute musical features as form, harmony, and texture had become sufficiently interesting in themselves that they could provide a complete musical experience. Although this Monteverdi aria is not purely instrumental, it nonetheless provides examples of the idiomatic virtuoso writing that is possible with instruments, especially at "Per me guerreggia."

♩ Opera

Preliminaries

Opera can be difficult to sell to a class of nonmajors. Most students know only the stereotypes from cartoons or commercials—buxom blond females shrieking in breastplates and horned helmets, faux-Baroque concertos emphasizing the timelessness of diamonds, or sensuous Puccini arias lending elegance to carpet commercials. In the popular mind, opera and musical theater are unrelated, opera fans are snobs, and going to the opera is a pastime of the wealthy. Students are surprised to discover that opera was incredibly popular in the Baroque period—in fact, opera was as popular then as movies are today. Opera was the original multimedia extravaganza, and it met with a commercial success unheard of in the history of early music. No matter what you do, you cannot make all students like opera, but the holdouts will leave with at least grudging respect for it if you convey enthusiastic appreciation for opera, if you can get them to a good operatic performance or show them a first-rate video, and if you constantly emphasize the story line and the dramatic situation whenever you discuss opera. It also helps to start with discussion of how opera came to be.

♩ Early Baroque Opera

The Renaissance saw renewed interest in the art and scholarship of ancient Greece and Rome. Classical influences on Renaissance music were minimal, however, because Renaissance musicians did not have direct access to ancient music—they could only study writings that discussed the effect of music from a philosophical standpoint.[1] These writings had little influence until the tail end of the Renaissance, when a group of scholars and musicians in Florence (the Camerata) became excited about Greek descriptions of music that had the power to reach into the heart and change people's emotions. What would such music sound like?

Composers who attempted to write such music must have drawn inspiration from Orpheus, a mortal who in Greek mythology played the lyre and sang so beautifully that he moved the shades and demons of the underworld to tears. One style that developed from these experiments was the recitative—an emotionally charged, dramatic style of singing for solo voice with simple accompaniment, often on the lute (the Monteverdi and Purcell examples both use lute as a continuo instrument). Based on principles of good oration, the music tried to match the natural rhythm and register of a speaking voice as it expressed different emotions. Anger called for high, loud pitches and rapid delivery; sadness called for low, soft notes with slow, even halting, delivery. Use of the solo voice created an intimacy and directness that had no equivalent in Renaissance music.

Ask the students to imagine a tragic poem about the loss of a loved one, remind them of Shakespeare's famous "To be or not to be," or provide them with a copy of the text from Monteverdi's "Lamento della Ninfa" (see Further Listening Examples below). Ask students which would be more moving—to have a choir read the poem in unison or to have a dramatic actor recite the poem alone. Communication between one person and an audience can convey emotions with greater directness and immediacy. The vocal ensemble that figured

---

[1]The fifteen surviving examples of Greek musical notation known to modern scholars were all discovered after the Renaissance.

so prominently in Renaissance Masses, motets, and madrigals proved un-wieldy and impersonal in the face of the dramatic demands made by Baroque composers. The recitative style quickly proved its aptness for the theater, and opera was born. The simple accompaniment fed into development of the basso continuo, which served as the foundation for most Baroque music.

MONTEVERDI *The Coronation of Poppea*

The earliest operas used recitative style heavily. Perhaps the intensity of emotional expression proved overwhelming; operas soon began to put more emphasis on solo songs mixed with other works, such as duets, trios, choruses, dances, instrumental interludes, and (of course) recitative. Monteverdi's *The Coronation of Poppea*, written when opera was only forty years old, includes just such a mixture of pieces.

Start with the text. This scene from *The Coronation of Poppea* captures a situation to which anyone in a significant romantic relationship can relate. This is Act I, and we are just getting to know the characters. As the preceding duet between the armed guards informs us, Nero and Poppea have just spent the night in each other's arms. Nero prepares to leave Poppea's chamber, but Poppea wants to know if he will come back. Each time she asks, he tells her how much she means to him, even breaking into an arioso to proclaim his love—but he never gives a direct answer. Finally her seductiveness is replaced by a tone of voice that says, "Look, buster! Are you coming back or not?" No sooner does he say yes than she, without dropping a beat, asks when. His response, "Soon," is not enough, and when she tries to exact a promise that he will return very soon, he throws up his hands and exclaims, "If I do not come, you'll come find me!" They say farewell, and Poppea is left alone to reflect on their tryst. In her aria it becomes clear that Poppea is fighting for Nero's love, along with the power and prestige that he can bring to her.

Once you have read through the text with the students, ask them to describe the personalities of Nero and Poppea. The dramatic situation reflects the changing emotions and ploys of each character as they interact. Poppea is seductive, insistent, and clear in her purpose; Nero is gladly seduced but not willing to commit too much.

Now play the music. Ask students to discover how the music reflects the personality and emotions of each character at different points in the drama. Poppea's lute continuo lends a subtly seductive character to her recitatives, and her lyric phrases turn back on themselves. Nero's harpsichord continuo supports his bluster with its sharp, abrupt attacks. Students may notice that some parts are more conversational and others more songlike.

In fact, this work offers an ideal demonstration of the differences between recitative and aria. Be prepared to cue up the beginning of each recitative and aria. Play a portion from the beginning of the recitative and then play Poppea's aria. Ask students to compare the two. In the discussion that follows, draw out these distinctions.

Recitative	*Aria*
free, speechlike rhythms	clear beat and meter
pitches follow natural patterns of declamation	pitches fall into melodic patterns and phrases
continuo accompaniment	orchestral accompaniment
prose text	poetic text, phrases often repeated
advances the action (movement, dialogue)	reflects on the action
free, spontaneous interaction	soliloquy, expresses single emotion

Once students are clear about the distinctive aspects and respective roles of recitative and aria, play the arioso ("Io non posso da te"). *Arioso* means "songlike." Nero's arioso demonstrates a clear beat and meter and the melodic character of an aria, but it is very short, briefly giving wings to Nero's declaration of love for Poppea. Now listen to the entire excerpt again. Ask students to notice how incredibly flexible Monteverdi's music is. It changes quickly from recitative to arioso to recitative to aria, adapting to an ever-changing dramatic situation.

PURCELL *Dido and Aeneas*

Monteverdi's operas were based on Greek and Roman history and mythology. The powerful themes of classical mythology continued to inspire Baroque composers just as they had inspired the Florentine scholars whose experiments helped to forge a new Baroque style. Mythology sometimes dealt with light, humorous subjects, but most often it dealt with life-and-death issues and heart-wrenching tragedy. The tragic tale of Queen Dido and the hero Aeneas, from Virgil's *Aeneid*, served as the basis for Henry Purcell's only opera, *Dido and Aeneas.*

By Purcell's time, the Baroque impulse to classify and systematize had reached opera as well. In place of Monteverdi's fluid response to the needs of the dramatic situation, we now find rigid alternation between recitative and aria. Recitative was inevitably used in scenes that called for action or dialogue; aria, which had become a powerful vehicle for emotional expression, allowed the soloist to turn away from the action and reflect on a single emotion. Such strict conventions made it difficult to tell a story, and reforms inevitably took place in the next century. Writing in an England with no operatic tradition of its own and far removed from Italy, Purcell was not bound by these constraints, and he wrote some of his most beautiful, most emotional music in this opera.

In the opera's final scene, Dido prepares to commit suicide. Cut to the quick by Aeneas's abandonment of her, even though he was tricked into it, she finds nothing left to live for. Purcell proves himself a master even of the rigid operatic conventions, turning them to his advantage. The recitative "Thy hand, Belinda!" is a farewell addressed to Dido's trusted confidante. Then Dido turns away from her friend and the dramatic situation, as one did to sing an aria, but she also turns away from life itself to sing her final aria and stab herself.

The aria "When I am laid in earth" is constructed over a descending, chromatic ground bass. Play the bass pattern several times at the keyboard or on the recording until students can recognize it. The somber ground shrewdly reflects Dido's state of mind. Suicidal depression causes one to focus only on the awful present. Dido cannot see her choices; she sees only the release that death offers. The ground bass reflects this single-mindedness. Above the ground, Purcell adds poignant harmonies and dissonances, especially the sighing melodic suspensions at the end.

Play the recitative and the aria. Ask students to listen for changes in the upper voices of the aria and to describe the emotional tone of the music. (If time permits, guide students through the subtle ornaments employed by the singer where she repeats the sections of her binary-form aria.) In the discussion that follows, point out that, mythological subject matter notwithstanding, Baroque composers sought to express the full range of human emotions and situations in their music.

Conclusions to Draw about Early Baroque Opera

Opera became the most significant new vocal genre to develop in the Baroque period. Its monumental size, lavish sets, stages (see the illustrations on textbook pages 101, 119, 124, and 155), and costumes make it the most extravagant genre in the history of early music. Its attention to human emotions rendered it a deeply expressive art form. The Baroque impulse to systematize created rigid schemes that organized the plot and the music. In opera, Baroque extravagance and control received fullest expression.

African Ostinatos 1

Just as in Chapter 5, it works best to weave in Global Perspectives materials where the connections are most obvious. The Gambian "minstrel" song fits well immediately after the Purcell example because they both employ solo voice and ostinato repetition. See the lecture suggestions following the Frescobaldi suite for ideas to use in presenting this material.

❼ The Rise of Instrumental Music

FRESCOBALDI Suite: Canzona, Balletto, Corrente, and Passacaglia

The rise of instrumental music manifested itself in many ways. We see it especially in the development of instrumental works that match the size and scope of major vocal works, most notably the Mass and the opera. Opera composers created a long work by linking together a series of short works (recitatives, arias, choruses, and so on). In the same manner, Baroque composers created large-scale instrumental works by linking together several short pieces called movements. Dance suites were created when composers linked several dances together; other combinations of short pieces created sonatas, concertos, and so on. Baroque extravagance shows itself in these processes.

The dance suite was one of the first multimovement genres of the early Baroque. Initially written for solo lute or keyboard or for small ensemble, it soon influenced the development of a variety of works, including the *sonata da camera* (chamber sonata) and orchestral suite. Many early dance suites were rather loose collections; the dances were not related to each other in any way except to provide a pleasing contrast with each other. Some composers, however, sought to provide musical links between the dances of their suites. These links were quite simple—perhaps a melodic head-motive or a bass line— but they provide evidence of the same architectural thinking we saw in Josquin's *Pange lingua* Mass.

Frescobaldi's suite reflects the trends described above. A virtuoso work for solo keyboard, it is typical of the early Baroque dance suite. As one would expect, it strings together several dances, or movements, of contrasting character, and it uses a common bass line to link them together in the manner described above. Two important concepts need to be introduced here. First, movements are separate pieces within a suite (or sonata or concerto). Each has its own themes and its own tempo; in fact, the word *movement* derives from the French term for tempo—*mouvement*. Second, this suite reinforces the textbook's discussion of sources for instrumental music on page 108: the last three movements show the influence of dance; every *movement* demonstrates idiomatic, virtuoso writing for keyboard; and the canzona epitomizes the fugal writing that derives from Renaissance vocal music (see Listening Idea 4 below).

The canzona had its roots in the Renaissance chanson. The chanson, like the madrigal, employed different melodic figures and textures for each new line of text. These contrasts carried over into the late Renaissance (and early Baroque) canzona, an instrumental work for worship based on the conventions of the chanson. In fact, some early canzonas were merely instrumental transcriptions of vocal chansons. By contrast, Frescobaldi's canzona is a newly composed work conceived for the keyboard. It contains the imitative texture and contrasting sections so typical of the canzona. Take time to help your students hear both of these features. Focus first on the imitation. The main melodic idea (or subject—about two measures long in this work) passes from voice to voice throughout this canzona. Hardly a measure goes by without it. The imitation can be heard best at the very beginning, but be sure to point out each reappearance of the subject. Next look at the two contrasting sections. The first section ends with a cadence, and the new section starts up at 0:27 with a new theme. Help your students hear this theme as the music plays. In spite of the new theme, note that the composer almost immediately reintroduces the original subject in counterpoint with it. As a result, the contrast between sections is rather subtle. If you would like your students to hear more obvious contrasts, play a recording of the complete canzona (see the Frescobaldi *Toccate, Partite, Capricci, and Other Works for Harpsichord* CD in Sound Recordings below). Subsequent sections of this canzona introduce new motives and provide greater variety of texture than we hear in the excerpt from the *Listen* set.

As Baroque church music continued to evolve, these contrasting sections grew longer and more distinct, transforming themselves into the contrasting movements of the *sonata da chiesa*. For an example of a church sonata, see Corelli in the Further Listening Examples below.

Now turn to the dance movements in our suite. Ask students to use the checklist of musical elements and structures (see Chapter 5) and to identify contrasts between movements as they listen to the second and third movements (balletto and corrente) played without pause. In the discussion that follows, students will most likely notice contrasts in tempo and meter, the balletto a slower duple-meter dance and the corrente with a quick triple feel, actually a compound meter. Point out that each movement attempts to portray a single emotion or mood, in the same way that Baroque opera arias reflect on a single emotion. This helps to reinforce the distinct qualities of each movement.

At this point it is helpful to reflect on the construction of dance suites and on the contrasts between these two dance types. In the late Renaissance and early Baroque, it was common practice to pair a slower dance with a faster one, like the pavan-galliard pair the authors mention in Chapters 6 and 7. In fact, the dance suite resulted from this practice of pairing dances, and a slow-fast pair served as the kernel for many early dance suites. The balletto was not frequently paired with other dances, but when it was, the second dance was inevitably a corrente. Typically, our Frescobaldi suite is built around this pairing. The Italian balletto itself likely originated as a German import with many similarities to the allemande (the French word for "German"). Like the allemande, the balletto was a duple-meter dance whose tempo could be slow or fast. When paired with a corrente, however, the balletto would be taken at the slower tempo. The corrente (the Italian word means "flowing") is generally viewed as an Italian variant of the French courante. By contrast with the balletto, a corrente moved at a quick tempo in either triple or compound meter. The triple feel with its recurring quarter note–eighth note rhythm supported this dance's typical hop-step foot pattern. The triple-meter corrente was rather simple in its construction, but the compound-meter version relished a degree of rhythmic ambiguity, likely derived from the French courante. Our Frescobaldi corrente fits in the latter category. Its rhythmic unpredictability surfaces immediately—what sounds like the first downbeat is actually right in the middle of a 6/4 measure. And although the first section pulls us inexorably toward the cadence, we're not exactly sure when we'll get there until we get there, about five measures later. This kind of asymmetry will recur again and again in Baroque music.

Continue your look at the balletto and corrente by focusing on two features they share—homophonic texture and binary form. Unlike the canzona, with its pervasive imitation, these dances rely primarily on homophonic texture. Yes, the bass line is quite active and the inner voices often add quickly moving motives to the texture, but our primary focus is on the melody in the top voice, which guides us securely through the work. Next, look at form. Binary form is far and away the most common form found in Baroque dances of any type, and because sections usually repeat in binary form, students find it easy to hear. These two dances were cut from the same cloth. Each begins with an **a** section lasting about nine seconds. After **a** repeats, the contrasting **b** section rounds out the dance, lasting about twice as long as the **a** section. Play the balletto until your students can hear both the repetition of **a** and the contrasts inherent in the **b** section. Then play the corrente to allow students to hear its nearly identical structure. These two dances provide excellent examples of the "inner" versus "outer" form described by the authors in Chapter 4.

Follow this with a look at the bass line the three dance movements share. On page 111 of the textbook, the *Listen* Guide for this suite provides notated examples of this bass line. Play these lines at the keyboard to help your students hear the similarities between them as well as their contrasts in meter, tempo, and rhythm (transpose down a half step if you want to match the organ's pitch). The balletto and corrente bass lines are nearly identical in their melodic contour, whereas the passacaglia rearranges the ending to make it into an authentic cadence.

Finally, spend some time with the passacaglia that concludes the suite. Compared to the other two dances, this movement is longer and more elaborate. Frescobaldi was likely the first composer to treat the passacaglia as a variation form, and listening both for the variety of figuration and for the recurring pattern can help your students stretch their ears. This passacaglia can prove tricky—you won't find the consistent ground bass repetition associated with famous examples such as "When I am laid in earth" from Purcell's *Dido and Aeneas* or Bach's Passacaglia and Fugue in C minor. Nonetheless, students can successfully follow the form simply by counting measures. The bass pattern in the *Listen* Guide lays out a four-measure pattern that ends on the dominant chord; the tonic in the fifth measure begins the next pattern. This dominant ending is perhaps the one feature used consistently—everything else is subject to variation. The bass line may move up or down, the chords that begin the pattern might change every time, and the melodic figures can and will renew themselves continuously, but so long as students count out the basic pattern, they can follow the variations of the passacaglia. Another feature that can help students grasp the form is the feeling of the strong cadence that both ends one pattern and begins the next. This structural elision helps give the passacaglia its self-renewing forward momentum.

Although the sense of variation in this passacaglia is continuous, one contrast stands out: the abrupt change of tempo and key at variation 14 (at 1:37). The shift from major to the relative minor key gives the closing variations an entirely new color, and the slower tempo and simpler rhythms contribute to the effect. After all the virtuoso figuration used earlier in the movement, these variations seem much simpler, more serious, more reflective—and almost anti-climactic.

This passacaglia also provides an interesting connection with the music we saw in the Global Perspectives module from Chapter 6. As twin examples of Baroque continuous variation forms, passacaglia and chaconne are often mentioned in the same breath. In modern usage, a passacaglia is based on a recurring bass line, the chaconne on a recurring chord progression; but in the works of many Baroque composers, these two terms are used interchangeably. The differences between them seem to have been based primarily on the origins of each work. The passacaglia originated in Spain as an improvised bridge between stanzas of a song. The chaconne, however, may have started life in New Spain (Mexico, specifically) as a wild, sensual dance. Once imported to Europe, this dance enjoyed a true *succès de scandale*. Frescobaldi was probably the first to cast both works in a more modern variation format, and although his treatment of each is similar, he also distinguishes the two. Whereas his passacaglias tend to be somewhat sedate minor-key works at moderate tempi, his chaconnes are often faster, wilder major-key works, as befits the scandalous dance from the New World. Frescobaldi himself, however, was not rigid about these distinctions, so it is not too surprising to find several features of the chaconne in the *Listen* passacaglia. The following items point toward the influence of the chaconne on this passacaglia: major key, frequent emphasis on the second beat of each group of three, and two 6/4 measures in each variation (*Listen* Guide notation notwithstanding). The sudden contrasts found at variation 14 can now be seen in another light altogether. It is as if we shift gears from the world of the chaconne to the world of the passacaglia. Perhaps Frescobaldi was playing a joke on us, using the closing variations to tell us he really meant to write a passacaglia after all.

◗ Global Perspectives 3: Ostinato Forms

Both examples included in this chapter come from Africa, a continent that harbors some of the most varied, diverse musical cultures on the planet. In spite of this incredible diversity, some features tend to appear in many different African cultures. Intricate rhythmic patterns are often associated with African music, but perhaps even more universal is the use of ostinato patterns—melodic and/or rhythmic patterns that repeat obsessively, over and over again. While both excerpts provide examples of ostinato, it is even more fascinating to note how different these musics are from each other—yet another example of "inner" versus "outer" form.

The first example comes from the Gambia, a tiny nation in the West African savanna that hugs the river from which it takes its name; the second from the Mbuti pygmies, who inhabit the Ituri rainforest in the heart of this enormous continent. This manual begins with background information on each culture and its musical traditions. Use it as you see fit for your own preparation or for class presentation. Following this you will find specific information about each example as well as teaching suggestions.

Music of the Gambia

Despite the fact that the Gambia is Africa's smallest nation, its 1.2 million people divide into at least five major ethnic groups. The largest of these, the Mandinka, once ruled the Mande Empire that controlled Saharan trade routes and most of the West African savanna from the thirteenth to the fifteenth centuries. Even though that empire has long since faded, descendants of the Mande are still widely dispersed throughout West Africa. In fact, they can be found today in virtually every West African nation, and they account for a significant percentage of the population not only in the Gambia, Guinea-Bissau, Mali, and Senegal (where they are the dominant group), but also in Burkina Faso, Côte d'Ivoire, Guinea, Liberia, and Sierra Leone. In spite of the many peoples and language groups found in West Africa, the broad dispersion of the Mande has resulted in a body of traditions shared by most nations in this region. The "praise song" is one of these. The instruments and terminology associated with this genre may vary from one nation, ethnic group, or dialect to another, but these songs and their singers form an important part of West Africa's cultural fabric.

It is difficult to talk about the Senegambian region without mentioning the role it played in the slave trade. As the Mande empire waned, European explorers and traders made progressively deeper inroads into West Africa. By 1544, the Portuguese were using the island of Gorée (now part of Dakar, Senegal) as a holding station for African prisoners destined for shipment to locations in the Caribbean or in North or South America. It would be convenient to place all of the blame on the Europeans, but sadly, many Africans were sold to the slave traders by other Africans. In some cases, prisoners-of-war were sold by their captors for a handsome profit; in others, bands of marauding thieves made a living by kidnapping the unfortunate souls who crossed their path. However it happened, a significant proportion of slaves in the New World came from the Senegambian region of West Africa. Sterling Stuckey, Samuel A. Floyd Jr., and many other scholars have long turned to this region when looking for the sources of African American musical styles such as spirituals, blues, and jazz. When Alex Haley was doing the genealogical research that resulted in his spectacularly successful book, *Roots,* he visited a small village in the Gambia. And the person he consulted in that village was a *jali*—a *griot!*

Griots and Griottes

Griot is the word used to denote the "praise singer" in West Africa. The word itself is problematic; not only is it a French word and thus not the original African term, but some scholars believe it fails to fully describe the roles these singers play in society. In spite of this, *griot* continues to be used widely as a generic term for the profession, in part because French remains an official language in many West African nations and in part for convenience—since different languages and regions have different names for the *griot*. Several examples should suffice: in the Senegambian Mande region (including the Gambia), the *griot* is a *jali*; in the central Mande area (in and around Mali), *jeli*; for the Wolof speakers of Senegal, *gewel*; for Soninke speakers, *geseré*; for the Songhay, *jeseré*; and for the Fulbe, *gawlo*.

Of course, the English term "praise singer" is also an inadequate descriptor, suggesting that the *griots* are masters at "sucking up" and little else. The very first chapter of Thomas Hale's excellent book *Griots and Griottes* (Indiana University Press, 1998) is titled "A Job Description for Griots." That chapter's subheadings make the varied and essential roles played by the *griot* painfully clear: genealogist, historian, adviser, spokesperson, diplomat, mediator, interpreter, translator, musician, composer, teacher, exhorter, warrior, witness, and praise singer. In addition, the *griot* frequently participates in or leads ceremonies that mark rites of passage, including the naming of a child, initiations, courtship, marriages, the installation of chiefs, and funerals. It comes as no surprise, then, that the services of the *griot* are in high demand, and these practitioners take great pride in their versatility—in their ability to provide precisely the right song for every occasion. According to Hale, "At events related to birth, initiation, marriage, family history, sports, music, and government, the griots and griottes are there to witness the occasion, to enliven it, to facilitate it, and to convey what happened to others."

Griots have been a fixture in West Africa for centuries. The first written description of the griots comes from Ibn Battuta, a fourteenth-century Moroccan visitor to the court of Mansa Sulayman, ruler of the powerful Mande Empire. His writings suggest that the profession was already highly developed, and it is likely that griots had been around for several centuries before that. It is interesting to note that even at this early stage, the griots were a class of professional musicians. Indeed, we should view their songs as a kind of classical music that enjoyed the patronage of the courts and in turn enhanced the prestige of those courts. Seen in this light, the griots were not so different from Renaissance and Baroque musicians such as Josquin, Weelkes, Monteverdi, or Purcell.

In past centuries, a *griot* would hold permanent employment at the court of a king or chief or some other noble personage. As a member of the court, the *griot* held a position of great prestige and was extravagantly rewarded for providing so many essential services. In fact, it was thought that the words and songs of the griots possessed an almost magical power. (Recall the reference to sacred Navajo songs as spiritual high-voltage wires.) The appropriate praises and exhortations were thought to prolong the life of the chief, ensure victory in battle, provide protection from curses, and so on. But the griot's songs had the power to cause harm as well as to bestow blessings, and so the griot was someone to be feared. In this light, it was crucial that the griot receive the best possible education. Incompetence was not an option; in fact, it was downright dangerous. The profession handled this through a system of hereditary guilds. Families became highly specialized in this craft, and they taught their sons and daughters the tricks of the trade as soon as they expressed an interest. Griots still take great pride in their lineage, and many griot families trace their roots both to the famous griots of the Mande Empire and to Muhammad himself (Islam is the dominant religion of the savanna).

In modern times, the *griot* has become more of a freelance artist who provides services to anyone who requests them—but always for a price. The role of the hereditary guilds remains strong. In the Gambia, family names such as Kuyateh, Jobarteh, and Suso retain a strong association with the profession. The singer of our minstrel song, Foday Musa Suso, belongs to one of these families, though he is only one of hundreds of griots with the Suso name. To ensure their livelihood, griots have also had to develop an entrepreneurial spirit. They have become expert at finding new ways to make themselves invaluable to the communities in which they live. The finest musicians among them have even found their way into international musical careers, including Foday Musa Suso—one of the most successful Gambian musicians. Suso immigrated to Chicago in the 1970s, and over three decades he has collaborated with many famous American musicians, including jazzers Herbie Hancock, Jack DeJohnette, and Pharoah Sanders; techno wizard Bill Laswell; and classical artists Philip Glass and the Kronos Quartet. For information on Suso's current activities, visit him online at www.fmsuso.com.

Such transformations are commonplace in the long history of the griots, and they dramatize the fact that this is a living tradition. Initially, the griots took the ancient bardic tradition and transformed it into something much more comprehensive and essential to their society. Such adaptations have continued in more recent times, as the world has changed in so many ways. That Foday Musa Suso reinvented his role by taking advantage of new opportunities offered by the West should come as no major surprise. Historically even more significant was the transformation of the griot into the blues singer of the early twentieth century. Several scholars have noted that the early blues singer fulfilled many of the same roles as the griot: as storyteller, spokesperson, professional musician, or social commentator. The evidence for these connections is sometimes tenuous, but Michael Coolen (*Black Music Research Journal,* 1991) has noted some striking similarities between the blues and the *fodet,* an instrumental genre practiced by the Wolof griots of Senegal. In any event, Africans in America adapted the traditions of the griot to their new context as slaves, and African Americans adapted them once again after Lincoln abolished the institution of slavery. Much research remains to be done, but many scholars are vigorously taking up the challenge—at long last.

The Kora

Much like the bards of old, griots accompany their songs with a variety of different instruments. Often they will sing only with their own accompaniment, but instrumental ensembles are also common. As we have seen, the choice of instruments varies according to region and family traditions. The most common instruments played by Mandinka griots of the Gambia are the *balo,* a seventeen- to twenty-one-keyed xylophone with gourd resonators; the *konting,* a five-stringed, oval-shaped lute; and the *kora,* a large, twenty-one-stringed bridge-harp. Neighboring regions may prefer the balo or the konting, but the kora is the instrument most often used by Gambian griots. It is no surprise, then, to find Foday Musa Suso accompanying himself on the kora in our *Listen* recording.

In appearance, the kora resembles a very large lute. Half of a large kettle gourd (calabash), some 16–20 inches in diameter, is used as the instrument's resonating chamber. The hollow side of the gourd is covered tautly with cowhide, and a tall bridge rests on this surface. A wooden pole just over four feet long pokes through the gourd, serving both as the instrument's neck and as the tailpiece on which the instrument rests. This pole and the bridge are most often made from African rosewood. Once made from animal hide, the twenty-one strings are now made of nylon fishing line. On the upper end, these are attached to the neck, and at the bottom, they are knotted to an anchor secured to the tailpiece. Unusually, these strings pass over notches on both *sides* of the bridge, rather than the top—half on the right side and half on the left.

In performance, the kora is more like a harp than a lute. The purpose of the neck is to support the strings. There is no fingerboard, and the player never "fingers" different notes or chords as one would with a guitar or lute. Instead, the strings are simply plucked in harplike fashion. For Western listeners used to seeing a bassist or cellist positioned behind the instrument, it comes as a surprise to see the griot seated in *front* of the kora, facing the strings, bridge, and "soundboard." The tailpiece rests securely on the ground, supporting the instrument's weight and providing the best possible resonance. With the smaller, outside fingers, the player grabs onto two handholds—rosewood sticks inserted into the gourd on each side of the bridge. The thumb and forefinger of each hand are then used to pluck the strings. The picture on page 112 in *Listen* should give you and your students a good idea of how this works. Better yet, use Roderic Knight's *Mande Music and Dance* DVD (see Video Recordings below); Part II includes several segments that allow students to watch Gambian kora players at work.

The tuning of the kora is a subject unto itself. Several tuning systems are in use, and preferences for one versus another vary from region to region, but the ones most frequently used share several common features. They all provide seven notes to the octave, as do most Western scales. Though these scales are not equal tempered, perfect intervals above the "tonic" pitch—fourths, fifths, and octaves, come very close to their Western equivalents. There is great variety in scale-steps 2, 3, 6, and 7, however. If you would like more detailed information on tunings, Eric Charry's excellent book *Mande Music* (University of Chicago Press, 2000) is a good place to start.

Laminba

This song represents one of the most prominent genres practiced by the griots of West Africa: the praise song. Titled "Laminba," this song was sung by Foday Musa Suso during a celebration at the home of Musa Koli. According to the liner notes from *Sounds of West Africa: The Kora and the Xylophone* (Lyrichord LYRCD 7308), this celebration "involved a continuous flow of food, money and music that lasted for nearly a week. A kora player could not leave the compound of any of these men without being laden down with gifts." Such songs might praise living patrons—the Lyrichord recording also includes a song praising Musa Koli himself—or they might praise great heroes of past generations (perhaps to encourage greater generosity in the here and now). Many of these praise songs are centuries old, and some are more recent—tailor-made for a specific patron. Sadly, there is no translation readily available for this song, so we cannot be certain of the precise context for "Laminba." One thing we can be sure of, patrons place great value on the role of the griot in celebrations such as the one described above.

In presenting this work to your students, begin by playing the music several times to introduce its features. Help them to listen for the sounds of the voice and kora, the ostinato pattern, the downward melodic motions described in the textbook, and the dissonances that become increasingly prominent near the end. To dig a bit more deeply, focus on the two specific aspects that contribute most to the overall shape of this song—the kora ostinato and the vocal melody.

The ostinato is frequently varied in this performance, but it retains the same basic shape throughout. The most commonly heard version is some six beats long: the kora's lowest string sounds on the first of four beats on "tonic" followed by two beats on "dominant." Encourage students to use the deep, resonant sound of that low string as an anchor point in following the ostinato as it repeats. Though occasionally omitted, it provides a useful point of orientation nonetheless. As students become familiar with this ostinato, point out two common features of almost every Gambian kora performance—*kumbengo* and *birimintingo*. Playing low notes with the two thumbs, the kora player lays down a basic ostinato, the *kumbengo*. The kora player uses specific techniques to vary this ostinato, but it remains recognizable in spite of these variations. In contrast, the two index fingers pick out high-pitched, virtuosic, rapidly descending scale patterns that have a very free, improvisational feel to them. These are called *birimintingo*. While these patterns can repeat, they do not occur one after another after another in the manner of a true ostinato; they are used infrequently and irregularly. You can hear examples of *birimintingo* at 0:00, 0:17, 0:32, 0:53, and 2:07. These instrumental episodes appear in the gaps between vocal phrases, and you can even hear Suso softly humming and singing along with the *birimintingo* starting at 0:57.

The vocal melody is also based on simple patterns that vary when repeated. In fact, two simple phrases serve as the basis for much of the melody, and we hear these clearly when the voice first enters at 0:22. The **a** phrase begins on scale step 3, jumps to scale step 5, and descends, mostly by step, to either scale step 1 or scale step 7. The **b** phrase begins on a higher pitch, usually scale step 7, and it also descends, mostly by step and most often to scale step 3. These phrases are the key to hearing the overall shape of the song, which can be diagrammed as follows:

intro	**a b**	gap	**a b**	gap	**a b**	a^2 a	a^2 a′ b′	a^3 a^3	coda
0:00	0:22	0:32	0:42	0:51	1:26	1:35	1:42	1:57	2:08

As the diagram suggests, this song starts out sounding like a typical strophic song, with two phrases per stanza and short instrumental interludes. About a minute into the song, however, we discover that the interludes have taken on a life of their own, and the string of variations on the **a** phrase that follows (1:26–2:08) signals an abrupt move away from simple strophic form. The repetitive nature of this extended vocal section is reminiscent of some of the sacred chant we heard in Chapter 5, especially the reciting tone formula in "Vere dignum" and the varied repetition of **a** and **b** phrases in "K′adnikini′ya′." These chant formulas provided a vehicle for expressing the sacred power of their texts simply and directly, and Suso seems to be doing something similar here. This repetition emphasizes and intensifies the words more than in any other part of the song. It is as if Suso is listing out the attributes of the patron in this section, and the extended interludes that frame it serve as emphatic punctuation marks—or perhaps a kind of halo.

Finally, take time to compare this work with "Dido's Lament." Both can trace their lineage back to the ancient Greek bardic tradition; both feature a solo voice with simple plucked-string accompaniment (plus bowed strings in Purcell); both spin out their melodies over a repeating instrumental ostinato, freely repeating simple motives; both differentiate clearly between the roles of melody and ostinato; both repeat their large structural units; both were intended as a public entertainment. Clearly they do not create the same mood, yet the similarities are compelling.

Pygmy Polyphony

Perhaps the oldest surviving group of native Africans, pygmy tribes inhabited the central African rainforests long before the ancient Egyptians recorded their presence there. Several millennia later, Stanley also reported encounters with the "Wambutti" people of the Ituri rainforest.[2] Today, approximately 168,000 pygmies reside in these extensive (but dwindling) forests. The lush rainforests they call home have seen political boundaries drawn and redrawn around them through the centuries. The regions they inhabit fall within portions of the modern-day Democratic Republic of Congo (Zaire), the Central African Republic, Gabon, Cameroon, and the Congo Republic. About 80,000 of them live in Zaire; 40,000 of these comprise the largest pygmy group—the Mbuti tribe of the Ituri rainforest.

Like other pygmy groups, the Mbuti are nomadic hunter-gatherers who rely on the forest for their every need. It is tempting to think of these "people of the forest" as the people who never left Eden. Their religious beliefs stem from the awe and respect they accord the forest and the spirit that guides life within it. The forest is their friend, and they cultivate a symbiotic relationship with it.

---

[2]Henry M. Stanley, *In Darkest Africa*. New York: Charles Scribner's Sons, 1890, 2: 100–09.

They take only what they need for their sustenance, and they never deliberately harm the forest in any way. Rich as the forest is, however, they must move their camps periodically to avoid overharvesting the fruits, berries, and game in a given area. Because of their nomadic existence, little value is placed on possessions—what good is something if you can't take it with you? What they have they share with everyone, especially the food they gather. This attitude of sharing and cooperation extends to their "political" organization as well. There are no chiefs. Individuals are valued for whatever expertise they possess, but everyone's contribution is needed, and a true egalitarian ethic dominates all interactions.

The Mbuti are not the only inhabitants of the Ituri region; other groups moved in more recently (though still many centuries ago), particularly Bantu peoples. The Bantu, with their hierarchical political and religious structures, settled primarily in villages. For a time, some of them attempted the Mbuti lifestyle but found themselves uncomfortable in the forest. For the Bantu, the forest was full of demons and evil spirits that needed warding off. They cleared the forest for their villages and plantations, creating clear lines of demarcation. The peaceable Mbuti have generally cultivated friendly relations with the Bantu villagers. In fact, the Mbuti will visit local villages periodically on trading expeditions. The Mbuti supply fresh meat and forest goods to the villagers even though the self-sufficient Mbuti need little from the villagers in return. Time in the village offers a brief respite from daily forest work and a chance to relax, make music on village instruments, and enjoy local alcoholic beverages. In spite of their rich musical culture, the Mbuti have few musical instruments of their own—they'd need to be carried during each move, after all. But their ingrained musicality allows them to quickly master Bantu instruments, and the Mbuti often surpass the skill of the village musicians. The Mbuti also come to the villages for certain rituals, including a male circumcision ritual that takes place near the time of puberty. For the Bantu, this ritual marks one's coming of age; uncircumcised males of any age are not accorded adult status by the Bantu. So the Mbuti make this concession to enhance their status with the villagers, even though they practice their own much more meaningful puberty rituals in the forest. This example summarizes many aspects of the relations between Mbuti and Bantu. To the forest dwellers, the constant rituals and divinations of the villagers seem unnecessary, but they tolerate them to maintain amicable relations. The villagers, on the other hand, suspicious (and ignorant) of anyone and anything from the forest, do their best to remake the Mbuti in their own image.

In the forest, however, the Mbuti are their own masters. Here they follow their own customs. Perhaps the richest and most distinctive Mbuti tradition is their music. Visitors to some camps have marveled at their seemingly constant music making; songs are often heard all day long—and well into the night. Songs accompany almost every activity of their lives, including elephant hunting, small-game hunting, honey gathering, male and female puberty rituals, and the sacred *molimo* observance (see Further Listening Examples below for teaching suggestions on an Mbuti *molimo* song).

A Hunting Song for Chorus

Start your presentation with some background material. Feel free to use any of the information presented immediately above. If you would like to know more about the Mbuti, consult the books of Colin Turnbull, such as *Wayward Servants: The Two Worlds of the African Pygmies* (Garden City, N.Y.: Natural

History Press, 1965). At the very least, use the notes below to help your students understand the significance and uniqueness of central African pygmy musical traditions.

Although the Bantu music of many villages in the Ituri basin reflects a broader African tradition found in other regions of the continent, the music of the central African pygmies comes out of a much different, and much older, tradition. The pygmy peoples may have adopted the Bantu language many centuries ago, but they did not adopt their music. One might expect an ancient tradition to be "simpler" than more recent ones, but the opposite proves true here. It is awe-inspiring to realize that this music—from what may be the oldest continuous musical tradition on the planet—remains more complex than many African styles that grew up around it.

What makes this music unique? It employs an elaborate vocal polyphony unlike anything else in African music. We heard ostinato patterns in the music of the Gambia, and we will hear rhythmic counterpoint from Yoruba drummers, but nowhere else do we hear such an elaborate layering of ostinatos or such a rich *melodic* counterpoint. In the Gambia we heard one ostinato at a time; Mbuti music is created from multiple ostinatos used simultaneously. Each voice sings his or her own melody, repeating it again and again. Some melodies are related to each other but start at different time intervals; others are the unique expression of individuals within the ensemble. Each melodic repetition begins and ends at a different point than the others, creating an effect reminiscent of the imitative texture and continuous motion found in Renaissance polyphony. These various repeating melodies—the *interlocking ostinatos* described in the textbook—thus interweave and overlap in surprising ways. In addition, some works employ techniques reminiscent of rounds, hocket, or call-and-response patterns. The result is a rich and beautiful polyphony unlike any other music.

Start with just a few preparatory comments. Call attention to the antiphonal (back-and-forth) singing between two solo voices that dominates the first minute or so. Gathered around the fire at the end of the day, these two young men take a "tag-team" approach in telling the story of the hunt earlier that day. This should prove easy to hear and follow once students can distinguish one solo voice from the other. Without giving away too much, alert them to the full-blown vocal polyphony that emerges around 1:30 or so. Now play the entire piece. Ask students to describe what they heard, especially toward the end. With such rich counterpoint, it is difficult to hear every voice after just one hearing. Students will have the same difficulty here as with Josquin's Renaissance polyphony—with so much going on and no single "lead" voice, it's hard to know what to listen for (see Listening Idea 7 below). Tell your students there is no one "right" voice to listen to; they should just sit back and enjoy the experience. Play from 1:30 to the end several times and ask your students to listen to a different part each time. If you wish, sing along with one or two different patterns with each playing. Once they become familiar with some of the melodic patterns and attuned to the rich texture, go back and play the entire excerpt, but this time ask them to listen with special care to what is going on behind the antiphonal solo voices. At first we hear only a few voices humming or singing softly, but gradually these voices grow in number and in strength, and from 1:30 to the end of the excerpt we can hear the vocal polyphony quite clearly. Suddenly the listening experience becomes much richer as students begin to hear individual voices emerging, adding their special sound to the mix. We become accustomed to following a single melody in most Western music, but this habit doesn't serve us well in this hunting song—the antiphonal melodies are probably the least interesting layers in this music.

Finally, to place this work in its context, provide your students with some information about the purpose of this music. Hunting songs serve a utilitarian function. As individuals fan out to hunt large game such as the elephant, they sing their own ostinato pattern. The patterns allow the hunters to keep track of each other's location as they move in on their prey. In fact, they may not even regard this as singing, in spite of the rich polyphony they create. The hunting song in the recorded set actually serves as an epilogue to the day's hunt. The hunters gather around the fire to tell the story of the hunt. On this particular occasion, two young men tell the story of the hunt and of the bravery of the hunters who participated. The polyphony that gradually emerges actually recalls the sounds and the atmosphere of the hunt itself, much like an automatic replay from a televised sports event or during the evening news.

What a rich musical experience—and how rich the culture that produced it! The Mbuti spirit of cooperation and egalitarianism has made a deep impression on researchers who have entered its sphere. (Louis Sarno, a New Jersey native, was so enchanted that he moved to Central Africa to live permanently with the Bayaka tribe.) Some of these scholars suggest that the vocal polyphony of these tribes mirrors their social interactions. Each singer's role is valued and necessary, and each singer makes a unique contribution—marvelous affirmation of both the individual and the community. Modern American suburbanites focus all too readily on the seemingly "primitive" living conditions of these tribes, an outlook echoed by anthropologists who placed pygmy groups at a "Stone Age" level of development. Nonetheless, modern "civilization," with its strife and world wars, has much to learn from this incredibly stable society—one that has managed to provide for the common welfare since before the dawn of recorded history.

Summary Thoughts

In spite of their differences, the essential feature that links these examples with music throughout the African continent is the ostinato. Uses of ostinato can differ strikingly: the ostinato in Purcell's lament creates a very different impression than the looser one of the passacaglia in Frescobaldi's suite. Still, in their search to fill an ever-larger canvas without sacrificing coherence, Baroque composers discovered what musicians in other parts of the world had long known—ostinato offers a powerful means for setting a mood and achieving coherence, yet it allows for meaningful play, both against its basic structure and alongside it. In these examples, ostinato reveals itself as a universal manifestation of the principle of variation described in Unit I.

Additional Teaching Suggestions

ʔ Lecture-Demonstration Ideas

1. Review Unit II by comparing medieval, Renaissance, and early Baroque motets. Machaut's "Quant en moi," Josquin's "Mille regrets" or the "Qui tollis" from his *Pange lingua* Mass, and Gabrieli's "O magnum mysterium" serve well. Draw on lists of style characteristics from Lecture Suggestions in Chapters 5, 6, and 7.

2. Read excerpts from the debate between Monteverdi and Artusi as found in *Strunk's Source Readings in Music History,* Vol. 4 (New York: Norton, 1997,

pp. 18–36). Two radically different styles coexisted in the transition between Renaissance and Baroque. Artusi labeled the old style good music and the new bad music; Monteverdi described them as two valid yet different styles that operate according to different principles. This unusual situation has parallels in the development of twentieth-century music (see Listening Idea 3). Nicolas Slonimsky's *Lexicon of Musical Invective*, 2nd ed. (Seattle: University of Washington Press, 1965) provides other examples of inexplicably harsh judgments made throughout music history. If you have time, play a recording of the madrigal Artusi condemns, Monteverdi's "Cruda Amarilli" (see Burkholder in the Sound Recordings below). Ask the students if they can hear what Artusi found so offensive.

3. Invite a singer to class who specializes in Baroque performance. Ask your guest to demonstrate Baroque ornaments and to sing seventeenth-century operatic excerpts—by Monteverdi and Purcell if possible. (Your guest may require an accompanist or two to play continuo.) Keep the session informal and involve students in the demonstration and discussion as much as possible. Come prepared with questions in case student participation lags. What problems do performers encounter in early Baroque music? How is this music different from other music you sing? What do you like best about it?

4. Invite a violinist to class who specializes in Baroque performance. If he or she has a Baroque violin, so much the better. Ask your guest to demonstrate Baroque ornaments and to play seventeenth-century works for violin—Corelli sonatas, for instance. Ask your guest to discuss the process of adding ornaments and the role of continuo. Keep the session informal and involve students in the demonstration and discussion as much as possible. Come prepared with questions in case student participation lags. Why is there so much improvisation in Baroque music? What problems do performers encounter in early Baroque music? What are the differences between Baroque and modern violins? How is this music different from other music you play? What do you like best about it?

5. Invite an African musician to class. If you can find someone who knows Gambian or pygmy traditions, great, but anyone who can help your students understand the use of ostinato will work well. If he or she can bring along African instruments, so much the better. Ask your guest to demonstrate different ways of using ostinato patterns. Depending on the guest, you may be able to draw out information about various African styles, instruments, customs, and rituals, and even reflections on the differences between written and oral traditions. As usual, involve students in the demonstration and discussion as much as possible, and come prepared with questions in case student participation lags.

6. Take your class on a trip up the Ituri River, a tributary of the mighty Congo River. Find and display slides, pictures, or digital images of the (endangered) rainforest and its (equally endangered) inhabitants. The library and the departments of anthropology, foreign languages, geography, and art at your school might prove good sources. Photographs can be found in Colin Turnbull's *Wayward Servants*[3] or in the booklet that accompanies the *Echoes of the*

[3]Colin Turnbull, *Wayward Servants: The Two Worlds of the African Pygmies.* Garden City, N.Y.: Natural History Press, 1965.

Forest CD (see Sound Recordings below). For an interesting twist, accompany your picture show with selected quotes from Turnbull's book—read aloud—as well as more extended recordings of this music (see Sound Recordings below).

7. If your department has a computer lab equipped with either *GarageBand* (Macintosh) or *Acid* (Windows), let your students experiment for themselves with the effect of layering ostinatos one on top of the other. These loop (ostinato)-based programs make it super-easy (and a lot of fun) to create short compositions without much training. All you need is a ten-minute tutorial and they'll be off and running. Toward the end of the period, give students time to share their compositions and make comparisons with ostinato-based works by Purcell, Frescobaldi, Foday Musa Suso, and the Mbuti tribe.

❦ Class Discussion Ideas

1. *What do you think of when you think of opera*? It helps when students can express their fears and misgivings about opera. A host of different images and prejudices will emerge. Follow up discussion with questions: *Why was opera so much more popular in the seventeenth century than it is today? Why does opera remain so popular in Italy but not in the United States?* (Many Italians are hard put if asked to choose between soccer and opera!)

2. *Why did male singers sing in a female range in Baroque operas?* Monteverdi's Poppea begs the question, though students who have seen the recent movie *Farinelli* may ask this question without prompting. In *The Development of Western Music*, 3rd ed. (McGraw-Hill, 1998, p. 243), K Marie Stolba provides a discussion of the role and importance of castrati in the Baroque period; this discussion touches on the role of female singers as well. Read portions to your class as a means of generating discussion. You can also use excerpts on the role of female singers and composers in the Baroque from *Women in Music: An Anthology of Source Readings from the Middle Ages to the Present*, edited by Carol Neuls-Bates (New York: Harper & Row, 1982). If you have time, show clips with singing from *Farinelli*, which created a hypothetical castrato voice on a computer by morphing together the sounds of countertenor and soprano voices.

3. Ask your students to search through their recording collections for songs that feature only solo voice with guitar accompaniment (or possibly piano, if you want to make it a bit easier). This usually means contemporary popular music, which means you can make important connections with the music they know and love. Have them bring their recordings to class and play as many as time permits. After each recording, ask students to compare the song with others from *Listen*—especially the Gambian minstrel song but also Bernart's troubadour song and the opera arias from this chapter. Make them go beyond quick value judgments; insist that they get at the musical features and structures that affect their responses to the music. This exercise can help students understand the communicative power that underlies the ancient and ongoing tradition of the solo song.

4. Share excerpts from Albert B. Lord's *The Singer of Tales* (Cambridge, Mass.: Harvard University Press, 1964) with your class. This classic work re-

veals the ancient bardic tradition as it survived into twentieth-century Muslim Yugoslavia. Lord examines the methods used to learn and practice the art of singing epic poems to simple instrumental accompaniment. His resulting insights into oral tradition are applicable to the study of many other oral traditions. You can use his ideas to generate an interesting, thought-provoking class discussion.

5. *Why does the rainforest matter*? Over the past twenty years, the news media have often reported on events, discoveries, and conferences related to this still-controversial issue. Students will have no trouble coming up with examples: its impact on the ecosystem, rare plants that may hold cures for deadly diseases, and so on. In fact, some of your students will likely know more about it than you do. Make sure to point out the significance of the rainforest to the pygmy tribes of central Africa. When one partner in a symbiotic relationship dies, the other suffers. Studies already confirm the disastrous psychological impact of uprooting the trees from these peoples' forests. The Belgian Jean-Pierre Hallet has long fought to save the rainforests of central Africa. Equally significant are his efforts to save displaced tribes by finding viable, hardy crops they can grow on former forest lands. His tireless work stabilized the once-dwindling population of the Efé tribe, earning him a Presidential End Hunger award in 1987. The potential loss of these tribes, their way of life, and their music heightens the poignance of this question about rainforests.

♩ Listening Ideas

1. Compare a Venetian motet with a High Renaissance selection. Gabrieli's "O magnum mysterium" and the "Qui tollis" from Palestrina's *Pope Marcellus* Mass serve well. Play both works and ask students to describe the difference in style between these sacred compositions. Palestrina inspires faith and devotion; Gabrieli, awe and celebration. Both use new musical ideas for each new phrase of text, and declamation is clear in each; but Gabrieli's use of sonority is more extravagant, and his use of imitation between choirs goes beyond Palestrina's use of imitation between voices.

2. Explore the differences between Renaissance word painting and Baroque text expression. Play Weelkes's "As Vesta Was from Latmos Hill Descending" and "Dido's Lament" from Purcell's *Dido and Aeneas*. Ask students to follow the words and describe the techniques each composer uses to express the text. Weelkes captures the images suggested by the words; Purcell expresses the emotions that underlie the words. Weelkes offers a wonderful entertainment, but Purcell engages modern listeners at a gut level in a way that Weelkes's madrigal cannot.

3. Like Beethoven, Monteverdi was a giant whose music straddled two eras— he had one foot planted securely in the Renaissance, the other squarely in the Baroque. Listen to three works—early, middle, and late—by Monteverdi. Choose an early madrigal ("Cruda Amarilli" if you use Lecture-Demonstration Idea 2 above), a continuo madrigal from Books VIII through X ("Lamento della Ninfa" from Further Listening Examples below), and the scene from *The Coronation of Poppea* used in the textbook. These works demonstrate the move from madrigal to opera, the shift from vocal ensemble to solo voice with continuo, and increasing flexibility and variety in response to the text.

4. Compare Baroque instrumental polyphony with Renaissance vocal polyphony. Play the "Qui tollis" from Josquin's *Pange lingua* Mass and the canzona from Frescobaldi's suite. The imitative procedures that had supported and organized large motets and Masses in the Renaissance were transposed to the Baroque sacred instrumental medium just when Baroque vocal music shifted to homophonic textures. The main difference is that where the Renaissance composer used a new melody for each new phrase of text, the Baroque composer used a single melodic idea more systematically, as if to catalogue all the ways a melody might be combined with itself through imitation. This exercise also serves to highlight differences between Renaissance and Baroque styles.

5. Compare Foday Musa Suso's minstrel song with an example of authentic Delta blues. The West African *griot* tradition is frequently cited as a significant influence on early blues. Play some recordings and ask students if they hear any similarities. Comparisons will be more meaningful if you avoid recordings of electrified urban blues. What you really want are recordings by early bluesmen from the 1930s that feature only a solo singer and an acoustic guitar. Recordings by Charley Patton, Blind Lemon Jefferson, or Robert Johnson are highly recommended. See Sound Recordings below for suggestions.

6. This manual and the *Listen* textbook both refer to Foday Musa Suso's many collaborations with Western musicians since his move to Chicago in the 1970s. Play examples of Suso's work with Herbie Hancock, Pharoah Sanders, Jack DeJohnette, Bill Laswell, Philip Glass, or the Kronos Quartet. Ask students to determine which features come from Western styles and which come from Gambian griot songs. See Sound Recordings below for suggestions.

7. Give your class a "big bite" of Mbuti polyphony to supplement the "nibble" provided in the recorded set. Longer excerpts allow students to experience more fully the spiritual qualities of this music, and they point to the nearly constant presence of music in the daily lives of these people. For some reason, recordings of elephant hunt songs often run longer than the others, but many other examples can also serve you well. Especially atmospheric is Colin Turnbull's recording of the "Men's Elephant-Hunting Song" on *Echoes of the Forest*; thunder crashes in the "background" convey the full reality of the rainforest. See Sound Recordings below for recommended CDs.

8. Compare pygmy polyphony with an example of European sacred polyphony—the Gloria from Josquin's *Pange lingua* Mass. The gentle rocking patterns and more continuous feel of Josquin's Gloria work better than the start-and-stop feel of his Kyrie's emphatic cadences. John Cage often quoted a favorite phrase from a Renaissance treatise, saying that the purpose of music is to quiet the soul and render it susceptible to divine influence. Both of these examples accomplish that purpose, and they do so by similar means. Both use overlapping melodies and subtle repetition or imitation to create a rich, continuous, polyphonic texture. Just as the divine presence cannot be fully grasped through human perception and reason, these complex musics defy our ability to hear them all at once.

9. Play popular music influenced by pygmy polyphony to help your students make closer connections with this music. Over the past twenty years, pop musicians have turned increasingly to world music as a source of inspiration. As mentioned in *Listen*, Zap Mama and Madonna have borrowed from central African pygmy music, but so have many others. To sample some tracks by Zap Mama, Madonna, Herbie Hancock, and the rap group Roots, see Sound Recordings below.

ʻʼ Further Listening Examples

GABRIELI "In ecclesiis"

Another Venetian motet on an even grander scale than "O magnum mysterium," this work calls for three choirs of voices and instruments with continuo. The form uses new music for each new phrase of text with a magnificent recurring alleluia. See Sound Recordings below for recommended performances, and Appendix II for complete text and translation.

MONTEVERDI "Lamento della Ninfa"

This continuo madrigal offers a fascinating example of a dramatic scene halfway between Renaissance madrigal and Baroque opera. The first section features three male voices with continuo accompaniment; they serve in the second section as a chorus that sets the scene and sings backup to the soprano's lament. Like Purcell's aria "When I am laid in earth," this lament (beginning where the soprano sings "Amor") is sung over a ground bass, though Monteverdi adds frequent sympathetic interjections from the male trio (like Gladys Knight and the Pips—right down to the "soul"). The final section returns to the three male voices, at "Si tra sdegnosi pianti." This beautiful work reflects Monteverdi's careful attention to the text, with extraordinarily wrenching dissonances (even today) where appropriate. For performances of this work, see Sound Recordings below. Complete text and translation can be found in Appendix II.

MONTEVERDI *L'Orfeo* (selection from Act IV)

This excerpt is drawn from the first great opera—one of the earliest ever written and one of many based on the Orpheus myth. This scene, with its typical mixture of chorus, aria, and recitative, shows Orpheus leading Eurydice out of the underworld. Unfortunately, he looks back, and Eurydice dies a second time. The best of recitative style can be found here. For CD and video performances of this work, see Multimedia Resources below. See Appendix II for text and translation.

CORELLI Trio Sonata in F Major, Op. 3, No. 1

Because the mid-Baroque church sonata grew out of the early Baroque canzona, this example provides a kind of "Where are they now?" follow-up to the canzona that began the Frescobaldi suite in the textbook. The short, barely distinguished sections that defined the canzona have now grown into four separate movements that create strong contrasts, and the influence of various dance rhythms makes these extremely attractive, listenable works. The notes below provide teaching suggestions for this work; recordings can be found either in the recorded set for *Listen: Brief Fourth Edition* or in Sound Recordings below.

   The notes on the Frescobaldi suite (see Lecture Suggestions above) describe the rise of instrumental music. Further signs of this trend can be found in the development of standard instrumental ensembles, most notably the orchestra, as well as in the development of new genres for these ensembles, including the dance suite, the trio sonata, and the concerto. This work by Corelli provides an excellent example of the trio sonata. Baroque trio sonatas came in two flavors, the *sonata da camera* (chamber sonata) and the *sonata da chiesa* (church sonata). The chamber sonata grew out of the traditions of the dance suite.

Essentially a collection of dances for two equal instruments (usually violins) and continuo, a typical chamber sonata might contain a prelude, an allemande, a sarabande, and a gigue. The church sonata, on the other hand, evolved from the canzona. The canzona we saw in the Frescobaldi suite was quite typical of the genre, with several contrasting imitative sections. As these individual sections grew longer and more distinct, they evolved into the contrasting movements of the *sonata da chiesa*. The trio sonata in turn exerted enormous influence on the concerto, which was to become the most significant orchestral genre of the late Baroque period.

Corelli's trio sonata is a church sonata that reflects the trends described above. It presents a combination of short movements of contrasting character. The last three movements show the influence of dance, while the second and fourth movements demonstrate idiomatic, virtuoso writing for violins as well as fugal writing. Note that the contrasts between the movements of this work are more striking than those in the Frescobaldi suite. Students can hear even more clearly the single emotion or mood of each movement.

Examine the movements one by one. The first movement provides the slow processional that often begins a church sonata. Ask students to listen for virtuoso elements and imitative polyphony in the second and fourth movements and for dancelike characteristics in the last three movements. For the third movement, point out the lilting triple meter and the competitive alternation between soloists. For the fourth movement, identify the quick compound meter and imitative entrances so typical of the gigue (jig) that concludes many Baroque suites and sonatas. If you have time, compare this movement with "Kemp's Jig" in the previous chapter. Corelli's jig demonstrates more sophistication by far than its Renaissance cousin and points to the increasing stylization of dance music in the Baroque era.

CORELLI Trio Sonata in E Minor, Op. 2, No. 4, I (Preludio: Adagio), II (Allemanda: Presto), III (Grave—Adagio), IV (Giga: Allegro)

For a contrast with the previous example and a slightly later dance suite for comparison with the Frescobaldi suite, present this complete chamber sonata. Chamber sonatas developed along quite different lines, resembling dance suites more than anything else. This trio sonata can serve as another example of the process of creating a large work by linking several dances together. You can use it to demonstrate contrasts between movements as well as between Baroque dance types. For a recording, see Sound Recordings below.

SUDAN Doogus Idris, A Minstrel's Song

Try this for another fascinating example of ostinato technique or if you would like to explore music from the Sudan. Background material and teaching suggestions follow; for recordings, use the *Listen: Brief Fifth Edition*.

Music of Sudan

Great diversity can be found in the musical styles of Sudan, not only because of its size but also because of its history, which was shaped by its geography. The Sahara Desert blankets most of the nation; only the Nile River and the southern sub-Saharan region provide relief from desert conditions. Not surprisingly, 60 percent of Sudan's twenty-six million residents live along the Nile, and another 30 percent populate the southern region. Traveling upstream (southward) on the Nile, you cross into Sudan at the Egyptian border and follow the river around two enormous bends before arriving at the city of Khartoum. At that point the river splits into its two main tributaries: the White Nile, which you could follow southward to the Ugandan border, and the Blue Nile, which you could follow in a southeasterly direction to the regions of the Ingassana and Berta tribes and finally to the Ethiopian border.

Except for easily defensible hill country in the south and southeast, most of the Sudan came under Islamic influence in the century after Muhammad. As a result, Arabic became (and remains) the *lingua franca*, but the retention of a large number of native languages has guaranteed the survival of indigenous, pre-Islamic customs among many of the peoples of Sudan. Nowhere is this more evident than in Sudanese music (once again we see a close link between word and music); even in regions where Islam is strongest, one can find music associated with pre-Islamic traditions and rituals. (Given Islam's theological ambivalence toward music of any kind, this retention is remarkable.) The diversity of Sudanese musics can be seen in the Ingassana and Berta tribes of the Blue Nile region, who, as close as they are geographically, reflect quite different traditions. Living close to the river, the Berta quickly came under the Islamic sphere of influence; located in the hill country farther away from the river, the Ingassana repelled Islamic (and other) invaders and have resisted outside influences in their music as well.

In spite of Sudan's great cultural diversity, some ancient traditions remain nearly universal. A prominent example is the lyre—a chordophone much like a small harp, which can be found throughout the country. The names given to such lyres, as well as the details of their construction, vary from region to region, but in each case the lyre is used to accompany the traditional secular songs of the region. As one might surmise, the tradition of the lyre derives from a bardic tradition going back at least as far as the ancient Greeks. Once the tradition came to Egypt, if it traveled up the river at all, it would have to reach the peoples of the White Nile and Blue Nile. As it happened, these Sudanese song traditions were well established before the advent of Islam.

Other traditions are particular to certain regions of Sudan. In the Blue Nile district, as in the rest of the country, each tribe has its own five-stringed lyre, again associated with secular song traditions. But this region is unique in the prevalence of unusual instrumental ensembles used to accompany rituals. These ensembles consist of like aerophones (wind instruments), each of which can play only a single pitch. In the Ingassana tribe it is an ensemble of five one-note bamboo flutes, called *bal*, a gourd trumpet, and a gourd rattle; in the Berta tribe it is the famed *waza* ensemble, consisting of ten to twelve gourd trumpets.

The Ingassana Tribes

Because of its size, Sudan encompasses the line of demarcation between Islamic Africa and "black" Africa. Traveling up the Blue Nile from Khartoum, the Ingassana peoples are the first non-Islamic "black" Africans one meets. Given their position on that line, they have absorbed influences from both the north and the south over the centuries. At the same time, their location in the Tabi Hills has made it possible to defend themselves from unwanted intrusion, Islamic or otherwise. The hills, fifty to seventy-five kilometers southwest of Ed Damazin, feed a tributary of the Blue Nile. The Ingassana refer to themselves as "people of the mountain" and to their language as "speech of the mountain," yet the word *Ingassana* (thankless ones) was first applied by the Arabs, supposedly when the people of the mountain refused to capitulate to Islam.

The Ingassana are mostly farmers living in small, close-knit villages. Given the importance of agriculture and family ties, the most significant rituals are marriages and harvest festivals. Just as we have seen in other cultures, music is an integral part of these rituals, especially that of the *bal* ensemble described above. *Bal* ceremonies are essentially fertility rites thought to bring blessings to both families and crops. They persist from spring's first rains until the final harvest, but they are forbidden by custom once the growing season is over.

The tradition of secular song with lyre accompaniment is as rich in the Tabi Hills as anywhere in Sudan. The lyre used by the Ingassana is called a *jangar* (or *shangar*). Two upright bars extend from a resonating sound box and are fastened to a crossbar at the top; five strings are stretched between the crossbar and the bottom of the sound box. Other regions have adopted modern steel strings for their lyres, but the Ingassana still use traditional gut strings, which give the instrument a softer, warmer sound. The use of a plectrum, following the northern style, helps give the sound greater definition. The *jangar* strings are tuned to five different pitches that make up a pentatonic scale, though not the pentatonic scale you can play on an equal-tempered piano. Whereas some of the intervals are, to Western ears, recognizable whole steps and minor thirds, others are very large whole steps (c. 240 cents).[4] If you listen carefully (with equal-tempered ears) to the interval between the bottom two notes of the *jangar*, it sounds like an out-of-tune whole step, the lowest note sounding flat. Be careful not to make the same mistake as did Spanish chroniclers of the Aztecs, alluded to in the previous chapter—the fact that our ears are trained one way doesn't make other possibilities wrong. In fact, the Ingassana tuning is quite precise, and to render its intervals in equal temperament would violate the intended sound.

A Minstrel's Song

Although the tradition of song with lyre is ancient, it is a living tradition as well. The singer of the Sudanese song on the *Listen,* Brief Fifth Edition, recordings, Doogus Idris, is also the composer, and one of the most famous singers in the Bau region of the Tabi Hills. In listening to his song, one quickly hears pronounced differences in the handling of the *jangar* and the vocal melody. Whereas the *jangar* is tuned to a pentatonic scale, the singer does not restrict himself to only five notes; and whereas the notes of the *jangar* ostinato span a fifth, the vocal range is much wider, reaching to a tenth. The *jangar* repeats an ostinato pattern throughout the song, with only slight variation. The voice, on the other hand, is much freer, its phrases constructed from simple motives that are varied and embellished throughout each stanza. The stability of the ostinato provides a nice foundation against which the melody can play. Listening more carefully, one realizes that voice and *jangar* share some features as well. Both fit easily and playfully into the same metric framework, and both share a soft-edged tone color. The primary melodic motion is downward, both in each phrase and in each stanza as a whole, from the highest note on the name "Kana" to the final cadence. This same downward motion is echoed in the *jangar* ostinato.

In presenting this work to your students, begin by playing the music several times to introduce its features. Help them listen for the sounds of the voice and *jangar*, the ostinato pattern, the downward motion, and the repeated stanza

---

[4]An equal-tempered half step equals 100 cents. Thus, a whole step equals 200 cents and the minor third, 300.

structure. Once they get a handle on the structure, point out the ways in which the melody plays with and against the ostinato pattern. Finally, as with Foday Musa Suso's "Laminba," take time to compare this work with "Dido's Lament."

DEMOCRATIC REPUBLIC OF CONGO (ZAIRE) Pygmy Polyphony

Try this for another example of music from the Ituri rainforest. This *molimo* song takes us into the spiritual life of the Mbuti tribe. Background material and teaching suggestions follow below; for recordings, use either the *Listen: Brief Fourth Edition* set or see *Mbuti Pygmies of the Ituri Rainforest* in Sound Recordings below.

A Molimo Song

In covering the hunting song from the current edition of *Listen*, you have already provided your students with some background material from the Lecture Suggestions above. In addition to the interlocking ostinatos that typify pygmy polyphony, the hunting song employed an antiphonal exchange between two solo singers; other songs may weave other devices into the prevailing polyphonic web, including rounds, hocket, or call-and-response patterns. The latter bears mention before you play the music for your students. Although vocal polyphony is unique to the central African pygmies, call-and-response patterns constitute a universal feature of African music. Scholars often cite call and response as one of the African retentions that figures prominently in black American music. The concept is simple enough; a soloist sings a phrase (the call) and other singers answer back (the response). The response tends to be a continuously repeated ostinato, while the more elaborate lead singer's part offers greater variety in both text and music. Many students can identify situations in which they participated in call and response, whether they were singing hymns and gospel songs at church or joining an audience-participation song at a folk or rock concert. Some may remember the song "Amen" from Christian worship services, campfire sing-alongs, or the recent movie with Whitney Houston, *The Preacher's Wife*. The "Amen" refrain, sung over and over again, becomes the response to the lead singer's phrases, inserted between each "Amen."

The *molimo* song is short enough that you can afford to play it several times, a necessity given the music's rich complexity. Start with a few preparatory comments. Call attention to the call-and-response pattern that dominates the first minute. Typical of many African traditions, this should prove easy to hear and follow. More important, warn them to listen with special care after the call-and-response pattern finishes. It is in the final thirty seconds that they can hear the vocal polyphony most clearly. Then play the entire piece. After their experience with the hunting song, students will immediately recognize many of the same features. The primary difference rests in the use of the solo voice in a call-and-response pattern here rather than the antiphonal singing in the hunting song.

Finally, place this work in its context; provide your students with some information about the purpose of this music. *Molimo* songs come out of the Mbuti's sacred *molimo* observance. I use the term *observance* in preference to *ritual;* the notion of a fixed ritual hardly fits with the Mbuti's nonhierarchical approach to life, and their religious observances possess a freshness and spontaneity often missing in more liturgical traditions. The *molimo* observance, a kind of spiritual "911" call, is used when troubles come. Perhaps the Mbuti experience bad luck in hunting, or a respected tribe member dies, or a bout of illness sweeps through the camp. Whatever the problem, the Mbuti never blame it on evil spirits. Instead, they assume the great forest spirit is asleep—after all, if the spirit were awake, their problems would be fixed. What is needed? They must wake up the forest spirit, and the *molimo* observance serves precisely that purpose. Depending on the nature and severity of the trouble, the Mbuti employ different types of observance, such as greater and lesser *molimo*, and the greater one requires at least a month to bring to completion.

The term *molimo* can refer to the observance itself, to the trumpet that is sometimes used, or to the men's association that participates in it. This sacred observance must be performed by the men alone; women should not even hear the songs that accompany the observance. So at night the men wait around a fire until everyone else has gone to sleep. Their music begins slowly, seemingly without enthusiasm, but after their preliminary songs have lulled to sleep any female night owls, they begin their singing and dancing in earnest. The *molimo* trumpet serves several purposes. It can be used to scare away women and children prior to the observance; during the *molimo* it can also be carried away from the camp by one of the singers as a means of broadcasting the songs further into the forest, thus increasing their chances of wakening the forest spirit. The *molimo* generally lasts until daybreak, not just for one night but for every night for at least several days—and for several months in extreme cases.

When you set this music alongside the "sophisticated" European music of this chapter, many comparisons come to mind. Outside of the use of ostinato patterns, many have more to do with social function than with musical features. Gabrieli creates a sense of awe with the very grandeur of his music. Pygmy songs can also inspire awe, but for very different reasons. Such a short *molimo* recording hardly conveys the full impact of this music; in context, the sounds of Mbuti polyphony washing over you can trigger a truly spiritual experience (see Listening Idea 7 above). The forest provides for and protects the Mbuti people. The superstitions of their neighbors seem ridiculous to them, and they live with far less fear than the inhabitants of "civilized" Western nations. Ironically, what the Mbuti fear most are the Western nations (and their African collaborators) who are driving them from "Eden" one tree at a time.

Multimedia Resources

ʔ Further Listening Charts and Texts

See Appendix II for texts and translations if you use these works from Further Listening Examples above:

Gabrieli, "In ecclesiis"

Monteverdi, "Lamento della Ninfa"

Monteverdi, *L'Orfeo* (selection from Act IV)

ʔ Sound Recordings

Burkholder, *History of Western Music,* 7th ed. New York: W. W. Norton, 2006. The CDs that accompany this standard music history textbook contain recordings of works suggested in Lecture-Demonstration Idea 2 and Listening Idea 3 above, especially Monteverdi's "Cruda Amarilli."

Corelli, *Sonatas for Strings*, Vol. 1. Purcell Quartet. Chandos CHAN 0516 (CD). Splendid period performances of Corelli's trio sonatas. Try this recording if you use suggestions from Further Listening Examples above for Corelli's Sonata in E minor, Op. 2, No. 4.

Corelli, *Sonatas for Strings*, Vol. 3. Purcell Quartet. Chandos CHAN 0526 (CD). More splendid period performances of Corelli's trio sonatas. Try this recording if you use suggestions from Further Listening Examples above for Corelli's Sonata in F major, Op. 3.

Echoes of the Forest: Music of the Central African Pygmies. Ellipsis Arts 4020 (CD). Sampler of music by the Mbuti, Efé, and Bayaka tribes recorded by Colin Turnbull, Jean-Pierre Hallet, and Louis Sarno, respectively. Contains examples of hunting songs, puberty songs, instrumental music, and so on. Accompanied by an excellent sixty-four-page booklet. Try this recording if you use Lecture-Demonstration Idea 6 or Listening Ideas 7 and 8 above.

Folk Music of Gambia. Smithsonian Folkways F-4521 (2-CD set). Sampling of various traditional instruments and styles from the Gambia. This makes a useful supplement to your presentation on the Gambian minstrel song.

Frescobaldi, *Toccate, Partite, Capricci, and Other Works for Harpsichord*. Louis Bagger. Titanic Ti–259 (CD). Vivid performances of selected keyboard works by this early Baroque master. Try this recording if you use Lecture Suggestions above for the complete canzona on track 14 (*Listen* uses an excerpt) or for other Frescobaldi examples.

Gabrieli, *Music for San Rocco*. Gabrieli Consort and Players. Deutsche Grammophon Archiv 449 180-2 (CD). Splendid, ideally balanced period performances of Gabrieli's magnificent polychoral motets, led by Paul McCreesh. Use this recording if you try suggestions for Gabrieli's "In ecclesiis" from Further Listening Examples above.

Glass, Philip, and Foday Musa Suso. *Music from the Screens*. Point/Philips 432-966-2 (CD). American minimalist and Gambian griot collaborated to create incidental music for a 1989 Guthrie Theatre revival of Jean Genet's last stage work. This collaboration mirrored the African-European tensions of a play set in 1960s Algeria. Try this recording if you try Listening Idea 6 above.

Hancock, Herbie. *Head Hunters*. Columbia Legacy 65123 (CD). Hancock's funky remake of the tune "Watermelon Man" for this 1974 album is often cited as an example of the influence of pygmy music on American popular music. That song replicates the sound of the *hundewhu* (or *hindewhu*), a three-holed bamboo flute used by the Baka and (Ba)Aka tribes. It's not exactly pygmy polyphony, but this classic album clearly demonstrates African influences on American popular (jazz fusion) music. Try this recording if you use Listening Idea 9 above.

Hancock, Herbie. *Sound System*. Columbia Legacy 65961 (CD). Hancock's sequel to *Future Shock* (the album that brought us "Rockit") continues to lay down a techno groove thanks to coproducer Bill Laswell. It also features Foday Musa Suso as composer and/or performer on four of its seven tracks. Try this recording if you use Listening Idea 6 above.

Jali Kunda: Griots of West Africa and Beyond. Ellipsis Arts CD3511 (CD). Foday Musa Suso supervised this fascinating recording of several West African griots doing traditional material alongside Suso's own collaborations with artists such as Philip Glass, Pharoah Sanders, and the Mandingo Griot Society—Suso's

Chicago-based fusion band. The edition with the fat booklet offers valuable background information and lots of glossy color photos. Try this recording if you use Listening Idea 6 above.

Jefferson, Blind Lemon. *Blind Lemon Jefferson: The Complete 94 Classic Sides Remastered.* JSP 7706 (4-CD set). Complete recordings of this early blues master from the late 1920s. JSP does a superb remastering job, and this four-disc set costs less than most two-CD sets. Try this recording if you use Listening Idea 5 above.

Johnson, Robert. *Robert Johnson: The Complete Recordings.* Columbia/Legacy C2K 64916 (CD). Complete recordings of perhaps the most famous early Delta blues master. Johnson represents even older traditions, those of the self-accompanied troubadour and the West African griot. Use this recording if you try Listening Idea 5 above.

Madonna, *Bedtime Stories.* Warner Brothers 9 45767-2 (CD). The tune "Sanctuary" is often cited as an example of the influence of pygmy music on American popular music. The song's accompaniment is perhaps somewhat polyphonic, but the pygmy influence is actually secondhand. Madonna uses a sample from "Watermelon Man," a tune from Herbie Hancock's *Head Hunters* (see above), that replicates the sound of a pygmy flute, the *hundewhu.* Even so, Madonna's superstar status can carry great weight with your students. Try this recording if you use Listening Idea 9 above.

Mbuti Pygmies of the Ituri Rainforest. Smithsonian Folkways SF 40401 (CD). Distinguished collection of music recorded by Colin Turnbull and Francis Chapman comes with detailed liner notes by Turnbull with an introduction by Michelle Kisliuk. Contains some instrumental music but consists mainly of songs for hunting (including the one in the *Listen* set), honey gathering, initiation, and puberty, as well as seven different *molimo* songs. Try this recording if you use Lecture-Demonstration Idea 6 or Listening Ideas 7 and 8 above.

Monteverdi, *L'incoronazione di Poppea.* English Baroque Soloists. Deutsche Grammophon Archiv 447 088-2 (CD). Intimate, expressive period performance of Monteverdi's late masterwork, conducted by John Eliot Gardiner. The cast features stars like Sylvia McNair, Anne Sofie von Otter, Dana Hanchard, and Michael Chance. If the *Poppea* excerpts in the *Listen* recordings left you wanting more, try this recording.

Monteverdi, *L'Orfeo.* Chiaroscuro, the London Baroque, and the London Cornett and Sackbut Ensemble. EMI Records CDMB 7 64947 2 (CD). Highly recommended. An intimate yet colorful performance of Monteverdi's first opera. Nigel Rogers remains the most compellingly virtuosic Orfeo ever recorded. Performed by Rogers, Patrizia Kwella, Emma Kirkby, and others; conducted by Nigel Rogers and Charles Medlam. Try this recording if you use the Act IV selection in Further Listening Examples above.

Monteverdi, *Madrigali Concertati.* Tragicomedia. Teldec Das Alte Werk 4509-91971-2 (CD). Heartfelt period performances of Monteverdi continuo madrigals, including a deeply moving performance of "Lamento della Ninfa." Use this recording if you try Listening Idea 3 or suggestions for this work in Further Listening Examples above.

Monteverdi, *Madrigali guerrieri et amorosi.* Consort of Musicke. Virgin Veritas CDVB 61570 (CD). Anthony Rooley leads his ensemble in committed, satisfying performances of madrigals from Book VIII. Try this recording if you use Listening Idea 3 or suggestions for "Lamento della Ninfa" in Further Listening Examples above.

Patton, Charley. *Charley Patton: Complete Recordings 1929–1934.* JSP 7702 (5-CD set). Complete recordings of perhaps the earliest Delta blues master. Patton influenced Robert Johnson and an entire generation of blues artists. JSP's careful remastering is state of the art, and these five discs sell for less than most two-CD sets. Try this recording if you use Listening Idea 5 above.

Pieces of Africa. Elektra/Nonesuch 79275-2 (CD). This adventuresome quartet presents a fascinating collection of works by African musicians and composers. It includes Foday Musa Suso's Tilliboyo. Use this recording if you try Listening Idea 6 above.

Purcell, *Dido and Aeneas.* Philharmonia Baroque Orchestra and Choir of Clare College, Cambridge. Harmonia Mundi HMU 907110 (CD). Complete performance on period instruments led by Nicholas McGegan. Lorraine Hunt sings beautifully in the title role. The *Listen* excerpts came from this recording; try it if you want to explore more of this work with your class. A bit of trivia: The Stradivarius violin played by the concertmaster belongs to Joseph Kerman.

Roots. *Things Fall Apart.* MCA MCAD-11948 (CD). Philadelphia-based hip-hoppers work with several guest artists on this album, including Marie Daulne of Zap Mama (see below). Her background vocals and the polyphonic layering on "Act Too (the Love of My Life)" move this song close to the spirit of pygmy music, especially in the lengthy introduction and coda (after the string interlude). If you're not put off by the language (sh**, f***, and n*****), use this recording with Listening Idea 9 above.

Sounds of West Africa: The Kora and the Xylophone. Lyrichord LYRCD 7308 (CD). Fine collection of music from Ghana, Senegal, and the Gambia includes a number of griot songs. The *Listen* recording of Foday Musa Suso's minstrel song was taken from this CD. The other griot songs on this disc offer a useful supplement to your classroom presentation.

Sudan: Music of the Blue Nile Province. Auvidis/UNESCO D 8073 (CD). Features recordings of music from the Ingassana and Berta tribes of Sudan, including the minstrel excerpt from Further Listening Examples. Try this recording if you want to introduce more of this music to your class or if you use teaching suggestions in Further Listening Examples above.

Suso, Foday Musa. *Kora Music from the Gambia.* Smithsonian Folkways F-8510 (CD). Fine early recording by Suso offers an entire disc of traditional West African griot songs. This CD allows you to explore several works by this Gambian master musician as part of your classroom presentation on his minstrel song.

Suso, Foday Musa, and Jack DeJohnette. *Music from the Hearts of the Masters.* Golden Beams GBP1112 (CD). Fascinating collaboration between the Gambian griot and the famous jazz drummer includes a mix of traditional and newer works. Try this recording if you use Listening Idea 6 above.

Zap Mama, *Adventures in Afropea 1.* Luaka Bop 72438-49046-2-3 (CD). Zap Mama is an African women's ensemble led by Marie Daulne. Recent albums demonstrate a strong pop orientation, but this, their first album, shows the clear influence of many indigenous African traditions, particularly the music of the central African pygmies with whom Daulne lived for a time. The songs "Mupepe," "Babanzélé," and "Ndje Mukanie" can serve as excellent supplements to your coverage of pygmy polyphony. Try this recording if you use Listening Idea 9 above.

⁷ Video Recordings

The Age of Reason. Man and Music Series. www.films.com (DVD or VHS, color, 53 minutes). This video focuses on the development of vocal music from the ensemble madrigal to virtuoso solo singing. Musical examples are drawn from early Baroque songs, opera, oratorio, and instrumental music, including a Frescobaldi toccata.

Baroque Art and Music. www.insight-media.com (VHS, color, 37 minutes). This still-image video provides a concise, visually appealing introduction to important artistic and musical trends in the Baroque. Part 1 covers the early Baroque, containing the artwork of Caravaggio, Rubens, and Bernini and music by Frescobaldi, Monteverdi, and Corelli.

The Birth and Life of Opera. Howard Goodall's Big Bangs: Turning Points in Music History Series. www.films.com (DVD or VHS, color, 51 minutes). Entertaining video about one of the most important new genres of the Baroque: opera. Includes the Florentine Camerata and a look at Monteverdi.

Cecilia Bartoli: Live in Italy. Decca 074 104-9 (DVD, color, 110 minutes). This live concert performance by the outstanding mezzo ranges widely in its program, but it begins with a set of three continuo madrigals by Giulio Caccini. These songs provide a wonderful supplement to Monteverdi's *Poppea*, and the sight of the theorbo that accompanies Bartoli will wow your students.

Dido and Aeneas. Image Entertainment (DVD, color, 56 minutes). Dance performance by the Mark Morris Dance Group that nonetheless provides a fairly complete, authentic performance of Purcell's score, featuring Jennifer Lane in the title role with the distinguished Toronto-based period instrument orchestra Tafelmusik. You may feel uncomfortable watching Mark Morris himself dance the part of Dido; otherwise this offers a creative, novel supplement to a presentation of *Listen* material on Purcell's opera.

Gabrieli, *O Magnum Mysterium: Music for Christmas.* Brilliant Classics (DVD, color, 71 minutes). It is virtually impossible to find Gabrieli on DVD (yet!), and to come across a video performance of this *Listen* motet can seem like a real *coup*! Sadly, this disc is not fully recommendable, even though conductor Matthew Best and his Corydon Singers are fine musicians with many excellent recordings to their credit. In spite of Gabrieli's frequent and explicit instructions, Best opts for exactly the same instrumental ensemble in every Gabrieli work on this disc, depriving the music of its richness, color, and grandeur. Further, Best's gestures and facial expressions were very distracting, if not a bit creepy. Use at your own risk!

The Golden Age. Man and Music Series. www.films.com (DVD or VHS, color, 53 minutes). This video program covers music in Rome during the seventeenth and early eighteenth centuries. Special emphasis on Corelli and his influence on later composers. Includes Corelli's Trio Sonata, Op. 1, No. 11; his Violin Sonata, Op. 5, No. 1; and music by Stradella, Alessandro and Domenico Scarlatti, and Handel.

The Golden Age. Music in Time Series. www.films.com (DVD or VHS, color, 60 minutes). James Galway covers the Elizabethan period in England and contemporary developments in Italy and France. The first half works well for Chapter 6: It includes madrigals and songs by Morley, Marenzio, Weelkes,

Dowland, and Gibbons; dances and other instrumental works by Holborn, Dowland, and Bull; and a motet by Byrd. The second half fits this chapter: It includes music by Caccini, Monteverdi (*L'Orfeo*), Marini, Adson, Lully, and Purcell. Helpful if you plan to cover Chapters 6 and 7 quickly.

The History of Music, Part 1. www.insight-media.com (VHS, color, 89 minutes). The section on the Baroque era covers opera, concerto, toccata, prelude and fugue, oratorio, and the music of Monteverdi, Gabrieli, Vivaldi, Handel, and Bach.

JVC Video Anthology of World Music and Dance. Tapes 17 through 19 from this excellent video series offer music from Africa. Although these tapes offer no examples of Sudanese music, they include many examples of minstrel songs simply accompanied by various plucked string instruments. Of particular interest is example 17-21, a dance of the Mbuti people. Highly recommended for your presentation of Global Perspectives materials for this chapter.

Mande Music and Dance. Lyrichord/Multicultural Media (DVD-R, color, 82 minutes). This is *the* video to use as a supplement to your presentation on the Gambian minstrel song. Part I features the music of warriors, hunters, and ordinary people played on a variety of instruments. Part II is especially valuable for its focus on music of professional Gambian griots. Members of several old griot families sing and play the kora, and there is even a kora-making demonstration. The accompanying CD-R includes color photographs and valuable, detailed background notes on every segment of the video. Highly recommended for your presentation of Global Perspectives materials for this chapter. Available from www.worldmusicstore.com.

Monteverdi in Mantua. *Man and Music* Series. www.films.com (DVD or VHS, color, 53 minutes). Considers Monteverdi's career with the Gonzaga family in Mantua, where he wrote madrigals, religious works, and his first opera. Includes Monteverdi's "Arianna's Lament," Chorus and Concerto VII from *Vesperae Mariae Virginis* (Vespers for the Virgin Mary), selections from *L'Orfeo*, and music by Salomone Rossi.

Monteverdi, *L'Incoronazione di Poppea*. Arthaus Musik 100 109 (DVD, color, 150 minutes). Concerto Köln performance of *The Coronation of Poppea*. Soloists include Patricia Schumann, Richard Croft, Kathleen Kuhlmann, Harry Peeters, and Dominique Visse; conducted by René Jacobs. Highly recommended supplement to any presentation of *Listen* material on *Poppea*.

Monteverdi, *L'Incoronazione di Poppea*. Kultur (DVD, color, 150 minutes). This older Glyndebourne performance on modern instruments (London Philharmonic) conducted by Raymond Leppard occasionally sounds clunky, but with Maria Ewing as perhaps the most seductive Poppea ever to take the stage, it is worth a look. A good supplement to your presentation of *Listen* material on *Poppea*.

Monteverdi, *L'Incoronazione di Poppea*. BBC Opus Arte (DVD, color, 219 minutes). Christophe Rousset leads an excellent cast and Les Talens Lyriques in this new Amsterdam Opera production of *The Coronation of Poppea*. Highly recommended supplement to any presentation of *Listen* material on *Poppea*.

Monteverdi, *L'Orfeo*. BBC Opus Arte (DVD, color, 140 minutes). Compelling period performance of Monteverdi's great first opera by Le Concert des Nations and La Capella Reial de Catalunya at Barcelona's Gran Teatre del Liceu. Soloists include Montserrat Figueras, Furio Zanasi, and Sara Mingardo;

conducted by Jordi Savall. Sets often evoke paintings in Mantua's ducal palace where *L'Orfeo* was premiered. Frequent close-up shots of the period instruments in the orchestra. Highly recommended if you use suggestions for this work in Further Listening Examples above.

Monteverdi, *L'Orfeo.* BBC Opus Arte (DVD, color, 140 minutes). Staging is simple and spare compared with the Savall production, but this is probably the finest period performance of *L'Orfeo* on DVD. This two-disc set features John Mark Ainsley in the title role, with Tragicomedia and Concerto Palatino led by Stephen Stubbs. Highly recommended if you use suggestions for this work in Further Listening Examples above.

Monteverdi, *Vespro della beata Vergine.* Deutsche Grammophon (DVD, color, 110 minutes). John Eliot Gardiner leads this splendid period-instrument performance of Monteverdi's 1610 Vespers in the historic setting of St. Mark's, Venice. This work combines the polychoral splendor of Gabrieli with the new expressive sensitivity and solo vocal virtuosity of opera. The opportunity to see gorgeous Byzantine mosaics as the music echoes through the basilica where Monteverdi worked for thirty years is extraordinary. Highly recommended supplement to any presentation of *Listen* materials on Gabrieli or *Poppea.*

New Voices for Man. The Music of Man Series. Home Vision (VHS, color, 58 minutes). Yehudi Menuhin narrates this survey of the Baroque period. Includes Monteverdi's *L'Orfeo,* instrumental music by Corelli, and works by Purcell and Handel.

Old Masters. Culture Fix Series. www.films.com (DVD or VHS, color, 29 minutes). Looks at the techniques and artists of the Renaissance and Baroque, including Leonardo, Michelangelo, and Rembrandt. Useful supplement to your study of Baroque music.

Opera: Words and Music. Understanding Music Series. www.films.com (DVD or VHS, color, 25 minutes). George Fenton and Judith Weir narrate this look at text expression and the techniques of recitative and aria. Three excerpts from Purcell's *Dido and Aeneas* provide the context for their discussion.

Powaqqatsi: Life in Transformation. MGM (DVD, color, 97 minutes). This visually rich sequel to Godfrey Reggio and Philip Glass's *Koyaanisqatsi* takes us to locations around the world. Using only fast- and slow-motion film clips, this movie takes progress and the human condition as its subjects. This was Glass's first collaboration with Foday Musa Suso, and you can hear the sounds of Suso's kora toward the end of track 15. Use this video if you try Listening Idea 6 above.

Venice and the Gabrielis. Five Centuries of Music in Venice Series. www.films.com (DVD or VHS, color, 60 minutes). This program offers a sumptuous portrait of the history, art, and architecture of sixteenth-century Venice. Covers Willaert, the Gabrielis, and the importance of the Basilica of San Marco with its resonant acoustics. Live performances of music by Gabrieli and Schütz in Venetian churches and palaces.

The World of Claudio Monteverdi. Five Centuries of Music in Venice Series. www.films.com (DVD or VHS, color, 60 minutes). This program offers a sumptuous portrait of the history, art, and architecture of seventeenth-century Venice. Covers Monteverdi, the art of the madrigal, the rise of women composers, and the world's first public opera house. Live performances of works by Monteverdi and Barbara Strozzi in Venetian homes and palaces.

7 Software

Art and Music: The Baroque. Zane Publishing (CD-ROM—Windows or Macintosh). The Baroque volume of this inexpensive CD-ROM series uses images and sound clips to survey important developments in art and music. Quality of screen images is variable, but it's quite inexpensive. Available from www.cdaccess.com.

GarageBand www.apple.com (Macintosh) or *Acid* www.acidplanet.com (Windows). These programs make it really easy (and a lot of fun) to create compositions by dragging ready-made loops (ostinatos) onto a sequencer-like screen. Some loops are MIDI-based, others use digital audio samples. Users can add or subtract instruments freely and even edit the ostinatos to create more interesting patterns. Try this if you use Lecture-Demonstration Idea 7 above.

The History of Music, Part 1. www.mccormicksnet.com (CD-ROM—Windows or Macintosh). CD-ROM version of the video listed above. The section on the Baroque era covers opera, concerto, toccata, prelude and fugue, oratorio, and the music of Monteverdi, Gabrieli, Vivaldi, Handel, and Bach.

History Through Art: The Baroque. Zane Publishing (CD-ROM—Windows or Macintosh). The Baroque volume of this inexpensive CD-ROM series contains several hundred full-screen images, including artwork by Rubens, Titian, and others. Much attention devoted to Louis XIV and his court. Quality of screen images is variable, but it's hard to argue with the price.

CHAPTER 8

Prelude
The Late Baroque Period

Chapter Outline

Important Terms

Baroque	court	festive Baroque orchestra	figured bass
absolutism	opera house	sequence	affects
Age of Science	walking bass	ornamentation	
theatricality	harmonic rhythm	ritornellos	
church	basic Baroque orchestra	continuo	

Teaching Objectives

ʏ **Overall Objectives**

This chapter will help students acquire familiarity with:

1. Late Baroque music as a reflection of the Baroque dualism between absolutism, extravagance, and theatricality, on one hand, and science and systematic control, on the other.

176

2. The three institutions that dominated music making in the late Baroque period: church, court, and opera house.

3. Typical late Baroque uses of rhythm, dynamics, tone color, orchestra, melody, virtuosity, improvisation, texture, continuo, and musical form.

4. Baroque interest in depicting a wide range of human emotions, or "affects."

⁊ Listening Objectives

After completing this chapter, students should be able to:

1. Hear how the elements of music are typically used in late Baroque music.

2. Identify basso continuo and the two types of Baroque orchestra.

Lecture Suggestions

⁊ Absolutism and the Age of Science

The music of the Baroque era was influenced by a complex series of events.

1. The ever-decreasing power of the church allowed the rise of the absolute monarch, who sought to celebrate himself in opulent, extravagant art, architecture, and music.

2. The public's increasing interest in human (rather than religious) expression led to a fascination with theater, where human emotions could be exposed, magnified, and experienced vicariously.

3. The scientific climate of the time led to a new intellectual emphasis on experimentation and observation, logic, and control, an emphasis we can see in the carefully controlled elements of Baroque music.

4. Finally, the rise of purely instrumental music illustrates that the structural elements of Baroque music became fully developed enough that they alone could create a viable musical statement, without the need for text or voices.

The Baroque period was characterized by two trends that seem mutually exclusive. On one hand, composers, writers, and audiences were fascinated with theater and the emotional extremes that could be portrayed theatrically. The ultimate Baroque manifestation of this fascination was opera, with its poetry, music, dance, spectacular stage designs, and exaggerated emotional content. On the other hand, the new, systematic approach to scientific inquiry manifested itself musically in carefully controlled musical forms and greater regularity in the elements of harmony, texture, rhythm, and meter.

Extravagance and Control in Other Arts

The dualism between extravagance and control characterized all the fine arts in the Baroque era. Examples from the textbook demonstrate how pervasive it was. Perhaps the ultimate example of Baroque extravagance (and absolutism) is the palace built by Louis XIV at Versailles. Ask the students to examine the illustration of Versailles on page 117 of the textbook. Describe this enormous complex to the class: more than 1,300 rooms, including the eighty-foot-long Hall of Mirrors, and formal gardens extending for miles. For all its incredible size, though, the impression one receives from the illustration—and it is accurate—is of the symmetry and form of this palace. Everything is balanced and symmetrical. The overall effect of the buildings and grounds is one of order and control.

Nowhere is the Baroque desire to quantify and control nature more clearly demonstrated than in the Baroque formal garden. Ask students to look closely at the landscaping in the painting of Versailles on textbook page 117. Tell students that this was typical of the period. Baroque landscape architecture exemplified absolute control of nature—bushes were clipped, lawns were tailored, all was carefully laid out in a symmetrical, geometrical plan.

Extravagance and Control in Music

Handel's Hallelujah Chorus from *Messiah* serves well as an example of extravagance and control (or theatricality and science). Write the headings "Extravagance" and "Control" on the blackboard. Ask students to write ideas in each column when they listen to the chorus. Extravagance can be found in the power and fullness of the chorus and orchestra, the dramatic effects created by sudden changes in dynamics, the variety of melodic ideas, and the long sequences that build to powerful climaxes. Control results from steady beat and meter, consistent association of specific motives and rhythms with specific phrases of text, masterful handling of functional harmony and modulation, and diverse elements united to express a single "affect"—profound, jubilant rejoicing. In the discussion that follows, ask students to compare features of the Handel chorus with features of the paintings and architecture discussed above. Intricate patterns of symmetry and freedom on a grand scale characterize both the paintings and the music.

❦ Musical Life in the Early Eighteenth Century

Call attention to Kerman and Tomlinson's discussion of music in church, court, and opera on textbook pages 123–25. It is not necessary to play examples of each right now, but you will want to make these connections as you look at individual works in Chapters 9 and 10.

❦ Style Features of Late Baroque Music

Elements of Baroque style were introduced and discussed in brief in Chapter 7. Chapter 8 is the first of three chapters on late Baroque music, so the elements of Baroque style will come up again and again. A solid grounding in this era's characteristic uses of musical elements and structures will help students enormously.

Begin with a listening exercise. Put the checklist of musical elements and structures from Chapter 5 on the board. Ask students to write comments about each item as they listen; then play the first movement of Bach's *Brandenburg* Concerto No. 5. In the discussion that follows, make these points.

> *Rhythm*—Melodic rhythm and meter become systematic and precise during the Baroque. Bach's melodic rhythms are exciting and energetic, and the steady meter is clearly expressed.

Dynamics—Subtle, expressive nuances aside, the overall dynamic level is also steady. The most pronounced dynamic change comes about through alternation between full orchestra and a small group of solo instruments, not by each musician playing louder or softer.

Tone color—The sound is bright and dynamic. The writing is appropriate for the instruments Bach uses; these melodies would not work well for voices. The long harpsichord cadenza stands out as an example of idiomatic instrumental writing. Further, Bach pits a small group of solo instruments—flute, violin, and harpsichord—against the colors of the full orchestral ensemble.

The Baroque orchestra—The string orchestra became the most significant large instrumental ensemble of the Baroque period. Bach's concerto employs first and second violins, violas, cellos, basses, harpsichord, and flute. This corresponds most closely to the basic Baroque orchestra (textbook page 127).

Melody—Bach's opening melody is typical of Baroque melodies: long, twisting lines, ranging quickly from high to low, with irregular phrase lengths. The frequent leaps of Baroque melodies stand in contradistinction to the "singing" quality of Renaissance melodies. This melody offers a dramatic profile.

Ornamentation—The extended harpsichord cadenza provides an excellent example of the virtuosity required of the Baroque musician. We heard nothing in Renaissance music to compare with this. Although Bach's cadenza is written out, it successfully captures the ornate, improvisational quality associated with much Baroque ornamentation.

Texture—Though the main theme is rather homophonic, most often we hear polyphony and imitation in this work. In general, Baroque music favors polyphony, with homophonic passages mixed in.

The continuo—The basso continuo is a uniquely Baroque invention. Continuo instruments play both the bass line and the accompanimental harmonies of a piece of music. The use of continuo provides a sense of order and control even during the most complex polyphonic passages. The continuo part usually requires two instruments: a bass-register melodic instrument—most often a cello—to play the bass line and a plucked string or keyboard instrument—often harpsichord or organ—to play the bass line *and* improvise chords according to figured bass symbols. In this concerto we hear cellos, basses, and harpsichord on the continuo line. Note the weight of the bass line as a result of this technique (and the dramatic change when the continuo strings drop out for a time at track 1, 0:19).

Musical form—Some students may hear the ritornello theme as it returns throughout the piece. Most remarkable is the length of this movement. Instrumental music had developed to the point where abstract musical elements—form, melody, harmony, texture, and so on—could provide and sustain a complete musical experience over long time spans. Instrumental music began to rival vocal music in significance.

Key, mode, and harmony—Major and minor scales and the well-tempered tunings that make modulation to any key possible were products of the systematic scientific thought of the Baroque. The Bach concerto uses the familiar major and minor scales and clearly begins in major. The systematized science of harmonic function, whereby each chord plays a specific role in relation to the tonic chord, also developed during the Baroque. As a result, the pull toward the tonic is strong in this concerto. Some passages (such as the harpsichord cadenza) create enormous tension as we wait for the return to the tonic.

❧ The Emotional World of Baroque Music

The possibilities for emotional expression in Baroque music have already been demonstrated in Purcell's "When I am laid in earth" from *Dido and Aeneas*. If you have not used it already, Listening Idea 2 from Chapter 7 works well here. It compares this aria with Weelkes's "As Vesta Was from Latmos Hill Descending" as a means of contrasting Renaissance word painting and Baroque emotional expression.

You can also discuss the concept of affect described by the authors on textbook page 130. Many Baroque compositions, opera arias and concerto movements alike, attempt to depict a single emotion. To portray an affect, composers would choose keys carefully and use similar rhythmic and melodic motives throughout. Some theorists even suggested that certain affects were best expressed by specific genres, rhythms, or keys. Listening Idea 2 in Chapter 9 and Class Discussion Idea 1 in Chapter 10 present Johann Mattheson's theories about the appropriate affects for certain instrumental and vocal genres. It was also thought that certain keys were appropriate for certain affects: D minor for serious discourse; E-flat major for heroic music; E minor for pathos or tragedy; F major for bucolic, pastoral moods; and so on. Of course, different keys did sound different before equal temperament came into common usage; even the well-tempered tunings of the late Baroque contained subtle differences in intonation from one key to the next. This "key symbolism" appears to have affected music as late as Beethoven's.

Ask students to identify the primary emotion expressed as they listen to "La giustizia" from Handel's *Julius Caesar* (2:21–3:53). Once they have reached a consensus on the emotion, use the checklist of musical elements and structures from Chapter 5 and ask them to list the techniques used to express that emotion. At the end of the discussion, have them turn to textbook page 159 for a look at the English translation to see how close they came. This discussion can reinforce the idea that Baroque composers used elements of music expressively.

Additional Teaching Suggestions

❧ Lecture-Demonstration Ideas

1. Create a slide show of Baroque paintings, architecture, and sculpture. Your school's art department and your local library are good sources for slides. Ten minutes' worth will convey concepts of absolutism, science, and theatricality more quickly than an hour-long lecture. In place of slides, see Multimedia Resources below for video CD-ROM resources.

2. Invite a harpsichord player to class. Your guest can discuss the construction of the harpsichord, differences between piano and harpsichord, and how to read figured bass. He or she can also provide insights into Baroque performance practice along with the other issues raised in Chapter 8. Ask students to come with questions and have some of your own ready if discussion flags.

3. If you are able, demonstrate figured bass for your class. Find a score and recording (use the anthologies of scores and recordings that accompany standard music history textbooks by Burkholder and others) with a basso continuo part and hand out photocopies (or project a transparency). At the keyboard, play two different realizations of the same continuo part (prepare these ahead

of time if necessary) and discuss the meaning of various figured bass symbols. If you spent time constructing scales in Unit I, or if you write out the scale tones for your figured bass example on the board, students can easily learn to find the third, fifth, and sixth scale steps above any given bass note. When you have finished, play a recorded performance of the score so that students can hear how the continuo part fits into the texture.

4. If you have a keyboard lab at your school, devise a simple exercise that allows your students to improvise chords above a figured bass. If you spent time in the lab playing scales in Unit I, or if you write out the scale tones for your figured bass example on the board, students can easily learn to find the third, fifth, and sixth scale steps above any given bass note. Choose a short example of recitative so that meter will not be a factor. Students will need lots of time to rehearse. Once they have mastered the first four or five chords, try a performance. Sing the solo melody while students play continuo.

⅋ Class Discussion Ideas

1. *What characteristics do Baroque art and music share?* This question can be used to continue the discussion of extravagance and control above. Ask students to study a Baroque painting (Tiepolo's ceiling painting on page 120 of the textbook, for example) and write a description of its line, color, texture, and balance. Then play a Baroque instrumental work (Bach's Air from Orchestral Suite No. 3 in D, for example) and have students write a description of its melody, timbre, texture, and form. Their written lists can be read aloud to begin discussion of similarities and differences between the painting and the music.

2. *Is it possible to hear absolutism, science, and theatricality in music?* This question can be used to continue the discussion of extravagance and control above. Begin discussion by clarifying each of these currents. Then play Bach's *Brandenburg* Concerto No. 5, I, and ask students to pick out elements that suggest absolutism, science, and theatricality. Absolutism reveals itself in this work's grand scale (its length and the size of the ensemble) and perhaps even in its clear tonal center. Science can be found in the way Bach examines the same few melodic ideas from many different perspectives: different keys and modes, different combinations of instruments, and varied polyphonic combinations of voices. Science can also be found in the regularity of rhythm and meter, the ordered recurrence of the main theme, and the carefully regulated harmonies. Theatricality is suggested by the vivacious, engaging quality of the main theme, the almost dramatic contrasts between full orchestra and solo ensemble, and the showy virtuosity of the harpsichord cadenza.

⅋ Listening Ideas

1. Play one example each of music for church, court, and opera house, according to the authors' discussion on textbook page 123. Appropriate examples might include Bach's "Christ lag in Todesbanden" (church), Bach's *Brandenburg* Concerto No. 5, I (court), and Handel's "La giustizia" from *Julius Caesar* (opera house). Ask students to compare the three works and to determine what makes each work appropriate for its setting. Bach's chorale prelude emphasizes the important role of the organist in Lutheran worship. The concerto

points to the wealth of many courts that could maintain an orchestra and hire composers to produce such music. Handel's opera offers dramatic expression of strong emotion.

2. Compare the basic Baroque orchestra with the festive Baroque orchestra as described on page 127 of the textbook. The first movement of Vivaldi's Concerto in G, Op. 4, No. 12, and the gavotte from Bach's Orchestral Suite in D work nicely. Ask students to identify differences in the orchestras and play the two back to back. The trumpets and timpani are fairly obvious in the Bach. After discussion of the listening, have students open to page 127 in the textbook and compare the two listed orchestras with what they heard. Play part or all of each movement again if necessary.

3. Compare basso continuo with the rhythm section in a jazz band. Play one example of each and ask the class to pick out similarities. "La giustizia" from Handel's *Julius Caesar* and Parker and Davis's "Out of Nowhere" work well. Most commonly, continuo and rhythm section both use a bass stringed instrument and a keyboard instrument (the rhythm section also uses a drum set); plucked string instruments could also be used in both. Both require some improvisation from chord symbols (figured bass in continuo, "pop" chord symbols in jazz). Both provide a foundation for the musical texture and lead the ensemble by keeping a steady tempo. If you can find a good recorded example of *inégales* (try Albert Fuller's Rameau recording in Sound Recordings below), you can even compare this Baroque rhythmic irregularity with swing rhythms.

4. The Swingle Singers recorded many of Bach's works in a jazz style, using scat syllables and swinging the rhythms. Find two recordings of the same work, one the original version, the other a Swingle Singers version (see Sound Recordings below). Ask students to compare the two. In the Swingle version, which elements sound Baroque? Which elements sound like jazz? This comparison reinforces the textbook's juxtaposition of the adaptability of much Baroque music with its new sensitivity to the sounds and capabilities of individual instruments (see textbook page 126).

Multimedia Resources

♪ Sound Recordings

Bach Hits Back/A Cappella Amadeus. The Swingle Singers. Virgin Classics 5 61472 2 (CD). Classic jazz vocal performances of well-known works by Bach and Mozart, including Bach's Air and excerpts from Cantata 140 and *Brandenburg* Concerto No. 3. Try this recording if you use Listening Idea 4 above.

Jazz Sebastian Bach, Vols. 1 and 2. The Swingle Singers. Philips 4542552 and 4542553 (CD). Jazz vocal performances of well-known Bach works. Vol. 1 includes a fugue from *The Art of Fugue* and a chorale prelude on "Wachet auf." Try this recording if you use Listening Idea 4 above.

Rameau, *Pièces de clavecin*. Albert Fuller. Reference RR 27 CD (CD). Harpsichordist Albert Fuller makes the rhythmic intricacies of French Baroque performance practices sound perfectly natural and musically effective. Try this recording if you use Listening Idea 3 above.

❦ Video Recordings

The Advent of Fashion. Music in Time Series. www.films.com (DVD and VHS, color, 60 minutes). James Galway narrates this look at the rise of public concerts and theaters during the late Baroque. Many examples of Baroque music: Handel's *Zadok the Priest, Music for the Royal Fireworks, Messiah, Orlando,* and Concerto for Organ in D Minor; Rameau's *Naïs;* Couperin's *Deuxième Ordre;* Telemann's Sonata in E Minor; Scarlatti's Sonata in B-flat Major; and Gay's *The Beggar's Opera.*

Baroque Art and Music. www.insight-media.com (VHS, color, 37 minutes). This still-image video provides a concise, visually appealing introduction to important artistic and musical trends in the Baroque. Part 2 covers the late Baroque and contains the artwork of Rembrandt and music by Bach and Handel.

Delaware Music Series (NEH Videodisc Project). Newark, Del.: Office of Computer-Based Instruction, University of Delaware (DVD). This exceptional video series is not as helpful for the Baroque as for later eras, but it does contain early instrument demonstrations.

The History of Music, Part 1. www.insight-media.com (VHS, color, 89 minutes). The section on the Baroque era covers opera, concerto, toccata, prelude and fugue, oratorio, and the music of Monteverdi, Gabrieli, Vivaldi, Handel, and Bach.

Music at the Court of Louis XIV. Man and Music Series. www.films.com (DVD and VHS, color, 53 minutes). Filmed largely at Versailles, this video looks at the extravagance associated with absolutism. Musical excerpts from works by DeLalande, Lully, and François Couperin.

❦ Software

Art and Music: The Baroque. Zane Publishing (CD-ROM—Windows or Macintosh). The Baroque volume of this inexpensive CD-ROM series uses images and sound clips to survey important developments in art and music. Quality of screen images is variable, but it's quite inexpensive. Available from www.cdaccess.com.

The History of Music, Part 1. www.mccormicksnet.com (CD-ROM—Windows or Macintosh). CD-ROM version of the video listed above. The section on the Baroque era covers opera, concerto, toccata, prelude and fugue, oratorio, and the music of Monteverdi, Gabrieli, Vivaldi, Handel, and Bach.

History Through Art: The Baroque. Zane Publishing (CD-ROM—Windows or Macintosh). The Baroque volume of this inexpensive CD-ROM series contains several hundred full-screen images, including artwork by Rubens, Titian, and others. Much attention devoted to Louis XIV and his court. Quality of screen images is variable, but it's hard to argue with the price.

CHAPTER 9

Baroque Instrumental Music

Chapter Outline

Boldface indicates works in the recording set.

Important Terms

concerto	basso ostinato	fugue subject	stretto	Baroque dance form
concerto grosso	chaconne	exposition	augmentation	binary form
concertare	passacaglia	subject entries	diminution	trio
movement	ground	episodes	inversion	French overture
ritornello form	ground bass	free and learned fugues	contrapunctus	overture
ritornello	double listening	fugato	suite	air
archlute	cadenza	fugal devices	gigue	walking bass
variation form	fugue	countersubject	gavotte	bourrée

Teaching Objectives

❦ Overall Objectives

This chapter will help students acquire familiarity with:

1. The essential difference in organization between vocal, text-based music and strictly instrumental music.

2. The features of Baroque instrumental genres (concerto, fugue, and dance suite) and the importance of contrast in multimovement works.

3. The features of important Baroque instrumental forms, each one the systematic, "scientific" expression of significant underlying principles:

> ritornello form—contrast and return
>
> ground bass—variation
>
> fugue—imitation
>
> Baroque dance form and French overture—repetition and contrast

4. The lives and music of Antonio Vivaldi and Johann Sebastian Bach.

❦ Listening Objectives

After completing this chapter, students should be able to:

1. Hear and identify how the elements of music are typically used in Baroque instrumental music.

2. Follow the genres of Baroque instrumental music, especially concerto, fugue, and dance suite.

3. Follow the forms of Baroque instrumental music, especially ritornello form, ground bass, fugue, and Baroque dance (binary) form.

4. Practice what Kerman and Tomlinson call "double listening"—that is, listen for the different, systematic ways in which:

> a. main ideas are stated and restated
>
> b. contrast is achieved.

Lecture Suggestions

❦ Introduction and Review

The emergence of purely instrumental music constitutes one of the most profound developments in Western music of the Baroque period (though Baroque Europe was hardly the first society to develop a substantial body of serious instrumental music). Reflecting the scientific temper of the age, Baroque composers systematized and standardized the elements of music—rhythm, dynamics, tone color, melody, texture, harmony, and especially form—to the point that these elements alone were sufficient to sustain a listener's interest. Each form provided a rational framework that permitted orderly presentation of musical materials, and the emergence of instrumental forms profoundly altered the course of Western art music. From the Middle Ages through the early Baroque, vocal music occupied the central position. Since the late Baroque, instrumental music has equaled and often displaced vocal music as the essential mode of musical discourse.

It is important that students grasp the magnitude of this rise of instrumental music during the Baroque. On a practical level, one of the best things you can do to help students attain the Listening Objectives for this chapter is acquaint them with one of the most important tools in the textbook: Listening Charts. Do your best to encourage students to use the Interactive Listening Charts available on the *Listen* Web site, but recognize that some students may be unwilling or unable to take advantage of this tool. For these students, listening to a piece of music while following a Listening Chart can be tricky, even with the timing designations indicated. At the very least, you need to review the suggestions from Chapters 1 and 4 of this manual concerning Listening Charts, lead the class through each Listening Chart in Chapter 9 of the textbook, and offer students some pointers for using the charts on their own.

When listening in class, always use whatever technology you have available to display the Listening Charts from the textbook. You must be able to point out the sections of music on the chart as they are heard. This allows students to focus on the chart and the music, and saves them from referring to a stopwatch. If your classroom is equipped for computer display, by all means use the Interactive Listening Charts as often as possible. If not, your Bedford/St. Martin's representative can still provide you with a packet of transparencies for display on an overhead projector. (If you use Further Listening Examples recommended in this manual, feel free to photocopy transparencies of charts and texts from Appendix I and Appendix II.) As a last resort, you can always write the large divisions of any work on the board and point these out instead.

Review: Repetition, Variation, Contrast, Return, and Imitation

Briefly review the role of memory in perceiving form (see Chapter 4 Lecture Suggestions) and emphasize the role of repetition and contrast in creating unity and variety. As discussed in Chapter 4 of this manual, consecutive sections of music, usually defined by melodic content and cadences, can relate to each other in three general ways.

1. One section of music can be an exact repetition of the other; this can be shown as

> **A A** or |: **A** :|

2. One section of music can be a variant of the other; this can be shown as

> **A A′**

3. One section of music can contrast with the other; this can be shown as

> **A B**

Review these three types of sectional relationships with the class along with a discussion of return and imitation. A demonstration like the following will help.

Repetition—Play "Happy Birthday," "Heart and Soul," or any short, simple tune. Keep repeating the tune and ask the students to tell you when they get bored. The point? Vital as repetition is in establishing a familiar point of reference, repetition alone cannot create the interest needed to sustain a piece of music.

Variation—Play your tune again. This time, follow it with one or more variations; for example, play the tune in minor, change the accompaniment, change the register, change the tempo, and so on. Ask students to describe how their experience of your variations differed from their experience of your repetition demonstration. Confirm the importance of the variation principle in many musical works.

Contrast—Play your tune again, but this time follow it with a different tune ("Twinkle, Twinkle, Little Star," for instance). Point out that contrast need not be as dramatic as your demonstration; more subtle contrasts might consist of a slightly different melody. Ask students to compare their experience of this demonstration with the other two. The principle of contrast is the most profound of the three, for once we depart from an original thematic idea, we anticipate and desire a return to that idea, especially when the original idea was made familiar through repetition.

Return—Play your "contrast" demonstration again. Follow it with a demonstration in which you play your first tune, play your contrasting tune, and end by playing the first tune again, in an **A B A** form. Ask the students which demonstration felt more complete. Describe return as repetition after contrast. Emphasize the importance of remembering primary melodic ideas and listening for their return. The principle of return figures prominently in instrumental forms.

Imitation—The principle of imitation is mentioned here because of its central role in the fugue and because students often confuse it with repetition. Use the example of a round (like "Row, Row, Row Your Boat") to point out that imitation requires at least two instruments or voices (one to state the melody, the others to imitate it) that *overlap* when stating the tune. Compare this with the repetition demonstration, in which a *single* instrument stated the entire tune and then repeated it. I tell students that I can repeat myself all day long, but I cannot imitate myself (that I leave to them!).

♩ Concerto and Concerto Grosso

Movements

Problem: You are an early Baroque composer. Your patron adores music for instruments—can't get enough of it. You want to create significant, substantial compositions without singers, but the only instrumental works you know are short and dancelike. *What do you do?*

Baroque composers discovered two solutions to this important problem. One solution was to develop and expand musical forms—using the principles of repetition, contrast, variation, return, and imitation—so that they could sustain interest over longer and longer time spans. This was the more difficult solution, and only in the late Baroque do we find forms that fill a big canvas— Bach's toccatas and fugues and the first movement of his *Brandenburg* Concerto No. 5 provide good examples. As we saw in the Frescobaldi suite from Chapter 7, an earlier, simpler solution was to take several short, contrasting works and string them together to create an instrumental composition of substantial length. These contrasting works were called movements because each followed its own tempo (*mouvement* was the French word for *tempo*). Baroque composers discovered this solution early on, and we see it in several new Baroque genres—first in the dance suite, then in the trio sonata, and later in the concerto. We looked at the dance suite in Chapter 7; this chapter takes up the concerto and revisits the dance suite.

The concerto became the most important orchestral genre of the Baroque period. As the textbook states, *concerto* comes from the Latin *concertare,* "to contend." The contrast between movements plays a significant role in shaping a concerto, but remind students that the "contention" in any concerto derives from the interplay between solo instruments and orchestra. In the Baroque concerto grosso, it is more precisely the element of contrast between one or more soloists and the orchestra that defines the genre's "contest."

The typical late Baroque concerto consists of three movements in a fast-slow-fast sequence. Let your students quickly hear the contrasts between movements in the Vivaldi Concerto in G. Use the skip button on your CD player to jump from movement to movement, playing the first fifteen or twenty seconds of each.

At this point you can look at individual movements of the concerto in detail. Each movement follows its own form; the first movement (and often the third) employs ritornello form.

Ritornello Form

The contest between solo (or solo group) and orchestra displays itself most vividly in the ritornello movements of a concerto grosso. The main theme of these movements is called the "ritornello" theme, from the Italian *ritorno,* or "return" (to return home), since it returns throughout the movement. Ritornello form is thus a systematic expression of the principles of contrast and return. Call attention to the textbook's diagram of ritornello form on page 134. It clearly shows the recurrent ritornelli with contrasting solo passages sandwiched in between.

VIVALDI Violin Concerto in G, *La stravaganza,* Op. 4, No. 12, I

Ritornello movements are usually easy to follow, especially once students familiarize themselves with the ritornello theme. Fortunately, ritornello themes tend to be attractive, memorable melodies, as in the *Brandenburg* Concerto movement introduced below. While students may be eager to hear the periodic return of the ritornello theme, don't let them forget to listen for the contrast between soloist(s) and orchestra; both features together distinguish the ritornello from the solo episodes. The first movement of Vivaldi's Concerto in G presents an interesting, rather unusual example.

1. Display Listening Chart 3 or write the following on the board:

Ritornello 1	*Solo*	*Ritornello 2*	*Solo*	*Ritornello 3*	*Solo*	*Ritornello 4*	*Solo*	*Ritornello 5*
beginning			end	free use of		freer yet		middle
middle				middle & end				end
end								

Even if you can display the chart by other means, you may want to write this on the board. It does not replace the Listening Chart, but it allows students to grasp the whole structure visually from left to right.

2. Emphasize the importance of recognizing each return of the ritornello. Play the ritornello theme until the class is familiar with it. This will take some time because the theme is not as tuneful or memorable as others by Vivaldi or Bach. You can use the time to your advantage, though, by helping students investi-

gate different elements of the music. Students like to follow the melody, but melody is not the most memorable element here—they must look elsewhere. The most striking aspects of this ritornello are the abrupt, staccato chords anchored by the continuo, and the churning motor rhythms of the violin arpeggios. Rhythm and texture dominate here. As you finish up, play the complete ritornello theme again and ask students to describe its character. As in many Baroque melodies, the rhythms and contour are complex, phrase lengths are irregular, and notes cover a wide range.

3. Play the first forty seconds of the movement (ritornello theme and first solo excursion). Ask students to describe the contrasts they hear between ritornello and solo. Point out the rapid, virtuosic figuration and light melody and accompaniment texture of the violin solo, as opposed to the steady motor rhythms and polyphonic give and take of the orchestral ritornello.

4. Call attention to the fact that the ritornello theme rarely returns in its entirety, but is used as a "quick reminder" or even as a basis for variation and development, as in Ritornelli 3 and 4. Play the entire movement. Point to each section on the Listening Chart display or the board as it occurs.

5. Point out changes of key. After the first ritornello or two, composers generally present the ritornello in new keys to provide variety and to prepare for a double return at the end—return of the ritornello and return of the original tonality. Vivaldi's concerto is no exception. Ritornello 3 begins in D major and Ritornello 4 in B minor. Students will have little trouble hearing the move to B minor; it begins at the end of Ritornello 3, and Vivaldi maintains the key all the way up to the beginning of Ritornello 4. Of course, the final ritornello makes a strong statement in the original key, returning to the original G Major tonality.

6. Note that Vivaldi employs progressively more freedom with each new solo and ritornello. At first he maintains clear roles—a stable ritornello theme presented by the orchestra versus a modulating solo for one violin and continuo. These roles begin to break down as orchestral strings accompany the violin in the second solo. Ritornello 3 finds Vivaldi treating the theme more freely with a sudden modulation to B Minor at the end. In a total flip-flop of expected harmonic function, the third solo employs *stable* harmonies affirming B minor, while frequent modulations create harmonic instability in Ritornello 4, where Vivaldi treats the theme even more freely than in Ritornello 3! The final solo again employs orchestral strings in the background, but this leads us smoothly into the final ritornello, where we welcome the stable, literal return of the main theme all the more intensely because of Vivaldi's unusual handling of ritornello form conventions.

7. If time permits, play the entire movement again. Point to each section on the Listening Chart display or the board as it occurs.

Conclusions to Draw about Ritornello Form

1. This form is based on the systematic exploration of contrast and return.

2. The principle of contrast plays a greater role in ritornello form than in most other Baroque forms. We find contrast not only between ritornello and solo themes but also between full orchestra and small ensemble.

3. Contrasts intensify the feeling of resolution when the ritornello theme returns.

Baroque Variation Form: The Ground Bass

In their discussion of Baroque variation forms on textbook page 137, the authors describe a "double listening" technique. For any work based on the principle of variation, the listener must simultaneously identify similarities and contrasts. Baroque variation forms ordinarily rely on a bass line ostinato (and its accompanying harmonic progression) as the constant element in each variation; contrast results from constantly changing lines and figures in the upper voices. Point out this work's similarity to the Frescobaldi passacaglia in Chapter 7, and remind the class that these ostinato-oriented variation forms go by several names, including *ground, ground bass form, passacaglia,* and *chaconne.*

VIVALDI Violin Concerto in G, *La stravaganza,* Op. 4, No. 12, II

The second movement of Vivaldi's concerto employs ground bass form. As in the other ostinato-oriented forms named above, a bass line ostinato—the ground bass or theme—is systematically repeated while the polyphonic voices above it weave ever-new lines about each other.

In this movement, the six-measure ground bass theme is initially stated with a simple melody in the first violins, followed by six variations and a recapitulation of the theme. During the course of the variations, the ostinato theme remains constant. Slight changes to the ground in Variations 5 and 6 adapt it to the minor mode but do not affect our ability to recognize the repeating bass line. The real contrasts result from the constantly changing voices above the bass line, especially the solo violin.

1. Display Listening Chart 4 or write "Theme" on the board followed by the numbers 1 to 6 and then "Theme" again at the end.

2. Notate the ground bass theme on the board, above or below the numbers 1 to 6.

Theme, Variations 1–4, 7

3. Play the bass ostinato theme at the keyboard or sing the theme while pointing to specific pitches on the board. Repeat until the class is familiar with the theme. Point out how the quickening motion in the last measure drives toward a cadence that is completed only when we reach the first measure of the next statement of the ground. This cadential overlap between variations creates the continuous motion associated with Baroque variation forms, quite different from the full cadence that *separates* variations in the Classical theme and variations form. Note also the instrumentation—a string orchestra with continuo (the basic Baroque orchestra)—and a solo violin.

4. Play the entire recording. Indicate each successive variation by pointing to the appropriate number on the Listening Chart display or the board. While each variation plays, alternate between pointing to each note of the theme on the board as it is heard and singing or playing the ground bass theme along with the recording. Singing or playing along is especially helpful in Variations 5–6, where the ostinato, slightly altered, moves to the upper voices. If your students like to sing, have them sing or hum, too.

5. Now that students are aware of the repeating ground bass and the sections that it demarcates, you can point out groupings of variations on the Listening Chart. Variations 1–4 feature the solo violin with continuo. Here the ostinato

remains constant, the solo violin plays increasingly virtuosic figures, and the orchestral strings fade into the background. An abrupt change occurs in Variations 5–6: The mode changes to minor, the continuo drops out, orchestral violins take over the ground, and the soloist turns from virtuoso figures to expressive ones. The final statement of the theme serves as a triple return: Vivaldi returns both to the major mode and to the original version of the ostinato theme, last heard in Variation 4, and he recapitulates the *tutti* theme statement that began the movement. This powerful conjunction of returns serves a dual function: It resolves the tensions created by Variations 5–6 and, like the concluding ritornello of the first movement, it ends the movement on a familiar note—we've come back home again.

6. These groupings of variations superimpose a larger level of structural organization on this movement. The changes in Variations 5–6 are so striking that we perceive them as a distinct, contrasting section within the movement. As a result, it is not difficult to hear the characteristic shape of three-part form here: statement, contrast, and return. The first section—the opening theme statement and Variations 1–4—relies on statement and variation. The second section—Variations 5–6—provides a sharp contrast. The last section—the final theme statement—returns to the world of the first section. Vivaldi's superimposition of three-part form over a variation form creates a fascinating interplay of structural principles. At one stroke, he heightens the level of contrast and enlivens the listening experience, successfully combating the potential for boredom inherent in the inexorable repetition of any ostinato theme.

Conclusions to Draw about Vivaldi's Violin Concerto in G, II

1. Ground bass form is based on systematic use of the principle of variation, with its continuous juxtaposition of ostinato repetition and contrast.

2. When listening to a ground bass form, our attention is so strongly drawn to the constantly changing upper voices that we are often unaware of the shaping effect of the repeating ostinato theme. Deliberate attention to both the ground bass and the variable upper voices is necessary to grasp this form aurally.

BACH *Brandenburg* Concerto No. 5, I

This work offers another example of both the Baroque concerto and ritornello form. There are many differences between Bach and Vivaldi. Bach tends toward greater complexity, as in his frequent polyphonic textures, and he uses an ensemble of solo instruments, not just one. On the other hand, Bach's ritornello theme, with its attractive, memorable melody and rhythmic vitality, will prove much easier for students to learn and recognize than the Vivaldi ritornello. To make comparisons more obvious, follow the same steps you used to present the Vivaldi concerto.

1. Display Listening Chart 5 or write the following on the board:

First Large Section

Ritornello 1	Solo	Rit. 2	Solo	Rit. 3	Solo	Rit. 4	Solo	Rit. 5	Solo
beginning		beginning		middle		middle		middle	central
middle									solo
end									(long)

Second Large Section					*Final Section*		
Rit. 6	Solo	Rit. 7	Solo	Rit. 8	Solo		Rit. 9
beginning		beginning		middle	long		beginning
		middle			harpsichord		middle
					cadenza		end

Even if you can display the chart by other means, you may want to write this on the board. It does not replace the Listening Chart, but it allows one to grasp the whole structure visually.

2. Help students recognize each return of the ritornello. Play the three phrases of the ritornello theme until the class is familiar with the beginning of each. Then play the recording of the complete ritornello theme and ask students to describe its character. As in Vivaldi's ritornello, the rhythms and contour are complex, phrase lengths are irregular, and notes cover a wide range. Note also the homophonic texture and the orchestral timbre.

3. Play the first forty-five seconds of the movement (ritornello theme and first solo excursion). Ask students to describe the contrasts they hear between ritornello and solo. Point out the delightful polyphonic exchange between soloists and the contrast in weight between solo instruments and full orchestra.

4. Through his handling of the ritornello theme, Bach divides the movement into three large sections. He defines these sections in two ways:

   a. Each large section begins with the first phrase of the ritornello theme. It is natural for the listener to identify these statements as important.

   b. These ritornello statements are preceded by extra-long solo passages that heighten anticipation of the ritornello's return.

5. Call attention to the fact that the ritornello theme, as in Vivaldi's concerto, rarely returns in its entirety but is used as a "quick reminder."

6. Although virtuosic solo cadenzas were commonplace in late eighteenth- and nineteenth-century concertos, the length of the extensive harpsichord cadenza just before the end was unusual in 1721.

7. Play the entire movement. Point to each section on the Listening Chart display or the board as it occurs.

Conclusions to Draw about Bach's Concerto No. 5, I

1. Bach's mastery of instrumental form is demonstrated by his ability to successfully extend a single movement to the length of ten minutes.

2. Bach's concerto operates at a more sophisticated level of structural intricacy and compositional technique than does Vivaldi's concerto.

Conclusions to Draw about the Baroque Concerto

1. The concerto was the most significant multimovement Baroque orchestral work. It often included parts for one or more solo instruments.

2. The typical Baroque concerto contains three movements in a fast–slow–fast sequence.

3. The principle of contrast functions on several levels in a concerto. Large-scale contrasts occur between movements, which usually differ in tempo, key

or mode, form, and overall mood. Contrast also plays a prominent role in the ritornello-form movements that begin and often end a concerto.

4. The principle of return also functions on different levels. At the largest level, the final movement of a concerto often returns to the same tempo (and sometimes the same form) as the first movement. At a lower level, frequent returns abound in the ubiquitous ritornello-form movements.

The Court Orchestra of Japan

Since the *Brandenburg* Concerto and *Etenraku,* both orchestral works, create extended forms using the principles of repetition, contrast, and return, this is an ideal place to introduce the Japanese *togaku* tradition. See the lecture suggestions in Global Perspectives from Chapter 13 for ideas to use in presenting this work.

♪ Fugue

Fugue is the most significant and surely the single most representative musical *procedure* to emerge from the Baroque period, for it epitomizes the Baroque genius for systematic organization, symmetry, and polyphonic manipulation.

Please note the italicized word above: "procedure." Although the fugue must be considered a musical form, it does not contain the predictable sections, repeats, returns, and variations found in other forms. The fugue is not a fixed form but a flexible polyphonic procedure. Because of the fugue's complex texture and its often-maddening flexibility, students frequently have trouble identifying the features of this form. Therefore, help your students do two things as your present this fugue to your class: (1) focus on the exposition, and (2) memorize the subject. The exposition stands as the most characteristic, identifiable part of the fugue—this makes it the easiest part to hear. Memorization remains the surest way to recognize each subject entry, especially once students get beyond the exposition. (See Listening Idea 4 in this chapter's Additional Teaching Suggestions for exercises in recognizing fugal expositions.)

BACH *The Art of Fugue,* Contrapunctus 4

A certain hushed awe surrounds this late compendium by Bach. Even in its unfinished state, *The Art of Fugue* stands as the composer's final summation of the form and its myriad possibilities. As if to drive home the point, Bach bases every work in this collection on exactly the same subject, subjecting this theme to every learned technique available, including ornamentation, augmentation, diminution, and inversion. (If you would like to present more of *The Art of Fugue* to your class, try Listening Idea 8 in Additional Teaching Suggestions below.) One of the "simple" fugues in this collection, Contrapunctus 4 serves as a useful introduction to the fugal art. Bach's organ and keyboard fugues can prove quite difficult for novices to follow, but the *Listen* recording of Robert Simpson's string quartet arrangement should make it easier to keep track of individual voices. Preparation for this presentation will go more smoothly if you can find a score to study.

Fugue Subject

1. Stated simply, a fugue is a composition built from a single theme—the fugue subject—and founded on the principle of systematized imitative polyphony.

2. At the keyboard, play the subject (mm. 1–4) of the Bach fugue for the class.

Ask students to describe the character of the melody. Play it often enough that students can recognize it easily. The slow initial rhythm and the melodic contour, with its distinctive arpeggio, scale, and neighbor figures, ensure that subject entries will be easily heard through the continuous polyphonic texture. Since there are variant versions of the subject, take time to play through the answer in mm. 5–8 and the expanded version as well.

Exposition

1. In the first section of a fugue—the exposition—the fugal voices take turns announcing the subject in imitation until all voices have joined in. It creates a cumulative effect; one voice starts and others join one by one until all voices are heard simultaneously. Remind students of the round they heard in the review above, where each voice entered independently with the same tune until all voices had joined in. Point out that the exposition is similar to a round, but once a voice has finished stating the subject, it is free to continue with its own melody, in free counterpoint. Play just the exposition of the Bach fugue several times, until students can hear these features.

2. The subject entries from the exposition of this Bach fugue are easy to follow, since they move from high to low. Put the following diagram on the board.

Soprano (Violin 1)	SUBJECT – – – – – – – – – – – – – – – – – –
Alto (Violin 2)	SUBJECT – – – – – – – – – – – – – –
Tenor (Viola)	SUBJECT – – – – – – – – –
Bass (Cello)	SUBJECT

SUBJECT represents fugue subject entrances. Dashes indicate free material in each voice after the subject has been stated. The exposition is over when the last voice to enter finishes stating the fugue subject. Play the exposition again.

Episodes and Subject Entries

After the exposition, Bach follows standard fugal procedure by restating the subject in various keys and modes. Subject entries can appear singly or in clusters; in this fugue, Bach clusters two to four entries at a time, usually heard one after another. These subject-entry clusters are separated from one another by episodes—modulatory passages built on motivic materials drawn from the subject. Use the keyboard to play through motives from one or more episodes for your students, especially to show the derivation of these ideas from the subject itself. One of the most remarkable features of a well-constructed fugue is its melodic economy—virtually every figure and motive derives in some way from the subject.

Now is a good place to work in some of the terms from the "Fugues, Free and Learned" box on textbook page 145, especially *inversion*, *diminution*, and *stretto*. If at all possible, play these lines at the keyboard. For inversion you need look no further than mm. 4–5 in the top voice, which presents a figure and its inversion back-to-back. Diminution can be a bit trickier, but check out the bass line in mm. 23–26 (in episode 1). These arpeggio figures clearly relate to notes 2–4 of the subject itself, but they move down rather than up (another example of inversion), and they move twice as fast—that's diminution! Stretto appears twice toward the end of this fugue. These examples give us unusually close stretto entrances, just one beat apart. The first stretto appears in mm. 107–110 (at track 7, 1:12), where tenor and bass state the subject; the second appears in mm. 111–15 (at track 7, 1:18), in the alto and soprano voices.

Just before you play the fugue, ask students to listen for contrasts between the sections outlined in Listening Chart 6—that is, between episodes and subject entry clusters. Play the fugue in its entirety. Using the Listening Chart display or the board, point out the sections as they go by. It also helps to sing or play along with the recording, but in this case playing requires transposition—Simpson's arrangement takes this fugue up a fourth. After listening, ask students if they could hear clear differences between the sections of the fugue. Chances are they had trouble telling one section from another. If you taught them the subject well (and played or sang it along with the recording), many will at least notice its presence or absence, and some may even notice typical features of the episodes: their instability and the intensifying effect of their sequences.

Conclusions to Draw about Fugue

1. The exposition of the fugue is fairly easy to perceive, owing to its cumulative texture.

2. This is important! Keeping track of the various subject entries and episodes is more difficult; the music seems to "wash together" in a steady stream of polyphony and rhythmic momentum. Sections look distinct on a Listening Chart, but we experience fugues as seamless entities, with voices and sections constantly overlapping. Further, the fugue composer's desire to build an entire work from a single melody means that motives from the subject must permeate every section of the work. In fact, this is a hallmark of good polyphonic writing. Point out that because of the continuous flow and motivic continuity, it is difficult to introduce anything more than subtle contrasts within a fugue. *Sharp contrasts in polyphonic compositions generally come between movements, not within them.* Tell students that repeated listening offers the best means of hearing the subtle contrasts between sections of this fugue, including the handful of strong cadences, the changing keys and modes of subject entries, and the stability of subject entries versus the instability of episodes.

3. The systematic treatment of the subject and the unrelenting energy of polyphonic presentation are typical of Baroque compositional thoroughness and rhythmic regularity. In its thorough examination of a single musical thought from many different perspectives, fugue is the most rigorous and "scientific" of all Baroque forms. As such, the fugue became the true test of a late Baroque composer's skill.

❦ The Dance Suite

The Baroque dance suite stands as one of the first multimovement instrumental genres. With the suite, composers learned techniques of combining short dances, often inconsequential by themselves, into a significant large-scale instrumental work. As we saw with Frescobaldi, even the earliest suites demonstrate judicious, effective use of contrast between dances, and some even use recurring headmotives (cf. Schein's *Banchetto musicale*—see Sound Recordings below) or bass lines (as in the Frescobaldi suite) to unify the work. Suites further exhibit the stylization of dances that began during the Renaissance. Stylized dances—compositions based on dance rhythms but intended more for listening than dancing—reached a high state of development during the Baroque. Collections of Baroque dances for keyboard or lute were called "partitas" or "suites"; dance collections scored for orchestra were called "orchestral suites." These stylized dances differ from other Baroque instrumental music in their clearly defined, steady rhythms; their light, often homophonic, texture; and their simple forms (most often binary), based on the principles of repetition and contrast.

BACH Air, Orchestral Suite No. 3 in D

Bach's famous air is not a dance, but it does follow the form of almost all Baroque dances—a simple two-part form in which each part is repeated. Play the piece and ask the class to listen for the repeats.

$$|: a :||: b :|$$

As the class listens, have them follow the authors' annotations of the melody on textbook page 152. The melody provides a prime example of Baroque irregularity. After hearing the air, ask students whether they heard a sharp contrast between the **a** and **b** sections. This is a good time to remind them that the contrast may be subtle in two-part form; sometimes only one musical element will change.

BACH Gavotte, Orchestral Suite No. 3 in D

Short dances, such as minuets or gavottes, were frequently paired and played back-to-back, with the first dance returning after the second. This resulted in a large-scale **A B A** form. To create contrast with the first dance (**A**), the second dance (**B**) was typically scored for only a few instruments and continuo. As a result, the second dance came to be known as the "trio."

Bach's gavotte follows this practice, and can be mapped as follows:

GAVOTTE	TRIO	GAVOTTE
A	**B**	**A**
|: a :||: b :|	|: c :||: d :|	|: a :||: b :|

Put the map on the board and point to it as the class listens. Before listening, play a few measures each of the gavotte's **a** and **b** themes. Point out the upbeat motive, Bach's use of inversion, the stately tempo, the dancelike sprung rhythms, and other similarities. After they hear the piece, ask the students to describe the contrasts between gavotte and trio. This list will be much longer than the list of contrasts between **a** and **b** themes of the gavotte (or the air above). Make sure the class understands that within each two-part dance, whether air, gavotte, or trio, similarities outweigh contrasts; but contrasts between dances in a larger three-part form are often striking and obvious. The air, gavotte, and trio offer a good opportunity to review the concept of inner versus outer form from Chapter 4.

Conclusions to Draw about Baroque Dance Suites

1. A variety of contrasting dances are often grouped together in large works called suites.

2. These dances employ short forms based on subtly contrasted short sections that repeat. Greater length and contrast are achieved by pairing like dances, as in the gavotte and trio.

3. Stylized or not, dance music depends on clearly heard melodies, uncomplicated textures, and sharply defined rhythms that support the dance steps.

Additional Teaching Suggestions

❦ Lecture-Demonstration Ideas

1. To introduce Baroque instrumental forms, review repetition, imitation, return, variation, and contrast; discuss their role in musical form (see Lecture Suggestions above).

2. If you have a dramatic flair, find a wig and impersonate Johann Sebastian Bach; talk about "yourself" and "your" music. Whether you do this or not, Bach letters and documents in David and Mendel's *Bach Reader* (rev. ed., New York: Norton, 1966) provide fascinating information you can share with your class, including salary receipts (pp. 62–63) and anecdotes of disagreements (pp. 137–49), fights (p. 51), and "jail" terms (p. 75). At the very least, read the letter Bach sent with his *Brandenburg* Concertos (pp. 82–83).

3. If you use Listening Idea 1 below, invite an organist to talk to your class about his or her experience with Bach's organ music and to describe how a pipe organ works. If possible, take your students to visit a real pipe organ nearby and have your guest demonstrate and play the instrument for your class. Just as in the Baroque era, the organ remains one of the most complex, fascinating instruments ever made.

4. "Write" a fugue in class as an alternative way to present the features of the fugue. If you can compose in the style, dare any student to offer you a tune, and use it as the subject of a fugue. If you are not a composer or are short on time, you can reproduce the same demonstration by taking a preexisting fugue and talking about it as if you were composing it on the spot. Once you have a subject, begin "writing" the main sections of the fugue (exposition, a later subject entry, and an episode to connect the two will do—you don't have to finish the fugue). At each point, introduce important terms as you talk about your compositional process. Keep the emphasis on listening, not on notation.

5. When studying and listening to Baroque dance music, invite a dancer to demonstrate dance steps for common Baroque dances. These dances take on new meaning when students can see for themselves the relationship between physical dance steps and the characteristic rhythms and tempi of dance music.

6. Invite a Baroque trumpet player to class (valveless trumpet, if possible). The art of playing in the high clarino register demands extraordinary skill and control. Cultivated in the Baroque period, this art was abandoned in the Classical period. Not until the last half of the nineteenth century did trumpeters and composers once again explore the trumpet's higher register. High trumpet parts were a hallmark of festive Baroque orchestral music. Your guest can offer insights into the technical problems of playing so high, the limitations imposed by the overtones of a tube of fixed length, and the music Baroque composers wrote for trumpet. Trumpeters love to tell the story of the player in Bach's orchestra who "blew his brains out"—the physical exertion from playing such high notes ruptured an aneurysm and the poor man died of a stroke.

❦ Class Discussion Ideas

1. *What was it like to be a composer or musician living and working in the early eighteenth century?* Prepare by assigning readings from *Listen* (Bach and Vivaldi biographies) or David and Mendel's *Bach Reader* (contracts and "salary" receipts) or by showing *J. S. Bach: A Documentary Portrait* (see Video Recordings below).

2. *How do large-scale works of the Baroque differ from those of the Renaissance?* Assign readings from the textbook on the Renaissance Mass and the concerto. Class discussion can focus on the purpose each genre served, the reasons for multiple movements and the relationships between them, or musical characteristics of each work. *What does this say about the difference between the Renaissance and the Baroque eras?*

3. *What effect did the main currents of the Baroque era—absolutism, science, and theatricality—have on music?* This question is useful in a review of Baroque music, as students reread Chapters 8 and 9. Following discussion of these currents, replay works like Vivaldi's Concerto in G or Bach's *Brandenburg* Concerto No. 5 and ask which characteristics students can hear in these works.

❦ Listening Ideas

1. Bring a recording of one of Bach's famous organ works to class. Many instructors feel they haven't done justice to Bach without covering at least one example of his virtuoso organ music. Obvious examples that also permit review of the fugue include the Toccata and Fugue in D Minor (compare an organ performance with Stokowski's orchestral transcription on the *Fantasia* video) or the Passacaglia and Fugue in C Minor (see Further Listening Examples below).

2. Introduce the class to the "Doctrine of Affections." The authors describe the Baroque composer's interest in depicting a different affect in each piece (textbook page 130). Johann Mattheson's *Der vollkommene Kapellmeister* of 1739 (Ann Arbor: UMI Research Press, 1981, pt. 2, chap. 13, secs. 79–142) describes the expected affect for a variety of dances and instrumental genres. Read aloud some excerpts from Mattheson that describe the genre your class is studying. Ask students if the affect of the musical work matches Mattheson's description. What elements create the affect?

3. P.D.Q. Bach recordings keep things from getting too deadly serious, and they provide clear, concise examples of forms from this chapter. The ground

from the cantata *Iphigenia in Brooklyn* serves as an example of ground bass form. The Fugue in C Minor (*Fuga vulgaris*) for calliope four hands from the *Toot Suite* makes a wonderful review of fugue. The "Song of the Volga Boatmen" is its subject, and exposition, episodes, and subject entries are easy to recognize (it even uses augmentation and stretto!). P.D.Q. Bach examples work best as review—the gags are funnier when students understand the clichés he spoofs.

4. Have students listen to a variety of fugal expositions when you teach fugue. The exposition is the first, most recognizable section of a fugue, and students can recognize fugal expositions with practice. Teach students to map out the entrances as they hear them—this also gives them practice identifying instruments and registers (high, middle, low). Look up "exposition (fugal)" in the *Index of Terms and Musical Examples* (Appendix III) to find recordings of expositions in the *Listen* anthology. Other recordings are readily available for Bach's *Brandenburg* Concerto No. 3, III; Bach's "Little" Fugue in G Minor for organ; Bach's Fugue No. 2 in C Minor from *The Well-Tempered Clavier,* Book I; Stravinsky's *Symphony of Psalms*, II; Bartók's *Music for Strings, Percussion, and Celesta*, I; and the "Shark Cage Fugue" from the movie *JAWS*. See Sound Recordings below for suggested performances of these works.

5. Compare two or more recorded performances of an appropriate work by Bach (such as *Brandenburg* Concerto No. 3)—one might use modern instruments, another original instruments, yet another a synthesizer (*Switched-On Bach*), and another voices (Swingle Singers). This exercise leads naturally into a discussion of performance practice and the durability of Bach's music. See Sound Recordings below for suggested CDs or use the *All That Bach* video described in Video Recordings below.

6. Compare the gavotte from Bach's Orchestral Suite No. 3 with the Renaissance galliard "Daphne" (both in the *Listen* anthology). Ask students to listen especially for melody, rhythm, texture, and timbre. Follow with discussion of characteristics of dance music and differences between Renaissance and Baroque styles.

7. Listen to the most popular example of ground bass (ostinato) variation form—Pachelbel's Canon in D. Many students already know and enjoy this work, but few have noticed either the canon (imitation) or the ground bass. Awareness of these features in a familiar work comes as a pleasant surprise. See Sound Recordings below for suggested performances.

8. Introduce your students to more fugues from Bach's *The Art of Fugue*. Contrapunctus 4 is one of the simple fugues in this collection, which also includes canons, double and triple fugues, mirror fugues, and even a quadruple fugue. The most remarkable feature of this collection is that every fugue is based on the same subject. You don't have to look far for good examples of the techniques of learned fugues, inversion, augmentation, diminution, and the like. For an especially good example of inversion—right in the exposition—try Contrapunctus 5. And for augmentation, the exposition of Contrapunctus 7 answers the subject first at half speed, then at quarter speed. Also of interest is the final incomplete contrapunctus, perhaps one of his last works, in which Bach musically signs his name with the pitches B flat, A, C, B (in the German musical alphabet, B equals our B flat and H our B natural). We first hear this motive at m. 193 (at 6:50 on the Delmé Quartet CD) as the subject for a fugal exposition, and we last hear it at m. 235, just moments before this incomplete work trails off into nothingness—a poignant moment if ever there was one. See Sound Recordings below for suggested performances.

❧ Further Listening Examples

BACH **Passacaglia, from Passacaglia and Fugue in C Minor**

Bach's monumental Passacaglia in C Minor for Organ (c. 1715) provides a marvelous introduction to his organ music. See Appendix I for a Listening Chart, and Sound Recordings below for suggested CDs.

The pipe organ was one of the most elaborate machines produced in the Baroque era, the equal of anything produced for industry or commerce in the late seventeenth century. Does one need further proof of the significance of instrumental music in the Baroque period? Begin by describing the organ's prominent features: keyboards, pedals, stops, and pipes.

Passacaglia is another name for a ground bass (ostinato) variation-form movement. In a passacaglia, a bass line—the ground bass, theme, or ostinato—is systematically repeated while the polyphonic voices above it weave ever-new lines about each other.

In Bach's passacaglia, an eight-measure ground bass theme is initially stated alone and then followed by twenty variations. During the course of the variations, the theme appears in various guises, but it is always recognizable. The free polyphonic voices above the theme are in a constant state of change.

1. Photocopy and display a transparency of the Listening Chart for the passacaglia (see Appendix I) or write "theme" on the board and the numbers 1–20.

2. Notate the ground bass theme on the board, above or below the numbers 1–20.

3. Play the ground bass theme at the keyboard or sing the theme while pointing to specific pitches on the board. Repeat until the class is familiar with the theme.

4. Before listening, point out the grouping of variations on the Listening Chart. In Variations 1–10, the theme remains in the bass and is fairly easy to hear; in Variations 11–13, the theme moves to the top voice; and in Variations 14–15, the theme is partially hidden. Variations 16–20 are recapitulatory, with the theme clearly heard in the bass.

5. Play the entire recording. Indicate each successive variation by pointing to the appropriate number on the Listening Chart display or the board. While each variation plays, alternate between pointing to each note of the theme on the board as it is heard and singing or playing the ground bass theme along with the recording. Singing or playing along is especially helpful where the theme is partially hidden, as in Variations 14–15.

Conclusions to Draw about Bach's Passacaglia in C Minor for Organ

1. Passacaglia form, like ground bass form, is based on systematic use of the principle of variation, with its continuous juxtaposition of repetition and contrast.

2. When listening to a passacaglia, our attention is so strongly drawn to the constantly changing upper voices that we are often unaware of the repetitious ground bass theme. Deliberate attention to both the repeating theme *and* the

variable upper voices (what Kerman and Tomlinson call "double listening") is necessary to come to grips with passacaglia form.

3. In Bach's hands, the passacaglia becomes a monumental form for musical expression.

BACH Fugue, from Passacaglia and Fugue in C Minor

This Bach fugue is longer and more complex than the textbook's example from *The Art of Fugue.* It offers insights into the variety and complexity possible in Baroque fugues, yet it uses the same basic procedures found in Bach's Contrapunctus 4. If you want to introduce the concept of countersubject to your students, this fugue provides an excellent example.

Fugue Subject and Countersubject

1. At the keyboard, play the subject of Bach's fugue. After hearing the passacaglia, students should find the fugue subject quite familiar, but point out that the subject is half the length of the passacaglia theme.

2. This fugue differs from Bach's Contrapunctus 4 in its use of a countersubject—a short melodic line written to be heard against the subject. Play the countersubject by itself. Ask students to describe its character and compare it with the subject. Then play subject and countersubject together. Ask students to describe the effect. Explain how the rhythm and articulation of one theme complement those of the other.

Exposition

1. This exposition uses successive imitative entries just as the fugue from *The Well-Tempered Clavier* did, but use the Listening Chart display or board to highlight the different order in which voices enter. On the board, copy just the subject entries from the diagram of the exposition given below. Play the exposition and ask students to listen only for the four subject entries.

Highest (soprano)		SUBJECT		
High (alto)	SUBJECT			
Middle (tenor)				SUBJECT
Pedals (bass)			SUBJECT	

2. The countersubject adds a new wrinkle. On the board, finish copying the diagram below. Point out the countersubject entries and the thicker texture that results. Play the exposition again and ask students to listen for the interplay of subject and countersubject as voices are added. Point to each on the diagram as it is played.

3. Here is a diagram of subject and countersubject entries in the exposition of the fugue from the Passacaglia and Fugue in C Minor.

Highest (soprano)	SUBJECT- - - Countersubject-------------------
High (alto)	SUBJECT - - - Countersubject------------------------------------
Middle (tenor)	Countersubject---SUBJECT
Pedals (bass)	SUBJECT - - - - - - Countersubject

The subject and countersubject are labeled; dashes indicate free material after the subject or countersubject has been stated. Although it is important to hear the effect of the countersubject, main emphasis must be placed on recognizing the subject each time it is stated.

Episodes and Subject Entries

Just as he does in *The Art of Fugue,* Bach restates the subject in various keys and modes after the exposition is over. Again, these subject entries are separated from one another by brief modulatory episodes. The fullness of the organ's timbre and the length of this fugue make it difficult to follow subject entries and episodes in this work. Learn the work in advance (find a score, if possible) and use a photo-copied transparency of the Listening Chart (see Appendix I) to point out each subject entry just before it is played; otherwise, the students will not hear half of them. It also helps to sing or play along with the subject each time it enters.

Conclusions to Draw about Bach's Fugue in C Minor for Organ

1. The larger number of subject entries and episodes makes this a longer, more complex fugue than the one from *The Art of Fugue,* though the structural elements are similar. The length of this fugue demonstrates the control late Baroque composers achieved in using and extending instrumental forms.

2. This fugue blends the "scientific" side of the Baroque approach to music with the equally prevalent Baroque extravagance. The virtuosity (and occasional theatricality) of Bach's writing and his mastery of the organ and its sonic capabilities are apparent in both the passacaglia and the fugue.

BACH Fugue in C-sharp Major, from *The Well-Tempered Clavier,* Book I

This fugue, reasonably short and clear, provides another example of a fugue with countersubject, this time for keyboard (see Sound Recordings below for both piano and harpsichord renditions). This presentation will go more smoothly if you study a score in advance and photocopy a transparency of the Listening Chart in Appendix I. (For ease of reading and playing, the music has been transposed down a half step into C major.)

Fugue Subject

At the keyboard, play the subject of the fugue for the class.

Ask students to describe the character of the melody. Play it often enough that students can recognize it easily. The rhythmic profile and the melodic contour, with its distinctive turns and leaps, ensure that subject entries will be easily heard through the continuous polyphonic texture.

Exposition

1. The subject entries from the exposition of this Bach fugue are easy to follow, since they move from high to low. Put the following diagram on the board.

High (Soprano)	SUBJECT —
Middle (Tenor)	SUBJECT — — — — — — — — — — — — — — —
Low (Bass)	SUBJECT

SUBJECT represents fugue subject entrances. Dashes indicate free material in each voice after the subject has been stated. The exposition is over when the last voice to enter finishes stating the fugue subject. Play the exposition so students can hear these entries.

2. Sophisticated listeners will take greater pleasure in this fugue if they know both the subject and the countersubject well. If you have time and confidence in your students, by all means take time to learn the countersubject; the Listening Chart from Appendix I provides a good guide to the locations of countersubject entries.

Episodes and Subject Entries

After the exposition, Bach follows standard fugal procedure. He restates the subject in various keys and modes, and his subject entries are separated from one another by shorter and longer episodes. In this fugue, motives drawn from both the subject and the countersubject are used to construct episodes.

Just before you play the fugue, display the Listening Chart from Appendix I and point out the sections of this fugue. Ask students to listen for these sections, and then play the fugue in its entirety. As the music plays, point to each section on the Listening Chart display as it goes by.

BACH Ouverture, Orchestral Suite No. 3 in D

The overture to this orchestral dance suite (described in *Listen* but not provided as a recording—see Sound Recordings below for suggested performances) offers an excellent example of the French overture that was so influential from the time of Lully onward. Played by the famed *Vingt-quatre violons du Roy*, this standard opening for Lully's lyric tragedies (French opera) probably accompanied the entrance of King Louis XIV (the "Sun King") into the theater. Composers all over Europe began to use a French overture, associated with the power and authority of Europe's most powerful monarchy, to begin instrumental works as well as opera. Examples include Purcell's *Dido and Aeneas*, Handel's *Julius Caesar* (among many other operas) and *Messiah*, Couperin's dance suites, Corelli's trio sonatas, and Bach's orchestral suites. Perhaps the most striking example comes from Bach's Cantata 61, "Nun komm, der Heiden Heiland," where Bach writes his opening chorus (labeled *Ouverture*) in the manner of a French overture. This cantata was written for the first Sunday of Advent, which is also the first Sunday of the church year. In this context, Bach's overture heralded the entrance of the King of Kings, as Bach understood it—one of many musical symbols that permeate Bach's sacred music.

The musical features of the French overture are easy to follow. These binary-form movements divide into two vividly contrasted sections. As you present this work, help your students hear these contrasts. The first section is a slow, serious, stately processional that uses homophonic (nearly chordal) texture and duple meter. Perhaps the overture's most characteristic feature, its sharply dotted rhythms emphasize the beat quite clearly. Louis XIV was a stickler for precision, and the uniformly short upbeats provide just enough warning to allow you to snap your foot down exactly on the beat. The second section does a complete about-face. Suddenly we move at a quick, lively tempo in a triple or compound meter (though Bach uses a fast duple meter here). Before, everyone attacked the beat together; now every part goes its own way in a busy, imitative polyphonic texture. It's hard to miss the contrasts between these two sections. In many French overtures, this one included, the very end of the second section briefly returns to the sound, tempo, and texture of the opening section.

Like the dances in this suite, this overture uses binary form with the normal repeats, but nowhere else in this suite do we hear such sharp contrasts between **a** and **b** sections. These two sound worlds could hardly be more different. Together they create a grand, imposing beginning for any work. As was typical of late Baroque composers, Bach adds to the impact in several ways. He uses the festive Baroque orchestra, replete with trumpets and timpani. He gives the texture a richer, more polyphonic flavor, especially in the more homophonic first section. He expands and lengthens both sections to create a more monumental structure. In every way, Bach envisions this work on a much grander scale than was typical of Lully's overtures.

BACH Bourrée, Orchestral Suite No. 3 in D

This short bourrée (described in *Listen* but not provided as a recording—see Sound Recordings below for suggested performances) offers another example of a Baroque dance. It exhibits the features the authors list in their chart of dance types on textbook page 148. Ask students to listen for the short, two-note upbeat figure, duple meter, and quick tempo. The two-part form is exactly the same as for other Baroque dances found in the Sixth Edition.

Multimedia Resources

⁊ Further Listening Charts and Texts

See Appendix I for Listening Charts for these works:

Bach, Passacaglia, from Passacaglia and Fugue in C Minor for organ

Bach, Fugue, from Passacaglia and Fugue in C Minor for organ

Bach, Fugue in C-sharp Major, from *The Well-Tempered Clavier,* Book I

⁊ Sound Recordings

Bach, *The Art of Fugue.* Delmé Quartet. Hyperion CDA67138 (CD). The first fourteen contrapuncti from Bach's late compendium, arranged for string quartet by composer Robert Simpson. This version can make it easier for students to follow each line, and the *Listen* recording of Contrapunctus 4 was taken from this album. Try this CD if you use Listening Idea 8 above.

Bach, *Complete Toccatas and Fugues*. David Schrader. Cedille Records CDR 90000 006 (CD). The first recording to feature all of Bach's toccatas and fugues on one CD; performed on a Jaeckel organ. Try this recording if you use Listening Idea 1. Available at http://www.cedillerecords.org/.

Bach, *Great Organ Works*. Peter Hurford. London 443485-2 (CD). Hurford was instrumental in establishing a more energetic, vital approach to Bach's organ music. Available at a bargain price, this impressive collection of famous pieces includes Toccata and Fugue in D Minor (BWV 565) and Passacaglia and Fugue in C Minor (BWV 582). Try this recording if you use Listening Idea 1 or 5 or suggestions for the Passacaglia and Fugue in C Minor in Further Listening Examples above.

Bach Hits Back/A Cappella Amadeus. The Swingle Singers. Virgin Classics 5 61472 2 (CD). Classic jazz vocal performances of well-known works by Bach and Mozart, including Bach's Air from Suite No. 3, Cantata 140, and *Brandenburg* Concerto No. 3. Try this recording if you use Listening Idea 5 above.

Bach, *Les Quatre Ouvertures*. Le Concert des Nations/La Capella Reial de Catalunya. Astrée E 9958 (CD). Complete recordings of the four orchestral suites on period instruments; conducted by Jordi Savall. Use the recording of Orchestral Suite No. 3 in D to demonstrate a French overture, to introduce the variety of dances in a late Baroque dance suite, or if you use suggestions in Further Listening Examples above for the ouverture or the bourrée.

Bach, *Les Six Concerts Brandebourgeois*. Le Concert des Nations/Capella Reial de Catalunya. Auvidis Astrée 9948 (CD). The *Brandenburg* recording used in the *Listen* set. This set includes all six concertos on period instruments; conducted by Jordi Savall. Useful if you want to present a complete *Brandenburg* Concerto or to demonstrate the typical contrasts between concerto movements. Use this recording if you try Listening Idea 4 or 5 above.

Bach, *Switched-On Bach*. Wendy Carlos. East Side Records ESD 81602 (CD). A best-selling album from the late 1960s reissued on CD with a track of commentary by Carlos. Contains performances of Bach's Air from Suite No. 3, *Brandenburg* Concerto No. 3, "Jesu, Joy of Man's Desiring," preludes and fugues from *The Well-Tempered Clavier*, Book I, and other works. Vol. 2 of the *Switched-On Bach* series (ESD 81622) contains Bach's *Brandenburg* Concerto No. 5. Telarc issued a millennium edition—*Switched-On Bach 2000* (Telarc CD 80323). Here Carlos does new performances of the same works, but using digital synthesis and a Bach tuning (not equal temperament). Try these recordings if you use Listening Idea 4 or 5 above.

Bach, *Das Wohltemperierte Klavier, Book I*. Masaaki Suzuki. BIS CD–813/814 (CD). The complete Book I beautifully played on a gorgeous Kroesbergen harpsichord. Highly recommended. Try this recording if you use Listening Idea 4 or suggestions for the Fugue in C-sharp Major in Further Listening Examples above.

P.D.Q. Bach, *The Wurst of PDQ Bach*. Peter Schickele and friends. Vanguard VCD2-719/20 (CD). A collection of P.D.Q. Bach favorites. Contains the cantata *Iphigenia in Brooklyn*, Fugue in C Minor from the Toot Suite, *New Horizons in Music Appreciation*, and more. Try this recording if you use Listening Idea 3 above.

Bartók, *Concerto for Orchestra: Music for Strings, Percussion, and Celesta*. Chicago Symphony Orchestra. RCA Victor 61504 (CD). Vividly atmospheric, superbly recorded performances of Bartók's music; conducted by Fritz Reiner. Try this recording if you use Listening Idea 4 above.

Handel, *Water Music; Music for the Royal Fireworks*. London Classical Players. Virgin Veritas CDC 545265 (CD). Roger Norrington leads attractive, buoyant period performances of these famous Handel suites for a festive Baroque orchestra. Use this recording to introduce students to a range of Baroque dance types in an idiom that contrasts with Bach's dance works.

Jazz Sebastian Bach, Vols. 1 and 2. The Swingle Singers. Philips 4542552 and 4542553 (CD). Jazz vocal performances of well-known Bach works. Vol. 1 even includes a fugue from *The Art of Fugue*. Try this recording if you use Listening Idea 5 above.

The Pachelbel Canon. Paillard Chamber Orchestra. RCA Red Seal 65468-2-RC (CD). Pachelbel's Canon was made famous by this recording when it was issued in the United States c. 1970 by the Musical Heritage Society; conducted by Jean-François Paillard. I prefer a period-instrument performance, but it's hard to argue with success when dealing with nonmusicians. Try this recording if you use Listening Idea 7 above.

Schein, *Banchetto musicale,* from *Dance Music of the High Renaissance*. Collegium Terpsichore. Boston Skyline BSD 118 (CD). This CD features dance works of the late Renaissance and early Baroque by Praetorius, Widmann, Schein, Gervaise, and others; directed by Fritz Neumeyer. Such rich "orchestration" of early instruments may not be totally authentic, but these delightful, engaging performances continue to see regular airplay on classical radio stations thirty-five years after they were recorded. Schein's musical banquet offers a feast of early dance suites, as well as early examples of cyclic unity in instrumental music. This recording is recommended for use with Lecture Suggestions on "The Dance Suite" above.

Stravinsky Conducts Stravinsky. CBC Symphony Orchestra and Columbia Symphony Orchestra. CBS Masterworks MK 42434 (CD). Definitive performances of Symphony in Three Movements, Symphony in C, and *Symphony of Psalms;* conducted by the composer. Try this recording if you use Listening Idea 4 above.

Vivaldi, *Il cimento dell'armonia e dell'inventione*. Europa Galante. Virgin Veritas 5 45465 2 (CD). By far the most exciting new recording of *Four Seasons* in recent memory. Using the composer's own manuscript scores, violinist Fabio Biondi leads energetic, driving period performances of the most popular of all Vivaldi concertos. Useful if you want to expose your students to other Vivaldi concertos and demonstrate typical features of Baroque concerto movements.

Williams, *JAWS: Anniversary Collector's Edition*. Decca 289467045 (CD). This recent release does a fine job of cleaning up the original soundtrack from the 1975 blockbuster. The eerie "Shark Cage Fugue" has more punch than ever. Try this recording if you use Listening Idea 4 above.

❦ Video Recordings

The Advent of Fashion. Music in Time Series. www.films.com (DVD or VHS, color, 60 minutes). James Galway narrates this look at the rise of public concerts and theaters. Many examples of Baroque instrumental music: Handel's *Music for the Royal Fireworks* and Concerto for Organ in D Minor, Couperin's *Deuxième Ordre,* and Telemann's Sonata in E Minor.

All That Bach. VAI (VHS, color, 50 minutes). Movie celebrated Bach's tercentennial (1985) with an eclectic mix of performances by Keith Jarrett, Maureen Forrester, the Cambridge Buskers, the Canadian Brass, Christopher Hogwood, and others. In addition to "straight" performances, Bach's music is transformed into jazz, synthesized, and even tap-dance versions. Try this video if you use Listening Idea 5 above.

Bach, *The Art of Fugue.* EuroArts (DVD, color, 70 minutes). Fine DVD recording of the Keller Quartet playing excerpts from Bach's late masterwork, interwoven with recent works by György Kurtág; as an added bonus, it includes Baroque cellist Anner Bylsma playing two Bach suites. This DVD includes Contrapunctus 4 from *Listen,* but it only includes one of the contrapuncti mentioned in Listening Idea 8 (the final one).

Bach, *Brandenburg Concertos.* EuroArts (DVD, color, 96 minutes). Excellent DVD recording of the Freiburg Baroque Orchestra performing on period instruments in the Spiegelsaal of the Castle Cöthen; led by Gottfried von der Goltz. Choose this over the newly released Richter DVD—your students need to *see* these instruments, and the added bonus of such wonderful music making in the residence of a Bach employer make this recording an invaluable adjunct to your class presentation. Use this for your presentation of the *Listen Brandenburg* movement or if you try Listening Idea 4 or 5 above.

Bach, *48 Preludes and Fugues: The Well Tempered Clavier.* EuroArts (DVD, color, 312 minutes). The complete *Well-Tempered Clavier* on DVD. World-class pianists Andrei Gavrilov, Joanna MacGregor, Nikolai Demidenko, and Angela Hewitt each take twelve preludes and fugues and perform them in locations as exotic as Venice, Barcelona, and the Wartburg in Eisenach (Bach's natal city). With four pianists to choose from, performance styles vary considerably, but that's part of this set's fascination. Highly recommended if you use Listening Idea 4 or suggestions for the Fugue in C-sharp Major in Further Listening Examples above.

Bach, *Four Bach Suites.* EuroArts (DVD, color, 85 minutes). DVD recording of the Amsterdam Baroque Orchestra performing on period instruments in the National Museum, Het Loo Palace (Apeldoorn, the Netherlands); conducted by Ton Koopman. Excellent performances by this renowned ensemble allow your students to see the instruments of the festive Baroque orchestra. Try this recording for another performance of the air or the gavotte covered in *Listen* or if you use suggestions for the ouverture and the bourrée in Further Listening Examples above.

Bach, *Greatest Organ Works,* Vols. 1 and 2. Pioneer Classics (DVD, color, 80 and 86 minutes). DVD recording Bach's organ music performed by Hans-André Stamm on the beautiful Baroque Trost organ in Waltershausen, Germany. While not as exciting to watch as Koopman's DVD above (Stamm is stiff and uninspiring), the performances are very good, and the program is more generous and varied than Koopman's. Both volumes offer a nice sampling of Bach organ works. For instance, Vol. 1 includes the Toccata and Fugue in D Minor, and the Passacaglia and Fugue in C Minor, among others. Try this recording if you use Listening Idea 1 or suggestions for the Passacaglia and Fugue in C Minor in Further Listening Examples above.

Bach, *J. S. Bach: Musical Offering in C Minor.* EuroArts (DVD, color, 53 minutes). Another late contrapuntal compendium comparable to *The Art of Fugue, Musical Offering* contains a fugue, two ricercars (one for six voices!), a set of puzzle canons, and a sonata for flute, violin, and continuo—all based on a theme given Bach by King Frederick of Prussia. Excellent period-instrument performances in Leipzig's historic Old Town Hall by Robert Kohnen and Barthold, Sigiswald, and Wieland Kuijken. It's fun to get such a good look at Wieland's viola da gamba. Highly recommended as a supplement to your coverage of *The Art of Fugue*.

Fantasia. Disney Studios (DVD, color, 120 minutes). Groundbreaking feature-length cartoon with soundtrack performed by Leopold Stokowski and the Philadelphia Orchestra. Includes Bach's Toccata and Fugue in D Minor (arranged by Stokowski) accompanied by abstract cartoon images. Musically, a curious amalgam of Baroque fantasy and fugue with Romantic performance practice. Try this recording if you use Listening Idea 1 above.

The Four Seasons: Kyoto Vivaldi. Kultur Video (VHS, color, 45 minutes). These complete performances of the four concertos by the Kyoto Ensemble work surprisingly well. Using Kyoto as the backdrop, this video superimposes a story over the music. Interesting way to introduce further examples of Baroque concertos, and also makes a fascinating comparison with the *gagaku* example from Chapter 13.

The Glenn Gould Collection: Greatest Hits. Sony Classics (VHS, color, 46 minutes). Collection of performances by the eccentric genius. Of particular interest is Gould's famous "So You Want to Write a Fugue" (also available in Vol. 4). Try this video if you use Lecture-Demonstration Idea 4 above.

The Glenn Gould Collection, Vol. 15: *An Art of the Fugue.* Sony Classics (VHS, color, 58 minutes). Features Glenn Gould discussing and playing the music of Bach. Gould was at his best with Bach, and this is perhaps the finest video in the Gould collection. He plays several fugues here, including Contrapunctus 4 (also available on Vol. 8) and two others from *The Art of Fugue* (including the unfinished final fugue). Use this video as a valuable supplement to your coverage of this fugue or if you try Listening Idea 8 above.

Handel, *Handel's Water Music.* BBC Opus Arte (DVD, color, 78 minutes). This fascinating film documents a painstaking re-creation of the original performance of Handel's best-known dance suite—on royal barges floating down the Thames! Andrew Manze leads the English Consort in this excellent period-instrument performance. As a bonus, the DVD allows the viewer to follow the river route as it looked in 1717 while listening to the music. This disc provides a useful way to introduce Baroque dances (bourrée, minuet, hornpipe, and so on) while experiencing the extravagance of the English royal court.

Johann Sebastian Bach. Harmonics: The Innovators of Classical Music Series. www.films.com (DVD or VHS, color, 27 minutes). Video survey of Bach's achievements, with musical selections from *Brandenburg* Concerto No. 1, *The Art of Fugue, The Well-Tempered Clavier,* and *St. Matthew Passion.*

J. S. Bach: A Documentary Portrait. www.films.com (DVD and VHS, color, 60 minutes). Chronological presentation of the places and documents of Bach's life.

Luther and the Reformation. Music in Time Series. www.films.com (DVD or VHS, color, 60 minutes). Music of Bach (Fugue in G Minor, Air from Orchestral Suite No. 3, and *Brandenburg* Concerto No. 3 are appropriate for this chapter), Buxtehude (Toccata and Fugue in F), and others presented in the context of the Reformation. James Galway narrates.

Musical Forms: The Fugue. www.insight-media.com (VHS, color, 19 minutes). Quick introduction to the fugue by way of Bach's Fugue in G Minor. Through live-action photography and animation, the viewer can learn to identify and diagram the structure of a fugue.

The Parts of the Suite: Baroque Music and Dance. www.insight-media.com (VHS, color, 44 minutes). A look at the world of Baroque dances, featuring costumed performances.

Ralph Kirkpatrick Plays Bach. www.films.com (DVD or VHS, color, 58 minutes). Performances by the great harpsichordist of Bach's Toccata in D, Chromatic Fantasy and Fugue, and Partita No. 5 in G. Useful for comparison with the Frescobaldi suite or if you try Listening Idea 4 above.

The Seasons and the Symphony. Music in Time Series. www.films.com (DVD or VHS, color, 60 minutes). This program offers an overview of eighteenth-century music. Beginning with Vivaldi's *The Four Seasons,* James Galway guides us through the music of the Mannheim symphonists, Gluck, and Haydn. Most useful in looking at the transition from Baroque to Classical styles.

Sounds Like Christmas. EuroArts (DVD, color, 82 minutes). This compilation offers a smattering of vocal and instrumental works in varied styles, but the real gems here are Corelli's Christmas Concerto and Vivaldi's Violin Concerto, RV 270 (*Per il S. Natale*). The outstanding period-instrument Freiburg Baroque Orchestra is led by Gottfried von der Goltz. Highly recommended if you want to present a complete Vivaldi concerto or to demonstrate the typical contrasts between concerto movements.

Ton Koopman Plays Bach. EuroArts (DVD, color, 80 minutes). DVD recording of two short Bach programs. The first features Koopman playing the spectacular Silbermann organ in Freiberg's St. Marien Church. Selections include the Toccata in D Minor (but not the fugue), the Fugue in G Minor (BWV 578), and some chorale preludes. The second program, *At Home with Bach*, features Koopman at the harpsichord playing lighter works from the notebook for Anna Magdalena Bach and other sources. Highly recommended if you use Listening Idea 1.

Venice and Vivaldi. Five Centuries of Music in Venice Series. www.films.com (DVD or VHS, color, 60 minutes). This program offers a sumptuous portrait of the history, art, and architecture of eighteenth-century Venice. Covers Vivaldi and his contemporaries. Live performances of music by Vivaldi, Albinoni, and Cimarosa in Venetian churches and conservatories.

Vivaldi. www.films.com (DVD or VHS, color, 55 minutes). Video biography directed by Lina Wertmüller. Includes music from Vivaldi concertos, opera, and sacred music. Italian with English subtitles.

Vivaldi. www.films.com (DVD or VHS, color, 105 minutes). Video biography uses actors on location to portray scenes from the composer's life. Includes music from many Vivaldi works, including *The Four Seasons*.

Vivaldi, Viva Vivaldi. Arthaus Musik (DVD, color, 106 minutes). The main attraction is Cecilia Bartoli singing Vivaldi opera arias (useful in Chapter 10), but the period-instrument orchestra on this disc, Il Giardino Armonico, is excellent in its own right, and is featured in two Vivaldi solo concertos that feature the flautino and the lute, respectively. Useful if you want to present a complete Vivaldi concerto or to demonstrate the typical contrasts between concerto movements.

❧ Software

Bach Toccata and Fugue Sketch. Time Sketch: Composer Series. ECS Media (CD-ROM—Windows or Macintosh). Program presents E. Power Biggs's CD recording of Bach's Toccata and Fugue in D Minor (and other works) with interactive arch map analysis and background information about the composer, his style, and the work. Useful if you try Listening Idea 1 above. Available at www.ecsmedia.com.

The Norton Masterworks CD-ROM. New York: W. W. Norton (CD-ROM—Macintosh). Authors Daniel Jacobson and Timothy Koozin provide a clever multimedia introduction to twelve important works, including Vivaldi's *Four Seasons* and Bach's Prelude and Fugue in C Minor from *The Well-Tempered Clavier,* Book I. For comparison, the Bach works are performed on harpsichord, clavichord, piano, and synthesizer (in a version by Wendy Carlos). Package offers animated, guided listening resources as well as information on the composers, eras, genres, and the works themselves.

CHAPTER 10

Baroque Vocal Music

Chapter Outline

Boldface indicates works in the recording set.

Important Terms

"affects"	secco recitative	oratorio	chorale prelude
coloratura	accompanied recitative	chorus	organ chorale
opera seria	aria	church cantata	
libretto, librettist	da capo (**A B A**) form	chorales	
recitative	*castrato*	gapped chorale	

Teaching Objectives

❼ Overall Objectives

This chapter will help students acquire familiarity with:

1. Baroque vocal music as the expression of strong emotions, or "affects."

2. Significant Baroque vocal genres:

opera seria	church cantata
oratorio	organ chorale

3. Baroque vocal forms and techniques, especially secco and accompanied recitative, da capo aria, chorus, chorale, and chorale prelude.

4. The life and music of George Frideric Handel.

❦ Listening Objectives

After completing this chapter, students should be able to:

1. Hear and identify how the elements of music are typically used to express strong emotions in Baroque vocal music.

2. Follow the genres of Baroque vocal music, especially opera seria, oratorio, church cantata, and organ chorale.

3. Follow the forms and techniques of Baroque vocal music, especially secco and accompanied recitative, da capo aria, chorus, chorale, and chorale prelude.

Lecture Suggestions

Sacred and secular vocal music, for solo voice or chorus, formed a major part of the output of virtually all Baroque composers. Chapter 8 provided opportunities for comparison between Baroque music and Renaissance music. In Chapter 10, emphasis can be placed on either the genres, forms, and techniques found in individual works or on the comparison between music and the political, religious, and social trends outlined in Chapter 8. The second option affords the possibility for fruitful comparisons between Baroque opera and Japanese *kabuki* theater (see Chapter 18) as social institutions. Either way, connections constantly must be made between words and music as you explore the role of affect in Baroque vocal music. If you omitted Unit II, consider using the Lecture Suggestions on Purcell's *Dido and Aeneas* (p. 146) and Listening Idea 2 (p. 161) from Chapter 7 of this manual as an introduction to Baroque opera.

❦ Opera

Baroque opera, with its intense emotions, larger-than-life characters, virtuoso singers, dancers, and extravagant set design, was the quintessential Baroque spectacle. It always helps when students can make connections between their studies and their own life experience; help the class make connections between Baroque opera and modern-day spectacles. Many of your students have gone to rock concerts. Ask them to describe the most spectacular rock concert they ever attended. What made it so? Draw out specific details about the staging, lighting, choreography, special effects, performance, instrumentation, amplification, and so on. (If you teach at a large school where football dominates, ask for detailed descriptions of a half-time show.) As you draw parallels between Baroque opera and today's rock concerts, make sure students understand that opera was every bit as popular in the Baroque era as rock concerts (or movies) are today. In fact, opera became the first musical genre that did not rely on the church or a wealthy patron for its existence. The opera house became an independent business that could support itself by selling season subscriptions. This sounds commonplace now, but in those days it represented a radical shift in the music business. The 1995 movie *Farinelli* drives home the point that opera singers toured Europe, sang to full houses, and lived turbulent lives in the public eye—just as rock stars do today.

Italian Opera Seria

The characters of Baroque operas were frequently the heroes and divinities of classical Greece and Rome. The two early Baroque operas discussed in Chapter 7—Monteverdi's *The Coronation of Poppea* and Purcell's *Dido and Aeneas*—offer perfect examples of the Baroque fascination with classical history and mythology. By the late Baroque, operatic procedures had evolved into a genre called *opera seria,* or "serious opera." Plots drew on dramatic, often tragic tales from classical history and mythology, but frequently a god descending in a machine (*deus ex machina*—see textbook page 101 for pictures of typical machines) would intervene at the last minute to conjure up a happy ending. Nonetheless, these ancient stories provided precisely the intrigues, life-and-death struggles, and emotional extremes that audiences demanded.

In the early days of opera, composers such as Monteverdi, always sensitive to dramatic ebb and flow, employed a fluid motion among recitative, arioso, and aria. By the late Baroque, the roles of recitative and aria became standardized. Recitative, a heightened form of emotional speech, was reserved primarily for action and dialogue; in arias, soloists stepped out of the action to express and reflect on their emotions. Lengthy arias served as vehicles for virtuoso display and found favor with singers and audiences. To accommodate the large number of arias that were demanded, a rigid alternation between recitative and aria became common. Good librettists had to come up with more plot twists than a soap opera to create situations that elicited the strong emotions appropriate to arias.

Recitative and Aria

Now is a good time to review the differences between recitative and aria. Refer to the chart in Chapter 7 of this manual (p. 145) for a quick comparison of these two singing styles. After a review of recitative and aria, introduce the distinction between secco and accompanied recitative. The word *accompanied* can be misleading because both types have accompaniment. Make sure students understand that secco ("dry") recitative uses only continuo accompaniment, whereas accompanied recitative is accompanied by the entire orchestra. Play a few examples to reinforce the concept. (Excerpts start at the beginning unless otherwise indicated.)

Secco recitative	Monteverdi, *The Coronation of Poppea,* Act I, "Tornerai?"
	Purcell, *Dido and Aeneas,* Act III, "Thy hand, Belinda"
	Handel, *Messiah,* "There were shepherds" (0:00–0:10, 0:33–1:01)
	Mozart, *Don Giovanni,* Act I, "Alfin siam liberati"
Accompanied recitative	Handel, *Messiah,* "There were shepherds" (0:10–0:33, 1:01–1:19)
	Verdi, *Aida,* Act IV, "La fatal pietra sovra me si chiuse"

HANDEL *Julius Caesar,* Aria, "La giustizia"

The biggest mistake you can make with opera is to overlook the dramatic context. If you are unfamiliar with *Julius Caesar,* you must at least take time to learn what the authors have to say about it. Better yet, share details of the following story with your students.

The plot hinges on two central conflicts. The first, between Roman leaders Caesar and Pompey, resolves itself in Caesar's favor just before the opera begins, but with consequences that play themselves out through the remainder of the story. The second conflict—between Ptolemy, king of Egypt, and his sister Cleopatra, queen of Egypt—finds no resolution until the opera's end. The story's many twists and turns result from the interactions between the participants in these two conflicts.

Act I opens as Caesar's legions celebrate their victory over Pompey, who had enlisted Ptolemy's assistance against Caesar. Ptolemy, trying to make the best of a bad situation, executes his ally Pompey and presents the head to Caesar as a peace offering. Pompey's wife Cornelia and their son Sextus, who had come to beg Caesar's clemency for Pompey, now find him dead. Cornelia is ready to kill herself, and Sextus vows vengeance. Back at Ptolemy's palace, Cleopatra plots to compete with her brother for Caesar's favor; meanwhile Ptolemy makes plans of his own, consenting to his general Achilla's offer to murder Caesar in exchange for Cornelia, Pompey's widow. At the Roman camp, a disguised Cleopatra meets with Caesar, who finds her irresistible. As she leaves, she speaks with Cornelia and Sextus and offers to help them in their revenge. Caesar then visits Ptolemy's palace with his retinue; when Caesar leaves, Cornelia and Sextus challenge Ptolemy to a duel. It backfires, however, when Ptolemy orders them imprisoned, Cornelia in his harem and Sextus in jail.

As Act II opens, Cleopatra continues her seduction of Caesar in a sensual, allegorical entertainment. Back in the harem, Cornelia must now fend off both Ptolemy and Achilla while Sextus strengthens his resolve. Returning to Cleopatra's palace, Caesar is about to proclaim his love when he is interrupted by news that Ptolemy's soldiers have come to kill him. He flees, leaving Cleopatra alone with her newfound feelings of love for Caesar. Back at the harem, Sextus dashes in to kill Ptolemy, only to be thwarted by Achilla, who brings news that Caesar escaped his soldiers but probably drowned in the harbor. After informing Ptolemy that Cleopatra's armies are marching against him, Achilla again asks for Cornelia. Ptolemy turns him down flat. Achilla leaves swearing his own revenge as Cornelia encourages Sextus to persevere in spite of his recent failure.

In Act III, Achilla defects to Cleopatra's side, but in vain. Ptolemy's army carries the day, and Achilla is mortally wounded. Back at the harbor, Caesar miraculously reappears alive and well, just in time to witness Sextus tending to Achilla's dying moments. As Sextus and Achilla discuss plans for revenge on Ptolemy, Caesar steps in to take charge. Finally, Sextus senses, justice will be done—at this point he sings the aria "La giustizia." Back at Cleopatra's palace, the queen prepares to go to prison following her defeat, but is instead reunited with her love Caesar when he marches in to liberate her. In the harem, Ptolemy again tries to win Cornelia's affection, but she pulls out a dagger. Before she can use it, Sextus rushes in again and kills Ptolemy himself. A grand celebration back at the harbor brings the opera to an end.

The two conflicts identified above resolve themselves. The Caesar-Pompey conflict should have alienated Caesar from Cornelia and Sextus, but Ptolemy's treachery puts them all on the same side against the Egyptian king. The Cleopatra-Ptolemy conflict appears to resolve in Ptolemy's favor, but her gambit to win Caesar's favor works out after all when Caesar escapes assassination. The work ends happily for everyone—except Ptolemy.

Once you have shared the story with your class, ask students to put themselves in Sextus's shoes. "Poor Sextus, Ptolemy just murdered your father and forced your mother into his harem. What will you do next?" Ask students how they would feel, how they would respond to this situation. Draw out as many details as you can. Next, ask your students to imagine what kind of music could express this feeling. What type of melody, rhythm, dynamics, and so on, would be appropriate? Prompt them as necessary, and take notes on the board. Once the class has conjured up a musical portrait, play the aria. If possible, play the return of **A**, from 2:14 to the end. The beginning (0:00–1:46) works well, too, but the ornamentation in the da capo conveys Sextus's rage even more forcibly. Once the excerpt has finished, ask the students how close they came. Some students may expect more volume, angst, or dissonance; take the opportunity to compare the modern world with the eighteenth century, when no amplification existed; an orchestra was loud, comparatively speaking; and the musical style of the day imposed some limits on chord types, expression, and so on.

Turn to the aria's da capo form (**A B A**), which offers an example of contrast and return. Once again, the words can aid student understanding. The *Listen* Guide on textbook page 159 maps out the frequent text repetition in the **A** section, the contrasting text of the **B** section, and the return to **A** immediately afterward. Ask students to listen for musical contrasts between **A** and **B** sections, then play the music. In the discussion that follows, ask the class how they could tell when one section ended and the next began. Not all students will catch this the first time, since, in many ways, the musical mood does not differ all that significantly as the music moves from section to section; tempo and general melodic character, for instance, remain much the same in both sections. Nonetheless, some features make it easy to identify the points of demarcation once students are made aware of them. In the **A** section, the descending octave scale in the voice's final phrase, made all the more emphatic by the pause just before it, momentarily creates a strong ending. But an even more striking feature demarcating sections is the instrumental ritornello. Musically, it belongs to the **A** section, but its positioning at the beginning and end of each **A** section provides an instrumental cushion before and after the voice's **B** section as well. Other features that make the **B** section stand out are its contrasting text, its major mode beginning (in the relative major), and its tone color—for the only time in the piece, the violins drop out and let the continuo instruments handle the accompaniment by themselves. As students become attuned to these contrasts, the return of the ritornello and the now-familiar **A** section proves more satisfying. Once **B** is over, the ritornello immediately signals the return of **A**.

Students may notice that the return of **A** is not exactly the same as the first **A**. The difference, of course, can be found in the voice part. Point out that when **A** returned (the da capo), the singer was expected to add improvised ornaments to the aria melody, an important feature of Baroque music described in Chapter 8. Baroque audiences considered these ornaments a significant, often exciting demonstration of vocal prowess and musical expression. This art was largely lost for many years, but many modern singers who specialize in music of the Baroque have revived the practice through careful study of Baroque writers on musical performance. Play the two **A** sections back to back (0:16–1:46 and 2:15–end) and ask students to describe any differences they hear in the vocal line. If you have time to prepare, phrase-by-phrase comparison is the most effective strategy (taped excerpts, digital excerpts ripped from CD, or computer control over the CD drive make this possible) for helping students hear the ornaments. Be sure to compare the endings for both **A** sections (1:10–1:46 and 3:16–3:53), where the soloist's cadenza offers an obvious addition. Ask students to describe the effect of the ornaments. In some cases, the phrases sound more florid; in others, more jarring and dramatic.

Finally, point out this work's use of virtuosity and improvisation. The ornamentation you just covered provides an excellent example of this, especially the frequent embellishments and the cadenza in the da capo. These were often improvised by the soloist on the spur of the moment, and this practice naturally requires great virtuosity. The role of virtuosity can be heard even apart from the ornamentation, of course. Dare students to try singing along with the melody. They will quickly admit that this is no simple tune; it's fast, unpredictable, and filled with long, melismatic *coloratura* passages that enliven key words in the text. Such vocal writing underscores the fact that Baroque opera was a singer's art. Audiences didn't come because of the composer, the story, or the producer; they came to hear star singers perform—virtuosos who could sing higher, faster, longer, and more beautifully than mere mortals. It reminds one of Michael Jordan. In his last year with the Chicago Bulls, the team's games sold out across the country. Fans didn't come because their team was likely to lose to the Bulls; they came to see a virtuoso who could think faster, soar more beautifully, score more often, and win more convincingly than the mere mortals who played against him. Baroque opera was just like that.

Japanese Musical Drama

An example of Japanese *kabuki* theater does not appear until Chapter 18 of the *Listen* textbook, but *kabuki* and Baroque opera grew up at about the same time, and there are compelling similarities between these two genres, both in their dramatic practices and their social contexts. This is an ideal moment to look at the *kabuki* play *Dojoji*. If you choose to do so, you can make use of several resources from Chapter 18, especially Listening Idea 8 and the teaching ideas from the Global Perspectives module (p. 456 in Lecture Suggestions).

♩ Oratorio

Although Baroque sacred music takes many forms, two broad generalizations can be made:

1. Baroque sacred music borrows heavily from Baroque operatic technique and procedures.

2. Many Baroque sacred works include a choir and give it a more prominent role than in Baroque opera.

The various names and functions of the many sacred Baroque vocal genres—oratorio, passion, church cantata, Mass, motet, magnificat—can be confusing to students. The authors mention most of these but focus primarily on oratorio and church cantata. Their choice is a practical one and is best observed. If students raise questions about the other genres, or if you have a special interest in this music, the following checklists may prove helpful.

Oratorio

1. An extended work for choir, solo voices, and orchestra.

2. Includes arias, recitative, choruses, occasional duets, and orchestral overture and interludes.

3. Based on a dramatic story drawn from Scripture.

4. Performed in theaters without action, costumes, or sets.

5. Not part of any church service.

6. Written for both Catholic and Protestant audiences.

Passion

1. A type of oratorio.

2. Includes arias, recitative, choruses, occasional duets, and chorales.

3. Based on one of the Gospel accounts (Matthew, Mark, Luke, or John) of Christ's passion—that is, the events of the last few days leading up to and including Christ's crucifixion.

4. Part of worship services for Holy Week (the week before Easter—usually Good Friday).

5. Written for both Catholic and Protestant (Lutheran) audiences.

Church Cantata

1. Shorter than an oratorio; for choir, solo voices, and orchestra (secular cantatas often for solo voice and continuo).

2. Includes arias, recitative, choruses, occasional duets, and chorale.

3. Performed without action, costumes, or sets.

4. The church cantata was part of the Sunday worship service, based on that week's Bible reading.

5. Written for Protestant (Lutheran) audiences.

6. Both church and secular cantatas were written.

Mass

1. Length and performing forces varied greatly.

2. Often includes arias, recitative, and choruses.

3. Based on traditional five sections (Kyrie, Gloria, Credo, Sanctus, Agnus Dei), though these were sometimes subdivided into several numbers to create massive works (Bach's B Minor Mass).

4. Part of worship services for church holidays and festivals.

5. Written for both Catholic and Protestant audiences.

Motet

1. A type of cantata for *a cappella* choir.

2. Part of worship services.

Magnificat

1. Sometimes like a cantata (Bach's *Magnificat*).

2. Often includes arias, recitative, and choruses.

3. Based on the canticle of the Virgin Mary from the Bible, Luke 1:46–55.

For all intents and purposes, the oratorio, which was not part of any church service, is an opera on a religious subject. Like operas, oratorios took place in several acts (or parts) and included arias, recitative, characters, and narrative action. Unlike operas, oratorios made considerable use of the chorus, and they were (and are) presented in concert form, not acted out on stage.

HANDEL *Messiah*

Without any introduction, play the beginning of the Hallelujah Chorus from *Messiah* (not *"The"* Messiah). Ask students to identify the music. Most, if not all, will be able to name it. Next to Beethoven's Symphony No. 5, the Hallelujah Chorus may be the most widely recognized piece of classical music—an icon of Western culture.

Messiah, the most famous oratorio ever written, includes the same operatic elements as other oratorios: recitative, arias, and choruses. It is atypical, however, in that it does not feature specific characters or plot action. Instead, it is written in three parts that reflect on the meaning and purpose of the Messiah's coming. Part I deals with prophecies of Christ's coming and their realization. Part II describes the passion and sacrifice of Christ for the redemption of humankind. Part III celebrates Christ's resurrection and humanity's consequent hope for eternal salvation.

HANDEL *Messiah,* Recitative, "There were shepherds"; Chorus, "Glory to God"

This may be the only portion of *Messiah* that tells a story. Start with the words. This recitative and chorus come from Part I. Together they form a small dramatic scene in which angels appear to the shepherds and announce the birth of Christ. The words for the recitative can be found on page 162 of the textbook. This text from the book of Luke (Luke 2:8–14) is one of the best-known passages from the Bible. Students who have never been to a Christmas Eve service may have heard Linus recite this passage in the *Peanuts* Christmas television special. "There were shepherds" is cast as a recitative in four sections, as the authors' notations on textbook page 161 indicate. It provides the best example in the anthology of Baroque accompanied recitative; it is especially useful because the alternation between secco and accompanied recitative permits direct comparison of the two. Ask the class to listen for the differences. Play the entire recitative and ask students to describe those differences. The viola da gamba and organ accompaniment in the secco recitative clearly distinguishes itself from the string orchestra used in the accompanied recitative. As part of the discussion, ask students to look again at the words and determine why Handel chose to alternate between secco and accompanied recitative. Point out that accompanied recitative highlights the appearance of the angel and later the appearance of a multitude of angels. Further, the dry recitative ("And the angel said") framed by the two accompanied sections receives extra emphasis *because* it contrasts with what surrounds it. Handel wants the all-important message of the angel to stand out clearly.

The text for the chorus is interspersed amid the textbook's discussion of "Glory to God." For your convenience, the full text is provided below. It is a good idea to print the words on the board, since each phrase is treated so distinctively. (Italics indicate phrases of text that are repeated.)

Glory to God in the highest!
And peace on earth.
Glory to God in the highest!
And peace on earth.
Good will toward men.

Glory to God in the highest!
And peace on earth.
Good will toward men.

Handel was much admired for his ability to marshal large musical forces. His unerring instincts for pacing and for judicious contrasts of melody, texture, timbre, and key resulted in an energetic sense of forward motion and huge, effective climaxes. Handel gives full expression to the vivid imagery of this text. Recitative cannot capture the effect of a choir of angels praising God, so the chorus and orchestra burst in after the shortest of pauses to proclaim "Glory to God"—perhaps the greatest segue in the history of music. Ask students to listen for contrasts in Handel's treatment of the three main phrases: "Glory to God in the highest," "and peace on earth," and "good will toward men." Then play the complete recitative and chorus so that students can take in the full effect of the entire scene.

In the discussion that follows, draw out the key elements of each phrase. "Glory to God" is pronounced in rhythmic unison by high voices (soprano, alto, and tenor) singing high pitches ("in the *highest*!") with energetic rhythms and full orchestral accompaniment. "And peace on earth" is sung quietly in calm, simple rhythms by low voices in unison—and they drop an octave to very low pitches to emphasize "on earth." "Good will toward men" calls for all sections of the choir to echo each other in imitative polyphony. The cumulative effect of overlapping entrances builds to a joyous climax, as if all creation joined in to proclaim God's good will for humankind.

The resources provided by full choir and orchestra create a grand effect. You can call attention to the authentic instruments and performance practice of this recording. Some period performances lack the overwhelming fullness of modern instruments and a large choir, but this one musters up plenty of weight where needed without sacrificing the vitality associated with period performances. As a result, the chorus truly dances with joy; its incisive rhythmic buoyancy and its clarity of balance and articulation allow us to savor every detail, even in the busiest polyphonic passages. Finally, note how Handel reveals his sensitivity to the dramatic situation by not giving in to the temptation to tack on a showy ending. Just at the point where we expect the choir to shout "Glory to God" once again, the voices drop out and the orchestral instruments thin out until a pair of high violins with continuo remains, as if to suggest that the angels have returned whence they came. Our puzzlement at such an ending leaves us to reflect on the shepherds' consternation—just as they begin to wonder if this overwhelming announcement was real or only a dream.

HANDEL *Messiah*, Hallelujah Chorus

The Hallelujah Chorus concludes Part II of *Messiah*. As you prepare to play the chorus, look carefully at the words on page 163 of the textbook, which celebrate the transformation of this world into God's kingdom. Just as in "Glory to God," phrases of text are associated with textural contrasts: between homophonic texture ("Hallelujah"), imitative polyphony ("and he shall reign for ever and ever"), and even monophony ("For the Lord God omnipotent reigneth"—the first two times). Handel uses these contrasts to heighten the effect of each section. Homophonic passages make polyphony sound more complex and rich—and polyphonic passages make monophony sound all the more direct and incisive. The same is true of other elements: quiet passages make loud passages sound more powerful; energetic rhythms in one passage make the slower rhythms of the next more peaceful. The performance in the *Listen* anthology brings out these contrasts admirably; its visceral, vibrant celebration is a far cry from many performances that can only manage loud, louder, and loudest. Ask students to listen for contrasts in texture and to pick out the musical elements Handel uses to convey the meaning of the words. One unusual effect that stands out is the sudden hush at "The Kingdom of this world is become," followed by *subito forte* at "The kingdom of our Lord and of his Christ," the very phrases that explain why the choir sings "Hallelujah" in the first place. Play the music. In the discussion that follows, work through the checklist of musical elements and structures from Chapter 5 and identify specific ways that the music expresses the words.

The ending is full of wonderful effects. One of the "King of Kings" sections (2:12–2:40) uses contrasts of key to heighten the effect—each time the phrase is repeated, the music moves to a higher key. This sequence places voices and instruments in successively higher registers. The frequency (cycles per second) increases, the sound becomes louder and more brilliant, the tension level rises— and the excitement mounts as well. One imagines that Handel would have gone higher if human limitations didn't stop him. At the very end, "Hallelujah" and "for ever" are repeated "for ever and ever," as if this song of praise had no end. The repetition does end (to the misery of the performer who stops counting here and loses his or her place!) with a moment of silence as the never-ending "Hallelujah" echoes into memory. The slow, broad concluding "Hallelujah" sounds all the more final due to its contrast with the lively section and pregnant pause that precede it.

♪ The Church Cantata

Well over two hundred of the cantatas Bach composed during his long career have survived to this day. These cantatas attest Bach's incredible compositional fecundity. Unfortunately, they are too rarely performed today, either in modern Lutheran services or in the concert hall. Nevertheless, the cantatas constitute some of Bach's most beautiful and dramatic music.

As the checklist of vocal genres above suggests, the church cantata was a kind of mini-oratorio designed for use in Lutheran worship. Bach's church cantatas would have been performed after the Scripture readings (Epistle and Gospel) but before the sermon.[1] In that position, the cantata served both as musical/theological reflection on the readings and as preparation for the sermon, the climax of Lutheran worship. Given this role, the words and music of the cantata necessarily expressed themes drawn from that day's Bible reading. Appropriate texts for cantatas were usually supplied by religious poets such as Lutheran clergyman Erdmann Neumeister.

Bach's church cantatas often followed a predictable format; they began with a substantial chorus, continued with recitatives and arias for solo voices, and concluded with a straightforward chorale harmonization. For the ending, Bach carefully selected chorales that were appropriate to the Bible readings for that Sunday. On many occasions, these familiar chorale tunes found their way into earlier movements of the cantata as well.

---

[1]Lutheran worship followed the order of the Catholic Mass closely but placed much greater emphasis on the sermon. For a clearer picture of the cantata's position, see the order of worship for the Mass on page 109 in Chapter 6 of this manual.

The Lutheran Chorale

The chorale provides a nice point of connection as you look into the varied genres of Bach's sacred music and the impact of both the Reformation and Lutheranism (then two centuries old) on Baroque music. Chorales were the hymns sung by Lutheran congregations in worship. In the sixteenth century, Luther made a point of building up the repertory of congregational song so as to engage laypeople more fully in the worship experience. By the eighteenth century, Luther's "new" hymns were as well known and well loved by Lutheran congregations as Christmas carols are by modern Christians. These hymns were used for worship in many ways—sung by congregation or choir; transcribed in organ preludes and other organ works; and incorporated into cantata, passion, and oratorio.

BACH Cantata No. 4, "Christ lag in Todesbanden"

In some cantatas, Bach used chorale melodies not only at the end but throughout the entire work. Cantata No. 4 is one of these. Even more unusual, each movement of Cantata No. 4 is based on a different stanza of Luther's original hymn text, so that the entire cantata becomes a novel recasting of the congregational hymn. Taken together, Bach's prelude and seven movements offer a compendium of different chorale settings—all based on the same tune. Although this cantata is not typical, the wisdom of the authors' choice becomes readily apparent when you consider that in this one work, students can hear the remarkably inventive contrasts Bach achieves in working with a single melody.

Stanza 7

In order for students to fully appreciate Bach's varied uses of the chorale in the cantata and the organ prelude from *Orgelbüchlein,* they must learn to recognize the tune. Stanza 7 ("Wir essen und leben wohl") provides a good starting point; students can hear the tune more easily here than in the other *Listen* stanzas. Play it through several times at the keyboard and play the recording until students can recognize the different phrases. Point out the repetition of the first two melodic phrases; the homophonic, four-voice texture (with some movement in the inner voices); and an orchestral accompaniment that doubles the choral voices. Most of Bach's cantatas end with precisely this type of reflective chorale setting, and his passions are filled with them. Finally, call attention to the "Hallelujah" at the end of the stanza. Note that every stanza ends with a "Hallelujah." Make a point of comparing this "Hallelujah" with the endings of the other stanzas when you get to them.

Ask students to describe the overall mood of this piece. For an Easter cantata, this work sounds surprisingly serious and stern. Most Easter music expresses joy over Christ's resurrection; this work seems to suggest the grim battle between Life and Death, good and evil. Then ask students to study the words to Stanza 7 on textbook page 167. Except for the "Hallelujahs" at the end, there are few images here that lend themselves to the kind of text painting we saw in Handel's *Messiah.* Of course, such a straightforward chorale harmonization presents limited opportunities for text painting, but we will find that Bach most often uses music not only to set an appropriate mood but also to emphasize important theological images and concepts. Bach's text setting concerns itself with meaning and interpretation, not with mere madrigalisms.

Stanza 3

This chorus is based on the same chorale melody as Stanza 7. This time, read through the words with the class before you turn to the music. Ask students to describe the mood and the main themes suggested by the words. The chorale verse states that Christ has "done away with our sins, thereby robbing Death" of its sting. These actions lie at the heart of a Lutheran theology of grace and offer cause for celebration. In response, Bach's music nearly dances with its engaging, vivacious motor rhythms, though we might still describe the overall mood as serious. Just before you play the music, ask the class to follow the text and listen for the chorale melody. Play the music and ask students to describe how the chorale was used. This is a "gapped" chorale, with instrumental interludes before and after each phrase of the chorale. Just as in Stanza 7, the music of the first two phrases repeats for the third and fourth phrases. Even more important, point out that each interlude uses the same melodic pattern; in fact, the recurring interludes sound much like a ritornello theme in a ritornello form. There is even a final complete statement of the ritornello after the tenor's last "Hallelujah." Bach creates a hybrid form, a cross between ritornello form and chorale setting. Play the work one more time so that students can focus attention on the instrumental ritornelli.

Now that students have listened to the music twice, ask them to identify the most unusual moment in the piece. That moment comes in the sixth phrase, "Da bleibet *nichts*—denn Tods Gestalt." For the first half of the movement, Bach's dancelike motor rhythm drives ahead ceaselessly. Just after the fifth phrase, the solo violin switches to rapid multiple-stopped chords. Halfway into the sixth phrase, the music stops abruptly at the word *nichts*—nothing—followed by the rest of the phrase in a slower tempo *ad libitum*. On first hearing, this sounds like a simple madrigalism, a musical image to match the word at hand. On closer examination, we see that this image points to the central message of the text—the utter powerlessness of the devil over Christ's resurrection.[2] After this momentary sidetrack the music resumes its dance, gaining further momentum in the "Hallelujah," which sounds positively jubilant. This movement offers a prime example of Bach's use of music both to set an appropriate mood and to emphasize central concepts of the text. When Bach does something unusual in a sacred vocal work, one need never look further than the words for a full explanation. We can see further evidence of his attentiveness to text in the recently discovered Calov Bible that belonged to Bach (see Lecture-Demonstration Idea 2). This Bible-with-commentary contains many handwritten comments added by Bach himself. His remarks emphasize and amplify points in the text in much the same way that his music emphasizes and amplifies concepts and images in Luther's hymn text.

Stanza 4

Stanza 4, "Es war ein wunderlicher Krieg," provides yet another approach to setting this chorale melody. Begin by playing the first section of Stanza 4, just up to the point where the alto voice finishes its longer, slower version of the first phrase (0:00–0:20). If you introduced Stanza 7 thoroughly, students will recognize the first phrase immediately when the tenor voice comes in. But soon after this the soprano also comes in with the first phrase, only to be followed by

---

[2]Interesting parallels can be found in the case of Hildegard of Bingen, who believed that the devil had no power to make music (and was thus given the only speaking role in her *Ordo virtutum*), and in the case of Liszt, whose Mephistopheles (in the *Faust* Symphony) had no power to create— only to distort.

the bass. In this movement, Bach uses imitative entries based on the phrases of the chorale. Once tenor, soprano, and bass have entered, Bach caps off the section by having the alto sing the complete phrase in longer, slower note values.[3] Each new phrase of Stanza 4 is treated in like fashion, so that each phrase serves as the basis for a new point of imitation. As usual, the music of the first two phrases is repeated for phrases three and four. Some phrases are harder to hear due to ornamentation, but students can follow this well enough if you spend some time with each phrase.

For the first six phrases, Bach sets up a pattern with six consecutive points of imitation. Not surprisingly, there comes a spot where Bach breaks the pattern. For the seventh phrase, soprano, tenor, and bass toss a two-note motive ("Ein Spott") back and forth at the same time that the alto sings the seventh phrase. Why? Again we must turn to the text. The first six lines describe how Christ's death destroyed Death itself in the war between Life and Death. Bach's music employs elaborate imitative entries to emphasize each detail of the story. The seventh line, however, turns from description of the victory to description of the consequences for the devil—Death becomes a mockery, since Christians need no longer fear the grave. Here Bach's music does not give Death (the devil) the dignity of imitative treatment. Instead, the two-note "Ein Spott" figures seem to mock Death's fate, reminiscent of Luther's suggestion that the devil hates nothing more than a good laugh at his expense.

Comparing Bach and Handel

It is fascinating to observe how differently Bach and Handel treat religious texts. Even a cursory comparison of Bach's cantata with Handel's oratorio brings us face to face with Bach's stern theological reflection and Handel's dramatic emotional appeal. Bach constantly asks, "What does this text mean for me?" His musical ideas and symbols all work together to express his personal theological interpretation. Handel asks, "What is this text's dramatic potential?" His music seeks to express the text's images and emotions as vividly and effectively as possible. Of course, these two works served entirely different purposes. Cantata No. 4 was written for use in Lutheran worship; *Messiah* was written for the theater (albeit without acting, costumes, or sets). In fact, *Messiah* was considered too theatrical for church performance during Handel's lifetime. Whereas Bach spent most of his career in the church, Handel owed his livelihood to the theater. It is ironic, then, that each found his greatness by incorporating something that the other possessed. Bach's greatest church music, the *St. Matthew Passion,* for instance, includes intensely dramatic scenes that borrow operatic elements. Handel's enduring fame, on the other hand, rests not on his operas but on monumental religious works such as *Messiah.* See Further Listening Examples below for a fascinating exercise that compares music by Bach and Handel—based on the same texts.

7 The Organ Chorale

Organ chorales, or chorale preludes, are organ compositions based on a chorale tune. They use many different techniques and forms similar to those found in Bach's Cantata No. 4—the textbook mentions ornamented and

---

[3]Textbooks on form and analysis call this common Baroque technique *Vorimitation* (fore-imitation), in which imitative entrances based on a particular melody precede the slower, full statement of the "real" melody.

"gapped" organ chorales—but they were all intended for use in worship and often served as a prelude to the congregational singing of a chorale. Within this new genre we come to our final example based on the chorale "Christ lag in Todesbanden."

BACH Chorale Prelude, "Christ lag in Todesbanden"

Ask students to identify the mood created by the prelude and to listen for ways the now-familiar chorale tune has been changed. (Even if they cannot read music, the chorale tune printed on page 165 of the textbook can serve as a helpful guide.) Without further introduction, play the music. In the discussion that follows, help students clarify the elements that create this music's blend of seriousness and vitality: the full contrapuntal texture, the constant motion of the stepping motives in the inner voices, and the vigorous bass line. This work clearly avoids the meditative quality associated with many other chorale preludes. Just as we saw in the cantata based on this melody, Bach creates a serious yet celebrative work for Easter morning. Finally, read the first stanza of the chorale text (see Appendix II) for the class and have students identify musical features that are appropriate to the words. Point out that Bach is just as attentive to the words in this instrumental work as he was in the settings from Cantata No. 4.

Additional Teaching Suggestions

❦ Lecture-Demonstration Ideas

1. Use *Messiah* arias to demonstrate the variety of emotional expression in Baroque music. You can play a rage aria ("But who may abide" or "Why do the nations"), arias that depict pastoral ("He shall feed his flock") or joyous ("Rejoice greatly, O daughter of Zion") moods, and so on. Sound recordings and video performances can be found in Multimedia Resources below.

2. Bring Bach's Calov Bible to class. If your library owns a copy (Howard Cox, *The Calov Bible of J. S. Bach,* Ann Arbor, Mich.: UMI Research Press, 1985), this facsimile of a recently discovered volume from Bach's own library offers fascinating insights into Bach's devotional life. The Calov Bible is a Luther Bible with commentary by Abraham Calov interspersed throughout. Comments in Bach's own hand appear on many pages. Howard Cox's preface provides description of a particle-induced x-ray emission procedure used by scientists at the University of California's Crocker Nuclear Laboratory to verify the authenticity of this discovery. Share Bach's handwritten comments with the class as a vehicle for understanding the composer better. Scholarly analysis of Bach's comments can be found in Robin Leaver's *J. S. Bach and Scripture* (St. Louis: Concordia, 1985), which also includes many pages in facsimile.

3. Invite a church choir director to class. Choose a director from a liturgically oriented tradition (Lutheran, Episcopalian, or Catholic) if you want someone whose experiences most closely parallel Bach's. Your guest can provide wonderful insights into problems of choosing music appropriate to each Sunday of the church year, dealing with pastoral staff, running rehearsals, and making a living. The director can also reflect on experiences conducting and performing choral works from *Messiah,* Bach cantatas, and other great Baroque choral works.

4. If you didn't try this in Chapter 9, invite an organist to talk to your class about his or her experience with Bach's organ music and to describe how a pipe organ works. Your guest can also discuss the art of accompanying hymns, a tradition linked with that of the chorale prelude. If possible, take your students to visit an organ nearby; have your guest demonstrate and play the instrument for your class.

ℐ Class Discussion Ideas

1. *Does music express human emotions?* Spend more time with the "Doctrine of Affections." Kerman and Tomlinson describe the importance of "affect" in Baroque vocal music (textbook pages 130 and 154). Johann Mattheson's *Der vollkommene Kapellmeister* of 1739 (Ann Arbor: UMI Research Press, 1981, pt. 2, chap. 13, secs. 1–78) describes the expected affect for a variety of vocal genres. Read aloud some excerpts from Mattheson that describe the genres your class is studying (aria, recitative, cantata, opera, and oratorio are included). Ask students if the affect of the musical work matches Mattheson's description. *What musical elements create the affect?*

2. Arrange for your class to attend a choral rehearsal—a local church choir or one of your college's choirs (especially if they are working on a Baroque cantata or oratorio) will do. At your next class meeting, invite questions and observations about the rehearsal. If your students have attended other concerts or rehearsals, invite comparisons.

3. *Whose music do you like better—Bach's or Handel's?* This question can work well if you spent lots of time with the music of these composers in Chapters 8–10, or if you use Listening Idea 1 or the exercise in Further Listening Examples that compares Handel's *Messiah* with Bach's *Christmas Oratorio.* Draw out the students' reasons for their preferences. Wherever possible, help them to specify elements of music that influence their decisions. For those who choose Handel, a good follow-up question is, *Then why do you think Bach is considered one of the greatest composers of all time?* Above all, don't take sides; that would inhibit open discussion.

4. *What difference does the middle class make?* Both European opera and *kabuki* theater relied on the merchant class—the bourgeoisie—for support. This question points to the complex interaction between musical style and social class structures. *How does middle-class support differ from aristocratic support? What advantages does one have over the other? How does music for the aristocracy differ from music for the lower classes?* A comparison of *gagaku* and *kabuki* might yield some answers. Ask students to draw on their own experiences, and if you chose to look at *kabuki* along with your coverage of Baroque opera, have them draw comparisons as well.

ℐ Listening Ideas

1. Compare Handel's *Messiah* with Bach's *Christmas Oratorio.* Appendix II provides side-by-side comparison of the texts Handel and Bach use to present the story of angels appearing to shepherds to announce Christ's birth. Plan an in-class exercise that allows students to compare the music as well. Lecture suggestions can be found in Further Listening Examples below; look for CDs and videos in Multimedia Resources below.

2. Many Lutheran chorale tunes had been in existence nearly two centuries by the time Bach used them in his sacred music. To provide a sense of this long tradition, play other versions of the Passion Chorale. Like many chorale tunes, the Passion Chorale was initially a secular song. Start with the sixteenth-century original, Hassler's "Mein G'müt ist mir verwirret" (from the anthology to accompany K Marie Stolba's *Development of Western Music*, 3rd ed.). If you can find early and mid-Baroque chorale preludes based on this tune (by Scheidt, Pachelbel, or Buxtehude), so much the better. In addition to chorale preludes such as "Herzlich tut mich Verlangen," Bach harmonizations include settings from the *Christmas Oratorio* and the four famous harmonizations from his *St. Matthew Passion*. Finally, Paul Simon's "American Tune" offers a contemporary setting of this time-honored chorale, which students enjoy. See Multimedia Resources below for suggested audio and video recordings.

3. Introduce the class to a complete cantata. You can finish the one you've already started (Bach's Cantata No. 4), use teaching suggestions for Bach's Cantata No. 140 in Further Listening Examples, or browse through Multimedia Resources below for other ideas. To place the cantata in its proper context, use *Johann Sebastian Bach: Masterpieces to Order*, a video that presents excerpts from a reconstructed eighteenth-century Lutheran worship service (see Video Recordings below).

4. Introduce the class to the contributions of women in Baroque music. Start with the textbook's box "Women in Music" on page 164. Then play recordings of Baroque music written by or for women musicians. For possible recordings, see Elisabeth-Claude Jacquet de la Guerre and *Concerto delle donne* in Sound Recordings below.

5. Listen to more da capo arias and expose your students to the art of the *castrato*. As good as the example from Handel's *Julius Caesar* may be, it hardly conveys the wide range of emotions and moods composers expressed within this highly adaptable form. Examples are plentiful. Late Baroque operas by Handel or any other composer are excellent sources, and even Bach's passions will yield many da capo arias (though not for *castrato*). See Multimedia Resources below for suggested audio and video recordings. If at all possible, use a video recording for this exercise. A particularly breathtaking example by Vivaldi can be found on the *Cecilia Bartoli: Live in Italy* DVD in Video Recordings below.

6. If you chose to study *kabuki* theater (from Chapter 18) along with your coverage of Baroque opera, compare Handel's "La giustizia" with *kabuki nagauta* music. Focus especially on the roles of instruments in relation to the voice as they pertain to our perception of both texture and form. Both consist of up to three textural components: vocal melody, violins, and continuo instruments in the Handel aria; voice/shamisen melody, flute countermelody, and percussion in the *nagauta* music. Both works feature instrumental introductions and interludes, both use changes in instrumentation to define sections, and both have one group that rhythmically leads and supports throughout (continuo and percussion). Both examples also share the main melody between the voice and instruments. In Handel's aria, violins and voice present the melody at different times, resulting in imitative counterpoint. In the *nagauta* excerpt, voice and shamisen (and sometimes flute) present the melody simultaneously—but since they are not quite synchronized, the result is heterophony. Finally, both examples employ polyphony. But whereas Handel favors imitative polyphony, the *kabuki* excerpt creates nonimitative polyphony—in Parts 1 and 4, where the flute adds a new melody.

❦ Further Listening Examples

HANDEL *Messiah* versus BACH *Christmas Oratorio*

Compare Handel's *Messiah* with Bach's *Christmas Oratorio*. This exercise provides a nice follow-up to Lecture Suggestions material (above) on *Messiah* and on the comparison of Bach and Handel. The announcement of Christ's birth to the shepherds (Luke 2:8–14) is included in both works (see Multimedia Resources below for suggested audio and video recordings).

Text first: A side-by-side comparison of the texts of these two versions is provided in Appendix II. Display or circulate this chart in class. It is fascinating to see how differently Bach and Handel treat the scene. Point out how Bach's librettist provided, in addition to the usual recitative and aria texts, several chorale verses. Interpolated among the evangelist's recitatives and the chorus "Glory to God," these verses offer reflection and commentary on the biblical narrative as it unfolds. Handel's version treats the story as a dramatic scene; Bach constantly asks, "What does this Scripture mean for me?"

Once students familiarize themselves with the texts, compare musical excerpts from *Messiah* and the *Christmas Oratorio*. Play enough of the Bach to demonstrate how the chorales interrupt and interpret the dramatic action. The two "Glory to God" choruses provide the most telling comparison between the approaches of these composers. The Lecture Suggestions above describe Handel's mastery of dramatic contrasts. Bach's approach, on the other hand, demonstrates his mastery of continuous, nonstop polyphonic textures. The mood of joyous ebullience eases for just a moment at "peace on earth," but the music plunges right back into the work's primary affect. Both examples contain wonderful music, but they also point up the fundamental differences between these composers.

One other fact bears mention: The *Christmas Oratorio* was originally not an oratorio but a set of six cantatas intended for six different worship services of the Christmas season (between Christmas and Epiphany). Like other oratorios, this work was written for chorus, soloists, and orchestral accompaniment. Unlike *Messiah* and other oratorios, the music of *Christmas Oratorio* was performed in church, as part of a series of worship services.

BACH *Christmas Oratorio*, "Wie soll ich dich empfangen," "Nun seid Ihr wohl gerochen"

BACH Chorale Prelude, "Herzlich tut mich Verlangen"

For further examples of Bach's varied uses of chorale melodies, present these three settings (see Sound Recordings below), all based on the famous Passion Chorale. Use the first one, "Wie soll ich dich empfangen," to introduce the melody to your class. Bach includes this chorale in Part I of the *Christmas Oratorio*, after Mary becomes pregnant but just before Jesus' birth. We know Christ is coming, but he has not yet arrived, and the chorale verse allows us to reflect on our feelings of expectation (see Appendix II for text and translation). As we have already seen, this is just the type of reflective chorale setting that concludes many Bach cantatas. The *Christmas Oratorio* is filled with them.

The second setting, "Nun seid Ihr wohl gerochen," concludes the final section of the *Christmas Oratorio*. Read through the words with the class before you turn to the music (see Appendix II). Ask students to describe the mood and the main themes suggested by the words. The chorale verse states that Christ's coming shatters "Death, the devil, sin, and hell," making possible a close relationship between God and humanity. These are the greatest triumphs Christendom can celebrate, and Bach's music conveys a mood of joyful celebration.

Before you listen, ask students which orchestral instruments would be appropriate for this verse. This affords an opportunity to review the distinction between basic and festive Baroque orchestras. Just before you play the music, ask the class to follow the text and listen for the chorale melody. Play the music and ask students to describe how the chorale was used. This is another gapped chorale, with long instrumental interludes before and after each phrase or two of the chorale. Play the work one more time so that students can focus attention on the instrumental ritornelli.

Finally, play the third setting, the organ chorale "Herzlich tut mich Verlangen." Ask students to identify the mood created by the prelude and to listen for ways that the chorale tune has been changed. Without further introduction, play the music. In the discussion that follows, help students clarify the elements that create the thoughtful, meditative mood and draw out comments on Bach's embellishment of the chorale melody. Finally, read the chorale text (see Appendix II) aloud and have students identify musical features that are appropriate to the words.

See Listening Idea 2 above for further examples of Passion Chorale settings.

BACH Cantata No. 140, "Wachet auf, ruft uns die Stimme"

This cantata (see Sound Recordings below) is based in large part on the chorale "Wachet auf, ruft uns die Stimme." These suggestions concentrate on Bach's treatment of this chorale in the cantata. The cantata is in seven sections. The first, fourth, and seventh sections correspond to the first, second, and third verses of the chorale.

> Part 1—Chorale (verse 1): Christians
> *Wachet auf, ruft uns die Stimme*
> ("Awake, a voice is calling us")
>
> Part 2—Recitative
>
> Part 3—Duet: The Soul and Jesus
> *Wann kommst du, mein Heil?*
> ("When wilt thou come, my Savior?")
>
> Part 4—Chorale (verse 2): Christians
> *Zion hört die Wächter singen*
> ("Zion hears the watchman singing")
>
> Part 5—Recitative
>
> Part 6—Duet: The Soul and Jesus
> *Mein Freund ist mein*
> ("My friend is mine")
>
> Part 7—Chorale (verse 3): Christians
> *Gloria sei dir gesungen*
> ("Glory to God")

Play one of Bach's harmonizations (in any complete Bach chorale collection) of this chorale at the keyboard until students are reasonably familiar with it, or play the recording of Part 7. Only in Part 7 is the chorale presented in a complete, straightforward manner, with simple, beautiful harmonization accompanied by the orchestra.

Next play Part 1 of the cantata, based on the first verse of the chorale. This is the most complex of all the sections of the cantata. The chorale itself is sung slowly by the sopranos, whose almost bell-like sounds frame the rest of the music. Within this framework, the other voices and instruments intone various other motives and melodies in imitative counterpoint.

Finally, play Part 4 for the class. Based on verse 2, Part 4 is an especially beautiful movement and a superb example of nonimitative counterpoint. The section opens with a warm, stately tune, derived from material first presented in Part 1 of the cantata and played richly by the violins and violas in unison. After a minute or so, the tenors (the rest of the choir remains silent) enter with the chorale tune. The striking effect of the nonimitative counterpoint is softened by the incredible ease with which these two melodies combine and intertwine.

Multimedia Resources

ʔ Further Listening Charts and Texts

See Appendix II for texts and translations for these works:

Bach, "Christ lag in Todesbanden"

Handel *Messiah* versus Bach *Christmas Oratorio*

Bach, *Christmas Oratorio,* "Wie soll ich dich empfangen" and "Nun seid Ihr wohl gerochen"

Bach, Chorale Prelude, "Herzlich tut mich Verlangen"

ʔ Sound Recordings

Bach, *Christ lag in Todesbanden,* BWV 4. Taverner Consort and Players. Virgin Classics CDC 5 45011 2 (CD). This lively performance on period instruments captures more of the celebration Bach wrote into this Easter cantata than most recordings; directed by Andrew Parrott. Especially useful if you want to explore more of this cantata in the recording used by Kerman and Tomlinson.

Bach, *Christmas Oratorio.* English Baroque Soloists and Monteverdi Choir. Deutsche Grammophon Archiv 423-232-2 (CD). A superb performance on period instruments that captures the exhilaration of this festive work; conducted by John Eliot Gardiner. Outstanding vocal soloists include Anne Sofie von Otter and Anthony Rolfe-Johnson. Try this recording if you use Listening Idea 1 or 2 or the Further Listening Examples exercise above for "Wie soll ich dich empfangen" or "Nun seid Ihr wohl gerochen."

Bach, *Complete Cantatas.* Amsterdam Baroque Orchestra & Chorus. Erato (CD). A recent project aiming to record all of Bach's extant cantatas on period instruments, directed by Ton Koopman. Currently in progress, twelve volumes have been completed (just over 100 cantatas). Avoiding the sometimes severe manner of the Teldec series, these performances capture the beauty and reverence of Bach's music. The first three volumes contain the cantatas Bach wrote before coming to Leipzig, volumes 4 and 5 record his Leipzig secular cantatas, and the remaining volumes contain his Leipzig sacred cantatas. Warmly recommended, especially if you need a complete recording of Cantata No. 4.

Bach, *Great Organ Works.* Peter Hurford. London 443485-2 (CD). Impressive collection of famous pieces includes Toccata and Fugue in D Minor (BWV 565) and Passacaglia and Fugue in C Minor (BWV 582). Try this recording if you use Listening Idea 2 or suggestions from Further Listening Examples above for the chorale prelude "Herzlich tut mich Verlangen."

Bach, *Kantatenwerk*. Teldec Das Alte Werk Series (CD). Various soloists and ensembles conducted by Gustav Leonhardt and Nikolaus Harnoncourt. Begun in the 1970s, this massive project has yielded recordings of nearly all of Bach's extant cantatas using authentic instruments and an informed modern understanding of Baroque performance practice. They are recorded in BWV order (starting with Cantata No. 1). Highly recommended, especially if you prefer the sound of boy sopranos. Try these recordings if you use suggestions for Cantata No. 140 from Further Listening Examples above.

Bach, *St. John Passion*. English Baroque Soloists and Monteverdi Choir. Deutsche Grammophon Archiv 419-324-2 (CD). One of the best period performances available; conducted by John Eliot Gardiner. Try this recording if you use Listening Idea 5 above or want an example of a late Baroque passion.

Bach, *St. Matthew Passion*. Bach Collegium Japan. Bis 1000/2 (CD). One of the best period performances available; conducted by Masaaki Suzuki. Suzuki studied with Ton Koopman and in several respects surpasses his teacher's work, especially in sheer beauty of sound. Contains four chorale harmonizations based on the Passion Chorale. Try this recording if you use Listening Idea 2 or 5 above or for an example of a late Baroque passion.

Concerto delle donne. The Consort of Musicke. Deutsche Harmonia Mundi 77154-2-RC (CD). The textbook's box "Women in Music" offers an opportunity to explore the many contributions women made to Baroque music. This recording, named for the crack ensemble of women's voices at the court of Ferrara, samples late Renaissance and early Baroque vocal works written (mostly by men) to display the talents of famous female vocalists. It includes works by Baroque composers Monteverdi, Barbara Strozzi, Carissimi, and Alessandro Scarlatti; directed by Anthony Rooley. Try this recording if you use Listening Idea 4 above.

Handel, *Giulio Cesare*. Concerto Köln. Harmonia Mundi HMC 901385.87 (CD). Finest complete recording available of Handel's famed opera. Superb cast includes Jennifer Larmore and Barbara Schlick; directed by René Jacobs. Highly recommended if you use Listening Idea 5 above or just want a further look at *Julius Caesar.*

Handel, *Messiah*. Les Arts Florissants. Harmonia Mundi HMC 901498.99 (CD). Of the many period performances of this late Baroque masterwork, this one captures both the dancelike energy of his competitors and the weight and grandeur associated with performances on modern instruments. Outstanding soloists, orchestra, and chorus; directed by William Christie. Especially useful if you want to explore more of *Messiah* in the recording used by Kerman and Tomlinson.

Handel, *Operatic Arias*. David Daniels and the Orchestra of the Age of Enlightenment. Virgin Veritas CDC 45326 (CD). Outstanding sampler by one of the finest countertenors to emerge in recent years; conducted by Roger Norrington. Includes *castrato* arias from *Julius Caesar, Serse, Rinaldo*, and other Handel operas. Try this recording if you use Listening Idea 5 above.

Jacquet de la Guerre, Elisabeth-Claude. *Pièces de Clavecin:* Suite in D Minor. Included in recordings to accompany Stolba's *Development of Western Music*, 3rd ed., McGraw-Hill, 1998 (CD). The textbook's box "Women in Music" offers an opportunity to explore the many contributions women made to Baroque music. Among these, the music of composer Jacquet de la Guerre stands out. This recording includes one of her many keyboard dance suites.

Simon, Paul. *There Goes Rhymin' Simon*. Warner Brothers WB 25589 (CD). This recording contains "American Tune," a contemporary setting of the ancient Passion Chorale melody. Try this recording if you use Listening Idea 2 above.

℣ Video Recordings

The Advent of Fashion. Music in Time Series. www.films.com (DVD and VHS, color, 60 minutes). James Galway narrates this look at the rise of public concerts and theaters. Many examples of Baroque vocal music: Handel's *Zadok the Priest, Orlando,* and *Messiah;* Rameau's *Naïs;* and Gay's *The Beggar's Opera.*

All That Bach. VAI (VHS, color, 50 minutes). Video celebrated Bach's tercentennial (1985) with an eclectic mix of Bach performances by Keith Jarrett, Maureen Forrester, the Cambridge Buskers, the Canadian Brass, Christopher Hogwood, and others. In addition to "straight" performances, Bach's music is transformed into jazz, synthesized, and even tapdance versions. Available in VHS format from other sources.

Bach, *An Advent Concert of Music by Bach*. Kultur (DVD, color, 81 minutes). This disc features atmospheric period-instrument performances of Bach Cantatas Nos. 61 and 147 as well as his magnificat in Austria's Kloster Melk Benedictine Monastery. An outstanding team of soloists includes Christine Schäfer, Bernarda Fink, and Ian Bostridge. The Arnold Schoenberg Choir and Concentus Musicus Vienna are led by Nikolaus Harnoncourt. Let your students *see* these instruments and experience cantata performances in a historic setting. Highly recommended if you use Listening Idea 3 above or for an example of a late Baroque church cantata.

Bach Cantatas. BBC Opus Arte (DVD, color, 127 minutes). A result of Gardiner's Bach cantata project and pilgrimage, this DVD includes complete performances of three cantatas: 179, 199, and 113. Filmed at various locations, these are superb period instrument performances with a marvelous team of soloists led by the radiantly expressive soprano Magdalena Kožená. Let your students *see* these instruments and experience cantata performances in European churches. Highly recommended if you use Listening Idea 2 or 3 above or for an example of a late Baroque passion.

Bach, *Greatest Organ Works*, Vols. 1 & 2. Pioneer Classics (DVD, color, 80 and 86 minutes). DVD recording of Bach's organ music performed by Hans-André Stamm on the beautiful Baroque Trost organ in Waltershausen, Germany. Several chorale preludes are included in each volume; Vol. 2 contains "Herzlich tut mich Verlangen" and the chorale from the end of *The Art of Fugue,* "Vor deinen Thron tret ich hiermit." Try these recordings for more organ chorales or use Vol. 2 with Listening Idea 2 above.

Bach, *St. John Passion*. EuroArts (DVD, color, 116 minutes). Superb new period performance of Bach's "other" passion by the Bach Collegium Japan; conducted by Masaaki Suzuki. This Japanese ensemble has quickly established itself as one of the foremost Bach ensembles in the world. Try this recording if you use Listening Idea 5 above or for an example of a late Baroque passion.

Bach, *The St. Matthew Passion*. www.films.com (DVD and VHS, color, 180 minutes). This masterwork was filmed in Leipzig at Bach's own church (the Thomas-Kirche). Performed by Peter Schreier and soloists with the Choir of

St. Thomas Church, Leipzig. Try this recording if you use Listening Idea 2 above or for an example of a late Baroque passion.

Bach, *Weinachtsoratorium (Christmas Oratorio)*. Arthaus (DVD, color, 198 minutes). At long last this marvelous period-instrument performance of Bach's six Christmas cantatas has been released on DVD. John Eliot Gardiner leads a superb team of vocal soloists, the Monteverdi Choir, and the English Baroque Soloists. Highly recommended if you use Listening Idea 1 or 2 or the Further Listening Examples exercise above for "Wie soll ich dich empfangen" or "Nun seid Ihr wohl gerochen" (the Baroque trumpet licks in the latter are amazing!).

Cecilia Bartoli: Live in Italy. Decca 074 104-9 (DVD, color, 110 minutes). This live concert performance by the outstanding mezzo ranges widely in its program, but the aria from Vivaldi's *Griselda,* "Agitata da due venti," will knock your socks off. One expects this kind of virtuoso writing—rapidly re-iterated notes and wide leaps at breakneck tempo—in a Vivaldi concerto, but not from a singer. Accompanied by a small period-instrument orchestra, Bartoli brings this off with incredible panache. Try this recording if you use Listening Idea 5 above.

Farinelli. Sony Pictures (DVD and VHS, color, 110 minutes). Fascinating "Hollywood" portrait of one of the great *castrati*. Includes encounters with Handel and a technologically engineered *castrato* voice (morphing software was used to blend countertenor and soprano voices). Especially useful are scenes from theatrical performances.

George Frideric Handel. Harmonics: The Innovators of Classical Music Series. www.films.com (DVD and VHS, color, 27 minutes). Video survey of Handel's achievements includes interviews with William Christie and Christophe Rousset as well as musical selections from *Julius Caesar, Orlando, Solomon, Water Music, Royal Fireworks Music,* and others.

Handel, *Giulio Cesare*. BBC Opus Arte (DVD, color, 295 minutes). David McVicar's new Glyndebourne production of Handel's great opera features an excellent young cast and the period-instrument Orchestra of the Age of En-lightenment; conducted by William Christie. This is now a clear first-choice recording of *Julius Caesar*. Highly recommended for your classroom presenta-tion of any music from *Julius Caesar*.

Handel, *Julius Caesar*. Image Entertainment (DVD, color, 180 minutes). Eng-lish National Opera production of Handel's great opera features Janet Baker in the title role; conducted by Charles Mackerras. This is about as good a modern-instrument performance as you will find. Highly recommended for your classroom presentation of any music from *Julius Caesar*.

Handel's *Messiah*. Image Entertainment (DVD, color, 140 minutes). Excellent period-instrument performance filmed at the Pieterskerk in Leiden, Holland. Beautiful singing from a strong team of soloists that includes Lynne Dawson and John Mark Ainsley, accompanied by the Brandenburg Consort and the Choir of King's College, Cambridge; conducted by Stephen Cleobury. Highly recommended for your classroom presentation of *Messiah* or if you use Lis-tening Idea 1 or the comparison of Bach and Handel in Further Listening Ex-amples above.

Handel's *Messiah*. Kultur (DVD, color, 136 minutes). Very fine period-instrument performance of the 1754 Foundling Hospital version, filmed at Westminster Abbey. Especially fine solo work from Emma Kirkby and David Thomas, but tenor Paul Elliott is no match for John Mark Ainsley on the Cleobury set, and the producer's preference for extreme close-up shots of the soloists is distracting. The excellent Westminster Abbey Choir and the Academy of Ancient Music are led by Christopher Hogwood. Recommended for your classroom presentation of *Messiah* or if you use Listening Idea 1 or the comparison of Bach and Handel in Further Listening Examples above.

Handel's *Messiah*. Norman: University of Oklahoma Foundation, 1990 (VHS). Charles Burney's reflections on the 1784 Westminster Abbey performance of *Messiah* are woven together with excerpts from Handel's oratorio.

Handel's *Messiah*. www.films.com (DVD and VHS, color, 114 minutes). Another fine performance available on video. Performed by Norma Burrowes, Helen Watts, Robert Tear, Willard White, the London Baroque Players, and the Cardiff Polyphonic Choir; conducted by Roger Norrington.

The Italian Connection. Man and Music Series. www.films.com (DVD and VHS, color, 53 minutes). A look at Italian opera in England. Emphasis on Handel's operas. Selections from Bononcini's *Griselda;* Gay's *Beggar's Opera;* and Handel's *Rinaldo, Acis and Galatea* (with Emma Kirkby), *Julius Caesar, Alexander's Feast,* and *Zadok the Priest.*

Johann Sebastian Bach: Masterpieces to Order. www.films.com (DVD and VHS, color, 80 minutes). Looks at Bach's life in Leipzig. Includes part of a reconstructed Lutheran service modeled on eighteenth-century practice. Performances of Bach's *Ascension Oratorio* and Cantata No. 11 by the Yorkshire Bach Choir and Baroque Orchestra. Try this video if you use Listening Idea 3 above.

Luther and the Reformation. Music in Time Series. www.films.com (DVD and VHS, color, 60 minutes). James Galway narrates this look at the effect of the Reformation on Bach and on the history of music. Baroque vocal excerpts come from a Schütz passion and Bach's "O Welt, ich muss dich lassen," Passion Chorale, and *St. Matthew Passion.*

The Voice of Britannia. Man and Music Series. www.films.com (DVD and VHS, color, 53 minutes). A look at mid-eighteenth-century English music. Handel's oratorios and the music of Arne and Boyce are covered. Selections from Handel's *Samson* and *Jephtha.*

⁊ Software

Bach Magnificat/Vivaldi Gloria. Time Sketch Series. ECS Media (CD-ROM—Windows or Macintosh). Program presents Robert Shaw's CD recording of Bach's *Magnificat* and Vivaldi's *Gloria* with interactive arch map analysis and background information about the composers, their styles, and the works themselves. Useful for a look at other sacred vocal works. Available at www.ecsmedia.com.

CHAPTER 11

Prelude
Music and the Enlightenment

Chapter Outline

Boldface indicates works in the recording set.

Suggested Listening

Haydn, Symphony No. 95 in C Minor, II
Mozart, *Don Giovanni*, Aria, "Ho capito"

Important Terms

the Enlightenment	Classical style	homophony
"The Pursuit of Happiness"	"natural"	repetition
Rococo	"pleasing variety"	cadence
divertimento	crescendo	sonata form
opera buffa	diminuendo	minuet form
novel	Classical orchestra	rondo
Neoclassicism	tune	theme and variations form
public concerts		

Teaching Objectives

⍦ Overall Objectives

This chapter will help students acquire familiarity with:

1. Classical style as a reflection of the Enlightenment ideals of "pleasing variety" and "natural" simplicity.

2. The social, economic, and musical changes associated with the rise of public concerts.

3. Typical Classical uses of rhythm, dynamics, tone color, melody, and texture, especially the roles played by the orchestra, tunes, homophony, and counter-point.

4. The importance of repetition, cadences, and standard formal patterns in the Classical approach to musical form.

⍦ Listening Objectives

After completing this chapter, students should be able to:

1. Hear and identify how the ideals of "pleasing variety" and "natural" simplicity affect typical use of the elements of music in Classical style.

2. Hear and identify the clarifying effect of repetition and cadences.

Lecture Suggestions

Modern concertgoers face a wonderful, diverse world of musical possibilities, ranging from popular to classical, from ancient to contemporary, and from Western traditions to music of the world. Even with this trend toward greater diversity, the majority of music performed by most classical music institutions (orchestras, opera houses, and the like) still comes from the Classical and Romantic periods of music history. Textbook Chapters 11 through 18 cover this repertory and must be given full attention to prepare students for the music they will most likely hear in the concert hall.

The Classical style was forged in musical centers across Europe during the mid-eighteenth century. Vienna, a cosmopolitan center much like New York City today, held a preeminent position for a variety of reasons:

1. Vienna stood at the midpoint between two great musical traditions of the eighteenth century: the operatic-vocal tradition of southern European Catholic countries—particularly the Italian states—and the instrumental-polyphonic tradition of northern, Protestant Europe—particularly the German states.

2. As the capital of the large, powerful Hapsburg empire, Vienna was exposed to the cultural and intellectual currents of the time and was involved in many conflicts as well. The "threat" of Islam just to the east often proved all too real. Use a map of Europe in 1800 (photocopy a transparency or borrow one from your school's history department) to illustrate the late eighteenth-century boundaries of the Hapsburg empire.

3. Emperor Joseph II of Austria, the most enlightened of the Hapsburg rulers, presided over a golden age in Viennese music, spanning the years 1780–1790.

4. Vienna became the adopted home of the greatest Classical composers: Haydn, Mozart, and Beethoven.

¶ The Enlightenment and Music

The late eighteenth century saw the rise of an intellectual and philosophical movement called the Enlightenment, which formed the basis for Western society as we know it today. The Enlightenment was characterized by a new concern for problems of public morality, promotion of universal education, the politics of plurality, a distrust of organized religion, and an abhorrence of social injustice.

Tremendous changes in Western society and politics took place during the Enlightenment—changes that profoundly affected Western art and music. These changes included:

Humanism—As the once absolute authority of the church continued to wane and the general standard of living continued to rise, the promise of an afterlife in Paradise became less important to the average person. People became more concerned with improving earthly existence. Most Enlightenment philosophy posited human reason as the measure of all things; in fact, some scholars and thinkers rejected the church altogether.

"The Pursuit of Happiness"—The notion emerged that the "common man" with "common sense" had the right to self-determination for the "common good." The idea that common folk could overthrow a hereditary monarchy was unthinkable in 1700, yet eighty years later such revolutions occurred, first in North America and then in France. The spirit of revolution that arose during the Enlightenment would continue to stir Europe throughout the nineteenth century and into the twentieth.

Cosmopolitanism—The ideal of brotherhood espoused by humanism was partly realized in a trend referred to as "cosmopolitanism," which saw the downplaying of national differences in favor of the common humanity of all people. Cosmopolitanism is seen in the use of "international" languages: Italian was the language of music, whether one was discussing music in England or Austria; French was the language of politics. J. J. Quantz, composer and music teacher to Frederick the Great of Prussia, wrote in 1752 that the ideal musical style of the Enlightenment was a composite of the best features of all European nations: "For a style of music that is received and approved by many peoples, and not just by a single land, a single province, or a particular nation, a style of music that, for the above reasons, can only meet with approbation, must, if it is also based on sound judgment and healthy feeling, be the very best" (*On Playing the Flute,* trans. Edward R. Reilly, New York: Schirmer, 1966; fuller quotation available in Grout and Palisca's *History of Western Music,* 7th ed., New York: W. W. Norton, 2006).

Musical consumerism—The movement toward universal education meant an ever more literate population that was also, to a degree, musically literate. The musically literate consumers of the Classical era were interested in music as a hobby, as a diversion; they wanted simple, easy, pleasant music to listen to and perform.

Music as entertainment—Here the Enlightenment ideals most decisive for Classical music come into focus. According to these ideals, music must be both pleasing and accessible in order to entertain. As a manifestation of the pursuit of happiness, "pleasing" meant music that could delight and amuse, and a certain amount of variety was needed to produce this. The ideals of "naturalness" and humanism that crystallized during the Enlightenment were manifested in a simpler, more accessible musical language. The resulting Classical style conformed to the twin principles of pleasing variety and natural simplicity.

To demonstrate the principles of pleasing variety and natural simplicity, play the exposition from the first movement of Mozart's Symphony No. 40 in G Minor (the first two minutes). Write "pleasing variety" and "natural simplicity" on the board and ask students to pick out features appropriate to each category as they listen. Pleasing variety is displayed in the many contrasts Mozart builds in, not only between sections but within the themes themselves. The first few bars of theme 1 contrast a halting, lyrical theme played by strings with a martial fanfare played by *forte* woodwinds, horns, and strings (at track 16, 0:19)—two contrasting moods in a single melodic unit. Even the repetition of theme 1 (at track 16, 0:24) offers a contrast; it begins to move to another key. The bridge offers a dramatic, extended *forte* outburst by the full orchestra that eventually gives way to theme 2. The quietly lyrical theme 2 contrasts markedly with the preceding bridge, offering delightful contrasts in tone color as the melody passes back and forth between woodwinds and strings. A typical symphony's first movement is often complex in construction, but we can hear "natural" simplicity in Mozart's tuneful melodies—his insistence on a simple rhythmic motive, clear duple meter, and simple homophonic textures, especially evident when he presents theme 1 and theme 2.

❼ The Rise of Concerts

The rise of public concerts went hand in hand with the growth of the middle class and the development of a simpler, more accessible musical language. The first hall built especially for concerts was constructed in Oxford, England, in 1748. The rise of the concert hall altered the sociology and economics of Western music in three profound ways:

1. The concert hall enabled composers to be supported by the general public rather than by an individual patron. Even though only fourteen years separated the births of Mozart and Beethoven, the increasing prevalence of the public concert hall gave Beethoven a greater degree of freedom from the patronage system than Mozart and his contemporaries could imagine.

2. Instrumental music became the staple of public concert halls. Thus, the rise of such halls gave impetus to the creation of orchestral music: symphonies and concertos.

3. The public concert hall eventually replaced the church, the court, and (to some extent) the opera house as the focal point of musical life.

❼ Style Features of Classical Music

The Enlightenment ideals of pleasing variety and natural simplicity colored the ways that Classical composers used the elements of music. Start with a listening comparison exercise; the contrast between Baroque and Classical music throws style features into sharp relief. The first movement of Bach's *Brandenburg* Concerto No. 5 and the last movement of Haydn's Symphony No. 95 serve well. To determine how variety and simplicity play a heightened role in Classical style, ask students to compare Baroque and Classical uses of rhythm, dynamics, tone color, melody, and texture. Play a minute or two of each work. In the discussion that follows, draw out the following points:

Rhythm—Rhythms become more flexible and less predictable than in Baroque music. Greater variety of durations is used, and off-the-beat accents become much more common.

Dynamics—Dynamics become more variable. Baroque music employed a fixed contrast between loud and soft, but Classical composers used a broad range of dynamics—very soft, soft, medium soft, loud, very loud, and so forth. Further, Classical composers began using *crescendo* and *diminuendo*. The harpsichord's inability to produce the dynamic shadings required by Classical composers and performers led to its eventual replacement by the piano.

Tone color—The size and instrumentation of the basic orchestra grew beyond that of the Baroque orchestra. Bach's orchestra in *Brandenburg* Concerto No. 5 consists of only strings, flute, and harpsichord continuo; Haydn adds more woodwinds, brass, and percussion (this recording does not use a keyboard instrument). Further, Bach uses a fixed contrast between full orchestra and a small group of solo instruments, but Haydn's ever-changing orchestral combinations are more flexible, more colorful, and less predictable.

Melody—Melody became the most highly prized musical element. Classical melodies are usually clearly stated, memorable tunes. Bach's ritornello melody twists and turns back on itself without phrase repetition or symmetry; Haydn's clean-lined, good-humored melody is based on a few repeating rhythmic motives, and his symmetrical phrases are often repeated, creating a sense of proportion and balance. This repetition alone makes Haydn's melody easier to grasp (though Bach's melody is one of his more memorable "tunes").

Texture—Melody and accompaniment texture (homophony) dominated Classical music. Bach's concerto begins with two-voice counterpoint between the upper string melody and the continuo, and it moves into imitative polyphony at track 1, 0:20. Haydn's symphonic movement begins with the melody and a simple accompaniment. The accompanying patterns often change, and Haydn tosses in bits of monophony and a fair amount of polyphony (episode 1) to keep the texture varied and interesting. Nonetheless, a single main melody stands out clearly at all times.

Baroque counterpoint worked well to create a single intense "affect" but proved unwieldy for the constantly changing, even composite, moods expressed by much Classical music (remember the frequent contrasts in the first movement of Mozart's Symphony No. 40). As a result, the prevailing texture of Classical music was homophony. Classical counterpoint, discussed by the authors on textbook page 179, was prized for its ability to create tension and contrast when used side by side with homophony.

Form in Classical Music

Chapters 12 and 13 deal with specific Classical forms; at this point it helps to provide an introduction to the characteristic features of these forms. The authors mention three aspects of melodic relationships in their discussion on textbook page 180: the repetition of themes, transition passages (used to lead into main themes), and distinctive cadences. Each of these features tends to emphasize the melody and make it more memorable. The following listening exercise can help students hear the concepts Kerman and Tomlinson discuss.

The first movement of Mozart's Symphony No. 40 serves well to demonstrate these concepts. Begin by reading or paraphrasing the first paragraph under the heading "Repetitions and Cadences" on textbook page 180, then play track 16, 0:00, to track 17, 0:54. Ask students to raise their hands each time they hear a melodic phrase or theme repeat. Hands will go up frequently during theme 1, infrequently during the bridge, and (we hope) up again during theme 2. In the discussion that follows, play through portions of the movement again as needed to highlight points where repetition is important. Make the point that repetition is used most heavily in the most important themes to highlight them—themes 1 and 2 are repeated, but the bridge's transitional function precludes the use of repetition.

The bridge provides a good example of a passage used to lead into a main theme. Read or paraphrase the second paragraph under the heading "Repetitions and Cadences" on textbook page 180. Play track 16, 0:33, to track 17, 0:28, so that the class can hear the sense of urgency in the bridge, then the sense of arrival at theme 2 (and its repetition).

Finally, consider the role of cadences in defining themes. Read or paraphrase the third and fourth paragraphs under the heading "Repetitions and Cadences" on textbook page 180, then play two examples. Start with Contrapunctus 4 from Bach's *The Art of Fugue* and follow that with the first movement of Mozart's Symphony No. 40 (track 16, 0:00, to track 17, 0:54). This time ask the students to raise their hands whenever they hear a strong cadence at the end of a phrase or section. If your students learned to identify cadences in Unit I, there will be few hands during the Bach fugue and many during the Mozart. Challenge students to explain why. In polyphonic music, voices overlap and phrase endings are staggered so that the motion of the texture as a whole never stops long enough to let us perceive a clear ending. Bach's work often creates the expectation of a cadence, but just at the cadence point, a new idea begins. In homophony, cadences are more clearly heard because our focus is on a single main melody. When that melody breathes or stops, we notice immediately. Mozart's melody is full of these points of articulation. Call attention to the cadence that ends the bridge section. Not only does it provide a clear ending for the transitional passage, but the pause also gives added significance to the beginning of theme 2. The stronger the sense of ending, the stronger the sense of a new beginning.

If you want further examples to demonstrate the authors' discussion of cadences, you would do well to use the two listening examples suggested on textbook pages 180–181. Taken from a Mozart aria and a Haydn theme and variations movement, they provide even clearer examples of cadences than Symphony No. 40. These forms rely on clearly constructed tunes far more than do sonata form movements.

The great artistic challenge for Classical era composers was the creation and expansion of homophonic, sectional forms based on the constant contrasts dictated by the ideal of pleasing variety. No longer did composers set out to create a single affect; they sought to express multiple moods, often within the space of a phrase or two. These contrasts created a greatly expanded range of possibilities for heightened drama and tension. As composers realized these possibilities, instrumental music finally achieved true equality with vocal music as a significant means of musical expression.

Additional Teaching Suggestions

⁊ Lecture-Demonstration Ideas

1. Invite a pianist to class. The piano replaced the harpsichord during the Classical period because it could produce fine dynamic shadings. Ask your guest to demonstrate the inner workings of the piano mechanism and to play Classical selections that show off the piano's dynamic flexibility. Ask your students to prepare questions for your guest.

2. Create a slide show of scenes from Vienna. Use your art department's collection to find as many pictures as you can of buildings associated with Classical music—the Burgtheater, St. Stephen's and St. Michael's, the Hofburg, the Freyhaus-theater, Schönbrunn Palace, and so on.

3. Compare Baroque and Neoclassical paintings, sculpture, and architecture. Use the pictures in *Listen* or prepare a slide show using your art department's collection. The ornate, dramatic quality of Baroque art contrasts sharply with the clean lines and elegant balance of Neoclassicism. Draw comparisons between these artworks and Baroque and Classical music.

4. Bring Baroque and Classical score pages to class. The first pages of a Baroque concerto grosso and a Classical symphony permit comparison of Baroque and Classical orchestras. Kerman and Tomlinson include the first page of Mozart's Symphony No. 41, IV, on textbook page 24. Review the Mozart score and its notational detail with the class—meter, tempo, duration, articulation, instrumentation, dynamics, and pitch are all indicated. Then examine the Baroque orchestral score (photocopy a transparency or handouts). Ask students which elements indicated in Mozart's symphony cannot be found in the Baroque score. Both scores indicate meter, duration, instrumentation, and pitch, but Mozart's tempo marking is more specific (*Molto* Allegro), his durations are more varied, and his orchestra is larger. The Baroque score may not include tempo indications (Bach includes them in most movements of his *Brandenburg* Concertos) or dynamic markings (if present, only *forte* and *piano* can usually be found). The Baroque score will not include articulation (slurs, staccato marks, and so on), though it may indicate some ornaments. This exercise permits review of musical notation as well as comparison of Baroque and Classical styles.

⁊ Class Discussion Ideas

1. *What was the purpose of music in the late eighteenth century?* To generate class discussion, read or hand out the following quotations, which make it clear that composers and audiences wanted pleasing, decorous, entertaining music.

> Music is an innocent luxury, unnecessary, indeed, to our existence, but a great improvement and gratification of the sense of hearing.
> —Dr. Charles Burney, *General History of Music*

> [Music is] the art of pleasing by the succession and combination of agreeable sounds.
> —Dr. Charles Burney, *General History of Music*

The mid-eighteenth century also saw an almost violent backlash against the complexities of polyphonic composition.

> [Music is] the art of inventing tunes and accompanying them with suitable harmonies. . . . To sing two melodies at once [polyphony] is like making two speeches at once in order to be more forceful.
>
> —Jean-Jacques Rousseau, *Dictionnaire de musique*

> The old composers were too much absorbed with compositional "tricks" and carried them too far, so that they neglected the essential thing in music, which is to move and please.
>
> —J. J. Quantz, *On Playing the Flute*

> [Bach has] been constantly in search of what was new and difficult, without the least attention to nature and facility. . . . [Bach could not give up] all unmeaning art and contrivance [and write] in a style more popular and generally pleasing.
>
> —Dr. Charles Burney, *General History of Music*

2. *What were public concerts like in the late eighteenth century?* Find a program from an eighteenth-century concert. Photocopy a transparency or copies for your class to read. Such programs can be found on pages 84–85 and 97 of Charles Hamm's *Music in the New World* (New York: Norton, 1983). If you have time, reconstruct such a concert for your class from video clips and sound recordings.

3. *What role did women play in music in the Classical era?* Several extracts from Carol Neuls-Bates's *Women in Music* (New York: Harper & Row, 1982, pages 73–88) can be assigned or read in class. Music was often regarded as a private "accomplishment," a mark of gentility that made women desirable prospects for marriage. The readings deal with this cultural expectation and with society's treatment of women who dared to go further by composing and presenting works in public performance. (Expectations notwithstanding, Mozart wrote some piano concertos for women students—Piano Concerto No. 17 in G, for instance.)

♩ Listening Ideas

1. Play the final movements (just the beginning of each) from three different Classical symphonies (for example, Haydn's Symphony No. 95 from the *Listen* anthology and, from other sources, Mozart's Symphony No. 41 and Beethoven's Symphony No. 1). Challenge students to determine whether these works were written by three different composers, two different composers, or the same composer. There are some differences among these pieces, but unless a student already knows all the excerpts, it is unlikely that anyone will be able to determine positively whether these works were written by the same or by different composers. This exercise can be used to demonstrate the cosmopolitan, "international" style common to many Classical composers. See Sound Recordings below for suggested performances.

2. Play recordings of the harpsichord, clavichord, and fortepiano. The last half of the eighteenth century saw the fortepiano gradually replace the harpsichord and clavichord. Ask students to first listen for the differences in instrumental timbre and then describe the different actions for each of the three instruments. See Sound Recordings below for suggested CDs.

3. The textbook mentions the influence of folk tunes on Classical melody in the discussion on textbook page 178. To drive home this point, play recordings that demonstrate these connections. Possibilities include Mozart's Variations on "Ah vous dirai-je, maman"; Haydn or Beethoven settings of folk songs from the British Isles; and Haydn and Beethoven symphonies (Haydn Symphonies 103 and 104, IV; Beethoven's Symphony No. 6, I), whose tunes were found among the folk songs ethnomusicologist Béla Bartók collected in the twentieth century in rural eastern Europe.[1] See Further Listening Examples in Chapter 13 of this manual for lecture-demonstration ideas on Mozart's Variations on "Ah vous dirai-je, maman." See Sound Recordings below for suggested performances.

❦ Further Listening Examples

Classical Homophony versus Baroque Polyphony

This exercise permits further comparison between Baroque and Classical styles as well as between organ and pianoforte. Recordings of both works can be found in the *Listen* anthology. Play the first thirty-five seconds of each work for the class:

FRESCOBALDI, **Suite: Canzona**

LEBRUN, **Sonata in F, II**

Ask students to list the differences between these two pieces. Most of the differences are indicative of the changes in musical style that separate the Baroque and the Classical eras. Draw out the following points:

1. The rhythms of the Frescobaldi canzona sound consistent and continuous in comparison with the more varied rhythms of the LeBrun sonata. Curiously, in spite of Frescobaldi's greater rhythmic consistency, the meter stands out more clearly in the LeBrun.

2. The canzona is polyphonic, the sonata homophonic.

3. The canzona is performed on the organ. The sustained timbre of the organ is richer but makes it harder to clearly hear the three polyphonic voices of the fugue. The sonata was written for violin and fortepiano; the latter's dynamically sensitive keyboard can be used to shade and add nuance to the music.

4. The sonata's opening theme—a lengthy, symmetrical (mostly eight-bar phrases), clearly defined tune with frequent phrase repetitions and extensions—remains in the piano's upper voice; Frescobaldi's subject—a short, distinctive melodic motive that is imitated, transposed, and fragmented—constantly moves from one voice to another. The sonata's homophonic texture helps to focus our attention on the single melody.

5. The fortepiano sounds less full-bodied and more sharply articulated than the organ. Though the fortepiano cannot sustain its notes as long as the organ can, its dynamic flexibility allows it to sing nonetheless, and it creates greater rhythmic energy as well.

---

[1]In some cases it is difficult to say whether these composers quoted preexisting tunes or whether their tunes were so popular that they were absorbed into the folk repertory; the former is more likely.

6. Due to the organ's limitation with respect to dynamics, Frescobaldi can only create greater loudness by adding more organ stops or simultaneous notes. LeBrun, on the other hand, need not rely on thick textures to create loud dynamics. Her fortepiano allows her to create an enormous variety of dynamic shadings.

Multimedia Resources

❦ Sound Recordings

Beethoven, *9 Symphonies*. Orchestre Révolutionnaire et Romantique. Deutsche Grammophon Archiv 2AH5 439 900 (CD). Vigorous, exciting performances of the complete Beethoven symphonies on period instruments; conducted by John Eliot Gardiner. Try this recording if you use Listening Idea 1 or 3 above.

Gluck, *Orfeo ed Euridice*. English Baroque Soloists and Monteverdi Choir. London 470 424 (CD). Excellent performance features Sylvia McNair, Derek Lee Ragin, and Cyndia Sieden; conducted by John Eliot Gardiner. Gluck's music embodies the "Neoclassic" label more fully than most music of the Classical era. He worked hard to purge his operas of the perceived excesses of late Baroque opera. The immediacy and power of his reform operas result from the lean simplicity of his melodic lines and his subjugation of musical form to the natural dramatic flow. These late Classical works retained their popular appeal well into the nineteenth century, where they had a profound effect on even modern composers such as Berlioz.

Haydn, *The London Symphonies*, Vol. 1. Royal Concertgebouw Orchestra. Philips 442 611-2 (CD). Fine modern-instrument performances of late Haydn symphonies; conducted by Colin Davis. Try this recording of Symphonies 103 and 104 if you use Listening Idea 3 above.

Mozart, *Complete Piano Variations*. Ronald Brautigam. Bis 1266/7 (CD). Part of Brautigam's outstanding Mozart series on fortepiano, this CD includes the Variations on "Ah vous dirai-je, maman," K. 265/300e. Try this recording if you use Listening Idea 2 or 3 above.

Mozart, *Symphonies Nos. 40 and 41*. Vienna Philharmonic. Deutsche Grammophon 445 548-2 (CD). Dramatic modern-instrument performances of Mozart's two late symphonies; conducted by Leonard Bernstein. Try this recording if you use Listening Idea 1 above.

❦ Video Recordings

Delaware Music Series. www.ecsmedia.com (DVD). This important collection includes period-instrument performances of works by several important Classical composers, including Haydn, Mozart, and Beethoven. It also includes demonstrations of eighteenth-century orchestral instruments.

Eighteenth-Century Art and Music. www.insight-media.com (DVD, color, 35 minutes). This still-image video provides a concise, visually appealing introduction to important philosophic, artistic, and musical trends in the Classical era. Part 1 covers the heart of the Classical era, containing the artwork of Hogarth and Fragonard and music by Gluck, Haydn, and Mozart.

The History of Music, Part 1. www.insight-media.com (VHS, color, 90 minutes). The section on the Classical era covers the symphony, sonata form, and music of Haydn, Mozart, and early Beethoven.

London: The Musical Capital. Man and Music Series. www.films.com (DVD or VHS, color, 53 minutes). Covers the transition from Baroque to Classical music in England. Includes music from J. C. Bach's Symphony Op. 18, No. 2; Clementi's Sonata Op. 24, No. 2; Haydn's Symphony No. 104; and songs by J. C. Bach, Webbe, and Haydn.

Music of an Empire. Man and Music Series. www.films.com (DVD or VHS, color, 53 minutes). A look at Vienna's growing musical importance during the eighteenth century. Includes musical excerpts from Cesti's *Il Pomo d'Oro,* Gluck's *Orfeo ed Euridice,* and other works.

Performance Practices in Classical Piano Music. www.insight-media.com (DVD, color, 60 minutes). Includes music of several important *Listen* composers, especially Haydn, Mozart, Beethoven, and Schubert. Looks at musical characteristics and several different keyboard instruments. Useful as a classroom supplement or if you use Listening Idea 2 above.

The Seasons and the Symphony. Music in Time Series. www.films.com (DVD or VHS, color, 60 minutes). James Galway narrates this look at the transition from Baroque to Classical music. Musical excerpts from Vivaldi's *The Four Seasons;* Gluck's *Orfeo ed Euridice;* J. C. Bach's Overture No. 2; Stamitz's Symphony in D Major; and Haydn's String Quartet Op. 77, Piano Trio, Symphony No. 100 (*Military*), *Lord Nelson* Mass, *Emperor* Quartet, and *Farewell* Symphony (No. 45). Performances by the Bach Orchestra, Choir of St. Paul's, Academy of Ancient Music, Takacs Quartet, and Mannheim Orchestra.

♩ Software

Art and Music: The Eighteenth Century. Zane Publishing (CD-ROM—Windows or Macintosh). The Classical volume of this inexpensive CD-ROM series looks at the Enlightenment and the Age of Revolution. Includes art by Fragonard and David as well as the music of Bach, Haydn, Mozart, and Beethoven. Quality of screen images is variable, but it's hard to argue with the price. Available from www.cdaccess.com.

The History of Music, Part 1. www.mccormicksnet.com (CD-ROM—Windows or Macintosh). CD-ROM version of the VHS tape above. The section on the Classical era covers the symphony; sonata form; and music of Haydn, Mozart, and early Beethoven.

CHAPTER 12

The Symphony

Chapter Outline

Boldface indicates works in the recording set.

Important Terms

symphony	development	minuet
symphony movement plan	retransition	trio
slow introduction	recapitulation	ternary form
sonata form	coda	rondo form
exposition	fragmentation	rondo
first theme	Classical variation form	rondeau
bridge (transition)	theme and variations	episodes
second group	slow movement	sonata rondos
second theme	minuet form (Classical dance form)	finale
cadence (closing) theme	stylized dances	

Teaching Objectives

❧ Overall Objectives

This chapter will help students acquire familiarity with:

1. Features of the Classical symphony genre and its associated musical forms, understood as expressions of the principles of "pleasing variety" and "natural" simplicity.

2. The symphony movement plan, a four-movement format that dominated Classical instrumental genres.

3. The internal structures of important Classical forms associated with the four-movement plan:

    a. sonata form   c. minuet form

    b. theme and variations   d. rondo form

4. The lives and music of Wolfgang Amadeus Mozart and Franz Joseph Haydn.

❧ Listening Objectives

After completing this chapter, students should be able to:

1. Hear and identify how elements of music are used in the Classical symphony genre and its associated musical forms.

2. Recognize and follow important features of the Classical symphony genre.

3. Recognize and follow the symphony's four-movement plan.

4. Follow the forms associated with the symphony, especially sonata, theme and variations, minuet, and rondo forms.

Lecture Suggestions

Chapters 12 and 13 function together, almost as a single, long chapter. Chapter 12 presents the basic four-movement plan and important Classical forms in the context of the symphony; Chapter 13 describes how the four-movement plan and Classical forms adapted themselves to the needs of the other significant Classical genres. This manual follows the textbook's order of presentation for several good reasons:

1. When students encounter Classical music, whether live, broadcast, or recorded, they encounter musical genres first: symphonies, sonatas, concertos, quartets, opera, and so on. The authors' focus on genre prepares students for these encounters.

2. The symphony provides an excellent starting point for a study of Classical genres. The most significant musical achievement of the Classical era, the symphony continues to enjoy enormous prestige even today. Further, many of its features carry over into other instrumental genres.

3. When students study the symphony genre, they learn its basic four-movement plan, a plan that also forms the basis for the instrumental genres covered in Chapter 13: sonata, concerto, and string quartet. Once students know the plan, they possess a tool that will enhance their enjoyment of most Classical instrumental music.

4. Students who know the four-movement plan can grasp more fully the role and significance of Classical musical forms, since they can place these forms in a familiar framework. When students encounter Classical music, they can recognize and follow these forms when they know where to look for them.

5. The encounter with the symphony genre and its related forms provides excellent preparation for Chapter 13's encounters with other venerable, influential orchestral traditions—Japanese *gagaku* and the Balinese *gamelan*. In fact, you may wish to cover these Japanese and Balinese orchestras alongside the examples from Chapter 12. Similarities and differences will stand out all the more clearly if you cover *gagaku* and *gamelan* immediately after the orchestral tradition of Haydn and Mozart.

6. Students get to know at least one complete Classical work, a Haydn symphony. A full understanding of Classical conventions proves especially useful in Chapter 14, where Beethoven's accomplishments in Symphony No. 5 stand out all the more clearly.

The Symphony: Background Information

The genre known as the symphony is, by definition, a large, multimovement work for orchestra. The symphony was the most significant new instrumental genre of the Classical era. The inherent drama of its sonata-form first movement, the pleasing succession of movements that followed (according to the four-movement plan), and its versatile handling of orchestral sonorities proved immensely satisfying and successful. The symphony quickly surpassed other instrumental genres in both size and importance. In fact, the symphony mounted an impressive challenge to opera's preeminent position as the most significant form of musical expression. As we shall see in Chapter 14, the symphony eventually surpassed opera in the hands of a composer named Ludwig van Beethoven.

❦ The Movements of the Symphony

Many different formats were used in early symphonies; some followed the three-movement plan of the Italian opera overture (or *sinfonia*), while others borrowed features from Baroque concertos and trio sonatas. By about 1770, a four-movement plan emerged as the most common format for the symphony. The symphonic four-movement plan proved so successful that composers began to use it or adapt it for most of their instrumental works, as we shall see in Chapter 13. In essence, the symphony was the testing ground where the four-movement plan was developed and refined.

Take a few moments to introduce the symphony's four-movement plan. The main textbook provides an outline of the movements of the symphony on pages 182–183; the outline can also be expressed in chart form. Put this chart on the board.

Movement	Form	Tempo	Character
I	sonata (optional slow introduction)	moderate to fast	complex, substantial, impressive
II	no fixed form (sonata, variation, rondo)	slow	lyrical, songlike
III	minuet (with trio)	moderate	dancelike, triple meter
IV	sonata or rondo	fast	often light, tuneful, brilliant

The four-movement plan must have been profoundly satisfying for eighteenth-century audiences, judging by the enormous success it enjoyed. This format dominated all primary instrumental genres during the Classical period and continued to influence symphonies, concertos, sonatas, and chamber music throughout the nineteenth century. It encapsulates the notion of pleasing variety—no two movements are alike. The succession of moods remains pleasing even for modern audiences. Put simply, the four-movement plan provides something thought provoking, even serious; something beautiful and lyrical; something to tap your foot or dance to; and a tune to whistle on the way out the door—something for everyone! In fact, the format fulfills most purposes for which humans "use" music. The first movement stimulates the intellect and satisfies a need for drama; the second satisfies a need for beauty; the third, a dance, invites a physical response; and the fourth offers the pleasure of a good tune and a brilliant conclusion.

Listening Exercise: The Four-Movement Plan

Students can begin to feel at home in the four-movement plan with the help of the following exercise, based on Haydn's Symphony No. 95 in C Minor. In random order, play just the first minute of each movement. Ask students to inventory characteristics of each movement and compare them with the chart on the board. Which movement does the first excerpt come from? the second? the third? the fourth? Draw out the reasons in class discussion. The excerpt with the fastest tempo and the clearest tune is probably the fourth movement; a slow tempo indicates the second movement; triple meter and a dancelike moderate tempo point to the third movement; and the more dramatic-sounding movement that remains must be the first movement. This exercise does not rely on form as a distinguishing feature; at first, surface features such as tempo, meter, and character will be most useful to students. Once they know which movement they are listening to, they can listen for the expected form. If you have time, try this exercise with other four-movement symphonies of your choice. Most students find they can identify movements successfully with just a few minutes of drill; this extra confidence will prove an asset when you tackle a more difficult task: following classical forms.

Classical Forms

One cannot understand the development of music after 1750 without knowledge of Classical forms. They form the basis of most music written between 1770 and 1830, but their influence reaches far beyond 1830. One must know the conventions of Classical forms to appreciate how Beethoven stretches and adapts them to suit his expressive purposes. Romantic composers either used or rejected Classical forms, but those who rejected them still borrowed many of their features. Even in the twentieth century, Classical forms were frequently used by Neoclassical and twelve-tone composers.

You cannot spend too much time with this material, but you must find a balance between the importance of this material and your desire to do justice to other parts of the book. Some instructors devote as many as twelve class hours to this chapter alone. That sounds excessive, since you can review and reinforce all of these forms as you study Beethoven, Romanticism, and the twentieth century, but it is hard to imagine using fewer than three class hours.

The ideals of pleasing variety and natural simplicity suggest two familiar concepts when applied to musical form: contrast and repetition (variety and unity). There can be no variety without contrast, but the contrast must be pleasing, judicious, and well proportioned—not too much, but not too little. "Simplicity" suggests relationships that can be heard easily, and repetition creates a familiarity that permits easy perception of musical form. Homophonic textures also simplify the task of hearing formal relationships. In polyphonic textures, one must listen intently to catch the simultaneous relationships between two or more melodies; but with homophonic textures, the melody is easy to find—one can listen instead for consecutive sections and the relationships between them. Most Classical forms consist of clearly defined sections related according to principles of repetition and contrast. The most notable exception is sonata form, whose dynamic, continuous development of ideas sets it apart from the others.

Sonata Form

Sonata form was unquestionably the most important new form developed by Classical composers. The first movement of most multimovement Classical compositions—symphonies, quartets, trios, piano sonatas, even opera overtures—was in sonata form. Many of these works have two or even three movements in sonata form. Sonata form stands apart from the other principal Classical forms because it treats contrasts of key and theme in a new, dramatic, combative manner.

Start with a diagram. This complex form makes more sense if students can follow a map. You can create a diagram on the board by following the instructions below, or you can prepare three transparencies modeled after the diagrams immediately below, each one more detailed than the last. Begin with the three main sections:

EXPOSITION   DEVELOPMENT   RECAPITULATION

The exposition introduces ("exposes") the main themes and presents the fundamental conflict between two different keys. The development section permits alteration of the main themes and interaction between them (the themes are "developed"), and frequent modulations heighten the conflict presented in the exposition. The recapitulation (*re-*, "again"; *capit-*, "the head"—the head again, or back to the beginning) restates the main themes in the same order as in the exposition, but this time all themes are stated in the home key; conflicts of theme and key are resolved. In a nutshell, the form can be described as statement-conflict-restatement (resolution).

Add tonal relationships to your diagram:

EXPOSITION   DEVELOPMENT   RECAPITULATION

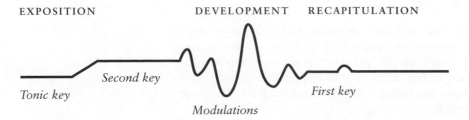

Second key

Tonic key

First key

Modulations

These key relationships define the primary conflicts within sonata form. The exposition establishes a fundamental conflict between two closely related keys. The themes associated with the tonic key and the second key are harmonically stable (horizontal lines), but the transition between the two keys (diagonal line) often provides a moment of dramatic conflict. That conflict works itself out at length in the development section, where frequent modulations create enormous instability. In the recapitulation, the conflict resolves in favor of the tonic key. This diagram of key relationships expresses Classical theorists' understanding of sonata form (even the terms *exposition, development,* and *recapitulation* were invented later).

In the early nineteenth century, theorists noticed that many Classical composers wrote a contrasting second theme to articulate the arrival at the second key in the middle of the exposition. As you add theme names to the diagram, the form suddenly begins to look more rigid. (This is a good place to refer students to the textbook's diagram on page 185.)

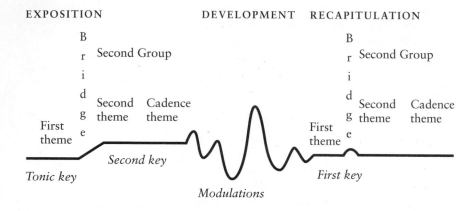

The first theme is a stable melody associated with the tonic key. The second theme sounds equally stable but is stated in the second key. The cadence theme, also associated with the second key, provides strong cadences and a sense of finality at its end. Bridge passages can present new thematic material, but their function is transitional, modulating from the key of the first theme to the key of the second. New themes are not usually presented in the development; here themes from the exposition can be fragmented, transposed, recombined, and transformed—according to the composer's sense of dramatic necessity. The recapitulation restates the themes from the exposition in the same order, but now entirely in the tonic key. The bridge threatens to move away from tonic again, but this time it returns to the first key. The thematic structure does not change the key structure in any way; rather, it serves to heighten our sense of the tonal structure, especially the contrast between tonic and the second key, the sense of conflict in the development section, and the sense of resolution in the recapitulation.

MOZART **Symphony No. 40 in G Minor, I**

Once students have a sense of what to expect in sonata form, display Listening Chart 7 (or refer students to textbook page 188) and play the entire first movement of Mozart's Symphony No. 40, pointing to each section as it is played. Note that the entire exposition repeats; this is typical of sonata-form movements. Once students have this broad overview under their belts, work through this movement one section at a time.

Exposition

In the exposition, play and discuss each theme individually. Use the checklist of musical elements and structures; ask students to describe each theme and to compare themes with each other. This exercise allows students to focus on the function of each theme in the exposition. The first theme must establish the tonic key securely; it introduces and often repeats an important melodic idea.

Mozart's first theme is based on a brief motive (short-short-long: ♪♪♩) that, unusually, appears in many guises later in the exposition and throughout the entire movement. The frequent appearances of this brief motive create an intensifying effect. The bridge serves a transitional function; its melodic content is secondary to the change of tonal center that defines it. Most students will not easily hear the modulation itself, but they can hear the instability it creates, especially in contrast with the stability of the first and second themes. (Students have a nice advantage in minor key movements; since the key change also involves a shift from minor to major mode, they can more easily hear the new key's arrival.) The bridge, as it often does, ends with cadence and a pause, a rhetorical device used to emphasize the arrival of both the new key and a new theme. To establish the new key securely, the second theme introduces and often repeats an important melodic idea. Mozart frequently favors a lyrical, gentle melody that contrasts with the first theme. The cadence theme serves a concluding function, since it must end both the exposition and the recapitulation. It usually accomplishes this by vigorously (and loudly) repeating strong cadence figures.

Development

Once you have finished with the exposition, work through the development one section at a time. The listening goal here is different, however, since the development does not follow a set pattern of thematic and tonal relationships. Instead of listening for the fixed order and the function of different themes, it is important to listen for techniques and procedures common to most development sections. The sequence of events differs dramatically from one development to another, but most developments have two aspects in common.

1. They are based on previously stated thematic material.

2. They convey instability, tension, and forward momentum.

These aspects result from characteristic uses of several musical elements and structures.

Melody—Strong cadences are avoided, creating constant movement. Frequently at least one of the principal themes will be "fragmented"—broken down into short motives. Further, motives drawn from these themes can be repeated again and again at different pitch levels (transposed); this technique is often used to modulate from one key to others. These unfamiliar uses of now-familiar melodies create a feeling of dislocation and disorientation.

Key—Development sections modulate freely and frequently, creating instability and tension; as a result, there is almost constant forward momentum. We feel no strong sense of tonic. In this respect, development sections are akin to modulating bridges.

Texture—Imitation and polyphony figure prominently in the development section. Polyphony's lack of strong cadences creates continuous motion. Its simultaneous melodies heighten the sense of complexity and disorientation, especially given the sharp contrast with the prevailing homophony of the exposition and recapitulation.

Form—In contrast with the exposition and recapitulation, the development comes without fixed expectations. Contrast outweighs repetition, but even repeated passages never sound secure—they are always varied in some way. The listener faces uncertainty, not knowing what will happen next.

Play through each of the development sections that the authors define in Listening Chart 7. Ask the class to identify the themes that are developed and the characteristic uses of melody, key, and texture for each section. For instance, the first section (track 18, 0:00–0:16) explores theme 1, using sequences to modulate frequently through different keys. In the second section (track 18, 0:16–0:42), imitation based on figures from theme 1 pervades the mostly polyphonic texture. A process of fragmentation, gradually reducing the first theme to its basic short-short-long motive, dominates the third section (track 18, 0:43–1:00). The final section, the retransition (track 18, 1:00–1:15), serves a different function. Here frequent modulations cease, and the music prepares for the double return of tonic and the first theme.

Note two unusual features of this development: It is relatively short, and Mozart only develops the first theme. Sensing the lack of thoroughness in this development, Mozart introduces unusual features into his recapitulation as well.

Recapitulation

The recapitulation resolves the tensions that were stated in the exposition and explored in the development. Several factors work together to create a sense of resolution and return: familiar themes return whole and complete; a single, stable key (the tonic) is restored; homophonic texture again prevails; and a sense of certainty and order is reestablished. There is one significant difference between exposition and recapitulation, however. In the exposition, the second and cadence themes are played in the second key, but this tonal conflict resolves itself in the recapitulation, where the second group is played in the tonic key. This change also allows the recapitulation to end in the proper key. (Again, students can hear this more easily owing to this work's minor key; the second group was played in a major key in the exposition—now we hear it in the minor mode.)

Play through the recapitulation so the class can hear the effect. One section in particular sounds quite different from the exposition: the bridge. As if to compensate for a short, narrowly focused development, the bridge section is expanded to an unusual degree; it sounds like a second development section. The overall mood of the second group also sounds changed. The minor mode contributes to this effect, but we still sense the overpowering instability of development and bridge lingering in the second group. A poignant, almost tragic mood is the result—we sense no triumph in this recapitulation.

Back up and play the entire movement again, pointing to each section on the display or transparency as it is played. Afterward, point out one final unusual feature: a brief coda-like passage at the end of the recapitulation. Instead of tacking on a coda after the cadence theme, Mozart interpolates the new material into the middle of the cadence theme.

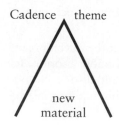

Cadence theme / new material

HAYDN Symphony No. 95 in C Minor, I

It is a good idea to offer students at least one more example of sonata form, so as to reinforce the concepts they have just learned. The first movement of Haydn's Symphony No. 95 serves well for several reasons. First, a comparison between sonata form movements by Mozart and Haydn provides a good opportunity to consider "outer" form versus "inner" form. Both movements employ the same "outer" form—sonata form. The "inner" forms of these two works differ considerably, however; Mozart's dramatic, brooding lyricism contrasts with Haydn's motivic ingenuity and frequently sunny good humor. Second, the whole point of Chapter 12 is the thorough study of a complete symphony, specifically Haydn's Symphony No. 95 in C Minor. Haydn's first movement is our point of entry into this delightful example of the Classical symphony and its typical four-movement plan.

The first movement of this particular symphony is surprisingly tricky, even for Haydn. In spite of the advertised C minor key, the first movement ends in C major, and deciding where the recapitulation begins is no easy matter. To make sense of all this for your students, be prepared to take a little extra time with this movement. Begin by playing and comparing the individual themes of this movement. The main themes, often constructed from recurring motives, are not included in the textbook. For your convenience, the main themes are provided below, but these should not replace your own score study. In light of the difficulties described above, plan on finding a score of this symphony to use in your class preparation. Before class, prepare listening examples based on the themes below so that you can guide your students more effectively. It is especially important to help students hear the motives from which these themes are constructed—motives that will be used again and again throughout the movement. Haydn sonata form movements are like a treasure hunt; half the fun is discovering his pervasive, ingenious uses of a mere handful of short motives. You can find examples under every rock as you search through the themes of the exposition, development, and recapitulation.

Theme 1, with its highly contrasted *staccato fortissimo* (theme 1a, mm. 1–2) and *dolce piano* (theme 1b, mm. 3–4) motives, provides an excellent example of the heterogeneous melodic construction so typical of Classical melodies. Right off the bat, this example of pleasing variety stands apart from the narrow focus on a single emotion found in Baroque music.

Theme 1

In his Symphony No. 40 Mozart employed an independent bridge theme, but Haydn simply reuses motives from his first theme to modulate to the dominant in the relative major key, adding triplet rhythms to energize his bridge. At first hearing, what the violins play at mm. 17–20 sounds like a new theme, but if you look closely you will find that the violins are simply ornamenting the main theme as heard in the flute (with a bit of octave displacement tossed in for good measure).

Bridge

Theme 2, in the relative major key, is an altogether jollier tune without the dramatic contrasts that marked theme 1. Nonetheless, it introduces three or four different motives that will serve as grist for the development section's mill. Like many Classical second themes, this one repeats in its entirety. In the Classical era, repetition is used to highlight important themes.

Theme 2

In his Symphony No. 40 Mozart introduced a new cadence theme, but whereas Haydn writes a clear cadential section to end the exposition, there is no clear theme—certainly nothing that repeats as did theme 2. Instead, Haydn's cadential section flows directly from the end of theme 2, repeating that theme's cadence formula as it launches into loud, energetic, triplet-driven figures that derive from previously heard themes, including theme 1. The closer we get to the end, the more strong cadences we hear, typical of the conclusion of many Classical-era sonata form expositions.

Cadential Section

When you play the entire movement, refer students to the *Listen* Guide on textbook page 191 and put the following diagram on the board so you can point to each section as it goes by.

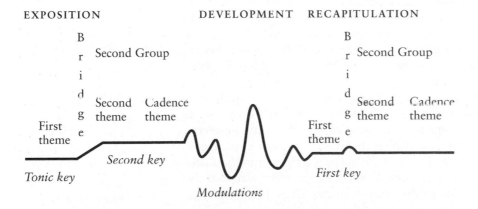

A comparison of first movements from Mozart's Symphony No. 40 and Haydn's Symphony No. 95 can help at this point. Both examples are minor-key sonata form movements, which typically modulate to the relative major. This minor-major contrast between themes 1 and 2 makes it easier for students to hear that the key has changed, even if they do not hear the new tonic. If you want your students to hear the new tonic clearly, use the recorded excerpts you prepared for the exercise above. Back-to-back comparisons of the first and second themes from the exposition can help students hear the different tonal centers. If students don't hear these relationships quickly, try playing along with the recorded examples at the keyboard. For example, in the first comparison above, play just *do* and *ti,* as appropriate, following the chord progression of the first theme. Picking out these two notes can help students home in on the tonic. When you play the second theme, continue to play *do* and *ti* in the old key of C minor. These patterns sounded so right in the first theme, but they sound out of place in the second theme. Now play the second theme again and plunk out *do* and *ti* in the correct key, E-flat major. Most students can hear the difference.

Some striking differences between this Haydn movement and the Mozart example must be pointed out, however. In your comparison, emphasize the following:

1. Mozart used one primary motive—the short-short-long pattern of the first theme—which appeared again and again in the cadence theme and throughout the movement. Haydn uses several motives pervasively. Mozart's single motive created a powerful intensifying effect; Haydn's multiple motives offer precisely the pleasing variety we associate with Classical music.

2. Haydn's development is more typical than Mozart's. Mozart only worked with one theme in an extremely brief development; Haydn works over both main themes as well as several important motives, and the overall length of his development section nearly equals that of the recapitulation. The moods created by these two development sections also differ. Mozart created an intense, brooding instability; Haydn balances moments of drama and uncertainty with moments of playfulness and good humor—the very contrasts implicit in themes 1 and 2. Each work is dramatic in its own way, but these pieces create two different moods.

3. In the hands of lesser composers, the recapitulation was often a routine, predictable affair. Not so for Haydn or Mozart; neither of them provides a literal reprise of the exposition. Mozart lengthened his bridge section to intensify the drama and instability of the recapitulation, but he left no question where the recapitulation begins; given his longer development section, Haydn actually shortens his bridge to avoid anticlimax, but where exactly does the recapitulation begin? The authors put it at track 24, 0:25 (m. 120), where it begins, curiously, with theme 1b, the *dolce piano* motive. On the face of it, this makes sense, because it begins in the tonic key after the customary rhetorical pause. But what happened to theme 1a, the *staccato forte* motive? If you back up to track 24, 0:09 (m. 110), there it stands—in the key of C minor! Haydn makes this a grippingly memorable moment in the simplest possible way: he reverts to running eighth notes to replace the triplets that dominate most of the movement. This moment stands out enough that the authors include it in the *Listen* Guide as the last item in the development. One could make the case that this moment is actually the beginning of the recapitulation. There is no rhetorical pause beforehand—it flows continuously out of the fabric of the development—but one can easily find similar examples in other symphonies. So which interpretation is correct? Probably both, and neither. Haydn certainly seems to relish the ambiguity. Theme 1a appears at track 24, 0:09 in the right key and with the grandeur appropriate to a recapitulation, but it quickly conveys a developmental feel, taking great pains to establish the dominant in C minor, as if still preparing for the recapitulation. And theme 1b's tonic outline answers that dominant after a brief pause, but it's the same brief pause we heard when it answered theme 1a in the exposition. On top of that, theme 1b is no longer followed by the theme 1a motive and the bridge, as it was in the exposition; instead it sequences downward, and three short measures later we arrive at theme 2. In such an abbreviated form, theme 1b is hardly long enough to stand in for all of theme 1. However you slice it, Haydn certainly does "sneak into" the recapitulation—a touch of creativity that can be frustrating at first but that finally points to form as a framework to be played with, not a rigid box.

4. Although both are minor-key movements, Haydn ends in the parallel major key of C major. Everything goes as expected in the exposition and development, and Haydn even begins the recapitulation in C minor, but when we get to theme 2, Haydn goes to C major and stays there until the end. At the same

point in his recapitulation, Mozart's expected minor-key statement completely transformed the mood of theme 2, evoking a sense of tragedy at that moment. Haydn does the unexpected, however, "breaking the rules" to retain the jolly, major-key quality of his second theme. In so doing he also retains the somber-jolly contrast created between themes 1 and 2 in the exposition. Given the recapitulation's abbreviated version of theme 1, he also ultimately places greater weight on the good-humored mood of the second theme. If this is a battle between C minor and C major, then C major wins.

5. Mozart sandwiched his coda in the middle of the cadence theme. In line with earlier discrepancies, Haydn's final measures feel more like an expanded ending for the cadential section than a true coda. Most striking is Haydn's clever use of the theme 1a motive in parallel thirds, a four-measure idea that repeats, finally providing the sense of a true cadence theme missing in the exposition. If there is a coda, it comes in the seven measures that follow this "cadence theme"—two measures of tonic-dominant alternation followed by five measures of nothing but tonic enlivened by a rapidly moving bass line. This movement offers an appealing example of Haydn's melodic invention, vigor, and good humor.

Introduction and Coda

Although many Classical symphonies provide full-blown examples of slow introduction at the beginning and coda at the end of the first movement, neither Mozart nor Haydn provides clear-cut examples of either in the *Listen* symphonies. When they appear, the introduction begins and ends *before* the beginning of the exposition, and the coda is tacked on *after* the end of the recapitulation. The slow introduction lends weight and dignity to the beginning of the symphony, and it also serves as a foil to the beginning of the exposition—the first theme sounds much livelier after the slow-tempo section that precedes it. For an example of a sonata form first movement with a slow introduction, see suggestions for Haydn's Symphony No. 88, I, in Further Listening Examples below.

The coda generally reinforces the tonic by repeating cadence formulas again and again, while playing with important motives from earlier in the movement. In spite of Symphony No. 95's eccentricities, the following experiment can emphasize the importance of a good coda. Play Haydn's recapitulation starting at theme 2, but stop right on the downbeat of m. 159 (at track 24, 1:31). Ask students if the piece sounds finished. Some may say yes, some will say no. Then play from theme 2 all the way to the end. Most students will get the point. The repeated cadence figures and *tutti* orchestration drive home a feeling of finality that the recapitulation's cadence theme cannot muster. That's the function of a typical coda. For an example of a typical coda, see suggestions for the Haydn symphony referred to at the end of the previous paragraph.

Concluding Remarks on Sonata Form

What makes sonata form special, no matter what mood it expresses, is its characteristic presentation, dramatic development, and restatement of principal themes. A useful simile: Sonata form movements are like stage dramas (or episodes of *Law and Order*) in which various characters (themes), once introduced (exposition), interact and even fight with each other (development), and ultimately disengage themselves from each other (recapitulation), sometimes altered by the experience of interaction, sometimes not.

It is amazing that this pattern was used so faithfully by so many composers who never saw a schematic diagram of sonata form. There must have been something deeply satisfying about this form for Classical audiences. The nature of its proportions, its conflicts, and its resolution can tell us something profound about late eighteenth-century culture. The intense drama inherent in sonata form permitted instrumental music to finally compete head-on with opera, and in Beethoven's hands, instrumental genres surpassed vocal ones in significance for the first time in Western music.

7 Classical Variation Form

In the second movement of Haydn's Symphony No. 95 we encounter theme and variations form. A theme and variations movement presents a theme and systematically modifies it in successive sections. Baroque variation forms, including ground bass form (covered in Chapter 9), conform to this definition, as does Classical theme and variations form. In both, each variation equals the theme in length and follows the same phrase structure. Nonetheless, there are significant differences between the two. For purposes of comparison, play the ground bass theme from Vivaldi's Concerto in G, II (0:00–0:19) and the theme from Haydn's Symphony No. 95, II (track 25). In the discussion that follows, draw out the following items:

Vivaldi ground bass theme	*Hadyn symphony theme*
short, just a single phrase	complete tune, several phrases
theme in bottom voice	theme in top voice
polyphonic texture in variations	homophonic texture predominates
no internal cadences	clear cadences separate phrases
final cadence overlaps with beginning of next variation	full cadence at end of theme
continuous motion	phrases and sections clearly defined

HAYDN Symphony No. 95 in C Minor, II

The second movement of the four-movement plan is typically a slow movement with a singing melody. For each of the other movements, we expect specific musical forms—sonata form for the first movement, minuet form for the third, and rondo or sonata form at the end—but there is no fixed, standard form for the second movement. Some slow movements use a "slow-movement" sonata form in which the development is omitted or reduced to a brief transition, some use a simple ternary form, and others use rondo or theme and variations forms. For Symphony No. 95, Haydn uses theme and variations form.

Begin by introducing important features of theme and variations form. Play Haydn's theme (track 25) once more for the class. Note these characteristics of a good variations theme:

1. It is memorable so that we can follow it easily in each variation.

2. It is presented simply—nothing distracts us from learning the tune.

3. The tune exhibits clear, symmetrical phrases and easily perceived cadences.

Ask the students to pick out the theme's structure and inventory its characteristics as they listen. Tell them that their inventory must be as thorough as possible, since composers can vary almost anything in theme and variations form. It will be easier to determine what elements the composer has altered in each variation if the theme's features have been clearly identified. Then play the theme several more times until students can recognize each phrase with ease. In the discussion that follows, draw out the tune's structure first. Since the phrase structure of the theme is repeated in each variation, it is useful to make a diagram. The structure of the theme can be expressed as:

|: a :||: b :|

Then work through a complete inventory of the tune's musical features. In your discussion, draw out the following characteristics:

> *Melody*—simple tune with regular phrases; mixes stepwise motion simple triad arpeggios that sequence downward
>
> *Articulation*—mostly *legato* with a bit of *staccato* for articulation
>
> *Mode*—major
>
> *Harmony*—relatively stable; **a** remains in tonic, **b** moves away briefly and returns to tonic
>
> *Rhythm*—simple, stays close to the beat; motives repeat regularly
>
> *Meter*—compound duple
>
> *Tempo*—slow, *Andante*
>
> *Dynamics*—*piano*
>
> *Tone color*—orchestra (strings only); melody played by violins
>
> *Register*—middle to low
>
> *Texture*—homophonic, melody and accompaniment texture in **a**; simple two-part polyphony in **b**
>
> *Accompaniment*—simple, *staccato* chords stay in the background in the **a** section

This list provides a more complete inventory of musical elements and structures than usual, and for good reason. If you want to create a list of variation techniques for your students, you need look no further than a list of musical elements and structures, because almost any element can be changed in theme and variations form. The one element that does not (usually) vary is the internal structure (form) of the theme.

Now play the variations one at a time. If students have trouble following the tune at any point, play the original theme at the keyboard while students listen to the recording. For each variation, make students compare what they hear with the list of characteristics for the theme. Ask them which elements were altered in each variation. Encourage students to be thorough—it is good to end up with long lists for each variation—but ask them to study the list and pick the one or two most significant changes for each variation. For instance, in Variation 1 the following elements are changed:

> *Melody*—decorative ornamentation added when **a** repeats and in the **b** section as well; ornamentation is used in lower countermelody at beginning of **b** but taken over by violins in second half
>
> *Rhythm*—ornamented lines move much faster
>
> *Tone color*—cello plays the theme in the first **a** section; chords in second **a** played *pizzicato*

Register—in first **a**, melody is an octave lower with accompaniment above it; violin decorations explore somewhat lower and higher registers

Articulation—ornamented lines somewhat more staccato

Accompaniment—first **a** accompanied with *legato* countermelody

Several elements change, but most significant are the decorated statements of the melody and some shifts in register. Of course, several other elements remain unchanged; composers don't vary everything in a single variation—that would be contrast, not variation.

Continue to work through each variation in this fashion. Listening Chart 8 (textbook page 193) highlights the most significant changes in each variation. Notice that the repetitions of **a** and **b** can be altered within a variation, as we already saw in Variation 1.

In the last variation, omit the coda the first time around. Ask students if the ending sounds "final" enough to end this movement. The third variation has pizzazz and might seem a more convincing ending than when we tried this trick in the first movement. Some students will say yes, the piece is over; some may say no. Ask students what Haydn could do to make the ending sound more final. Encourage comments, even if some seem irrelevant. Then play from Variation 3 to the end of the movement and ask the class what Haydn did to make the ending sound more final. Of course, this exercise was a setup. Haydn does just the opposite of what we might expect in a coda: he brings back the main theme at a quiet dynamic, deliberately reminiscent of the movement's opening bars. Haydn wants us to hear this as a fourth variation, not as a coda. But soon enough we move into a passage that sounds like new, cadential material. It seems as if this coda might behave counterintuitively, fading into nothingness. Just when Haydn finally convinces us that this is the case, he hits us with the surprise—two loud chords. Just as you set up your class a moment ago, Haydn sets up the listener. First he tries to convince us that it's Variation 4, not a coda; then he tries to convince us that he's going to fade out at the end. These two "gotcha" moments provide excellent examples of "Papa" Haydn's wit and charm.

Display Listening Chart 8 (or refer students to textbook page 193) and play the entire movement for the class. Point out each phrase and variation as it is played. Ask students to describe the overall effect of theme and variations form.

The art of a theme and variations movement lies not in altering the theme past the point of recognition but in artfully and cleverly re-dressing the theme. In a typical theme and variations movement, the theme is always present to some degree in the listener's ear. Draw the following conclusions about Classical theme and variations form:

1. It is a sectional form, characterized by clear cadences and distinct sections.

2. The principle of variation, with its simultaneous repetition and contrast, defines the relationships between sections (and sometimes phrases).

3. The theme is a good tune with symmetrical phrases and clear internal cadences.

4. The following scheme is typical of Classical theme and variations movements:

$$\text{A} \quad \text{A}^1 \, \text{A}^2 \, \text{A}^3 \, \text{A}^4 \ldots \text{Coda}$$

If you want another example of theme and variations form for your class, see suggestions for Mozart's "Ah vous dirai-je, maman" variations in Further Listening Examples for Chapter 13. For an example of a ternary form slow movement, see suggestions for Haydn's Symphony No. 88, II, in Further Listening Examples below.

⁊ Minuet Form (Classical Dance Form)

Stylized dances—compositions based on dance rhythms but intended more for listening than dancing—reached a high state of development during the Classical era. Much dance music continued to be written for the express purpose of dancing, but the minuet and trio movements that became standard in Classical symphonies, quartets, sonatas, and so on were not. These pieces used the same overall structure as real dance music, but they were often longer and more elaborate. Composers of stylized minuets often worked with lengthier, more substantial melodic ideas, inserted transitions between sections, and added cadential extensions at the end.

HAYDN Symphony No. 95 in C Minor, III

Use this work to review principles of repetition and contrast and to practice diagramming formal relationships. Without referring to Listening Chart 9 in the textbook, work through the entire minuet and trio by ear; start with the first **a** and then add one or two more sections with each playing. If you would like to start with a simpler minuet and trio movement—one more typical of Classical dance music—try the third movement of Mozart's *Eine kleine Nachtmusik* (see Sound Recordings below).

Play the **a** section of Haydn's minuet until students can easily recognize it. Label the first section as **a** on the board. Then play the first two sections and ask students if the second section demonstrates repetition or contrast. The answer is repetition; write a second **a** on the board. Play the first three sections and ask if the third section demonstrates repetition or contrast. The third section offers a contrast; add **b** to your diagram on the board. At this point, possibilities for the next section become more complex. It could demonstrate a return of **a** or a repetition of **b,** or it could contrast with both. Continue to work through the entire piece in this fashion. When you get to the end, your diagram should look like this:

a a b a′ b a′ c c d c′ d c′ a b a′

Ask students to point out phrases or groups of phrases that show repetition. The following phrase clusters can be observed.

a a   b a′ b a′   c c   d c′ d c′   a   b a′

Finally, explain repeat signs and condense your diagram as follows:

|: a :||: b a′ :||: c :||: d c′ :| a b a′

Ask students to study this diagram and point out larger patterns of repetition or contrast. Some students will notice the group of **a** and **b** sections at the beginning and end with a contrasting group of **c** and **d** sections in the middle. This overall three-part (ternary) form is based on the principles of contrast and return and can be expressed as "statement-contrast-restatement," or **A B A**. The **A** section is the minuet, and the **B** section the trio. As you write this information on the board, the completed diagram of the form of Haydn's minuet will look like the one on the following page.

MINUET	TRIO	MINUET
A	**B**	**A**
|: a :||: b a′ :|	|: c :||: d c′ :|	a b a′

Point out that the internal structure of the minuet is identical to that of the trio—two sections, each repeated—and the second section of each concludes with a return of its opening theme. This structure is somewhat different from the structure of Baroque dances. As we learned in Chapter 9, the typical Baroque dance was a simple binary form, with both sections repeated. Similarly, Classical dance form uses binary form, with both sections repeated, but now the theme of a dance's first section returns at the end of the dance's second section to create a rounded binary form, just as we see in Haydn's minuet.

Review Baroque minuet and trio form with the class. (It appears as gavotte-trio-gavotte form in Bach's Orchestral Suite.) Put the diagram of Baroque minuet-and-trio form (see below) on the board right next to the completed Haydn minuet diagram (see above), or refer students to textbook page 197.

MINUET	TRIO	MINUET
A	**B**	**A**
|: a :||: b :|	|: c :||: d :|	a b

Ask the class to compare this Baroque dance form with its Classical equivalent. The internal structure of individual dances changed, but the large **A B A** (minuet-trio-minuet) form of the Baroque minuet and trio was retained during the Classical era. As a result of these internal changes, the Classical minuet and trio looks somewhat more complex and often runs longer than its Baroque predecessor. This seeming complexity proves misleading, however; the Classical form is actually easier to hear—and more satisfying musically. The return of **a** at the end of the minuet (and **c** at the end of the trio) provides a strong sense of resolution and closure—like a return home. For purposes of comparison, play just the minuet section (**A**) and ask students to focus on the effect of the **a′** at the end of the second section. Have them describe this effect. Then play just the gavotte from Bach's Orchestral Suite in D. Ask students to describe the effect when **a** does not return at the end.

Now display Listening Chart 9 (or refer students to textbook page 198); use it to explain how Haydn employs techniques associated with stylized dances: lengthy, substantial melodic ideas; transitions and other insertions between and within sections; and cadential extensions added at the end. First, in a simple minuet, **a**, **b**, **c**, and **d** would represent single phrases; but in Haydn's symphony, they represent groupings of two or more phrases (note the length of each section on the chart). Second, Haydn inserts passages that disrupt the "normal" flow, as in the Neapolitan insertion just before the **a′** cadential passage and the violins' interruption of the cello solo in **d′**, both examples of Haydn's wit. Finally, Haydn repeats the cadence figures at the end of both the **a** and **a′** sections. All three techniques work together to create a more substantial musical work as they expand the basic structure of these simple dances.

Finally, ask students to focus on the differences between minuet and trio—these are, after all, two contrasting minuets put together to create a longer piece. These differences offer another excellent example of "inner form" versus "outer form"; minuet and trio share the same outer form, but the content, or "inner form," of each is so different that we would never mistake one for the other. Remind students that form was a structure to be played with, to the surprise and delight of the audience. Now play the entire third movement and point out each section on the transparency as it is played. In the discussion that follows, draw out the following comparisons:

Minuet	*Trio*
more somber and dramatic	more lighthearted and *galant*
melody *staccato,* many small leaps, grace note figures	melody more *legato,* exaggerated arpeggios
triple meter	triple meter
moderate tempo	moderate tempo
durations emphasize beat	shorter, quicker note values
dynamics alternate between soft and loud	dynamics mostly soft
alternates between strings and full orchestra	solo cello and *pizzicato* strings
minor mode	major mode, same tonic
b develops grace note motive	**d** develops **c** materials
homophonic texture (melody and accompaniment)	homophonic texture (melody and accompaniment)
(oom)-pah-pah to start, then varied accompaniment	*pizzicato* accompaniment on beats 3 and 1
b much shorter than **a**	**d** exactly as long as **a**, trio half as long as minuet

Conclusions to Draw about Minuet and Trio Form

1. It is a sectional form, characterized by clear cadences.

2. Repetition and contrast define the relationships between phrases and sections.

3. Triple meter and moderate tempo characterize this aristocratic dance.

4. The following scheme is typical of virtually all Classical minuet and trio movements:

MINUET	TRIO	MINUET
A	**B**	**A**
|: a :||: b a′ :|	|: c :||: d c′ :|	a b a′

⁊ Rondo Form

Rondo form is based on the principles of contrast and return. A principal theme is stated at the beginning and returns periodically in alternation with contrasting episodes. Rondo-form movements run the gamut from simple to complex and from short to long. Rondo movements are typically light and engaging in character, though this is by no means always the case. Rondo form is less standardized than minuet and trio or theme and variations form. In fact, it is more a process than a rigid form.

Although similar in many respects to Baroque ritornello form, the Classical rondo grew out of the Baroque *rondeau,* a simple homophonic-textured musical form often encountered in Baroque dance suites. A typical rondeau followed an alternating formal pattern such as **A B A C A** or **A B A C A D A,** and the return to **A** most often repeated that theme literally. Classical composers kept or expanded these formal patterns, but in their hands the rondo became a more complex yet flexible formal procedure.

Rondo form most commonly appears in the final movement of the four-movement plan. Haydn's Symphony No. 95 provides a rather sophisticated example of rondo form, its episodes containing the elaborate transitions, cadence formulas, and developmental sections that the authors describe on textbook page 199. For further examples of rondo form, turn to Chapter 13 for both the Lecture Suggestions for LeBrun's Sonata in F and notes in the Further Listening Examples for Mozart's Piano Sonata in B-flat.

HAYDN Symphony No. 95 in C Minor, IV

It is essential that the listener recognize the rondo theme quickly in order to perceive rondo form. Play just the rondo theme (track 33) several times, until students can identify the first phrase consistently. Ask students to map out the structure of the theme and inventory its characteristics. The structure of the theme, a simple binary form, can be expressed as:

$$\text{|: a :||: b c:|}$$

In your discussion, draw out the following characteristics:

Melody—simple tune based on rhythmic motives

Rhythm—varied, fast moving

Meter—duple

Tempo—fast

Dynamics—soft

Tone color—orchestra (strings; later flute, oboe, bassoon, and horns)

Register—middle to high

Articulation—mix of *staccato* and *legato*

Texture—homophonic

Accompaniment—simple, mostly *staccato* figures; little to distract from the melody

Mode—major

If you take time to help your students hear the tune's main rhythmic motives—the first the *legato* turn and leap figure at m. 1, the second a *staccato* three-quarter-note figure with a distinctive grace note turn, the third the four-eighth-note figure that follows the second motive—they will be better prepared to recognize not only the return of the rondo theme but also Haydn's playful use of the theme in the developmental episodes. Once students have identified the primary characteristics of the rondo theme, play the second and third statements of the rondo theme. For each one, ask the class to identify differences between these **A** sections. Except for the fact that we hear the theme without repeats, the second **A** section presents us with a literal return, without changes of any kind. The third rondo statement is an entirely different matter, however. Here Haydn recomposes the theme completely, transforming it into a coda-like section just a few bars later. Listening Chart 10 shows this as an **A** section that last only three seconds—the merest evocation of the rondo theme—followed immediately by the coda. As this implies, we hear only the first phrase of the **A** theme, but Haydn cunningly elides the two sections by starting the coda with the three-quarter-note motive, the normal follow-up to the first phrase. In spite of the sudden, blaring orchestral *tutti,* it feels like a logical continuation of the rondo theme. And it provides a rousing conclusion to the entire symphony as well; for once, it's everything we expect of a coda.

Next, explore the contrasting episodes. Play the **B** section (track 34). Ask the class to identify contrasts between the rondo theme (**A** section) and the **B** section. There are quite a few differences:

Melody—new melody based on the initial motive of the rondo theme

Dynamics—loud

Tone color—full orchestra (including brass and timpani)

Register—expanded

Texture—imitative polyphony—a fugue!

Accompaniment—simple figures in nonfugal sections

Tonality—unstable developmental section moves through several keys, including C major, G major, D major, G minor, F major, and A minor, some for an extended period, some for only a few bars

Significant differences reveal themselves in the polyphonic texture, the weight of the full orchestra, the tonal instability, and the continuous nature of this **B** section. Unlike the rondo theme, the **B** section provides a nice, sectional tune with clear phrase relationships and cadence points; this heightens the sense of satisfaction when the rondo theme returns. Also note the brief passage (track 34, 0:55–1:07) that prepares for the rondo theme's return. A Phrygian cadence on dominant in the key of A minor, it sets us up for the wrong key—C major's relative minor! The return of the rondo theme in C major comes as a surprise. If you can, help your students hear the wrong key; play a bit of this cadence at the keyboard and follow it with the **A** theme in A minor. Bear in mind that this is not Haydn's innovation; Baroque music provides hundreds of examples of this same progression. However, in the context of the fugue—another Baroque invention—it sounds perfectly natural. Haydn does not hesitate to draw on these conventions of an earlier style when it can heighten the dramatic impact.

Play the second contrasting episode, labeled as **B C** in the Listening Chart (track 35, 0:28–1:09). Again, ask the class to identify contrasts between the rondo theme and this new section. The **B** part of this episode is similar to the first episode, only shorter and more stable (we never leave C major). However, the **C** section contains quite a few differences:

Melody—new ideas, lots of tremolo and running eighth-note figures

Dynamics—very loud

Tone color—full orchestra (including brass and timpani)

Register—expanded

Texture—homophonic

Mode—first half minor with chromatic, unstable harmonies; then back to major over dominant harmony

As the authors describe it in the textbook, Haydn plays with our expectations. When he starts the second episode with **B** material, we think we know what's coming, and the stormy **C** section comes as a total surprise. But the storm subsides and the sun comes out as we return to C major. Point out the long, teasing passage that prepares for the rondo theme's final return (track 35, 0:54–1:09). Once we "catch on" that the movement is in rondo form, the return of the rondo theme is no longer a surprise—in fact, we begin to anticipate its return. Haydn, acutely aware of audience expectation, plays with the anticipation, almost as if to say, "You think you know where the rondo theme will start? Gotcha! Listen again!"

Display Listening Chart 10 or refer students to textbook page 200. Point out the features that were part of class discussion. Then play the entire movement so that students can hear these sections in context, but omit the coda. Ask students if the ending sounds "final" enough to end a long four-movement symphony. Of course, this quiet little snippet of the **A** theme with its tentative harmonies feels completely unfinished. Then play from this final rondo theme statement (track 36) to the end of the movement. Haydn demonstrates his immaculate timing and wit—only twenty seconds long, this "surprise" coda sounds just right, as an ending to both this movement and the entire four-movement symphony.

Conclusions to Draw about Rondo Form

1. Rondo form is sectional, characterized by clear cadences and distinct sections. Even when Haydn's symphony movement blurs final cadences—starting a new section right at the cadence for the old one—we hear a clear contrast between the two sections.

2. The principles of contrast and return define the relationships between sections; in fact, composers often play with the audience's expectation of return.

3. The theme is a simple, easily recognized tune, usually at quick tempo, with symmetrical phrases and clear internal cadences.

4. The following scheme is typical of Classical rondo-form movements:

A B A C A (Coda)

Conclusions to Draw about the Symphony

1. The symphony is a large multimovement work for orchestra.

2. The symphony originated and came to prominence in the Classical period.

3. The Classical symphony typically uses the four-movement plan:

Movement I	moderate to fast tempo; sonata form
Movement II	slow tempo; no fixed form
Movement III	moderate tempo in triple meter; minuet form
Movement IV	fast tempo; sonata or rondo form

4. There are no deliberate melodic or rhythmic connections between movements; each movement is a separate, complete musical work. The four movements work together only because of the tasteful, calculated contrasts between them.

5. In its use of form and other musical elements, the symphony offers the ultimate embodiment of pleasing variety in Classical music.

Additional Teaching Suggestions

❦ Lecture-Demonstration Ideas

1. Invite a music theorist to class to discuss the importance of form. A second perspective on the nature and significance of musical form can provide valuable insights. Further, students can learn about a major discipline within the realm of music: *What is music theory? What does a music theorist do? How does music theory relate to other musical activities and professions?*

2. Compare Haydn's use of rondo form in Symphony No. 95, IV, with Bach's use of ritornello form in the *Brandenburg* Concerto No. 5, I. Both forms are based on the principles of contrast and return, but there are several differences between them. Display Listening Charts 5 and 10 and draw out the following comparisons:

Melody—Bach's ritornello theme exemplifies Baroque melody with its lack of repetition and irregular phrase lengths. It differs sharply from Haydn's symmetrical phrases and clear cadences. Play the opening themes of both works to clarify the differences.

Return—Bach's ritornello returns much more frequently, but often only part of the theme returns. Classical composers most often use the entire rondo theme at each return. Play several returns from each piece to demonstrate.

Tone color—Bach's ritornello form follows a rigid alternation between full orchestra (for the ritornello theme) and solo instruments (for the contrasting episodes). There are no equivalent guidelines for Classical rondo form. Play the first three sections (**A B A**) from each piece to demonstrate.

Key and mode—Bach's ritornello theme returns in different keys and even in minor mode; Haydn's rondo theme always returns in the tonic key. Play several returns from each piece to demonstrate.

Finally, play both examples all the way through so that students can hear these differences in context.

ᛞ Class Discussion Ideas

1. *What was it like to be a composer in Vienna in the late eighteenth century?* Read excerpts aloud from Mozart's engaging letters,[1] ask students to read the textbook's biographies of Mozart and Haydn (textbook pages 189 and 195), or even have them watch the movie *Amadeus* in preparation for discussion. (Students remain fascinated by this movie about Mozart and have many good observations and questions about it.) This question offers a good opportunity to delve into the lives of Haydn and Mozart and to draw comparisons between them. Point out that the old system of patronage, which had provided a living for composers for centuries, still held Haydn and Mozart in its grip, even though it was starting to crumble.

2. *Why was sonata form so popular?* There are no simple answers to this question, but it does afford an opportunity to define the nature of sonata form once again and to compare it with other phenomena in late eighteenth-century European and American cultures. Encourage students to come up with examples from their own majors. How do the drama and proportion of sonata form compare with the novel? other Classical art forms? the system of checks and balances in the U.S. Constitution? Hegel's dialectic mode of thought?

3. *How did Mozart die?* Speculation has always run wild concerning Salieri's rumored role in Mozart's death; *Amadeus* helped refuel that speculation. You can prime the pump by encouraging students to watch *Amadeus* outside of class or by watching relevant scenes in class. Ask students what they've heard about Mozart's death, whether it fits with the movie version or not. Finally, read the pages from the end of H. C. Robbins Landon's *1791: Mozart's Last Year* (New York: Schirmer, 1988), which contain Dr. Peter J. Davies's sobering diagnosis of the conditions leading to Mozart's death.[2] You may need to ask a nursing or pre-med student to decipher some of the terminology. Ask students how this compares with their preconceptions.

---

[1]Look for Robert Spaethling's excellent translation of selected letters, *Mozart's Letters, Mozart's Life* (New York: W. W. Norton, 2000). More than any other translator, Spaethling conveys the sense, meaning, and playfulness of Mozart's language. Highly recommended.

[2]Originally published in *Musical Times* 125 (1984).

⁊ Listening Ideas

1. For an unusually clear example of a four-movement plan, play part or all of Mozart's *Eine kleine Nachtmusik* for your class (see Sound Recordings below). You can play just the beginning of each movement to review features of the four-movement plan, though individual movements provide textbook examples of specific musical forms as well. The third movement offers an ideal introduction to minuet and trio form, and you can use the first movement to review sonata form once your students have an example or two under their belts. Many of them will be surprised to discover that they can follow this sonata form on first hearing (it is a remarkably clear example). For those who recognize the music, it is a double pleasure to understand the work at a deeper level.

2. Compare Classical forms with Romantic and twentieth-century uses of the same forms. This exercise permits review of the four forms covered in this chapter and points up the importance of these forms beyond the Classical era. Most examples come from the recorded anthology for this textbook; for the others, see Sound Recordings below.

> *Sonata form*—Compare the first movement of Mozart's Symphony No. 40 or Haydn's Symphony No. 95 with the overture to Mozart's *Don Giovanni;* the first movement of Mozart's Piano Concerto in A Major, K. 488; the first or fourth movement of Beethoven's Symphony No. 5; Liszt's Transcendental Etude No. 10 in F Minor; the fourth movement of Berlioz's *Fantastic* Symphony; Tchaikovsky's *Romeo and Juliet;* or the second movement of Bartók's *Music for Strings, Percussion, and Celesta.*

> *Classical variation form* (see Chapter 13)—Compare the second movement of Haydn's Symphony No. 95 with the second movement of Beethoven's Symphony No. 5; the *Listen* DVD excerpt from Beethoven's Symphony No. 9; the final movement of Brahms's Violin Concerto in D; Section 5 of Copland's *Appalachian Spring;* Parker and Davis's *Out of Nowhere;* or Part 4 of Reich's *Tehillim.*

> *Minuet form*—Compare Haydn's Symphony No. 95 in C Minor, III, with the third movement of Beethoven's Symphony No. 5; the second movement of Beethoven's Quartet in F, Op. 135; the fourth movement of Berlioz's *Fantastic* Symphony; or the third movement of Mahler's Symphony No. 1.

> *Rondo form*—Compare the fourth movement of Haydn's Symphony No. 95 with Schubert's *Moment Musical* No. 2 in A-flat; "The Great Gate at Kiev" from Musorgsky's *Pictures at an Exhibition;* or the fourth movement of Bartók's *Music for Strings, Percussion, and Celesta.*

3. Play the expositions from several different Classical sonata-form movements. This exercise offers practice in listening for the different functions served by different sections of the exposition: stability (first and second themes), instability (bridge passage), and conclusion (cadence theme). The first movements of most Mozart and late Haydn symphonies will work well. You can also use first movements from string quartets or piano sonatas if you want to begin making connections between the symphony's four-movement plan and the genres presented in Chapter 13.

4. Play a guessing game. Prepare excerpts from one or more sonata-form movements. You should have examples of a first theme, a bridge, a second theme, a cadence theme, and a development section. The excerpts can be taken from examples in the recorded anthology or from any sonata-form movement.

Play the excerpts out of order and ask students both to put them in the right order and to determine whether they sound like the first or the second theme (both sound stable; in some movements the first theme might be more dramatic and the second more lyrical), the bridge (unstable, ending with a cadence and usually a pause), the cadence theme (stable, repeats cadence figures again and again), or development (unstable like a bridge but longer, often polyphonic, repeats motives in different keys, and so on). This exercise can help students find their way around in sonata form with greater ease and comfort. See Sound Recordings below for suggested performances.

¶ Further Listening Examples

HAYDN Symphony No. 88, I

For a good clear-cut example of a sonata form first movement with a slow introduction, try this example from Haydn's Symphony No. 88 in G. See Appendix I for a Listening Chart.

Begin by playing and comparing the individual themes, included below. Before class, prepare listening examples so that you can easily play through these themes for your students.

It is especially important to help students hear the motives from which these themes are constructed—motives that will be used again and again throughout the movement.

When you play the entire movement, display the Additional Listening Chart for this work (see Appendix I) and point to each section as it goes by. Several interesting features of this Haydn movement must be pointed out in the discussion that follows:

1. Just as in the vast majority of Haydn's late symphonies, this movement begins with a slow introduction. The themes of this introduction bear no resemblance to melodies heard later in the movement; rather, Haydn uses the introduction to add weight and significance to the symphony's beginning. Further, the con-

trast posed by a slow introduction makes the exposition's first theme sound all the more lively and buoyant.

2. The movement begins in G major. In the exposition, the bridge modulates to D major, the key of the second group. In the recapitulation, however, the second group returns in the tonic key, G major.

3. Haydn uses several motives pervasively, offering precisely the pleasing variety we associate with Classical music.

4. In the development, Haydn works over both main themes as well as several important motives so thoroughly that the overall length of his development section equals that of the recapitulation. Haydn balances moments of drama or uncertainty with moments of playfulness and wit.

5. Although this recapitulation proves much easier to hear than that in Symphony No. 95, Haydn still resists writing a literal return of the exposition. Here Haydn shortens his bridge section to keep the music fresh and well paced, constantly surging toward the conclusion.

6. Haydn provides a fairly typical coda, with repeated cadence figures supporting motives derived from important themes. That being said, nothing can prepare us for Haydn's outpouring of melodic invention. He constantly finds fresh ways to state the first theme's opening motive, even in the final ten seconds. This movement offers an appealing example of Haydn's vigor and wit.

HAYDN Symphony No. 88, II

Unlike its companion movements, the slow movement of a Classical symphony can use any of several forms; it does not have a "fixed" form of its own. Try this example for a slow-movement form that contrasts with the theme and variations in Symphony No. 95—an "irregular" ternary form. See Appendix I for a Listening Chart.

We find several formal principles at work in this movement. First, we find the principle of return after contrast. The **a** material comes back again and again—after the **b** phrase in the theme itself, and after contrasting transitions and trumpet figures later on. So that your students can recognize the **a** theme when it returns, play it through once or twice.

These frequent returns suggest rondo form, as this diagram shows.

a a b a′ c a b a′ d a″ d′ a′ c

Second, we find the principle of variation. Each time the **a** material returns, Haydn adds a new accompanimental figure or countermelody. This procedure is not far removed from Haydn's usual slow-movement adaptation of theme and variations form. Finally, we find the principle of statement-contrast-return. This movement offers its most significant contrast in the developmental minor-mode **B** section. The subsequent return to the major mode and the primary theme, at **A′**, rounds off the form nicely. Viewed in this way, the overall structure can be interpreted as a lopsided ternary form: **A B A′**.

With so many formal principles at work simultaneously, the relationships between sections lend themselves to multiple interpretations. While tantalizing to ponder, the ambiguities of this work's form make it difficult to understand and follow. If you have time, you can work through the movement one principle at a time, but it works just as well to focus on the large-scale statement-contrast-return pattern. Display the Listening Chart or put the following diagram on the board (just the letters for now; add the labels as you discuss this with the class).

a a b a′ c	a b a′	d a″ d′	a′ c
Main Theme	Main Theme	Contrasting	Main Theme
	repeated	section	returns

Ask students to pick out the section (or sections) that create the most significant contrast in the entire work; then play the entire movement. Much of the first three-fifths of the movement inhabits the same sound world; there are frequent contrasts but no truly dramatic changes until the **B** section. Sudden minor-mode trumpet figures move us into darker, more developmental material that poses a stark contrast to the rest of the work. Even the **a″** in the middle of this **B** section stands apart from other **a** statements in this movement. These contrasts help to define the **d a″ d′** sequence as a separate section, followed by one last return of **a′**.

The overall statement-contrast-return pattern—the **A B A** structure of ternary form—finally emerges from this fascinating web of thematic interrelationships. Given the different formal principles at work here, there can be no single correct interpretation of this movement's form. There is no shame in presenting this as a problematic work; rather, the ambiguities offer fertile ground for class discussion. Your students may well offer valid interpretations of their own if you give them room to ask questions and ponder these issues.

HAYDN Symphony No. 88, III

This minuet and trio form provides an excellent contrast with the examples in Lecture Suggestions above. (See the Additional Listening Chart for this movement in Appendix I.) Similar in outer structure, this movement nonetheless differs in the moods it creates—an excellent example of "inner" versus "outer" form.

Rather than work section by section as you did with the Symphony No. 95 minuet above, start by focusing on the similarities between these two dance movements. Remind students that the principles of repetition, contrast, and return predominate in this form. Put the diagram for Classical minuet and trio form on the board.

MINUET	TRIO	MINUET
A	**B**	**A**
|: a :||: b a′ :|	|: c :||: d c′ :|	a b a′

Remind the class that the internal structure of the minuet is identical to that of the trio—two sections, each repeated—and the second section of each concludes with a return of its opening phrase.

As you prepare to play this movement, display the Listening Chart for this work (see Appendix I) and ask students to listen for contrasts between the minuet and trio sections. Play the entire minuet and trio, and point out each section as it is played. In the discussion that follows, work through an inventory of musical elements and structures to draw out the differences between minuet and trio.

Minuet	Trio
melody accented *staccato,* many small leaps	melody more *legato,* moves by step
durations emphasize beat	shorter note values
dynamics mostly loud	dynamics mostly soft
major mode	major mode, same key (Lydian flavor)
motivic development in **b**	**d** transposes **c** materials
homophonic texture (rhythmic unison)	homophonic (melody and drone accompaniment)
b a bit longer than **a**	**d** almost as long as **a**, trio shorter than minuet

Most of these changes center around the different characters of these two dances: the minuet, a stately, courtly dance; the trio, a rustic peasant dance— a further example of Haydn's wit.

HAYDN Symphony No. 88, IV

This finale provides another rondo-form movement to contrast with the example in Lecture Suggestions above. You can find an Additional Listening Chart for this movement in Appendix I.

Play just the rondo theme several times, until students can identify the first phrase consistently.

Then map out the structure of the theme, the now-familiar Classical dance form (rounded binary):

|: **a** :||: **b a′** :|

As you discuss this theme, call attention to its tunefulness, quick tempo, and simple accompaniment. All of these make for a memorable tune, easy to spot when it returns later on. If you take time to help your students hear the tune's two rhythmic motives—the first a staccato two-eighth-note upbeat figure, the second a legato four-sixteenth-note upbeat figure—they will be better prepared to recognize not only the return of the rondo theme but also Haydn's playful use of the theme in the developmental episode.

Once students have identified the primary characteristics of the rondo theme, display the Listening Chart (see Appendix I). Play through the entire movement and point out each section as it goes by. In the discussion that follows, point out these interesting features:

1. Unlike the rondo theme, the first episode (**B**) does not state a clearly defined, easily recognized tune. In this often dramatic section, the music is much more continuous, polyphonic, and unstable harmonically. New melodic ideas are introduced, though these are often based on motives from the rondo theme. Point out the "false" restatement of the rondo theme about halfway through **B**, a gesture typical of Haydn's wit. Also note the brief passage that prepares for the rondo theme's return, based on the opening motive of the **a** phrase.

2. Outside of changes in orchestration, the main differences in the second statement of the rondo theme rest in its form. In this **A′** section we only hear **a** and **b** phrases. There are no repeats, and the final **a′** is omitted when the music moves directly (and surprisingly) into the second contrasting episode.

3. Bursting in with a bang before the second rondo statement can finish, the second episode (**C**) is much more developmental than the first, almost entirely polyphonic with frequent modulations. Especially entertaining is the long, teasing passage that prepares for the rondo theme's final return.

Acutely aware that by now we will not be surprised by the rondo theme's return, Haydn plays with the anticipation (as in Symphony No. 95), almost as if to say, "You think you know where the rondo theme will start? Gotcha! Listen again!"

4. Compared with the final rondo theme statement in Symphony No. 95, this one is much more complete and straightforward. In this **A″** section the entire tune is presented, but without repeats: **a b a′**.

5. Haydn provides a full and robust coda to end this symphony. He sets up the coda with an inconclusive extension of the rondo theme's cadence to guarantee that we will not mistake this for the end of the movement. After a pregnant pause, the orchestra plunges in with a flurry of activity led by the violins—it all sounds like the Classical version of a barn dance! Haydn uses the last twenty seconds to bring back the opening motive of the rondo theme, transposing and repeating it while he reinforces the tonic key with strong repeated cadence progressions. Haydn again demonstrates his immaculate taste and timing—this forty-second-long coda sounds just right, both as an ending to this movement and for the entire four-movement symphony.

MOZART **Symphony No. 40 in G Minor, K. 550, III**

This minuet and trio form provides an excellent contrast with the examples in Lecture Suggestions above. (See the Additional Listening Chart for this movement in Appendix I.) Diagram the phrase structure for the first minuet on the board.

|: a :||: b a′ codetta :|

Play the first minuet and ask students to inventory its musical characteristics. Point out phrases on the diagram as they are played. In the discussion that follows, draw out the following characteristics:

Rhythm—marked by syncopation; strong third beat accents in measures 1, 4, and 7

Meter—triple (characteristic of a minuet)

Dynamics—loud

Tone color—scored for the entire orchestra

Mode—minor

Call attention to the surging, dark, restless quality of this minuet (no longer a courtly dance in Mozart's hands) and the marvelous, quiet codetta that puts the minuet's unpredictable energy to rest.

Ask students to list ways that the trio section might contrast with the minuet. The mode could be major, the rhythm smoother, the orchestral timbres lighter, the dynamics more *piano,* the spirit more subdued, and so on. In fact, Mozart creates a highly contrasting trio by doing all of these and more.

Diagram the phrase structure for the trio on the board.

|: c :||: d c′ codetta :|

Play the trio and ask students to inventory its musical characteristics. Point out phrases on the diagram as they are played. In the discussion that follows, draw out the following characteristics:

Rhythm—on the beat, no syncopation

Meter—triple

Dynamics—soft

Tone color—scoring highlights woodwinds, French horns, and strings; a trio section was often written for just three instruments in the Baroque period, but Classical composers did not observe this practice. At the most, they scored trio sections for a smaller ensemble than in the minuet.

Mode—major

As you did with the minuet, point out the quiet codetta at the end of the trio.

Finally, display (or hand out photocopies of) the Additional Listening Chart for this piece from Appendix I. Play the entire work and point out sections as they occur. When listening to the movement, ask students if there is any moment of drama in which they get an emotional rush above and beyond an appreciation of the melodies. There will be many responses to this subjective question, but many students often agree on two special moments: the beginning of the trio and the return of the minuet. The trio's change of mood, mode, rhythm, dynamic, and tone color creates a sense of dislocation and departure from the minuet and a sense of relief from the minuet's dark urgency. The return to the minuet constitutes the dramatic high point of the piece. We return to familiar territory, a thematic home base, and the moment of return is an especially satisfying one. This sort of dramatic moment occurs frequently in music that emphasizes contrast in the relation between sections.

MOZART Symphony No. 40 in G Minor, K. 550, IV

This sonata-form movement offers another opportunity to familiarize your students with sonata form. (See Additional Listening Chart in Appendix I.)

Copy the complete diagram of sonata form onto the board (see Lecture Suggestions above for the first movement of Mozart's Symphony 40). Note that this movement has no introduction or coda. Play theme 1 (mm. 1–16) for the class and ask students to inventory its musical characteristics.

Mood—dramatic (typical for the first theme in a sonata-form movement)

Melody—wide melodic leaps and an upward-reaching motive

Dynamics—contrasts between *forte* and *piano*

Tone color—theme played by entire orchestra

Mode—minor

Phrase structure—|: **a** :||: **b a′** :|

Remind students that the themes of a sonata-form movement will often contrast, sometimes to an extreme degree. Play theme 2 (mm. 55–85) and ask students to inventory its characteristics. Point out the ways that these characteristics contrast with those of theme 1.

Mood—quiet and lyrical (typical for a second theme in many sonata-form movements)

Melody—stepwise melodic motion, with occasional leaps

Dynamics—*piano*

Tone color—theme played by strings and winds

Mode—major

Phrase structure—**a a′**

Remind students that themes 1 and 2 also contrast in key.

If the listener is to perceive the gentle and lyrical theme 2 as important in its own right, it cannot appear immediately after the dramatic theme 1, which would overpower it. The two themes are separated and connected by the bridge. Play the bridge (mm. 16–54) and ask students these questions:

Why doesn't the bridge sound like part of theme 1?

Why doesn't the bridge sound like a new theme?

How does it sound transitional?

In the discussion that follows, draw out these points:

1. The harmony is unstable as we modulate from the tonic key to a new key, an effect that is amplified by the bridge's continuous motion and lack of strong cadences.

2. No clear tune is stated—there are only brief motives, scales, and sequences.

3. This section conveys excitement, anticipation, and tension—it does not create the sense of stasis and melodic interest that characterize a theme.

Point out the strong cadence and pause just before theme 2 enters; these are like a giant arrow pointing to the beginning of theme 2. When theme 2 begins, we have a satisfying sense of arrival and relief.

Now play the entire exposition for the class. Note the cadence theme immediately after theme 2. As is customary, the exposition repeats, which allows the listener to become better acquainted with the primary themes.

The development section of this movement can be divided into five parts. Play each part separately, then play the entire development section at least twice, pointing out each part as it goes by.

Part 1 (mm. 109–118): Remind the class that the exposition ended with a strong cadence in the second key. Mozart begins this development with an extraordinary section of music that obliterates our sense of tonic and meter. Taken out of context, this passage could sound like something from twentieth-century music.

Part 2 (mm. 119–130): Having swept the second key clean out of our ears, Mozart now begins the development in earnest. Part 2 explores the rising motive of theme 1.

Part 3 (mm. 131–158): Mozart continues to explore the rising motive of theme 1, but now with imitative polyphony. The dynamics build in volume.

Part 4 (mm. 159–174): Mozart switches back to homophonic texture. Bass instruments insistently reiterate the rising motive from theme 1. Note that each part of development has grown out of the previous one. Part 4 gradually builds to a *fortissimo* for the entire orchestra, the loudest passage in the movement. Just when we expect the tension to resolve (m. 171), the resolution is diverted.

Part 5 (mm. 175–190): This retransition begins the motion back to the tonic key to prepare for the return of theme 1 in the recapitulation. The rising motive of theme 1 is stated in imitation between low and high instruments. Part 5 begins quietly but quickly builds to a dramatic high point—a widely spaced cadence followed by a pause. The onset of the recapitulation comes as a marked relief.

The recapitulation brings back the themes from the exposition in their original order and entirely in the key of G minor. The main difference between the exposition and the recapitulation is that theme 2 and the cadence theme must now appear in the tonic key. Play theme 2 from the exposition (B-flat major, mm. 55–84) and from the recapitulation (G minor, mm. 231–60). This juxtaposition of the two versions dramatically demonstrates the change of mode and mood—from the lyric, major-key version of the exposition to the darker, more tragic version in the recapitulation.

Finally, display (or hand out photocopies of) the Additional Listening Chart for this piece in Appendix I. Play the entire movement and point out themes and sections as they are played.

Multimedia Resources

❧ Further Listening Charts and Texts

See Further Listening Examples in Chapter 13 to explore the use of Chapter 12 forms (sonata, Classical variation, minuet, and rondo forms) in other genres, such as string quartet, piano sonata, and piano concerto. Appendix I contains Listening Charts for many of these works.

See Appendix I for Listening Charts for these orchestral works:

Haydn, Symphony No. 88 in G, I, II, III, and IV. See Further Listening Examples above for lecture suggestions on each movement of this complete symphony.

Mozart, Symphony No. 40 in G Minor, K. 550, III and IV. See Further Listening Examples above for lecture suggestions on these minuet- and sonata-form movements.

Mozart, *Don Giovanni,* Overture. See Further Listening Examples in Chapter 13 of this manual (p. 318) for lecture suggestions on this sonata-form work.

⁷ Sound Recordings

Bartók, *Concerto for Orchestra: Music for Strings, Percussion, and Celesta.* Chicago Symphony Orchestra. RCA Victor 61504 (CD). Vividly atmospheric, superbly recorded performances of Bartók's music; conducted by Fritz Reiner. Movement IV features vivacious folk melodies in free rondo form. Try this recording if you use Listening Idea 2 above.

Berlioz, *Symphonie fantastique.* Orchestre Révolutionnaire et Romantique. Philips 434 402-2 (CD). This recording of Berlioz's masterwork uses the original 1830 orchestration on period instruments; conducted by John Eliot Gardiner. Gardiner is one of the most successful conductors of nineteenth-century repertory on period instruments, and he draws bold colors and vitality from his players. Movement IV features terrific, raucous orchestral writing in an ambiguous form (see the Listening Chart in Appendix I). Try this recording if you use Listening Idea 2 above.

Haydn, *The London Symphonies*, Vol. 1. Royal Concertgebouw Orchestra. Philips 442 611-2 (CD). First-class modern-instrument performances of late Haydn symphonies, including 95, 96, 98, 102, 103, and 104; conducted by Colin Davis. Try this recording if you use Listening Idea 3 or 4 above.

Haydn, *Symphonies Nos. 88, 89, and 90.* Tafelmusik. Sony Classical Vivarte SK 66253 (CD). Outstanding period-instrument performances of three late Haydn symphonies supervised by H. C. Robbins Landon; conducted by Bruno Weil. Try this recording if you use Listening Idea 3 or 4 or suggestions for Symphony No. 88 in Further Listening Examples above.

Liszt, *Complete Piano Music,* Vol. 2. Jenö Jandó. Naxos 8.553119 (CD). Intense, committed performances from one of the finest living Liszt specialists. Vol. 2 contains the 12 Transcendental Etudes. Transcendental Etude No. 10 in F Minor features virtuoso writing for piano in loose sonata form. Try this recording if you use Listening Idea 2 above.

Mozart, *Don Giovanni.* English Baroque Soloists. Deutsche Grammophon Archiv 445 870-2 (CD). Excellent recording of Mozart's great opera on period instruments; conducted by John Eliot Gardiner. The overture features a wonderfully clear example of sonata form with slow introduction and coda. Try this recording if you use Listening Idea 2, 3, or 4 above.

Mozart, *Eine kleine Nachtmusik [The Great Serenades].* Academy of St. Martin in the Fields. Philips 464 022–2 (CD). Fine performances of Mozart serenades on modern instruments; conducted by Neville Marriner. Includes *Eine kleine Nachtmusik,* K. 525. Try this recording if you use Listening Idea 1 above.

Mozart, *Symphonies Nos. 39 and 40.* Bamberg Symphony Orchestra. Orfeo C 045 901A (CD). Fine performance on modern instruments (the one used in the *Listen* set); conducted by Eugen Jochum. Try this recording if you use Listening Idea 3 or 4 or suggestions from Further Listening Examples above for the later movements of Mozart's Symphony No. 40.

ʹ Video Recordings

Amadeus. Warner Brothers (DVD or VHS, color, 160 minutes). The award-winning movie (1984 Academy Award for Best Picture), based on Peter Shaffer's Tony Award–winning play, has done more to rekindle interest in Mozart than any other event of the past twenty-five years. It follows the broad outline of Mozart's final years but is not a factual story. In fact, most of the material on Salieri is fictitious—but the movie is highly recommended nonetheless. It presents Mozart's music in period settings, with fascinating insights into the compositional process and political maneuvering in eighteenth-century Vienna. A twenty-minute-longer "Director's Cut" version is now available, but outside of making explicit Mozart's infidelities and Constanze's willingness to do whatever it takes to help Wolfie's career, it adds little. You can use this movie with Class Discussion Idea 3.

Haydn. BBC Opus Arte (DVD, color, 83 minutes). Superb DVD features Cecilia Bartoli and conductor Nikolaus Harnoncourt performing the music of Haydn. Especially useful for Chapter 12 is the excellent Concentus Musicus Wien period-instrument performance of Haydn's Symphony No. 92 (*Oxford*). Though not written expressly for Haydn's first trip to England (as was No. 95), Symphony No. 92 *was* performed at Oxford University when Haydn received his honorary doctorate. Highly recommended if you use Listening Idea 3 above or for a video performance of a complete Haydn symphony.

Haydn and Mozart: Symphony No. 87 and Symphony No. 39. Sounds Magnificent: The Story of the Symphony Series. Image Entertainment (DVD, color, 88 minutes). André Previn narrates this look at the composers and their music. The video includes complete performances of these two symphonies by the Royal Philharmonic Orchestra.

Haydn and the Esterházys. Man and Music Series. www.films.com (DVD or VHS, color, 53 minutes). Reports on Haydn's forty years in the service of the wealthy Esterházy family. Music from Haydn's Piano Sonatas in D and F; Baryton Trio No. 48 in D; Quartet Op. 20, No. 2; Symphonies 44 in E Minor and 65 in A; *Il mondo della luna;* and the *Lord Nelson* Mass.

Haydn, *Haydn/Pergolesi*. Immortal (DVD, color, 74 minutes). Fine performances of Haydn's Symphony No. 77 and Pergolesi's *Stabat Mater*. This fairly late Haydn symphony (1780s) provides an excellent example of the standard four-movement format. Under Christopher Hogwood's direction, the modern-instrument Ensemble Orchestral de Paris uses period manners to produce a lively, often dramatic performance. Recommended if you use Listening Idea 3 above or for a video performance of a complete Haydn symphony.

[Haydn, Symphony No. 94 (*Surprise*), II.] *Delaware Music* Series. www.ecsmedia.com (DVD). Performance by the University of Michigan Orchestra, conducted by Gustav Meyer. This important collection includes a scrolling two-line score with harmonic reduction analysis. Superb resource for lecture-demonstration on Haydn and theme and variations form.

In Rehearsal with Christoph von Dohnányi and the Philharmonic Orchestra. Image Entertainment (DVD, color, 58 minutes). In this recent release, the renowned conductor rehearses Haydn's Symphony No. 88 with the orchestra. Try this video for a look at the Classical symphony from the performer's vantage point, especially if you use suggestions for Symphony No. 88 in Further Listening Examples above.

Joseph Haydn: The Famous Composers Series. Kultur Video (VHS, color, 35 minutes). A look at Haydn's life, with musical excerpts performed by the Elysian Ensemble.

London: The Musical Capital. Man and Music Series. www.films.com (DVD or VHS, color, 53 minutes). This intriguing look at London in the late eighteenth century includes musical excerpts from Haydn's Symphony No. 104 and from other works by Clementi, Webbe, and J. C. Bach.

Mozart. BBC Opus Arte (DVD, color, 112 minutes). Superb DVD features Cecilia Bartoli and conductor Nikolaus Harnoncourt performing the music of Mozart. Especially useful for Chapter 12 is the excellent Concentus Musicus Wien period-instrument performance of Mozart's Symphony No. 38 (*Prague*). This work was premiered while Mozart was in Prague for what turned out to be incredibly successful performances of *Le nozze di Figaro,* resulting in the commission for *Don Giovanni.* Unusual for late Mozart, this symphony has only three movements (no minuet)—a good reminder that there are always exceptions to the "rules." Highly recommended if you use Listening Idea 3 above or for a video performance of a complete Mozart symphony.

Mozart: A Genius in His Time. Man and Music Series. www.films.com (DVD or VHS, color, 53 minutes). Covers the last five years of Mozart's life and looks at his troubles with patrons and audiences. Musical excerpts from the String Quintet in G Minor, K. 516; *Eine kleine Nachtmusik;* Violin Sonata in A, K. 526; Symphony No. 41 in C (*Jupiter*); *Così fan tutte;* and *Die Zauberflöte.*

Mozart: Dropping the Patron. Man and Music Series. www.films.com (DVD or VHS, color, 53 minutes). Looks at Mozart's employment with the Archbishop of Salzburg and his departure for Vienna to further his career. Includes musical excerpts from Mozart's Wind Serenade in E-flat, K. 375; Violin Sonata in G, K. 379; *Die Entführung aus dem Serail;* Terzet, K. 436; Piano Concerto in E-flat, K. 449; String Quartet in B-flat (*Hunt*), K. 458; and *Le nozze di Figaro.*

[Mozart, Quintet for Clarinet and Strings, K. 581, I.] *Delaware Music Series.* www.ecsmedia.com (DVD). Performance by clarinetist Peter Hill with the Delos String Quartet. The DVD includes scrolling full score with harmonic analysis, melodic contour map, and analysis of melodic ornaments. Superb resource for lecture-demonstration on Mozart and sonata form.

Mozart, Symphonies 40 and 41. Philips (DVD, color). Riccardo Muti leads the Vienna Philharmonic through Mozart's final two symphonies at a Salzburg concert during the 1991 Mozart bicentennial. These are modern-instrument performances, of course, but Muti ensures that the music speaks with passion and urgency. Recommended as a supplement to your presentation of the first movement of Symphony No. 40, if you use Listening Idea 2 or 3 above, or if you use Additional Listening Suggestions for movements 3 and 4.

Mozart, Symphony C Major "Jupiter" and Symphony C Major "Linz." Arthaus Musik (DVD, color, 70 minutes). Superb performances of two late Mozart symphonies by the English Chamber Orchestra; conducted by Jeffrey Tate. Both works provide excellent examples of the Classical four-movement format. Recommended if you use Listening Idea 3 above or for a video performance of a complete Mozart symphony.

The Seasons and the Symphony. Music in Time Series. www.films.com (DVD or VHS, color, 60 minutes). This program offers an overview of eighteenth-century music. Beginning with Vivaldi's *Four Seasons,* James Galway guides us through the music of the Mannheim symphonists, Gluck, and Haydn. Most useful in looking at the transition from the Baroque to the Classical style. Relevant musical excerpts come from Haydn's Symphonies 45 and 100.

200 Years of Mozart. www.insight-media.com (DVD, color, 27 minutes). A look at the composer's life, with excerpts from *Marriage of Figaro,* Piano Concerto No. 21, *Eine kleine Nachtmusik, Magic Flute,* and the Requiem.

Vienna. Music in Time Series. www.films.com (DVD or VHS, color, 60 minutes). Looks at Vienna in the late eighteenth and early nineteenth centuries. Special emphasis on operas and symphonies by Mozart. Many Schubert works also included. Music by Mozart includes excerpts from the Requiem ("Dies irae" and "Lachrymosa"); Andante in C Major; Piano Concerto, K. 414; the *Haffner* Serenade; Piano Concerto, K. 459; *Don Giovanni;* Symphony No. 38 in D (*Prague*); and *Così fan tutte* (Act I Finale).

Wolfgang Amadeus Mozart. Harmonics: The Innovators of Classical Music Series. www.films.com (DVD or VHS, color, 27 minutes). Video survey of Mozart's life and achievements includes interviews with Mozart scholars as well as musical selections from *Don Giovanni, Marriage of Figaro, Magic Flute, Ave Verum Corpus,* the Requiem, Piano Sonata No. 9, and Piano Concertos 9 and 14.

♪ Software

Great Composers: Mozart, Mendelssohn, and Dvořák. Zane Publishing (CD-ROM—Windows or Macintosh). 45-minute multimedia presentation and four hundred photos illustrating the lives of these three composers. Available at www.cdaccess.com.

Mozart, Symphony No. 40. Time Sketch Composer Series. www.ecsmedia.com (CD-ROM—Windows or Macintosh). Program presents a CD recording of Mozart's Symphony No. 40 and other works, with interactive arch map analysis and background information about the composer, his style, and the work.

CHAPTER 13

Other Classical Genres

Chapter Outline

Boldface indicates works in the recording set.

Important Terms

sonata	double-exposition form	opera buffa
piano sonata	orchestra exposition	ensemble
violin sonata	solo exposition	duet
sonata movement plan	cadenza	*gagaku*
rondeau	string quartet	*togaku*
Classical concerto	string quartet movement plan	*komagaku*
Classical concerto movement plan	chamber music	*hichiriki*

ryuteki	*gakuso*	*gangsa*
heterophonic texture	*gamelan*	*gongan*
sho	metallophones	stratified polyphony
kakko	gong	*ostinato*
tsuridaiko	*gamelan pelegongan*	
biwa	*legong*	

Teaching Objectives

❦ Overall Objectives

This chapter will help students acquire familiarity with:

1. Features of other important Classical genres, understood as expressions of the principles of "pleasing variety" and "natural" simplicity:

   a. sonata   c. string quartet

   b. concerto   d. opera buffa

2. The four-movement plan that dominated Classical instrumental genres and the three-movement plans derived from it.

3. The internal structures of other important forms associated with Classical genres:

   a. double-exposition form (concerto only)

   b. ensemble (opera buffa only)

4. Universal principles of form in instrumental music and their manifestation in music of different cultures, especially Japan and Bali.

5. Important features of the Japanese *gagaku* tradition and the *togaku* orchestra.

6. Important features of Balinese *gamelan* music, especially *gamelan pelegongan*.

❦ Listening Objectives

After completing this chapter, students should be able to:

1. Hear and identify how elements of music are used in other Classical genres and their associated musical forms.

2. Recognize and follow important features of other primary Classical genres:

   a. sonata   c. string quartet

   b. concerto   d. opera buffa

3. Recognize and follow the three-movement plans of Classical sonatas and solo concertos.

4. Recognize and follow the four-movement plan in Classical string quartets.

5. Follow other important forms associated with Classical instrumental genres, especially double-exposition form.

6. Listen for dramatic continuity and musical characterization in opera buffa.

7. Recognize and follow important forms of opera buffa: aria, recitative, and especially the ensemble.

8. Hear important features of music for the Japanese *togaku* orchestra and compare them with features of Classical orchestral music.

9. Hear how elements and structures of music contribute to the sense of form in *gamelan pelegongan*.

Lecture Suggestions

Chapter 12 introduced and examined the Classical symphony and its essential forms—sonata, Classical variation, minuet, and rondo—using Haydn's Symphony No. 95 and the first movement of Mozart's Symphony No. 40. Chapter 13 studies the other primary genres of Classical music—sonata, concerto, quartet, and opera buffa—along with ensemble works from Japan and Bali that belong to traditions even older than the Classical symphony. At this point, you must make a decision. What's the problem? If you covered Chapter 12 thoroughly, you probably don't have time to look at complete sonatas, concertos, quartets, and operas; for that matter, the recorded anthology does not provide complete recordings of these works. The two Global Perspectives examples put even greater time pressures on your coverage of Classical genres. Perhaps the most compelling non-Western works in the entire *Listen* set, you really can't skip them, and they beg comparison with the Classical symphony. Fortunately, the principal features of the symphony's four-movement plan carry over into the other significant Classical instrumental genres with only slight modification. There are several creative ways to use this to your advantage. Here are a few solutions for dealing with Classical genres:

Option 1   Use the authors' approach. You covered the four-movement format within a complete symphony in Chapter 12; now explain how each genre in Chapter 13 adapts the symphony's four-movement plan. Use one movement from each genre to demonstrate its characteristic sounds, forms, and techniques. The lecture suggestions below correspond to this approach.

Option 2   Assemble your own mix-and-match four-movement plan by borrowing movements from four different works. Make sure that each instrumental genre is represented; include as many listening examples as you can from this chapter.

Option 3   Assign a complete sonata, concerto, and/or string quartet as an out-of-class listening assignment; after all, Kerman and Tomlinson discuss complete works in the textbook. Use only Further Listening Examples from Chapter 13 in class.

Option 4   Do it all! Cover all of LeBrun's Sonata in F, Op. 1, No. 3; Mozart's Piano Concerto in A, K. 488; and Beethoven's String Quartet in F, Op. 135 (from Chapter 14). Again, the textbook discusses each movement of these works, though you will need to find your own complete recordings (see Sound Recordings below). You may regret it later, when you must leave out important Romantic or twentieth-century works, but your students will possess a thorough knowledge of the forms, genres, and conventions of Classical music.

Option 5   Make no attempt to cover other instrumental genres in Chapter 13—you covered the symphony thoroughly in Chapter 12. Provide brief verbal comparisons between the symphony and the other genres and let it go at that.

Option 6   Try any combination of Options 1–5.

Whichever option you choose, you simply must make room for Global Perspectives examples. Japanese *gagaku* remains the oldest continuous orchestral tradition anywhere in the world, and Balinese *gamelan* music's attractive, distinctive timbres prove as intriguing to modern students as they did to Debussy. Since both are "classical," not folk, traditions, they provide many points of comparison with Western music. The authors focus primarily on the elements of form, specifically the principles of repetition, contrast, and variation. These familiar, universal principles provide the means of understanding and appreciating unfamiliar, non-Western musics; at the same time, knowledge of these traditions helps us to appreciate Western music in new and different ways. For further suggestions on how you can integrate the Global Perspectives examples into your coverage of Chapters 12 and 13, turn to the notes on these pieces toward the end of the Lecture Suggestions for this chapter.

The options above suggest approaches to *instrumental* genres, both Classical and non-Western, but one other significant Classical genre remains unmentioned: opera buffa. Its position at the end of the chapter places it in grave danger of neglect. You can omit anything else in Chapter 13, but it would be a major mistake to leave out opera buffa. Nonsingers often "pooh-pooh" vocalists and opera with glee, but before you delete opera buffa from your syllabus, consider the following:

1. Mozart's most substantial, significant works were his operas. To talk about Mozart without mentioning his operas is like lecturing on Beethoven without mentioning his symphonies.

2. Students often relate to music more easily when there are words. The interplay between verbal-dramatic meaning and musical meaning gives added depth to their listening experience. This deeper understanding helps when they encounter purely instrumental works by the same composer. Remember: The most effective musical scenes in *Amadeus* were associated with text-based works—Mozart's operas and his Requiem.

3. In spite of American culture's negative preconceptions about opera, many students come to opera with an open mind, especially when you don't impose your own prejudices on them. It also helps enormously to point out the similarities between American musicals and comic opera. I go so far as to tell my students that musicals like *Rent, Chicago, Phantom of the Opera,* and *Wicked* are modern operas. Whether you agree or not, they are clearly modern descendants of comic opera traditions.

Four-Movement Plan Review

Before you look at specific genres, review the symphony's four-movement plan. Put this chart from Chapter 12 on the board and keep it handy for discussion of each of the instrumental genres in this chapter. A clear understanding of the four-movement plan will help your students absorb other instrumental genres more quickly and more thoroughly.

Movement	Form	Tempo	Character
I	sonata (optional slow introduction)	moderate to fast	complex, substantial, impressive
II	no fixed form (sonata, variation, rondo)	slow	lyrical, songlike
III	minuet (with trio)	moderate	dancelike, triple meter
IV	sonata or rondo	fast	often light, tuneful, brilliant

⁊ The Sonata

The genre known as the sonata is, by definition, a chamber work in several movements. In the Classical period, the sonata was typically a work for solo instrument, with or without accompaniment. The most important Classical sonatas were solo sonatas for piano alone; others were written for violin with keyboard accompaniment, flute with keyboard accompaniment, cello with keyboard accompaniment, and sometimes even for keyboard with violin accompaniment, as we shall see. The symphony's four-movement plan forms the basis for most Classical piano sonatas, but the sonata adapts the plan in various ways. Some Beethoven sonatas use the four-movement plan literally, but the majority of Classical sonatas create a three-movement plan by omitting the minuet. Other interesting options can be found without looking too far. Mozart's Piano Sonata in A, K. 331 (see Further Listening Examples below) creates a three-movement format by omitting the opening sonata-form movement, beginning instead with a slow theme-and-variations movement. Most commonly, however, Classical sonatas contain a sonata-form first movement; a slow second movement; and a fast third movement using sonata, rondo, or even theme and variations form. (If some students are still confused about the difference between genre and form, this is the place to clear it up; otherwise, the distinction between sonata *form* and the sonata *genre* will create endless confusion.)

LEBRUN **Sonata in F, Op. 1, No. 3**

We don't know a great deal about Francesca LeBrun; most of the significant details of her biography are mentioned in the *Listen* textbook. She took the one avenue open to women who wanted to pursue a career in music in the eighteenth century—she became an opera singer. It was her great success in this profession that allowed her both the freedom and the opportunity to compose. Bear in mind that female composers were rare at this time, and many men *and* women assumed that it was not possible for a woman to compose as well as a man. These LeBrun sonatas may not have the sophistication of those by Mozart (very few Classical composers can withstand comparison with Mozart), but their quality equals that of countless sonatas written by a multitude of other Classical composers.

This sonata is representative of the style and technique of many other Classical sonatas, but it is a rather unusual work in two crucial aspects. First, this sonata contains only two movements, an allegro in sonata form and a rondeau marked allegretto. While the rondeau is similar to the rondo-form movements that end many Classical instrumental works, the allegro takes a rather free approach to the standard first-movement sonata form. In a move reminiscent of Haydn's later Symphony No. 95, LeBrun begins her recapitulation with theme 2—theme 1 is nowhere to be found. Second, this sonata belongs to a somewhat unusual (by today's standards) subgenre: the sonata for piano with violin accompaniment. When the piano plays with another instrument, we are conditioned to hear the piano as accompaniment, but the title page for the 1780 London publication of LeBrun's sonatas makes it clear that this is *not* the case. Her Opus 1 sonatas are titled *Six Sonatas for the Harpsichord or Piano Forte with an Accompaniment for a Violin*. The violin part, which has been omitted from the *Listen* recording, is rather uninteresting—it is the piano that carries the main melody. The violin is often relegated to accompanimental arpeggio patterns, and when it does play the melody, it merely doubles or imitates the piano melody.

The *Listen* recordings have included many period-instrument performances up to this point, yet this is the first time we have heard a fortepiano. This "beta" version of the piano has distinctive sound all its own; take some time to point out its unique features. More delicate than the modern piano, some students may find that the fortepiano sounds similar to a harpsichord. What it lacks in power it makes up for with its wide range of tone colors. Each register of the pianoforte creates its own unique timbre, and Classical composers took advantage of these differences.

Rondeau: Allegretto

This rondeau contains some unique features that require special treatment. In most respects it is a typical Classical rondo-form movement, but it also bears a striking resemblance to third-movement minuet and trio form. (Perhaps Le-Brun decided to roll features of the final two movements into one, given that she only had two movements to work with.) In either case, the rondeau theme itself is the place to begin. Play it until students can recognize it easily, and ask them to map out the structure of the theme and inventory its characteristics. The structure of the **A** theme, a simple parallel period, can be expressed as:

a a′

Note that these two phrases are as neat and symmetrical as you could ever hope to see, and LeBrun continues to use pairs of straightforward eight-measure phrases throughout this movement. In your discussion, draw out the following characteristics:

Melody—simple tune based on a quick, sixteenth-note motive

Rhythm—varied, fast moving

Meter—duple

Tempo—quick

Dynamics—alternates between softer and louder

Tone color—piano

Register—piano middle to high

Articulation—mix of *staccato* and *legato*

Texture—homophonic

Accompaniment—simple chord arpeggiations; little to distract from the melody

Mode—major

Once students are comfortable with the rondeau theme, introduce the contrasting episodes. The **B** section, based on motives from **A**, sounds very similar to the rondeau theme. If it were not in the dominant key, we would almost mistake it for a continuation of **A**. The first significant contrast comes at the beginning of the **C** section. Since the **C** section also returns once in rondo-like fashion, play it a couple of times and ask students to describe how it differs from the rondeau theme.

Melody—also a simple tune based on rhythmic motives, but with longer note values

Rhythm—longer note values make it feel slower

Dynamics—softer overall

Register—higher overall

Articulation—a more *legato* feel

Accompaniment—simple chords without arpeggios

Mode—minor

As you introduce the **D** section, note how the **C D C** sections together form a large, D-minor middle section for this movement. LeBrun's first **C** section ends in the "wrong" key, the relative major; as a result, it feels incomplete, and **D** feels like a natural and necessary continuation. The return of **C** restores the minor mode (and finally does cadence in D minor this second time), giving this large **C D C** middle section the feel of a self-contained rounded binary form. The modulation that ends the **C** section and the synchronized return of both the **C** theme and the D-minor tonic provide exactly what we would expect in the trio of a minuet movement! The subsequent return of **A B A** as a large structural unit only confirms this impression.

Once the second **C** section has finished, LeBrun needs to return to the rondeau theme. We haven't heard it for a while, but she has a problem. The **C D C** middle section is so self-contained and makes such a strong impression that a simple return to **A** might seem glib, especially since listeners are expecting it. Thinking now like a true rondo-form composer, she inserts an entirely new transitional section. This minor-mode passage, easily the most dramatic moment in the piece, gives full expression to the darker implications of the **C** section's minor key. Further, the transition captures our attention so completely that we forget about the **C D C** sections. By the time it finishes, we are truly ready to hear the rondeau theme again, and the stability and familiarity of the **A B A** sections that conclude the work are doubly satisfying because of this extra bit of drama.

If you have time, a quick look at LeBrun's use of phrase relationships can offer fascinating insights into the craft of the Classical composer. As noted above, the rondeau theme is a simple parallel period—two eight-measure phrases that begin with the same tune, the first ending with a half cadence, the second with an authentic cadence. Of course, every major theme in this piece uses that same basic structure, providing a sense of regularity and consistency. Further, the repetition within each theme says to the listener, "This is an important theme," at the same time helping the listener to hear it more clearly. The most interesting sections, however, are the ones where LeBrun breaks that pattern. Two examples should suffice.

The first example is the transition mentioned above, from the last **C** section back to the **A** section. Its minor mode and rhythmic energy certainly contribute to the drama, but so does the cadential elision that begins this transition. Without waiting for the final **C** phrase to come to a full stop, the transition barges in right at the start of that phrase's eighth measure. (Recall that Haydn used this same technique to begin both **B** sections in movement IV of Symphony No. 95.) To further enhance the sense of disorientation, the transition is grouped into three *four*-measure phrases, the second a varied repetition of the first, and the third clearly transitional. Along with the elision, these shorter units serve to intensify the drama—everything seems to happen faster here.

The second example comes in the final bars of the piece. LeBrun wants to end with a flurry of activity, and her coda begins with exactly the same type of cadential elision we heard in the transition. The result here? The music surges ahead with nervous energy and excitement. The frenetic phrase groups that begin this coda are the most unusual in the entire piece—two *three*-bar groups. The first of these groups gives us a typically strong Classical cadence, but just as we are about to reach the final chord, LeBrun again uses cadential elision, interrupting with a repetition of this three-bar cadence formula. This time the cadence reaches completion, and the reassuringly symmetrical four-bar group that follows repeats a simple, descending cadential motive four times before stating the final chord three times. In fact, LeBrun ends this movement with the Classical equivalent of a fade-out. The final four-bar group defuses the tension of the two three-bar groups, and a palpable sense of relaxation is provided by the simultaneous use of the descending motive and longer note values in the piano, regular repetition of a simple V-I chord progression, and a gradual decrescendo. In spite of this relaxation, LeBrun does not allow things to get dull. As the textbook points out, this final descending motive provides a touch of syncopation, just enough to keep things interesting to the very end.

❼ The Classical Concerto

The genre known as the Classical concerto is, by definition, a large, multi-movement work for solo instrument and orchestra. The Classical concerto retained several of the elements that made the Baroque *concerto grosso* successful: alternation between solo instrument(s) and orchestra and a three-movement plan based on contrasting tempos (fast-slow-fast). Nonetheless, the success of the symphony's four-movement plan rubbed off on the concerto during the Classical period. In the resulting format, the typical first movement was an adaptation of sonata form, the second movement corresponded to the slow movement of a symphony, and the fast third movement was like the symphony's final movement except that it favored rondo (or theme and variations) form. In short, the Classical concerto was much like a symphony without minuet, adapted to accommodate interaction between the soloist and the orchestra—a hybrid that combined the best features of the Baroque concerto and the Classical symphony.

If you have access to a complete recording of Mozart's Piano Concerto in A, K. 488 (see Sound Recordings), play excerpts from all three movements in random order, just as you did for the symphony. As students have come to expect, the quickest excerpt comes from the final movement, the slowest excerpt from the second movement, and the remaining excerpt must be the first. This short exercise can help students hear how each movement conforms to the concerto's typical three-movement plan, described above.

The adapted sonata form used for the first movement of a Classical concerto is often called double-exposition form. Copy the diagram of sonata form from Chapter 12 of this manual (page 250) onto the board. Ask the class to compare the textbook's diagram of double-exposition form (page 205) with the sonata form diagram on the board. Have students pick out the differences between the two forms. In the discussion that follows, draw attention to these points:

1. There are two expositions in the concerto, the first for orchestra alone and the second for piano with orchestra. The length of the two expositions encouraged composers to introduce more than just two main themes. The second group is often just that—a long string of related themes.

2. The modulating bridge is saved for the second exposition; the second group in the orchestral exposition remains in the tonic key.

3. The second group in the solo exposition rarely repeats the second group of the orchestra exposition literally—the solo instrument will often mix in new themes along with the old. Consequentially, the single second group in the recapitulation must be a composite of both expositions.

4. A solo cadenza is added at the end of the recapitulation, and the coda often brings back cadential material from earlier in the movement.

MOZART **Piano Concerto in A, K. 488, I**

This movement provides an excellent, easy-to-follow example of double-exposition form. Since double-exposition form is essentially a modified sonata form, you can use the same procedures you followed in Chapter 12 for sonata form.

1. Examine the main themes. Focus primarily on theme 1, theme 2, and the cadence theme, but don't overlook the response to theme 1 (a theme in itself) or the "deflection" passage, which contains more than one theme. Take an inventory of their musical characteristics, their internal phrase structures, and the differences between them.

2. Play the main themes in two versions: as performed by the orchestra in the first exposition and as performed by the pianist in the second exposition.

3. Play the first exposition. Call attention to the main themes as they appear and point out the relative stability of this section's harmonies.

4. Play the second exposition. Point out how the solo exposition differs from the orchestral exposition, especially in its ornamentation, the reduced role of the orchestra, and the instability of its bridge. Most striking of all is the flurry of new material following the "deflection" passage: a solo virtuoso passage, another statement of the response theme, and a brand new closing theme.

5. Work through the development—one section at a time—and observe the devices Mozart uses to develop his themes. Like the development in his Symphony No. 40 (but unlike that in Haydn's Symphony No. 95), this development is rather short, and it works with just one theme. Curiously, the theme Mozart develops is *not* one of the main themes—it's the new theme he introduced just before the development began. Even the retransition is based on the new theme, and it stands apart only because of the relative stability created by the E pedal in the bass. Mozart only abandons the new theme in the cadenza-like passage toward the end of the retransition, a rhetorical shift that prepares us for the recapitulation.

6. Play the recapitulation and note its significant features: the restatement of theme 2 in the tonic key, the piano's solo excursions and thematic extensions (typical of double-exposition form but not of sonata form), and the solo cadenza. Ask students to identify the theme or themes used in the cadenza. Briefly compare the recapitulation with the two expositions; it looks more like the piano exposition, retaining the new theme as its cadence theme.

7. Play the entire movement so that students can hear these relationships in the proper context.

Once students have experienced at least this one movement of a Classical concerto, review by making the following points:

1. The Classical concerto's three-movement format derives from the four-movement plan of the symphony. We see this clearly in the derivation of double-exposition form from sonata form.

2. Some features of the Classical concerto remind us of the Baroque concerto, especially the alternation between solo instrument and orchestra and the recurring cadence theme that functions much like a Baroque *ritornello* theme.

3. The Classical concerto is far from "derivative," however. The profusion of themes, the almost operatic writing for solo piano, and the dramatic interplay between piano and orchestra all make this genre unique.

4. Call attention to the cadenza. Improvisation does not play a significant role in most classical music. Cadenzas provide one of several major exceptions to general practice. Mozart wrote out cadenzas for some of his students, but he himself would have improvised a cadenza on the spot in live performance. Even when the cadenza is written out (as is the case in the *Listen* recording), it still retains the spontaneous, playful quality of a real improvisation.

5. The qualities that made the Classical concerto popular in the eighteenth century—the pleasing variety implicit in its three-movement format, the possibility of virtuoso display by the soloist, and the often dramatic contest between soloist and orchestra—helped guarantee its continued success in the nineteenth and twentieth centuries.

♩ The String Quartet

The genre known as the string quartet is, by definition, a multimovement work for two violins, viola, and cello. Goethe described it as a conversation between four intelligent adults. During the Classical era, the string quartet replaced the trio sonata as the primary chamber-music genre. Like other instrumental genres, the string quartet was influenced by the symphony's four-movement plan. Unlike the sonata and concerto genres, the string quartet often follows this format literally, without adaptation—the diagram of the string quartet's typical four-movement plan on textbook page 209 corresponds almost word for word to the symphony plan diagram on textbook page 202. There are two main differences between string quartet and symphony: The string quartet ensemble is far smaller and more intimate in nature, and the second and third movements occasionally trade places—the minuet can come before the slow movement. Beethoven's Quartet in F, Op. 135, provides an example of precisely this change.

The textbook offers an overview of the string quartet and Classical chamber music in general, but it provides no quartet listening examples—at least not in this chapter. The authors offer the possibility of turning ahead to Chapter 14 for a look at Beethoven's String Quartet in F, Op. 135, or turning back to Schubert's String Quartet in A Minor (*Listen* DVD). You must decide whether to use a quartet example now or wait for the Beethoven example in Chapter 14. There are good reasons for either choice. If you look at a quartet now, students can make a direct comparison between the quartet and other Classical genres. Both Beethoven and Schubert have advantages and disadvantages.

Beethoven—Students do get another example of minuet form, but you will have to explain Beethoven's late style (far removed from eighteenth-century Classicism) and his transformation of minuet into scherzo, all before you introduce your students to Symphony No. 5.

Schubert—Students get to revisit this lovely, already-familiar example in a new context. It's only an excerpt, however, so you can't use it as an example of form, and Schubert's early Romantic lyricism (like Beethoven's late style) has moved beyond Classical style.

Whatever you decide, this manual can help. If you choose to cover the Beethoven now, turn to Lecture Suggestions on the String Quartet in F, Op. 135, in Chapter 14 of this manual (p. 357). If you opt for Schubert, it will be enough to ask students to listen for the sound of the four solo stringed instruments and the interaction between them. With either example, take a moment and use the same guessing game you played with the concerto above. Find a complete recording of either the Beethoven or the Schubert quartet (see Sound Recordings below) or any other quartet by Haydn or Mozart. Play the movements in random order and ask students to figure out where they are in the quartet's four-movement plan.

♩ Opera Buffa

The advent of *opera buffa,* or "comic opera," was one of the most important developments of the Classical era. Opera buffa developed during the Enlightenment for the same reasons that other new musical procedures did: to create a more flexible, realistic, more "natural" vehicle for musical expression.

During the late Baroque era, the main type of opera was *opera seria,* or "serious opera." The plots of these operas were derived mostly from mythology or ancient history. Baroque audiences loved extremes in emotional display, and opera seria served up all the strongest emotions—love, rage, grief, triumph, and so on—by the bushel. By the late Baroque, the formal procedures of opera had become standardized; certain types of arias followed certain types of recitatives with absolute predictability. Market pressures also had an impact; the operatic "star system" required frequent arias to keep the incredibly popular (and highly paid) soloists and their audiences happy. This in turn affected composers and librettists. Since arias asked singers to step outside the action to express and reflect on a strong emotion, opera plots were contrived to create countless situations in which extreme emotions were plausible, and the momentum of the story was constantly halted for the next aria. Opera seria's mythological, over-dramatic, and constantly interrupted stories were far from natural or realistic.

One of the great thinkers and authors of the Enlightenment, Jean-Jacques Rousseau, launched a devastating attack on the aristocratic opera seria of the late Baroque. In attacking serious opera—the most important, substantial, and glamorous musical (and entertainment) genre of the time—Rousseau called into question the basic esthetic assumptions of the Baroque era and indirectly attacked the aristocracy that supported opera as well. Rousseau believed that Baroque opera plots and characters were as hopelessly artificial as their complicated music. He suggested that the only opera relevant to the humanist spirit of the Enlightenment was an opera that portrayed real people in real-life situations.

For this reason, Rousseau embraced an opera by Italian composer Giovanni Battista Pergolesi titled *La serva padrona* (The Servant as Master, 1733). The direct, simple, lively music of this opera (*intermezzo,* actually) serves an equally direct plot in which a cunning servant girl tricks an old bachelor into marriage. Such an opera had a much greater appeal to the "common" person, cost less to produce, and, as a result, reached a much wider audience than the ornate, costly serious operas. Out of this opera and others like it grew a new genre called opera buffa.

Opera buffa did not traffic in ancient heroes, their idealized feats, and extreme emotions; instead, it dealt with contemporary middle- and lower-class folk expressing themselves in a clear and natural way. The characteristics of opera buffa can be compared as follows with features of Baroque opera seria.

	Opera Seria	*Opera Buffa*
Story	from ancient history or mythology	based on contemporary subjects—often on plays or novels
Characters	ancient heroes and nobility	often ordinary middle- and lower-class folk
Singers	*castrati,* sopranos, and tenors common, few basses	no *castrati,* bass voice common
Musical numbers	recitative and arias	ensembles, recitative, and arias
Acts	three or four (long operas)	two or three (shorter operas)
Pacing	slow, drawn out	quicker, much livelier, more lifelike
Atmosphere	serious, tragic	light, comic
At its best	gripping, profound drama; powerful expression of emotions; timelessness of myth	fast-paced, nonstop entertainment; pointed social commentary; realistic story and characters
At its worst	far-fetched, stilted plots; exaggerated emotions; no dramatic continuity	trivial plots and music, comic situations not believable

An important new element in opera buffa was the ensemble. Whereas opera seria consisted of solo arias alternating with recitative, opera buffa added frequent ensembles—numbers in which two or more characters sing at the same time. In a Baroque aria, the action is interrupted whenever a character stops to sing, but because of the natural dramatic interaction between characters in an opera buffa ensemble, the action moves ahead more naturally and effectively. The operatic ensemble transformed Classical opera into a much more dynamic genre than its Baroque counterpart.

MOZART *Don Giovanni*

There are compelling reasons to spend class time with this opera. First, *Don Giovanni* ranks among the greatest operas ever written. Further, Mozart's operas and operatic procedures—and opera buffa itself—provide important links between Baroque opera and the Romantic masterworks of Verdi and Wagner. You can determine for yourself how much time to commit to *Don Giovanni.* The scene on the *Listen* DVD offers a clear example of an ensemble and of opera buffa style; lecture suggestions for this scene are provided in the following paragraphs. If you want to demonstrate Mozart's unique combination of comic and tragic elements in this *dramma giocoso,* you can also play the overture and/or scene XV from the Act II finale in which the stone guest confronts Don Giovanni and drags him to hell; lecture suggestions are provided in Further Listening Examples below, and the text is provided in Appendix II. Of course, you can add any other scenes you like.

Once you decide to devote time to this work, give yourself the best possible means for presenting it to your class—find a complete DVD or videotape performance of *Don Giovanni* (see Video Recordings below). Sound recordings can be very good, but opera was never a purely musical genre. Students unfamiliar with opera cannot make the mental leap needed to imagine the action, sets, costumes, and so on. In my experience, even a mediocre video recording does more to enhance student appreciation for opera than a superb audio recording. It's worth the effort.

Dramma giocoso

Just a quick note on *dramma giocoso* before we get too far. The librettist Goldoni claims to have invented the genre in his operatic collaborations with Galuppi in Venice in the 1750s. Goldoni's first "smash" hit in this genre was with Piccinni's *La buona figliuola*, a 1760 opera based on Samuel Richardson's 1740 novel *Pamela*. Viewed as an offshoot of opera buffa, *dramma giocoso* blends features of serious and comic opera. *Dramma* points to the opera seria influence, giocoso to its opera buffa characteristics. The blend happens character by character:

Parti serie (serious roles)—These parts, usually written for high voices (soprano, tenor, or even *castrato*), infuse the opera with some of the passion (or at least melancholy) associated with opera seria, and with that genre's typical forms as well. These characters are most likely to sing accompanied recitative and da capo arias. In *Don Giovanni*, the noble couple, Donna Anna and Don Ottavio, falls into this category.

Parti buffe (comic roles)—These parts, often for bass or baritone voice, draw on the stock *commedia dell'arte* character types that populate most eighteenth-century opera buffa. These characters are most likely to sing dry recitative, ensembles, and shorter, more contemporary aria forms. In *Don Giovanni*, the servant Leporello and the peasant couple, Zerlina and Masetto, fall into this category.

Parti di mezzo carattere ("middle" or mixed roles)—These complex characters typically experience a conflict that requires them to move between features of the buffa and seria roles described above. A common example finds a noblewoman (or nobleman) disguised as a servant—their true personality expresses itself in seria conventions, but their assumed disguise demands buffa affectations. In *Don Giovanni*, Donna Elvira and Don Giovanni himself fall into this category, Donna Elvira because of the conflict between her noble station and the "inappropriately" intense emotions (love and hate mixed) she feels toward Giovanni, and the Don because of his chameleon-like propensity to meet every woman at her own level, whether peasant or noble-born.

In spite of his reputation as one of the great composers of comic opera, Mozart expressed a preference for the older opera seria genre on several occasions. And in correspondence with his librettists, he always insisted on fully fleshed-out, fully human characters—not the cardboard caricatures common in opera buffa. It is not surprising, then, to find that Mozart often mixes seria and buffa elements in his comic operas. This mixture gives Mozart latitude to express the full range of human emotion.

Characters and Plot

Start with plot, writing names of characters on the board as you go along. Don Giovanni (Don Juan translated into Italian) is the infamous, irresistibly attractive womanizer and "noble"-man of Spanish legend. This opera allows us to follow his exploits during his last days on earth. From the first note, this "comic" opera blends comic and serious elements. Even the overture begins with two minutes of dark, foreboding introduction before turning to a lighter opera buffa style in its exposition—a gripping example of *dramma giocoso*. The opera's first scene offers another good example of this comic-tragic blend. The curtain opens to reveal Leporello (Don Giovanni's manservant) pacing back and forth, keeping watch while his master keeps busy with a noblewoman (Donna Anna). Suddenly, Donna Anna and Don Giovanni enter arguing. They have dallied after a masked ball, and Don Giovanni still has his mask on. We cannot tell whether Donna Anna has encouraged or resisted the Don's attentions (rape cannot be ruled out here), but now she wants to know this man's identity, and Don Giovanni refuses to reveal himself. The commotion rouses the Commandant (Donna Anna's father), who insists on protecting his daughter's honor. In the ensuing duel, Don Giovanni murders the commander and escapes, his identity still a mystery, with Leporello. The comic mood of this first scene suddenly turns tragic with the duel and murder. Mozart lets us know up front that this is not a typical opera buffa. (See Multimedia Resources below for recordings that include this first scene.)

In the scenes that follow, Mozart introduces two new characters: Don Ottavio, a nobleman betrothed to Donna Anna who swears revenge on the commander's murderer (whoever he may be), and Donna Elvira, a noblewoman who wants to find Don Giovanni and tear out his heart after being loved and abandoned by him. Just before the *Listen* excerpt, Mozart introduces a young, simple peasant couple about to marry—Zerlina and Masetto. Don Giovanni rides into town just in time to see a chorus of peasants celebrating, and he takes an immediate fancy to Zerlina. He takes the bride and groom under his "protection" and invites the company to a party. He offers to escort Zerlina and instructs Leporello to distract Masetto. When Masetto balks, uncomfortable at the thought of leaving Zerlina and Don Giovanni alone together, the Don threatens him with his sword.

MOZART *Don Giovanni:* from Act I, scene iii

In the *Listen* excerpts from *Don Giovanni* we primarily see the buffa side of *dramma giocoso*. Zerlina and Masetto are peasants, after all, and although the Don can swing both ways, here he adopts lowbrow mannerisms in his efforts to woo Zerlina.

The first aria in the textbook constitutes Masetto's response to Don Giovanni's thinly veiled threat. Before you play any music, call attention to the libretto on textbook pages 215–16. Ask students to study the text for the entire scene and to describe the three characters.

Masetto—Not surprisingly, he is full of anger and jealousy, but he cannot risk antagonizing a nobleman. He adopts a superficially compliant but bitterly sarcastic manner and turns his anger on Zerlina instead.

Zerlina—She cannot believe that a nobleman would take an interest in a poor peasant, but in her naiveté she is overwhelmed by his promises and his attentions.

Don Giovanni—He wants Zerlina badly, but always maintains a suave, gallant, amorous manner. He constantly monitors her state of mind to determine just the right phrase or promise to win her.

Once the class has a sense of the characters, ask for volunteers with a dramatic bent. Assign the roles of Masetto, Don Giovanni, and Zerlina and ask the students to do a "reader's theater" presentation of the entire scene on textbook pages 215–16. The rest of the class can evaluate their performance and point out spots where the readers captured (or failed to capture) the appropriate mood.

What happens in this scene? Masetto registers his blustery but ineffective complaint and leaves Don Giovanni and Zerlina together. In the recitative and duet that follows, we have an opportunity to watch Don Giovanni at work. When flattery fails to break her resolve, he promises to marry her; when recitative is not persuasive enough, he resorts to song. Zerlina thinks better of it many times, but in the end she relents.

Ask students to listen for the ways Mozart uses music to depict characters and to advance the drama; then play the entire scene. One of the extraordinary aspects of this opera is Mozart's gift for characterization. We hear Masetto's stubbornness and simple nature in the static harmonies that accompany him and in his tendency to repeat simple, short motives over and over. Play the first phrases of his aria again to make the point. Don Giovanni is a chameleon—he will say anything or adopt any role if it will get him what he wants. With noblewomen, he assumes a noble, gallant manner and spouts lofty rhetoric. With Zerlina, he sings a simple, folklike tune, precisely the type of melody Zerlina sings throughout the opera. (At the end of Act I, Don Giovanni invites Zerlina to do a contredanse, a middle-class dance. This is a great honor and a step up for Zerlina; it is also a gracious step down by the aristocratic Don.) Play the first few phrases of "Là ci darem la mano" to make the point.

As for advancing the drama, note that whether Mozart employs aria, recitative, or ensemble, the action constantly moves forward. Masetto expresses emotion in his aria, just as singers did in Baroque opera seria, but he expresses several emotions. Most important, he does not step out of the action to do so. Masetto constantly interacts with the other characters on stage: he shows a passive-aggressive face to the Don and then curses out Zerlina on the side. The action continues to move forward in the ensemble "Là ci darem la mano," a duet between Don Giovanni and Zerlina. The action does not stop while they reflect on their attraction for each other. Don Giovanni uses the song to woo Zerlina, and we watch him slowly overcome her resistance.

Mozart uses a musical device to depict their gradual motion toward emotional synchronization. Don Giovanni begins the duet by singing two phrases; Zerlina responds with two phrases that express her doubts. The two singers continue to pass the melody back and forth, but their "lines" get shorter and shorter until Zerlina gradually gives in. Finally, she consents, and just at that point the Don and Zerlina sing together in precise rhythmic unison. For good measure, Mozart also picks up the tempo and switches to compound meter. Play the ensemble one more time so that students can assimilate the different aspects of this duet.

Conclusions to Draw about Opera Buffa

In this listening example we see the importance of the ensemble. The drama no longer stops while the soloist sings; characters now interact and the story advances. Mozart used this type of interaction to create dramatic continuity in every musical number of his operas. As a result, he stands out as one of the great dramatists in the history of opera. Mozart's strides toward greater realism and dramatic continuity were carried even further by the composers of Romantic opera (Chapter 17). In this way, the techniques of opera buffa revolutionized opera.

Listening Exercise: Review

Try this listening exercise to review both the four-movement plan and the four instrumental genres covered in Chapters 11–13. Play a guessing game with your class: Have them listen to four excerpts from four works in random order. Each movement of the four-movement plan must be represented, as well as each instrumental genre (symphony, piano sonata, piano concerto, and string quartet). Ask students to determine the genre and the movement number for each excerpt. Encourage them to listen for tempo and character in order to determine the movement number, just as they did in the exercise at the beginning of this chapter. Genre should be even easier—instrumentation is the key here. If students can distinguish among orchestra alone, solo piano, piano with orchestra, and string quartet, they can identify the symphony, piano sonata, piano concerto, and string quartet, respectively. After the strenuous listening exercises in Chapters 12 and 13, this review can restore confidence to students who struggled with Classical forms.

You can expand this exercise to include opera buffa. Add three more excerpts to the four above, from an ensemble, a recitative, and an aria.

♪ Global Perspectives 4:
Musical Form: Two Case Studies from Asia

In the final three units of *Listen,* Global Perspectives materials have been clustered at the end of each unit. At first glance, this configuration offers the possibility of reflecting on an entire unit's worth of material from another perspective, and you can certainly use it that way. Or you can take advantage of the enormous flexibility this arrangement offers. When you introduce Vivaldi, Bach, and the eighteenth-century court orchestra tradition in Chapter 9, why not expose your students to the oldest continuous court orchestra tradition in the world: Japanese *gagaku*? As you explore Classical forms in Chapter 12, why not compare them with the intricate construction of Balinese *gamelan* music? When you consider the role of ornamentation in Baroque opera (Chapter 10) or improvised cadenzas in the Classical concerto (Chapter 13), why not contrast these practices with improvisation in a north Indian *raga* or a south Indian *kriti* (see Further Listening Examples below)? And the list goes on, limited only by your imagination (and the restrictions imposed by your syllabus!). There is no wrong approach here; use these examples wherever they make most sense to you.

The two modules presented below all follow the same overall format. Each begins with detailed background information on the country and the musical traditions under consideration, and each concludes with practical teaching suggestions for the work itself. Feel free to use the background material for your own study or as part of your classroom presentation. The order of these modules follows the order in the textbook, but don't let that influence your decision about where to present these examples. In the belief that a comparative approach works best, I again encourage you to use these non-Western examples where you believe they offer the most interesting mix of similarities and contrasts. Each module suggests possible comparisons with *Listen* examples from Chapters 8 to 13, but these are suggestions rather than prescriptions. Above all, have fun exploring this music, and let it jog your own creativity.

Sadly, it was impossible to include the Ravi Shankar/Ali Akbar Khan *raga* performance found in the Fifth Edition. *Do not* let this stop you from using an example from India. Most Americans know little about the music of Islam, Hawai'i, The Gambia, Japan, or Bali, but the same cannot be said for music of the Indian subcontinent. The Beatles' much-publicized trip to India and Ravi Shankar's subsequent exposure in the West contributed to growing interest, and today many Americans have at least heard of the sitar or of Ravi Shankar. As a result, students are willing to go deeper with Indian music than with other traditions, and you can use that energy to craft powerful learning experiences. I cannot encourage you enough to use either the north Indian *raga* or the south Indian *kriti* included in Further Listening Examples below.

1. Japan

The tradition of the Japanese court orchestra began one thousand years before Vivaldi or Bach began playing in European court orchestras of the eighteenth century. In fact, *gagaku* may be the oldest continuously practiced orchestral tradition in existence today. A good place to introduce this music is immediately after you present the concertos of Vivaldi and Bach, where you can compare the role and functions of these orchestras as courtly institutions. You can also study this music alongside the symphony; the more public nature of this orchestral tradition makes for interesting comparisons with *gagaku*. Of course, whatever similarities there may be, profound differences exist as well. The material below provides background information on the history of *gagaku* in Japan before it moves to lecture suggestions for *Etenraku*.

History of *Gagaku* in Japan   Japan's history as a nation dates back to the Nara period (710–794 C.E.). Late in the Yamato period (300–710 C.E.), Japanese clan leaders came under the spell of the magnificent Sui (589–618 C.E.) and T'ang (618–907 C.E.) dynasties of China. The obvious way to consolidate power in Japan was to imitate successful Chinese models. A constitution, modeled after Chinese documents, was introduced in 604 by Prince Shotoku, the most powerful clan leader. Buddhism, introduced to Japan in the sixth century C.E., was encouraged as a means of centralizing authority. All in all, a host of Chinese-influenced reforms were instituted, but the establishment of a permanent capital in Nara in 710 marked the true beginnings of the Japanese nation. Not surprisingly, the new capital itself was modeled after the Chinese capital of Chang'an (Xian).

Just as in politics, Japan's leadership borrowed extensively from China's music, especially the *gagaku* music associated with Chinese and Korean courts. Chinese courtly music and dance, initially ritual traditions, were themselves an international mixture of influences from as far away as India and Persia. The renowned Chinese court orchestras combined many different types of instruments whose materials were thought to reflect the balance of nature. The importance and depth of Chinese influence on Japan is clearly illustrated in one of the most spectacular imperial celebrations of the Nara period, the 752 dedication of the enormous bronze Buddha at the Todaiji monastery in Nara. All of the Nara dignitaries, many thousands of Buddhist monks, and hundreds of musicians and dancers participated. Music for the festivities consisted primarily of *gagaku* and Buddhist chant. The *gagaku* was performed in the Chinese tradition, mostly by foreign musicians. Seventy-five of the instruments used for these festivities have been preserved in excellent condition in the

Shosoin, Nara's imperial treasury. The variety of Asian instruments in this collection suggests the breadth of China's sphere of influence, and the artistry of their construction points to the wealth of the T'ang dynasty.

In the Nara period, the music for courtly entertainments and rituals came primarily from the Chinese *gagaku* tradition. Most musicians employed by the imperial court were of Chinese origin, and all musical activities were overseen by a new governmental department of music, the Gagakuryo. The formation of musicians' guilds, responsible for *gagaku* and Shinto ritual music, also dates back to this period. But Japan began to turn away from Chinese influence in the Early Heian period (794–897 C.E.), which began when the capital was moved to Heian (Kyoto). In Heian the Chinese *gagaku* tradition flourished, but now it was performed by Japanese musicians, both members of the musicians' guilds and nobles of the court who fell in love with the music. Signs of the tradition's vitality can be seen in the establishment of a permanent imperial *gagaku* orchestra and the standardization of the *gagaku* repertory. The repertory was now split into two categories: *togaku,* the T'ang court music that blended Chinese, Indian, and Persian influences; and *komagaku,* derived from Korean and Manchurian court traditions. As direct contact with China diminished, however, the music gradually acquired more Japanese features.

The Late Heian period (897–1185 C.E.) saw the decline of the emperor's power and the rise of powerful warrior families, the *samurai.* Finally the Genji family seized power in 1185, marking the beginning of the Kamakura shogunate. For the next seven centuries, Japan was a feudal society. The new ruling families had little interest in the courtly lifestyle of the previous Nara and Heian periods, and traditional *gagaku* was used only for important rituals and ceremonies. The shogunate did provide nominal support for the imperial family, now completely powerless, and this support enabled three guilds to continue their activities over the centuries. In spite of their best efforts, however, the art of *gagaku* declined, owing to a gradual drop in both the number of pieces in the repertory and the level of expertise of its practitioners. Further, the repertory underwent subtle changes. When the aristocracy guided the tradition in the Heian period, *gagaku* performers relied on written notation, but when the guilds became keepers of the flame, transmission from one generation to the next appears to have relied more on oral tradition, in some cases altering and obscuring the old T'ang melodies that served as the basis for this repertory.

The Meiji restoration of imperial rule (1868 C.E.) saw the reunification of the traditional music guilds in the new capital of Edo (Tokyo), supervised by the new Imperial Household Agency. As a result, the imperial *gagaku* orchestra was reestablished, and *gagaku* has been well supported in the modern era, even with the onslaught of modern Western styles. Naturally, the Japanese take great pride in being heirs to the oldest continuously maintained orchestral tradition in the world.

Etenraku   *Etenraku* comes out of the *togaku* tradition of *gagaku,* the repertory most directly influenced by T'ang dynasty courtly music from China. Take a look at the background material provided in the textbook, especially the description of instruments in the *togaku* orchestra. The original Chinese melodies can still be found in *togaku* music, though they are buried in the music for *biwa* and *sho.* What now sounds like the main melody is the result of ornamentation and changes typical of the mode of oral transmission that kept this tradition alive during Japan's Middle Ages. Still, the modern version represents a long and venerable tradition, and the music retains a unique expressive power.

The experience of listening to this work can prove a real challenge for students. The *Listen* textbook does an excellent job of introducing the instruments of the *togaku* orchestra, whose distinctive sounds can help guide students through this work. Familiarity with two focal points helps enormously in unlocking the secrets of this work: its melodic structure and its rhythmic (colotomic) structure. Anything you can do to help students hear these structures will deepen their listening experience.

Starting with melody: The *Listen* Guide outlines what appears to be a straightforward melodic structure: **A A B B C C A A B B.** In spite of this clear pattern of repetition, hearing these relationships proves a difficult feat, especially since the piece begins so slowly and freely. In fact, these note durations are so long and irregular that most students will not be able to follow simple motives the first time through, to say nothing of entire phrases. Two strategies can help here. First, since the melody is hard to follow at the beginning, don't start at the beginning! Start instead at 5:25, where the **A** section returns for the first time. Once students grasp the **A** and **B** sections at a quicker tempo, go back to the beginning and lead them through the slow, free version. Second, display the melody for your students so you can guide them through it.

Melody of *Etenraku*

Though most students cannot read music notation, the concepts you introduced in Unit I will allow them to follow along, especially at such a slow tempo. The important thing is to offer some kind of visual representation. Of course, just to be safe, point out each note as the music plays.

If you have time, you can use the notated version to introduce a few features of *gagaku* scales. When the Japanese imported *gagaku*, they imported the Chinese music theory that accompanied it. Chinese theory employs diatonic scales derived from seven adjacent notes in the circle of fifths. The bottom line: Chinese scales look much like Western scales, and any note of the scale can theoretically serve as the first scale step (just as in the European church modes). Of these seven pitches, five serve as primary notes and the other two, less important, serve as exchange notes—variants of other scale degrees. This construction lends *gagaku* melodies a strong pentatonic flavor. In *Etenraku* the five primary pitches are D, E, F sharp, A, and B, with C serving an expressive, embellishing function above the pitch B in the C phrase. The pitch E serves as the final, appearing prominently throughout the melody as well as at the ends of the **A** and **B** phrases. The Japanese call this scale *hyojo*.[1]

Once students become familiar with the melody, they can begin to hear phrase repetitions and contrasts more easily, and their new sense of structure will permit them to notice the effect of the gradual accelerando. Now is also the time to point out the subtle, simultaneous differences between the *ryuteki* and the *hichiriki* versions of the melody—the heterophony referred to in the

---

[1]Liner notes for *Gagaku: The Imperial Court Music of Japan.* Lyrichord LYRCD 7126 (CD).

textbook. Note also the increasing participation of the *gakuso* and *biwa* in the main melody, especially from the C sections to the end.

Rhythmic structure provides a second point of entry into this work. The central rhythmic focus is the pattern played by the lowest-sounding drum (*tsuridaiko*), consisting of a weaker stroke (*mebachi*—tender stroke) followed two beats later by the main stroke (*obachi*—venerable stroke). This pattern repeats at regular intervals throughout this piece, every sixteen beats in the first four sections (**A A B B**) and every eight beats from there to the end. As students become aware of this pattern, point out the other patterns in the music that flow from these drum strokes.The single notes and chords played by the *biwa* are coordinated with the main strokes, and the three-note motives played by the *gakuso* consistently come immediately after each main stroke. Even the wind instruments depend on the drum strokes to coordinate their performance of the main melody. You can mark *X*'s in the score you displayed for your students to show the precise, unchanging points where the drum strokes occur in relation to the melody. Finally, the *kakko* fills in the long gap between *obachi* and *mebachi* with accelerando patterns that help suggest the pacing and tempo in between these strokes.

Just as in the court orchestras of the European Baroque, no professional conductor waves a baton to keep everyone together. The strokes of the *tsuridaiko* partially fill the need for coordination, but they do not replace the need for musicians to listen to each other intently and feel the beat together. Of course, the sense of beat found in *gagaku* does not conform to Western notions of metronomic precision. William Malm describes the Japanese principle of "breath rhythm" as follows: "one . . . finds sections—like the opening of any *gagaku* piece—in which the beat simply cannot be conducted. The melody moves from beat to beat in a rhythm more akin to that of a breath taken in deeply, held for an instant, and then expelled."[2] This points to the other rhythmic processes that shape this piece: the ever-so-gradual acceleration from very slow tempo to moderate tempo and a parallel motion from the very free treatment of the beat described above to a more regular, distinct statement of beats. To make these processes clear, you can count aloud along with the melody near the beginning and again near the end. Students will hear these aspects readily once they have a handle on the melodic structure. More subtle aspects of this work and its musical expression require you to undertake a more profound study of Japanese music and culture, though such study offers many rewards. One such reward is an appreciation for the concept of *ma,* "the space between events,"[3] especially relevant at the beginning of *Etenraku.* The moments of silence—that which is *not* heard—become incredibly significant for the manner in which they frame what we *do* hear.

Concepts such as *ma* point to the marvelous subtleties of Japanese esthetic awareness. The textbook, describing this music's "aura of quiet, inward-looking Buddhist contemplation," points to the strong Buddhist influence on *gagaku.* *Etenraku* reflects other aspects of Japanese esthetics as well in its purity, refined taste, and elegance. Yet underlying the contemplative exterior is a haunting, subdued passion that gives life to the whole. How else could such a music endure for so many centuries?

---

[2]William Malm, *Music Cultures of the Pacific, the Near East, and Asia.* Englewood Cliffs, N.J.: Prentice-Hall, 1967, pp. 139–41.

[3]William Malm, *Six Hidden Views of Japanese Music.* Berkeley: University of California Press, 1986, p. 43.

2. Indonesia

The sounds of the gamelan orchestra have intrigued and enchanted Westerners ever since they first wrote of this music in the early 1800s. The gamelan music that inspired Debussy and Ravel at the 1889 Paris Exposition has inspired increasing numbers of Western composers over the past century. This interest has advanced to the point that one can now attend concerts of works written by Western composers for gamelan orchestra.

With its large-scale patterns of sixty-four beats, this music elevates rhythm to a structural level; from that perspective you might consider presenting this work alongside the Classical forms presented in Chapter 12. The frequent use of ostinato layers, on the other hand, suggests fruitful comparisons with the Baroque variation forms discussed in Chapter 9. Either way, the material below will help you with a brief overview of Balinese history and culture, a look at the main types of gamelan orchestra and the instruments they require, and lecture suggestions for the work in the *Listen* recordings: I Lotring's *Bopong*.

Bali   Bali is located in the Malay-Indonesian archipelago, a large group of islands that have shared cultural elements over the centuries. Throughout the island chain, one finds frequent examples of ensemble music for bronze idiophones—music constructed of faster- and slower-moving rhythmic layers. Bali's location has also rendered it susceptible to many Asian influences; Indian influence came to the region in about 800 C.E., and Islam spread through much of southeast Asia from 1290 on. When Islam gained a foothold in neighboring Java in about 1400, many Javanese nobles fled to Bali (with their gamelan orchestras). As Islam spread through the islands, Bali stood firm, becoming the strongest remaining bastion of Hinduism in the archipelago. To this day, many Balinese continue to practice their unique blend of Saivite Hinduism and local ancestor worship.

Traditionally, music and religion were intertwined to the degree that religious observance without artistic expression was inconceivable. Thus, training in music and the arts became a natural part of Balinese education, leading foreigners to observe that everyone was "both artist and farmer (or nobleman)."[4] The statistics in the textbook also point to widespread artistic activity—one gamelan orchestra for every 350 citizens adds up to between 5,000 and 6,000 such ensembles in Bali. This high level of activity also suggests the reverence tendered toward artistic expression, especially toward music and dance. Playing and dancing were sacred activities, beneficial and even healing for the individual and the community. The gamelan instruments themselves were held to possess sacred properties, and their sounds made those properties tangible. The placement of the gamelan orchestra during rituals and festivities suggests their religious function and their significance. The instruments were positioned somewhere between the site of the most sacred rituals and the areas where people congregated for festivals, thus marking off the boundary between sacred space and secular space. Further, the music itself was constructed to transport the listener into a sacred, cyclic experience of time, apart from the linear flow of human time.

Gamelan orchestras were originally associated with the temples and the princely courts. In the courts they served as symbols of a ruler's spiritual authority.

---

[4]David Harnish, "Bali." *Garland Encyclopedia of World Music,* Vol. 4: *Southeast Asia.* New York: Garland Publishing, 1998, p. 729.

Powerful rulers owned many gamelans; lesser nobles were happy to acquire even one. Gamelan music accompanied virtually all ritual activities associated with temples or courts, whether they related to agriculture, temple festivals, or rites of passage such as birth, marriage, or death. Gamelans could even accompany and sanctify everyday activities of the noble family. Given the many functions of this music, many gamelan types developed over the centuries, at least twenty-five of them still in common use. Some were so sacred that they could only be used once or twice a year for the holiest of rituals. Others were associated with specific historic courts; playing them invoked the spirit of that time and place. Yet others served recreational functions as accompaniment to theater or dance. The *Gamelan Semar pegulingan* that played in palace courtyards afternoons and evenings was named for Semar, the god of love; the full phrase means roughly "gamelan of the god of love of the sleeping chambers." At major festivals, many gamelans and musical ensembles might set up and make music throughout the day and night, sometimes performing simultaneously.

Dutch influence in the archipelago increased from the early 1600s on. Dutch trading interests took control of the spice trade by the late 1700s, and Bali finally succumbed to Dutch military forces, becoming a Dutch colony in the first decade of the 1900s. During the colonial period, the revenues that once supported the courts now flowed out of Bali. As the courts declined, so did their ability to support gamelan orchestras. Instruments were often sold or pawned or simply gathered dust. Fortunately, many instruments came into the hands of villagers, who quickly formed clubs to promote the performance of gamelan music. Suddenly this music took on a new vitality in Bali. Dissociated from its courtly functions, gamelan orchestras took on a more "populist" complexion, drawing players from all social classes. The tradition also saw a new infusion of creativity as composers sprang up in many village gamelan clubs. The music they composed kept many elements of traditional Balinese music but added a new, exciting virtuosic element that appealed especially to younger players. This new *kebyar* style has spread and developed since its inception in about 1915. *Bopong*, from the *Listen* recordings, was composed by one of the most popular gamelan composers of the twentieth century, I Lotring.

Balinese Gamelan Ensembles   The differences between gamelan types extend beyond the diverse functions they served. Each type is also characterized by its instrumentation and its tuning. Even within a type, instrumentation might vary somewhat from region to region, and the tuning of the instruments varies from ensemble to ensemble. Gamelan orchestras are built as matched sets; instruments constructed for use with one set most often cannot be played in another gamelan—the tuning would not match.

Another aspect of tuning is the scale type associated with each gamelan. Balinese music borrows two scales from Javanese music: the five-tone *sléndro* scale, known in Bali as *saih gendèr wayang,* and the seven-tone *pélog* scale, known as *saih pitu. Saih gendèr wayang* employs roughly equal intervals between its pitches, approximating an equipentatonic scale. *Saih pitu* mixes larger and smaller intervals, and—as in Japanese music—five of its pitches are primary, the remaining two auxiliary. A popular variant on *saih pitu* is *selisir,* a five-tone scale that omits the auxiliary pitches of *saih pitu.* Less common is *saih angklung,* an old four-tone variant of the *saih gendèr wayang* scale. One small complicating factor: Some ensembles that traditionally used *saih pitu* have more recently adapted their music to simpler *selisir* tuning.

Tuned gongs and metallophones of various sizes constitute the heart of almost every gamelan. The exact instrumentation varies with the type of gamelan, and many types may incorporate additional drums, flutes, and the occasional string instrument as well. The following list identifies some of the important gamelan types.

Gamelan gong—the largest, most popular, most commonly encountered gamelan type is the gamelan gong. It subdivides into *gong gedé,* formerly associated with the courts, and *gong kebyar,* a recent adaptation favored for gamelan music in the new style. *Gong kebyar* represents a blending of gamelan gong and the legong orchestra (*gamelan pelegongan*) described below. The new combination of instruments results in a more brilliant sound, and the preference for instruments that use the more flexible one-handed playing technique permits more virtuosic effects. Both types generally employ the five-tone *selisir* scale.

Gamelan Semar pegulingan—a smaller ensemble with a lighter sound that formerly provided music for royal families. It almost died out, but the conservatories and a few villages continue to perform on this gamelan. Complete orchestras still use *saih pitu* tuning, but one most often encounters smaller ensembles that employ the *selisir* scale.

Gamelan pelegongan—a smaller ensemble similar to the *gamelan Semar pegulingan,* but it replaces the *trompong* (a row of ten kettle-shaped gongs) with a pair of large metallophones (*gendèr*). It accompanied *legong* dancing when princely courts held sway; now it sees other uses as well. The rich polyphony created by this gamelan's rapid figuration has had an enormous influence on Balinese gamelan music in general. The ensemble is tuned to the five-tone *selisir* scale.

Gamelan angklung—another smaller ensemble that, surprisingly, now rarely uses the pitched rattle-like instruments that give the ensemble its name. The music of this ensemble employs the four-tone *saih angklung* scale.

Gamelan gambang—features xylophone-like instruments with bamboo bars. Noted for its short, eight-beat rhythm (5 + 3) and a unique playing style, *gambang* music has influenced *kebyar*-style composers. This music generally uses seven-tone *saih pitu* tuning.

Gamelan selundeng—possibly the oldest Balinese gamelan, it predates Hindu influence. It features metallophones made of iron and a unique musical repertory. Its age and rarity make it especially sacred—so sacred that its storage location is kept secret, and only copies are used for public performance. It is also an endangered species. This music is based on seven-tone *saih pitu* tuning.

Gamelan gambuh—the orchestra associated with courtly *gambuh* theater. It is unusual in its omission of metallophones; instead, it relies on an ensemble of flutes (*suling*), a stringed instrument (*rebab*), and several small gongs and cymbals. This ensemble employs seven-tone *saih pitu* tuning.

Gendèr wayang—a delicate ensemble that accompanies both plays from the Hindu shadow puppet tradition and cremation rituals. The five-tone *saih gendèr wayang* scale derives its name from its association with this repertory.

Gamelan Pelegongan   Because of its association with *legong* dancing, music for this ensemble developed a free musical structure that could reflect the frequent changes in mood and tempo required by the dance. Sections in free rhythm might be followed by slow, lyric sections or by the rapid, ostinato-based sections that accompany especially active dancing. A hallmark of *gamelan pelegongan* style, these ostinato-based sections with their fast tempo and rich polyphony have exerted a significant influence on Balinese music in general.

I Lotring, one of the most famous Balinese composers associated with new gamelan styles in the 1920s and 1930s, wrote much of his music for the *legong* orchestra played by the gamelan club in the village of Kuta. Colin McPhee provides much valuable information about the instrumentation of the Kuta *gamelan pelegongan.*[5]

Gangsa jongkok—Gangsa is Balinese for *bronze.* These single-octave metallophones consist of five bronze keys on a soundbox that are struck with a single mallet.

- two *gangsa jongkok chenik*—the smaller *gangsa,* pitched from D^3 to B flat^3
- two *gangsa jongkok gedé*—the large *gangsa,* pitched from D^2 to B flat^2

Single-octave *genders*—These metallophones consist of five suspended keys.

- four *kantilans*—the smallest *gendèr,* pitched from D^3 to B flat^3
- four *penyachahs*—one octave higher than the *jublag,* pitched from D^2 to B flat^2
- four *jublags*—the second largest *gendèr,* pitched from D^1 to B flat^1
- two *jegogans*—the largest *gendèr,* pitched from D to B flat

Thirteen-key *genders*—These metallophones cover a range of two octaves and a fourth. The thirteen keys, suspended over resonator tubes, are played with two mallets, often in octaves.

- two *gendèr barangan* 13—follows the *gendèr gedé's* lead, pitched from F^1 to B flat^3
- two *gendèr gedé* 13—lower pitched *gendèr,* pitched from F to B flat^2

Gongs—These bronze idiophones tend to be perpendicularly mounted, with the exception here of the *kelenang.* Arranged from high to low, each one possesses a distinctive sound.

- *kelenang*—a small horizontally mounted gong, pitched at D^2
- *kemong*—a small perpendicularly mounted gong, pitched at G flat^1
- *kajar*—a small gong with a sunken boss, pitched at D^1
- *kempur*—the largest gong in the *legong* ensemble, pitched at F

Percussion—These include various instruments serving different roles in the ensemble.

- two *kendangs*—membranophones, often played with a drumstick
- *rinchik*—a small cymbal with a light sound, used to accompany dance and theater
- *gentorak*—a rack containing a number of small bells

Flute—The flute is little used in the *gamelan pelegongan* because its pitches are so frequently out of tune with the ensemble.

- *suling gambuh*—the large bamboo flute associated with the *gamelan gambuh*

Note that the metallophones listed above come in pairs. This deliberate pairing allows for a special effect. In the construction process, metallophone pairs are

---

[5]Colin McPhee, *Music in Bali.* New Haven: Yale University Press, 1966, p. 153.

not tuned exactly the same—one will be just a bit out of tune with its mate. This slight mistuning creates an acoustic phenomenon known as "beats"—a vibrato-like effect. The number of beats per second is equal to the difference in frequency between the two pitches. The beats give the sound extra warmth and resonance, qualities that are highly prized.[6] If you listen carefully to the last chord of *Bopong,* you can hear the beating effect.

Each instrument plays a more or less fixed role in the performance of gamelan music. A closer look at the function of the instruments in I Lotring's *gamelan pelegongan* at Kuta can help us understand the layered textures found in Balinese music as a whole. The rhythmic layers prove easy enough to hear: the higher an instrument's pitch, the more rapid its figuration. Textural layers, pointing to distinct elements and their relationships in the sonic weave, require more preparation. The essential layers found in the music of this *legong* ensemble can be described as follows:

Colotomic structure—Not merely timekeeping, this refers to the marking of major structural units and their subdivisions. Western musicians often speak of rhythmic relationships only at the level of the measure or lower; larger rhythmic groupings tend to be referred to as melodic units—phrase, period, section, and so on.[7] Not so in Balinese music, where melodic structures must conform to large-scale, cyclic rhythmic units called *gongan. Bopong*'s largest rhythmic units are 64 beats long; some works are based on 128-beat units. The *gongan,* equivalent to the duration of the nuclear melody (a period), is generally subdivided, first in half, then in quarters, and so on. The gongs mark off these units and their subdivisions. The lowest gong, the *kempur,* sounds only once at the beginning of each *gongan.* Coupled with the *kempur* is the *kemong,* which often plays at the midpoint of each *gongan.* Subdividing the gongan even further is the *kajar,* which marks off *palets*—the main units within each period. (In faster passages the *kajar* beats time, aligning itself more with the drums than with the gongs.) The highest-pitched gong, the *kelenang,* usually plays on secondary beats (2, 4, 6, and so on). The higher the pitch, the faster the rhythm.

Nuclear melody—The principal melody, the *pokok,* serves as the core of the musical work as a whole. The colotomic structure described above flows from the fixed length of the *pokok,* and the metallophones also derive their roles from prescribed proportional rhythmic relationships to it. Primary responsibility for the *pokok* falls to the four *genders.* The two *gendèr gedé* play a lightly ornamented version of the *pokok* in octaves. The *gendèrs barangan,* playing an octave higher, can double the *pokok* or create a faster-moving paraphrase. Other instruments also derive their roles directly from the nuclear melody. When used, the *suling gambuh* plays a freely ornamented version of the *pokok.* Finally, the *jublags* and *jegogans* play abstracted versions of the *pokok,* picking out and playing only primary notes of the *pokok* (much like playing through a Schenkerian reduction analysis). Generally, the *jublags* play one pitch every two beats, and the *jegogans* one pitch every four beats. (In reference to the colotomic structure, they divide the *pokok* into sixteenths and thirty-seconds, respectively.) Once again, the lower the pitch, the slower the rhythm.

---

[6]Piano tuners use much the same technique in tuning double- and triple-stringed pitches, looking to give each pitch the right amount of "motion."

[7]Many song forms in Western music do rely on large-scale rhythmic units—thirty-two-bar (A A B A) song form, twelve-bar blues, and so on. Nonetheless, Westerners still think of these as melodic or formal constructions, not as rhythmic structure.

Figuration—The *kotekan*—the rapid, interlocking figuration patterns played by the highest metallophones—is one of the distinguishing features of the *gamelan pelegongan*. Other gamelan ensembles use similar figuration, but the higher pitch of the *legong* orchestra's *gangsas* gives the *kotekan* a lightness and brilliance not matched by the others. Although the *kotekan* sounds like a single melody, in fact it is created by two melodic parts that interlock and overlap in a hocketlike manner. Given the *kotekan*'s fast speed—anywhere from four to eight notes per beat—these patterns require no small degree of virtuosity in their performance, which is all the more remarkable, since these parts are given to the youngest performers, sometimes as young as nine or ten years old. In the *gamelan pelegongan*, the *kotekan* parts are performed by the *gangsas, kantilans,* and *penyachahs*.

Percussion—The actual leadership of the gamelan ensemble falls to the *kendangs*. Although the drum patterns are often intricate, the other performers look to them to set the tempo and guide them through tempo changes. Of course, when the *gamelan pelegongan* accompanies dance, the *kendang* players must coordinate their patterns with the dancers. As was mentioned above, the *kajar* joins in with the *kendang* patterns in faster passages. The *rinchik* provides accentuation, while the *gentorak* provides a continuous jingling background color.

I LOTRING *Bopong*

Originally composed for *gamelan pelegongan, Bopong* has also been adapted for performance by other gamelan orchestras, including the *gamelan Semar pegulingan*—a sign of its popularity. The composer of *Bopong,* I Lotring, was one of the most celebrated Balinese gamelan composers from the 1920s on. According to Colin McPhee, who worked with the composer on numerous occasions, I Lotring was born around 1900,[8] early enough that he could begin his training while the Balinese princely courts still functioned independently. I Lotring studied dance and music at the court of Blahbatu, no longer in existence. Later he relocated to Kuta, a fishing village in south Bali, where he led two ensembles, the *gamelan pelegongan* and the *gendèr wayang*. When these ensembles disbanded, he trained dancers for other villages and wrote occasional works for festivals. While in Bali, McPhee himself also provided I Lotring with work opportunities.

Typical of music for the *legong* orchestra, this work consists of several contrasting sections. These sections include an introduction (0:00–0:29) that almost imperceptibly drifts into the second section. Based on cyclic repetition of a sixty-four-beat nuclear melody, the second section (0:29–2:41) is the most traditional portion of this work. The third section (2:41–4:04), full of dramatic *kotekan* flourishes, builds momentum above an eight-beat ostinato that repeats fourteen times. The work's final section (4:04–end)) offers a fast, syncopated, virtuosic unison melody that ends the work with a burst of energy.

When you present this work to your class, start with some background on Balinese history and culture; feel free to use any materials above that interest you. The information on instruments and layers in *gamelan pelegongan* works best when woven into your class discussion of *Bopong*, where students can immediately hear what you're talking about. Once you complete your introduction, proceed directly to the music. As you guide your students through *Bopong,*

---

[8]McPhee, *Music in Bali,* p. 308.

introduce just one section at a time. Once students can hear the salient features of each section, they can identify the contrasts between them more easily.

Start with the introduction (0:00–0:29). This work begins a bit tentatively; a few *gangsas* play initially, but once the gong stroke sounds (0:04), other instruments such as the *genders* and flute soon find their way in. Point out the fast *gangsa* patterns (at 0:04) in which they play eight notes per beat (the equivalent of thirty-second notes in the textbook's transcription). If you follow carefully, you will also hear that the introduction concludes with Phrase 4 of the nuclear melody. It evolves so naturally from the melodic phrases of the introduction that we hardly notice it at first.

Spend some time with the second section (0:29–2:41). This portion best exemplifies the colotomic, layered structures of gamelan music in general. To make it easier to guide students through this section, display the nuclear melody (*pokok*) so everyone can see it.

Point out the melody's length, sixty-four beats, and note how successive division by two gives us progressively smaller structural units. The entire period divides into thirty-two-beat units, and these units divide into sixteen-beat phrases, and so on. Play this section several times, but focus on a different layer each time. The first time through, ask students to listen for the instruments playing the *pokok* (*genders* and bamboo flute) and point out each note as the music plays. The second time through, ask students to listen for the gongs that mark the colotomic structure—the lowest gong sounds only at the beginning of Phrase 1, secondary gongs at the beginning of the other phrases, and a preparatory stroke on the downbeat of m. 15. Point out how the gongs articulate the largest divisions of this sixty-four-beat structure, and draw attention to the slight slowing of tempo that occurs at phrase beginnings, especially in Phrases 1 and 3. When these gongs are struck, all activity stops momentarily, as if paying reverence to the sound of the gong. The third time through, ask students to listen for the *kotekan*, the rapid figuration played by the *gangsas* at the top of the texture. It is easy enough to hear them play *subito forte* at measure 10 of each *pokok* repetition, but call attention to the softly played version heard through much of this section. Point out the four-notes-per-beat rhythm (sixteenth notes as per the textbook's transcription), and explain that no one instrument plays the entire *kotekan* pattern. Rather, it is shared between pairs of instruments that play simpler melodies that interlock, hocketlike, to create the impression of a single melody. Finally, for the fourth play-through, ask students to listen for the drums (*kendang*)—the ensemble leaders. Point out the active, shuffle-like rhythmic patterns they play.

Once the students acclimate themselves to the stratified polyphony of section two, move on to the third section (2:41–4:04). This section offers a good example of the dance-related, ostinato-based music so characteristic of *gamelan pelegongan*. No need to play this four times through—once or twice through the fourteen ostinato repetitions provides sufficient opportunity to trace the same four layers successfully. Once again, display the nuclear melody for your students.

This time, ask students to tell you what was happening in each layer. In the discussion that follows, draw out these points. The *pokok* is only eight beats long this time, and it continues to be played by *gendèrs* and flute. With just eight beats to play with, the colotomic structure is less elaborate. The low gong sounds at the beginning of each pattern, a secondary gong on beat 5, and a preparatory stroke on beat 7. The *kotekan* instruments now pull out the stops with many dramatic contrasts in dynamics (note repetitions 4, 5, 9, 10, and 14) and a fast eight-notes-per-beat rhythm (sixty-fourth notes!). Between the double-time *kotekan* and the short ostinato, this third section sounds much faster than the previous two sections. Finally, the *kendang* players continue to maintain their elaborate, supportive rhythmic patterns. Note the cumulative effect of this ostinato section, both its growing activity and its increasing excitement.

Although the third section maintained the layering and even the colotomic structure (though simplified) of the second section, the fourth section (4:04–end) presents a surprising contrast. Ask students to tell you what is so different here. Of course, there is still a primary melody, but what a melody it is—fast, rhythmically unpredictable, conveying the feel of elaborate syncopations. As expected, the melody is played by *gendèrs* and flute, but the *kotekan* has suddenly disappeared, the *gangsas* now playing along on the primary melody. Students who try to keep the beat in this passage will discover that the colotomic structure has disappeared as well. Our safety net is gone—no longer can we divide by two again and again. The gongs now punctuate the primary melody at erratic intervals; the *kendangs* play in rhythmic unison with the main melody, abandoning their previous sixteenth-note shuffle patterns. These changes create a radical contrast with the earlier sections of *Bopong*. Let students know that this kind of virtuoso, unison writing is characteristic of the modern *kebyar* style that changed gamelan music so dramatically in the twentieth century.

Now play the entire work without pause and ask students to describe the work's overall form. In the discussion that follows, draw out these points. Just as in the Classical symphony, the elements of repetition and contrast figure prominently here. Repetition occurs primarily within each section, and contrast, between sections. The introduction nicely anticipates some of the melodic figures heard later in sections two and three. The second section presents the main argument, the third section paraphrases the argument with greater concision and excitement, and the final section serves as a coda, playing out and releasing the energy that was built up in the previous section. The structure is not identical to any encountered in the Classical symphony, but it uses many of the same elements—repetition, contrast, variation, and coda—to create a satisfying musical form. In addition, *Bopong*'s suitelike structure affords the opportunity to hear several important aspects of gamelan music, ranging from traditional cyclic, ritual constructions (section two) to a modern virtuoso, recreational style (section four).

Additional Teaching Suggestions

⁊ Lecture-Demonstration Ideas

1. Show excerpts from *Amadeus*. Many scenes lend themselves to classroom presentation. You can use scenes to demonstrate different Viennese operatic traditions (serious and comic Italian opera or the *Singspiel*), different operatic performance venues (the Imperial Opera on one hand, the lowly *Singspiel* house on the other), differences between German and Italian opera (Mozart's argument with the emperor and his advisers), Mozart's compositional process (the scene where Constanze brings Mozart's scores to Salieri, or Mozart's death-bed dictation to Salieri), or any other topic that strikes you as appropriate. Many of your students have at least heard of the movie, and it raises important musical issues in a format that hits home. *Caution*: Tell the class that Shaffer's story is *not* real. It was based on a hypothetical question: "What if Salieri tried to hasten Mozart's death?"[9] The playwright adapted historical facts and characters to make the *if* plausible. As a result, you cannot use the movie alone to demonstrate Mozart's biography or the personalities of Mozart, Constanze, Leopold, or Salieri. You must do some research, issue a strong disclaimer, and be prepared to tell it the way it really happened. If you want the facts on Mozart's death, consult H. C. Robbins Landon's excellent book *1791: Mozart's Last Year* (New York: Schirmer, 1988). See Video Recordings below for suggested DVD or VHS recordings.

2. Introduce students to the controversies that surrounded opera in the eighteenth century. Excerpts from Strunk's *Source Readings in Music History* (New York: Norton, 1950) offer fascinating, sometimes entertaining insights. To understand the problems that plagued late Baroque opera seria, select passages from Benedetto Marcello's scathing satire on "modern opera," *Il teatro alla moda* (1720). Heated reactions to the introduction of opera buffa in Paris (1752) stirred one of the most famous controversies, the "War of the Buffoons/(*Querelle des Bouffons*)." There seemed to be no middle ground between supporters of older serious opera and proponents (the "bouffons") of the new opera buffa. To understand the bouffons, read selected passages from F. W. von Grimm's *Little Prophet of Boehmischbroda* (1753) or Jean-Jacques Rousseau's *Lettre sur la musique française* (1753). Ask students if they can think of similar controversies in popular music today. (Eminem's apparent misogyny and homophobia? rap versus "family values"? the ascendance of rave culture? Older students will remember disco versus punk rock or even rock'n'roll versus swing.)

3. Introduce your class to contemporary music for string quartet—written by African composers! *Pieces of Africa,* a Kronos Quartet CD (see Sound Recordings below), offers precisely this meeting of cultures. It features new works by composers from Zimbabwe, Morocco, Gambia, Uganda, Ghana, Sudan, and South Africa. Many of these works add voices or indigenous African instruments to the traditional string quartet, and some use elaborate rhythms and ostinato patterns. You can also use this music to make connections with Global Perspectives segments on West Africa and South Africa (see Chapters 7 and 23 in *Listen*).

---

[9]Rumors that Salieri poisoned Mozart have their own distinguished history, including a play by Pushkin and a mention in Beethoven's conversation books, but other historical documents suggest otherwise.

4. To bring Japanese culture to life for your students, create a Japan "travelogue." Show slides that depict important cities, shrines, artworks, architecture, and music making. You can make direct connections with material from this chapter if you can find images of the bronze Buddha and instrument collection from Nara, or of *gagaku* performers and instruments. Further connections can be found in images of the Japanese tea ceremony and in other examples of art and ritual that reflect the elegant, meditative (Buddhist-influenced) Japanese esthetic. Play appropriate music while students study the images on the screen.

5. Create a slide show for your presentation of Balinese music. Colin McPhee's *Music in Bali* (New Haven: Yale University Press, 1966) contains 110 black-and-white photos, and the departments of art, geography, or anthropology at your school may have slides you can borrow. These images will make your lecture-demonstration much more vivid for your students.

❦ Class Discussion Ideas

1. *What was commedia dell'arte? What influence did it have on comic opera?* Read the description of this "comedy of artisans" on page 350 of Stolba's *Development of Western Music,* 3rd ed., or consult *New Grove.* Ask students to compare the stock characters of *commedia dell'arte* with the characters found in Mozart's *Don Giovanni.* Take Mozart's characters one by one to see where they might fit. For instance, the Commandant corresponds to the elderly guardian, and Leporello to the *zanni* (zany male servants). Don Giovanni is not a typical Scaramuccio, but he is certainly an adventurer with conquests to boast of.

2. *What ever became of Mozart's sister?* A child prodigy and talented composer like her brother, she traveled with Wolfgang, performing throughout Europe at a young age. After that—except for Mozart's letters to her—she disappears from view. Read the brief biography of Maria Anna Mozart on page 380 of Stolba's *Development of Western Music,* 3rd ed., or consult *New Grove.* This information can help the class reflect on the different treatment accorded to male and female performers and composers in the eighteenth century.

3. *Is borrowing a sign of respect or just a gimmick?* Present several examples of Classical-era borrowing and ask students what they think. Haydn used eastern European folk tunes in some late symphonies; the enlightened Masons borrowed from many ancient religions going back to the time of the pharaohs; and Mozart, particularly in his operas, often borrows from "exotic" faraway lands, most often Turkey. Each case is different, of course. The Classical predilection for good tunes quite naturally took composers into the largest tune repertory in existence: folk songs. Haydn liked them so much that he included some in Symphonies 103 and 104, IV—score one for respect. Mozart incorporates melodies with a "Turkish" flavor into his Piano Sonata in A, K. 331 (see Further Listening Examples below) and his Violin Concerto No. 5, but his most thought-provoking examples come from *Die Entführung aus dem Serail* (see Sound Recordings below). Here Mozart employs piccolo, triangle, cymbals, and bass drum to evoke the Janissary bands of the Turkish military. He also creates parts for two Turkish characters: Pasha Selim, the harsh, unyielding ruler; and Osmin, captain of the guard, a stereotypical "barbaric" Muslim who would as soon torture as kill unbelieving infidels—score one for gimmick. But that judgment might be premature; in the end Pasha Selim proves the magnanimous tyrant by refusing to perpetuate the wrongs done him by Christians. In

spite of these ambiguities, however, the verdict in Mozart's case must be this: good theater, bad ethnology. This question offers no simple answers; try it for a good, open-ended class discussion.

4. *What is the "Mozart Effect"?* In 1993, a study by Fran Rauscher (University of Wisconsin—Oshkosh) suggesting that Mozart's music could assist in the development of spatial thinking and abstract reasoning made quite a stir. Drawing on the research of Rauscher and many others, Don Campbell wrote a book titled *The Mozart Effect* (Avon Books, 1997), and by late 1997 he had issued *Music for the Mozart Effect* CDs, which made it onto the Billboard charts by early 1998. You can use either the book or the CD liner notes for more background information. Many of your students have at least heard news reports about these books and studies, and those with children of their own are often genuinely curious. Of course, the jury is still out; two 1999 studies, one conducted by Christopher Chabris (Harvard University), failed to duplicate Rauscher's results. Rauscher claims the new studies looked at broader indicators of intelligence than her much more specific study.[10] See Sound Recordings below for more information on Campbell's CDs.

5. *Why does one culture borrow from another?* Japanese *gagaku* was borrowed from China, which in turn borrowed elements from other cultures. In Europe, the French overture was borrowed by German composers like Handel and Bach, and dance types crossed borders with regularity. In its youth, the United States borrowed European traditions. Paul Simon borrowed from South African and Brazilian traditions in the *Graceland* and *Rhythm of the Saints* albums, respectively. World history is filled with examples of such borrowing. Ask students to name other examples. Follow up with further questions: *What do borrowers hope to find or gain? What makes a culture attractive to borrowers?*

6. *Is change good?* When Bali became a Dutch colony (1908), the gamelan tradition quickly moved from the princely courts into the villages. The new *kebyar* style—faster, flashier, louder—quickly emerged, and many of the old court gamelans were melted down to make new *gong kebyar* instruments. With fewer of the court gamelans, older traditions are in danger of being lost. As the villages that support ancient temple gamelans dwindle in population, their traditions also become endangered. The conservatory programs that attempt to preserve the older traditions send out graduates who also know the latest styles. Guess which styles they prefer to teach when they return to their villages? Change is natural—inevitable—but not without consequences. *What do we lose when old traditions die out? What do we gain from change? How much change is beneficial—or harmful?* These questions raise issues that students face here as well. Ask students to identify changes, musical or otherwise, that concern them today.

♪ Listening Ideas

1. Compare a Baroque concerto grosso with either a Classical concerto or a Classical symphony; you can examine the evolution of the concerto or compare principal orchestral genres from these two eras. Use examples from the recorded anthology or choose your own examples. Play short excerpts to compare both

---

[10]"More Discord on 'Mozart Effect': Two Studies Challenge Sonata's Benefit to IQ." *Chicago Tribune,* August 26, 1999, Section 1, p. 20.

first movements, both slow movements, or both final movements. Ask students to compare the characters of these movements and to identify different ways solo instruments are used with the orchestra. This exercise also offers an opportunity to compare features of Baroque and Classical styles. See Sound Recordings below for suggested recordings.

2. Compare a da capo aria from Baroque opera seria with an ensemble from Classical opera buffa. "La giustizia" from Handel's *Julius Caesar* and the Act II Finale ("Don Giovanni! a cenar teco") from Mozart's *Don Giovanni* work well. Play both excerpts. In the discussion that follows, draw out comments about the character of each work, but point out the different dramatic functions they serve. As powerful as Handel's aria is, it remains a statement of the emotions experienced by one character who reflects on actions that took place earlier. No action occurs during the aria. Mozart's ensemble, on the other hand, is pure action—the music drives the drama forward with fantastic intensity.

3. Compare Mozart and Beethoven string quartets. You can find especially interesting links between Beethoven's String Quartet in A, Op. 18, No. 5 and the work Beethoven used as a model, Mozart's Quartet No. 18 in A, K. 464. Beethoven so greatly admired the Mozart quartet that he copied out its final rondo by hand, showing it to his pupil Czerny as an example of a great musical work. Among the many superficial similarities between these scores are their key (A major); the reversed order of the middle two movements (minuet first, then slow movement); the same key (D), meter (2/4), and form (theme and variations) for the slow movement; rondo form for the final movement; and the use of chromaticism. How many other similarities can you and your students find? See Sound Recordings below for complete recordings of these Beethoven and Mozart quartets.

4. Compare *Etenraku* with Haydn's Symphony No. 95 (from Chapter 12). You can compare the two orchestral ensembles. Which instruments carry the primary melody? Which ones keep the beat? Which instruments serve primary, secondary, and supporting roles? Or compare the form of *Etenraku* with that of Haydn's slow movement, since both feature slow tempo and sectional form. Which principles are most important in each work—repetition, contrast, return, or variation? How is tempo handled in the different sections of each work? How do these features contribute to the different moods these pieces create?

5. Compare *Etenraku* with another work in which the basic pattern gets faster and faster. Bill Evans's "Blue in Green," from the Miles Davis *Kind of Blue* album (see Sound Recordings below), is based on this ten-chord progression:

gm   A$^+$ dm   F   B flat   A$^+$ dm   E$^+$ am   dm
                    C

At the beginning we hear one chord per measure in a free tempo. Further into the piece, the chords change every two beats, and then on every beat. The effect is easily heard, especially since the changes are not gradual, but the principle is similar.

6. Compare *Etenraku* with a work that conveys a strikingly similar mood. "Little Church," from the Miles Davis *Live-Evil* album (see Sound Recordings below), creates an unusual tone poem that layers an expressive, understated melody over a hazy, sustained accompaniment. A remarkable coincidence that two such different cultures could produce works that share such a keen sensitivity to the eloquence of sound and space.

7. Compare different gamelan orchestras. The textbook focuses only on *gamelan pelegongan,* but a wealth of gamelan ensembles and styles can be found on other recordings. This manual's section on Balinese gamelan ensembles (see Lecture Suggestions above) provides brief descriptions of several important types. The Sound Recordings section below lists useful recordings. Two recordings can serve you well: *Bali: Gamelan and Kecak* (Elektra/Nonesuch) serves up music for *gendèr wayang, gong kebyar,* and the rare *gamelan selundeng; Gamelan Music of Bali* (Lyrichord) features recordings of *gong kebyar* and *gamelan angklung* ensembles. These recordings generally demonstrate the layered textures (stratified polyphony) and colotomic structure of *gamelan pelegongan,* but each type is unique.

8. Compare Lou Harrison's Suite for Violin and American Gamelan with Baroque music from the *Listen* set. Just as in a Baroque suite, we find a variety of dances, but as is so typical of Harrison, this suite borrows dances from different historical and international traditions. Harrison's "Estampie" uses a medieval dance type. His "Air" offers interesting comparisons with Bach's Air from Orchestral Suite No. 3 in D. A series of movements titled "Jhala" draw from the rhythmical north Indian style. The concluding "Chaconne," with its nine-beat ostinato, borrows from the Baroque ground bass tradition that produced Vivaldi's Concerto in G, II, and Purcell's "When I am laid in earth" from *Dido and Aeneas.* A recording can be found on a CD titled *La Koro Sutro* (see Sound Recordings below).

9. Compare gamelan-influenced works by Western composers with real gamelan music. The Lou Harrison works mentioned in Listening Idea 8 above can serve well; so can works by ethnomusicologist Colin McPhee, Benjamin Britten, and others. See Sound Recordings below for suggested performances.

♪ Further Listening Examples

MOZART **Piano Sonata in B-flat, K. 570, III**

This piano sonata follows the usual three-movement plan described above. Mozart's sonata-form first movement moves in triple meter at moderate speed; the slow second movement offers a melodious rondo form; and the quick final movement uses an unusual **A B C A** rondo form. See Sound Recordings below for a charming rendition on a modern copy of a German fortepiano (Louis Dulcken, Munich 1790) much like the ones Mozart played.

The rondo form of Mozart's final movement is somewhat unusual. His rondo theme only returns once, and there are no sophisticated developmental transitions. Here, Mozart relies on his own remarkable gift for melodic invention, churning out one good tune after another. Be sure to focus on the contrasts between the three main tunes that constitute this movement. A comparison of the three tunes yields an opportunity to study "inner" versus "outer" form. Taken by themselves, all three fit into the same outer form, Classical dance: |: **a** :||: **b a′** :|. Yet the inner form, the unique mood created by each individual tune, differs as we move from section to section in this movement.

Begin by writing the formula for Classical dance form on the board:

|: **a** :||: **b a′** :|

As you introduce each theme, ask students to inventory musical elements as they listen; then play the theme and point to each phrase as it goes by. After playing each theme, draw out student observations. Call special attention to these features of the **A** theme:

Melody—a jaunty, *staccato* tune; regular phrases; **a** moves mostly by step, **b** by leap

Harmony—harmonies reinforce tonic; **a** extremely stable, **b** less stable

Rhythm—clear beat and duple meter, some syncopation in the melody

Dynamics—moderately soft

Texture—strictly homophonic; a clear melody and accompaniment texture

Color—delicate fortepiano timbre; medium to high register

Form—no repeats, just **a b a**

Call attention to these differences in the **B** theme:

Melody—more majestic, with quick ornamental scale figures; regular phrases; mixture of steps and leaps

Harmony—harmonies still reinforce tonic; **c** stable, **d** includes excursion to minor mode

Dynamics—louder than in **A**

Texture—fuller texture than in **A**

Color—explores higher and lower registers than any other section; melody goes up to the top note on Mozart's piano: f^3

Call special attention to these differences in the **C** theme:

Melody—more delicate *staccato* articulations

Harmony—new key (subdominant); stable harmonies in **e**, but **f** extremely unstable

Dynamics—often quiet dynamics with some *staccato* accents

Texture—thin, delicate texture

Color—explores slightly lower registers than in **A**, particularly the melody

Now that you have drawn out the distinct personalities of each tune, you are ready to play the entire movement. Before you do, display the Additional Listening Chart for this work (see Appendix I) and point out the connecting and concluding sections Mozart adds: short, modulating transitions from **B** to **C** and from **C** back to **A**, and a coda at the end. Now play the movement through, but stop just before the coda. This final **A** is barely long enough to sound like a return, and it hardly sounds conclusive. Now play the final **A** and the complete coda. This spirited conclusion begins abruptly and forcefully with allusions to themes from the **B** and **C** sections, the first real development in the entire movement; then Mozart brings the music to a close with the same profuse melodic inventiveness that characterizes the rest of the movement.

Is this rondo form or not? While one brief return of **A** hardly constitutes the multiple returns after contrast that we expect, nothing else fits! Sonata form? There is no development section and the harmonic structure is entirely wrong. Minuet? This has too many themes. Theme and variations? The principle of variation is nowhere in evidence. This is no "textbook" example, but we can at least cite this movement's tunefulness and its token use of return as qualifications for the rondo-form label. This movement provides further evidence that Classical composers were not slaves to abstract musical forms; they approached form with the same creativity they brought to other elements of music.

MOZART **Piano Sonata in A, K. 331, III—Rondo "alla Turca"**

This movement provides an additional example of both the sonata genre and rondo form. In this unusual sonata, Mozart omitted the first movement of the four-movement plan. Mozart's first movement corresponds to the slow movement with its andante tempo; the second movement is a minuet; and the last movement is a rondo in a quick tempo. To compensate for the unusual omission of the sonata form movement, Mozart lengthens the minuet and makes it more elaborate than usual. Play short excerpts from each movement so that students can hear the unusual format of this sonata (see Sound Recordings).

Use the same procedure with this work as with the fourth movement of Haydn's Symphony No. 95, but note that Mozart's rondo contains only one return of the opening rondo theme and two returns of the contrasting **B** section. Once again, rondo form is more a flexible procedure than a rigid form, as Mozart demonstrates in this charming, fashionably "Turkish" piano piece.

MOZART **Variations on "Ah vous dirai-je, maman" for piano, K. 265**

This piece works especially well to reinforce the understanding of theme and variations form—most students already know the tune ("Twinkle, twinkle, little star" or "Baa, baa, black sheep"). (See Appendix I for an Additional Listening Chart, and Sound Recordings below for a performance.)

If you have some keyboard proficiency, play the composition yourself; if not, recordings can easily be found. As before, play the theme several times and ask students to map out its structure and inventory its characteristics. The structure of theme can be expressed as:

$$\|: a :\|\|: b\ a :\|$$

The theme exhibits these characteristics:

Rhythm—simple, on the beat

Meter—duple

Tempo—moderate

Dynamics—medium soft

Register—medium high

Articulation—staccato

Texture—homophonic

Accompaniment—simple

Mode—major

Play several variations. As before, have the class compare each variation with the list of characteristics for the theme. Ask them which elements were altered in each variation. Again, encourage students to be thorough, but ask them to pick the one or two most significant changes for each variation. For instance, thematic elaboration in Variation 1, new accompaniment in Variation 2, thematic elaboration and compound duple meter[11] in Variation 3, minor mode and imitative polyphony in Variation 8, adagio tempo and thematic ornamentation in Variation 11, and triple meter with new accompaniment in Variation 12.

If you can play these variations yourself, or if you have software that gives you control over a CD-ROM drive, try this interesting alternative presentation.

---

[11]Triplets, actually, but without the score to look at, compound duple is the better answer.

Prepare excerpts so that you can play any variation at any time. Once students know the theme thoroughly, ask them to pretend they are composers. "If you were the composer, what element would you vary?" When a student chooses the tempo, you can say "Is this what you had in mind?" and play the adagio Variation 11; if another student chooses mode or texture, play Variation 8; if one chooses meter, play Variation 12; if another chooses accompaniment, play Variation 2; and so on.

Finally, display (or hand out photocopies of) the Additional Listening Chart for this piece found in Appendix I. Play the entire work and point out phrases and variations as they are played.

MOZART Piano Concerto No. 17 in G, K. 453, III

This delightful theme and variations movement provides another good example of that form as well as a good introduction to the Classical concerto finale. See Appendix I for an Additional Listening Chart, and Sound Recordings below for a suggested CD.

As with previous theme and variation movements, start with the theme. This extremely attractive tune demonstrates all of the characteristics of a good variations theme: it is memorable and presented simply, and its structure is easy to follow. Ask students to inventory its characteristics as they listen. If you find it helpful, put the melody on the board and play the theme once or twice.

In your discussion, draw out the following characteristics:

Melody—simple tune with regular phrases; mostly stepwise motion with some leaps

Articulation—mostly *staccato*

Mode—major

Harmony—relatively stable; **a** moves away from tonic, **b** returns

Rhythm—simple, stays close to the beat; rhythmic motives repeat regularly

Meter—duple

Tempo—moderate

Dynamics—moderate

Tone color—orchestra (woodwinds and strings)

Register—middle

Texture—homophonic, melody and accompaniment texture

Accompaniment—simple, stays in the background

Form—simple binary: |: **a** :||: **b** :|

Now play the variations. If students have trouble following the tune at any point, play the original theme at the keyboard while students listen to the recording. Make students compare what they hear with the list of characteristics for the theme. Ask them to pick out the one or two most significant changes for each variation. For instance, in Variation 1 the following elements are changed:

Melody—decorative ornamentation added

Rhythm—faster-moving melody

Tone color—piano

Register—piano decorations explore slightly higher register

Articulation—somewhat more *legato*

Continue to work through the variations in this fashion, as time allows. Display the Additional Listening Chart for this work (see Appendix I); it highlights the most significant changes in each variation. Notice that the repetitions of **a** and **b** can be altered within a variation, as we see starting with Variation 2. Play through the variations and point out each phrase and variation as it is played. Ask students to describe what they hear.

Mozart does some interesting things to make the coda sound more final. After the short transition at the end of Variation 5, the orchestra plunges in with the coda, increases the tempo, and introduces a brand-new theme; these last two are rather unusual in a Classical coda. Mozart does not abandon his primary theme, however; a minute later we hear a new, faster version of the original tune and several strong cadential passages. A two-and-a-half-minute coda seems like a lot to end a modest theme and variations movement, but it serves to conclude not only this movement but the entire three-movement concerto.

BEETHOVEN String Quartet in A, Op. 18, No. 5, II

This early Beethoven quartet movement offers a short and sweet example of minuet form and the quartet genre in late Classical style. The Op. 135 quartet from Chapter 14 works equally well to introduce the quartet, but its style had advanced well beyond the eighteenth-century Classical idiom. See Appendix I for an Additional Listening Chart for this work, and Sound Recordings below for a suggested CD.

Find a complete recording of this quartet and play excerpts from all four movements in random order, just as you did for symphony, sonata, and concerto. As students have come to expect, the quickest excerpt comes from the final movement, the slowest excerpt and the dancelike triple meter excerpt constitute the two middle movements, and the remaining excerpt must be the first. Point out that while all four movements of the plan are present, the order of the middle two movements is reversed—Beethoven's minuet comes second, his slow movement third. This short exercise can help students hear how each movement conforms to the quartet's typical four-movement plan, described above.

The detailed coverage given to single movements in Chapters 12 and 13 is not needed here. Put the structure of Classical dance form on the board:

MINUET	TRIO	MINUET
A	**B**	**A**
|: a :||: b a′ :|	|: c :||: d c′ :|	a b a′

Play just the **a** section and ask students to identify the role each instrument plays in the texture. Initially the first violin carries the tune over a simple moving accompaniment in the second violin, but in the second half of **a**, the viola takes over the melody while the first violin and cello join the second violin in its accompanimental figures. Throughout this movement, Beethoven continues to pass the melody from one instrument or instrumental pair to another, including playful yet genuine imitative polyphony near the end of the **A** section. In some quartets, the first violin dominates throughout, but this Beethoven work is truly a conversation among equals.

Now ask students to create an inventory of musical elements as they follow the form, then play the entire **A** section and point out each section on the board as it goes by. In the discussion that follows, draw out significant musical features. The structure of the **A** section offers several interesting twists: point out the written-out repeat of the **a** section (so the viola can take over the tune), the long **b** section, the surprise return of **a′** after **b**'s strong cadence in the wrong key and full pause, two statements of the main theme in the **a′** section (the second in the wrong key), and a brief codetta at the end for greater emphasis. As for other musical elements, point out the melodic motive that climbs as it repeats in the first phrase, the gentle accompaniment figures that begin on beat two, the steady beat, the prevailing soft dynamics that make Beethoven's loud thrusts even more effective, and the variety of colors and textures as the melody moves around the ensemble, including the imitative section just after the first statement of the theme in **a′**.

Ask students to repeat the same exercise and play the **B** section. Structurally, the trio pulls no punches—its brief, symmetrical sections repeat according to the diagram, with a clear return of **c′** at the end of the second section. In the discussion that follows, call attention to other significant elements: the melody's constant quarter-note patterns; the accents on beat three in the **c** phrases that contrast with generally soft dynamics; the full, unchanging homophonic texture; and the varied colors as the melody moves from one instrument to another. Outside of the expected melodic contrasts, the most striking differences between the minuet and the trio can be found in their treatment of texture and form. Beethoven's minuet loves to investigate different textural weights and combinations, unusual keys, and interesting melodic extensions and developments. These elements conspire to create a huge second section bent on exploration rather than exposition, far removed from real dance music. By comparison, the trio sounds safe and predictable—almost square. Its full-sounding chordal texture contrasts with the clean lines of the minuet.

Finally, play the entire movement; ask students to focus on the features that are typical of the minuet. This movement exemplifies all of the surface features we associate with the minuet movement: moderate tempo, triple meter, dance-like character, and contrasted minuet and trio sections. Only the internal structure of the minuet is atypical.

MOZART *Don Giovanni*, K. 527, Overture

This example provides a wonderfully clear example of sonata form with a slow introduction. See Appendix I for an Additional Listening Chart, and Multimedia Resources below for suggested audio and video recordings.

Display (or photocopy handouts of) the Additional Listening Chart for this overture (see Appendix I) and play from the *Molto Allegro* (just after the slow introduction) to the end, pointing to each section as it is played. Once students have this broad overview under their belts, work through the overture one section at a time.

Exposition—In the exposition, play and discuss each theme individually. Use the checklist of musical elements; ask students to describe each theme and to compare the themes with each other. The first theme establishes the tonic key securely; it introduces and repeats an important melodic idea. The bridge serves a transitional function; its melodic content is secondary to the change of tonal center that defines it. Again, most students will not easily hear the modulation itself, but they can hear the instability it creates, especially in contrast with the stability of the first and second themes. The second theme establishes the new key securely; it introduces and repeats a contrasting melodic idea. The cadence theme serves a concluding function, bringing the exposition to a decisive end.

Development—Once you finish with the exposition, work through the development one section at a time. Play through each of the development sections identified in the Additional Listening Chart. Ask the class to identify the themes that are developed and the characteristic changes of melody, key, and texture that define each section. For instance, the first section explores theme 2, breaking up the theme and using sequences to modulate frequently. Imitation pervades the mostly polyphonic texture. The final section—the retransition—serves a different function. The frequent modulations cease, and the music prepares for the double return of tonic and the first theme.

Recapitulation—The recapitulation resolves the tensions that were stated in the exposition and explored in the development. Familiar themes return whole and complete; a single, stable key (the tonic) is restored for both the first and second theme groups; homophonic texture again prevails; and a sense of certainty and order is reestablished. Play through the recapitulation so that the class can hear the effect. Then back up and play from the *Molto Allegro* to the end again, pointing to each section on the transparency as it is played.

Introduction and Coda—Following the example of Haydn's symphonies, this Mozart overture also begins with a long, slow introduction and ends with a brief coda. Play the entire overture for the class and ask them to describe how the introduction and coda affect their perception of the form and mood of the piece as a whole. In the discussion that follows, point out that an overture is an orchestral piece at the beginning of an opera, and that the introduction to this overture contains music that will be played again in a dramatic scene at the end of *Don Giovanni* in which a ghostly statue appears to take Don Giovanni to hell. (This music also figures prominently in the first scene of the movie *Amadeus*, when Salieri attempts suicide.) The introduction's ominous, foreboding atmosphere stands in stark contrast with the light, almost comic flavor of the exposition. If you have time, play the recapitulation with and without the coda and ask students to determine which ending is more satisfying and conclusive.

MOZART *Don Giovanni,* Act II Finale, Scene 15

This example provides another sampling of music from a Classical opera buffa; it also provides a superb example of an ensemble. During the nineteenth century this scene was considered so powerful that many performances of *Don Giovanni* ended here, omitting Mozart's large concluding ensemble. See Appendix II for the text for this scene; see Multimedia Resources below for recommended video and audio recordings.

Display (or photocopy handouts of) the text for this scene (see Appendix II). Ask students to study the scene and size up each of the characters. The stone guest—the statue from the Commandant's grave—comes to Don Giovanni's hall. The voice of doom itself, he offers the Don one last chance to change his ways. Don Giovanni refuses to repent; he will die as he has lived, fearlessly and without remorse. Leporello cares more for life than for principles; he is scared out of his wits and constantly begs the Don to back down and repent. Play the music and ask students to comment on Mozart's musical characterizations.

The stone guest—The ghost of the commander does indeed sound like the voice of fate. He sings at a constant forte dynamic in even, measured tones. His infrequent changes of pitch suggest the slow but inexorable motion of his stone body. When he finally makes his pronouncement of doom (*Ah, tempo più non v'è!*), the harmonies suddenly destroy any sense of tonal center; it is as if the bottom has dropped out. Mozart even uses trombones when the commander sings—and not just to add weight. In Mozart's day, trombones were not part of the orchestra but were associated with church music. In this scene, they suggest the power of divine judgment, adding a supernatural flavor.

Don Giovanni—Except at the end, when he feels the flames and ice of hell, the Don matches the commander's resolve note for note. He sings in the same measured tones, though his confident bravado permits him to change pitches more readily. Don Giovanni is an almost unstoppable force that meets an immovable object.

Leporello—His stark terror is reflected in the stammering patter he keeps up whenever he speaks.

As in the earlier duet, the action never lets up for a minute. Due to the statue's pace, the music does not move quickly at first (perhaps this is Mozart's way of suggesting that the Don faces eternity in this scene), but the interaction between the three characters is continuous. Don Giovanni is offered the opportunity to repent, he refuses, and a chorus of demons drags him to hell. No one stops to reflect here; this is the dramatic high point of the entire opera.

This makes a curious ending for a "comic" opera, but the mixture of comic and tragic elements is part of what makes this opera fascinating. Point out how the long, serious introduction to the overture anticipates the statue's entrance in this scene. Play the first thirty seconds of the overture and the first thirty seconds of the scene, starting at the statue's entrance. By anticipating Don Giovanni's ultimate downfall at the beginning of the opera, the otherwise light overture becomes a microcosm of the entire work: an opera buffa with dark, sinister overtones. Mozart blends the powerful expressive possibilities of opera seria with the fast pace and dramatic continuity of opera buffa in one of the greatest operas ever written.

India

Thanks to the Beatles and their friendship with Ravi Shankar, many Americans know a little something about Indian music. You can expect that at least some students will come into your course already fascinated by this unfamiliar yet somehow very familiar tradition. Use this to your advantage!

You will find lecture suggestions below for two examples from India. The first is a north Indian *raga,* a genre that stands squarely at the center of India's classical music tradition; the second is a Carnatic *kriti* by Tyagaraja, the "Beethoven" of south India who transformed this genre sometime around 1800. The next few pages offer distinctions between Hindustani (northern) and Carnatic (southern) streams of India's "Great Tradition," along with background information on essential concepts in Indian music (especially *raga* and *tala*) and some thoughts on Indian music as a "classical" tradition. Following that are notes specific to each musical work, including background on the genres, performers, and composers as well as concrete teaching suggestions. For more detailed information on Indian music, see the list of suggested resources in Appendix V.

Hindustani and Carnatic Music   Indian musicians refer to their classical music as the Great Tradition, a tradition whose roots extend back into ancient Hindu religious practice. Adherents to the Great Tradition must conform to accepted theoretical principles and demonstrate a master-pupil lineage going back several generations. While the entire subcontinent shares this ancient tradition, more recently it has divided into Hindustani (northern) and Carnatic (southern) streams. Current wisdom says the split between the two resulted from Islamic (largely Persian) influence in the north, particularly during the period of the Mughal emperors (c. 1500–1707 C.E.), though many differences between them had already emerged before that point. We explored the Muslim ambivalence toward music in Chapter 5; Hinduism, in contrast, embraced music and dance as profound expressions of religious devotion. This split shaped the social parameters of music making as well. Hindustani musicians tended to be lower-caste virtuoso performers focused more on development of their craft than on theory; their Carnatic colleagues, who included many high-caste Brahmins, valued composition and theory alongside a well-developed performance practice. Today, Carnatic musicians like to believe they preserve the older Hindu traditions, but significant changes have occurred in both streams over the centuries.

The two streams share many essential features but generally vary in the interpretation and use of those features. One can best appreciate the differences between these streams by looking at their common elements. Both streams share the concept of *raga,* but while some *ragas* are shared, each stream has developed its own repertory. In general, the Carnatic stream employs a somewhat more detailed, systematic classification of *ragas*—one that has been adopted by some northern Indian musicians, including Ravi Shankar. At the same time, Carnatic performances tend toward more elaborate melodic ornamentation, often obscuring the principal pitches of a *raga.* Thus, while Hindustani *ragas* are classified less rigorously, the performers take greater care to make the *raga* clearly audible in performance. This stems from the greater importance attached to improvisation in the northern tradition—the *raga* provides the primary structure for improvisation. Carnatic performers, on the other hand, often rely on preexisting compositions to establish the *raga,* allowing them to treat the melody much more freely. In turn, greater reliance on compositions has freed some Carnatic composers from the associations, developed in the Middle Ages, between *raga* and time of day or year.

Performance traditions offer another point of comparison. Both streams rely on specific roles in performance: a melody instrument (or voice), a secondary instrument that can play with or against the primary melody, a drummer who provides rhythmic counterpoint, and a drone. The instruments that fill these roles differ, however. The melody is most often taken by the sitar in the north, while a solo voice or a *vina* is favored in the south. Note the predilection for plucked string instruments! While voice figures prominently in some Hindustani genres, vocal performance is cultivated to a much higher degree in Carnatic regions. The harmonium often fills the secondary role in the north, while southern musicians prefer the violin. (Both of these instruments were British imports adopted by Indian musicians.) Hindustani drummers favor a pair of *tabla,* Carnatic drummers a double-headed *mrdangam.* (The more recent invention, dating from the seventeenth century, *tabla* were created by splitting the *mrdangam* in two!) The playing surfaces of these drums are elaborately prepared with various vegetable pastes to give them just the right tone quality, and a playing technique that uses all of the performer's fingers permits rhythmic patterns of extraordinary difficulty and complexity. The drone instruments, usually sounding scale steps 1 and 5, are the *tanpura* in the north and the *tambura* in the south.

Raga* and *Tala   The term *raga* can be viewed from two different perspectives: *raga* as theoretical concept and *raga* as performance genre. On the theoretical side, the *raga* is much more than just a scale or mode; it can be understood as a musical kit, or seed, from which a work is constructed, or grows. On the genre side, we can speak of the performance of a particular *raga* by a specific performer, such as Ravi Shankar. Of course, these two understandings are not mutually exclusive; the *raga* as performance genre must follow principles implicit in the *raga* as kit.

A *raga* lies somewhere on a spectrum between our notions of scale and tune, and its position on that spectrum can vary somewhat. Like Western scales, many *ragas* are based on seven primary pitches, but the concept of *raga* goes much further than its interval relationships. If you used Class Discussion Ideas 3 and 4 from Chapter 5 of this manual (page 90), you discovered that the Arabic modes (*maqamat*) and even European medieval modes are richer than the modern Western concept of scale. So it is with the *raga* as well. Any specific *raga* has its own melodic gestures, ascending and descending patterns, and an association with specific emotional states and times of day; these point to a comprehensive relationship between the *raga* and musical works derived from that *raga.* In less than an hour, a Western music student can learn a C-major scale and begin to improvise simple tunes at the keyboard; some might sound elementary or awkward, and some might sound good. But in the Indian tradition, it takes years to acquire the depth of understanding required to improvise within a *raga.*

Depending on who does the counting, approximately seventy-two *ragas* are in common use in north Indian music, but many others are also available. For purposes of classification, Indian musicians have developed the concept of parent *ragas* (*thata ragas*). The history of this concept may be convoluted, but the current understanding is not hard to grasp. *Ragas* are grouped into families according to their basic scale pattern. The chart below shows the basic pattern for each of the ten parent *ragas.* A note on the letter names: Using a system remarkably similar to *solfège,* Indian musicians name their scale tones *sa re ga ma pa dha ni,* the equivalent of *do re mi fa sol la ti.* Essentially a movable-*do* system, musicians can transpose the tonic (*sa*) to any pitch that best suits their instrument. When translating scale degrees into Western letter names, Indian musicians generally equate *sa* with C, but purely for convenience—in performance they still transpose tonic to the most suitable pitch, be it C, D, or B flat![12]

1. *Kalyan*   C D E F sharp G A B c

2. *Bilaval*   C D E F G A B c

3. *Khamaj*   C D E F G A B flat c

---

[12]Walter Kaufmann, *The Ragas of North India.* New York: Da Capo Press, 1984, p. 14.

4. *Bhairav*   C D flat E F G A flat B c

5. *Purvi*   C D flat E F sharp G A flat B c

6. *Marva*   C D flat E F sharp G A B c

7. *Kafi*   C D E flat F G A B flat c

8. *Asavari*   C D E flat F G A flat B flat c

9. *Bhairavi*   C D flat E flat F G A flat B flat c

10. *Todi*   C D flat E flat F sharp G A flat B c

All *ragas* within a family share the same pattern of whole steps and half steps, but the similarity ends there. While a parent *raga* is essentially an abstract seven-note construction created for purposes of classification, the individual *ragas* in each family are living, breathing musical entities, each with their own unique features. One mode in a family might omit scale-step 2 (*re*) in an ascending pattern; another will omit scale-step 6 (*dha*). One mode in a family might raise scale-step 4 (*ma*) in an ascending pattern; another will instead lower scale-step 7 (*ni*) on the way down. In addition, each *raga* emphasizes different scale tones (*vadi* and *samvadi*) than those emphasized by its other family members. *Vadi* designates the most important tone in a *raga,* and *samvadi* the second most important tone. (Note: These two pitches are *melody* tones that receive special emphasis throughout a *raga*; don't confuse them with tonic and dominant!) Thus, one mode in a family might emphasize scale-steps 3 (*ga*) and 5 (*pa*); another will instead emphasize 2 (*re*) and 6 (*dha*). *Ragas* can further be distinguished on the basis of characteristic phrases, ornaments, and microtonal inflections.

Tala, the Indian equivalent of meter signature, refers to time lengths that repeat cyclically. As short as a couple of seconds or as long as forty seconds, these time lengths subdivide into various groupings of beats. Examples from the Hindustani tradition include 2 + (2) + 2 + (2) + 2 + 2 (*Ektal*); 2 + 3 + (2) + 3 (*Jhaptal*); 3 + 4 + (3) + 4 (*Jhumra*); and 4 + 4 + (4) + 4 (*Trital*), the latter used in Rag *Mauj-Khammaj* (see below). Examples from the Carnatic tradition include 2 + 4 (*Rupaka*); 3 + 2 + 2 (*Triputa*); and 4 + 2 + 2 (*Adi*), the latter used in "Marakata manivarna" (see below). As you can see, some *tala* patterns resemble Western asymmetric meter signatures. Although some *talas* are only three beats long, beat groupings can be strung together to an overall *tala* length of 35 beats in the Carnatic formal system. Such long patterns have inspired Western jazz and popular musicians, notably Don Ellis, whose "27/16" and "33 222 1 222"—based on 27- and 19-beat *talas* respectively—can be heard on his *"Live" at Monterey* CD (see Sound Recordings below). Some *talas* are thought to be more appropriate for slow tempos, some for fast tempos, while others can be used in various tempos.

Indian Music as Classical Music   It cannot be said strongly enough that the music of the Great Tradition is *classical* music! India's traditional music evidences all of the hallmarks of a classical tradition:

❧ It is a centuries-old tradition that has developed distinctive, often elaborate, genres and practices.

❧ It relies on a class of professional, trained musicians; it is not something that everyone participates in.

❧ It is not "everyday" music; rather, it is set apart in formal performances that maintain a clear performer-audience relationship.

ア Its level of difficulty is such that amateurs do not generally perform at a professional level.

ア A rigorous training system has been developed to ensure high-quality musical performances.

ア It uses a system of music notation; thus, it is not a purely oral tradition.

These are remarkable points of similarity with Western classical music. And in the highly developed genres of the Great Tradition, we can hear the same principles that undergird Western classical music—repetition, variation, contrast, return, and development.

In spite of these similarities, crucial differences remain between Indian and Western classical traditions. For instance, the mixture of composed and improvised sections in both Rag *Mauj-Khammaj* and "Marakata manivarna" below points to a concept of the musical work that differs from what we find in the Western classical tradition. Mozart wrote out every note of his symphonies, and performers do their best to play them according to his specifications. In the Indian tradition, however, even composed portions of a musical work are subject to embellishment and variation. The *pakar* in the first and second *gats* of Rag *Mauj-Khammaj* offer a case in point. The composed portion serves as a tune to be varied and a set of motives to be developed, just as the *raga* itself serves as a performance framework rather than a fixed work. This fact in no way diminishes the respect accorded great performers like Ravi Shankar or Ali Akbar Khan, creative musicians whose contributions to Indian music can be compared to those of Mozart or Bach in the Western tradition. It simply reflects a different understanding of the relationship between the musical performance and the musical work, and it offers yet another opportunity to reflect on the "voice of the other."

A *Hindustani* Raga—*Rag* Mauj-Khammaj

Ravi Shankar   Admired and revered worldwide as one of the great musicians of the twentieth century and the world's most visible ambassador for Indian music, Ravi Shankar (b. 1920) was perhaps an unlikely candidate to become a great *sitar* player. As a Hindu and the son of an internationally distinguished, well-to-do, high-caste scholar and lawyer, young Shankar hardly fit the stereotypical image of north Indian musicians: lower-class Muslim journeymen, sacrificing years of their lives to study with a guru and hone their craft. As an adolescent, Ravi moved even further away from that stereotype, traveling around the world with his oldest brother's dance troupe, staying in the finest hotels, and hanging out with the glitterati of the day. On the other hand, his unconventional upbringing probably contributed to the often startling innovations that helped make him one of the greatest *sitar* virtuosos of all time, and his early travels abroad gave him a confidence and ease bridging cultural divides—personal qualities that enabled him to carry Indian music to all corners of the globe. The following notes provide a brief biographical sketch; for further information, consult Shankar's recent autobiography, *Raga Mala*.[13]

Born in the city of Varanasi (Benares), Shankar was raised primarily by his mother, Hemangini Shankar. In fact, Ravi did not even meet his father, Shyam Shankar, until he was eight years old. Shyam, a member of the Brahmin caste (the highest social level in India), was a lawyer, statesman, scholar, philosopher, writer, and amateur musician. His career, which included positions with the

---

[13]Ravi Shankar, *Raga Mala: The Autobiography of Ravi Shankar,* ed. George Harrison. New York: Welcome Rain Publishers, 1997.

League of Nations, Columbia University, and so on, took him away from India for years at a time. Despite being part of such a prestigious family, Ravi grew up in extremely modest circumstances. Shyam and Hemangini separated shortly before Ravi's birth, and though Shyam arranged an annual pension for the family, they received only 30 percent of the stipend due to widespread corruption in pre-independence India's financial sector.

At age ten, Ravi met his oldest brother, Uday Shankar, for the first time. Twenty years Ravi's senior, Uday had left India in 1920 to study in London at the Royal College of Art. An overnight success in performances with Anna Pavlova, Uday launched a career as a dancer. In 1929 he returned to India to tour with his troupe, do some research, and find musicians to provide traditional Indian music for his dancers. Uday convinced his family to share his dream of carrying Indian music and dance (his personal synthesis, at least) to the rest of the world, and in 1930 Ravi found himself traveling to Paris with his mother and brothers. Over the next few years Ravi traveled the globe with his brother's company, playing *sitar* and learning to dance as part of the troupe.

Shankar might have continued for many years as a dancer in his brother's troupe, but tragedy intervened. His father was fatally attacked in London in 1935 while the troupe was in Singapore, and his mother died at home of pneumonia in 1936 while Ravi was in Paris. Shankar took some time off, but in 1938—deciding he could no longer ignore music's call—he entered a traditional student-guru relationship with the great *sarod* master Allaudin Khan, known to Shankar as Baba. Baba had traveled with Uday's troupe for a time, watching over Ravi at his mother's request. When she died, Baba continued to take his promise to her very seriously, and he became a second father to Ravi. Shankar had to live simply during his apprenticeship, which was quite a contrast to his years of travel, but he emerged from this seven-year period a fully formed Indian classical musician; husband to Baba's daughter, Annapurna; and good friend to Baba's son, Ali Akbar Khan.

The rest is history, as they say. Shankar's career slowly but surely took on greater significance as he gave concerts, made recordings, worked in theater and radio, traveled with cultural delegations to the U.S.S.R. and Japan, and so on. He also gradually forged more and more ties with the West. Even before the Beatles, Shankar befriended the great British violinist Yehudi Menuhin in 1952. Their friendship yielded many opportunities for collaboration, bringing Ravi into close contact with the Western classical tradition. In the late 1950s, Shankar determined to revisit many of the countries he had visited in his youth, but with the goal this time of bringing Indian music to the West. In 1956–57 he embarked on his first solo tour to Europe and the United States, an event that saw his first Western solo recordings.

Menuhin was the first of many famous Western musicians to befriend Shankar. In the years following his solo tour, he came to know and work with performers and composers such as John Coltrane, Zubin Mehta, André Previn, Jean-Pierre Rampal, Philip Glass, and, of course, George Harrison and the Beatles. Shankar's humility and his openness to other traditions made him an ideal, much sought-after collaborator. And from the vantage point of international renown, Shankar has become synonymous with Indian music for much of the world.

Before moving on, it is important to reflect on Shankar's achievements as a musician. None of his accomplishments on the world stage would have been possible had not his musical skills been of the highest order. Western listeners cannot fail to hear the virtuosity in his lightning-fast performances of a *gat* or *jhala*, but an understanding of the innovative nature of Shankar's music requires a deep knowledge of the Great Tradition. Stephen Slawek's assessment helps us understand Shankar's Mozart-like ability both to absorb many different traditions and genres, and to blend and transform them to create something new, exciting, and expressive.

> Drawing inspiration from the rhythmic practices of South Indian classical music, Shankar fashioned a unique approach to elaborating the Indian raga system. He synthesized his knowledge of numerous instrumental and vocal genres gained during the broad-based training that he received from his *guru* to develop a distinctive approach to the concert format. In his repertory he maintains a *dhrupad*[14] approach to the solo *alap-jor-jhala*, a *khayal*-inspired[15] approach to slow instrumental compositions (*vilambit gat*), and a late-19th century instrumental approach to fast compositions (*drut gat*). Beyond this core of his repertory, Shankar draws heavily on the light-hearted and erotic themes of *thumri*[16] in the closing numbers of his performances.[17]

In the search for his own unique sound, Shankar encouraged improvements in *sitar* construction and explored new performance techniques, especially in the use of the plectrum (*mizrab*). Needless to say, Shankar's innovations have had an enormous impact on classical musicians of north India.

Ali Akbar Khan   Ali Akbar Khan was born in 1922 in East Bengal. Having Allaudin Khan—one of the most influential performers and teachers in India—for a father, the young Khan's musical training on *sarod* began at age three. For twenty years he studied and practiced, alongside Ravi Shankar when Shankar took Baba (Allaudin Khan) as his guru and still later when Shankar became his brother-in-law. In his early twenties, Khan followed the time-honored path of many classical musicians and took a position as a court musician—and he also made his first recordings! After India's independence, Khan also met Yehudi Menuhin and found his way to the West. Khan's impact was no less significant than Shankar's; he made the first Western LP recording to feature Indian classical music, and he became the first Indian musician to perform on Western television. After several years of teaching and touring, Khan decided that American interest was strong enough to start a school in the United States. In 1967 he established the Ali Akbar College of Music in Berkeley. Still a going concern, the college moved to San Rafael in 1974. When he is not touring or recording, Khan still teaches and oversees the school. In recent years, Khan has devoted much effort to the exploration and preservation of his father's many innovations. Alongside Shankar, Khan remains one of the most important classical Indian musicians of the twentieth century.

***Raga* Performance**   The instrumental performance of a *raga* by north Indian musicians provides yet another excellent example of the concept of inner versus outer form discussed in Chapter 4. In spite of (or perhaps because of) the impor-

---

[14]The *dhrupad* is a classical, revered vocal style of composition, which first achieved popularity in the fifteenth century. Its lyrics praise deities, rulers, or nature, and its mood is one of great solemnity, seriousness, and nobility. (These words serve equally well as a description of another genre that emerged in the fifteenth century—the Renaissance motet!)

[15]The *khayal* is the dominant vocal style in Indian classical music today. Dating from the thirteenth century, it takes the *dhrupad* as its basis, but allows greater flexibility in its treatment. This freedom extends to the performer's use of ornamentation, dramatic contrasts, and virtuoso display. The flavor of this genre is embodied in its name, which translates as "imagination."

[16]The freest of all vocal genres, the very popular *thumri* permits the unusual practices of modulating and bringing in other *ragas* or even folk tunes. Given its light, almost popular tone, it tends to favor light rather than serious *ragas*.

[17]Stephen Slawek, "Shankar, Ravi," *The New Grove Dictionary of Music Online*, ed. L. Macy (Accessed 3 March 2003), http://www.grovemusic.com.

tant role improvisation plays in this tradition, the outer form breaks down into several standard sections that remain remarkably consistent in format from one *raga* to another. With a healthy dose of improvisation and so many *ragas* to choose from, the inner form can vary enormously; this explains why it takes years for practitioners to learn their craft. In spite of these contrasts, however, when you compare equivalent sections from different *raga* performances, you find striking similarities in texture, register, accompaniment, tempo, and meter (or lack thereof), all features that point toward the *raga*'s outer form. The basic *raga* format consists of two primary sections. The slow, nonmetric opening section—the *alap*—serves much the same function as an exposition in sonata form: it introduces the *raga* and carefully lays out that mode's basic motivic material. The faster, clearly metric closing section—the *gat*—serves as a rondo-like finale, whose tune may return at ever-faster tempos. The notes below describe features of each large section as well as its important subdivisions.

> *Alap*—Almost all metered Indian music begins with a slow, free, nonmetric section called the *alap* (*alapana* in Carnatic music). Played by only the solo instrument(s) and *tambura* (no *tabla*), this introductory material consists of improvised, free sections that end only when the performers decide to end them. The *alap* serves the significant function of introducing the *raga* on which the work is based. Indian musicians believe that the *alap*'s free rhythm and slow speed provide the best context for exploring and exposing both the emotion (*rasa*) and the most delicate melodic-structural features of a particular *raga*; metered sections leave no time for such subtleties. The very beginning of the *alap*, called the *asthayi*, explores the lower register of the *raga*; the *antara* that follows moves into the upper register (some *ragas* begin in the upper register and move down). Typical events in the *alap* include the establishment of the most significant melodic pitches (*vadi* and *samvadi*) of the *raga*, traversal of the *raga*'s typical ascending (*aroha*) and descending (*avaroha*) melodic patterns, and exploration of the entire melodic range. In a recent DVD recording, *Ravi Shankar in Portrait*, the sitarist compares the *alap*'s process of revealing the *raga* to that of painting a beautiful woman, one body part at a time. Shankar also describes several different *alap* styles, ranging from leisurely to short in time frame and from straightforward to gradual and coy in its manner of exposition.[18]

>> *Jor*—Indian musicians do not agree whether the *jor* is a new section or a continuation of the *alap*, but it definitely sounds more like *alap* than *gat*. Even though the music in this section remains nonmetric, its rhythms feel faster and more deliberate, creating an overall sense of increased rhythmic activity.

>> *Jhala*—This final section before the *gat* is also the fastest and most active so far. The *jhala* almost feels metric, but its main identifying feature is a series of fast strokes going back and forth between the main strings and the two "drone" strings. *Jhala* can also refer to a similar section at the end of the *gat*. When used in this manner to conclude the *raga*, it is clearly metric, extremely fast, and virtuosic in its intricacy. Naturally, we hear the *jhala*'s defining fast strokes in either location.

> *Gat*—While it can prove tricky to discern the subsections of the *alap*, no one can miss the beginning of the *gat*, thanks to the entrance of the *tabla* and the simultaneous establishment of a clear meter. The *alap* is almost entirely improvised, but the *gat* uses a fixed composition as the basis for improvisation.

---

[18]*Ravi Shankar in Portrait*. BBC Opus Arte OA 0864 D (2 DVDs, color, 190 minutes), 2002.

The beginning of the *gat* generally announces this preexisting melody (*pakar*), a tune that can reappear several times. Like the *alap,* the *gat* subdivides into sections that follow a similar progression from slower to faster rhythms and tempo. Each *gat* goes faster than the previous one, and each tends to begin with a statement of the main melody or a variant. This gradual increase of tempo creates a marvelous climax of activity that sweeps us toward the end. Once again, at the very end another *jhala* may be used, further increasing the excitement with its rapid, intricate plucking patterns.

Raga and Tala in the Rag *Mauj-Khammaj*   Light and even somewhat erotic in mood, *Mauj-Khammaj* (or *Manj-Khammaj*) is a late evening *raga* designed to convey both pathos and joy. Devised by the great Allaudin Khan, this hybrid *raga* presents many challenges to the inexperienced listener. Specifically, this *raga* mixes features of several *ragas*—especially Khammaj, Mand, and the Bilaval *thata* variant of the Bhatiyar *raga*. Based on the Khamaj *thata* described above, this *raga*'s core scale is equivalent to the Western Mixolydian mode, essentially a major scale with lowered scale-step 7.

C   D   E   F   G   A   B flat   c

Mauj-Khammaj is similar to the Khammaj *raga* in its tendency to omit scale-step 2 (*re*) and raise scale-step 7 (*ni*) in ascending patterns, but where Khammaj tends to emphasize scale-step 3 (*ga*), the hybrid *raga* emphasizes scale-steps 4 (*ma*) and 6 (*dha*). For trained Western musicians, the emphasis on *ma* is perhaps the single most disorienting aspect of this *raga*. Why? Take the Khamaj *thata* scale above and play melodic patterns that consistently emphasize F. What happens? Since this pattern of whole steps and half steps starting on F corresponds to an F-major scale, our well-trained ears tell us that we *are* in F major. In the same way, when we listen to the Mauj-Khammaj *raga,* our Western ears tell us that *ma,* not *sa,* is tonic, especially when the drone pitches of the *tambura* also oscillate between scale-steps 1 and 4. And when we hear scale-step 7 raised in ascending patterns, our focus on scale-step 4 may lead us to (mistakenly) describe this as a Lydian inflection.

The *tala* used in this performance is very common, in part due to its versatility. Unlike some other *talas, trital* (or *tintal*) is appropriate at slow, medium, or fast tempo. *Trital* is a 16-*matra* pattern, *matra* being very close to the Western concept of a beat. Some *talas* group the beat asymmetrically, but *trital* uses binary groupings that feel quite normal to Western listeners: 4 + 4 + (4) + 4. On the other hand, the pattern of accented beats in this *tala* is not quite as symmetrical. As we might expect, *trital* puts primary emphasis on the first beat, but where we might expect another accent on the ninth beat, *trital* places secondary accents on the fifth and thirteenth beats. In other words, it places accents on the first notes of the first, second, and fourth group of four beats—thus the parentheses around the third "4."

Rag *Mauj-Khammaj*   Begin your presentation of this work with some background material. Feel free to use any of the information above, but at the very least be sure to both include a bit of Ravi Shankar's biography and introduce the concept of *raga* and important features of *raga* performance. Once you finish with the preliminaries, call attention to the sections outlined in the Additional Listening Chart for this work (see Appendix I). Put the checklist of musical elements and structures on the board, play the first minute of the *alap* (beginning) and the first *gat* (at 3.31), and ask students to compare them with each other. In the discussion that follows, draw out these essential points.

Melody—Melodic features can be heard by following the *sitar* and *sarod* throughout. The phrases in the *alap* seem tentative and searching, and they vary greatly in length. The melodic style is rather ornate, with frequent embellishments of specific notes in the *raga*. Some notes are also subjected to a vibrato-like effect (*gamaka*) created by pulling back and forth on the string with the left hand (after plucking with the right hand). This initial section explores the lower and middle registers of the *raga*. The *gat* presents a more tunelike melody (*pakar*) that repeats several times in whole or in part with various ornaments, sounding sometimes like variations and sometimes like motivic development. This section explores somewhat higher and lower registers than we heard at the *alap*'s beginning.

Harmony—This music does not use harmony in the Western sense, though the *tambura* drone, heard throughout the example, keeps us anchored on tonic as it alternates between the two main pitches of the *raga*. In many *ragas*, those pitches are scale-steps 1 (*sa*) and 5 (*pa*), but in *Mauj-Khammaj*, they are 1 (*sa*) and 4 (*ma*). As noted above, this makes it easy to mistake *ma* for the tonic.

Rhythm—While the *gat* demonstrates a clear beat and a sense of duple meter, the *alap* employs free rhythms in a nonmetric environment. Of these sections, the *alap* feels slower, and the *gat* faster. The metered sections of this work are in *trital*, but this virtuoso performance does not provide aural cues that make it easy for novices to spot. If students hear duple meter, that's close enough.

Color—Both sections feature *sitar, sarod,* and the drone (*tambura*). The pair of drums (*tabla*) appears only in the *gat*. Note differences between the sounds of the *sitar* and the *sarod*, the former higher and "twangier," the latter lower and more guitarlike. The cascading zither-like sounds at the very beginning are the sympathetic strings of the two plucked-string instruments the ascending pattern on *sarod*, the descending on *sitar*. After these cascades, the *sarod* initially leads and the *sitar* follows, but after that the alternation can happen in any order, and often both play simultaneously. This duet style (*jugalbandi*) was popularized by Shankar.

Texture—These two sections demonstrate the roles described above under *Raga* Performance. The *alap* offers a sometimes quasi-imitative interplay between *sitar* and *sarod*. Either instrument can take the role of leader, and sometimes both instruments play simultaneously in a kind of two-voice nonimitative polyphony. Only the *tambura* accompanies this interplay. The *gat* finds *sitar* and *sarod* in a somewhat different relationship. They may still alternate on occasion, but when they present the main melody (*pakar*), a heterophonic doubling—often at the octave—occurs. Of course, this section also adds the *tabla,* which provide an elaborate rhythmic counterpoint, and they establish the beat and the tempo. The *tambura* drones on in the background. The texture throughout the work centers around a primary melody, but it would be a mistake to describe this music as monophonic. The interaction between plucked-string instruments and the sophistication of the drum parts suggest a much more active texture. "Melody with accompaniment" comes closer—as long as one acknowledges the quasi-imitation (and occasional two-voice polyphony) of the *alap* and the heterophony and intricate rhythmic counterpoint of the *gat*.

Improvisation—It is easy to overstate the role of improvisation in *raga* performance. Certainly the performers do not know ahead of time exactly what they will play from one moment to the next, but the *raga* framework in which they improvise is surprisingly strict. Some notes must be omitted or chromatically altered in ascending or descending patterns. Certain motivic patterns are encouraged; others are discouraged. Some ornaments can only be used on specific scale tones; others cannot be used at all. Important scale tones must be emphasized using specific melodic patterns; others must be de-emphasized or relegated to an ornamental role. Microtonal inflections are permitted with some scale tones, but not with others. The list goes on and on, and of course the list is different for every different *raga*! One cannot improvise just any tune that comes into one's head; the parameters of the *raga* must be observed. Here one begins to appreciate the years of practice this classical discipline requires. On the other hand, the improvisation is free enough to have an impact on the duet style (*jugalbandi*). The frequent alternation noted above is a practical response to this improvisatory environment. Since neither soloist knows for sure what the other will play next, alternation guarantees a more successful result than playing simultaneously throughout, and the virtuoso cat-and-mouse between two great soloists is in itself a source of pleasure for the listener.

Form—At this point, students will possess a clear understanding of the two main sections of a north Indian *raga*. The performance from the fifth edition of *Listen* contained only two excerpts from an already abbreviated performance of *Mauj-Khammaj*; the full recording can be found on the *Anthology of Indian Classical Music* (see Sound Recordings below). Neither version contains distinct *jor* or *jhala* sections such as one might find in a complete *raga* performance, but such a performance would run anywhere from twenty-five minutes to a full hour. Still, for a first introduction to north Indian music, these *alap* and *gat* excerpts offer plenty for your students to absorb.

Once you and your students come to a clear understanding of the musical features of this music, put them in context. Display the Additional Listening Chart and play through both excerpts for your students (If you use the complete recording, play only the first five minutes and the final two minutes). Point out important sections as they go by. Afterwards, ask students to describe what they heard. In the discussion that follows, draw out the following.

Alap—The comparison exercise above should make it possible for students to describe this in some detail. Point out the *alap*'s main purpose—to present and explore the structure of the *raga* and its characteristic melodic patterns, ornaments, emphasized and de-emphasized pitches, and so on. Students may first find this section more tedious than the *gat,* so remind them that the *alap* is the expressive heart of the *raga*, the place where we here its specific emotion (*rasa*) most clearly. The faster tempo of the *gat* leaves no time for such subtlety and expression. Finally, call attention to the subtle increase in tempo that precedes the *gat*.

First Gat—Once again, students should have a good handle on features of the *gat* after the comparison exercise above. Remind the class that the main melody (*pakar*) is a composed, preexisting tune. Call attention to the frequent heterophonic passages and point out that two soloists can only play in unison if they both know the tune already. If necessary, play through the first *gat* again to help students hear the *pakar* and its frequent repetitions and development. The recurring motives of the *pakar* give this section a greater sense of organization and structure than we heard in the *alap*. In fact, the differences between *alap* and *gat* are much like the contrasts we hear between recitative and aria in Baroque and Classical operas.

Second Gat—The second excerpt was not part of the comparison exercise above, but its features are very similar to the first *gat*. Preceding the second *gat* we hear another gradual increase in tempo, and as the music speeds up, the interplay between soloists becomes progressively more virtuosic. Note the unison playing on a cadence-like figure that immediately precedes the second *gat*. This figure derives from the end of the *pakar* as we heard it in the first *gat*, but now it has much more rhythmic energy. The second *gat* begins as did the first *gat*, with a heterophonic statement of the *pakar*, but the tempo is faster. Consequently, the element of virtuoso display comes through even more strongly, and the treatment of the *pakar* now sounds more like development and less like variation.

As you wrap up your discussion, remind your students that music of the Great Tradition is *classical* music (see notes on Indian Music as Classical Music above). Discussion of this connection can sharpen students' understanding of both the similarities and the differences between Indian and Western classical music. And by listening for the same principles that inform Western classical music, students can readily appreciate the virtuosity, structure, and other musical elements that give such expressiveness to this great tradition.

A *Carnatic* Kriti *"Marakata manivarna"*

If you want to introduce your students to an example of south Indian music, this *kriti* by Tyagaraja provides an excellent example. The notes on Hindustani and Carnatic music above provide useful comparisons between these two traditions, and the notes below offer a look at Tyagaraja's life, an outline of important features of the *kriti*, and teaching suggestions for "Marakata manivarna." See Appendix I for an Additional Listening Chart; you can find recordings in the set that accompanied *Listen: Brief Fourth Edition* or in Sound Recordings below.

Further resources may prove useful as you introduce Tyagaraja, especially if you want to give your students greater insight into the man himself. Tyagaraja lived a life of religious devotion, refusing to sing the praises of anyone but Rama. Use Tyagaraja's poetry to help students savor his essence, especially the texts of his *kriti* and *kirtana*. Just as finding a Beethoven score poses few difficulties in Western culture, finding the writings of Tyagaraja proves easier than you might think. His song texts, preserved and published widely in India, have often been translated into English. (If your college library doesn't have them, use interlibrary loan.) Especially useful is William J. Jackson's *Tyagaraja: Life and Lyrics* (Delhi: Oxford University Press, 1991), which includes information on Tyagaraja's life and southern Indian cultural history in addition to translations of 160 song texts. Especially interesting are the songs that describe his view of the relationship between music and the divine. Chapter 4 of Jackson's book contains sections titled "The Divine as the Embodiment of Music" (pages 117–20), "Music and Devotion" (pages 120–23), and "Music as the Meeting Place of the Human and the Divine" (pages 126–29), and his translations of "Nada sudharasambilanu" (page 262), "Raga sudharasa" (page 297), "Sangita sastrajnanamu" (page 315), "Moksamu galada" (page 260), "Nadatanumanisam" (page 263), and "Intakanna anandamemi" (page 236) provide excellent examples of this relationship. Read some of these song texts for your students as prelude to a discussion of Tyagaraja.

Tyagaraja

Revered equally as a musician and saint, Tyagaraja (1767–1847) has been the single most dominant figure in Carnatic music for the past two centuries. His life spanned a period of great turmoil in southern India. In his adolescence he witnessed the siege of Tanjore by Muslim armies from Mysore. As an adult he watched the British presence grow into a dominant force. These external events had no apparent effect, however, on his spiritual growth—after all, the illusory events of the material world (*samsara*) can only distract from the truth within. He followed the path of *bhakti,* of devotion (to Rama), without wavering, and it is said he repeated his mantra nearly a billion times in twenty years, so constant was his meditation. For Tyagaraja, music itself was a form of meditation, a form of immediate and joyous contact with the divine.

Tyagaraja, which translates as "king of self-renunciation," was born into a Brahmin family of musicians and poets. His father, an authority on the Ramayana, moved to Tanjore to take a position at court, and Tyagaraja grew up there. As a youth, he undertook musical studies with Sonti Venkataramanayya, one of the greatest musicians of his day. Tyagaraja saw his music as a joyous act of devotion, and he refused to practice his art in praise of anyone but Rama, his god. Since positions in princely courts would require him to sing songs honoring his patron, Tyagaraja never served at court. He refused to misuse his divine gifts, much as Mahalia Jackson in the twentieth century refused to sing secular music. Following the path of self-renunciation, he would accept only a bowl of rice for his performances. His reputation as a singer and composer quickly spread throughout southern India, and invitations for performances poured in from many rulers, but Tyagaraja refused them all. Unlike other Hindu saints, Tyagaraja undertook few pilgrimages to holy places until near the end of his life, but his passing was fully consistent with saintly expectations—it is said that he did not die; rather, his spirit was absorbed directly into the divine presence, thus ending his cycle of reincarnation.

Tyagaraja left as his legacy thousands of *kriti* and *kirtana* (both poetry and music), his countless acts of devotion, and the memory of an extraordinary performer and improviser. So valuable was his life's contribution that the first few generations of his students went far beyond the usual oral transmission of learning from master to pupil; they wrote his biography (twice), notated his compositions, and translated and published his music and his song texts. They also perpetuated the use of the Telugu language in their instruction and compositions. Note that Tamil, not Telugu, was the native language in Tanjore. Telugu-speaking Nayak viceroys brought their language to Tanjore long before Tyagaraja was born, and they encouraged Telugu poetry at court. Tyagaraja himself grew up in a Telugu-speaking family, so it was natural that he write song texts in his native tongue. Given his desire to speak directly to everyday folk, one might wonder why he chose Telugu over Tamil. Familiarity, certainly, but the soft lilt of the Telugu tongue must have appealed to his musical sensibilities, and he wrote the vast majority of his song texts in that language. Because of Tyagaraja's choice, Telugu remains the language of southern Indian classical musicians to this day, much as Italian long served as the language of European musicians. These examples speak to the breadth of Tyagaraja's influence, but to understand the significance of his work as a musician, we must take a look at the genre that he transformed and made his own, the *kriti.*

The Kriti

The Carnatic *kriti* originated as a type of sacred song about two hundred years before Tyagaraja. Initially the *kriti* bore a strong resemblance to the *kirtana,* a work with poetic text set syllabically, intended as a hymn for group singing. In fact, the *kriti* appeared in many different forms, making a specific definition difficult. Tyagaraja literally transformed the genre, creating a tight, expressive structure that many regarded as the height of perfection. Further, his *kriti*s successfully merged classical and devotional traditions. What had been devotional music now acquired the full weight and sophistication of the classical tradition. Tyagaraja's *kriti*s maintained a devotional stance, but he paved the way for later composers to produce *kriti*s in the tradition of absolute music, separate from their devotional roots. Apart from its subject matter, the current definition of *kriti* corresponds precisely to the genre Tyagaraja practiced two hundred years ago.

The structure of Tyagaraja's *kriti*s can be grasped by studying the texts themselves. Overall, Tyagaraja tightened up the form's structure, making it more concise, succinct, and consistent. Each *kriti* begins with the *pallavi*, a short opening section that serves as a refrain. The *pallavi* sets the mood and defines the poetic themes for the entire work. The *anupallavi*, the second section, serves as the continuation of the *pallavi*, amplifying its central ideas. Both *pallavi* and *anupallavi* can return later in the manner of a refrain. The *caranam*, or verse, typically follows. Some *kriti* contain only one verse, others include many, but in either case a refrain generally follows the verses. Although this structure may sound formulaic, in fact it provided an enormously expressive vehicle that spoke to Tyagaraja's audiences with immediacy and power.

The musical structure of the *kriti* echoes that of the text. The *pallavi* typically begins in the lower register of the *raga*, establishing the mood of both song and *raga* (the two should ideally match). In the same way that the text of the *anupallavi* amplifies the meaning of the *pallavi*, its music intensifies the mood by moving into a higher register. The *caranam*, somewhat longer poetic structures than the *pallavi* and *anupallavi*, allow for more varied expression. A verse will often begin at a lower intensity level than the preceding *anupallavi* and build to its own climax toward the end. The musical return of *pallavi* and/or *anupallavi* at the end provides the same sense of satisfaction experienced in European ternary-form works. As we shall see below, other sections are frequently inserted into this framework by skilled musicians—not only the customary slow, free *alapana* that introduces the *raga*, but also later improvised sections that heighten the musical experience.

The affective side of Tyagaraja's *kriti*s deserves comment as well. Some observers have criticized Tyagaraja's lack of poetic sophistication. Although it is true that he often chose simple words or metaphors, these often reflect the blending of poetic and prose styles in his *kriti*, giving him a broader expressive palette. At the same time, he employed devices such as *yati* (initial syllable rhymes) and *prasa* (alliteration), which reveal poetic sensitivity and craft. More to the point, his apparent simplicity permitted him to communicate with an unparalleled directness. Tyagaraja could make his audiences laugh, cry, or ponder deeply as no previous Carnatic composer had. In this regard, Tyagaraja begs comparison with Beethoven. The great European composer often used rhythms and melodies that were trite, brusque, or otherwise inelegant, yet his music could convey terror, joy, sadness, hope, or triumph like the music of no European composer before him. Both the words and music of a *kriti* by Tyagaraja instantly conveyed the full flavor of its mood, and listeners could immediately share the master's joy in creation.

Musically no less inventive, Tyagaraja knew how to find the perfect link between text and music. In some cases this meant the invention (or revelation) of new *ragas* that captured hitherto unexpressed musical moods. Some *ragas* are still associated with Tyagaraja today. Another device, *sangati*, allowed the composer to juxtapose several possible understandings of the same text. *Sangati* refers to a specific type of variation procedure in which a phrase is stated and immediately repeated more than once, each time emphasizing words differently, each time embellishing specific notes (and therefore specific words) differently. A particularly good sequence of variations introduces surprise twists in meaning that can delight or amuse the audience or, better yet, lead the listeners toward profound new revelations. Usually associated with the *pallavi* and *anupallavi*, *sangati* offers the possibility for creativity within the *kriti*. Tyagaraja himself toyed with different variations in his *kriti*s. When a new variation worked especially well, he made it part of the composition. This performance practice continues to the present day, and the variations one hears in a modern *pallavi* often reflect several generations of additions—with one or two new ones at the end of the string.

Another seemingly simple device—Tyagaraja's frequent use of melisma— reaped enormous benefits. The older *kirtana*, set simply and syllabically, relied on its poetry to give the music structure and regularity. But with Tyagaraja's new *kriti* structure, he no longer needed poetic conceits to create shape and coherence. Once strict syllabic text setting was abandoned, Tyagaraja could use the melismas that gave Carnatic classical music its enormous expressive range; and once melismas were adopted, he could effectively blend prose and poetic styles, as described above. Note the significance of these developments. By making the full range of melodic styles available for his *kriti*, Tyagaraja brought the genre squarely into the mainstream of Carnatic classical music. Through Tyagaraja's combined gifts as musician, lyricist, and composer, the *kriti* became the most significant classical genre in southern India, capable of expressing the full range of human emotions with force and immediacy. Once again, Tyagaraja begs comparison with Beethoven, who single-handedly elevated the symphony to a position of prominence in European music—a position it maintained well into the twentieth century.

TYAGARAJA "Marakata manivarna"

Begin your presentation of this work with some background material. Feel free to use any of the information above, but at the very least include a bit of Tyagaraja's biography, identify important features of Carnatic music, and review the concept of *raga*. Once you finish with the preliminaries, call attention to the three large sections outlined in the Additional Listening Chart (see Appendix I). Put the checklist of musical elements and structures on the board, play the first minute of each section, and ask students to compare them with each other. In the discussion that follows, draw out these essential points.

Melody—Melodic features can be heard by following the voice throughout. The phrases in section 1 seem tentative and searching, and they vary greatly in length. Starting in a low register near the beginning, they explore higher and higher registers. Section 2 presents a basic, regular phrase that repeats several times with only minimal ornamentation before we hear variations on the phrase. This section also begins in a low register, gradually moving into higher territory. The final section seems freer and more irregular in its phrase structure, but it now moves along much more rapidly than in any previous section, approaching the feel of a *perpetuum mobile*. This section maintains a higher *tessitura* than the others.

Harmony—This music does not use harmony in the Western sense.

Rhythm—Whereas sections 2 and 3 demonstrate a clear beat and a sense of duple meter, section 1 employs free rhythms in a nonmetric environment.

Of the three sections, the first feels slowest, the third fastest. The metered sections of this work are based on *adi tala,* but this performance does not provide aural cues that make it easy to spot. If students hear duple meter, that's close enough. (If you want to follow it for your own satisfaction, start an eight-count pattern on the cadence tone at the end of the first phrase, where the drums enter.)

Color—All three sections feature solo voice, two double-headed drums (*mrdangam*), and the drone (*tambura*). The violin appears only in sections 1 and 2.

Texture—These three sections demonstrate the roles described in Lecture Suggestions above under "Hindustani and Carnatic Music." Section 1 offers a quasi-imitative interplay between voice and violin; the voice, the primary instrument, leads, and the violin, the secondary instrument, follows. Only the *tambura* accompanies this interplay. Section 2 finds the voice and violin in a different relationship—a heterophonic doubling of the main melody. The voice still dominates our attention, but the violin no longer waits to hear the voice before it plays. This section also adds the drums which both provide an elaborate rhythmic counterpoint and establish the beat and the tempo. The *tambura* drones on in the background. Section 3 quickens the pace but simplifies the textural interaction. Now the voice alone carries the primary melody, accompanied by the drums and drone. The texture throughout the work centers around a primary melody, but it would be a mistake to describe this music as monophonic. The interaction between voice and violin and the sophistication of the drum parts suggest a much more active texture. "Melody with accompaniment" comes closer—as long as one acknowledges the quasi-imitation of section 1, the heterophony of section 2, and the rhythmic counterpoint throughout.

Text—Only section 2 is based on the words of the *kriti* by Tyagaraja. This becomes clearer when students can follow the words in the Additional Listening Chart. In section 1 the voice uses syllables that supposedly derive from sacred phrases like "Om Anantam" (*Om,* "Infinite"). This opening section carves out, in a sense, a sacred space in which the performance can occur. In place of a text, section 3 employs the note-name syllables used by Indian musicians, *sa ri ga ma pa da ni,* in a fast, virtuosic improvisation.

Once you and your students come to a clear understanding of the musical features of this music, put them in context. Describe each section one at a time.

Section 1—This introductory *alapana* (the Carnatic equivalent of the *alap*) falls into the category of *anibaddha*—improvised, free sections that end only when the performers decide to end them. The improvised nature of this section accounts for the free use of rhythm and phrase relationships described above. Since the *alapana* is improvised, the violin in our performance has no way of knowing what the voice will sing—thus the leader-follower arrangement. The voice improvises according to the guidelines of the *raga,* and the violin imitates what the voice sings. The *alapana* serves another significant function: it introduces the *raga* on which the work is based. Just as we saw in the north Indian *alap,* the *alapana*'s free rhythm and slow speed provide the best context for exploring and exposing the most subtle features of a particular *raga.* Typical events in the *alapana* include the establishment of the most significant pitches of the *raga,* traversal of the *raga*'s typical ascending and descending melodic patterns, and exploration of the entire melodic range. Once students grasp these concepts, play all of section 1.

If you have time, this is a good place to introduce the primary pitches of the *varali raga,* on which this piece is based. The Western equivalents of these pitches are as follows:

F   G flat   G   B   C   D flat   E   F

Play through the entire scale, but home in on the most interesting notes—the first three scale steps. This half-step pattern gives the work a distinctive flavor, and the singer often approaches her cadences by descending from G to G flat to F, sometimes at slow speed, as if delaying the arrival of the F. After introducing the *raga* pitches, sound out the bottom three pitches along with the singer as you play the recording of section 1.

Section 2—Here the singer introduces the *kriti.* (Many of the terms used here were described in greater detail in the material above titled "The *Kriti.*") Call attention to the text as printed in the Additonal Listening Chart. Point out the sections labeled "refrain" and "verse," and note the return of the *pallavi* following the *anupallavi* (at 2:18). This *pallavi-anupallavi-pallavi* grouping is typical of the first section of a *kriti* composition. As described above, the *pallavi* inhabits a somewhat lower register than the *anupallavi;* thus, the return of the *pallavi* relaxes some of the tension built up by the *anupallavi.*

Make sure students hear the effect of *sangati* in the *pallavi.* As described above, *sangati*s are the varied repetitions of the basic phrase. Each new statement of the phrase becomes more elaborate. First the singer introduces more and more florid ornamentation, then she layers new and more extended motives over the basic phrase framework. *Sangati*s are a significant feature of the *kriti,* and students can hear their effect without much difficulty. Play through the beginning of section 2 until students grasp the concept.

Make students aware that section 2 is the one precomposed section of this work. Point out how this explains many of the features you discovered in the initial listening exercise for this piece. The use of heterophony between voice and violin now makes sense. When the violin followed vocal improvisation, it had to hear the voice before playing. Now both voice and violin know the tune; the violin can play along. The use of words and the more regular phrase lengths also point to the composed nature of this section.

Section 3—Here the music returns to a freely improvised section, another example of *anibaddha.* The addition and interpolation of such sections remains a common feature of Indian musical performances. This section requires great virtuosity on the part of the performer; not only must she improvise an elaborate melody at fast tempo, but she must also sing the appropriate scale names for the main pitches of her melody. This style of vocal improvisation is known as *kalpana svara,* the term *svara* referring to scale degrees. Given this section's speed and improvised nature, it is nearly impossible for the violin to participate as it did in the previous two sections. It drops out, and it has barely begun an elaborate solo improvisation of its own when the excerpt from *Listen: Brief Fourth Edition* fades out. Note one last detail: Just at the end of the vocal improvisation, the singer returns to the opening phrase of the *anupallavi,* "Parama-purusha!" In this case, the *anupallavi,* not the *pallavi,* serves the role of a refrain.

Once students sense the overall context of this work, play the entire performance one more time. Call attention to each feature from the Additional Listening Chart as it goes by.

Whether you use the recording from the fourth edition of *Listen* or the CD from Sound Recordings below, you will not hear Tyagaraja's entire *kriti*—even the "complete" recording below fails to present his *caranam* (verse). This version more closely resembles an actual Carnatic *raga* performance, in which the singer often quotes a well-known *kriti* in the metered section immediately following the *alapana,* using it as the melodic basis for further improvisation. Of course, even a complete *kriti* performance would begin with an *alapana* and interpolate improvised sections like the *kalpana svara* heard here.

As we learned in looking at the north Indian *raga,* even composed portions of a musical work are subject to embellishment and variation. The *sangati*s based on the first phrase of the *pallavi* offer an example of this, reflecting the input of several generations of performers, including the current one. This additive approach can be disconcerting to Western musicians. A composition thus serves more as a performance framework than a fixed work, and this fact in no way diminishes the respect accorded a great composer like Tyagaraja. Once again, we find an unfamiliar understanding of the relationship between a musical performance and a musical composition.

Multimedia Resources

¶ Further Listening Charts and Texts

See Appendix I for Listening Charts for these works:

Mozart, Variations on "Ah vous dirai-je, maman" for piano, K. 265. See Further Listening Examples above for lecture suggestions on this example of theme and variations form.

Mozart, Piano Concerto No. 17 in G, K. 453, I. See Listening Idea 1 above if you use this alternate example of classical double-exposition form.

Mozart, Piano Concerto No. 17 in G, K. 453, III. See Further Listening Examples above for lecture suggestions on this example of the Classical concerto and theme and variations form.

Beethoven, String Quartet in A, Op. 18, No. 5, II. See Further Listening Examples above for lecture suggestions on this example of the string quartet genre.

Mozart, *Don Giovanni,* Overture. See Further Listening Examples above for lecture suggestions on this example of an opera overture.

Rag *Mauj-Khammaj.* See Further Listening Examples above for lecture suggestions on this Hindustani *raga.*

Tyagaraja, "Marakata manivarna." See Further Listening Examples above for lecture suggestions on this Carnatic *kriti.*

See Appendix II for texts and translations for this work:

Mozart, *Don Giovanni,* Act II Finale, Scene 15, "Don Giovanni! a cenar teco." See Further Listening Examples above for lecture suggestions on this example of an operatic ensemble.

♩ Sound Recordings

Anthology of Indian Classical Music: A Tribute to Alain Daniélou. Auvidis/ UNESCO D 8270 (CD). Excellent collection of north and south Indian music features performances by great artists such as Ravi Shankar, Ali Akbar Khan, and D. K. Pattamal. Detailed, informative booklet included. Highly recommended for *any* Indian music collection; it also contains both of the Indian examples in Further Listening Examples above—Rag *Mauj-Khammaj* and Tyagaraja's "Marakata manivarna."

Bach, *Les Six Concerts Brandebourgeois.* Le Concert des Nations/Capella Reial de Catalunya. Auvidis Astrée 9948 (CD). The *Brandenburg* recording used in the *Listen* set. This set includes all six concertos on period instruments; conducted by Jordi Savall. Try this recording if you use Listening Idea 1 above.

Bali: Gamelan and Kecak. Various ensembles. Elektra/Nonesuch Explorer Series 9 79204–2 (CD). Sampling of music for several gamelan ensembles, including *gamelan selundeng, gendèr wayang, gong kebyar,* and a vocal *kecak* ensemble. Try this recording if you use Listening Idea 7 above.

Beethoven, *Quatuors Opus 18 No. 5 & 6.* Quatuor Mosaïques. Astrée Auvidis E 8541 (CD). Gracious, charming period-instrument performances enlivened by a gentle yet firm rhythmic "spring" and crafted so that each detail of the score can be heard. Beethoven's Classical heritage speaks clearly in these works, yet the performers make sure we hear those moments of tension and drama with equal aplomb. Use this complete recording of Op. 18, No. 5 to demonstrate Beethoven's use of the quartet's four-movement plan, or if you use Listening Idea 3 or suggestions for this work in Further Listening Examples above.

Britten, *The Prince of the Pagodas.* London Sinfonietta. Virgin EMI VCD7 59578-2 (CD). Brilliant recording of an orchestral work influenced by the gamelan orchestras Britten heard on his 1955 trip to Bali: conducted by Oliver Knussen. Try this recording if you use Listening Idea 9 above.

Chine: Musique Ancienne de Chang'an [China: Ancient Music of Xian]. Ensemble of the High Conservatory of Xian. Inedit W 260036 (CD). Modern recreation of orchestral music from the T'ang dynasty, the same music that influenced the beginnings of the Japanese *gagaku* tradition. This music underwent many changes during Japan's feudal era, and modern *gagaku* sounds rather different than its Chinese forebear, but it is fascinating to make comparisons nonetheless.

Davis, Miles. *Kind of Blue.* Miles Davis Sextet. Columbia/Legacy CK 64935 (CD). Classic modal-jazz recording is on every jazz critic's ten-best list. Use this recording if you try Listening Idea 5 above.

Davis, Miles. *Live-Evil.* Columbia/Legacy C2K 65135 (CD). Jazz-rock fusion classic. Use this recording if you try Listening Idea 6 above.

Don Giovanni. Great Operas at the Met Series. New York: Metropolitan Opera Guild Video Service (CD or cassette). Highlights from great Metropolitan Opera productions of *Don Giovanni.* Singers include Della Casa, Farrar, Gadski, Gigli, Lehmann, Pini-Corsi, Pinza, Price, Ramey, Sayão, Scotti, Siepi, Steber, Sutherland, Welitsch, and others. This series permits comparison of different performances; students can compare singers, styles of singing, and different approaches to acting and interpretation.

Ellis, Don. *"Live" at Monterey*. Don Ellis Orchestra. Blue Note 94768 (CD). Don Ellis's experiments with electronics and rhythm constitute an important chapter in jazz history. Especially interesting are the works on this album that use *tala*-like meters: "33 222 1 222" and "27/16." Try this recording if you use Further Listening Example Rag *Mauj-Khammaj* above.

Gagaku: The Imperial Court Music of Japan. Kyoto Imperial Court Music Orchestra. Lyrichord LYRCD 7126 (CD). Performances of *Etenraku* (from the *Listen* recordings) and seven other works from the *gagaku* repertory. Try this recording if you want to explore this style.

Gagaku: Japanese Traditional Music. Kunaicho Gakubu. King Record Co. KICH 2001 (CD). Excellent, authentic performances by the Music Department of the Imperial Household Agency, the Japanese government orchestra chiefly responsible for maintaining this ancient tradition for use in official ceremonies. Recording includes another performance of *Etenraku* and four other extended examples. Extensive liner notes in Japanese; three worthwhile pages in English by expert Allan Marett. Good CD if you want to explore more of this music with your students.

Gamelan Music of Bali. Lyrichord LYRCD 7179 (CD). Features recordings of two Balinese ensembles, the older *gamelan angklung* and the more recent, more virtuosic *gong kebyar*. Try this recording if you use Listening Idea 7 above.

Harrison, Lou. *La Koro Sutro*. American Gamelan & U.C. Berkeley Chorus. New Albion Records NA 015 (CD). Associated with Cage and the percussionists in the 1930s, Harrison incorporates many world musics into his own unique style. This CD includes two works that feature the American Gamelan ensemble, and his suite offers fascinating comparisons with Baroque music. Use this recording if you try Listening Idea 8 or 9 above.

Haydn, *The London Symphonies*, Vol. 1. Royal Concertgebouw Orchestra. Philips 442 611-2 (CD). First-class modern-instrument performances of late Haydn symphonies, including 95, 96, 98, 102, 103, and 104; conducted by Colin Davis. Try this recording if you use Class Discussion Idea 3 or Listening Idea 1 above.

Haydn, *Symphonies Nos. 88, 89, and 90*. Tafelmusik. Sony Classical Vivarte SK 66253 (CD). Outstanding period-instrument performances of three late Haydn symphonies supervised by H. C. Robbins Landon; conducted by Bruno Weil. Try this recording if you use Listening Idea 1 above.

McPhee, Colin. *Balinese Ceremonial Music*. Colin McPhee and Benjamin Britten. Pearl PEA 9177 (CD). More recent performances are available, but this one is an important historical document. Try this recording if you use Listening Idea 9 above.

Mozart, *Complete Piano Variations*. Ronald Brautigam. Bis 1266/7 (CD). Part of Brautigam's outstanding Mozart series on fortepiano, this CD includes the Variations on "Ah vous dirai-je, maman," K. 265/300e. Try this recording if you use suggestions for this set of variations from Further Listening Examples above.

Mozart, *Concerti 17 and 18*. Murray Perahia and the English Chamber Orchestra. CBS Masterworks MK 36686 (CD). One of the best modern-instrument performances available; conducted by the soloist. Perahia, who plays with great sensitivity, is one of the finest Mozart interpreters around. Try this recording if you use Listening Idea 1 or suggestions on the third movement of Piano Concerto No. 17 from Further Listening Examples above.

Mozart, *Don Giovanni*. Orchestra of the Royal Opera House. Philips 422 541-2 (CD). Featured on the *Listen* set, this excellent recording from the 1970s boasts a starry cast that includes Ingvar Wixell, Kiri Te Kanawa, and Mirella Freni. To top it off, conductor Sir Colin Davis leads an exceptionally dramatic reading. Recommended if you try Listening Idea 2 or suggestions on *Don Giovanni* from Further Listening Examples above.

Mozart, *Die Entführung aus dem Serail*. English Baroque Soloists. Deutsche Grammophon Archiv 435 857-2 (CD). Recommended recording of Mozart's "Turkish" *Singspiel* on period instruments; conducted by John Eliot Gardiner. Use this recording if you try Class Discussion Idea 3 above.

Mozart, *Don Giovanni*. English Baroque Soloists. Deutsche Grammophon Archiv 445 870-2 (CD). Excellent recent recording of Mozart's great opera on period instruments. Singers include Rodney Gilfry, Andrea Silvestrelli, Luba Orgonasova, Christoph Prégardien, Charlotte Margiono, Ildebrando D'Arcangelo; conducted by John Eliot Gardiner. Highly recommended. Use this recording if you try Listening Idea 2 or suggestions on *Don Giovanni* from Further Listening Examples above.

Mozart, *The Piano Concertos*. English Baroque Soloists. Deutsche Grammophon Archiv 463 111-2 (CD). Concertos 5 to 27 in excellent period instrument performances by soloist Malcolm Bilson; conducted by John Eliot Gardiner. Try this recording to compare with the modern-instrument recording in the *Listen* set or if you use Listening Idea 1.

Mozart, *Les Quatuors dédiés à Haydn III: K. 464 & K. 465*. Mosaïques Quartet. Astrée Auvidis E 8845 (CD). Wonderful period-instrument performances of two of the quartets Mozart dedicated to Haydn. Beethoven, in turn, modeled his Op. 18, No. 5 quartet after Mozart's Quartet No. 18 in A, K. 464. Try this recording if you use Listening Idea 3 above.

Mozart, *Sonatas, Volume I*. Malcolm Bilson. Hungaroton HCD 31009-10 (CD). Stylish performances of Mozart's complete piano sonatas by one of the foremost fortepiano specialists. Try volume I if you use Class Discussion Idea 3 or suggestions from Further Listening Examples above on the Piano Sonata in A, K. 331. If you want to hear the Piano Sonata in B-flat, K. 570 from Further Listening Examples above, try volume II (Hungaroton HCD 31011-12).

Mozart, *Symphonies Nos. 40 and 41*. Vienna Philharmonic. Deutsche Grammophon 445 548-2 (CD). Dramatic modern-instrument performances of Mozart's two late symphonies; conducted by Leonard Bernstein. Try this recording if you use Listening Idea 1 above.

Music for the Mozart Effect, Vol. 1: *Strengthen the Mind*. Spring Hill Music SHM 6501-2 (CD). Recordings compiled and sequenced by Don Campbell, author of the best-selling book, to take full advantage of the "Mozart effect." Multiple volumes and spin-off recordings are now available. Try this recording if you use Class Discussion Idea 4 above.

Music of Bali: Gamelan Semar Pegulingan. Village of Ketewel Gamelan Club. Lyrichord LYRCD 7408 (CD). Devoted to music by a gamelan associated with Balinese princely courts. Contains the recording of *Bopong* found in the *Listen* set. Some inaccuracies in the liner notes.

Pieces of Africa. Kronos Quartet. Elektra/Nonesuch 9 79275-2 (CD). Fascinating recording offers music for traditional string quartet written by contemporary composers from Zimbabwe, Morocco, Gambia, Uganda, Ghana, Sudan, and South Africa. Many of these works add voices or indigenous African instruments to the traditional string quartet, and some use elaborate rhythms and ostinato patterns. Use this recording if you try Lecture-Demonstration Idea 3 above.

Schubert, *Quatuors D 87 & D 804 "Rosamunde."* Quatuor Mosaïques. Astrée Auvidis E 8580 (CD). Lovely performances by this superb period-instrument ensemble. Highly recommended if you want a complete recording of the String Quartet in A Minor for the guessing game described above in Lecture Suggestions.

Shankar, Ravi. *The Sounds of India.* Columbia CK 9296 (CD). Older, monaural recording of Shankar playing northern Indian ragas. Especially valuable for Shankar's four-minute "Introduction to Indian Music." He mixes words and musical examples to introduce important concepts such as *raga* and *tala.* Shankar further introduces the specific *tala* and the ascending and descending patterns for each *raga* he plays. Highly recommended as a supplement to the Indian *raga* and *kriti* in Further Listening Examples above.

♪ Video Recordings

Amadeus. Warner Brothers (DVD or VHS, color, 160 minutes). The award-winning movie (1984 Academy Award for Best Picture) based on Peter Shaffer's Tony Award–winning play has done more to rekindle interest in Mozart than any other event in recent memory. It presents Mozart's music in period settings, with fascinating insights into the compositional process and political maneuvering in eighteenth-century Vienna. A twenty-minute-longer "Director's Cut" is now available, but outside of making explicit Mozart's infidelities and Constanze's willingness to do whatever it took to help Wolfie's career, it adds little. Try this video if you use Lecture-Demonstration Idea 1 above.

Bach, P. D. Q., *Abduction of Figaro.* Video Arts International (VHS, color, 144 minutes). Performed by the Minnesota Opera, Chorus, and "Corpse" de Ballet; conducted by Peter Schickele. This modern spoof offers a buffo look at opera buffa. Plays with the conventions and characters of Classical opera buffa and of Mozart's operas in particular. This may prove too much to sort through for a music appreciation course, but you could easily substitute an audio recording of P. D. Q. Bach's half-act opera *The Stoned Guest,* a take-off on Mozart's *Don Giovanni* (subtitled *The Stone Guest*).

Baraka. MPI Home Video (DVD, color, 104 minutes). This movie tries to do for the rest of the world what *Koyaanisqatsi* did for the United States. It offers spectacular photography and even several examples of music making. Most of these music clips are too brief to be useful, but the longest one—a fascinating example of Balinese *kecak* singing—can work well here.

Colin McPhee: The Lure of Asian Music. (VHS, color, 58 minutes). Video follows the life and work of musicologist and composer Colin McPhee, one of the leading experts on Balinese music. Highly recommended.

Discovering the Music of Japan. www.insight-media.com (VHS, color, 22 minutes). 1967 film provides a brief introduction to the music and instruments of Japan.

Gagaku: The Court Music of Japan. University of Oklahoma (VHS, color, 29 minutes). Wonderful introduction to the world of *gagaku.* Narrated by William Malm and Sidney Brown, the program features demonstrations on each instrument and performances of several works, including an excerpt from the *Listen* example, *Etenraku.* Usually gregarious, Malm seems a bit uncomfortable in front of the camera, but that does not diminish the value of this video; use it if at all possible! Available from www.worldmusicstore.com.

The Isle of Temples: Bali. www.insight-media.com (VHS, color, 30 minutes). Filled with examples of gamelan music, this video offers folk songs and dance-dramas.

JVC Video Anthology of Japanese Classical Performing Arts. Barre, Vt.: Multicultural Media (VHS, color, 25 tapes). This landmark anthology contains examples of all major genres from the Japanese classical tradition, including *gagaku, noh,* and *kabuki.* Two accompanying videos cover Japanese musical instruments, and two large books (in Japanese) provide background material and describe each performance.

JVC Video Anthology of World Music and Dance. Tapes 9 and 10 from this excellent video series offer music from Bali. Tape 9 provides examples of different gamelan ensembles; of particular interest is example 9-4, a *legong* dance. Highly recommended for your presentation of Global Perspectives materials for this chapter.

Koto: Music in Praise. www.films.com (VHS, color, 48 minutes). Interviews with Hideaki Kuribayashi cover the history and techniques of koto music. Video also includes concert footage.

Mozart, *Concerto for Flute and Harp, K. 299. Concerto!* Series. www.films.com (DVD or VHS, color, 60 minutes). Dudley Moore narrates this look at the Classical concerto. Contains rehearsal footage, discussions between soloists and conductor, and a complete performance of the concerto. Soloists James Galway and Marisa Robles perform with the London Symphony; conducted by Michael Tilson Thomas. Try this video if you use Listening Idea 1 above.

Mozart, *Don Giovanni.* Deutsche Grammophon (DVD, color, 180 minutes). The highlight of this Metropolitan Opera production is Bryn Terfel's assumption of the title role. In the very first scene he murders Donna Anna's father with a relish that is truly frightening, and he continues to command the stage throughout the opera. James Levine draws a dramatic reading from his Met orchestra. Try this video whether you use Lecture Suggestions or Further Listening Examples above.

Mozart, *Don Giovanni.* Columbia Tristar (DVD or VHS, color, 177 minutes). Losey's movie version films *Don Giovanni* on location in Vicenza, Italy. Some viewers will appreciate the movie-like feel; others may miss the immediacy of the stage experience. Performed by Ruggiero Raimondi, Kiri Te Kanawa, Edda Moser, and José Van Dam; conducted by Lorin Maazel. Try this video whether you use Lecture Suggestions or Further Listening Examples above.

Mozart, *Don Giovanni.* Arthaus Musik (DVD, color, 187 minutes). Zurich Opera production of Mozart's classic *dramma giocoso* features soloists Rodney Gilfry, Laszlo Polgar, Isabel Rey, Cecilia Bartoli, and Matti Salminen; conducted by Nikolaus Harnoncourt. This production highlights the compulsiveness of Giovanni's actions, and Bartoli brings a deep humanity to Donna Elvira, fully conveying her conflicting emotions. Recommended for use with Lecture Suggestions or Further Listening Examples above.

Mozart: Dropping the Patron. Man and Music Series. www.films.com (DVD or VHS, color, 53 minutes). Looks at Mozart's employment with the Archbishop of Salzburg and his departure for Vienna to further his career. Includes musical excerpts from Mozart's Wind Serenade in E-flat, K. 375; Violin Sonata in G, K. 379; *Die Entführung aus dem Serail*; Terzet, K. 436; Piano Concerto in E-flat, K. 449; String Quartet in B-flat (*Hunt*), K. 458; and *Le Nozze di Figaro*.

Mozart: A Genius in His Time. Man and Music Series. www.films.com (DVD or VHS, color, 53 minutes). Covers the last five years of Mozart's life; looks at his troubles with patrons and audiences. Musical excerpts from the String Quintet in G Minor, K. 516; *Eine kleine Nachtmusik*; Violin Sonata in A, K. 526; Symphony No. 41 in C (*Jupiter*); *Così fan tutte*; and *Die Zauberflöte*.

Mozart, *The Magic Flute*. The Criterion Collection (DVD or VHS, 135 minutes, color). Ingmar Bergman's charming, acclaimed 1975 film version of Mozart's greatest *Singspiel*. Performed by Håkan Hågcgard, Ragner Ulfung, et al.; conducted by Eric Ericson. *Note:* It is sung in Swedish, and Bergman made several cuts, changed the order of scenes, abbreviated the dialogue, and in some instances altered the libretto (always interested in family dynamics, Bergman makes Sarastro the Queen of the Night's ex-husband and Pamina's father!). Nonetheless, Bergman never loses sight of the essence of Mozart's *Singspiel,* and this remains one of the most convincing movie opera performances ever released.

Mozart, *Le Nozze di Figaro*. Deutsche Grammophon Archiv (DVD, color, 169 minutes). Students love this lively, witty production of *Figaro,* as well acted as it is well sung! Part of conductor John Eliot Gardiner's series of wonderful period performances of Mozart operas, it features soloists Alison Hagley, Hillevi Martinpelto, Rodney Gilfry, and Bryn Terfel. Performed by the English Baroque Soloists. Highest recommendation.

Mozart: Overture to "The Marriage of Figaro." The Score Series. www.films .com (DVD or VHS, color, 15 minutes). This brief video focuses on orchestral colors and effects used to create contrast and enrich the texture. Excerpts performed by the Scottish Chamber Orchestra; conducted by William Conway.

Mozart, Beethoven, and Brahms, *Piano Concertos*. Deutsche Grammophon (DVD, color, 180 minutes). This two-DVD set offers a bonanza of Classical and Romantic piano concertos. Especially useful for *Listen* are the Mozart Concerto in A, K. 488, and Beethoven's *Emperor* Concerto (*Listen* DVD). Pianist Maurizio Pollini offers a polished performance with fire where needed. Karl Böhm leads the Vienna Philharmonic in typically magisterial performances. Recommended for your presentation on this concerto from *Listen* or if you use Listening Idea 1 above.

[Mozart, Piano Concerto in G Major, K. 453, I.] *Delaware Music Series* www.ecsmedia.com (DVD). Performance by fortepianist Penelope Crawford with Ars Musica; conducted by first violinist Lyndon Lawless. This important collection includes a complete performance of the first movement on period instruments with two of Mozart's own cadenzas, a reduced four-line scrolling score, color-coded formal analysis, and demonstrations of period instruments. Superb resource for lecture-demonstration on the concerto and double-exposition form. Highly recommended if you use Listening Idea 1 or as a companion to suggestions for the third movement from Further Listening Examples above.

[Mozart, Quintet for Clarinet and Strings, K. 581, I.] *Delaware Music Series* (NEH Videodisc Project). www.ecsmedia.com (DVD). Performance by clarinetist Peter Hill with the Delos String Quartet. This important collection includes a scrolling full score with harmonic analysis, a melodic contour map, and analysis of melodic ornaments. Superb resource for lecture-demonstration on chamber music genres.

Mozart, *Die Zauberflöte*. Deutsche Grammophon (DVD, color, 160 minutes). There are no ideal video recordings of Mozart's final *Singspiel,* but this one is as good as any with its strong cast, attractive staging, and abundant charm. The singers include such distinguished Mozarteans as Kurt Moll, Edita Gruberova, Lucia Popp, and Francesco Araiza; conductor Wolfgang Sawallisch leads the Bavarian State Opera Orchestra in a simply superb performance. The one thing that might give offense is the minstrel-show-style blackface used for Monostatos and the servants. Try this video to show another side of Mozart's operatic personality.

Ravi Shankar in Portrait. BBC Opus Arte (DVD, color, 190 minutes). A DVD to treasure! Disc 1, "Ravi Shankar Between Two Worlds," provides a video documentary of Shankar's life filled with interviews and historic archival footage going back to the 1930s. Disc 2, "Ravi Shankar in Concert," features a 2002 live performance with daughter Anoushka, Bikram Ghosh, and Tanmoy Bose. Extras include Shankar's excellent twenty-minute introduction to the sitar and Indian music, and footage of Shankar working with a student. Highly recommended.

Vienna. Music in Time Series. www.films.com (DVD or VHS, color, 60 minutes). Looks at Vienna in the late eighteenth and early nineteenth centuries. Special emphasis on operas and symphonies by Mozart. Schubert works also included. Music by Mozart includes excerpts from the Requiem ("Dies irae" and "Lachrymosa"); Andante in C Major; Piano Concerto, K. 414; the Haffner Serenade; Piano Concerto, K. 459; *Don Giovanni;* Symphony No. 38 in D (*Prague*); and *Così fan tutte* (Act I Finale).

♪ Software

The Norton Masterworks CD-ROM. New York: W. W. Norton (CD-ROM—Macintosh). Authors Daniel Jacobson and Timothy Koozin provide a clever multimedia introduction to twelve important works, including Mozart's *Eine kleine Nachtmusik.* Features animated, guided listening resources as well as information on the composers, eras, genres, and the works themselves.

Raga: An Interactive Guide into Indian Classical Music. Navras (CD-ROM—Windows). This package offers video demonstrations, text, sound clips, and an instruction module. You can sample the sounds of fifty-four different *ragas,* fifteen *talas,* and twelve instruments. Available from the World Music Institute (www.heartheworld.org).

CHAPTER 14

Beethoven

Chapter Outline

Boldface indicates works in the recording set.

Important Terms

French Revolution	motivic consistency	fragmentation
Eroica Symphony	psychological progression	rhythmic motive
rhythmic drive	scherzo	third-period style

Teaching Objectives

Overall Objectives

This chapter will help students acquire familiarity with:

1. The transition from Classicism to Romanticism and the ideological impact of the French Revolution.

2. The life of Ludwig van Beethoven.

3. Beethoven's transformation of the symphony.

4. The music of Beethoven's three style periods.

❧ Listening Objectives

After completing this chapter, students should be able to:

1. Hear and identify features of Beethoven's style, especially rhythmic drive, motivic consistency, and psychological progression.

2. Follow a Beethoven symphony and identify a scherzo.

3. Recognize important features of Beethoven's "third-period style."

Lecture Suggestions

❧ Between Classicism and Romanticism

In the words of Donald Grout, "Beethoven was one of the great disruptive forces in the history of music."[1] Beethoven was at once a child of the Classical age and a man of the Romantic era. His basic artistic tenet—that music was a mode of *self-expression*—changed forever the face of Western art and music and helped to spur the development of Romanticism.

The Baroque composer thought of himself or herself as a craftsperson, with a job to do and a master to satisfy. Like other artisans—bricklayers, window makers, chefs—he or she produced on demand to fill a particular requirement. During the Baroque, there were three institutions where a composer could make a living. These were the church, the court, and the opera house.

The late eighteenth century was a period of transition for composers. While the church, the court, and the opera house were still the main employers, new possibilities for support were emerging. The rise of the public concert hall proved a significant boon for composers. Mozart, despite guaranteed church employment through the Archbishop of Salzburg, chose to move to Vienna, where he tried to support himself through public concerts and private teaching. Haydn, after a long period of court employment at the Esterházy estate, scored tremendous successes in both England and Vienna through public concertizing. Unfortunately, public concerts were not a resource for Haydn until late in his career, and they were not adequate to sustain Mozart in the 1780s.

Would Beethoven have been able to function in the patronage system as it existed in the 1770s and 1780s? Probably not. It is hard to imagine Beethoven dining at the servants' table, as Haydn did for decades with the Esterházy family. It is equally difficult to imagine Beethoven taking orders from an archbishop who disdained music, as Mozart did before leaving Salzburg. After leaving Salzburg, Mozart depended on Viennese aristocrats for his support, and his career's downturns resulted from their casual rejection of his music. Mozart was powerless to change the situation when he "fell out of style"—he was, after all, just a writer of music, a servant to the upper classes. Sadly, Mozart's failing health ended his life just when his career was changing for the better.

Beethoven also depended on the Viennese aristocracy for financial support, but his relationship with the upper class was very different from Mozart's. This resulted from Beethoven's personality, his shrewd business sense, and the

---

[1]Donald Grout and Claude Palisca, *A History of Western Music*, 5th ed. New York: W. W. Norton, 1996, p. 560.

changing times. Before the French Revolution, the patron-composer relationship was a master-servant relationship. After the Revolution, Beethoven, the creator, granted his patrons limited friendship. In fact, Beethoven insisted on being called a *Tondichter* ("tone-poet") instead of a *Komponist* ("composer"). As a poet he could demand the respect and esteem accorded to writers such as Goethe; as a composer he would have been doomed to eat with the butlers, maids, and cooks. It worked; the Viennese upper class tripped over each other scrambling to help Beethoven.

Could Beethoven have sustained such a relationship with the upper classes before the French Revolution? Probably not. Beethoven was able to write slowly, to express himself, and to try out new modes of musical expression because he lived in a society that provided him the means to do so. Vienna was imbued with a heady sense of freedom, hope, danger, and newness brought about by the French Revolution and the new century. Beethoven found himself the right man in the right place at the right time.

Beethoven and the Symphony

Perhaps you took the time to work through an entire symphony in Chapter 12. If so, your students can measure Beethoven's deviations from Haydn's "norm." If not, now is the time. In a textbook such as this one, breadth is necessarily emphasized over depth, but it is important for students to have the experience of digging deeply into at least one composer or one work; Beethoven must be that composer, and his Symphony No. 5 must be that work. The first movement illustrates Beethoven's motivic consistency, rhythmic drive, and expansion of sonata form; the slow movement employs an unusual theme and variations form; the third movement illustrates the scherzo; and the four movements together demonstrate the psychological progression of movements within the four-movement plan that characterizes Beethoven's mature work. It is entirely appropriate to spend at least three class hours on Beethoven.

A list of basic orchestral repertoire would be unthinkable without Beethoven's nine symphonies. Starting with Symphony No. 3 (*Eroica*), Beethoven completely transformed the genre into a more monumental, more cohesive, more powerful, and more personal mode of musical expression than it had been during the eighteenth century. The three elements that Beethoven brought to the genre of the symphony and to much of his music were a new, incredibly intense rhythmic drive, motivic consistency, and a psychological progression from movement to movement.

BEETHOVEN Symphony No. 5 in C Minor, Op. 67, I

Before you begin, write two diagrams on the board:

Sonata-form diagram from Chapter 12 of this manual (page 250)

Symphony four-movement plan diagram from Chapter 12 of this manual (page 248)

Rhythmic Drive

Play the following two excerpts from the recorded anthology:

Mozart, Symphony No. 40 in G Minor, K. 550, I (track 16, 0:00–0:32)

Beethoven, Symphony No. 5 in C Minor, Op. 67, I (track 5)

Both of the excerpts constitute the first theme of a sonata-form movement. Each theme is "dramatic" relative to its composer's compositional language. Each theme comes from the first movement of the symphony. Each symphony is considered a "tragic" work. Both themes are in minor mode. Yet with so much in common, these two works differ sharply in their dramatic impact. Ask the following questions:

How are they different?

How does each composer create a sense of drama?

Which theme seems more dramatic to our ears? Why?

In the discussion that follows, draw out these points: Mozart's darkly elegant theme creates a sense of unsatisfied yearning and anxiety. Beethoven's theme, on the other hand, produces a palpable physical impact. Its primal ferocity grows from the insistent reiteration of the opening four-note motive. Play or sing this motive for the class. What makes it so powerful? It is the *rhythm*—three short, repeated notes followed by a longer one—that gives this motive its incredible power. Compared with Mozart's elegant, melodic theme, Beethoven's is like a series of hammer blows.

Motivic Consistency

Beethoven's extraordinary motivic consistency is nowhere more easily demonstrated than in the first movement of his Symphony No. 5. Take time to work through the entire exposition and point out motivic relationships. Beethoven begins by stating the motive as directly and forcefully as possible—using strings (and clarinets) without accompaniment of any kind. Note that there are two aspects to Beethoven's motive: rhythm and pitch. The motive's rhythmic shape (short-short-short-long) is more obvious and easier to recognize than its pitch shape.

The musical examples from textbook page 231 do a nice job of pointing out the appearance of the rhythmic motive in each main section of the exposition:

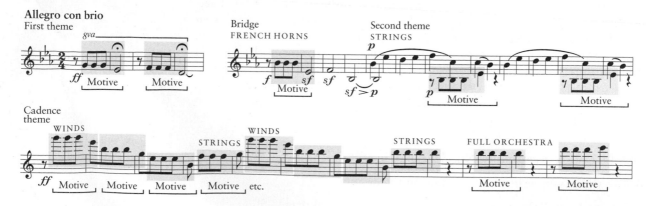

First Theme—The first theme begins with two statements of the rhythmic motive, and its continuation creates a melody as the motive is tossed from violin 2 to viola to violin 1 (mm. 6–9). Play the first phrase for the class (track 5, 0:00–0:07). It is easy to hear how these three separate, distinct motivic statements make up the first phrase of theme 1. Beethoven continues to build all of theme 1 using statements and variations of the basic motive. Play all of theme 1 (track 5).

Bridge—Only six notes long, it states the rhythmic motive once and tacks on two notes at the end. Play the bridge (track 6, 0:00–0:02).

Second Theme—Here, Beethoven uses the rhythmic motive more subtly, as accompaniment to the theme at cadence points (*sol-sol-sol-do*). Play theme 2 (track 6, 0:02–0:30).

Cadence Theme—Like theme 1, it consists of many statements of the rhythmic motive strung together, with especially forceful statements at the very end (mm. 117–22). Play the cadence theme (track 7, 0:00–0:08).

As you can see, the rhythmic motive pervades the entire exposition.

The pitch shape of the motive leads to more subtle but equally important thematic connections. In the first statement of the rhythmic motive, it is easy enough to hear that the short notes repeat the same pitch (G) and the long note states a lower pitch (E flat). In subsequent statements of the rhythmic motive, we often leap down (but not always the same distance) to the fourth note, we sometimes leap or step up, and we sometimes repeat the same note four times. This tells us that the rhythmic shape is the primary element defining the motive for the listener, and that Beethoven treats pitch as a more plastic, adaptable element.

If we limit the pitch motive to the four notes of the rhythmic motive alone, we miss important motivic-thematic connections, as theorist Heinrich Schenker pointed out in his analysis of this movement.[2] The pitch component of Beethoven's motive is a four-pitch group taken from the first two statements of the rhythmic motive: G–E flat–F–D. Note the sequential repetition—the last two pitches repeat the pattern of the first two pitches, but a step lower.

First theme

Play these four pitches until students hear their relationship clearly. The many permutations of this motive take us into advanced musical analysis far beyond the ability or interest of most in an appreciation class, but the motive affects one passage of particular interest. The bridge and theme 2 are both based on the four-pitch motive.

Play this passage for the class. As stated above, Beethoven treats pitch as a plastic, adaptable element. Consider the shape of the original four-pitch motive: The outer two intervals (G to E flat and F to D) are descending leaps, an example of sequential repetition; the middle interval steps up (E flat to F). Consider the bridge theme: The outer two intervals (B flat to E flat and F to B flat) are descending leaps, again an example of sequential repetition; and the middle interval steps up (E flat to F). The only difference? The descending leaps are larger in the bridge theme, but note that they hinge on the same E flat to F step that we heard in measures 2–3! To help us make this connection between theme 1 and the bridge theme, Beethoven begins the bridge with theme 1's

---

[2] This analysis is contained in Elliot Forbes's *Norton Critical Scores* edition of Beethoven's Symphony No. 5, New York: Norton, 1971, pp. 164–82.

rhythmic motive (after a short, pregnant pause).³ It is interesting to note that when the pitch sequence repeats (the third and fourth pitches, F to B flat), Beethoven does not repeat the rhythmic motive, as if to lessen the rhythmic urgency in preparation for theme 2's more relaxed lyricism.

Beethoven is not content to stop with the bridge, however; he shapes an even more subtle permutation. Once he has stretched the intervals of theme 1 to create the bridge, he takes the bridge theme and embellishes it to create theme 2. The pitches of the bridge theme are virtually the same as the pitches of the first four measures of theme 2 (the first interval is inverted). Play this passage for the class again. The rhythm and mood of the two themes are entirely different, but Beethoven only needed two embellishing pitches to effect the transformation, as the following diagram shows:

Bridge theme:　　**B flat–E flat– – – – – – –F– – – – –B flat**

Second theme:　　**B flat–E flat–(D)–E flat–F–(C–C)–B flat**

Incredible! Every major theme in the exposition is based on the first four measures of the piece. No matter how deeply we delve into the music, the motive is present. It is as if Beethoven challenged himself to see how much music he could make out of four short measures—a rhythmic motive and four pitches. The resulting music guides us from transformation to transformation according to its own internal, commonsense logic. Beethoven constructs his musical argument so carefully that we can almost follow his thought process as he moves from one idea to the next. Leonard Bernstein pointed out that every move Beethoven makes feels right. No other options would work as well; that's where the music *should* go next! One can talk all day about Beethoven's rhythmic drive, motivic consistency, or carefully constructed musical forms—these terms certainly describe Beethoven's music, though they describe many pieces by Haydn as well—but that brings us no closer to understanding the eternal "rightness" of Beethoven's music or the inexplicable force that draws us back to it again and again.

Work through the first movement of Beethoven's Symphony No. 5, following the guidelines for sonata-form movements discussed in Chapter 12. Refer to your diagram of sonata form on the board as necessary.

1. Compare and contrast theme 1 and theme 2.

2. Play the bridge and the cadence theme. Remind students that these themes are manifestations of the opening motive.

3. Play the entire exposition and ask students to listen for harmonically stable (thematic) sections and harmonically unstable (transitional) sections.

4. Work through the development section part by part, observing themes used and the various developmental processes. Note particularly the process of fragmentation, by which Beethoven reduces his motive to a single note.

5. In the recapitulation, note that the new oboe cadenza (between the two continuations of theme 1) provides yet another embellished statement of the opening four-pitch motive. Call special attention to the second group. Though the

---

³If you are skeptical about this relationship, consider mm. 228–31 in the development or mm. 398–408 in the coda. The development passage adapts the bridge theme in preparation for the return of theme 1. The coda passage (see example on textbook page 234) combines the pitches of mm. 1–4 with the rhythm of the bridge to begin an important new section of the coda. This coda passage does not merely develop theme 1 or develop the bridge; Beethoven wants to clarify the relationship between these two themes.

second group is reconciled to the original tonic (C), it does not use the original mode (C minor). (If you have keyboard facility, play theme 2 for the class in C minor. It sounds wrong!) Beethoven always follows the logic dictated by his musical ideas, even if it means disregarding traditional procedures.

6. Examine the massive coda, more a development section than a coda. Here Beethoven erases our sense of C major to reestablish the minor mode and turbulent mood of the first theme. In the development proper, Beethoven subjected the bridge theme to fragmentation, almost dissolving it. In the coda, Beethoven takes the theme 1/bridge theme (the four-pitch motive—G–E flat–F–D—combined with the bridge theme's rhythm) and expands it to create a significant new section of the coda.

STRINGS, FRENCH HORNS

7. Play the entire movement for the class. Project the transparency for Listening Chart 14 (or refer students to textbook page 233) and point out themes and sections as they go by. In the discussion that follows, draw out the ways in which Beethoven expands and adapts traditional sonata form.

Psychological Progression

In Beethoven's hands, the symphony stood transformed from a series of discrete movements related only by key into a four-act narrative, with each movement progressing dramatically and inevitably to the next. The four movements of Beethoven's Symphony No. 5 exhibit just such a psychological progression. (In fact, the progression from movement III to movement IV is more than just psychological.) The dramatic transformation of mood—from the tragic, dark first movement to the celebratory and triumphant fourth—is discussed on textbook pages 234–237.

Beethoven supposedly referred to the opening motive as "fate knocking at the door," a notion that casts the struggle between C minor and C major in apocalyptic terms. How does this struggle affect the four movements of the symphony? (If you have time, play short excerpts from each movement as you present the following outline.) In the first movement, C major almost triumphs over C minor at the end of the recapitulation, but the stormy, turbulent C minor material reasserts itself with a vengeance in the coda. The second movement alternates between a gentle, lyric theme in A-flat major and a stirring fanfare in C major. It ends in A-flat, but we are left with the possibility of a triumphant C major. The third movement's scherzo section is in C minor with a C major trio. The two keys almost seem to coexist here, though this is by no means a typical scherzo and trio movement. The third movement plays a pivotal role in the transition to the fourth movement. The final movement provides a jubilant ending to the symphony—C minor disappears entirely. Light has triumphed over darkness, the human spirit over tragic fate. Symphonies by Mozart or Haydn were rarely discussed in such cosmic terms, but Beethoven's work invites such description. Turn now to the remaining movements.

BEETHOVEN Symphony No. 5 in C Minor, Op. 67, II

As we discovered in looking at Haydn's Symphony No. 95, the slow movement in the four-movement format has no specific form associated with it.

Haydn's slow movement used a fairly straightforward theme and variations form; Beethoven takes the same form, but instead of using just one theme, he introduces two themes of contrasting character—a most unusual approach! Begin by introducing just the first theme. Prepare excerpts ahead of time so that you can play the first theme and its six variations back-to-back, as if this were a typical theme and variations movement. These would make a nice enough slow movement for a Haydn symphony, but they lack the dramatic contrasts we expect from Beethoven.

Now introduce the second theme. Play both theme 1 and theme 2 and ask the class to describe the differences between them. Theme 1 is a lyric, long-lined melody presented initially by violas and cellos; theme 2 offers a modest contrast when played *piano* by woodwinds and even more contrast in the eerie, questioning transition that follows. But *fortissimo* brass turn the second statement into a triumphant fanfare. In just a few short bars, the transition moves from *pianissimo* questioning to unbearable tension when suddenly the full orchestra bursts in *fortissimo*. Beethoven's resolution of that tension comes with the force of a startling revelation, moving us into a new key far removed from A-flat major: the "new" key of C major, the key of light and triumph. The subsequent retransition back to A-flat sounds far more disorienting than the transition *to* C, as if Beethoven's transcendent vision of C major has left our senses reeling. Beethoven's modulations here are not mere key changes; they are musical revelations—Beethoven's discovery of marvelous new tonal regions, *terra incognita*. Display Listening Chart 15 (or refer students to textbook page 236) and point out the alternation between themes. Note that the variations affect only theme 1; theme 2 functions more as an interlude between variations of theme 1. Play the entire movement and point out themes as they go by.

The motive from movement I makes a subtle appearance in this movement. If you ignore the upbeat, the first two measures of theme 2 present a variant of Beethoven's motive. The short-short-short-long rhythmic pattern is clear enough, and the melody presents the original interval—the descending third—inverted and filled-in, just as it appears in mm. 146–59 of the first movement.

BEETHOVEN Symphony No. 5 in C Minor, Op. 67, III

As we saw in Haydn's Symphony No. 95, the third movement in the four-movement plan is a dance movement—a minuet and trio. Beethoven adapted minuet form to fit his own needs (after the model of some Haydn string quartets), calling his third movement form "scherzo." Of the four primary Classical forms, minuet and trio is the most predictable, the most standardized. Beethoven's esthetic cared little for standardization or the eighteenth-century elegance of the minuet. His scherzo and trio movements retain the triple meter, the playful quality, and (usually) the large-scale **A B A** form of Haydn's minuet movements, and he still calls the middle section (**B**) a trio—but the resemblance ends there. The two primary differences between minuet form and scherzo form relate to tempo and internal structure. Beethoven's tempo for the scherzo is so quick that the meter feels compound instead of triple. Further, the phrase structure and content of Beethoven's scherzo movements cannot be reduced to a consistent formula—they vary from piece to piece according to the psychological progression he envisioned.

Display Listening Chart 15 (or refer students to textbook page 236) and point out the internal structure of the scherzo and the trio. Note that the trio looks almost like the trio in minuet and trio form—|: c :| d c′ d′ c″—except that Beethoven writes out the repeat of the d c′ section because he wants to re-orchestrate it the second time through. The first scherzo section, on the other hand, looks quite different. Here Beethoven states two short, contrasting ideas, **a** and **b,** and repeats them twice with some variation (**a b a′ b′ a″ b″**).

As you play the following sections, point to each theme as it goes by. Play the first scherzo (track 16). In the discussion that follows, draw out the following points.

1. The music alternates between a quiet, ominous, ascending phrase (**a**) followed by an explosive, *forte* theme in the horns (**b**).

2. The key is C minor, though the tragic mood of the first movement is replaced with a sort of anxious restlessness.

3. The rhythmic motive from movement I (short-short-short-long) makes several appearances in this movement. The **b** theme in the scherzo is the most obvious example.

Play the trio (track 17, 0:00–1:29). In the discussion and comparison that follow, draw out the following points.

1. An energetic, fugal trio in C major immediately changes the mood of the music. Once again, the confrontation between C minor and C major comes to the forefront.

2. Call attention to the humor in this section. *Scherzo* means "joke," of course, and Beethoven gives the solo opening statement of the fiendishly fast **c** theme to instruments not noted for their agility—the basses (with cellos). We expect them to blow it, and Beethoven makes it sound as if they *do* blow it at the beginning of the **d** section, when they stop twice to repeat the opening motive. Anyone who tries to count out the basic beat pattern along with the first eight measures of **d** will discover a more subtle joke. Beethoven nearly destroys our sense of meter with a rhythmic pattern that sounds more like **6/8** than **3/4.**

3. Note the striking difference in mood between the first and second repetitions of the second section (**d c′**). The first repetition builds to a powerful climax; the second repetition fades out to a *pianissimo* ending, preparing us for the return of the scherzo.

Play the second scherzo (track 17, 1:36–2:53). In the discussion and comparison that follow, draw out the following points.

1. The scherzo undergoes an incredible metamorphosis. Though still in C minor, it is played by hushed *pizzicato* strings and quiet woodwinds. The soft, brittle texture creates tremendous anticipation and tension. Say a few sentences to your class *sotto voce* (or whispered), pointedly. They will have to lean forward to hear you. Point out that Beethoven draws special attention to this passage in just this way, heightening our anticipation.

2. Just at the point where we expect a cadence, Beethoven begins a new section in a strange key. This deceptive ending plunges us into an unexpected musical world, without a strong tonic or downbeat.

Play the second scherzo and the transition to movement IV (from track 17, 1:36, in the third movement up to track 18, 0:24 or so, in the fourth movement). In the discussion that follows, draw out these points.

1. The unexpected world referred to above begins the transition section. (This world centers around A flat, the tonal center for movement II!) We gradually regain our bearings as ghostly motives (drawn from the third movement) begin to appear.

2. The music gets louder and louder as a single harmony is reached. (The harmonic progression in this passage closely resembles the progression that took us from A-flat major to C major in theme 2 of the second movement! Beethoven took only five measures to accomplish the transformation in movement II; here he takes well over fifty measures to extract every last ounce of tension from these chords.)

3. In one of the great moments in Western art, the music emerges from anxious anticipation into a brilliant, triumphant wash of sound. Beethoven's struggle between darkness (C minor) and light (C major) ends with the victorious emergence of C major; the final movement celebrates the triumph.

This hyperbole can help the class understand the gut-wrenching drama played out in the four movements of this symphony. Beethoven's scherzo, written to fit the dramatic context of this symphony, plays a pivotal role in its overall psychological progression.

BEETHOVEN **Symphony No. 5 in C Minor, Op. 67, IV**

By now, most students can follow sonata form without much prompting. Project the transparency for Listening Chart 15 (or refer students to textbook page 236). For the most part, Beethoven's use of sonata form is routine here; even his struggles against conventional forms resolve themselves. Point out the following unusual features.

1. The rhythmic motive from movement I makes several appearances in this movement. Most significant are the triplet rhythm of theme 2 and the low string accompaniment in the *Presto* section of the coda (at m. 362).

2. Something extraordinary happens in the development section's retransition. The transition section that ended the third movement and led into the fourth worked so well the first time that Beethoven uses it again to lead from development to recapitulation! To take material from one movement and use it in another was an earth-shattering innovation. Movements had always been separate musical entities, but Beethoven began to break down the walls that separated one movement from another.

3. Note the enormous length of the coda—two to three times as long as any previous section of the movement. A symphony as dramatically supercharged as Beethoven's Fifth needs time to resolve the tension and create a strong ending.

4. The development section worked over theme 2 but left the other themes untouched; development of the bridge, cadence theme, and theme 1 is reserved for the coda.

5. To increase the effectiveness of the ending, Beethoven employs an accelerando in the middle of the coda (starting at m. 353), and the tempo marking for the final section is *Presto* (m. 362)!

So that students can weigh the impact of the transition to the fourth movement and the long coda, play movements III and IV without a break. Point out important sections and themes on the transparency as they go by.

Concluding Remarks on Beethoven's Symphony No. 5

In his Fifth Symphony, Beethoven uses a musical style whose dramatic strength and rhythmic power go far beyond orchestral music of previous eras. Less obvious but equally profound are the techniques Beethoven develops to unify four disparate movements into a cohesive whole.

1. Musical ideas appear in more than one movement: Beethoven uses the short-short-short-long rhythmic motive in each movement, and the transitional material from the end of the third movement appears again in the middle of the fourth movement. These techniques formed the basis of cyclic procedures used by later composers to unify long multimovement works.

2. Movements can be connected without pause: In previous symphonies, each movement ended with a strong cadence. After a short wait, the musicians began the next movement. In this symphony, no pause separates the third and fourth movements. The transitional material builds tension that only the first theme of the fourth movement can resolve.

Beethoven single-handedly changed the nature of the symphonic genre with his nine magnificent symphonies. Composers after Beethoven would never again view the symphony as a simple entertainment.

✻ The "Third Period"

Beethoven's music divides into three periods. In the first period (up to 1802), Beethoven mastered the style, forms, and procedures of Classical music. He found his own unique, powerful voice in the often heroic works of his second period (up to 1814), including his Fifth Symphony. Composition slowed for Beethoven during the 1815–1820 court battles for custody of his nephew Karl. When he resumed composing more actively in the 1820s, his style was much changed. These third-period works reflect an introspective, meditative, spiritual quality that was absent in most earlier works. Beethoven did not reject his earlier style—on the contrary, he expanded his palette of expressive techniques and skipped from one mood to the next spontaneously, regardless of the effect on form. This freedom and spontaneity of expression was well described by Friedrich Johann Rochlitz in his account of a visit with Beethoven in 1822:

> During the entire visit he was uncommonly gay and at times most amusing, and all that entered his mind had to come out. ("Well, it happens that I am unbuttoned to-day," he said and the remark was decidedly in order.) His talk and his actions all formed a chain of eccentricities, in most part peculiar. Yet they all radiated a truly childlike amiability, carelessness, and confidence in every one who approached him. Even his barking tirades—like that against his Viennese contemporaries, which I already have mentioned—are only explosions of his fanciful imagination and his momentary excitement. They are uttered without haughtiness, without any feeling of bitterness and hatefulness—and are simply blustered out lightly, good-humoredly, the offsprings of a mad, humorous mood.[4]

For a clear example of the meditative, introspective quality associated with many of Beethoven's late works, turn to the movement from his Piano Sonata No. 31 in A-flat, Op. 110, described in Further Listening Examples below. In the quotation above, however, Rochlitz could have been talking about the *Vivace* movement from Beethoven's Op. 135 quartet—as unbuttoned as any piece of music could ever hope to be.

---

[4]O. G. Sonneck, ed., *Beethoven: Impressions by His Contemporaries.* New York: Dover, 1954, pp. 127–28.

BEETHOVEN **String Quartet in F, Op. 135, II**

The third period frequently finds Beethoven stretching Classical forms and genres, at times beyond recognition. During these twilight years he wrote a seven-movement string quartet, a two-movement piano sonata, and a few massive fugues, so we naturally keep our eyes open for anything out of the ordinary when we look at a late work such as the Op. 135 quartet! On the surface, this work looks disappointingly ordinary. It stays close to the Classical quartet's four-movement plan throughout, close enough that you can use it for a quick review. If you have time and a complete recording (see Sound Recordings below), play just the beginning of each movement. In the discussion that follows, you can point out several discrepancies but no genuine innovations. Beethoven does reverse the order of the middle two movements—the "minuet" appears second and the slow movement third—but even Haydn does that in some of his string quartets. If we look a bit more closely, we see something more unusual: a slow introduction attached to the fourth movement instead of the first one. Although this passage offers a bit of Beethoven's humor—the introduction's G–E–A flat motive (*Muss es sein?*—"Must it be?") inverts as A–C–G to become the movement's main theme (*Es muss sein!* "It must be!")—it is not without precedent. Beethoven used a slow introduction to the fourth movement in his Symphony No. 1, way back in his "first" period. Where then do we look to find the unusual and even bizarre features of Beethoven's late style? We must look to the music itself.

The scherzo from Beethoven's Fifth was too spooky to really convey the playful quality that we hear in so many Beethoven third movements from the *Eroica* on, but *this* is a scherzo! In fact, with its bizarre, sudden mood shifts and its offbeat accents that threaten to derail the meter altogether, this movement carries the "joke" to an entirely new level. You probably reviewed the features of minuet and trio when you worked through Symphony No. 5; no need to do that again here. Instead, focus on the musical jokes Beethoven plays in this movement. Work through the sections of this work one at a time so that your students can savor its idiosyncrasies.

In the scherzo itself, the jokes are primarily rhythmic. Although the surprise E-flat of the **b** section counts as a "wrong pitch" joke (enhanced by the purely diatonic, repetitive **a** section), it is Beethoven's use of rhythm that makes the joke truly subversive. Let's start at the beginning. In the first six bars, the violins and viola each play on a different beat; we wouldn't know which one was playing the downbeat if it weren't for the clearly defined rhythms of the cello melody. When the four instruments finally agree to play simultaneously at the beginning of **b,** not only do they play the wrong pitch (E flat), they're on the wrong beat! Here they play rhythms that insist so strongly on beat 2 (in mm. 17, 19, and 21–24) that we can't be sure where the downbeat is. And no sooner does Beethoven reestablish the beat than the end of the **a′** section calls it back into question. The texture's two-part counterpoint couldn't be simpler, but the violins emphasize beat 1 while the viola and cello play as if beat 2 were the downbeat (see the notated example on textbook page 238). Your ear can't tell for sure whether to trust the upper or the lower instruments! Perhaps this is why Beethoven added a **c** section to conclude the scherzo—he needed at least one section to establish the beat clearly. In other works, we have seen dissonances that needed to resolve or development sections that needed recapitulations to restore melodic and tonal order; similarly, Beethoven needs rhythmic stability to resolve the rhythmic tensions of **a, b,** and **a′.**

The jokes in the trio have more to do with the order of events, that is, its form. With the exception of the added **c** section, the scherzo's form was a conventional rounded binary form. Not so with the trio! In fact, its structure is so free that the *Listen* Guide (textbook page 238) doesn't even assign letters to the trio's subsections. The first melodic idea here appears to be a five-note-long eighth-note motive that starts with a lower neighbor and then goes up the scale; immediately following is a second melodic idea, a simple scale in quarter notes that just keeps going up and up. If the joke in the scherzo was too many misplaced accents, the rhythmic joke in the trio's quarter-note-scale figures is no accents at all. We go up to four bars at a time without a chord change, and the lack of accents momentarily suspends our sense of meter, even though the beat keeps on chugging.

The trio's rhythmic stability is offset, however, by the instability of its sudden key changes. The first three subsections of the trio present these two melodic ideas in three different keys: F major, G major, and A major, a chromatic mediant away from our starting point. Think about that for a moment . . . when we change key in the Classical period, we usually head for the dominant or the relative minor. Here we move up by step—twice. Why? If your students read the textbook carefully, they may recall the reference to "Three blind mice" (A–G–F) in the very first paragraph on this quartet. The **a** section's violin melody goes down and up the scale between A and F several times. That Beethoven should take the F–G–A portion of this motive and turn it into a succession of keys is unusual indeed. One might suspect pure coincidence if we didn't find Beethoven doing precisely the same thing in other works of the third period. In fact, Beethoven's innovative integration of melodic motive and tonal plan anticipates the "unity of musical space" that figures so prominently in twentieth-century musical thought. This scheme of keys further accomplishes something that every Broadway composer knows instinctively—raising the key by a step increases the excitement level. Each time Beethoven bumps the key up a step, that interminable scale motive goes higher yet. The third statement pushes it as high as it seems it can go, but when Beethoven does a thing three times, he's setting you up for the biggest surprise yet—in this case the *fortissimo* explosion at 1:31. Bold and raucous, the first violin saws away at a rough fiddle tune while the others play the first melodic motive over and over again in three different octaves. No problem hearing the beat here, but what a madcap sound! This goes on for nearly half a minute, finally fading out into a unison that slips down chromatically toward F and slows into the rhythms of the **a** section. After such a shock, even the subversive rhythms of the now-familiar scherzo bring a sense of relief as the **A** section returns.

Before you play the entire work for your students, read aloud the Rochlitz quotation above and ask students to identify passages that fit his description of Beethoven's behavior and personality. As you play the music, call attention to the events listed in the *Listen* Guide on textbook page 238. In the discussion that follows, draw out these phrases from Rochlitz.

> *Chain of eccentricities*—This certainly describes the overall form. Each subsection contains at least one peculiarity, whether of rhythm, meter, melody, pitch, texture, dynamics, or tonality, but even more eccentric is the overall succession of events. Take just the scherzo, the **A** section. The pitches of the violin's **a** melody are childishly simple, if rhythmically ambiguous. Then the rude interruption of the **b** section's accents on all the wrong beats, an effect immediately mollified by the beginning of **a'**, a radiant *legato* passage that completely transforms the mood—from the ridiculous to the sublime! Finally the disorientation of two colliding meters at the end of **a'** followed by the satisfying resolution of the **c** section's dance rhythms. And all of this in less than a minute, even *with* repeats!

Barking tirades—This describes both the **b** section and the trio's *fortissimo* explosion. Both pass quickly enough, however, and Beethoven goes on to the next idea. Jarring though they may be, they do not express anger. "They are uttered without haughtiness, without any feeling of bitterness and hatefulness—and are simply blustered out lightly, good-humoredly."

Fanciful imagination and . . . momentary excitement—Unlike the Fifth Symphony, this quartet no longer takes a motive and works it over until its possibilities have been exhausted. It's not that Beethoven doesn't use motives heavily in this movement, but now it's not work—it's play! Beethoven is having fun with these ideas, taking them wherever his next whim carries him. One might accuse Beethoven of a short attention span if the overall structure of this movement were not so satisfying. This music clearly lives in the moment, and it expresses the same unstoppable, unbuttoned zest and joy that Rochlitz saw in Beethoven on that day late in the composer's life, "the offsprings of a mad, humorous mood."

A Note on Beethoven's Deafness

Just a few years before Beethoven wrote this quartet, his deafness had reached its peak. It is actually not so amazing that Beethoven could compose while deaf. Composers write down the music that they "hear" internally. Beethoven had tested his remarkable "inner hearing" against the reality of live performance countless times—and forty-odd years of experience cannot be forgotten quickly. What *is* amazing is that Beethoven's inner ear remembered the sound of the piano, the bowed strings, and other instruments so well that he could create entirely *new* sonorities—some raucous and irreverent, some beautifully delicate and exquisite. His miraculous compositional skills continued to grow and mature after he lost his hearing.

Additional Teaching Suggestions

♪ Lecture-Demonstration Ideas

1. Introduce your class to Beethoven as he was seen by his contemporaries. *Beethoven: Impressions by His Contemporaries* (ed. O. G. Sonneck, New York: Dover, 1954) reprints stories about the great composer told by those who knew him. Thayer's famous biography of Beethoven includes similar eyewitness accounts and other fascinating documents. You can start by asking your class to describe what they know of Beethoven's personality. (Most have seen pictures of him.) Then read quotations that address different aspects of Beethoven's personality and ask for student reactions.

2. Try the same approach with Beethoven's Symphony No. 5. Elliot Forbes's wonderful critical edition of Beethoven's Fifth (New York: Norton, 1971) includes historical background materials filled with quotations from Beethoven and his contemporaries; a study of Beethoven's sketches for Symphony No. 5; analyses of the symphony by Tovey, Hoffmann, and Schenker; and comments on the symphony by such famous musicians as Berlioz, Mendelssohn, Wagner, and Cone. These materials can be used in countless ways to enhance your presentation of the Fifth.

3. Changes and improvements in the piano had an enormous effect on music written for that instrument. Beethoven took full advantage of the latest develop-

ments when writing piano music. Read excerpts from Stolba's discussion of early nineteenth-century pianos on page 404 of her *Development of Western Music,* 3rd ed. (McGraw-Hill, 1998). Compare the piano she describes with the modern piano, emphasizing the features that influenced Beethoven's music. This can be especially helpful if you use suggestions for the Piano Sonata in A-flat, Op. 110, in Further Listening Examples below. (See Sound Recordings below for suggested performances.)

♩ Class Discussion Ideas

1. *Why is Beethoven's music still so popular today, nearly two centuries later?* This question raises an even larger question: *How can any piece of music have meaning beyond its immediate culture and generation?* Students can speak from experience; they face this difficulty in their encounters with Global Perspectives materials. Use Beethoven as a case study. To deal with this question, ask students to list situations where they have heard music from Beethoven's Fifth (commercials and so on), to discuss their own reactions to Beethoven's music, and to identify elements in the music that elicit these reactions. Some aspects of these questions may prove unanswerable, and students need to wrestle with these aspects as well. Excerpts from Leonard Bernstein's "Why Beethoven?" (in *The Joy of Music,* New York: Simon & Schuster, 1959, pp. 21–29) address Beethoven's greatness with deftness, insight, and creativity.

2. *How did Beethoven react when he discovered he was going deaf?* Read Beethoven's *Heiligenstadt Testament* to the class or make it assigned reading. (Some instructors play "third period" Beethoven quartets or sonatas in the background while they read.) In this letter to his brothers, Beethoven bares his soul with directness and eloquence. Many students find this letter moving; it puts a human face on the ubiquitous caricature of Beethoven's scowl. Students often have questions about Beethoven's deafness and its impact on his music. This question allows the class to deal with such issues.

3. *What is the relationship between the musical work and the musical performance?* Display a score page so students can see it clearly. Ask them how they like this music! Apologize profusely for "forgetting" they don't read music. Play a few lines at a keyboard to help them out, and when that doesn't work so well, play a recording. Of course, the point is not their opinion of the music; this demonstration serves, rather, to highlight the importance of the score. For students who don't read music, the score can seem meaningless, just as an American novel would seem meaningless to someone who doesn't read English. But for someone who reads scores, the musical work can exist *independent* of its performance, just as a novel possesses meaning even when you don't read it out loud—through an internal reading (or internal performance). This concept lies at the heart of the relationship between the work and the performance in the Western classical tradition. *Can you think of any music with a different relationship between the work and the score?* Use this follow-up question to draw out examples that don't fit the Western classical tradition. Many exist, including blues works and others for which no notation exists— the work cannot exist independent of its performance (except perhaps in memory or a recording). To further discussion, bring both a lead sheet and two different recordings of the same tune—an old "standard" works best. Recordings of "standard" pop tunes by jazz and popular artists are plentiful, and someone in your department surely owns a "fake" or a "real" book. Display

the lead sheet for your students. Compared to the score you displayed earlier, it looks incomplete—just a tune and some chord symbols. At the keyboard, play the tune and, if you can, sound out some of the chords as well. Then play the two recordings back to back and ask students to compare them. Same tune, maybe the same chords, but the accompaniments differ! The rhythm section, ubiquitous in popular music and jazz, operates according to its own mix of oral and written traditions, and two performances of the same work played by the same rhythm section can differ dramatically. The lead sheet guides both performances, but it is no score in the classical sense. Understanding the range of possible relationships between the work and its performance in our Western traditions helps prepare students to understand a similar range of relationships around the world.

♪ Listening Ideas

1. Compare the quality of rhythmic drive in different historical styles. Play excerpts from Bernart's "La dousa votz"; Weelkes's "As Vesta Was from Latmos Hill Descending"; Bach's *Brandenburg* Concerto No. 5; Haydn's Symphony No. 95, IV; and Beethoven's Symphony No. 5, I. Ask students to describe and compare the use of rhythm and the sense (or lack) of rhythmic drive in each of these works. Do students hear a progression from Bernart to Beethoven? Alternatively, mix in some Global Perspectives examples from Chapters 5 through 13. Excerpts from the Gambia and Bali offer the clearest sense of beat and meter; the others use rhythm differently. This exercise offers a good chance to review rhythmic principles.

2. For another brief demonstration of Beethoven's rhythmic drive, play two versions of the first movement of Beethoven's Symphony No. 5. In the first version, play measures 1–21 at the keyboard (or create a MIDI version) and reduce the three eighth notes of Beethoven's motive to a single quarter-note upbeat each time it appears. In the second version, play a real recording of the same passage. Ask the class to compare the rhythmic drive conveyed by each version.

3. Compare Beethoven's sketch materials with his completed scores. For one of his *Omnibus* television broadcasts, Leonard Bernstein presented a fascinating comparison of Beethoven's sketches and his finished score for Symphony No. 5. The script of Bernstein's broadcast, complete with simple piano reductions of Beethoven's sketches, makes it possible to reconstruct this demonstration for your class. This exercise brings Beethoven's anguished compositional process to life, and students can hear for themselves why Beethoven kept some ideas and rejected others. The script is published on pages 73–93 of Bernstein's *The Joy of Music* (New York: Simon & Schuster, 1959). (The audio portion of that broadcast is now available; see Sound Recordings below.)

4. Play the classic P. D. Q. Bach version of the first movement of Beethoven's Symphony No. 5 (see Sound Recordings below). In a comedy sketch titled "New Horizons in Music Appreciation," radio announcers Pete Schickele and Bob Dennis broadcast a performance of Beethoven's symphony as if it were a sports event (conductor Heilige Dankgesang versus the New York Mills Philharmonic). Don't be fooled by this humorous, novel approach—Schickele draws attention to all of the key elements in Beethoven's use of sonata form. This example works best at the end of a lesson on the first movement of Beethoven's Fifth. Students appreciate Schickele's humor, and you will appreciate his thorough analytical commentary.

5. Compare examples from all three Beethoven style periods. The second movement of String Quartet in A, Op. 18, No. 5, serves well for the first period, in which Beethoven mastered Classical style (for lecture suggestions, see Further Listening Examples on page 317 in Chapter 13 of this manual; for teaching resources, see Further Listening Charts and Texts, and Sound Recordings below). Of course, Symphony No. 5 presents the quintessential example of the second period, in which Beethoven defined his own unique style. The Quartet in F, Op. 135, provides an excellent example of third-period style, but if you want an example of the reflective, introspective quality some late works offer, try either the third movement of the Op. 135 quartet, the third movement of the Ninth Symphony, or the piano sonata movement in Further Listening Examples below. See Multimedia Resources below for suggested recordings.

⁊ Further Listening Examples

Compare Minuet and Trio with Scherzo

Compare the third movement of Haydn's Symphony No. 95 with the third movement of Beethoven's Symphony No. 3 (*Eroica*). Play the first minute or so of each movement. Ask the class to compare the excerpts in terms of meter, tempo, and "danceability." In the discussion that follows, draw out these points:

1. Haydn's minuet and trio are in triple meter at a moderate tempo. Though stylized, the music is still clearly dancelike in character. This majestic minuet is the sort of dance one might encounter in a royal ballroom.

2. Beethoven's scherzo goes so quickly that its triple meter sounds more like compound meter. In many passages it is difficult to identify the meter clearly because Beethoven places strong accents on beats two or three, or even groups his beats in twos instead of threes. Moreover, this music has lost any association with the minuet. The rhythmic excitement generated by this movement is completely divorced from the formal, elegant dance of the minuet.

3. These two works have many elements in common: triple meter, playful use of syncopation, and "minuet" form (though greatly expanded by Beethoven). The primary difference is tempo; Beethoven's faster tempo not only increases the disruptive force of the syncopation, but also changes the mood of the music entirely.

BEETHOVEN **Piano Sonata No. 31 in A-flat, Op. 110, I**

Try this movement for an example of the more introspective side of Beethoven's third-period style. See Sound Recordings below for suggested performances. Like the quartet above, this sonata looks fairly conventional in format, but its content is full of surprises. If you have time, play just the first minute of the first two movements and enough of the last so that students can hear the alternation between arioso and fugue. In the discussion that follows, draw out relationships between this work and the Classical sonata's usual three-movement plan: a sonata-form movement that concerns itself more with free development and flights of fantasy than with clear-cut melodic statements or dramatic urgency; a second movement whose fierce, almost manic scherzo contains a gentle trio that recalls the feathery arpeggios of the first movement; and a final movement that sounds like two movements in one, interleaving arioso sections (typical of a slow movement) with fast fugal sections (typical of the concluding movement). These unconventional features point to the freedom and spontaneous expression that characterize the music of Beethoven's third-period style.

This movement reflects the spontaneity of Beethoven's third-period approach. The very first theme of this sonata-form movement is unconventional and introspective—a meditative, expressive melody; simple chords carefully placed; a slow tempo compared with other first movements—hardly comparable to the dramatic tension we have come to associate with sonata form. If you have time, you can use this movement as yet another example of sonata form, but the main goal here is to offer another example of Beethoven's third-period style. Whether you emphasize the form or not, put this diagram of sonata form on the board and guide students through the different themes; this piece is difficult to follow without points of reference. Play the movement and indicate themes and sections as they go by.

Exposition				*Development*	*Recapitulation*				*Coda*
First theme	Bridge	Second theme	Cadence theme		First theme	Bridge theme	Second theme	Cadence	
m. 1	m. 12	m. 28	m. 31	m. 39	m. 56	m. 70	m. 87	m. 90	m. 97

This intimate work relies on spontaneity rather than dramatic tension. In the discussion that follows, point out its unconventional uses of sonata form.

1. The bridge is the longest section in both the exposition and the recapitulation, whereas the second theme and cadence theme are short. Long, stable sections do not figure prominently here; Beethoven changes key as quickly as he changes mood.

2. Beethoven uses sequence to modulate in the development section but uses none of the other development techniques he is famous for (fragmentation, for instance). Only the first theme is developed.

3. The arpeggios from the bridge accompany the first theme in the recapitulation—Beethoven merges contrasting ideas.

4. The first theme and bridge are longer in the recapitulation. Beethoven repeats phrases to linger awhile in these sections. The bridge modulates to several keys (including E major) before it returns to A-flat major, the tonic key.

These unconventional features point to the freedom and spontaneous expression that characterize the music of Beethoven's third-period style.

Multimedia Resources

❡ Further Listening Charts and Texts

See Appendix I for Listening Charts for these works:

Beethoven, String Quartet in A, Op. 18, No. 5, II. See also Listening Idea 5 above or teaching suggestions in Further Listening Examples from Chapter 13 of this manual (page 317).

❡ Sound Recordings

Bach, P. D. Q. *The Wurst of PDQ Bach*. Peter Schickele and friends. Vanguard VCD2-719/20 (CD). A collection of P. D. Q. Bach favorites. Contains the cantata *Iphigenia in Brooklyn*, Fugue in C Minor from the *Toot Suite*, and more. Peter Schickele's classic routine "New Horizons in Music Appreciation" treats a performance of Beethoven's Symphony No. 5 as if it were a sports event.

Provides a funny yet cogent analysis of the first movement. Most successful when used for review, after students know the work. Try this recording if you use Listening Idea 4 above.

Beethoven, *The Late Sonatas*. Richard Goode. Nonesuch 79211 (CD). A complete collection of Beethoven's third-period piano sonatas: No. 28 in A, Op. 101; No. 29 in B-flat, Op. 106 (*Hammerklavier*); No. 30 in E, Op. 109; No. 31 in A-flat, Op. 110; and No. 32 in C Minor, Op. 111. Goode's recordings stand among the best by contemporary pianists. Recommended if you use Lecture-Demonstration Idea 3, Listening Idea 5, or suggestions from Further Listening Examples above for the first movement of Op. 110.

Beethoven, *The Late String Quartets*. Lindsay Quartet. ASV DCS403 (CD). Perhaps the finest modern recordings of Beethoven's late quartets and *Grosse Fuge*. Try this recording if you use Listening Idea 5 above.

Beethoven, *Nine Symphonies*. Orchestre Révolutionnaire et Romantique. Deutsche Grammophon Archiv 439 900-2 (CD). Raw, powerful performances of Beethoven's complete symphonies. These period-instrument recordings permit us to hear the ferocious intensity Beethoven achieved by pushing the instruments of his day to their limits, yet they more than hold their own in comparison with modern-instrument performances. Period-instrument performances of Classical music have truly come of age! (Symphonies 3, 5, and 9 are also available separately.) Highly recommended. Try this recording to present Symphony No. 5 or if you use Listening Idea 5 and the suggestions from Further Listening Examples above that compare a Haydn minuet with the scherzo from the *Eroica*.

Beethoven, *Ode to Freedom: Symphony No. 9*. Deutsche Grammophon 429 861 2 (CD). This historic international performance (Christmas Day, 1989) of Beethoven's masterpiece in what was East Berlin celebrated the demise of the Berlin Wall. The performers restored Schiller's original wording at the beginning of the "Ode to Joy," substituting the word *Freiheit* (freedom) in place of *Freude* (joy). (After the French Revolution, *freedom* was a dangerous word, threatening to those who held political power.) Soloists Anderson, Walker, König, and Rootering perform with musicians from many of the world's major orchestras; conducted by Leonard Bernstein. Highly recommended. The *Listen* DVD contains some of the "Ode to Joy" variations; try this recording to explore more of "the Ninth" or if you use Listening Idea 5 above.

Beethoven, *Quatuors Opus 18 No. 5 & 6*. Quatuor Mosaïques. Astrée Auvidis E 8541 (CD). Today's finest period-instrument string quartet offers gracious, charming period-instrument performances enlivened by a gentle yet firm rhythmic "spring" and crafted so that each detail of the score can be heard. Use this recording if you try Listening Idea 5 above or suggestions for the second movement of Op. 18, No. 5, in Further Listening Examples from Chapter 13 of this manual (page 317).

Bernstein Talks about Beethoven's Symphony No. 5. New York Philharmonic. Sony Royal Edition SXK 47645 (CD). This recording begins with an audio recording of Bernstein's famous *Omnibus* broadcast, "How a Great Symphony Was Written," and concludes with a performance of Beethoven's Fifth Symphony. In the spoken portion, Bernstein compares excerpts from Beethoven's sketchbooks with the finished product, illustrating his points with excerpts performed at the piano and by members of the Columbia Symphony Orchestra. Provides a fascinating look into the composer's workshop. Highly recommended, but it goes in and out of print (your library might even have the old LP release). Try this recording if you use Listening Idea 3.

⁊ Video Recordings

Beethoven by Barenboim Series. www.films.com (DVD or VHS, color, 28 minutes each). Thirteen-part series explores various aspects of Beethoven's life and music, narrated by pianist/conductor Daniel Barenboim. Series includes *Beethoven the Promethean, Minuet into Scherzo, The Appassionata, The Working Process, Beethoven and the Sonata Form, The Comprehensive Vision, Orpheus Taming the Furies, Amid Tears and Sorrow, The Eroica, The Symphonist, The Late Works, The Last Piano Sonata,* and *The Fifth Symphony.* These can be useful for your presentation of Symphony No. 5 or for sugestions from Further Listening Examples above.

Beethoven: The Age of Revolution. Man and Music Series. www.films.com (DVD or VHS, color, 53 minutes). Looks at Beethoven's early career, tracing his development from Haydn's classicism to the *Eroica* Symphony. Includes insights from Beethoven's sketchbooks and highlights his unique contributions—for instance, the scherzo. Musical excerpts from Haydn's *Creation* and Beethoven's Piano Trio in C Minor Op. 1, No. 3; Piano Sonata in C Minor (*Pathétique*); String Quartet in B-flat, Op. 18, No. 6; Violin Sonata in F (*Spring*), Op. 24; and Symphony No. 3 in E-flat (*Eroica*).

Beethoven: The Composer as Hero. Man and Music Series. www.films.com (DVD or VHS, color, 53 minutes). Looks at Beethoven's growing deafness and the political turmoil caused by French invasions. Includes excerpts from his most famous works: Symphony No. 5 in C Minor, Op. 67; Cello Sonata in A, Op. 69; *Fidelio;* Piano Sonata in C Minor, Op. 111; String Quartet in E-flat, Op. 127; and Symphony No. 9 in D Minor, Op. 125 (*Choral*).

Beethoven. The Great Composers Series. www.films.com (DVD or VHS, color, 23 minutes). Video biography includes music from Beethoven's *Moonlight* and *Pathétique* Sonatas, *Egmont* Overture, Symphonies 5 and 9, and *Emperor* Concerto.

[Beethoven, Piano Sonata, Op. 13 (*Pathétique*), III.] *Delaware Music Series.* www.ecsmedia.com (DVD, color). Performance by Michael Steinberg. The DVD includes full score with harmonic reduction and analysis, performance of the harmonic reduction, examples of harmonic reduction procedure, color-coded scrolling score, and formal analysis.

Beethoven String Quartets, Vol. 3. EMI Classics (DVD, color, 172 minutes). The Alban Berg Quartet has recorded superb performances of all sixteen Beethoven quartets on DVD, maintaining the same high standards throughout the early, middle, and late works. Vol. 3 contains six quartets, including Op. 18, No. 5, and Op. 135. Highly recommended as a supplement to your presentation of Beethoven's Quartet in F Major, if you use Listening Idea 5 above, or if you use suggestions on the Op. 18, No. 5 Quartet in Further Listening Examples from Chapter 13 (see page 317).

Beethoven: Symphonies 2 and 5. EuroArts (DVD, color, 75 minutes). Claudio Abbado leads the Berlin Philharmonic in superb performances of Beethoven symphonies. These are modern-instrument performances, but Abbado has clearly learned much from period orchestras. I prefer Abbado, but you can't go too far wrong with Karajan's older recordings on Sony and Deutsche Grammophon. Many critics complain that Karajan is too polished, but his recordings of the Fifth are often grippingly dramatic. Highly recommended supplement to your presentation of Beethoven's Fifth Symphony. Students learn better when they can match up the sound and the image of specific instruments.

Beethoven: Symphony No. 7 and Symphony No. 5. The Story of the Symphony Series. Image Entertainment (DVD or VHS, color, 86 minutes). André Previn narrates this look at Beethoven, his ideals, his deafness, and his music. The video features a complete performance of Symphony No. 7 and excerpts Symphony No. 5. Especially useful is a discussion of the motivic construction of the Fifth, but you must go elsewhere for a complete performance. All performances are by the Royal Philharmonic Orchestra.

Beethoven: Symphonies 3 and 9. EuroArts (DVD, color, 75 minutes). Claudio Abbado leads the Berlin Philharmonic in superb performances of these Beethoven symphonies. The Ninth features the always superb Eric Ericson Chamber Choir and a fine team of soloists that includes Karita Mattila and Thomas Moser. Highly recommended if you use Listening Idea 5 or if you want to study the Ninth—a third-period work—as an example of Beethoven's thematic unity (cyclic form) and his expansion of traditional forms. The Third is especially useful if you compare minuet and scherzo (see Further Listening Examples above).

Eighteenth-Century Art and Music. www.insight-media.com (DVD, color, 35 minutes). This still-image video provides a concise, visually appealing introduction to important philosophic, artistic, and musical trends in the Classical era. Part 2 covers the period following the French Revolution, containing the artwork of Goya and David and music by Beethoven.

The History of Music, Part 1: *Origins Through the Classical Period.* www .insight-media.com (VHS, color, 90 minutes). The section on the Classical era covers the symphony; the sonata form; and the music of Haydn, Mozart, and early Beethoven. Part 2: *Romanticism Through Modern,* looks at late Beethoven and his influence on Romantic composers.

Ludwig van Beethoven. Against the Odds Series. www.films.com (DVD or VHS, color, 10 minutes). Brief biography of Beethoven. Starts with his childhood in Bonn and ends with his third-period works in Vienna.

Ludwig van Beethoven. Harmonics: The Innovators of Classical Music Series. www.films.com (DVD or VHS, color, 27 minutes). Letters, paintings, and scholarly commentary are used to explore Beethoven's life and musical innovations. Karl Böhm, Herbert von Karajan, and Leonard Bernstein conduct excerpts from Piano Concerto No. 4 and Symphonies 3, 5, 8, and 9.

The Revolutionary. Music in Time Series. www.films.com (DVD or VHS, color, 60 minutes). James Galway narrates this look at Beethoven's life and major works. Performances by the Los Angeles, Berlin, and Vienna Philharmonics led by Giulini, von Karajan, and Böhm. Excerpts from Beethoven's Quartets Op. 18, No. 1, and Op. 135; Symphonies 3, 6, and 9; *Fidelio;* and the *Appassionata* Sonata.

❼ Software

Art and Music: Romanticism. Zane Publishing (CD-ROM—Windows or Macintosh). CD-ROM version of the video above. This inexpensive volume draws parallels between the paintings of Delacroix, Goya, and Turner and the music of Beethoven, Berlioz, Chopin, Liszt, Mendelssohn, and Wagner. Available from www.cdaccess.com.

Beethoven. www.films.com (CD-ROM—Macintosh and Windows). Multimedia guide to Beethoven's life and music contains video and audio performances, scores, early criticism of Beethoven's music, works lists, and so on.

Beethoven Pathétique Sonata. Time Sketch Piano Series. www.ecsmedia.com (CD-ROM—Windows or Macintosh). Program presents a CD recording of Beethoven's *Pathétique* Sonata and other works, with interactive arch map analysis and background information about the composer, his style, and the work. Recommended for a look at a work from the composer's first-period style.

Beethoven Piano Concerto No. 3. Time Sketch Piano Series. www.ecsmedia.com (CD-ROM—Windows or Macintosh). Program presents a CD recording of Beethoven's Third Piano Concerto and other works, with interactive arch map analysis and background information about the composer, his style, and the work. Recommended.

Beethoven's 5th: The Multimedia Symphony. Future Vision Multimedia (CD-ROM—Macintosh and Windows). This multimedia guide offers many of the features found in other CD-ROM packages: a biography of Beethoven, an introduction to instruments of the orchestra, a structural map of the symphony, and a listening guide that provides running commentary while the music plays. Distinctive features of this package include an attractive, user-friendly interface, short QuickTime movies that demonstrate instruments, and an interesting time-line presentation of Beethoven's biography, which is peppered with quotations from Beethoven and his contemporaries. Highly recommended. Try this CD-ROM if you use Class Discussion Idea 2 above. Available from www.cdaccess.com.

Beethoven Symphony No. 5. Time Sketch Composer Series. www.ecsmedia .com (CD-ROM—Windows or Macintosh). Program presents a CD recording of Beethoven's Symphony No. 5 and other works, with interactive arch map analysis and background information about the composer, his style, and the work. Highly recommended supplement to your presentation of the Fifth.

Great Composers: Beethoven, Grieg, and Hanson. www.mccormicksnet.com (CD-ROM—Windows or Macintosh). This inexpensive CD-ROM includes a multimedia presentation, photographs, quizzes, and sound clips. Available from www.cdaccess.com.

The History of Music. www.mccormicksnet.com (CD-ROM—Windows or Macintosh). CD-ROM version of the videos above. The section on Classicism covers early Beethoven, and the one on early Romanticism covers late Beethoven, Schubert, Berlioz, Liszt, Chopin, Schumann, and Verdi.

The Norton Masterworks CD-ROM. New York: W. W. Norton (CD-ROM—Macintosh). Authors Daniel Jacobson and Timothy Koozin provide a clever multimedia introduction to twelve important works, including Beethoven's Symphony No. 5. Features animated and guided listening resources as well as information on the composers, eras, and genres, and the works themselves.

CHAPTER 15

Prelude
Music after Beethoven: Romanticism

Chapter Outline

Boldface indicates works in the recording set.

Suggested Listening

Tchaikovsky, *Romeo and Juliet*

Berlioz, *Fantastic* Symphony
R. Schumann, "Im wunderschönen Monat Mai"

Wagner, *The Valkyrie*, Prelude

Important Terms

Romanticism	*rubato*	"inner form"
cult of individual feeling	Romantic melody	miniatures
revolt	chromaticism	grandiose compositions
the supernatural	Romantic orchestra	thematic unity
artistic barriers	instrumental combinations	thematic transformation
the public	program music	

Teaching Objectives

❧ Overall Objectives

This chapter will help students acquire familiarity with:

1. Recurrent themes in music and the arts during the Romantic era: the cult of the individual, revolt, the supernatural, artistic freedom, and a restless boundlessness.

2. The problem of the growing gap between composers and concert audiences.

3. Typical Romantic uses of rhythm, melody, harmony, tone color, and the orchestra.

4. Romantic formal procedures as solutions to the conflict between artistic freedom and the need for meaningful structures: miniatures, grandiose compositions, program music, and thematic unity.

❧ Listening Objectives

After completing this chapter, students should be able to:

1. Hear and identify how the recurrent themes of Romanticism affect typical uses of the elements of music in Romantic style.

2. Hear how Romanticism derives from aspects of Classical style and the music of Beethoven.

Lecture Suggestions

The Romantic themes of artistic freedom and the cult of individual feeling worked against the existence of a uniform "period" style. Self-expression was prized above all else, and each composer sought to define a unique style. In spite of this tendency, broad, general characteristics of Romantic style can be identified. Like Chapters 8 and 11, this chapter introduces the trends and themes of a major historical period. The following three chapters—on early Romanticism, Romantic opera, and late Romanticism—demonstrate the different ways these tendencies influenced individual works. The primary task in this chapter is to clarify important Romantic themes and style features. The lecture suggestions below can help you work with students to develop a checklist of Romantic themes and style features. This checklist will prove useful when you study the musical examples in Chapters 16–18.

Less than a century separated late Baroque and early Romantic styles. Enormous changes took place in that turbulent period. Quickly review the stages on the way to Romanticism.

1. The Baroque period was characterized by scientific investigation and systematic observation of natural phenomena as well as by extravagance and theatricality. The musical manifestation of the Baroque genius for systematic, ordered thought was instrumental polyphony. Baroque opera developed as a powerful vehicle for the systematic portrayal of human emotions in drama and music.

2. The Classical style was shaped by the Enlightenment, a period that saw human values elevated above those of church and state. The Enlightenment valued humanism, not science. The music of the Enlightenment was simpler and more "natural." Classical composers preferred homophonic textures, and they created new musical forms to exploit the dramatic possibilities presented by homophony. Classical opera developed a more realistic, natural approach in its portrayal of character types, emotions, and dramatic momentum.

3. Beethoven imbued the homophonic forms of Mozart and Haydn with new force and emotion. He stretched these forms to the breaking point in his search for new modes of expression. Through Beethoven, music became a mode of explicit self-expression, a tenet that grew out of the Enlightenment's emphasis on the importance of the individual.

In these three stages, the following trends can be observed:

1. An ever-increasing emphasis on "natural" human values and self-expression in music.

2. The creation of musical forms that exploit the dramatic possibilities inherent in contrast.

3. A continuing movement away from sacred music toward secular music (including a more secular reinterpretation of the sacred).

4. The transformation of the symphony and other instrumental genres into significant modes of emotional self-expression.

5. A growing reliance on instrumental music for presentation of the most profound musical ideas.

These trends are reflected in the themes of Romanticism: the cult of individual feeling and individual style; revolt; artistic freedom; and a restless, endless search for higher experience and higher expression. These themes grew out of Classical music, the Enlightenment, a new social consciousness, and the response to Beethoven. Romanticism does not represent a complete break with Classicism; rather, it transformed the elements and structures of Classical style according to the themes that dominated the new era.

Romanticism

Work through the themes described by the authors on textbook pages 240–44: the cult of individual feeling, revolt, the supernatural, the breakdown of artistic barriers, and the endless search for new forms of expression. These themes characterize culture and the arts in the nineteenth century. They are not important as abstract concepts, but for the insights they offer into Romantic culture. From the beginning, these themes must be compared with and tested against nineteenth-century historical events, artworks, and musical compositions.

Start by making Kerman and Tomlinson's discussion of these themes (textbook pages 240–44) assigned reading. Ask students to make a checklist of themes and to identify the primary features of each theme. Use the following exercise to clarify these themes. The textbook illustrates these pages with several nineteenth-century artworks. Divide the class into small groups and assign a different painting to each group. Ask the groups to study their assigned artworks and compare them with the checklist of Romantic themes. Each group should choose a person to take the minutes of their discussion. Once the small groups have finished, ask the recorder from each group to report the results of their discussions to the class. As class discussion winds down, point out the frequent depiction of nature in these paintings. Nature was a source of endless fascination for Romantic artists and thinkers, and it is reflected in many Romantic themes.

Cult of individual feeling—In Romantic artworks, nature often served as a mirror for the individual's feelings. At the same time, the Industrial Revolution left many city dwellers feeling helpless ("rage against the machine") and nostalgic for the "natural" surroundings they left behind.

The supernatural—The Enlightenment philosopher Rousseau found nature a condition to aspire to, but Romantic artists often focused on the malevolent side of nature. If nature could mirror sublime feelings, it could also mirror the dark recesses of the human soul.

Artistic barriers—As North American explorers opened up the interior to settlers, the image of the wilderness, with its freedom from human boundaries and restrictions, appealed greatly to Romantic artists. Nature's power and vastness were intriguing.

ϒ Concert Life in the Nineteenth Century

As the authors point out, the dominance of the concert hall revolutionized music making. Composers were no longer bound to satisfy the whims of a single patron, but the paying concert audience created a new set of difficulties. Audiences wanted works of "value," masterpieces produced by great geniuses, such as Beethoven's symphonies. This cult of genius, or cult of the masterpiece, pulled in two directions at the same time. On the up side, these circumstances hastened the development of an esthetic that valued self-expression and individual styles; on the down side, Romantic audiences became leery of anything too new or too novel, whose value was not yet established. One sort of "value" that could easily be perceived was virtuosity; virtuoso performers such as Paganini, Liszt, Jenny Lind, and Gottschalk toured Europe and the Americas to great acclaim. In this age of the virtuoso, the overall technical proficiency of the performing musician improved by leaps and bounds.

ϒ Style Features of Romantic Music

As you work through the style features of Romantic music, add a list of these features to your checklist of Romantic themes. Use your checklist of Romantic themes when you cover each style feature; ask students to determine which themes influenced each style feature.

Rhythm: Rubato

Rubato was an expressive Romantic performance technique of slightly slowing and speeding the tempo of a piece of music. Its effect, when well performed, is to create a breathlike sense of rising and falling, an almost conversational sense of line. The speeding up balances the slowing down so that the overall duration of the piece is much the same whether it is performed "straight" or with *rubato*. *Rubato* reflects the themes of individual freedom (self-expression for the performer), revolt (against the tyranny of the beat), artistic freedom, and the restless quality associated with the search for higher expression.

Play the first minute or so of the following pieces. Ask students to listen for the different uses of rhythm, meter, and tempo in these three excerpts. Encourage them to tap their feet with the beat.

Haydn, Symphony No. 95, IV (track 33)

Schumann, *Carnaval,* "Eusebius" (0:00–0:52)

Schumann, *Carnaval,* "Florestan" (entire piece)

Ask the class to describe what effect these uses of rhythm, meter, and tempo create in each piece. Draw out these points in the discussion that follows.

1. Haydn's symphony movement has a clear, consistent beat. The meter is duple. The music creates a sense of constant forward motion.

2. Schumann's "Eusebius" presents a different character. The melody moves so freely that it is difficult to find a beat; the left-hand accompaniment provides a more constant pulse. In spite of the extraordinary rhythmic freedom of the melody, the performer in this recording actually keeps a rather steady beat; she mostly slows it down at cadence points. Play this example again and count along with the left-hand accompaniment so that students clearly perceive the tempo changes. This subtle *rubato* does not create the constant motion of Haydn's rondo; rather, it sets each phrase apart from the other as an expressive entity with its own ebb and flow.

3. Schumann's "Florestan" displays extreme fluctuations in tempo—far more extreme than those of "Eusebius." It is easy to spot the tempo changes, but they are more drastic than one would expect of *rubato.* In fact, Schumann wanted this exaggerated effect and wrote contrasting tempo indications into the score itself. The tempo changes create inconsistent, mercurial moods. At one moment the music surges forward; at the next, it draws back. This dramatic, wavelike motion makes for a vivid contrast with Haydn's constant forward motion.

Romantic Melody

Romantic melody, like Romantic rhythm, takes on a speechlike eloquence. Ask the class to compare the following two melodies.

Mozart, *Don Giovanni,* "Là ci darem la mano" (0:00–0:40)

Tchaikovsky, *Romeo and Juliet* (track 27, 0:56–2:01)

Mozart's duet between the two would-be lovers is charming and expressive in its own way, but it sounds tame next to Tchaikovsky's surging, passionate love theme. In the discussion that follows, draw out these comparisons.

Mozart	*Tchaikovsky*
short, equal phrases	long, irregular phrases
clear cadences at regular intervals	cadences not clearly articulated
stable harmonic underpinning	unstable, ever-shifting harmony
restricted registral space	wide range, nearly two octaves
expresses the text	expresses a story, but without words

Tchaikovsky's melody expresses an impassioned yearning, a marvelous statement of individual feeling, freedom from artistic barriers, and a restless boundlessness. Call attention to the following paragraph from textbook page 247.

When one thinks of Romantic melody, what comes first to mind is the grand, exaggerated emotionality of Tchaikovsky or Mahler. Some Romantic melodies are more intimate, however—and they are no less emotional for sparing the handkerchief, as it were. Each in an individual way, Romantic composers learned to make their melodies dreamy, sensitive, passionate, ecstatic, or whatever shade of feeling they were able to express.

Melody was one of the primary expressions of individual feeling. According to the whim of the composer, melody was capable of expressing any of the themes associated with Romanticism.

Romantic Harmony

Used to support Romantic melody or "savored for its own sake," Romantic harmony underwent enormous changes and advances during the nineteenth century. The authors describe Romantic harmony as the most potent tool used by composers to create specific moods. In Classical sonata forms, we focused on the use of harmony to create either stability or instability; Romantic composers—discovering new and unusual chords or using tools such as chromaticism, dissonance, and frequent modulation to distant keys—created an incredible variety of different moods on a wide spectrum between stability and instability.

Play the first minute or so of the following pieces. Ask students to listen for stability and instability in each excerpt.

Mozart, Piano Concerto in A, K. 488, I (track 37, 0:00–0:32)

Berlioz, *Fantastic* Symphony, V (track 2, 0:00–0:50)

In the discussion that follows, draw out these comparisons.

	Mozart concerto	*Berlioz symphony*
Tonality	tonic clearly established, easy to find	ambiguous, searching, often hard to find
Modulation	one brief modulation to a closely related key	hard to tell when tonality is so ambiguous
Chords	simple, triadic sonorities; consonant	unstable, often dissonant
Consonance	consonant, stable	dissonant, strong pull to resolve
Chromaticism	diatonic, based on major scale	complete chromatic scale used
Mood	simple, stable, lovely tune	eerie sound effects, unstable, never really resolves

Romantic harmony expressed individual feeling with great sensitivity, and its advances broke down many older rules and principles (artistic barriers) for its use. Like melody, it could express any of the themes associated with Romanticism.

The Expansion of Tone Color

As mentioned earlier, Romantic virtuoso performers explored new and dazzling techniques for their individual instruments. Similar developments took place in compositions for orchestra. The size and instrumental variety of the orchestra grew during the Romantic period. In addition, Romantic composers combined instruments in novel ways to create entirely new orchestral timbres. As composers attempted to express more and more of their feelings and imaginations musically, they constantly invented new sounds appropriate to their ideas. With its endlessly flexible palette of color combinations, the orchestra became the quintessential musical ensemble of the Romantic era.

Play the following two excerpts. Ask students to describe the type of instruments and relative size of the orchestra in each excerpt.

Mozart, Symphony No. 40 in G Minor, I (track 16, 0:00–track 17, 1:08)

Berlioz, *Fantastic* Symphony, V (track 2, 0:00–track 3, 0:36)

Only forty years separate these two works, but what a difference forty years can make! In the discussion that follows, draw out these points:

1. Berlioz's *Fantastic* Symphony is written for an ensemble well over twice the size of Mozart's.

2. The principal timbre in Mozart's orchestra is the string family, augmented by oboes, flutes, bassoons, and horns. Berlioz's coloristic variety is stunning. No single family of instruments dominates the texture—strings; various solo brass and winds; and various combinations of brass, winds, and percussion move in and out of the texture, creating an incredibly rich experience of sounds.

One further distinction relates to the problem of form in Romantic music. Mozart's symphony falls into the category of absolute music; Berlioz's is program music. Mozart's music consists of themes, transitions and cadences, stable and unstable harmonies, and homophony and imitation. The orchestration is important insofar as it clearly expresses the absolute musical characteristics of the movement. Berlioz's incredible sounds immediately evoke extramusical images. In this movement, Berlioz portrays a witches' sabbath; the eerie music at the beginning sets the tone for the midnight festivities. The motives, harmonies, cadences, and textures are vehicles for the supernatural timbral effects—in other words, the orchestration *is* the central point of the piece.

¶ Form in Romantic Music

The spontaneity, individualism, and creative freedom treasured by Romantic composers were at odds with the notion of preordained musical forms. Early Romantic composers who used traditional Classical forms often twisted and altered them almost beyond recognition. Many Romantic composers, particularly the early ones, abandoned Classical forms altogether. It was almost as if composers lived in fear of the shadow cast by Beethoven. Most early Romantic composers avoided works that would beg comparison with Beethoven's— especially symphonies, string quartets, and piano sonatas. When they did write such works, composers went beyond the traditional restrictions imposed by these genres, instead following paths suggested by the music of Beethoven, especially that of his third period. All of the categories that the authors list have parallels in Beethoven's music. Beethoven's late bagatelles and folk-song arrangements were miniatures; chorus, soloists, and large orchestras make his Ninth Symphony and *Missa Solemnis* grandiose; his Sixth Symphony (*Pastoral*) was the first great program symphony; and thematic unity is manifest in the Fifth and Ninth Symphonies.

You have no need (or time) to play complete song cycles, symphonies, or operas here—this final section of the chapter simply alerts the reader to important structural, formal aspects of works about to be covered. As these aspects reveal themselves in the next three chapters, make sure you point them out. For now, identify the formal principles the authors discuss and list several upcoming listening examples that demonstrate each principle.

Miniatures	Schubert, "Erlkönig"
	Schubert, Moment Musical No. 2 in A-flat
	R. Schumann, *Dichterliebe*
	C. Schumann, "Der Mond kommt still gegangen"
	R. Schumann, *Carnaval*
	Chopin, Nocturne in F-sharp, Op. 15, No. 2
Grandiose compositions	Berlioz, *Fantastic* Symphony, V
	Verdi, *Aida*
	Wagner, *The Valkyrie*
	Tchaikovsky, *Romeo and Juliet*
	Musorgsky, *Pictures at an Exhibition*
	Mahler, Symphony No. 1
Program music	R. Schumann, *Carnaval*
	Berlioz, *Fantastic* Symphony, V
	Tchaikovsky, *Romeo and Juliet*
	Musorgsky, *Pictures at an Exhibition*
	Mahler, Symphony No. 1, III
The principle of thematic unity	R. Schumann, *Carnaval*
	Berlioz, *Fantastic* Symphony, V
	Wagner, *The Valkyrie*
	Musorgsky, *Pictures at an Exhibition*

Additional Teaching Suggestions

❧ Lecture-Demonstration Ideas

1. To provide your students with a sense of the fullness and variety of the fine arts in the Romantic era, create a slide show to supplement the illustrations in the textbook. Borrow some slides from the art department (or see Multimedia Resources below for video and CD-ROM supplements) and show Romantic paintings and historic sites to your class. Ask the students to look for Romantic themes in these artworks. Encourage students who are majoring in humanities such as literature or philosophy to contribute from their own majors.

2. If you have a historical bent, look at revolts in the nineteenth century. The French Revolution of 1789 was decisive, but Paris saw further revolts in 1830 and 1848—a year of revolutions throughout Europe. Discuss the impact of these revolts on nineteenth-century culture and music.

3. Look for Romantic features in Beethoven's music. Work through the checklists of Romantic themes and style features and see how closely they fit Beethoven's music. Beethoven insisted on self-expression, stretched artistic barriers, and took inspiration from nature and from other arts. He explored chromatic harmonies and expanded the size and constitution of the symphony orchestra. He anticipated grandiose compositions (Symphony No. 9), program music (Symphony No. 6), and cyclic form (Symphonies 5 and 9). In many areas, Beethoven served as a model for Romantic composers.

ꙮ Class Discussion Ideas

1. *Do the themes of self-expression and expression of emotions show up before the Romantic era? If so, how do earlier manifestations differ from Romantic uses?* Self-expression may not be so easy to find before Beethoven, but the Baroque period was based on the idea of depicting emotions. Ask students how Baroque emotional depiction differs from Romantic expression of individual feeling.

2. *What are the differences between the Classical and the Romantic styles?* This question works well at the end of Chapter 15 as a review of this chapter and of Classical style. Create two columns on the board under which to write student ideas. Musical examples can help stimulate discussion.

3. *Were women accepted as legitimate composers in the nineteenth century?* Read excerpts from Carol Neuls-Bates's *Women in Music* (New York: Harper & Row, 1982). The section titled "The 'Woman Composer Question'" contains several readings (from the late nineteenth and early twentieth centuries) that attempt to answer the once-burning question, Can women compose great music? Many perspectives are represented and can be used to generate an interesting discussion.

4. *How does cyclic form differ from other multimovement genres?* This question requires a brief review of cyclic form. Several other questions need to be raised as part of the discussion. *How were movements connected with each other before the development of cyclic form? What effect does cyclic form create in a multimovement work?* In the discussion, draw a clear distinction between traditional multimovement formats (which generally have no thematic connections between movements) and cyclic form. Supplement your discussion with musical examples (see Multimedia Resources below).

ꙮ Listening Ideas

1. Demonstrate the theme of individual feeling. Play short excerpts by different Romantic composers and ask students to describe the differences between them. Any of the examples from Chapters 16–18 can be used, including Schumann's "Im wunderschönen Monat Mai," Chopin's Nocturne, the fifth movement of Berlioz's *Fantastic* Symphony, Tchaikovsky's *Romeo and Juliet,* and Mahler's Symphony No. 1. If you have time, try a similar exercise with Classical style. Play two unfamiliar excerpts, one by Haydn and one by Mozart. Ask students if it was easier or harder for them to find significant differences between these two composers than among the Romantics.

2. Compare the use of chromaticism in different historic eras. Play examples from the Baroque ("When I am laid in earth" from Purcell's *Dido and Aeneas*), Classical (theme 2 from the first movement of Mozart's Symphony No. 40), and Romantic (Berlioz's *Fantastic* Symphony) eras. Note that the Purcell remains entirely within a single key and Mozart's decorative chromaticism remains mostly in one key (with a surprise move away at the end of the second repetition), but Berlioz's chromaticism exerts a profound effect on the melody, harmony, and tonal center.

3. Demonstrate the historic importance of thematic transformation by playing listening examples from the textbook. Play brief examples of thematic trans-

formation in Beethoven's Symphony No. 5, Berlioz's *Fantastic* Symphony, Wagner's *The Valkyrie,* and Bernstein's *West Side Story.* The styles differ, but the technique serves a similar function in each case.

Multimedia Resources

❧ Sound Recordings

Beethoven, *Nine Symphonies.* Orchestre Révolutionnaire et Romantique. Deutsche Grammophon Archiv 439 900-2 (CD). Raw, powerful performances of Beethoven's complete symphonies. These period-instrument recordings permit us to hear the ferocious intensity Beethoven achieved by pushing the instruments of his day to their limits, yet they more than hold their own in comparison with modern-instrument performances. Period-instrument performances of Classical music have truly come of age! (Symphonies 3, 5, and 9 are also available separately.) Highly recommended. Try this recording if you use Lecture-Demonstration Idea 3, Class Discussion Idea 4, or Listening Idea 3 above.

Berlioz, *Symphonie fantastique.* Orchestre Révolutionnaire et Romantique. Philips 434 402-2 (CD). This recording of Berlioz's masterwork uses the original 1830 orchestration on period instruments; conducted by John Eliot Gardiner. Gardiner is one of the most successful conductors of nineteenth-century repertory on period instruments, and the bold colors and vitality of this performance vividly convey the composer's audacity. Try this recording if you use Listening Idea 3 above.

Bernstein, *West Side Story.* Kiri Te Kanawa and José Carreras. Deutsche Grammophon 457 199-2 (CD). Bernstein's final recording of his classic musical. Operatic voices jar a bit at first, but the results are often strikingly beautiful. Try this recording if you use Listening Idea 3 above.

Wagner, *Die Walküre.* Vienna Philharmonic Orchestra. London 414 105-2 (CD). Sir Georg Solti's 1960s *Ring* cycle for London was perhaps the finest ever recorded. *The Valkyrie* features the great Wagnerian soprano Birgit Nilsson with Hans Hotter, Christa Ludwig, James King, Régine Crespin, and Gottlob Frick. The Wagner *Listen* recording was taken from this CD set. Try this recording if you use Listening Idea 3 above.

❧ Video Recordings

Age of the Individual. Music of Man Series. Home Vision (VHS, color, 60 minutes). Yehudi Menuhin narrates this look at the Romantic era. Includes material on Chopin, Liszt, Verdi, Wagner, Brahms, and Tchaikovsky.

Classical and Romantic Music: Keys to Authentic Interpretation. www.films .com (DVD or VHS, color, 60 minutes). Video follows Evelyn Tubb and John Potter as they rehearse songs by Haydn, Dibdin, R. Schumann, and Lady Arthur Hill. Through the medium of the solo song, we see how these performers work to re-create the sound worlds of Classical and Romantic music.

Delaware Music Series. www.ecsmedia.com (DVD). This important series includes many resources for introducing Romanticism. For example, excerpts from Berlioz's *Fantastic* Symphony with scrolling score can be used to demonstrate thematic unity. All in all, this set comprises a superb resource for lecture-demonstrations introducing Romanticism.

The History of Music, Part 2: *Romanticism Through Modern.* www.insight-media.com (VHS, color, 92 minutes). The section on early Romanticism covers Beethoven, Schubert, Berlioz, Liszt, Chopin, Schumann, Verdi, and others.

Nationalism and Revolution. Music in Time Series. www.films.com (DVD or VHS, color, 60 minutes). James Galway narrates this look at the effect of political changes and revolt on Romantic music. Heavy emphasis on Romantic opera. Musical excerpts from Berlioz's Requiem; Liszt's *Légend* and *Fantasia on Hungarian Folk Themes;* Verdi's *Nabucco, Aida,* and Requiem; and Wagner's *Tannhäuser, Siegfried Idyll*, Prelude to *Tristan und Isolde,* and *Meistersinger.* Performances at La Scala and Bayreuth.

The Romantics. Music in Time Series. www.films.com (DVD or VHS, color, 60 minutes). James Galway narrates this look at the Romantic century. Musical examples include character pieces by Chopin (Polonaise in A-flat, Prelude), Schumann's "Im wunderschönen Monat Mai" (and Symphony No. 3), and other works by Mendelssohn, Brahms, and Bruckner.

The Spirit of Romanticism. www.insight-media.com (VHS, color, 26 minutes). This video looks at the Romantic movement in literature, art, and music. It covers significant events and some important figures of early Romanticism (1789–1838), including Wordsworth, Delacroix, Shelley, Byron, Beethoven, and Chopin.

♪ Software

Art and Music: Romanticism. Zane Publishing (CD-ROM—Windows or Macintosh). This inexpensive volume draws parallels between the paintings of Delacroix, Goya, and Turner and the music of Beethoven, Berlioz, Chopin, Liszt, Mendelssohn, and Wagner. Available from www.cdaccess.com.

The History of Music. www.mccormicksnet.com (CD-ROM—Windows or Macintosh). CD-ROM version of the video above. The section on early Romanticism covers Beethoven, Schubert, Berlioz, Liszt, Chopin, Schumann, and Verdi.

CHAPTER **16**

The Early Romantics

Chapter Outline

Boldface indicates works in the recording set.

Important Terms

lied, lieder

accompaniment

poetry

mood

through-composed song

strophic song

song cycle

étude

character pieces

nocturnes

program music

concert overture

program symphonies

idée fixe

Dies irae

col legno

Teaching Objectives

❦ Overall Objectives

This chapter will help students acquire familiarity with:

1. Principal genres of the early Romantic period as individual solutions to the problem of form, each creating thematic unity in either miniature or grandiose contexts:

    a. German lied and the song cycle

    b. Character pieces for piano

    c. Program music, especially the program symphony

2. The lives and music of Franz Schubert, Robert Schumann, Clara Wieck Schumann, Frédéric Chopin, and Hector Berlioz (*optional*: Franz Liszt, Felix Mendelssohn, and Fanny Mendelssohn).

❦ Listening Objectives

After completing this chapter, students should be able to:

1. Hear how the elements of music are typically used in early Romantic music.

2. Identify and follow the genres of early Romantic music, especially the lied, character piece, and program symphony.

3. Hear different techniques used to create thematic unity in early Romantic music.

Lecture Suggestions

The music of the early Romantic era offers an embarrassment of riches. As the textbook points out, the years 1797 to 1813 saw the births of Schubert, Robert Schumann, Liszt, Chopin, Mendelssohn, Berlioz, Wagner, and Verdi. Because the Romantic era is characterized by individual styles, each of these composers created a unique body of work. This manual presents lecture outlines for each of the genres covered in Chapter 16. You must face a difficult decision here: which composers and compositions to discuss in class and which to omit. There are no right or wrong choices; in fact, it is best to choose the works you know and like and can teach effectively. Students respond best if they sense you are enthusiastic about what you teach.

❦ The Lied

The early Romantic era saw a great outpouring of German Romantic poetry by Goethe, Müller, Heine, and many others. Composers like Schubert and Schumann were fascinated by these poems and keenly sensitive to the meaning of the words. They turned out songs by the hundreds, both singly and in collections called song cycles.

Through-Composed and Strophic Songs

Start with discussion of the techniques composers use to set poetry to music. Two types of settings stand at opposite ends of a spectrum of possibilities: strophic settings, which use the same music for each stanza of text (like a hymn), and through-composed settings, which use different music for each stanza.

strophic ◄ ----------------------- ► through-composed
A A A A   A A A B   A B C A   **A B C D**

One can usually predict whether a song setting will be strophic or through-composed by looking at the poem. Poems with constantly changing emotions, like "Erlkönig," will be through-composed; poems with parallel stanzas, like "Im wunderschönen Monat Mai," strophic. Introduce each song you use by asking students to scan the poem as if they were composers setting words to music. Ask if they would use strophic or through-composed structure. Then ask which images and emotions they would express musically. What mood would they create? Often, the class will come close to describing the song, though they have not heard it yet. At this point, play the song and summarize its main features.

The order in which songs are presented here differs from the order in the *Listen* textbook. I have found it most effective to start with clear examples of through-composed and strophic songs and then to proceed to mixed settings that combine features of both. The two songs that follow are clear examples of through-composed and strophic settings.

SCHUBERT "Erlkönig"

1. It has a through-composed setting, with motives and phrases used throughout to create unity and tension. Nervous, hammering repeated notes throughout the song suggest the horse's pounding hooves, and the boy's "Mein Vater, mein Vater!" is higher-pitched each time it returns.

2. Schubert's characterization of father, boy, Erlking, and narrator must be mentioned. The father's phrases are low and gruff; the boy's, frightened and frantic; and the Erlking's, ominously sweet (the Erlking's stanzas take us out of the reality of the frantic ride through the night). Try asking four students to take these roles in a dramatic reading of the poem.

3. Tension builds through the whole song, reaching a peak in the quicker tempo of the last stanza. When the buildup stops abruptly, the narrator informs us bluntly, without sentiment ("like a recitative"!), that the child is dead. All ends with a final cadence.

ROBERT SCHUMANN *Dichterliebe* ("A Poet's Love")

"Im wunderschönen Monat Mai" ("In the wonderfully lovely month of May")

Dichterliebe is a cycle of sixteen songs based on a cycle of poems by Heinrich Heine. "Im wunderschönen Monat Mai" is the first song in the cycle. It exhibits the following features:

1. It is a strophic song, reflecting parallelism between the stanzas. Note the similar construction and phrasing of each stanza.

2. At first reading, poetic imagery suggests a spring scene at odds with Schumann's ambiguous, unresolved harmonies. Even the solo voice matches the hesitant mood of Schumann's harmonies. A more careful reading reveals that Schumann got it right after all. Yes, "Love broke through" and "I confessed to her my longing and desire," but the poem's ending does not tell us how the beloved responds to the poet's confession. We are left to experience the poet's ambiguous, unresolved feelings, which *are* at odds with images of spring.

Mixed Settings

The next two songs are not purely strophic or through-composed but mix elements of each. The first is mostly strophic with a through-composed ending, and the second is mostly through-composed with strophic features introduced (some stanzas repeat).

CLARA SCHUMANN *"Der Mond kommt still gegangen"* ("The moon has risen softly")

1. It starts off as a strophic song, in response to the similar mood and imagery of the poem's first two quatrains. The changed mood that the authors point to in the third quatrain leads us to suspect (correctly) a different musical treatment. While the third stanza starts out like a literal repeat of the other stanzas, Schumann quickly intensifies the musical expression. Following the poet's lead, she begins her second phrase in the middle of the stanza's first line, then extends the phrase by a measure to emphasize the first syllable of "Liebchens," the climax of the entire song. A lesser composer might make sure to synchronize musical phrases with the lines of the poem's stanzas; Schumann's more imaginative approach shows the expressive touch of a master.

St. 1: ¹The moon has ri - sen soft - ly ²With gleaming rays of gold ³Be - neath its shin - ing splendor ⁴The wea - ry earth's at rest.
St. 2: ¹And on the drifting breez-es ²From man - y faith - ful minds ³Endearing thoughts by the thousand ⁴Waft down on those who sleep.

St. 3: ¹Und drun-ten im Ta-le, die funkeln ²Die Fenster von Lieb - chens Haus; ³Ich a - ber blikke im Dunkeln Still . . .
      ¹And down in the val-ley, the window's ²A - light in my loved - one's house ³But I keep staring in darkness silently

The final two phrases are entirely new, and their emphasis on the word "Still" gently mirrors Schumann's treatment of "Liebchens." The song ends with a brief piano coda. The final stanza and coda introduce through-composed elements into a predominantly strophic setting.

2. The slowly falling, gently throbbing piano figures may suggest the moon's "gleaming rays" or the "drifting breezes" that "waft down" in the first two stanzas. These alluring images give way to a vision of darkness and loneliness in stanza 3. This poem, like hundreds of other Romantic poems, paints idyllic images of nature only to contrast them with the poet's bleak, lonely interior landscape. The music must reflect these changes, of course. The previous paragraph describes musical changes in the third stanza, but the coda also testifies to this changed mood. The same falling, throbbing piano figures reappear in the brief coda, but with a minor-mode flavor that suggests the poet's emotional bruises.

ROBERT SCHUMANN *Dichterliebe* ("A Poet's Love")

"Die alten, bösen Lieder" ("The bad old songs")

1. The song is mostly through-composed, though the music of the first stanza returns in stanza 5, and the music of stanza 2 is used in varied form in stanzas 3 and 4. The form of the song might be expressed as follows:

	A	B	B′	B″	A′	C	coda
Stanzas:	1	2	3	4	5	6	piano solo
	0:04	0:22	0:40	0:58	1:17	1:48	2:35

2. Thematic unity is preserved by repeating motives and phrases and even stanzas (a strophic element).

3. The singer and pianist work together as equal partners in an artistic unit, changing tempo and expression freely, sometimes dramatically.

4. A lengthy coda offers a pensive, lyric contrast to the prevailing sadness and drama of the song itself.

Conclusions to Draw about Lieder

1. The lied, a type of miniature work, does not rely on elaborate musical forms. Songs juxtapose two levels of meaning: verbal and musical. Musical form usually follows the structure of the poem, with the composer left to evoke the emotional world of the poem in musical terms.

2. Thematic unity is achieved when the same music repeats in the stanzas of a strophic setting and also when motives or phrases return throughout a through-composed song.

3. Lieder were a significant, intimate form of musical expression in the early Romantic era.

4. Song cycles grouped songs that told a story or dealt with similar themes. These works permitted composers to probe subjects and emotions in greater depth yet retain the intimacy of the solo song.

❦ The Character Piece for Piano

Briefly outline the development of the piano since Mozart. The pianos of Mozart's time were fragile instruments; their frames could not support great string tension. As a result, the thin, light strings used in early pianos produced a quiet, slightly metallic sound (see the *Listen* recording of LeBrun's Piano Sonata in F). By the beginning of the Romantic era, pianos had become larger and more durable. Cast-iron frames, which could support much greater string tension, allowed the use of heavier, wrapped-wire strings. These metal-frame pianos produced a richer, more sonorous tone than their ancestors. Further, more notes were added to the piano keyboard during the nineteenth century. The highest note in Mozart's and LeBrun's day, f^3, was one-and-a-half octaves below the high c^5 on a modern piano.

Early Romantic composers exploited the emotional power and expressive capabilities of these ever-larger pianos. The piano is sometimes called "the instrument of Romanticism."

Character pieces—short piano works that convey a certain mood or character—were written by the thousands in the Romantic era. They are known by a host of vague, atmospheric titles: preludes, ballades, nocturnes, études, *musical moments, Album Leaves, Songs without Words, Pictures at an Exhibition, Scenes from Childhood,* and so on.

Musical examples can be presented as follows:

1. Introduce each character piece by describing its title: what it means and what mood one can expect.

2. Help students follow the form of each work, usually a simple, sectional form. Outline the form on the board and point to it while the music plays.

3. Identify unique characteristics of the composer's piano music.

After playing, ask students both to describe the mood each piece creates and to identify the musical elements used to create that mood.

SCHUBERT Moment Musical No. 2 in A-flat

Schubert's music underwent an enormous transformation during his brief life. We see this most clearly in large-scale pieces, notably his symphonies and chamber works. In these genres, early works partake fully of the Viennese Classical idiom, but under the spell of Beethoven, his late works add drama and gravitas to his usual outpouring of beautiful melody. Schubert's brand of lyric Romanticism shows up most consistently, however, in his miniature works, especially his lieder and character pieces. These works offered a freedom of expression and harmonic exploration that inspired Schubert to create some of his finest music. Moment Musical No. 2 provides an excellent example of Schubert's work in the character piece genre.

1. A French phrase, *moment musical* translates quite literally as "musical moment." The title is picturesque and poetic. Unlike the nocturne or the étude, it does not refer to any particular type of character piece, nor does it create any particular musical expectation, except perhaps that of brevity. Any mood is possible. In fact, the delicate lyricism and nostalgia of this musical moment stand in stark contrast with Moment Musical No. 3 in F Minor (see Further Listening Examples below for teaching suggestions on this minor-key example).

2. The form of this character piece is:

A	B	A′	(coda)	B′	A″	coda
0:00	1:20	2:23	3:17	3:57	4:54	5:36
m.1	m. 18	m. 36	m. 48	m. 56	m. 74	m. 83

Ternary (**A B A′**) form was probably the most frequently used form for a character piece. Schubert creates more of a rondo form here, but not without first trying to fool us into thinking it is ternary. The middle **A′** section even adds a coda to enhance the sense of finality—one could easily end the piece in m. 55 and no one would be the wiser. What follows this comes as a total surprise. Having been lulled by the gentle finality of the coda, we can now be shocked with a surprise *forte* worthy of Haydn. One further touch makes the surprise even more jarring, however. With none of the careful preparation Schubert gives to all other transitions in this piece, the **B′** section begins abruptly in the distant key of F-sharp minor! In fact, the word *distant* is not strong enough here. Compared with A-flat major, F-sharp minor is *really* remote, nearly all the way around the circle of fifths. This wrenching surprise creates a mood of genuine pathos that is only partially mitigated by the return of **A″**. Curiously, when Schubert ends the work with a coda *identical* to the one after the middle **A′**, we can't help but wonder if he will grab us by the throat again. In spite of the coda's obvious lyric beauty, this is not a comforting ending.

3. This work alternates between a beautifully lyric **A** theme tinged with melancholy and a more extroverted, emotive **B** that basks in a feeling of sadness. **A**'s mix of rocking figures and long chords makes it rhythmically ambiguous, but there can be no mistaking **B**'s clear-cut meter and drive. These contrasts energize the piece while they heighten the pathos of this beautiful yet disturbing music, giving it a genuinely Romantic flavor.

ROBERT SCHUMANN *Carnaval*

This is a collection of twenty character pieces. These vignettes are whimsical, intimate portraits that depict the personalities of people (some real, some fictitious) close to Schumann.

If you have time, you can describe the thematic relationships that make *Carnaval* an example of cyclic form. Schumann wrote these pieces during a youthful romance with a woman from Asch. Delighted that the letters in Asch were also in his last name, the composer translated these letters into three- and four-note motives that figure prominently throughout this work. *Asch* became A–E flat (Es in German)–C–B (Germans read "H" as the pitch B and "B" as B flat), or A flat (As in German)–C–B; *Scha* (from Schumann) became E flat–C–B–A.

"Eusebius"

1. Eusebius and Florestan are the names of Schumann's two fictitious alter egos. These strikingly different characters appear in many of Schumann's reviews for *Die Neue Zeitschrift für Musik*. The reviews are written as a dialogue, often heated, between Eusebius and Florestan, who often sound like a nineteenth-century Ebert and Roeper. Eusebius is a thoughtful dreamer and idealist who often seems to be in a world of his own. The music, with its unusual rhythms, rubato, and soft dynamic levels, captures the introspective, ethereal qualities of Eusebius's character.

2. This work is constructed simply from just two phrases, the second one a variant of the first. The form can be described as follows:

a a	**a′ a**	**a′ a**	**a′ a**
0:00	0:23	0:52	1:19
m. 1	m. 9	m. 17	m. 25
		(8ves)	

"Florestan"

1. Florestan is impetuous and mercurial, prone to severe mood shifts. The music captures Florestan's personality with its energetic first theme and abrupt changes of tempo, dynamics, register, and mood.

2. The form can be described as follows:

a	**a′**	**a″**	**a‴**
0:00	0:11	0:26	0:51
m. 1	m. 11	m. 23	m. 45

Each **a** section begins with the same melody, but each is extended differently, the last two sections much longer than the first two. The contrast provided by the extensions is enough that each new **a** section almost sounds like a return.

3. The **a** theme in this piece is based on one of the *Asch* motives, A–E flat–C–B.

CHOPIN **Nocturne in F-sharp, Op. 15, No. 2**

No composer better exploited the tone color and expressive capabilities of the piano, or wrote more idiomatically for the instrument, than Frédéric Chopin. Chopin's music is ideal for general music appreciation classes since it is almost universally liked and easily recognized.

1. Nocturnes are literally "night pieces." In Chopin's hands, this nocturne conveys a relaxed, beautiful singing quality. (Try turning down the lights while you play this.)

2. The form of the nocturne is:

a	a'	b	c	a''	coda
0:00	0:26	0:57	1:27	2:13	2:54
m. 1	m. 9	m. 17	m. 25	m. 37	m. 46

The **a** sections are varied through use of embellishment.

3. The elegant, lyric melody is freely embellished, often using chromatic lines. Slow tempo and liberal use of rubato provide a relaxed atmosphere.

Conclusions to Draw about Character Pieces

1. Character pieces, a representative miniature genre, do not rely on elaborate musical forms. They use a variety of simple, sectional forms to accomplish a primary goal: to express and sustain a single, distinctive mood.

2. Thematic unity is achieved through use of recurring motives and figures and through similarity of mood.

3. Character pieces account for the majority of piano music written in the Romantic period, an era in which the piano became enormously popular.

Early Romantic Program Music

Program music—instrumental music associated with a story or extramusical idea—assumes great significance in the Romantic era. In program symphonies and symphonic poems, an ever more colorful orchestral palette is used to convey an extraordinary range of moods and images.

BERLIOZ *Fantastic* Symphony

Hector Berlioz's *Fantastic* Symphony provides a spectacular example of the program symphony. It adapts the Classical four-movement plan to the purpose of telling its story, and displays the Romantic preoccupation with thematic unity.

Background

As fantastic as the symphony's program sounds, it does reflect real-life events. While watching her perform with a Shakespeare troupe, Berlioz fell hopelessly in love with the great actress Harriet Smithson. She refused all his advances, and this symphony was "inspired" by his feelings of rejection. The music expresses Berlioz's love in many ways but contains an element of revenge as well. As it turned out, Smithson attended one of the first performances and was moved to discover that the music was inspired by Berlioz's love for her. She returned Berlioz's attentions and the two were soon married. Love did not conquer all, however. Their marriage proved disastrous and ended in divorce.

The Program

At the first performance of the *Fantastic* Symphony, a program written by Berlioz himself was distributed to the audience. The program (which begins on textbook page 269 and continues in the margins on pages 272–73) outlined the "story" of each movement. As you introduce the symphony and individual movements, take time to read the program to the class—Berlioz's colorful language stands well by itself—and add any necessary comments or clarifications.

Thematic Unity: The "Fixed Idea"

Thematic unity is achieved in the *Fantastic* Symphony through use of an *idée fixe,* or fixed idea, which is the artist's musical image of his beloved. This melody, representing the unattainable beloved, is heard in each movement of the symphony but changes each time according to the emotional state of the artist and the dramatic action of the particular movement.

Play the fixed idea as it first appears in Movement I for the class.

Note the character of this melody:

1. The fixed idea is a long, typically discursive Romantic melody.

2. At the beginning of the symphony, the fixed idea reflects a beloved who is "at the same time noble and shy."

3. The melody's expressive quality can be gauged by observing the many dynamic, expressive, articulation, and tempo markings found in the music. Ask students to examine the melody as printed on textbook page 271.

The obvious thing to do before you go to Movement V is explore uses of the *idée fixe* in the first four movements. See Additional Teaching Suggestions below for several possible approaches. For example, the exercise in Further Listening Examples uses the fourth movement for a creative introduction to program music, and Listening Idea 5 follows the *idée fixe* through all five movements.

Fifth Movement: "Dream of a Witches' Sabbath"

This movement is described in detail in the textbook on pages 273–75. Here are some guidelines for presenting this movement to the class.

1. Read Berlioz's program for this movement.

2. At the center of the movement is a parody of the Catholic chant for the dead, the *Dies irae* ("Day of Wrath"). The declining power of the church is nicely illustrated by this movement. If Berlioz, a French Catholic, had written

such a devilish parody two hundred years earlier, he would probably have been burned at the stake; one hundred years earlier he might have been excommunicated. In 1830 this movement created a scandal, but that was all.

3. Play the *Dies irae* as it was heard in the Catholic liturgy until students can recognize at least the beginning of each phrase. (Some students may recognize it from the movies *K-19: The Widowmaker* or *Sleeping with the Enemy;* see Sound Recordings and Video Recordings for suggested performances.)

4. Compare this with the *Dies irae* portion of the fifth movement, track 4, 0:00–1:34. Explain how Berlioz repeats each phrase at three different tempos, as if the witches could hear the *Dies irae* melody sung at the artist's funeral and poke fun at it as part of their revels.

5. Point out the extraordinary orchestral effects Berlioz creates in this movement. Real Halloween music, this. Take special note of the sound effects created in the following sections:

Introduction (track 2, 0:00–1:37)—Filled with ominous sounds, including eerie, *sul ponticello* violins and violas, rumbles in the low strings, falling winds, and dissonant, sustained harmonies; fantastic images are conjured up.

Funeral bells (track 3, 1:12–1:37)—These bells set the stage for the *Dies irae;* they toll the witching hour and announce the funeral of the artist.

Col legno "skeleton dance" (track 7, 0:28–0:42)—By having the strings play *col legno* (with the stick of the bow), Berlioz creates an eerie clacking effect that suggests bones rattling.

6. Display Listening Chart 16 or write the large divisions of the movement on the board as follows:

Introduction	Mysterious effects	Fanfare	Fanfare
Fixed Idea Transformed	Prefatory statement	Riotous response	*Idée fixe*
Dies irae	Phrase 1 slow–faster–fastest	Phrase 2 slow–faster–fastest	Phrase 3 slow–faster–fastest
Witches' Round Dance	Exposition/Episode 1/Subject Entries/Episode 2/Subject Entry/Subject plus *Dies irae*/Subject Entry with *col legno*/*Dies irae*/Conclusion		

Play the movement, indicating each section as it is heard.

Conclusions to Draw about "Dream of a Witches' Sabbath"

1. Each large section ends with the equivalent of a theatrical blackout; the music simply stops and the next section begins. The lack of transitional music does not bother us a bit, since the movement is conceived theatrically. All aspects of a stage play are present: the scene is set (Introduction), characters are introduced (*idée fixe*), the artist's death is celebrated (*Dies irae*), and action builds to a climax in a devilish orgy (Witches' Round Dance).

2. Berlioz's use of instrumental timbre is phenomenal. The novel instrumental sounds, combinations, and playing methods create original, extraordinary sound effects.

3. How different this music is from that of Viennese Classical composers just forty years earlier! The fifth movement uses bizarre sound effects to tell an extramusical story. Symphonies by Haydn or Mozart do not "tell a story" but derive meaning, coherence, and drama from purely musical means.

Conclusions to Draw about the Fantastic *Symphony as a Characteristic Early Romantic Work*

The *Fantastic* Symphony clearly demonstrates a number of important early Romantic trends:

1. It tells a story through instrumental music—program music.

2. It blurs the lines between music, literature, and theater (and autobiography, here).

3. Thematic unity is realized through use of cyclic form, in which a theme is used in several movements as a unifying device.

4. It exhibits a fascination with the macabre and supernatural.

5. Its expanded orchestra and new orchestral timbres create new expressive effects.

6. Its forms are created in response to the dramatic context of each movement.

See Further Listening Examples below for lecture suggestions on another work that uses the *Dies irae*—Franz Liszt's *Totentanz.*

Additional Teaching Suggestions

ʔ **Lecture-Demonstration Ideas**

1. Invite a singer to class. Choose someone conversant with German Romantic songs who can perform works by Schubert or the Schumanns for your class. Interview your guest with questions about the experience of singing these songs, the life of a singer, or anything else that may interest the class. Leave time for student questions and discussion.

2. Invite a pianist to class. Choose someone conversant with Romantic piano literature who can perform works by Schubert, the Schumanns, Chopin, or Liszt for your class. Interview your guest using questions about the experience of playing this music, the life of a pianist, or anything else that may interest the class. Leave time for student questions and discussion.

3. Compare Classic and Romantic use of the piano. LeBrun's Sonata in F might be compared with Schubert's *Moments musicaux,* Schumann's *Carnaval,* or Chopin's Nocturne in F-sharp. Discussion might focus on physical changes in piano construction (pedals, metal frame), the expansion of the piano's range, and the development of virtuoso techniques used to play the instrument.

4. Compare Berlioz's *Fantastic* Symphony with a Classical symphony by Mozart, Haydn, or Beethoven. Comparisons can focus on the differences between Classical and Romantic musical style, between Classical and Romantic orchestras and orchestration, and between the Classical four-movement plan and the ways Berlioz adapts that format. Berlioz's first three movements are close to the Classical formula—sonata form, triple-meter dance movement, and slow movement. If you have time, you can also compare the Berlioz symphony with Beethoven's Symphony No. 6, a five-movement program symphony that influenced Berlioz. See Sound Recordings below for suggested performances of these works.

❼ Class Discussion Ideas

1. *Can music really tell a story?* Play a short example of program music by composers from Chapter 16—Mendelssohn's *Hebrides* Overture, Liszt's *Mazeppa* or *Les préludes,* excerpts from Schumann's *Carnaval* or Berlioz's *Romeo and Juliet* Symphony, or movements from Berlioz's *Fantastic* Symphony will do—without describing the program! Ask students to take their best guess at what the story is and write it down in half a page. Play the music a second time if necessary. Have them read their stories aloud and compare the results. How were the stories different? How were they similar? Then reveal the program intended by the composer. After comparison of student stories with the original, ask what the music was able to express. What was it not able to express? See Sound Recordings below for suggested performances of these works.

2. *What did music express for nineteenth-century musicians?* Read quotations by Romantic composers on music and expression. Especially good examples include E. T. A. Hoffman's essay on Beethoven's Fifth Symphony (Elliot Forbes, ed., *Beethoven: Symphony No. 5 in C Minor, Norton Critical Scores* Series, New York: Norton, 1971) and Franz Liszt's discussion of music as direct expression (Grout and Palisca's *History of Western Music,* 5th ed., New York: W. W. Norton, 1996, p. 564). Ask students to compare this with attitudes toward music in the Classical era or in earlier historical periods.

3. *What was it like to be a composer or musician living and working in the early nineteenth century?* Prepare by assigning readings from *Listen* (biographies of Schubert, Robert and Clara Schumann, Chopin, Liszt, and Berlioz). Additional readings (assigned or in class) from Berlioz's *Memoirs* or *Evenings with the Orchestra* can be highly entertaining. Many modern stereotypes about composers come from the Romantic period—the starving artist misunderstood in his or her own time, for example. According to Alexandre Dumas, "It was the fashion to suffer from the lungs; everyone was consumptive, poets especially; it was good form to spit blood after every emotion in any way sensational, and to die before reaching thirty."

4. *Why were there so few women who composed and performed music in the early Romantic period?* To provide specific issues to comment on, read a few quotations from diaries and letters written by Fanny Mendelssohn Hensel or Clara Schumann. *Women in Music: An Anthology of Source Readings from the Middle Ages to the Present,* edited by Carol Neuls-Bates (Harper & Row, 1982), provides many such resources. Page 154 gives the following:

> *Clara in her diary, November 1839:*   [Leipzig]
>
> I once thought that I possessed creative talent, but I have given up this idea; a woman must not desire to compose—not one has been able to do it, and why should I expect to? It would be arrogance, though indeed, my father led me into it in earlier days.

> *Robert in the joint diary, February 1843:*   [Leipzig]
>
> Clara has written a number of smaller pieces, which show a musicianship and a tenderness of invention such as she has never before attained. But children, and a husband who is always living in the realms of imagination, do not go well with composition. She cannot work at it regularly, and I am often disturbed to think how many tender ideas are lost because she cannot work them out.

❡ Listening Ideas

1. Compare Renaissance word painting with Romantic emotionality. Play Weelkes's "As Vesta Was from Latmos Hill Descending" and Schubert's "Erlkönig." Ask students to contrast how each composer "expresses" the text. Draw out the distinction between word painting, which expresses the meaning of the words, and Romantic expression of the feelings and characters suggested by the words.

2. Compare a song by Robert Schumann to a song by Clara Schumann. For additional songs by Clara Schumann, see Sound Recordings below or use her "Liebst du um Schönheit" from the anthology that accompanies K Marie Stolba's *Development of Western Music*, 3rd ed. (McGraw-Hill, 1998). Ask students to ponder these questions as they listen. Which expresses the text more faithfully? Which contains more distinctive musical ideas? How do you account for differences between the two?

3. Listen for uses of the *Asch-Scha* (A–E flat–C–B, A flat–C–B, or E flat–C–B–A) motives in Schumann's *Carnaval*. Bring a complete recording to class (see Sound Recordings below) and play the beginnings of preselected pieces. Conversation may center on the effect of these motives: Can they be heard? Do they create a sense of unity?

4. Compare two works based on the same melody. Comparison of "Là ci darem la mano" from Mozart's *Don Giovanni* with Chopin's Variations on "Là ci darem la mano," Op. 2 (for piano and orchestra), leads into discussion of differences in Classical and Romantic style. Comparison of the fifth movement of Berlioz's *Fantastic* Symphony with Liszt's *Totentanz* (see Listening Chart in Appendix I), both based on the traditional *Dies irae* plainchant, leads into discussion of the individual styles of Berlioz and Liszt and characteristics of Romantic style. See Sound Recordings below for suggested performances.

5. Play brief excerpts from all five movements of the *Fantastic* Symphony so that students can hear how Berlioz uses his *idée fixe* in each movement (see Sound Recordings below for suggested performances; for ready-made examples, see the *Delaware Music Series* in Video Recordings below). This effectively demonstrates Berlioz's use of cyclic form to achieve thematic unity. Before class you will need to determine cue points on your CD (manually or computer-assisted) or prepare MP3 excerpts or a cassette tape. In class, read the program for each movement before playing the excerpt. Ask students to compare these different versions of the same melody.

> *Movement 1* (mm. 72–111): introduces fixed idea as a main theme—"noble and shy"
>
> *Movement 2* (mm. 120–62): he sees her at a dance—triple meter, waltzlike version
>
> *Movement 3* (mm. 90–111): can't get her out of his head—stormy, fragmented version
>
> *Movement 4* (mm. 164–68): on the scaffold—clarinet solo version cut short by guillotine
>
> *Movement 5* (mm. 40–67): she becomes a witch—grotesque transformation of *idée fixe*

◥ Further Listening Examples

SCHUBERT "Der Jüngling an der Quelle" ("The Youth at the Spring")

Try this for another example of a mostly strophic lied. See Appendix II for text and translation, and Sound Recordings below for suggested performances. Follow the same procedures recommended for the other songs above. Read through the text with your students. Ask them to decide whether they would use a strophic or through-composed setting, and have them explain why. Then play the music and make the following observations.

1. This starts off as a strophic song, in response to the similar mood and imagery found in each of the poem's two quatrains. Those expecting the second stanza to be a literal repeat of the first will be surprised by Schubert's ending, which dwells on the sighing image in the last line. Schubert extends the ending by repeating the last two lines of the second quatrain and adding a short codetta that ends with a sighing motive on the word "Luise." The ending introduces a through-composed element into a predominantly strophic setting.

2. The rippling, arpeggiated piano accompaniment picks up on images from stanza 1 of a "rippling spring" and "whispering poplars," images that reappear in stanza 2—"leaves and brook are sighing." The poet, though he wishes to forget his loved one, is constantly reminded of her by the sounds of nature around him.

SCHUBERT Moment Musical No. 3 in F Minor

This character piece offers a fascinating contrast with the Moment Musical No. 2 in Lecture Suggestions above, emphasizing the expressive freedom such a vague title gives the composer. The marchlike Moment Musical No. 3 could hardly be more different than its A-flat major companion.

1. Once again, this moment musical does not create any particular musical expectation. This work creates a very different mood than the moment in A-flat. In spite of contrasts of melody and key, this work's jaunty march rhythms push forward relentlessly from beginning to end.

2. The form of this character piece can be represented as follows:

intro	‖: a :‖	‖: b :‖	‖: c :‖	a	d	a′
m. 1	m. 3	m. 11	m. 19	m. 27	m. 35	m. 45
Fm	Fm	A-flat	Fm to A-flat	Fm	Fm to FM	FM

This surprisingly quirky short work is simpler than the diagram makes it appear. The regular eight-bar sections and repeat signs confuse things at first, but one can boil this down to a ternary form with coda (**A B A coda**). Taken together, the **b** and **c** sections form a nice little unit in the key of A-flat major, and when you discover that the end of **c** brings back **b**'s opening motive, you realize that these two sections make a nice little rounded binary form. Looking more closely at the **d** section, we see that it uses **a** section motives over a repeating cadence formula that leads to a dominant pedal; this is a cadential extension, pure and simple. Tossing in a bit of thematic transformation, the concluding **a′** recasts our march theme in F major, changing its mood from mock seriousness to good-natured warmth as it hugs close to the tonic and fades out to the cadence. Thus, the form could be boiled down to the following:

	A	**B**		**A**	ext.	coda
intro	‖: a :‖	‖: b :‖	‖: c :‖	a	d	a′

3. Nowhere near as dramatic or harmonically adventurous as his Moment Musical No. 2, this little march depicts yet another side of Schubert's personality. Mock seriousness, playfulness, and warmth all emerge in this tuneful work, quite a contrast with the lyric beauty, melancholy, and pathos of Moment Musical No. 2. This work, along with the other character pieces included in this chapter, demonstrates the enormous variety of moods possible in this diminutive yet infinitely expressive genre.

SCHUBERT **String Quartet in A Minor, II**

Try this movement if you'd like to include an example of early Romantic chamber music. The second movement of this Schubert quartet offers an excellent example of an often-used adaptation of sonata form, the so-called slow-movement sonata form. This beautiful work allows students to review principles of sonata form and simultaneously explore another form associated with second movements. See Appendix I for an Additional Listening Chart, and Sound Recordings below for recommended performances.

Schubert wrote his late string quartets at roughly the same time that Beethoven was finishing his last quartets, including Op. 135, and Schubert was ever conscious of Beethoven's recent work in the genre. His A-minor quartet (*Rosamunde*), however, shows less of Beethoven's influence than the later quartets in D minor and G major. It clearly follows the Classical quartet's four movement plan, and only its Romantic lyric tunefulness prevents us from mistaking it for a late Classical work.

Begin by playing and comparing individual themes. Before class, use the Additional Listening Chart (see Appendix I) to prepare excerpts so that you can play themes 1, 2, and 3 for your students. It is especially important to help students hear the theme 1 motive, since that motive figures prominently in the cadence theme transition and coda.

Ask students to compare the three themes. The first theme is by far the most tuneful, most easily recognized melody of the three—deliberately so, since Schubert will reuse this theme and its motives more than any other. To make it even more memorable, Schubert casts theme 1 in a binary form that closely resembles Classical tune form, rather unusual for a sonata-form theme. In the Additional Listening Chart, the theme's structure is labeled as follows:

a a′   b c   b c   or   a a′ |: b c :|

The only thing missing is an **a** phrase to follow the **b** phrase, but if you listen carefully you will note that the second half of the chart's **c** phrase sounds almost identical to the second half of the **a′** phrase; only the cadence is different. By contrast, themes 2 and 3 sound ambiguous and tentative; theme 2 starts by simply repeating a single note on successive offbeats; and as theme 3 starts, we're not sure at first which violin has the melody. As a result, students will find themes 2 and 3 much harder to recognize than theme 1, and Schubert must have planned it that way.

Once students can distinguish the three main themes from each other, play the entire movement. Display the Additional Listening Chart and point to each section as it goes by. Some significant differences between this Schubert movement and the more typical sonata-allegro movement must be pointed out in the discussion that follows:

1. This work's slow tempo and unabashed lyrical quality distinguish it from the much more dramatic use of sonata form in typical first movements.

2. The bridge between themes 1 and 2 (from C major to G major) provides some wonderful harmonic progressions and modulates as expected to the dominant key, but it hardly creates the dramatic conflict between tonic and dominant keys that we expect in first-movement form.

3. The traditional development that separates exposition and recapitulation has disappeared! Schubert replaces it with a short "cadence theme transition" that takes us back to the original key just in time for the recapitulation.

4. The return of theme 1 in the recapitulation is not the literal return we hear in so many sonata-form movements. Melody and bass lines sound much as they did before, but the inner voices enliven the texture here.

5. As if to apologize for "omitting" the development section, Schubert completely rewrites the bridge in the recapitulation. He works over theme 1 using standard development techniques: thematic fragmentation, unstable harmonies, and a more polyphonic texture.

6. Themes 2 and 3 return, now in the tonic key, just as we expect in the recapitulation. Theme 2 sounds much as it did before, but theme 3 is reduced to only five measures in length.

7. The "cadence theme transition" that replaced the development section now serves as the coda, or at least as the coda's beginning. Schubert extends the coda by adding materials heard earlier in the piece, modified to stay close to tonic and dominant harmonies in the home key, C major.

Just as the square peg doesn't fit into the round hole, the intense drama inherent in first-movement sonata form has no place in a typical slow movement. Beauty and a relaxed lyricism are required at this point in the four-movement plan, not a second high-powered showdown. Therefore Schubert mollifies or even omits potentially dramatic sections such as bridges, transitions, and the development. He also reduces thematic tension; theme 1 has no well-defined tunes to fight against! With its teeth removed, this form proves the perfect vehicle for Schubert's extraordinary melodic gifts, well suited to the Schubertian mix of sweetness and melancholy.

CHOPIN Étude in C Minor, Op. 10, No. 12 ("Revolutionary" Étude)

This work offers an excellent, fire-eating example of the Romantic character piece. Follow the procedures recommended above for character pieces in the recorded set. See Sound Recordings below for suggested performances.

1. Describe études for your students. These works aid mastery of a particular technical problem. No particular mood is implied, and each étude attacks a different problem of technique. To play this étude, the pianist must learn techniques for playing melody in the right hand in octaves, and develop facility and speed in the left hand.

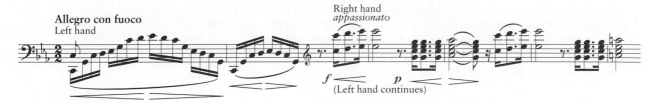

2. Outline this work's form for your students. This étude falls into two large sections; the second is similar to the first, but it adds embellishments to the main themes, and a″ turns out somewhat differently than a′. The form of the étude can be diagrammed as follows. Display the diagram for your students and point out each section as the music plays.

A				A′				
intro	a	a′	b	intro	a	a″	b′	(explosion)
m. 1	m. 9	m. 19	m. 29	m. 41	m. 49	m. 59	m. 65	m. 81

3. Point out significant features of Chopin's piano music. For instance, here Chopin uses the entire keyboard, top to bottom, and takes advantage of the sustaining, sonorous capabilities of the piano.

After playing the work, ask students to describe its mood and to identify the musical elements used to create that mood. A furious, turbulent mood is created through use of minor mode, quick tempo, nervous rhythms, swelling, abrupt changes from *forte* to *piano,* rushing left-hand arpeggios, and an explosive melody in octaves in the right hand.

CHOPIN **Polonaise in A, Op. 40, No. 1**

Try this stylized Polish dance if you want another character piece, more music by Chopin, or an early example of the nationalism that became so prominent in the later eighteenth century. See Sound Recordings below for recommended performances.

1. As its name suggests, the polonaise is a dance from Chopin's native country, Poland. Polish dances took on great significance for Chopin during his self-imposed exile in Paris, and he even wrote a grand polonaise for piano and orchestra (see Sound Recordings below). The most obvious feature of the polonaise is the dance's characteristic rhythm, given below. The left-hand accompaniment maintains this energetic pattern throughout.

2. Not too surprisingly, the polonaise uses a variant on Classical dance form, just as we saw in the minuet and trio movement of Haydn's Symphony No. 95. Quickly review that structure with your students for comparison with Chopin's dance. The Classical dance form is given here:

MINUET	TRIO	MINUET
A	**B**	**A**
|: a :||: b a′ :|	|: c :||: d c′ :|	a b a′

In comparing the structure of Chopin's dance with minuet and trio form, we find Chopin's **b** section repeats for emphasis, his **c** section (in the subdominant key of D major) is greatly expanded, and the second half of the trio fails to repeat; other than that, no significant differences exist between them. The form of Chopin's polonaise can be diagrammed as follows:

POLONAISE	TRIO	POLONAISE
A	**B**	**A**
|: a :||: b b′ a′:|	|: c c′:| d c c′	a b b′a′

1st time:	m. 1	m. 17	m. 49	m. 81	m. 105 m. 113
Repeat:	*m. 9*	*m. 33*	*m. 65*		

3. Chopin uses the entire keyboard, top to bottom, taking full advantage of the sustaining, sonorous capabilities of the piano.

A grand yet energetic mood is created through use of major mode, moderate tempo, dancing left-hand rhythms, sonorous *forte* dynamics, full chords in right and left hands, and a propulsive rising **a** motive that rides right up the scale.

LISZT Transcendental Étude No. 10 in F Minor

This work provides another example of the étude while introducing one of the great virtuosi of the nineteenth century. Follow the procedures recommended above for character pieces in the recorded set. See Sound Recordings below for suggested performances.

1. Although this work shares the name of étude with Chopin's, above, Liszt's étude is more a virtuoso showpiece than an intimate (if fiery) character piece. The Transcendental Études were so difficult that the technical proficiency needed to play them went beyond what was expected of pianists at that time. In short, these études represent a quantum leap in the development of virtuoso piano technique.

2. Map out the form for your students. Joseph Kerman once described the structure as a "loose, Romantic form." The main theme includes **a**—an accompanimental cadencelike figure with rapid, alternating hand chords—and **b**—a nervous, off-the-beat melody that turns around scale-step 5. The second theme (**c**) is printed below; it alternates with the accompanimental figure (**a**) from the main theme.

The diagram below fleshes out melodic relationships in some detail. Display the diagram for your students, and point out each section as the music plays.

Section	**A**										Transition	**A′**				Coda	
Theme	Theme 1				cadence th.							Theme 1	cadence th.				
Motive	a	b	a	b	a	b	c	a	c	b b′		a	b	c	a	c b″	c′
										LH						LH	
m. #:	1	3	4	6	13	21	31	42	54	61 78		86	90	100	136	148 160	170

3. Point out several significant features of Liszt's music. This fast, bravura showpiece is full of virtuoso piano writing—melody in octaves (**b** and **c**), hands rapidly alternating back and forth (**a**), quick arpeggios up and down the keyboard for both hands, and occasional melodies in the left hand (**c** second time). Add to that Liszt's chromaticism and frequent modulation and the effect overwhelms the listener.

LISZT *Totentanz*

Liszt's *Totentanz* is half symphonic poem and half piano concerto. It is subtitled "Paraphrase on the *Dies irae*" and is, indeed, a variations piece of sorts that uses the *Dies irae* as its main theme. Try this work for an unusual example of the Romantic themes of the supernatural or artistic barriers, or for comparison with character pieces and the program symphony.

The program of *Totentanz* is loosely based on a series of fifty-four Renaissance woodcuts by Hans Holbein of the *Dance of Death,* which appealed deeply to the Romantic fascination with the supernatural. These grisly woodcuts depict Death as the leveler confronting all kinds of people—young and old, powerful and humble. Liszt's use of the *Dies irae* tune was undoubtedly a result of the poem's description of the horrors of Judgment Day. Liszt was also aware that Berlioz's use of the *Dies irae* had caused a sensation in the *Fantastic Symphony* twenty years earlier.

Liszt's incredible pianistic abilities are apparent in his spectacular use of the instrument in *Totentanz,* just as we discovered immediately above in his Transcendental Étude No. 10 in F Minor. *Totentanz,* like the woodcuts on which it is based, is fascinating, sometimes vulgar, brutal, and exciting—a perfect example of Romantic artistic excess.

Photocopy the Additional Listening Chart in Appendix I and distribute it to the class. Display the Additional Listening Chart or write the large divisions of the movement on the board as follows. Then play the movement, pointing to each section as it is heard.

Theme: *Dies irae*					Cadenza 1					
Variations on *Dies irae* theme:	1 2 3 4 5 6 7 8 9									Cadenza 2
New Theme & Horn Calls	Variations on new theme: 1 2 3 4 5 6									Cadenza 3
Variation 10 on *Dies irae* theme					Conclusion					

BERLIOZ *Fantastic* Symphony

Fourth Movement: "March to the Scaffold"

It is strongly recommended that you look at this march when you introduce the fifth movement of Berlioz's audacious program symphony to your class. At the very least, show them how the *idée fixe* is used at the end of this movement. To do more, try the suggestions below, starting with form.

Form

Do not read the program for this movement yet. The fourth movement contains two themes of contrasting character, but its form is ambiguous—a cross between sonata form and the expected march–trio–march with coda. The ambiguities are presented in the chart below. If you treat it as sonata form, you must explain why there is no bridge, no development in the development section, and no theme 2 in the recapitulation (unless mm. 140–164 counts as theme 2). If you treat it as a ternary-form march, you must explain a repeat sign that seems to connect part of the trio with the first march section and a fragmented return of the march theme (twice) in the middle of the trio. Display the Additional Listening Chart from Appendix I, or put the following chart on the board. (You can also make photocopies to hand out in class.)

		A	B								A'			

Sonata Form

Intro.	Exposition		Development							Recap	Coda		
	61 m.		45 m.							17 m.	38 m.		

Intro.	Th 1 three times	Th 2 :|	Mod.	Th 1 div. orch.	Th 2	Mod.	Th 1 div. orch.	Trans.	Th 1	dotted rhythm of Th 2	fixed idea	chop & cheers
	45 m.		27 m.			27 m.		7 m.	17 m.	38 m.		

Intro.	March	Trio			Trio repeated			Trans.	March	Coda		

March Form

m1	17	62	78	82	89	105	109	114	123	140	164	169
0:00	0:26	0:00	0:24	0:31	0:42	1:06	1:12	1:20	1:34	0:14	0:48	1:00

Though the form may be ambiguous, the two main themes are well defined and easy to follow. Play both themes until students can distinguish between them. Then play the entire movement for the class, twice if necessary. Ask them to (1) decide which makes more sense to them—sonata form or march form—and to (2) write down the story the music seems to be telling. Brief discussion of the form allows you to draw out these points:

1. Freedom of expression and individual spontancity are more important than strict adherence to traditional forms.

2. Traditional forms provided coherence and meaning. Romantic composers relied on thematic unity and/or an extramusical program to provide coherence when they adapted or abandoned traditional forms. Berlioz uses both.

The Program

Now ask the students to share the stories they wrote while listening to the movement. After hearing a few, ask them to compare stories. Usually, the stories will differ greatly, but the general atmosphere they describe and the adjectives they use will be very similar. Raise these questions as part of your discussion:

1. Can music really tell a story?

2. What does the music really express? (What can the *whole* class agree on as a description of this music?)

Now read the program of the fourth movement. Those who have read (or seen) *A Tale of Two Cities* will have a point of reference. Suggest that the first two themes might depict a march to the scaffold through streets brimming with innocent bystanders and rowdy curiosity seekers. Most interesting, of course, is the coda's end. A solo clarinet plays the fixed idea, but it is interrupted after only seven notes by the fall of the guillotine (a loud chord) and the head bouncing off the block (string *pizzicato*).[1] Such executions are a public entertainment, of

---

[1]If you use the on-screen reduced score of this ending from the *Delaware Music Series* DVD, students can see as well as hear the guillotine stroke and bouncing head. Very effective!

course, and the crowd cheers (drum rolls and brass fanfares). Play this excerpt from the coda and, if time permits, play the entire movement one last time so that students can judge how well the music fits Berlioz's intended program.

Conclusions to Draw about "March to the Scaffold"

1. The dramatic content of the movement is more important than the form.

2. Two main themes and their associated motives tie this movement together; the fixed idea at the end connects this movement with the other four.

3. The size of Berlioz's orchestra, his unusual instrumental combinations, and techniques of divided orchestration (m. 82; you may know this as *Klangfarbenmelodie,* but you need not inflict this word on nonmusicians) differ dramatically from orchestral music of the Viennese Classical period.

Multimedia Resources

ʔ Further Listening Charts and Texts

See Appendix I for Listening Charts for these works:

Berlioz, *Fantastic* Symphony, fourth movement. See Further Listening Examples above for lecture suggestions for this movement.

Liszt, *Totentanz.* See Further Listening Examples above for lecture suggestions for this work.

ʔ Sound Recordings

Beethoven, *Nine Symphonies.* Orchestre Révolutionnaire et Romantique. Deutsche Grammophon Archiv 439 900-2 (CD). Raw, powerful performances of Beethoven's complete symphonies on period instruments; conducted by John Eliot Gardiner. Highly recommended. Try this recording of Symphonies 1, 2, or 6 if you use Lecture-Demonstration Idea 4 above.

Berlioz, *Roméo et Juliette.* Orchestre Révolutionnaire et Romantique. Philips 289 454 454-2 (CD). Recent period-instrument performance of all the music Berlioz composed for his dramatic symphony after Shakespeare; conducted by John Eliot Gardiner. Berlioz combines his love for both grand opera and the symphony in this large-scale hybrid work, one of his finest. Try this recording if you use Class Discussion Idea 1 above.

Berlioz, *Symphonie fantastique.* Orchestre Révolutionnaire et Romantique. Philips 434 402-2 (CD). A complete recording of Berlioz's masterwork that uses the original 1830 orchestration on period instruments; conducted by John Eliot Gardiner. Gardiner is currently one of the most successful conductors of nineteenth-century repertory on period instruments, and he brings out the bold colors and vitality of this symphony. Try this recording for a period-instrument alternative if you use Lecture-Demonstration Idea 4, Class Discussion Idea 1, Listening Idea 5, or suggestions for the fourth movement from Further Listening Examples above.

Berlioz, *Symphonie fantastique.* Cincinnati Symphony Orchestra. Telarc CD-80578 (CD). A complete recording of Berlioz's masterwork on modern instruments; conducted by Paavo Järvi. The last two movements from this excellent modern digital recording were used on the *Listen* set. Try the first three movements if you use Lecture-Demonstration Idea 4, Class Discussion Idea 1, or Listening Idea 5.

Chopin, *The Chopin I Love.* Jean-Yves Thibaudet. Decca 289 466 357-2 (CD). Intriguing program mixes various Chopin character pieces including mazurkas, waltzes, preludes, études, nocturnes, and a polonaise, four of them played on Chopin's own 1848 Broadwood piano. Try this recording for more examples of the genre, or if you use Lecture-Demonstration Idea 3 or suggestions for the "Revolutionary" Étude in Further Listening Examples above.

Chopin, *Études for Piano, Op. 10 and Op. 25.* Vladimir Ashkenazy. London 414 127-2 (CD). Distinguished performances from Ashkenazy's complete traversal of Chopin's solo piano music. Try this recording if you use suggestions from Further Listening Examples above for Chopin's "Revolutionary" Étude.

Chopin, *4 Ballades.* Murray Perahia. Sony Classical SK 64 399 (CD). Beautifully poetic performances of solo piano works by Chopin. Features his ballades, which transform the character piece into dramatic narrative, but also includes a sampling of mazurkas, waltzes, and études, as well as a nocturne. Try this recording if you want to share more character pieces with your students.

Chopin, *Nocturnes, Opp. 9, 15, 27, 32.* Brigitte Engerer. Harmonia Mundi HMT 7901430 (CD). The recording featured in the *Listen* set. Try this CD to explore more of these lovely character pieces.

Chopin, *Piano Concerto No. 1/Variations on Mozart's "Là ci darem la mano."* Emanuel Ax & Orchestra of the Age of Enlightenment. Sony Classical SK 60771 (CD). Emanuel Ax's second period-instrument Chopin recording; conducted by Sir Charles Mackerras. This early set of variations earned Schumann's rave review, "Hats off, gentlemen, a genius." Try this CD if you use Listening Idea 4 above.

Chopin, *Piano Concerto No. 2/Grand Fantasia/Grande Polonaise.* Emanuel Ax & Orchestra of the Age of Enlightenment. Sony Classical SK 63371 (CD). With this recording Emanuel Ax becomes the first great Chopin interpreter of the modern era to perform this music on a period instrument. He uses a restored 1851 Érard piano much like the instruments Chopin used. It balances perfectly with the period-instrument orchestra conducted by Charles Mackerras, and its more variegated colors make the music deliciously vivid. The *Grand Fantasia on Polish Airs* offers another example of Chopin's devotion to his heritage.

Dies irae, in Stolba, *Development of Western Music Anthology,* 3d ed. Boston: McGraw-Hill, 1998. The CDs that accompany this standard music history textbook contain a recording of the *Dies irae* chant quoted by Berlioz in his *Fantastic* Symphony and by Liszt in *Totentanz* (see Further Listening Examples above for lecture suggestions). Use this recording to compare the original melody with Berlioz's or Liszt's use of it.

Haydn, *The London Symphonies,* Vol. 1. Royal Concertgebouw Orchestra. Philips 442 611-2 (CD). First-class modern-instrument performances of late Haydn symphonies, including 95, 96, 98, 102, 103, and 104; conducted by Colin Davis. Try this recording if you use Lecture-Demonstration Idea 4 above.

Liszt, *Complete Piano Music*, Vol. 2. Jenö Jandó. Naxos 8.553119 (CD). Intense, committed performances from one of the finest living Liszt specialists. Vol. 2 contains the 12 Transcendental Études. Use this recording if you try suggestions for Transcendental Étude No. 10 in F Minor from Further Listening Examples above.

Liszt, *Piano Concertos Nos. 1 and 2/Totentanz*. Zimerman and the Boston Symphony. Deutsche Grammophon 423 571-2 GH (CD). Definitive recordings of Liszt's virtuoso works for piano and orchestra; conducted by Seiji Ozawa. *Totentanz* echoes Berlioz's *Fantastic* Symphony in its *Dies irae* quotations, thematic transformation, and fantastical orchestra writing. Try this recording if you use Listening Idea 4 or suggestions for *Totentanz* from Further Listening Examples above.

Liszt, *Symphonic Poems*. Berlin Philharmonic. Sony Classical SK 66834 (CD). Full-blooded performances of several Liszt symphonic poems, including *Les préludes, Orpheus,* and *Mazeppa;* conducted by Zubin Mehta. Recommended if you want to cover one of Liszt's symphonic poems as part of your survey of Romantic program music or if you use Class Discussion Idea 1 above.

Liszt, *Symphonic Poems,* Vol. I. Georgia and Louise Mangos. Cedille Records CDR 90000 014 (CD). World-premiere recordings of Liszt's four-hand piano versions of his symphonic poems. Before the advent of recording technology, composers commonly made keyboard arrangements of their orchestral works. In this case, though, Liszt may have first conceived these works for piano, only later "arranging" them for orchestra. These long-lost piano works were recently discovered by the duo performers, who turn in splendid performances of *Les préludes, Orpheus, Tasso,* and *Ce qu'on entend sur la montagne*. What these works lose in timbral variety (compared with the orchestra, at least—though Liszt nearly makes the pianos sound like an orchestra) they gain in intimacy and expressive flexibility. These recordings can help students make connections between Romantic piano music and orchestral music, and they highlight Liszt's orchestral approach to the piano. Highly recommended, especially if you use Class Discussion Idea 1 above.

Mendelssohn, *Works for Orchestra*. Hanover Band. Nimbus NI 1765 (CD). This inexpensive period-instrument recording contains several program works by Mendelssohn, including the *Hebrides* Overture mentioned in the textbook; conducted by Roy Goodman. Try this recording if you use Class Discussion Idea 1 above.

Mozart, *Symphonies Nos. 40 and 41*. Vienna Philharmonic. Deutsche Grammophon 445 548-2 (CD). Dramatic modern-instrument performances of Mozart's two late symphonies; conducted by Leonard Bernstein. Try this recording if you use Lecture-Demonstration Idea 4 above.

Schubert, *The Impromptus: Moments musicaux*. András Schiff. London Double Decker 289 458 139-2 (CD). Gorgeous performances of the *Moments musicaux* and other Schubert character pieces. Try this recording for additional examples of this genre, or if you use Lecture-Demonstration Idea 3 or suggestions from Further Listening Examples above.

Schubert, *Lieder*. Anne Sofie von Otter and Bengt Forsberg. Deutsche Grammophon 453 481-2 (CD). Gorgeous performances of well- and lesser-known Schubert songs. Use this recording if you try suggestions for "Der Jüngling an der Quelle" in Further Listening Examples above.

Schubert, *Quatuors D. 87 & D. 804 "Rosamunde."* Quatuor Mosaïques. Auvidis Astrée E 8580 (CD). Superb recording by this most extraordinary period-instrument string quartet. Try this recording if you use suggestions for this work in Further Listening Examples above.

Schubert, *Trout Quintet/Arpeggione/Notturno.* L'Archibudelli with Jos van Immerseel. Sony SK 63361 (CD). New period-instrument performance surpasses many on modern instruments. In no work is the influence of Schubert's songs on his instrumental music more obvious than in his *Trout* Quintet. Schubert added an extra movement to the four-movement plan just to make room for a set of variations on his lied "The Trout." Highly recommended.

Schumann, Robert. *Carnaval, Bunte Blätter, Kreisleriana, Papillons.* Youri Egorov. EMI Classics *double fforte* 74191 (CD). Poetic, volatile performances of important character piece cycles. Useful if you want to provide students a more complete look at *Carnaval* or if you want to introduce several examples of Schumann's *Asch–Scha* motives (start with "Sphinxes"!). Try this recording if you use Lecture-Demonstration Idea 3, Class Discussion Idea 1, or Listening Idea 3 above.

Schumann, Robert. *Dichterliebe.* Fritz Wunderlich and Hubert Giesen. Deutsche Grammophon—*The Originals* 449 747-2 (CD). Recording contains performances of *Dichterliebe* and other Schumann lieder by the same artists as in the *Listen* recordings. Try this recording to sample more of Schumann's song cycle or if you use Listening Idea 2 above.

Schumann, Robert and Clara. *Lieder.* Barbara Bonney and Vladimir Ashkenazy. London 452 898-2 (CD). Finally, internationally renowned performers have turned their attention to Clara Schumann's lieder! Lovely renditions of eleven of Clara's songs, including a performance of "Der Mond kommt still gegangen" superior to the one in the *Listen* set. Music by Robert includes ten miscellaneous songs and his *Frauenliebe und -leben* cycle. Highly recommended if you want to give extra attention to Clara Schumann or the role of women in Romantic music. Try this recording if you use Listening Idea 2 or Class Discussion Idea 4 above.

♩ Video Recordings

The Art of Piano: Great Pianists of the Twentieth Century. Elektra/Asylum (DVD or VHS, color, 108 minutes). Interviews with and performances by the great pianists of the past century. Music by Chopin, Schumann, Liszt, and many others. Recommended for a look at both the character piece and the art of performance.

Arthur Rubinstein Plays Chopin and Rachmaninov. Video Artists International (DVD, black & white, 50 minutes). Taken from 1950s telecast performances, these performances offer a nice sampler from one of the great Chopin interpreters of the twentieth century. Better yet, this DVD includes the *Listen* nocturne. Highly recommended for your presentation on the Romantic character piece.

Barbara Bonney. Voices of Our Time Series. TDK (DVD, color, 91 minutes). The highlight on this disc is a complete performance of Robert Schumann's *Dichterliebe.* This song cycle is normally sung by a man, but in the hands of a master interpreter like Bonney, the music yields fresh insights at every turn. Highly recommended for your presentation on the Romantic lied.

[Berlioz, *Fantastic* Symphony, fifth movement.] *Delaware Music Series.* www .ecsmedia.com (DVD). Performance of the fifth movement of Berlioz's *Fantastic* Symphony by the Oberlin Conservatory Orchestra conducted by Ken Moore. This important collection also includes a scrolling reduced score, statements of the *idée fixe* from all five movements, and on-screen excerpts from Berlioz's program for the symphony. It also contains a performance of the *Dies irae* chant by students at Catholic University, on-screen notated comparison of the chant and its use in the symphony, and quick access to quotations of the *Dies irae* in the symphony for aural comparison. Highly recommended, especially if you use Listening Idea 5 above.

Berlioz, *La Damnation de Faust.* Arthaus Musik (DVD, color, 146 minutes). Powerful new modern production of one of Berlioz's hybrid genres that blends the symphony and elements of grand opera. Performed by Paul Groves, Willard White, Vesselina Kasarova, and the Berlin State Opera Orchestra; conducted by Sylvain Cambreling. Try this recording if you use Class Discussion Idea 1 above.

Berlioz, Symphonie Fantastique/Harold en Italie. Bel Air Classics (DVD, color). This new DVD goes right to the top of the list. The Orchestre de Paris relishes every last ounce of the idiosyncratic vitality Berlioz put into this music, and conductor Christoph Eschenbach knows how to whip them into a frenzy whenever necessary. Just one complaint—the producer's preference for off-kilter camera angles and extreme close-ups (the clarinetist's left hand or the business end of the bass drum mallet) can make it difficult for students to really see how the instruments are played. If you need a good view of the musicians, use the excellent Berlin DVD with Jansons, but for a truly exciting, fully idiomatic Berlioz performance, go with Eschenbach. Whichever DVD you use, take time to cue up all of the *idée fixe* statements in advance! Highest recommendation for your presentation on Romantic program music.

Berlioz, Symphonie Fantastique. Sounds Magnificent: The Story of the Symphony Series. Image Entertainment (DVD or VHS, color, 86 minutes). André Previn narrates this look at Berlioz's *Fantastic* Symphony. Discussion and rehearsal of the music, followed by a complete performance of the symphony by the Royal Philharmonic. Use this video to present the fifth movement or if you try Lecture-Demonstration Idea 4, Class Discussion Idea 1, Listening Idea 5, or suggestions from Further Listening Examples above for the fourth movement.

Chopin. The Great Composers Series. www.films.com (DVD or VHS, color, 25 minutes). Video biography includes music from Chopin's two piano concertos, nocturnes, waltzes, preludes, mazurkas, and a barcarolle.

Chopin Piano Music. BBC Opus Arte (DVD, color, 135 minutes). A mixed bag, this DVD features performances by three different pianists. Alfredo Perl gives us all of the Op. 28 Preludes, and Freddy Kempf gives us the complete Op. 10 *and* Op. 25 Études. Perhaps the best segment is Angela Hewitt's rendition of the Sonata in B-flat Minor, including Chopin's famous funeral march. Try this DVD if you want to explore additional examples by Chopin or if you use suggestions for the "Revolutionary" Étude in Further Listening Examples above.

[Chopin, Polonaise, Opus 53.] *Delaware Music Series.* www.ecsmedia.com (DVD). Performance of Chopin's character piece by Leon Bates. This important collection also includes a full score with color-coded harmonic analysis, full score with harmonic reduction and formal analysis, and full performance of the harmonic reduction.

Chopin, *24 Etudes for Piano*. Valal (DVD, color, 75 minutes). The complete etudes for solo piano performed by Valentina Lisitsa. Recommended if you use the "Revolutionary" Étude in Further Listening Examples or as a supplement to your classroom presentation of the Chopin Nocturne.

Claudio Arrau. Classic Archive Series. EMI Classics (DVD, black & white, 113 minutes). This fine package includes performances of works by Schumann and Beethoven that were telecast between 1963 and 1970. Where *Listen* is concerned, the main attraction is Arrau's sterling rendition of Robert Schumann's *Carnaval*. An especially nice touch: each character piece in the set is prefaced with a close-up of the piano score. You can pause the DVD and point out Schumann's ASCH-SCHA motives before you play the music! Highly recommended for your presentation on the Romantic character piece.

Code and Cypher. www.films.com (VHS, color, 51 minutes). A look at composers who translated letters and names into musical themes, including Schumann (*Asch-Scha*), Brahms, and Elgar.

Delaware Music Series. www.ecsmedia. com (DVD). This important collection covers several important early Romantic works and composers. See other entries in this section for teaching resources on Berlioz's *Fantastic* Symphony; Chopin's Polonaise, Op. 53; and Schubert's "Erlkönig."

European Concert from Istanbul. EuroArts (DVD, color, 104 minutes). Mariss Jansons leads the Berlin Philharmonic in a Classic/Romantic program at the historic St. Irene Church in Istanbul. The program begins with Haydn's *Surprise* Symphony and Mozart's Flute Concerto No. 2, but the rousing finale is a complete performance of Berlioz's *Fantastic* Symphony. The camera does a decent enough job of calling attention to specific instruments where appropriate; this allows students to watch musicians creating the many colors and special effects Berlioz demands of the orchestra. With the right DVD player you can also cue up all of the *idée fixe* statements in advance! The old Munch telecast performance on EMI Classics is another wonderful performance by one of the great Berlioz conductors, but this one comes with color and modern stereo sound. Highly recommended for your presentation on Romantic program music.

Frederic Chopin. Harmonics: The Innovators of Classical Music Series. www .films.com (DVD or VHS, color, 27 minutes). Video biography of Chopin includes commentary and performances by pianists such as Arthur Rubinstein, Byron Janis, and Martha Argerich.

Horowitz in Moscow. Sony Classical (DVD, color, 104 minutes). Emotional 1986 "homecoming" concert by one of the great "old school" virtuosos of the twentieth century captured on film. His recital includes many character pieces by Schubert, Chopin, Schumann, and Liszt. Highly recommended.

Ian Bostridge. Voices of Our Time Series. TDK (DVD, color, 91 minutes). Known for his intimate, insightful, and occasionally idiosyncratic recital performances, Bostridge is one of today's finest young lieder singers. Here he turns his attention to Schubert and Wolf. "Erlkönig" is included on the program, and Bostridge brings a delicious malevolence to the Erlking's stanzas. The disc also includes interviews with Bostridge and pianist Roger Vignoles. Highly recommended for your presentation on the Romantic lied.

Impromptu. MGM Home Entertainment (DVD, color, 108 minutes). Lyric yet amusing portrayal of the romance between nineteenth-century feminist George Sand (Judy Davis) and her lover, composer Frédéric Chopin (Hugh Grant); released in 1991. Director James Lapine includes plenty of Chopin's music in one of the better movies about famous composers. Recommended supplement to a study of Chopin and Liszt in Paris.

In the Steps of Chopin: A Portrait by Byron Janis. www.films.com (VHS, color, 58 minutes). Biographical portrait of Chopin as composer and virtuoso pianist with performances by Janis.

Liszt at Weimar. Man and Music Series. www.films.com (DVD or VHS, color, 54 minutes). Video focuses mostly on Liszt's later period but provides a good overview and excerpts from some earlier works, such as the virtuosic *Années de pélèrinage* for piano solo.

Mendelssohn Gala Concert. Arthaus Musik (DVD, color, 82 minutes). Excellent performances by Mendelssohn's own Leipzig Gewandhaus Orchestra; conducted by Kurt Masur. Try this to introduce your students to Mendelssohn or for further examples of programmatic works such as the overture to *A Midsummer Night's Dream* or the *Scottish* Symphony.

The Piano: King of Instruments. Howard Goodall's Big Bangs: Turning Points in Music History Series. www.films.com (DVD or VHS, color, 51 minutes). Entertaining video views the invention of the piano as one of the major discoveries of the eighteenth century, and looks at its impact on Western music. Try this video if you use Lecture-Demonstration Idea 3.

The Romantics. Music in Time Series. www.films.com (DVD or VHS, color, 60 minutes). Character pieces by Chopin (Polonaise in A-flat, Prelude), Schumann's "Im wunderschönen Monat Mai" (and Symphony No. 3), and other works by Mendelssohn, Brahms, and Bruckner, with commentary.

[Schubert, "Erlkönig."] *Delaware Music Series.* www.ecsmedia.com (DVD). Three different settings of Goethe's poem composed by Schubert, Karl Loewe, and Johann F. Reichardt; sung by Reginald S. Pindell, baritone. Also includes demonstration of alternate interpretations of the Schubert setting, scrolling score with harmonic analysis, and audio performance of the Schubert in English.

Schubert. The Great Composers Series. www.films.com (DVD or VHS, color, 25 minutes). Video biography includes music from Schubert songs such as "Erlkönig," "Gretchen am Spinrade," and "Ave Maria" as well as his *Rosamunde* Overture and *Unfinished* Symphony.

Schubert, *Winterreise.* Deutsche Grammophon (DVD, color, 83 minutes) or TDK (DVD color, 73 minutes). Two excellent new releases feature Schubert's late, great song cycle—a chilling winter's journey into the dark recesses of the human soul. The first features Thomas Quasthoff with Daniel Barenboim in a live 2005 performance at the Berlin Philharmonie. Some students may be taken aback at first by Quasthoff's thalidomide syndrome, but the music making is exceptional—probably the best video performance now available! The TDK disc gives us Dietrich Fischer-Dieskau with Alfred Brendel. Fischer-Dieskau was past his prime in this 1979 recording, but he more than makes up for his aging voice with an extraordinary artistry honed over several decades. Both recordings are highly recommended if you want to explore further examples of Romantic lieder with your students.

Schubert: The Young Romantic. Man and Music Series. www.films.com (DVD or VHS, color, 53 minutes). Schubert's life and music are the subject of this video. Discussion of Schubert lieder. Musical excerpts from Symphonies 5 and 8, Piano Trio in B-flat, and String Quintet in C.

Schwarzkopf/Seefried/Fischer-Dieskau. Classic Archive Series. EMI Classics (DVD, black & white, 85 minutes). With its heavy dose of Mahler and R. Strauss, this disc is more appropriate for Chapter 18, but the bonus recordings of Fischer-Dieskau singing Schubert lieder accompanied by the great Gerald Moore make this well worth a listen. Best of all, your students can watch these fine artists performing "Erlkönig"! Highly recommended for your presentation on the Romantic lied.

Vienna. Music in Time Series. www.films.com (DVD or VHS, color, 60 minutes). Much material is more appropriate for Chapters 11 and 12, but the last half of the video deals with Schubert. Excerpts include Schubert songs ("Seeligkeit" and "Frühlingsglaube") and instrumental works as well as music of Mozart (see Chapters 12 and 13).

Vladimir Horowitz: A Reminiscence. Sony Classical (VHS, color, 120 minutes). A video remembrance of one of the last great pianists from the grand Romantic tradition, hosted by his wife, Wanda Toscanini Horowitz. Includes home movies, concert performances, and other memorabilia. Recommended supplement to your presentation on Romantic character pieces.

❦ Software

Great Composers: Bach, Schumann, and Rakhmaninov. Zane Publishing/Selectsoft (CD-ROM—Windows or Macintosh). This inexpensive CD-ROM includes a multimedia presentation, photographs, quizzes, and sound clips. Available from www.cdaccess.com.

Great Composers: Handel, Chopin, and Debussy. Zane Publishing/Selectsoft (CD-ROM—Windows or Macintosh). This inexpensive CD-ROM includes a multimedia presentation, photographs, quizzes, and sound clips. Available from www.cdaccess.com.

Great Composers: Schubert, Brahms, and Strauss. Zane Publishing/Selectsoft (CD-ROM—Windows or Macintosh). This inexpensive CD-ROM includes a multimedia presentation, photographs, quizzes, and sound clips. Available from www.cdaccess.com.

The Norton Masterworks CD-ROM. New York: W. W. Norton (CD-ROM—Macintosh). Authors Daniel Jacobson and Timothy Koozin provide a clever multimedia introduction to twelve important works, including Schubert's "Erlkönig" and Chopin's Polonaise in A-flat Major (see Further Listening Examples above). Features animated, guided listening resources as well as information on the composers, eras, and genres, and the works themselves.

Schubert Unfinished Symphony. Time Sketch Composer Series. www.ecsmedia .com (CD-ROM—Windows or Macintosh). Program presents a CD recording of Schubert's Symphony No. 8 and other works, with interactive arch map analysis and background information about the composer, his style, and the work. Highly recommended supplement to your presentation of Schubert.

CHAPTER 17

Romantic Opera

Chapter Outline

Boldface indicates works in the recording set.

Important Terms

early Romantic opera	exoticism	thematic transformation
bel canto opera	*arioso*	*The Ring*
German Romantic opera	music drama	psychological drama
Italian opera	*Gesamtkunstwerk*	declamation
Verdian recitative, aria, and ensemble	leitmotiv	

Teaching Objectives

⁊ Overall Objectives

This chapter will help students acquire familiarity with:

1. Romantic opera as a supreme reflection of the recurring themes of Romanticism.

2. Stylistic features of the important categories of Romantic opera—especially Italian opera and Wagnerian music drama.

3. The lives and music of significant operatic composers of the nineteenth century, especially Verdi and Wagner.

❦ Listening Objectives

After completing this chapter, students should be able to:

1. Hear and identify how elements of music are typically used in different categories of Romantic opera, especially Italian opera and Wagnerian music drama.

2. Hear and identify how Romantic opera departs from the traditional recitative-and-aria format.

Lecture Suggestions

This chapter looks at nineteenth-century operatic traditions from Italy and Germany; the Global Perspectives section of the next chapter looks at operatic traditions from Japan and China. The obvious place to study *kabuki* drama and Beijing opera, however, is right here alongside the operas and music dramas of Verdi and Wagner. The similarities between these traditions are often striking, and the history of Japanese *kabuki* begins within ten years of the first Italian operas. Teaching suggestions for these Asian theatrical works can be found in Chapter 18 of this manual. There you will find information and ideas that can help you make interesting connections and comparisons between Japanese, Chinese, Italian, and German operatic traditions.

Earlier discussions of opera took place within larger contexts of period styles and musical genres. This chapter, however, devotes itself entirely to Western opera. The two sections of this chapter juxtapose the operas of Verdi and Wagner. This pairing highlights the great differences between Italian and German opera in the Romantic era. The Italian genius for melody and glorification of beautiful singing took precedence over the increasing role of the orchestra in Italian Romantic opera. The German predilection for counterpoint and motivic development and Wagner's leitmotiv techniques enabled the opera orchestra to rival and even surpass the importance of the singers. For suggested teaching approaches and an outline of the problems instructors face when presenting opera, refer back to Lecture Suggestions in Chapter 7 of this manual (p. 144).

In order to convince students that opera is a valid expressive artistic medium, you must focus on the story (first and foremost!), relate historical background and musical features to the story, and convey enthusiasm. When presenting an opera scene to the class, follow these guidelines.

1. Give a quick synopsis of the opera. Find a good synopsis, but do not simply read it to the class. Learn it well enough that you can tell the story of the opera just as you would tell a good story to a friend.

2. Ask students to read through the translation of the scene. Assign parts to students and encourage the players to ham it up. Choral parts can be assigned to the entire class. Keep the action moving! Let students sense the drama of the scene before they hear the music.

3. Play the scene straight through using video recordings if at all possible. When a scene is presented in an interesting and exciting manner, the class could insist on seeing more.

7 Verdi and Italian Opera

Comic opera (*opera buffa*) dominated the theater at the turn of the nineteenth century, but serious, often tragic opera enjoyed a resurgence in the 1820s. This new tragic genre borrowed the realism and fast pacing of comic opera, resulting in greater dramatic intensity. In addition, a singing style called *bel canto* ("beautiful song") came to dominate both comic and serious opera during this time. *Bel canto* style emphasized long, Romantic melodies and beautiful, virtuoso singing.

Verdi's first operas were firmly rooted in the *bel canto* tradition. Throughout his career, Verdi's commitment to beautiful melody and singing never flagged; the human voice was always the most important musical element in his operas. But as Verdi matured compositionally, he began to exploit the orchestra more fully and blur traditional distinctions between *secco* recitative and aria. Abandoning the rigid either/or of Classical opera, Verdi explored new musical possibilities: lightly accompanied lyric *ariosos* and bold new recitatives augmented by the full power of the Romantic orchestra. By adding these expressive tools to his palette, Verdi could respond to the dramatic situation with greater flexibility and naturalness. We can hear the result in his later operas—Verdi's orchestra, now exploited for both its dramatic and coloristic possibilities, combines in countless new ways with the singers to create a sense of continuous momentum and dramatic urgency.

VERDI *Aida*

Play the following examples of recitative. Ask the class to follow the texts and listen for differences between them.

> Mozart, *Don Giovanni,* "Alfin siam liberati" (entire piece)
>
> Verdi, *Aida,* Act IV, scene ii (Tomb Scene), Recitative Parts 1–3 (track 9)

Ask students to describe the differences between these examples. In the discussion that follows, draw out these points:

1. The recitative from *Aida* is more dramatic by far. The plot has something to do with it. In *Aida,* the two main characters are about to die together in a sealed tomb, whereas in *Don Giovanni* we are witnessing a seduction. Nevertheless, point out how the orchestra in *Aida* heightens and reinforces the impact of the scene. Whereas the recitative from *Don Giovanni* is accompanied only by the harpsichord (*secco* recitative), the recitative from *Aida* is accompanied by a large Romantic orchestra.

2. Verdi's recitative is more sung than spoken; the opposite is true for Mozart's. Verdi's recitative moves forward melodically, with the orchestra creating a quiet, mournful mood. By the time Verdi composed *Aida,* he had abandoned *secco* recitative in favor of this newly dramatic, orchestrally accompanied recitative.

Play two more excerpts from the same two operas—this time two ensembles. Again ask the class to follow the texts and listen for differences between them.

> Mozart, *Don Giovanni,* "Là ci darem la mano" (entire piece)
>
> Verdi, *Aida,* Act IV, scene ii (Tomb Scene), "O terra, addio" (track 12, 0:00–2:11)

Ask students to describe the differences between these examples. In the discussion that follows, draw out these points:

1. Mozart's duet is characterized by a simple, elegant, clearly proportioned tune—a typical Classical melody. The gentle mood evoked by the tune pleases but does not deeply move the listener.

2. Verdi's duet is cut from different cloth altogether. The two doomed lovers, Aida and Radames, bid farewell to the sorrows of earth and greet the prospect of eternity. This incredibly beautiful Romantic melody covers a tremendous musical range; point out the extreme high notes on the words "the heavens open" (*schiude il ciel*) and "ray" (*raggio*). The listener feels as much as hears the yearning of the characters for heavenly peace. Anyone unmoved by this duet has a heart of stone!

Once students can hear and identify these significant features of Verdi's mature style, it is time to present the entire scene to the class. Start with this quick synopsis of *Aida,* adapted from textbook page 280.

> Acts I and II introduce a young Egyptian general, Radames, and a captive Ethiopian slave girl, Aida, who are secretly in love. The Egyptians don't know that Aida is the daughter of Amonasro, king of Ethiopia. Unfortunately, Radames has also attracted Amneris, a passionate and jealous Egyptian princess.
>
> In Act III, Radames is tricked into revealing his country's battle plan to Aida. Amneris has eavesdropped on their tryst, and she turns Radames over to the all-powerful priests for judgment as a traitor. Aida escapes in the confusion.
>
> In Act IV Amneris offers to save Radames if he will return her love. To her dismay, he says he would rather die than live without Aida. Amneris realizes too late that she has assured the doom of the man she loves. His trial by the priests, which she witnesses, is the most dramatic scene in the entire opera (see Further Listening Examples below for lecture suggestions). Radames makes no defense and is condemned to be buried alive in a tomb under the temple, sealed by a huge stone.
>
> In Act IV, scene ii, Radames is entombed. His hopes that Aida will be spared a similar fate are dashed when he discovers that Aida has hidden in the tomb, so as to see him once again and die with him. To the sounds in the temple above—chanting priests and a sorrowful, pathetic Amneris asking for peace for the lovers—Aida and Radames sing their final duet.

Assign roles to individual students (the entire class can be the chorus) and have them read aloud the libretto for this final scene on textbook pages 282–83. Then play through the entire scene for the class. In the discussion that follows, ask them to describe their reactions. Try to draw out specific musical features that contributed to those reactions.

♪ Wagner and Music Drama

German Romantic opera had its roots in the eighteenth-century genre of *Singspiel,* a type of German opera in which there was both music and spoken dialogue (no recitative). *Singspiel* stories were most often comic, based on characters drawn from folklore. Although Mozart usually wrote operas using the Italian language and Italian styles, he also created two of the greatest eighteenth-century *Singspiele: The Abduction from the Seraglio* and *The Magic Flute.* With its fanciful, mythical plot, *The Magic Flute* looks forward to the supernatural plots of German Romantic opera, the first great example of which was *Der Freischütz* (The Magic Bullet) by Carl Maria von Weber.

Next to Beethoven, Wagner was the most influential composer of the nineteenth century. Wagner rejected the recitative-and-aria conventions of French and Italian opera, claiming that arias were hopelessly artificial and that opera had degenerated into mere "concert in costume." Instead, he set forth the concept of the *Gesamtkunstwerk,* the "total work of art." He proposed that opera should be an all-encompassing human experience employing music, drama, literature, art, dance, philosophy, mythology, religion, and politics.

Wagner was an extraordinary orchestrater. No one before him had used the orchestra so effectively. Wagner's ability to create intoxicating new orchestral sounds and textures that could convey the entire range of human emotions was legendary. With the recent invention of valves for the brass family, he showed the world how one could use these newly chromatic instruments, and he made the brass choir an equal partner to the strings and winds in the orchestra. Wagner also elevated the opera orchestra to a whole new level of importance. Taking Beethoven as his guide, Wagner incorporated the scope and motivic development of the older master's symphonies into his music dramas. In place of traditional opera's alternation of recitatives, arias, and ensembles, each act in Wagner's "music dramas" creates one long, unbroken musical web, with orchestral and vocal strands cleverly interwoven. Through the use and transformation of these intertwining leitmotivs, he gave the orchestra the ability to *tell* the story, not simply embroider it!

Wagnerian Music Drama versus Italian Opera

Although Italian Romantic opera composers blurred Classical distinctions between recitative and aria, they did not erase them altogether. The motion between them can be more fluid, but we can still easily detect sections that correspond to aria, *arioso,* recitative, ensemble, and chorus. The same cannot be said for the operas of Wagner. Ask students to listen for the nature and character of the melody as you play the first minute or two of the following excerpts.

Verdi, *Aida,* Act IV, scene ii (Tomb Scene), "O terra, addio" (track 12, 0:00–2:11)

Wagner, *The Valkyrie,* Act I, scene i

In the discussion that follows, ask students to describe differences in each composer's use of melody. Draw out these points:

1. In Verdi's duet, a soprano and then a tenor sing a lovely, poignant tune over a subdued orchestral accompaniment. The voice is clearly in command; the orchestra provides a coloristic, supportive accompaniment—a homophonic texture. If the singers dropped out, the orchestral music would make little sense by itself. Moments of quiet passion alternate with passages of peaceful resignation.

2. The best word to describe Wagner's melodic material in this scene (and in most of his mature works) is *continuous.* This melody lacks the strong cadences that help define clear musical sections. Note that the orchestra does far more than merely accompany the voices; Wagner gives the orchestra its own melodic material, different from that of the singers. The orchestral writing is so perfectly conceived and self-contained that the singers would barely be missed if they dropped out. The polyphony, both within the orchestra and between orchestra and singers, creates a full, lush musical texture.

Der Ring des Nibelungen

Twenty-six years in the making, Wagner's magnum opus is without question his *Ring* cycle—*The Nibelung's Ring*. Though rooted in Norse myth (the same myths Tolkien drew on for his *Lord of the Rings* trilogy), Wagner's sixteen-hour, four-opera cycle is in many ways a critique of the society in which he lived, espousing the revolutionary ideals that led to his exile from Dresden in 1849. In his hubris, Wagner also envisioned his *Ring* as an agent for social change, a work that could help to unite a German people separated by "arbitrary" political divisions into countries such as Saxony, Bavaria, and Prussia. As part of this vision, Wagner went so far as to build an opera house in Bayreuth specifically for performances of the *Ring*. The unification of Germany was ultimately accomplished, not by Wagner's *Ring* but through Bismarck's adroit combination of diplomacy and military action. Nonetheless, the annual festival performances at Bayreuth continue to the present day, and they attract Wagner fans from around the world.

In a nutshell, the *Ring* is a story about the devastation wrought by an unholy lust for wealth and power—the curse of the ring—and love's power to redeem that curse. As always, you will need to start with the story, but with a tale of such magnitude you will have to decide how much of the story you have time to tell! Here is as brief a synopsis as you are likely to find.

Das Rheingold (*The Rhine Gold*)—In scene i, Alberich the dwarf steals the Rhine gold from the Rhinemaidens and forges a ring of power. In scene ii, the giants who built Valhalla demand payment from the gods. Wotan promised them the goddess Freia, but the other gods find this unacceptable. Wotan stalls for time. In scene iii, Wotan and Loge take Alberich into custody by trickery. When they take away the ring and his accumulated treasure, Alberich curses the ring. In scene iv, Wotan uses the treasure to pay off the giants, and immediately one giant kills the other for the ring—the curse's first victim! As a result, the gods' triumphal entry into Valhalla is rather hollow.

Die Walküre (*The Valkyrie*)—(See the synopsis in Lecture Suggestions for this work below.)

Siegfried—In Act I, Mime the dwarf (Alberich's brother) has rescued and raised Siegfried after Sieglinde died in childbirth. When Mime is unable to do it, Siegfried forges a sword from the fragments of his father's sword. In Act II, hoping to win the ring, Mime tricks Siegfried into slaying a dragon (the giant from *Das Rheingold* in disguise). Inadvertently tasting the dragon's blood, Siegfried finds he can understand the birds, who warn him about Mime. When the dwarf tries to poison him, Siegfried kills Mime. Now the birds sing of a "sleeping beauty," and Siegfried sets off to find her with the ring in hand. In Act III, Siegfried encounters a weary Wotan who tries to block his way. With his sword, Siegfried breaks Wotan's staff, symbol of the god's power. Siegfried marches through the flames to awaken Brünnhilde, and the two fall madly in love.

Götterdämmerung (*Twilight of the Gods*)—In the Prologue, the rope of fate breaks. Brünnhilde bids Siegfried farewell as he sets out in search of adventure. In Act I, he makes new "friends," who give him a forgetfulness potion. He falls in love with Gutrune and agrees to help his new blood brother Gunther find a wife. Disguised as Gunther, Siegfried forces Brünnhilde to become Gunther's bride. In Act II, there is a double wedding for Siegfried and Gutrune, and Gunther and Brünnhilde. Brünnhilde is horrified when Siegfried gives no sign of recognizing her. Brünnhilde's protests are twisted by Hagen (Alberich's son) into a plot to murder Siegfried. In Act III, while on a hunting expedition, Hagen gives Siegfried a potion to restore his memory. As Siegfried describes his joyous marriage to Brünnhilde, Hagen murders him on the pretext of defending Gutrune's honor. In scene ii Hagen also murders Gunther to gain the ring, but Brünnhilde now stands in his way. She builds a blazing funeral pyre for Siegfried and jumps in with her horse—and the ring. The Rhinemaidens reclaim the gold, and Hagen makes one last mad dash for the ring and drowns in the flood. Valhalla burns, the curse is undone, and a new day dawns for humankind.

WAGNER *The Valkyrie*

Whether or not you introduced the story of the entire *Ring* cycle, you need to introduce the story of *The Valkyrie* to your class. Feel free to use all or part of this synopsis of *The Valkyrie,* but make sure you at least cover all of Act I.

Act I—Seeking shelter in a ferocious storm, Siegmund meets Sieglinde and they feel an immediate attraction. Not wanting to inflict his misfortune on her, he prepares to leave. Sieglinde's husband, Hunding, enters and asks about Siegmund's past. Siegmund tells how his mother was killed and his twin sister carried off; how his father raised him in the woods; and how this very day he championed a young woman forced into marriage against her will, but was forced to flee after killing several attackers. The dead were Hunding's kinsmen, however, and Hunding demands vengeance in the form of a duel in the morning. Sieglinde mixes a drug into Hunding's evening drink. While he sleeps, she shows Siegmund a sword buried to the hilt in a tree trunk. Falling ever more deeply in love, they soon realize they are the twins separated at birth. Siegmund claims Sieglinde as his bride and pulls the sword from the tree. The lovers rush into the night.

Act II—At first, Wotan commands Brünnhilde to defend Siegmund in his duel with Hunding. Fricka enters and demands that Wotan uphold the laws on which the gods' power rests (including marriage vows) and withdraw protection from Siegmund. When Brünnhilde returns, she finds Wotan discouraged that his plans for his son Siegmund cannot be realized. He orders her to make sure Hunding wins the duel. When she protests, Wotan threatens punishment if she disobeys. In scene ii, Sieglinde collapses in anguish as she and Siegmund flee Hunding. While she sleeps, Brünnhilde appears and tells Siegmund he must die. He accepts his fate gladly until he discovers that Sieglinde will not join him in death. Deeply moved by the depth of his love, Brünnhilde promises to help them. Siegmund goes to face Hunding, and Brünnhilde protects him. Wotan himself is now forced to intervene. He shatters Siegmund's sword with his spear, and Hunding kills Siegmund. Brünnhilde flees with Sieglinde. Anguished over the death of his son, Wotan kills Hunding out of contempt. He exits swearing he will punish Brünnhilde.

Act III—Her sister Valkyries are surprised when Brünnhilde appears with Sieglinde asking for protection from Wotan. In despair, Sieglinde wants to die until she learns that she carries Siegmund's unborn son. The Valkyries recommend a hiding place, and Sieglinde leaves. Wotan arrives, and Brünnhilde bravely comes out of hiding. Wotan banishes her from Valhalla. When the other Valkyries complain, he threatens them with the same fate—to sleep on the Valkyries' rock until the first man who awakens her claims her for his wife. Left alone with Wotan, Brünnhilde begs him to surround her with a fire that will repel all but the most fearless hero. Moved, he relents. Sadly bidding her farewell, he kisses her immortality away. She sinks into sleep as flames encircle the mountain.

The Prelude and Act I, scene i, give us the very beginning of the story. If you would like to use the final scene, Wotan's Farewell, see Further Listening Examples below. Set to some of Wagner's most enchanting music, this scene also conveys Wotan's anguish. First he lost his son Siegmund, the hero he hoped would undo the ring's curse; now he loses his favorite daughter, Brünnhilde.

Prelude

Your students got to know this music at the beginning of Unit I. Now it's time to revisit this work and put it in its dramatic context. Before you play the entire Prelude (overture), play the first forty seconds or so and ask the class to describe the music. What mood is created, and what musical means create the mood? Draw out these points:

1. Ominous and foreboding, the mood is one of great tension and energy.

2. Wagner creates the sense of tension using surprisingly simple musical elements: basically diatonic (unusual for Wagner), the music creates instability by emphasizing high-tension notes in the scale, especially the flat 6 and raised 7; in spite of the strong pulse, the 3/2 meter is not so easy to catch at first, and Wagner uses frequent, strong accents at unexpected points in the measure; the music is continuous, avoiding the regular cadences that divide phrases and sections in more traditional music; the dark, brusque tone of the basses and the fierce tremolo in the upper strings give this passage an unsettled, nervous quality. To top it off, we never hear anything that qualifies as a real melody. We hear motives and a quasi-ostinato in the bass line, but nothing that ever turns into a complete melody. Texture, color, and rhythm come to the foreground in the Prelude. All in all, this makes for a disturbing beginning.

3. As always, the music reflects the story. Siegmund is fleeing for his life in the middle of a thunderstorm. As we learn later in Act I, Siegmund has interfered with the forced marriage of an unwilling bride and earned the wrath of the groom's family and friends. In the ensuing battle the bride herself is killed and Siegmund kills many of the wedding party, but he is forced to flee when his sword and shield are hacked to bits. The raging thunderstorm is only a pale reflection of the inner turmoil Siegmund is experiencing.

Draw a clear connection between Siegmund's inner anguish and the music's constantly restless, churning character—its surging, "formless waves of emotion." Now play the entire Prelude. Display Listening Chart 1 or ask students to follow the chart on textbook page 5. When you play the Prelude, call attention to each theme as it goes by. As you finish, call attention to Wagner's effective use of the orchestra, especially his use of brass and percussion in building to the climax about two minutes in.

Act I, scene i

Set the scene: Exhausted, Siegmund collapses in the home of Hunding and Sieglinde. Home alone, Sieglinde enters to find a strange man on the floor. Both are cautious at first, but as they talk they feel an immediate bond. They have both led lonely, loveless lives, and this is the first tenderness either one has experienced in a very long time. Unknown to either of them, they are twins who were separated at birth. By the time they figure this out (much later in the act), they have fallen deeply in love. This scene portrays the first few steps in this budding love relationship.

If you have time, stage the scene with two volunteers from the class. Use the libretto on textbook pages 291–92. Take time to talk through various interpretations of some of the subtleties in the libretto. For instance, when Siegmund asks Sieglinde to take the first drink of honeyed mead, is it out of suspicion (could it be poison?) or generosity (offering her a privilege she has never enjoyed?)? As a nice touch, play the corresponding motives as the "cast" reads through the scene (in the margins on textbook pages 291–92) at the keyboard or prepare recorded excerpts in advance.

You may want to take time to deal with the question of incest. Of course, Siegmund and Sieglinde don't discover their family relationship until it's too late, and given their loveless lives up to this point, one can almost forgive them for giving in to the nurturing intimacy they find in each other. This was no accident on Wagner's part, however. The notion that one must break nature's rules to learn its secrets occurs again and again in late Romantic thought. Made explicit in Nietzsche's writings, this theme reveals itself throughout Wagner's *Ring* cycle. Siegfried, the great hero who plays a part in undoing the ring's curse, is the bastard child of this illicit union between Siegmund and Sieglinde. (If you want other examples, find out where Wotan's staff comes from or how he came to lose one of his eyes!) Given the lush orchestral music that accompanies the two lovers throughout this act, Wagner clearly wants us to sympathize with these characters. However one interprets it, some viewers will come to Act I with a mixture of sympathy and revulsion.

Before you play Act I, scene i, take time to introduce the motives that accompany this scene. Explain that these motives represent characters, objects, actions, emotions, or thoughts. Through the use of these "leading motives," called leitmotivs, the orchestra can comment continually on the action and inner thoughts of the characters. Play these motives often enough that students can recognize them. Point out that Wagner will combine two or more motives at a time (polyphony). This can make them trickier to hear.

Now that students have learned some specific leitmotivs, help them place these in a broader context. Students must understand that Wagner's orchestra does not merely embroider the action that takes place onstage; the orchestra becomes an independent agent that can tell us more than we see on the stage. Try a simple demonstration. Play a few motives from movie scores by John Williams—the "Indiana Jones" motive or the "Darth Vader" motive work well.[1] Many students can still quickly identify the characters associated with the motives. Point out that Williams uses Wagner's leitmotiv technique throughout his film scores (though without Wagner's subtlety). Williams often uses the foreboding "Darth Vader" motive when we see his character on the screen, but ask the class what it would mean to hear the "Darth Vader" motive when only Luke Skywalker and Princess Leia were onscreen, with Darth Vader light years away. Suddenly the orchestra no longer simply amplifies the action taking place on the screen; it causes us to reflect, to reinterpret this scene completely. We must ask ourselves what connection Darth Vader has with these characters in this scene. Through the technique of leitmotivs, the orchestra plays an entirely new, independent role in telling the story.

---

[1]*Star Wars* will remain current for a while, especially now that George Lucas has released three prequels to the original *Star Wars* epic.

Now your students are ready to see this scene! Ask them to follow the libretto on textbook pages 291–92. Then play a video recording of the entire scene (see Multimedia Resources below for suggested DVDs). Call attention to the leitmotivs as they go by; singing or playing them along with the recording can be especially helpful. In the discussion that follows, ask students to describe their reactions. Try to draw out specific musical features that contributed to their reactions.

Conclusions to Draw about Romantic Opera

1. Italian and German Romantic operas share several common features. Both took full advantage of the large Romantic orchestra. Both broke down recitative/aria distinctions to follow the drama's changing moods more naturally. From Classical comic opera, both types learned the value of realism and dramatic pacing.

2. In spite of their similarities, Italian and German operas speak with their own unique voices. The chart below summarizes significant differences between the chief exponents of these national styles: Verdi and Wagner.

	Verdi's Operas	*Wagner's Music Dramas*
Stereotypes	Italian passion	German philosophy
Story	drawn from popular plays or novels, even historical plots seem modern; believable, realistic stories based on the passions of real people	drawn from German history, legends, or mythology; improbable stories rely on magical or supernatural elements yet convey eternal truths
Characters	princes and prostitutes, poets and peasants, parents and progeny; characters are equally red-blooded and human whether the story is set in Egypt or Italy	gods, giants, dragons, dwarves, kings, knights, Minnesingers, pilgrims, and princesses; usually Germanic or Norse in derivation
Singers	sopranos and tenors steal the show, but many juicy roles for low voices	heroic roles for sopranos and tenors; altos and basses also prominent
Musical numbers	recitative, ariosos, arias, ensembles, and choruses	each act is a long, unbroken symphonic poem with voices
Melody	tuneful with often regular phrases	irregular phrases skate on top of the harmony; "infinite" melody
Harmony	functional harmony with decorative chromaticism	chromaticism often destabilizes tonal centers
Texture	homophonic: vocal melody with orchestral accompaniment	polyphonic: elaborate web of vocal and orchestral lines
Pacing	fast-paced, razor-edged drama	deliberately slow but inexorable
Focal point	singers carry the show	orchestra tells the story (leitmotivs)
At its best	fast-paced, nonstop drama; powerful expression of emotions; realistic story and characters	gripping, psychological drama, profound revelations, timelessness of myth

Additional Teaching Suggestions

❧ Lecture-Demonstration Ideas

1. Take a closer look at Verdi and Wagner. The comparison of Verdi's operas with Wagner's music dramas (see Lecture Suggestions above) reveals sharp differences, but their personalities and lifestyles differed just as profoundly. Ask students to read biographies of the two composers (textbook pages 279 and 284) beforehand.

2. Create a slide show with pictures of La Scala, Bayreuth, and other significant locations in the lives of Verdi and Wagner. Help bring these operatic cultures to life for your students. See Video Recordings below for useful resources.

3. Introduce your students to the unstable political climate of mid-nineteenth-century Europe, and show them how it affected music and musicians. Both Verdi and Wagner were controversial political figures in their own time. Wagner's radical views on German nationalism (Germany was splintered into many independent states) led to his exile in Switzerland in the 1850s. Verdi's name became associated with the Italian independence movement (much of Italy was under Austrian rule), and some of his operas contained veiled references to captivity and foreign domination. This presentation can help students understand that musicians are both affected by and have an impact on world events. For useful information on this subject, consult any of the standard biographies of Verdi and Wagner, or see Appendix V for suggested resources.

4. Invite an opera singer to class. Choose someone conversant with Romantic opera who can perform excerpts from operas by Verdi, Wagner, or other Romantic opera composers for your class. Interview your guest using questions about the experience of singing this music, the life of an opera singer, or anything else that may interest the class. Leave time for student questions and discussion.

5. Arrange for your class to attend a rehearsal or take a backstage tour at a local opera house. These activities help bring opera down to earth as students see how it works from the inside.

❧ Class Discussion Ideas

1. *What makes Verdi's music so different from Wagner's?* This discussion works best as a review of this chapter, once students have experienced the music of these two composers.

2. *How much is soap opera like real opera?* Soap operas depict good, bad, and ordinary people whose lives are constantly turned upside down by fate or the unscrupulous actions of others. In their twisting plots one finds stories of love, betrayal, manipulation, and deceit. These stories are not that different from those of *Aida, Madama Butterfly,* or *Der Rosenkavalier.* If you have the time, tell the story of Verdi's *Rigoletto* or Berg's *Lulu.* For handy plot summaries of most major operas, see *The New Kobbé's Complete Opera Book,* edited by the Earl of Harewood, New York: G. P. Putnam's Sons, 1976.

3. *What is verismo? How realistic can opera be? Verismo* was an important movement in late nineteenth-century opera. *Verismo* operas by Mascagni and Leoncavallo sought to be true to life, showing real people in real-life situations.

These operas were realistic in the sense that their heroes were no longer decent, moral people—sordid, seamy aspects of human experience could now be presented. By modern standards, however, they were no more realistic than soap operas. Review the operas covered in this chapter and ask students to determine which one seems most realistic and explain why. (It's no problem if some decide that none seem particularly realistic.) Small groups work well to initiate discussion, and their reports can generate further class discussion, especially if groups disagree with each other. If you wish, you can use this question to address some of opera's affectations—especially its reliance on singing rather than the spoken word.

♩ Listening Ideas

1. Find a way for your class to watch one entire opera! If you cannot arrange a field trip to a local opera company performance, find a DVD or videotape (with subtitles!) and play the entire opera for the class (they can even bring popcorn). Many students *think* they hate opera (even those who enjoy musicals) but have never watched an opera from start to finish. Choose an opera with proven appeal; you want to make a good first impression. Puccini's *La Bohème* (introduced in Chapter 21) works especially well, and it's not too long. Take time beforehand to talk through important features of the opera and take time afterward to help students process their reactions. Most students will not suddenly turn into opera lovers, but at least they will gain a more complete understanding of the genre. This exercise takes an enormous amount of time, but consider that many of your students will never see an opera unless you make it possible. See Video Recordings below for suggested performances.

2. Take your students on a galloping tour of Italian opera and *bel canto* from Mozart to Verdi. Draw attention to the turn to tragic subject matter found in Bellini's operas. Musical examples by Rossini and Bellini can be found in the score and recording anthologies for standard music history textbooks by Stolba (*Development of Western Music,* 3rd ed.) or Grout and Palisca (*A History of Western Music,* 6th ed.). These anthologies also include excerpts from early nineteenth-century German and French operas by Weber and Meyerbeer. If you have time, continue your tour with a look at late nineteenth-century Italian opera *verismo* and the operas of Puccini (introduced in Chapter 21). See Multimedia Resources below for suggested audio and video recordings.

3. Compare Act I, scene i, of *The Valkyrie* with the Presentation of the Rose scene in Strauss's *Der Rosenkavalier* (introduced in Chapter 21). Both depict the precise moment a man and woman fall in love, though the circumstances that bring each couple together differ. Play recordings of the two scenes and compare the two opera plots up to the scenes in question. See Multimedia Resources below for suggested audio and video recordings.

4. Take your class on a galloping tour of the entire story of *The Nibelung's Ring.* Find a good summary of the libretto, and illustrate plot points with recordings of important leitmotivs. See Multimedia Resources below for useful audio and video recordings. Now that the movie version of J. R. R. Tolkien's epic trilogy *The Lord of the Rings* is complete, many students are pleasantly surprised to discover that Wagner and Tolkien drew on many of the same Norse myths. Both works deal with the corrupting influence and ultimate destruction of a ring of power, and both feature unusual creatures: dwarves, giants, dragons, and the like.

5. Compare Qur'anic recitation with the chorus (invoking the Egyptian deity Ftha) woven into the duet that ends Verdi's *Aida*. Verdi's prevailing scale is major, but the chorus introduces flatted scale degrees 2 and 6, and sometimes 7, creating an occasional augmented second between scale degrees 7 and 6 and a diminished third between scale degrees 7 and 2. These intervals are often associated with Middle Eastern scales; play them at the keyboard to help your students hear their distinctive sound. While the recitation from Chapter 5 doesn't use these intervals, it does use similar melodic figures. It's not an exact correspondence, but students can see where Verdi got some of his ideas.

♪ Further Listening Examples

VERDI *Aida,* Act IV, scene ii—Judgment Scene

Use this example to give your students a vivid example of Verdi's dramatic intensity. In the opera, the Judgment Scene immediately precedes the Tomb Scene described above. Together they form the largest portion of Act IV. To provide more complete coverage of *Aida,* follow the Lecture Suggestions above and insert this scene just before the Tomb Scene. See Multimedia Resources below for CD or video recordings; if at all possible, use the latter.

After you tell the story of the complete opera (see the synopsis in Lecture Suggestions for *Aida* above), introduce this tense scene as the dramatic high point of the opera. The priests, led by Ramphis, try Radames on three counts, pronounce him a traitor, and condemn him to death. Amneris finds herself helpless to stop the process of judgment that she has set in motion. Photocopy handouts or display the words for this scene (see Appendix II) and ask for volunteers to read the different parts. The entire class can play the chorus of priests. After a discussion of the libretto, play the entire scene.

WAGNER *The Valkyrie,* Act III, Wotan's Farewell

The Wagner excerpts in *Listen* give us the beginning of the second music drama from Wagner's *Ring* cycle; this scene (five hours later!) gives us the ending. Though set to some of the most enchanting music ever written, this scene shows us Wotan as a truly tragic and very human figure—if one can say that of a god! See Multimedia Resources below for suggested CD and video recordings; if at all possible, use the latter.

Your students already know how the story begins. If you did not do so when you worked through Act I, scene i, start by telling the story of the entire opera (see notes in Lecture Suggestions above). Draw attention to Wotan's dilemma. Wotan possesses a power far greater than any of the other gods, a power that resides in his role as enforcer of contracts. But when his human children, Siegmund and Sieglinde, fall in love and flee from Hunding, Wotan has no choice but to uphold the marriage contract between Hunding and Sieglinde by allowing Hunding to kill Siegmund—the son he hoped would undo the ring's curse. Wotan rightly describes himself as the "least free of all beings." The pain has only just begun, however. His sorrow and anger are compounded when he discovers that the Valkyrie Brünnhilde, who read his heart but disobeyed his orders, has decided to protect Siegmund in his battle with Hunding. Once Siegmund is dead, Wotan is compelled to punish his favorite daughter and confidante by stripping her of her immortality and putting her to sleep until a great hero comes to awaken her. Powerless to do anything to stop the turn of events, Wotan has lost two children in one day.

There is no dialogue in this final scene—only Wotan's monologue as he puts Brünnhilde to sleep on a mountaintop and rings it with flames. The marvelous orchestral music simultaneously conveys the enchantment of the magical fire, Wotan's infinite tenderness toward the daughter he loves so dearly, and his own feelings of loss and grief. Photocopy handouts or display the text (see Appendix II). Read the words to the class—including the stage directions, which are Wagner's own. There are several passages where action continues onstage even when the singers are silent. Finally, play this scene.

WAGNER *Tristan and Isolde*

Filled with some of the most yearningly beautiful music ever written, this music drama transformed Wagner's harmonic language and took the use of leitmotivs to a new level of sophistication. Try the excerpts below if you want to explore another great music drama with your students.

As always, start with the story! This brief synopsis can serve well.

Tristan and Isolde derives from medieval legend. Act I opens on shipboard. The victorious knight Tristan returns to his English homeland with Isolde, the daughter of a vanquished king. Isolde is to marry Tristan's king and uncle, Mark of Cornwall. Isolde has other plans. She decides to poison Tristan (her fiancé's murderer) and herself, and she instructs her maidservant Brangaene to prepare the poison. Instead, Brangaene prepares a love potion; Tristan and Isolde fall madly and hopelessly in love.

In Act II, love overcomes chivalrous morality, and the couple meets adulterously in the longest unconsummated love scene in all opera. The tryst is discovered, and Tristan—faced with the impossibility of his relationship with Isolde and feeling truly hopeless—allows himself to be mortally wounded.

In Act III, Tristan has escaped to a distant coast where he undergoes a profound transformation, finally understanding the truth of his life and his love for Isolde. He refuses to die until he has seen her one last time. She comes to him and he dies in her arms, whereupon Isolde herself sinks down in a rapturous vision of love's fulfillment beyond the grave and expires. For both of them, death is not a defeat but an ecstatic expression of eternal love.

Note the surface resemblance to the Tomb Scene in Aida—star-crossed lovers united finally in death. However, Verdi's characters die out of dramatic necessity; Wagner's die out of philosophical necessity.

Prelude

Before you play the entire Prelude (overture), play the first fifteen measures and ask the class to describe the music. What mood is created, and what musical means create the mood? Draw out these points:

1. The mood is one of great tension and yearning.

2. Wagner creates the sense of yearning by omitting certain expected musical elements: The music has no detectable beat or meter; the harmony is strangely unstable; we have no sense of tonic; there are long silences; and an ever upward-moving motive never turns into a complete melody. Chromaticism characterizes the melodic and harmonic motion.

3. The unsatisfied yearning the listener feels reflects the unconsummated love that Tristan and Isolde experience throughout the drama. From the first measure, Wagner creates the state of nonresolution that characterizes the entire dramatic action of the opera.

4. The strangely disturbing opening motive, repeated three times, is called the Love-Death Motive. Whenever Wagner wants to evoke the hopeless yearning and ill-fated love of Tristan and Isolde during the opera, the orchestra plays this motive in the background.

5. After the first fifteen measures, the music finally settles on a meter, and the melody sounds more complete and conventional. Even so, point out that the harmony remains unstable and the tonic elusive; Wagner judiciously avoids strong cadences or expected resolutions (note the deceptive cadences in the Listening Chart from Appendix I). The music takes on a constantly restless, churning character—surging, "formless waves of emotion."

Display the Listening Chart from Appendix I. When you play the Prelude, call attention to each theme as it goes by.

Act I, "Philter" Scene

Set the scene: Isolde, aboard a ship with her maidservant Brangaene, bewails her fate, complaining that her marriage to King Mark will be loveless. At this point, as the "Philter" Scene begins, Brangaene reminds Isolde of her many secret potions, including aphrodisiacs. Isolde makes several cryptic remarks, but only near the scene's end do we learn Isolde's plan. She chooses not the love potion but a death potion—poison.

If you have time, stage the scene with volunteers from the class. (All of the men can take the part of the offstage sailors.) Display or photocopy the libretto from Appendix II. Keep the action moving. As the "cast" reads through the scene, play the corresponding motives at the keyboard (or prepare recorded excerpts in advance). If you covered excerpts from *The Valkyrie* carefully, students will be familiar with the concept of the leitmotiv. Remind them that these motives represent objects, actions, or thoughts, and help them pick out motives that were also used in the Prelude—the Love-Death Motive, for instance. As we saw earlier, these "leading motives" allow the orchestra to go beyond mere decoration. Now the orchestra can help "tell the story" as it comments continually on the action and inner thoughts of the characters.

Ask students to follow the libretto (from Appendix II). Then play a recording (video is best) of the entire "Philter" Scene. Call attention to the leitmotivs as they go by; singing or playing them along with the recording can be especially helpful. In the discussion that follows, ask them to describe their reactions. Try to draw out specific musical features that contributed to their reactions.

Act III, "Liebestod"

This famous music accompanies the concluding scene of the opera. For an interesting twist, compare this scene with the tomb scene from Verdi's *Aida*—they both end with the deaths of both lovers, and they contain the most rapturous music either composer ever wrote. Both audio and video recordings of the concert version (without voice) can be found in Multimedia Resources below, but you would do better with a video recording of a staged performance (see Video Recordings below). See Appendix II for complete text and translation.

Photocopy handouts or display the words (from Appendix II) and read through the scene with the class. Isolde sings this lengthy aria just before she dies. She describes a transcendent vision of Tristan waiting for her in death—the one place where their love can finally be consummated. Play the music for the class. Its endless sequences and modulations build unbearable tension that resolves in one of the most glorious climaxes ever written. At the very end, point out the final occurrence of the Love-Death Motive (in the oboes and English horn), which resolves *for the first time* in the entire opera in the closing tonic chords.

PUCCINI *Madama Butterfly,* Act II aria, "Un bel dì"

This beautiful, poignant aria offers an excellent example of Italian Romantic opera after Verdi. For lecture suggestions and recordings, see Further Listening Examples and Multimedia Resources in Chapter 21 of this manual; text and translation can be found in Appendix II.

STRAUSS *Der Rosenkavalier,* The Presentation of the Rose

For lecture suggestions and recordings for this neo-Romantic, traditionalist work, see Further Listening Examples and Multimedia Resources in Chapter 21 of this manual; text and translation can be found in Appendix II.

Multimedia Resources

⅋ Further Listening Charts and Texts

See Appendix II for texts and translations for these works; see Further Listening Examples above for teaching suggestions.

> Verdi, *Aida,* Act IV, scene ii—Judgment Scene
> Wagner, *The Valkyrie,* Act III, Wotan's Farewell
> Wagner, *Tristan and Isolde,* Prelude
> Wagner, *Tristan and Isolde,* "Philter" Scene from Act I
> Wagner, *Tristan and Isolde,* "Liebestod"

⅋ Sound Recordings

Puccini, *La Bohème.* Philharmonia Orchestra. EMI Classics 5 56120 2 (CD). One of the finest recordings ever released of Puccini's most popular opera. Features Leontina Vaduva, Roberto Alagna, Ruth Ann Swenson, Thomas Hampson, Simon Keenlyside, and Samuel Ramey; conducted by Antonio Pappano. This enhanced CD also contains several goodies worth exploring—text, photos, video, and the like. Try this recording if you use Listening Idea 2 above.

Puccini, *Madama Butterfly.* Vienna Philharmonic Orchestra. London 417 577-2 (CD). Great recording of Puccini's Japanese tragedy features Mirella Freni, Luciano Pavarotti, and Christa Ludwig; conducted by Herbert von Karajan. Try this recording if you use Listening Idea 2 above.

Strauss, *Der Rosenkavalier.* Vienna Philharmonic Orchestra. London 417 493-2 (CD). Strong performance of Richard Strauss's most popular opera. Performed by Régine Crespin, Yvonne Minton, Manfred Jungwirth, Helen Donath, and Otto Wiener; conducted by Sir Georg Solti. Try this recording if you use Listening Idea 3 above.

Verdi, *Aida*. Vienna Philharmonic Orchestra. EMI Classics CDMC 69300 (CD). Classic recording of *Aida* features Mirella Freni, José Carreras, Agnes Baltsa, Piero Cappuccilli, and José Van Dam; conducted by Herbert von Karajan. This excellent all-around recording is recommended over the rest, especially if you use suggestions in Further Listening Examples above for the Judgment Scene.

Wagner, *The Opera Collection: Tristan und Isolde*. Vienna Philharmonic Orchestra. London 470 814-2 (CD). Classic recording features the great Wagnerian soprano Birgit Nilsson with Fritz Uhl, Regina Resnik, and Tom Krause; conducted by Sir Georg Solti. Try this recording if you use Listening Idea 3 or suggestions on *Tristan and Isolde* from Further Listening Examples above.

Wagner, *Orchestral Excerpts from Der Ring des Nibelungen, Die Meistersinger, Tristan und Isolde*. Cleveland Orchestra. Sony Classical Essential Classics SBK 48175 (CD). This excellent older recording remains one of the finest Wagner orchestral CDs available. Try this recording to explore the *Ring* or if you use suggestions for the *Tristan and Isolde* Prelude or "Liebestod" in Further Listening Examples above and prefer the orchestral version.

Wagner, *The "RING" without Words*. Berlin Philharmonic. Telarc CD-80154 (CD). One of several single-disc surveys of the *Ring* cycle, this recording offers many of the best-known leitmotivs and orchestral scenes played by one of the world's great orchestras; arranged and conducted by Lorin Maazel. Particularly useful if you use Listening Idea 4 above.

Wagner, *Die Walküre* (from *The Nibelung's Ring*). Vienna Philharmonic Orchestra. London 455 559-2 (CD). Perhaps the most gripping performance of this work ever recorded, from Solti's classic early 1960s *Ring* cycle. Incredible cast features Hans Hotter, Birgit Nilsson, and Christa Ludwig; conducted by Sir Georg Solti. Try this recording (the one used in *Listen*) if you use suggestions for "Wotan's Farewell" from Further Listening Examples above, and use Solti's whole set if you try Listening Idea 4 above.

♪ Video Recordings

Age of the Individual. Music of Man Series. Home Vision (VHS, color, 60 minutes). Yehudi Menuhin narrates this look at the Romantic era. Includes material on Verdi and Wagner, as well as Chopin, Liszt, Brahms, and Tchaikovsky.

Bellini, *Norma*. Kultur (DVD, color, 153 minutes). Bellini's masterpiece was one of the first Romantic operas to move in the direction of tragedy. This video features superstar Joan Sutherland with the Australian Opera; conducted by Richard Bonynge. The performance is stronger than Sutherland's later recording with the Canadian Opera, but the recording is sadly uneven. Try this recording if you use Listening Idea 2 above.

Bizet, *Carmen*. Image Entertainment (DVD or VHS, color, 163 minutes). Royal Opera House production of Bizet's masterpiece, an early example of "realism" in opera. Superb acting and singing from Maria Ewing, Luis Lima, Leontina Vaduva, and Gino Quilico; conducted by Zubin Mehta. Try this video if you use Listening Idea 1 above.

Donizetti, *L'elisir d'amore*. Decca (DVD, color, 125 minutes). Recent recording of Donizetti's comic masterpiece features opera's hottest couple, Angela Gheorghiu and Roberto Alagna. Performed by the Lyon National Opera orchestra; conducted by Evelino Pido. Try this video if you use Listening Idea 2 above.

Donizetti, *Lucia di Lammermoor*. Deutsche Grammophon (DVD, color, 155 minutes). Metropolitan Opera production of one of Donizetti's most famous tragic *bel canto* operas. Performed by Joan Sutherland, Alfredo Kraus, Pablo Elvira, and Paul Plishka; conducted by Richard Bonynge. Try this video if you use Listening Idea 2 above.

Mascagni and Leoncavallo, *Cavalleria Rusticana/I Pagliacci*. Philips (DVD, available separately on VHS, color, 142 minutes). Zeffirelli filmed the first of these *verismo* classics on location in Sicily. They feature Plácido Domingo, Teresa Stratas, Elena Obraztsova, Juan Pons, and Renato Bruson. Performed by La Scala Orchestra; conducted by Georges Prêtre. Try this recording if you use Listening Idea 2 above.

Nationalism and Revolution. Music in Time Series. www.films.com (DVD or VHS, color, 60 minutes). James Galway narrates this look at the effect of political changes on Romantic music. There is a heavy emphasis on Romantic opera. Includes musical excerpts from Berlioz's Requiem; Liszt's *Légend* and *Fantasia on Hungarian Folk Themes;* Verdi's *Nabucco, Aida*, and Requiem; and Wagner's *Tannhäuser, Siegfried Idyll*, Prelude to *Tristan und Isolde*, and *Meistersinger*. Performances at La Scala and Bayreuth.

Die Nibelungen. Kino Video (DVD, color, 291 minutes). Fritz Lang's five-hour silent movie version of the same Norse myths Wagner used in his *Ring* cycle. First released in 1924, Lang's two-part epic includes both *Siegfried* and *Kriemhild's Revenge* (equivalent to Brünnhilde) and is filled with state-of-the-art (for 1924) special effects. Lang was reportedly *not* influenced by Wagner's *Ring*, though you will find many similarities between these movies and the last half of Wagner's tetralogy, *Siegfried* and *Götterdämmerung*. This DVD release uses the Munich Film Archive restoration with the original 1924 score performed by the Munich Radio Orchestra. If you use Listening Idea 4, try a few scenes to supplement your presentation.

Puccini, *La Bohème*. Deutsche Grammophon (DVD, color, 103 minutes). There are many lovely video performances of *La Bohème*, including a wonderful Met version with Teresa Stratas and José Carreras, and an often-touted San Francisco Opera video with two aging stars, Mirella Freni and Luciano Pavarotti. Even so, this classic 1965 performance from La Scala is probably the finest of all. This production made Mirella Freni a star, and her gorgeous singing sets the standard for a cast that includes Gianni Raimondi, Rolando Panerai, and Adriana Martino; conducted by Herbert von Karajan. Add Franco Zeffirelli's inspired direction and the visual beauty of the sets, and the result is magical. Highly recommended if you use Listening Idea 1 or 2 above.

Puccini, *La Bohème*. Kultur Video (DVD, color, 117 minutes). A close second to the Karajan version above, this more intimate Covent Garden production is absolutely charming. For once, we have an aptly youthful cast that can act as well as sing—and how beautifully they sing! Principals include Ileana Cotrubas, Neil Shicoff, Thomas Allen, and Marilyn Zschau; conducted by Lamberto Gardelli. Highly recommended if you use Listening Idea 1 or 2 above.

Puccini, *Madama Butterfly*. Deutsche Grammophon (DVD or VHS, color, 144 minutes). Jean-Pierre Ponnelle's beautifully filmed version of Puccini's tragic opera. Performed by Mirella Freni, Plácido Domingo, and Christa Ludwig; conducted by Herbert von Karajan. Try this video if you use Listening Idea 2 above.

Rossini, *Barber of Seville.* Arthaus Musik (DVD, color, 157 minutes). This amusing Cologne Opera production's chief attraction is a young Cecilia Bartoli, already in full command of a difficult role. Rounding out the fine cast are Gino Quilico, Carlos Feller, David Kuebler, and Robert Lloyd; conducted by Gabriele Ferro. Try this video if you use Listening Idea 2 above.

Strauss, *Der Rosenkavalier.* Deutsche Grammophon (DVD, color, 213 minutes). Beautiful performance of Richard Strauss's most popular opera, produced by Otto Schenk. Performed by Felicity Lott, Anne Sofie von Otter, Barbara Bonney, Kurt Moll, and Gottfried Hornik with the Vienna State Opera Orchestra; conducted by Carlos Kleiber. Try this recording if you use Listening Idea 3 above.

Verdi, *Aida.* Deutsche Grammophon (DVD, color, 158 minutes). Metropolitan Opera recording of the Verdi opera used in the *Listen* textbook. Performed by Aprile Millo, Plácido Domingo, Dolora Zajick, Sherrill Milnes, Paata Burchuladze, and Dimitri Kavrakos; conducted by James Levine. Try this video to supplement teaching ideas on *Aida* in Lecture Suggestions or Further Listening Examples above.

Verdi, *Aida: Busseto 2001.* RAI Cinema (DVD, color, 188 minutes). To celebrate the centennial of Verdi's death, several operas were performed by the Arturo Toscanini Foundation at the small theater in Verdi's hometown. Using young singers, Zeffirelli produced an intimate, lovely performance of Verdi's grand opera. Performed by Adina Aaron, Scott Piper, and Kate Aldrich; conducted by Massimiliano Stefanelli with artistic direction by Carlo Bergonzi. Try this video to supplement teaching ideas on *Aida* in Lecture Suggestions or Further Listening Examples above.

Verdi and Venetian Theatre. Five Centuries of Music in Venice Series. www.films .com (DVD or VHS, color, 60 minutes). This program offers a sumptuous portrait of the history, art, and architecture of nineteenth-century Venice. Covers Rossini, Verdi, and Wagner's death in Venice. Live performances of music by Rossini, Verdi, and Wagner in the salon of La Fenice Theater.

Giuseppe Verdi. www.films.com (DVD or VHS, color, 53 minutes). Fascinating video biography follows Verdi's career using reenactments, photos, archival footage, and rare recordings from La Scala and the National Institute of Verdi Studies. Features interviews with stage directors Mortier and Visconti and musical excerpts from *Nabucco, Rigoletto, La Traviata, Aida, Otello,* and *Falstaff.* Conductors include Solti and Karajan. Recommended.

Giuseppe Verdi. Harmonics: The Innovators of Classical Music Series. www .films.com (DVD or VHS, color, 27 minutes). Video biography of Verdi features interviews with stage directors Mortier and Visconti and musical excerpts from *Nabucco, La Traviata, Rigoletto, Don Carlo, Aida, Otello,* and other works. Conductors include Solti and Karajan. Recommended.

Verdi, *Otello.* Deutsche Grammophon (DVD, color, 140 minutes). Excellent recording of this dark tragedy, probably the best currently available. Performed by Plácido Domingo, Renée Fleming, and James Morris at the Metropolitan Opera; conducted by James Levine. Try this video if you use Listening Idea 2 above.

Verdi, *Rigoletto.* BBC Opus Arte (DVD, color, 169 minutes). David McVicar's Covent Garden production of this great middle-period opera captures the debauchery and cynicism of the Mantua court better than any other, including full frontal nudity in Act I—talk about *verismo!* The cast is outstanding: Paolo

Gavanelli makes an extraordinarily effective, expressive Rigoletto; Christine Schäfer an affectingly naïve, pure-toned Gilda; and Carlos Alvarez a callously cynical Duke; conducted by Edward Downes. Try this video if you use Listening Idea 2 above.

Verdi, *La Traviata*. Decca (DVD, color, 135 minutes). Royal Opera House production of this Verdi classic captures Angela Gheorghiu's stunning debut as Violetta. Performed by Gheorghiu, Frank Lopardo, and Leo Nucci; conducted by Sir Georg Solti. Recommended if you use Listening Idea 2 above.

Wagner, *Der Ring des Nibelungen*. Deutsche Grammophon (DVD, color, 937 minutes—4 operas available separately or as a set). Viewers who are tired of modernist reinterpretations of an older opera can always count on the Metropolitan Opera to do it in the traditional manner—and to do it very well indeed. The 1990 Met production of Wagner's *Ring* remains one of the best available. Special effects such as the crashing pillars at the end of *Götterdämmerung* are effective in class, especially on something larger than a TV screen. A strong cast includes James Morris, Christa Ludwig, Siegfried Jerusalem, Matti Salminen, Hildegard Behrens, Jessye Norman, and Kurt Moll; conducted by James Levine. Try these videos to augment your presentation of *The Valkyrie* or if you use Listening Idea 4 or suggestions on *The Valkyrie* from Further Listening Examples above.

Wagner, *Der Ring des Nibelungen*. Deutsche Grammophon (DVD, color, 7 discs—4 operas available singly or as a set). Originally released on the Philips label, this set is now available from Deutsche Grammophon. First mounted in the *Ring*'s centennial year, Patrice Chéreau's innovative Bayreuth production holds pride of place both as the first complete *Ring* to be telecast (on PBS in 1982) and as the earliest *Ring* currently available on DVD. The updated Industrial Revolution setting doesn't seem as radical as it once did, and the performance has held up very well in the face of recent stiff competition. The cast includes Donald McIntyre, Peter Hofmann, and Gwyneth Jones; conducted by Pierre Boulez. Try these videos to augment your presentation of *The Valkyrie* or if you use Listening Idea 4 or suggestions on *The Valkyrie* from Further Listening Examples above.

Richard Wagner. Harmonics: The Innovators of Classical Music Series. www .films.com (DVD or VHS, color, 27 minutes). Video biography of Wagner follows his innovations from *Der Fliegende Holländer* to *Parsifal*. Conductors Solti and Boulez are featured in excerpts recorded in various theaters, including Bayreuth. Recommended.

Wagner, *Lohengrin*. Image Entertainment (DVD or VHS, color, 219 minutes). The Vienna State Opera production of this important German Romantic opera. Performed by Plácido Domingo, Cheryl Studer, Dunja Vejzovic; conducted by Claudio Abbado.

Wagner, *Parsifal*. Deutsche Grammophon (DVD, color, 264 minutes). Otto Schenk's Metropolitan Opera production of Wagner's late music drama. Performed by Siegfried Jerusalem, Waltraud Meier, Bernd Weikl, Franz Mazura, and Kurt Moll; conducted by James Levine.

Wagner: The Complete Epic. Kultur Video (DVD or VHS, color, 540 minutes). This documentary starring Richard Burton as Wagner and Vanessa Redgrave as Cosima was broadcast by PBS some years ago. The nine-hour series takes up Wagner's life in great detail. Excerpts can be useful in lectures on Wagner.

Wagner, *Die Walküre*. After years of slim pickings, we suddenly have more DVD recordings of Wagner's *Ring* than we can use! With so many options, which DVD should you use to supplement your presentation of *The Valkyrie*? That depends on how adventurous your tastes are. Here are your options:

❧ Barenboim, Bayreuther Festspiele. Warner Classics (DVD, color, 2 discs). Part of the finest new *Ring* cycle released in years, this is my top recommendation. Barenboim leads the orchestra in some extraordinary music making. The sound recording is immediate and vivid, the acting is superb, and Harry Kupfer's direction sheds new light on many scenes. Even the Prelude is staged, with spectacular effects and transitions highlighting Siegmund's flight through the ferocious storm. The staging is spare, but the monolithic, stylized tree at center stage gives it an epic feel. In the *Listen* scene, Siegmund and Sieglinde look for once as if they could be twins, and we quickly sense the mix of emotions sparked by their chance encounter, not least of which is their growing passion for each other. Wotan's Farewell offers a stunning example of the laser lighting effects that give this production such a distinctive look—Brünnhilde seems to float in mid-air at the very end!

❧ Levine, Metropolitan Opera. Deutsche Grammophon (DVD, color, 2 discs). This excellent 1989 production "out-traditionals" all of the others, with Siegmund and Sieglinde dressed in fur and skins in a spacious yet rustic deepwoods hut. Looking very much like stereotypical heavy-set Wagnerian singers, there is no way that Gary Lakes and Jessye Norman will be mistaken for twins! Their acting is a bit stagey (the down side of tradition), but they sing beautifully, and we "get" what the scene is about without difficulty. Wotan's Farewell is very effective, again with a red-smoke-filled stage. Overall, this is a luxurious, well-recorded performance, beautifully sung and played. It can be recommended without hesitation.

❧ Boulez, Bayreuther Festspiele. Deutsche Grammophon (DVD, color, 2 discs). Patrice Chéreau's 1976 production once seemed oh-so-modern, but it now looks much more traditional. Hunding's woodsy hunter's home has become a palatial country estate that dwarfs the two lovers. Even more than in Barenboim's *Ring*, Siegmund and Sieglinde look like twins. Emotionally, however, this scene has a cooler feel than the others. The recorded sound does not help the situation, as it lacks the impact of more recent recordings. That's a shame, because the music making is first-rate throughout. Wotan's Farewell is very moving indeed, supported by a smoke-filled stage that glows and shimmers from the inside—a very effective "magic fire."

❧ Zagrosek, Staatsoper Stuttgart. EuroArts (DVD, color, 2 discs). Set in a spare, dumpy 1950s-style kitchen, this "trailer trash" version of Act I of *The Valkyrie* gives us Sieglinde in a slinky, tight-fitting, see-through dress and Siegmund in jogging sweats and a tank top that shows a paunchy midriff. This is lust at first sight, and within two minutes, Siegmund has buried his face in Sieglinde's crotch. This sounds off-putting, but in fact it is thoroughly recommendable. Scene i is well sung and well acted, and it makes very effective theater! Wotan's Farewell is rather bizarre, on the other hand. Wotan puts Brünnhilde to sleep at a tacky kitchen table, and Loge's "magic fire" is a stage light that Wotan wheels in to illuminate the Valkyrie.

❧ de Billy, Barcelona Gran Teatre del Liceu. BBC Opus Arte (DVD, color, 3 discs). This highly regarded *Ring* cycle features the same director as Barenboim's Bayreuth *Ring*, but this is a rather different production. It starts off full of promise with the most energetic Prelude of any; unfortunately the

Barcelona brass lack the polish of their Bayreuth colleagues, and other orchestral weaknesses become evident in the slower, more tender passages of Act I. Siegmund and Sieglinde seem older and more world weary than in other productions, but the moment when Siegmund offers Sieglinde the first drink is especially tender. Wotan's Farewell gives us a flickering red neon checkerboard on the back wall. The same could be said for this effect as for the entire production—decent enough, but not as memorable as some of the others.

⁊ Haenchen, Amsterdam Opera. BBC Opus Arte (DVD, color, 3 discs). The most recent complete *Ring* on the market has much to commend it. This is not a big-budget production, and the staging is often minimal, but it is visually striking. The resulting lack of clutter puts the focus on human relationships, and this is one of the most touchingly intimate versions avaliable. The simultaneous hesitation and growing attraction of Siegmund and Sieglinde are well caught, and Wotan has never seemed more vulnerable (and human!) in bidding farewell to Brünnhilde. The cast is strong; the orchestral playing is quite fine; and the costumes, special effects, and lightling are very effective indeed. This DVD makes a good alternative to the others.

⁊ Software

The Norton Masterworks CD-ROM. New York: W. W. Norton (CD-ROM—Macintosh). Authors Daniel Jacobson and Timothy Koozin provide a clever multimedia introduction to twelve important works, including Leoncavallo's *I Pagliacci*. Features animated, guided listening resources as well as information on the composers, eras, and genres, and the works themselves.

CHAPTER **18**

The Late Romantics

Chapter Outline

Important Terms

realism	nationalism	Classicism
symphonic poem	exoticism	double stops
theme transformation	*kuchka*	cross-rhythms
Romantic nostalgia	*shamisen*	*jinghu*
parody	*kabuki*	*erhu*
round	*nagauta*	*yueqin*
noh drama	Beijing opera (*jingju*)	heterophony
bunraku	*jing*	

Teaching Objectives

❦ Overall Objectives

This chapter will help students acquire familiarity with:

1. Features of late Romantic music as a reflection of the tension between Romanticism and realism.

2. Features of late Romantic program music and the symphonic poem.

3. The role of nationalism in late Romanticism, especially in the music of the Russian *kuchka*.

4. Classicism and nostalgia as late nineteenth-century responses to Romanticism.

5. The lives and music of Pyotr Ilyich Tchaikovsky, Modest Musorgsky, Johannes Brahms, and Gustav Mahler.

6. The Japanese traditions of musical drama, especially *kabuki,* and the similar societal roles played by Western opera and the *kabuki* theater.

7. The conventions and musical features of Beijing opera.

8. Similarities in the social contexts, musical structures, and theatrical features of European and Chinese opera.

❦ Listening Objectives

After completing this chapter, students should be able to:

1. Comprehend and follow important genres of late Romanticism, especially the symphonic poem and other types of program music, the concerto, and the symphony.

2. Hear and identify the effect of trends in late Romantic music, especially realism, program music, nationalism, classicism, and nostalgia.

3. Hear and identify important features of Japanese *nagauta* music and compare them with those of European opera.

4. Hear vocal styles and other important musical features associated with Beijing opera and compare them with those of Romantic opera.

Lecture Suggestions

This chapter provides an embarrassment of riches: four examples from the core repertory of late Romanticism and excerpts from two of the world's important theatrical traditions. The paragraphs below provide teaching suggestions for all of these works, but you should seriously consider presenting Japanese kabuki and Beijing opera with the Verdi and Wagner examples in Chapter 17, as suggested in the previous chapter. The placement of Global Perspectives examples at the end of each unit in no way implies that you must present them after everything else is said and done. Rather, this arrangement provides maximum flexibility—you can plug them in wherever it seems most appropriate. And although this manual urges frequent comparisons between Western and non-Western music, the clustering of Global Perspectives examples also facilitates comparisons between different world traditions.

The lecture suggestions below follow the order of the *Listen* textbook, beginning with Tchaikovsky, Musorgsky, Brahms, and Mahler and concluding with *kabuki* and Beijing opera. As usual, each Global Perspectives segment begins with a historical overview and background information on the traditions represented, followed by teaching suggestions for the musical examples themselves. These suggestions also include ideas for comparing Japanese and Chinese musical theater with Chapter 17 examples.

Late Romanticism

The variety, richness, and quantity of late Romantic music are staggering. These qualities have ensured that much of this music remains in the modern concert repertoire. Four examples hardly suffice to provide a full picture, yet time constraints will limit your ability to use additional listening examples. This chapter contains comprehensive lecture suggestions for each listening example in the textbook. If you need to streamline your presentation of Chapter 18, try the following three procedures:

1. Initiate a quick and general discussion of the nature of Romanticism after 1848 (discussed on textbook pages 293–94).

2. Use the introductory notes in each section below to discuss the trends of late Romanticism: realism, the development of the symphonic poem, nationalism, the return to Classical forms, and Romantic nostalgia.

3. Use Listening Charts and recordings for any three works to illustrate these trends. Make sure you include one example each of symphonic poem, nationalism, and classical form. (Additional Listening Charts for favorite works not found in *Listen* can be found in Appendix I.)

Romanticism and Realism

The year 1848 saw failed revolutions in France, Italy, and various German states. The failure of these revolutions symbolized for the Romantics the failure of their aspirations for political freedom. After 1848, Romantic art lived on, not as a revolutionary movement but as nostalgia.

♪ Late Romantic Program Music

Descriptive music increasingly became the norm during the late Romantic era. The symphonic poem emerged. Franz Liszt pioneered this new genre, writing many tone poems during the 1850s. Richard Strauss, Tchaikovsky, and nationalist composers such as Smetana, Musorgsky, and Rimsky-Korsakov wrote many more in the late nineteenth century. (For an interesting example of Chinese program music, see suggestions for *The Drunken Fisherman* in Further Listening Examples below.)

This is a good time to redefine important orchestral Romantic genres.

Program music—This generic term describes *instrumental* compositions associated with poems, stories, and the like. All of the genres below are types of program music.

Program symphony—These *multimovement* works for orchestra follow some sort of literary program. Berlioz's *Fantastic* Symphony offers a prime example.

Concert overture—These *single-movement* works for orchestra, written in sonata form, became popular in the early nineteenth century. They were called *concert* overtures because they were intended for concert (not operatic) performance; they were called overtures because they used sonata form—the usual form for opera overtures in Classical and early Romantic music. The symphonic poem evolved from the concert overture.

Symphonic (tone) poem—These *single-movement*, free-form works for orchestra were based on a poem, a story, or a literary-philosophic model. They often borrowed features of sonata form or the four-movement format of the symphony, but they are essentially free-form works with no predetermined formal plan.

TCHAIKOVSKY *Romeo and Juliet*

Nearly nineteen minutes in length, this is the longest single movement in the *Listen* anthology. Students need special preparation to follow this long, free-form composition. To do justice to this work, plan on a full class hour.

Shakespeare's plays enjoyed a tremendous revival in the nineteenth century, and many composers wrote works based on Shakespeare, including Berlioz, Mendelssohn, Verdi, and Tchaikovsky. Ask your class to tell *you* the story of *Romeo and Juliet*. (This exercise also sets up your presentation of *West Side Story* in Chapter 23.) Call attention to the details that figure most prominently in Tchaikovsky's music:

1. Two warring families in Verona, Italy—the Montagues and Capulets—behave more like street gangs than wealthy aristocrats.

2. Romeo and Juliet, one a Montague and the other a Capulet, fall hopelessly in love with each other despite the enmity between their families.

3. Friar Laurence attempts (and fails) to mediate between the two families and arranges for Romeo and Juliet to marry secretly. But Romeo is exiled from Verona after killing Juliet's cousin, so the friar devises another plan. Juliet drinks a potion to help her feign death. She plans to rejoin Romeo once her family believes her dead.

4. The plan goes awry—Romeo, unaware of the deception, receives a message that Juliet is dead. He goes to her tomb, finds her dead (or so she appears), and poisons himself. Juliet awakens, finds Romeo dead, and stabs herself.

5. The deaths of the two lovers shock their families into calling a truce. Out of tragedy comes hope for reconciliation.

Display Listening Chart 17 (or refer students to textbook page 297). The main themes of the piece match up nicely with different characters and themes in the story. Play the main themes until students can recognize them consistently. Describe the links between the themes and the story.

Hymn theme (track 19, 0:00–0:33)	often associated with Friar Laurence mixture of solemnity and foreboding (the most Russian-sounding theme!)
Vendetta theme (track 22, 0:00–1:17)	associated with the warring families powerful theme based on a short, accented rhythmic motive syncopation

Love theme
(track 23, 0:36–
track 24, 0:58)

associated with the love between Romeo and Juliet
lyric, soaring, rhapsodic theme

Talk through the sequence of events in this symphonic poem. Point out how closely the work follows sonata form:

The Hymn theme serves as a slow introduction.

The Vendetta theme and the Love theme function like themes 1 and 2 in an exposition.

The development works over the Vendetta and Hymn themes.

A free recapitulation restates the Vendetta and Love themes, though in a more abbreviated and developmental fashion.

The coda presents a tragic version of the Love theme, a new theme, and a transformed version of the Love theme.

In the body of the piece, the Love theme is always heard against the backdrop of the Vendetta theme. The intensity and conflict of these themes increase throughout the exposition, development, and recapitulation, reaching a climax near the end of the recapitulation, where the Love theme is actually interrupted by the Vendetta theme—as if the vendetta wins out over love. But the Vendetta theme's victory is short-lived; the subsequent coda is dominated by the Love theme. The coda begins with a funereal version of the Love theme that suggests the tragic deaths of the two lovers. A new theme changes the mood from tragedy to hope, and the final transformation of the Love theme suggests love's victory and the hope for reconciliation between the two families.

Thematic Transformation

The earliest symphonic poems by Liszt relied on the technique of thematic transformation; Tchaikovsky also uses that technique here. Thematic transformation is a variation technique whose goal is the complete alteration of a given theme's mood and character. In *Romeo and Juliet,* the introduction's low, solemn Hymn theme (track 19, 0:00–0:33) becomes a loud, menacing march with syncopated accompaniment (track 26, 0:22–0:50) in the development section. The Love theme undergoes two transformations, both of them in the coda. For the funereal version (track 29), Tchaikovsky fragments the theme; puts it in minor mode; and accompanies it with solemn, muffled drum beats. The final transformation (track 30, 0:55–1:40), accompanied by strumming harp, returns to major mode and puts to rest the yearning quality of earlier versions of the theme. This "transcendent" version remembers the lovers' deaths, but it points to hope in spite of the tragedy. Play these transformations if you have time.

Conclude your presentation of *Romeo and Juliet* by playing the entire symphonic poem for the class.

⁊ Nationalism and Exoticism

The revolutions and the spirit of nationalism that swept nineteenth-century Europe were manifestations of the Romantic search for freedom and individual (national) identity. The search for national identity gave rise to an equivalent movement in music called nationalism. Wagner and Verdi both embodied the nationalist aspirations of their own people, but their musical styles grew out of mainstream European traditions. Their music sounds German and Italian, respectively, but no more so than the music of mainstream German and Italian composers before them. The great German-Italian musical tradition continued to dominate mainstream European music until the end of the nineteenth century. What made the nationalist movement unusual was the number of composers from countries outside of the mainstream who tried to evoke the character of their native lands musically. In so doing, they often broke away from mainstream traditions. If the nationalists took any inspiration from German or Italian composers, it was from "radical" composers like Berlioz or Liszt, whose program music and colorful orchestration offered the nationalists many useful techniques. The list of Romantic nationalist composers is a long one. It includes:

Bohemia—Dvořák, Smetana

Denmark—Nielsen

England—Elgar, Vaughan Williams

Finland—Sibelius

Norway—Grieg

Russia—Musorgsky, Rimsky-Korsakov, Borodin, Balakirev, Glinka

Spain—Granados, Turina, Falla

United States—Gottschalk, MacDowell

Because of the late nineteenth-century fascination with exoticism, the music of nationalist composers often enjoyed a wide audience beyond their native lands. This taste for the foreign and the exotic was satisfied not only by nationalist music from foreign lands but also by mainstream composers who imitated foreign styles—consider the Japanese flavor of Puccini's *Madame Butterfly*, the Egyptian flavor of Verdi's *Aida*, the Spanish flavor of Bizet's *Carmen*, or the eastern European flavor of Brahms's *Hungarian Dances*.

The Russian Kuchka

In an era of censorship and artistic repression, Russian artists in many fields banded together for mutual support and encouragement. One such group was the *moguchaya kuchka*, a close group of radical Russian composers (some of them amateurs) who rejected the conservative, European style of their colleagues at the St. Petersburg Conservatory. They sought to create a uniquely Russian music, and they borrowed the techniques of radical Romantic composers such as Berlioz, Liszt, and Wagner in their quest. Two composers stand out because of their music and their influence on twentieth-century composers mentioned later: Rimsky-Korsakov, mentor to Stravinsky, and Musorgsky, who influenced the impressionist composers Debussy and Ravel.

MUSORGSKY *Pictures at an Exhibition*

Begin with a question. *If you wanted to depict your native land in a musical composition, how would you do it?* If you were born in the United States, what could you put into the music so that listeners would say, "That sounds like something from the United States!" What kinds of music would you write? Write student responses on the board; encourage comments, even if some are irrelevant. When comments peter out, summarize the answers on the board. You may need to add an item or two, but make sure these categories appear in your summary:

Use indigenous music or imitate its style features. Examples could include folk songs, patriotic songs, hymns, spirituals, dance music, jazz syncopation, and so on.

Write program music that evokes national history, landmarks, geographical features, stories, or legends.

Write vocal music (songs or operas) based on national poetry, literature, history, stories, or legends.

Musorgsky was the most radical nationalist in the *kuchka*—he used all of the techniques listed above, and he sought to express even the rhythm of Russian speech in his music. *Pictures at an Exhibition* provides one of the most novel, effective examples of nationalist music available. Like Schumann's *Carnaval,* Musorgsky's composition was a cycle of character pieces for piano. (Ravel orchestrated the cycle in 1922.) Musorgsky provided a unique twist, however, by creating the musical equivalent of a visit to an art gallery. Each character piece depicts a different painting by the Russian painter Victor Hartmann. (The entire composition was inspired by an exhibition of Hartmann's paintings shortly after the painter's death.) Musorgsky even gives the listener time to mull over one painting and walk to the next in the "Promenade" music inserted between character pieces.

These features make Musorgsky's character pieces program music, but what features make *Pictures at an Exhibition* a nationalist work? To start with, several of Hartmann's paintings depict scenes from Russian culture and lore; but there is more. Play the theme of the opening "Promenade" (0:00–0:34).

Allegro giusto

Several features mark the influence of Russian folk song on this melody: use of irregular meter (**5/4**); use of changing meter (alternates between **5/4** and **6/4**); and unusual, angular melodic contours (a pentatonic scale forms the basis of the first five measures). The brass accompaniment suggests the low, rich sound of Russian Orthodox choral music for worship. From the first, Musorgsky imitates the style features of indigenous Russian music. He also uses two Russian melodies in "The Great Gate at Kiev" (0:00–1:01 and 1:01–1:37) (see textbook page 301); depicts a Russian folk-art nutcracker in "Gnomus" (see the nutcracker on textbook page 300); and employs the sound of the bells that rang in every village and town across Russia—a powerful symbol ("The Great Gate at Kiev" [5:17–end]).

The comments below provide teaching suggestions for all four *Listen* examples from *Pictures at an Exhibition.* You can pick and choose according to your time and interest.

"Promenade [1]"

Built on the Russian-sounding melody described above, this short piece of "walking music" moves through several contrasting sections before it ends with a return of the opening melody.

"Gnomus"

This unusual piece paints a macabre portrait of a Russian folk-art nutcracker (refer students to the picture on textbook page 300). Three primary ideas alternate in this free-form work. The first (**A**) is a forceful, frantic seven-note scrambling motive that ends with a long, sustained note (0:00–0:05). The second (**B**) features a quieter, descending stepwise melody with some sharp dissonances (0:16–0:24). It uses remarkably colorful orchestral effects (mutes, *pizzicato, glissando,* harmonics, trills, and stopped notes for horn), and the orchestration transforms itself each time the theme returns. The powerful, angular third theme (**C**) features awkward leaps and chromatic motion in an odd two-voice counterpoint (0:46–1:07).

section:	A	B	A	C	A	C	A	C	A	C	B	A'
timing:	0:00	0:16	0:33	0:46	1:07	1:11	1:33	1:36	1:42	1:45	2:24	2:40
measure #:	1	19	39	48	55	57	64	66	68	70	82	104

"Promenade [2]"

The second statement of the "Promenade" is much softer and more lightly scored (horn and winds) than the first. This version also inverts the texture—the horn melody sounds below the accompanying chords. These changes create a subtle thematic transformation.

"The Great Gate at Kiev"

This work paints a grand, brilliant portrait of Hartmann's fanciful artwork (reproduced on textbook page 301—note the bells in the tower!). The first four sections alternate between two contrasting Russian melodies. The majestic first theme (**A**, 0:00–1:01) features the brass section and builds to an orchestral tutti. The quiet, reflective second theme (**B**, 1:01–1:37) creates the sound of a delicate organ stop by using only clarinets and bassoons. Its minor-mode sound contrasts with the major mode of the **A** theme. The bell first tolls in the **C** section, which provides a surprise contrast to both **A** and **B** themes and builds tension that can only be resolved by the shattering final statement of the **A** theme. Halfway through the **C** section, the Promenade theme appears (3:17), affirming the cyclic unity this theme provides throughout Musorgsky's *Pictures.* The final **A** section employs the entire orchestra (a large Romantic orchestra—percussion instruments include timpani, triangle, cymbals, bass drum, tam-tam, and bells) and slows the theme to half-speed to eke out every last bit of grandeur. Novel chord progressions herald one final statement of the **A** theme, and *Pictures* comes to an end.

A	B	A	B	C	A
0:00	1:01	1:37	2:13	2:47	3:50
m. 1	m. 30	m. 47	m. 64	m. 81	m. 115

❧ Responses to Romanticism

In the wake of the widespread disillusionment that followed the failure of the 1848 revolutions, a mood of realism settled in during the late nineteenth century. The dashed hopes and dreams of Romanticism no longer seemed fully appropriate, yet many composers were not ready to give them up completely, and they responded to Romanticism in many ways. Brahms responded by tempering his Romanticism with the meaningful structures of older music; Mahler responded by exploring Romanticism's nostalgic appeal.

The Renewal of Classicism: Brahms

The prominent position accorded to musicians and composers in the late nineteenth century had several side effects. Among them was the birth of musicology; music had become so important that it had to be studied scientifically. German musical scholars looked back to discover how music (German music, specifically) had evolved to its present state of perfection. Fascinated by this research, Brahms befriended several important musicologists and developed a deep respect for traditions of the past, absorbing these newly rediscovered styles into his own work.

Brahms used the best of the past in his music—Beethoven's relentless motivic development, for instance—yet it would be a mistake to call him a conservative composer. He did not pursue chromaticism to the degree that Wagner or Liszt did, but no one explored metric displacement and regrouping to the extent that Brahms did. Further, Brahms's distinctively rich, dark-hued orchestration clothed his compositional ideas perfectly.

BRAHMS Violin Concerto in D

One can quickly see Brahms's allegiance to the past in the forms and genres he employed. Brahms wrote concert overtures, for instance, but never a symphonic poem; in fact, program music of any kind held little interest for Brahms. He turned to the concerto genre four times in his career, writing a violin concerto, two piano concertos, and a concerto for violin and cello. Three of these works exhibit the three-movement plan associated with the Classical concerto, whereas the fourth work, Brahms's second piano concerto, follows a four-movement plan. Brahms's three-movement concertos employ the standard fast-slow-fast tempo scheme, and a study of individual movements reveals the same forms we would expect to find in Classical concerto movements. It comes as no surprise, then, to discover a rondo-form movement at the end of Brahms's Violin Concerto in D, the example in the *Listen* textbook. These choices place Brahms squarely in the tradition of Haydn, Mozart, and Beethoven. Nonetheless, Brahms does not use Classical forms slavishly, as we shall see in a moment.

Brahms was a pianist, not a violinist, but he knew the violin and its capabilities intimately. In his late teens in Hamburg, Brahms heard much Hungarian music from refugees who came through Hamburg after a failed Hungarian nationalist uprising. A few years later, on a concert tour with violinist Eduard Reményi, Brahms had to learn to play Hungarian gypsy rubato authentically. At about the same time he met violinist Joseph Joachim, who became a lifelong friend and introduced the young Brahms to many important composers, including Liszt and Robert and Clara Schumann. All of these influences color Brahms's violin concerto—a gracious, sunny work that demonstrates mastery of the instrument's virtuoso possibilities and a knowledge of Hungarian fiddle music.

Display Listening Chart 18 (or refer students to textbook page 307). As with previous rondo-form movements, play the rondo theme (track 1, 0:00–0:45) until students can recognize it readily. Point out the motive on which Brahms bases his rondo theme, both its rhythmic aspect (short-short-short-long!) and its melodic contour. Note also the tunefulness of the theme and its traditional **a a b a′** structure. Brahms wrote many beautiful melodies, but not many qualify as tunes; this one does. Some listeners also hear echoes of Hungarian gypsy violin in this theme.

Look through the rest of the Listening Chart with your students. If you have time, play later appearances of the rondo theme; if not, even a glance at the chart suggests that Brahms alters and varies each new statement of the rondo theme. Point out the episodes as well, and take time to play at least the **B** section now, since it returns at several points in the movement. Once students acquaint themselves with these themes, you can play the entire movement for them. While they listen, have the class write down any changes they hear when the main themes return in this movement. Brahms abbreviates these returns and plays with our sense of return, but the most interesting changes come in the coda, where Brahms changes to compound meter to give the rondo theme a marchlike character—an example of true thematic transformation. Before you finish, point out just a few other features of the music, especially the lyric contrast provided by the C theme, the solo violin cadenzas, and the coda, with its playful treatment of earlier themes.

How could a late Romantic composer continue to work happily within traditional Classical forms? Brahms's profound, exhaustive manipulations of motives and rhythms at many structural levels, referred to by some analysts as "continuing variation," acquired greater urgency and impact when housed in the context of traditional forms. With his intimate knowledge of older music, Brahms understood as well as anyone the power and durability of the principles of contrast and return, yet his predilection for "continuing variation" guarantees that we will not find the literal restatements of the rondo theme that Classical composers used so often. Further, his control over his themes and over tonal stability and instability provides several moments where we experience the same powerful sense of recapitulation associated with sonata form. Yes, Brahms used traditional forms, but never for their own sake. He appropriated the forms that provided the most forceful vehicles for expressing his musical ideas, and he adapted those forms creatively to enhance the music's overall impact.

Romantic Nostalgia: Mahler

For Mahler, Romanticism represented something naive, pure, and innocent—like the lost innocence of childhood. His music expresses a nostalgic yearning for something lost forever, something whose memory is in constant danger of being crowded out by the realities and disillusionment of the harsh present. Mahler embraced Romanticism with full awareness of the broken dreams it symbolized. He used the Romantic style in a nostalgic manner that pitted its lost innocence against a cynical realism.

Mahler's symphonies followed the grandiose Romantic tradition. Even when his works were not specifically programmatic, they expressed aspects of his own life experiences. Some followed the traditional four-movement plan (though with the slow movement *after* the dance movement), and others included as few as two movements (Symphony No. 8) or as many as six (Symphony No. 3). Most were long symphonies (50–100 minutes) for large Romantic orchestras. Mahler used an enormous variety of orchestral colors—he conducted for a living and knew the orchestra inside out. The textbook refers to the kaleidoscopic effect of Mahler's creative handling of orchestration.

MAHLER Symphony No. 1

Refer students to the children's illustration reproduced on textbook page 310, *The Huntsman's Funeral Procession*. Ask them what is wrong with this picture. The picture looks so innocuous that it takes time to recognize the incongruities. Yes, it is a funeral and the animals are crying, but why would animals cry over the death of their tormentor? We see a banner, a choir, solemn gowns, torches, pallbearers, a bell, and a complement of mourners. Why go to such great lengths to honor the death of the huntsman? Slowly the droll, tongue-in-cheek humor of this print sinks in. The childhood imagery and mock seriousness appealed to Mahler, and he based the slow third movement of his Symphony No. 1 on this artwork.

Play the first theme of this movement for the class (track 7, 0:00–0:33). Ask students if they recognize the tune. If they cannot, go to the keyboard, play "Frère Jacques," and ask students if they can recognize the tune. (It doesn't hurt to sing the words as you play the tune.) Go back and play Mahler's first theme again. Ask the class if they hear a connection between the two melodies. Make the point that Mahler *wants* the listener to hear the connection; what better way to express the imagery of this painting than to take a children's tune and turn it into a solemn march? This bold move reproduces the same mock-serious atmosphere in purely musical terms. Note that Mahler even treats the tune as a round (imitative polyphony), just as "Frère Jacques" is usually sung.

Display Listening Chart 19 (or refer students to textbook page 311). Call attention to the four sections identified on the chart, and relate this form to Classical march and trio form. March and trio form, covered in Chapter 16 of this manual (in suggestions for the fourth movement of Berlioz's *Fantastic Symphony* under Further Listening Examples on p. 397), is virtually the same as minuet and trio form from the Classical period. As the diagram below shows, the funeral march theme and the dance-band phrases function as do the **a** and **b** sections in a Classical minuet. (Don't confuse the **a** and **b** in minuet form with the authors' labels for the two dance-band phrases!)

	Section 1			*Section 2*	*Section 3*		*Section 4*		
	a			b a′			a	b	a′
			March (**A**)		Trio (**B**)			March (**A′**)	
	0:00			2:09 4:12	5:01		7:02	7:59	8:37
track timings:	7—			8— 9—	9—		12—	13—	14—
	0:00			0:00 1:19	2:08		0:00	0:23	0:19

The primary difference is the lack of Classical balance and proportion in this movement; the final section condenses material from the first two sections.

Play each of the main themes for the class (use either the recording or the keyboard)—"Frère Jacques," the two dance-band phrases, the trio, the "additional" fragment, and the new trumpet counterpoint to the march (Section 4)—until students can recognize each one. Point out the exaggerated qualities of the dance-band melodies and the naive, folklike innocence of the trio. Then play the entire piece and point out each section on your display as it goes by. In the discussion that follows, ask students to describe the relationship between the illustration and the music.

♩ Global Perspectives 5: Musical Drama Worldwide

No matter where you go, opera is opera. Inevitable stylistic differences exist between the traditions of different nations, but they also share many features. These features can and do include the following: fusions of song, dance, and drama; emotional expression through music; wide popular support; distinctive styles of singing; differentiation between songs (arias) and narrative singing (recitative); and "stock" roles or plots. This segment looks at two operatic traditions: the *kabuki* theater that originated in Japan just as Italian composers were writing their first operas, and the nineteenth-century Beijing opera tradition. Both Japan and China developed classical traditions with roots deep in the past.

The best place to introduce this music is right alongside the nineteenth-century operatic works of Verdi and Wagner. All four examples share many of the features listed in the paragraph above, and they all represent traditions that go back at least two centuries (if not much earlier). Alternatively, you could present *kabuki* along with Handel's *Julius Caesar* in Chapter 10, where you can compare *kabuki* and Baroque opera as social institutions that served a lower class than did older courtly entertainments. Wherever you decide to cover this material, the suggestions below offer comparisons with most theatrical works prior to Chapter 18.

Japanese Drama

This segment on Japanese *kabuki* drama begins with background information on the history of Japanese theater. If necessary, review the discussion of Japan's early history in the Lecture Suggestions for Chapter 13. It continues with a discussion of *kabuki* theater and concludes with specific lecture suggestions for *Dojoji.*

History of Theater in Japan   The roots of the Japanese theater extend deep into Japan's past, long before *gagaku* was imported from China. Shinto, and later Buddhist, religious rituals mixed the elements of acting, mime, music, and dance in various combinations. When *gagaku* came to Japan, *bugaku* necessarily came along with it. Stemming from the oldest masked theater tradition in the world, *bugaku* was a Chinese theatrical tradition that emphasized dance and music. *Gagaku* and *bugaku* together provided the core repertory for religious ritual, ceremony, and entertainment at the imperial court.

As the power of samurai lords eclipsed that of the emperor, the imperial court declined, and *bugaku* along with it. Given the Japanese love for theater, it was only a matter of time before a new genre emerged, one more attuned to the stoicism of the warrior class: *noh* theater. Realistic expression is deliberately avoided in this highly stylized genre; instead, it relies on the merest of suggestions to convey its meaning. A mask, or even a costume's pattern, points to a character's inner nature. A simple, subtle gesture expresses the deepest emotion. A small shrub signifies a forest. Outright emotional expression would offend the warrior's sensibility, but emotions need to be expressed somehow. Simple, elegant, and austere, the *noh* theater's symbolic, ritualized expression met that need in a profound way.

While *bugaku* and *noh* traditions developed according to the needs of the aristocracy, two new genres, *kabuki* and *bunraku,* began quite differently. In much the same way that Europe's growing middle class made possible the public theaters that supported opera's rapid growth, the growing wealth of Japan's artisan and merchant classes (at the bottom of the class structure) fueled the growth of popular theatrical genres.

Bunraku—puppet theater—began near the end of the sixteenth century, when Menukiya Chozabura, who practiced the popular art of storytelling accompanied by the *shamisen,* decided to dramatize his stories through the incorporation of puppets. The new genre took hold with astonishing rapidity, and several conventions were established as it evolved. The story itself, elevated to the level of literature, remained primary in *bunraku.* The singer-narrator always read from a book, and even blind singer-narrators kept the book open in front of them. Each puppet came to be manipulated by three puppeteers: one to carry the puppet and move the right arm, another to operate the left arm, and a third to move the legs. All three wore black hooded gowns to minimize their presence behind the puppet. The singer-narrator, just as in the storytelling tradition from which *bunraku* evolved, had to narrate the story, sing the songs, and provide the voices for every character. Consummate acting and singing skills were required to convey the quirky personalities and varied emotions of the puppet-characters. All in all, the fantastical mix of elements, vivid emotional expression, and visual beauty of the puppet theater appealed directly to the artisans and merchants who became its champions. As we shall see, *bunraku* soon influenced other theatrical genres around it, and it continues to exert its influence even today—a notable example can be found in the legacy of Jim Henson of *Muppets* fame.

History of Kabuki in Japan   Kabuki originated when Okuni, a Shinto priestess, danced and sang on a *noh*-style stage on a Kyoto riverbed in 1596 (as Peri was finishing the music for the first opera, *Dafne!*). Derived from a Buddhist festival dance, her lively dance was accompanied by a *noh* flute and drums and combined with short sketches and popular songs. Her performances were an instant hit, and the label *kabuki,* a word meaning "unconventional," quickly attached itself to this new form of entertainment. With women singers and dancers as the featured attraction, kabuki spread across the country. As the government became aware of the practice of prostitution by some companies, women's kabuki was banned in 1629. A rival form of kabuki that featured boys became popular once it had no competition, but the government banned this as well in 1642, for much the same reason. But kabuki was not to be stopped. A new form was cultivated featuring more wholesome singing and dancing as well as adult male actors who took both male and female roles; in this form it has continued to the present day.

Kabuki shares several elements with *bunraku*: elaborate, sumptuous sets; beautiful costumes; and especially a vivid expression of emotions. The subtle suggestion of *noh* meant little to merchant and artisan audiences; realistic representation was now required. In most other ways, however, kabuki is strikingly different from *bunraku*. First and foremost, kabuki is actors' theater, in much the same way that European Baroque opera was singers' opera—audiences come to see their favorite actors. There is no literary script as in *bunraku*; much of the kabuki dialogue is improvised onstage. In fact, sometimes actors interact spontaneously with the audience, introducing political jokes and other topical humor (as was the case with the wildly popular lowbrow *Hanswurst*-style theater in Classical Vienna). In the early days of kabuki, the songs and dances of solo entertainers were far more important than the story element. Though many genuinely dramatic works were created as the form evolved, some works retain kabuki's original flavor, the story serving as a loose framework to showcase the skills of the actors.

The history of kabuki includes several important developments that bear mentioning. Theaters were gradually enlarged and modified, moving away from *noh* stage design. Special stage effects were explored, including multiple platforms, trapdoors, and revolving stages. By the end of the seventeenth century, a tradition of written plays emerged within kabuki, introducing greater complexity and depth of expression. In the eighteenth century, faced with *bunraku*'s surging popularity, kabuki theater borrowed many devices from the puppet theater in order to compete with it. It proved simple to borrow *bunraku*'s stories and musical elements; other changes were more difficult. Puppets, of course, can be manipulated and even "damaged" in ways that are impossible for live human performers. Kabuki actors took on the challenge, nonetheless, creating choreography that required incredible flexibility and athleticism, and perfecting the art of the onstage costume change. The work in the recorded set, the 1753 *Musume Dojoji*, resulted from precisely these changes.

The kabuki repertory divides itself into categories on the basis of many criteria. One such division reflects kabuki's many influences over the centuries:

some plays were written specifically within the kabuki tradition, whereas *noh-torimono* includes plays adapted from *noh* theater, and *gidayu kyogen* includes those from *bunraku*. Another division hinges on the story's time period: *jidaimono* plays are based on historical subject matter; *sewamono* plays present contemporary characters and stories (similar to the eighteenth-century European distinction between opera seria and opera buffa). Other divisions may be based on a play's place of origin, its content, its subject, its use of dance, or the type of *shamisen* music used.

Nagauta Music from the Kabuki Play *Dojoji*   *Dojoji* originated as a play in the *noh* theater but was adapted more than once for use in the kabuki theater. The excerpt in the recorded set is taken from *Musume Dojoji*, the most popular adaptation (*noh-torimono*) and the one that remains in the current repertory. This version, a one-act dance play, was a smash hit when first performed by dancer Nakamura Tomijuro in 1753. Created when kabuki was in competition with *bunraku*, the virtuosic choreography features an often stunning athleticism and many quick onstage costume changes. Currently one of the classic works in the kabuki repertory, it has become a test piece for dancers embarking on a career. As a kabuki dance piece, *Musume Dojoji* provides good examples of the "long song" most often used to accompany dance—*nagauta*.

Given kabuki's eclectic beginnings, it should come as no surprise that the music of kabuki derives from many sources, including the *noh* tradition, the puppet theater, and the song literature that grew up around the *shamisen*—a three-stringed lute that arrived in Japan in the sixteenth century. *Nagauta* music first appeared as one of the song-types with *shamisen* accompaniment. It quickly found its way into the kabuki theater and grew to encompass both dance and lyric music as well as both poetic and narrative types. Various forms can be employed, but most consist of songs strung together with instrumental introductions and interludes.

When you present this work to your class, begin with the story.

All *Dojoji* plays were based on an old legend in which a samurai lord informs his daughter that he has arranged her marriage to a Buddhist priest who often visits with them on his annual pilgrimage to the shrine. She tells the priest of her love, but fearing for his soul, he flees and hides under the bell in *Dojoji*, a Buddhist temple. When flood waters prevent her from following, she turns into a serpent, crosses the waters, and encoils the bell. The heat of her fire melts down the bell, killing the priest. *Musume Dojoji* takes place in the temple; its large bronze bell dominates the stage. Ceremonies are under way to dedicate the new bell. Hanako, a young woman dressed as a courtesan (played as usual by a male actor—*onnagata*), approaches the temple gate and asks to be admitted. The priests refuse her until she agrees to perform sacred dances. Once inside, she begins a long sequence of varied dances around the bell. Through a series of costume-change transformations, her appearance and dance become increasingly menacing. In the final dance, to the horror of the priests, she is revealed in the guise of the serpent.

Briefly introduce your students to the structure of this excerpt. The *Listen* Guide nicely labels the major sections of the work; one can easily find the instrumental introduction and interlude typical of many *shamisen* songs. The guide frequently refers to a main melody, suggesting a texture similar to what we found in *gagaku*. It also mentions many details of instrumentation.

Acquaint your students with the instruments used in this excerpt. As the textbook points out, up to three groups of musicians participate in kabuki performances. Not heard in our recording are the offstage group (*geza*) and the narrator/*shamisen* pair (*chobo*) associated with *bunraku* adaptations. We hear the group of musicians seated at the back of the stage (*debayashi*). Of this group, up to eight singers and *shamisen* players sit on a platform; seated on the floor in front of them are the *hayashi,* borrowed from *noh* theater, consisting of several types of drums and one *noh* flute (*nokan*). The drums include one *otsuzumi* (the lead drum), up to four *kotsuzumi,* and up to two *taiko.* The *otsuzumi* and *kotsuzumi* are hourglass-shaped drums with tension ropes that, when squeezed, permit the performer to play up to four different pitches; the *taiko* are played with a stick.

Whereas the flute player sometimes uses the simple bamboo flute associated with folk traditions, our performance employs the *noh* flute. It, too, is constructed of bamboo, but the wood is cut into strips and turned upside down so that the bark lines the bore of the instrument. The strips are then bound together with cherry bark, giving the flute a distinctive appearance. In between the seven finger holes and the mouth hole is another small hole that interferes with the normal overblown octaves produced on any flute, causing the octaves to sound nearly a whole step flat in some cases. This, coupled with a playing style that favors sliding into notes with a gush of air, makes the flute sound out-of-tune to Western ears.

Whereas kabuki employs several singing styles, including a *parlando* style reminiscent of European recitative, the style of *nagauta* singing is unique. The desired *nagauta* vocal timbre avoids falsetto even in the upper register, has little or no vibrato, and produces a powerful, edgy sound that can cut through the full instrumental ensemble. A good *nagauta* voice is highly prized, and singers train for years to master this style—note the parallels with European operatic singing.

Start with the main melody as you help students hear the different strands in the texture. Note that the *shamisen* plays the melody throughout the excerpt. Thus, the singer always doubles the *shamisen,* though alert listeners will notice that voice and *shamisen* are frequently out of sync with each other. Congratulate them on discovering another example of heterophony, and reassure students that this is no mistake—it is a deliberate effect, typical of *nagauta* singing. How it came to be so is not known, but the practice ensures that the singer's words can be easily understood. The role of the flute proves less predictable; it often provides a second textural strand. In parts 2 and 3 it participates in the heterophony between voice and *shamisens,* but in parts 1 and 4 it plays a different melody altogether, creating an often dissonant-sounding nonimitative counterpoint with the main melody. Both the flute and its seeming lack of synchronization (rhythmically, melodically, and harmonically) reflect aspects of the *noh* theater tradition. Note that the rhythmic dissonance between these melodic strands does resolve at cadence points. The third strand consists of parts for the drums, which often rely on stock patterns. In addition to the colors they provide, the drums keep time for the main melody. The drummers also add an expressive touch, the upward-gliding exclamations that are so prominent at the beginning. Make sure students don't confuse these exclamations with the main melody!

Conclude by summarizing the many points of connection between kabuki theater and European opera from the Baroque era onward.

1. Both were new art forms that fused song, dance, and drama.

2. Both expressed emotions much more vividly than previous musical genres.

3. Both appealed to and were supported by a growing merchant class with newfound wealth.

4. Both inspired new public theaters to be built to support them.

5. Both prized distinctive singing styles that required years of training.

6. Both employed one singing style for narrative passages and another style for songs.

7. Both used "cross-dressing" roles: male singers in female roles or vice versa.

8. Both developed a "star" system; audiences came to see their favorite actors or singers.

Chinese Opera

Beijing opera has roots in various Chinese theatrical traditions. In fact, one of the strengths of the Chinese theater has always been its openness to new influences. Each new genre draws on earlier theatrical styles as well as current ones, often drawing on outside influences from the worlds of music, dance, or poetry. Even existing genres routinely transform themselves through the same processes. Several centuries of integration and transformation led to the birth of Beijing opera at the tail end of the eighteenth century, and this new genre reached its heyday in the last half of the nineteenth century. Thus, Beijing opera is exactly contemporary with Romantic opera, which makes comparisons with the work of Verdi and Wagner especially fruitful.

China represents an ancient, venerable classical music tradition that goes back roughly three millennia. This Global Perspectives segment can give only a taste of the Chinese tradition's riches. If you want to explore further, another example of that tradition can be found in Further Listening Examples below. Teaching suggestions for *The Drunken Fisherman* look at ancient Chinese history beginning with the Confucian era as they follow the development of music for the *qin*, a seven-stringed instrument variously described as a lute or a zither. *The Drunken Fisherman* itself offers a fascinating example of Chinese program music, suitable for comparison with character pieces from Chapter 16 or examples above by Tchaikovsky, Musorgsky, or Mahler. (For a more comprehensive study of Chinese music, refer to the sources described in Appendix V.)

This segment on Chinese opera begins in the twelfth century C.E., during the Song dynasty, and traces the development of Chinese theater. The following pages provide a survey of Chinese theatrical traditions from the twelfth to the eighteenth century; detailed information on the origins, history, and traditions of the Beijing opera; and lecture suggestions on *The Prince Who Changed into a Cat*.

A Brief History of Chinese Theater   Chinese history is filled with examples of "mixed" entertainments: various combinations of song, dance, instrumental music, and so on. Given that fact, it is surprising that a true Chinese theatrical tradition emerged as late as it did, if the admittedly incomplete historical records can be trusted. One of the earliest quasi-theatrical genres, the *nanxi*, or southern play, emerged c. 1125 C.E., at the beginning of the southern Song dynasty. The first reported example of the *zaju* genre came about a century later, though it is assumed that *zaju* and its cousin, *yuanben*, were popular through much of the late Song (southern) and Jin (northern) dynasties.

In 1234 the Mongols swept through northern China and deposed the Jin dynasty; the conquest of the Song dynasty took longer, but by 1280 Kublai Khan ruled all of China. Many changes took place at the hands of this Yuan dynasty. The scholars, poets, dancing girls, and others associated with the theater suddenly found themselves at or near the bottom of the social ladder. In spite of that, theater prospered under the Mongols, and a new genre, Yuan *zaju,* emerged. These northern-style dramas borrowed from earlier theatrical types and from the *qu* song repertory, creating a more substantial, more sophisticated dramatic work. As a result of these changes, the Yuan *zaju* far surpassed the simpler *yuanben* that had been its cousin. After a long period of gestation, a true Chinese theatrical tradition was born in the Yuan *zaju.*

As the Mongols' grip on China weakened, local theatrical types suppressed by the Yuan dynasty, such as the *nanxi,* found renewed popularity. A *nanxi* variant that emphasized literary quality—the *chuanqi*—also emerged in the mid-1300s. With the founding of the Ming dynasty in 1368, the Chinese reasserted self-rule. Once again, the change of regime influenced theatrical developments. Under the Mongols, Chinese theater had been relatively free to lampoon governmental cruelties, but the Ming emperors insisted that plays instill morality and loyalty to the government. Not only were the new rulers repressive; their punishment of offenders was swift and harsh. When the Ming leadership moved the capital north to Beijing in 1421, the Yuan *zaju* enjoyed a brief revival of popularity in the hands of some Ming princes, but its association with the hated Mongols probably contributed to its demise.

Over the next few centuries, several theatrical genres emerged and grew in popularity, only to be replaced by newer genres. Southern styles played a key role in these developments, due to their vitality, vibrant colors, frequent sophistication, and sure sense of what "worked" onstage. One good example was the *chuanqi* that emerged in the mid-1300s. It quickly became the dominant theatrical genre of the Ming era. Its strict structures and literary quality made it popular with the Beijing aristocracy, and the genre saw the creation of many new works from the mid-1400s on. Unfortunately, this sophisticated, essentially southern genre was saddled with a less sophisticated northern musical style when it came to the capital. Southern theater troupes noticed this disparity, and a fresh burst of creativity resulted in many new regional styles. Many of these styles used folk songs to meet the needs of the lower classes, but the Kunshan style, or *kunqu,* was destined for greater importance. In the hands of Wei Liangfu and Liang Chenyu—two popular playwrights of the mid-1500s—*kunqu* moved far beyond its simple roots. In its literary emphasis, it was strikingly similar to *chuanqi,* but its music was far more sophisticated. Wei Liangfu borrowed instruments from other traditional theatrical ensembles and added the flutes that became a *kunqu* hallmark. As *kunqu* came to national prominence, its southern musical style fused with the older theatrical style of *chuanqi,* giving birth to a new national art form that kept the southern name, *kunqu.* The new *kunqu* saw its first masterpieces written by Tang Xianzu in the late 1500s, among them *The Peony Pavilion (Mudan Ting*—see Video Recordings below) in 1598. By the early 1600s, *kunqu*—and the wide new variety of southern styles in general—came to dominate all Chinese theaters. As heir to the *chuanqi, kunqu* soon became the style most favored by the aristocracy, reaching its peak in the mid-1600s.

As the Qing dynasty came to power in 1644, *kunqu* was in its heyday, and it retained pride of place through the end of the next century. As before, regional styles continued to develop. The Yiyang style, which grew up alongside *kunqu,* grew dramatically in popularity during the Qing era, especially in the 1700s. Eventually, even the aristocracy overcame its revulsion toward Yiyang, and this style dominated Beijing theaters in the 1770s. Another variety from the northern provinces became known simply as clapper opera, due to the wooden clappers that provided rhythmic accompaniment. Clapper opera matured and spread early in the Qing era, and by the 1700s it had worked its way into south China, where it was absorbed into local dramatic forms. The Szechwan province's version of clapper opera found its way to Beijing in 1779, where the great Szechwan actor Wei Cheng-sheng met with instant and overwhelming success. In short order, his new *qin-qiang* style effectively replaced the Yiyang style recently favored by Beijing theaters. When the more lascivious aspects of Wei Cheng-sheng's productions met with censure by the mid-1780s, it created a void that the venerable old *kunqu* style no longer had the vitality to fill. Enter the Beijing opera.

The Beijing Opera   As we saw above, two older regional forms, the cultivated *kunqu* and the lowbrow Yiyang styles, had competed for some time. Their popularity seesawed from time to time, but both were showing their age in the Qing dynasty of the late 1700s. The short-lived, lascivious *qin-qiang* was popular in the 1780s, but it, too, was replaced in the 1790s by a new southern style brought to the capital in 1790 by Anhwei troupes, a style called *p'i-huang*. While Beijing audiences had argued the merits of *kunqu* and Yiyang styles, southern provinces had merged the *erh-huang* style from the southern Kiangsi province with the *hsi-p'i* style, a clapper variant from the Shensi province to the north. The resulting hybrid form, *p'i-huang*, became widely popular in the southern provinces during the eighteenth century, especially in Canton, Hupeh, and Anhwei. Acting troupes from Anhwei brought this new style to Beijing for the first time in 1790, for festivities surrounding Emperor Ch'ien-lung's eightieth birthday. The exciting new *p'i-huang* style blended the lyricism of *erh-huang* with the vitality of *hsi-p'i*, a combination that proved enormously successful. Within a few short years, the new "Four Great Anhwei Companies" became the heart of Beijing's theatrical scene, and their *p'i-huang* style soon became known as the "theater of the capital," or *jingju*—the Beijing opera.

What features contributed to *jingju*'s ascendance over *kunqu*? To begin with, *p'i-huang* offered a more colorful, more acrobatic theatrical experience. The literary qualities of *kunqu* often made for profoundly thought-provoking theater, but its use of movement and choreography paled beside the more athletic *p'i-huang* style. *Kunqu* developed its plots carefully; some extended to fifty acts in length. *Jingju*, on the other hand, relied on popular historical novels and romances; since audiences knew the stories already, these plays offered just a few acts portraying only the most stageworthy moments. Musically, *p'i-huang* provided much more exciting tunes and instrumental sounds than the older *kunqu*. *Kunqu* favored the *ti tzu*, a bamboo flute, to accompany the singers; *p'i-huang* made use of the louder, more vibrant *jinghu*, a small two-string bowed instrument. Concerning the tunes, the wider spectrum of poetic types in *kunqu* led to more subtlety and variety of musical construction. *P'i-huang*, on the other hand, used a repertory of stock tunes drawn from both *erh-huang* and *hsi-p'i* styles. Tunes for a specific scene were chosen according to the emotion required, whether happy, sad, serious, or angry. The smaller repertory meant greater audience familiarity and appreciation, and the style's overt expressiveness spoke to audiences with greater immediacy. Even the singing styles differed. Whereas *kunqu* focused on perfect enunciation and polished vocal technique, *p'i-huang* singers employed a wide range of vocal colors and dynamics. In every comparison, *jingju*'s brilliant, expressive theatrical values took center stage away from *kunqu*'s thoughtful, well-crafted literary values. As A. C. Scott put it, the rise of *jingju* reflected "the triumph of the art of the boards over the art of the book."[1]

----

[1]A. C. Scott, *The Classical Theatre of China*. London: George Allen & Unwin, 1957, p. 37.

Kunqu did not disappear overnight; in fact, it saw several revivals in the early nineteenth century. But in the great Chinese tradition of assimilation, *jingju* took over many of *kunqu*'s best features, making it even more expendable. Each act of a *kunqu* drama was carefully constructed as a self-contained unit; this made it easy for *jingju* playwrights to incorporate entire *kunqu* acts into their entertainments. A healthy dose of *kunqu*'s strengths guaranteed *jingju*'s popularity well into the next century and helped make it more palatable to the aristocracy who so frequently condemned it. *Kunqu*'s death knell was sounded with the Taiping uprisings, 1853–1864, in *kunqu*'s home province of Kiangsu. This sophisticated, literary theater stood for everything the antiaristocratic rebels opposed, and without its base of support "back home," it soon passed away.

The fixed roles of Beijing opera point once more to its assimilation of previous styles. Such roles were a standard feature of most Chinese theatrical genres going back at least as far as the birth of *nanxi* in the twelfth century. Kerman and Tomlinson briefly list some of the roles, but given their importance, a fuller list is provided here. Unlike European categories based on voice type, these roles define themselves in terms of the character type portrayed. In most categories, we find a further division into civilian and military roles.

Tan—Just as we saw in Japanese kabuki drama, female roles are taken by male actors. Known as *tan* actors, these specialists portray a wide variety of female roles. Wei Cheng-sheng, who brought *qin-qiang* to Beijing in 1779, was a *tan* actor, and *tan* actors continued to be overwhelmingly popular through *jingju*'s first fifty years. One of the lead characters in the 1993 movie *Farewell, My Concubine* played a *tan* specialist.

- *ch'ing-i*—a virtuous woman, usually a daughter or wife. Gestures and costumes convey modesty. Sings delicately with a high falsetto voice.
- *hua-tan*—a flirtatious young woman, perhaps a prostitute. Wears colorful costumes and uses lively gestures. Sings with a high falsetto voice in an alluring or suggestive manner.
- *wu-tan*—a young woman warrior, skilled in acrobatics and swordplay.
- *lao-tan*—an old woman with a staff. Walks with difficulty, hunched over. Sings with both power and sadness, befitting her dignity and age.

Sheng—These actors specialize in major male roles. Initially far less popular than *tan* actors, they came to dominate the stage in the mid-1800s.

- *hsiao-sheng*—a young male without a beard, perhaps a prince, scholar, or lover. Is equivalent to the *ch'ing-i* in grace of movement. Sings delicately using both falsetto and normal vocal qualities.
- *lao-sheng*—a middle-aged or older man with a beard, perhaps a general, member of the royal family, or prime minister. Is dignified in dress and bearing, but the *lao-sheng* must be a skilled acrobat and swordsman as well. Sings vigorously with a full-throated sound.
- *wu-sheng*—a warrior with a beard. Even more than the *lao-sheng*, must be expert in acrobatics and swordplay. The *wu-sheng* sings, but vocal quality matters less than physical abilities.

Jing—More than personality, the significant feature of a *jing* role is the face paint. Different colors and patterns suggest different personalities. White indicates deceit; scarlet, integrity; black, strength; and so on. These roles are often characterized by bravura.

❦ *jeng-jing*—a male of high character, perhaps a general or statesman. Sings forcefully with a full-throated sound. The general in *Farewell, My Concubine* fits this category.

❦ *fu-jing*—the "bad guy." This character places more emphasis on movement and dramatic speech than on singing quality.

❦ *wu-ching*—a warrior, perhaps a soldier, bandit, or rebel. Is similar to the *wu-sheng*, but with makeup.

❦ *Ch'ou*—These roles are filled by quick-witted comics and clowns. They wear a characteristic white patch around the eyes and nose, and they must be skilled acrobats to handle the physical humor required of them. Unlike the others, *ch'ou* actors may improvise freely, inserting topical humor, gags, or pratfalls at will. An exaggerated quality typifies their speech and their occasional singing.

In the nineteenth century, the Beijing opera perpetuated itself through a new system of training young actors. The four main companies took responsibility for the care and training of young boys from the south who were brought to Beijing as indentured servants. The boys, who studied with leading actors in the company, were mostly trained to fill still-popular *tan* roles. Once they served out the term of their contract, they generally became members of the company that trained them. When the Taiping rebellion cut off the supply of young students from the south, boys were brought in from Beijing itself. By the time of the Boxer Rebellion in 1900, young actors had begun to form their own troupes upon "graduation." The rebellion forced the disbanding of the last surviving Anhwei theater in Beijing. To provide for the continued training of new actors, independent schools in Beijing replaced the old system of indentured servitude. One of these newer schools is portrayed in the 1993 movie *Farewell, My Concubine.*

Nineteenth-century changes in the style of Beijing opera resulted from periodic absorption of new influences and the changing skills of the actors themselves. The great *lao-sheng* actor Ch'eng Chang-keng almost single-handedly brought about the incredible surge in the popularity of *sheng* roles in the mid-1800s. This was perhaps the inevitable consequence of the heroic stories that served as Beijing opera plots, and a string of strong *lao-sheng* actors followed in Ch'eng's footsteps. Not surprisingly, heroic rather than romantic plays came to the fore at mid-century. *Jingju* had always been popular with the masses, but the prominence of *sheng* roles in the last half of the century made *jingju* more palatable to the aristocracy. Even Empress T'zu-hsi became a big fan in the final years of the Qing dynasty, and command performances became a frequent feature of imperial court life from 1884 to 1912.

Although Beijing opera reached its peak in the nineteenth century, it maintained its viability as a theatrical genre throughout the twentieth. Once the Chinese republic replaced the old dynastic system in 1912, mixed troupes of male and female actors gradually began to appear. A new system of training schools prepared young actors for many different roles. The internationally renowned *tan* actor Mei Lanfang revived the popularity of *tan* roles in the 1920s, and his versatility raised professional standards for all Chinese actors. The Japanese occupation saw a temporary reduction of theatrical activity; actors like Mei refused to perform for the Japanese. But the Communist era that followed World War II saw a new surge of activity in *jingju*. Its history as a popular art form and its emphasis on patriotic heroes of the past fit in perfectly with Communist ideologies. Some adaptations were needed, of course: women were featured more prominently; the use of scenery became common;

new "revolutionary" operas entered the repertory; training schools broadened their curriculum; and, with class structure abolished, actors were no longer forced into homosexual prostitution by virtue of their low station in life. In this new format, Beijing opera has maintained its popularity. Starting in 1964, *jingju* was suppressed by Mao's wife, Chiang Ch'ing, and her "gang of four," but with her downfall in 1976 the genre quickly revived. It continues to be practiced today.

The Prince Who Changed into a Cat   Start your presentation with some background material. Feel free to use any of the information immediately above. At the very least, introduce the typical roles played by *jingju* actors. Since this theatrical genre is unfamiliar to most of your students, you must "set the stage" for them. Beijing opera was performed in many situations, ranging from large rooms in imperial buildings to specially constructed outdoor theaters to informal teahouse theaters. The atmosphere was frequently informal—theatergoers often sipped tea and chatted with acquaintances while the performance took place. The stage was often raised, with a decorative "fence" surrounding it. As in Japanese *noh* theater, no scenery was used. Specific costumes, gestures, words, song types, and instrumental styles helped to set the scene in the minds of the viewers. The actors wore distinctive, often beautiful clothes, with colorful makeup for *tan* and *jing* roles. The orchestra sat onstage alongside the actors.

Invite your students to look more carefully at the orchestra. Describe the mix of instruments enumerated on textbook page 316: the drums, gongs, cymbals, woodwinds, and bowed and plucked stringed instruments. The orchestral instruments serve two major musical functions, that of melody (strings and winds) and that of rhythm (percussion). The string instruments used in our recording are as follows:

- *jinghu*—The principal bowed stringed instrument. Often featured as a virtuoso solo instrument, it generally plays the melody along with the singer. Its body is a piece of bamboo roughly the size of a Campbell's soup can. Like a banjo, its face is covered with skin. An eighteen-inch bamboo neck, two silk strings tuned in fifths, and two tuning pegs complete the instrument. The stick of the bow is also made of bamboo. The hair of the bow passes between the two strings, thus permanently affixed to the instrument, and the player must stroke the front side of one string but the back side of the other. Its bright, even piercing sound dominates the ensemble.

- *erhu*—Similar in shape and construction to the *jinghu*, but larger and lower-pitched. Made of redwood, its tone quality is more mellow. It, too, doubles the main melody, but an octave lower than the *jinghu*. This instrument was added to the ensemble only in the 1920s, by Mei Lanfang's *jinghu* player.

- *yueqin*—A plucked stringed instrument, the "moon guitar." Its circular face is fourteen inches in diameter and made of rosewood. The rest of the body uses *wu-t'ang* wood, and the ten-inch redwood neck has ten frets. Four silk strings are tuned with pegs. The *yueqin* also doubles the vocal melody, playing sustained notes in a quick, strumming fashion.

Wind instruments see much less use in Beijing opera. *Ti-tzu* flutes continue to be used in melodies borrowed from *kunqu,* and the double-reeded *so-na* is reserved for special ceremonial or festive occasions.

The most frequently used instruments in the opera orchestra are the percussion instruments. Various patterns and instrumental combinations can indicate a character's status or emotional state. The ensemble often provides rhythmic "punctuation," adding percussive commas or periods and underlining or enlivening important words, names, or phrases. They accompany combat scenes, grand entrances and exits, dance and gesture, and interludes, and they even provide sound effects.

The leader of the orchestra sets the beat on the *hsiao-ku,* a small round drum played with bamboo sticks. The leader also plays the *pan,* the clapper associated with *hsi-p'i,* much like a large (ten-inch by two-inch) wooden pair of castanets. A second, larger drum, the barrel-shaped *ta-ku,* is used most commonly in military plays. Gongs and cymbals round out the percussion ensemble. Made of bronze, both large (*ta-lo*) and small (*hsiao-lo*) gongs are used, ranging in diameter from twelve to six inches. The most commonly used cymbals are the *po,* a pair of small brass cymbals struck together.

Once you have "set the stage," introduce students to the story at hand. Textbook page 317 provides some background information on the plot. The tradition of *jingju* favored the presentation of important scenes from well-known stories, not the entire story. The scene in our recording depicts just such a stageworthy moment. A fair and just Prime Minister happens to encounter the banished Empress on a trip in the south. Not sure if he can believe her story, he tests her by bowing low in her presence. A commoner would be embarrassed by such treatment from a superior, but the true Empress accepts it graciously. By the end of the scene the Prime Minister, satisfied that he has discovered the Empress and distressed by the story of her exile from the capital, returns to Beijing to demand justice. Our recorded excerpt provides only the very beginning of this scene, as the Prime Minister enters and addresses the Empress.

Without further explanation, display the checklist of musical elements and structures, play the music, and ask your students to describe what they heard. In the discussion that follows, draw out the following points.

1. The percussion instruments provide a sonorous introduction to the song. Note the *accelerando* and *decelerando* at the very beginning. Following this somewhat free introduction, the stringed instruments—*jinghu, erhu,* and *yueqin*—and the clapper enter in duple meter at a moderate tempo. Soon the Prime Minister enters, singing his melody in heterophony with the stringed instruments.

2. Note that this is a *luo-sheng* role—the Prime Minister is a bearded, dignified older man who sings in a high baritone or tenor range reflecting his age. The percussion ensemble that accompanies his entrance signifies his importance. Students may notice the somewhat nasal quality typical of this singing style.

3. Given the heterophonic texture, no harmony is present.

4. Although the melody often sounds pentatonic, it uses a seven-note scale with much ornamentation and pitch bending.

5. At the very end of our excerpt, we hear a brief example of the exaggerated, sliding speech style typical of important characters. Just as singing styles differ according to character type and social standing, so do speaking styles. Unfortunately, the *Listen* recording cuts out just before the Empress responds to the Prime Minister. If you would like to play more of this scene for your students and demonstrate the sound of a *tan* actor's speech and song, use the CD described in Sound Recordings below.

Conclude your presentation by comparing the conventions of Chinese opera with those of nineteenth-century Italian and German opera. Ask students to share their own comparisons first, but be sure to draw out the following points.

1. All three forms catered to the general public, not the aristocracy.

2. Verdi and *jingju* writers often based their plots on popular historical novels and romances; only Wagner relied on more mythological sources. Interesting trivia: the play on which Verdi based *La Traviata,* Dumas's *La dame aux camélias,* became popular in twentieth-century Chinese spoken theater.

3. *Jingju* doesn't tell the entire story; instead, it mounts only the most stage-worthy scenes. Verdi never goes quite that far, but his libretti do condense the story to its most essential dramatic elements. Wagner, on the other hand, gives you all five or six hours of his story.

4. All three distinguish between songs (arias) and stylized forms of speech (recitative), though European composers, especially Wagner, begin to break down these categories.

5. All three types, each in its own way, require unique singing styles that require special training.

6. Roles in European opera are assigned on the basis of voice type; *jingju,* on the basis of character type. Each type requires special training. Verdi's soprano, tenor, baritone, and bass roles are nonetheless quite similar in many different operas, and Wagner's *heldentenor* voice type implies a heroic role.

7. Some sources compare the stock tune repertory in *jingju* to Wagner's technique of *leitmotiv*s. The Chinese correspondence between tune and emotional state is perhaps somewhat similar to Wagner's web of associative motives, though Wagner's technique appears more sophisticated. In both cases, audience familiarity with the tunes is considered a plus. The *jingju* repertory more closely resembles the books used by organists in silent movie theaters, filled with appropriate music for every occasion and emotion.

8. The orchestra helps tell the story in both Beijing and Wagner operas. The *jingju* ensemble must make up for the lack of scenery; Wagner uses his *leit-motiv*s to give the orchestra heightened storytelling powers. In both cases, the orchestra points to something the audience does not necessarily see onstage. Verdi's orchestra provides color, mood, and dramatic emphasis.

9. The orchestra in Beijing opera is much smaller than the European orchestras but still includes strings, winds, and percussion.

10. Beijing opera is not "composed" in the same way as Wagner or Verdi operas. Chinese actors play a much greater role in choosing the music and shaping the drama than is the case in European Romantic opera.

11. All three types provide powerful insights into characteristic features of the nineteenth-century cultures they represent.

Additional Teaching Suggestions

♩ Lecture-Demonstration Ideas

1. Invite an orchestra conductor to class. Chapter 18 is devoted entirely to the orchestral music of an era when orchestras had grown to their largest size ever. The art of conducting with a baton developed during the Romantic era (see the sketch of Mahler on textbook page 310), and conductors can provide valuable

information about the nature and purpose of rehearsals, the role of the conductor, and problems of orchestral performance. Ask students to come prepared with questions, and bring several questions of your own in case discussion flags.

2. Arrange for your class to observe a rehearsal of a college orchestra, a community orchestra, or a professional orchestra. Ask students to observe the interaction between the conductor and the instrumentalists and to listen to the sounds of different instruments, singly and in combination. Afterward, take class time to elicit student reactions and comments.

3. Compare the symphonic poem with the symphony. Even though the symphonic poem adopted a free form that followed a program, many tone poems borrowed the features that made the symphony's four-movement plan successful (something thought provoking, even serious; something beautiful; something to tap your foot or dance to; and something to whistle on the way out the door). Liszt's symphonic poem *Les préludes* offers an excellent example (see Multimedia Resources below for sound and video recordings), weaving features of sonata form and the four-movement plan into a grand symphonic tapestry. Play the following excerpts for the class. The introduction (mm. 1–34) corresponds to the slow introduction found in many symphonies' first movements. The next three transformations of the theme evoke the first three movements of a symphony: the first (mm. 35–46) is majestic, forceful, and deliberate; the second (mm. 47–69) slow and lyrical; and the third (mm. 70–90) light and dancelike. The next section (starting at m. 109) sounds like the development from a sonata-form movement. Near the end (starting at m. 344), the tempo picks up to create a fast, marchlike mood, reminiscent of the quick tempo of a typical fourth movement. The final section (starting at m. 405) brings back the first transformation of the main theme; this "recapitulation" reinforces the cyclic unity of the work. You can also use this exercise to point out Liszt's use of thematic transformation.

4. Try different techniques for presenting Tchaikovsky's *Romeo and Juliet*. After reviewing the story with your students, play different themes from the story and ask them what Tchaikovsky wants to portray with each one. This provides a good opportunity to ask how effective program music is; students often have no problem with the Love theme, but the hymn that starts off the introduction often eludes them. Or, ask your students to play composer. What portions of the story would they set to music, and what specific elements of music would they use to depict these portions? Then play portions of the music to compare their suggestions with Tchaikovsky's solution. Students often come surprisingly close to the mark.

5. Explore Brahms's relationship with Clara Schumann. Nancy B. Reich provides valuable insights in Chapter 9 of *Clara Schumann: The Artist and the Woman* (Ithaca, N.Y.: Cornell University Press, 1990, pp. 187–207) and in her essay in *Brahms and His World*, edited by Walter Frisch (Princeton, N.J.: Princeton University Press, 1990, pp. 37–47). She cites several letters between Johannes and Clara; further correspondence can be found in Grace E. Hadow's translation of Berthold Litzman's *Clara Schumann: An Artist's Life from Diaries and Letters* (New York: Vienna House, 1972). Also see *Johannes Brahms: But for Women . . .* in Video Recordings below.

6. Invite a musicologist to class. Ask your guest to describe the development of musicology as a discipline, to discuss the importance of musicology, and to talk about what a musicologist does. You can prepare your class by reading

K Marie Stolba's brief insight into musicology on page 515 of her *Development of Western Music,* 3rd ed. (Boston: McGraw-Hill, 1998). Ask students to come prepared with questions, and bring several questions of your own in case discussion flags.

7. Share nineteenth-century criticism of Romantic music with students. Eduard Hanslick was the most powerful music critic in late nineteenth-century Vienna. His strong musical convictions led him to champion Brahms and condemn Wagner, views that were unpopular with Wagner's legions of supporters. A sampling of his reviews can be found in *Hanslick's Music Criticism,* translated and edited by Henry Pleasants (New York: Dover, 1988; this is a reprint edition of *Music Criticisms 1846–99,* Baltimore: Penguin, 1963). For classroom presentation, select and read aloud interesting passages from Hanslick's reviews of works and composers treated in the textbook. Start with reviews of Wagner's *Tristan und Isolde* (pp. 243–45). The book also contains reviews of performances by Clara Schumann and Liszt and of various works by Tchaikovsky, Brahms, Richard Strauss, Liszt, Wagner, and Verdi—and even Handel's *Messiah.*

8. Read more criticism of nineteenth-century music. In his *Lexicon of Musical Invective* (Seattle: University of Washington Press, 1965), Nicolas Slonimsky compiled deliciously caustic reviews of the music of great composers. You can find reviews of almost every composer dealt with in Unit IV, from Beethoven to Mahler. (You can also use this resource in Unit V; it contains reviews of Schoenberg, Webern, Debussy, Stravinsky, Bartók, Berg, Gershwin, Copland, and Varèse.) One word of caution: Use this lexicon only for works that students seem to like. To supply invective for works they dislike might perpetuate misunderstanding.

9. Invite a Chinese musician to speak to and play for your class (this may prove easier than you think). Players of the *pipa erhu* or other common Chinese instruments can offer fascinating insights into Chinese instrumental music. (If you can find a *qin* player, consider using suggestions for *The Drunken Fisherman* in Further Listening Examples below.) Ask students to prepare questions in advance and encourage discussion between the class and your guests. Be ready with some of your own in case discussion flags.

10. Find video or images to bring your presentation of kabuki theater to life. *Kabuki,* by Masakatsu Gunji (Tokyo: Kodansha International, 1969), is essentially a kabuki photo album that even includes images associated with *Musume Dojoji,* showing costume changes, advertisements, and so on. Thomas Immoos's *Japanese Theatre* (New York: Rizzoli International Publications, 1977) provides beautiful photo coverage of Japan's four historic traditions: *bugaku, noh, bunraku,* and kabuki. Moving pictures or still images can help convey the myriad sensory experiences that make kabuki theater unique.

11. Bring Chinese opera to life for your students with a slide show or "travelogue." Many departments at your school are likely to have images you can borrow, including the departments of art, foreign languages, geography, and anthropology. Pictures of artwork, architecture, musical instruments, theaters, and Chinese cities and countryside can help bring this material to life. Alternatively, show clips from the 1993 movie *Farewell, My Concubine,* a shattering tragedy about two Beijing opera singers and a prostitute caught up in twentieth-century China's turbulent changes. It vividly portrays the importance and vitality of Beijing opera in its heyday. In addition to short scenes from the opera that gave the movie its name, this film also offers insights into master-pupil relationships, operatic training schools, and backstage politics.

↻ Class Discussion Ideas

1. *How does late Romantic music compare with the ideals of early Romanticism?* This question can be used to review Unit IV. Ask students to help you regenerate the list of Romantic characteristics from Chapter 15. Then ask them to compare the list against the four works covered in this chapter and pick out features of Romanticism in each work.

2. Compare Classical and Romantic use of Classical musical forms. Play and map out, with student help, the structure of two works in using the same form. This exercise helps students visualize how Classical proportion and balance and Romantic freedom of expression affect musical structure. For sonata form, Tchaikovsky's *Romeo and Juliet* can be compared with any Classical sonata-form movement (Mozart's Symphony No. 40, I, or Beethoven's Fifth, IV, for instance). For minuet form, compare the third movement of Mahler's Symphony No. 1 with the third movement of Haydn's Symphony No. 95. For rondo form, compare the final movement of Brahms's Violin Concerto in D or Musorgsky's "The Great Gate at Kiev" with the final movement of Haydn's Symphony No. 95. For theme and variations form, compare Liszt's *Totentanz* (see Further Listening Examples in Chapter 16) with Haydn's Symphony No. 95, second movement.

3. *Who were the moguchaya kuchka?* To delve more deeply into Musorgsky's music and Russian nationalism, read César Cui's own description of this group to generate discussion about the "mighty handful." His quotation can be found in Richard Taruskin's article "Some Thoughts on the History and Historiography of Russian Music" (*Journal of Musicology* 3 [1984], p. 335) and on page 667 of Grout and Palisca's *History of Western Music,* 5th ed. (New York: Norton, 1996). Follow-up questions might include: *Why would composers need to band together? Why were nationalist ideas so important to the Five? Why was Tchaikovsky not a nationalist composer?*

4. *What is exoticism? What examples of exoticism can you find in Romantic music? Does it still exist today?* Exoticism refers to a fascination with unfamiliar, perhaps mysterious cultures "long ago" or "far away." In Mozart's *Abduction from the Seraglio* and Rondo *"alla Turca"* we find instances of the Turkish music Viennese audiences found so exotic. The Lecture Suggestions for this chapter briefly allude to the late Romantic fascination with exoticism, evidenced in works such as Verdi's *Aida,* Puccini's *Madama Butterfly,* Bizet's *Carmen,* Tchaikovsky's *Nutcracker,* Brahms's *Hungarian Dances,* and Mahler's *Das Lied von der Erde*—even Gilbert and Sullivan's *The Mikado.* Ask students to name recent (or not-so-recent) examples of popular music that suggest "exotic" influences. Some examples might include Paul Simon's *Graceland* (South Africa) or *Rhythm of the Saints* (Brazil), the Beach Boys' "Kokomo" (Caribbean islands), the reggae-tinged sound of Sting and the Police (Jamaica), *South Pacific* (for those with long memories), or *Miss Saigon* (a modern retelling of *Madama Butterfly*). Exoticism appeals to twentieth-century Americans just as it did to late nineteenth-century Europeans. See Multimedia Resources below for suggested audio and video performances.

5. Read Schumann's final review for the class. Schumann had been editor and critic for the *Neue Zeitschrift für Musik* (*New Music Journal*) for many years, but he turned the work over to others in the 1840s. In 1853, Schumann picked up his pen one last time to present a brilliant young composer to the music world: Johannes Brahms. Read this brief review for your class (in *Schumann*

on Music: A Selection from the Writings, New York: Dover, 1988, pp. 199–200, or in *On Music and Musicians,* New York: Norton, 1946, pp. 252–54). This announcement raises several questions: *What was Schumann's motivation in writing this article? What does this say about the relationship between older and younger composers? What effect might this have on a young, sensitive, self-critical composer like Brahms?*

6. *What was it like to be a Jewish musician living and working in Vienna at of the 1900s?* Anti-Semitism cast its shadow on the careers of many Jewish artists and thinkers. Most tragic was the story of Otto Weininger (1880–1903), a brilliant intellectual who committed suicide because he believed the myth of Jewish inferiority (propagated by German culture) and saw no hope of producing meaningful scholarly work. Mahler's confrontations with anti-Semitism are chronicled in Chapter 4 ("The Jewish Presence," pp. 47–52) of Egon Gartenberg's *Mahler: The Man and His Music* (New York: Schirmer, 1978) and in Chapter 3 ("The Eternal Jew," pp. 43–65) of Henry A. Lea's *Gustav Mahler: Man on the Margin* (Bonn: Bouvier, 1985). The story of one of Wagner's conductors at Bayreuth is told in Chapter 4 ("Hermann Levi: A Study in Service and Self-Hatred," pp. 189–230) of Peter Gay's *Freud, Jews, and Other Germans* (New York: Oxford University Press, 1978). Read passages from these writings aloud to generate class discussion.

7. For a closer look at Chinese culture, compare Plato and K'ung Fu-tzu, especially if you use suggestions for *The Drunken Fisherman* in Further Listening Examples below. Your school's library almost certainly contains Plato's *Republic* and the writings of K'ung Fu-tzu (Confucius). Select passages that describe the ideal state, the ideal person, and the relationship between the two. If you can find passages that deal with music, so much the better, since both men believed that music possessed the power to improve or undermine the balance between body and mind.

8. *What difference does the middle class make?* Both European opera and kabuki theater relied on the merchant class—the *bourgeoisie*—for support. This question points to the complex interaction between musical style and social class structures. *How does middle-class support differ from aristocratic support? What are the advantages of one over the other? How does music for the aristocracy differ from music for the lower classes?* A comparison of *gagaku* and kabuki might yield some answers. Ask students to draw on their own experiences with American culture as well.

9. How are *commedia dell'arte* and Beijing opera similar? Read the description of this "comedy of artisans" on page 350 of Stolba's *Development of Western Music,* 3rd ed. Ask students to decide which stock characters from *commedia dell'arte* correspond with the character types described for *jingju.* If you used Class Discussion Idea 1 from Chapter 13 of this manual, you can extend the comparisons to include roles from Classical opera buffa.

♩ Listening Ideas

1. Listen to more symphonic poems. Offer a sampling of excerpts from different types of tone poems. For a nationalist tone poem that depicts natural phenomena, use Smetana's *The Moldau* (see Further Listening Examples below). For a literary program, use Strauss's *Don Juan* or *Don Quixote.* For a poetic program, use Liszt's *Les préludes.* For a philosophical program, use Strauss's *Also sprach*

Zarathustra. For a depiction of historic events, use Tchaikovsky's *1812 Overture.* For each example, ask students to pick out descriptive elements. Try this: Play the music first and ask students what story they hear in the music; then share the program with them and compare results. See Multimedia Resources below for suggested recordings.

2. Compare Musorgsky's character pieces with Robert Schumann's. When Musorgsky wrote *Pictures at an Exhibition,* he produced a cycle of character pieces in the tradition of Schumann. Play excerpts from *Carnaval* and *Pictures;* if at all possible, bring a recording of Musorgsky's original version for solo piano to contrast with the *Listen* recordings (see Sound Recordings below). Ask students to compare the two. Most of the differences they pick out will define the contrasts between early Romanticism and late Romantic Russian nationalism. *How do the programs of these two works compare? Which composer creates more vivid musical images? Why?*

3. Listen to more examples of Russian nationalism. Sample works by Musorgsky (*Boris Godunov*), Rimsky-Korsakov (see Further Listening Examples below), Borodin, Balakirev, Cui, or even Stravinsky (*The Firebird*). Once you have established characteristic features of Russian nationalism (see discussion of *Pictures at an Exhibition* above), compare these works with the music of Tchaikovsky, a nonnationalist Russian composer (most of the time). See Sound Recordings below for suggested performances.

4. Listen to examples of nationalism from other countries. To save time, choose short examples—Sibelius's *Swan of Tuonela* or *Finlandia,* a movement from Grieg's *Peer Gynt* Suites or the *Holberg* Suite, Vaughan Williams's *Fantasia on Greensleeves,* one of Dvořák's *Slavonic Dances,* piano music of Granados, and excerpts from Falla's ballets (*El amor brujo* or *Nights in the Gardens of Spain*) work well. As you play each example, ask students to identify features that suggest each composer's native country. See Multimedia Resources below for suggested audio and video performances.

5. Listen to examples of exoticism by mainstream (or other) European composers, especially if you use Class Discussion Idea 4. Bizet's *Carmen* and Rimsky-Korsakov's *Capriccio Espagnol* reflect Spanish music; Puccini's *Madama Butterfly* and Gilbert and Sullivan's *The Mikado* reflect Japanese music; Mahler's *Das Lied von der Erde* reflects Chinese music; and Dvořák's *New World* Symphony reflects American music. Tchaikovsky's *Nutcracker* contains many dances with an exotic flavor, including Dance of the Sugar-Plum Fairy from the *Listen* DVD (see Further Listening Examples for Chapter 1). Pick out the exotic elements in each of these pieces. See Multimedia Resources below for suggested recordings.

6. Compare Brahms's concerto movement with the first movement of Mozart's Piano Concerto in A, K. 488. These examples use different forms, but they both offer clearly defined tunes and the concerto's characteristic interplay between soloist and orchestra. Play excerpts from these works and ask the class to compare them. Help students hear for themselves both the traditional and the progressive features of Brahms's music. This exercise also affords an opportunity to compare features of Classical and Romantic styles.

7. Compare two Romantic marches. Play portions of the fourth movement of Berlioz's *Fantastic* Symphony and the third movement of Mahler's Symphony No. 1. Both marches are stylized, and both serve a program. Ask students to compare the programs and the music for these two works.

8. Compare Handel's "La giustizia" with kabuki *nagauta* music. Focus especially on the roles of instruments in relation to the voice as they pertain to our perception of both texture and form. Both consist of up to three textural components: vocal melody, violins, and continuo instruments in the Handel aria; voice/*shamisen* melody, flute countermelody, and percussion in the *nagauta* music. Both works feature instrumental introductions and interludes, both use changes in instrumentation to define sections, and both have one group that rhythmically leads and supports throughout (*continuo* and percussion, respectively). Both examples also share the main melody between the voice and instruments. In Handel's aria, violins and voice present the melody at different times, resulting in imitative counterpoint. In the *nagauta* excerpt, voice and *shamisen* (and sometimes flute) present the melody simultaneously, but since they are not quite synchronized, the result is heterophony. Finally, both examples employ polyphony. But whereas Handel favors imitative polyphony, the kabuki excerpt creates nonimitative polyphony—in parts 1 and 4, where the flute adds a new melody.

9. Listen to Toshiko Akiyoshi's "Kogun" (see Sound Recordings below) and the *nagauta* music from *Dojoji* side by side. Akiyoshi, a jazz pianist and composer who played with Charles Mingus in the early 1960s, went on to front a big band with husband Lew Tabackin. She became the first woman and the first Asian to win Down Beat awards in the best composer, best arranger, and best band categories. Her most interesting work reflects her Japanese heritage, and the opening of "Kogun" employs *otsuzumi* and *kotsuzumi* in the manner we hear in *Dojoji*. In addition, Lew Tabackin plays flute in a style that blends Western and *noh* flute sounds. All in all, this work offers a fascinating blend of Japanese and African American traditions. "Kogun" was inspired by the story of the Japanese soldier who hid in a Philippine forest for nearly thirty years, not knowing the war had ended.

10. For a review of *gagaku* and kabuki, introduce your students to excerpts from Benjamin Britten's *Curlew River*. Britten was profoundly influenced by Japanese music during his trip to the Far East in 1955–56—he even went to *two* performances of the *noh* play *Sumidagawa*. William Plomer adapted the story of this *noh* play for Britten, setting it in England during the Middle Ages, and Britten's musical setting shows the clear influence of Japanese music. From the *noh* tradition Britten borrowed masks, stylized gestures, an all-male cast (even for female roles), and the flute in heterophony with the voices. The chamber organ captures the clusterlike sounds of the *sho* from *gagaku*. Play excerpts for your class and ask them to identify features influenced by kabuki and *gagaku*. (Remember that our kabuki example borrowed not only the story of the *noh* drama *Dojoji* but many features of its musical style as well.)

11. Compare Beijing opera with Japanese kabuki theater. Play both excerpts from the recorded set and ask students to draw comparisons. Look at vocal quality, scales used, rhythmic features, texture, instrumentation, orchestral accompaniment, and any other striking features. This exercise offers an opportunity to compare East Asian cultures.

12. If you use suggestions for *The Drunken Fisherman* in Further Listening Examples below, compare Chinese music for *pipa* and for *qin*. The *pipa* developed much more recently than the *qin*—a mere fifteen centuries ago. Yet the *pipa* never managed to dethrone the *qin* as the favored instrument of the *literati*. Originally associated with dance and entertainment, the *pipa*'s music was often showy and virtuosic, exactly the opposite of the more contemplative

music favored for the *qin*. *Qin* players tended to label both the *pipa* and its music barbaric. Play examples of both *qin* and *pipa* music for your students and let them decide which they like better. See Sound Recordings below for suggestions.

❦ Further Listening Examples

SMETANA "Vlatava" ("The Moldau"), from *Ma Vlast*

This work is highly recommended as an example of both nationalism and the symphonic poem. As the music follows the course of the Moldau River, Smetana depicts Bohemian scenes, history, and folk customs. This tone poem—one of the most beautiful ever written—is one of a cycle of six that portrays different aspects of the composer's beloved country (*Ma Vlast*—"My Home" or "My Country"). The musical form for "The Moldau" (see Additional Listening Charts in Appendix I) follows Smetana's own program, reprinted here:

> This composition pictures the course of the Vlatava river [the Moldau]. It catches the sound of its first sources, the warm and the cold Vlatava, then pursues the union of both streams and the course of the river through meadows and woods and through regions where the inhabitants celebrate in joyful festivals. In the silver moonlight water-nymphs perform their dances; proud castles and mansions and venerable ruins which have grown into the wild rocks pass by. The Vlatava foams and eddies at the St. John's rapids, then flows broadly on towards Prague, until the castle of Vysehrad comes into sight along its banks. It then moves majestically onwards till it disappears from view, flowing finally into the Elbe.

The main theme of the movement (the River Theme on the Additional Listening Chart) represents the Moldau itself. In its first appearance, the phrase structure of this Bohemian-sounding tune is:

a a b a′ b a′

On the way from its trickling tributaries to the Elbe, Smetana's Moldau passes, respectively, a hunt, a peasant wedding, moonlit water nymphs, the rapids of St. John, and the Vysehrad (a rock outcropping around which various myths have sprung up and the subject of another tone poem in *Ma Vlast*). If time permits, play the opening measures of each of these episodes for the class. These episodes are easy to perceive due to the clearly descriptive, programmatic nature of the music (and are also clearly marked in the score). The hunt includes hunting horns; a peasant dance evokes the rustic wedding festivities; delicate, fluid gestures and sound effects portray the water nymphs; and the rapids call up a maelstrom of rapid musical motion. Beyond the rapids, we hear a major-key variation of the river theme that suggests the Moldau's growling size and power. The tempo broadens in a grandiose section that reflects the Moldau at its widest and most majestic point, as the ancient promontory comes into view. Finally the river disappears in the distance and the tone poem ends with two jarring chords that nearly destroy the delicious poignance of Smetana's fade-out. As a music appreciation teacher once said of the ending, "If only Smetana had been a greater composer . . . "

Display (or photocopy handouts of) the Additional Listening Chart in Appendix I or outline the chart on the board. When you play the piece, point to each section as it goes by. See Multimedia Resources below for suggested recordings.

SMETANA *The Bartered Bride*

The Bartered Bride provides an accessible, tuneful example of Czech nationalism and an excellent vehicle for comparisons with Russian nationalism. Because Smetana was older than most other nationalists we have encountered, we find fewer radical elements in his music than in, say, Musorgsky's. Smetana's musical style advanced little beyond that of early Romantic composers such as Mendelssohn or Schumann; Joseph Kerman once observed that Smetana "poured his new nationalistic wine into a rather old bottle." Even Berlioz, who premiered his *Fantastic* Symphony when Smetana was six, sounds modern and radical next to the Czech nationalist. Nonetheless, we can see many of the techniques of nationalism at work in *The Bartered Bride*—the frequent use of folk dances and a story that glorifies peasant life in Bohemia, to name two. Smetana's tuneful, lively music and colorful orchestration proved so successful that *The Bartered Bride* became the foundation for almost all subsequent Czech nationalist works.

The teaching suggestions below cover two instrumental numbers from *The Bartered Bride:* the overture and the furiant. As a result, knowledge of the opera's plot is not required to appreciate the music. Still, if you have time, a brief review of the story can provide a deeper sense of Smetana's nationalist sources of inspiration.

Act I opens with a group of Bohemian villagers celebrating in anticipation of the upcoming holidays. We are soon introduced to two young lovers, Jenik and Marenka, who have just learned that Marenka's parents will arrange a marriage for her—to another man. As the lovers exit, we see Marenka's parents negotiating with a marriage broker, Kecal, who suggests a marriage to Vasek, the son of their neighbor, Tobias Micha. Marenka's father, Krusina, agrees quickly, but her mother, Ludmila, thinks Marenka ought to have some say in the matter. Marenka walks in on the negotiations to announce her engagement to Jenik. An argument ensues; Krusina is angry that no one asked his permission, and Marenka throws the contract on the floor and leaves.

Act II begins in an inn where Kecal, Jenik, and a group of villagers have gone for a beer. Kecal is trying to figure out how to save his commission from Marenka's marriage, and Jenik is trying to save his engagement. The drinkers dance the Furiant and leave. Next we meet Vasek, the slow-witted, stuttering son of Tobias Micha and Marenka's unwanted husband-to-be. When Marenka comes into the inn and finds Vasek there, she takes advantage of the fact that Vasek does not know her. To scare him off, she tells Vasek that Marenka is a flighty, domineering woman who will make his life miserable; to sweeten the deal, she tells him about another, more attractive woman who has fallen in love with him from afar. In the next scene, Kecal brings Jenik to the inn for a drink, hoping to persuade Jenik to abandon Marenka. When Jenik refuses, Kecal offers a large sum of money. After some hesitation, Jenik consents to stand aside, but only in favor of the eldest son of Tobias Micha. Kecal leaves gloating over his good fortune. Now we learn that Jenik is Tobias Micha's long-lost first son, the issue of Tobias's first marriage. Jenik rejoices in this stroke of luck—he can marry Marenka, claim a sizable nest egg, and hoodwink Kecal and his father's second wife. Kecal returns to the inn with Krusina and many villagers to boast of his success and formalize his arrangement with Jenik. To the accompaniment of music from the overture, Kecal reads the legal contract between himself and Jenik, Jenik signs the document, and the villagers express their anger at Jenik's apparent callousness.

Act III finds Vasek mourning the disappearance of the woman who gave him such good advice, but he quickly forgets her when a circus troupe bursts on the scene. Vasek is enthralled by the beauty of a circus dancer, Esmerelda, and when the ringmaster informs her that her dance partner is too drunk to perform that evening, they ask Vasek if he will step in. Just as Vasek agrees, his parents come in to introduce him to his bride-to-be. When Vasek learns that it is Marenka, he runs away in terror. Marenka enters, fuming over Jenik's faithlessness. Vasek decides to come back and is overjoyed to discover that the woman who gave him good advice is Marenka after all. Marenka asks for time to make up her mind. When the others leave, she sings a sad lament. Jenik enters and his lightheartedness makes Marenka all the more furious, especially when he urges her to sign the marriage contract so that he can collect his money. The villagers gather to celebrate the betrothal of Marenka and the "elder son of Tobias Micha." Tobias and his wife gasp when they recognize Jenik as Tobias's son, and Jenik turns triumphantly to Marenka, asking her to choose between himself and Vasek. Without hesitation she chooses Jenik. While Kecal does a slow burn, Vasek breaks the ice as he bumbles in, trying to get out of a dancing bear suit. The opera ends with general rejoicing over the good fortune of the two lovers.

Overture to The Bartered Bride

Use the information above to provide as much or as little background as seems appropriate. As you work through this sonata-form overture, display (or photocopy handouts of) the Additional Listening Chart from Appendix I. In your discussion of this work, help students with the following items.

1. Familiarize students with the two primary themes before you play the entire work. The first theme offers a vivacious example of fugal imitation far removed from the counterpoint of J. S. Bach. The second theme, a boisterous polka for full orchestra, dances along with offbeat accents and a simple accompaniment. These folklike melodies reflect eastern European traditions and lend a distinctive folk flavor to Smetana's early Romantic language—with little of the sprawling, surging restlessness that characterizes Romantic melody.

2. Help students hear features of sonata form in this work. Like many Classical operas, this one begins with a sonata-form overture, but Smetana treats the features of this time-honored form with great flexibility, as did Tchaikovsky in his *Romeo and Juliet*. Following the two themes of the exposition, Smetana rearranges the form completely, with developmental sections wedged in between portions of the recapitulation and a substantial coda. His first development modulates far more than it develops themes, and the recapitulation has barely gotten under way when Smetana decides to develop the first theme in an extended contrapuntal section. The second theme proceeds much as before, while the coda starts with another developmental section, reminiscent of the first one but with motives from the second theme. Finally, Smetana weaves together the flurry of the first theme and a full, climactic statement of the second. In this one bold stroke, Smetana ties together all the threads of the overture and carries them to a brilliant conclusion.

3. Point out the role of the raucous fanfare-like motive that begins the overture. It functions almost as a rondo theme that constantly returns after contrasting sections, and Smetana also uses it to announce or conclude the most important sections of this work—like a set of bookends. After the first statement, this fanfare returns as closing material at the end of the exposition, to announce the beginning of the recapitulation, and as closing material again at the end of the recapitulation. The abbreviated final statement comes at the very end, just before the chords that conclude the coda.

Furiant from **The Bartered Bride**

Several delightful rhythmic irregularities characterize this Czech folk dance. Spend some time with the first thirty seconds of this work; count out the changing duple and triple patterns with your students until they can catch Smetana's playful rhythms. Underneath the nationalist veneer—the rhythmic intricacy and folkish quality of this dance—lies an old, familiar friend: Classical minuet form. Ask the class to help you construct this diagram on the board.

MINUET	TRIO	MINUET
A	**B**	**A**
|: a :||: b a′:|	|: c :||: d c′:|	a b a′

Smetana employs the minuet's triple meter as well as its two sharply contrasted dances—a furiant and trio here. Play excerpts from the furiant and the trio, and ask students to describe the differences. Note especially the contrasts in rhythm, articulation, and tonal stability. The furiant's resemblance to the minuet even carries over into the internal structure of each section. Just substitute "furiant" for "minuet"!

FURIANT	TRIO	FURIANT
A	**B**	**A**
a |: b a :|	c |: d c′:|	a b a′

Though he follows this old dance form more closely than many Romantic composers, Smetana does not use minuet form slavishly. For instance, the **a** and **c** sections do not repeat, and the **c′** sections in the trio bring back only the end of the **c** section, making this return difficult to hear.

Finally, Smetana makes this simple dance form less predictable by interpolating transitional material around each major section. Add these to your diagram so that it looks like this:

INTRODUCTION	FURIANT		TRIO		FURIANT	CODA
	A	trans.	**B**	trans.	**A**	**A′ & B′**
a′	a |: b a :|		c |: d c′:|		a b a′	

Note the introduction's variant on the **a** phrase and the codetta-like first transition. More interesting are the other new sections. The second transition's slow crescendo makes the furiant's return more compelling, and the coda combines both dances freely, bringing the whole to a sparkling conclusion. Play through the entire work so that students can hear the effect of these connecting materials.

MUSORGSKY *Pictures at an Exhibition*

If you want to expose your students to more music from this exciting, colorful, distinctive nationalist work, "The Hut on Fowl's Legs" provides an excellent example. See Sound Recordings below for suggested performances.

"The Hut on Fowl's Legs"

This strange-sounding structure comes straight out of Russian folklore—it is the bizarre, even frightening home of Baba Yaga, the witch! In its depiction of Baba Yaga's home, this movement, like "Gnomus," paints a bold, evocative, highly colored portrait. The first section of this simple three-part form (**A**) begins with a bang. Orchestral unison highlights a muscular, angular theme, whose intervals suggest no scale we've encountered so far. Energy builds to a brass fanfare that eventually gives way to an even more frantic version of the orchestral unison.

The second section (**B**) provides a near-complete contrast; it is as soft and eerie as the first section was brash and energetic. Point out the delicate, colorful orchestral effects: rapid fingered *tremolos,* harmonics, and mutes. The melody is based on an unusual scale similar to the one in **A,** and it sounds almost like a transformation of the **A** section's orchestral unison theme, especially if you follow its rhythmic profile.

The concluding **A** section follows the same sequence as the first, but the final orchestral unison builds to an even greater frenzy that leads directly into the last picture, "The Great Gate at Kiev."

A	B	A
m. 1	m. 97	m. 125

RIMSKY-KORSAKOV *Russian Easter* Overture

This bold, colorful work is recommended as an example of both Russian nationalism and a concert overture. See Sound Recordings below for a suggested performance, and Appendix I for an Additional Listening Chart.

Though a concert overture, ostensibly in quasi-sonata form, this work is too irregular to use as a sonata-form example. Focus instead on its specifically Russian features, and use the program itself (see Additional Listening Chart) as a guide to this work's structure. Rimsky-Korsakov's brilliantly orchestrated music depicts a festive Russian Easter day that starts with early morning prayers and ends with a jubilant, clangorous celebration.

Russian Easter Overture is based on four melodies from the *Obichod,* an early collection of Russian liturgical music: "Let God Arise," "An Angel Wailed," "Let Them Also That Hate Him Flee before Him," and "Christ Is Arisen." Introduce these hymn tunes one at a time.

"Let God Arise," a serious melody that evokes the sound of plainchant, is played prayerfully by winds and then strings when it first appears at the beginning. Play "Let God Arise" (mm. 1–6). Compare this version with a later return of the theme: during the only subdued moment of the *Allegro* (mm. 291–302), the trombone plays a strikingly solemn, stentorian variation that heightens this hymn's ancient, chantlike quality.

"An Angel Wailed"—a lyric, melancholy melody—first appears in a cello solo. Play this hymn (mm. 10–14).

The *Allegro* begins with an agitated, syncopated version of the hymn tune "Let Them Also That Hate Him Flee before Him." Play this tune (mm. 82–156).

"Christ Is Arisen," the most important theme of the *Allegro,* returns in varied guises. Near the end of the overture it returns grandly, surrounded by celebratory bells and a fast, ornamental accompaniment. Play "Christ Is Arisen" (mm. 661–75).

Give your students a broad overview of this overture's two sections. The introduction consists of alternations between "Let God Arise," "An Angel Wailed," and a series of light, graceful violin and flute solos. This section evokes at once the early morning prayers and the dawning of a cold but bright Easter day. The *Allegro* section consists of various appearances of "Let Them Also That Hate Him Flee before Him" and "Christ Is Arisen," as well as a trombone reprise of "Let God Arise." Alternating with these thematic appearances is a bridgelike passage that creates great momentum and excitement.

Display (or photocopy handouts of) the Additional Listening Chart from Appendix I, or outline the chart on the board. Play the piece and point to each section as it goes by.

BRAHMS Symphony No. 4, IV

This work provides another example of Brahms's devotion to German musical traditions of the past. With minor adjustments, Brahms followed the Classical four-movement plan in this symphony, as in each of his four symphonies. In another nod to tradition, Brahms used variation form in the final movement of his Fourth Symphony, just as Beethoven did in his Third and Ninth Symphonies. Brahms did not use Classical theme and variations form, however; he followed an even older tradition by using the *passacaglia,* a Baroque variation form. (See Sound Recordings below for suggested recordings.)

Display (or photocopy handouts of) the Additional Listening Chart for this movement in Appendix I. Play the *passacaglia* theme (mm. 1–8) until students can recognize it readily. Point out how the thirty variations are grouped into three larger sections, **A, B,** and **A′.** Ask students to determine what distinguishes the two **A** sections from the **B** section, and play the entire work. Point out sections on the display as they go by, or play the *passacaglia* theme at the keyboard along with each variation. In the discussion that follows, ask students to describe the differences between the **A** and **B** sections. Significant differences include:

Dynamics—**A** section dynamics are variable, often loud; the **B** section is mostly *piano*

Tone color—the scoring is much lighter in the **B** section

Tempo—the **B** section is twice as slow as **A**

Melody—**B** section melodies are less angular, more stepwise, than in the **A** section

Mode—most **B** variations use major mode; the **A** sections are minor

Mood—the volatile, urgent, dramatic character of the **A** section is replaced by a pensive, halting, lyric quality in the **B** section

With his intimate knowledge of older music, Brahms understood as well as anyone the power and durability of the principles of contrast and return. Brahms was not content to construct a set of thirty variations without a clear sense of the overall shape and direction of the piece. By superimposing a large-scale **A B A′** form on the *passacaglia,* Brahms created a new level of meaning within the old variation form. In so doing, he provided the same "powerful sense of recapitulation" that we experience in sonata form or minuet and trio form, an experience not normally associated with variation forms. As we saw above, Brahms never used traditional forms for their own sake. He chose forms that expressed his musical ideas most directly and adapted them creatively and expressively.

CHINESE PROGRAM MUSIC *The Drunken Fisherman*

For a more intimate example of Chinese music and an intriguing example of program music from a non-Western tradition, this work from the *qin* literature is highly recommended. *The Drunken Fisherman* offers opportunities to rethink European program music from another culture's vantage point and to reflect on the subtlety and variety of program music around the world. It also protects students against the mistaken notion that program music was invented by nineteenth-century Romanticism. Europe's music history is itself filled with examples that contradict this notion, but a three-thousand-year-old tradition of program music is another matter altogether. You can use the recording from *Listen:* Brief Fourth Edition or see Sound Recordings below.

The European music above offers several different approaches to program music: Tchaikovsky's poignant dramatics, Musorgksy's *grotesquerie* and grandeur, and Mahler's ironic naïveté. In contrast, *The Drunken Fisherman* offers a thoughtful whimsy. And this *qin* piece achieves on a single instrument what the Europeans needed a full orchestra to accomplish. Comparisons almost seem irrelevant, so great is the awe one feels when faced with a tradition three millennia old. To study music for the *qin* we must go back to the very roots of that tradition, back before even Confucius, who came to be so strongly associated with this Chinese zither.

Once again, three thousand years of history cannot fit themselves into so small a space; thus, the next few pages focus on the *qin*'s origins, the importance of the *qin* in the Confucian era, and the subsequent development of the instrument and its literature. This segment concludes with teaching suggestions for *The Drunken Fisherman*. For further information on the *qin* or other Chinese plucked stringed instruments, refer to sources suggested in Appendix V.

The Qin *in Chinese History*

Distinctive in its appearance and playing technique, the *qin* belongs to the zither family. A long (four feet), narrow (six inches), and rather flat (two to three inches) wooden box is constructed of a curved soundboard over a flat-bottomed board with sound holes, with strings running from one end to the other. Unlike related instruments such as the *cheng* or the Japanese *koto,* the *qin* has only seven silk strings and uses no movable bridges. It rests on a playing stand in front of the performer. The performer uses the left hand, palm down, to finger different pitches; since the instrument has no frets, left hand finger positions are judged in relation to thirteen studs that mark divisions of the strings. The right hand plucks, snaps, and strums the strings in at least sixteen prescribed manners to achieve the appropriate tone quality for each pitch.

The precise age of the *qin* is unknown. Chinese tradition places its origins as early as the third millennium B.C.E., but no reliable evidence points to such an early birth. The earliest references appear in Chou dynasty sources (1050–255 B.C.E.), and most scholars agree that the instrument probably came into being during the fifteenth or fourteenth century B.C.E. Tradition points to several early uses for the *qin*—as an orchestral instrument, in duets with the larger twenty-stringed *cheng* zither, as accompaniment for poetry, and as a solo instrument for personal recreation. In the orchestra, it was used for temple celebrations and courtly entertainments. In this context the *qin* came to Japan as part of the Chinese orchestra that played for the dedication of the great bronze Buddha at Nara, Japan, in 752 (described in Chapter 13 of this manual). A beautifully crafted *qin* used in those ceremonies has been preserved to this day in the Shosoin collection in Nara. The *qin* could not hold its own against louder instruments of the orchestra, however. Its role was thus deemphasized, and it was assigned very simple parts to play. The *qin-cheng* duets disappeared sometime before the Eastern Chin dynasty (317–420 C.E.), when the *cheng* fell out of favor. It was in the contexts of poetry and personal recreation that players of the *qin* developed techniques for elaborate, sophisticated performances as a solo instrument. The following notes will focus on the *qin* in its solo context.

A remarkable body of lore grew up around the *qin,* quite unlike that associated with other Chinese instruments. By the time the *qin* was first mentioned in the *Wu-ching* (*Five Classics*) attributed to K'ung Fu-tzu (Confucius) and his followers, much of this lore was already well established. One of the mythical ancient emperors was said to have brought his empire into harmony through playing the *qin.* The *qin-cheng* duet was likened to a happy relationship between husband and wife. And the icing on the cake: K'ung Fu-tzu himself loved music and played the *qin.* Playing the *qin* became associated with great rulers and scholars and with a cosmic harmony between heaven and the Chinese people.

K'ung Fu-tzu (551–479 B.C.E.) might have expressed surprise at becoming the object of religious worship after his death. He spent his life as a scholar, teacher, public servant (at times), and moral philosopher. He taught his pupils to strive for goodness, righteousness, sincerity, reciprocity, and devotion to duty. An expert in ceremony, he believed that proper rituals symbolized and promoted proper harmony between heaven and the state as well as between the rulers and the people. Apparently he proved an able administrator in his brief stints in public service. For K'ung Fu-tzu the sign of good government was a happy populace. His philosophy of the state and the relationship between the rulers and the governed is filled with eerie similarities to Plato's Republic. But K'ung Fu-tzu's ideas came first; he died before the birth of Socrates (469–399 B.C.E.) or Plato (427–347 B.C.E.), and he postulated the Golden Rule five centuries before Christ. The following summation of a Confucian understanding of music appears in the *Yueh-chi* (*Annotations on Music*)—a part of the *Li-chi* (*Book of Rites*), one of the *Five Classics* of Confucianism: "Therefore, when music flourishes, human relations are clarified, eyes and ears are made more susceptive, body and mind are in balanced harmony, good customs prosper and morals are improved, and peace reigns everywhere under Heaven."[2]

K'ung Fu-tzu's ideas and writings quickly spread throughout China following his death. Many rulers found justification for strong government in his ideas, and they were quick to encourage the Confucian religious practices that sprung up. During this time the *qin* became increasingly popular among scholars, poets, and aristocrats who followed the example of K'ung Fu-tzu. Confucianism encountered a bump in the road in the middle of the short-lived Qin dynasty (221–206 B.C.E.) when the first emperor, Ch'in-shih-huang-ti, decided that K'ung Fu-tzu's ideas were dangerous. Not only did he burn all the Confucian books he could find, but he buried forty scholars alive for continuing to spread K'ung Fu-tzu's teachings. Fortunately, rulers of the Han dynasty (206 B.C.E.–220 C.E.) immediately set out to rectify the situation, collecting as many Confucian volumes as possible for safekeeping in the major centers of learning. They saw Confucian ideals as a strong connection with the past that would strengthen their authority over the state, and they wanted to establish a true Chinese heritage that would instill national pride and distinguish them from the outsiders who periodically attacked China. In this new climate, the *qin,* with its numerous connections to the past, flourished.

In the Han era, the *qin* quickly became the favored instrument of the literati, including scholars, poets, and the aristocracy. Not only was it prized for its distinguished history and lore, but it was thought to purify and harmonize body, mind, and spirit for the player. Suddenly the *qin*'s use as a solo in-

---

[2]R. H. van Gulik, *The Lore of the Chinese Lute: An Essay in the Ideology of the Ch'in.* Tokyo: Sophia University and Charles E. Tuttle, 1968, p. 25.

strument for private recreation mushroomed. References to the instrument appear frequently in poems of the Han dynasty, and many of the early *qin* treatises and compositions date from that era. One's education was incomplete if it failed to include lessons on the *qin*. Even with all this activity, the *qin* never became a "popular" instrument in the broadest sense. Some commoners managed to learn the instrument, but many teachers refused to take students of low social standing, and the instrument itself was an expensive one.

Confucianism's influence on the development of the *qin* and literature was crucial, but Taoism also played a significant role. In fact, Confucian lore includes apocryphal stories of meetings between K'ung Fu-tzu and Lao-Tzu, Taoism's "saint." Their outlooks differed fundamentally: Whereas K'ung Fu-tzu emphasized a moral philosophy, Lao-Tzu followed a spiritual path toward enlightenment. Lao-Tzu had little patience with the artificial structures of a governing state; humans needed only return to their natural state and follow the Tao (the way). The following quotation from Chapter 38 of the *Tao Te Ching* is filled with jabs at K'ung Fu-tzu's teachings.

The Progress of Morality Is Really Regress

Losing wholeness and naturalness (*Tao*) man comes to particularize his view (*te*). Losing the particular applications of virtue he comes to a theoretical concept of Goodness (*jen*). Losing the ideal of Goodness man's highest value becomes Righteousness (*yi*). When he loses even that he sinks to the level of Ceremony (*li*). Now ceremony is evidence that Conscientiousness (*chung*) and Sincerity (*hsin*) have worn thin, and that moral breakdown is imminent.[3]

For the literati swayed more by Taoism than by Confucianism, the *qin* still proved popular. Confucians might play to achieve harmony; for the Taoists, the *qin* became a path to wisdom, an instrument for following the Tao. Hsi K'ang (223–262 C.E.) rejected the Confucian understanding altogether, emphasizing music's expressive, imaginative qualities. Under Taoist influences, many *qin* players carried their instruments into the woods and along the streams to play in communion with nature, reflecting on the natural state of being that was so important to Lao-Tzu.

During the period of international influences (exemplified by the *ya-yueh* orchestra that played in Nara, Japan, in 752), especially in the Sui, Tang, and Five Dynasties eras, the *qin* tradition fell off somewhat. Small court circles kept it alive, however, and the *qin* enjoyed another rebirth of interest in the Song dynasty (960–1279 C.E.). During this time, a new system of tablature notation was developed. Even more impressive was the incredible surge of *qin* activity during the Ming dynasty (1368–1644 C.E.), which expressed a renewed interest in "pure" Chinese culture. More *qin* compositions and treatises come from this era than any other. The *qin* became such a status symbol that many up-and-coming members of the newly wealthy middle class owned the instrument—whether they could play it or not. Many performance practices were standardized at this time, including the "twenty-four touches" and "fifty-four finger techniques" related to proper uses of the right and left hands. Treatises dealt with elaborate systems of *qin* symbolism found in the construction of the instrument, playing techniques, *qin* compositions, and even the tones themselves. Whereas the treatises of earlier eras dealt with cosmic and theoretical matters, Ming-era treatises sought to bring theory and performance practice together.

---

[3]Laurence G. Thompson, *The Chinese Way in Religion*. Encino, Cal.: Dickenson Publishing, 1973, p. 48.

Always the province of the highly literate classes, the *qin* has always had more difficulty surviving than popular art forms like the Beijing opera. The *qin* continued to maintain its prestige through the Qing dynasty (1644–1912), but publications came to focus more on the traditional repertory than on new compositions. In the twentieth century, musicological research on the *qin* reached an all-time high, but musical performance fell off significantly. Not surprisingly, the *qin*'s association with the aristocracy worked against it during the Cultural Revolution of the 1960s. Its ultimate fate remains to be seen.

The Drunken Fisherman

In his treatise on the *qin* (*The Lore of the Chinese Lute,* Tokyo, 1968), R. H. van Gulik lists five types of *qin* compositions found in the Ming repertory: tunes that describe a mystic journey (Taoist), tunes of semihistorical character (Confucian), musical versions of literary works, tunes that describe nature, and tunes that describe literary life. Categories often overlap, especially in the case of nature, which figures prominently in the Taoist and Confucian categories. *The Drunken Fisherman* (*Zui yu chang wan*) appears to fall into the first group. Many Taoist-influenced *qin* compositions make reference to fishermen and to the "drunkenness" one experiences following true insight into the Tao. The image of the fisherman (or fuel gatherer) also figures prominently in Chinese lore; it is said that K'ung Fu-tzu once encountered a fisherman (the madman mentioned in the Confucian *Analects*?) who showed him the right way (Tao?) and then disappeared. The image of drunkenness might be taken more literally at times—the great *qin* artist Hsi K'ang reportedly used wine to help him achieve a spiritual consciousness. In any event, the custom of carrying the *qin* into the woods and mountains makes it easy to envision a scholar-fisherman meditating on the beauties of nature.

Start your presentation with some background material. Feel free to use any of the information immediately above. At the very least, provide a physical description of the instrument and information about Confucianism and Taoism. Then introduce the four sections of a typical *qin* composition. The opening—a free, nonmetric section similar to the north Indian *alap*—establishes the important notes of the scale. The metrical second section introduces the main melody and supporting motives, all of which are subject to variation. The third section slows down, sometimes restating motives from the second section. The final section, a brief coda, slows down even further and restates important scale tones in harmonics. The chart below includes section headings that correspond to the four sections described above, and it lists thematic/motivic repetitions in order of appearance. You may find it useful to display this chart for your class (or photocopy and distribute handouts).

If you have time, introduce the scale on which this work is based. First, a bit of background: The Chinese pitch system is remarkably similar to the Western system; students will sense nothing odd about the intonation. Chinese music theory describes a twelve-pitch system nearly identical to the Western chromatic scale. The original derivation was based on perfect fifths, like Western Pythagorean tuning. In practice, most Chinese musicians have used well-tempered tunings for centuries, though one later Chinese theorist described equal temperament a century or two before that practice became common in the West. (For that matter, the Chinese were concerned with absolute pitch many centuries before A-440 became standard in the West.) Now for the scales themselves. Whereas the overall sound of much Chinese music is pentatonic, most of it is based on seven-note scales much like Western scales. This work is based on the Chinese equivalent of a Western Mixolydian mode. There are five primary pitches; the other two are treated as secondary pitches. In fact, one of the secondary pitches, scale degree 7, only appears once (at 2:43). Play the notes of a B Mixolydian scale at the keyboard to introduce the sounds. Then play the two interlocking pentatonic scales that account for the primary pitch patterns used in *The Drunken Fisherman:* B–C sharp–D sharp–F sharp–G sharp and E–F sharp–G sharp–B–C sharp. Improvise a few motives in each five-note group to give students the flavor of these pitch patterns.

Before you play *The Drunken Fisherman,* play its three main ideas separately: the basic melody, the three-note motive in octaves, and the rocking theme with repeated notes. Once students recognize the differences between them, display the chart below and play the music. Point out each main idea as the music plays.

Section 1

0:00	Introduction

Section 2

0:09	**Basic melody** introduced and developed
0:46	Three-note motive in octaves
0:56	**Basic melody** repeated, faster
1:04	*Rocking theme* with repeated notes
1:12	Three-note motive repeated
1:31	*Rocking theme* repeated
1:38	Three-note motive repeated
1:53	Three-note motive repeated
2:00	Rhythms gradually become quicker and quicker
2:04	*Rocking theme* repeated
2:09	Three-note motive repeated
2:25	*Rocking theme* repeated
2:30	Three-note motive repeated

Section 3

2:42	Abrupt slowdown, return to beginning of **basic melody**
2:50	Irregular, "staggering" theme

Section 4

3:02	Harmonics

Afterward, ask students to describe this work's overall impression and to identify specific musical elements and structures that create such an impression. Draw out the following points.

1. This is indeed very personal, intimate music. The solo instrument and its range of articulation and ornamentation make for a delicacy of expression. Call attention to the variety of techniques used by the right and left hands to vary the basic color of the instrument.

2. The melody is constructed from a small group of motives that repeat and return frequently. Point out the use of variation in these frequent returns.

3. Apart from some fifths, drone pitches, and the frequent octave doublings that give depth and resonance to specific pitches, there is no harmony to speak of; the overall impression is that of a monophonic texture.

4. The rhythm moves between metric and nonmetric, and between faster and slower tempos. Note the gentle stagger of the theme at 2:50 and its connection

with the drunkenness implied by the title; as the notes under "The *Qin* in Chinese History" suggest, this music was never intended to portray an all-night "bender."

5. Finally, call attention to the sound of the harmonics at the end. Violin and guitar harmonics create a more "glassy," eerie sound, but with its long strings (four feet!), the *qin*'s harmonics create a rich yet delicate harplike sound that proves quite lovely.

Conclude by playing *The Drunken Fisherman* one last time. The first time through you focused on melodic relationships. This time ask students to listen for the colors created on the instrument itself. The following notes by van Gulik can help set up a different context for listening. Read it to your students and then play the music.

> The lute [*qin*], on the contrary, is not so easy to appreciate, chiefly because its music is not primarily melodical. Its beauty lies not so much in the succession of notes as in each separate note in itself. "Painting with sound" might be a way to describe its essential quality. Each note is an entity in itself, calculated to evoke in the mind of the hearer a special reaction. The timbre being thus of the utmost importance, there are very great possibilities of modifying the colouring of one and the same tone. In order to understand and appreciate this music, the ear must learn to distinguish subtle nuances: the same note, produced on a different string, has a different colour; the same string, when pulled by the forefinger or the middle finger of the right hand, has a different timbre. The technique by which these variations in timbre are effected is extremely complicated: of the vibrato alone there exist no less than 26 varieties.
>
> The impression made by one note is followed by another, still another. There is thus a compelling, inevitable suggestion of a mood, an atmosphere, which impresses on the hearer the sentiment that inspired the composer.[4]

Van Gulik's final sentence could just as easily describe the character pieces from Chapter 16. Those solo piano pieces offer perhaps the most interesting comparisons with music for the *qin*. Ask students to identify points of similarity between these genres. Gentler works like Chopin's Nocturne or Schumann's "Eusebius" match the intimacy and delicacy of this most personal genre of Chinese music. For Romantic composers, music was unique in its ability to directly express inner experience or even the great truths of existence. For the *qin* player, music could at the very least harmonize mind, body, and soul; some even saw it as a path to spiritual enlightenment. Both *qin* music and character pieces often achieved a tantalizing blend of music and poetry, each seeking to express something beyond the purely musical—what we call program music.

Multimedia Resources

¶ Further Listening Charts and Texts

See Appendix I for Listening Charts for these works; see Further Listening Examples above for teaching suggestions.

Smetana, "Vlatava" ("The Moldau"), from *Ma Vlast*

Smetana, Overture to *The Bartered Bride*

Rimsky-Korsakov, *Russian Easter* Overture

Brahms, Symphony No. 4, IV

---

[4]Van Gulik, *Lore of the Chinese Lute*, pp. 1–2.

❦ Sound Recordings

Akiyoshi, *Kogun*. The Toshiko Akiyoshi–Lew Tabackin Big Band. RCA BVCJ 35001 (CD). Five extended works by the Japanese jazz pianist/composer/arranger. Akiyoshi's most fascinating works bring sounds and concepts from Japanese music into the big band jazz environment. Use this recording if you try Listening Idea 9 above.

Beating the Dragon Robe: A Traditional Peking Opera. Smithsonian Folkways (CD). Extended scenes from this Beijing opera (the *Listen* recording came from this CD). Try this CD for further examples of this genre. Available from www.worldmusicstore.com.

Bizet, *Carmen: RCA Opera Treasury*. Vienna Philharmonic Orchestra. RCA Red Seal 39495 (CD). Features Leontyne Price as perhaps the finest Carmen of the twentieth century. Other cast members include Mirella Freni, Franco Corelli, and Robert Merrill; conducted by Herbert von Karajan. Try this recording if you use Class Discussion Idea 4 or Listening Idea 5 above.

Brahms, *Hungarian Dances*. Budapest Symphony Orchestra. Naxos 8.550110 (CD). Sparkling recording of Brahms arrangements of his piano music; conducted by István Bogár. Perhaps the finest recording available, and at a bargain price. Try this recording if you use Class Discussion Idea 4 above.

Brahms, *Isaac Stern: A Life in Music—Beethoven and Brahms Concertos*. Isaac Stern with the New York Philharmonic. Sony Classical SM2K 66941 (CD). Latest re-release of the recording used in the *Listen* set; conducted by Zubin Mehta. Use this recording of the complete Brahms Violin Concerto in D to demonstrate Brahms's use of the classical concerto's three-movement format.

Brahms, *Symphony No. 4*. Berlin Philharmonic. Deutsche Grammophon 435349 (CD). Outstanding recording of Brahms's final symphony on modern instruments; conducted by Claudio Abbado. Try this recording if you use suggestions for Symphony No. 4 from Further Listening Examples above.

Britten, *Curlew River*. London 421 868-2 (CD). Wonderful recording of Britten's Japanese influenced "parable for church performance" features John Shirley-Quirk and Peter Pears; supervised by the composer himself. Try this recording if you use Listening Idea 10 above.

China: The Art of Qin. Li Xiangting. Ocora 560001 (CD). Several selections performed by this modern *qin* virtuoso. Try this CD for additional examples of *qin* music if you use Listening Idea 12 or suggestions for *The Drunken Fisherman* in Further Listening Examples above.

China: The Art of the Qin Zither. Dai Xiaolian. Ethnic 6765 (CD). Eleven selections performed by this modern *qin* master. Try this CD for additional examples of *qin* music if you use Listening Idea 12 or suggestions for *The Drunken Fisherman* in Further Listening Examples above.

China: Music of the Pipa. Lui Pui-yuen. Elektra/Nonesuch Explorer Series 9 72085-2 (CD). Collection of works for the *pipa*, an instrument associated more with entertainment than with meditation. Wide variety of moods require virtuoso technique and frequent special effects. Includes informative liner notes in English. Try this recording if you use Listening Idea 12 above.

China: The Peking Opera. PlayaSound PS 65197 (CD). Extended scenes from two Beijing operas: *The Swimming Dragon Pays Court to the Phoenix* and *The Prince Who Changed into a Cat* (The *Listen* recording came from this

CD). Try this CD for more extended examples of *tan* and *lao-sheng* roles. Available from www.heartheworld.org.

The Chinese Cheng. Liang Tsai-Ping. Lyrichord LYRCD 7302 (CD). Music for the *cheng*, the ancient Chinese sixteen-stringed zither. Recording mixes classical works and new compositions by the performer. If you use suggestions for *The Drunken Fisherman* in Further Listening Examples above, try this recording to demonstrate the sound of the instrument, whose partnership with the *qin* in ancient times was compared to a harmonious relationship between husband and wife.

Dvořák, *Slavonic Dances.* Chamber Orchestra of Europe. Teldec 8573-81038-2 (CD). Delightful recent recording gives these dances new vitality. Highly recommended if you use Listening Idea 4 above.

Dvořák, *Symphony No. 9 (New World).* London Symphony Orchestra. Penguin Classics 460 604-2 (CD). One of the finest stereo recordings of this symphony, written to show American composers what they were missing by ignoring indigenous American musics; conducted by István Kertész. Includes *Carnival Overture*. Try this recording if you use Listening Idea 5 above.

Emotions for the Weishui River: Instrumental Music from China. Guizhou National Arts Ensemble. Pan Records 149CD (CD). Recording features an ensemble of Chinese instruments, including *pipa, cheng, yueqin*, and *erhu*. Two are newly composed works, but the others are classical works from the Han dynasty or traditional music and dances from southern China. Liner notes are brief but to the point. Try this recording for more extended examples of instruments used in Beijing opera (*yueqin* and *erhu*).

Excursions in World Music. Prentice-Hall (CD). This CD anthology that accompanies Bruno Nettl's world music textbook includes three arias from Beijing opera that demonstrate *hsi-p'i* and *erh-huang* styles as well as *ch'ing-i* (*tan*), *jing*, and *lao-sheng* roles.

Falla, *El amor brujo; Nights in the Gardens of Spain.* Montreal Symphony Orchestra. London 430 703-2 (CD). Superb performances of Spanish nationalist works with soloists Alicia de Larrocha and Huguette Tourangeau; conducted by Charles Dutoit. Also includes Rodrigo's evocative *Concierto de Aranjuez*. Try this recording if you use Listening Idea 4 above.

Grieg, *Peer Gynt Suites.* Berlin Philharmonic. Deutsche Grammophon Galleria 419 474-2 (CD). Classic recordings of Grieg's best-known nationalist works; conducted by Herbert von Karajan. Also includes the *Holberg Suite* and the suite from *Sigurd Jorsalfar*. Try this recording if you use Listening Idea 4 above.

Guqin: The Art of Yao Gongbai. Yao Gongbai. World Music Library KICC 5232 (CD). Album devoted to music for the *qin* includes some of the oldest tunes in the instrument's repertory. Accompanying booklet includes photographs and useful notes in English and Chinese. Try this recording for additional examples of music for *qin* if you use Listening Idea 12 or suggestions for *The Drunken Fisherman* in Further Listening Examples above.

Japan: Kabuki and Other Traditional Music. Ensemble Nipponia. Nonesuch Explorer Series 9 72084-2 (CD). Effective performances of excerpts from several works from the kabuki repertory, including *Musume Dojoji*. Try this recording if you want to introduce your students to more kabuki music or if you want an alternative performance of Part 2 of the *nagauta* from *Dojoji*.

Japanese Noh Music. The Kyoto Nohgaku Kai. Lyrichord LYRCD 7137 (CD). Nine excerpts from representative works in the *noh* theater tradition. Strikingly similar in style and instrumentation to the *Listen* excerpt from *Dojoji*, originally derived from the *noh* repertory. Good liner notes in English.

Kabuki: Japanese Traditional Music, Kanjincho. King Record Co. KICH 2003 (CD). Complete recording of the kabuki dance drama *Kanjincho,* in live performance at the Minami-za in Kyoto. You can hear the whole range of vocal expression, including *nagauta* songs and stylized speech. Thorough Japanese liner notes include the complete libretto; unfortunately, only two pages of notes in English are included.

Liszt, *Piano Concertos Nos. 1 and 2/Totentanz.* Zimerman and the Boston Symphony. Deutsche Grammophon 423 571-2 GH (CD). Definitive recordings of Liszt virtuoso works for piano and orchestra; conducted by Seiji Ozawa. Use this recording if you try Class Discussion Idea 2 above.

Liszt, *Symphonic Poems.* Berlin Philharmonic. Sony Classical SK 66834 (CD). Full-blooded performances of several Liszt symphonic poems, including *Les préludes, Orpheus,* and *Mazeppa;* conducted by Zubin Mehta. Recommended if you want to cover one of Liszt's symphonic poems as part of your survey of Romantic program music or if you use Lecture-Demonstration Idea 3 or Listening Idea 1 above.

Mahler, *Orchestral Songs including "The Song of the Earth."* Janet Baker and James King, Royal Concertgebouw Orchestra. Philips Duo 454 014-2 (CD). Bargain set includes a classic recording of *Das Lied von der Erde,* a sublime work from Mahler's twilight years, performed by the great Mahlerian mezzo Janet Baker; conducted by Bernard Haitink. Use this recording to demonstrate Mahler's successful fusion of song and symphony or for an example of late Romantic tonal language just at the time when Schoenberg moved into atonality. Try this recording if you use Class Discussion Idea 4 or Listening Idea 5 above.

Mahler Plays Mahler. Yvonne Kenny, Claudine Carlson, and Gustav Mahler. Golden Legacy Recorded Music GLRS 101 (CD). Fascinating recording of performances by Mahler himself on a modern concert grand; via the turn-of-the-century Welte-Mignon piano roll technology, capable of capturing dynamic inflections and pedaling as well as the pitches. Mahler performs two of his songs and one movement each from his Fourth and Fifth Symphonies. You can use this recording as a window to the past, both to provide contact with a flesh-and-blood composer from an era when we don't expect sound recordings and to demonstrate the exaggerated tempo changes that marked late Romantic performance practice.

Mahler, *Symphony No. 2.* Ruth Ziesak, Charlotte Hellekant, and the San Francisco Symphony Orchestra and Chorus. London 443 350-2 (CD). Committed, expressive orchestral playing in this fine performance of Mahler's Resurrection Symphony; conducted by Herbert Blomstedt. Use this recording if you want to demonstrate the extremes grandiose compositions had reached by the late nineteenth century.

Miss Saigon: Original London Cast. Geffen 224 271 (CD). Original cast recording for this remake of Puccini's *Madama Butterfly.* Try this recording if you use Class Discussion Idea 4.

The Monkey King: The World of Peking Opera. JVC World Sounds VICG–5016 (CD). Extended excerpts from *The Monkey King* with two other works. Try this CD for more extended examples of the genre.

Mozart, *Die Entführung aus dem Serail*. English Baroque Soloists. Deutsche Grammophon Archiv 435 857-2 (CD). Recommended recording of Mozart's Turkish *Singspiel* on period instruments; conducted by John Eliot Gardiner. Use this recording if you try Class Discussion Idea 4 above.

Mozart, *Sonatas, Volume I*. Malcolm Bilson. Hungaroton HCD 31009-10 (CD). Stylish performances of Mozart's complete piano sonatas by one of the foremost fortepiano specialists. Try this recording of the Rondo "alla Turca" from Sonata in A, K. 331, if you use Class Discussion Idea 4 above.

Musorgsky, *Boris Godunov*. Kirov Opera and Orchestra. Philips 462 230-2 (CD). Recent recording by one of today's finest Russian opera companies features powerful, idiomatic performances of both Musorgsky's 1869 and 1872 versions of the greatest Russian nationalist opera; conducted by Valery Gergiev. Bargain pricing offers five CDs for the price of three. Try this recording if you use Listening Idea 3 above.

Musorgsky, *Pictures at an Exhibition/Night on Bare Mountain*. Vienna Philharmonic. Philips 289 468 526-2 (CD). Recent recording of a live performance of *Pictures;* conducted by Valery Gergiev. Try this recording if you use Listening Idea 2 or 3 or suggestions for "The Hut on Fowl's Legs" in Further Listening Examples above.

Musorgsky, *The Sofia Concert 1958*. Sviatoslav Richter. Philips 464 734-2 (CD). Remastered recording of a live recital includes *the* definitive recording of *Pictures at an Exhibition* in the original version for solo piano. It goes in and out of print, but it's worth finding. Try this idea if you use Listening Idea 2 above.

Nagauta Kabuki Theater Music. Kineya Ensemble. Ocora 560144 (CD). Excerpts from four kabuki works: *Kurama Yama, Niwaka Jishi, Reimei,* and *Ninin Wankyu*. Useful for further exploration of kabuki music.

Nogaku: Japanese Traditional Music. Nakatani Akira, Kakihara Takashi, and various artists. King Record Co. KICH 2002 (CD). Excellent recording of instrumental music, generally the dances that end each play, from nine different *noh* dramas. Extensive liner notes in Japanese; four worthwhile pages by Richard Emmert in English. Try this recording to explore more music from the Japanese theater with your students.

The Peking Opera: The Forest on Fire, The Princess Hundred Flowers. Dalian Troupe. Buda Musique du Monde 92618-2 (CD). Superb performances of Beijing operas by a troupe that keeps the old traditions alive. Includes the first and last scenes of *The Forest on Fire* but presents *The Princess Hundred Flowers* complete and unabridged. Excellent liner notes in English even identify song styles so your students can compare *hsi-p'i* and *erh-huang* songs.

The Police. *The Very Best of Sting and the Police*. UTV 493 252 (CD). Greatest hits collection includes many reggae-tinged songs such as "Roxanne." Try this recording if you use Class Discussion Idea 4.

Puccini, *Madama Butterfly*. Vienna Philharmonic Orchestra. London 417 577-2 (CD). Great recording of Puccini's Japanese tragedy features Mirella Freni, Luciano Pavarotti, and Christa Ludwig; conducted by Herbert von Karajan. Try this recording if you use Class Discussion Idea 4 or Listening Idea 5 above.

Rimsky-Korsakov, *Scheherazade, Capriccio espagnol, etc.* Various orchestras. Deutsche Grammophon Panorama 469 187-2 (CD). Bravura recordings of many Russian nationalist showpieces by Rimsky-Korsakov, including a splendid performance of *Russian Easter* Overture by Igor Markevitch with the

Royal Concertgebouw Orchestra. Try this recording if you use Listening Idea 3 or 5 or suggestions for the *Russian Easter* Overture in Further Listening Examples above.

The Ruse of the Empty City: A Traditional Peking Opera. Smithsonian Folkways (CD). Extended scenes from this Beijing opera. Try this CD for further examples of this genre. Available from www.worldmusicstore.com.

Schumann, Robert. *Carnaval, Bunte Blätter, Kreisleriana, Papillons*. Youri Egorov. EMI Classics *double fforte* 74191 (CD). Poetic, volatile performances of important character piece cycles. Try this recording of *Carnaval* if you use Listening Idea 2 above.

Sibelius, *Finlandia*. Berlin Philharmonic. EMI Classics CDM 64331 (CD). Collection of Finnish nationalist works; conducted by Herbert von Karajan. Includes Sibelius's *Finlandia, En Saga, Tapiola*, and *The Swan of Tuonela*. Try this recording if you use Listening Idea 4 above.

Simon, Paul. *Graceland*. Warner Brothers 46430 (CD). Landmark 1986 album features collaborations with many South African artists, including Joseph Shabalala and Ladysmith Black Mambazo. Try this recording if you use Class Discussion Idea 4.

Smetana, *The Bartered Bride*. Czech Philharmonic. Supraphon 10 3511-2 (CD). Marvelously idiomatic performance of Smetana's nationalist opera by a Czech cast; conducted by Zdenek Kosler. Use this recording to introduce this opera to your class if you use suggestions from Further Listening Examples above for the overture and furiant.

Smetana, *Ma Vlast*. London Classical Players. Virgin Veritas CDC 45301 (CD). Period instrument performances of Smetana's famous cycle of nationalist tone poems; conducted by Roger Norrington. Includes Smetana's *The Moldau* and the Czech Republic's national anthem. Try this recording if you use Listening Idea 1 or 4 or suggestions from Further Listening Examples for *The Moldau*.

The Sounds of Kabuki: Traditional Music and Drama of Japan. National Kabuki Company. Legacy CD 423 (CD). Extended excerpts from two kabuki works: *Lion Dance from Echigo Country* and *The Noble Pine*. Useful for further exploration of kabuki music. Minimal liner notes.

South Pacific: Original Soundtrack. RCA 67977 (CD). The score for this famous musical is filled with examples of musical exoticism. Try this recording if you use Class Discussion Idea 4.

Strauss, *Also sprach Zarathustra*. Berlin Philharmonic. Deutsche Grammophon Originals 447 441-2 (CD). Recording conducted by one of the great Strauss interpreters, Herbert von Karajan. Includes *Don Juan* and *Till Eulenspiegel*. Try this recording if you use Listening Idea 1 above.

Strauss, *Don Quixote*. Berlin Philharmonic. Deutsche Grammophon Originals 457 725-2 (CD). Conducted by one of the great Strauss interpreters, Herbert von Karajan. Try this recording if you use Listening Idea 1 above.

Stravinsky, *The Great Ballets*. London Philharmonic. Philips Duo 438 350-2 (CD). Excellent performances of famous Stravinsky scores; conducted by Bernard Haitink. Includes *The Firebird Suite, Rite of Spring, Petrushka*, and *Apollo* on two discs for the price of one. Try this recording of *Firebird* if you use Listening Idea 3 above.

Sullivan (& Gilbert), *The Mikado*. D'Oyly Carte Opera Company and the Royal Philharmonic. London 425 190-2 LM2 (CD). Authentic performance (but without dialogue!) of one of the great Gilbert and Sullivan operettas; conducted by Royston Nash. Try this recording if you use Class Discussion Idea 4 or Listening Idea 5 above.

Tchaikovsky, *Ballet Suites*. Berlin Philharmonic. Deutsche Grammophon 449 726-2 (CD). Superb performances of suites from *The Nutcracker, Swan Lake,* and *Sleeping Beauty;* conducted by Rostropovich. Use this recording if you try Class Discussion Idea 4 or Listening Idea 3 or 5.

Tchaikovsky, *Tchaikovsky Festival*. Royal Philharmonic Orchestra. Naxos 8.550500 (CD). Another gem from the Naxos catalogue. Excellent performances of classic works by Tchaikovsky; conducted by Adrian Leaper. It contains *1812 Overture, Capriccio italien, Romeo and Juliet,* and *Marche Slave.* Try this recording if you use Listening Ideas 1, 3, or 5.

Vaughan Williams, *Fantasia on a Theme by Thomas Tallis*. Academy of St. Martin-in-the-Fields. Argo 414 595-2 ZH (CD). Fine collection of English nationalist works by Vaughan Williams; conducted by Sir Neville Marriner. Includes the title track; *Fantasia on Greensleeves; Variants of "Dives and Lazarus";* and *The Lark Ascending.* Try this recording if you use Listening Idea 4 above.

Yangguan San Die (Parting at Yangguan). Liang Mingyue. Wergo 1706 (CD). Eight selections performed by this modern *qin* performer. This CD contains a performance of *The Drunken Fisherman,* titled here as *Drunken Fisherman's Evening Song.* Use this CD if you try Listening Idea 12 or suggestions for this work in Further Listening Examples above.

♩ Video Recordings

Akiyoshi, Toshiko. *Jazz Is My Native Language*. Rhapsody Films (VHS, color, 60 minutes). Documentary portrait of the life and music of Japanese composer, arranger, and pianist Toshiko Akiyoshi. Leonard Feather compares her with Ellington and Kenton. Filled with interview, rehearsal, and performance clips. Try this recording if you use Listening Idea 9 above. Available at www.worldmusicstore.com.

Bizet, *Carmen*. Image Entertainment (DVD or VHS, color, 163 minutes). Royal Opera House production of Bizet's masterpiece, an early example of "realism" in opera. Superb acting and singing from Maria Ewing, Luis Lima, Leontina Vaduva, and Gino Quilico; conducted by Zubin Mehta. Try this video if you use Class Discussion Idea 4 or Listening Idea 5 above.

Brahms, *Complete Symphonies*. Hänssler Classic (DVD). These fine recordings of all of Brahms's symphonies use "period" manners on modern instruments; conducted by Roger Norrington. Highly recommended if you use suggestions for Symphony No. 4 from Further Listening Examples above.

Brahms. *Johannes Brahms: But for Women . . .* www.films.com (DVD or VHS, color, 58 minutes). Video biography focuses on Brahms's inner life and relationships using letters, diaries, photos, manuscripts, reviews, and even a rare recording of Brahms playing his own *Hungarian Dance* No. 1. Actors are used as the voices of Brahms and Clara Schumann. Highly recommended if you use Lecture-Demonstration Idea 5 above.

[Brahms, *Schaffe in mir, Gott,* Op. 29, No. 2.] Delaware Music Series. www .ecsmedia.com (DVD). Oberlin Conservatory Chorus performance of Brahms's motet for mixed five-part chorus. The DVD also includes a scrolling full score with color-coded formal analysis.

Brahms, Symphony No. 4. Sounds Magnificent: The Story of the Symphony Series. Image Entertainment (DVD or VHS, color, 85 minutes). André Previn narrates this look at Brahms and his music. The video includes a complete performance of Symphony No. 4 by the Royal Philharmonic Orchestra. Highly recommended if you use suggestions for the fourth movement from Further Listening Examples above.

[Brahms, Violin Concerto.] *Europa Konzert from Palermo.* EuroArts (DVD, color). Gil Shaham is an outstanding soloist in this performance of the Brahms Violin Concerto with the Berlin Philharmonic; conducted by Claudio Abbado. Itzhak Perlman's rendition with the same orchestra on EMI Classics is also very fine, but Shaham's performance is more stylish all around. As an added bonus, the Europa Konzert disc also includes Dvořák's *New World* Symphony. Highly recommended supplement to your coverage of the Brahms concerto or if you use Listening Idea 5 above.

Chinese Cracker: The Making of The Peony Pavilion. www.films.com (DVD or VHS, color, 53 minutes). Video follows efforts to stage this nineteen-hour *kunqu* (ancestor to the Beijing opera) classic from the sixteenth century. Director Chen Shi-Zheng's production of *The Peony Pavilion* (see video below) was ultimately premiered by the Shanghai Kunju Troupe at Lincoln Center.

Delaware Music Series. www.ecsmedia.com (DVD). This important collection covers several important late Romantic composers. See the entry in this section for teaching resources on Brahms's *Schaffe in mir, Gott.*

Discovering the Music of Japan. www.insight-media.com (DVD, color, 22 minutes). This 1967 film provides a brief introduction to the music and instruments of Japan.

Dvořák: Symphony No. 9, "From the New World." Herbert von Karajan: His Legacy for Home Video Series. Sony Classical (DVD or VHS, color, 44 minutes). Karajan leads the Vienna Philharmonic in a strong 1985 performance of this favorite symphony, but the more recent Abbado version with the Berlin Philharmonic is better yet (see the Europa Konzert DVD for Brahms's Violin Concerto above). Try this video if you use Listening Idea 5 above.

Farewell, My Concubine. Miramax Classics (DVD or VHS, color, 172 minutes). Chen Kaige's powerful story of the lives of two Beijing opera actors, a *tan* and a *jing,* caught up in twentieth-century China's turbulent changes. Many scenes depict Beijing opera performances and the social institutions that supported *jingju.* Stars Leslie Cheung, Zhang Fengyi, and Gong Li. Chinese with English subtitles. Highly recommended if you use Lecture-Demonstration Idea 11 above.

Heritage of Chinese Opera. www.insight-media.com (DVD, color, 38 minutes). Looks at the history of Chinese opera as well as its characteristic features, including stage props, face paint, acrobatics, costumes, and orchestral accompaniment. Good supplement to your coverage of Beijing opera.

The History of Music, Part 2: *Romanticism Through Modern.* www.insight -media.com (VHS, color, 92 minutes). The section on later Romanticism covers Brahms versus Wagner, nationalism, Freud, Tchaikovsky, Dvořák, Puccini, Mahler, and Strauss.

JVC Video Anthology of Japanese Classical Performing Arts. (VHS, color, 25 tapes). This landmark anthology contains examples of all major genres from the Japanese classical tradition, including *gagaku, noh,* and kabuki. Two accompanying videos cover Japanese musical instruments, and two large books (in Japanese) provide background material and describe each performance.

JVC Video Anthology of World Music and Dance. (VHS, color). Tapes 3 through 5 from this excellent video series offer music from China. Of particular interest is example 3-10, from the Beijing opera "The king's parting with his favorite." Other examples include 3-3, instrumental music for *erhu,* and 3-2 and 3-4, which feature music for Chinese plucked stringed instruments—the *pipa* and *zheng,* respectively. Highly recommended for your presentation of Global Perspectives materials and Further Listening Examples for this chapter.

Kabuki. www.films.com (DVD or VHS, color, 36 minutes). Wonderful introduction to the world of kabuki. Mixes information on the history and traditions of the art with rehearsal and performance footage. Recommended supplement to your presentation of kabuki.

Land of Our Fathers. Music in Time Series. www.films.com (DVD or VHS, color, 60 minutes). James Galway narrates this look at nationalism in the late nineteenth century. Features excerpts from Ives's *Three Places in New England* (see Further Listening Examples in Chapter 20) and music of Smetana, Dvořák, Janacek, Grieg, Falla, Vaughan Williams, Kodály, and Sibelius. Try this video if you use Listening Idea 4 above.

Liszt at Weimar. Man and Music Series. www.films.com (DVD or VHS, color, 60 minutes). Liszt is introduced in Chapter 16, but his influence on late Romanticism is incalculable. The Weimar years begin at midcentury and include many of Liszt's most significant works. The film includes excerpts from *Années de Pélèrinage;* Symphonic Poems 2, 6, and 8; the *Faust* Symphony; Piano Sonata in B Minor; and *Bénédiction de Dieu dans la solitude.*

Mahler, *Gustav Mahler. Harmonics: The Innovators of Classical Music* Series. www.films.com (DVD or VHS, color, 27 minutes). Video biography of Mahler features expert commentary and musical excerpts from *Kindertotenlieder* and Symphonies 2, 5, 8, and 9. Musical excerpts feature Brigitte Fassbaender, Janet Baker, and Leonard Bernstein. Recommended.

Mahler, *The Symphonies/Das Lied von der Erde.* Deutsche Grammophon (DVD, color, 9 discs—also available separately). Leonard Bernstein was the first to record the complete Mahler symphonies on LP, and this belated release gives us the first complete Mahler cycle on DVD. These recordings are not to be missed. Where Symphony No. 1 is concerned, this is the one to use in class. Recent releases by Haitink and Tennestedt are also very fine, but Bernstein captures the simultaneous irony, verve, and schmaltz of the dance sections better than anyone else. Highly recommended.

Mahler, *Symphonies 1 and 8.* EMI Classics (2 DVDs, color, 156 minutes). Known as a fine Mahler interpreter, Klaus Tennestedt leads a fine Mahler orchestra (Chicago Symphony) in the First Symphony (disc 2 features the London Philharmonic playing the *Symphony of a Thousand*). The slow movement doesn't quite capture the *klezmer* verve of the Bernstein DVD, but this is fine playing all around, and highly recommendable. If you can't find Bernstein, use this DVD to supplement your Mahler presentation.

The Mighty Fistful. Music in Time Series. www.films.com (DVD or VHS, color, 60 minutes). James Galway narrates this look at Russian nationalism. Features excerpts from music by Glinka, Tcheshnikov, Musorgsky (*Boris Godunov*), Borodin, Rimsky-Korsakov, Tchaikovsky (Violin Concerto, *Swan Lake,* and Symphony No. 6), Scriabin, and Stravinsky (*The Firebird*). Try this video if you use Listening Idea 3 above.

Music for a Nation. Man and Music Series. www.films.com (DVD or VHS, color, 53 minutes). Covers Russian music in the last twenty years of the nineteenth century. Looks at the Rubinsteins, the Mighty Fistful, and Tchaikovsky. Music by Tchaikovsky (Violin Concerto, String Quartet No. 1, *Eugene Onegin, Swan Lake,* and Symphony No. 6), Balakirev, Borodin, and Musorgsky (*Boris Godunov*). Try this video if you use Listening Idea 3 above.

Musorgsky, *Boris Godunov.* Philips (DVD, color, 221 minutes). Director Andrei Tarkovsky's production of Musorgsky's greatest work by the Kirov Opera Orchestra and Chorus. Singers include Olga Borodina, R. Lloyd, A. Steblianko, Sergei Leiferkus, and A. Morosov; conducted by Valery Gergiev. Try this video if you use Listening Idea 3 above.

Musorgsky, *Pictures at an Exhibition.* Sony Classical (DVD, color, 37 minutes). Herbert von Karajan and the Berlin Philharmonic turn in powerful performances of this blockbuster score. Karajan's meddling with camera angles is often distracting, but the music making is first rate. For an equally fine rendition that *feels* like a live performance, see the Ormandy DVD below (under Tchaikovsky, *Violin Concerto*). This disc makes a handy supplement to your presentation of the *Listen* selections from Musorgsky's *Pictures* or if you use suggestions in Further Listening Examples above for "The Hut on Fowl's Legs."

Modeste Mussorgsky: Towards New Shores. Great Composers and Musicians Series. www.films.com (DVD or VHS, color, 78 minutes). A look at the development of Musorgsky's style. Useful supplement to *Pictures at an Exhibition* or if you use Listening Idea 3 above.

Nagauta: The Heart of Kabuki Music. University of Oklahoma (VHS, color, 30 minutes). Wonderful introduction to the world of kabuki. Narrated by William Malm and Sidney Brown, the program features analytical commentary, demonstrations by singers and instrumentalists (students at the National University of Fine Arts and Music in Tokyo), and a performance of *nagauta* music from *Sue Hirogari.* Use this video if at all possible! Available from www.worldmusicstore.com.

New Year's Gala 1997. Arthaus Musik (DVD, color, 85 minutes). Claudio Abbado leads the Berlin Philharmonic in a concert filled with examples of nationalism and exoticism, including Brahms's *Hungarian Dances,* Falla's *El amor brujo,* Bizet's *Carmen,* and Ravel's *Rhapsodie espagnole.* Try this video if you use Class Discussion Idea 4 or Listening Idea 4 or 5 above.

No: Music of Noh Drama. University of Oklahoma (VHS, color, 30 minutes). Video contains excerpts filmed by torchlight at Nara's Kofukuji Temple during the 1996 Takigi Onoh festival. Narrated by William Malm and Sidney Brown, the program also offers demonstrations of flute, drum, and vocal techniques mixed in with historical and cultural background. Because *noh* drama exerted such an influence on kabuki theater, this can add useful insights to your study of *Dojoji.* Available from www.worldmusicstore.com.

The Peking Opera Company in The Perfumed Handkerchief. Kultur Video (VHS, color, seventy minutes). One of few examples of Beijing opera on video. Performance takes place on location in the Imperial Summer Palace of Beijing. In 70 minutes you only get selections, but it's enough to tell the story and gives a good feel for the genre. Many funny moments in this comedy! Narration for the original television broadcast by Steve Allen and Jayne Meadows is well-meaning but corny. Recommended supplement to your presentation of Beijing opera.

The Peony Pavilion (Mudan Ting). Image Entertainment (DVD or VHS, color, 122 minutes). Live performance of this sixteenth-century *kunqu* classic by Tang Xianzu—an ancestor to Beijing opera but with many similarities. Many cuts were needed to squeeze this nineteen-hour-long drama into a two-hour video, and the editors tended to favor comic or acrobatic scenes that would appeal to Western audiences. Otherwise a splendid achievement. Includes a one-hour video on the making of *The Peony Pavilion.* Highly recommended supplement to your presentation of Beijing opera.

Pictures at an Exhibition: Collectors Edition. DVD Company Ltd. (DVD, color, 42 minutes). This digitally remastered release of Emerson Lake & Palmer's 1970 live concert performance provides a fascinating alternative performance of Musorgsky's character pieces. ELP stays surprisingly close to the original, and it's a lot of fun to watch Keith Emerson twiddle the knobs on his filters, random signal (noise) generators, and the like—this was the first generation of performance synthesizers, after all—and "The Great Gate at Kiev" features a mixture of theatricality and feedback effects. In some songs, psychedelic Marvel animation is laid over the live images, but happily this does not affect any of the *Listen* examples. You can also find the *Listen* excerpts in a 1996 performance on ELP's *Live at the Royal Albert Hall* DVD. Try this as a supplement to your presentation of *Pictures at an Exhibition.*

Puccini, *Madama Butterfly.* Decca (DVD or VHS, color, 144 minutes). Jean-Pierre Ponnelle's film version of Puccini's tragic opera. "Un bel dì" is included in Further Listening Examples for Chapter 17 of this manual (p. 421). Performed by Mirella Freni, Plácido Domingo, and Christa Ludwig; conducted by Herbert von Karajan. Try this video if you use Class Discussion Idea 4 or Listening Idea 5 above.

The Romantics. Music in Time Series. www.films.com (DVD or VHS, color, 60 minutes). James Galway narrates this look at the Romantic century. The first and largest portion of the video is devoted to composers from early Romanticism (Chopin, Mendelssohn, and Schumann), but it also includes music of Bruckner and excerpts from Brahms's Symphony No. 2, "Lullaby," *German Requiem,* and Clarinet Quintet.

Sibelius. *Jean Sibelius: A Giant from the North.* www.films.com (DVD or VHS, color, 90 minutes). Video biography of this Finnish nationalist features expert commentary and musical excerpts from various works.

Sibelius, Violin Concerto; De Falla, Nights in the Gardens of Spain. Arthaus Musik (DVD, color, 87 minutes). This bonanza of nationalist music also offers *El amor brujo* and other works by Falla. Live concert performances by Maxim Vengerov, Daniel Barenboim, and the Chicago Symphony Orchestra; conducted by Barenboim and Plácido Domingo. Try this video if you use Listening Idea 4 above.

Simon, Paul. *Graceland: The African Concert.* Warner Brothers (DVD or VHS, color, 90 minutes). Video record of Paul Simon's live concert in Harare, Zimbabwe. Includes performances by Hugh Masekela, Miriam Makeba, and Ladysmith Black Mambazo. Try this recording if you use Class Discussion Idea 4 above.

Smetana, *The Bartered Bride.* Qualiton Imports (DVD, color). Authentic, idiomatic Czech performance of Smetana's important nationalist opera features the Czech Philharmonic Orchestra with Zdenek Kosler as the ideal conductor. Highly recommended if you use suggestions for this work from Further Listening Examples above.

[Smetana, *The Moldau.*] *Great Conductors in Rehearsal and Performance: Karel Ancerl and Hermann Scherchen.* CBC Home Video/VAI (DVD, color). The segment on *The Moldau* in rehearsal and performance is especially useful. These 1969 telecasts are on the older side, but still work well in class. Try this recording if you use Listening Idea 1 or 4 or suggestions from Further Listening Examples for *The Moldau.*

South Pacific. Twentieth Century Fox (DVD or VHS, color, 157 minutes). The 1958 movie version of this famous musical is filled with examples of musical exoticism. Try this video if you use Class Discussion Idea 4.

Strauss, *Richard Strauss: Erich Leinsdorf.* Pioneer (DVD, color, 86 minutes). Idiomatic video performance of two Strauss tone poems, *Don Juan* and *Ein Heldenleben,* by the Berlin Staatskapelle; conducted by Erich Leinsdorf. Try this recording if you use Listening Idea 1 above.

Stravinsky, *The Firebird/Les Noces.* BBC Opus Arte (DVD, color, 108 minutes). Excellent performances of two early Stravinsky ballets using choreography from the original Diaghilev productions. Try this recording of *The Firebird* if you use Listening Idea 3 above.

Sullivan (and Gilbert), *The Mikado.* Acorn Media (DVD or VHS, color, 150 minutes). Live (and lively) performance of one of the great Gilbert and Sullivan operettas at Canada's Stratford Festival. Try this video if you use Class Discussion Idea 4 or Listening Idea 5 above.

Taming a 100-Headed Dragon. The Art of Conducting Series. www.films.com (DVD or VHS, color/black and white, 31 minutes). A program that explores the development of conducting in the nineteenth century. Contains footage of famous conductors in rehearsal and performance, including Arthur Nikisch, Sir Thomas Beecham, Richard Strauss, Felix Weingartner, and Bruno Walter, among others. Most relevant to the *Listen* textbook are the portions devoted to Walter, who conducts Mozart's Symphony No. 40 and Brahms's Symphony No. 2.

Tchaikovsky, *Nutcracker.* Kultur Video (DVD and VHS, color, 100 minutes). Recent rerelease of this 1968 recording of the Royal Ballet at Covent Garden features the incomparable Rudolf Nureyev and Merle Park. Try this video if you use Class Discussion Idea 4 or Listening Idea 3 or 5 above.

Tchaikovsky, *Nutcracker.* Kultur Video (DVD and VHS, color, 105 minutes). Recent rerelease of this 1978 recording features the renowned Bolshoi Ballet with dancers Yekaterina Maximova and Vladimir Vasiliev. Try this video if you use Class Discussion Idea 4 or Listening Idea 3 or 5 above.

Tchaikovsky, *Symphony No. 6. Sounds Magnificent: The Story of the Symphony* Series. Image Entertainment (DVD or VHS, color, 87 minutes). André Previn narrates this look at Tchaikovsky and his music. The video includes a complete performance of Symphony No. 6 (*Pathétique*) by the Royal Philharmonic Orchestra. Try this video if you use Listening Idea 3 above.

Tchaikovsky, *Violin Concerto/Romeo and Juliet.* EuroArts (DVD, color, 89 minutes). At long last, a DVD with *Romeo and Juliet*! Eugene Ormandy leads the Philadelphia Orchestra in a dramatic, beautifully played performance. This disc also includes a terrific rendition of Musorgsky's *Pictures at an Exhibition*—

half of the Chapter 18 selections on a single DVD! This makes a thoroughly recommendable supplement to your presentation of Tchaikovsky and Musorgsky or if you use suggestions in Further Listening Examples above for "The Hut on Fowl's Legs."

Tsugaru Shamisen: The World of Michihiro Sato. www.insight-media.com (DVD or VHS, color, 48 minutes). Video portrait of one of Japan's most important shamisen virtuosos. Good supplement to your coverage of kabuki or *gagaku.*

Turn of the Century. Man and Music Series. www.films.com (DVD or VHS, color, 53 minutes). A close look at late Romanticism and the transition to the twentieth century in Vienna. Special emphasis on Mahler (Symphonies 4 and 5 and *Kindertotenlieder*), but also includes some of Wolf's songs and Schoenberg's works (see Chapter 20).

The Turn of the Century. Music in Time Series. www.films.com (DVD or VHS, color, 60 minutes). James Galway narrates this look at music in transition. Hard to decide whether this works best in this chapter or in Chapter 20. Late Romantic examples include Puccini's *Madama Butterfly,* Mahler's *Das Lied von der Erde* and Symphony No. 10, Schoenberg's *Verklärte Nacht,* Wagner's Prelude to *Tristan and Isolde* (Chapter 17), and Richard Strauss's *Till Eulenspiegel.* Early twentieth-century examples include Debussy's *Syrinx* and *La Mer* and Richard Strauss's *Salome.* Performers include Galway and the Vienna Philharmonic, conducted by Bernstein, Böhm, and von Karajan.

The Waltz City. Man and Music Series. www.films.com (DVD or VHS, color, 53 minutes). Looks at music in Vienna in the last half of the nineteenth century. Includes excerpts from Johann Strauss waltzes (*Emperor* and *Blue Danube*) and *Die Fledermaus;* Wagner's *Die Meistersinger;* Brahms's Piano Waltz, Clarinet Quintet, Symphony No. 1, and *German Requiem;* and Bruckner's Symphony No. 3 and a motet. Useful supplement to a presentation on Brahms and Mahler.

♪ Software

Brahms Symphony No. 3. Time Sketch Composer Series. www.ecsmedia.com (CD-ROM—Windows or Macintosh). Program presents a CD recording of Brahms's Symphony No. 3 and other works, with interactive arch map analysis and background information about the composer, his style, and the work. Highly recommended supplement to your presentation of Brahms.

Dvořák: New World Symphony. Time Sketch Composer Series. www.ecsmedia .com (CD-ROM—Windows or Macintosh). Program presents a CD recording of Dvořák's *New World* Symphony with interactive arch map analysis and background information about the composer, his style, and the work. Highly recommended supplement to your presentation of nationalism.

Great Composers: Haydn, Tchaikovsky, and Ravel. Zane Publishing (CD-ROM—Windows or Macintosh). This inexpensive CD-ROM includes a multimedia presentation, photographs, quizzes, and sound clips. Available from www.cdaccess.com.

Great Composers: Schubert, Brahms, and Strauss. Zane Publishing/Selectsoft (CD-ROM—Windows or Macintosh). This inexpensive CD-ROM includes a multimedia presentation, photographs, quizzes, and sound clips. Available from www.cdaccess.com.

The History of Music. www.mccormicksnet.com (CD-ROM—Windows or Macintosh). CD-ROM version of the video above. The section on later Romanticism covers Brahms versus Wagner, nationalism, Freud, Tchaikovsky, Dvořák, Puccini, Mahler, and Strauss.

Moussorgsky: Pictures at an Exhibition. Time Sketch Composer Series. www.ecsmedia.com (CD-ROM—Windows or Macintosh). Program presents a CD recording of Musorgsky's *Pictures at an Exhibition* with interactive arch map analysis and background information about the composer, his style, and the work. Highly recommended supplement to your presentation of *Pictures*.

CHAPTER 19

Prelude
Music and Modernism

Chapter Outline

Important Terms

modernism	impressionism	octatonic scale
traditionalism	symbolism	quarter-tone scale
avant-garde	expressionism	serialism
progress	*fauves*	"emancipation of dissonance"
uncertainty	pentatonic scale	atonal
objectivity	whole-tone scale	

Teaching Objectives

❧ Overall Objectives

This chapter will help students acquire familiarity with:

1. Features of early twentieth-century musical styles as reflections of major scientific, philosophical, literary, and artistic trends in that century.

2. The changes and features associated with twentieth-century modernist music before World War I, especially changes in melody, harmony, and tonality.

ꝟ Listening Objectives

After completing this chapter, students should be able to:

1. Hear and identify typical uses of the elements of music in early twentieth-century styles.

2. Hear and identify the effect of changing features associated with modernist music before World War I, between the world wars, and after World War II, especially changes in melody, harmony, and tonality.

Lecture Suggestions

ꝟ Preliminary Suggestions

Some Thoughts on Presenting Twentieth-Century Music

As you begin Unit V, be aware that presenting twentieth-century music to undergraduate nonmajors poses a number of problems. Happily, these problems can be overcome.

Problem—Many students (and even some instructors) don't like twentieth-century music, particularly music written after World War II.

Solution—You cannot force students to like what they do not enjoy, but you must help them understand what the music is about. Challenge them to give the music a chance and to listen as much as possible, since repeated listening provides the surest means to appreciation and understanding of an unfamiliar style. If all else fails, help students pinpoint features they don't like. Some suggestions:

ꝟ Present twentieth-century music as an outgrowth of nineteenth-century music, as the logical "next step" in the expressive development of Western music. As much as possible, build on familiar concepts.

ꝟ Place this music in the context of larger cultural events: the growth of technology, mass media, and communications; the rapid rate of change in Western society; Freud and psychoanalysis; the world wars; nuclear weapons; and so on.

ꝟ Present twentieth-century styles as solutions to an artistic problem: how to create music that expresses the spirit as well as the technical and sociological changes of the century.

Problem—The tremendous stylistic variety of music written since 1900 makes it difficult to decide what to focus on.

Solution—It is hard to imagine a music appreciation course that does not cover Debussy, Stravinsky, Schoenberg, and Copland; for that matter, each listening example in the textbook demonstrates an important aspect of twentieth-century music. But you cannot do it all; you need to pick and choose. The chief consideration must be your own interests; choose the music you know best and can present effectively. If students sense that you are covering a piece because you "have" to, your lecture is doomed to fail. (Think twice before you omit jazz, Global Perspectives materials, or Adams's *El Niño*. Jazz, a uniquely American tradition, and world music examples provide an antidote to the European styles studied throughout the course; Adams's music offers a taste of current directions in contemporary music.)

Problem—Many teaching assistants in large music appreciation classes don't feel comfortable discussing twentieth-century music.

Solution—Many resources are available for teaching assistants (or anyone else) who need to bone up on twentieth-century music. Standard music history textbooks provide a wonderful refresher. The final chapters of J. Peter Burkholder's new revision of the industry-standard Grout textbook (W. W. Norton, 2006) is superb—Burkholder is a fine Ives scholar, after all. The last three chapters of K Marie Stolba's *Development of Western Music,* 3rd ed. (Boston: McGraw-Hill, 1998) are also recommended, especially since they divide the century according to the world wars just as *Listen* does. For those who need more comprehensive coverage, Eric Salzman's *Twentieth-Century Music: An Introduction,* 4th ed. (Englewood Cliffs, N.J.: Prentice-Hall, 2002) provides an excellent survey just over 300 pages in length.

Problem—Instructors typically save twentieth-century music, for the end of the term, when little time or energy remains for something new.

Solution—Reserve at *least* two weeks for Unit V, time enough for students to absorb new concepts and new sounds. If you are tempted to let earlier units run overtime, remember that you will pay a price at the end; let it go and move on—no matter what unit you are in, there is never enough time.

Some Thoughts on Presenting Unit V

Before you look at musical characteristics of twentieth-century music, consider how to present the chapters of Unit V. For the Sixth Edition, Kerman and Tomlinson continue to use a chronological approach. This makes good sense, given a student's tendency to equate lecture sequence with historical chronology. This chapter offers a prelude to early twentieth-century music, and Chapters 20, 21, and 22 look at the three "eras" of twentieth-century music in turn: before World War I, between the wars, and after World War II.

Chapter 23 suggests two possible modes of presentation, however. One possibility is to cover jazz, American musical theater, and popular American musical styles in precisely the order suggested by the textbook—at the end of the course. Students who were turned off by the atonal music in Chapters 20 and 22 will heave a big sigh of relief when the course ends with more familiar American musical styles. A second possibility is to parcel out portions of Chapter 23 in an effort to create a totally chronological survey of twentieth-century music. This approach offers advantages of its own: Students can see where American musical styles fit in alongside the examples of Western "art" music presented in Chapters 20–22, they can see the similarities and differences between these musics, and they can see how these musics influenced each other. The following is a suggested chronology:

Before World War I
Chapter 19—all
Chapter 20—sections on Debussy, Stravinsky, and expressionism
Chapter 23—the sections on early American music and the box on ragtime
Chapter 20—the section on Ives

Between the Wars
Chapter 20—the section on Schoenberg and serialism
Chapter 23—Global Perspectives 6: African Drumming
Chapter 23—sections on Wallace, Armstrong, Ellington, and Gershwin
Chapter 21—sections on Ravel, Bartók, Copland, and Prokofiev

After World War II

Chapter 22—sections on postwar modernism, Ligeti, Varèse, and Cage

Chapter 23—sections on Parker, Davis, and Bernstein

Chapter 22—the section on Reich, Saariaho, and Adams

Chapter 23—the section on popular music since the 1950s

Chapter 23—Global Perspectives 7: Global Music

Although it may look a bit confusing, this second approach offers several amenities. It positions Ives *after* a look at the early American musics that figure so prominently in his music. We encounter Gershwin before Copland. We can directly compare bebop and Bernstein with the postwar avant-garde. The Global Perspectives segments allow us to look at African drumming and swing-era jazz side by side, and they force us to recognize the considerable influence of world music on American popular music since the 1950s—and vice versa.

The first approach offers two trips through the twentieth century—once to look at Western "art" music, and again to look at American jazz and musical theater. The second approach permits a more concentrated focus on style features and diverse musical expressions within each period.

♪ Progress and Uncertainty

This chapter presents a plethora of terms, ideas, and artistic movements. The years prior to World War I saw the rise and fall of a confusing number and variety of artistic movements. These movements engendered a rich variety of pre–World War I modernist music, and many later twentieth-century styles grew out of these developments.

Discuss the following twentieth-century events and concepts with your class. Students can better understand the radical changes in twentieth-century art music if you make them aware of the extreme degree of change that characterized the century. Two pivotal periods stand out: the turn of the century and the years immediately after World War II. Save the years after World War II for Chapter 22.

Change—The philosophical, technological, and social changes of the twentieth century established a new and faster rate of change in Western culture. Such rapidity was unheard-of up to that time.

Ideas—Einstein's theory of relativity, Darwin's theory of evolution, and Freud's psychological theories threw traditional understandings of science and religion into crisis, changing the way we think about the world, our relationships, and ourselves.

Technology—Ask the class to name some of the new inventions that were developed at and around the turn of the century. This list can include:

the automobile	the lightbulb and household electricity
the airplane	electric appliances
the telephone	the record player
the motion picture	

The rise of technology also brought with it a dark side. The invention of the machine gun, the tank, and poison gas ensured death on an unimaginable scale during World War I. That scale increased by several levels of magnitude during World War II, as we will see in Chapter 22.

Nationalist movements—Nationalism in Germany and Italy ultimately united those countries into sovereign states during the 1870s and 1880s.

The Russian Revolution of 1918 affected the twentieth century in much the same way that the French Revolution affected the nineteenth. Nationalism played a role in both world wars.

The spirit of the new century—Now that it's happened, ask the class how they feel about the turn of the twenty-first century. Not so long ago we were constantly bombarded with retrospectives of the old century and constant hype for the new. What has it felt like to close the book on one century and begin afresh? Clearly, the specter of 9/11 and the war on terrorism will haunt this discussion. The turn of the twentieth century was an equally anxious and exciting time of turmoil and new beginnings.

⁊ The Response of Modernism

Ask the class to imagine that they are young composers living in the year 1900. They are inspired by the spirit of the new century. They are surrounded by new technological wonders that seem to change the very nature and pace of life. Recent developments include instant voice communication via the telephone and the beginnings of mass media via the record player and motion pictures. Freud's profoundly disturbing ideas shed new light on the nature of the human mind. Young composer friends are listening to the music of Wagner and Mahler, music that stretches melody and harmony to the breaking point. Will they be satisfied to write music in the tradition of Bach, Mozart, Beethoven, and Tchaikovsky? Or will this spirit of newness, energy, and inventiveness also affect the language of musical composition? (As Debussy once said, "The century of airplanes has a right to its own music.")

These are loaded questions. Composers react to the mood of their time, as do all other artists. Young composers at the turn of the century could no more continue writing "tonal music as usual" than we could ride a horse and buggy to school every morning. The rapid changes of the twentieth century are reflected in each of the fine arts. Visual artists abandoned representation, writers abandoned conventional grammar and syntax, and many composers abandoned traditional tonality. People working in each of the arts sought new languages that could create meaning from the havoc of modern life (and would wreak havoc with traditional structures of meaning).

⁊ Literature and Art before World War I

The striking parallels between art and music just before World War I offer valuable insights into the musical examples in this chapter. Spend time with your class looking at the illustrations on textbook pages 324–26. Ask students to identify the unique features of impressionism, expressionism, cubism and *les fauves,* and abstract art in general (textbook page 324–28). List student observations on the board. When working through Chapter 20, refer back to these observations as you compare Debussy's music with impressionism, Stravinsky's with the fauves and cubism, and Schoenberg's with expressionism.

⁊ Modernist Music before World War I

The principal changes prior to World War I affected melody, harmony, and tonality. The following demonstrations can be used to present concepts from the *Listen* textbook.

Experiment and Transformation: Melody

The authors describe the disintegration of traditional melody. Melody had long been the primary bearer of musical information, but in the hands of many twentieth-century composers, melody became only one of several elements that could express musical meaning. Play several examples; ask the class to describe each and compare Classical and Romantic melodies with early twentieth-century melodies. The following examples work well.

Haydn, Symphony No. 95, IV (track 33)

Tchaikovsky, *Romeo and Juliet* (track 27, 0:56–2:01)

Debussy, Three Nocturnes, *Clouds* (track 15, 0:00–0:34)

Stravinsky, *The Rite of Spring*, Introduction (track 21, 0:00–1:02)

Schoenberg, *Pierrot lunaire*, "The Moonfleck" (entire piece)

Melody dominates the texture in the first two examples. Haydn's melody fits the definition of a tune, with its symmetrical phrases and memorable contour; Tchaikovsky's surging, soaring melody makes up for a lack of symmetry with its dramatic sweep. Melody is handled quite differently in the last three examples, however. Debussy's opening melody consists only of short motives that repeat, and toward the end there is no discernible melody at all. Stravinsky uses short melodic fragments that resemble a Russian folk tune, but he repeats and varies them in unpredictable, asymmetric phrases. Schoenberg seems to abandon traditional melody altogether. In fact, it is difficult to identify *any* clear melody in Schoenberg's use of *Sprechstimme*; the vocal part sounds more spoken than sung, and the pitch successions in the instrumental parts fly by too quickly to cohere. As Kerman and Tomlinson describe it, this is "an explicit—indeed aggressive—denial of melody."

New Scales

Several examples from *Clouds* in Debussy's Three Nocturnes can be used to compare the sound worlds created by three different scale types. Play these excerpts for the class:

Whole tone   (track 17, 0:00–0:13)—with chromatic passing tones!

Pentatonic   (track 19, 0:00–0:19)

Octatonic   (track 17, 0:36–1:06)

Ask students to compare these three scales.

Whole-tone scales are constructed entirely from whole steps; they are completely symmetrical. The interval relationships surrounding scale-step **1** correspond precisely to the interval relationships surrounding any other scale step. As a result, music based on the whole-tone scale lacks a strong sense of tonal center. Whole-tone passages sound unstable; they suggest tension.

The five tones of the pentatonic scale correspond to five of the seven pitches in the major scale. Music based on pentatonic scales sounds tonal and stable, and students may perceive a faintly oriental quality—hardly surprising given the prevalence of the pentatonic scale in many of our Global Perspectives examples. (Debussy heard musicians from East Asia and the Pacific islands at the Paris World Exposition in 1889.)

The octatonic scale is constructed of alternating whole and half steps. Like the whole-tone scale, it is symmetrical—and suggests instability and tension. Because of the presence of half steps, however, the octatonic scale sounds a bit more stable than the whole-tone scale. The half steps duplicate the effect of the leading tone in the major scale (*ti* to *do*), and they exert a subtle pull toward the upper pitch.

"The Emancipation of Dissonance"

Schoenberg's famous phrase described the end result of a trend he observed in music history. Throughout the nineteenth century, Romantic composers introduced more and more dissonance into their works, but the dissonances usually resolved. Remind students that by the early twentieth century, dissonance was used constantly and freely, and its resolution was so prolonged that many passages seemed to contain unresolved dissonance. Finally, composers decided not to worry about dissonance resolution; they used dissonances for their unique color. "Emancipation of dissonance" meant the freedom to use unresolved dissonance. Play these two examples for your class.

> Tchaikovsky, *Romeo and Juliet* (track 20, 0:26–1:21)
>
> Stravinsky, *The Rite of Spring,* Dance of the Adolescents (track 23, 0:00–track 24, 0:17)

Ask students to describe the use of dissonance in these two excerpts. Tchaikovsky uses several harsh dissonances to convey tension, but each dissonance resolves. There is a constant ebb and flow of tension and relaxation. In Stravinsky's music, however, the opening dissonant chords create a constant tension that energizes this passage. Stravinsky lowers the tension level by abruptly changing the texture, but we never sense that his dissonances resolve.

Taking things even further, Schoenberg argued that it was a small (but inevitable) step from the constant chromaticism, modulation, and high-level dissonance of late Romantic music to the atonality of his early twentieth-century music. Play the excerpts below and ask the class to describe similarities and differences between them. (You will need to find your own recording of Wagner's *Tristan and Isolde,* but there is no better example of late Romantic chromaticism!)

> Wagner, *Tristan and Isolde,* Prelude (first minute or two)
>
> Schoenberg, *Pierrot lunaire,* "Night" (0:00–1:02)

Neither excerpt gives us a clear, stable sense of tonality, except perhaps at the very end of the Wagner. In the first minute, Wagner creates tensions that resolve, but they resolve to chords that only set up further tension. The entire excerpt builds tension that resolves around 1:32 (in m. 17), but Wagner rests for hardly more than a moment even there. Wagner does not rely on a stable tonic in this music, and neither does Schoenberg. But Schoenberg takes the instability even further—the tensions in the second excerpt *never* resolve. A brief sense of relaxation at the very end of the excerpt results more from both rhythmic slowing and sinking melodic figures than from tonal stability. Wagner plays with our expectation that the tonic is just around the corner; Schoenberg creates tension as well, but without expectation of the tonic.

Additional Teaching Suggestions

❦ Lecture-Demonstration Ideas

1. Create a slide show of early twentieth-century art. Borrow slides from the art department (or use CD-ROM sources described in Software below) to demonstrate the artistic movements described in the textbook. Include the principal movements before World War I: impressionism, expressionism (include some of Schoenberg's paintings if you can), fauves, and cubism. In

preparation, ask students to read textbook pages 324–27 carefully. In class, ask them to pick out features in the artworks that correspond to concepts from their readings.

2. Take the class to your school's keyboard lab for hands-on experience with twentieth-century musical materials. Introduce the interval patterns for whole-tone, pentatonic, and octatonic scales, and ask students to construct these scales from different given starting pitches. Once they find the notes of a scale, ask them to improvise simple melodies in each scale. (They can use the black keys for pentatonic scale improvisations.) As always, ask them to listen carefully to the sounds they make.

Class Discussion Ideas

1. *How do you listen when there is no melody?* In homophonic music (most of the music that students are familiar with), it is possible to listen primarily to melody—to ignore the other elements of music. If you have demanded that students listen for other elements throughout the course, students will be prepared to follow music that has no melody. The experience is disorienting at first, but as students become attuned to changes in texture, tone color, and so on, they can begin to follow avant-garde music. Ask students to name any works heard earlier in the course in which they could identify nonmelodic elements that played a significant role in the music. These earlier experiences with more familiar examples can help to reassure students. Good examples include Varèse's *Ionisation,* Schoenberg's *Farben* from his Op. 16 set, and one of the études from Carter's Eight Études and a Fantasy for Woodwind Quintet. See Sound Recordings below for suggested recordings.

2. *Why did Schoenberg abandon tonality and develop serialism?* Read excerpts (or assign readings) from the article "Composition with Twelve Tones (1)" in Schoenberg's *Style and Idea* (New York: St. Martin's, 1975, pp. 214–44). Schoenberg describes the historical necessity of the "emancipation of dissonance" and provides an explanation of his method of "composing with twelve tones related only to each other." Students can still disagree with Schoenberg's choices, but they will come face to face with the composer's integrity and determination. See Video Recordings below for suggested resources.

Listening Ideas

1. Listen to music based on the quarter-tone scale. Recordings can be found of Ives's *Three Quarter-Tone Pieces* and Penderecki's *Threnody.* The Ives work requires two pianos tuned a quarter-tone apart. Penderecki writes for a string orchestra and asks the ensemble to play massive tone clusters built out of quarter tones. Compare these works with short examples based on diatonic and chromatic scales and ask students to describe the different effects of each of these pieces. See Multimedia Resources below for suggested recordings.

2. Compare the twentieth-century orchestra with the orchestra of earlier periods. Play excerpts from Debussy's Three Nocturnes, Copland's *Appalachian Spring,* Ellington's *Conga Brava,* and Reich's *Music for 18 Musicians;* compare them with typical Baroque (Vivaldi's Concerto in G), Classical (Haydn's Symphony No. 95), and Romantic (Berlioz's *Fantastic* Symphony) orchestras. Use the

following questions to generate discussion. *Which orchestra was largest? Which used the greatest variety of instruments? Which instrument family dominated each excerpt? Do these changes suggest any overall trends in the development of the orchestra?*

3. Debussy once said, "The century of airplanes has a right to its own music." Play examples of music that glorifies progress. These are not always easy to find, but Antheil's *Ballet mécanique,* Mosolov's *The Iron Foundry,* and Honegger's *Pacific 231* (a type of locomotive) can serve you well. Varèse was also fascinated with science and technology, as the titles of many of his works suggest: *Ionisation, Intégrales,* or *Density 21.5.* His compositional method was more akin to the manipulation of geometric shapes than to traditional composition, and the percussive rhythms and dissonances of his scores reflect a fascination with the vitality of America's urban landscapes. *Ionisation* provides the perfect example of music that abandoned melody, harmony, and tonality, being one of the first works written for percussion ensemble. See Sound Recordings below for suggested recordings.

4. Play Schoenberg's first atonal work, the fourth movement of his String Quartet No. 2, Op. 10 (1907–1908). In the final two movements, Schoenberg takes the unusual step of adding a soprano voice to the quartet. The text for the fourth movement, by the German poet Stefan George, suggests why Schoenberg chose to abandon tonality; it begins, "I feel the air of another planet." If you take time to read the poem to the class and point out its unusual imagery, students can come away with some sense of "why atonality?" Nonetheless, Schoenberg's quartet movement maintains some ties to tonality; a coda returns us to F sharp, the tonal center of the first movement. See Sound Recordings below for suggested recordings.

Multimedia Resources

⅂ Sound Recordings

Antheil, *Ballet mécanique and Other Works for Player Pianos, Percussion, and Electronics.* University of Massachusetts-Lowell Percussion Ensemble. Electronic Music Foundation EMF CD 020 (CD). World première recording of the original version (with sixteen player pianos) of *Ballet mécanique,* never performed during Antheil's lifetime due to technological limitations; conducted by Jeffrey Fischer. Includes *Ballet mécanique, Double Music* by John Cage and Lou Harrison, and other works by Grayson and Roldán. Try this recording if you use Class Discussion Idea 1 or Listening Idea 3 above.

[Carter, Eight Études and a Fantasy for Woodwind Quintet.] *The Best of the New York Woodwind Quintet,* Vol. 1. Boston Skyline BSD 137 (CD). Recordings of this work go in and out of print, so grab this CD while it's available. These are very fine performances. Use this recording of Carter's *Klangfarbenmelodie* étude if you try Class Discussion Idea 1 above.

Honegger, *Pacific 231.* Zürich Tonhalle Orchestra. Decca 455 352-2 (CD). Recording contains *Pacific 231,* Honegger's famous depiction of a locomotive, as well as his Symphony No. 2, *Rugby, Pastorale d'été,* and other works; conducted by David Zinman. Try this recording if you use Listening Idea 3 above.

Ives, *Three Quarter-Tone Pieces for Two Pianos*. G. Bouwhuis and C. van Zeeland. Channel Classic CCS 4592 (CD). Try this recording of Ives's microtonal experimentation if you use Listening Idea 1 above.

[Mosolov, *The Iron Foundry.*] *Prokofiev/Varèse/Mosolov*. Royal Concertgebouw Orchestra. London 436 640–2 (CD). Sadly, recordings of *The Iron Foundry* go in and out of print. One of only a few good modern recordings, you can still buy a used copy of this one through Amazon.com (search "prokofiev chailly"). This intriguing album contains several works influenced by industrial, scientific, and technological advances: Prokofiev's Symphony No. 3, Mosolov's *The Iron Foundry*, and Varèse's *Arcana*; conducted by Riccardo Chailly. Mosolov's glorification of Russian industrialization earned him instant celebrity and later notoriety when conservatives denounced his work as "naturalistic." The Varèse orchestral work boasts harsh dissonances, driving marchlike rhythms, and a huge percussion battery. Try this recording if you use Listening Idea 3 above.

Penderecki, *Anaklasis, etc*. Polish Radio National Symphony Orchestra and London Symphony Orchestra. EMI Classics CDM 5 65077 2 (CD). Collection of significant Penderecki orchestral works from 1959 to 1974, including the famous *Threnody for the Victims of Hiroshima;* conducted by the composer. Use this recording of *Threnody* if you try Class Discussion Idea 1 Listening Idea 1 above.

Schoenberg, *Arnold Schoenberg 2*. Arditti String Quartet and Dawn Upshaw. Auvidis Montaigne MO 782135 (CD). Definitive performances of Arnold Schoenberg's four string quartets. The final movement of Quartet No. 2 was Schoenberg's first genuinely atonal work. Highly recommended if you use Listening Idea 4 above.

Schoenberg, *Verklärte Nacht, etc*. Los Angeles Philharmonic, Cleveland Orchestra, and Vienna Philharmonic. London 448 279-2 (CD). This Decca Double offers a mix of Schoenberg's works in one inexpensive package; conducted by Zubin Mehta and Christoph von Dohnányi. Includes fine performances of Five Orchestral Pieces, Op. 16, Chamber Symphony No. 1, and *Erwartung*. Try this recording of Op. 16 if you use Class Discussion Idea 1 above.

Varèse, *The Complete Works*. Royal Concertgebouw Orchestra. London 289 460 208-2 (CD). Definitive recent release contains nearly all of Varèse's works in editions supervised by the Chinese composer and Varèse protégé Chou Wen-Chung; conducted by Riccardo Chailly. Includes *Density 21.5*, *Offrandes*, *Octandre*, *Intégrales*, and other works. *Ionisation*, for a large percussion ensemble, represents one extreme in the motion away from traditional melody, harmony, and tonality. Try this recording if you use Class Discussion Idea 1 or Listening Idea 3 above.

❧ Video Recordings

The History of Music, Part 2: *Romanticism Through Modern*. www.midiworkshop.com (DVD, color, 92 minutes). The section on the early twentieth century covers new approaches to tonality in the music of Debussy, Schoenberg, Stravinsky, and Bartók.

Impressionism in Art and Music. www.insight-media.com (DVD, color, 34 minutes). This still-image video provides a concise, visually appealing introduction to important philosophic, artistic, and musical trends in the early twentieth century. Contains the artwork of Monet, Renoir, and Pissarro and music by Debussy, Ravel, and Respighi. Try this video if you use Lecture-Demonstration Idea 1 above.

Ives, *Twentieth Century Music for Two Pianos*. Pioneer (DVD, color, 84 minutes). Worth it primarily to hear Ives's *Three Quarter-Tone Pieces*. The rest of the program consists of the Paratores' own arrangements of Gershwin's *Rhapsody in Blue* and Concerto in F and Stravinsky's *Rite of Spring*. Try this video if you use Listening Idea 1 above.

The New Music. Man and Music Series. www.films.com (DVD or VHS, color, 53 minutes). Looks at atonal music and the development of twelve-tone techniques in the music of the Second Viennese School. Musical excerpts taken from Schoenberg's *Erwartung* and Op. 25 for piano, from Berg's *Wozzeck* and Violin Concerto, and from Alexander Goehr's Quartet. Try this video if you use Class Discussion Idea 1 above.

Pablo Picasso. Against the Odds Series. www.films.com (VHS, color, 13 minutes). Brief look at one of the seminal artists of the early twentieth century. Try this video if you use Lecture-Demonstration Idea 1 above.

Recorded Sound: The Dream Becomes a Reality. Howard Goodall's Big Bangs: Turning Points in Music History Series. www.films.com (DVD or VHS, color, 51 minutes). Entertaining video looks at the impact of recording technologies on music making, beginning in 1877 with Thomas Edison.

Schoenberg, *Arnold Schoenberg. Harmonics: The Innovators of Classical Music* Series. www.films.com (DVD or VHS, color, 27 minutes). Video biography of Schoenberg features expert commentary and musical excerpts from *Moses and Aaron, Transfigured Night, Survivor from Warsaw,* Piano Pieces, Op. 25, Chamber Symphony No. 1, and *Pierrot lunaire*. Musical excerpts feature Pierre Boulez, Glenn Gould, and Erich Leinsdorf.

Schoenberg, *Arnold Schoenberg: My Evolution*. www.films.com (DVD or VHS, color, 50 minutes). Recorded Schoenberg lecture at UCLA serves as narration. Offers a fascinating look at the composer, atonality, and music in the twentieth century. Try this video if you use Lecture-Demonstration Idea 1 or Class Discussion Idea 1 above.

Turn of the Century. Man and Music Series. www.films.com (DVD or VHS, color, 53 minutes). A look at cultural contradictions in turn-of-the-century Vienna. Covers Freudian psychoanalysis, expressionist paintings by Klimt and Kokoschka, and the transition from nineteenth- to twentieth-century sensibility in Vienna. Includes excerpts from Schoenberg's *Pierrot lunaire*.

The Turn of the Century. Music in Time Series. www.films.com (DVD or VHS, color, 60 minutes). James Galway narrates this look at music in transition. It's hard to decide whether this works best in Chapter 18 or in this chapter. Late Romantic examples include Puccini's *Madama Butterfly,* Mahler's *Das Lied von der Erde* and Symphony No. 10, Schoenberg's *Verklärte Nacht,* Wagner's Prelude to *Tristan and Isolde* (Chapter 17), and Richard Strauss's *Till Eulenspiegel*. Early twentieth-century examples include Debussy's *Syrinx* and *La Mer* and Richard Strauss's *Salome*. Performers include Galway and the Vienna Philharmonic conducted by Bernstein, Böhm, and von Karajan.

Twentieth-Century Artistic Revolutions. www.insight-media.com (DVD, color, 32 minutes). This still-image video provides a concise, visually appealing introduction to important philosophic, artistic, and musical trends of the early twentieth century. Part 1 covers turn-of-the-century Paris and features the art-work of Matisse, Picasso, and Braque and music by Satie. Part 2 covers expressionism, with artwork by Kandinsky and Klee and music by Schoenberg, Berg, and Webern. Try this video if you use Lecture-Demonstration Idea 1 above.

❧ Software

Art and Music: Impressionism. Zane Publishing (CD-ROM—Windows or Macintosh). This inexpensive volume draws parallels between impressionist painters such as Monet and early twentieth-century music of Debussy, Ravel, Griffes, and Stravinsky. Available from www.cdaccess.com.

Art and Music: The Twentieth Century. Zane Publishing (CD-ROM—Windows or Macintosh). This inexpensive volume draws parallels between early twentieth-century artistic styles and the music of Stravinsky, Schoenberg, Berg, and Webern. Available from www.cdaccess.com.

The History of Music. www.mccormicksnet.com (CD-ROM—Windows or Macintosh). CD-ROM version of the video above. The section on the early twentieth century covers new approaches to tonality in the music of Debussy, Schoenberg, Stravinsky, and Bartók.

History Through Art: Pre-modern Era. Zane Publishing (CD-ROM—Windows or Macintosh). The turn-of-the-century volume of this inexpensive CD-ROM series contains several hundred full-screen images, including artworks by Monet, Renoir, Van Gogh, Cézanne, and others. Includes sound clips by Debussy, Ravel, Mahler, Schoenberg, and Stravinsky. Quality of screen images is variable, but it's hard to argue with the price. Try this CD-ROM if you use Lecture-Demonstration Idea 1 above. Available from www.cdaccess.com.

CHAPTER 20

The Twentieth Century: Early Modernism

Chapter Outline

Boldface indicates works in the recording set.

Important Terms

impressionism	*Sprechstimme*	inverted
nocturne	passacaglia	Second Viennese School
ballet	serialism	ragtime
fauve	twelve-tone system	"master rhythm"
ostinato	twelve-tone row	quotation
Neoclassicism	twelve-tone series	hymn
expressionism	transposed	
"emancipation of dissonance"	backwards (retrograde)	

Teaching Objectives

❧ Overall Objectives

This chapter will help students acquire familiarity with:

1. Musical features of important early twentieth-century styles, especially impressionism, expressionism, the Second Viennese School, and American modernism.

2. The influence on music of other art forms, such as ballet, theater, and the visual arts.

3. Features of twentieth-century American art music as they reflected and influenced European music before World War I.

4. The lives and music of Claude Debussy, Igor Stravinsky, Arnold Schoenberg, Alban Berg, and Charles Ives.

❧ Listening Objectives

After completing this chapter, students should be able to:

1. Hear and identify typical uses of the elements of music in early twentieth-century modernist styles.

2. Identify and follow important twentieth-century genres, especially program music, ballet, song cycle, and opera.

3. Hear and identify features of important styles in early twentieth-century art music, especially impressionism, expressionism, and American modernism.

Lecture Suggestions

We saw the devastating impact of European colonialism on the New World in Global Perspectives 2 from Chapter 6. As with all things, however, some good came of this often shameless (remember the "scramble for Africa") imperialism. It hastened a "meeting of cultures" that had a profound and ultimately beneficial impact on Western culture. Through events like the Paris Exposition of 1889, the first of several such expositions to occur in Paris over the next twenty years, many Europeans became acquainted with distant cultures for the first time. Composers came to know the music of Indonesian gamelan orchestras, painters came to know African tribal art, and they all began to incorporate these influences into their work.

As a result, the period from 1895 to 1913 became one of the most interesting and varied in the entire history of Western music. Modernist composers grappled with a great dilemma and challenge: to create a "new" music relevant to the spirit and technological growth of the new century. Although the music created by each of the modernist composers was very different, composers from Paris to Vienna to Budapest to Danbury, Connecticut, agreed on one thing: The traditional tonal system had little place in the melody, harmony, and rhythm of the new century's music. In their search for a new language, they began to look to cultures outside the mainstream for inspiration. Paradoxically, the Romantic cult of individual expression became even more important during the twentieth century as composers cultivated the ideal of originality not only in the avoidance of a uniform period style but also in the avoidance of stylistic repetition in their own music. A look at the expressionist composers of the Second Viennese School reveals that even when composers shared similar artistic goals, they could still produce strikingly different music. This chapter explores several original styles. Each example, in its own way, reflects a meeting of cultures that infuses new life into the European classical tradition. Debussy's music shows the influence of the Far East, Stravinsky brings in ancient Russian folk tunes, Schoenberg borrows from the more popular style of the cabaret, and Ives weaves the whole spectrum of cultivated and vernacular American styles into his crazy quilt. The international style of the Classical era, weakened by the emphasis on individualism in the nineteenth century, was now a thing of the past.

♩ Debussy and Impressionism

> The century of airplanes has a right to its own music. As there are no precedents,
> I must create anew.
> —Claude Debussy

Claude Debussy was a mature thirty-eight years old when the twentieth century began. His traditional training at the Paris Conservatory was steeped in the music of the Classical and Romantic periods. Nevertheless, Debussy was one of the most stunningly original composers in the history of music. Though he was a child of Romanticism, his compositional voice belonged to the twentieth century.

Debussy represented a radical departure from nineteenth-century tonal music. His music is frequently associated with the French artistic movement called impressionism. Impressionist painters were primarily concerned with the effects of light, color, and atmosphere. Water and watery reflections were favorite subjects; they permitted painters to focus on the effect of light and movement, slight differences of shade, and subtle changes of color.

Impressionist painters were not concerned with "significant" subject matter; they drew their subject matter from everyday scenes. In fact, the true "subject" of an impressionist painting is not the object or person depicted but the play of light, color, and shade on and around the object. Impressionist images of people and things seem to shimmer, lacking the hard edges characteristic of artistic styles that preceded them. The most noticeably "impressionistic" qualities of Debussy's music parallel the painting style: a lack of strong articulation and a reliance on tone color to create musical movement. Like impressionist painting, Debussy's music favors content over form and tone color over narrative. Debussy was further influenced by the French language, with its long vowels, highly developed timbral character, and lack of hard accentuation.

DEBUSSY Three Nocturnes, *Clouds*

Use the following exercises to demonstrate musical characteristics of Debussy's style and of *Clouds*.

Timbre

Debussy's most enduring contribution to twentieth-century music was his use of timbre. He elevated tone color to a position equal to that of melody, harmony, and rhythm. Play track 15, 0:00–0:34, for the class.

This opening section presents the main thematic material of the piece. Ask the class to determine what exactly the theme consists of: a tune? a chord progression? something else? The movement opens with gently undulating clarinets and bassoons, followed by a chromatic English horn motive, and then a quiet drum roll accompanied by icy-sounding strings. There is no distinctive melody in this passage. Neither is there a sense of harmonic progression; the harmonic material is atmospheric and vague in the extreme. What then is thematic about this music? What makes it special, even remarkable?

Tone color. The colors of the woodwinds' undulating "cloud theme," the chromatic English horn motive, and the icy strings with drum roll are the main timbral elements that together constitute the "theme" of this movement. Indeed, the composition as a whole is a progression of rich coloristic effects, with ideas linked via timbre rather than through melodic development or harmonic function (compare the R. van Gulik quotation that concludes Further Listening Examples materials on the *qin* in Chapter 18 of this manual, p. 468).

It is interesting to note that although Debussy's scores call for a large Romantic orchestra, he avoided the excesses of his predecessors by using carefully chosen combinations of only a few (or even solo) instruments at a time to achieve specific coloristic effects (for example, solo English horn at track 16, 0:33; or solo flute and harp at track 19).

Melody

The same excerpt can be used here. Ask the class if they noticed any traditional melodies, any harmonic progressions, any cadences, or a tonal center. The answer to this question is no. Beneath the lovely surface of this music are some extremely original compositional devices—devices that replace traditional approaches to melody and harmony.

Debussy rarely wrote long, traditional-sounding melodies. He favored short motives, which afforded a much greater degree of compositional freedom. Debussy abhorred musical excess; nowhere is this more evident than in his approach to melody. Indeed, his use of short, compact motives was a reaction against the long, overblown melodies of late Romantic composers. Debussy also preferred nontraditional scales as sources for his melodic material, frequently drawing on exotic modes such as the whole-tone, pentatonic, and octatonic scales as well as the ancient church modes.

The melodic content of *Clouds* is typical of Debussy's mature works. It exhibits the use of fragmentary, motivic melodic material and several exotic scales, including whole tone (the beginning of the first **b** section), pentatonic (the **B** tune), and octatonic scales (the English horn motive in the **A** sections). If you did not use them in Chapter 19, play these excerpts from *Clouds* now.

Whole tone   (track 17, 0:00–0:13)—with chromatic passing tones!

Pentatonic   (track 19, 0:00–0:19)

Octatonic   (track 17, 0:39–1:06)

Harmony

Debussy once said that "one must drown the sense of tonality." Although tonal centers appear in most of Debussy's music, they are not determined through functional harmony (that is, through the use of tonic and dominant chords). Rather, these tonal centers are created by repeating or insisting on a particular note. In the absence of traditional scales, twentieth-century composers used alternative techniques to establish tonality and create chord progressions. Three important techniques were pedal tones, ostinato, and parallelism.

Pedal tone—a single pitch, sustained or repeated underneath (occasionally above) the music. Debussy frequently used pedal tones as harmonic under-pinnings, avoiding the need for traditional chord progressions and estab-lishing a tonal center by sheer repetition. *Clouds* (track 19, 0:00–0:20) provides an example.

Ostinato—a motive or brief melody repeated over and over. We heard os-tinatos in the music of West Africa (Chapter 7). The ground-bass themes of Vivaldi's Concerto in G (second movement) or Purcell's *Dido and Aeneas* ("When I am laid in earth") are also ostinatos, as are boogie-woogie bass lines. Along with pedal tones, Debussy frequently used ostinatos to establish the tonal center and the prevailing harmony. *Clouds* (track 17, 0:36–1:06) provides an example.

Parallelism—Often Debussy used long successions of similar chords to create a tonal haze. This technique is called parallelism. These chord streams create long splashes of harmonic color that lack the sense of tension and resolution typical of functional harmony, yet they provide a harmonic motion nonethe-less. *Clouds* (track 16, 0:00–0:15 and 1:02–1:21) provides examples.

Before you play *Clouds* in its entirety, point out the following elements:

1. The movement is impressionistic in the truest sense, consisting of carefully balanced, fleeting, luminescent tone colors. The music lacks sharp articulation and is characterized by blurred edges. The listener has no problem conjuring up the image of nocturnal clouds, which are in themselves imprecise and ephemeral in character. The opening, undulating cloud theme seems neither a tune nor a series of functional chords; it makes no strong thematic declaration, nor does it seem to lead anywhere in particular. The cloud theme is atmospheric and vague, a musical impression of the clouds it represents.

2. Form results from the periodic return of the undulating cloud theme and the English horn motive; naturally, these elements are in a continual state of flux, as one would expect of gently moving clouds. That form is given shape and movement through judicious contrasts of color and scale type.

3. Section **B** features a pentatonic tune that contrasts with the chromaticism of the undulating cloud theme and the English horn motive. Point out De-bussy's extraordinary scoring of section **B**. The solo flute and harp, which first play the melody, seem to become a single instrument—a flute with a sharp, pointed attack.

4. The movement does not end so much as it just fades away, as befits clouds scudding across a darkened sky.

Play the movement. Display Listening Chart 20 (or refer students to text-book page 335) and point out each section as it goes by.

Conclusions to Draw about Debussy

Debussy was the first great twentieth-century modernist composer. Unlike the typically polyphonic, narrative German music of the late nineteenth century, Debussy's music is coloristic and pictorial. Debussy went beyond traditional melody and functional harmony, creating a wholly original approach to musical composition. In place of traditional melody, he used motives and melodies based on exotic pitch collections. In place of traditional tonality and func-tional harmony, he used pedal tones, ostinato, and parallelism. As a result, his music often has a static quality that forces us to listen to individual sounds and colors "in the moment." His solution to the compositional challenge of the new century was to elevate tone color to the same level as melody, harmony, and form.

ʔ Stravinsky: The Primacy of Rhythm

Stravinsky's long creative career spanned nearly sixty years. His first master-work, *The Firebird,* was written in 1910; his last, *Requiem Canticles,* in 1966. Although he passed through a number of distinct style periods during his ca-reer, his music was always uniquely "Stravinskyan."

In 1902, at the age of twenty, Stravinsky began a relationship with his mentor, the great Russian nationalist composer Nicolai Rimsky-Korsakov (whose *Russian Easter* Overture was included under Further Listening Examples in Chapter 18 of this manual). Rimsky-Korsakov was a member of the *kuchka*—the group of five Romantic composers dedicated to making Russian music "Russian" (for more information on the *kuchka* see notes on Musorgsky's *Pictures at an Exhibition* in Chapter 18 of this manual). Many of Stravinsky's youthful works are typical Russian Romantic compositions that demonstrate the brilliant orchestral style of his mentor. The rhythmically asymmetrical character of Russian music made a lasting impression on Stravinsky and inspired his most enduring contribution to twentieth-century music: his manipulation of rhythm.

During the first decade of the twentieth century, Paris was swept by a fervor for "primitive" art, particularly African tribal art. It is vital to point out that there is nothing primitive about this art. African tribal sculpture is character-ized by sophisticated, stylized depictions with tremendous power and energy. Many young artists were attracted to the elemental power of this art, using its techniques to escape the overrefinement of European art. In Paris, a group of artists called the fauves (or "wild beasts") celebrated "primitive" images to defy the decadence they perceived in Western art. Ask the class to study Picasso's painting of five prostitutes, *Les demoiselles d'Avignon* (see textbook page 328). After he completed the painting, Picasso went back and painted African masks over the faces of two of the women. The masklike faces create a powerful, striking effect; the painting hums with primal, exotic energy.

Sergei Diaghilev, *impresario extraordinaire,* was well aware of popular artistic currents in Paris. He made his fame and fortune by keeping his Ballets Russes on the cutting edge of Parisian (and Western) culture; his motto was "Astonish me!" Diaghilev decided that for the 1912–1913 season, a ballet steeped in primitive, pagan energy would capture the public's fancy. He hired Igor Stravinsky to compose music for *The Rite of Spring,* subtitled "Scenes from Pagan Russia." The ballet is a series of pre-Christian Russian fertility rites that culminate in a human sacrifice (a chosen maiden dances herself to death, "du-bious anthropology but effective theater"—*Listen 3*).

STRAVINSKY *The Rite of Spring*

The Rite of Spring belongs to Stravinsky's first style period, 1906 to 1920, often called his "Russian" period. Even though Stravinsky's later music moved away from the distinctly Russian-flavored music of this first period, the com-positional techniques and priorities he established during these years remained present throughout his career.

Several of Stravinsky's early scores also showed the influence of Debussy's style. In turn, Debussy, already a great admirer of Musorgsky, was mightily impressed with the young Russian composer's work; Debussy called Stravinsky's

Petrushka "orchestrally perfect." Even Stravinsky's more radical *Rite of Spring* contains echoes of Debussy's timbral sensitivity and shifting colors. Play the first part of the introduction for the class (track 21, 0:00–1:02), a passage that inhabits the same world of color and texture as the opening of Debussy's *Clouds,* though at a higher level of dissonance. Note especially the color and asymmetry of the high bassoon "fanfare" at the beginning. Modern bassoonists possess the proficiency to handle it smoothly, but in 1913 a bassoonist trying to play these "unheard-of" high notes would have sounded strained and awkward—precisely the "primitive" effect Stravinsky wanted.

Use the following exercises to introduce students to the style features of Stravinsky's *The Rite of Spring,* especially his use of rhythm, melody and harmony, and texture.

Rhythm

Stravinsky's enduring contribution to twentieth-century music was his manipulation of rhythm. Play this excerpt for the class and ask students to decide which element is most significant.

"Dance of the Adolescents" (track 23, 0:00–track 24, 0:27)

1. Rhythm, rhythm, and more rhythm! The sense of musical motion, tension, and excitement in this music is almost entirely created by the driving, irregular rhythm. The brutal, elemental E-flat^7/F-flat major chord that begins this dance could be altered somewhat (but why?), yet the effect of the passage would be much the same as long as the rhythms were unchanged.

2. The listener is acutely aware of the irregular accentuation created by the pounding chord. Given such a complex rhythmic pattern, it is difficult to believe that Stravinsky uses duple meter throughout.

3. The syncopated E-flat^7/F-flat major chord gives this music a violent, elemental character. Ask the class if they were aware of any traditional melody or harmonies while they listened to this music. No indeed! It is rhythm—driving, asymmetrical, and unpredictable—that moves this music forward.

Play another excerpt for the class:

"The Game of Abduction" (track 25)

1. The whirlwind of rhythms is always asymmetric.

2. As in the "Dance of the Adolescents," the musical momentum is created essentially through rhythmic manipulation.

3. Point out in particular the incredible ending passage (track 25, 0:54–1:15) that articulates the following swirl of irregular accents:

3 + 10 + 3 + 9 + 11 + 2 + 6 + 6 + 6 + 6 + 2 + 6 + 2 + 2 + 6 + 6 + 2 + 2 + 6 + 6 + 6 + 4 + 2

(Count this pattern along with the music to demonstrate it for the class. Take a deep breath!)

Melody and Harmony

Play the following excerpt and ask the class to describe Stravinsky's use of melody and harmony.

"Dance of the Adolescents" (tracks 23–24)

1. Stravinsky uses brief, irregular motives—folk-song fragments—to create an angular, jagged, asymmetrical melodic surface.

2. Like Debussy, Stravinsky relies heavily on pedal tones and ostinatos to create harmonic underpinnings.

Back up a bit so that students can hear one of these ostinati more clearly. Play this excerpt.

"Omens of Spring," "Dance of the Adolescents" (track 22, 0:36–track 24, 0:27)

Point out the D flat–B flat–E flat–B flat ostinato that first appears in the "Omens of Spring" and continues to surface whenever the primal E-flat⁷/F-flat major chord stops in the "Dance of the Adolescents." Sing or play the ostinato along with the recording (over and over again) to highlight it for the students. Whatever sense of tonality Stravinsky establishes in the listener's ear is the result of ostinato repetition—insistence on a single pitch—rather than functional harmony.

Texture

Stravinsky builds his musical textures by stacking different ideas on top of each other, a procedure called layering. Play the following example and ask the class to observe how Stravinsky builds to a climax at the end.

"Dance of the Adolescents" (track 24, 0:40–2:23)

1. The music, loud to start with, becomes louder as more and more instruments join in.

2. Point out how Stravinsky achieves a sense of climax by layering—that is, by stacking various ostinatos, motives, and rhythms one atop the other. He starts with one or two ideas and gradually adds more and more until the confusion is almost overwhelming. His music doesn't "go" anywhere during climactic moments; there are just more elements present at the same time.

3. Stravinsky uses layering in place of any sort of development. He does not change his melodic ideas much, but he constantly alters the context in which he repeats them. The layered elements—asymmetric melodic and rhythmic materials of different lengths—rarely line up the same way twice. This layering creates a tremendous rhythmic complexity.

When you are ready to play the entire Part I *Listen* selection, by all means take advantage of the video footage on the *Listen* DVD. This excellent performance offers a wonderful opportunity for students to *see* the instruments that create Stravinsky's unique sound world. Verbally call attention to each section as it goes by—be prepared to shout!

Conclusions to Draw about Stravinsky

Stravinsky started his compositional career as a Romantic Russian nationalist composer. Though his musical style quickly departed from the clichés of nineteenth-century Russian Romanticism, the asymmetrical, irregular rhythms of Russian folk music had a lasting influence on his music.

Stravinsky's pre–World War I music was deeply influenced by Debussy, particularly in its use of ostinato, pedal tones, and timbral effects. However, Stravinsky's distinctive use of rhythm sets his music apart from that of his contemporaries. Stravinsky's new approach to rhythm constitutes his greatest contribution to twentieth-century music.

❡ Expressionism

Essentially self-taught as a composer, Schoenberg believed that his atonal music was the logical "next step" in the German musical tradition, which had been a significant force in European music since the early Baroque. However, many of Schoenberg's contemporaries did not hear his music that way. As early as 1900, several of his songs provoked a nasty scene at a concert, and in Schoenberg's own words, "since that day the scandal has never ceased."

Toward the end of the nineteenth century, German music had become increasingly complex. Composers such as Wagner and Mahler, in their desire to express emotion more and more intensely, pushed tonality to its very limits. Wagner used chromaticism to avoid a sense of tonality in the prelude to *Tristan and Isolde* to create the proper emotional mood for the opera. In his Symphony No. 9, Gustav Mahler wrote an extraordinary passage that depicts his diseased heart having a massive coronary. In both examples, the composers felt that the major and minor chords of traditional tonality could not create the appropriate mood. Tonality became weaker and weaker as motivic manipulation, development, and transformation increasingly dominated German Romantic music (in the name of greater thematic unity and expressivity).

Schoenberg's vision led him to free German Romanticism completely from the bonds of tonality, so as to explore further possibilities in motivic development and emotional expression. By the mid-1920s, he had created an entirely new musical system based on motivic development and transformation—the twelve-tone method. This new context for pitch relationships was Schoenberg's most enduring contribution to Western music.

Schoenberg found many parallels between his work as a composer and the work of painters in the German expressionist movement. By the first decade of the twentieth century, German artists had taken Romantic emotionalism to its furthest reach, exploring and portraying extreme emotional states, including hysteria, nightmares, and even insanity. Schoenberg, a gifted amateur painter, associated with expressionist painters of the "Blue Rider" group. He adopted their principles and color theories in much of his music, becoming the leading composer of the expressionist movement. In his pre–World War I music, we hear the dark, mysterious, sometimes nightmarish atmosphere that was the essence of expressionist art.

SCHOENBERG *Pierrot lunaire*

Pierrot lunaire is Schoenberg's Opus 21; given the composer's superstition about numbers, it is no coincidence that there are twenty-one songs in the piece, divided into three groups of seven songs each. Approach these songs via their texts and expressionist style. Before you begin, make sure the students have read the textbook's discussion of this song cycle (textbook pages 340–42).

Use the following exercises to introduce features of Schoenberg's style. Play the example below for the class. The students' first exposure to *Pierrot lunaire* will typically provoke strong reactions. Be specific about what you want students to listen for in this music.

No. 18: "The Moonfleck" (voice, piano, piccolo, clarinet, violin, cello)

Use this song to introduce important stylistic features of Schoenberg's expressionist song cycle. Play "The Moonfleck." Ask students to determine the mood of the music and describe Schoenberg's use of melody, harmony, and tonality. In the discussion that follows, draw out the following points:

1. The mood can be described as "weird," "bizarre," or "totally strange." The half-sung and half-spoken vocal part (*Sprechstimme*) lends a particularly eerie sound to this music. These settings, written as melodramas for a German actress, belong to the literary cabaret tradition. If you have time, note the connections between *Sprechstimme* and German cabaret style (see Lecture-Demonstration Idea 3 below). This song's bizarre humor inhabits a strange emotional world far removed from that of nineteenth-century Romantic music.

2. There is no sense of traditional melody, functional harmony, or tonic. Remind the class that in the music of Debussy and Stravinsky, there were long passages that established tone centers through pedal tones or ostinatos. No tonal center can be detected in Schoenberg's "Moonfleck," however. The music is freely atonal—that is, it ranges freely across the chromatic spectrum without emphasizing any single pitch.

3. The song is filled with imitative devices. The piano part is a three-voice fugue with expositions at mm. 1, 8, and 15. The woodwinds and strings present a double retrograde canon; the second half of the song is exactly the same as the first half—but backward (m. 10 is the midpoint; its last two beats are a retrograde of the first two). Students will not hear all of these contrapuntal devices, but they must understand that Schoenberg was a superb craftsman. The compositional procedures he used in the twenty-one songs of *Pierrot lunaire* are varied and highly original. His complete command of musical forms and technique enabled him to create striking and original musical textures.

Ask students to open to textbook page 342. Read "The Moonfleck" aloud as they follow along. Point out elements that characterize the entire poetic cycle.

1. Like Debussy's *Clouds,* this is night music. The twenty-one poems that make up *Pierrot lunaire* (*lunaire* = "lunar" = "of the moon") are full of night-time images. In "The Moonfleck," we find *moonlight, black, evening,* and *till dawn comes up.* Note that Schoenberg's night is a darker, stranger, and more mysterious place than Debussy's.

2. These poems contain images that range from playful to disturbing to malevolent, much like "Twilight Zone" or Terry Gilliam's bizarre cartoon images for Monty Python. Lighter in mood, "The Moonfleck" depicts a spot of moonlight that can't be rubbed off. But "Night" (No. 8) portrays a dark terror descending on humanity, and "Beheading" (No. 13) paints images of decapitation.

3. Each poem employs the same thirteen-line structure, the *rondeau* form that was so popular in the late Middle Ages. The first two lines repeat as the last two lines of the second quatrain (lines 7 and 8), and the first line alone reappears at the very end (line 13). This poetic structure is comparable to (used in place of?) the tonal structure that Schoenberg eschews.

No. 8: "Night" (voice, piano, bass clarinet, cello)

Expressionist art exaggerates and distorts outer reality—its images, colors, and perspective—to plumb the depths of inner reality, especially the dark, disturbing corners of the human psyche. With its bizarre, ironic humor, "The Moonfleck" doesn't quite fit this understanding of expressionism, in spite of its musical language. "Night," on the other hand, fits perfectly. This grim, nightmarish song provides an excellent example of the dark, disturbing side of Schoenberg's expressionistic language. Have the class open to textbook page 341 and read this poem to them. Ask students to think of the somber, shadowy darkness described by the poem as the dark depths of the human psyche. How can such a mood of psychological darkness and terror be depicted? With major and minor modes? With tonic and dominant chords? Of course not—extremes in emotional content call for extreme means of depiction!

Play this song for the class. Ask the students to note how perfectly the music creates the dark, nightmarish mood suggested by the text.

After listening, point out that this song's subtitle is "Passacaglia." In fact, Schoenberg uses this Baroque variation form as the structural basis for this song. Constant repetition and imitation of a short motive at various speeds pervade the texture of the entire song.

Of course, Schoenberg always uses such a device for expressive purposes, never as an end in itself. His passacaglia echoes the obsessive quality found in Stravinsky's ostinato repetition (*The Rite of Spring*) or Purcell's ground bass structure (*Dido and Aeneas*). As motive statements follow or pile on top of each other in ever-quicker rhythms, the music's emotional impact becomes more and more intense. Through these means, Schoenberg creates an ominous, oppressive mood that fits the poem perfectly.

Conclusions to Draw about Schoenberg

Schoenberg was a child of German Romanticism. In his pre–World War I compositions, he continued the Romantic tradition of depicting emotions by plumbing ever deeper into the human psyche. Schoenberg's works of this period are expressionistic; they depict dark, fantastic, sometimes nightmarish glimpses into the human mind and soul.

Schoenberg dispensed entirely with functional harmony, traditional melody, and tonality in his search for new expressive means. Motivic development and transformation were the essential compositional processes used by Schoenberg in his music. The expansion of pitch relationships—the elevation of motivic development and transformation above and beyond the restraints of tonality—constitutes Schoenberg's great contribution to twentieth-century music.

Schoenberg and Serialism

After spending several editions in Chapter 19, the material on serialism has moved to Chapter 20. You can cover this topic now, alongside atonal, expressionist examples by Schoenberg and Berg. Since the twelve-tone system was not invented until the early 1920s, you can also save it and present it with other music from the period between the two world wars (Chapter 21).

Twelve-tone music can prove a trying experience for many listeners (even for musicians!). The best thing you can do is help students understand why composers would choose to write such music. For some students, it helps to know that many composers of horror-film scores (beginning with Bernard Herrmann) have used serial techniques; for others, it helps to hear Schoenberg's thoughts on the matter (see Class Discussion Idea 2 in Chapter 19); and for still others, seeing the similarities between twelve-tone techniques and time-honored fugal procedures helps them understand that this music is not random after all. Surprisingly, some students may have heard of the twelve-tone system, and there is a natural curiosity about it. This can also work in your favor.

Start with some historical background. Developed in the early 1920s, serialism was one of the most radical new musical languages of the twentieth century. As we saw in the sonata form examples of Chapters 12 through 14, tonality was perhaps the most significant structural element. Atonal composers initially struggled to find techniques that could provide the same degree of coherence and architecture. The twelve-tone system provided precisely the meaningful context they sought, and it permitted the construction of coherent large-scale forms in an atonal idiom. Though serialism never achieved wide popularity (or understanding), many people have at least heard of it—and anyone who loves horror movies has probably heard several film scores composed using twelve-tone techniques. Take time to clarify the information in "Schoenberg and Serialism" on textbook pages 346–47.

1. *What is a row?* A row consists of all twelve pitches of the chromatic scale put into a particular order. Each pitch is used once and only once; thus, the row is twelve notes long.

2. *How is a row constructed?* Like a scale, the row provides a collection of pitches available for composition; unlike a scale, the notes of the row must be used in a specific order. Composers who construct a twelve-tone row start by juggling the twelve pitches of the chromatic scale (like tiles in a Scrabble game) until they find the order that works best for the piece they envision.

3. Once the order of the row is set, the row can be modified using the prescribed techniques ever-so-briefly described on textbook page 346. These techniques include:

> *inversion*—the basic series played upside down, like the mountain range reflected in the alpine lake
>
> *retrograde*—the basic series played backward, from end to beginning
>
> *retrograde inversion*—the inverted series played backward
>
> *transposition*—the series, its inversion, its retrograde, or its retrograde inversion transposed to start on any pitch

Demonstrate these modifications. It can be difficult for students if you start with a complete row. Instead, start with a phrase from a familiar melody. Pick one with a distinctive contour—the first phrases of "Twinkle, Twinkle, Little Star" or "Frère Jacques" work well. Play a basic phrase several times. Once students are familiar with it, play modified versions of the phrase: inverted, retrograde, retrograde inversion, and transposition. After several examples, you can even quiz the class—play a modification and ask them which technique they hear. (You can give the students a hint by repeating the original version.) Once they catch on, try the sample row in the textbook (page 346) or suggestions for the main theme of Schoenberg's Concerto for Piano and Orchestra in Further Listening Examples below.

4. *How does a composer use a row to compose a piece?* The pitches of the row must be used in order. The composer can use a single row statement to construct melody, chords, or both melody and chords. Use a phrase from Schoenberg's Concerto for Piano and Orchestra to demonstrate several possibilities at the keyboard. Refer students to the example on textbook page 346 and play the series for the class as if each note were a half note. To demonstrate melodic use of the row, use Schoenberg's rhythms and play the first phrase of the concerto's main theme in tempo.

1 2 3 4 5 6 7 8 9 10 11 12

Next, use the row to generate chords. Divide Schoenberg's basic series into four three-note chords (pitches **1-2-3**, **4-5-6**, **7-8-9**, and **10-11-12**) and play them as a chord progression. Write this diagram on the board before you play:

1	4	7	10
2	5	8	11
3	6	9	12

Finally, use the row to generate both melody and chords. Play pitches **1-2-3** and **7-8-9** as melody. Play pitches **4-5-6** and **10-11-12** as chords to support pitches **1-2-3** and **7-8-9**, respectively. Write this diagram on the board before you play:

```
1          2          3            7          8          9
4 ——————————————        10———————————————
5 ——————————————        11———————————————
6 ——————————————        12———————————————
```

Once the composer states all twelve pitches of the row, she or he moves to another statement of the row (or any desired modification of the row). A twelve-tone composition is thus a string of statements of the twelve-tone series.

5. *Why is the order important?* Using the pitches in order limits the number of possible melodic patterns and chordal combinations. These limitations create a consistent context that permits meaningful melodic and harmonic relationships and avoids random construction. Twelve-tone composers must create their own context in each new piece; they cannot fall back on the preexisting context created by traditional tonal harmony and melodic development. As the motives and chords of a twelve-tone work become more familiar, it is easier for the listener to make sense of the music. Since relationships among adjacent pitches in the row determine the context for the entire piece, composers typically spend a great deal of time constructing a row that creates precisely the melodic figures and chords they have in mind.

6. Serial composers after World War II applied serial techniques not only to pitch but also to rhythm, dynamics, articulation, and so on.

The Second Viennese School

Schoenberg first experimented with atonality in 1907–1908 and by 1909 was composing completely atonal music. His most famous students, Alban Berg and Anton Webern, worked closely with him in developing an expressionistic, atonal language. Webern's music was characterized by extreme brevity, austerity, and long silences (see the listening example in Chapter 22, textbook page 374). Berg, on the other hand, was a completely expressionistic composer who maintained subtle ties to tonality. The three of them came to be known as the Second Viennese School.

Shortly after Arnold Schoenberg formulated his motivic-developmental procedures into the compositional technique known as the twelve-tone system, Berg and Webern both adopted this method. Some of the most impressive twelve-tone music composed between the wars was written by Berg and Webern. Webern's precise, distillate music was to have an incredible influence on the post–World War II generation of composers. Berg joined the twelve-tone system to a hyper-Romantic mode of expression; his Violin Concerto (1935) provides an excellent example of an accessible, moving twelve-tone composition.

BERG *Wozzeck*

Berg's opera *Wozzeck* was written while Schoenberg was still developing his twelve-tone method; thus, the opera does not use twelve-tone techniques but employs the freely atonal expressionistic language Berg had pioneered before World War I. For many, *Wozzeck* is the ultimate expressionistic composition. Wozzeck is a pathetic, Kafkaesque character. A soldier abused by his superiors and cuckolded by his common-law wife, he finally goes mad, murders his wife, and kills himself. Berg's expressionistic music not only allows the listener to follow the action of the opera but draws us into Wozzeck's tormented mind.

Present this opera just as you presented Romantic operas in Chapter 17. Berg himself supplied the following chart, which lays out this work's fascinating structure. If you emphasize opera in your course, you can share this chart with your students and supplement your classroom presentation with scenes of your choice, perhaps all of Act III.

ACT I

Wozzeck and his surroundings		*Five Character Pieces*
Wozzeck and the Captain	Scene i	Suite
Wozzeck and Andres	Scene ii	Rhapsody
Marie and Wozzeck	Scene iii	Military March and Lullaby
Wozzeck and the Doctor	Scene iv	Passacaglia
Marie and the Drum major	Scene v	*Andante affettuoso (quasi Rondo)*

ACT II

Dramatic development		*Symphony in Five Movements*
Marie and child, later Wozzeck	Scene i	Sonata form
Captain and Doctor, later Wozzeck	Scene ii	Fantasy and Fugue
Marie and Wozzeck	Scene iii	*Largo*
Beer-garden	Scene iv	Scherzo
Sleeping quarters (Barracks)	Scene v	*Rondo con introduzione*

ACT III

Catastrophe and Epilogue		*Six Inventions*
Marie and child	Scene i	Invention on a theme
Marie and Wozzeck	Scene ii	Invention on one note
Inn	Scene iii	Invention on a rhythm
Wozzeck's death	Scene iv	Invention on a chord of six notes
	Orchestral Interlude	Invention on a key
Children at play	Scene v	Invention on an eighth-note figure

Begin with a synopsis of the plot:

Act I introduces Wozzeck in interaction with the characters who inhabit his miserable daily life. We see Wozzeck as servant to a pompous, moralizing, judgmental captain; overstressed, paranoid colleague of another soldier in hard, manual labor; common-law husband and father whose work permits little time with his family; and paid participant in the odd experiments of a doctor who cares more for his fame than his patients. Wozzeck's wife, Marie, has an eye for handsome soldiers, and in the final scene she invites into the house a drum major whose advances she can no longer resist.

In Act II Wozzeck slowly learns of Marie's infidelity. He wonders at her secrecy over having "found" a pair of earrings, and when he meets the captain and the doctor in the street, they taunt him with coarse innuendo—Marie's affair is common knowledge to everyone but Wozzeck. When Wozzeck confronts Marie and threatens to strike her, she responds, "Better a knife in my breast than a hand on me." The image of blood is reinforced throughout the rest of the act. Wozzeck goes to a beer-garden, where he finds Marie dancing with the drum major. In the midst of Wozzeck's jealous rage, a fool tells him in passing that it "reeks of blood." Wozzeck goes back to the barracks, where he tries to sleep, but cannot. The drum major stumbles in drunk. He boasts of his conquest and insists that Wozzeck go drinking with him. They fight and Wozzeck is knocked down bleeding, in his own cryptic words, "One after the other!"

Act III opens with Marie reading her Bible and praying for forgiveness. Later that night, Wozzeck takes Marie to a pond where he slits her throat. In scene iii Wozzeck goes to a tavern to drink, pick up a woman, and start a fight. At the height of his abusive behavior, the woman notices blood on his hand. As customers crowd around, Wozzeck flees the room. In scene iv he returns to the pond to find and hide the murder weapon. As he watches the knife sink into the water, Wozzeck is seized with the conviction that he (and the whole world) is covered in blood. He wanders into the pond to throw the knife further from shore, but as he distractedly tries to wash off the blood, he drowns. The captain and the doctor, walking nearby, hear the sounds of the drowning but rush off to avoid any unpleasantness. In the poignant final scene, children are playing near Marie's house. When they hear the news that Marie's body has been found, they rush off to see what they can see. Marie and Wozzeck's child, however, is too young to understand what has happened. As the curtain closes, he continues to play his game alone—then follow the others.

Next, refer students to the libretto for Act III, scenes iii and iv (textbook pages 346–48). Assign students to take different roles. Four students will be needed to play Wozzeck, Margret, the captain, and the doctor; the rest of the class can be the apprentices. Have the "actors" do a dramatic reading of these scenes. Even without the music, this makes a disturbing story. Before you play the music, point out a few musical devices Berg uses to enhance the impact of these scenes. As Berg's chart indicates, each scene in Act III is an invention, a free structure based on a single musical idea. Scene iii is based on a rhythm, scene iv on a chord, and the subsequent interlude on a key.

Scene iii is an invention based on a rhythmic pattern (see textbook page 345). Take time to familiarize the class with this "master rhythm." Introduced by the timpani during the scene change and then by a ragtime piano at the beginning of the scene, the rhythm appears in virtually every measure. Most stunning is the passage where Margret notices blood on Wozzeck's hand, starting at m. 185 (track 31 or DVD track 5). Every vocal and instrumental line from here to the end of the scene uses and repeats the rhythmic pattern. As more and more customers come over to see the blood, the counterpoint between accumulating, overlapping statements of the rhythm builds to fever pitch. The rhythm is everywhere, accusing Wozzeck of his crime. Play the scene.

Scene iv is an invention on a six-note chord, B flat–D flat–E flat–E–F–G sharp. The chord is first stated—both simultaneously and in various figurations—at the beginning of the scene as Wozzeck searches for the knife. Take time to familiarize the class with the chord. When you play this scene, students can hear the chord more readily if you play the notes of the chord at the keyboard along with the recording. Note the incredible ascending parallel chords that accompany Wozzeck's drowning (track 32, 2:30–track 33, 0:34, or DVD track 6).

The interlude between scenes iv and v is an invention on the key of D minor. Unlike the previous inventions, this one is tonal. Although the music is highly chromatic, it inhabits the same sound world as Wagner's *Tristan and Isolde* and Mahler's late symphonies, especially Nos. 9 and 10. This is perhaps the only moment in the opera where Berg addresses the audience directly; here he reflects on the tragedy of Wozzeck's life and death. Interestingly, Berg chooses a key rich in associations. D minor has long been used to express serious or tragic emotions, as in Bach's Toccata and Fugue in D Minor, Mozart's *Don Giovanni* (the Don's fatal encounter with the statue), Beethoven's Symphony No. 9, Bruckner's Symphonies Nos. 0, 3, and 9, and Mahler's Symphonies No. 1 and 3. The music fades out about halfway through the interlude in the recorded set.

Berg's inventions, with their single-minded focus on one idea, masterfully reflect Wozzeck's obsessive thoughts and compulsive behaviors. After you have covered each scene individually, play straight through both scenes and the interlude.

Once again, you need go no further than the *Listen* DVD to find video footage for the *Listen* selections. Sadly, the much-revered Abbado *Wozzeck* DVD is out of print (see Video Recordings below for more information). Fortunately, the *Listen* clips were taken from the Frankfurt Opera disc that remains in print. The modernist staging will not suit every taste, but this is a very fine performance overall.

❡ Modernism in America: Ives

Charles Ives's incredibly original music represents the first truly great musical body of work produced by an American. Though most of his music was written between 1900 and 1920, the great bulk of it remained unperformed until the 1940s, 1950s, and beyond. As a result, Ives's influence was not truly felt until after World War II. With Ives, play the music first and let the students experience his often bewildering array of sounds and tunes. Save the Listening Chart and explanations for the discussion that follows.

IVES Second Orchestral Set, "The Rockstrewn Hills Join in the People's Outdoor Meeting"

Ask your students to jot down their impressions of this music by Ives; then play this work. In the discussion that follows, draw out the following.

1. The music is extremely eclectic, consisting of many different kinds of music: ragtime, revival hymns, and marches—all under one compositional roof (or tent meeting). These different musics somehow blend together to create a larger whole.

2. The musical multiplicity re-creates the confusion of a large, diverse, celebratory crowd of people, perhaps at a revival meeting.

3. The title further suggests the intrusion of nature (a favorite transcendentalist theme) into this celebration. This imagery reflects Ives's philosophy that all things are related to a deep, underlying reality and are therefore compatible with one another, no matter how incongruous they seem.

4. The music possesses tremendous rhythmic energy.

5. The climaxes are created with the same sort of layering observed in Stravinsky's *Rite of Spring*. Point out that Ives wrote this music in 1909, four years *before* the Stravinsky ballet.

6. The ending subsides into a quiet, reflective, mystic atmosphere. Ives loved such endings, and they almost seem to suggest an ever-present spiritual reality underlying the transitory confusion of his music.

A brief discussion of Ives's life and musical concerns can help at this point. Ives's father was a professional musician from whom Ives received a thorough and remarkably liberal music education. Ives was also a talented athlete who excelled in baseball. A few years after graduation from Yale, Ives chose to go into the insurance business, a business that he idealistically saw as a way of helping common people achieve economic security. Ives maintained two entirely different lives: by day he was a successful insurance agent, by night a reclusive composer, deeply committed to American folk music (understood in the broadest possible way) and his personal musical ideals. Ives's life as a composer was in many ways a microcosm of the struggle between art and economics, music and manhood, that characterized American music at that time. Ives was torn between the nineteenth-century American view of music—a hobby for women and a job only for "prissy" men—and his own desire to create and compose. Ives's dual life almost killed him. A series of heart attacks in the early 1920s seriously impaired his ability to work and compose, and Ives composed little new work after the 1920s. Reasonably well off, he used his money in a variety of ways to support new music, and he lived long enough to hear on the radio (by the 1950s he was too frail to travel) some of his orchestral works premiered by Leonard Bernstein and the New York Philharmonic.

Ives's music reflects his life struggle between music and manhood. Driven to compose, he nonetheless refused to write "pretty," "sissy" music or kowtow to foreign (European) musical styles. For Ives, dissonance was a masculine attribute, and he filled his music with uncompromisingly harsh sonorities. This was music for real men, not for wimps who wanted soothing background music. Ives himself, speaking in the third person, provided the following story—a wonderful statement of his attitudes and personality.

> At this concert he [Ives] sat quietly through the "boo" and jeers at his own music—but when that wonderful orchestral work "Men and Mountains" of Carl R[uggles] was played, a sound of disapproving hiss was heard near him. Ives jumped up and shouted: "You g–ddarn, sissy-eared mollycoddle—when you hear strong masculine music like this, stand up and use your ears like a man—and don't 'flibby' faint over backwards."[1]

Ives also relished the dissonances inherent in the multiplicity and diversity of American life and culture, and he captured this energy in his compositions. Ever the fiercely independent Yankee, Ives wrote a profoundly personal yet genuinely "American" music. His often collagelike canvas is filled with folk songs, hymns, and patriotic tunes. Sometimes he used this material structurally, as an intrinsic part of the composition; sometimes he used it to evoke a nostalgic sense of time and place. The moving text of one of Ives's many songs—"The Things Our Fathers Loved (and the greatest of these was Liberty)"—offers one explanation for the frequent quotations in his music.

> I think there must be a place in the soul
> all made of tunes, of tunes of long ago . . .

---

[1]Frank R. Rossiter, *Charles Ives and His America*. New York: Liveright, 1975, p. 225.

In the middle of the song, Ives's lyrics describe the types of tunes—organ music, gospel hymns, band music—and their locations, physically and temporally: Main Street, an aunt humming as she works around the house, the town square on the Fourth of July, or a lazy summer evening. After a brief exhortation to listen to all of these songs (all at once?), Ives ends with these words:

> I know not what are the words
> But they sing in my soul
> of the things our Fathers loved.

Eclectic, wild, filled with life energy, Ives's music rarely fails to evoke a response from the listener. Play the music one more time. Display Listening Chart 22 and point out each section as it goes by.

IVES *The Unanswered Question*

This well-known work provides another, more accessible example of Ives's music. See Appendix I for an Additional Listening Chart.

This chamber piece, subtitled "A Contemplation of a Serious Matter," represents Ives at his metaphysical, solemn best. The composition is scored for strings, trumpet, and winds. Ives's own program best describes the music (students can find this on textbook page 352).

> The strings play *ppp* throughout, with no change in tempo. They represent "The Silences of the Druids" who know, see, and hear nothing. The trumpet intones "The Unanswered Question of Existence" and states it in the same tone of voice each time. But the hunt for the "Invisible Answer" undertaken by the flutes [with clarinets and oboes ad lib] and other human beings gradually becomes more active and louder. The "Fighting Answerers" seem to realize a futility, and begin to mock "The Question"—the strife is over. . . . After they disappear, "The Question" is asked for the last time, and the "Silences" are heard in "Undisturbed Solitude."

Play through this work several times: once just to listen, a second time after reading Ives's program, and a third time with the Additional Listening Chart from Appendix I displayed for your students to see. In class discussion, call attention to the three levels (or layers) that the authors describe. The solo trumpet (layer 1) asks the "Unanswered Question of Existence," and the woodwinds (layer 2) contentiously offer their own answers. Most fascinating, however, is the third (the background) layer. The strings play quiet, hymnlike material that repeats throughout the work. I have always equated this layer with the "music of the spheres," an underlying truth that we can sense only if we listen hard enough. We can hear echoes of this layer briefly at the end of many other Ives works as well, even in cacophonous scores like "The Rock-strewn Hills Join in the People's Outdoor Meeting." Ives creates the illusion that this quiet layer was present throughout the entire piece, only we couldn't hear it because of the hodgepodge of other events that clamored for our attention. *The Unanswered Question* clearly articulates this transcendentalist vision of music.

With Ives, musical sounds, ideas, or forms never seem to exist for their own sake; rather, they are vehicles for the expression of experiences, memories, or truths—or all three. In *The Unanswered Question*, Ives points to important philosophical issues familiar to anyone who has wrestled with the "why" of human existence—the unanswerable (trumpet question), the meaningless (woodwind responses), and the unknowable (the strings).

Additional Teaching Suggestions

❦ Lecture-Demonstration Ideas

1. Invite a dancer or dance historian to class. In addition to demonstrating the differences between classical ballet and modern dance, your guest can discuss the role of dancers like Nijinsky (from Diaghilev's Ballets Russes, choreographer for *The Rite of Spring*) or Martha Graham (choreographer for Copland's *Appalachian Spring*—see Chapter 21) in the development of modern dance.

2. Spend more time with the Second Viennese School. Who were Schoenberg, Berg, and Webern? How did their music differ? Play music of each composer and ask students to compare features of these works. Use the examples from the textbook or find other recordings to augment your presentation. For instance: *Farben,* from Schoenberg's Five Orchestral Pieces, Op. 16, demonstrates the composer's keen interest in coloristic patterns; Berg's Violin Concerto is one of the most accessible, achingly beautiful twelve-tone works ever written; and the first movement of Webern's *Symphonie* reveals the cool, abstract polyphony and the reliance on traditional forms that characterize the composer's mature work. See Sound Recordings below for suggested recordings.

3. Compare *Sprechstimme* with German cabaret vocal style. Use "Night" from Schoenberg's *Pierrot lunaire,* Schoenberg's own cabaret songs (*Brettllieder*), and Kurt Weill's *Threepenny Opera* or recordings by Ute Lemper (see Multimedia Resources below for suggested sound and video recordings). These recordings demonstrate a free intermingling of sung and spoken vocal qualities. Students can hear that Schoenberg was not just "being weird" but that he drew on the conventions of another style. After all, *Pierrot lunaire* was written for German literary cabaret singer Albertine Zehme.

4. Here is an exercise for the keyboard lab. Ask students (or groups) to compose their own twelve-tone rows. They can put the twelve tones of the chromatic scale in any order they choose. Ask them to listen carefully and put the tones in an order that pleases them. When they finish, take one of their rows and compose a short piece with it on the spot (three or four row statements will do). Map out the compositional procedures you want to demonstrate on the board. Then walk students through the compositional process. Explain each step as you invert, retrograde, or transpose the row. Make it a class project; ask for student input at decision points in the process. At the end, perform the composition for the class.

5. Compare serialism with the Baroque fugue. Fugue VIII from Bach's *Well-Tempered Clavier,* Book I, offers interesting parallels to the techniques of serialism used by Schoenberg and other twelve-tone composers. At various points in the fugue, Bach states his fugue subject in inversion and transposition—even in augmentation. Statements of the subject can be compared to melodic statements of a twelve-tone row, and Bach's frequent *stretti* demonstrate how his subject pervades the texture. Even the episodes and "free" material are based on motives drawn from the subject, just as Schoenberg's accompaniment in his Concerto for Piano and Orchestra draws on fragments from the row. See Multimedia Resources below for suggested recordings.

6. Study an example of total serialism with your class. The first of Babbitt's *Three Compositions for Piano* is often used for this purpose; his serial procedures are easy to pick out and understand. Babbitt's rhythmic series undergoes

several modifications and is applied in a variety of ways. Specific dynamic markings correspond to specific modifications of the tone row. The score can be found in several anthologies, but Charles Burkhart's *Anthology for Musical Analysis*, 3rd ed. (New York: Holt, Rinehart and Winston, 1979, pp. 578–84) includes detailed analytical notes and a chart that spells out the row and its modifications.[2] The CDs that accompany K Marie Stolba's *Development of Western Music*, 3rd ed. (Boston: McGraw-Hill, 1998) include a recording. See Sound Recordings below for other recordings.

❧ Class Discussion Ideas

1. *What did Debussy say about his own music?* Like Berlioz, Schumann, and other composers, Debussy engaged in music criticism from time to time. Many of his writings are collected in *Debussy on Music* (New York: Knopf, 1977). Articles describe a wide range of topics, including Wagner and other composers, the Prix de Rome, and interviews with Debussy about his music. A thorough index permits easy access to topics of interest. Read selections to the class and ask students to share their reactions.

2. *Can you imagine anything that would cause a riot during a modern Classical concert? Why did Stravinsky's* Rite of Spring *create a riot?* American concert audiences are incredibly placid; it is difficult to imagine a riot today (except perhaps at an outdoor rock festival). Jacqueline Maskey's *"Le sacre* Restored" in *Musical America* (May 1988, pp. 16–19) tells a fascinating story. Her article describes the years of painstaking research that went into Millicent Hodson's re-creation of the original choreography for Stravinsky's *Rite.* In mounting this production in the 1980s and again in 2003, the Joffrey Ballet has provided new insights into the radical nature of Nijinsky's choreography. Further information is contained in Stravinsky's account of the riot at the première, found in *Expositions and Developments* (New York: Doubleday, 1962, pp. 159–69). Ask students to hypothesize why the riot took place, given the information you provide.

3. *What was Stravinsky like?* Stravinsky's writings and interviews with Robert Craft provide fascinating insights into the composer's life and thought. These books range over many topics, but you can use the index in each volume to find comments on specific pieces. Some examples include comments on the role of imagination and freedom in the compositional process in *Poetics of Music* (New York: Vintage, 1956, pp. 66–69 and other passages); a description of the riot at the première of *The Rite of Spring* in *Expositions and Developments* (New York: Doubleday, 1962, pp. 159–69); and Stravinsky's comparison of himself with Schoenberg in *Dialogues and a Diary* (New York: Doubleday, 1963, pp. 56–58). If possible, use the excellent 1965 *Stravinsky* documentary, first telecast just a few years before the composer's death (see Video Recordings below). It contains interviews and behind-the-scenes footage of Stravinsky with friends and colleagues, which help to put a human face on this great composer. Ask students to share their reactions to Stravinsky's comments.

4. *Why did Schoenberg write such difficult music?* Read excerpts from *Style and Idea* (Berkeley: University of California Press, 1975), a collection of

---

[2]Burkhart omits Babbitt's *Three Compositions for Piano* in his fifth edition.

Schoenberg's own writings. Articles describe a wide range of topics, including his musical evolution and his twelve-tone method. Ask students to share their reactions to Schoenberg's comments. See Video Recordings below for suggested video resources.

5. *What is the connection between Ives and transcendentalism?* Ives provided his own answer to this question in *Essays Before a Sonata and Other Writings* (New York: Norton, 1962). Read excerpts from his essays and play corresponding portions of the *Concord* Sonata. This exercise can help acquaint students with the ideas that underlie (in this work, at least) Ives's often difficult style. See Sound Recordings below for suggested recordings.

6. *What do modern American composers say about their music?* After listening to examples from the *Listen* recordings, read comments by the composers and ask for student reactions. Several books contain interviews with and articles by important composers, both Americans and others. *Contemporary Composers on Contemporary Music* (New York: Holt, Rinehart, and Winston, 1967) by Elliot Schwartz and Barney Childs is a collection of writings by Debussy, Stravinsky, Berg, Bartók, Shostakovich, Copland, Varèse, Cage, and others.

♪ Listening Ideas

1. Compare nocturnes by Debussy and Chopin. Play examples from the *Listen* set and ask students to describe the differences between them. Do they both capture the same nightlike qualities? In what ways are they similar? How do they differ?

2. Listen for similarities between Debussy's music and Balinese gamelan music or Chinese traditional music. Play *Bopong* or *The Drunken Fisherman* (see Further Listening Examples in Chapter 18) side by side with examples by Debussy. Ask students to identify features these excerpts share. The **B** theme in *Clouds* (from Three Nocturnes) resembles traditional Chinese pentatonic melodies, and the clangor of sections in "La Cathédrale engloutie" (see Further Listening Examples below) could be related to gamelan music. See Sound Recordings below for suggested recordings.

3. Listen for the influence of Russian folk melodies in Stravinsky's music. Play excerpts from Stravinsky's *Rite of Spring* (Introduction and "Dance of the Adolescents") and Musorgsky's *Pictures at an Exhibition* ("Promenade" and "The Great Gate at Kiev"). Point out the changing meters, nontraditional scales, and angular melodic shapes. This exercise also allows you to compare features of old and new nationalism in Russian music.

4. Compare Stravinsky's *Rite of Spring* with dance music of earlier composers. Play excerpts from "Daphne," "Kemp's Jig," Bach's Orchestral Suite in D, the minuet from Haydn's Symphony No. 95, or the Dance of the Sugar-Plum Fairy from Tchaikovsky's *Nutcracker* (*Listen* DVD). What makes Stravinsky's dance music so radically different? What kind of dance or bodily movement does each example suggest?

5. Debussy favors three-part (**A B A**) form in *Clouds* and in the other nocturnes as well. Ask students to name pieces from earlier chapters that used this tried-and-true old form. Some examples include Bach's Orchestral Suite No. 3 in D (Gavotte), Haydn's Symphony No. 95 (III), Beethoven's Symphony No. 5 (III) and Quartet in F (II), and Mahler's Symphony No. 1 (III). (See Appendix

III for a complete list.) Play a few examples. Ask students to compare features of each work and to describe how each composer handles the return of the **A** section.

6. Compare Berg's *Wozzeck* with Mozart's *Don Giovanni* ("Là ci darem la mano") and Wagner's *The Valkyrie,* Act I, scene i. How do these composers differ in their handling of ensembles? Do Berg's scenes more closely resemble Mozart's or Wagner's?

7. How does twentieth-century orchestral music differ from earlier orchestral music? Compare Debussy's Three Nocturnes, Stravinsky's *Rite of Spring,* or Ives's "Rockstrewn Hills" with Vivaldi's Concerto in G, Haydn's Symphony No. 95, Beethoven's Symphony No. 5, Berlioz's *Fantastic* Symphony, or Tchaikovsky's *Romeo and Juliet.* Who uses the largest orchestra? Which piece offers the most varied colors? Students may note a progression toward increased size and variety between the Baroque and Romantic periods. What becomes of that trend in the twentieth century?

8. Compare traditional and twentieth-century vocal techniques. Play excerpts from opera recitative, Schubert songs, Romantic opera, Schoenberg's *Pierrot lunaire,* and/or Berg's *Wozzeck.* Ask students to find differences in vocal production, melodic shape, and phrase relationships.

❦ Further Listening Examples

DEBUSSY **Three Nocturnes,** *Festivals*

Festivals, the vivacious middle movement of Debussy's Three Nocturnes, provides a delightful contrast to the searching ambiguity of *Clouds. Clouds; Festivals;* and the third nocturne, *Sirens,* all share the same **A B A′** form, but whereas the materials and structure of *Clouds* feels vague and uncertain, *Festivals* brings everything into sharp focus. See Appendix I for an Additional Listening Chart, and Multimedia Resources below for sound and video recordings.

Start with the **A** section. It goes off like a shot, immediately establishing a clear meter and a quick tempo. The opening accompanimental figure sets up an energetic dancelike rhythm, and the melody that follows rushes up the scale only to tumble back down again in a sequence of neighbor figures. We can easily recognize this melody as a real melody, something that was often hard to find in the vague motives of *Clouds.* Still, we do not find a real *tune* in this melody. The opening motive is easy to hear every time it returns, but that motive and its extension are really the only melody we have, and Debussy varies that by changing the scale each time we hear it (church modes and whole-tone scales are all available to Debussy). Curiously, even though the texture is much busier and the color and mood are more vivacious, the main emphasis remains on color, texture, and mood. The recurring melody becomes an island of stability in a sea of frenetic activity that builds in energy and intensity, right up to the end.

The **B** section's beginning provides immediate relief from the near-chaos that ends the **A** section. A simple pulse in the harp sets in motion a quiet if slightly ominous march rhythm. Then comes the melody—a real tune! Here Debussy writes the most sustained melody in all of the Three Nocturnes. It divides into several clear phrases, and for once we don't hear huge gaps between statements of melodic fragments. This melody unfolds continuously and calls attention to itself. In fact, the structure of the **B** section is simplicity itself: three complete statements of this new melody. We're not used to such clear-cut relationships in Debussy. Each statement is louder than the previous one, and the third statement weaves in the main melody of the **A** section as a counterpoint to the **B** theme, bringing the middle section to an overpowering climax.

The final **A′** returns to the world of the first section, but not literally. Rather, we hear echoes of events from the first section in a new context, with a few new themes and motives tossed into the mix, including a bit of the trumpet's march from the **B** section. Eventually, however, this festive occasion begins to wind down, slowing and "rumbling" to a halt, where we can hear the oboe playing the main motive from *Clouds*. The tempo picks up again, we hear fragments of melodic ideas, and finally the movement ends with a very soft cymbal crash.

Display (or hand out photocopies of) the Additional Listening Chart for this work and play through this movement, pointing out events as they go by. Conclude by pointing out Debussy's progression from ambiguity to clarity and back again. We saw this in *Clouds,* where the **B** section's melody and form were easier to follow than the **A** section's. Debussy repeats this pattern in *Festivals,* though he starts from a point of greater clarity than in *Clouds*. Most fascinating of all is the way this three-part format plays out at different structural levels. Recall the division of the **B** section into three statements of a main melody—in both *Clouds* and *Festivals*. And even though we haven't encountered *Sirens*, note the contrast between the ambiguity of *Clouds* and the clarity of *Festivals*. Debussy's progression from ambiguity to clarity (and back again) plays out not only in the structure of each movement but in the relationship between the three movements as well—wheels within wheels. Debussy's incredible ability to balance profound musical ambiguities against such far-reaching structural thinking is part of his genius and one of the reasons his music remains so tantalizing nearly one hundred years later.

DEBUSSY "La Cathédrale engloutie" (Preludes, Book 1)

This piano prelude makes a wonderful example of an impressionist character piece. See Appendix I for an Additional Listening Chart, and Sound Recordings below for suggested performances.

Before you display (or hand out photocopies of) the Additional Listening Chart for this work, play the first twenty-eight measures of "La Cathédrale engloutie." Ask students to jot down their impressions of the music. What sort of picture does this music paint?

1. Students may describe this music as "mysterious," "fluid," and "flowing." It evokes a "beginning" of some sort: sunrise, birth, or even the Creation.

2. Tell students what this music is "about." "La Cathédrale engloutie" describes an old Breton legend in which the ancient cathedral of Ys rises from the sea on certain mornings. As it rises from the mists, its priests intone their prayers and, at midday, its bells ring. As the day ends, the cathedral slips back into the sea, quietly disappearing from sight.

Now display or distribute the Listening Chart. Before you play the entire piece, point out the following elements.

Measures 1–15—The organum-like parallel chords create a mysterious, religious atmosphere.

Measures 16–21—The rolling left-hand arpeggios create a watery image. As the music quickens and gets louder, the listener senses the emergence of the cathedral from the mists.

Measures 28–40—A clangorous, celebratory mood prevails as the bells of the now-risen cathedral toll out across the water.

Measures 72–83—Like a distant echo of mm. 28–40, the bells of the cathedral are muffled as they are swallowed by the rolling waters.

Play "La Cathédrale engloutie." On the display, point out sections of the music as they go by.

The title and descriptive nature of "La Cathédrale engloutie" are clearly Romantic in their impulse. Indeed, most of Debussy's works have descriptive titles, and the music itself is quite pictorial, though not in the "photographic" fashion of nineteenth-century Romanticism. Ask the class if the program of this piece is as easy to perceive as that of Smetana's "The Moldau," for example. "La Cathédrale engloutie" offers a much more personal, less specific, more *impressionistic* vision of its subject than does Smetana's tone poem.

SCHOENBERG *Pierrot lunaire*

For further examples from Schoenberg's expressionistic song cycle, try the songs below. Texts and translations for these songs can be found in Appendix II; see Multimedia Resources below for suggested sound and video recordings.

As you introduce these songs, read and discuss the imagery and mood of each poem with the class. After you play each song, point out significant features and ask the class to describe the relationship between words and music. Note how different each song is from the others; students may not notice at first because the idiom is so unfamiliar, but Schoenberg expresses a wide variety of different moods in this music.

No. 1: "Moondrunk" (voice, piano, flute, violin, cello)

Display (or photocopy handouts of) the poem for this song and read it to the class. Point out the following elements of the poem.

1. As in the other poems of *Pierrot lunaire*, nighttime imagery figures prominently.

2. "Moondrunk" equates moonlight with a heady, intoxicating wine. "Liquid" associations permeate the text of this poem: *wine, drink, pours, waves, springflood, swimming, flood waters, drunken, sips,* and *swallows.*

Play the song for the class and ask students to listen for the relationship between words and music. In the discussion that follows, draw out the following:

1. Accumulating repetitions of the song's quasi-ostinato figures build to a climax during lines 9 and 10, "The poet, by his ardor driven / Grown drunken from the Holy drink . . . "

2. The strange, liquid, nighttime mood of the poem is evoked perfectly by the nontraditional musical elements and the sound of the *Sprechstimme.*

No. 19: "Serenade" (voice, piano, cello)

Display (or photocopy handouts of) the poem for this song and read it to the class. Point out the following elements of the poem.

1. The text first sets the scene—Pierrot plays a nighttime serenade, plucking and scraping on his viola with a monstrous bow.

2. When Cassander arrives to complain about the racket, Pierrot grabs him and plays on his bald spot as if he were a musical instrument (the same Cassander as in No. 16, who screamed in pain as Pierrot drilled a hole in his head and smoked him like a pipe). Here we see the same bizarre humor as in "The Moonfleck."

Play the song for the class and ask students to listen for the relationship between words and music. In the discussion that follows, draw out the following:

1. In Schoenberg's hands, Pierrot's viola and monstrous bow become a cello playing a swooping, exaggeratedly sentimental melody with ornaments and a slow waltz feel.

2. The cello melody provides a typically expressive Romantic melody, but the exaggeration and "wrong notes" make it hard to hear as such.

No. 20: "Journey Home" (voice, piano, flute, clarinet, viola, cello)

Display (or photocopy handouts of) the poem for this song and read it to the class. Point out the following elements of the poem.

1. After all the bizarre imagery and activity of this moonlit night, "Journey Home" proves surprisingly gentle and lyrical. This poem describes a fanciful sea voyage home; Pierrot steers his waterlily boat with a moonbeam.

Play the song for the class and ask students to listen for the relationship between words and music. In the discussion that follows, draw out the following:

1. The opening pizzicato ostinato suggests the gentle rocking of the boat, and the song depicts the restless motion of Pierrot's nocturnal voyage.

No. 21: "O ancient scent" (voice, piano, flute, piccolo, clarinet, bass clarinet, violin, viola, cello)

Display (or photocopy handouts of) the poem for this song and read it to the class. Point out the following elements of the poem.

1. Here the poet relives the magical, lost days of fairy lore. This poem paints an appealing picture of an innocent place, long ago and far away, similar to Mahler's Romantic nostalgia.

2. It could represent the lost innocence of childhood or the crushed dreams of Romanticism—perhaps the latter, given the quasi-traditional music in this song.

Play the song for the class and ask students to listen for the relationship between words and music. In the discussion that follows, draw out the following:

1. Unlike the other songs in this cycle, Schoenberg's music here consists of quasi-traditional harmonies, melodic figures, and form.

2. For the first time in the cycle, Schoenberg acknowledges the *rondeau* form of the poetry in his music. He uses the same melody each time the opening couplet recurs. A small rondo form is the result:

a   b   a′   c   a″

The traditional principles of contrast and return help create a reassuring familiarity.

3. The quasi-traditional language used in this song seems to acknowledge a powerful nostalgia for traditional Romantic tonality, but the text of the poem labels this longing a "scent from days of fairy lore." A powerful, comforting image, to be sure, but ultimately out of touch with present realities—childish, even escapist—as Schoenberg knows full well.

SCHOENBERG Concerto for Piano and Orchestra, Op. 42, beginning

If you would like to further explore the section on Schoenberg and serialism discussed above, this excerpt provides a good introduction to Schoenberg's twelve-tone method. See Sound Recordings below for suggested performances of this work. You'll only need the first two minutes of the recording, in which Schoenberg states the main theme of the first movement. This four-phrase melody is played twice, once by the piano and again by the orchestra.

In this short excerpt, students can see how one composer used twelve-tone technique. The four phrases of this concerto's main theme are as follows:

*Indicates notes that do not follow the order of the SERIES.

Display the melody for your students and point out these features:

1. The row is stated melodically.

2. Each phrase states a different modification of the series. In order, we hear the basic series (**P–0**), a retrograde inversion (**RI–5**), the retrograde (**R–0**), and an inversion (**I–5**).

3. Note the following relationships in this melody. The retrograde phrase uses the basic series backward, untransposed. The inverted phrase *is* transposed, however; it starts five half-steps above (same as seven half-steps below) the "zero" pitch, **E flat**. The retrograde inversion uses the same transposition as the inversion; thus, its pitches are exactly the same as the inversion's, but backward.

4. Free use of recurring rhythmic motives provides another means of coherence.

5. The four-phrase melody is stated twice—first by piano with orchestral accompaniment, then by orchestra with piano accompaniment.

6. The accompaniment uses pitch patterns freely derived from the row.

Play the example for the class and point out each phrase as it goes by. Fade out the recording at the end of the orchestra's statement of the theme (at approximately 2:00). The melody is easy to hear when the piano plays it, but the orchestral statement can be hard to follow. If your keyboard is in tune with the recording, you can help students by playing the melody along with the orchestra, but please note that this second theme statement is not identical to the first. Ever the practitioner of continuing variation, Schoenberg transposes each phrase of the orchestral statement differently, using **P–7**, **RI–4**, **R–2**, and **I–6**, respectively. For your convenience, the orchestral theme statement is printed below.

*Indicates notes that do not follow the order of the SERIES.

BERG *Wozzeck,* Act III, scene ii

This scene can be used to supplement your coverage of scenes iii and iv (see Lecture Suggestions above). To depict the murder scene, Berg wrote an invention on a single note. He sustains the pitch **B** in various registers throughout the scene. We tend not to hear it at first, but as we become aware of it, the obsessive fixation on **B** creates an eerie foreboding. Finally, in the scene change, the **B** takes over the entire texture, associated with the rhythm that dominates the next scene. Ask two students to act out the scene (the libretto is available with almost all recordings); then play the music. See Multimedia Resources below for suggested sound and video recordings.

IVES *Three Places in New England*

One of Ives's best-known works, this orchestral set provides an excellent vehicle for further exploration of Ives's music. Ives wrote *Three Places in New England* between 1908 and 1914. He preceded each of the movements with a printed statement that provides insights (often poetic) into the music that follows. If at all possible, find a score and read these statements aloud as part of your presentation. See Sound Recordings below for suggested performances.

II "Putnam's Camp, Redding, Connecticut"

The statement preceding the second movement outlines the story of a small boy who goes to a Revolutionary War memorial park on a picnic. Read the story aloud for the students. They will find this program music fairly easy to follow once they know Ives's program. Like "The Rockstrewn Hills Join in the

People's Outdoor Meeting," it is filled with quotations and frenetic energy. Write the following chart on the board and point to each section as it goes by when you play the music.

March ("Exposition")

Introduction	Main March	March elaborated	Children's song	Boy wanders away
m. 1	m. 6	m. 27	m. 37	m. 46

Trio (Dream Sequence)

Dream Idea	"Goddess of Liberty" March (opposed by "British Grenadiers" fragments)	"The British Grenadiers" March	Putnam's music	Soldiers' cheers
m. 64	m. 67	m. 88	m. 103	m. 107

March ("Recapitulation"—rearranged)

Children's song	Main March	"The British Grenadiers" March	Main March (climactic statement)	Final Climax (collage)
m. 114	m. 126	m. 134	m. 144	m. 157

III "The Housatonic at Stockbridge"

The score for the third movement of *Three Places in New England* is preceded by a quotation from a Robert Underwood Johnson poem. This meditative, thoughtful music sets the flowing, watery rhythms of the strings against a beautiful, hymnlike tune (Ives again quotes an old hymn tune—"Dorrnance"). The music builds in intensity as the river flows toward the sea. After an acutely dissonant climax, the music ends, suddenly and beautifully, on a quiet, profoundly spiritual note. Write the following chart on the board and point to each section as it goes by when you play the music. (See Sound Recordings below for suggested recordings.)

A				A′		
Introduction	**a**	**a′**	**a″**	*Introduction*	**a‴**	**a⁗**
"mist-water" texture	Hymn ("Dorrnance")			"mist-water" reorchestrated	Hymn	
m. 1	m. 7	m. 11	m. 17	m. 21	m. 23	m. 25

A″			A‴	
Introduction	**a** fragments developed		**a⁗**	
"mist-water" texture	"mist-water" texture builds into collage	climax	short return and cadence	
m. 31	m. 34	m. 42	m. 44	

Multimedia Resources

✌ Further Listening Charts and Texts

See Appendix I for Listening Charts for these works; see Further Listening Examples above for teaching suggestions.

Debussy, Three Nocturnes, *Festivals*

Debussy, "La Cathédrale engloutie" (Preludes, Book 1)

Ives, *The Unanswered Question*

See Appendix II for texts and translations for these works; see Further Listening Examples above for teaching suggestions.

> Schoenberg, *Pierrot lunaire*, No. 1 "Moondrunk," No. 19 "Serenade," No. 20 "Journey Home," and No. 21 "O ancient scent"

7 Sound Recordings

Babbitt, *Piano Music*. Taub. Harmonia Mundi HMC 905 160 (CD). Recording of all of Babbitt's piano works up to 1985. Try this recording of Babbitt's *Three Compositions for Piano* if you use Lecture-Demonstration Idea 6 above.

Bach, *Das Wohltemperierte Klavier, Book I*. Masaaki Suzuki. BIS CD–813/814 (CD). Book I beautifully played on a beautiful Kroesbergen harpsichord. It contains Fugue No. 8 (in E-flat Minor), useful if you try Lecture-Demonstration Idea 5 above.

Berg, *Violinkonzerte*. Anne-Sophie Mutter and the Chicago Symphony Orchestra. Deutsche Grammophon 437 093-2 (CD). Excellent, impassioned performance of Berg's great twelve-tone work, the Violin Concerto; conducted by James Levine. Try this recording if you use Lecture-Demonstration Idea 2 above.

Berg, *Wozzeck*. Royal Stockholm Opera Orchestra. Naxos 8.660076/7 (CD). Strong, vivid new recording of Berg's expressionist classic; conducted by Leif Segerstam. Carl Johan Falkman and Katarina Dalayman head the cast. Try this recording if you use suggestions for this work in Further Listening Examples above.

Berlin Cabaret Songs. Ute Lemper and Matrix Ensemble. London 452 849 (CD). This recording from London's superb *Entartete Musik* ("Degenerate Music") series captures the biting satire and ironic humor of Berlin's intellectual underground between the two world wars. Of course, they deal with subjects made taboo by the Nazis: jazz, gender reversal, and gay/lesbian concerns. The translations Lemper uses are not always exact, but they marvelously capture the spirit of the original texts. (For the original German texts, look for London 452 601.) Try this recording if you use Lecture-Demonstration Idea 3 above.

Debussy, *La Mer/Nocturnes/Jeux*. Cleveland Orchestra. Deutsche Grammophon 439 896-2 (CD). Beautiful performances conducted by one of the finest living Debussy interpreters, Pierre Boulez. Try this recording if you use Listening Idea 5 or suggestions for *Festivals* (from Three Nocturnes) in Further Listening Examples above.

Debussy, *Orchestral Works*. Philharmonia Orchestra. Sony Classical 52K 68327 (CD). The recording featured in the *Listen* set; conducted by Pierre Boulez. Recording also includes *La Mer*, *Prélude à l'après-midi d'un faune*, and *Jeux*. Try this recording for further examples of Debussy or if you use Listening Idea 5 or suggestions for *Festivals* (from Three Nocturnes) in Further Listening Examples above.

Debussy, *Preludes for Piano, Books 1 and 2*. Krystian Zimerman. Deutsche Grammophon 435 773-2 (CD). Superb, intensely atmospheric performances of favorite Debussy piano works. Try this recording if you use Listening Idea 2 or suggestions for "La Cathédrale engloutie" from Further Listening Examples above.

Ives, *The Orchestral Music of Charles Ives*. Orchestra New England. Koch International Classics 3-7025-2 H1 (CD). Delightful collection of world premieres and first performances of new Ives Society critical editions; conducted by James Sinclair. Includes *Three Places in New England, Four Ragtime Dances,* Set for Theatre Orchestra, *Calcium Light Night, Country Band* March (one source of materials Ives used in the second movement of *Three Places*), and other assorted works. Try this recording if you use materials from Further Listening Examples above for *Three Places in New England*.

Ives, *Sonata No. 2 for Piano ("Concord, Mass., 1840–1860")*. Gilbert Kalish. Elektra/Nonesuch 71337-2-J (CD). Good, readily available recording of Ives's greatest piano work. Try this recording if you use Class Discussion Idea 5 above.

Schoenberg, *Piano Concerto*. Mitsuko Uchida and the Cleveland Orchestra. Philips 468 033-2 (CD). Perhaps the most beautiful recording of this work ever made; conducted by Pierre Boulez. In addition to the concerto, Uchida plays solo piano works by Schoenberg, Berg, and Webern. Highly recommended if you use Lecture-Demonstration Idea 5 or suggestions for the Schoenberg Concerto in Further Listening Examples above.

Schoenberg, *Pierrot lunaire*. Christine Schäfer and Ensemble InterContemporain. Deutsche Grammophon 457 630-2 (CD). Superb new performance of Schoenberg's song cycle; conducted by Pierre Boulez. Recording also includes *Ode to Napoleon* and *Herzgewächse*, the work published by the group of expressionist painters known as the "Blue Rider." Try this recording of *Pierrot lunaire* if you want to compare the approaches of two different singers to *Sprechstimme* or if you use suggestions from Further Listening Examples above for No. 1 "Moondrunk," No. 19 "Serenade," No. 20 "Journey Home," or No. 21 "O ancient scent."

Schoenberg, *Urban Cabaret*. Maria Tegzes and Geoffrey Burleson. Neuma 45083 (CD). Performances of cabaret songs by Schoenberg and Hanns Eisler. The *Brettllieder* (*Cabaret Songs*) provide especially good examples of the tradition Schoenberg parodied in *Pierrot lunaire* ("Mahnung" works well). Try this recording if you use Lecture-Demonstration Idea 3 above.

Schoenberg, *Verklärte Nacht, etc.* Los Angeles Philharmonic, Cleveland Orchestra, and Vienna Philharmonic. London 448 279-2 (CD). This Decca Double offers a mix of Schoenberg's works in one inexpensive package; conducted by Zubin Mehta and Christoph von Dohnányi. Includes fine performances of Five Orchestral Pieces, Op. 16; Chamber Symphony No. 1; and *Erwartung*. For an example available of pure, unadulterated musical expressionism, you can't do better than *Erwartung* with its portrayal of psychosis and hysterical behavior. Try this recording of Op. 16 if you use Lecture-Demonstration Idea 2 above.

Stravinsky, *Le sacre du printemps*. Chicago Symphony Orchestra. RCA Silver Seal 60541-2-RV (CD). The recording featured on the *Listen* set; conducted by Seiji Ozawa. Try this recording if you want to share more of this work with your students, especially the concluding "Danse sacrale."

Webern, *Boulez Conducts Webern III*. Berlin Philharmonic Orchestra. Deutsche Grammophon 447 765-2 (CD). Exquisite new performances give an easy expressiveness to Webern's often austere style; conducted by Pierre Boulez. Includes Five Pieces for Orchestra (1913); the two cantatas; Variations for Orchestra; and Symphony, Op. 21. Also available in the new Deutsche Grammophon *Complete Webern* box set. Try this recording if you use Lecture-Demonstration Idea 2 above.

Weill, *The Threepenny Opera*. CBS MK 42637 (CD). Recording from the 1950s supervised by Lotte Lenya. It goes in and out of print but wears an air of authenticity rarely matched in newer recordings. "Der Song vom Nein und Ja" provides a particularly good example of the vocal style Schoenberg parodied in *Pierrot lunaire*. Try this recording if you use Lecture-Demonstration Idea 3 above.

❼ Video Recordings

The American Way. The Music of the 20th Century: Leaving Home Series. www.films.com (DVD or VHS, color, 52 minutes). Simon Rattle narrates this look at American music, from hymns, band music, country dances, and jazz to the music of such twentieth-century composers as Ives, Gershwin, Copland, Cage, and Bernstein.

Berg, *The Secret Life of Alban Berg*. www.films.com (DVD or VHS, color, 50 minutes). This video follows soprano Kristine Ciesinski as she tracks down people and documents to shed light on the relationship between Berg's life and his music. Excerpts from *Wozzeck, Lulu, Seven Early Songs,* and other works are performed by the BBC Symphony, Ciesinski, Norman Bailey, and the Mc-Capra String Quartet.

Berg, *Wozzeck*. Image Entertainment (DVD, color, 97 minutes). Profoundly moving video performance features Franz Grundheber, Hildegard Behrens, and Philip Langridge; conducted by Claudio Abbado. Also available in VHS on Kultur Video. Highly recommended for comparison with the clips on the *Listen* DVD or if you use suggestions for additional selections from this work in Further Listening Examples above.

Berg, *Wozzeck*. Kultur Video (DVD, color, 102 minutes). Clips from the *Listen* DVD came from this video, the only *Wozzeck* currently in print. Fortunately, the singing and acting are strong, but some will find the modernist staging hard to stomach. Performance features Dale Duesing and Kristine Ciesinski; conducted by Sylvain Cambreling. Try this DVD if you use suggestions for additional excerpts from this work in Further Listening Examples above.

Berlioz/Debussy/Ravel. VAI (DVD, black and white, 96 minutes). Known as a Berlioz conductor, Charles Munch leads the Boston Symphony Orchestra in wonderfully idiomatic 1962 performances of two masterworks of French impressionism: Debussy's *La Mer* and Ravel's *Daphnis et Chloé* No. 2. The disc also includes Berlioz's *Fantastic* Symphony, but the Eschenbach DVD recommended in Chapter 16 gives us all of Munch's passion—in modern video and stereo! Try this DVD for further examples of impressionism.

Georg Büchner: Woyzeck. www.films.com (DVD or VHS, color, 49 minutes). A look at the fragmentary play, first published in 1879 and premiered in 1913, on which Berg based his opera.

Bunin Plays Chopin and Debussy. Pioneer Video (DVD, color, 75 minutes). Recital performance by Stanislav Bunin includes several Debussy piano works, including the first *Arabesque* and *Images*, Set 1. Useful supplement to your classroom presentation.

Color. The Music of the 20th Century: Leaving Home Series. www.films.com (DVD or VHS, color, 52 minutes). Simon Rattle narrates this look at revolutionary uses of color in the music of twentieth-century composers, especially Debussy, Stravinsky, Schoenberg, Boulez, and Takemitsu.

Debussy, *Britten/Debussy/Ravel/Rihm*. Image Entertainment (DVD, color, 79 minutes). Claudio Abbado and the Berlin Philharmonic perform four twentieth-century works: Britten's *Serenade; Clouds* and *Festivals* from Debussy's Three Nocturnes; Ravel's La Valse; and Rihm's *In doppelter Tiefe*. Try this recording to augment your presentation of *Clouds* or if you use Listening Idea 5 or suggestions for *Festivals* (from Three Nocturnes) in Further Listening Examples above.

Debussy, *Claude Debussy. Harmonics: The Innovators of Classical Music* Series. www.films.com (DVD or VHS, color, 27 minutes). Video biography of Debussy features a look at the techniques of his musical language with musical excerpts from *La Mer, Prélude à l'après-midi d'un faune,* Preludes for Piano, and other works. Featured performers include Herbert von Karajan, Leonard Bernstein, and Arturo Benedetti Michelangeli. Try this video if you use Class Discussion Idea 1 above.

Debussy, *La Mer*. Image Entertainment (DVD, color, 89 minutes). Daniel Barenboim and the Chicago Symphony perform this important impressionist work along with de Falla's *Three-Cornered Hat* and Boulez's *Notations*. Try this recording for further examples of Debussy's impressionism.

[Debussy] *Mists, Fairies, and Fireworks*. Amadeus Press (DVD, color, 90 minutes). Pianist Paul Roberts hosts this thoughtful look at Debussy's *Préludes*. His often-illuminating analysis gets at the heart of impressionism and is easily understood by non-musicians. Further, he illustrates his points with many excerpts. The disc includes complete performances of five preludes: *The Girl with the Flaxen Hair, What the West Wind Saw, Footsteps in the Snow, Sails,* and *Minstrels*. I much prefer Roberts's performances to Michelangeli's—Roberts is fully engaged in the music and gives us lovingly detailed performances. Recommended if you want further examples of Debussy and impressionism.

[Debussy, *Prelude to the Afternoon of a Faun*.] *Delaware Music Series*. www.recsmedia.com (DVD). Complete performance by the Oberlin Conservatory Orchestra; conducted by Ken Moore. DVD also includes a scrolling reduced two-line score and color-coded formal analysis. Superb resource for lecture-demonstration on Debussy and impressionism.

Debussy. *Ravel, Daphnis et Chloe. Herbert von Karajan: His Legacy for Home Video*. Sony Classical (DVD or VHS, color, 54 minutes). Impressionist music contained in this recording includes Debussy's *La Mer* and *Prélude à l'après-midi d'un faune* and Ravel's second suite from *Daphnis et Chloé*. Performances by the Berlin Philharmonic Orchestra; conducted by Herbert von Karajan.

Ives, *Charles Ives: A Good Dissonance Like a Man*. www.insight-media.com (VHS, color, 61 minutes). This Peabody Award winner blends words from Ives's *Memos* with photographs and music to create a unique portrait of a unique composer. Frequent dramatizations seem somewhat amateurish.

Michelangeli Plays Debussy. BBC Opus Arte (DVD, black and white, 84 minutes). Performances from 1962 by this legendary pianist feature impressionist piano works by Debussy. Michelangeli is not emotive, but his pianism is extraordinary. His delicate touch produces sonorities of great beauty, and even small details stand out clearly. Try this recording for further examples of Debussy and impressionism.

Music for the World. Man and Music Series. www.films.com (DVD or VHS, color, 53 minutes). A look at Stravinsky, Scriabin, Rachmaninoff, and Prokofiev in the context of the generation of Russian composers that preceded them.

The New Music. Man and Music Series. www.films.com (DVD or VHS, color, 53 minutes). Looks at atonal music and the development of twelve-tone techniques in the music of the Second Viennese School. Musical excerpts taken from Schoenberg's *Erwartung* and Op. 25 for piano, from Berg's *Wozzeck* and Violin Concerto, and from Alexander Goehr's Quartet. Try this video if you use Class Discussion Idea 4 above.

Rhythm. The Music of the 20th Century: Leaving Home Series. www.films .com (DVD or VHS, color, 52 minutes). Using Stravinsky's *Rite* as a springboard, Simon Rattle narrates this look at revolutionary uses of rhythm in the twentieth century.

The Roots of 20th-Century Music. Dancing on a Volcano: Leaving Home Series. www.films.com (DVD or VHS, color, 52 minutes). Simon Rattle narrates this look at the music of turn-of-the-century Viennese composers, especially Schoenberg, Webern, and Berg. Try this video if you use Lecture-Demonstration Idea 2 above.

Schoenberg, *Arnold Schoenberg. Harmonics: The Innovators of Classical Music* Series. www.films.com (DVD or VHS, color, 27 minutes). Video biography of Schoenberg features expert commentary and musical excerpts from *Moses and Aaron, Transfigured Night, Survivor from Warsaw,* Piano Pieces, Op. 25, Chamber Symphony No. 1, and *Pierrot lunaire.* Musical excerpts feature Pierre Boulez, Glenn Gould, and Erich Leinsdorf. Try this video if you use Class Discussion Idea 4 above.

Schoenberg, *Arnold Schoenberg: My Evolution.* www.films.com (DVD or VHS, color, 50 minutes). Recorded Schoenberg lecture at UCLA serves as narration. Offers a fascinating look at the composer, atonality, and music in the twentieth century. Try this video if you use Class Discussion Idea 4 above.

Schoenberg (and R. Schumann), *Pierrot lunaire/Dichterliebe.* Arthaus Musik (DVD, color, 126 minutes). Probably the best performance of *Pierrot* currently available, but couched in an MTV-style music video gone mad! The movie presents a bizarre nightscape dominated by an overbearing full moon, but the filmic images have little or nothing to do with the words we hear at any given moment. We see cockroaches, nightmares (No. 8), the making of a witch's brew, a peep show, a live corpse in a forensic medicine classroom (No. 18), a murder. These images are often profoundly disturbing, even menacing; at least in that sense they capture the flavor of the poetry. Musically this is top drawer. Soprano Christine Schäfer is probably today's finest *Pierrot* practitioner, and Pierre Boulez leads his crack Ensemble InterContemporain in committed, persuasive performances of literature they excel in. If you dare, use this video to supplement your presentation of *Listen* excerpts or Further Listening Examples from *Pierrot lunaire. Parental advisory:* Some songs contain nudity. Of the songs described in this manual, beware Nos. 18 and 19.

Stravinsky. VAI (DVD, black and white, 50 minutes). This fascinating 1965 documentary follows Stravinsky through a week in his life. Rehearsal footage shows Stravinsky conducting *Symphony of Psalms.* Try this video if you use Class Discussion Idea 3 above.

Stravinsky, *Aspects of Stravinsky.* Kultur Video (VHS, color, 166 minutes). Video biography with commentary by Robert Craft, George Balanchine, Nadia Boulanger, and others. Includes footage of Stravinsky on stage in Paris and performance footage from *Les Noces.*

Stravinsky, *Boulez Conducts Stravinsky.* Image Entertainment (DVD, color, 57 minutes). Pierre Boulez conducts the London Symphony Orchestra in performances of *The Rite of Spring* and *Symphonies of Wind Instruments. Listen* DVD clips from *The Rite of Spring* came from this recording. This disc is an excellent choice if you want to introduce your students to more of this landmark work.

Stravinsky: Devil's Dance from A Soldier's Tale *and Vivo and Finale from* Pulcinella. *The Score: Classical Music Appreciation through Listening* Series. www.films.com (DVD or VHS, color, 15 minutes). This brief video focuses on Stravinsky's use of rhythm and color. Excerpts performed by the Scottish Chamber Orchestra; conducted by William Conway.

Stravinsky: The Final Chorale/Schoenberg: Five Orchestral Pieces. JuxtaPositions Series. Ideale Audience International (DVD, color, 104 minutes). This DVD gives us the commercial release of two fine films available since the early 1990s.

- *The Final Chorale* (49 minutes)—In the Stravinsky film, Robert Craft weaves archival footage from Stravinsky's estate into a study of the composition, instrumentation, and history of Stravinsky's *Symphonies of Wind Instruments*. Includes a complete performance by the Dutch Wind Ensemble.

- *Five Orchestral Pieces* (54 minutes)—In the Schoenberg film, Michael Gielen, Charles Rosen, and Carl E. Schorske analyze Schoenberg's Op. 16 from several perspectives using archival footage, photographs, artwork, biographical information, and a complete performance by the Netherlands Radio Philharmonic. Try this video if you use Lecture-Demonstration Idea 2 or Class Discussion Idea 4 above.

Stravinsky, *The Firebird/Les Noces*. BBC Opus Arte (DVD, color, 108 minutes). Recent video contains Royal Ballet re-creations of two Ballets Russes productions: Stravinsky's *Firebird* and *Les Noces*. They use the original choreography by Fokine and Nijinska, respectively. Use this video to supplement your presentation of Stravinsky.

Stravinsky, *Return of the Firebird*. Decca (DVD, color, 120 minutes). New video contains filmed re-creations of three Ballets Russes productions: Stravinsky's *Petrushka* and *The Firebird* and Rimsky-Korsakov's *Scheherazade*. This Russian production features famous ballet dancers accompanied by the Bolshoi State Academic Theatre Orchestra. They all seem faithful to the original choreography by Michael Fokine, though they use a film studio rather than a stage to create a more naturalistic setting. Use this video to supplement your presentation of Stravinsky.

Stravinsky's Rite of Spring. Keeping Score: Revolutions in Music Series. San Francisco Symphony (DVD, color). Michael Tilson Thomas travels to many locations associated with Stravinsky's life as he narrates this look at Stravinsky's landmark work. The DVD gives a good feel for the sources of Stravinsky's inspiration and the riot that greeted the *Rite*'s première. Also included is a complete performance of *The Rite of Spring* and three excerpts from *The Firebird*. Highly recommended as a supplement to your presentation of *The Rite of Spring* or to introduce your students to more of this groundbreaking work.

Today and Tomorrow. Music in Time Series. www.films.com (DVD or VHS, color, 60 minutes). James Galway narrates this look at music of our own time. Most appropriate for Chapter 22 but includes excerpts from Stravinsky's *The Firebird, The Rite of Spring*, and Symphony in C.

Turn of the Century. Man and Music Series. www.films.com (DVD or VHS, color, 53 minutes). A look at cultural contradictions in turn-of-the-century

Vienna. Covers Freudian psychoanalysis, expressionist paintings by Klimt and Kokoschka, and the transition from nineteenth- to twentieth-century sensibility in Vienna. Includes excerpts from Schoenberg's *Pierrot lunaire*.

The Turn of the Century. Music in Time Series. www.films.com (DVD or VHS, color, 60 minutes). James Galway narrates this look at music in transition. Also appropriate for Chapter 18. Excerpts taken from Debussy's *La Mer* and *Syrinx,* Schoenberg's *Verklärte Nacht,* Berg's String Quartet, and Strauss's expressionistic opera *Salome.* Performers include Galway and the Vienna Philharmonic, conducted by Bernstein, Böhm, and von Karajan.

Twentieth-Century Artistic Revolutions. www.insight-media.com (DVD, color, 32 minutes). This still-image video provides a concise, visually appealing introduction to important philosophic, artistic, and musical trends of the early twentieth century. Part 1 covers turn-of-the-century Paris and features the artwork of Matisse, Picasso, and Braque and music by Satie. Part 2 covers expressionism, with artwork by Kandinsky and Klee and music by Schoenberg, Berg, and Webern.

20th-Century Music in Venice. Five Centuries of Music in Venice Series. www.films.com (DVD or VHS, color, 60 minutes). This program offers a sumptuous portrait of the history, art, and architecture of twentieth-century Venice. Covers Stravinsky, Schoenberg, Hindemith, Bartók, and the postwar avant-garde. Live performances of music by Schoenberg and Stravinsky in Venice.

Weill, *The Threepenny Opera.* Home Vision or Bel Canto Society (DVD, black and white, 110 minutes). The bitingly satirical musical by Kurt Weill and Bertolt Brecht, turned into a 1931 movie by G. W. Pabst. In 1933, Hitler ordered every print of the film destroyed; fortunately, one survived. Lotte Lenya is one of the featured performers. Try this video if you use Lecture-Demonstration Idea 3 above.

Weill, *Ute Lemper Sings Kurt Weill.* Universal (DVD, color, 150 minutes). The acclaimed cabaret-revival singer performs twenty-one songs, some from *The Threepenny Opera.* Try this recording if you use Lecture-Demonstration Idea 3 above.

❦ Software

Great Composers: Handel, Chopin, and Debussy. Zane Publishing (CD-ROM— Windows or Macintosh). This inexpensive CD-ROM includes a multimedia presentation, photographs, quizzes, and sound clips. Available from www.cdaccess.com.

The Norton Masterworks CD-ROM. New York: W. W. Norton (CD-ROM— Macintosh). Authors Daniel Jacobson and Timothy Koozin provide a clever multimedia introduction to twelve important works, including Stravinsky's *Petrushka* and Schoenberg's *Pierrot lunaire.* Features animated, guided listening resources as well as information on the composers, eras, and genres, and the works themselves.

CHAPTER 21

Alternatives to Modernism

Chapter Outline

Boldface indicates works in the recording set.

Important Terms

traditionalism

Neoclassicism

jazz

blues

breaks

concerto first
   movement form

nationalism

folk music

recapitulation

sonata form

square dance

hymn

film music

leitmotivs

theme and variations

totalitarianism

cantata

Teaching Objectives

⅋ Overall Objectives

This chapter will help students acquire familiarity with:

1. Musical features of important traditionalist twentieth-century styles before 1945, especially Neoclassicism, nationalism, and film music.

2. Various alternatives to modernism explored by twentieth-century traditionalist composers and their reasons for rejecting modernism.

3. The influence on music of other art forms, such as ballet, modern dance, and film.

4. Features of twentieth-century American music as they reflected and influenced European music between the world wars.

5. The lives and music of Maurice Ravel, Béla Bartók, Aaron Copland, and Sergei Prokofiev.

6. The impact of totalitarianism on twentieth-century music, especially in the former Soviet Union and Nazi Germany.

7. (*optional*) Traditionalist opera of the early twentieth century, especially the works of Puccini and Strauss.

⅋ Listening Objectives

After completing this chapter, students should be able to:

1. Hear and identify typical uses of the elements of music in traditionalist twentieth-century styles before 1945.

2. Identify and follow important twentieth-century orchestral genres, modern dance scores, and film music.

3. Hear and identify features of important styles and trends in twentieth-century art music, especially Neoclassicism and nationalism.

Lecture Suggestions

⅋ Twentieth-Century Traditionalism

Composers retreated from modernism at many times and in many places during the twentieth century. Composers such as Richard Strauss and Sergei Prokofiev began their careers as "wild-eyed" modernists, but turned toward more traditionalist idioms midway through their careers. The reasons for this retreat were as individual as the composers themselves, yet each example in this chapter flows from trends between the two world wars that affected most composers in the Western world. The spirit of invention and innovation that characterized the years prior to World War I morphed into a devil-may-care attitude in the 1920s, right after the war, which then gave way to profound disillusionment and suspicion of "progress" and technology when the effects of economic depression were felt in many parts of the world. All of these factors deeply affected the music of the late 1920s and 1930s. The period between the wars was characterized by music that was often more conservative and more accessible.

The "traditionalist" neoclassical music of this period was first pioneered by Stravinsky, Prokofiev, and several French composers *(Les Six)* in the early 1920s (see Further Listening Examples below for notes on Stravinsky's first neoclassic work, *Pulcinella,* and for the second movement of *Symphony of Psalms* as well). Composers from other countries, most notably Paul Hindemith in Germany and Walter Piston in the United States, soon followed suit. Modernism was still alive in the newly invented (1920–1923) twelve-tone music of the Second Viennese School (discussed in Chapter 20), and the musical scene quickly polarized into two opposing camps—Schoenberg and the serialists on one side and Stravinsky and the neoclassicists on the other. Neoclassicism was easily the more popular style, and it is no surprise that the composers represented in this chapter—Ravel, Bartók, Copland, and even Prokofiev—each took something from Stravinsky's Neoclassicism. In the end, however, each of these composers developed a unique fusion of styles, blending features of the neoclassical idiom with something else. Ravel fused neoclassicism with impressionism; Bartók, with eastern European folk music; Copland, with American (broadly defined) folk and popular styles; and Prokofiev, with Russian folk themes—with a dash of satire thrown in for good measure. These fusions gave their musical styles a profoundly individual flavor.

♩ Maurice Ravel

Maurice Ravel is often lumped in with Debussy and a few lesser-known composers as an example of French impressionism. Ravel certainly wrote many impressionist works—*Daphnis and Chloe* and any number of piano works come to mind—but this classification overlooks the profound differences between Debussy and Ravel. Kerman and Tomlinson astutely separate the two, placing Debussy alongside other modernist composers in Chapter 20 and Ravel with the traditionalists in this chapter. This doesn't explain all of their differences, nor does it account for the similarities between them, but it does point us in the right direction. A few comparisons between Debussy and Ravel can help clarify these differences:

Melody—With its focus on texture and color, Debussy's music often sounds anti-melodic, using short motives and melodic fragments. Ravel was a melodist through and through. We can almost always find the melody, and its clear, arching phrases often swell to a climax and back down again, much like many of the Romantic melodies we looked at in Unit IV. Ravel's melodies also tend to be modal and diatonic.

Harmony—Debussy used a mix of chord types ranging from simple triads and seventh chords to upper tertian sonorities (ninth, eleventh, and thirteenth chords) to chords stacked in fourths or fifths. Ravel uses all of the above, though he tends to favor triadic and upper tertian sonorities. The most striking difference can be found in their chord progressions. Debussy's chords move with enormous freedom, but Ravel, in spite of his rich harmonic vocabulary, sticks with functional harmony and a clear bass line. In later works, such as the Piano Concerto in G, we hear occasional sharp dissonances (chords with split thirds) and bitonal effects, but these can often be traced to the influence of jazz and its blue notes.

Rhythm—Debussy's rhythms can be as vague as his melodic material, but sharply defined rhythms are Ravel's life blood. Beat and meter tend to be clear, and Ravel is far more likely to move in quick tempo and to use dance rhythms.

Texture—Ravel is as likely as Debussy to use rich, multilayered textures. Ravel places more emphasis on the melody, however, and we often hear melody-and-accompaniment texture. Even so, Ravel manages to retain a multilayered feel with accompanimental textures that are rhythmically more active than the melody itself.

Color—Simply put, Ravel's orchestrations are brilliant—in every sense of the word. Ravel knew the orchestra backwards and forward, and he knew instinctively how to use color to clarify the harmony, texture, and form—and to ravish the ear as well. His orchestration of Musorgsky's *Pictures at an Exhibition* provides a remarkable example. Nonetheless, note that these attributes could describe many Romantic composers as well. By contrast, Debussy did not simply use color to clarify other elements; for Debussy, color *was* the primary element.

Form—Debussy favored **A B A** forms and other simple structures that could be treated ambiguously. The phrase "literal return" was simply not in his vocabulary. Ravel turns to the past for his forms, using sonata, rondo, and other forms from the Classical era. Ravel treats these forms freely, of course, but their derivation remains clear.

We find many points of similarity between Debussy and Ravel, especially in their harmonic vocabulary and use of texture, but where they differ, Ravel tends to be the more traditional of the two. This does not mean that Ravel's music avoids modernism at all costs. Ravel's use of bitonality, chords with split thirds, or materials borrowed from jazz and popular styles all point to a modernist sensibility. Even his cool, classical objectivity resonated with anti-Romantic modernists in the neoclassical camp. Still, his predilections became evident in the 1920s when he and Stravinsky evolved in different directions, and Ravel found his music rejected by the younger generation of French composers, *Les Six*. Ravel never went out of his way to be modernist or traditionalist, but his sin in the eyes of his younger colleagues was his unwillingness to reject Romanticism completely. Today we can be more objective and appreciate the often ravishing qualities of Ravel's music on their own merits.

RAVEL **Piano Concerto in G**

Ravel liked to work on more than one piece at a time, but these simultaneous creations were often polar opposites. Examples from earlier in his career paired the impressionistic *Miroirs* with the Neoclassical *Sonatine* or the childhood fantasy of *Mother Goose* with the fiendishly difficult, often disturbing *Gaspard de la Nuit*. Late in his career, from 1929 to 1931, Ravel was working on two piano concertos: the dark, weighty Concerto for the Left Hand (written for Paul Wittgenstein, brother of philosopher Ludwig, who lost an arm fighting in World War I and commissioned one-handed concertos from many major composers), and the light, mercurial Concerto in G.

Like any good concerto from the Classical era, and like most from the Romantic, the Concerto in G employs the typical three-movement, fast-slow-fast format associated with the genre. Ravel's outer movements are fast and jazzy, full of fizz, panache, and exquisite orchestral colors. In the slow movement, the spirit of Mozart hovers over some of the most sublimely beautiful music ever written; even here, however, "blue" notes add a dissonant bite to the harmonic language. In fact, the influence of jazz permeates this work more than any other by Ravel; we hear it in the blue notes, the dissonant jazz harmonies, the syncopated rhythms, the muted trumpet "breaks" and "fills," and the trombone *glissandi*. As the authors point out, Ravel uses jazz idioms without sacrificing the "delicacy and elegance" so typical of his music. Ravel's unique mix of modern sounds and classical forms, of jazz and Mozart, makes for an intoxicating, exquisitely spiced *ragoût*.

First Movement

Where to begin? The authors point out Ravel's free use of sonata form—his omission of an orchestral exposition and a proper development—and even though we find three themes that might correspond to first, second, and closing themes, sonata form is hardly the point here, at least not in the way it would be in a Beethoven symphony. In fact, the three themes afford so much pleasure in and of themselves that we might easily forget about form. We must not ignore form, however; Ravel uses the principles of repetition, contrast, return, and variation throughout, and the three themes divide this movement into clearly demarcated, easily recognized sections. Further, the very clarity of these themes makes Ravel's digressions all the more special, most notably the dreamlike episode. Use these themes as the key that will unlock this movement for your students. Introduce them one at a time, playing them and pointing out their characteristic features. As you do so, be sure to help students hear the inflections of jazz, blues, and popular music in this music.

Theme 1—By far the quickest theme, this jaunty tune clearly demonstrates the diatonic nature of many of Ravel's melodies. It almost sounds pentatonic until we add a sixth pitch in m. 6, and only once does Ravel slip in the leading tone, thus retaining a modal flavor. The authors note that this tune is *not* jazzy, but it definitely evokes the flavor of popular music of the 1910s and 1920s, especially with the irregular, syncopated chords in the accompaniment.

Theme 2—At once the most introspective and the jazziest of the three themes, theme 2 moves much more slowly than theme 1. The alternation between the opening triplet and the sustained note that follows gives this theme a searching quality, an effect amplified by the frequent "blue" notes in the melody's quarter-note continuation. Ravel creates these blue notes by pitting a major-key accompaniment against a minor-key (actually Dorian mode, usually, with the occasional Phrygian flatted 2) melody—a bimodal effect. Demonstrate by playing an F-sharp major chord with your left hand and any melodic patterns that include the pitch A natural with your right. Finally, make sure students hear the other notable jazz feature of theme 2, the frequent use of breaks. These are the instrumental fills that we so often hear between phrases in a jazz or blues performance, and they interrupt theme 2 every time it appears. In fact, these breaks take on a life of their own later on, in the middle of the "driving music for piano," for instance.

Theme 3—A broad, rising theme capable of building to a genuine climax, this theme, more than the others, evokes the world of Gershwin's popular music. It even has a dancelike little fill of its own in between phrases, a staccato two-eighth-note figure on the weak beats that lasts for two measures. Like theme 1, it sounds pentatonic at first, until Ravel adds the other two scale tones. More thoughtful in its first statement by the piano, it swells to a climax in the orchestral statement once the brass section takes over.

Once students are familiar with these themes, display Listening Chart 23 and play this movement. Point out each of the main themes and sections as they go by. Call attention to contrasting sections, particularly the "vigorous, driving music," approach to the cadence, and retransition in the exposition's second group as well as the "dreamlike episode," cadenza, and coda in the movement's second half. Note that many of these sections use previously heard themes that have been subjected to the Lisztian technique of thematic transformation. The "dreamlike episode" is especially interesting. Ravel's delicately impressionistic harp colors here are so evocative that we almost don't recognize this as a transformation of theme 2 until the break interrupts with a vengeance, this time adding flutter-tongue effects (in the piccolo, piccolo clarinet, and trumpet) and string *glissandi* to the trombone smear—like something straight out of 1920s jazz. No less striking is the subsequent horn statement of theme 2. It takes the horn way up to the top of its register at a *piano* dynamic, accompanied by Ravel's trademark super-scale, passing from low bassoon to flute and then to piccolo before coming back down again.

As you wrap things up, briefly note the special color the trills provide in the cadenza's transformation of theme 2. Finally, take some time with coda. Theme 3, the "vigorous, driving music," and the cadence idea work well to build up a head of steam, but this driving music's surging unpredictability won't work for the coda. Instead, Ravel wants something fast, tuneful, flashy, and brilliant to take us down the home stretch. The obvious place to go? Theme 1. Ravel borrows several short motives from this tune, trading them back and forth between trumpet and a flute/piccolo clarinet pair in best jazz fashion. The concluding measures borrow another motive from theme 1, this time an accompanimental figure first played by the strings (mm. 14–15) just before the piccolo drops out and the clarinet starts "trading twos" with the flute. Violins and violas play simple triads descending in parallel motion. Ravel reuses this same idea at the very end, but now with full orchestra *fortissimo,* moving from G down an octave to G using a bizarre scale that includes a raised leading tone but lowers scale steps three and two—our blue notes from theme 2. Parallelism was one of the principle devices used by impressionist composers, but Ravel's use of *staccato* articulation, orchestral *tutti,* and altered tones at a *fortissimo* dynamic create a cheeky sound with a sharp clarity that is anything but impressionistic. The final three bars give us Ravel the Neoclassicist at work.

This superb example pays homage to all of the streams that feed into Ravel's personal musical fusion: impressionism and Neoclassicism as well as popular and jazz styles. Modernist and traditionalist, ravishing and prickly—often all at the same time—Ravel's novel, individual music provides a most attractive alternative to modernism.

7 Béla Bartók

Béla Bartók presents a rather different situation than neoclassical colleagues who looked to the Classical and even the Baroque eras for models. Bartók found significant alternatives to Romanticism in the folk music of his native Hungary and neighboring regions, music that remains unfamiliar to many Western listeners. Still, the very folk traditions that allowed him to break free of Romanticism guaranteed that his music would retain a degree of accessibility—unlike the music of many other modernists. Overall, Bartók's music was not as groundbreaking as the music of Debussy, Stravinsky, or Schoenberg, especially when it mellowed in the late 1930s and the 1940s. Nonetheless, even these late works could never be mistaken for the music of Romanticism, and Bartók's music has come to occupy a position of great importance in the twentieth-century repertoire. The following features characterize Bartók's musical language:

1. Bartók's music absorbed the sounds and rhythms of his native Hungarian folk music. This ancient, often unusual music provided Bartók with evocative alternatives to traditional tonal structures. He came by his nationalism honestly, having listened to, collected, and studied central European folk music to the point where it became a natural language for him. His published collections of Hungarian, Rumanian, Bulgarian, Turkish, and even north African folk songs fill three library shelves.

2. Bartók's rhythmic language, closely allied to the powerful rhythms of Hungarian folk music, owes much to Stravinsky's rhythmic innovations as well.

3. Bartók's incredible motivic development and unity are worthy of Schoenberg (and Liszt and Beethoven). Bartók's String Quartet No. 4 (1926) is a motivic tour de force that few composers could hope to achieve.

4. Bartók worshiped the music of Debussy. Debussy influenced Bartók's approach to orchestration and his manipulation of tone color.

5. Bartók often used the forms of the Classical era. In this way, he was sympathetic with such late Romantic composers as Brahms and Dvořák, who felt that the compositional impulse had to be reined in and controlled in order to create music of lasting value. This sympathy naturally allied him with neoclassical composers between the world wars. (See notes on the *Pulcinella* Suite and the second movement of *Symphony of Psalms* in Further Listening Examples below for teaching suggestions for Stravinsky's Neoclassicism.)

BARTÓK Music for Strings, Percussion, and Celesta

This twentieth-century masterpiece comes as close to a symphony as any work Bartók wrote. Its four movements contain the careful formal design, Hungarian-influenced melody and harmony, exciting rhythm, and rigorous compositional construction that characterize Bartók's best music. Suggestions in Further Listening Examples below offer tools for a presentation of this complete four-movement work. Use them if you would like to explore Bartók's creative use of the Classical four-movement plan and the many motivic links between movements that make this a cyclic work. The notes immediately below focus on the second movement.

Bartók's second movement employs the fast tempo and sonata form that we expect at the beginning of a symphony. From the outset we realize that Bartók takes some liberties with the Classical four-movement format. Some other unique features of this work include its instrumentation, its antiphonal effects, and its special effects. The title itself points to the unique instrumentation of this work. Unlike most symphonies, this work includes no brass or woodwind instruments, and the percussion section employs greater diversity of instruments than any work in the recorded set prior to this chapter. The score calls for two string orchestras, piano, harp, timpani, xylophone, a battery of unpitched percussion instruments—and celesta. The two orchestras are often used antiphonally, a throwback to the antiphonal choirs of Gabrieli (be sure to play this in stereo!). In an interesting role reversal, Bartók often uses *pizzicato* string sounds to increase the percussiveness of the overall sound, while his percussion instruments, notably timpani and xylophone, sometimes take over melodic material. In the midst of these percussive and plucked sonorities, even the piano sounds like a percussion instrument. The most striking colors in this music, however, appear in the slower, atmospheric movements when the celesta enters or when we hear the xylophone or the rolling timpani *glissandi* (see Further Listening Examples below).

Second Movement

Bartók offers one contrast after another in the frenetic second movement. Even when he brings themes back throughout the movement, they are often varied and transformed. That sounds like a recipe for cacophony, but the composer holds it all together within a sonata-form structure and tosses in a few good folklike tunes along the way to maintain interest. Treat this movement as you would any other sonata-form movement. Acquaint the students with the main themes first. Since Bartók transforms several themes in the recapitulation, take extra time to play both the exposition and the recapitulation versions of each major theme. If you use suggestions for this work from Further Listening Examples below, note the similarities between theme 1 and the fugue subject from movement I: Both begin on a primary pitch, move up to the pitch a tritone higher, and return to the primary pitch (C to F sharp and back to C in this movement's theme). Once students are familiar with the main themes, play through the entire movement. Display Listening Chart 24 and point out each theme and section as it goes by. Make a note of the *pizzicato* scales in section 2 of the development; these figures anticipate the rondo theme of the final movement.

In the discussion that follows, relate what students heard to the list of Bartók's style features above.

1. Even the Listening Chart clearly labels several themes with a folklike character. These tunes often use unfamiliar scale patterns, but they do help to establish tonal centers more clearly than do some examples from Chapter 20. Even when the melodies are hard to sing back accurately, their tuneful character makes them distinctive, memorable, and inviting. In some ways, these tunes hark back to Haydn's inclusion of eastern European folk melodies in many of his late symphonies.

2. Bartók's rhythms often dance with energy and vitality. Irregular accents and rhythms often keep us off-balance, but we can often rely on a secure, stable beat. Again we can thank folk-song influences for rhythms with so much character.

3. Bartók's use of motives and motivic development remind the listener of the symphonies of Haydn or Beethoven. Underlying this movement's sense of contrast and variety are several distinctive motives that bind the whole structure together.

4. No one will mistake this work for one by Debussy, but Bartók uses tone colors just as effectively as his French counterpart. That feat becomes even more remarkable given the limited instrumentation Bartók imposes on himself in this work. He accomplishes this task through the use of reverse typecasting. Strings are supposed to play lyrical melodies; Bartók turns them into percussion instruments that pluck and scrape. Percussion instruments are supposed to provide splashes of color, but only at the high points of the piece; Bartók gives them melodies and keeps them busy continuously. The piano is supposed to project Chopin's smooth lyricism; Bartók makes the instrument pound out ferocious rhythms and percussive melodies.

5. Bartók uses the sonata form of the Classical era, and he stretches and adapts the form creatively just as Beethoven did. He then fills the form with strikingly original melodic, harmonic, and rhythmic materials. His music takes

full advantage of sonata form's implicit dramatic qualities; at the same time he imbues it with the tensions and dissonances typical of twentieth-century styles. The result is a vivacious yet powerfully dramatic work that successfully rethinks the symphony in modern terms.

❦ Aaron Copland

COPLAND *Appalachian Spring*

Aaron Copland was born to Jewish immigrant parents in Brooklyn, New York. He received a solid musical education, and at the age of twenty he traveled to Europe to study in Paris with Nadia Boulanger. After his return to the United States, he began to develop strong ideas about the directions American music should take. Copland felt that as an American, he should write music that said something to his compatriots. Additionally, like many artists who experienced the Depression, he felt his music should be relevant to common folk. To this end, Copland drew freely upon various vernacular idioms during his compositional career. In *Appalachian Spring,* he based an entire section of the ballet on a Shaker hymn tune called "Simple Gifts." In his ballet *Rodeo* (see Further Listening Examples below), he used cowboy songs and square-dance tunes to evoke a period and a locale.

The textbook provides commentary on each of the ballet's six sections; the recorded set includes the first two and the last two sections. These four sections reveal the fascinating web of motivic relationships Copland conceived to bind the entire work together. If you cannot take time to present all of them, focus your attention on section 5, the best-known portion of the ballet. The suggestions below cover sections 1, 2, 5, and 6; you can use them in whole or, if time is short, in part. In your presentation, take time to describe Copland's style, set the scene (a ballet tells a story, just as an opera does), point out motivic connections between sections, and then consider each section individually.

Copland's music possesses a unique, identifiable sound; his orchestral sonorities have an open quality that some students associate with America's wide-open spaces. In fact, many musicians regard Copland as the dean of American composers, the one who finally answered Dvořák's challenge to write genuinely American music inspired by rich native folk traditions. To achieve this characteristic sound, Copland uses musical elements as follows:

Texture—thin, with lots of space between instruments

Tone color—pure, bright, vivid

Melody—tuneful, often with a folk quality

Tonality—clearly established tonal centers

Harmony—simple triadic chords, sometimes juxtaposed, with mild dissonance mixed in

Rhythm—jauntily irregular jazz-influenced rhythms

Appalachian Spring, perhaps Copland's most famous dance work (choreographed by modern dance pioneer Martha Graham), depicts what the composer described as a "pioneer celebration of Spring in a newly built farmhouse in Pennsylvania in the early 1800's." In section 1 of the ballet suite, we meet the main characters: a bride and groom, a preacher, and their neighbor. The celebration turns out to be part wedding reception and part housewarming. The festivities include several square dances (section 2), dances for the bride and groom, a revival sermon, and hymns (section 5). In section 6, the guests leave, and the final scene shows the newlyweds entering their new home together. Textbook pages 363–65 set the scene nicely for the individual sections described below.

Copland uses free musical forms that follow the story and the dance (except in section 5, which uses theme and variations form), just as Stravinsky and other ballet composers did. Nonetheless, Copland's music is never aimless; to create a sense of thematic unity, he employs an ingenious web of motives that recur throughout the ballet. The scenes in the recorded set serve well to demonstrate this cyclic procedure. In the four analytical diagrams provided below, motives are labeled consistently so that you can easily find restatements in later sections. Note especially the **a** motive in sections 1, 2, and 6 and the **d** motive in sections 2 and 6.

Section 1

The opening suggests the stillness of dawn and the spaciousness of a "vast landscape." The motives used in this section include:

a   simple triadic motives, includes Copland's well-known juxtaposition of A and E major triads, introduces ♫♩ rhythm (slow)

b   slow, lyric melody, first introduced by violins

Copland's use of chord juxtaposition creates a strikingly different effect from the polychords Stravinsky uses in *The Rite of Spring* (Dance of the Adolescents). Compare the two at the keyboard. Stravinsky's E-flat[7]/F-flat major chord (F flat–A flat–c flat–f flat/g–b flat–d flat[1]–e flat[1]) sounds dense and harshly dissonant; Copland's E major/A major chord (c sharp[1]–e[1]–a[1]/b[1]–e[2]–g sharp[2]) sounds light, spacious, and slightly ambiguous—a lovely sonority.

The form of this section can be diagrammed as follows:

a	b	a′	b′	a
clarinet	strings		flute, oboe, bassoon	clarinet
0:00	0:44	1:10	1:26	2:15

Section 2

This music, with its fiddle tunes, quick tempo, and frequently changing meters, depicts a square dance. The motives used in this section include:

c   hoe-down theme—octave skips, angular arpeggios, and jaunty rhythms

a   same triadic motives used in section 1 (♫♩ rhythm), but much faster

d   slower, an arching, lyric hymnlike melody; begins with a slow **a** motive

The form of this section is outlined below. As the diagram suggests, the hoe-down tune (**c**) reveals itself bit by bit—first just the motive, then a phrase, and finally the whole melody. The hymnlike motive (**d**) mingles with the square dance in the **B** sections.

A					B	
c	a	c	a	c	d′	c and d
motive		phrase		tune		hymn-tune mingles
strings		strings		flutes		with the hoe-down
m. 1	m. 5	m. 12	m. 16	m. 19	m. 24	m. 30
0:00	0:09	0:19	0:25	0:30	0:37	0:46

A						B	A	
c	a	c	a	c	a	c and d	c	a
motive flute		phrase strings		tune flute	developed	hymn added	motive flute	
m. 48	m. 49	m. 56	m. 61	m. 62	m. 69	m. 85	m. 97	m. 99
1:13	1:15	1:27	1:33	1:35	1:45	2:09	2:32	2:35

Section 5

This section must surely be the best-known portion of the ballet suite. Copland offers a theme and variations on the eighteenth-century Shaker hymn "Simple Gifts." The motives used here include:

e   first phrase of "Simple Gifts"

e′   second phrase of "Simple Gifts"

f   third phrase of "Simple Gifts"

e″   fourth phrase of "Simple Gifts"

As the letters suggest, "Simple Gifts" uses the **a a b a** structure typical of many tunes. Mozart often embellishes the tune beyond recognition in his theme and variations movements, but Copland hardly varies the theme. Instead, he alters the accompaniment, the texture, and even the phrase structure in order to vary the mood, a procedure that closely resembles thematic transformation.

The form of this section can be diagrammed as follows:

Theme				Variation 1				Variation 2		
e	e′	f	e″	e	e′	f	e″	e	e′ imitation	e′ imitation
clarinet				oboe				trombone and strings		
m. 1	m. 9	m. 17	m. 25	m. 20	m. 24	m. 28	m. 32	m. 36	m. 46	m. 55
0:00	0:08	0:16	0:23	0.36	0.43	0:50	0:56	1:03	1:17	1:30

Interlude	Variation 3				Interlude		Variation 4	
	e	e′	f	e″	f	e′	e	e′
	brass				woodwinds		tutti	
m. 63	m. 69	m. 77	m. 85	m. 93	m. 101	m. 109	m. 117	m. 126
1:42	1:51	1:56	2:02	2:08	2:14	2:22	2:30	2:41

Section 6

After bidding their guests farewell, the newlywed couple enters the house to begin their life together, and the music recalls the simple spaciousness of the ballet's opening moments. The motives used in this section include:

g   simple lyric theme, "like a prayer," according to the program; Copland's favorite passage—he said it should sound like a church organ

d   arching, lyric hymnlike melody; begins with a slowed-down **a** motive

a   triadic motives from section 1 (♪♪♩ rhythm)

The form of this section can be diagrammed as follows:

g	g′	g″	g′	d	a
strings	strings	winds	*tutti*	flute	clarinet
m. 1	m. 10	m. 19	m. 27	m. 36	m. 52
0:00	0:22	0:43	0:57	1:20	2:14

❣ The Rise of Film Music

The year 1926 saw the release of the first-ever "talking picture," *Don Juan,* with Mary Astor and John Barrymore. The very next year, *The Jazz Singer* with Al Jolson became the first megahit in the new genre, and there was no turning back. Movie moguls who imagined they could continue producing silent movies found that no one was interested in anything but "talkies." What followed was a mad scramble to update equipment and produce talking pictures as fast as was humanly possible. Not surprisingly, music was an important part of this new kind of movie, and many composers involved themselves in the industry. Kerman and Tomlinson provide a nice overview of the rise of film music, and they rightly point out Wagner's connection to movie music. Wagner's leitmotiv technique had a huge impact on all of the arts. Even major literary figures— from Thomas Mann to the French symbolists (friends of Debussy) to F. Scott Fitzgerald—applied this technique to their writings. It should come as no surprise that the techniques Wagner used to help the orchestra tell the story in his music dramas proved equally effective in film.

In looking at Sergei Prokofiev's forays into film music, one must always be aware of the undercurrents created by the political system in which he lived and worked. On the one hand, there was the Comunist Party dogma concerning the arts, called socialist realism. These principles made it clear that art must serve the people while avoiding the extremes of "bourgeois decadence" (Western modernism). On the other hand, there was Stalin, a dictator who ruled with an iron hand but who was notoriously capricious where music and the arts were concerned. Interpreting the guidelines of socialist realism was tricky in the best of circumstances, but even when composers could make a good case for themselves, it made no difference whatsoever if Stalin didn't like their music. The *Listen* textbook clearly spells out the consequences for composers such as Prokofiev who ran afoul of His Arbitrariness. As you present Prokofiev to your students, don't stray too far from these undercurrents. For traditional college-age students, the Cold War is ancient history, but the situation in the former Soviet Union raises profound and enduring questions about the role of the artist in society and the appropriate role of the government as arbiter of public taste. You can use this opportunity to spark some good discussion (see Class Discussion Idea 6 below).

PROKOFIEV *Alexander Nevsky*

We're talking movie music here, and it makes no more sense with film than it does with opera to simply sit and listen to the music. Students need to *see* the relationship between the sounds, the action, and the dialogue, and your class discussion will be much richer when they can see the "big picture." If at all possible, you *must* use the Sergei Eisenstein movie *Alexander Nevsky* as part of your classroom presentation, and the Criterion Collection edition is the one to get. To top it off, the story of how Eisenstein and Prokofiev came to create this movie is an epic in its own right, weaving together threads from the history of American cinema, the drama of World War II, and menacing tales of Stalin and his "art police."

The Criterion Collection DVD contains a truly fascinating twenty-minute documentary on the making of *Alexander Nevsky*. You may not have time to play it for your class, but take the time to watch it for yourself—it's the best preparation you can have to teach this excerpt. What follows is a brief summary of the highlights, organized by topic.

American film history—You might expect the director of a 1930s Russian historical epic to borrow ideas from American cinema, but would you expect the biggest influence to be Mickey Mouse? Walt Disney Studios were pioneers in developing precise synchronization between sound and video, and both Eisenstein and Prokofiev visited the studios while visiting the United States. Eisenstein was not able to take full advantage of these techniques (it was his first talking picture, after all), but some of the sound effects in *Nevsky* are frankly cartoonish—for example, the descending trombone *glissandi* as the last German soldier drowns after the ice has given way.

Stalin—In 1937, both Eisenstein and Prokofiev were in great danger. The film director had produced a string of unsuccessful movies, and Prokofiev, recently back in Russia after years of living in the West, was viewed with great suspicion. Both needed to score a hit with *Alexander Nevsky* to rehabilitate their standing with Stalin. For his part, Stalin was so convinced they would botch the project that he placed spies in the production crew. As the movie neared completion, Stalin arranged for a private midnight showing of the movie (Prokofiev and Eisenstein were not invited)—and he really liked what he saw. Sadly, once it had Stalin's seal of approval, it wouldn't have been prudent to make any changes. Given time to do it right, further edits would have been made, a suddenly "missing" reel might have been restored, Prokofiev would have rerecorded the orchestral score in state-of-the-art sound, and so on.

World War II—The movie proved very successful when it was released in 1938, a real crowd pleaser. Stalin went on record in support of the movie, and even conferred the Order of Lenin on the filmmaker. Less than a year later, however, Russia signed a nonaggression treaty with Germany. Not wanting to ruffle German feathers, Stalin had the movie yanked from theaters. The tables turned again when the Nazis invaded Russia, and *Nevsky* was played throughout the country as a powerful propaganda tool in the Soviet war effort.

Alexander Nevsky's legacy—The justly famous Battle on Ice sequence was unlike anything ever seen on the big screen. Even New York audiences at the 1939 U.S. première were bowled over. As film critic J. Hoberman describes it on the Criterion Collection Web site, "this strategically undercranked and brilliantly edited mix of massing soldiers and slashing close combat—alternately horrifying and carnivalesque—would serve as a prototype for the battlefield scenes in Laurence Olivier's *Henry V*, Akira Kurosawa's *Seven Samurai*, and Stanley Kubrick's *Spartacus*." Whatever its flaws, this film became a legitimate landmark in the history of cinema.

The Battle on Ice

Just as with any opera, plot comes first! Alexander Nevsky was a great hero of Russia's Middle Ages. At the age of only nineteen he had defeated Swedish invaders, and now he is being called on to fight off a Teutonic invasion. The decisive battle takes place on the frozen ice of Lake Chudskoe, which Nevsky hopes will place the Germans and their heavy armor at a disadvantage. His ill-prepared army of soldiers and peasants cannot match the training, precision, or technology of the German knights in their full battle armor, but after a battle of epic proportions, the Russians somehow carry the day with a combination of heroic bravery and shrewd strategy. In the end, goodness is rewarded and evil-doers are punished.

Given *Alexander Nevsky*'s role as a propaganda vehicle, this movie deals more in stereotypes than in character study (though the reel that mysteriously disappeared after Stalin's midnight viewing might have given us something more!). Nevsky himself is a tall, blond, unflappable hero given to grand pro-nouncements ("He who comes to Russia with a sword will die by the sword!"), and his ragtag Russian army shows spunk, grit, and courage in spite of their all-too-human flaws. The Germans wear helmets that cover enough of their faces to give them a depersonalized, menacing appearance (the foot soldiers' helmets closely resemble Nazi gear). They make formidable, even terrifying adversaries, but in the end they are no match for the Russians. The Germans who survive the battle run like cowards, only to plunge to their deaths in freezing water when the ice breaks up underneath them.

Nearly half an hour in length, this battle on the ice is the movie's *raison d'être*, but since no recording of the soundtrack is available, both of our *Listen* excerpts come from the cantata Prokofiev wrote to piggyback on the movie's success. To bring us closer to the movie itself, Kerman and Tomlinson have wisely pared away material that was newly composed for the cantata, leaving us with music very nearly identical to the soundtrack that accompanies this epic battle scene. The first excerpt corresponds to track 13 on the Criterion Collection DVD, and the second excerpt gives us the music from track 15.

The first *Listen* excerpt begins with the German and Russian troops in battle formation at opposite ends of the lake. This menacing music portrays a sense of dread in anticipation of the battle, and the motives in the brass evoke the terrifying sounds of German battle trumpets. Halfway through the excerpt, the tempo picks up as the German army begins its advance across the ice. The camera cuts between close-ups of various Russian soldiers and the faceless Germans riding across the ice in their formidable wedge formation. The battle itself begins just at the point where this excerpt ends, and Eisenstein gives us only the clanking of metal for the first few minutes of the battle. In fact, the director continues to alternate between music and the noises of battle through-out this scene.

After the German wedge has driven deep into the Russian line, Russian troops that Nevsky has held in reserve are ordered to charge. With cries of "For Russia!" the Russian reserves attack both sides of the wedge to the ac-companiment of the second *Listen* excerpt, in effect surrounding this first wave of German soldiers. This jaunty music appears to symbolize Russian cheek and chutzpah—a kind of optimistic, "Here I am to save the day" theme. Once you've heard this tune, you know the Germans don't stand a chance. In fact, Prokofiev brings this same theme back at the end, once the battle has turned into a rout.

In the movie, the battle goes on for another twenty minutes. Except for the novel percussion sounds that accompany the Germans as they thrash about in the lake's freezing waters, there is not much that is new, musically speaking. Prokofiev reuses and reworks the music from these two excerpts throughout the battle scene. This makes your job much easier! You only need to introduce a few themes and motives—the ones identified in Listening Chart 25 will do nicely. If possible, use short clips from the movie so students can hear these in context. After each clip, ask students what each theme expresses, and what it adds to the overall effect of the clip. (As an interesting exercise, play these clips twice, first without sound and then with. How does Prokofiev's score change one's understanding of what is happening on the screen?)

Once your students are familiar with these motives, explain that they are similar to Wagner's leitmotivs. They will recur throughout the scene, and each one has its own associations with specific emotions, characters, symbols, props, and/or events. In this case, some are linked to the Germans and some to the Russians; some are ominous and some optimistic; and so on. But like all good leitmotivs, they are subject to transformation over time. The German horn-call motives that sounded so threatening and dangerous at the beginning of the battle are reduced to a weak caricature twenty minutes later. When your students are clear on these concepts, they are ready to watch the battle. If you have time, play the entire scene. Leave some time for discussion at the end.

Additional Teaching Suggestions

❣ Lecture-Demonstration Ideas

1. Invite an ethnomusicologist to class. The work of early twentieth-century ethnomusicologists proved invaluable to the development of twentieth-century nationalism; Bartók himself was a distinguished ethnomusicologist, Stravinsky's *Rite of Spring* drew on a collection of Russian folk melodies, and Copland's music is full of folk tunes from the Americas. Your guest can talk about the influence of folk music on art music, field questions about Global Perspectives examples from the textbook, and provide refreshing insights into the complex relationship between music and culture. Many ethnomusicologists take a hands-on approach to teaching, which makes for especially interesting classroom sessions.

2. Invite a dancer or dance historian to class. In addition to demonstrating the differences between classical ballet and modern dance, your guest can discuss the role of dancers like Nijinsky (choreographer for *Rite of Spring*—see Chapter 20) or Martha Graham (choreographer for Copland's *Appalachian Spring*) in the development of modern dance.

3. Read criticism of twentieth-century music. In his *Lexicon of Musical Invective* (Seattle: University of Washington Press, 1965), Nicolas Slonimsky compiled deliciously caustic reviews of the music of great composers. You can find reviews of many composers in Unit V, including Schoenberg, Webern, Debussy, Stravinsky, Bartók, Berg, Gershwin, Copland, and Varèse. Students learn to take these with a grain of salt when even Copland's tame, appealing music comes under fire.

4. Look at more facets of Ravel's musical personality. Over the course of his career, Ravel demonstrated a preference for certain sources of inspiration— themes that he revisited time and time again. Examples include his childhood fantasy-themed works: *Mother Goose* Suite or *L'enfant et les sortileges* (*The Child Bewitched*); works that feature Spanish exoticism: *Rapsodie espagnole* or *L'heure espagnole* (*The Spanish Hour*); or his Baroque- or Classical-influenced works: *Le tombeau de Couperin* or *Menuet antique*. See Sound Recordings below for suggested performances.

5. Introduce your students to "golden section" proportions and the Fibonacci series. Ernö Lendvai, in his article from *Bartók Studies* (pp. 40–61), takes the

"golden section" proportions frequently found in nature and applies them to specific works by Bartók. Bartók himself was interested in such matters, as seen in his "overtone" scale (see Further Listening Examples below), and Lendvai has demonstrated the presence of these proportions in the structure of several Bartók works, including the first movement of Music for Strings, Percussion, and Celesta. The article also includes fascinating information about Bartók's chords, scales, and polar tonality.

6. Explore the often tense, sometimes dangerous relationship between Shostakovich or Prokofiev and the totalitarian Russian regime under which they worked. These composers never knew from one concert to the next when they might incur Stalin's wrath. A number of useful video documentaries deal with this topic. See Video Recordings below for resources.

♪ Class Discussion Ideas

1. *What did Ravel think about all the changes taking place in contemporary music?* Arbie Orenstein's *A Ravel Reader: Correspondence, Articles, Interviews* (New York: Columbia University Press, 1990) provides a fascinating collection of Ravel's own writings. Read excerpts for the class, especially those that discuss *Listen* composers such as Chopin, Wagner, Musorgsky, Debussy, and Stravinsky. Ask your students whether they agree or disagree—and why.

2. *How does Bartók's Music for Strings, Percussion, and Celesta compare with the Classical symphony?* Have the students help you reconstruct the Classical symphony's four-movement plan as you write on the board. Ask them to compare the outline of Bartók's movements on the Additional Listening Chart from Appendix I with the diagram on the board. How are they similar? How do they differ? Play excerpts from Bartók and from Haydn's Symphony No. 95. Ask students to describe differences in timbre (articulation and special coloristic effects), form, and rhythm. Point out that though Bartók uses traditional forms, his musical language is far removed from that of Classical music. (See Further Listening Examples below for more detailed lecture suggestions on this work.)

3. *Does Copland's music sound American?* In Chapter 18 we looked at Russian nationalism, but with Copland we have an example of nationalism that really hits home for many American students. Play portions of *Appalachian Spring*, especially section 5, or find a recording of "Hoe-down" from *Rodeo*. Many students will agree that these sound "American," but make them pinpoint specific musical features that create this impression. See Sound Recordings below for suggested performances.

4. *Who was Nadia Boulanger?* In the twentieth century, women gradually gained acceptance as performers and composers. Nadia Boulanger, one of the most compelling teachers of the century, helped to change attitudes toward women musicians. Don G. Campbell chronicles her impact on young American composers in *Master Teacher: Nadia Boulanger* (Washington, D.C.: Pastoral Press, 1984, pp. 31 and following). Read excerpts from this book to generate discussion. The following questions can help, especially if you discuss popular music: *What roles do women play in music today? How many women do you know in musical careers? What do they do?*

5. *What was the effect of the Depression on American music and culture?* Display paintings by Wyeth and other artists of the 1930s. Ask students to recount stories they heard from their parents or grandparents about the Depression.

Show clips from Depression-era movies that are filled with glitzy production numbers and peopled by suave, urbane American aristocrats who lead perfectly happy lives—entertaining escapist fare. You can contrast this with excerpts from Steinbeck novels such as *The Grapes of Wrath*. Use these images and stories to paint a picture of American life during the Depression. This material makes a good backdrop against which to view Copland's *Appalachian Spring*.

6. *What was it like trying to compose with Stalin looking over your shoulder?* The Stalin years in Russia were a frightening time for composers whose music fell out of favor. Share examples with your students from some of the standard collections of primary source materials. Weiss and Taruskin's *Music in the Western World* (Schirmer, 1984) contains a Soviet denouncement of Western modernism ("Music and Ideology," pp. 495–98) and Prokofiev's 1948 response after he was officially censured for writing music that was too radical ("A Composer on Trial," pp. 499–502). Burkholder's *A History of Western Music* (Norton, 2006) includes the *Pravda* review (p. 879) that condemned Shostakovich's too-modernist opera, *Lady Macbeth;* and Fisk's *Composers on Music* (Northeastern University Press, 1997) contains Shostakovich's reflections on writing Symphony No. 5, his "response" to that public censure (pp. 359–60). This raises a host of questions that are well worth pursuing: *Do composers have a right to self-expression? Do composers have an obligation to their audience? What happens when that right and that obligation conflict with each other? Why do we get "warm, fuzzy" feelings when Copland chooses to write accessible, enjoyable music, but feel horrified when Prokofiev and Shostakovich are punished for not writing accessible, enjoyable music?* Some students who absolutely hated Chapter 20 examples by Schoenberg, Berg, or Ives will now find themselves in the awkward position of defending a composer's right to create such music.

♪ Listening Ideas

1. Play Stravinsky's Neoclassical works for your class and compare them with the works on which he drew. Some possibilities follow:

   a. Compare Stravinsky's *Pulcinella* with the Gallo and Pergolesi chamber works on which he drew.

   b. Compare the second movement of *Symphony of Psalms* with a Bach organ fugue, fugal cantata movement, or *The Art of Fugue*.

   c. Compare the *Dumbarton Oaks* Concerto with Bach's *Brandenburg* Concerto No. 3.

   d. Compare *The Rake's Progress* with Mozart's *Don Giovanni*.

Point out both classical and modern features of these works. See Sound Recordings below for suggested performances.

2. To follow up on the "Opera in the Early Twentieth Century" box on textbook page 354, play examples from Richard Strauss's *Der Rosenkavalier* or Giacomo Puccini's *Madame Butterfly*. Turn to Further Listening Examples below for lecture suggestions and to Sound Recordings below for suggested performances. See Appendix II for texts and translations.

3. If you didn't use suggestions for Ravel's *Boléro* in Further Listening Examples for Chapter 3, present this work now. A bold, colorful, accessible orchestral work, *Boléro* offers a superb example of Ravel's awesome skills as an orchestrator.

Turn to Chapter 3 for teaching suggestions and to Sound Recordings below for suggested performances.

4. Listen to another jazz-influenced work by Ravel. His Sonata for Violin and Piano includes a slow movement titled "Blues." Ravel uses many special effects in this fascinating movement, including blue notes, chords with split thirds, rhythmic *pizzicato* strumming effects, and pitch bending. This work clearly demonstrates the influence of blues, jazz, and popular music, yet it remains a recognizable example of Ravel's music. See Sound Recordings below for suggested performances.

5. Bartók uses many traditional forms in his Music for Strings, Percussion, and Celesta. These range from the fugue to sonata form to rondo form. Ask students to name pieces from earlier chapters that used these tried-and-true forms. Examples of fugue include Frescobaldi's Canzona and Contrapunctus 4 from Bach's *The Art of Fugue*. Examples of sonata form include Mozart's Symphony No. 40 (I), Haydn's Symphony No. 95 (I), Beethoven's Symphony No. 5 (I and IV), and Tchaikovsky's *Romeo and Juliet*. Examples of rondo form include Haydn's Symphony No. 95 (IV), LeBrun's Sonata in F (II), and Brahms's Violin Concerto in D (III). (See Appendix III for a complete list.) Play a few examples. Ask the students to compare features of each work and to describe how each composer handles these forms.

6. Have the students listen to other examples of twentieth-century nationalism:

Hungary—Kodály's *Háry János* or *Dances of Galanta*

England—Vaughan Williams's *Fantasia on a Theme by Thomas Tallis* or *Fantasia on Greensleeves*

United States—Copland's *Rodeo, Billy the Kid,* or *Old American Songs*; Roy Harris's *Folksong* Symphony

Brazil—Villa-Lobos's *Bachianas Brasileiras* or *Chôros*

Mexico—Carlos Chávez's *Sinfonia India* or Revueltas's *Sensemayá*

As you play each example, ask students to identify features that suggest each composer's native country. See Multimedia Resources below for suggested sound and video performances.

7. Explore music written by composers who experienced the effects of totalitarianism on their music and/or careers. Possibilities include composers forced to seek exile in the United States in the 1930s, such as Bartók, Stravinsky, Schoenberg, and Kurt Weill, and composers who lived under totalitarian regimes, such as Strauss, Shostakovich, and Prokofiev. See Multimedia Resources below for suggested sound and video recordings.

8. Listen for similarities between Ravel and Gershwin. We don't encounter Gershwin until Chapter 23, but thanks to United Airlines, most everyone knows a bit of *Rhapsody in Blue*. Ravel took a four-month tour of the United States in 1928. He spent hours listening to jazz in Harlem nightclubs, and he got to know Gershwin as well. Gershwin's most famous works for piano and orchestra, *Rhapsody in Blue* (1924) and Concerto in F (1925), were both written before Ravel's visit. It can be a fascinating exercise to listen for similar harmonies, blue notes, orchestral colors and effects, and so on. See Sound Recordings below for suggested performances.

9. Compare Haydn's Symphony No. 95 with one of Prokofiev's earliest Neoclassical works, his *Classical* Symphony from 1918. In describing this work,

Prokofiev compared his approach to Haydn's—remaining faithful to tradition, yet putting in something new. Prokofiev follows the Classical four-movement format quite closely. The first and final movements give us sonata form in a fast tempo; the second movement is the slowest of the four; and the third movement gives us a dance in moderate tempo. While the dance is a gavotte rather than a minuet, its trio serves up a peasant drone worthy of Haydn. Sample excerpts from both the Haydn and the Prokofiev symphonies and ask students to describe what they hear. Which elements sound traditional? Which ones sound modern?

10. Explore the often fascinating, complex relationships between music and image. Bring in examples of film music from a variety of twentieth-century movies. *Alexander Nevsky* comes from the early days of talking pictures, but a lot has happened since. For a look at contemporary uses of leitmotivs, any of John Williams's scores work well—*Jaws, Star Wars, Indiana Jones,* and so on. For further information and ready-made examples, a number of excellent recent books can help. Roy Prendergast's *Film Music,* Roger Hickman's *Reel Music,* and Anahid Kassabian's *Hearing Film* provide three different perspectives on this fascinating art form.

✸ Further Listening Examples

PUCCINI *Madame Butterfly,* Act II, aria, "Un bel dì"

This beautiful, poignant aria offers an excellent example of Italian Romantic opera after Verdi. For this or further excerpts from this tragic late Romantic opera, you can find suggested audio and video recordings in Multimedia Resources below.

Plot first! Here is a brief synopsis of *Madame Butterfly:*

In Act I, we meet Lieutenant Pinkerton of the U.S. Navy. In spite of warnings from the American consul, he is about to marry a young Japanese woman for a diversion—but he has no intention of honoring the marriage once he leaves Japan. His bride-to-be, Cio-Cio-San (Madame Butterfly), deeply in love with Pinkerton, has renounced her religious faith. The two are married in a traditional Japanese ceremony, but during the subsequent festivities, Cio-Cio-San's family discovers her renunciation and calls down curses on her head. Pinkerton throws them out and comforts his bride. The act ends with an extended love scene.

Act II opens three years later. Cio-Cio-San and her son await Pinkerton's return. When her maid expresses doubts, Cio-Cio-San responds with "Un bel dì." But Pinkerton has married an American woman, and he sends the American consul to Cio-Cio-San to inform her. Cio-Cio-San will hear nothing of it; her misguided faith is so strong that the consul cannot convince her of the truth. When Pinkerton's ship comes to the harbor, she decorates the house and watches the harbor, waiting for Pinkerton's return.

In Act III, Pinkerton arrives with his American wife and the American consul while Cio-Cio-San sleeps. Only now does Pinkerton realize the tragedy of the situation he has created. Overwhelmed, he leaves before Cio-Cio-San awakes. She wakes up in time to meet Pinkerton's American wife and the consul. Finally, she understands Pinkerton's betrayal, but she accepts it with stoic grace. She wishes Pinkerton's wife well and tells her that Pinkerton can take his son. Once they leave, Cio-Cio-San stabs herself with a sword and dies just as Pinkerton arrives for the child.

The bittersweet aria "Un bel dì" appears near the beginning of Act II. The audience already knows of Pinkerton's faithlessness; thus Cio-Cio-San's blind denial of the truth carries deeply tragic overtones. Photocopy handouts or display the words (see Appendix II) and read them for the class. Ask students to listen especially for the effect Puccini creates at the following three phrases; then play the music. In the discussion that follows, draw out these points about the three passages:

1. *Chiamerà: "Butterfly" dalla lontana*—This moment of great beauty highlights the alluring, lovely fantasy Cio-Cio-San has constructed around Pinkerton's return.

2. *Per non morire al primo incontro!*—The full orchestra bursts in on the word *morire*, a tragic gesture that foreshadows Cio-Cio-San's death.

3. *Tutto questo avverà*—The final three lines attest to the strength of Cio-Cio-San's faith that Pinkerton will return for her. The music takes on a dramatic quality here, yet not without more turbulent undertones.

For an interesting twist, compare this with the *kabuki* example in Chapter 18.

STRAUSS *Der Rosenkavalier,* Act II, Presentation of the Rose

Use this excerpt as an example of German opera after Wagner. Strauss was regarded as the most radical German modernist of his generation. His operas *Salome* and *Elektra* could fairly be classified as early examples of expressionism, and his symphonic poems included some of the boldest, most audacious sounds heard anywhere in the 1890s. Some of these works were also controversial for their subject matter—his tone poem based on Nietzsche's *Thus Spake Zarathustra,* for instance. Yet just at the time when Schoenberg was beginning to experiment with atonality, Strauss turned his back on the modernism that brought him fame and notoriety, turning first to an unabashedly post-Romantic style in the opera *Der Rosenkavalier,* then moving progressively further back toward Classical models for his music. If you want to use this or further excerpts from this charming late German Romantic opera, you can find suggested sound and video recordings in Multimedia Resources below.

As usual with any opera, begin with the story. Here is a brief synopsis of *Der Rosenkavalier*:

> Act I opens at the end of a night of lovemaking between the Marschallin and young Count Octavian. Their talk is interrupted (Octavian hastily disguises himself as a maid) by the entrance of Baron Ochs, who (when he's not trying to seduce the "maid") asks the Marschallin to help him arrange his upcoming marriage to young Sophie. The Marschallin offers her lawyer and promises to find him a "Knight of the Rose" (in this libretto, anyway, the knight delivers a "traditional" silver rose to a young woman and proposes marriage on behalf of his sponsor). She arranges for Octavian to serve as knight.
>
> In Act II, at Herr von Faninal's house, Octavian presents Sophie with the silver rose, but the two youngsters fall in love at first sight. Baron Ochs arrives to present himself to Sophie, but she is immediately repulsed by his coarse manner. When the baron leaves the room to sign the papers, Sophie falls into Octavian's arms. She swears that she can never marry the baron, and Octavian promises to protect her. The baron returns to find them embracing. An argument between Octavian and the baron turns into a duel, which ends with a minor injury to the baron. As the commotion subsides, Octavian and Sophie make plans. The baron receives a note promising a tryst with the Marschallin's maid (Octavian in disguise).

Act III takes place in a room in an inn. Octavian's note lures the baron, who comes looking for an evening of love, but Octavian intends to trap him in a compromising situation. By the time the confusion subsides, the police are on the scene, Herr von Faninal wants nothing more to do with the baron, and everyone has a lot of explaining to do—only the surprise appearance of the Marschallin saves the day. She calls off the police, gets rid of the baron, and pushes Octavian into Sophie's arms. The three then sing one of Strauss's great trios. The opera ends with the two young lovers united and the Marschallin on Herr von Faninal's arm.

Now ask students to look at the libretto for this scene. Photocopy handouts or display the text and translation provided in Appendix II. In this scene near the beginning of Act II, young Count Octavian enters to present Sophie with a silver rose on behalf of old Baron Ochs. The two are instantly attracted to each other and feel flustered and embarrassed. This scene begins as Octavian presents the rose. Ask for two volunteers to read the words aloud. This scene captures the confusion and wonder of the precise moment when the two fall in love. In the last half of the scene, they are so caught up in their feelings that they can hardly speak—the words they sing are spoken to themselves, as if we can hear their thoughts.

Before you play the music, warn the students that a woman sings the part of Octavian, but for a different reason than we saw with Monteverdi's *Coronation of Poppea*. Artificial though it may seem to modern audiences, the roles of young men barely out of puberty have often been assigned to a woman's voice in opera, going back well before Mozart gave Cherubino's role to a woman in *Marriage of Figaro*. (We also saw examples of men taking female roles in Chinese and Japanese theater.) Besides, the female voice does have the advantage of sounding more youthful than many male operatic voices.

Play the music for the class. In the discussion that follows, point out the perfect match between the music and the emotions experienced by Octavian and Sophie: the magical charm of the moment, the mutual attraction, a light-headed giddiness, and moments of pure rapture. (Joseph Kerman once described the "magical tinkling" effect of the Silver Rose motive by suggesting that the lovers might be "seeing stars.") The ever-changeable music flits from one idea to another and from one key to another, but the beautiful orchestration and the suave handling of musical materials create a charming grace and elegance that is absolutely gorgeous.

BARTÓK Music for Strings, Percussion, and Celesta

The Bartók materials under Lecture Suggestions above deal with only the second movement of this masterwork. The second movement offers an excellent example of the creative use of sonata form in the twentieth century, but it provides no insights into Bartók's carefully crafted multimovement structure or the many links he creates between the four movements. The notes below, when used with the lecture suggestions above, permit you to cover all of Music for Strings, Percussion, and Celesta, one of the most intriguing and ingenious works of the twentieth century. See Sound Recordings below for a suggested performance.

So that students can orient themselves to this work more readily, start by quickly comparing Bartók's four movements with the Classical symphony's four-movement plan. Play just the beginning of each movement in random order and ask students to guess which movement is which. Two are fast and two are slow—already the comparison with the symphony breaks down somewhat, but for now assume that one of the slow movements is the second movement.

Of the two fast movements, the fourth movement is both the most tuneful and the most dancelike—assume that this movement is the last, or possibly the third. At this point we have a problem making it fit the symphony's four-movement plan. Try out some permutations with your class, keeping these "rules" in mind: We can't end with a slow movement, and we can't have two slow movements in a row. Suddenly we have an impossible situation—but remind students that Beethoven and Haydn occasionally reversed the order of the middle two movements. If one of the slow movements came third, we could put the dancelike movement at the end and avoid two slow movements in a row. The resulting tempo scheme—*slow–fast–slow–fast*—still doesn't look like a Classical symphony, though it does correspond to some of Haydn's early symphonies.

Now display the Additional Listening Chart from Appendix I to give students a look at Bartók's forms. Although the order is "wrong," three of Bartók's movements correspond to movements we expect to see in a Classical symphony. His second movement employs the fast tempo and sonata form expected at the beginning of a symphony; his third movement employs the slow tempo typical of the second movement of a symphony; and his final movement employs the fast tempo and rondo form that conclude many symphonies. All in all, this comes closer to the Classical symphony's plan than we suspected at the beginning of this exercise. Again, we can compare this to many other works, but it remains a unique work to be encountered on its own terms.

Before you launch into a survey of individual movements, take time to acquaint students with the cyclic nature of this work. Like Beethoven, Bartók links these four movements together with a tightly knit web of themes and motives. The main theme of the first movement appears in various guises in each of the other three movements; scalar motives in the second movement anticipate the rondo theme of the fourth; and the final movement echoes themes from each of the previous three movements, especially toward the end.

Take time to familiarize students with each phrase of the subject for the first movement.

VIOLAS, muted

The melody's chromatic twists and turns make it difficult to catch at first. Once students begin to hear the shape of this melody, play examples of this theme as it appears in later movements. Start with the third movement. In between the primary sections of this movement, Bartók brings back individual phrases of the fugue subject. (These entrances are labeled "Background cues" on the Additional Listening Chart from Appendix I.) Note that each of the phrases appears with accompaniment that makes the subject sound like an eerie memory. Next, go to the fourth movement; play the theme labeled "Original fugue subject" in the Additional Listening Chart (at m. 203). This statement of the subject, near the end of the final movement, qualifies as a transformation of the theme. Most startling is the absence of the chromaticism that characterized the subject throughout the work. Bartók gives us a diatonic version of the chromatic melody. Remember that Bartók constructed the original subject from the following sequence of scale steps taken from a chromatic scale on A.

First phrase pitches:	A–B flat–D flat–C–B
First phrase scale steps:	1 2 5 4 3

If we apply this same sequence of scale steps to the scale Bartók uses at m. 203 in the final movement (C–D–E–F sharp–G–A–B flat–C), we end up with the following pitch sequence.

First phrase pitches: C–D–G–F sharp–E

First phrase scale steps: 1 2 5   4   3

Note the unusual interval structure of Bartók's scale, one that he sometimes called an "overtone" scale. Starting on C, the complete scale would be spelled C–D–E–F sharp–G–A–B flat–C. When compared with the major scale, we find that it includes raised scale-step four (corresponding to the eleventh partial in the tonic's overtone series) and lowered scale-step seven (corresponding to the seventh partial in the tonic's overtone series). Bartók regarded this as a "natural" scale, more closely in tune with nature than major, minor, or chromatic scales, and he often pitted his "overtone" scale against other scales to create conflict in his music. In Music for Strings, Percussion, and Celesta, the conflict between the chromatic scale and the "overtone" scale reminds us of the conflict between C minor and C major in Beethoven's Symphony No. 5. Just as C major won out at the end of Beethoven's Fifth, the "overtone" scale triumphs in the fourth movement of Bartók's work.

First Movement

The most striking colors in Music for Strings, Percussion, and Celesta appear in the slower, more atmospheric movements. The remarkable first movement also offers a startling motivic consistency and intensity that can only be compared to Bach's fugues or the first movement of Beethoven's Symphony No. 5. Not only does Bartók derive from this theme all of the melodic material in the first movement, but he derives structural ideas from it as well. The subject's motion from A to E flat and back to A again foreshadows the primary tonal relationships of this movement. The chart below summarizes the tonal structure of the work.

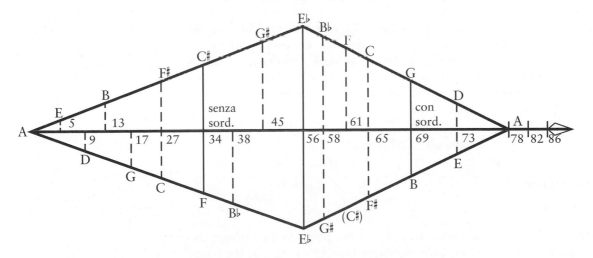

In a traditional fugue, the subject entrances in the exposition alternate between the tonic and dominant keys. Bartók takes that principle a step further. Following a first subject statement on A (tonic) and a second a fifth higher on E (dominant), Bartók's third entrance comes in a fifth lower than A (on D), and the next a fifth higher than E (on B), and so on, until the ascending and descending entrances at the fifth converge on E flat—a tritone away from A—at the movement's climax (m. 56). The pitches A and E flat stand at opposite poles of the circle of fifths, and this work provides an example of what some theorists call Bartók's "polar" tonality. Once we reach E flat, the pattern of fifths continues, but more quickly, and the celesta entrance at m. 78 marks the point where the ascending and descending fifth entrances finally return to A, having traversed the entire circle of fifths in both directions.

The chart above clarifies the mirroring that takes place in this movement—as one set of entrances goes up by successive fifths, the other set goes down by successive fifths. Bartók uses that mirroring in two other significant ways in this movement. First, in the opening fifty-six measures, each phrase of the fugue subject moves up and then turns back down on itself. From m. 56 to m. 78, however, each phrase of the fugue subject moves down and turns back up on itself—a mirror inversion of the original subject. Play this for the students, starting right at the Listening Chart's second climax in m. 56. Second, Bartók uses the final eleven measures (mm. 78–88) to make the mirroring explicit. From the celesta entrance to the end, each statement of the original subject is paired with its mirror inversion. Play this for the students, starting with the celesta entrance (at m. 78). Most fascinating is the pair of voices we hear in the final three measures (at m. 86). Both voices start together on A, move away from each other until both arrive on E flat, and then move back toward each other to reunite on A at the very end of the movement. In three brief measures, Bartók summarizes the tonal motion and the mirroring that characterize the entire movement.

Third Movement

This movement offers one of Bartók's most beautiful, evocative sound worlds. This study in tone color offers many unusual sounds. From the opening xylophone strokes to the rolling timpani *glissandi* to the string trills and *glissandi* to the celesta entrances, Bartók offers unforgettable colors in perhaps his most famous example of "night music." To heighten the eerie night-time mood, Bartók writes his **A** theme in the freely expressive *rubato* manner of a Hungarian *tárogató* melody.

Of special interest in this movement is the form. This is the only movement of this cycle that fails to use a classical form, and Bartók chooses one of his favorites: arch form. Arch form creates a kind of musical palindrome in which the order of sections in the last half matches the order of the first half, except backwards. The following chart reveals the "arch" in arch form.

$$\text{C}$$
$$\text{(fugue a}')\qquad\text{(fugue b)}$$
$$\text{B}\qquad\qquad\qquad\qquad\text{B}$$
$$\text{(fugue a)}\qquad\qquad\qquad\qquad\text{(fugue b}')$$
$$\text{A}\qquad\qquad\qquad\qquad\qquad\qquad\text{A}$$

If you move forward or backward from **C**, the midpoint, you encounter the same sections in the same order, each separated here by phrases of the fugue subject from the first movement. (Bartók also applied this structure to the sequence of movements in String Quartets 4 and 5.) Take time to familiarize the students with each of the three main sections, **A**, **B**, and **C**; then project a photocopied transparency of the Additional Listening Chart from Appendix I and play through the entire movement, pointing out sections as they go by. Ask students to note the effect of the fugue subject phrases throughout the movement.

Fourth Movement

The final movement concludes and sums up the entire cycle. The chromaticism of movements I and III is replaced with diatonic overtone scales and the exciting, asymmetric meters associated with Bulgarian folk music. Take time to play through the rondo theme and several of its transformations. The version labeled **A′** in the Additional Listening Chart from Appendix I (at m. 74) bears some attention, since it alters the melodic contour somewhat. Take some time with the various transformations in **A‴** as well, especially the harp version in even rhythmic values.

When you play the movement, turn it into a guessing game. Ask students to make a note of passages where they hear themes from the first three movements. If you photocopy the Additional Listening Chart from Appendix I, they can pencil in ideas directly on the chart. When the music ends, see what they found. Some references are subtle, such as the opening timpani strokes and *pizzicato* that recall the beginning of movement II, or the transition at m. 181 that resembles movement II's coda; others are more obvious, such as the diatonic return of the first movement's fugue subject, or the cello solo at **F** that recalls **A** materials from movement III. Bartók takes great pains to write four movements that create a single grand cycle with carefully planned contrasts and links. One can enjoy individual movements of this cycle on their own merits, but to appreciate the fullness of Bartók's achievement one must listen to all four movements.

Finally, make sure students grasp the incredibly rhythmic energy of this music. This movement is at once rhythmically exciting, nationalistic in flavor, Classical in form, and thoroughly modernist in terms of compositional detail. In rethinking the orchestra and in weaving a complex web of relationships between the movements, Bartók created a masterpiece that ultimately stands by itself—*sui generis*.

BARTÓK **String Quartet No. 2, II**

Bartók wrote his most important music from the 1920s to the 1930s, yet the early String Quartet No. 2 (1915–1917), the second movement in particular, offers an excellent example of Bartók's musical language. See Appendix I for an Additional Listening Chart, and Multimedia Resources below for suggested audio and video performances. Timings below and in the chart are approximate.

This movement mixes features of sonata form and minuet and trio form. You can present this movement just as you presented sonata form movements in Chapter 12. Work through the following features one at a time:

1. Play theme 1 (mm. 1–48) until students are familiar with it.

2. Play theme 2 (mm. 118–39) until students are familiar with it.

3. Play the transformations of themes 1 and 2 where they appear in the recapitulation (mm. 391–445).

4. Work through the development section (mm. 234–390). Point out the new material (mm. 304–37) called a trio in the Additional Listening Chart and ask students to compare it with the surrounding developmental materials.

5. Play the coda (m. 481–end).

Display the Additional Listening Chart for this work (see Appendix I). Play the entire movement and point out each section of the music as it goes by (or write large divisions on the board and point these out instead).

Make students aware of the incredibly rhythmic energy of this music. This movement is at once rhythmically exciting, nationalistic in flavor, Classical in form, and thoroughly modernist in terms of compositional detail.

COPLAND *Rodeo:* "Buckaroo Holiday," "Corral Nocturne," "Saturday Night Waltz," and "Hoe-Down"

The ballet *Rodeo* was written for the Ballets Russes de Monte Carlo in 1942. The ballet tells the story of a tomboyish girl's attempt to attract the attentions of a handsome cowboy. When performed in concert, *Rodeo* is presented as a four-part suite. Although this is not a symphony, you can point out interesting parallels between these four pieces and the Classical four-movement plan. Copland drew freely on folk song and square-dance melodies in composing *Rodeo,* fitting these tunes smoothly into the overall musical structure. "Buckaroo Holiday" quotes two cowboy tunes—"Sis Joe" and "If He'd Be a Buckaroo." "Hoe-Down"—the best known of these movements—is built from a square-dance tune called "Bonyparte."

"Hoe-Down" makes a wonderful demonstration of American nationalist music. In this short movement (just over three minutes), Copland imbues a square-dance tune with a very personal rhythmic energy. Whether or not the Brooklyn-born Copland had ever been to a rodeo is immaterial; this music epitomizes the eclecticism and rhythmic energy that are the essence of American society and spirit. (See Sound Recordings below for suggested performances.)

STRAVINSKY *Pulcinella* Suite

Neoclassicism was a musical movement initiated by Stravinsky in the early 1920s. It can be viewed as an attempt to create order from the spiritual chaos created by World War I. For many, Neoclassicism is an aspect of post–World War I traditionalism; however, the artistic impulse that drove Neoclassicism was a manifestation of modernism. For our purposes, Neoclassicism can be defined quite specifically. It was a movement inspired by Stravinsky in which traditional musical genres, forms, and techniques were adapted and used in a modern tonal idiom. Note that the harmonic aspect of Neoclassicism was based on harmonic advances in the music of Debussy and Stravinsky and in American popular music. Although the melodic and formal makeup of Neo-classical music might seem a throwback to an earlier time, the harmonic element was strictly twentieth century.

Stravinsky's Neoclassical phase began with the composition of *Pulcinella* in 1919. Written at Diaghilev's request, *Pulcinella* was based on the music of the pre-Classic composer Pergolesi (and several contemporaries). In *Twentieth-Century Music: An Introduction,* Eric Salzman says this of Stravinsky's ballet:

> To the extent that material by Pergolesi (or whoever really wrote the music Stravinsky used as source material) actually appears, the work might be said to be tonal in the old way. Heard in these terms, *Pulcinella* becomes an eccentric set of arrangements of and intrusions on eighteenth century style. But it is nothing of the sort, of course; Pergolesi has been transformed at every moment into something quite new. The Baroque progressions are no longer representatives of musical direction and motion; they are literally sound objects or blocks of sound which gain new meanings from new contexts. A progression or melodic pattern may begin from the middle, so to speak, or stop at some point short of a satisfactory "resolution"; such patterns are set into the typical overlapping cycles of repetition with shifting accents and

metrical values; and all of this is reinforced by a clear and brilliant if restrained orchestration in which color functions analogously to rhythm and phrase.[1]

Display (or photocopy handouts of) the Additional Listening Chart from Appendix I. This chart outlines sections of the *Pulcinella* Suite, arranged by the composer in 1920. The movements of the suite can be easily distinguished from each other. If you do not have time for the entire suite, use dances 2 ("Serenata"), 4 ("Tarantella"), 7 ("Vivo"), and 9 ("Finale"). See Video Recordings below for recorded performances of the complete ballet.

Before listening, point out the following:

1. The element of rhythmic manipulation—unexpected accents; changing meters; overlapping, asymmetrical rhythmic patterns—dominates *Pulcinella*. From a rhythmic point of view, this piece is pure Stravinsky.

2. The harmony is extremely static. Underneath the eighteenth-century melodic surfaces are a considerable number of twentieth-century pedal tones and ostinatos.

Display the Additional Listening Chart or write large divisions of each movement on the board. Point out each section as it goes by.

STRAVINSKY *Symphony of Psalms,* II

The crowning achievement of Stravinsky's Neoclassical period is his *Symphony of Psalms,* written for the fiftieth anniversary of the Boston Symphony Orchestra. This double fugue offers an excellent demonstration of Stravinsky's technique of adapting pre-twentieth-century forms to fit a twentieth-century context. The *Listen* DVD contains the first exposition of this movement; for a complete performance see Sound Recordings below.

The chart below offers a useful diagram of important sections in the fugue. Rehearsal numbers from Stravinsky's score are provided at the very bottom, and important keys are indicated just above that. Display the chart for your students so that you can point out important sections as they go by. Then play the complete movement.

Exposition 1	Exposition 2	1st Subject	2nd Subject	1st Subject	Climax
(instruments)	(voices)	motives	Stretto	Stretto	Final Subject Statements
S A T B	S A T B				
c g c g	e♭ b♭ e♭ b♭		f	b♭ c	g E♭
[1] [2] [3] [4]	[5] [6] [7] [8]	[9]	[10] [11]	[12] [13]	[14] [15] [16] [17]

In the discussion that follows, call attention to several important features of this work.

---

[1] Eric Salzman, *Twentieth-Century Music: An Introduction,* second edition. Englewood Cliffs, N.J.: Prentice-Hall, 1974, p. 46.

ᵞ Stravinsky writes two expositions that use contrasting subjects, keys, and performing forces.

ᵞ The movement progresses from C minor to its relative major key, E-flat major.

ᵞ Stravinsky encapsulates that motion in the simple four-note motive he uses to build the subject of Exposition 1: C–E flat–B–D.

ᵞ Stravinsky gives his Exposition 1 motive a more dissonant twentieth-century flavor through the use of octave displacement.

ᵞ The Exposition 1 motive appears throughout the fugue in various contexts.

ᵞ Stravinsky's orchestration of Exposition 1 recalls the wind sonorities of the Baroque organ.

ᵞ Stravinsky's work includes many standard fugal features, including expositions, episodes, and stretto.

Multimedia Resources

ᵞ Further Listening Charts and Texts

See Appendix I for Listening Charts for these works; see Further Listening Examples above for teaching suggestions.

Bartók, Music for Strings, Percussion, and Celesta, complete work

Bartók, String Quartet No. 2, II

Stravinsky, *Pulcinella* Suite

See Appendix II for texts and translations for these works; see Further Listening Examples above for teaching suggestions.

Puccini, *Madame Butterfly*, Act II aria, "Un bel dì"

Strauss, *Der Rosenkavalier*, Act II, Presentation of the Rose

ᵞ Sound Recordings

Bach, *Complete Toccatas and Fugues*. David Schrader. Cedille Records CDR 90000 006 (CD). The first recording to feature all of Bach's toccatas and fugues on one CD; performed on a Jaeckel organ. Try the fugues on this recording if you use Listening Idea 1 above.

Bach, *Les Six Concerts Brandebourgeois*. Le Concert des Nations/Capella Reial de Catalunya. Auvidis Astrée 9948 (CD). The *Brandenburg* recording used in the *Listen* set. This set includes all six concertos on period instruments; conducted by Jordi Savall. Try this recording of *Brandenburg* Concerto No. 3 if you use Listening Idea 1 above.

Bartók, *The 6 String Quartets*. Takács String Quartet. London 455-297 (CD). Perhaps the most outstanding Bartók quartet recording available today. Try this recording if you use suggestions for the second movement of Quartet No. 2 from Further Listening Examples above.

Bartók, *Concerto for Orchestra—Music for Percussion, Strings, and Celesta*. Chicago Symphony Orchestra. RCA Victor 61504 (CD). Vividly atmospheric, superbly recorded performances of Bartók's music; conducted by Fritz Reiner. Try this recording if you use Listening Idea 7 or suggestions for Music for Percussion, Strings, and Celesta from Further Listening Examples above.

Chávez, *Musica Mexicana, Vol. 2*. Mexico City Philharmonic and Royal Philharmonic Orchestra. ASV 866 (CD). Recordings of several Mexican nationalist works, including Chávez's Symphony No. 2 (*Sinfonia India*), based on native Indian tunes; conducted by Enrique Bátiz. Try this recording if you use Listening Idea 6 above.

Copland, *Appalachian Spring/Rodeo/Billy the Kid*. New York Philharmonic. Sony Classical (Bernstein Century Edition) SMK 63082 (CD). Brilliant, vital performances of Copland Americana; conducted by Leonard Bernstein, for decades a staunch supporter of Copland and his music. Useful for an alternative performance of *Appalachian Spring* or to provide other examples of Copland's American music. Try this recording if you use Class Discussion Idea 3, Listening Idea 6, or suggestions for *Rodeo* from Further Listening Examples above.

Copland, *Old American Songs/Appalachian Spring*. William Warfield and Aaron Copland/London Symphony Orchestra. CBS Masterworks MK 42430 (CD). Classic recordings of these Copland settings coupled with recordings of *Appalachian Spring* and *Rodeo*; conducted by the composer. The *Listen* set uses this recording of *Appalachian Spring*. Try this recording if you use Class Discussion Idea 3, Listening Idea 6, or suggestions for *Rodeo* from Further Listening Examples above.

Gershwin, *Rhapsody in Blue/American in Paris/Concerto in F/Porgy and Bess*. Aalborg Symphony. Virgin Classics Special Import VIR 562056 (CD). Sparkling performances of Gershwin's best-known works for piano and orchestra featuring Wayne Marshall as conductor and pianist. Try this recording of *Rhapsody in Blue* or Concerto in F if you use Listening Idea 8 above.

Harris, *Symphony No. 3/Symphony No. 4 "Folk Song Symphony."* Naxos 8.559227 (CD). It is good to see these symphonies back in print, and on a label that won't discontinue this disc any time soon. Your library may have older recordings by the Eastman Orchestra led by Howard Hanson. Try this recording of Harris's *Folksong* Symphony if you use Listening Idea 6 above.

Kodály, *Háry János Suite/Dances of Galanta*. Budapest Festival Orchestra. Philips 462 824 (CD). Definitive performances of great examples of Hungarian nationalism; conducted by Iván Fischer. Try this recording if you use Listening Idea 6 above.

Mozart, *Don Giovanni*. English Baroque Soloists. Deutsche Grammophon Archiv 445 870-2 (CD). John Eliot Gardiner's excellent recording of Mozart's great opera on period instruments. Use this recording if you try Listening Idea 1 above.

Prokofiev, *Suites*. Czecho-Slovak State Philharmonic Orchestra. Naxos 8.550381 (CD). Excellent recordings of well-known ballet suites in this Prokofiev sampler; conducted by Andrew Mogrelia. Includes *Lieutenant Kijé*, *Cinderella*, and others. Try this recording if you use Listening Idea 7 above.

Prokofiev, *Symphony No. 1/Symphony No. 4*. Scottish National Orchestra. Chandos 8400 (CD). This may be the most exciting performance of the *Classical* Symphony on disc; conducted by Neeme Järvi. Highly recommended if you use Listening Idea 9 above.

Puccini, *La Bohème*. Philharmonia Orchestra. EMI Classics 5 56120 2 (CD). One of the finest recordings ever released of Puccini's most popular opera. Features Leontina Vaduva, Roberto Alagna, Ruth Ann Swenson, Thomas Hampson, Simon Keenlyside, and Samuel Ramey; conducted by Antonio Pappano. This enhanced CD also contains several goodies worth exploring: text, photos, video, and the like. Try this recording to supplement your study of early twentieth-century opera.

Puccini, *Madama Butterfly.* Vienna Philharmonic Orchestra. London 417 577-2 (CD). Great recording of Puccini's Japanese tragedy features Mirella Freni, Luciano Pavarotti, and Christa Ludwig; conducted by Herbert von Karajan. Try this recording if you use Listening Idea 2 or suggestions for "Un bel dì" in Further Listening Examples above.

Ravel, *Boléro*. Orchestre symphonique de Montréal. Decca 289 460 214–2 (CD). Brilliant recordings of works by Ravel in an inexpensive "Double Decca" release; conducted by Charles Dutoit. CD includes *Mother Goose* Suite, *Rapsodie espagnole, Le tombeau de Couperin, Menuet antique,* and other works. Try this recording if you use Lecture-Demonstration Idea 4 or Listening Idea 3 above.

Ravel, *L'enfant et les sortileges/L'heure espagnole.* French National Radio Orchestra. Deutsche Grammophon: The Originals 449 769 (CD). Vintage recordings of Ravel's two operatic works in an inexpensive release; conducted by Lorin Maazel. Try this recording if you use Lecture-Demonstration Idea 4 above.

Ravel, *The Twentieth Century Violin.* Christian Tetzlaff and Leif Ove Andsnes. Virgin Classics Special Import 45122 (CD). Superb recordings of sonatas by Ravel, Nielsen, and Janácek. Try this recording of Ravel's Sonata for Violin in G if you use Listening Idea 4 above.

Revueltas, *Sensemayá*. Los Angeles Philharmonic. Sony Classical SK60676 (CD). An entire disc of music by Silvestre Revueltas, a Mexican nationalist composer who deserves to be better known. This Grammy-nominated CD features his greatest hit, *Sensemayá*; conducted by Esa-Pekka Salonen. Try this recording if you use Listening Idea 6 above.

Schoenberg: A Survivor from Warsaw/Webern: Orchestral Works. Vienna Philharmonic. Deutsche Grammophon 431 774-2 (CD). Gripping performance of Schoenberg's *Survivor from Warsaw*; conducted by Claudio Abbado. Try this recording if you use Listening Idea 7 above.

Shostakovich, *Lady Macbeth of Mtsensk.* London Philharmonic Orchestra. EMI Great Recordings of the Century CMS 67779 (CD). Landmark recording of the opera that incurred Stalin's ire features Galina Vishnevskaya, Nicolai Gedda, and others; conducted by Mstislav Rostropovich. Try this recording if you use Lecture-Demonstration Idea 6 or Listening Idea 7 above.

Shostakovich, *Symphony No. 5.* Vienna Philharmonic. EMI Classics Special Import 56442 (CD). First-class, electric recording of the symphony that restored Shostakovich to Stalin's good graces (for the time being, at least); conducted by Mariss Jansons. Try this recording if you use Lecture-Demonstration Idea 6 or Listening Idea 7 above.

Strauss, *Der Rosenkavalier.* Vienna Philharmonic Orchestra. London 417 493-2 (CD). Strong performance of Richard Strauss's most popular opera. Performed by Régine Crespin, Yvonne Minton, Manfred Jungwirth, Helen Donath, and Otto

Wiener; conducted by Sir Georg Solti. Try this recording if you use Listening Idea 2 or suggestions for the "Presentation of the Rose" in Further Listening Examples above.

Stravinsky Conducts Stravinsky. CBC Symphony Orchestra and Columbia Symphony Orchestra. CBS Masterworks MK 42434 (CD). Definitive performances of Symphony in Three Movements, Symphony in C, and *Symphony of Psalms*; conducted by the composer. Recommended if you want to present Stravinsky's greatest Neoclassical symphonic works. Try this recording if you use Listening Idea 1 or 7 or suggestions for *Symphony of Psalms* from Further Listening Examples above.

Stravinsky, *Ebony Concerto, Dumbarton Oaks, etc.* Ensemble InterContemporain. Deutsche Grammophon: The Originals 447 405-2 (CD). Fine performances of Stravinsky's Neoclassical works and Berg's Chamber Concerto; conducted by Pierre Boulez. Try this recording if you use Listening Idea 1 or 7 above.

Stravinsky, *Le sacre du printemps/Petrushka/Pulcinella.* Philadelphia Orchestra and Academy of St. Martin-in-the-Fields. EMI Classics *double fforte* 74305 (CD). Fine performances of Stravinsky's most famous works, including the *Pulcinella* Suite; conducted by Neville Marriner. Try this recording if you use Listening Idea 1 or suggestions for *Pulcinella* from Further Listening Examples above.

Stravinsky, *The Rake's Progress.* Royal Philharmonic. Sony Classical SM2K 46299 (CD). Definitive complete recording of Stravinsky's last great Neoclassical work; conducted by the composer. Try this recording if you use Listening Idea 1 or 7 above.

Vaughan Williams, *Fantasia on a Theme by Thomas Tallis,* etc. Academy of St. Martin-in-the-Fields. Argo 414 595-2 ZH (CD). Fine collection of English nationalist works by Vaughan Williams; conducted by Sir Neville Marriner. Includes the title track, *Fantasia on Greensleeves, Variants of "Dives and Lazarus,"* and *The Lark Ascending.* Try this recording if you use Listening Idea 6 above.

Villa-Lobos, *Bachianas Brasileiras* (selections). Victoria de los Angeles and the Orchestre National de France. EMI Classics (Great Recordings of the Century) CDU 66964 (CD—mono). Warm performances by de los Angeles come across in spite of monaural sound; conducted by the composer. Includes Nos. 1, 2, 5, and 9. Try this recording if you use Listening Idea 6 above.

Weill, *The Threepenny Opera.* CBS MK 42637 (CD). Recording from the 1950s supervised by Lotte Lenya. It goes in and out of print but wears an air of authenticity rarely matched in newer recordings. Try this recording if you use Listening Idea 7 above.

ʏ Video Recordings

Aaron Copland: A Self-Portrait. www.films.com (DVD or VHS, color, 58 minutes). Copland himself talks about his life and music in a video that includes ballet sequences with Agnes de Mille dancing in *Rodeo* and Martha Graham dancing in *Appalachian Spring,* scenes of Copland conducting, and interviews with Leonard Bernstein and Ned Rorem.

After the Storm: The American Exile of Béla Bartók. Kultur Video (DVD or VHS, color and black and white, 76 minutes). The story of the last five years of Bartók's life, spent as a refugee in the United States. The program draws on archival footage, musical performances, journals, letters, and personal reminiscences from family and friends. Musical excerpts from Bartók's Concerto No. 3 for piano and orchestra and Concerto for Orchestra. Try this video if you use Listening Idea 7 above.

The American Way. The Music of the 20th Century: Leaving Home Series. www.films.com (DVD or VHS, color, 52 minutes). Simon Rattle narrates this look at American music from hymns, band music, country dances, and jazz to the music of twentieth-century composers. Works best for Chapter 20 or 23 but includes a section on Copland.

Bartók, *Europa-Konzert from Lisbon*. EuroArts (DVD, color, 120 minutes). Excellent live concert by the Berlin Philharmonic; conducted by Pierre Boulez. This disc features two Neoclassical works appropriate to Chapter 21: Ravel's *Le tombeau de Couperin* and Bartók's famous Concerto for Orchestra. Highly recommended if you use Lecture-Demonstration Idea 4 or Listening Idea 7 above.

Bartók, Shostakovich, Lutoslawski: *Three Journeys through Dark Landscapes*. *Leaving Home* Series. Arthaus Musik (DVD, color, 52 minutes). Simon Rattle narrates this look at the effect of political upheaval on the music of these three composers. Try this video if you use Lecture-Demonstration Idea 6, Class Discussion Idea 6, or Listening Idea 7 above.

Bartók, *String Quartets 2, 3 and 6*. Decca (DVD, color, 92 minutes). Definitive performances of three of Bartók's six quartets. Highly recommended if you use suggestions for the second movement of Quartet No. 2 from Further Listening Examples above.

Copland and the American Sound. Keeping Score: Revolutions in Music Series. San Francisco Symphony (DVD, color). Hosted by conductor Michael Tilson Thomas, this fascinating series features visits to locations associated with the composer and lots of background material, as well as complete live performances by the San Francisco Symphony. This installment focuses on Copland's *Appalachian Spring*. Recommended as a supplement to your presentation of this work.

Copland: Appalachian Spring. The Score Series. www.films.com (DVD or VHS, color, 15 minutes). This brief video focuses on the spacious quality in Copland's orchestration. Excerpts performed by the Scottish Chamber Orchestra; conducted by William Conway.

Copland, *Fanfare for America: The Composer Aaron Copland*. www.films.com (DVD or VHS, color, 59 minutes). Video documentary examines Copland's search for an American voice through expert commentary, interviews with Copland and others, and historic recordings of Copland conducting Benny Goodman in the composer's Clarinet Concerto.

Copland, *Martha Graham in Performance*. Kultur Video (DVD or VHS, black and white, 93 minutes). This video paints a portrait of a leading dancer and choreographer in the twentieth-century modern-dance movement. In addition to photos, text, and commentary by Graham collaborators, the disc contains two complete Graham works, *Night Journey* and *Appalachian Spring*. Use this disc if you want students to see the *Listen* excerpts from *Appalachian Spring* in their original context. *Warning:* Copland's theme and variations cannot be heard as a self-contained entity in the original version of *Appalachian Spring*.

When he created the later concert suite, Copland cut several minutes of music in Section 5 to form the theme and variations we all know and love. Highly recommended.

Hungarian Connections. London (VHS, color). Performances of Kodály's *Háry János* Suite, Bartók's Romanian Folk Dances, and other works by the Vienna Philharmonic; conducted by Sir Georg Solti. Try this recording if you use Listening Idea 6 above.

The Known and the Unknown. The Music of Man Series (VHS, color, 60 minutes). Yehudi Menuhin narrates a look at music between the world wars—jazz and twelve-tone. Features music of Louis Armstrong, Gershwin, Copland, and Schoenberg.

Milhaud: Boeuf sur le toit. The Score: Classical Music Appreciation through Listening Series. www.films.com (DVD or VHS, color, 15 minutes). This brief video focuses on Milhaud's use of bitonality and popular music. Excerpts performed by the Scottish Chamber Orchestra; conducted by William Conway. Try this video for a look at this French Neoclassicist composer, one of *Les Six*.

Mozart, *Don Giovanni.* Arthaus Musik (DVD, color, 187 minutes). Zurich Opera production of Mozart's classic *dramma giocoso* features soloists Rodney Gilfry, Laszlo Polgar, Isabel Rey, Cecilia Bartoli, and Matti Salminen; conducted by Nikolaus Harnoncourt. Production highlights the compulsiveness of Giovanni's actions; this makes for particularly fascinating comparisons with Stravinsky's *The Rake's Progress.* Use this recording if you try Listening Idea 1 above.

Music for the World. Man and Music Series. www.films.com (DVD or VHS, color, 53 minutes). A look at Stravinsky, Scriabin, Rachmaninoff, and Prokofiev in the context of the generation of Russian composers that preceded them. Try this video if you use Class Discussion Idea 6 or Listening Idea 7 above.

Of Mice and Men. Image Entertainment (DVD or VHS, color, 106 minutes). Copland wrote the score for this 1939 movie based on Steinbeck's great novel. Try this video if you use Class Discussion Idea 5 or Listening Idea 10 above.

[Prokofiev] *Alexander Nevsky.* Criterion Collection (DVD, black and white, 108 minutes). Packaged with *Ivan the Terrible,* this box set gives us two major collaborations between Prokofiev and director Sergei Eisenstein. This set is up to Criterion's usual high standards, with lots of fascinating bonus material. Of special interest is a twenty-minute documentary on the making of *Nevsky.* Highly recommended as an integral part of your presentation on Prokofiev and film music.

Prokofiev: The Prodigal Son. www.films.com (DVD or VHS, color, 92 minutes). Video documentary examines Prokofiev's life and music using photos, video footage, reenactments, and musical performances. Try this video if you use Class Discussion Idea 6 or Listening Idea 7 above.

Puccini, *La Bohème.* Deutsche Grammophon (DVD, color, 103 minutes). There are many lovely video performances of *La Bohème,* including a wonderful Met version with Teresa Stratas and José Carreras, and an often-touted San Francisco Opera video with two aging stars, Mirella Freni and Luciano Pavarotti. Even so, this classic 1965 performance from La Scala is probably the finest of all. This production made Mirella Freni a star, and her gorgeous singing sets the standard for a cast that includes Gianni Raimondi, Rolando Panerai, and Adriana Martino; conducted by Herbert von Karajan. Add Franco Zeffirelli's inspired direction and the visual beauty of the sets, and the result is magical. Highly recommended as a supplement to your study of early twentieth-century opera.

Puccini, *La Bohème*. Kultur Video (DVD, color, 117 minutes). A close second to the Karajan version above, this more intimate Covent Garden production is absolutely charming. For once, we have an aptly youthful cast that can act as well as sing—and how beautifully they sing! Principals include Ileana Cotrubas, Neil Shicoff, Thomas Allen, and Marilyn Zschau; conducted by Lamberto Gardelli.

Puccini, *Madama Butterfly*. Decca (DVD or VHS, color, 144 minutes). Jean-Pierre Ponnelle's beautifully filmed version of Puccini's tragic opera. Performed by Mirella Freni, Plácido Domingo, and Christa Ludwig; conducted by Herbert von Karajan. Try this video if you use Listening Idea 2 or use suggestions for "Un bel dì" in Further Listening Examples above.

Ravel, *Bernstein in Paris: The Ravel Concerts*. Kultur Video (DVD or VHS, color, 87 minutes). Video includes performances of Ravel's Piano Concerto in G, *Boléro, La Valse,* and other works by the National Orchestra of France; conducted by Leonard Bernstein. Highly recommended supplement to your presentation of the Ravel Concerto in G. You can also use this video if you try Lecture-Demonstration Idea 4 or Listening Idea 3 above.

Ravel, *Britten/Debussy/Ravel/Rihm*. Image Entertainment (DVD, color, 79 minutes). Claudio Abbado and the Berlin Philharmonic perform four twentieth-century works: Britten's *Serenade, Clouds* and *Festivals* from Debussy's Three Nocturnes, Ravel's *La Valse,* and Rihm's *In doppelter Tiefe.* Try this recording to augment your presentation of Ravel's Piano Concerto or if you use Lecture-Demonstration Idea 4 above.

Ravel, *Herbert von Karajan: Ravel: Daphnis et Chloe. His Legacy for Home Video* Series. Sony Classical (DVD or VHS, color, 54 minutes). Video performance of the second suite from Ravel's most ravishing ballet score, written for Diaghilev's Ballets Russes in 1912. Recording also includes Debussy's *La mer* and *Prélude à l'après-midi d'un faune* performed by the Berlin Philharmonic; conducted by Herbert von Karajan. Try this video if you use Lecture-Demonstration Idea 4 above.

Ravel, *Herbert von Karajan—His Legacy for Home Video: New Year's Eve Concert 1985*. Sony Classical (VHS, color). Video includes performances of Ravel's *Boléro,* Weber overtures, Liszt's Hungarian Rhapsody No. 5, and excerpts from Puccini's *Manon Lescaut* and Leoncavallo's *I Pagliacci* by the Berlin Philharmonic; conducted by Herbert von Karajan. Try this video if you use Listening Idea 3 above.

Ravel: Pavane pour une infante défunte. The Score: Classical Music Appreciation through Listening Series. www.films.com (DVD or VHS, color, 15 minutes). This brief video focuses on Ravel's use of melody and color. Performed by the Scottish Chamber Orchestra; conducted by William Conway. Try this video if you use Lecture-Demonstration Idea 4 above.

Shostakovich Against Stalin. Philips (DVD, color). This fascinating recent documentary looks at Shostakovich's Symphonies 4 through 9 as the composer's commentary on Stalin and his atrocities. Recommended if you use Lecture-Demonstration Idea 6, Class Discussion Idea 6, or Listening Idea 7.

Shostakovich, *Bernstein in Japan: Symphony No. 5*. Kultur (DVD, color, 90 minutes). Finally we have a video performance of the Fifth by a top-ranked

Shostakovich interpreter. Leonard Bernstein leads the New York Philharmonic in this gripping 1979 Tokyo concert. Symphony No. 5 was Shostakovich's "answer" to criticism of *Lady Macbeth of Mtsensk*. Try this video if you use Lecture-Demonstration Idea 6, Class Discussion Idea 6, or Listening Idea 7.

Shostakovich, *Lady Macbeth of Mtsensk*. EMI Classics (DVD, color, 187 minutes). Petr Weigl's screen adaptation of the Rostropovich recording (see Sound Recordings above) served well for many years, but this recent release from the Barcelona Opera finally gives a real staged version of Shostakovich's controversial opera, the one censured in *Pravda*—and what a seedy, sordid tale it is! Try this video if you use Lecture-Demonstration Idea 6, Class Discussion Idea 6, or Listening Idea 7 above.

[Shostakovich] *Testimony*. Kultur (DVD, color, 151 minutes). New DVD release of the powerful 1988 film reenacts Shostakovich's life and his often bitter run-ins with the Soviet regime. Ben Kingsley plays the composer. Recommended if you use Lecture-Demonstration Idea 6, Class Discussion Idea 6, or Listening Idea 7.

Strauss, *Richard Strauss: Between Romanticism and Resignation*. www.films.com (DVD or VHS, color, 58 minutes). Video documentary focuses on the last fifteen years of Strauss's life, examining the difficulties and contradictions he faced working in Hitler's Germany. Try this video if you use Listening Idea 7 above.

Strauss, *Der Rosenkavalier*. Deutsche Grammophon (DVD, color, 213 minutes). Beautiful performance of Richard Strauss's most popular opera, produced by Otto Schenk. Performed by Felicity Lott, Anne Sofie von Otter, Barbara Bonney, Kurt Moll, and Gottfried Hornik with the Vienna State Opera Orchestra; conducted by Carlos Kleiber. Try this recording if you use Listening Idea 2 or the suggestions for the "Presentation of the Rose" in Further Listening Examples above.

Stravinsky: Devil's Dance from A Soldier's Tale *and* Vivo *and* Finale *from* Pulcinella. *The Score: Classical Music Appreciation through Listening* Series. www.films.com (DVD or VHS, color, 15 minutes). This brief video focuses on Stravinsky's use of rhythm and color. Excerpts performed by the Scottish Chamber Orchestra; conducted by William Conway. Try this video if you use Listening Idea 1 or 7 or suggestions for *Pulcinella* in Further Listening Examples above.

Stravinsky, *Pulcinella/Soldat*. Elektra/Nonesuch 40165-6 ZV (VHS, color, 65 minutes). Stravinsky's first Neoclassical ballet. Dancers from the Rambert Dance Company perform Ashley Page's choreography. Useful resource for Listening Idea 1 or suggestions for *Pulcinella* from Further Listening Examples above.

Stravinsky, *Pulcinella*. Deutsche Grammophon (DVD, color, 42 minutes). Fine new recording of Stravinsky's first Neoclassical ballet. This is not the original *Ballets Russes* choreography, but this version does give us the authentic *commedia dell'arte* characters that inspired this ballet. A superb team of soloists with a chamber orchestra cap things off nicely; conducted by Sir Neville Marriner. Recommended resource for Listening Idea 1 or suggestions for *Pulcinella* from Further Listening Examples above.

Stravinsky, *The Rake's Progress*. Arthaus Musik (DVD, color, 146 minutes). Finally we have something besides the Large/Cambreling DVD on Image! If you want a cinematic version, you'll find lovely singing on the Barbara Hendricks/ Hakan Hagegard disc for Kultur, but I recommend the somewhat older Glyndebourne production with Leo Goeke, Felicity Lott, and Samuel Ramey; conducted by Bernard Haitink. The production has a totally appropriate eighteenth-century look and feel (helped by David Hockney's striking sets), and the characters are portrayed in a sympathetic manner that brings out their humanity. Use this recording if you try Listening Idea 1 or 7 above.

Surrealism in Art and Music. www.insight-media.com (DVD, color, 38 minutes). This still-image video provides a concise, visually appealing introduction to important philosophic, artistic, and musical trends in the twentieth century. Contains the artwork of Ernst, Magritte, and Dalí; music by Ravel, Stravinsky, Satie, Bartók, Milhaud, and Cage.

Today and Tomorrow. Music in Time Series. www.films.com (DVD or VHS, color, 60 minutes). James Galway narrates this look at music of our own time. Most appropriate for Chapter 22 but includes excerpts from Copland's *El salón México.*

War and Peace. Music in Time Series. www.films.com (DVD or VHS, color, 60 minutes). James Galway narrates this look at the many trends in music between the world wars. Covers many composers and styles. Works of composers discussed by the textbook include Stravinsky's *Rite of Spring* and *Ragtime,* Bartók's Sonata for Two Pianos and Percussion, Ravel's Piano Concerto in G, Shostakovich's Symphony No. 7 (*Leningrad*), Prokofiev's Quintet in G Minor, Weill's *Kleine Dreigroschen Musik,* Joplin's "Maple Leaf Rag," and Gershwin's *American in Paris* (the last two in Chapter 23). Other examples by Elgar, Satie, Hindemith, Milhaud, and Britten. Try this video if you use Lecture-Demonstration Idea 6 or Listening Idea 7 above.

❼ Software

Art and Music: Surrealism. Zane Publishing (CD-ROM—Windows or Macintosh). CD-ROM version of the video above. This inexpensive volume draws parallels between the paintings of Dalí, Ernst, and Miró and the music of Ravel, Stravinsky, Bartók, Satie, Milhaud, and Cage. Available from www.cdaccess.com.

CHAPTER 22

The Late Twentieth Century

Chapter Outline

Boldface indicates works in the recording set.

Important Terms

total serialism	chance (aleatoric) music	musical process
new sound materials	postwar avant-garde	new expressionism
multiphonics	sound complexes	IRCAM
electronic music	noise	postmodernism
musique concrète	minimalism	multiculturalism
sampling	gamelan	da capo aria
synthesizers	organum	
computer music	symmetrical musical forms	

Teaching Objectives

⁊ Overall Objectives

This chapter will help students acquire familiarity with:

1. Late twentieth-century styles as reflections of historical events in this century.

2. The changes and features associated with modernism in music after World War II, especially new sound materials, electronic music, new uses of musical time, and chance music.

3. Musical features of important twentieth-century styles, especially of the postwar avant-garde and more recent styles.

4. The relationship between music and other art forms, such as film, architecture, and literature.

5. Features of twentieth-century American art music that reflected and influenced European music after World War II.

6. The lives and music of György Ligeti, Edgard Varèse, John Cage, Steve Reich, Kaija Saariaho, and John Adams.

⁊ Listening Objectives

After completing this chapter, students should be able to:

1. Hear and identify typical uses of the elements of music in late twentieth-century styles.

2. Hear and identify important aspects of the second phase of modernism in late twentieth-century music, especially new sound materials, electronic media, and new uses of musical time.

3. Identify and follow important twentieth-century (and more recent) genres, especially chamber, choral, electronic, and vocal genres, including the oratorio.

4. Hear and identify features of important styles and trends in late twentieth-century (and more recent) music, especially sound complexes, electronic music, chance, minimalism, new expressionism, and postmodernism.

Lecture Suggestions

In Chapter 19 we made a list of technological advances at the turn of the century. The list of new developments since World War II is equally impressive: nuclear energy, mass media, computer technology, digital recording, television, space exploration, satellite communication networks, and so on. We reflected on the dark side of technology in Chapter 19, yet the magnitude of death and destruction during World War I was easily surpassed during World War II. The machinery of the Holocaust and the nuclear weapons developed during the second war provoked unthinkably nightmarish visions of a human-made hell on earth. More recently, the Internet has fueled an information explosion—the World Wide Web provides instant access to databases and Web sites around the world.

⁊ Modernism in Music: The Second Phase

The generation of composers who appeared immediately after World War II reacted in a manner opposite to that of their post–World War I colleagues. Whereas many of the latter looked on modernism with distrust, falling back on more traditionalist Neoclassical styles, the post–World War II generation looked upon this Neoclassical music with disgust. Wanting nothing to do with the past, they sought to create an entirely new musical aesthetic. In the process, they revived musical modernism, a movement cut off forty years earlier by the onset of World War I.

The principal changes after World War II affected tone color, rhythm, and form. The following demonstrations can be used to present concepts from the textbook.

New Sound Materials

After World War II, composers developed an insatiable appetite for new and unusual sounds, both acoustic and electronic. On the acoustic side, musicians explored new ways of producing sounds on traditional instruments, and they added new or unusual instruments to their ensembles (especially percussion instruments). Play these two examples for the class, and ask students to listen for any unusual sounds.

> Debussy, *Clouds* (track 15, 0:00–track 16, 0:32)
>
> Saariaho, *From the Grammar of Dreams*, Song 1

Ask students to describe any unusual sounds they heard. Debussy was known for his novel use of orchestral sonorities, but his music sounds tame compared with Saariaho's song. Saariaho asks her two sopranos to make sounds Verdi could never have imagined, including grunts, vocal *glissandos*, buzzing noises, various guttural sounds, and hard consonants that are literally spit out. Hardly any of Saariaho's tone colors sound like those of traditional singing. Composers after World War II developed similar techniques for most conventional instruments as well.

Electronic Music

Electronic-music technologies have mushroomed since World War II. The development of the tape recorder permitted composers to record and manipulate both noises and musical sounds for compositional purposes. The development of the electronic oscillator opened up possibilities for electronically generated music, and the synthesizer offered more flexibility in timbre, articulation, speed, and composer control than any acoustic instrument ever invented. Many composers were attracted to electronic music because it offered precise control of musical elements; further, they could now fully and directly realize their inspirations without the performer as intermediary.

The textbook describes three main categories of electronic music:

Musique concrète—natural sounds recorded and manipulated

Synthesizers—sounds produced by electronic instruments

Computer music—via software or MIDI interface, the computer can duplicate or control the functions of a synthesizer or recording studio

Both *musique concrète* and electronically generated sounds can be heard in Varèse's *Poème électronique* (0:00–1:43). The first minute contains *musique concrète,* whereas the last forty-three seconds mix in electronically generated sounds. (See Multimedia Resources below for examples of computer music.)

On the Boundaries of Time

Since music occurs in time, it can express the many ways humans experience time. On different occasions, a moment can seem like an eternity, or an hour can pass by in a flash. Twentieth-century composers often explored these extreme experiences of time.

WEBERN Five Orchestral Pieces, Op. 10, No. 4

Play this movement for the class, and ask students how they experienced time as they listened to it. This brief piece challenges the listener to think about melody, color, form, and other elements in entirely different ways. Webern was not interested in taking time to create long-range melodic or formal relationships, and the succession of colors almost seems more important than the succession of pitches. The music captures a brief, precious moment of ambiguity and soft tension.

RILEY *In C*

If you have a recording available (see Sound Recordings below), play a few minutes of this work for your class, and ask students how they experienced time as they listened to it. Like the Webern work above, this piece uses only a few musical ideas. Instead of using them once, however, Riley repeats his ideas again and again over a long time span. We experience time quite differently—changes occur slowly, so there is time to drift and examine each instrument, each motive, and each combination at leisure.

Chance Music

The most challenging, even subversive trend of the 1950s and 1960s was the development of chance music, music that leaves one or more musical elements (or the compositional process itself!) to chance—that is, to be determined by the performers at the moment of performance. Morton Feldman, one of John Cage's colleagues in the 1950s, used these procedures in several works (see Sound Recordings below):

Durations—pitches are specified, but not their durations

Intersections—durations, registers, and timbres are specified, but not specific pitches or dynamics

Intermission 6—musical ideas are written out completely, but the order of events (form) is not specified

John Cage carried these procedures even further. In many of his "indeterminate" works, he used the *I Ching* (*Book of Changes,* an ancient Chinese oracle from the time of K'ung Fu-tzu) to make compositional decisions. The scores for works such as *Fontana Mix* are do-it-yourself kits that provide materials and instructions that tell performers how to create their parts.

Riley's *In C* also uses chance procedures. Each player reads a score that contains fifty-three melodic motives. Performers must play all of the motives in order, but individual performers can repeat any motive as many times as they like before they move to the next one. This freedom to repeat means that simultaneous combinations of motives at any given moment are left to chance. Further, the performers finish at different times and the overall length of the piece varies from performance to performance.

7 The Postwar Avant-Garde

Even for trained musicians immersed in the music of the Western classical tradition, serialist and postwar avant-garde music can seem difficult and unfamiliar. Only with patience and careful study does it (slowly) yield its secrets and beauties. Your experience may be different from your students' experiences, however. Some students entered your class with a love for Bach, Mozart, and Beethoven; they may proclaim that what Schoenberg, Ligeti, and Reich write is not music. On the other hand, most of your students began your course with no more knowledge of the Classical era than of postwar modernism. For them the whole course has been a journey into unfamiliar territory; you can use this to your advantage. Much of this music is based on fascinating concepts that are easy to explain and understand. Challenge your students to listen beyond the dissonance for the patterns (generated by the concepts) that can make sense of their experience of the music. Point out the changes in tone color, rhythm, and form that move this music even further away from traditional conventions.

For many postwar modernists, the influence of electronic music was decisive. Even composers who spent little time in electronic studios were excited and challenged by the sounds and concepts of this new medium.

Electronic media created entirely new sounds. These sounds inspired composers to demand new and unusual tone colors from conventional instruments as well (e.g., Ligeti's sound complexes).

Magnetic tape offered new ways to combine sounds. Composers began to manipulate taped sounds in fascinating ways, cutting, pasting, changing speed, playing sounds backwards, and so on. Soon composers began to rethink conventional scoring as well (e.g., Varèse).

Sounds and tone colors replaced conventional melody almost entirely. Composers began to abandon the metric structures that gave traditional melodies coherence. Sounds could now exist for their own sake, without traditional rhythmic relationships to other sounds (e.g., Ligeti).

Electronic instruments encouraged virtuosic effects. The range, coloristic variety, and speed of electronic instruments far exceeded those of conventional musical instruments, and composers demanded an entirely new level of virtuosity from human performers as well (e.g., Saariaho).

Sound synthesis drew attention away from melody, harmony, and tonality. When you build sounds from the ground up, primary attention must be given to tone color, texture, dynamics, shapes, and durations. Composers found the means to create musical coherence and structure from these elements; melody, harmony, and tonality were often irrelevant.

Sounds came to be treated as objects. Always ahead of his time, Varèse had composed at a drafting table even before the days of electronic music, manipulating sounds as if they were three-dimensional objects. In the graphic score for Stockhausen's postwar *Elektronische Studie Nr. 1,* we clearly see sounds conceptualized as objects—bold new images for a new era.

Thus, the models for composition began to change.

LIGETI *Lux aeterna*

In the past, composing was analogous to painting; sounds were brushed onto an empty canvas. Now composers sought new analogies. Some worked more like sculptors; they started with a massive block of sounds and chipped away different portions in different sections of the piece. Ligeti was one who worked with large, slowly moving "sound blocks," "sound masses," or, in the authors' words, "sound complexes."

Written for sixteen-voice chorus (four parts each for sopranos, altos, tenors, and basses), *Lux aeterna* draws on a text from the ancient Requiem Mass. Ligeti's choral work offers a wonderful mix of new and old techniques. The liturgical Latin text, polyphonic texture, beautiful *a cappella* sound, and strict canonic writing suggest the influence of the Renaissance Mass. The dissonant sound complexes (tone clusters built in half steps) and avoidance of beat and melody are typical of the postwar avant-garde.

Display Listening Chart 26 (or refer students to textbook page 378). Point out the four main sections. Explain the authors' symbols as graphic analogies for the slow-moving sound events in Ligeti's music. Play the music and, on the display, trace the motion of the sound on the symbols themselves. In the discussion that follows, ask students to identify elements and structures that do not play a significant role in this music (beat, melody, scale, and so on). Texture and register, on the other hand, assume primary roles in shaping the music coherently. Interestingly, one of the most powerful unifying ideas in this work is a single pitch (the sopranos' highest). It stands out because Ligeti places it in an infrequently used (in this piece) high register. Further, its position in the first and last sections of the piece creates a sense of statement and return (with intervening contrast)—an old formula in new clothes.

Due to the tone clusters and the dense canonic writing, it is often impossible to hear the words clearly; nonetheless, students need to know the text. The traditional text from the Requiem Mass is therefore included here:

Lux aeterna luceat eis, Domine,	May everlasting radiance shine upon
Cum sanctis tuis in aeternum,	them, Oh Lord, with thy saints in eternity,
quia pius es.	for you are merciful.
Requiem aeternam dona eis, Domine,	Give them eternal rest, Lord,
et lux perpetua luceat eis.	and let perpetual light shine on them.

(Students may recognize this music from Stanley Kubrick's movie *2001: A Space Odyssey*, where the music's "light eternal" is associated with the monolith—a device created to nurture the spark of intelligence.)

VARÈSE *Poème électronique*

This classic work from the early days of electronic music created a sensation at the 1958 Brussels World Fair. Varèse constructed a rich collage of sounds to fill the novel, sail-shaped Philips Pavilion, designed by the modernist architect Le Corbusier. The piece freely mixes *musique concrète* and electronically generated sounds. The excerpt in the recorded set is too short to clarify the long-term motivic relationships Varèse built into the music, but it serves well to demonstrate the sound world of electronic music. The first minute and a half consists primarily of electronic sounds and well-disguised *musique concrète;* from that point on we also notice undisguised recordings of a drum, human voices, an organ, and so on. The principal sounds can be listed as follows:

Electronic crash	0:00	Roar	1:52
Random rustles	0:07	Bells	1:56
⌈Low sliding groans	0:13	Soprano solo	2:04
|Rattles	0:16	Men's voices	2:18
⌊Bell-like noises	0:17	⌈Sharp punctuations	2:25
Vocal hum	0:19	⌊Organ sounds	2:30
Drum rhythms	0:40	Three-note motive	2:47
Sustained chord	1:04	Siren	2:58
(climax)	1:11	Violent noise	3:14
Isolated rhythms	1:19		
⌈Snare drum	1:29		
⌊Isolated pitches	1:31		

CAGE *4'33"*

My favorite music is the music we hear all the time if we sit quietly and listen.
—John Cage

For a fascinating and controversial classroom project, perform Cage's 4'33" live. Tell the students you are going to play the work for them, walk to the tape deck, put on a blank tape, and let it run for four and a half minutes. If you have a dramatic bent, make this a theatrical experience by pointing out sections (Cage's score indicates three sections, 33", 2'40", and 1'20", respectively) on the board as they go by. It works best if you point them out using your usual classroom manner. Or you can imitate David Tudor's premiere performance of this work—he placed a stopwatch on the piano, opening and closing the piano lid to mark the beginning and end of each section (Tudor reproduces this performance in the excellent video *I Have Nothing to Say and I Am Saying It*—see Video Recordings below). In the discussion that follows, draw out these points.

1. Some students will say that the piece is a big joke, that it consists of nothing but silence. Of course this is untrue. Any or all of these sounds were present: laughter, snickers, talking, whispering, coughs, sneezes, tape hiss, the air-circulation system, breathing sounds, people shifting in their seats, pencils tapping, hearts beating. Cage reminds us that there is no such thing as silence—there is always something to listen to.

2. Every performance of 4'33" will be different. The piece is based on the changing circumstances of each performance rather than on any fixed series of sounds. Thus, this is chance music.

3. 4'33" is an experience that raises important philosophical questions about the nature of music.

4. Cage called into question the assumptions on which Western art music is based; in fact, he questioned our definitions of music. What is a "musical" sound? What is a "nonmusical" sound? If music is a collaborative, communicative human experience, why must it be limited to the traditional audience/performer context? Can't everyone participate? If life is unpredictable and full of surprises, why can't music be the same way?

5. Like many of Cage's compositions, 4'33" is conceptual art—the idea behind the piece is just as important as an actual performance of the piece.

6. Cage's musical thinking and many of his works were deeply influenced by world music. Non-Western music provided models and philosophies that helped Cage rethink his own musical ideas—as well as the entire Western tradition. Such influences are obvious in *The Seasons,* the String Quartet, and the prepared piano works, but in *4'33"* they remain more subtle. Even so, Eastern influences are suggested by this work's rhythmic structure and its Zen-like sensibility. In his famous statement, "I have nothing to say and I am saying it," Cage is not describing any kind of creative impoverishment. Rather, he voices a profound humility (rare in a modern composer!) and asks why "accidental" or "chance" sounds can't be just as interesting as the composer's inspiration. (Why *do* we Westerners accord godlike status to the composer?)

Cage's ideas about the nature and function of music have been extremely influential in shaping the postwar avant-garde. But Cage's ideas have proved equally seminal for many musicians outside of the classical sphere, especially for practitioners of house music and many other popular styles that rely on "noise," chance procedures, or a world music perspective (for more information, see Mark Prendergast and Brian Eno's *The Ambient Century: From Mahler to Trance: The Evolution of Sound in the Electronic Age,* Bloomsbury, 2001). Composer, author, and critic Andrew Stiller once likened Cage to a prospector who discovered one new claim after another, but in his fascination with exploration he never stayed in one place long enough to do the mining. Cage's discoveries will keep composers busy for generations as they seek to realize the possibilities he opened up.

♪ Music at the End of the Millennium

Some Thoughts on Postmodernist Music

In the first years of the new century, composers have begun to consolidate the incredible number of innovations, ideas, and compositional techniques created by composers over the past hundred years. From the 1960s on, a new, diverse body of music has begun to emerge, refined to variously postmodernist, minimalist, Neoromanticist, new age, or new tonality. Whatever the title, much of this music seeks to create the same sort of communicative, visceral musical experience as pre–World War II (and even nineteenth-century) music, without necessarily falling back on the melodic and tonal languages of earlier musical periods.

The great compositional problem of our time is a complex one. How can a composer write music that is relevant to today's society—a society defined by constant change, instant communication, nuclear peril, terrorist threats, wars, and general uncertainty—and at the same time create music that audiences will respond to, appreciate, and even like? (David Del Tredici reflects on the problem in a box on page 802 of Grout and Palisca's *History of Western Music,* 5th ed., New York: W. W. Norton, 1996.) The musical dogma that characterized postwar modernism has given way, from the late 1960s on, to an increasing number of individual styles—a number unheard of in the history of music. The three examples that follow range from 1974 to 2000 and derive from two continents. Rather than try to seek common threads, let students encounter each of these works as a unique experience.

REICH *Music for 18 Musicians*

Along with Philip Glass, Steve Reich remains one of the best-known composers in the minimalist idiom. A postmodernist movement that first emerged in the late 1960s and early 1970s, minimalism quickly became one of the most popular classical styles of the twentieth century. It is difficult to pin down any single, decisive influence on the style, since minimalist composers have drawn on such varied sources for their inspiration. Clearly the ethnic musics of Bali, India, and West Africa have been influential, but so have the chance music of the 1960s avant-garde, electronic music, and Pérotin's medieval Notre Dame organum. Minimalism has been hailed both as the "savior" of twentieth-century art music and as "musical wallpaper," yet there can be no doubt that this appealing style has deeply influenced many recent composers—minimalist or not.

Minimalism is based on repetitive, slowly shifting patterns. Minimalist composers generally use only a few patterns, thus the word *minimal*. The near-obsessive repetition associated with the style is sometimes used to create a trancelike feel, but more often the patterns are gradually varied, creating a slow yet inevitable transformation in the music. In some works this process of transformation can be followed quite easily by the listener; thus, minimalism has often been called process music. Even when the process holds few surprises, the textural shifts it causes are frequently interesting in and of themselves. Perhaps the most gratifying element of minimalist music is its return to tonality. The major and minor triads of this attractive sound world have endeared minimalism to many listeners who could not endure the atonal world of modernist music.

Steve Reich's early work in electronic music led him to some intriguing discoveries. *Come Out* (1966—see Sound Recordings below) used a short musical idea, recorded on several tracks and repeated continuously, that gradually moved out of phase with itself. Reich was so fascinated by the intricate rhythms that resulted from phase shifting that he wrote several pieces exploring this technique. But phase shifting proved too limiting, and Reich changed course.

Reich liked the close imitation of this early technique, so he began to use quasi-canonic procedures. Using short motives that repeat over and over, often with constantly changing meter, each voice followed the others only one or a few beats later. The resulting rich tapestry of percussive color and hypnotic rhythms was a far cry from the imitative polyphony of Josquin or Ligeti. Reich explored this new technique in works such as *Drumming* and *Music for Mallet Instruments, Voices, and Organ*. Typical minimalist works, these pieces gradually altered repeating patterns according to an often-audible process—for example, gradually shortening or lengthening the sustained chords in the background. Such changes took place slowly enough that the listener could focus on the incredibly rich cross-rhythms within the texture.

Reich gradually adapted this quasi-canonic technique to larger and larger ensembles. One important result was *Music for 18 Musicians* (1974–76), written for Reich's biggest ensemble to date. Not surprisingly, this piece possesses a richness and variety of color beyond that of his earlier works. This mixed ensemble includes strings, winds, voices, and percussion, but the largest group by far is the percussion section, numbering four pianos, three marimbas, two xylophones, and a vibraphone. As a result, rhythm remains the hallmark of Reich's style in this work. This emphasis on rhythm leads to an interesting inversion of "orchestral" relationships. In the past, bowed string instruments were the heart of the orchestra; percussion, used but sparingly, added color. In Reich's orchestration, the percussion instruments are constantly busy while the strings either count rests or play sustained chords or repeated notes in the background.

Pay attention to one further aspect of Reich's evolution. In *Drumming* there was often no attention paid to the melodic element; rhythm, texture, and color were the primary building blocks. Ten years later, Reich's *Tehillim* (see Further Listening Examples below) exhibited a highly developed melodic sense, so much so that we can talk about theme and variations form in the final movement. *Music for 18 Musicians* falls midway between these two works, and we can hear this emerging melodicism most clearly in what the textbook calls the main theme—the short, angular motives that repeat throughout Section 1 in the clarinet and voices. Although these are only short motives that repeat with little variation, they stake out a position in the foreground, relegating everything else to the background. This is melody and accompaniment texture at its most basic level.

Start by playing short excerpts from the Introduction and Section 1, mostly to draw comparisons between them. In the Introduction, call attention to the constant pulse, the slowly changing chords, and the long crescendo/decrescendo patterns that allow different instruments to fade in and fade out at different times. The chords may not follow a traditional chord progression, but these are simple triadic harmonies that stay in the same diatonic scale throughout. Note how the pulse continues in Section 1, but now mostly in the marimbas and pianos, and how the harmony (a single chord!) is even more static than in the Introduction (*Listen* compares this to Pérotin's organum). To avoid monotony, Reich adds several new layers over the basic pulse, each with its own rhythmic feel. Point out the main theme that gradually emerges from the pulse. It creates a syncopated feel by using alternating groupings of one, two, or three eighth notes. We hear it first in the clarinets (doubled by one of the pianos), and then the voices join in. The third marimba contributes a countermelody. Periodically the vibraphone adds a very slow-moving melody, and the strings play long slow chords in the background, signaling the new subsections referred to in the textbook (similar to the deep gongs in the Balinese gamelan example).

Once students can hear the different elements in the texture, you are ready to play the entire excerpt. Display Listening Chart 27 and point out the overall structure of these two sections. Play the music and point out each section as it goes by. In the discussion that follows, ask students how they experienced time in these two sections. This is bright, energetic, contagiously cheery music, but for all of its rhythmic energy, the overall pace or rate of change is quite slow (this can take some getting used to!). As a result, our perception of the time-frame widens, and we are invited to listen more closely to the individual threads that create the rich tapestry of this work's texture. If you have time, try asking students to draw connections between the Riley artwork in the textbook (p. 384) and Reich's music.

A New Expressionism

Minimalism was perhaps the most important new style to emerge in the latter half of the twentieth century, but it was not the only one. Composers such as George Crumb rejected the coolness of early minimalism, seeking a style that expressed emotions more vividly. As the *Listen* textbook suggests, these works often express the same dark emotions found in the early twentieth-century expressionism of Schoenberg and Berg, but with a difference. These newer works take full advantage of the new virtuoso performance techniques pioneered by postwar modernists. Further Listening Examples below provide suggestions for two significant works by Crumb, *Black Angels* and *Ancient Voices of Children*. But here we take up the music of Kaija Saariaho (kah –yuh sah –ree–ah–ho), perhaps the most important living Finnish composer. As we shall see, her *From the Grammar of Dreams* uses the human voice in striking and original ways.

If they know Finnish music at all, most Americans know only the music of Sibelius, the great nationalist and "patron saint" of Finnish classical music. Nonetheless, the twentieth century saw an ever-increasing vitality in Finland's musical life, especially following the influx of modernist music by Ligeti, Stockhausen, and others in the 1960s. Several young composers allied with the Ears Open! society came to international prominence in the 1980s, including Magnus Lindberg, Esa-Pekka Salonen (best known today as a world-class conductor), and Kaija Saariaho. In the past ten years, Saariaho has become one of the most important composers of our day.

Since Saariaho is not yet a household name, the notes that follow provide a bit more background material than usual. The following biographical sketch and notes on her musical style are provided to give you a better sense of Saariaho as a person and as a composer. Feel free to use this as you see fit. Much of the information that follows comes from Saariaho's excellent *Prisma* CD-ROM, published with her *Private Gardens* CD on the Montaigne naïve label in 1999. Other useful sources include the *New Grove Dictionary of Music and Musicians,* www.saariaho.org, an interview in Anders Beyer's *The Voice of Music,* the Finnish Music Information Centre (www.fimic.fi), IRCAM (mediatheque .ircam.fr), and her U.S. publisher's Web site (www.schirmer.com/composers/).

Although she learned several instruments in her childhood and adolescence, Saariaho (b. 1952) first pursued a career as an artist. When she found she could no longer ignore her musical inclinations, she entered the Sibelius Academy at the relatively late age of twenty-four, studying with Paavo Heininen. With her classmates Magnus Lindberg and Esa-Pekka Salonen, she became one of the founding members of Ears Open! (*Korvat auki!*), a society dedicated to the performance and propagation of new music that was being ignored by the "establishment." Following her studies with Brian Ferneyhough in her first summer course at Darmstadt in 1980, she chose to study with Klaus Huber at the Musikhochschule in Freiburg, completing her diploma in 1983. The computer music courses she undertook at IRCAM in 1982 proved decisive, grounding her in techniques and ways of thinking that have dominated her music for the last twenty years; 1982 was also the year she settled permanently in Paris. By the late 1980s Saariaho had carved an international reputation for herself, and the 1990s have seen a steady increase in commissions, recordings, and awards. The recent work that has caused the biggest sensation is her 2000 opera, *L'Amour de loin* (Love from Afar), based on Amin Maalouf's retelling of the story of medieval troubadour Jaufré Rudel.

Though a Finn, Saariaho has lived in Paris for the past twenty years, and she maintains a cautious relationship with her homeland. A rather shy person, she originally left Finland not only to broaden her horizons but to pursue her studies in relative anonymity, as she found it difficult to work while drawing constant attention as a "promising young woman composer." Saariaho recently spent a happy year as visiting professor at the Sibelius Academy, but she was glad to return to Paris—the pride Finns take in her achievements meant she was constantly in the limelight, something she does not enjoy even now. This cautious relationship spills over into her music as well. Finnish listeners tend to hear the European influences in her style, while European listeners hear more clearly its Scandinavian features. In any event, Saariaho's style is never deliberately Finnish or French. She writes the music that she feels within her, and often has trouble explaining what makes her music work.

Descriptions of Saariaho's musical style most often focus on her use of color. In fact, Saariaho herself often sounds more like a painter than a composer when describing her music, using words like "degree of pigment," "luminosity," and "smooth" or "rough-textured." But her understanding and use of color differs markedly from that of Debussy or other earlier composers noted for their coloristic music. Through her work with electronic media at IRCAM, Saariaho acquired an extremely sophisticated set of tools and concepts for the analysis, conceptualization, and synthesis of sounds. She frequently begins her compositional process with a detailed analysis of the sounds she intends to use. This additive analysis breaks down sounds according to their pitch, loudness, and duration, with emphasis on overtone content as well as the sounds' perceived pitches and their respective weights. This analysis also helps Saariaho separate the harmonic and "noisy" aspects of the sounds she uses. (Recall the noise component discussed under Sound Vibrations in Lecture Suggestions for Chapter 1 of this manual.) This information can be fed into the computer to provide parameters for sound synthesis; it can also be used to guide the composer's compositional choices. As she composes, Saariaho then uses strategies derived from electronic music to manipulate the components of these sounds and textures—whether or not she is composing an electronic work. The following strategies, many of them derived from the techniques of *musique concrète,* are described in further detail on Saariaho's *Prisma* CD-ROM (see Software below):

Interpolation—A kind of metamorphosis or "development" used by Saariaho to make transitions from one section or texture to another.

Cross-synthesis—A type of interpolation in which Saariaho combines the overtone spectra of different sounds to create new sounds. For instance, fusing a sustained, *legato* sound with a rhythmic, *staccato* idea makes for a striking new sonority.

Sound processing—Many types of sound effects are used in modern electronic music, but Saariaho favors two main types of sound processing: harmonization and reverberation. Harmonization is a process of thickening the sounds by as much as a quarter tone up and down. Reverberation lengthens the sounds, making for a denser texture. Varying the amount of harmonization or reverberation can create the illusion of motion within the performance space.

Spatialization—The process of moving sounds around, whether by moving the human performers or by panning from one speaker to another. Saariaho is not interested in motion for its own sake, however, but in its ability to give a unique ambience to the performance space—to set the scene, as it were.

Amplification—The modification of the "natural" balance of sounds. Amplification can bring out delicate sounds that might otherwise be faint or inaudible. In Saariaho's music, where the various lines and other elements of her textures do not remain in a fixed relationship, amplification (or the acoustic equivalent of *crescendo* or *forte* markings—or *decrescendo* and *piano*) can also allow lines to come to the foreground and just as readily fade to the background again.

Temporal expansion—A specific type of transformation that involves slowing down the sound without changing the pitch. Most fascinating to Saariaho is the manner in which this technique emphasizes a sound's noise components—its attack, its articulation, or, in the case of vocal music, its consonants. As an electronic technique, this requires the use of digital equipment; in the "bad old days" of analogue tape, slowing down the sound resulted in a lower pitch. Of course, this technique can also be approximated in acoustic music, as in Song 4 of *From the Grammar of Dreams.*

Vocal music has always been a source of fascination for Saariaho, but her interest in the voice is not limited to classical *bel canto* technique. Two important musical influences include Lakshmi Shankar and Billie Holiday. Holiday needs no introduction; Shankar is one of today's finest singers in the north Indian style.[1] In these two singers, Saariaho found vocal styles that are rich, direct, and expressive, yet do not treat the voice in an operatic or instrumental manner. In her vocal music, Saariaho does not imitate these singers directly, but their influence shows up clearly in the composer's willingness to use varied, sometimes unconventional vocal timbres expressively. In the 1990s, Saariaho's vocal music led her increasingly in new directions, especially in her collaborations with soprano Dawn Upshaw. Works such as *Château de l'âme* (1995–96), *Lonh* (1996), and *L'Amour de loin* (2000) have moved from a purely color-centered style toward an idiom that relies more on melodic lines. Written in 1988, *From the Grammar of Dreams* precedes these developments, but its use of the unusual vocal sonorities and compositional strategies listed above results in a set of striking, fascinating songs.

SAARIAHO *From the Grammar of Dreams*

From the Grammar of Dreams is based on excerpts from the often deeply disturbing writings of Sylvia Plath (1932–1963), the brilliant yet troubled author whose career ended in suicide at the age of thirty. Saariaho grew up in a Finland where women composers were virtually unknown. Early in her career she needed to find female artists she could use as role models. Plath became one of her "mentors." Saariaho uses two Plath sources in this work: "Paralytic," a poem from Plath's *Ariel* collection, and *The Bell Jar*, a novel.[2]

The core text for this song cycle is a ten-stanza poem Plath wrote only two weeks before her death, "Paralytic." As the authors point out, this poem re-creates the experiences and sensations of a patient in an iron lung. An iron lung is a mechanical contraption that "breathes" for patients who cannot breathe on their own. Iron lungs were used widely to treat polio patients during the epidemic of the mid-twentieth century, but gradually fell out of use after Salk developed a vaccine in the 1950s. The patient in Plath's poem is an older man, paralyzed and totally immobile ("Dead egg"), for whom the days pass by mechanically ("like ticker tape"). Even his own body becomes part of a mechanism, his lungs now vacuum cleanerlike "dust bags." In an ironic twist, Plath associates the condition of this patient, whose wants and desires have been forcibly stripped from him ("a whole world I cannot touch"), with spiritual enlightenment ("I smile, a buddha, all / Wants, desire / Falling from me"). In this poem, Plath could be exploring her own sense of claustrophobia and paralysis, or she could be envisioning spiritual transcendence (nirvana) in a context that

---

[1]Lakshmi Shankar is also Ravi's sister-in-law. Born in Madras (southern India), she started her career as a dancer in the troupe run by Uday Shankar, Ravi's older brother. When an attack of pleurisy ended her dancing career, she trained instead as a singer. Today she is one of the most famous traditional Indian singers, both in India and around the world. See Sound Recordings below for a recommended performance; for an example of the south Indian style of singing, see notes on Tyagaraja's "Marakata manivarna" under Further Listening Examples in Chapter 13. The recorded set that accompanied *Listen: Brief Fourth Edition* featured a performance by D. K. Pattamal.

[2]If you want further information on Plath's writings, you will have no trouble finding material on *The Bell Jar*. Little has been written about "Paralytic," however. The following sources offer more than most: Tracy Brain's *The Other Sylvia Plath* (Longman, 2001) and Judith Kroll's *Chapters in a Mythology: The Poetry of Sylvia Plath* (Harper & Row, 1976).

resonated with her experiences. The closing image ("The claw / Of the magnolia") suggests a defiant posture (or the desire for it) and once again the possibility of transcendence: the magnolia's buds point upward all winter long, indomitable and indifferent, waiting for the spring days when they will bloom in full glory.

Against this poetic text Saariaho juxtaposes short prose excerpts from Plath's best-known novel, *The Bell Jar* (1962). In *The Bell Jar,* Plath chronicles the experiences of her protagonist, college student Esther Greenwood. The novel tracks Esther's gradual slide from reality into madness, her attempted suicide, and her extended hospital stay, and ends on the day of her discharge. The novel's title is a metaphor for both the confinement and the distortion of Esther's madness; trapped inside the jar like a dead scientific specimen, her view of reality is thoroughly skewed by the preserving fluid and the curved, thick glass. Because *The Bell Jar* is a thinly disguised retelling of her own experiences while a Smith College student, Plath can describe Esther's experiences with near-scientific clarity. But the novel is far more than a patient's medical chart. By turns frankly honest, chillingly surreal, and even darkly funny, this work ultimately presents Esther as a sympathetic, believable, profoundly human character.

Saariaho's juxtaposition of these two texts from the last year of Plath's life, one poetic and the other prose, creates fascinating verbal and musical counterpoints. We shall examine these as we look at each song in turn. If you have time, play the same game that you played when you presented Romantic lieder in Chapter 16. Read the texts aloud and ask students to guess what the music might sound like.

Song 1

In Song 1 Saariaho superimposes the first four stanzas of "Paralytic" (see textbook page 386) with a short excerpt from the final chapter of *The Bell Jar*: "A bad dream. I remembered everything." The passage from which those sentences were taken follows.

A bad dream.

To the person in the bell jar, blank and stopped as a dead baby, the world itself is the bad dream.

A bad dream.

I remembered everything.

. . .

Maybe forgetfulness, like a kind snow, should numb and cover them [my memories].

But they were part of me. They were my landscape.[3]

This text looks back at the "bell jar" experience from the vantage point of recovery, but the paralyzed patient in the iron lung cannot look forward to any change in his condition. The first four stanzas of "Paralytic" set the scene, describing the grim realities and daily drudgery of the patient's predicament. The iron lung, like the bell jar, signifies a kind of entrapment—all the more horrendous because there is no escape. These two very different perspectives are reflected in Saariaho's treatment of these texts. Soprano 2 takes the part of Esther,

---

[3]Sylvia Plath, *The Bell Jar: The 25th Anniversary Edition.* New York: Harper Collins, 1996, p. 265.

reflecting in hindsight on her "bad dream"; Soprano 1 takes the role of the hopeless patient in the iron lung. Soprano 2 sings her long, *legato* lines rather calmly, if with a rather wide *vibrato* (the vocal equivalent of the "harmonization" described above)—shaken by her experiences, but not beaten. By contrast, Soprano 1 is all over the gamut with her grunts and swooping *glissandi*. Suggesting the patient's inner rage, her exaggerated musical expression is as hyperactive as the paralytic is motionless. Her manner of singing further echoes the electronic techniques listed above. Temporal expansion is especially prominent—Saariaho slows down the words, sounding out each vowel and consonant in turn. The result is a fiercely buzzing "s," a harshly guttural "ck," a long rolled "r," or a "t" spit out with vehemence. This dramatic rendition, as much spoken (or grunted) as sung, cannot help but command attention.

The end of Song 1 relaxes somewhat. The two sopranos share material for the first time. Both voices play off of the (0,1,4) interval set introduced by Soprano 2 earlier in the song. At the end, this motive sounds nearly like a "blue note" inflection. They also trade off on a long high note (suggesting the reverberation effect described above) with their final phrases softly spoken, almost whispered, underneath. Especially striking is Soprano 2's last statement in a moment of silence: "I remembered everything."

Song 3

Only in this song and Song 5 do the two sopranos have the same text—and only in this song do they sing throughout! Here Saariaho uses the eighth and final stanza of "Paralytic" (see textbook page 386). This stanza, with its image of defiance, supreme indifference, and transcendence, calls for a different treatment than the previous nine. Saariaho obliges with slowly intertwining *legato* lines that pass motives back and forth in imitative fashion, sounding almost tonal at times. Because it is sung, this song has the feel of two-voice counterpoint. Various intervals are used, but Saariaho's predilection for tritones and half steps (emphasized both harmonically and melodically) guarantees that this will not sound like the imitative polyphony of Josquin or Palestrina. The dissonances may point to defiance more than transcendence, but by avoiding the hyperactive timbral variety of Song 1, Song 3 achieves a quiet serenity all its own.

Song 4

In Song 4 Saariaho juxtaposes two snippets from *The Bell Jar,* one from Chapter 13 and the other from Chapter 20, the final chapter. Chapter 13 deals with Esther's growing preoccupation with suicide, and the first excerpt (Soprano 1—see textbook page 386) describes one of several failed attempts. Esther swims out to a faraway rock in the hope that she will drown when she becomes too tired to swim to safety. But she tires of trying before she reaches the point of exhaustion, and several attempts to dive to the bottom and drown are short-circuited when her body bobs back up. The beating of her heart's "I am I am I am" (iamb?)[4] symbolizes her body's will to survive, seeming to spite the elaborate plans her mind hatches. The passage from Chapter 20 (Soprano 2—see textbook page 386) deliberately echoes the Chapter 13 excerpt, but now in the far happier context of Esther's recovery and impending discharge from the hospital. As in Song 1, memories of terrible events cannot (should not?) be

---

[4]A pun, perhaps? The short-long rhythm of the iamb is precisely the rhythm of the heartbeat.

covered over; in the words of the old proverb, you don't burn the bridge that carried you across.

In Saariaho's setting, there is no "playing nice" with Esther's suicide attempt. You cannot help but hear her gasping for every breath she takes; each intake and exhalation of air becomes a painful experience (perhaps echoing the image of Song 1's iron lung—always a noisy contraption). The panting that opens this song gives way to a rocking, slow half-step trill motive that, once introduced, quickly expands to extremely high and low notes (the two-voice equivalent of one of Ligeti's expanding wedge shapes). Now the sopranos take turns stating the words of their respective texts, "singing" in a manner reminiscent of Song 1, but not so extreme. Their lines continue to play off the half-step motive, accompanied by more of the opening passage's heavy breathing. The song gradually builds intensity, working into higher and higher registers until it reaches a climax on the words "I am." Added tension is achieved by overlapping, repetitive statements of the "I am" motive, an effect reminiscent of close imitation. Like Song 1, this song ends with a gentle coda-like passage, echoing the climactic cluster of "I am" motives in a lower register and at a much softer dynamic.

And what do we make of the heartbeat now? Do we celebrate its ultimate victory over Esther's mental illness? Does it point to the "great I Am" (God, or the ultimate life force) referred to by Plath in the earlier short story *Johnny Panic and the Bible of Dreams*? Or does it mock her even in her recovery?

Final Thoughts on Saariaho

Taken as a set, these works challenge conventional notions of what a song should be. Songs 1 and 4 are clearly not "beautiful" in the manner of a song by Schubert or Schumann. Nonetheless, they retain the same vivid expression of the text that we associate with earlier German lieder. In Saariaho's music, any vocal sound can be used, but never for its own sake—expression and communication remain paramount in this music. Saariaho's unique blend of the intellectual and the visceral make her one of the most prominent and accessible composers working today.

Back to the Future

The new expressionism of Saariaho or Crumb was not the only answer to the emotional coolness of early minimalism. Some composers of the past two decades sought new means to express emotions frankly and directly, in ways that an audience would find more accessible and enjoyable. Saariaho herself turned to a more conventional lyricism in her recent opera, *L'Amour de loin*, but the "man of the hour," the one whose music speaks to contemporary concert-going audiences like no one else's, is John Adams.

ADAMS *El Niño*

John Adams was initially a minimalist composer in the mold of Steve Reich, but with works such as *Harmonielehre* (see Further Listening Examples below), he broke free of the dogmatic elements of that style. Adams kept minimalism's pulsing rhythmic energy and pattern repetition, but he added rich, shifting harmonic textures and long, Romantic melodic lines. Adams's dramatic and frankly pleasing musical textures offer the listener a greater degree of musical narrative and contrast than does the minimalist music of Reich.

This flair for the dramatic has made Adams the most important opera com-poser of the last twenty years, and in his collaborations with Peter Sellars and Alice Goodman, he has not shied away from troubling contemporary issues such as the Cold War, terrorism, or the nuclear threat. His growing operatic catalogue includes important, topical works such as *Nixon in China* (1987), *The Death of Klinghoffer* (1991), and *Dr. Atomic* (2005).

Like Handel before him, Adams brings his dramatic, operatic style into other vocal genres, especially the oratorio. In fact, Handel's *Messiah* seems to lurk in the background throughout *El Niño,* not so much as a model but as a theme for improvisation (and even debate)—one that triggers new ideas, new approaches, and a more contemporary handling of the story and the meaning of Christ's birth.

This work exhibits many points of similarity with Handel. Both *Messiah* and *El Niño* use full orchestra, soloists, and chorus. Both use recitative, arias (some da capo), and choruses. Both deal with the birth of Christ. Both weave together newly written texts with verses from both the Old Testament and the gospel accounts of Christ's life. Both include reflections on the meaning and significance of Christ's birth. But the differences between them are much more interesting:

❧ Adams's orchestra is much larger, capable of huge, richly textured climaxes that overwhelm the listener. Adams also uses the very unusual (in contem-porary music, at least) sound of three countertenors. Sometimes he uses them independently and sometimes, as in "When Herod Heard," as a trio to back up the soloist (think Gladys Knight and the Pips). In either case, this trio tends to provide either narration or commentary.

❧ Adams's use of form is more varied than Handel's. On the face of it, "Pues mi Dios" uses that most traditional of Baroque forms, the da capo aria, but the return of the first section is far from literal in Adams's **A B A** form, and the chorus frequently inserts itself in dialogue with the mezzo, horning in on what would have been the soloist's "star turn" in Handel's day. The chorus, "Woe unto Them," provides another example. Partway through, once we have decided that this is a clear-cut chorus, Adams cleverly weaves in phrases from the recitative-like "When Herod Heard" as a counterpoint to the cho-rus's condemnation of Herod's murderous plot.

❧ Handel took on a big task in *Messiah,* reflecting not only on Christ's birth but on prophecies of his coming, life, death, and resurrection, and on the meaning of the resurrection for believers—eternal life. Adams looks more narrowly on the events surrounding Christ's birth, giving him the opportu-nity to include details often omitted, such as Herod's slaughter of the inno-cents and the Holy Family's flight to Egypt. Adams also changes the focus in this oratorio. In all of *Messiah,* Handel never mentions the Virgin Mary by name, but part one of *El Niño* is devoted almost entirely to this sixteen-year-old unwed mother, including the Annunciation, the Magnificat, Joseph's reaction to her pregnancy, and so on.

❧ Most striking of all, Adams and Peter Sellars turn this oratorio into a more theatrical work. Handel's oratorios were concert works, performed without sets or costumes and without action or choreography of any kind, but right off the bat, the *El Niño* excerpts on the *Listen* DVD give us the video projections (a movie created specifically for *El Niño*); the simple dance choreography; and the brightly colored, everyday-casual costumes that are part of a live performance of this work. Even more controversial, Adams and Sellars place the entire story in southern California. Mary and Joseph become Mexican immigrants (talk about a hot-button issue!) who have their baby on a beach on the Pacific. This gives them a social standing closer to that of the real Mary and Joseph, outsiders who were forced to stay the night and give birth in a stable in Bethlehem. All of these changes give this oratorio a more contemporary, relevant, theatrical feel.

Plan to spend time with all three excerpts from *El Niño*. Students will be reassured that music history doesn't end with the harsh dissonance and atonality of modernist music. And those who found Reich's minimalism too cool emotionally are often caught up in the melodic beauty and dramatic sweep of Adams's compelling and very accessible sound world. Once you finish your introduction to Adams and to *El Niño*, take time to look at these examples separately.

Of course, you *must* use the video performances of the three *El Niño* numbers found on the *Listen* DVD. The visual aspect of this work is just as powerful as the music, and you owe it to your students to give them the full experience. In addition, it is well worth your while to grab a copy of the commercial DVD of the entire work (see Video Recordings below). Especially valuable is the bonus twenty-eight-minute documentary on the making of *El Niño*. It includes background information on Adams and his musical style as well as interviews with Adams, director Peter Sellars, and conductor Kent Nagano. Selected clips from the documentary can make an effective addition to your classroom presentation, and you can even explore other scenes from this oratorio with your students if you have the time.

"Pues mi Dios ha nacido a penar"

This song text, written by a Mexican nun in the seventeenth century, gives voice to Mary's thoughts as she gazes at her newborn son. Adams and Sellars deliberately chose texts by women to supplement those taken from the Bible. They wanted to emphasize Mary's perspective in this story, and they felt that women's writings about Mary might have greater insight and authenticity than those by male authors. (They even use a text by Hildegard of Bingen!) The *Listen* textbook provides text and translation (and information on the poet). On the face of it, deciding whether the baby should sleep or stay awake is no big deal, but at some level Mary knows what is in store for her son later in life. She associates waking with the love he will share with the world, and she links sleeping to his death. Take time to make students aware of Mary's ambivalence as she ponders the future.

Musically this is a dialogue between mezzo soloist and choir that takes the form of a da capo aria. The soloist sings the lines that argue for keeping *el niño* awake; and the choir, those that argue for letting him sleep. This song opens with a haunting, beautiful, angular melody over the rich sound of low strings—evoking the tenderness of a mother gazing at her newborn—and the choir answers in a similar vein. The textbook describes the contrasting **B** section well. This more agitated section begins at 1:38, when the violin enters and the mezzo begins line 3 (overlapping with the choir as they finish line 2). At 2:15 the sense of agitation is heightened when the low strings drop out, giving greater prominence to the nervous solo violin. The return of the **A** section (at 3:07) restores the comforting sounds of the opening, but a new addition works hard to contradict that sense of comfort. The solo violin from the **B** section continues to interject its nervous, staccato *perpetuum mobile,* as if to suggest Mary's ultimate ambivalence about her son's fate.

A curious coincidence—the mezzo soloist in this performance, Lorraine Hunt Lieberson, is the very same woman who sang another da capo aria in the

Listen set, "La giustizia" from Handel's *Julius Caesar*. Her beautifully expressive singing here is all the more poignant for those who know that she died of cancer in July 2006.

"When Herod Heard" and "Woe unto Them That Call Evil Good"

These two numbers act very much like the recitative and chorus pair that we heard with "There were shepherds" and "Glory to God" in Handel's *Messiah*. In "When Herod Heard," the baritone and countertenors tell the story from the Gospel of Matthew; in "Woe unto Them," the chorus extracts a moral lesson from the story using verses from the Old Testament book of Isaiah. The musical links between these two numbers derive from this relationship.

Take a moment to clarify the story before you go any further. Three wise men from the east come to King Herod asking about a newborn King of the Jews. This is news to Herod, who is not kindly disposed to any competitors for his throne. He tells the wise men that he himself would like to worship this new king, and would they please let him know when they find the baby. As the later "slaughter of the innocents" makes all too clear, Herod plans to take advantage of the good graces of the wise men to further his secret plans to murder the baby.

One advantage Adams found in the oratorio genre was the possibility of giving a single singer multiple roles. In "When Herod Heard," the three countertenors take the roles of the three wise men, but just as frequently they serve as a backup ensemble for the baritone soloist, echoing and amplifying his words. The baritone soloist serves primarily as the narrator here, but at the point where Herod actually speaks, the baritone takes over the role of Herod, and the three countertenors sing with him in strict rhythmic unison—an eerie sound that suggests the unbelievable nature of Herod's true plans. All of this is accompanied by the constant chugging rhythms heard in the basses, bassoons, and low brass—a discomforting undercurrent that gives the lie to Herod's hypocritical "sweet talk."

Without a pause, the chorus bursts in over a new, driving diminished-triad bass ostinato, punctuated by orchestral "hits" that recur at irregular intervals. The words from the book of Isaiah condemn hypocrisy in its many forms, and their target in this context is Herod, who greets the wise men with honey on his lips but murder in his heart. This energetic music is organized in three large sections, each one swelling to an overpowering climax, and each one more anxious and turbulent than the last.

The first section is for choir and orchestra, but the second and third sections add the baritone soloist to the mix. He recaps Herod's words from the previous number, dramatically placing Herod's hypocrisy in direct counterpoint with the choir's words of condemnation. One of the nicest juxtapositions comes toward the end of the last section. One of the verses from Isaiah reads as follows:

> Woe unto them that seek deep to hide their counsel from the Lord, and their works are in the dark, and they say, Who seeth us? and who knoweth us?
> —Isaiah 29:15

The chorus introduces this verse's first phrase in the second section, and they add "their works are in the dark" in the third section. Up to this point the baritone has been repeating Herod's words again and again, "Go and search diligently . . ." But at the midpoint of the third section it is the baritone, not the choir, who sings the final questions, "Who seeth us?" and "Who knoweth us?" Adams chooses to put these words in Herod's mouth. This Herod who imagines that he can plot murder in secret without anyone seeing or knowing becomes precisely the person God condemns in Isaiah. As the baritone sings these new words, the choir spells out the punishment God will inflict on such evildoers: "I will also choose their delusions, and will bring forth their fears upon them" (Isaiah 66:4). Strong stuff!

Take time to decompress with your students. This strong music and the rich, often provocative counterpoint between video, choreographic, visual, textual, and musical elements will leave your students with many loose ends in need of tying up. Music has always had the power to make us not only hear but also understand things differently. Adams and Sellars take this old, familiar story, encrusted with centuries of accumulated meaning and tradition, and force us to look at it with fresh eyes. We find things that we missed, and we come to see characters such as Mary with new understanding. In the end, the old story becomes contemporary in the fullest sense, taking on a new significance, urgency, and poignancy.

In Chapter 5 we saw sacred Navajo songs compared to high-voltage electrical wires. In a sense, music was the original medium for "shock and awe," as we readily see from the religious music of many ancient peoples. Much of the modernist music we have studied managed to shock well enough, but John Adams has restored a tangible, visceral sense of awe as well. His high-energy, eclectic music and his insistence on dealing with contemporary issues have proven enormously popular with audiences—if not always with his critics and fellow composers. Few recent composers write music that speaks to an audience the way Adams's music does. No wonder the authors call Adams the "premier concert music composer in America today." To this pronouncement one might also add, one of the great composers of the past fifty years.

Additional Teaching Suggestions

❼ Lecture-Demonstration Ideas

1. Create a slide show of late twentieth-century art. Borrow slides from your school's art department to demonstrate representative artworks from after World War II as well: abstract expressionism, avant-garde, and so on. In preparation, ask students to read textbook pages 371–72 (up to "New Sound Materials") carefully. In class, ask them to pick out features in the artworks that correspond to concepts from their readings. See Multimedia Resources below for video and software resources.

2. Invite an avant-garde musician to class. Whether they sing or play an instrument, these musicians can demonstrate the incredible variety of performance techniques available to contemporary performers. Vocalists can speak about the experience of performing works such as Schoenberg's *Pierrot lunaire,* Berg's *Wozzeck,* Ligeti's *Lux aeterna,* Cage's *Aria,* or Saariaho's *From the Grammar of Dreams;* pianists about music by Debussy, Ives, Schoenberg, Ravel, Bartók, Copland, Crumb, or Reich; string players about Bartók's Music for Strings, Percussion, and Celesta or Crumb's *Black Angels*; and percussionists about the music of Varèse, Cage, Crumb, or Reich.

3. Take your students to the keyboard lab to play with "sound complexes." Ask them to play tone clusters in different registers using white keys only, black keys only, or both white and black keys. How do the sounds of these clusters differ from one another? Refer to textbook page 377 and ask students

to improvise cluster patterns that re-create the sounds suggested by the symbols in the textbook. This exercise can be used to introduce Ligeti's *Lux aeterna*.

4. Demonstrate Elliott Carter's technique of metric modulation. Find scores and recordings of Carter's String Quartet No. 1, Cello Sonata, or "Canaries" from *Eight Pieces for Timpani*. (The score for "Canaries" can be found in Burkhart's *Anthology for Musical Analysis*, 5th ed., Fort Worth: Harcourt Brace, 1994.) See Sound Recordings for suggested performances.

5. Perform Cage's *Imaginary Landscape IV* in class. You will need to find a score and twelve radios. Each radio requires two performers, one to control the volume and the other to change the stations. Students do not need to read conventional music notation to perform, so everyone in class can (should!) participate. If your class is larger or smaller than twenty-four people, you can double or omit parts as necessary. This unusual experience of sound and the random elements in this composition offer plenty of fuel for discussion once the performance is over.

6. Bring twentieth-century score pages to class. Both John Cage and George Crumb created handwritten scores of great beauty. Cage's scores have even been exhibited in modern art galleries. Works by Penderecki and Stockhausen also provide music notation with an entirely different look. In some cases, new sounds and new concepts require new notational symbols. In other cases, the notation reflects images central to the music or the text (compare Crumb's scores with Baude Cordier's fourteenth-century chansons). If your library does not own individual scores by these composers, seek out anthologies that contain twentieth-century scores. Stolba's *Development of Western Music: An Anthology*, vol. II, 3rd ed. (Boston: McGraw-Hill, 1998) includes scores by Ives, Cowell, Crumb, and Reich. Charles Burkhart's *Anthology for Music Analysis*, 5th ed. (Fort Worth: Harcourt Brace, 1994) contains scores by Ives, Cowell, Cage, Crumb, Riley, and Saylor. These scores can be used to generate discussion about the function of notation from a new perspective.

7. Invite a percussionist or a new music ensemble to class. These performers have a wealth of practical, firsthand experience. They can discuss and demonstrate new sound materials, chance music, and the virtuosity this music often requires. Further, this music makes an entirely different impression in live performance than it does on a recording. Ask students to prepare questions to bring to class, and bring some of your own in case discussion wanes.

8. Visit an electronic music studio or a music store that specializes in MIDI sound synthesis and music software (or bring a synthesizer, a sampler, or a computer to class—whatever you understand and can demonstrate successfully). Many schools have an electronic studio; if yours does not, music stores are usually happy to demonstrate equipment for potential customers. Musicians and nonmusicians alike are fascinated to watch as sounds are recorded into a sampler or sequencer and manipulated and edited using various software packages. *Musique concrète* has never been easier. It's hard to believe that MIDI is only twenty-five years old!

❦ Class Discussion Ideas

1. *How do you listen when there is no melody?* In homophonic music (most of the music that students are familiar with), it is possible to listen primarily to melody—to ignore the other elements of music. If you have demanded that

students listen for other elements throughout the course, students will be prepared to follow music that has no melody. The experience is disorienting at first, but as students become attuned to changes in texture, tone color, and so on, they can begin to follow avant-garde music. Ask students to name any works heard earlier in the course in which they could identify nonmelodic elements that played a significant role in the music. These more familiar experiences can help to reassure students.

2. *What was it like to be a European composer right after World War II?* Ask students to read textbook page 371 in preparation. In class, ask them to list several of the tragic events of World War II: Pearl Harbor, the Holocaust, and the atomic bomb may come to mind. Ask students to imagine themselves in Europe—many cities and villages bombed or destroyed, friends and relatives dead. *What connections can you have with the past? New technologies enable you to move ahead, but where are you emotionally? How do you deal with what has happened? What kind of music is appropriate to express the tragedy and hopelessness that surround you?*

3. Read Cage's prophetic Credo to stimulate discussion. Cage's *Silence* (Middletown, Conn.: Wesleyan University Press, 1973) contains the text for a 1937 talk titled "The Future of Music: Credo." It is hardly surprising that Cage's prophecies describe his personal developments in subsequent years, but his prophecies also outlined the course of avant-garde music after World War II. Read this creed to the class and ask the students to compare Cage's predictions with the authors' summary of musical developments since World War II. This provides a useful review of the chapter and gives Cage, a major figure in contemporary music, more visibility in the classroom.

4. *Is chance music really music? Why should music be different from the sounds of life? Why "musical" sounds, rather than noises?* Read excerpts from Cage's *Silence* (cited in Class Discussion Idea 3 above) to the class. Cage's writings are engaging and thoughtful as they challenge conventional notions about music and composition. *How much influence did Zen Buddhism have on John Cage's chance music?* Cage studied Zen with Daisetz Suzuki in the late 1940s, but the precise connection between Zen and Cage's ideas about intention and nonintention are unclear. He tells a few good Zen stories in *Silence*—and few can tell a story as well as Cage. If you want to let Cage himself tell some of his stories, grab a copy of the recently reissued *Indeterminacy* on CD (see Sound Recordings below).

5. *What does it mean to be an American composer?* For Virgil Thomson, it was enough to be both a composer and an American, but others have demanded more than that. Henry Cowell's *American Composers on American Music* (Ann Arbor, Mich.: Books on Demand, 1933) includes writings by many composers describing what it means to be an American composer. Read excerpts for your students and ask for their reactions.

6. *What do contemporary composers say about their music?* After listening to the *Listen* examples, read comments by the composers and ask for student reactions. Several books contain interviews with and articles by important composers. Richard Dufallo's *Trackings* (New York: Oxford University Press, 1989) includes conversations with Crumb, Cage, Copland, Ligeti, and others; *Contemporary Composers on Contemporary Music* (New York: Holt, Rinehart, and Winston, 1967) by Elliot Schwartz and Barney Childs is a collection of writings by Bartók, Shostakovich, Copland, Varèse, Cage, and others; *The*

Voice of Music: Conversations with Composers of Our Time (Burlington, Vt.: Ashgate, 2000) by Anders Beyer is a collection of interviews with Ligeti, Gubaidulina, Stockhausen, Schnittke, Glass, Xenakis, Saariaho, and others.

⅄ Listening Ideas

1. Listen to music based on the quarter-tone scale. Recordings can be found of Ives's three *Quarter-Tone Pieces* and Penderecki's *Threnody*. The Ives work requires two pianos tuned a quarter tone apart. Penderecki writes for a string orchestra and asks the ensemble to play massive tone clusters built out of quarter tones. Compare these works with short examples based on diatonic and chromatic scales and ask students to describe the different effects of each of these pieces. See Sound Recordings below for suggested performances.

2. Compare the twentieth-century orchestra with the orchestra of earlier periods. Play excerpts from Debussy's Three Nocturnes, Stravinsky's *The Rite of Spring,* Ravel's Concerto in G, Bartók's Music for Strings, Percussion, and Celesta, Copland's *Appalachian Spring,* or Adams's *El Niño;* compare them with typical Baroque (Vivaldi's Concerto in G), Classical (Mozart's Symphony No. 40), and Romantic (Berlioz, *Fantastic* Symphony) orchestras. Use the following questions to generate discussion. *Which orchestra was largest? Which used the greatest variety of instruments? Which instrument family dominated each excerpt? Do these changes suggest any overall trends in the development of the orchestra?*

3. Take your class on a galloping tour of electronically generated music from the following periods. See Sound Recordings below for suggested recordings.

Stage I—The classic studio synthesizer: huge, expensive, difficult and time-consuming to use, no real-time performance possible (use Stockhausen's *Gesang der Jünglinge* or Babbitt's *Vision and Prayer*).

Stage II—Voltage-controlled synthesizers by Moog and Buchla: smaller, modular, less expensive, real-time performance possible, but time-consuming to construct and change individual sounds (use Subotnick's *Silver Apples of the Moon, 4 Butterflies,* or *The Wild Bull*).

Stage III—Digital sound synthesis and the MIDI revolution: sophisticated digital synthesis computer programs and portable, versatile, affordable synthesizers for studio or live performance that work with sequencers and computers (use Charles Dodge's *Any Resemblance Is Purely Coincidental,* Morton Subotnick's *All My Hummingbirds Have Alibis,* Saariaho's *Six Japanese Gardens,* or recordings of works by composers at IRCAM).

4. Compare serialism with chance music. Find recordings of Boulez's *Structures* and Cage's *Music of Changes.* Boulez used the techniques of total serialism; Cage used chance procedures. Play two or three minutes from each one and ask students to describe the differences between them. Cage surrounds his sounds with more space (more silence), but otherwise the sound world created by these two works is remarkably similar—curious, since one is "totally" controlled and the other "totally" random. In fact, most compositional work in "total serialism" is devoted to creating the series of pitches, durations, dynamics, articulations, and so on. Once these series are in place, the composer has little control over the note-to-note succession of events. Cage, on the other hand, used serial sets in composing the music but consulted the *I Ching* to make compositional decisions about the note-to-note succession of events. See Sound Recordings below for suggested performances.

5. Compare Ligeti with Josquin. As the lecture notes above suggest, Ligeti followed many Renaissance procedures in his setting of *Lux aeterna*. Play excerpts from Ligeti's choral work and from Josquin's *Pange lingua* Mass. In what ways are they similar? How do they differ?

6. Play the famous third movement of Berio's *Sinfonia*. Play the third movement of Mahler's Symphony No. 2 to prepare the students. This incredible collage is one of the most stunningly virtuosic compositional achievements of the twentieth century. See Sound Recordings below for suggested performances.

7. Compare Adams's *El Niño* (2000) with Handel's *Messiah*. The Lecture Suggestions above suggest many parallels between these two works, and it can prove fascinating to explore them more fully. Good examples include comparing Handel's "He was despised" with Adams's "Pues mi Dios ha nacido a penar" (both da capo arias, Handel giving us the reason for Mary's anxiety in Adams's setting); Handel's "Thus saith the Lord" with Adams's "Shake the Heavens" (this will be obvious); Handel's "But who may abide the day of His coming" or "Why do the nations so furiously rage" with Adams's "Woe unto Them That Call Evil Good" (Handel's great rage arias transposed to the choral medium); or Handel's "Surely He hath borne our griefs" with Adams's "In the day of the great slaughter" (choruses whose texts deal with anger and suffering). The textbook suggests that "Woe unto Them That Call Evil Good" might be Adams's answer to Handel's Hallelujah Chorus, but this is not so much an example of Handel's direct influence as it is of Adams rethinking and reinterpreting Handel in a new context. See Multimedia Resources below for suggested CDs and DVDs.

8. Play other examples of minimalism. This exercise suggests the range of expressive possibilities in this style. Good examples include Reich's *The Cave*, *Tehillim*, or *Different Trains*; Philip Glass's *Metamorphosis* (see Further Listening Examples below) or *Koyaanisqatsi*; Terry Riley's *A Rainbow in Curved Air*; and John Adams's *Harmonielehre* (see Further Listening Examples below) or *The Death of Klinghoffer*. See Multimedia Resources below for suggested recordings.

9. Compare Steve Reich with Pérotin. Reich has identified Pérotin as a composer who shares many of his techniques and concerns. Find a recording of an organum quadruplum by Pérotin (see Sound Recordings below) for side-by-side comparison with Reich's *Music for 18 Musicians*. The counterpoint and slowly changing harmonies sound remarkably similar. This demonstration pulls together the opposite ends of this book's historical survey quite nicely.

10. Compare Saariaho's successful recent opera, *L'Amour de loin* (2000), with the music of the medieval troubadours, especially Jaufré Rudel and Bernart de Ventadorn. Now available on DVD, this work is a modern retelling of Jaufré Rudel's tale of his distant love, Clémence. (You can substitute Saariaho's *Lonh* [1996], for solo voice and electronics—the work she wrote in preparation for the opera.) The more conventionally lyric treatment of the human voice offers fascinating comparisons with *From the Grammar of Dreams*, precisely because the sound world of the opera is so different. Some passages use drone accompaniments reminiscent of the Middle Ages, while others provide excellent examples of Saariaho's electronic techniques, described in Lecture Suggestions above. See Multimedia Resources below for suggested Rudel and Saariaho CDs and DVDs.

11. Play works that reflect on the often troubled relationships between Jews, Arabs, and Christians over the centuries. Two outstanding examples include

Steve Reich's *The Cave* and John Adams's *The Death of Klinghoffer. The Cave,* one of Reich's recent word-based works, uses sound bites from interviews with Jews, Arabs, and Christians from the Middle East and the United States. As speakers reflect on the story of Abraham/Ibrahim (buried in the Cave of Machpelah), striking differences emerge in the historical understandings of these three traditions. *The Death of Klinghoffer* portrays the 1985 terrorist hijacking of the *Achille Lauro.* In the premiere production, all characters were dressed similarly and given a chance to tell their stories without prejudice or condemnation (one reason we have not seen U.S. performances of this work since 9/11, sadly). Both works avoid taking sides (not easy to do), and all parties have their say. See Sound Recordings below for suggested performances.

℣ Further Listening Examples

JOHN CAGE *Aria* and *Fontana Mix*

Aria is written for voice. In Cage's unconventional score, the words are indicated, but the actual pitches and rhythms are left up to the performer (see textbook page 380). The performer also chooses styles of singing from a variety of options offered by Cage, ranging from operatic to baby talk. The performer can choose to sing the piece with or without accompaniment; Cage once offhandedly remarked that his own *Fontana Mix,* an electronic work written a few years earlier, offered a suitable accompaniment.

An actual performance of *Aria,* with or without *Fontana Mix,* will yield any number of randomly arrived-at moments. Like *4'33",* this piece makes a statement about the nature of music, the human voice, and our perception of both. See Sound Recordings below for suggested performances.

BABBITT *All Set*

Milton Babbitt was born in Philadelphia in 1916 and is professor emeritus at Princeton University. As a composer and teacher, Babbitt remains one of the most influential figures of his generation.

Babbitt was the first composer to take Schoenberg's "method of composing with twelve notes" to its logical extreme. In 1948 Babbitt wrote *Three Compositions for Piano,* in which not only pitches but rhythms and dynamics were systematically predetermined using serial procedures. In such absolutely unified, predetermined music, there is a great risk of creating dry, uninteresting music, precomposed according to formula and therefore unresponsive to dramatic pacing or the expressive needs of the moment. Babbitt's music consistently avoids this pitfall.

All Set, for jazz ensemble (1957), is a rigorously serial composition that takes advantage of the instrumentation, rhythmic drive, timbral combinations, and soloistic character of a 1950s-style jazz ensemble. As in a jazz group, the instruments in *All Set* take turns rising to the surface to take their "solos." Ensemble sections punctuate these solos, and the whole is accompanied by a jazzlike rhythm section. With this work, Babbitt joined a long list of composers whose music was influenced by jazz. Although *All Set* is structurally a product of postwar modernism, it is clearly American in its expressive flexibility, rhythmic energy, and wit. Even the punning title of this piece reflects this duality, referring both to the twelve-tone set that shapes this work and to the informal idiomatic expression. See Sound Recordings below for suggested performances.

BERIO *Sinfonia*, II

Berio helped to establish Italy's first electronic music studio in 1955, but he did little work with electronic music after the 1950s. He came of age as a serialist in a rationalist age, but he always retained an instinctive approach to music. Like Verdi and Puccini before him, Berio favored the human voice and never lost sight of the performer. He combined theatricality and virtuosity in his often breathtaking musical tapestries.

Sinfonia, a multimovement work for eight amplified vocalists and large orchestra, was one of Berio's most spectacular achievements. The title has multiple meanings. In Italian, *sinfonia* can mean "sounding together," a reflection on the mix of vocal and instrumental timbres that characterizes Berio's work. And so *Sinfonia* is not exactly a symphony, yet Berio knew full well that such a title would create expectations, and he acknowledges them here and there. For instance, the first version of *Sinfonia* employed the expected four movements. Further, some aspects of the second and third movements suggest the traditional four-movement plan. The second movement is a slow movement, and its funereal quality begs comparison with funeral-march slow movements by Beethoven and Mahler. The famous third movement takes as its framework a Mahler scherzo with a quick Ländler (an Austrian peasant dance that Mahler often substituted for the minuet in the four-movement plan). Mahler's name comes up often in connection with this work, and Berio followed Mahler's lead in one other respect. Mahler was the first to use voices in every movement of a symphony, and Stravinsky (*Symphony of Psalms*) and Berio (*Sinfonia*) were two among many twentieth-century composers who followed suit.

The second movement of *Sinfonia* uses several elements to create a subtle dramatic curve. Berio begins with a few sounds that at first seem random and unconnected. Gradually the spaces between sounds get shorter, consonants are added to the vowels, and our ears can connect these sounds into patterns. The initially inchoate vowels become syllables that eventually form the words "O Martin Luther King." In short, the music moves from softer to louder, from randomness to forward motion and intensity, and from ambiguity to greater clarity.

Although the motion is continuous and changes take place gradually, subtly defined sections can be discerned.

Section 1 (mm. 1–52)—Introduces the main materials: accented instrumental outbursts, sustained vowels in the voices, and occasional *glissando*s. Vocal parts use the pitches of a specially constructed scale (see musical example below). Constant reiteration of these scale tones creates a static quality that approximates the leaden effect of grief, randomly punctuated by stabs of various instrumental colors. Some syllables gradually emerge as intensity increases.

Section 2 (mm. 53–78)—The drive toward the climax. The palette of pitches gradually expands, especially in the instrumental parts. Intensity increases, especially after m. 68, and the syllables finally form into the words "Martin Luther King" at mm. 74–79.

Section 3 (mm. 79–93)—Climax and unwinding. The first two sections depict a grief that can hardly find words to express itself. Only when it finds the words—"O Martin Luther King"—can it begin to mourn more fully, as it does in the final section. Joseph Kerman described this mourning well on page 346 of *Listen: Third Brief Edition:*

A slow snare drum tattoo evokes a military funeral, as though King were a general [king!] felled in battle. The soprano follows this with little sobs; then the music dies down with quiet—but strikingly new—sounds (the organ is prominent). The movement ends with the men's voices mouthing the one word "Martin" [m. 93]: a haunting lullaby effect.

This movement was written in 1968–69 to lament the loss of the Rev. Dr. Martin Luther King Jr., the civil rights leader who was assassinated in 1968.

CRUMB *Black Angels*

George Crumb's unique musical world is a synthesis of many diverse influences. These include Asian music and philosophy, Debussy, Webern, Bartók (especially the evocative "night music"—see Music for Strings, Percussion, and Celesta in Chapter 21), and the poetry of Federico García Lorca (in works such as *Ancient Voices of Children*—see below).

Black Angels is subtitled "Thirteen Images from the Dark Land," images that Crumb groups in three large sections—"Departure," "Absence," and "Return." According to Crumb, the images portray "a voyage of the soul," a set of profoundly disturbing reflections on good and evil in the troubled years of the Vietnam War. The five numbers below comprise the first section, "Departure."

Scored for amplified string quartet, this work offers a prime example of the new virtuosity, incorporating a virtual catalogue of special effects. Crumb asks his musicians to play behind the bridge, *pizzicato, col legno,* and *sul ponticello* and to produce harmonics and *glissandi*; he also asks them to scratch with the bow, strum the strings, rap their knuckles on the instruments, whistle, count aloud in foreign languages, whisper, click their tongues, and play percussion instruments such as the maracas, water goblets, and the tam-tam (on which Crumb calls for crashes and bowed harmonics). The amplified string instruments offer incredible dynamic range, from ear-shattering assaults to delicate sounds that would normally be inaudible in the concert hall.

Find a score if at all possible when you present this piece (and the Kronos Quartet DVD as well—see Video Recordings below). Crumb's handwritten scores are beautiful to look at, and the visual design often conveys Crumb's symbolism as effectively as the music.

No. 1, Threnody I: Night of the Electric Insects

A threnody is a song of lamentation for the dead—another reflection on the Vietnam War. This amplified music for two violins, viola, and cello closely matches the mood of Penderecki's *Threnody* (for fifty-two string instruments), written in memory of atomic bomb victims at Hiroshima. It's hard to miss the sound of the electric insects—a menacing tremolo with sharp dynamic contrasts that pervades the entire section. Like a motive, this idea appears in later sections as well. At two points in the movement, "crying" *glissandos* are added to the texture. These events can be diagrammed as follows:

Insect sounds	Crying sounds	Crying sounds	Fades away
0:00	0:33	0:46	1:10

No. 2, Sounds of Bones and Flutes

The title says it all. This section for two violins and cello alternates between percussive sounds (bones) and flutelike melodies. Percussive sonorities include tongue clicks, bouncing the bow *col legno, pizzicato glissando,* and soft chanting;

the "flute" is a violin bowed *col legno*—with the stick of the bow. This movement is filled with number symbolism—thirteen-beat phrases and meter signatures that create groups of seven and thirteen notes—but these relationships are difficult to follow without the score. The alternation between bones and flute occurs as follows:

bones	flute	bones	flute	bones	flute	bones	flute (slows)
0:00	0:07	0:11	0:18	0:23	0:32	0:36	0:44

No. 3, Lost Bells

The longest portion of this duo for violin II and cello creates bell-like sounds through the use of harmonics and multiple stops. This portion is framed by the distinctive sound of a tam-tam—not struck but bowed to bring out its harmonics. The section concludes with melodic fragments much like the flute sounds in the previous piece. These relationships can be diagrammed as follows:

bowed tam-tam	bell sounds (harmonics)	bowed tam-tam	fragmentary melodies
0:00	0:14	0:46	0:59.

No. 4, Devil-Music

In the score, Crumb labels the first violin part *Vox Diaboli*—voice of the devil. This grotesque solo cadenza is accompanied by violin II, viola, and tam-tam (played by the cellist), who offer an obscene, retching, virtually unrecognizable rendition of the *Dies irae* chant. Pitch relationships further complement the diabolic sounds. The primary interval cell (**E, A, D sharp**) is constructed by counting down seven and thirteen half steps from **E**. Not only are these intervals highly dissonant, but the interval between **A** and **D sharp** is a tritone, known to early theorists as the *diabolus in musica,* the devil in music. The main sections can be diagrammed as follows:

Cadenza	"Retching" *Dies irae*	Cadenza	"Retching" *Dies irae*	Siren effect	"Retching" *Dies irae*	Siren effect	Electric insects
0:00	0:30	0:41	0:54	1:05	1:19	1:31	1:46

No. 5, Danse Macabre

Having encountered this devil music, we continue our descent into evil with the devil's dance. This section pits a principal duo (violin II and viola) against a "Duo Alternativo" (violin I and cello) that plays the *Dies irae* melody again. The principal duo establishes a clear, dancelike rhythm and weaves in another musical quotation—of Saint-Saëns' *Danse Macabre*—answered by the other duo's ancient funeral chant. This section employs unusual special effects: the principal duo plays *pizzicato,* with knuckles on wood, and *sul ponticello*; the alternate duo adds maracas, whistling, harmonics, and whispering in Hungarian (counting from one to seven). The alternation occurs in the following pattern:

Duo I Dance rhythm	Duo II *Dies irae*	Duo I Saint-Saëns	Duo II *Dies irae*	Duo I Dance rhythm	Duo II *Dies irae*	Duo I Saint-Saëns	Duo II Chanting (in Hungarian)
0:00	0:07	0:10	0:17	0:20	0:27	0:34	0:44

CRUMB *Ancient Voices of Children*

No. 1, "The Child Is Looking for His Voice"

Crumb asks his singer to perform a vocalise—a sung passage without words. The texture is often monophonic but unlike any monophony heard in the *Listen* recordings. The singer is required to use various vowels, warbles, melismas, and guttural sounds, which give this music a primitive and earthy sound. Crumb further instructs the soprano to sing into an open, amplified piano. At the same time, the pianist is told to depress the sustaining pedal, removing all the dampers from the strings. The undamped strings vibrate sympathetically with the singer's voice; their vibrations are picked up and amplified by a contact microphone. The product of this amplification is a subtle but definite echo that helps to create the ageless, ethereal atmosphere of this opening.

Crumb's atonal pitch structure is based on strict interval patterns. One of the patterns used is the pentatonic scale, an ancient and very simple scale. This further imbues the opening of *Ancient Voices of Children* with a primitive, almost ritualistic atmosphere. See Sound Recordings below for suggested performances.

No. 4, "Each Afternoon in Grenada"

This hauntingly beautiful song is elegantly and simply constructed. The soprano sings, mournfully and with a certain Spanish folk sound, two brief lines about the death of children. The musical setting behind the soprano includes a barely perceptible hum created by marimba and harmonica as well as the appearance of a toy piano playing a Bach(?) song, "Bist du bei mir" ("If You Abide with Me"), that deals with the acceptance of death. The theatrical effect of the slowing toy piano, like a child's toy winding down, is quite touching. The cutting and pasting of outside musical ideas into a composition is called *pastiche*, a common procedure during the 1960s and 1970s. See Sound Recordings below for suggested performances.

STEVE REICH *Tehillim*

Tehillim signaled a new direction for Reich. There is still plenty of repetition, but the slow, hypnotic rate of change is replaced with a more vital sense of motion and direction while the phase shifting gives way to an elaborate canonic web. Reich moved beyond the pure minimalism of *Music for 18 Musicians* in this work and in so doing created one of the masterpieces of minimalism.

Rhythm remains the hallmark of Reich's style in this work. The fourth section reveals the irregular, frequently changing meters that Reich favors; he knows that some irregularity is needed to sustain interest when musical ideas repeat again and again.

With this work, we again see the inversion of orchestral relationships discussed above in relation to *Music for 18 Musicians*. Here the percussion instruments are constantly busy while the strings count rests or play sustained chords in the background.

Other elements of Reich's style include simple triadic harmonies and diatonic scales and melodies (to the delight of listeners who hate atonality!). Reich handles tonality masterfully in the final movement of *Tehillim*; the music pulls the listener inexorably toward the final cadence, very much a true ending—unlike the simple cessation of activity that concludes many minimalist works.

Photocopy a transparency or handouts of the text and translation for this movement from Appendix II. Read the text for your class. The words come from Psalm 150—the last psalm—and they call up images of percussion instruments, flutes, strings, and dancing. As you prepare to play Part 4, take time to familiarize the students with the four phrases of the theme, just as you did with theme and variations works in earlier chapters. Play from rehearsal letter A to rehearsal letter B several times, until students can recognize each phrase. Note the relationships between phrases of the theme and phrases from the psalm.

Display the Additional Listening Chart for this work from Appendix I and point out the overall structure of this theme and variations movement. Play the music and point out each section as it goes by.

GLASS *Metamorphosis*

Although the rhythms of *Metamorphosis* are not as intricate as those in works by other minimalists, or even in other works by Philip Glass himself, rhythm remains a significant feature of Glass's style. As in much of his music, two or three simple ideas alternate throughout the work, distinguished from each other primarily by their rhythmic patterning. In *Metamorphosis 1,* Glass's **a** theme emphasizes quarter and dotted half notes; and his **b** theme, eighth notes.

This apparent simplicity carries over into other elements of Glass's style as well. The phrase structure, based on almost exclusive use of four-bar phrases, seems out of place in the twentieth century. Not since Chopin have we heard such regular phrase relationships. Glass provides variety in only a few places: in the gap that follows every **a** phrase (a gap that seems to widen a bit after each set of **c b** phrase repetitions), in the extra measure added to each **a′** phrase at the end, and in the gradual slowing that occurs toward the end. Further, triadic chords based on a diatonic scale (E minor) characterize the harmonies of this work. In fact, for the first time in the past hundred years of our historical survey, Roman numeral analysis suffices to describe most of the chords Glass uses! The chord progression of the **a** phrase could be analyzed as follows:

i	III$^6_4$	VI^7	It^{+6}
(em)	(GM)	(CM^7)	(C^7)

The entire **b** phrase consists only of a minor tonic chord—thus the eighth-note motion to compensate for the lack of harmonic activity. The **c** phrase uses the same basic progression as the **a** phrase, but the melodic motive at the top of the texture adds a seventh to the i chord and a ninth to the VI chord, and Glass substitutes a major triad built on the leading tone (E-flat major) for the augmented sixth chord. Finally, the **a′** phrases at the end add a French augmented sixth chord in the fifth measure, just after the Italian one. Even with the intrusion of occasional chromatic chords (the E-flat major or the augmented sixth chords), this style of tonal writing has contributed enormously to minimalism's popularity.

Play the basic patterns of this piece—the **a, b, c,** and **a′** phrases—one at a time to introduce them to your students. If you have any keyboard facility at all, you can probably pick out the basic patterns by ear and play them for your students. Call special attention to rhythmic differences between phrases, but make sure students can also hear the harmonic stability of the **b** phrase relative to the motion of the other three. Put the following diagram on the board for students to see. Point out the seemingly simple patterns of repetition and contrast in this work. Then, play the music and point out each section as it goes by.

‖: a b a b	c b c b c b :‖	a′ a′ a′ b b b
0:00	0:38	4:26
1:29	2:08	
2:58	3:36	

(repeated three times)

In the discussion that follows, make sure students understand the context—this is only the first movement of a five-movement work that lasts for half an hour. *Metamorphosis 1* establishes a slow-moving time frame for the rest of the work. The very stability of the first section makes the bigger changes in the middle sections—sections that introduce greater variety, especially in their rhythmic patterns—sound more effective. But even in the middle of the piece, the overall rate of change remains slow. One cannot come to Glass expecting Adams's spine-tingling drama. Glass's soundscapes are more like sonic meditations, possibly a reflection on the Buddhist faith he practices. We come to know his phrases intimately and perhaps even hear them differently by the time the piece is over.

Perhaps it is the simplicity of his patterns, the rhythmic energy of his faster pieces, or his preference for pop-music instrumentation (saxophones and electronic keyboards, among others) that makes Glass's music so popular. Whatever the reason, Glass has reached a wider audience than any of his minimalist colleagues. In fact, his music has attracted a large following among young people with little interest in "classical" music. Not surprisingly, Glass has been commissioned to write a number of film scores. Students may have seen one or more of the recent movies featuring his music—*The Hours, The Source,* or *Kundun* (and some of his music was featured in *The Truman Show*)—but *Mishima* and especially *Koyaanisqatsi* (see Multimedia Resources below) provide outstanding examples from the 1980s. The nature of Glass's musical language and the popularity of his music raise tantalizing questions about the direction of classical music in the twenty-first century.

ADAMS *Harmonielehre*

Adams's *Harmonielehre* offers an excellent example of the synthesis that characterizes much postmodern music. This earlier orchestral work also provides a nice contrast with the *Listen* example, *El Niño*. Even at this early stage, Adams breaks free of the dogmatic elements of minimalism. Minimalist elements are used to create rhythmic momentum and rich textures, but Adams adds long, Romantic melodic lines and never shies away from sudden dramatic contrasts. His unique compositional voice can be clearly heard.

Harmonielehre was written in three movements. In the opening moments of Part I, a throbbing, powerful E minor chord is drummed into the listener's head; this moment is reminiscent of the opening of both Beethoven's Symphony No. 3 and Stravinsky's *Symphony of Psalms*. Part II, "The Anfortas Wound" (the Anfortas from the Grail legends used in Wagner's *Parsifal*), is a commanding, mournful Adagio. Of the three movements, Part III, "Meister Eckhardt and Quackie" (a fantasy inspired by the medieval mystic and the composer's baby daughter), relies most heavily on minimalist textures, though the music never succumbs to pure minimalism—simple repetition of melodic patterns and harmonies at a fixed tempo. See Sound Recordings below for suggested performances.

Multimedia Resources

ˀ Further Listening Charts and Texts

See Appendix I for Additional Listening Charts for these works; see Further Listening Examples above for teaching suggestions.

Reich, *Tehillim,* fourth section

ˀ Sound Recordings

Adams, *The Death of Klinghoffer.* Orchestra of the Opéra de Lyon. Elektra/Nonesuch 9 79281-2 (CD). Premiere recording of Adams's opera about the Arab hijacking of the *Achille Lauro* in 1985. Singers include James Maddalena and Sanford Sylvan; conducted by Kent Nagano. Highlights include extended choruses that reflect centuries of troubled relations between Jews and Arabs. Try this recording if you use Listening Idea 8 or 11 above.

Adams, *Harmonielehre.* City of Birmingham Symphony Orchestra. EMI Classics CDC 5 55051 2 (CD). Recent recording of orchestral works by Adams, conducted by Simon Rattle. Recording also includes *Short Ride in a Fast Machine.* Try this CD if you use Listening Idea 8 or suggestions for *Harmonielehre* from Further Listening Examples above.

Babbitt, *Spectrum: New American Music.* Contemporary Chamber Ensemble. Elektra/Nonesuch 9 79222-2 (CD). CD reissue includes one of Babbitt's more unusual works, *All Set,* for jazz ensemble. Try this recording if you use suggestions for this work from Further Listening Examples above.

Babbitt, *Vision and Prayer.* Bethany Beardslee. Composers Recordings CRI 521 (CD). Sampler of works spanning Babbitt's career. Try this recording of *Vision and Prayer,* for soprano and tape, if you use Listening Idea 3 above.

Berio, *Sinfonia/Eindrücke.* Orchestre National de France and New Swingle Singers. Erato 2292-45228-2 (CD). *Sinfonia* represents one of the greatest virtuoso achievements of the 1960s. The spectacular third movement layers sung and spoken words and dozens of quotations from twentieth-century works over the scherzo movement from Mahler's Symphony No. 2. Try this recording if you use Listening Idea 6 or suggestions from Further Listening Examples above for the second movement.

Boulez, *Structures for Two Pianos.* Alfons and Aloys Kontarsky. Wergo WER 6011-2 (CD). Recording of one of Boulez's first serialist works (Book I, 1952) and its companion piece (Book II, 1962), performed by two brothers who have made a career in avant-garde music. Try this recording if you use Listening Idea 4 above.

Cage, *Daughters of the Lonesome Isle.* Margaret Leng Tan. New Albion Records NA070CD (CD). Exquisite performances of some of Cage's most accessible works for prepared piano, toy piano, string piano, and bowed piano.

Cage, *Indeterminacy.* John Cage and David Tudor. Smithsonian Folkways SF40804/5 (CD). Recent CD reissue of the classic Folkways recording. (Smithsonian is gradually reissuing the Folkways catalog on CD.) Cage tells ninety stories in ninety minutes while David Tudor plays excerpts from *Concert for Piano and Orchestra* and *Fontana Mix.* Try this recording if you use Class Discussion Idea 4 above.

Cage, *Music for Eight*. Salome Kammer. MD+G MDG 613701 (CD). One of only two recordings currently available for *Aria*, Cage's 1958 work for solo voice. Try this CD (if you can't find Cathy Berberian's recording) when you use suggestions for this work from Further Listening Examples above.

Cage, *Music of Changes*. Joseph Kubera. Lovely Music LCD 2053 (CD). Complete recording of Cage's first significant work based on the *I Ching*. Try this recording if you use Listening Idea 4 above.

Cage, *The 25-Year Retrospective Concert of the Music of John Cage*. Earle Brown, John Cage, Michael Colgrass, Merce Cunningham, Paul Price, David Tudor, and others. Wergo WER 6247-2 (CD). CD release documents a significant concert just at the point when Cage was veering into indeterminacy, a step beyond the *I Ching*–based work of the early 1950s. Useful if you want to document Cage's journey from quasi-serial works (*Six Short Inventions*—influenced by his teacher, Schoenberg) to percussion orchestras (*First Construction in Metal*) to prepared piano (*Sonatas and Interludes*) to musique concrète (*Williams Mix*) to chance music (*Concert for Piano and Orchestra*).

Carter, *Double Concerto/Sonata for Cello and Piano*. Contemporary Chamber Players/Joel Krosnick and Paul Jacobs. Elektra/Nonesuch 79183-2 (CD). Recording includes Carter's early *Sonata for Cello and Piano*. Try this recording if you use Lecture-Demonstration Idea 4 above.

Carter, *The Four String Quartets*. Juilliard Quartet. Sony Classical S2K 47229. Perhaps the greatest additions to the quartet literature after Bartók. These 1991 recordings were supervised by the composer. Try this recording of Quartet No. 1 if you use Lecture-Demonstration Idea 4 above.

Carter, *The Music of Elliott Carter, Vol. 4*. Speculum Musicae. Bridge BCD 9111 (CD). Performance on Carter's *Eight Pieces for 4 Timpani* and other works. Try this recording of "Canaries" if you use Lecture-Demonstration Idea 4 above.

Crumb, *Ancient Voices of Children/Music for a Summer Evening (Makrokosmos III)*. Jan DeGaetani and the Contemporary Chamber Ensemble. Elektra/Nonesuch 9 79149-2 (CD). CD release of a classic recording by Jan DeGaetani, one of the great virtuosos of new music in the 1970s; conducted by Arthur Weisberg. Try this recording if you use suggestions from Further Listening Examples above for *Ancient Voices of Children*.

Crumb, *Black Angels*. Kronos Quartet. Elektra/Nonesuch 9 79242-2 (CD). Complete recording of Crumb's eerie work for amplified string quartet by one of the premiere avant-garde ensembles. Highly recommended if you use suggestions for this work from Further Listening Examples above.

Dodge, *Any Resemblance Is Purely Coincidental*. New Albion NA 043 (CD). Collection of works by Charles Dodge employing computer sound synthesis. Tongue-in-cheek title track plays with resynthesis of Caruso's voice; other works include *Speech Songs*, *Viola Elegy*, and *The Waves*. Try this recording if you use Listening Idea 3 above.

Early Modulations: Vintage Volts. Caipirinha Records CAI 72027 (CD). Collection of works by significant pioneers in *musique concrète* sound synthesis, including Pierre Schaeffer, Luening and Ussachevsky, Cage, Morton Subotnick, and Max Mathews. Try this recording if you use Listening Idea 3 above.

Feldman, *First Recordings: 1950s*. Turfan Ensemble and Philipp Vandré. Mode 66 (CD). New recordings of early chance works by a colleague of John

Cage, including *Intersection, Intermissions 1–6,* and *Extensions 1, 3,* and *4.* Try this recording if you use this manual's Lecture Suggestions on "Chance Music" above (under "Modernism in Music: The Second Phase").

Glass, *Koyaanisqatsi* (see Video Recordings below).

Glass, *Solo Piano.* Philip Glass. CBS 45576 (CD). Complete performance by the composer of *Metamorphosis* as well as *Mad Rush* and *Wichita Sutra Vortex.* Try this recording if you use Listening Idea 8 above or if you use suggestions for *Metamorphosis* in Further Listening Examples above.

Glass and Shankar. *Passages.* Private Music 2074-2-P (CD). Fascinating collaboration between Philip Glass and Hindustani musician Ravi Shankar. Collection includes Glass works based on Shankar's themes, Shankar works on Glass's themes, and original works by both. Use this recording to explore fascinating connections between minimalism and the Indian music we studied in Chapter 13.

Handel, *Messiah.* Les Arts Florissants. Harmonia Mundi HMC 901498.99 (CD). This period performance combines dancelike energy with an appropriate weight and grandeur. Outstanding soloists, orchestra, and chorus; directed by William Christie. Recommended if you use Listening Idea 7 above.

Ives, *Three Quarter-Tone Pieces for Two Pianos.* G. Bouwhuis and C. van Zeeland. Channel Classic CCS 4592 (CD). Try this recording of Ives's pieces if you use Listening Idea 1 above.

Ligeti, *The Ligeti Edition,* Vol. 2. London Sinfonietta Voices. Sony Classical SK 62305 (CD). Album of choral music by Ligeti; conducted by Terry Edwards. The *Listen* set features this recording of *Lux aeterna.*

Mahler, *Symphony No. 2.* San Francisco Symphony Orchestra and Chorus. London 443 350-2 (CD). Committed, expressive orchestral playing in this fine performance of Mahler's *Resurrection* Symphony; conducted by Herbert Blomstedt. Try this recording if you use Listening Idea 6 above.

New World Records (701 Seventh Ave., New York, N.Y. 10036). This record label was created at the time of the U.S. bicentennial to record hitherto unavailable works by American composers and performing musicians. Recordings document many important types of American music, past and present. Most relevant to this chapter are the many recordings of recent American music. New World recordings are a treasure trove of Americana—often hard to find, but worth the effort.

OHM: The Early Gurus of Electronic Music, 1948–1980. Ellipsis Arts 3670 (CD). Collection of works by significant pioneers in *musique concrète* as well as analog, digital, and computer sound synthesis, including Pierre Schaeffer, Cage, Babbitt, Stockhausen, Morton Subotnick, Charles Dodge, Jean-Claude Risset, and others. Try this recording if you use Listening Idea 3 above.

Penderecki, *Anaklasis etc.* Polish Radio National Symphony Orchestra and London Symphony Orchestra. EMI Classics CDM 5 65077 2 (CD). Collection of significant Penderecki orchestral works from 1959 to 1974, including the famous *Threnody for the Victims of Hiroshima;* conducted by the composer. Penderecki's work shares many of the concerns found in Ligeti's *Lux aeterna.* Try this recording of *Threnody* if you use Listening Idea 1 above or if you want to compare threnodies by Penderecki and Crumb (*Black Angels,* No. 1— see Further Listening Examples above).

Pérotin. *The Hilliard Ensemble*. ECM Records New Series 837751 (CD). The preeminent early music ensemble turns in wonderful performances of several of Pérotin's most famous organa. Try this recording if you use Listening Idea 9 above.

Reich, *The Cave*. Steve Reich Ensemble. Elektra/Nonesuch 9 79327-2 (CD). Landmark multimedia work (1993) created in collaboration with video artist Beryl Korot; conducted by Paul Hillier. Reich uses recorded voice much as he did in *Different Trains,* but here he asks Jews, Arabs, and Christians in the Middle East and the United States to talk about Abraham/Ibrahim and his family. The resulting work offers fascinating insights into the historical misunderstandings between these peoples without taking any sides. Try this recording if you use Listening Idea 8 or 11 above.

Reich, *Different Trains*. Kronos Quartet. Elektra/Nonesuch 9 79176-2 (CD). This Reich work (1988) marked his first use of recorded voice since *It's Gonna Rain* and *Come Out. Different Trains* mixes string quartet sounds with spoken reminiscences of 1940s train trips—some taken by free Americans in the United States, others taken by Jewish prisoners in Nazi-controlled Europe. Reich brings out the musical quality of the spoken word, and the recorded voices add immediacy to this poignant Holocaust remembrance. Try this recording if you use Listening Idea 8 above.

Reich, *Early Works*. Steve Reich and other performers. Elektra/Nonesuch 9 79169-2 (CD). This collection of Reich's early works includes *It's Gonna Rain* (1965), *Come Out* (1966), *Piano Phase* (1967), and *Clapping Music* (1972). Invaluable if you want students to understand the evolution of minimalism. These works demonstrate the phase shifting that influenced the canonic writing in *Tehillim. Come Out* was mentioned in Lecture Suggestions for *Music for 18 Musicians* above.

Reich, *Music for 18 Musicians*. Steve Reich Ensemble. Elektra/Nonesuch 9 79448-2 (CD). Colorful, engaging work for large ensemble from the 1970s, not as directional as *Tehillim*. Try this recording if you use Listening Idea 9 or if you want a complete recording.

Reich, *Tehillim/Three Movements*. Schönberg Ensemble and London Symphony Orchestra. Elektra/Nonesuch 9 79295-2 (CD). Recent recordings of significant Reich works from the 1980s; conducted by Reinbert de Leeuw and Michael Tilson Thomas. Try this recording if you use Listening Idea 8 above.

Riley, *In C for Saxophone and Instrumental Ensemble*. Riley and SUNY at Buffalo Center for the Creative and Performing Arts. CBS MK 07178 (CD). CD reissue of the first recording of *In C*. Use this recording if you want students to hear the work the textbook describes in the section of this chapter titled "On the Boundaries of Time" (see Lecture Suggestions above under "Modernism in Music: The Second Phase").

Riley, *A Rainbow in Curved Air*. Terry Riley. CBS MK 07315 (CD). CD reissue of hypnotic, appealing minimalist works from the late 1960s. Try this recording if you use Listening Idea 8 above.

Rudel, *Distant Love: Songs of Jaufré Rudel and Martin Codax*. Paul Hillier and Andrew Lawrence-King. Harmonia Mundi France 907203 (CD). Recordings of all surviving songs by medieval troubadour Jaufré Rudel by early music specialist Paul Hillier. Includes the song Saariaho used as a source for *Lonh* and the inspiration for *L'Amour de loin*, "Lanquan li jorn son lonc en may." Try this recording if you use Listening Idea 10 above.

Saariaho, *From the Grammar of Dreams*. Anu and Piia Komsi, Avanti!, and others. Ondine ODE 958-2 (CD). Recent CD contains various chamber works including the song cycle in the *Listen* set, *From the Grammar of Dreams*. Try this recording to sample further examples of Saariaho's music or if you want a complete recording of the song cycle.

Saariaho, *Private Gardens*. Dawn Upshaw and others. Montaigne Naïve MO 782087 (CD). Recent recording of four works for soloist with electronics offers excellent introduction to the Finnish composer's work in the electronic sphere. CD includes *Lonh* (for soprano and electronics) and *Six Japanese Gardens* (for percussion and electronics). Try this recording if you use Listening Idea 3 or 10 above.

Shankar, Lakshmi, *Evening Concert*. Ravi Shankhar Music Circle RSMC-D-102 (CD). Performances of a *khyal, thumri,* and two *bhajans* by this prominent Indian singer. Kaija Saariaho lists Lakshmi Shankar as an influence on her own music. Try this recording to explore connections between the two and to make connections with the Ravi Shankar materials from Chapter 13.

Stockhausen, *Elektronische Musik 1952–1960*. Stockhausen-Verlag 3 (CD). Recordings of the composer's electronic works of the 1950s, including *Etude, Elektronische Studie I* and *II, Gesang der Jünglinge,* and *Kontakte*. Like most of Stockhausen's music, this CD is available only via mail order: Stockhausen-Verlag, Kettenberg 15, 51515 Kürten, Germany. Try this recording if you use Listening Idea 3 above.

Stockhausen, *"In the Sky I Am Walking..." (American Indian Songs)*. Voxnova. Mode 68 (CD). Recent recording of Stockhausen's vocal work based on song texts from Margot Astrov's *American Indian Prose and Poetry: An Anthology* (New York: Capricorn Books, 1946), including texts of the Pawnee, Chippewa, Nootka, Teton Sioux, Ayacucho (Peruvian), and Aztec peoples. No authentic tunes are borrowed; the music is pure Stockhausen, with many extended vocal techniques (including multiphonics). European avant-garde meets native America!

Subotnick, *All My Hummingbirds Have Alibis*. California EAR Unit. New World Records NW 80514-2 (CD). Fascinating 1991 multimedia composition based on the collage novels of Max Ernst. Features elaborate interactions between computer and MIDI instruments. Recording also includes *And the Butterflies Began to Sing*. The CD-ROM version (see Software below) is preferred, but if it's unavailable, use this recording when you try Listening Idea 3 above.

Subotnick, *Silver Apples/The Wild Bull*. Wergo WER 2035-2 (CD). CD reissues of two classic works from the age of the voltage-controlled synthesizer. *Silver Apples of the Moon,* the first electronic work commissioned for release on an LP, helped establish the viability of the synthesizers developed by Buchla and Moog. These relatively small, affordable synthesizers went on to revolutionize electronic music making. Try this recording if you use Listening Idea 3 above.

Varèse, *The Complete Works*. Royal Concertgebouw Orchestra. London 289 460 208-2 (CD). This recent release contains nearly all of Varèse's works in editions supervised by the Chinese composer and Varèse protégé Chou Wen-Chung; conducted by Riccardo Chailly. Includes his electronic works *Poème électronique* and *Déserts*. Try this recording if you use Listening Idea 3 above.

Webern, *Boulez Conducts Webern III*. Berlin Philharmonic Orchestra. Deutsche Grammophon 447 765-2 (CD). Exquisite new performances give an easy expressiveness to Webern's often austere style; conducted by Pierre Boulez. Includes *Five Pieces for Orchestra* (1913), the two cantatas, *Variations for Orchestra*, and *Symphony*, Op. 21. Also available in the new Deutsche Grammophon *Complete Webern* box set. Try this recording if you want your students to hear more of *Five Pieces for Orchestra*.

♩ Video Recordings

Adams, *El Niño*. Arthaus Musik (DVD, color, 119 minutes). John Adams's modern-day Christmas oratorio, produced in collaboration with Peter Sellars. Featured performers include Dawn Upshaw, Lorraine Hunt Lieberson, and Willard White; conducted by Kent Nagano. An excellent example of Adams's richly musical brand of minimalism. Includes an excellent twenty-eight-minute documentary on the making of *El Niño*. Highly recommended if you want a complete recording or if you use Listening Idea 7 above.

Adams, *Hail Bop! A Portrait of John Adams*. Kultur (DVD, color, 98 minutes). Tony Palmer's documentary provides an excellent overview of Adams's life and music up to 1998 (just shy of *El Niño*). His first two operas, *Nixon in China* and *The Death of Klinghoffer*, receive special emphasis. The film relies heavily on video clips from performances and interviews—not a problem with someone as articulate and thoughtful as Adams. Highly recommended as a supplement to your presentation of Adams or if you use Listening Idea 8 above.

Adams, *John Adams: Minimalism and Beyond*. www.films.com (DVD or VHS, color, 52 minutes). A study of composer John Adams and his *Harmonium* for chorus and orchestra on poems by Donne and Dickinson. The program weaves Adams's own commentary with rehearsal footage featuring conductor Simon Rattle and the City of Birmingham Symphony Orchestra. A useful supplement to the textbook's material on Adams. Try this video if you use Listening Idea 8 above.

Adams, *John Adams: A Portrait and a Concert of American Music*. Arthaus Musik (DVD, color, 134 minutes). The portrait provides a fascinating look at Adams and his concerns using interviews and other video footage. The concert features the Ensemble InterContemporain performing Reich's *Eight Lines*, Nancarrow's *Studies for Player Piano Nos. 1 and 7*, and Adams's *Gnarly Buttons* and *Chamber Symphony*; conducted by Jonathan Nott. Highly recommended. Try this video to supplement your Adams presentation or if you use Listening Idea 8 above.

Berio, *Luciano Berio*. www.films.com (DVD or VHS, color, 60 minutes). A living biography of this important Italian composer woven around the composition of his *Cronaca del Luogo*. Try this video if you use suggestions for *Sinfonia* in Further Listening Examples above.

Boulez, *Notations*. Image Entertainment (DVD, color, 89 minutes). Daniel Barenboim and the Chicago Symphony perform this modernist work along with de Falla's *Three-Cornered Hat* and Debussy's *La mer*. Try this recording if you use Listening Idea 4 above.

Cage/Cunningham. Kultur Video (VHS, color). Documentary explores the longtime relationship between composer John Cage and choreographer Merce Cunningham. A useful supplement to your coverage of Cage.

[Cage] *Cursive II.* BBC Opus Arte (DVD, color, 147 minutes). Lin Hwai-min choreographed this striking example of modern dance inspired by the esthetics of Chinese calligraphy; performed by the Cloud Gate Dance Theatre of Taiwan. He uses the music of John Cage, a composer who was also fascinated by words and script, as we see clearly in his many word pieces from the 1970s on. Excerpts were taken from Cage's *Sixty-eight, Seventy-four* for orchestra, *Ryoanji,* and *Five* series. Lin Hwai-min's combination of music, sets, motion, and gesture is quite beautiful. DVD extras include two documentaries: one introduces *Cursive II* and the other focuses on the dance company, its history, and its production of *Cursive II.* Highly recommended as a supplement to your presentation on Cage.

Cage, *From Zero.* Mode (DVD, color, 50 minutes). These four films on Cage tend to be more arty than informational, and chance procedures were introduced into the filmmaking process. Try this for a different approach to Cage and his esthetic.

Cage, *John Cage: I Have Nothing to Say and I Am Saying It.* Kultur Video (VHS, color, 56 minutes). Excerpts from Cage's music are woven between interviews with Cage and his colleagues, including Yoko Ono, Laurie Anderson, Merce Cunningham, and Robert Rauschenberg. A fascinating introduction to Cage, his ideas, and his music.

Crumb, *Kronos on Stage:* Black Angels *and* Ghost Opera. Image Entertainment (DVD, color, 56 minutes). Excellent concert performances of Crumb's *Black Angels* and Tan Dun's *Ghost Opera* by one of today's finest avant-garde string quartets. It makes such a difference when students can actually see the bowed tam-tams and goblets along with all the other special effects. Highly recommended! You *must* use this video if you use suggestions in Further Listening Examples for *Black Angels.*

Culture Fix Series. www.films.com (DVD or VHS, color, 29 minutes each). Fourteen-part series looks at various topics in the history of art and culture, with particular emphasis on the twentieth century. Particularly useful with Chapter 22 are *Abstract Art, Surrealism, Postmodernism, Installation Art,* and *Propaganda.*

Cunningham, *Merce Cunningham: A Lifetime of Dance.* WinStar Video (DVD, color/black and white, 90 minutes). Excellent documentary chronicles the career of this important modernist dancer/choreographer. John Cage figures prominently due to his long association with Cunningham's dance troupe, but this video really lets you see what made Cunningham's work so influential. Recommended as a fascinating supplement to your study of Cage, especially if you have dancers in your class.

Glass, *Koyaanisqatsi—Life Out of Balance.* MGM (DVD, color, 87 minutes). Fascinating collaboration between director Godfrey Reggio and composer Philip Glass. Stunning fast- and slow-motion sequences of landscapes and cityscapes blend cleverly with Glass's minimalist music. The title is a Hopi word meaning "Life out of balance," and the movie gives poignancy to Hopi prophecies. This video was released in 2002 after being out of print for many years. Buy it now before it disappears again! Try this video if you use Listening Idea 8 above.

Glass, *Looking Glass.* Ideale Audience (DVD, color, 103 minutes). This 2004 documentary provides a portrait of one of the leading minimalist composers. DVD extras include several interviews and a performance of Study No. 2 by the composer himself. Try this video if you use Listening Idea 8 or suggestions for Glass's *Metamorphosis* in Further Listening Examples above.

Glass, *Satyagraha*. Image Entertainment (DVD, color, 166 minutes). Along with *Einstein on the Beach* and *Akhnaten,* one of the works in Philip Glass's opera trilogy of the late 1970s and early 1980s. This opera portrays events in the life of Mahatma Gandhi intercut with scenes from the Bhagavad-Gita and the lives of Leo Tolstoy, Rabindranath Tagore, and Martin Luther King Jr. This unabashedly modernist version avoids the visual beauty of the original 1980s production, but this video offers a fine musical performance nonetheless; conducted by Dennis Russell Davies. Try this video if you use Listening Idea 8 above.

The History of Music, Part 2: *Romanticism through Modern.* www.midiworkshop .com (DVD, color, 89 minutes). The section on the postwar years covers serial, aleatoric, electronic, and minimalist techniques in the music of Varèse, Cage, Reich, and Glass.

Music Today. Leaving Home Series. Arthaus Musik (DVD, color, 52 minutes). Simon Rattle narrates this look at avant-garde composers of the late twentieth century, especially Berio, Henze, Gubaidulina, Kurtág, Turnage, Knussen, and Birtwistle.

Musical Outsiders: An American Legacy: Harry Partch, Lou Harrison, and Terry Riley. www.insight-media.com (DVD, color, 58 minutes). Intriguing profiles of three American originals, including the composer of *In C,* discussed on textbook page 375.

Post-War Music: After the Wake. Leaving Home Series. Arthaus Musik (DVD, color, 52 minutes). Simon Rattle narrates this look at the music after World War II, focusing on Stravinsky's turn to serialism.

Saariaho, *L'Amour de loin.* Deutsche Grammophon (DVD, color, 139 minutes). Peter Sellars has created a stylized but effective staging of Saariaho's impressive first opera, based on a song by twelfth-century troubadour Jaufré Rudel. The composer takes a profoundly lyrical approach in setting Amin Maalouf's thought-provoking libretto. Gerald Finley and Dawn Upshaw turn in powerful performances as the troubadour and his distant love; conducted by Esa-Pekka Salonen. Highly recommended if you use Listening Idea 10 above.

Sound of Unsound. The Music of Man Series (VHS, color, 60 minutes). Yehudi Menuhin explores the impact of LP recordings, radio, and television on Western music. The video moves from early jazz into folk, rock, and electronic music.

Subotnick, *Electronic Works I: Touch; A Sky of Cloudless Sulphur; Gestures.* Mode (DVD, color, 73 minutes). Fascinating package includes DVD audio performances of three recent electronic works, video footage of interviews with Subotnick, and a DVD-ROM that lets you play with an interactive version of *Gestures* (and a CD-ROM version of same just in case your computer doesn't support DVD-ROM). Recommended. Try this video if you use Listening Idea 3 above.

Surrealism in Art and Music. www.insight-media.com (DVD, color, 38 minutes). This still-image video provides a concise, visually appealing introduction to important philosophic, artistic, and musical trends in the twentieth century. Contains the artwork of Ernst, Magritte, and Dalí; music by Satie, Bartók, and Cage. Try this video if you use Lecture-Demonstration Idea 1 above.

Today and Tomorrow. Music in Time Series. www.films.com (DVD or VHS, color, 60 minutes). James Galway narrates this look at music of our own time. Musical excerpts by composers from this chapter include Ligeti's *Melodien,* Varèse's *Ionisation,* and Cage's "Improvisations" from *Songbooks.* Other composers include Lennon and McCartney, Tippett, Messiaen, Berio, Stockhausen, Boulez, Nono, and Henze.

2001: A Space Odyssey. Warner Home Video (DVD, color, 139 minutes). This edition includes an interview with author Arthur C. Clarke and theatrical trailers. Of course, the soundtrack contains music by Johann Strauss, Richard Strauss, and György Ligeti, including the *Listen* example *Lux aeterna.*

❦ Software

Art and Music: Surrealism. Zane Publishing (CD-ROM—Windows or Macintosh). CD-ROM version of the video above. This inexpensive volume draws parallels between paintings of Dalí, Ernst, and Miró and the music of Ravel, Stravinsky, Bartók, Satie, Milhaud, and Cage. Available from www.cdaccess.com.

The History of Music. www.mccormicksnet.com (CD-ROM—Windows or Macintosh). CD-ROM version of the video above. The section on the postwar years covers serial, aleatoric, electronic, and minimalist techniques in the music of Varèse, Cage, Reich, and Glass.

Saariaho, *Prisma.* Montaigne Naïve (CD-ROM—Macintosh and Windows). Packaged with the *Private Gardens* CD, this CD-ROM offers an excellent introduction to this Finnish composer's life, music, and career. Various modules offer performances of Saariaho's music, an interactive biography, a musicological analysis, information about her compositional methods and electronic techniques, and so on. This package was produced with Saariaho's cooperation and participation, so it provides a genuine encounter with this fascinating composer. Highly recommended supplement to your study of Saariaho. Try this recording if you use Listening Idea 3 or 10 above.

Subotnick, *All My Hummingbirds Have Alibis.* Voyager (CD-ROM—Macintosh). Once on the cutting edge, this multimedia package now works only in System 9. The CD-ROM provides performances of several Subotnick works augmented by Max Ernst's visual images, recorded by the EAR Unit. Best of all are the extras, including interviews with the composer and his associates, as well as a full description of Subotnick's MIDI equipment and Interactor software—software that follows the live performers and triggers MIDI sound events at the right moments. Highly recommended for Listening Idea 3 above.

Subotnick, *Electronic Works I: Touch; A Sky of Cloudless Sulphur; Gestures.* Mode (DVD-ROM/CD-ROM—Macintosh or Windows). Fascinating package includes DVD audio performances of three recent electronic works, video footage of interviews with Subotnick, and a DVD-ROM that lets you play with an interactive version of *Gestures* (and a CD-ROM version of same just in case your computer doesn't support DVD-ROM). Recommended. Try this interactive package if you use Listening Idea 3 above.

CHAPTER 23

Music in America: Jazz and Beyond

Chapter Outline

Boldface indicates works in the recording set.

Important Terms

cultivated music	polyrhythm	doo-wop
vernacular music	bebop	girl groups
Bay Psalm Book	jazz-rock	Motown
fuguing tunes	fusion	soul
Boston School	Jazz Age	funk
minstrel show	blues scale	British invasion
call and response	Broadway	folk rock
spiritual	operetta	singer-songwriter
jazz	musical comedy	acid rock
improvisation	musical	jam band
breaks	popular song	heavy metal
syncopation	cha-cha	art rock
rhythm section	"voice-over"	MTV
beat syncopation	thematic transformation	punk rock
ragtime	fugue	indie rock
blues	cool jazz	grunge rock
twelve-bar blues	"standards"	hip-hop
gospel music	rock'n'roll	rap
New Orleans jazz	rock	gangsta rap
collective improvisation	early rock'n'roll	post-rock
"jamming"	hillbilly music	globalism
big bands	country music	homogenization
swing	rhythm and blues	reggae
sidemen	electric guitar	localized music making
conga	rockabilly	*isicathamiya*
drumming	"covers"	choral declamation

Important People

William Billings	Ornette Coleman	Eric Clapton
Anthony Philip Heinrich	Wynton Marsalis	The Beach Boys
Louis Moreau Gottschalk	George Gershwin	Bob Dylan
John Knowles Paine	Paul Whiteman	Woody Guthrie
Arthur Foote	Johann Strauss Jr.	Pete Seeger
Henry Chadwick	Arthur Sullivan (Gilbert & Sullivan)	Paul Simon
Edward MacDowell	Victor Herbert	Simon and Garfunkel
Amy Beach	Jerome Kern	Bruce Springsteen
Stephen Foster	Richard Rodgers	Elvis Costello
John Philip Sousa	Oscar Hammerstein	Joan Baez
Antonin Dvořák	Leonard Bernstein	Joni Mitchell
Scott Joplin	Jerome Robbins	Tori Amos
W. C. Handy	Stephen Sondheim	k. d. lang
Sippie Wallace	Andrew Lloyd Webber	Missy Elliott
Mamie Smith	Bing Crosby	The Grateful Dead
Ma Rainey	Frank Sinatra	Jimi Hendrix
Bessie Smith	Elvis Presley	Carlos Santana
Louis Armstrong	Jerry Lee Lewis	The Who
Joe "King" Oliver	Buddy Holly	Cream
Fletcher Henderson	Fats Domino	Led Zeppelin
Lil Hardin	Little Richard	Pink Floyd
Count Basie	Chuck Berry	Patti Smith
Jimmie Lunceford	Bill Haley	The Ramones
Chick Webb	Ray Charles	The Sex Pistols
Duke Ellington	The Drifters	Nirvana
Juan Tizol	The Shirelles	Sugarhill Gang
Ben Webster	Berry Gordy Jr.	Grandmaster Flash
Benny Goodman	The Supremes	Public Enemy
Glenn Miller	The Temptations	Queen Latifah
Artie Shaw	Aretha Franklin	Eminem
Charlie Parker	James Brown	Slint
Dizzy Gillespie	Otis Redding	Godspeed You Black Emperor!
Miles Davis	Sly and the Family Stone	Radiohead
Thelonious Monk	George Clinton and Funkadelic	Ladysmith Black Mambazo
Sun Ra	The Beatles	Orpheus McAdoo
John Coltrane	The Rolling Stones	Solomon Linda and the Evening Birds

Teaching Objectives

❧ Overall Objectives

This chapter will help students acquire familiarity with:

1. Important musical developments, composers, and performers in cultivated and vernacular traditions before 1900.

2. The roots and stylistic development of jazz, especially ragtime, blues, New Orleans jazz, swing, bebop, and jazz-rock fusion.

3. The influence of jazz and blues in the concert hall.

4. The evolution of the American musical from operetta to the 1990s.

5. The styles of popular music since the 1950s.

6. The lives and music of Scott Joplin, Sippie Wallace, Louis Armstrong, Duke Ellington, Charlie Parker, Miles Davis, George Gershwin, and Leonard Bernstein.

7. West African drumming and South African choral music and their impact on American music.

❧ Listening Objectives

After completing this chapter, students should be able to:

1. Hear and identify important style features of jazz, especially improvisation, jazz instruments and instrumental roles, syncopation and swing rhythms, and jazz ensembles (combos and big bands).

2. Hear and identify important styles of jazz, especially ragtime, blues, New Orleans jazz, swing, bebop, and jazz-rock fusion.

3. Follow the structure of important jazz works, especially twelve-bar blues and thirty-two-bar song forms.

4. Hear the influence of jazz and blues in music written for the concert hall.

5. Follow scenes and musical relationships in an American musical.

6. Hear significant features of Yoruba drumming and *isicathamiya* choral singing.

Lecture Suggestions

American music deserves a special place in music appreciation courses in the United States. Since this music is a product of American culture . . . hmm, American culture . . . what does that mean? By now, even your students would stop to question such a statement if you have faithfully taken them through the Global Perspectives materials. American culture was once thought of as a "melting pot." Through a process of assimilation, immigrants and their traditions were somehow blended (or blanded) into a stew from which they emerged as Americans, indistinguishable from other Americans. Of course the stew was tastier as a result, but this process no longer describes the experience of immigrant or minority groups in this country. And it no longer describes American music, either.

American music was never a stylistically unified, readily identifiable phenomenon. The fact is, we all came from someplace else, and we all brought our own musics with us. Some of those musics have changed little over the years, some have fallen by the wayside, and some have merged with or borrowed from others to create fresh, new styles and genres. This latter case describes the syncretism we have observed in Peru and around the globe—a normal occurrence wherever cultures collide. The result? There is no such thing as a purely American music. And Americans revel in musical diversity as never before. Flip through the radio stations on your FM dial and you will hear an incredible variety of musical styles—especially compared with what was available thirty years ago. Walk into any large CD store and you find music from thousands of years ago and thousands of miles away.

This chapter considers our diverse musical history, and the Global Perspectives materials look at two traditions that changed our history forever. Unfortunately, the diversity of American styles identified in this chapter is such that you cannot do full justice to each one. Some topics must be glossed over or omitted; for that matter, musical examples for many styles named by the authors are mentioned by name only, if at all. Nonetheless, this material is too important to skip over altogether. I strongly recommend devoting at least the last three class hours to this chapter. If that sounds excessive, consider the following. Most of your students have lived through at least the past twenty years of American music history; they know some parts of that history at least as well as you do. American students can identify with those parts whether their families came to the New World last year or three centuries ago. You can further increase your students' sense of involvement if you let the class choose one or two favorite styles from Chapter 23 for special emphasis. You must pick and choose anyway, and this will give them something to look forward to at the end of a long, hard term.

❦ Early American Music: An Overview

The textbook provides no listening examples for the first section of Chapter 23. If you have time, consider playing examples of early American music for your class; listening examples can be found in Multimedia Resources below, and ideas for introducing this literature can be found in Additional Teaching Suggestions below. If you don't have time, textbook pages 391–95 and the lecture suggestions below provide the minimum background needed before you cover the twentieth-century examples.

In an earlier edition of *Listen,* Joseph Kerman asked, "Why did the United States produce no world-famous composers in the nineteenth century, when we produced such great writers as Herman Melville, Emily Dickinson, and Mark Twain, and such painters as Thomas Eakins, Mary Cassatt, and John Singer Sargent?" Ask the class the same question. The answers go directly to the heart of American culture. In the discussion that follows, draw out these points.

1. *The American mosaic*—Successive waves of foreign immigration left the United States with an incredible array of ethnic groups. If the soul of American society is its rich ethnic and cultural diversity, then no single ethnic group could create a genuine American art music by itself. Only a music that somehow combined aspects of these diverse cultures—or was influenced by the energy of the young, diverse American culture—could be called uniquely "American."

2. *Economics*—First and foremost, we are a mercantile society, as the World Wide Web is proving all over again. The notion that the streets were "paved with gold" was certainly an exaggeration, but immigrants even now are attracted by

the economic opportunities offered in the United States. The creation and pursuit of art or art music as a profession was not particularly compatible with the tenets of American economic opportunism. As a result, art music lagged behind the other arts. After all, one can invest in a painting and possess it, but one cannot "own" a good tune in the same way. In a developing country where "manhood" and success were measured by financial advancement and security, professional musicians ranked rather low on the social scale.

3. *Cultural heritage*—Much of the music we have studied was the product of centuries of historical continuity. Compared with other cultures, America's musical heritage was still in its infancy in the 1800s. Original and lasting art is often the product of a mature society, one that can provide financial support, stability, educational opportunities, and a set of shared esthetic principles. Such was not the case in the 1800s. Music education was just getting under way, and the first professor of music in American higher education was not appointed until 1875—John Knowles Paine at Harvard University. Further, an indigenous American art music could not develop until the incredible cultural diversity stabilized and congealed into a society that was somehow uniquely, though never purely, "American."

The Romantic trend of nationalism first became apparent in American music during the 1880s and 1890s. Many European and American-born composers felt that Native American and African American musics were distinctively American and should, therefore, be incorporated into art music. During a two-year stay in the United States, the great Czech composer Antonin Dvořák was deeply impressed by these musics, and he encouraged American composers to draw inspiration from these sources instead of copying European music. Slowly, American composers began to throw off German domination.

See Additional Teaching Suggestions below for ideas if you would like to cover popular music and African American music before 1900.

⅋ Jazz: The First Fifty Years

Around the turn of the century, classically trained composers of "art music" wrestled with the problem of how to write "American" music. While they struggled to answer the challenge—"Who will write the great American symphony?"—gifted black musicians were already at work developing a great, uniquely American art form: jazz. These African Americans blended European and African elements to create an identifiably American music. Jazz drew elements from many sources: field hollers, work songs, spirituals and other religious music, marching-band tunes, blues, and ragtime.

What makes jazz unique?

Performance orientation—In the listening examples in Chapters 1–22 we focused on composers and their compositions; with jazz we must look instead at performers and their performances.

Improvisation—One important aspect of this performer's art is improvisation. Jazz musicians cultivate the ability to compose while they play, to make it up as they go along. Few jazz works are completely improvised, but almost all jazz is at least partly extemporized. So that the collaboration of several improvising musicians does not collapse in confusion, the performers establish some ground rules before they play. Most often, the players agree to base their improvisation on a preexisting melody. Performers are free to play any melodic or harmonic patterns that fit with this tune's supporting harmonies. Further, specific instruments are often assigned specific roles within a piece.

Structure—The tune is usually played through several times—each chorus (that is, stanza) is different due to the improvisation. As a result, the structure of most jazz pieces closely resembles Classical theme-and-variations form.

Rhythm—Almost all jazz includes syncopation, the placement of accents on weak beats or between beats. In the swing era and beyond, jazz rhythms became even more sophisticated. Beat syncopation—anticipating strong beats by a fraction of a beat—became standard practice, and musicians began to swing" their rhythms by slightly lengthening the eighth note at the beginning of a beat and shortening the one at the end. The effect is almost like a fast compound meter, as the example shows.

Rhythm section—The heartbeat of any jazz ensemble, large or small, is the rhythm section. Each instrument serves a slightly different function. Early jazz styles used the drummer primarily as a time keeper, but later jazz styles have used the drums in a coloristic role as well. The bass (upright at first, later electric) provides the foundation for the texture; it plays a bass line that supports the chords and fits with the melody. The piano fills out the texture, improvising chord voicings that fit with the tune's supporting harmonies. Sometimes a guitar is used as well.

As you present each listening example in this section and in the "Later Jazz" section:

1. Help students hear the structure behind the improvisation by guiding them through the listening charts provided below for each piece. All of your students can count measures, and many of them, with assistance, can even hear the chord changes in a blues progression.

2. Identify the style of each work and point out characteristic features of each style.

Additional Teaching Suggestions below provide further ideas for covering the roots of jazz.

The following chart summarizes style features for the principal styles of jazz.

Ragtime

Dates—late 1890s–1918; peak popularity 1910–1915

Instruments—Solo piano

Syncopation—Left hand plays even "oom-pah" accompaniment; syncopation in the right-hand melody

Form—Several contrasting sixteen-bar sections strung together; composed, not improvised

Frequent ragtime structure:

Sections	A	A	B	B	A	C	C	D	D
Tonal Centers	I	—	—	—	—	IV	—	I	—
Bars	1		33		65	81		113	

LISTENING EXAMPLE—Scott Joplin, "Maple Leaf Rag" (*Listen* DVD)

The Blues

Dates—Began a decade or two before 1900

Vocal music—Evolved from slow chants or laments, later taken up by instruments

Blue notes—Unequal-tempered pitches from African scales

Pitch bending—In both the voice and the instruments

Improvisatory nature

Twelve-bar structure:	*Phrase 1*	*Phrase 2*	*Phrase 3*
Text	line **a**	line **a** repeated	line **b**
Harmony	I — — —	IV — I —	V — I —
	(tonic)		
Bars	1 2 3 4	5 6 7 8	9 10 11 12

LISTENING EXAMPLE—Sippie Wallace, "If You Ever Been Down" Blues

New Orleans Jazz

Dates—Before World War I; many New Orleans musicians in Chicago by the 1920s

Instruments—Small ensemble: trumpet, clarinet, trombone, and rhythm section (banjo, tuba, and drums at first; later string bass, drums, and piano)

Polyphony—Everyone can improvise simultaneously because instrumental roles are well defined—trumpet plays melody; clarinet, a high descant; trombone, the bass; and rhythm instruments, the chords and the beat

Rhythm—Four beats to the bar, even and heavy, with mild syncopation

Structure—Most often based on ragtime or blues structures

LISTENING EXAMPLE—Sippie Wallace, "If You Ever Been Down" Blues

Swing

Dates—c. 1930–1945

"Big band" jazz—Developed along with dance bands

Popularity—In the swing era, jazz *was* popular music

Swing—Rhythmic quality with a light grace and forward momentum; resulting syncopation much more sophisticated

Instruments—three to four trumpets, four to five saxophones (sometimes a clarinet), three trombones, and rhythm section (piano, guitar, bass, drums)

Arrangements—Emphasis on playing arrangements with occasional solo improvisation (ensemble was too large for the collective improvisation of New Orleans jazz)

Tone color—Arrangements often pitted sections against each other

Thirty-two-bar structure—Based on popular songs, usually with four eight-bar phrases, diagrammed **a a b a**

LISTENING EXAMPLE—Duke Ellington, "Conga Brava"

Bebop

Dates—c. 1944–1950; bebop-influenced styles flourished in the 1950s and after

Combos—Return to small ensembles

Instruments—Trumpet, saxophone, and rhythm section (piano, bass, drums)

Improvisation—Heavy emphasis on virtuoso solo improvisation (except first and last choruses)

Virtuosity—Complex melodies, chords, and rhythms, often played at breakneck speed

Afro-Cuban influence—Afro-Cuban rhythms and instruments used

Humor—Scat singing; quotation; and surprise, off-beat accents—especially by drummer

Thirty-two-bar structure—Based on popular songs, often with four eight-bar phrases, diagrammed **a a b a**

LISTENING EXAMPLE—Charlie Parker and Miles Davis, "Out of Nowhere"

Cool

Dates—c. 1949–1955

"Cool"—Everything understated and thoughtful, at times cerebral; influenced by classical music, especially impressionism; pastel colors and light, straight tone (little *vibrato*) favored

Improvisation—More orchestral conception, with emphasis on arrangements with limited solo improvisation

Tone Color—Neutral colors preferred; addition of vibraphone and orchestral instruments (flute, French horn, oboe, tuba, and so on); small or large ensembles used

Structure—Sophisticated treatment of form and phrases, based on advanced harmonies

LISTENING EXAMPLE—Leonard Bernstein, *West Side Story,* "Cool"

Jazz after Bebop

Dates—After 1950, many jazz styles were explored, including hard bop, modal jazz, free jazz, and jazz-rock fusion

Improvisation—New techniques for simultaneous improvisation explored

Structure—New structures (or no structure) substituted for preexisting songs or chord changes

Instruments—Electronic instruments added; expanded percussion and winds

Fusion—Influence of other popular styles, especially rock and funk

LISTENING EXAMPLE—Miles Davis, *Bitches Brew*

WALLACE "If You Ever Been Down" Blues

The blues has gone through many stages. Initially blues was more of a folk style, but this recording captures the blues in the 1920s, when it was enjoying its first big commercial successes. "If You Ever Been Down" Blues, for blues singer, piano, trumpet, and clarinet, provides interesting insights into jazz history as well.

Pitch bending—Many jazz scholars claim that instrumentalists learned to bend pitches by imitating the expressive devices of blues singers. This instrumental practice originated with the blues, but it became part of jazz early on. Play the recording and ask students to note how closely Louis Armstrong's trumpet lines match the expressive inflections of the singer, Sippie Wallace.

Development of swing—Count out loud along with the recording and invite students to compare the rhythms played by the clarinet and trumpet, especially in the third chorus. Which sounds more "square"? The clarinet emphasizes the beat consistently—the customary practice of New Orleans jazz musicians. Armstrong, on the other hand, plays much more varied rhythmic patterns; at times he even uses the beat syncopation typical of the swing era. By 1927 Armstrong was exploring a new rhythmic language that would make him one of the leading figures in the development of swing. In this recording, we can hear old and new rhythmic practices used simultaneously!

Display the following chart. Play the recording at least two more times. Play it once to demonstrate the harmonic structure of the twelve-bar blues; if you can, play I, IV, and V chords at the keyboard along with the recording. Play it again to focus on the relationship between the words and the music; point out sections on the chart as they go by. Take time afterward to compare this work with the features of blues and New Orleans jazz listed in the jazz-styles chart above.

LISTENING EXAMPLE—Sippie Wallace, "If You Ever Been Down" Blues

Introduction (0:00–0:10)

4 bars

1st chorus (0:10–0:45)

If you ever been down, you know just how I feel.   (*trumpet fill*)

    I |IV V |I | |

If you ever been down, you know just how I feel.   (*trumpet fill*)

        IV | |I | |

Like a tramp on a railroad, ain't got a decent meal. (*trumpet fill*)

        V | I | |I   V|

2nd chorus (0:45–1:18)

I'm a real good woman but my man don't treat me right.   (*clarinet fill*)

        I |IV |I | |

I'm a real good woman but my man don't treat me right.   (*clarinet fill*)

        IV |IV   V |I | |

He takes all my money and stays out all night. (*clarinet fill*)

        V | |I |I   V|

3rd chorus (instrumental chorus, 1:18–1:50)

trumpet solo   (*clarinet countermelody*)

I |IV |I | |

trumpet solo   (*clarinet and vocal countermelodies*)

IV |IV   V |I | |

trumpet solo   (*clarinet and vocal countermelodies*)

V | |I |I   V |

4th chorus (1:50–2:24)

I'm down today but I won't be down always.   (*trumpet fill*)

I |IV   V |I | |

I'm down today but I won't be down always.   (*trumpet fill*)

IV |IV   V |I | |

'Cause the sun's going to shine in my back door some day.   (*trumpet fill*)

            V | |I |I   V|

5th chorus (2:24–end)

Yes one thing papa, I've decided to do.   (*clarinet fill*)
   I |IV || | |

Aw pretty daddy, I've decided to do.   (*clarinet fill*)
  IV |IV V || | |

I'm gonna find another papa, then I can't use you.   (*trumpet and clarinet*)
     V | || IV || ||

ELLINGTON "Conga Brava"

Duke Ellington was one of the great innovators of the swing era. The diverse range of his compositions, his ear for unusual colors, and his ability to draw out the creativity of his band members set him apart from other bandleader-composers. "Conga Brava," composed by Ellington and Juan Tizol, is just one of many compositional collaborations between Ellington and members of the band. Some critics complain that Ellington's band did not swing as consistently as Basie's or that his music was harder to dance to, but Ellington's band was not just a dance band. Many of Ellington's works—*Concerto for Cootie,* his *Sacred Concerts,* or *Black, Brown, and Beige*—begin to blur the line between dance hall and concert hall, between jazz and "art" music. Ellington was, in fact, one of the great composers of the twentieth century.

Display the chart below. When you play the recording, count out loud along with the music, and point out important sections as they go by. After listening, compare this work with the features of swing listed in the jazz-styles chart above. Point out the unusual structure of this work's basic tune, and note the Afro-Cuban rhythms of the conga.

LISTENING CHART—Duke Ellington, "Conga Brava"

1st chorus

Intro	**a**			**a**			**b¹**		**b²**
	muted trombone melody —————————————————————————						clarinet solo		tutti
				riff (*muted trumpets*) ————————————					
			(*clarinet*)			(*clarinet*)			
4 bars	16	+	4	16	+	4	8	+	6
0:00	0:04		0:20	0:23		0:40	0:44		0:51

2nd chorus

a			**a**			**b¹**	
tenor sax solo ————————————————————————————						muted trumpets	
16	+	4	16	+	4	8	
0:59			1:18			1:39	

3rd chorus

a			**a**		**b²**
sax section melody			trumpets		tutti
muted trumpet solo					
		(*piano*)			
16	+	4	16		6
1:46		2:02	2:07		2:22

4th chorus

Intro	**a**		
	muted trombone solo		
			(fadeout)
4	16	+	5
2:28	2:32		2:48

‍ Global Perspectives 6: African Drumming

The influence of African drumming on music in the New World cannot be underestimated. Wherever Africans found themselves, under whatever circumstances, they left their mark on the music of that region. Jazz, rock, reggae, minimalism, and a host of contemporary popular styles would be unthinkable without the influence of African drumming. And that's just North America. The effect of African drumming on Latin or South American music has been no less profound.

Jazz was the first significant American style to develop from the roots of a genuinely African rhythmic sensibility. This is therefore the perfect place to look at African drumming—right in the middle of our survey of American jazz. The *Listen* recording takes us into the Yoruba region of West Africa. Since a disproportionate number of slaves were shipped from this region to the New World, the Yoruba influence proved especially strong in Brazil, the Caribbean, and the United States. The notes below begin with historical and cultural background materials on the Yoruba people, continue with information on Yoruba drumming, and conclude with specific teaching suggestions for "Ako," a performance by a Yoruba *bata* ensemble.

Yoruba History and Ritual

Today the Yoruba people live in western Nigeria, southern and central Benin (formerly Dahomey), and eastern Togo. The largest group, about fifteen million, lives in Nigeria, but a significant number live in Benin as well. The large urban buildup around Lagos and the resulting influx of Western influences have profoundly affected the course of traditional Yoruba music in Nigeria. In Benin, however, the lack of a natural ocean port created a more stable rural environment in which indigenous customs have flourished. Although Nigerian Yoruba music has lost much of its ritual significance, in Benin we can still see drumming in its original sacred contexts.

The first significant Yoruba kingdom was established at Ife in the eleventh century C.E. The more northerly Oyo kingdom emerged by the fifteenth century and became the dominant Yoruba kingdom by about 1600. Spain began shipping black slaves to its colonies in the Americas beginning in 1517. With the "help" of some local rulers, the Yoruba region quickly became a major hub of the slave trade, and by the 1700s about thirty-five thousand slaves a year were shipped out from this region of West Africa's "Gold Coast." Meanwhile, the Oyo kingdom continued its domination in this region up until the nineteenth century. During Europe's mad "scramble for Africa" at the end of the 1800s, portions of Yoruba land were grabbed up indiscriminately by Germany, France, and Great Britain. Germany's colony was passed to France after World War I, but when all three colonies were granted independence in 1960, they retained their old colonial boundaries. These arbitrary boundaries have caused no end of strife because they randomly group together peoples of very different languages and cultures.

The religious practices of the Yoruba region are of special interest. A good number have adopted Christianity, and Islam has made significant inroads, especially in Nigeria, where nearly half the population is Muslim. In Benin, however, two-thirds of the people still practice indigenous religious rituals. Many of these rituals center around cult practices, with each cult devoted to a specific deity. Curiously, no cults directly worship the chief god—Olorun, the sky god—though Eshu, the divine messenger, is thought to mediate between mortals, Olorun, and the other gods. Some lesser gods include Ifa, the god of divination; Odua, creator of the earth; Orishala, creator of humankind; and Ogun, god of iron (or war). Interestingly, the Yoruba have divinized many of their ancient kings, conferring on them the mythic qualities that most closely approximate their human personality traits. Odua was also the first king of Ife (the first recorded Yoruba kingdom), and Yoruba kings up to the present day must be able to trace their lineage to one of Odua's sixteen sons. One of those sons, Oranmiyan, became the first king of Oyo and ruled Ife after the death of Odua. Oranmiyan's son, Shango, was noted for his violent temper and his skill as a great warrior. Like his predecessors, Shango was also divinized, becoming the god of thunder (and lightning and fire).

The word *orisha* applies to any of these divinized ancestors of the Yoruba people, and most *orisha* cults choose one primary *orisha*. In the practice of its rituals, a cult can also invoke other deities in order to strengthen its own *orisha*. The principle *orisha* rituals involve a complex mix of specific dances, songs, rhythms, instruments, costumes, and so on, but the most characteristic feature of many rituals is a trancelike possession. Each cult's practices differ somewhat. In Ifa and Odua cults, possession never occurs, divination being the preferred method of communication with the *orisha*. In the popular Shango cults, possession tends to occur at the end of the initiation ceremony, after several weeks of seclusion and training in a shrine. And at the annual festivals of cults devoted to Yemoja or Oshun—two river goddesses—dozens can become possessed simultaneously.[1]

When many Yoruba were sold into slavery, the *orisha* cults were transplanted to the New World. In this new setting, they formed the basis of important religious practices: the *candomblé* in Bahia (Brazil), the *santería* in Cuba, and *vaudou* in Haiti (and elsewhere). These New World cults worship many gods, not just one, for fear that one god or another might otherwise get lost in the shuffle. Shango (Xango in Bahia, Changó in Cuba) remains especially popular, and he is saluted with the ritual greetings "Kabiesile" ("Your Majesty") in Bahia and "Kabiosile" in Cuba (both resemble the original "Kawo kabiye sile" used in Nigeria).[2] In some locations, including Cuba, *bata* ensembles continue to accompany this ritual. Apparently there is now a Shango temple in New York City as well. In all cases, drumming (with gourds or drums) and possession trances remain a significant part of these transplanted rituals.

Somewhat different from the *orisha* cults are the popular Egungun cults. Like the cults described above, Egungun cults are secret societies, but Egungun rituals do not call upon a divinized ancient ancestor. Rather, they invoke the spirits of ancestors from their own town, benign spirits who mediate between the dead and the living. Various explanations account for the origin of the Egungun ceremonies. One story attributes it to the god Amaiyegun, who taught

---

[1]William Bascom, *The Yoruba of Southwestern Nigeria*. New York: Holt, Rinehart and Winston, 1969, p. 78.

[2]William Bascom, *Shango in the New World*. Austin: Occasional Publication of the African and Afro-American Research Institute, University of Texas at Austin, 1972, p. 17.

the Yoruba the use of costumes and dances that could protect them from death. In yet another story the goddess Oya, after bearing Shango eight speechless children, made sacrifices that enabled her to bear a son, Egungun. Egungun could speak, but only in a distorted manner. Both stories explain aspects of the Egungun ceremonies, the first the notion of death's impermanence, the second the distorted voices used by Egungun ritual dancers.

Egungun festivals also have a public side. The cult carefully prepares and rehearses its rituals in private, but the actual "performance" of the ritual takes place in public, and "repeat performances" are often given at different locations around the city. Central to the ritual are costumed dancers who represent the Egungun, the ancestral spirits. Their costumes—long swirling robes—cover the entire body, with masks or veils that disguise each dancer's identity. As the dancers enter they speak or sing in a characteristic distorted manner. The dancers synchronize with an ensemble of *bata* drums in an elaborate choreography. Because these drums are small and portable, the lead drummer can interact closely and often theatrically with the dancers. Several types of Egungun dancers commonly participate in each ritual, including the "trickster" Egungun. While the other dancers evoke specific religious associations, the "trickster" group exists purely to entertain the crowd; in fact, they can ply their trade as street entertainers independent of an official Egungun festival. The entertainment aspect distinguishes Egungun performance from the more purely sacred rituals of many *orisha* cults.

Yoruba Drumming

Drums play a significant role in virtually all Yoruba religious rituals. Although they can serve to entertain or provide rhythmic accompaniment for public processions, their sacred nature makes them the preferred instruments for *orisha* and Egungun cult ceremonies, including those that involve trance possession. Each god requires specific sacrifices, carvings, symbols, taboos, and so on— and each god responds to specific rhythmic patterns. The drummers take the responsibility for invoking the right god by playing the correct rhythms. The patterns become equally important for the initiates; they are trained in such a way that the rhythms themselves help trigger their trance states.

Many different drums are used by the Yoruba, and each different type has its own specific religious associations. Drums typically perform in an ensemble of like instruments that include an *iya ilu* ("mother drum" or lead drum) and several support drums. Most commonly used are the *dundun* and *bata* drums. *Dundun* drums are hour-glass-shaped tension drums; though they are double-headed, only one head is used. The mother drum is configured so that the performer can produce different pitches by pressing the tension string. *Bata* drums are two-headed, cone-shaped drums. In the *bata* ensemble, support drums play on just one head, but the mother drum plays on both. *Bata* drums are associated with the god Shango and the rituals of Shango cults. According to one of the stories mentioned above, Egungun was the son of Shango and Oya; thus, *bata* drums are commonly used for Egungun festivals as well.

In both *dundun* and *bata* ensembles, the ability of the mother drum to sound multiple pitches points to a significant aspect of Yoruba drumming. These are talking drums. They not only duplicate the rhythms of Yoruba speech but follow the pitch contours of its words as well. The Yoruba language, which belongs to the Kwa family, is a tonal language with three basic pitch inflections: high, medium, and low. Further, the drums do not merely imitate speech, they actually speak—in words and sentences that Yoruba speakers recognize immediately. Egungun *bata* drummers often "recite" rather sophisticated poetry as part of the Egungun rituals. The following story from Mickey Hart's *Drumming at the Edge of Magic* makes the point in a more humorous way.

> [John] Chernoff tells a story of how he was sitting one afternoon with a drum master, learning some basic rhythms, when suddenly the man deviated from the rhythm he was playing, just for a few seconds, then returned to the lesson. A few minutes later a man who had been walking by at the time returned with two beers. That little rhythmic deviation had actually been the equivalent of a shouted, "Hey, friend, get us a couple of cold ones."[3]

Before turning to "Ako," let us follow a brief digression, especially since it bears on the syncretic nature of the "global music" discussed in Global Perspectives 7. Christopher Waterman has done much research in the area of Nigerian popular music, especially the *juju* music that originated in Lagos in the 1930s.[4] In its earliest form, *juju* served up a fusion of traditional Yoruba songs, Western percussion instruments, Western African urban music, and a guitar style that borrowed from American country music as well as Cuban and Liberian styles. Essentially an urban popular style for the working class, the music appealed little to rural Yorubans recently moved to the big city. That changed significantly with the arrival of electronic amplification, a Western invention. African drums would have drowned out the *juju* ensemble in its original form, but with the arrival of amplification, voices and guitars could now compete. In 1949 the talking *dundun* mother drum was added to the *juju* ensemble, followed shortly thereafter by various Afro-Cuban percussion instruments. The use of a mother drum with its typical support drums, coupled with frequent use of call-and-response patterns, changed *juju* dramatically. The result was an incredibly popular style that resonated with Yoruba peoples throughout Nigeria. Surprisingly, Western technology (amplification) made it possible for *juju* to sound *more* like indigenous music, not less. Nigeria's growing urbanization fostered the slow decline of traditional music; for once, Western influence helped reverse that trend.

Yoruba Drumming, "Ako"   "Ako," a work from the Egungun festival repertory, features the ensemble of five *bata* drums typical in Egungun ceremonies. Like all Yoruba drum ensembles, the *bata* ensemble is led by the *iya ilu*, or mother drum. As mentioned above, the player uses both heads of the drum and interacts with the dancers in the Egungun rituals. As befits its lead role in the ensemble, the *iya ilu* often plays highly varied soloistic patterns that interact with the support drums to create elaborate cross-rhythms. Unlike most other African drums, the heads of the *bata* mother drum produce pitches both higher and lower than the pitches of any other drums in the ensemble. Unfortunately, this can make it more difficult to follow the mother drum part in performance.

The second most important drum in the *bata* ensemble is the *ako*, which can also be played on both heads. Its small head produces the second highest pitch in the ensemble, but the pitch of its large head falls right in the middle of the ensemble's range. The *ako* mediates between the support drums and the mother drum; it generally provides steady support patterns for the *iya ilu*, but it can break away at specific places to interact with the mother drum.

---

[3]Mickey Hart, *Drumming at the Edge of Magic: A Journey into the Spirit of Percussion.* San Francisco: Harper Collins, 1990, p. 200.

[4]Christopher Waterman, "Juju." From Bruno Nettl, *The Western Impact on World Music.* New York: Schirmer Books, 1985, pp. 87–90.

The remaining three drums constitute the support drums of the *bata* ensemble, and they play only on one drumhead. From highest to lowest, they are the *omele ako*, the *omele abo*, and the *eki*. The two *omele*, close to each other in pitch, fall into a middle register. The *eki* is much lower; in fact, it provides the second-lowest pitch in the *bata* ensemble, low enough to be confused with the bottom pitch of the *iya ilu*. The support drums are given less freedom than the mother drum or the *ako;* they must repeat *ostinato* patterns throughout each piece. On occasion they can vary their rhythms as long as they preserve the feel of the assigned *ostinato*.

When you present "Ako" to your class, start with some background material. Feel free to use any of the information above, but at the very least explain the nature of Egungun ceremonies, describe the role of the drums in those ceremonies, and talk about the five drums of the *bata* ensemble. Make sure your class has read the pages on African drumming (textbook pages 404–05); then refer students to textbook page 405. The authors don't provide a listening chart for this piece, but they do provide some useful notated examples, and any bit of notation can help students see and hear the complex polyrhythms of this work. You will almost certainly need to play "Ako" several times for your students. With each playing, help them listen for just one or two patterns at a time. As you work your way through, try to draw out each of the main features described below.

Call attention first to the "main pulse," a constant sixteenth-note pattern played by the *omele ako*. This constant pulse provides the basis for the entire work. Note that the sixteenth-note pattern does not appear in the highest-sounding voice but in the middle. The basic *ostinato* for the *omele abo* and the *eki* is a constant eighth-note pulse that supports the main pulse. While these repeated *ostinato*s constitute the bulk of their playing, all three support instruments occasionally break out and play other patterns, each one at different times. The *omele ako* is the one that briefly speeds up to play six notes per beat instead of four, as the authors describe. The sixteenth-note/eighth-note pattern, written out just under the main pulse on textbook page 405, is played by the *eki*. Although not described, the *omele abo* occasionally substitutes a two-sixteenth-note/eighth-note pattern for its usual constant eighth notes.

The other two instruments play irregular patterns. The *ako* is difficult to hear because its pitches fall in the middle of the ensemble, where its slower *ostinato* patterns easily get lost. The mother drum proves much easier to hear since its two pitches provide both the highest and the lowest sounds in the ensemble. Show students how the combination of its high register and elaborate, irregular rhythms makes the *iya ilu*'s top line sound almost like a solo melody over the regular accompaniment of the support drums. If your speakers offer a good bass response, you may also be able to point out the mother drum's low pitch at the bottom of the ensemble's range. As described above, the mother drum's part is much more soloistic than that of the other drums. It is the *iya ilu* that provides the triplet rhythm the authors describe at 0:41–0:44, and it plays many other rhythmic motives with an almost melodic feel.[5]

The triple feel reappears briefly near the end, this time in the support drums. But at the very end, just before the rhythms peter out, a little codetta finds every instrument using triple and sextuple divisions. These triplet sec-

---

[5]Do yourself a favor and pick up a copy of the CD from which "Ako" was taken—*Yoruba Drums from Benin, West Africa* (Smithsonian Folkways SF 40440). The excellent liner notes include a nearly complete transcription of the mother drum part that can help you feel more at home with this complex music.

tions provide just one of the many polyrhythmic patterns that pervade this music. Other cross-rhythms weave in slower 3 + 3 + 2 patterns. Help students understand that polyrhythms involve the simultaneous use of two or more rhythms different enough that they sound as if they were using two different meters (3 + 3 + 2 vs. 4 + 4) or tempos (triplets vs. sixteenths). That they all fit together stands as a tribute to the virtuosity of these Yoruba percussionists.

⁊ Later Jazz

PARKER AND DAVIS "Out of Nowhere"

If your students have ever been to a club with a small jazz combo providing background music, chances are they have heard bebop or a style influenced by it. Bop was created by players who wanted to stretch beyond the confines of big band jazz and its limited opportunities for improvisation. Often too fast and unpredictable to dance to, this virtuosic style never enjoyed the popularity of big band swing, but its influence on subsequent jazz styles has been enormous.

Display the chart below. When you play the recording, count out loud along with the music and point out important sections as they go by. After listening, compare this work with the features of bebop listed in the jazz-styles chart that appears earlier in this chapter. Point out the unusual structure of this work's basic tune, Bird's impromptu quotation of "Kerry Dancers" in his solo, and the (deliberately) humorous classical-sounding folk-tune quotation that ends the work.

1st chorus

A	A′	
saxophone melody ————————————————		
16 bars	16	
0:00	0:24	

2nd chorus

A	A′	
trumpet solo ————————————————		
16	16	
0:48	1:12	

3rd chorus

A	A′	
sax solo ————————————————		
	("Kerry Dancers," 2:02–2:06)	
16	16	
1:36	2:00	

4th chorus

A	A′	Coda
piano solo	sax melody with trumpet countermelody	
16	14	2
2:24	2:49	3:11

DAVIS *Bitches Brew*

As the jazz-styles chart (earlier in this chapter) indicates, jazz after bebop underwent significant changes; in fact, it split into a variety of different, important styles, and Miles Davis pioneered many of them from the 1950s to the 1980s. As we heard in "Out of Nowhere," a young Davis got his start in bebop. Davis soon broke new ground in the development of cool jazz through his collaboration with arranger Gil Evans on albums such as *The Complete Birth of the Cool* and *Porgy and Bess*. If Davis had stopped there, he would have earned an important place in jazz history, but the restless musician moved on to explore modal jazz (*Kind of Blue*, 1959), a highly interactive style influenced by free jazz (*Sorcerer*, 1967), and jazz-rock fusion (*Bitches Brew*, 1969). In the process, Davis became one of the dominant forces in jazz, with major contributions as an improviser, composer, and bandleader. He was never easy to work with, and the personnel in his bands changed at least every four or five years. Nonetheless, the list of musicians who played under Davis reads like a jazz "Who's Who" for the past forty years; it includes Bill Evans, John Coltrane, "Cannonball" Adderley, Herbie Hancock, Ron Carter, Tony Williams, Wayne Shorter, Chick Corea, Keith Jarrett, John McLaughlin, and Josef Zawinul.

Bitches Brew was one of several albums from the late 1960s that found Davis trying to infuse jazz with rock's vitality. He turned increasingly to electronic instruments such as electric guitar and bass, electric pianos and other keyboards, and electronic devices used to manipulate live sounds. He also encouraged the use of repetitive bass patterns and the straight-ahead, driving rhythms of 1960s rock. The title track, *Bitches Brew*, finds Davis playing into an Echoplex in the introduction (before the *Listen* excerpt). The Echoplex was a specially designed tape recorder that allowed the user to create echo effects by feeding sound from the playback head back to the record head. The Echoplex also allowed the user to adjust the time between sound and echo by controlling the distance tape had to travel between the two heads.

The *Listen* excerpt offers Davis's second extended solo, starting about eight minutes into a twenty-six-minute track. The sounds in the introduction are fascinating, but not particularly rocklike; the *Listen* recording cuts straight to a section where we can hear rock elements clearly alongside Davis's solo. When you play this excerpt, help your class distinguish between rock and jazz elements. Students must listen for the electric bass and drum parts if they want to hear the rock influence clearly. The bass offers an *ostinato* that repeats throughout the excerpt, and the drums play straight-ahead rhythmic patterns that decidedly do *not* swing. This excerpt also uses several instruments associated with rock: electric guitar, electric bass, and the drum set. The remaining elements of this work reflect a jazz sensibility. The electric guitar, electric piano, and trumpet all improvise freely over the constant rhythm and *ostinato* of the drums and bass. The electric piano itself became ubiquitous in jazz fusion, though it never caught on in mainstream rock. Finally, Davis's trumpet work represents an extension of his work through the 1960s. But when compared with his 1950s style, Davis's fusion style presents some clear differences. He abandoned the Harmon mute that had become his trademark in the 1950s, and his solos exploit a more brilliant tone and a higher register than most of his earlier trumpet work.

Refer students to the *Listen* Guide on textbook page 408 when you play the recording. After listening, compare this work with the features of jazz after bebop listed in the jazz-styles chart that appears earlier in this chapter. Ask students to pick out features that apply to this work: The bass *ostinato* replaces the preexisting tunes and chord progressions that earlier jazz musicians used as a basis for improvisation; this brief *ostinato* provides an entirely new, more flexible structure for improvisation; electronic bass, guitar, and piano are used; and a rock element is present, especially in the bass and drum patterns.

Be sure to draw connections between this work and the example of Yoruba drumming in the *Listen* set. Davis deliberately turned to African influences with increasing frequency in the 1960s, and *Bitches Brew* surpassed his previous albums in this regard. Some of the song titles point to Africa—*Pharaoh's Dance* and *Miles Runs the Voodoo Down* (as we saw above, voodoo derives from Yoruba religious practices)—and even the cover art (bring the album along if you can) demonstrates a clear African influence. But the most striking connection can be found in Davis's rhythm section. In a remarkable departure from standard jazz conventions, Davis calls for an ensemble of drummers that includes two drum sets and a third player on auxiliary percussion—comparable to our Yoruba *bata* ensemble! Invite students to listen for the dense polyrhythmic ebb and flow these drummers create as they interact with the rest of the ensemble. Later jazz-rock fusion bands achieved greater popularity than Davis's, especially the bands formed by Davis's own former sidemen: Weather Report (Josef Zawinul and Wayne Shorter), Headhunter (Herbie Hancock), and Return to Forever (Chick Corea). Nonetheless, Davis always remained the jazz musician's musician, a thoughtful improviser who always seemed to know exactly what had to happen next. *Bitches Brew* remains a difficult work for musical neophytes, yet its many-layered textures, prolific inventiveness, and rhythmic energy become more and more apparent the more one listens. This music's haunting restlessness cannot easily be forgotten.

Jazz in the Concert Hall

GERSHWIN **Prelude No. 1**

George Gershwin and Aaron Copland were born to Jewish immigrant parents in Brooklyn, New York, within two years of each other. Their musical paths diverged early, though. Copland received a solid education in music, whereas Gershwin did not begin piano lessons until the age of ten. Although he studied the well-known classics of the nineteenth century, his heart lay with American popular music and jazz. He entered the music profession as a song demonstrator ("plugger") at a New York music-publishing house. Gershwin's own songs began to attract attention, and by the early 1920s he was a popular composer of musical comedies. Gershwin's first attempt at a concert work was his *Rhapsody in Blue,* composed in 1924 (see Further Listening Examples below for teaching suggestions). Despite the fact that Gershwin did not orchestrate the work and, by his own admission, knew no more about harmony than could be obtained "in a ten-cent harmony manual," its imaginative, youthful energy and brittle, jazzy melodies make *Rhapsody* a favorite to this day. By the time he wrote the Concerto in F, Gershwin had learned a great deal more about the classical side of composition, and the final movement presents as tight an example of rondo form as you could hope to find (see Further Listening Examples below for teaching suggestions).

Less well known than *Rhapsody* or the Concerto, Gershwin's three Preludes for Piano share the same concern as these larger works: the blending of jazz and classical sounds and techniques. Both larger works make use of traditional forms: *Rhapsody in Blue,* the Romantic free-form rhapsody (cf. Rachmaninov's *Rhapsody on a Theme by Paganini* from the *Listen* DVD), and Concerto in F, the three-movement Classical concerto format. As the authors point out, the Preludes for Piano also follow an earlier model: the Romantic miniature, specifically the character piece for piano. When you present Prelude No. 1, follow the same procedure we used for Romantic character pieces in Chapter 16.

1. The prelude is typically a short work with a simple structure that may or may not feel complete all by itself. By definition, a prelude should precede something, just as each prelude in Bach's *Well-Tempered Clavier* leads into a fugue. Starting with Chopin, however, preludes came to be written in sets—modeled after Bach as they traverse the twenty-four major and minor keys, but ignoring the expectation of a fugue or other companion work. Debussy followed Chopin's lead with two sets of twelve preludes; Gershwin himself planned a set of twenty-four but ended up with only three.

2. Gershwin uses a simple ternary structure, a form found in many preludes by Chopin and other composers. The **A** section's jaunty melody emphasizes a bluesy inflection of scale-step 3, accompanied by a 3 + 3 + 2 rhythm that sounds like a drunken oom-pah-pah waltz. While the **A** section stays close to B flat as its tonal center, the **B** section modulates frequently, using one sequence after another. Gershwin mates this tonal ambiguity with a motive-based melody aptly fitted to the sequences, but these motives, though energetic, serve primarily as building blocks, lacking the tunefulness of the **A** theme. Note the buildup to the return of **A′**. Just at the point where we start to miss having a real tune to listen to (m. 42—1:04), Gershwin gives us one. Due to the minor mode, students may not notice it, but this tune gives us the rhythmic motive of the **A** theme, preparing us for the real return at m. 50 (1:19). As part of the buildup, Gershwin also gives us the "drunken waltz," but much fuller sounding, with full right-hand chords to enliven the texture. This *crescendo* of activity leads directly into the return of the **A** theme (**A′** in the *Listen* Guide on textbook page 410), now an octave higher with octave doublings for fullness. Gershwin repeats the final motive three times, in successively lower octaves and gradually slowing. A brief surprise codetta, a rising flurry of parallel fourths *decrescendo* capped off with two *fortissimo* chords, brings the prelude to a convincing close.

3. Even in this less familiar work, the rhythms, harmonies, and melodies immediately suggest Gershwin. Point out the jazz elements of this work: the frequent blue notes (especially lowered scale steps 3 and 7), the ubiquitous syncopated rhythms (e.g., the "drunken waltz"), and the jazz harmonies. Note also the essentially rhythmic nature of the **B** theme.

Play the whole prelude. Refer students to the *Listen* Guide for this work on textbook page 410 or write the large divisions of the prelude on the board and point these out as they go by.

Point out that Gershwin's use of jazz elements—syncopation, blue notes, and jazz harmonies—was considered quite modern in the 1920s and 1930s. The initial shock has worn off, however, and today we realize that the melodic, harmonic, and formal aspects of this music make it quite traditional in nature. The net result: Gershwin succeeded in his ambition to unite jazz elements with classical forms and procedures. What he lacked in training and skill he more than made up for in energy and instinct.

The American Musical

It is curious that many students enjoy musicals but claim to dislike opera. They have never made a connection between the two and are surprised to discover that the American musical falls squarely in a comic-opera tradition that dates back to the eighteenth century. Both employ spoken dialogue in the vernacular and contemporary subjects and characters. Use textbook pages 410–12, which trace the development of the musical from late nineteenth-century European operetta on, to help students make these connections. If you have time to flesh out this evolution in class, look for ideas below in Additional Teaching Suggestions and Multimedia Resources.

BERNSTEIN *West Side Story*

Leonard Bernstein's classic *West Side Story* (1957) presents a full-blown, sophisticated example of the American musical. It may seem unlikely for a "classical" composer with Bernstein's credentials to write a smash-hit musical, just as it was for a "popular" composer like Gershwin to write a great American opera (*Porgy and Bess*). Both composers freely crossed the boundaries between "serious" and popular music; in so doing, they provided wonderful role models for succeeding generations of American composers.

In your presentation of *West Side Story,* draw out as many connections as possible between this musical and the operas you covered in earlier chapters. Just as you would with any opera, begin with a plot synopsis. As the textbook points out, the story is an updated version of Shakespeare's *Romeo and Juliet.* The synopsis below outlines the original stage version of Bernstein's musical; the movie version contains a somewhat different sequence of events.

Act I begins with a fight between members of two rival New York City street gangs, the Sharks (Puerto Rican—Capulets) and the Jets (white—Montagues). After the police break it up, the Jets decide to recruit Tony, a former gang member, to help them beat the Sharks. Jets member Riff asks Tony to come to a dance where he expects trouble with the Sharks. Next we meet Maria, sister of Sharks leader Bernardo, who looks forward to her first dance in America. At the dance, there is tension between the gangs, but when Tony and Maria meet, they have eyes only for each other. The dance momentarily fades into the background. When Tony kisses Maria, Bernardo forcibly separates the two lovers. Tony leaves, repeating Maria's name while the gang leaders schedule a war council.

Later that night, Tony comes to Maria's window but must leave when she is called by her family. Bernardo warns her to stay away from Tony. As he rejoins the Sharks, he and Anita (Bernardo's woman and Maria's friend) argue about the poor treatment accorded to Puerto Ricans in "America." Meanwhile, the Jets prepare for the war council at Doc's drugstore. The Sharks arrive, and Tony convinces the gangs to agree to a fair fight instead of a rumble. Just as they finish their plans, they are interrupted by a police lieutenant, Schrank, who kicks out the Sharks and cynically tells the Jets to finish each other off if they plan to rumble.

The next day, Tony meets Maria at the bridal shop where she works. Tony wants to take her home, but Maria insists that he stop the fight between the gangs first. They stage a mock wedding that turns serious. The next scene is a large ensemble—"Tonight"—that highlights the different expectations of the characters as they anticipate marriage, romantic encounters, or the fight that the evening will bring. This scene leads directly into the encounter between the two gangs. Tony tries to stop the fight, but his intervention leads to the death of his friend Riff. In a fit of rage, Tony grabs the knife and kills Bernardo.

Act II begins with Maria telling her friends that she will be married. Chino, a Sharks member, enters to tell her that her brother Bernardo is dead. She cannot believe it, and when Tony enters she strikes him and calls him a murderer. She relents when she sees that he is also devastated by the killing. After making plans to go far away, they spend the night together. Meanwhile, the Jets consider their situation following police interrogation. Following Officer

Krupke's exit, they make a hash of psychological explanations of their delinquent behavior.

Back at Maria's house the next morning, Anita comes in just in time to see Tony leaving. She is enraged, but as she and Maria grieve Bernardo's death, Anita agrees to help them leave the city. Anita goes to the drugstore where Doc is hiding Tony. She intends to tell Doc where and when Tony should meet Maria for their escape. Doc is out when Anita arrives, and the Jets take the opportunity to taunt and harass her. They are about to rape her when Doc walks in; in her anger she tells them that Chino found out about Tony and murdered Maria. Doc brings the sad news to Tony, who races out into the street shouting for Chino to come and kill him, too. Maria sees Tony first, but as she and Tony run to embrace each other, Chino shoots Tony. Tony dies in Maria's arms. Maria confronts the assembled gang members with their complicity in the tragic killings. She bids Tony good-bye; Sharks and Jets alike carry his body away.

Bernstein's classical training shows up in many aspects of *West Side Story*. Not only does he tackle Shakespeare in a musical,[6] but he uses the technique of thematic transformation to unify contrasting musical elements. The score also demonstrates his eclectic musical tastes; he borrows from Romantic opera, the American musical, Latin American music, Beethoven string quartets, big band swing, and cool jazz.

The three excerpts chosen by the authors show off Bernstein's use of thematic transformation. Each one is based on the same three-note motive (C–F sharp–G), but each one creates a remarkably different mood. In addition, the scenes demonstrate different types of musical numbers characteristic of the musical.

"Cha-Cha"

This scene takes place after the extended dance sequence in Act I. Tony and Maria notice each other for the first time, and the music of the dance fades around them—they only have eyes (and ears) for each other. The purely instrumental music for this brief number (just three phrases) uses the rhythm of a Cuban dance, the cha-cha. The textbook describes the delicate, halting quality of this lightly scored dance; the music nicely captures the charm and tentativeness of the first encounter between the two lovers.

Point out the three-note motive in the opening of the cha-cha melody. This number also offers an example of dance music—one of several examples in *West Side Story*. Modern dance had been discouraged in musical comedy until Agnes De Mille's stunningly choreographed scenes in *Oklahoma!* convincingly demonstrated the viability of artistic dance numbers in a genre designed to entertain.

"Meeting Scene"

This scene follows immediately after the cha-cha just described. Maria and Tony have been dancing; now they speak to each other for the first time. Tony can hardly believe this is happening, but they are fascinated with each other. Tentative hand-holding quickly leads to an innocent kiss.

Point out how the cha-cha's light, syncopated version of the three-note motive is transformed into questioning *legato* figures that accompany the spoken

---

[6]Bernstein is hardly the first to borrow from Shakespeare in a musical, though. A famous earlier example is Cole Porter's *Kiss Me, Kate*, based on *Taming of the Shrew*.

dialogue between Tony and Maria. This number offers an example of *melo-drama*—a musical number that consists of spoken dialogue with instrumental accompaniment. Melodrama was an important part of the *Singspiel*, the German comic opera genre that dates back to the eighteenth century (not to mention its use in American theater, where "sweet Nell" is tied to the tracks by the mustachioed villain).

"Cool"

In the original stage version, this ensemble came near the end of Act I as the Jets were preparing for a rumble with the Sharks. In the movie version, however, it appears in the middle of the second act—following the tragic rumble that went all wrong and subsequent police interrogations. In this position, the ensemble acquires a new urgency; it becomes a desperate plea for survival in the face of the anger and fear the Jets are experiencing. In his song, Riff tells the Jets that they must play it cool if they want to live. The gang responds with an extended modern-dance sequence.

Point out that the notes of the three-note motive are repeated again and again in the vibraphone introduction and the first two lines of Riff's song. This motive is once again heard in an entirely new context: the hard-edged world of cool jazz. "Cool" is an example of an ensemble and a production number. It begins with two stanzas of a song by Riff, turns into a long dance accompanied by a cool-jazz fugue, and ends with Riff's song, first played by the band and then sung by all of the Jets. The structure can be mapped as follows:

Riff's song	(0:00)	Introduction: based on three-note motive, features the electric bass
	(0:14)	first stanza
	(0:38)	second stanza
	(0:59)	Interlude: same motive as introduction
Fugue		
Exposition	(1:12)	subject; muted trumpet
	(1:33)	answer
	(1:51)	subject; muted trombone
	(2:09)	answer; strings in octaves
Episode	(2:25)	long episode
Subject entry	(2:40)	subject embellished; tutti
Riff's song	(2:56)	instrumental statement of introduction; brass
	(3:10)	first stanza, swing version performed by the "band"—climax
	(3:39)	second stanza, sung by the Jets
	(3:58)	Coda: return of introduction, features xylophone, vibraphone, and bass

Note that the introduction and the first stanza of Riff's song return in full-blown transformations that flow directly from the fugue. Not until the Jets sing the second stanza do we hear a clear return to the sound world of this number's beginning. Note also the relationship between this music and cool jazz. The vibraphone, sharply muted brass instruments, sophisticated harmonies and melodic contours, and fugal style (influenced by classical music) all suggest cool jazz.

❧ Rock: The First Fifty Years

This section surveys many of the styles associated with rock music since the 1950s, and although the textbook identifies many songs by name, the recorded set provides no listening examples. If you have time left at the end of the term to cover this material, by all means do so. Students love it when you validate the music they know best. There are countless ways to present these styles to your class; be creative. As always, focus on music you know best; your evident love and enthusiasm will strengthen your presentation. Still, don't hesitate to explore at least some new pieces, especially those that mean something to your students. If you need to bone up on this material, you can find resources in Appendix V. You can also find useful ideas, CDs, and videos (DVD and VHS) in Additional Teaching Suggestions and Multimedia Resources below.

❧ Global Perspectives 7: Global Music

Many early ethnomusicologists took it as their mission to record and preserve indigenous cultures around the world before "evil" Western influences changed them forever. As it has turned out, the reality of international musical interactions proves much more complex than that. In fact, efforts to "preserve" are themselves often misguided, imposing a false rigidity on living traditions that are by nature dynamic and fluid. In our look at Yoruba drumming we saw how African styles were transplanted to the New World and then returned, by way of Cuban popular music and the phonograph record, to influence a new Nigerian popular style called *juju*. Many other indigenous musics have certainly felt the impact of Western styles, but rarely has Western music replaced another music completely.

There is no question that Western popular music has saturated the globe and that many musicians have turned away from "pure" regional traditions to cultivate styles that blend Western and indigenous elements. But in a world as interconnected as ours, influence no longer travels one way only. Because of the efforts of popular musicians like Paul Simon and Peter Gabriel in the 1980s, the sounds of world music now pervade Western popular music, and musicians from around the world tour the United States regularly. The term *exoticism* seemed appropriate when international influences were the exception rather than the rule—the word itself often suggested a condescending, "colonialist" attitude toward world music—but not today. The reciprocity that characterizes the current "world-beat" phenomenon points to a new paradigm for understanding global music.

Our final Global Perspectives example pinpoints the locus of an especially fascinating chain of influences and counterinfluences: South African *isicathamiya* music. As we will discover, this music emerged from an intriguing and complex web of musical, social, and economic influences, and in turn it has influenced music around the globe. The material below begins with two brief histories of South Africa, followed by a look at indigenous Nguni music and several syncretic genres that emerged during the colonial era. After considering the roots, history, and style features of *isicathamiya,* these notes will conclude with specific teaching suggestions for "Anoku Gonda," as performed by Solomon Linda and the Evening Birds.

A European History of South Africa

The impact of Europe on South Africa goes back further than for many African nations. In 1652 the Dutch East India Company established a shipping station at the Cape of Good Hope that soon became the heart of a small Dutch colony. Like Spanish settlers in the New World, the Dutch made Cape Colony a home away from home. By 1676 the governor in Cape Town had even put together an orchestra made up of African slaves. Dutch settlers gradually moved eastward along the coast, coming into conflict with the indigenous Xhosa peoples.

English settlers first arrived in 1795. When the Netherlands was overrun by Napoleon's armies in the early 1800s, the English took advantage of the situation. By 1806 they had taken control of Cape Colony, and the 1814 Congress of Vienna gave official control to Great Britain. Starting in 1820, British settlers arrived in large numbers; for the most part they came to take advantage of new economic opportunities along the coast, but some came to set up missionary stations in the interior.

The Dutch residents quickly became dissatisfied with this increasing interference with their way of life, and in 1836 they left Cape Colony. Some moved to Natal, initially settled by the British in 1824, but most moved north and northeast into the interior, where they established independent republics, the Orange Free State and the South African Republic, later known as Transvaal. This move brought the *voortrekkers* into the homelands of the Zulu and the Xhosa peoples, and many battles were fought as the Boers sought to carve out a new home for themselves.

British and Boers might have coexisted in this uneasy tension for some time had it not been for the discovery of diamonds and gold in the 1870s and 1880s. New cities sprang up overnight: Kimberley in the diamond mining region in 1871 and Johannesburg near the gold mines in 1886. Great Britain desperately wanted its piece of the pie, and several British-backed uprisings escalated tensions into an all-out war, the South African War of 1899–1902. The British won, and in 1910 Great Britain granted dominion status to the new republic of South Africa, which merged the British colonies with the former Boer republics. The first prime minister, Louis Botha, was a moderate Afrikaner (Dutch South African) willing to cooperate with the British.

The republic's early years went smoothly, but the Depression of the 1930s affected everyone, and nationalist movements began. Segregationalist policies gradually became more restrictive, and when the Afrikaner-led Nationalist Party was voted into power in 1948, apartheid became the law of the land. New laws were passed restricting contact between white and nonwhite citizens, and new "homelands" were created for black citizens (74 percent of the population), who were assigned to homeland districts whether they lived in those regions or not.

An African History of South Africa

The original residents of South Africa were Khoikhoi and San hunter-gatherers; Bantu peoples moved into the region sometime between 1000 and 1500 C.E. The South African Bantu are known collectively as the Nguni, though they divide into several subgroups, primarily the Zulu, the Xhosa, and the Swazi. The Xhosa were the first Bantu peoples to come in contact with the Europeans, and their conflicts with the Dutch and the English settlers left them too weak to form strong kingdoms like those of the Zulu or Swazi peoples. The Zulu kingdom was actually a rather late development. The original Zulu peoples were a collection of separate, independent clans, but Shaka Zulu united them as a nation in 1816. His cruel military campaigns caused many Zulu peoples to flee north, and he was murdered by his subjects in 1828. The Zulu kingdom continued as a viable political entity for many years, though it came into frequent conflict with British and Boer settlers moving east and north from the Cape. The Zulu were finally defeated in 1879, with most of their lands taken from them. The Swazi kingdom fared somewhat better, since it lay to the east of lands contested by the British, the Boers, and the Zulu. It ultimately became a British protectorate known as Swaziland.

When the mining boom hit in the 1870s and 1880s, many black South Africans found themselves working the mines in the new cities of Kimberley and Johannesburg. Some came voluntarily, looking for work and wealth; others were "recruited" by large mining companies who used a variety of tactics to acquire necessary labor. These instant cities quickly became a hodgepodge of peoples representing different races, countries, languages, colors, social classes, and levels of education, all living in close proximity under crude conditions. Historically, the Zulu and the Xhosa had been rural peoples, but large new urban black communities faced the challenges of a new environment and new lifestyles. As the cities grew and stabilized, black residents were gradually moved from the center of town to more and more distant townships. In the meantime, these urban centers spawned the creation of many new musical genres.

With the defeat of the last Zulu uprising in 1908 and the end of colonial rule in 1910, conditions slowly worsened for black South Africans. Political power was turned over to white South Africans who continued to take a "colonialist" view of their black neighbors. The Land Acts of 1913 and 1936 required the separation of black and white residences. Other segregationist practices heightened as the Depression saw rural blacks moving to the cities for work in increasing numbers. Matters only worsened when the Nationalist Party won a majority in the 1948 elections—legislation was quickly enacted to make apartheid official government policy. As groups like the African National Congress mounted a campaign of resistance beginning in the 1950s, many new laws were passed to further restrict the activities of black South Africans. Devastating to black musicians were 1960s regulations that made it illegal to perform with white musicians or in white nightclubs. Worse yet, the 1966 Group Areas Act sought to move most black South Africans into newly designated "homelands"—often undesirable lands without the resources to support such a large population. Both sides often resorted to violence, and the international community gradually lifted their voices to protest the situation in South Africa. After a generation of failed attempts to repair a system that was dysfunctional from the outset, President F. W. de Klerk gave up and committed himself to the abolition of apartheid in 1990. He released Nelson Mandela after twenty-six years in prison, reinstated the long-banned African National Congress, and in 1991 signed the repeal of the Group Areas Act. In the first true popular elections in South African history, Nelson Mandela was elected president in a landslide victory. He initiated a process of national healing that continues today.

Nguni Traditional Music

The music of the indigenous Nguni peoples of South Africa presents a sound world quite different from that of the Yoruba. The examples from the Gambia and the Mbuti notwithstanding, we tend to think of percussion instruments as the dominant medium in African music. Nguni traditional music uses no percussion instruments to speak of other than body-rattles for dancing or occasional beating on shields. The primary musical medium is the choral ensemble, and the Nguni cultivate a style of vocal polyphony somewhat similar to that of the Mbuti and using as few as two parts or as many as four. Most voice parts sing repeating *ostinato* patterns, just as we heard in Mbuti music. Additional voice parts often double the main two or three parts at the interval of a fourth or a fifth. The soloist, who sings the top part, is given the most freedom to depart from the *ostinato* pattern in an improvisatory fashion. These *ostinato* patterns, especially the bass, continue to figure prominently in syncretic African vocal styles as well as indigenous ones.

Nguni polyphony differs enormously from Western polyphony. The overlapping voices initially feel a bit like imitation as the texture builds from one voice to several, but of course the voices do not have the same melodic material. They favor a responsorial (call-and-response) manner, which helps to explain in part why the voices overlap. Further, their harmonies give preference to the intervals of the fourth and the fifth. Further, no two parts begin or end their phrases at the same time; thus, the music has a fascinating overlapping effect. The music is often performed *a cappella*; accompaniment, when present, is often provided by a musical bow.

Other features of this vocal music can be attributed to the languages of the Nguni. Though they belong to the same Bantu language group, Zulu, Swazi, and Xhosa are not mutually understandable, but they have some features—including clicking sounds—inherited from even earlier South African peoples and a tendency to glide on syllables that contain voiced consonants (*d, k, t,* and so on), gliding up on initial consonants and down on final ones. In fact, Nguni languages are tonal languages, but not to the degree that Yoruba is. The primary influence of spoken language on song is the practice of *glissando* described above. This type of *glissando* is scrupulously avoided in Western classical music but is regarded as perfectly normal and natural in the Nguni tradition.

Roots of Isicathamiya

The long road from Nguni vocal polyphony to *isicathamiya* is full of interesting twists and turns. Probably the first European music to have a significant influence on the Nguni was the hymn tradition carried by English missionaries into the interior early in the 1800s. Given their traditions, it is not surprising that black South Africans found four-part Christian choral singing attractive, but the melodic contours of these hymn tunes rarely fit the speech contours of the translated texts. In short order, the composition of new hymn tunes and texts began; by 1816 the prophet Ntsikana had composed a number of Afro-Christian hymns. This new hymn tradition gradually inspired other genres as well. In the 1880s John Bokwe developed a new South African vernacular choral style called *makwaya*, modeled on four-part hymn-singing practices.

Perhaps the most curious influences came from overseas. Starting in the 1880s, a number of touring minstrel shows came over from the United States. Minstrel shows began after the Civil War when white entertainers in blackface parodied the music and dance of black entertainments from plantation days. Responding to this condescending rip-off of their traditions, many black entertainers formed minstrel troupes of their own (often in blackface!) in the late 1800s. The group that made the deepest impact in South Africa was McAdoo's Virginia Jubilee Singers, a black troupe modeled after the internationally successful Fisk Jubilee Singers. They first toured South Africa in 1890, and they proved enormously popular both with white audiences and with middle-class blacks who had great admiration for the accomplishments of Americans like George Washington Carver. Soon black South Africans formed similar troupes of their own, giving rise to a new style called *isikhunzi* (literally, "coon" style). The choral style associated with *isikhunzi* features four-part choral singing in a moderate to low range at a low intensity level (compared with *isicathamiya*, at least). Initially this music reflected the taste of the urban middle-class fans who first adopted this music, but as it traveled throughout the country, it soon assimilated features of rural styles as well.

These rural styles included *ngoma* dances and wedding songs. The vigorous steps and gestures associated with *ngoma* dances were especially popular with rural farmworkers. As in traditional Nguni dancing, the dancers accompanied themselves by singing. *Ngoma* songs tended to be simple, light unison songs. Much more complex were traditional wedding songs (*izingoma zomtshado*) that demonstrated the influence of four-part Western hymns. These developed especially in regions where traditional Zulu choral songs had first come in contact with the missions. Many of these songs were indigenous wedding songs adapted to a four-part Western style; they became known as *boloha* in the 1930s.

As was mentioned above, many rural black South Africans came to the new mining cities in the 1870s and 1880s. That number only increased after 1910, when more restrictive residential policies were enacted. Thus, urban musical styles also made significant contributions to the development of *isicathamiya*. Ragtime dancing, influenced by American ragtime, became popular in the 1910s and 1920s. Known as *ukureka*, this slower dance style quickly became associated with wedding songs in urban areas. American ragtime and jazz styles also influenced an urban piano music known as *marabi*. *Marabi* developed in the urban centers of the mining districts, and although it involved little improvisation, it captured much of ragtime's vitality. Much of its popularity stemmed from its merger of American and South African elements; it employed the chord voicings of traditional choral part songs and the I–IV–I$^6_4$–V *ostinato* pattern already common in South African choral music. One of the most popular attractions of the 1910s and 1920s was Reuben Caluza's Ohlange Choir. Mixing a mission-influenced choral sound with dance, action, and topical texts in the Zulu tongue, Caluza's group traveled to England around 1930.

All in all, the development of *isicathamiya* presents quite a bundle of varied threads. We see English styles influenced by South African music, and South African styles influenced by English music. We see South African styles influenced by American styles that were originally created by African Americans. Urban styles influenced rural music, and rural styles influenced urban music. This incredibly elaborate web of cross-fertilization created a musically rich environment that ultimately led to the birth of *isicathamiya*.

Some of the early *isicathamiya* ensembles came from Durban, an urban center on the Natal coast (in the former Zulu kingdom). The Crocodiles, likely the first group, emerged around 1914, and the Durban Evening Birds appeared by 1920. Gradually more groups were formed in Johannesburg as well, and by the 1930s *isicathamiya* had become one of the most popular new styles. At first these groups borrowed many songs from the repertories mentioned above, including *makwaya, isikhunzi,* and wedding songs. *Ukureka* dance steps and songs soon became associated with the entry procession of the singers at their performances. Out of these varied styles and this mix of music and dance, *isicathamiya* began to develop its own distinctive features.

"Mbube"

With their first recordings, Solomon Linda and the Evening Birds finally defined the distinctive features of *isicathamiya* style; they remained its most popular advocates until they disbanded in 1948. Lead singer Solomon Linda was born near Pomeroy in the Natal province, where he grew up herding cattle. He sang with a group called the Evening Birds, run by his uncle, but he soon left for Johannesburg to get a better job. In 1933 he formed his own version of the Evening Birds with his two employers and other friends from "back home."

Linda took the soprano part, and he was backed up by one alto (also male), one tenor, and three basses. Though all of the members came from rural South Africa, they always maintained a sophisticated urban manner—after all, they were in the big city now. Their music quickly caught on in Johannesburg, and in 1938 they began to wear uniforms at their performances, often striped suits. Linda got a new job in 1939 as a packer at the pressing plant for Gallo's, a South African record label. One of the talent scouts quickly caught wind of Linda's group and brought the Evening Birds into the studio for their first recording session. Their maiden release, "Mbube," based on a wedding song, was an instant hit, so popular that the name *mbube* became attached to the entire *isicathamiya* genre.

What made "Mbube" so revolutionary—and so popular? First, Solomon Linda was the first to use more than one singer on the bass line in such a small ensemble. Most *isikhunzi* musicians favored quartet singing, with one voice to a part. This strong emphasis on the lowest voice actually made it sound more like traditional Nguni polyphony, sure to appeal to a rural audience. Further, it used the I–IV–I$^6_4$–V *ostinato* pattern already common in much South African music, providing a link to Western-influenced genres popular with middle-class blacks. This pattern quickly became standard in *isicathamiya* music. In addition, they were the first group to adopt the uniforms mentioned above, and the sophistication of their dress carried over into the slow, smooth step movements that accompanied their singing. Finally, their Zulu-language texts dealt with real-life experiences, often criticizing or protesting current events.

Once Solomon Linda's Evening Birds discovered this successful formula, they were quickly imitated by many other groups. Just as in traditional Nguni choral singing, dance remained an important element, though *isicathamiya* dancing was always less vigorous than earlier *ngoma* dances. Most common was a dance style known as *isicathamiya* (from which the musical style took its name), in which a straight back and arms contrasted with active, elaborate motions of the feet. The Crocodiles were especially well known for this dance style. An interesting *mbube* variant featured extremely high *falsetto* lines, high-pitched yells, and choral shouts. During World War II these sounds reminded audiences of air-raid sounds, so they named it *mbombing*. Since *mbombing* came out of mission-choir traditions, these groups tended not to dance as they sang. Riding the popularity of the *mbube* style, groups frequently gathered to compete with each other, and Solomon Linda's group was a frequent winner. These competitions fostered camaraderie, creativity, and a large common repertoire—in addition to singing their own songs, groups had to perform specified contest pieces for each competition.

By 1940 the *mbube* style was well established; it changed little until the 1970s. More recently the style has broken away somewhat from the traditional *mbube* manner, and it is now referred to by the more generic term *isicathamiya*. These changes have not affected the style's popularity, however; it continues to be a vital, versatile form of musical expression in the hands of practitioners like Joseph Shabalala and Ladysmith Black Mambazo, today's leading *isicathamiya* ensemble.

"Anoku Gonda"

When you present "Anoku Gonda" to your class, begin with some background material. Feel free to use any of the ideas above, but at the very least point out the historical importance of *a cappella* singing in South Africa, outline characteristic features of *mbube* style, and point to the fascinating web of African, American, and European influences that led to the creation of *isicathamiya.* Since South Africa has often found its way into the news over the past twenty years, you may also want to touch on South African history. Make sure students have read Global Perspectives materials on textbook pages 422–24 and refer them to the *Listen* Guide on textbook page 424.

One further note before you begin. Call-and-response patterns were mentioned above as a feature of Nguni polyphony, and this same responsorial technique figures prominently in "Anoku Gonda." In fact, call and response constitutes a universal feature of African music, found in many nations across the continent. Scholars often cite call and response as one of the African retentions that figures prominently in black American music. The concept is simple enough; a soloist sings a phrase (the call) and other singers answer back (the response). The response may be a continuously repeated *ostinato,* while the more elaborate lead singer's part offers greater variety in both text and music. Many students can identify situations where they participated in call and response, whether they were singing hymns and gospel songs at church or joining in on an audience-participation song at a folk or rock concert. Some may remember the song "Amen" from Christian worship services, campfire singalongs, or the Whitney Houston movie *The Preacher's Wife.* The "Amen" refrain, sung over and over again, becomes the response to the lead singer's phrases, inserted between each "Amen."

Begin by picking out specific passages for comparison. Start with **a** at the very beginning. Note that it consists of two halves, an ascending *do-re-mi-do* pattern, followed by a slightly faster descending pattern. This choral declamation is nonmetrical, but it provides a basic framework for the contrasting sections that follow. Next play the **b** material. This sounds more nearly metric, but each phrase again includes the ascending/descending pattern we heard in **a.** Interestingly, this pattern continues through the end of the piece. Now play the metrical call-and-response pattern led by Solomon Linda (0:57–1:11). This section consists of a basic refrain that could be diagrammed as **c c d d.** Note that **c** sounds much like the first half of **a,** and **d** like **a**'s second half. When you play the second metrical call-and-response pattern, the one led by the basses (1:26–1:42), call attention to a similar structure, **e e f f.** Once again, **e** sounds much like the first half of **a,** and **f** like **a**'s second half. Throughout the piece we hear the same ascending/descending pattern established at the beginning; the rest of the piece simply provides successively more elaborate variations on that basic contour.

Once you have introduced these basic materials, play the entire song for your students. Display the *Listen* Guide from textbook page 424, play the music, and call attention to each event as it goes by. Note that the first call-and-response pattern (0:57–1:11) repeats once at 1:12; the second call-and-response pattern (1:26–1:42) repeats four more times, at 1:42, 1:58 (suddenly quieter here), 2:14, and 2:31. In the discussion that follows, ask students if they heard any typical features of Nguni polyphony or *isicathamiya.* The use of four parts, Western-influenced harmonies, male voices, and heavy doubling on the bass are probably the most identifiable features associated with *isicathamiya,* since this performance does not provide an example of the commonly used I–IV–I$^6_4$–V progression. Nguni traditions can also be heard in several of this work's features. The *a cappella* choral ensemble points to old traditions, as does the use of *glissando* on many pitches; note especially the downward slide on some bass notes in the bass-led call-and-response choruses. Further, the performance as a whole exhibits the Nguni tendency to go sharp during a performance. Of course, students won't catch this unless you show them. All you have to do is play to the end of the CD track and immediately jump back to the beginning; the difference is nearly a half step—not nearly the distance observed by David Rycroft in some Nguni songs he recorded.

We have looked at the complex web of influences that led to the creation of *isicathamiya*; of course, the story doesn't end there. Once defined, *mbube* music exerted tremendous influence on folk music in the United States, especially through performances of "Mbube" by folk musicians Pete Seeger and the Weavers. This song, variously known as "Wimoweh," "In the Jungle," "The Lion Sleeps Tonight," and so on, has been recorded nearly fifty times by as many musicians in the past forty years. And Paul Simon, a folk musician himself, brought a later version of *isicathamiya* into the spotlight when he featured Ladysmith Black Mambazo on his 1986 album *Graceland*. What a remarkable set of connections! African music travels to the United States. Transformed by the encounter, it comes back to Africa, where it merges with European, South African, and syncretic genres. This new fusion travels back to the United States, where it entertains and influences generations of listeners. Wouldn't you just love to find out what happens next? Keep your ears open, and we'll all find out together.

Additional Teaching Suggestions

ꙮ Lecture-Demonstration Ideas

1. Arrange for your class to attend a jazz band or concert band rehearsal. These bands are venerable American institutions (now—though it wasn't always so), and either experience provides insight into the inner workings of these ensembles. Further, in a jazz band rehearsal, students can see for themselves how much is written out in advance and how much is improvised. The opportunity to witness improvisational music making in a lab setting can be exciting.

2. Hold a hands-on jazz improvisation session in the keyboard lab. If you have taken your students to the lab throughout the term, they are ready for a challenge—and some fun. Start with a blues scale (a major scale in which *mi, sol,* and *ti* are often lowered a half step). Then introduce a basic blues progression; have them find chord tones and improvise melodic figures for each chord separately (I, IV^7, and V^7). Once students are comfortable with individual chords, play complete blues progression (you are the rhythm section) and ask students to try improvising melodic phrases. If your lab has headphones, students can all improvise simultaneously while you play, or students can take turns (trade fours) with their speakers on. Go slowly and keep it simple—don't ask them to play chords along with their melodies unless they are ready for it.

3. Leonard Bernstein provided a wonderful introduction to jazz on his *Omnibus* television series. You can play the old LP recording of the broadcast if your music library has it. If not, you can re-create his presentation from the transcript of "The World of Jazz" (with piano reductions of the musical examples) in Bernstein's *Joy of Music* (New York: Simon and Schuster, 1959, pp. 94–119).

4. Take your class on a galloping tour of the history of American popular song. The Smithsonian Institution offers a recorded anthology titled *American Popular Song: Six Decades of Songwriters and Singers*. The accompanying booklet provides concise but thorough information about important singers and songwriters. See Sound Recordings below for more information about this wonderful resource.

5. Take your students on a galloping historical survey of American musical theater. Play as many musical examples as you can (video recordings, if possible). Many resources are available. Gerald Bordman provides a chronology of the genre in *American Musical Theatre,* expanded edition (New York: Oxford University Press, 1986). A transcript of Leonard Bernstein's "American Musical Comedy" broadcast is included in *The Joy of Music* (New York: Simon and Schuster, 1959, pp. 152–79). For sound and video recordings of musicals, see Multimedia Resources below.

6. Invite to class a musician associated with various aspects of musical theater—singing, acting, or producing, for instance. Musicals differ from most other kinds of music making, and these musicians have often been involved in many aspects of production, not just performance. As a result, your guest can describe the whole range of activities required to bring a musical to the stage. These musicians are knowledgeable, they enjoy being in front of an audience, and they often tell good stories, too.

7. Introduce your students to Leonard Bernstein. Composer, conductor, performer, television personality, and author, Bernstein brought visibility and vitality to art music for many years. He shattered once and for all the notion that American musicians had to earn their credentials in Europe. Play musical examples that suggest the range of his work—*Prelude, Fugue and Riffs,* the *Jeremiah* Symphony, *Chichester Psalms,* and *Mass* work well. Bernstein's own writings provide good sources of information: look for *The Infinite Variety of Music* (New York: Plume Books, 1970), *The Joy of Music* (New York: Simon and Schuster, 1959), and *The Unanswered Question: Six Talks at Harvard* (Cambridge, Mass.: Harvard University Press, 1976). See Multimedia Resources below for suggested audio and video performances.

8. Introduce your students to the full range of Miles Davis's accomplishments in modern jazz. Use recorded examples to demonstrate the progression of Davis's style. Three albums stand out as touchstones in the evolution of important jazz styles: *The Complete Birth of the Cool* for cool jazz, *Kind of Blue* for modal improvisation, and *Bitches Brew* for jazz-rock fusion. For further information, consult Ian Carr's *Miles Davis: A Biography* (New York: William Morrow, 1982). See Sound Recordings below for suggested performances.

9. Invite a pop, rock, or jazz musician or arranger to class. These performers and composers have firsthand experience with commercial music making and often bring a healthy supply of anecdotes as well. Ask them to describe studio work, music production, and the problems of live performance, locally or on the road. If they can play or sing for your class, so much the better. Have students bring questions for your guest, and bring some of your own in case discussion flags.

10. Invite someone in the music business to class. These guests pursue careers in various fields, including sound engineering and production, music publishing and merchandising, and arts administration. They can discuss the wide range of musical careers available, as well as the day-to-day life of a working musician.

11. One of the fascinating relationships in the twentieth century was the friendship between Gershwin and Schoenberg. To the casual observer, they appeared to inhabit different worlds, but the two shared an interest in music, painting, and tennis—they even painted each other's portraits! Schoenberg often expressed his admiration for Gershwin (see Schoenberg's *Style and Idea,* Berkeley: University of California Press, 1975). Consult biographies of Schoenberg and Gershwin for further details.

12. Create a slide show for your study of the Yoruba region and South Africa. Your school's departments of art, foreign languages, geography, or anthropology may have images you can borrow. Pictures of artwork, architecture, musicians and musical instruments, the West African rainforest, the Transvaal, and the cities of Lagos and Johannesburg can help bring this material to life.

⁊ Class Discussion Ideas

1. *What roles do women play in jazz?* Like other musical institutions, jazz has historically been dominated by males. Nonetheless, women have been important as vocalists, instrumentalists, and composers throughout the history of jazz. For more information, consult Linda Dahl's *Stormy Weather: The Music and Lives of a Century of Jazzwomen* (New York: Pantheon Books, 1984) or the bibliography of women in jazz in Mark Gridley's *Jazz Styles: History and Analysis,* 3rd edition (Englewood Cliffs, N.J.: Prentice-Hall, 1988, p. 411).

2. *Is rap music?* Bring examples to class and ask students to identify characteristic uses of musical elements in rap. Since rap does not rely on traditional melodic relationships to give it shape and meaning, some students don't know how to listen to it analytically. This exercise helps students understand that they must stretch to understand some popular styles just as they had to stretch to understand avant-garde music. This question can also spark heated controversy—many listeners have already formed strong opinions about rap. To follow up on the discussion, play Herbie Hancock's serious yet playful response to this question, "The Melody," from his *Dis Is Da Drum* album.

3. *Is there a split between classical music and popular music? What are the differences?* Many genres of art music are commonly regarded as highbrow or elitist. *How do you perceive these differences? Can you think of any musicians you once respected who "sold out" to make a buck?* Even in commercial music, we have trouble deciding whether songs are commodities to be bought and sold or works of art that express important truths. These questions can begin a discussion of the place of music in contemporary culture.

4. *Should the government provide funding for the arts?* This question has been asked by many politicians in recent years; some students remember the uproar over Mapplethorpe's art or 2 Live Crew's music. This is a controversial question, but it can work well if you can relate current issues raised to past examples from the textbook—Beethoven's hard-earned artistic freedom, for instance.

5. *What does it mean to be an American composer?* For Virgil Thomson, it was enough to be both a composer and an American, but others have demanded more than that. Henry Cowell's *American Composers on American Music* (Ann Arbor, Mich.: Books on Demand, 1933) includes writings by many composers describing what it means to be an American composer. Read excerpts for your students and ask for their reactions.

6. *What do contemporary American composers say about their music?* After listening to the examples in the *Listen* recordings, read comments by the composers and ask for student reactions. Several books contain interviews with and articles by important composers, both Americans and others. Richard Dufallo's *Trackings* (New York: Oxford University Press, 1989) includes conversations with Crumb, Cage, Copland, Ligeti, and others; *Contemporary Composers on Contemporary Music* (New York: Holt, Rinehart, and Winston, 1967) by

Elliott Schwartz and Barney Childs is a collection of writings by Debussy, Stravinsky, Berg, Bartók, Shostakovich, Copland, Varèse, Cage, and others.

7. *What do jazz musicians say about themselves and their music?* Nat Hentoff's *Hear Me Talkin' to Ya* offers a collection of oral histories recorded by the author. Contributors include many of the earlier jazz musicians mentioned by the authors. Read excerpts along with appropriate musical examples and ask students for their reactions.

8. *How do you feel about the unprecedented fusion of cultures represented by "world-beat" and other recent popular musical styles? What will this mean for traditional music from cultures around the globe? Are these changes good or bad?* The following quotation from the work of anthropologist Claude Lévi-Strauss can help stimulate ideas.

> It is not enough to nurture local traditions and to save the past for a short period longer. It is diversity itself that must be saved; not the outward and visible form in which each period has clothed that diversity, and which can never be preserved beyond the period that gave it birth. We must therefore hearken for the stirrings of new life . . . ; we must also be prepared to view without surprise, repugnance or revolt whatever may strike us as strange in the many new forms of social expression. Tolerance is not a contemplative attitude. . . . It is a dynamic attitude, consisting in the anticipation, understanding and promotion of what is struggling into being.[7]

9. *What did the* Graceland *album mean to South African whites, South African blacks, and the rest of the world?* To prepare, read Louise Meintjes's excellent article on these complex questions.[8] Select some of her passages or her quotations by musicians involved to share with your class. This article makes it clear that the meeting of cultures is not always an easy process, and your students will benefit from wrestling with these issues.

♩ Listening Ideas

1. Take your class on a galloping tour of early American music. Find recordings of the composers and works identified in the first section of this chapter (textbook pages 391–95): Billings, Heinrich, Gottschalk, MacDowell, Beach, the "Boston School," Foster, Sousa, and spirituals, as well as other forms of African American music. Place each example in its context in American history. Some of this music is already familiar to your students. This exercise is useful in fleshing out the discussion in the textbook. You can easily extend this demonstration to include influences on early jazz, especially blues and ragtime, or to prepare a presentation on Ives, whose music quotes most of these styles. See Multimedia Resources below for suggested sound and video recordings.

2. Put jazz improvisation in historical context. Compare it with other forms of improvisation, especially Baroque continuo and ornamentation, Classical concerto

---

[7]Claude Lévi-Strauss, "Race and History," from *The Race Question in Modern Science.* Paris: UNESCO, 1956, p. 162. Quoted in David Rycroft, "Evidence of Stylistic Continuity in Zulu 'Town' Music," from *Essays for a Humanist: An Offering to Klaus Wachsmann.* New York: Town House Press, 1977, pp. 256–57.

[8]Louise Meintjes, "Paul Simon's *Graceland,* South Africa, and the Mediation of Musical Meaning." *Ethnomusicology* (winter 1990), pp. 37–73.

cadenzas, and chance music. Point out similarities and differences in each type. *Which elements are predetermined and which are improvised in each example?*

3. Compare Bernstein's fugue—"Cool" in *West Side Story*—with Beethoven's Grosse Fuge, Op. 133. Play Beethoven's slow introduction, especially mm. 1–30, and compare this with Bernstein's fugue subject (at 1:12, 1:33, 1:51, and 2:09). This exercise reveals Bernstein's sophistication in handling a "popular" genre. See Sound Recordings below for suggested performances.

4. Make a list of popular music categories and ask your students to bring to class their favorite recordings in one or more categories. Include rock (or several types of rock), rap, music videos, and any other category of your (and their) choice. Ask students to list musical features of each category as they listen to these examples in class. This exercise allows students to apply listening skills to the music they live with.

5. Take your class on a galloping tour of rock history. Flesh out the textbook's material on popular music since the 1950s and play examples of blues, early 1950s rhythm and blues, 1950s rock'n'roll, and later developments in rock (Motown, soul, the Beatles, folk rock, acid rock, heavy metal, punk, rap, and so on). Just as with jazz, the music of African Americans has had a decisive influence on popular music. The textbook mentions many songs, musicians, and bands for you to pick and choose from. See Multimedia Resources below for useful sound and video recordings.

6. Compare traditional Yoruba *bata* drumming with other musical styles. You can start by comparing *bata* and *dundun* ensembles from Nigeria or Benin. You can also bring in recordings of Brazilian *candomblé* or Cuban *santería* music, both derived from Yoruba musical and religious practices. Or you can play examples of popular Nigerian *juju* music to hear a modern transformation of the mother drum with support drums. See Sound Recordings below for recommended CDs.

7. Compare "Anoku Gonda" with other examples of *mbube* music. *Mbube Roots* provides an exceptional introduction to *mbube* recordings from 1932 to 1969. It includes Solomon Linda's classic recording of "Mbube," a classic example of the characteristic I–IV–I$^6_4$–V progression. Once you've played "Mbube" for your class, you really must compare it with more recent versions in many different styles (thanks to Chris Waterman of UCLA for this idea!). Under the name "Wimoweh" you can find recordings by Pete Seeger with the Weavers (this folk group popularized the song in the United States; studio and live versions available), the Kingston Trio (folk), Chet Atkins (country), and Ledernacken (German techno/punk). Under the name "The Lion Sleeps Tonight" look for the Tokens (1960s rock—the best-known version) and the Nylons (1980s *a cappella*). As "Mbube" it has been recorded by Miriam Makeba (South African pop) and Ladysmith Black Mambazo (*isicathamiya*—sixty years later!). These examples help students connect "Anoku Gonda" with music they probably already know, and they point to an incredibly complex web of cross-cultural influences. See Sound Recordings below for recommended CDs.

8. On textbook page 395 the authors ask, "What was the slaves' music like?" We can never know for sure, but the musicians of the Georgia Sea Islands, a region largely abandoned by white Americans after the Civil War, have kept this old traditional style alive ever since. Recordings made by the Lomax family from the 1930s to the 1960s preserve the shouts, spirituals, and work songs

that characterize this repertoire. Many of these recordings have been reissued in the *Georgia Sea Island Songs* CD issued by New World Records (see Sound Recordings below). It is especially fascinating to compare these songs with the similar *isicathamiya* tradition from South Africa.

9. Paul Simon borrows from the *isicathamiya* tradition in his *Graceland*, but he borrows from other African popular musics as well. Explore some of these styles with your class. The Ellipsis album *Africa: Never Stand Still* provides a fascinating collection of popular music from around Africa (see Sound Recordings below). Several specific examples serve well for comparison with *Graceland*. "Ngingenwe Emoyeni" by Ladysmith Black Mambazo offers many similarities to Simon and Shabalala's "Homeless." "Ndiri Bofu" by Oliver Mtukdzi of Zimbabwe offers interesting parallels to "Diamonds on the Soles of Her Shoes" starting at 0:59. Most direct of all is the comparison between Lulu Masilela's "Six Mabone" and Simon and Masilela's "Gumboots." Finally, the guitar timbre on the Soul Brothers' "Bayeza" closely matches the instrumental sonority in "I Know What I Know." In addition, both the Masilela and Soul Brothers songs represent another significant South African contemporary popular style, *mbaqanga*. This exercise can help students appreciate the diversity of contemporary African music.

10. Compare Ella Fitzgerald's jazz-and-pop inflected 1959 performance of "Who Cares?" (*Listen* DVD) with the original version from Gershwin's 1931 musical *Of Thee I Sing*. Several fascinating differences emerge from a comparison of the two, including singing styles, orchestration, and even tempo. Some differences can be attributed to the styles (Broadway versus jazz and popular music) and others to the time period (1931 versus 1959). It is also interesting to reflect on the circumstances of Fitzgerald's collaboration with arranger Nelson Riddle (who also worked with Sinatra) and this relatively "straight" performance by the queen of scat singing. It is also instructive to note Gershwin's importance to later jazz and popular music. His most popular songs became standards, at the core of the jazz repertory for decades after his death. See Sound Recordings below for suggested CDs.

11. Explore the role of "covers" in 1950s rock'n'roll. "Covering" is not necessarily a bad thing—black and white musicians perform ("cover") each others' songs all the time. Not so long ago Whitney Houston had a bigger hit with "I Will Always Love You" than did its composer, Dolly Parton. But in the 1950s it was assumed by many that "race records" were not appropriate for young white listeners. In this environment, many white "teen idols" (Pat Boone and Paul Anka, for instance) made their careers by recording sanitized versions of rhythm and blues hits. Even Elvis borrowed much of his material from black artists, but he made few attempts to "clean up" the originals (much to the horror of middle-class white parents), such was his respect for rhythm and blues musicians. For a lively discussion, play and compare cover versions with the original recordings. Good examples include Pat Boone and Wynonie Harris on "Good Rockin' Tonight"; Boone and Little Richard on "Tutti Frutti"; Elvis and Arthur Crudup on "Love Me Tender"; or Elvis and "Big Mama" Thornton on "Hound Dog." (And if you want students to find out why those white parents were so terrified, listen for Wynonie Harris's "definition" of rock'n'roll in "All She Wants to Do Is Rock.") See Multimedia Resources below for suggested recordings.

12. Take your class on a treasure hunt. Ask your students to find examples of African influence in contemporary music. Either have your students bring

recordings to class or play examples of jazz or popular music and ask students to pick out features that might exhibit African influence. Possible examples include Brian Eno and David Byrne's *My Life in the Bush of Ghosts,* Joni Mitchell's "Jungle Line" from *The Hissing of Summer Lawns,* Paul Simon's *Graceland* (see Listening Idea 9 above) or *Rhythm of the Saints* (Africa by way of Brazil), Herbie Hancock's "Watermelon Man" from *Head Hunters* or "Juju" from *Dis Is Da Drum,* the Bud Powell Trio's performance of "A Night in Tunisia," and countless others—even Disney's *The Lion King!* See Multimedia Resources below for suggested recordings.

13. Explore jazz-rock fusion with your students. In *Bitches Brew,* Miles Davis fuses rock with a very free jazz that not all students will enjoy, but later fusions explore many unique combinations that proved enormously popular in the 1970s and beyond. Many examples can serve well. Try the Mahavishnu Orchestra's fusion with high-decibel hard rock on *Birds of Fire* ("Birds of Fire"); Herbie Hancock's fusion with funk on *Head Hunters* ("Chameleon"); Chick Corea's soft, Latin-tinged fusion on *Light as a Feather* ("Spain"); Weather Report's eminently danceable pop fusion on *Heavy Weather* ("Birdland"); or Herbie Hancock's fusion with hip-hop and world-beat on *Dis Is Da Drum* ("Dis Is Da Drum"). See Multimedia Resources below for suggested recordings.

♪ Further Listening Examples

GOTTSCHALK *Bamboula*

Use this example to flesh out your presentation of early American music. The first significant American composer of art music was Louis Moreau Gottschalk (1829–1869). Born in New Orleans, he was the son of an Englishman and a Creole (colonial French) woman. Gottschalk's talent as a pianist and composer showed itself early; at the age of thirteen he was sent to Paris to study. He quickly came to the attention of composers such as Berlioz and established himself as one of Europe's most popular performers while still a teenager. Gottschalk never forgot his roots, though; he was first and foremost a child of the tropics. The New Orleans of Gottschalk's youth was undoubtedly the most colorful, exotic city within the borders of the United States. It was a combination of colonial Spanish, French, Caribbean, Latin, and African cultures. (This same racial and ethnic diversity would influence the birth of jazz sixty years later.) The titles and rhythmic energy of much of Gottschalk's music reflect the influences of the Caribbean-African music he heard as a child living just a few blocks away from Congo Square (a plaza in New Orleans where blacks gathered on Sundays). Such titles include *Bamboula, Danse de Nègres, Le Bananier, Chanson Nègre, La Savane, Ballade Creole, The Banjo, American Sketch, La Gallina, Dance Cubaine, Souvenir de Porto Rico,* and *Souvenir de la Havane.*

Bamboula was one of Gottschalk's first major compositions, and it remains his most famous. It could pass for sophisticated ragtime except for the fact that it was composed fifty-four years before the term *ragtime* was ever applied to a musical genre. Like many of Gottschalk's compositions, *Bamboula* is a stylized dance: The *bamboula* was a frantic, frenzied African dance that he reportedly witnessed numerous times in Congo Square.

Bamboula employs a sort of rondo form that can be diagrammed as follows:

Sections:	A	B	A	B	A'	C	A''	D	C'	B'	A'''
Measure nos.:	1	65	84	116	136	147	224	232	252	317	336

What makes this piece (and much of Gottschalk's music) so interesting is not its form but the way Gottschalk blends European tonal language and pianistic technique with the rhythmic intensity of African-Caribbean music.

Play *Bamboula* for the class. Ask students to note the syncopations and energy that characterize the rhythm of the piece. If "American" music must account for the ethnic diversity and rhythmic energy of American society, then this piece is indeed American. Gottschalk's music—a strange but wonderful blend of European, Caribbean, and African elements—constitutes a significant step in the development of American art music.

GERSHWIN *Rhapsody in Blue*

George Gershwin wrote *Rhapsody in Blue* for the Paul Whiteman Orchestra, a famous dance band of the 1920s. Gershwin did not orchestrate the original version of *Rhapsody in Blue*; that was left to Whiteman's arranger, Ferde Grofe. The work has subsequently been arranged for orchestra and any number of other combinations, including accordion ensemble and solo xylophone. *Rhapsody in Blue* fixes an entire age—the Jazz Age—in our ears. The "roaring twenties" was the post–World War I, pre-Depression era during which the United States came into its own as a country with a unique musical heritage. That heritage was jazz, a synthesis of African and Caribbean rhythms with European pitch structures and instruments.

Rhapsody in Blue consists of two large sections, each divided into various melodic episodes. As the title implies, the piece follows no particular musical form but rather the intuition of the composer. Play the first half (approximately eight minutes). Ask the class to reflect on the "mood" of this music—youthful, brash, jazzy, and brittle. That this music still sounds contemporary to our ears indicates that the spirit of energy and exuberance that produced it in the 1920s is still part of our American culture today.

GERSHWIN **Concerto in F**

When you present the third-movement rondo of Gershwin's Concerto in F for piano and orchestra, prepare recorded excerpts that let you follow the same procedure as with any rondo form.

1. Play the rondo theme, **A,** several times until students can recognize it readily. Point out the essentially rhythmic nature of this jazzy, syncopated theme.

2. Play the contrasting episodes, **B, C, D,** and **E,** once or twice each. Identify the character of these sections as the class listens.

3. Play the coda.

Just as you did with Prelude No. 1, point out Gershwin's use of jazz elements, especially syncopation, blue notes, muted trumpets, and jazz harmonies. In this work Gershwin succeeded in his ambition to unite jazz elements with the classical concerto genre.

Play the whole movement. Display the Additional Listening Chart for this work (see Appendix I) and point out each section as it goes by, or write the large divisions of the movement on the board and point these out instead.

Multimedia Resources

ꝰ Further Listening Charts and Texts

See Appendix I for Additional Listening Charts for these works; see Further Listening Examples above for teaching suggestions.

Gershwin, Piano Concerto in F, III

ꝰ Sound Recordings

Significant Recording Labels

New World Records (701 Seventh Ave., New York, N.Y. 10036). This record label was created at the time of the U.S. bicentennial to record hitherto unavailable works by American composers and performing musicians. Recordings document many important types of American music, past and present, including the evolution of various jazz styles and rock'n'roll; music of Heinrich, Paine, and other eighteenth-century Romantic composers; and songs of the Georgia Sea Islands (one of the most authentic recordings we have of the music of black American slaves). These recordings are a treasure trove of Americana—hard to find, but worth the effort.

Smithsonian Folkways Recordings (600 Maryland Ave. SW, Suite 2001, Washington, DC 20024). Folkways Recordings built up a huge inventory of American and ethnic music under its founder, Moses Asch. In 1987, the Smithsonian took over the Folkways archive and has begun to release new recordings as well as reissue selected titles in CD format. In addition, the label will custom-produce a CD of *any* recording in the archive on a special-order basis (allow 1-2 weeks). A gold mine if you are willing to do some digging. Search online at www.folkways.si.edu.

African Music

Africa: Never Stand Still. Ellipsis Arts CD3300 (CD). Fascinating compilation of contemporary popular music from many African nations, including Nigeria, South Africa, Sudan, and Zaire. All demonstrate Western influences, but all show the influence of indigenous styles and instruments as well. (Currently out of print, but you can buy a used copy.) Try this recording if you use Listening Idea 9 above.

Georgia Sea Island Songs. Georgia Sea Island Singers. New World Records 80278-2 (CD). A treasure from the New World discography. Mostly isolated from white influence after the Civil War, musicians on the sea islands have kept nineteenth-century (and earlier?) musical traditions alive. These spirituals, work songs, and dances are as close as any recording can hope to come to the music making of African American slaves before the Civil War. Also available on Rounder as Vols. 12 and 13 of their *Southern Journey* series. Highly recommended if you use Listening Idea 1 or 8 above.

Juju Music. King Sunny Adé and His African Beats. Mango 162-539 712-2 (CD). Nigerian *juju* music performed by one of its leading proponents. Fascinating mix of instruments and styles from Western and Yoruba traditions. Liner notes are "lite" but helpful—in English. Try this recording if you use Listening Idea 6 above.

Ladysmith Black Mambazo, *Shaka Zulu*. Warner Brothers 9 2558-2 (CD). Paul Simon's *Graceland* introduced many Western listeners to this ensemble's *isicathamiya* music for the first time. Obviously they liked what they heard; this album, released one year after *Graceland*, sold far more copies than any of their previous recordings. Try this recording if you use Listening Idea 7 or 9 above.

Ladysmith Black Mambazo, *The Ultimate Collection*. PolyGram 55666822 (CD). Recent release contains most of this *isicathamiya* ensemble's biggest hits. If you can buy only one of their recordings, this makes a good choice. Includes their recording of "Mbube," the song that started the *isicathamiya* movement sixty years earlier. Try this recording for further examples of this style or if you use Listening Idea 7 or 9 above.

Makeba, Miriam. *Africa*. Novus Series '70 3155 (CD). Compilation of important recordings made from 1960 to 1966 by this major South African artist, including her 1960 recording of "Mbube." Try this recording if you use Listening Idea 7 above.

Mbube Roots: Zulu Choral Music from South Africa, 1930s–1960s. Rounder CD 5025 (CD). Collection documents the history of *isicathamiya* in South Africa, up through the earliest recordings of Ladysmith Black Mambazo. Includes Solomon Linda's "Mbube." Use this recording if you try Listening Idea 7 above.

Sabar: The Soul of Senegal. Omar Thiam and Jam Bugum ensemble. White Cliffs Media WCM 9915 (CD). Sabar drumming of the Serer peoples of Senegal. Try this recording if you want to look at another excellent example of West African drumming. Available from www.worldmusicstore.com.

Sacred Rhythms of Cuban Santería. Smithsonian Folkways SF 40419 (CD). Collection of music from Yoruba religious traditions as transplanted to Cuba. *Bata* drums continue to be used, and this music is used in worship of many of the gods from the Yoruba tradition. Excellent liner notes in English and Spanish. Use this recording if you try Listening Idea 6 above.

Singing in an Open Space: Zulu Rhythm and Harmony, 1962–1982. Rounder CD 5027 (CD). Collection of Zulu popular music from recent decades. Useful for a look at more recent South African popular music in the wake of the *mbube* tradition. Detailed liner notes in English. Try this recording if you use Listening Idea 9 above.

The Yoruba/Dahomean Collection: Orishas across the Ocean. Library of Congress Endangered Music Project, Ryko RCD 10405 (CD). Collection of Yoruba sacred music as transplanted to Brazil, Haiti, Cuba, and Trinidad. Excellent liner notes. Try this recording if you use Listening Idea 6 above.

Yoruba Drums from Benin, West Africa. Smithsonian Folkways SF 40440 (CD). Excellent collection of *bata* and *dundun* ensemble music, including "Ako" from the *Listen* recorded set. Superb liner notes contain background information, detailed analysis, and even some transcriptions. Use this recording if you try Listening Idea 6 above.

American Music History—The Cultivated Tradition

Beach, *Symphony in E Minor, "Gaelic Symphony."* Detroit Symphony. Chandos CHAN 8958 (CD). Amy Beach blends nineteenth-century Romanticism with her own personal style in this work; conducted by Neeme Järvi. Try this recording if you use Listening Idea 1 above.

Beethoven, *The Late String Quartets*. Lindsay Quartet. ASV DCS403 (CD). Perhaps the finest modern recordings of Beethoven's late quartets and Grosse Fuge. Try this recording if you use Listening Idea 3 above.

Bernstein, *Chichester Psalms/Symphonies Nos. 1 and 2*. Israel Philharmonic Orchestra. Deutsche Grammophon 028945-77572-2 (CD). Excellent recordings of several of Bernstein's most important works; conducted by the composer. Fascinating mixture of influences, including Neoclassicism, jazz, and Copland. Recommended if you use Lecture-Demonstration Idea 7 above.

Bernstein, *Mass*. Alan Titus with Norman Scribner Choir and Berkshire Boys' Choir. Sony Classical (Bernstein Century Edition) SM2K 63089 (CD). Reissue of the first recording of this eclectic, theatrical work from 1971; conducted by the composer. Some scenes succeed brilliantly while others fall flat. Try this recording if you use Lecture-Demonstration Idea 7 above.

Billings, et al., *Trav'ling Home: American Spirituals 1770–1870*. Boston Camerata. Erato 12711 (CD). Collection of traditional American hymnody by Billings, Ingalls, and others contains some fuguing tunes; conducted by Joel Cohen. Try this recording if you use Listening Idea 1 above.

Black Composers Series. Missoula, Mont.: College Music Society (LP). Nine LPs of musical works by many significant African composers who lived and worked in Western cultures, including T. J. Anderson, David Baker, Roque Cordero, Jose Mauricio Nunes Garcia, Adolphus Hailstork, Talib Rasul Hakim, Ulysses Kay, the Chevalier de Saint-Georges, Hale Smith, Fela Sowande, William Grant Still, George Walker, Jose White, and Olly Wilson. An accompanying booklet provides helpful information about each composer and musical work.

Foster, *Stephen Foster Songs*, Vol. 1. Jan DeGaetani, Gilbert Kalish, and others. Elektra/Nonesuch 79158-2 (CD). Delightful performances of nineteenth-century American songs. Try this recording if you use Listening Idea 1 above.

Gottschalk, *The Banjo*. Eugene List. Vanguard Classics OVC 4050 (CD). List reintroduced this repertory to the concert going public in the 1960s, and his recordings remain riveting. This CD includes many of Gottschalk's best-known works for solo piano. Try this recording if you use Listening Idea 1 or suggestions for *Bamboula* in Further Listening Examples above.

Heinrich, *The Ornithological Combat of Kings*. Syracuse Symphony. New World Recordings 80208-2 (CD). Fascinating work by an eccentric early nineteenth-century American composer paired with Gottschalk's colorful *Night in the Tropics*, arranged for two pianos. Try this recording if you use Listening Idea 1 above.

MacDowell, Piano Concertos 1 and 2. Donna Amato and the London Philharmonic. Olympia OCD 353 (CD). Superb recordings demonstrate MacDowell's full-blown Romantic piano writing; conducted by Paul Freeman. Try this CD if you use Listening Idea 1 above.

New World Jazz. New World Symphony. RCA Red Seal 09026-68798-2 (CD). Excellent collection of jazz-influenced works by classical composers; conducted by Michael Tilson Thomas. Includes Bernstein's *Prelude, Fugue, and Riffs*; Gershwin's *Rhapsody in Blue*; and other classic works by Stravinsky, Adams, Milhaud, Hindemith, and Antheil. Try this recording if you use Lecture-Demonstration Idea 7 or suggestions for Gershwin's *Rhapsody in Blue* from Further Listening Examples above.

Sousa, *"Under the Double Eagle": The Marches of John Philip Sousa*. Sousa's Band. Pearl GEMM CD 9249 (CD—mono). Fascinating collection includes the complete electrical recordings and many acoustical recordings from 1928 to 1930; conducted by Sousa and other conductors who worked with him. Try this recording if you use Listening Idea 1 above.

Blues, Ragtime, Jazz, and Gospel

Armstrong, Louis. *Portrait of the Artist as a Young Man: 1923–1934*. Columbia/Legacy 85670 (CD). Four-CD set surveys the pivotal years in the development of Armstrong's style; they also demonstrate Armstrong's extraordinary influence on jazz musicians everywhere in the transition from early jazz to the swing era. Try this recording if you use Listening Idea 1 or 2 above.

Big Band Jazz: From the Beginnings to the Fifties. Smithsonian Recordings RD 030 (CD). Outstanding historical anthology of big band jazz from the 1920s to the 1950s. Won two Grammys; comes with excellent fifty-two-page booklet. Includes music of Louis Armstrong, Fletcher Henderson, Benny Goodman, Count Basie, Duke Ellington, Woody Herman, Dizzy Gillespie, Stan Kenton, and others. (Currently out of print.)

Corea, Chick, and Return to Forever. *Light as a Feather*. Verve 827 148 (CD). 1973 album features Spanish-tinged jazz-rock fusion with a soft pop sound. Use this recording if you try Listening Idea 13 above.

Davis, Miles. *Bitches Brew*. Columbia/Legacy 65744 (CD). A landmark in the development of jazz-rock fusion. Performers included many who went on to form their own fusion bands: Wayne Shorter, Joe Zawinul, Chick Corea, John McLaughlin, and others. Also available in *Complete Bitches Brew*, a four-disc set that adds previously unreleased studio takes and other material recorded around the same time. Use this recording to present more of *Bitches Brew* (especially Davis's use of the Echoplex at the beginning) or if you try Lecture-Demonstration Idea 8 above.

Davis, Miles. *The Complete Birth of the Cool*. Capitol Jazz 94550 (CD). Classic recordings from 1949 and 1950 document early stages in the development of cool jazz. In addition to the nonet's studio takes, this recent release also includes thirteen tracks recorded live at the Royal Roost. Use this recording if you try Lecture-Demonstration Idea 8 above.

Davis, Miles. *Kind of Blue*. Columbia/Legacy 64935 (CD). One of the greatest jazz albums ever recorded; contains lyric, understated performances by an all-star ensemble that included John Coltrane, Julian Adderley, Bill Evans, Paul Chambers, and James Cobb. The first jazz album to use mode-based improvisation throughout. Recent remastered release adds an alternate take of *Flamenco Sketches*. Use this recording if you try Lecture-Demonstration Idea 8 above.

Ellington, *The Blanton-Webster Band*. RCA/Bluebird 5659-2-RB (CD). Some of the finest recordings Ellington ever made, from 1940 to 1942, when bassist Jimmy Blanton and tenor sax Ben Webster played with Duke. Excellent liner notes. Use this recording for a closer look at Ellington's music or if you use Listening Idea 2 above.

Fitzgerald, *Ella Fitzgerald Sings the George and Ira Gershwin Songbook*. Verve 314 539 759-2 (CD). Four-CD set features Ella Fitzgerald singing Gershwin's songs to the accompaniment of big-band arrangements by Nelson Riddle. Try this recording to explore more examples of Gershwin's art or if you use Listening Idea 10 above.

The Gospel Sound. Columbia/Legacy C2K 57160 (CD). Historical anthology of gospel classics by Rev. J. M. Gates, the Golden Gate Jubilee Quartet, the Angelic Gospel Singers, the Dixie Hummingbirds, Mahalia Jackson, the Abyssinian Baptist Gospel Choir, and others. Try this recording if you want to explore gospel music with your class.

Hancock, Herbie. *Dis Is Da Drum.* Mercury 522 681 (CD). Important 1995 jazz fusion album blends jazz with both hip-hop and world beat. Try this recording if you use Class Discussion Idea 2 or Listening Idea 12 or 13 above.

Hancock, Herbie. *Head Hunters.* Columbia/Legacy 65123 (CD). Significant 1974 jazz-rock fusion album melds jazz with funk, as in the Sly-inspired "Chameleon." Use this recording if you try Listening Idea 12 or 13 above.

Joplin, *Scott Joplin (Original Piano Rolls Played by the Composer).* Dejavu Retro Gold Collection R2CD 40-13 (CD). Recordings of twenty rags by the most important ragtime composer, with twenty other historic recordings (1901–1921) featuring early ragtime and jazz ensembles. Try this recording if you use Listening Idea 1 above.

Mahavishnu Orchestra. *Birds of Fire.* Columbia/Legacy 66081 (CD). 1973 John McLaughlin album features jazz-rock fusion with a high-decibel, hard-rock edge. Use this recording if you try Listening Idea 5 or 13 above.

Parker, Charlie. *Charlie Parker Memorial,* Vol. 1, Savoy SV-0101; *The Immortal Charlie Parker,* Savoy SV-0102; *Charlie Parker Memorial,* Vol. 2, Savoy SV-0103; *The Genius of Charlie Parker,* Savoy SV-0104 (CD). These four recordings offer perhaps the finest collection of Parker's music currently available. Recorded between 1945 and 1948, they document his work with Miles Davis, Dizzy Gillespie, Bud Powell, Max Roach, John Lewis, and others. Use these recordings if you try Lecture-Demonstration Idea 8 or Listening Idea 2 above.

The Smithsonian Collection of Classic Jazz. Smithsonian Recordings RD 033 (CD). The best single-volume, comprehensive historical jazz anthology available anywhere. Comes with excellent notes in a 120-page booklet. If you don't own it—get it! (Currently out of print, but you can buy a used copy.) Includes classic recordings by Louis Armstrong, Duke Ellington, Charlie Parker, Miles Davis, Bud Powell, and many others. Use this recording if you try Lecture-Demonstration Idea 8 or Listening Idea 2 or 12 above.

Wallace, *Sippie Wallace: Complete Recorded Works in Chronological Order,* Vol. 1, 1923–1925. Document Records DOCD-5399 (CD). The earliest recordings by this important blues singer, in collaboration with early jazz greats Louis Armstrong, Clarence Williams, Sidney Bechet, King Oliver, and others. Try this recording if you use Listening Idea 1 or 5.

Weather Report. *Heavy Weather.* Columbia/Legacy 65108 (CD). Possibly the most influential and successful jazz-rock fusion album ever released. With synth-based sounds and Latin percussion, its tracks range from colorful and impressionistic to infectious and danceable. Use this recording if you try Listening Idea 13 above.

Gershwin and Musical Theater

American Musical Theater: Shows, Songs, and Stars. Smithsonian Recordings. Historical anthology contains recordings of Broadway productions from the turn of the century (*The Fortune Teller*) to 1964 (*Fiddler on the Roof*).

(Currently out of print.) Try this recording if you use Lecture-Demonstration Idea 5 or Listening Idea 3 above.

Bernstein, *West Side Story*. Kiri Te Kanawa and José Carreras. Deutsche Grammophon 457 199-2 (CD). Bernstein's final recording of his classic musical. Operatic voices jar a bit at first, but the results are strikingly beautiful. Try this recording to sample more of *West Side Story* with your class or if you use Lecture-Demonstration Idea 7 above.

Gershwin, *Fascinating Rhythm—The Complete Music for Solo Piano by George Gershwin*. Angela Brownridge. Hyperion Helios CDH55006 (CD). Excellent performances of everything Gershwin wrote, including early ragtime-influenced materials and the three Preludes for Piano. Try this recording to present all three preludes or if you use Listening Idea 1 above.

Gershwin, *Of Thee I Sing/Let'em Eat Cake*. CBS M2K 42522 (CD). Bracing, entertaining performances of two of Gershwin's Broadway musicals, by far the best available on CD. Singers included Maureen McGovern, Larry Kert, and Jack Gilford; conducted by Michael Tilson Thomas. Use this recording to explore another side of Gershwin's art or if you use Listening Idea 10 above.

Gershwin, *Rhapsody in Blue/American in Paris/Concerto in F/Porgy and Bess*. Aalborg Symphony. Virgin Classics Special Import VIR 562056 (CD). Sparkling performances of Gershwin's best-known works for piano and orchestra featuring Wayne Marshall as conductor and pianist. Try this recording of *Rhapsody in Blue* or Concerto in F if you use Listening Idea 1 or suggestions for these works in Further Listening Examples above.

Rock, Pop, and Folk Music

American Popular Song: Six Decades of Songwriters and Singers. Smithsonian Recordings (CD). Historical anthology of popular song; includes music of Berlin, Gershwin, Kern, Porter, Rodgers, and others. (Currently out of print.) Try this recording if you use Lecture-Demonstration Idea 4 above.

Amos, Tori. *Little Earthquakes*. Atlantic 7 82358-2 (CD). This 1992 album was the first solo recording by this important contemporary artist. More recent albums include *From the Choirgirl Hotel* (1998) and *To Venus and Back* (1999). Try these recordings to supplement the textbook's discussion of the role of singer-songwriters in American pop music or if you use Listening Idea 5 above.

Atkins, Chet. *My Favorite Guitars/It's a Guitar World*. One Way Records OW 35121 (CD). Rerelease of two albums from the 1960s by this major country guitarist. Includes an interesting instrumental recording of "Wimoweh." Try this recording if you use Listening Idea 5 or 7 above.

Baez, Joan. *The First Ten Years*. Vanguard VCD 6560/1 (CD). This 1970 album offers a retrospective collection of performances by this important folk singer. Try this recording to supplement the textbook's discussion of the role of singer-songwriters in American pop music or if you use Listening Idea 5 above.

The Beach Boys. *The Greatest Hits: 20 Good Vibrations*. Capitol/EMI 21860 (CD). Collection of twenty hits by the group that exemplifies the 1960s "surfing" sound. Includes the two songs mentioned in *Listen*, "I Get Around" and "Good Vibrations." Try this recording if you use Listening Idea 5 above.

The Beatles, *Abbey Road*. Capitol/EMI 46446 (CD). The Beatles' final album (recorded after *Let It Be*, though released earlier) is a classic that offers little to suggest the tensions that tore the band apart. *Listen* mentions "Maxwell's Silver Hammer," but this CD contains many other great songs. "And in the end, the love you take is equal to the love you make." Try this recording if you use Listening Idea 5 above.

The Beatles, *The Beatles (The White Album)*. Capitol/EMI 46443 (CD). The two-disc set that signaled a return to basic rock . . . and dispersion in four individual directions. This incredibly diverse, powerful album contains songs mentioned in *Listen,* including "Blackbird" and an alternate version of "Revolution." Try this recording if you use Listening Idea 5 above.

The Beatles Live at the BBC. Capitol Records (Apple) CDP 7243 8 31796 2 6 (CD—mono). Recordings from 1962 to 1965 document the early Beatles' heavy reliance on American rhythm and blues as well as rock'n'roll. Try this recording if you use Listening Idea 5 or 11 above.

The Beatles: 1962–1966. Capitol/EMI 97036 (CD). Chock-full of classic Beatles hits, the "Red Anthology" contains several songs mentioned in *Listen,* including "She Loves You," "Help!" and "Yesterday." Try this recording if you use Listening Idea 5 above.

The Beatles: 1967–1970. Capitol/EMI 97039 (CD). Chock-full of classic Beatles hits, the "Blue Anthology" contains several songs mentioned in *Listen,* including "Hey, Jude," "A Day in the Life," "Strawberry Fields," and "Revolution." Try this recording if you use Listening Idea 5 above.

The Beatles, *Sgt. Pepper's Lonely Hearts Club Band.* EMI Records (Apple) CDP 7 46442 2 (CD). Perhaps the Beatles' most famous album. With *Sgt. Pepper,* audiences began to view rock albums as a total artistic statement—a song cycle, if you will. Full of effects that could only be achieved in the recording studio, it includes several songs associated with mid-1960s "psychedelic" rock. *Listen* mentions "When I'm 64" and "A Day in the Life." Try this recording if you use Listening Idea 5 above.

The Beatles, *With the Beatles.* Capitol/EMI 46436 (CD). This early album contains several "cover" versions of U.S. hit songs from 1950s rock'n'roll and Motown traditions, including Chuck Berry's "Roll Over, Beethoven," Barrett Strong's "Money," "Please Mister Postman" by the Marvelettes, and "Devil in His Heart" by the Donays. Try this recording if you use Listening Idea 5 or 11 above.

Berry, Chuck. *His Best,* Vol. 1. Chess 9371 (CD). 50th anniversary rerelease of rock'n'roll classics by the man who defined the sound of rock guitar in the 1950s. Try this recording if you use Listening Idea 5 or 11 above.

Boone, Pat. *Pat's 40 Big Ones.* Connoisseur Collection SDVSOPCD 328 (CD). Collection includes "covers" of several hits by black artists, including "Tutti Frutti" and "Good Rockin' Tonight." Try this recording if you use Listening Idea 5 or 11 above.

Brown, James. *20 All-Time Greatest Hits.* Polydor 314 511 326-2 (CD). Known as "Soul Brother Number One," Brown oversaw the transition from 1960s soul to 1970s funk. This historical sampler traces Brown's music from about 1956 to 1974, including recordings of "I Got You (I Feel Good)," "Cold Sweat, Pt. 1," "Say It Loud (I'm Black and I'm Proud)," "Mother Popcorn, Pt. 1," "Super Bad," and others. Try this recording if you use Listening Idea 5 above.

Costello, Elvis. *My Aim Is True.* Warner Archives 74285 (CD). Remastered rerelease of Costello's 1977 Columbia debut recording with alternate takes and other goodies. Important, provocative songs in a punk idiom. Try this recording to supplement the textbook's discussion of the role of singer-songwriters in American pop music or if you use Listening Idea 5 above.

Cream, *Disraeli Gears*. Polydor 31453 1811-2 (CD). Classic 1967 album by Eric Clapton's group pioneers the new hard-rock sound, virtuoso guitar technique, and electronic effects. Includes "Sunshine of Your Love" (mentioned in *Listen*). Try this recording if you use Listening Idea 5 above.

Crudup, Arthur. *That's All Right, Mama*. RCA Bluebird 61043-2 (CD). Recordings from 1941 to 1954 by the artist whose "electrified" country blues made a deep impression on the young Elvis Presley. Try his recording of "That's All Right, Mama" if you use Listening Idea 5 or 11 above.

Drifters. *The Very Best of the Drifters*. Rhino Records R2 71211 (CD). Best-of collection features 1959–1964 hits by this doo-wop group, including "Under the Boardwalk" (mentioned in *Listen*). Try this recording if you use Listening Idea 5 above.

Dylan, Bob. *Bob Dylan's Greatest Hits*. Columbia CK 65975 (CD). This 1967 retrospective album offers a sampling of early hit songs by this important folk-rock artist, including "Blowin' in the Wind" and "The Times They Are A-Changin'." Try this recording to supplement the textbook's discussion of the role of singer-songwriters in American pop music or if you use Listening Idea 5 above.

Dylan, Bob. *Bob Dylan Live 1966—The Royal Albert Hall Concert* (*The Bootleg Series,* Vol. 4). Columbia Legacy C2K 65759 (CD). This CD captures a fascinating moment from Dylan's career. This 1966 tour was the first time Dylan had taken his new "electric" sound on the road. The first set is all acoustic, and you can hear folk purists in the audience boo when Dylan brings out electric instruments for the second set! Try this recording to supplement the textbook's discussion of the role of singer-songwriters in American pop music or if you use Listening Idea 5 above.

Eno, Brian, and David Byrne. *My Life in the Bush of Ghosts*. Warner Brothers 45374 (CD). With this album, these two artists led the way in developing the "world-beat" sound. This album uses "found sounds" and rhythms to create a richly layered sonic tapestry, a funky electronica version of the interlocking *ostinato*s found in many African traditions. The sampled sounds used as raw material come from many nations, and both Eno and Byrne acknowledge a strong African influence on this album. Try this recording if you use Listening Idea 12 above.

Franklin, Aretha. *30 Greatest Hits*. Rhino 81668 (CD). Collection of songs by the premiere female soul singer of the 1960s and one of the most remarkable voices in twentieth-century popular music. Includes "Respect," mentioned in *Listen,* as well as "(You Make Me Feel Like) a Natural Woman" and "Chain of Fools." Try this recording if you use Listening Idea 5 above.

From the Vaults: Decca Country Classics 1934–1973. MCA MCAD3-11069 (CD). Three-CD anthology provides a fascinating look at the development of country music. Though limited to recordings on the Decca label, this collection nonetheless features music of country greats such as the Carter Family, Tex Ritter, Sons of the Pioneers, Ernest Tubb, Bill Monroe and His Blue Grass Boys, Brenda Lee, Patsy Cline, Loretta Lynn, and Conway Twitty. (Currently out of print.) Try this recording to acquaint your students with country music traditions.

Funkadelic. Westbound Records WBCD-2000 (CD). George Clinton album (1971) makes clear the unmistakable influence of acid rock on early funk. Performances are incredibly loose but always maintain a funk groove. Try this CD if you use Listening Idea 5 above.

Godspeed You Black Emperor! *"lift yr. skinny fists like antennas to heaven!"* Kranky Records krank043 (CD). Two-disc set from this Canadian post-rock group. Like a large-scale symphonic poem, the music ebbs and flows, creating a wall of sound at climaxes. It's not labeled anywhere, but "Storm" (mentioned in *Listen*) is the first track on CD 1. Try this recording if you use Listening Idea 5 above.

Grandmaster Flash. *The Best of Grandmaster Flash, Melle Mel and the Furious Five.* Rhino Records R2 71606 (CD). Collection by one of the groups that pioneered rap in the late 1970s and early 1980s. Includes "The Message" (mentioned in *Listen*) and ten other songs. Try this recording if you use Listening Idea 5 above.

The Grateful Dead, *Aoxomoxoa.* Warner Brothers 1790-2 (CD). 1969 album by a band whose popularity remained undiminished until Jerry Garcia's death in 1995. Their eclectic approaches make it difficult to choose a representative album; their third album captures their experiments with electronic sound manipulation—their acid rock phase. Try this recording if you use Listening Idea 5 above.

Haley, Bill, and His Comets. *The Best of Bill Haley and His Comets—20th Century Masters: The Millennium Collection.* MCA Records 11957 (CD). Single-disc collection by an influential 1950s rockabilly group. Includes "(We're Gonna) Rock around the Clock" (mentioned in *Listen*) and eleven other songs. Try this recording if you use Listening Idea 5 above.

Harris, Wynonie. *Bloodshot Eyes: The Best of Wynonie Harris.* Rhino R2 71544 (CD). Recordings from 1947 to 1954 by "Mr. Blues," a rhythm and blues shouter whose reputation rested on some of the most risqué songs of the time. Try his recordings of "All She Wants to Do Is Rock" or "Good Rockin' Tonight" if you use Listening Idea 5 or 11 above.

Hendrix, Jimi. *Are You Experienced?* MCA MCAD-11602 (CD). First solo album by the guitar virtuoso, and an instant classic. Hendrix moved guitar technique to an entirely new level, much as Liszt did for the piano a century earlier. Several songs, including "Purple Haze" (mentioned in *Listen*) and the title track, influenced the development of acid rock, and Hendrix's guitar style influenced generations of metal guitarists. Try this recording if you use Listening Idea 5 above.

Hitsville USA: The Motown Singles Collection 1959–1971. Motown Records 636 312 (CD). Excellent four-CD anthology of significant Motown singles from this Detroit-based label's first dozen years, tracing the development of soul music and the Motown genre. Includes "My Girl" (mentioned in *Listen*) and other hits by the Temptations, Smokey Robinson and the Miracles, Mary Wells, Marvin Gaye, Martha and the Vandellas, Diana Ross and the Supremes, the Four Tops, Stevie Wonder, Gladys Knight and the Pips, the Jackson 5, and many others. Try this recording if you use Listening Idea 5 above.

The Kingston Trio/From the Hungry i. Capitol/EMI 96748 (CD). Rerelease of two albums by this important folk trio. Includes an early (1959) U.S. recording of "Wimoweh." Try this recording if you use Listening Idea 5 or 7 above.

Ledernacken, *Wheelin' and Dealin'*. Strike Back Records SBR 26 CD (CD single). German techno-punk band's 1989 release contains an especially raw, hard-rocking version of "Wimoweh." You're on your own finding this one—I was lucky to get it by mail order from an underground metal shop in Salt Lake City. If you can find it, use this recording with Listening Idea 5 or 7 above.

Led Zeppelin II. Atlantic Recordings 82633-2 (CD). 1969 album contains "Whole Lotta Love" (mentioned in *Listen*) and other classic examples of the emerging hard-rock sound (soon to be called metal). See their first album for "covers" of urban blues songs that influenced their music. Try this recording if you use Listening Idea 5 above.

Little Richard, *The Georgia Peach*. Specialty Records 7012 (CD). Great rock'n'roll tracks from the 1950s and 1960s by one of rock music's great vocalists. Try this recording if you use Listening Idea 5 or 11 above.

Mitchell, Joni. *Court and Spark*. Asylum 1001-2 (CD). This 1974 album was the highest-charting album by this significant folk-rock artist. It also shows the increasing influence of jazz fusion on her work. Try this recording to supplement the textbook's discussion of the role of singer-songwriters in American pop music or if you use Listening Idea 5 above.

Mitchell, Joni. *The Hissing of Summer Lawns*. Elektra/Asylum 1051-2 (CD). Experimental 1975 album by this folk-rock artist uses Burundi drumming in "The Jungle Line." Try this recording to supplement the textbook's discussion of the role of singer-songwriters in American pop music or if you use Listening Idea 5 or 12 above.

Mitchell, Joni. *Mingus*. Asylum 505-2 (CD). This excellent 1979 album was not well-received, but it documents the close relationship between Mitchell and Charles Mingus, the jazz artist who became her mentor at the end of his life. In addition to writing new songs of her own, Mitchell wrote lyrics for several classic tunes by Mingus (with his consent and cooperation) and recorded them with leading jazz fusion artists, including Herbie Hancock, Wayne Shorter, and Jaco Pastorius. "Goodbye Pork Pie Hat" is a special highlight. Try this recording for a fascinating look at interactions between jazz, folk, and rock styles if you use Listening Idea 5 or 13 above.

Morissette, Alanis. *Jagged Little Pill*. Maverick/Reprise 9 45901-2 (CD). This Grammy-winning 1995 album introduced this artist's searing intensity to a wide audience. Try this recording to supplement the textbook's discussion of the role of singer-songwriters in American pop music or if you use Listening Idea 5 above.

Nirvana, *Nevermind*. Geffen DGCD 24425 (CD). Grunge rock classic from Kurt Cobain's Seattle-based band. Contains both songs mentioned in *Listen*, "Lithium" and "Smells Like Teen Spirit." Try this recording if you use Listening Idea 5 above.

N.W.A. (Niggaz with Attitude), *Straight Outta Compton*. Ruthless CDL 72435-37936-3-2 (CD). This 1989 rap album, with lyrics as murderous and misogynist as you please, signaled the emergence of gangsta rap. Includes the song "F_ _ _ tha Police," which prompted a letter from the F.B.I. to the label's distributor. If you can handle the class discussion, try this recording when you use Listening Idea 5 above.

Nylons, *The Best of the Nylons*. Open Air Records 10308-2 (CD). Collection from the sophisticated pop *a cappella* group includes "The Lion Sleeps

Tonight," yet another cover version of Solomon Linda's classic hit, "Mbube." Try this recording if you use Listening Idea 7 above.

Pink Floyd. *Dark Side of the Moon.* Capitol/EMI 46001 (CD). 1973 art-rock classic (mentioned in *Listen*) pioneers a synth-driven sound. Try this recording if you use Listening Idea 5 above.

Presley, Elvis. *Elvis's Golden Records.* RCA 67462 (CD). Most of Elvis's No. 1 hits on a single CD. Indispensable in any survey of 1950s rock'n'roll. Get it before it goes out of print! Try this recording if you use Listening Idea 5 or 11 above.

Presley, Elvis. *Sunrise.* RCA 67675 (CD). Two-CD set contains most of Elvis's early recordings for Sun Records. Try this recording of "That's All Right, Mama" if you use Listening Idea 5 or 11 above.

Public Enemy, *It Takes a Nation of Millions to Hold Us Back.* Def Jam 314-527-358-2 (CD). Perhaps the finest rap album ever released, this 1988 recording captures the unapologetic anger and poetry of this significant group. Includes "Don't Believe the Hype" (mentioned in *Listen*). Try this recording if you use Listening Idea 5 above.

Queen Latifah. *She's a Queen—A Collection of Hits.* Motown Records 440 064 415-2 (CD). Essential collection from this female rapper. Includes "Latifah's Had It Up 2 Here" (mentioned in *Listen*) and eleven other hits. Try this recording if you use Listening Idea 5 above.

Radiohead. *Amnesiac.* Capitol Records CDP 7243 5 32764 2 3 (CD). This album by this popular alternative band shows them moving toward a post-rock sound with songs like "Pyramid Song" (mentioned in *Listen*). Try this recording if you use Listening Idea 5 above.

The Ramones. *Ramones.* Warner Archives/Rhino R2 74306 (CD). Important album by this influential punk-rock group. This rerelease includes "Blitzkrieg Bop" (mentioned in *Listen*) and adds eight bonus tracks. Try this recording if you use Listening Idea 5 above.

Redding, Otis. *The Very Best of Otis Redding.* Rhino Records R2 71147 (CD). Superb collection by this important soul artist. Includes "(Sittin' On) The Dock of the Bay" (mentioned in *Listen*) and twenty-four other hits. Try this recording if you use Listening Idea 5 above.

Rites of Spring. Dischord Records DIS 16 CD (CD). One of the most influential Emo albums available. *Listen* mentions this style in the preface ("To the Student") but provides no examples. Try this recording to learn about Emo or if you use Listening Idea 5 above.

The Rolling Stones. *Singles Collection—The London Years.* ABKCO Records 1231-2 (CD). Excellent three-disc collection contains all the great 1960s hits by the British "bad-boy" group. Includes "(I Can't Get No) Satisfaction," "Honky Tonk Women" (mentioned in *Listen*), and fifty-six other songs. Try this recording if you use Listening Idea 5 or 11 above.

Ross, Diana, and the Supremes. *The Ultimate Collection.* Motown Records 314 530 827-2 (CD). Excellent single-disc collection by the ultimate girl group. Includes "Where Did Our Love Go?" (mentioned in *Listen*) and twenty-four other hits. Try this recording if you use Listening Idea 5 above.

Santana. *Abraxas.* Columbia/Legacy 65490 (CD). Important 1970 album put this major guitar artist on the map. Includes "Black Magic Woman" (mentioned in *Listen*) and eleven other songs. Try this recording if you use Listening Idea 5 above.

Seeger, Pete. *Pete Seeger's Greatest Hits*. Columbia/Legacy CK 65711 (CD). Collection of often familiar songs by one of the most important figures in American folk music. Includes "Little Boxes," "Wimoweh," "Where Have All the Flowers Gone?," "Turn! Turn! Turn!," Woody Guthrie's "This Land Is Your Land," and nine others. Try this recording if you use Listening Idea 5 above.

The Sex Pistols. *Never Mind the Bollocks, Here's the Sex Pistols*. Warner Brothers 3147-2 (CD). Punk rock from the most cynical group of the late 1970s—you remember Johnny Rotten and Sid Vicious! Try this recording of "Anarchy in the U.K." (mentioned in *Listen*) if you use Listening Idea 5 above.

The Shirelles Anthology: 1959–1964. Rhino Records R2 75897 (CD). Collection of great songs by one of the great girl groups. Includes "Will You Love Me Tomorrow?" (mentioned in *Listen*) and fifteen other hits. Try this recording if you use Listening Idea 5 above.

Simon and Garfunkel. *Sounds of Silence*. Columbia/Legacy 65998 (CD). 1966 album was one of the best by this socially aware folk duo. Try this recording for an example of the singer-songwriter tradition or if you use Listening Idea 5 above.

Simon, Paul. *Graceland*. Warner Brothers 46430 (Enhanced CD). Landmark 1986 album features collaborations with many South African musicians, including Joseph Shabalala and Ladysmith Black Mambazo, General M. D. Shirinda and the Gaza Sisters, Lulu Masilela, and Stimela. Use this recording if you try Class Discussion Idea 9 or Listening Idea 5, 9, or 12 above.

Simon, Paul. *The Rhythm of the Saints*. Warner Brothers 26098 (CD). 1990 album features collaborations with Brazilian musicians such as Milton Nascimento and Nana Vasconcelos. Use this recording if you try Listening Idea 5 or 12 above.

Slint. *Spiderland*. touch and go records 64 (CD). Important album by this post-rock group. Includes "Good Morning Captain" (mentioned in *Listen*). Try this recording if you use Listening Idea 5 above.

Sly and the Family Stone. *Greatest Hits*. Epic EK 30325 (CD). Twelve songs by one of the groups who made the transition from soul to funk. Includes "Thank You (Falettinme Be Mice Elf Agin)" (mentioned in *Listen*). Try this recording if you use Listening Idea 5 above.

Smith, Patti. *Horses*. Arista 07822 18827-2 (CD). Perhaps the finest album by this important punk rocker. Includes "Gloria" (mentioned in *Listen*). Try this recording if you use Listening Idea 5 above.

Springsteen, Bruce. *Born to Run*. CBS CK 33795 (CD). This important 1975 album was a landmark in the career of this emerging artist. Even more famous was his *Born in the U.S.A.* (1984), though the title track's protest element was often overlooked by flag-waving fans. Try this recording to supplement the textbook's discussion of the role of singer-songwriters in American pop music or if you use Listening Idea 5 above.

Sugarhill Gang. *Rapper's Delight: The Best of Sugarhill Gang*. Rhino Records R2 71986 (CD). Collection of songs by one of the groups that pioneered rap in the late 1970s. Includes "Rapper's Delight" (mentioned in *Listen*) and ten other songs. Try this recording if you use Listening Idea 5 above.

Thornton, Willa Mae. *Hound Dog/The Peacock Recordings*. MCA Records MCAD-10668 (CD). "Big Mama" Thornton's rhythm and blues artistry from the 1950s. It is fascinating to compare her original version of "Hound Dog" with Elvis's cover. Try this recording if you use Listening Idea 5 or 11 above.

The Tokens. *Wimoweh! The Best of the Tokens.* RCA Records 66474 (CD). Collection notable mainly for what became the most popular and best known recording of "Mbube" in the United States, "The Lion Sleeps Tonight" (1961). Try this recording if you use Listening Idea 5 or 7 above.

The Weavers at Carnegie Hall. Vanguard Theatre Showcase VMD-73101 (CD). Collection of classics by the premiere folk ensemble of the 1950s, recorded live in 1955. Includes "Wimoweh," with Pete Seeger taking Solomon Linda's lead line in the South African hit "Mbube." Use this recording if you try Listening Idea 7 above.

The Who. *Tommy.* MCA Records 11417 (CD). This 1969 rock opera (mentioned in *Listen*) attempted to put rock music on a par with the classical tradition. It's hard to say if it succeeded, but the music is memorable, and it sounds better than ever in this remastered edition. Good example of both hard rock and art rock. Try this recording if you use Listening Idea 5 above.

Woodstock. Atlantic Recordings 82636-2 (CD). Live recordings from the most heavily mythologized festival in rock history. Includes performances by Joan Baez, Jimi Hendrix, Jefferson Airplane, Janis Joplin, Sly and the Family Stone, The Who, and others. Documentary significance overrides the often rough sound quality. Also provides a sampling of 1960s rock styles, including folk rock, blues, acid rock, rock'n'roll revival, soul music, country rock, and hard rock. Try this recording if you use Listening Idea 5 above.

Video Recordings

African Music

African Wave: South African Music and Its Influences. www.films.com (DVD or VHS, color, 13 parts, 25 minutes each). Fascinating series looks at South African musical traditions and contemporary practitioners. Especially relevant is the segment on Ladysmith Black Mambazo; performances by the group and explanations from leader Joseph Shabalala provide a good introduction to contemporary *isicathamiya*.

Babatunde Olatunji: African Drumming. Warner Brothers (DVD, color, 60 minutes). Features drumming "lessons" with this Nigerian master drummer. Several drums are used, including "talking" drums. Available from www.worldmusicstore.com.

Djabote: Senegalese Drumming and Song from Doudou N'Daye Rose. Multicultural Media (VHS, color, 43 minutes). "Indie" award–winning video captures this master drummer and his ensemble performing on the island of Gorée, a center for the West African slave trade. The final performance captures an especially rich example of rhythmic polyphony. Available from www.worldmusicstore.com.

Graceland: The African Concert. Warner Brothers (DVD or VHS, color, 90 minutes). Video record of Paul Simon's live concert in Harare, Zimbabwe. Includes performances by Hugh Masekela, Miriam Makeba, and Ladysmith Black Mambazo. Highly recommended if you use Class Discussion Idea 9 or Listening Idea 9 above.

Juju Music. Rhapsody Films (VHS, color, 51 minutes). Performance documentary includes excerpts from an all-night concert in Lagos featuring *juju* "stars" King Sunny Adé and Ebenezer Obey.

JVC/Smithsonian Folkways Video Anthology of Music and Dance of Africa. Excellent three-video set provides numerous examples of West African drumming from Senegal, Gambia, and Ghana and also Nigerian highlife and *juju* music. From South Africa come traditional and syncretic music and dance of the Zulu peoples, including several examples of *isicathamiya*. Highly recommended for your presentation of Global Perspectives materials for this chapter.

JVC Video Anthology of World Music and Dance. Tapes 17 through 19 from this excellent video series offer music from Africa. Of particular interest are examples 19-2 (drum language from the Baule people of the Ivory Coast) and 19-14, 19-18, and 19-19 (South African music of the Zulu and San peoples). Also interesting for their connections with Yoruba traditions are examples 28-6 and 28-9 from the tape on Brazil, which contain examples of a voodoo gathering and a *candomblé* religious observance, respectively. Highly recommended for your presentation of Global Perspectives materials for this chapter.

Konkombe: The Nigerian Pop Music Scene. Shanachie Entertainment (DVD or VHS, color, 60 minutes). This *Beats of the Heart* film, a PBS documentary, features the range of musical styles heard in 1980s Nigeria, including *juju*, Afro-pop, highlife, and street music. An interesting supplement to your study of Yoruba drumming.

Ladysmith Black Mambazo: Live at the Royal Albert Hall. Shanachie Entertainment (DVD or VHS, color, 75 minutes). Excellent live-concert video features this *isicathamiya* ensemble performing many of their hit songs, including "Homeless" from Paul Simon's *Graceland*. Highly recommended supplement to the final Global Perspectives segment.

Listening to the Silence: African Cross Rhythms. www.films.com (DVD or VHS, color, 33 minutes). Introduction to Ghanaian percussion music of the Ewe Ashanti, Ga, and Frafra peoples. Musical examples include religious trance dances, children's games, and so on.

Repercussions: A Celebration of African-Influenced Music. www.films.com (DVD or VHS, color, seven parts, 56–60 minutes each). Seven-part series looks at African influences on many musical styles, including jazz, rhythm and blues, gospel, and reggae. Segments include *Born Musicians: Traditional Music from the Gambia; The Drums of Dagbon; On the Battlefield: Gospel Quartets; Legends of Rhythm and Blues; Sit Down and Listen: The Story of Max Roach; Caribbean Crucible;* and *Africa Come Back: The Popular Music of West Africa.* Many of these are useful for Chapter 23.

Rhythm of Resistance: Black South African Music. Shanachie Entertainment (DVD or VHS, color, 50 minutes). This *Beats of the Heart* film, a PBS documentary, features performances by a wide range of popular musicians, including Johnny Clegg, the Mahotella Queens, and others. *Isicathamiya* is represented by Ladysmith Black Mambazo.

American Music History—The Cultivated Tradition

Amazing Grace: The Story of a Song That Makes a Difference. www.films.com (DVD or VHS, color, 90 minutes). Performances and reflections on the importance of this song by American musicians from all parts of the musical spectrum. Performers include Judy Collins, Jessye Norman, Johnny Cash, Jean Ritchie, and the Boys Choir of Harlem. A fascinating sample of music in American culture. Try this video for an unusual approach to Listening Idea 1 above.

The American Way. The Music of the 20th Century: Leaving Home Series. Arthaus Musik (DVD or VHS, color, 52 minutes). Simon Rattle narrates this look at American music from hymns, band music, country dances, and jazz to the music of twentieth-century composers such as Ives, Gershwin, Copland, Cage, and Bernstein.

Leonard Bernstein: Reaching for the Note. WinStar (DVD or VHS, color, 117 minutes). Superb video biography of this composer, conductor, and media presence incorporates interviews with Jerome Robbins, Stephen Sondheim, Isaac Stern, Michael Tilson Thomas, and others.

The Known and the Unknown. The Music of Man Series. Home Vision (VHS, color, 60 minutes). Yehudi Menuhin narrates a look at music between the world wars—jazz and twelve tone. Features music of Louis Armstrong, Gershwin, Copland, and Schoenberg.

Music of Williamsburg. Colonial Williamsburg Series. Williamsburg, Va.: Colonial Williamsburg, 1961 (VHS, color, 53 minutes). Director Sidney Meyers captures the variety of music found in a typical day in eighteenth-century colonial Williamsburg. Includes European chamber music, a glass harmonica, work songs of African Americans (sung by the Georgia Sea Island Singers), dance music, and church music. Filmed entirely in Colonial Williamsburg. Excellent resource if you use Listening Idea 1 above.

The Parting of the Ways. The Music of Man Series. Home Vision (VHS, color, 60 minutes). Yehudi Menuhin contrasts the music of Stephen Foster, Scott Joplin, and John Philip Sousa with the music of their counterparts in Europe—Debussy, Strauss, Mahler, and Stravinsky.

War and Peace. Music in Time Series. www.films.com (DVD or VHS, color, 60 minutes). James Galway narrates this look at the many trends in music between the world wars. Covers many composers and styles. More appropriate for Chapter 21 than for Chapter 23, but does include Joplin's *Maple Leaf Rag,* Gershwin's *American in Paris,* and a look at the influence of jazz on European composers Stravinsky, Milhaud, Ravel, and Weill.

Blues, Jazz, and Gospel

Against the Odds Series. www.films.com (DVD or VHS, color, 10 minutes each). Brief biographies of important figures in music history. Most relevant for Chapter 23 are videos on Bessie Smith, Woody Guthrie, Sarah Bernhardt, and Martin Luther King Jr.

Armstrong, Louis. *Satchmo: Louis Armstrong.* Columbia Music Video (DVD or VHS, 86 minutes). Excellent video biography of the greatest jazz trumpet player of all time. It contains interviews with friends, family, and colleagues as well as numerous archival clips and performances. Highly recommended.

At the Jazz Band Ball: Early Hot Jazz, Song and Dance. Yazoo (DVD or VHS, 60 minutes). Great jazz musicians from 1925 to 1933 captured on early sound films, including Louis Armstrong, Bessie Smith, and Duke Ellington. Just the music—no overdubbed commentary. Recommended.

The Blues: A Musical Journey. Columbia Music Video (Seven DVDs, color, 13 hours). Martin Scorsese's excellent series of films on the blues, each one with a different director. A gold mine for any presentation on the blues. Highly recommended.

Blues Masters: The Essential History of the Blues. Rhino Home Video (DVD or VHS, color/black and white, 103 minutes). Early video footage of many important blues artists, though not always singing the blues! Especially useful for this chapter are performances by early blues singers Bessie Smith and Mamie Smith; urban blues artists Muddy Waters, Buddy Guy, and B. B. King; and rhythm and blues singer Big Joe Turner. Recommended.

Davis, Miles. *The Miles Davis Story.* Columbia Music Video (DVD, 125 minutes). Excellent video biography of the innovator who changed jazz four or five times. It contains interviews as well as archival clips and performance footage. Highly recommended.

Deep Blues: A Musical Pilgrimage to the Crossroads. WinStar (DVD, color, 90 minutes). Robert Palmer takes us on a pilgrimage to the Mississippi Delta. Part historical documentary, this video also introduces us to modern-day Delta blues musicians such as R. L. Burnside and Lonnie Pitchford. Recommended.

Ellington, Duke. *Memories of Duke.* MVD (DVD or VHS, 90 minutes). Video alternates between interviews with long-time band members Russell Procope and Cootie Williams and concert footage of the band on tour. If you want complete performances of classic Ellington chart toppers like "Black and Tan Fantasy," "Mood Indigo," and "Take the 'A' Train," this is the one to get. Highly recommended.

Ellington, Duke. *On the Road with Duke Ellington.* Docurama (DVD or VHS, 62 minutes). Intriguing behind-the-scenes look at the great artist on tour, in concert, in the studio, and in private. Louis Armstrong drops in for a chat at one point. Highly recommended.

Hancock, Herbie. *Future 2 Future—Live.* Columbia Music Video (DVD, 104 minutes). 2002 live concert retrospective of Hancock's jazz-rock fusion hits from the 1970s to the 1990s, including the funky *Chameleon* and his first hit music video, *Rockit.* Highly recommended if you use Listening Idea 12 or 13.

Imagine the Sound. Home Vision (VHS, color, 92 minutes). A documentary that looks at contemporary (1980s) jazz through live performances and interviews with Cecil Taylor, Archie Shepp, Bill Dixon, and Paul Bley.

Jazz: A Film by Ken Burns. PBS DVD Gold (DVD or VHS, color/black and white, ten parts, about 114 minutes each). Superb, richly detailed look at the history of jazz, using archival footage wherever possible. Especially good at examining the social contexts in which jazz musicians lived and worked. With such an embarrassment of riches, it takes time to find the clips you want, but the DVD format makes this much easier. Highly recommended.

The Jazz Collection Series. www.films.com (DVD or VHS, color, ten parts, 49–58 minutes each). A series of ten biographies, each dealing with a major figure in jazz history. Includes segments on Louis Armstrong, John Coltrane, Fats Waller, Count Basie, Gerry Mulligan, Bill Evans, Gil Evans, Max Roach, B. B. King, and Dee Dee Bridgewater.

Jazz Heroes: Monk, Ella, and Dizzy. www.films.com (DVD or VHS, color, three parts, 25 minutes each). A close-up look at three postwar jazz greats: Thelonious Monk, Ella Fitzgerald, and Dizzy Gillespie.

Johnson, Robert. *Can't You Hear the Wind Howl? The Life and Music of Robert Johnson.* WinStar (DVD or VHS, color and black and white, 76 minutes). Danny Glover narrates this video portrait of Johnson's life and music. Includes tasteful reenactments (Keb' Mo' as Johnson) and interviews with Eric

Clapton, Keith Richards, and others who were influenced by this early blues master. Fascinating look at the man who influenced Muddy Waters, the Rolling Stones, Led Zeppelin, and countless others.

The Land Where the Blues Began. Vestapol (VHS, color, 60 minutes). This documentary looks at the Mississippi Delta (between the Mississippi and Yazoo Rivers in the state of Mississippi—*not* in Louisiana) and the living conditions that led to the formation of the blues. Legendary folk-song collector Alan Lomax narrates the film and conducts interviews with many musicians. Recommended.

Marsalis, Wynton. *Wynton Marsalis: All That Jazz.* www.films.com (DVD or VHS, color with black and white, 56 minutes each). A look at the life and career of one of today's most important trumpet players, both in jazz and classical arenas. Video is filled with interviews, performances, and reflections on jazz history and New Orleans, his hometown.

Parker, Charlie. *Bird.* Warner Brothers (DVD or VHS, color, 160 minutes). Clint Eastwood directs this unblinking yet sympathetic look at one of the greatest jazz artists of all time. The Oscar-winning film features performances by Forest Whitaker and Diane Venora. Sound engineers did a miraculous job with authentic Parker recordings; Parker's lines sound as if he recorded them in the studio last year.

Parker, Charlie. *Bird Now.* WinStar (VHS, color, 90 minutes). Video documentary looks at Parker's life and music. Includes archival footage and interviews.

Parker, Charlie. *Celebrating Bird: The Triumph of Charlie Parker.* Pioneer Artists (DVD or VHS, 59 minutes). This "authorized" documentary looks at Parker's life and music. It contains interviews with friends, family, and colleagues as well as archival clips and footage of many performances, including "Confirmation" and "A Night in Tunisia." Highly recommended.

'Round Midnight. Warner Home Video (DVD or VHS, color, 131 minutes). Jazz saxophonist Dexter Gordon stars in a semi-autobiographical story about a jazz musician in Paris in 1959. Bertrand Tavernier directs, with a film score by Herbie Hancock. Gordon also performs much of his own material in this great jazz film.

The Songs Are Free: Bernice Johnson Reagon and African-American Music. www.films.com (DVD or VHS, color, 58 minutes). Bill Moyers interviews the Smithsonian Institution curator and founder of Sweet Honey in the Rock. Their fascinating conversation focuses on the role of music in the history of the African American community. Includes archival and recent performances.

The Story of Jazz. BMG Special Products (DVD or VHS, color/black and white, 97 minutes). Covering musicians from Louis Armstrong to Miles Davis, this narrated history of jazz weaves in firsthand accounts. Recommended.

Straight, No Chaser. Warner Home Video (DVD or VHS, color, 89 minutes). A documentary about jazz great Thelonious Monk. Contains twenty-five of his songs, interviews with colleagues, and video footage of Monk backstage, on the road, and at home. Directed by Charlotte Zwering; jazz fan Clint Eastwood was executive producer.

Times Ain't Like They Used to Be: Early American Rural and Popular Music. Yazoo (DVD, color/black and white, 70 minutes). Archival footage from 1928 to 1935 captures real old-timey music, the roots of bluegrass, and modern country music. "Name" artists include Jimmie Rodgers and Bob Wills' Texas Playboys, but many tracks feature unknown rural musicians. Recommended.

Too Close to Heaven: The History of Gospel Music. www.films.com (DVD or VHS, color, 3 parts, 51 minutes each). Three-part series looks at the last two hundred years of black American church music. Includes many performances and interviews by gospel singers and other key figures.

Wallace, Sippie. *Sippie—Sippie Wallace: Blues Singer and Song Writer.* Rhapsody Films (VHS, color, 23 minutes). Short film includes extensive interviews with Wallace along with recent performance footage. Interesting look at a still vital eighty-three-year-old (in 1986) blues singer.

Waters, Muddy. *Can't Be Satisfied.* Wellspring (DVD, color/black and white, 54 minutes). Fine documentary gives us the life and music of this blues legend in a reasonably unvarnished fashion. Recommended.

Waters, Muddy. *Got My Mojo Working: Rare Performances 1968–1978.* Yazoo (DVD, color/black and white, 54 minutes). Live concert footage of the Delta bluesman who helped pioneer electric urban blues in Chicago. Video quality is not first-rate, but it's like listening to a scratched LP—the music comes through in spite of the defects. Recommended.

Gershwin and Musical Theater

Die Fledermaus. Image Entertainment (DVD or VHS, color, 197 minutes). Famous Strauss operetta that influenced the development of American musical theater. John Cox produced the film version of this superb Royal Opera House performance; conducted by Richard Bonynge. Try this video if you use Lecture-Demonstration Idea 5 above.

George Gershwin Remembered. A&E Home Video (VHS, color, 90 minutes). Interesting video documentary. Friends and colleagues tell the story of George Gershwin's life and music.

Gershwin, *Porgy and Bess.* EMI Classics (DVD or VHS, color, 184 minutes). Outstanding Glyndebourne recording of Gershwin's great "folk opera." Strong cast led by Cynthia Haymon and Willard White. Performed by the London Philharmonic and the Glyndebourne Chorus; conducted by Simon Rattle. Highly recommended.

The King and I. 20th Century Fox (DVD or VHS, color, 133 minutes). Classic Rodgers and Hammerstein musical briefly mentioned by the authors in their discussion of the American musical. Film version features Deborah Kerr (with singing by Marni Nixon) and Yul Brynner. Try this video if you use Lecture-Demonstration Idea 5 above.

The Mikado. Acorn Media (DVD or VHS, color, 150 minutes). Live (and lively) performance of one of the great Gilbert and Sullivan operettas at Canada's Stratford Festival. Try this video if you use Lecture-Demonstration Idea 5 above.

Oklahoma! 20th Century Fox (DVD or VHS, color, 145 minutes). Classic Rodgers and Hammerstein musical briefly mentioned by the authors in their discussion of the American musical. Film version features Gordon McRae and Shirley Jones; includes landmark dance sequences by Agnes de Mille. Try this video if you use Lecture-Demonstration Idea 5 above.

Show Boat. Warner Studios (VHS, black and white). Far more complete than the 1951 movie incarnation, this 1936 James Whale extravaganza remains the classic version of this great musical, featuring Irene Dunne, Hattie McDaniel, and Paul Robeson. Use this video to survey American musicals or if you use Lecture-Demonstration Idea 5 above.

The Sound of Music. 20th Century Fox (DVD or VHS, color, 172 minutes). Classic Rodgers and Hammerstein musical briefly mentioned by the authors in their discussion of the American musical. Film version features Julie Andrews and Christopher Plummer. Try this video if you use Lecture-Demonstration Idea 5 above.

South Pacific. 20th Century Fox (DVD or VHS, color, 157 minutes). Classic Rodgers and Hammerstein musical briefly mentioned by the authors in their discussion of the American musical. Film version features Mitzi Gaynor and Rossano Brazzi (with singing by Giorgio Tozzi). Try this video if you use Lecture-Demonstration Idea 5 above.

West Side Story. MGM/United Artists (DVD or VHS, color, 151 minutes). Bernstein and Sondheim collaboration resulted in one of the great musicals of all time. Film version features Natalie Wood (with singing by Marni Nixon), Russ Tamblyn, and Rita Moreno. Strongly recommended.

West Side Story: The Making of the Recording. Deutsche Grammophon (DVD, color, 89 minutes). Not a performance but a behind-the-scenes look at the 1985 production with Kiri Te Kanawa, Tatiana Troyanos, José Carreras, and Kurt Ollmann; conducted by Leonard Bernstein. This video provides a fascinating opportunity to watch Bernstein at work—and to hear his last thoughts on this famous work.

Rock, Pop, and Folk Music

The Beatles Anthology. Capitol (DVD or VHS, color/black and white, eight parts, 85 minutes each). Comprehensive documentary examines the lives and careers of the four Beatles. Extensive use of interviews and performance footage. Try this video if you use Listening Idea 5 above.

The Beatles' First U.S. Visit. Apple (VHS, black and white, 85 minutes). Unvarnished behind-the-scenes look at the Beatles' first trip to the United States. No narration—you see it as it happens. Includes their performances on Ed Sullivan and a live concert in Washington, D.C. Captures the mania of February 1964 as no other video can.

Complete Monterey Pop Festival. Criterion Collection. (DVD or VHS, color, 270 minutes). This rockumentary chronicles the important 1967 festival with performances by important rock musicians of the 1960s: Jimi Hendrix, Janis Joplin, Jefferson Airplane, the Mamas and the Papas, Otis Redding, Simon and Garfunkel, Ravi Shankar, and the Who. Try this video if you use Listening Idea 5 above.

Grateful Dead Movie. Monterey Video (DVD, color, 131 minutes). Video includes concert footage and behind-the-scenes events featuring the late Jerry Garcia and his crew. An interesting look at a rock phenomenon.

The History of Rock and Roll. Warner Home Video (DVD, color, 5 discs, 560 minutes). PBS's ten-hour rockumentary is now available. Set includes interviews, archival footage, and 250 songs from the 1940s to the present covering styles such as Memphis, Motown, the British invasion, psychedelia, reggae, disco, punk, and alternative.

The Last Waltz. MGM/United Artists (DVD or VHS, color, 117 minutes). Superb rock-concert video captures the final concert by the Band, an event that featured guest artists such as Bob Dylan, Eric Clapton, Joni Mitchell, Muddy Waters, and Ringo Starr. Try this video if you use Listening Idea 5 above.

Legends of Rock'n'Roll Live. Image Entertainment (DVD, color, 59 minutes). Concert video features several legendary musicians performing live in 1989. In addition to 1950s rock'n'roll, the track list also includes music from soul, gospel, and blues traditions. Featured performers are James Brown, Bo Diddley, Ray Charles, Little Richard, Jerry Lee Lewis, Fats Domino, and B. B. King. Try this video if you use Listening Idea 5 above.

Mitchell, Joni. *Joni Mitchell: Painting with World and Music*. Image Entertainment (DVD, color, 98 minutes). Video captures a 1998 live performance by this important folk-rock vocalist, featuring songs from throughout her career. She may have lost a couple of notes on top, but she still knows how to put a song across. Try this video for an example of the singer-songwriter tradition or if you use Listening Idea 5 above.

Pop Lyrics. *Culture Fix* Series. www.films.com (DVD or VHS, color, 29 minutes). Fourteen-part series looks at various topics in the history of art and culture, with particular emphasis on the twentieth century. Most useful with Chapter 23 is *Pop Lyrics*.

Radiohead. *Meeting People Is Easy*. Capitol (DVD, color, 95 minutes). Stream-of-consciousness film looks at this young post-rock band suddenly thrust into the limelight. Try this video if you use Listening Idea 5 above.

Rap: Looking for the Perfect Beat. www.films.com (DVD or VHS, color, 53 minutes). Fascinating documentary looks at rap's history and its styles, with footage from music videos and commentary by many practitioners—from Grandmaster Flash to the present day. It should probably come with a parental advisory. Try this video if you use Listening Idea 5 above.

The Rolling Stones. *Gimme Shelter*. Criterion Collection (DVD or VHS, color, 91 minutes). Documentary follows the Rolling Stones on their 1969 tour and includes chilling footage of a fan killed by Hell's Angels hired to handle security at the Altamont Festival. On the plus side, this film includes extensive live-concert-performance footage. Try this video if you use Listening Idea 5 above.

Seeger, Pete. *Pure Pete Seeger*. www.films.com (DVD or VHS, color, 60 minutes). Bill Moyers interviews Pete Seeger, one of the best-known folk singers in the United States. Seeger sings many of the songs that have meant the most to him, and Moyers draws out fascinating information about Seeger and the people and political events that have filled his life. Try this video if you use Listening Idea 5 above.

Sound of Unsound. *The Music of Man* Series. Home Vision (VHS, color, 60 minutes). Yehudi Menuhin explores the impact of LP recordings, radio, and television on Western music. The video moves from early jazz into folk, rock, and electronic music.

The Who. *The Kids Are Alright—Special Edition*. Pioneer (DVD, color, 200 minutes). The Who were one of the seminal bands in rock history. If you only buy one Who DVD, this is the one to get. The beautifully remastered 109-minute rockumentary offers an extraordinary collection culled from live performances that span The Who's career, from the mid-1960s to the late 1970s.

The special edition adds another 150 minutes of not-to-be-missed goodies. Use this DVD if you try Listening Idea 5 above.

Woodstock. Warner Home Video (DVD or VHS, color, 225 minutes). Director's cut of the Academy Award–winning documentary. Features performances by Canned Heat; Jimi Hendrix; Janis Joplin; Crosby, Stills, and Nash; Jefferson Airplane; and others. Use this video if you try Listening Idea 5 above.

♩ Software

Bob Marley: Soul Almighty: the Formative Years. Graphix Zone (CD-ROM—Windows or Macintosh). This inexpensive CD-ROM includes a video interview, discography, photographs, and many songs, some never before released. Available from www.cdaccess.com.

Brubeck Music Analyzed! Time Sketch: Piano Series. www.ecsmedia.com (CD-ROM—Macintosh and Windows). Program presents a CD recording of Dave Brubeck's famous album *Time Out* with interactive arch-map analysis and background information. Recommended for your presentation of American jazz.

Davis Music Analyzed! Time Sketch: Piano Series. www.ecsmedia.com (CD-ROM—Windows or Macintosh). Program presents a CD recording of Miles Davis's seminal *Kind of Blue* with interactive arch-map analysis and background information. Highly recommended supplement to your presentation of Miles Davis.

History of Folk Music. (CD ROM—Macintosh and Windows). Interactive introduction to music of Native Americans, early settlers, and African Americans. Also touches on country music. Includes many musical examples and rare images. Available from www.midiworkshop.com.

History of Jazz. (CD-ROM—Macintosh and Windows). A multimedia package that looks at jazz roots, important jazz musicians, jazz history, and how jazz is made. Includes many photographs and sound clips. Available from www.midiworkshop.com.

The Norton Masterworks CD-ROM. New York: W. W. Norton (CD-ROM—Macintosh). Authors Daniel Jacobson and Timothy Koozin provide a clever multimedia introduction to twelve important works, including several versions of the old standard "My Funny Valentine": the version from the original musical, jazz arrangements by Chet Baker and Gary Burton, and a rock version by Jerry Garcia. Features animated, guided listening resources as well as information about the composers, eras, and genres, as well as the works themselves.

Under the Covers of Classic Rock. Graphix Zone (CD-ROM—Macintosh and Windows). A look at music from the 1960s and 1970s through interviews, performances, video footage, and artist profiles. Available from www.cdaccess.com.

APPENDIX I

Additional Listening Charts

To facilitate photocopying for display or distribution, thirty-four Additional Listening Charts are contained in this separate appendix. The timings indicated on these Listening Charts are approximate; thus, measure numbers are provided for many charts. When you see "5th ed." in the heading, those Listening Chart timings correspond to the recordings for *Listen,* Brief Fifth Edition; "4th ed." indicates timings that correspond to the recordings for *Listen,* Brief Fourth Edition; and "3rd ed." indicates timings that correspond to the recordings for *Listen,* Brief Third Edition. For suggested CD or video recordings, see Multimedia Resources for the chapter indicated in the heading for each chart below.

Pyotr Ilyich Tchaikovsky, *Nutcracker* Suite, Op. 71a (Chapter 1)

Dance suite

OVERTURE MINIATURE

| 00:00 | | Played initially by the strings, softly. Moderately fast
Other featured timbres are the flute, triangle, and pizzicato strings. The tempo is allegro. The meter is duple. |

CHARACTERISTIC DANCES

03:30	**March**	Heard initially as a dialogue between the brass/winds and the strings. The middle section features very fast flutes. The dynamic ranges freely between *f* (loud) to *p* (soft). There are numerous crescendos from *p* to *f*.
05:50	**Dance of the Sugar-Plum Fairy**	Delicate, quiet dance Featured timbres are pizzicato strings and the celesta. The tempo is andante. Note the celesta arpeggios at the center of the dance.
07:25	**Russian Dance**	Exciting, rhythmic dance Powerful accents push the rhythm forward. The dance is played by the full orchestra and eventually rises to a dynamic of *fff* (fortississimo).
08:35	**Arabian Dance**	Slower, mysterious, quasi-Arabic-sounding dance The low strings play a hypnotic ostinato accompaniment. The meter is triple; the mode changes to minor. At the end of the dance there is a gradual decrescendo to *ppp* (pianississimo).
11:20	**Chinese Dance**	Faster, initially quiet dance features the piccolo, flute, and glockenspiel. The accompaniment consists of a pedal played by pizzicato basses and an ostinato played by the bassoons. A crescendo brings the dance to a *ff* conclusion.
12:35	**Dance of the Pan-Pipes**	Sweet, "pipe"-like flutes play the main tune. The brass instruments enter in the middle of the dance.
15:00	**Waltz of the Flowers**	Introduction Wind choir and harp. Note the brief harp cadenza and the ritardando at the end of the cadenza.

16:05		Waltz of the Flowers Theme
		    Lovely triple meter tune played initially by the horns
		    Major mode

18:15		New Tune 1 Played initially by the flutes and oboes

18:50		New Tune 2
		    Dramatic new tune, played by the violas and cellos
		    Minor mode

19:20		New Tune 1 In violins, major
19:45		Waltz of the Flowers Theme Heard initially in the French horns
20:50		The brass instruments enter and initiate a long accelerando and crescendo to *fff* by the end of the movement.

A Peruvian Raftpipe Ensemble: Centro Social Conima, "Manuelita" (Chapter 6; 4th ed.)

0:00	**a**	Note the strong syncopation
0:12	**a**	
0:23	**b**	
0:34	**b**	
0:45	**a'**	
0:53	**a'**	
1:00	**aa**	Full melody repeats
1:22	**bb**	
1:44	**a'a'**	

Johann Sebastian Bach, Passacaglia in C Minor for organ (Chapter 9)

Variation (passacaglia) form

0:01	**Theme**	In the organ pedals; unaccompanied	*5 variations: increasing*
0:27	**Var. 1–2**	Theme accompanied by broken chords	*complexity of texture*
1:13	**Var. 3–4**	More contrapuntal	
1:57	**Var. 5**	Theme in the pedals is broken up.	
2:21	**Var. 6–8**	Scale figures of various kinds	*5 variations:*
3:25	**Var. 9**	Theme in the pedals is broken up.	*scales and scale figures*
3:48	**Var. 10**	Theme, played detached, with chords above it	
4:08	**Var. 11–12**	Bass goes up into the high treble register.	*5 variations:*
4:49	**Var. 13**	Quieter: bass broken up	*PEDALS DROP OUT*
5:10	**Var. 14–15**	Bass broken up into quiet arpeggios—var. 15 is quieter.	*(except in var. 12)*
5:48	**Var. 16–17**	Theme back in the pedals: brilliant variations	*5 variations:*
6:30	**Var. 18**	Theme in the pedals is broken up.	*PEDALS RETURN:*
6:52	**Var. 19–20**	Two final variations, running directly into the Fugue	*Climax*

Johann Sebastian Bach, Fugue, from Passacaglia and Fugue in C Minor for organ (Chapter 9)

Fugue form

0:00	Runs in directly from the Passacaglia (Listening Chart on p. 668)			
0:00	FUGAL EXPO- SITION	Four **Subject entries** (with two countersubjects): *high* *higher* corresponding to *pedals* *middle*		(alto) (soprano) (bass) (tenor)

0:57 Strong cadence, followed by
another **Subject entry,** modulating to the major mode
(From now on, there are short episodes between all the subject entries.)

1:12 Strong cadence, in a major key, followed by
Subject entry   ***ORGAN PEDALS***

                                      DROP OUT

1:40   **Subject entry,** major mode

2:10   Strong **Subject entry,** minor mode   ***PEDALS RETURN***

2:41   **Subject entry,** minor mode—seems headed for a cadence

2:54 Episode with unexpected new upward scale figure

3:09   **Subject entry**

3:27 Strong cadence, followed by
            Subject entry in the pedals: the lowest yet

4:00 Strong cadence, scale figure, and expectant trill

4:12 Climactic high **Subject entry**—the highest yet

4:44 Dramatic stop, prior to a grandiose final cadence

Johann Sebastian Bach, Fugue in C-sharp Major, from *The Well-Tempered Clavier,* Book I (Chapter 9; 4th ed.)

Fugue form

		subject	counter-subject		
0:00	**Exposition**	S ——— ∿ ····		S = soprano (high range)	
		T ——— ∿		T = tenor (middle range)	
		B ———		B = bass (low range)	
0:15	**Episode 1**				
0:26	**Subject**	S ———			
		CADENCE Cadence in minor key			
0:36	**Subject entries**	B ———		minor mode	
		(delayed) T ———		minor mode	
		CADENCE Cadence in another minor key			
1:00	**Episode 2**	Brief sequence on the first half of the subject, leading to the entire subject—			
1:05	**Subject entries**	S ——— ∿			
		T ———			
1:16	**Episode 3**				
1:32		Longer sequences on the first half of the subject, leading to the entire subject—			
1:52	**Subject entries**	S ——— ∿ ····		} same as the exposition	
		T ——— ∿			
		B ———			
2:09	**Episode 1 (again)**				
2:18	**Final subject**	S ———			

Franz Joseph Haydn, Symphony No. 88 in G, I (Chapter 12; 4th ed.)

Sonata form

SLOW INTRODUCTION

0:00	First phrase
0:38	Second phrase, preparing for theme 1

EXPOSITION

1:18	**Theme 1** (main theme)	Theme 1, *p*
1:26		Theme 1 repeated, *f*; extension runs into the bridge
1:44	**Bridge**	Built out of motive *x*
		CADENCE

Second Group

2:04	**Theme 2**	Theme 2
		CADENCE
2:19	**Cadence theme**	Cadence theme: woodwinds, then strings
2:44	*Exposition repeated*	

DEVELOPMENT

4:09	**Opening passage**	Strings only; tentative modulations using theme 1 with motive *y*, *p*
4:35	**Main**	Full orchestra; modulations continue
4:51	**Development**	– momentary appearance of theme 2, *f*
4:56		– momentary imitation (canon)
5:09		– music seems to settle in a minor key
5:22		Expectant stop, again using motive *y*

RECAPITULATION

5:24	**Theme 1**	Theme 1, *p,* with added flute counterpoint
		Theme 1, *f,* with a different, shorter extension
5:47	**Bridge**	Mostly rewritten
		CADENCE

Second Group

6:11	**Theme 2**	Even shorter than before
6:23	**Cadence theme**	Shortened
		CADENCE

CODA

6:37	Theme 1; motive *x* divided between winds and strings

Franz Joseph Haydn, Symphony No. 88 in G, II (Chapter 12; 4th ed.)

Irregular ABA form. 5 min., 28 sec.

0:00	**A** (major	**a** (oboe and solo cello)	
0:33	mode)	**a** (pizzicato strings added)	
1:06		**b** (strings)	
		a′ (with new string figure) ⟶ *ff*	
1:52		**New cadences** *ff* trumpets and drum	
		Transition: woodwinds, then strings	
2:25	**A**	**a** (violins and flute with held note in the oboe; slightly compressed, and in a new key)	
2:46		**b**	
2:58		**a′** (oboe, with faster string figure) ⟶ *ff*	
3:32	**B** (minor	Begins by overlapping the cadence of **a′**	
	mode)	**Trumpet figure** *ff* recalls the "new cadences"; modulates	
3:53		**a″** starts in a new key, and then modulates	
		Trumpet figure *ff*	
4:25	**A′** (major		
	mode)	**a′** (oboe, with new woodwind figure) ⟶ *ff*	
5:00		**New cadences** *ff* trumpets and drum (as before)	
5:10		New ending: woodwinds	

a (first phrase)

a (second phrase)

b

Franz Joseph Haydn, Symphony No. 88 in G, III (Chapter 12; 4th ed.)

Minuet and trio form

MINUET (A)

0:00	**a**	Includes several statements of motive *x*, in various versions
0:15		Two repeated cadences: both *p*
0:20	**a**	*repetition*
0:41	**b**	Motive *x*, turning into continuous motion. Modulates to a new key
1:01		Return passage, momentarily in the minor mode
1:08	**a′**	Similar to **a,** but the last cadence is *f*
1:25	**b a′**	*repetition*

TRIO (B)

2:10	**c**	
2:24	**c**	*repetition*
2:39	**d**	Begins like **c**, higher, in the minor mode
		runs right in, without a stop ⟶
2:52	**c′**	Similar (not identical!) to *just the end* of **c**
3:02	**d c′**	*repetition*

MINUET (A)   *repetition of a b a′*

Franz Joseph Haydn, Symphony No. 88 in G, IV (Chapter 12; 4th ed.)

Rondo form

0:00	**A (Tune)**	a	The entire tune is presented by the strings with bassoon and	
0:07		a	then flute, starting *p*.	
0:15		b		
0:30		a′		
0:37		ba′	*repetition*	
			Leads into episode 1	
0:59	**B (Episode 1)**		Transitional passage, *f;* modulation	
1:18			A new melodic unit, *p,* derived from the tune's first motive; strings. Repeated in the minor mode	
1:30			Cadential passage, *f*	
1:44			Upward leaps—still *f*—emphasizing the note D in preparation for the return of the tune, which starts on D	
1:49	**A′ (Tune)**		Part of the tune (**a b**) is presented, starting *p*; French horns accompany **a**. Leads into episode 2	
2:11	**C (Episode 2)**		A developmental episode, *f;* contrapuntal, modulating	
2:42			Another preparation passage, this time *p,* harping on two Ds	
			Strings alternate with French horns.	
2:57	**A″ (Tune)**		The entire tune is presented, but without repeats (**a b a′**).	
3:26	**Coda**		A brief break in the rhythm, *f,* followed by exuberant runs	
3:47			Final cadence, including echoes of the tune's opening motive Trumpet fanfares	

Wolfgang Amadeus Mozart, Symphony No. 40 in G Minor, K. 550, III (Chapter 12)

Minuet and trio form

MINUET (A)

| 0:00 | m. 1 | **a** | Dramatic, disjunct, syncopated tune |
| | | | Stop. |

0:20		**a**	Repeat
			Stop.
0:40	m. 15	**b**	Groups of three repeated notes emphasized
0:55	m 28	**a′**	Polyphonic version
			Stop.
1:05	m. 37	**codetta**	Quiet ending based on **a**, *p*
			Stop.
1:15		**b**	Repeat
1:30		**a′**	Repeat
			Stop.
1:40		**codetta**	Repeat
			Stop.

TRIO (B)

| 1:50 | m. 43 | **c** | Sweet, lyric tune in major |
| | | | Stop. |

2:15		**c**	Repeat
			Stop.
2:40	m. 61	**d**	In low strings and winds

2:50	m. 69	**c′**	In strings, horns, and winds
			Stop.
3:15		**d**	Repeat
3:25		**c′**	Repeat
			Stop.

MINUET (A)

3:50	m. 1	**a**	Dramatic, disjunct, syncopated tune
			Stop.
4:05	m. 15	**b**	Groups of three repeated notes emphasized
4:25	m. 28	**a′**	Polyphonic version
			Stop.
4:35	m. 37	**codetta**	Quiet ending based on **a**, *p*
			Stop.

Wolfgang Amadeus Mozart, Symphony No. 40 in G Minor, K. 550, IV (Chapter 12)

Sonata form

EXPOSITION

| 0:00 | m. 1 | **Theme 1** | Dramatic, rising theme in G minor, alternates between *p* and *f* |
| | | |: a :||: b a′ :| | |

| 0:30 | m. 32 | **Bridge** | Sequential. Based initially on the final motive of **a** of theme 1, *f* |
| | | | Open cadence/pause |

| 1:10 | m. 71 | **Theme 2** | Smooth, lyric theme in major, played by strings (**a**) and winds (**a′**), *p* |
| | | a a′ | |

| 1:40 | m. 101 | **Cadence theme** | Based on the same theme 1 motive that initiated the bridge, *f* |

| 2:00 | m. 124 | **Exposition** | Exposition repeats |

DEVELOPMENT

4:05	m. 125	**Part 1**	Mode, meter, and tonic are annihilated in a brief passage built from the opening, rising motive of theme **a**, *f*.
4:15	m. 135	**Part 2**	Theme 1 rising motive is imitated, *p*.
4:25	m. 146	**Part 3**	Theme 1 rising motive is imitated polyphonically as the music becomes denser and louder, *f*.
4:55	m. 175	**Part 4**	Theme 1 rising motive is imitated in bass instruments; big buildup to . . .
5:05	m. 187		Deceptive cadence, *f*

| 5:10 | m. 191 | **Part 5** | Theme 1 rising motive is imitated between high and low instruments, *f*. |
| | | | Pregnant pause |

RECAPITULATION

5:25	m. 207	**Theme 1**	As before, though without inner repeats
		|: a :||: b a′ :|	
5:40	m. 222	**Bridge**	Much as before, although the harmonic goal is now G minor, *f*.
6:05	m. 247	**Theme 2**	In G minor, *p*
		a a′	
6:35	m. 277	**Cadence theme**	Slightly extended from before, in G minor

Wolfgang Amadeus Mozart, Variations on "Ah, vous dirai-je, Maman" for piano, K. 265 (Chapter 13)

Theme and variations form

Theme	Also known as "Twinkle, Twinkle, Little Star," the theme is presented simply, with minimal accompaniment and simple harmonies. ǀ: **a** :ǁ: **b a** :ǀ

Variation I	The theme is embedded in an elaborate melody.

Variation II	The theme is supported by denser, more complex harmonies and a fast, boogie-woogie-like accompaniment.
Variation III	The theme is embedded in an elaborate melody in steady triplets, which effectively change the meter to compound duple.
Variation IV	The triplets move into the left-hand accompaniment.
Variation V	Hocket-like variation in duple meter

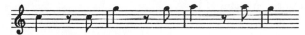

Variation VI	**a** Percussive chords and a fast, left-hand accompaniment **b** Chords move into the left hand, fast accompaniment into the right hand.
Variation VII	Fast, scalar variation; note the increasingly complex harmonies at the end of **a**.
Variation VIII	Minor mode, imitative polyphony
Variation IX	Major mode, imitative polyphony
Variation X	Virtuosic "crossed-hands" variation, harmonically the most complex variation in the set
Variation XI	Adagio, ornate, quite aria-like
Variation XII	Allegro, triple meter, fast left-hand accompaniment

Coda	After repeating the last phrase of Variation XII, the coda proceeds to reinforce the tonic and dominant harmonies.

Wolfgang Amadeus Mozart, Piano Sonata in B-flat, third movement (Allegro)
(Chapter 13; 5th ed.)

A B C A form

0:00	**A**	a	
0:14		b	
0:24		a	
0:38	**B**	c	
0:52	**(Episode 1)**	c	*repetition*
1:06		d	
1:14		c'	
1:28		d c'	*repetition*
1:50			Short transition
1:54	**C**	e	In a new key
	(Episode 2)	e	*repetition*
2:07		f	
2:14		e'	
2:21		f e'	*repetition*
2:34			Short transition = end of **b**
2:45	**A**	a	Back in the tonic key
2:58	**Coda**		Refers to **d** (or **c**), then **f**
3:19			⟨CADENCE⟩ Trill and strong cadence
New cadence motive

Wolfgang Amadeus Mozart, Piano Concerto No. 17 in G, K. 453, I (Chapter 13)

Double-exposition form

EXPOSITION 1 — ORCHESTRAL EXPOSITION

| 00:00 | **Theme 1** | Elegant, chipper theme, heard in the violins, *p* |

| 00:25 | **Bridge** | Bold, energetic theme, heard *f*. A sudden drop of dynamics to *p* anticipates theme 2. |

| 01:00 | **Theme 2** | Lyric theme, initially heard in minor |

Deceptive cadence

| 01:25 | **Cadence material** | Consists of three distinct melodic units |

Unit 2 (bridge)

Unit 3 (cadence theme)

EXPOSITION 2 — SOLO EXPOSITION

02:10	**Theme 1**	More ornamental version of theme in piano, *p*
02:45	**Bridge**	In violins and flute, then extended by piano
03:10	**Theme 3**	Light, graceful theme heard exclusively in the piano, *p*

03:40	**Bridge/solo episode**	Another bridgelike passage features rapid arpeggios in the piano.
04:00	**Theme 2**	Heard in the piano, then the piano and winds
04:25	**Solo excursion**	Scales, arpeggios, and passage work in the solo piano, accompanied by orchestra; ends with a trill
04:55	**Cadence material**	Units 2 and 3 of the cadence material played by tutti, *f*

DEVELOPMENT

| 05:20 | **Part 1** | Long, modulatory arpeggios in the piano while winds develop unit 1 of the cadence material |

| 06:05 | **Part 2** | Opening phrase of theme 1 sequenced in the piano |

RECAPITULATION

06:30	**Theme 1**	In violins, more or less as in first exposition, *p*
07:00	**Bridge**	As in the first exposition, *f*
07:30	**Theme 3**	In the piano, *p,* as in the second exposition
08:00	**Bridge/episode**	Features rapid piano arpeggios, as in the second exposition
08:20	**Theme 2**	Played at first by piano, then by piano and winds, as in the second exposition
08:45	**Solo excursion**	As in the second exposition
09:10	**Cadence material**	Unit 1 (as in the first exposition)
09:30	**Cadenza**	Piano only; ends with a trill
10:40	**Cadence material**	Units 2 and 4 finish the movement

Wolfgang Amadeus Mozart, Piano Concerto No. 17 in G, III (Chapter 13; 4th ed.)

Theme and variations form

Theme		Orchestra alone. Note the woodwind and horn figure at the cadences of **a** and **b**.	
0:00	|: **a** :|		
0:23	|: **b** :|		
Variation 1		Mainly piano, *p*; orchestral part is subsidiary.	
0:48	|: **a¹** :|	Piano enters; plays theme with melodic decorations	
1:11	|: **b¹** :|		
Variation 2		Mainly piano, more brilliant; woodwinds	
1:35	**a²**	Fast right-hand runs	
1:46	**a²′**	Fast left-hand runs	
1:58	**b²**	Right-hand runs	
2:10	**b²′**	Left-hand runs	
Variation 3		Woodwinds alternating with piano	
2:22	**a³**	Songlike dialogue in woodwinds	
2:35	**a³′**	Piano answers with its own version of the woodwind dialogue.	
2:48	**b³**	Woodwinds	
3:01	**b³′**	Piano	
Variation 4		Minor mode; strings alternating with piano, *p*	
3:14	**a⁴**	Strings play mysterious, syncopated counterpoint.	
3:26	**a⁴′**	Strings answered by piano version; more expressive	
3:40	**b⁴**	Orchestra	
3:54	**b⁴′**	Piano	
Variation 5		Major mode; full orchestra alternating with piano, *f*	
4:08	**a⁵**	Strongly metrical march played by the orchestra	
4:20	**a⁵′**	Piano counters with original theme, under a trill.	
4:33	**b⁵**	March continues in orchestra.	
4:45	**b⁵′**	Piano	
5:57		Short transition and slowdown	
Coda		Faster; orchestra in free, often rapid dialogue with the piano	
5:21		Orchestra plays new theme and insistent cadential passage.	
5:39		Piano and orchestra play the new theme with new continuations.	
6:24		New version of the original theme (only |: **a″** :| and cadential passages)	
7:32		Ends with theme fragments echoed	

Wolfgang Amadeus Mozart, Overture to *Don Giovanni* (Chapter 12 or 13)
Sonata form

SLOW INTRODUCTION

| 0:00 | | Solemn music in the minor mode. Rich orchestration; notice the low trumpets. Mysterious harmonies, heavy cadences. Leads into theme 1 |

EXPOSITION

2:11	**Theme 1** (main theme)	In the major mode, *p;* throbbing accompaniment in the strings; brief wind and brass fanfare, *f*
2:20		Theme 1 repeated. Crescendo, brass instruments help make a strong cadence.
		Stop.
2:35	**Bridge**	Bridge theme, *f,* modulates to new key; includes brief, quieter, more melodic section in the woodwinds.
		Stop.

Second Group

2:55	**Theme 2**	Theme 2 alternates between stern *f* fragment and faster, quieter answer. Contrapuntal treatment of theme 2 in the woodwinds
3:16	**Cadence theme**	Cadence theme, *f,* and repeated cadences
		Stop.

DEVELOPMENT

3:37	**Theme 2 developed**	Modulations: the two parts of theme 2 are alternated, then developed simultaneously in the woodwinds and strings.
3:56	**Theme 1**	Strings, *p,* in an unsettled-sounding key (including the wind-instrument fanfares)
		A tentative stop.
4:12	**Theme 2 developed**	Solemn feeling recalls the slow introduction; further modulations, to minor keys
4:34	**Retransition**	Crescendo prepares for return of theme 1.

RECAPITULATION

4:46	**Theme 1**	Theme 1 played twice, exactly as before.
		Stop.
5:09	**Bridge**	Bridge is in the tonic key, otherwise much as before.
		Stop.

Second Group

| 5:29 | **Theme 2** | In the tonic key, otherwise much as before |
| 5:49 | **Cadence theme** | In the tonic key, much as before, but leading without a stop to the brief coda |

CODA

| 6:05 | | Brief, emphatic coda makes the final cadence. |
| | | Stop. |

Ludwig van Beethoven, String Quartet in A, Op. 18, No. 5, Menuetto
(Chapter 13 or 14; 3rd ed.)

Minuet and trio form

MINUET (A)

0:00	**a**	Two instruments only: violins 1 and 2
0:12	**a**	The violins' music moved to viola and cello
0:25	**b**	For violin 1, with quiet accompaniment
		[CADENCE] in a minor key; low cello; *cresc.* → *ff*
0:49	**a'**	Violins 1 and 2
1:01	**a"**	Dialogue: violins 1 and 2 and viola
1:18	**coda**	Chordal, homophonic style
1:29	**b a' a" coda**	*repetition*

TRIO (B)

2:30	**c**	Melody in violin 2 and viola
2:40	**c**	*repetition*
2:50	**d**	Melody in viola and cello, then violins and cello
3:00	**c'**	Melody in violins 1 and 2
3:09	**d c'**	*repetition*

MINUET (A) *repetition of a a b a' a" coda*

Franz Schubert, String Quartet in A Minor, II (Andante) (Chapter 13 or 16; 4th ed.)

Slow-movement sonata form

EXPOSITION

0:00	**Theme 1**	a a′		
0:22		b		
0:35		c		Motive *x*
0:46		b c (exact repetition)		
1:10	**Bridge**	Dialogue: violin 1, violin 2, cello		
1:34	**Theme 2**			
1:53		Free shortened repetition of theme 2 in the minor mode		
2:08	**Theme 3**	Includes several sforzandos (*sf:* See page 12 of *Listen*)		
2:34	**Cadence theme/ transition**	Dialogue: violin 2, viola, cello, etc.		Motive *x*

RECAPITULATION

2:59	**Theme 1**	a a′	Variation: added sixteenth notes in violin 2	
		b c	Variation continues (sixteenth notes)	
3:47		b′ c′	In a further variation: minor mode, modulation	
4:13	**Short development**	*f:* uses material from the end of **c** and from the cadence theme/transition		Motive *x*
4:40	**Retransition**			Motive *x*
5:00	**Theme 2**			
5:35	**Theme 3**	Shorter and simpler than before		
5:50	**Cadence theme/ transition**	But this time not modulating		Motive *x*

CODA

6:15	**Bridge**	Also not modulating		Motive *x*, reduced

Rag *Mauj-Khammaj* (Chapter 13; 5th ed.)

First Excerpt

0:00   **Alap:** tambura, then sarod, then sitar

3:15   Rhythms quicken as the alap ends.

3:32   **First Gat:** tune played by sitar and sarod in heterophony; tabla enter.

Second Excerpt

0:23   Tempo quickens as **second gat** begins.

0:35   Tune from the first gat returns, faster.

Tyagaraja, "Marakata manivarna" (Chapter 13 or 22; 4th ed.)

0:00	**Section 1**	Improvised section, unmetered and without drum; violin follows voice's phrases in exploring rag.
2:34	**Section 2**	Main body of song begins with refrain; not improvised, voice and violin together; metered, with drum.
3:49		Verse, higher in pitch than refrain
4:53		Return to refrain
5:27	**Section 3**	New improvised section, on note syllables; violin drops out; metered, with drum.

REFRAIN:

Marakata manivarna! Rama!   Oh Rama, charming emerald-colored god!
Nannu maravaka, nayanna.   My beloved brother, do not forget me!

VERSE:

Parama-purusha! Binna brovumu,   You are the supreme being!
devara! Sharanukonna.   Protect me! Be my refuge!

Hector Berlioz, *Fantastic* Symphony, IV, "March to the Scaffold" (Chapter 16; 5th ed. CD-ROM)

Sonata form				March form
0:00	m. 1	**Introduction**	Incredible buildup as drums approach	

EXPOSITION   MARCH

0:25	m. 17	**Theme 1**	Powerful, falling minor scale, heard twice in the low strings, then twice in the violins, *ff*	

1:15	m. 49		Theme 1 inverted, played by strings, pizzicato, *pp*. Crescendo . . .	

1:35	m. 62	**Theme 2 (Scaffold March)**	Blaring march scored for brass and winds *f* :| (repeat sign rarely observed)	TRIO

DEVELOPMENT

2:00	m. 78	Vicious, percussive chords, *ff*	
2:05	m. 82	Divided orchestration of theme 1	

2:15	m. 89	Theme 2 in its entirety, with strings added	TRIO (repeated)
2:35	m. 105	Vicious, percussive chords, *ff*	
2:40	m. 109	Divided orchestration of theme 1	
2:50	m. 114	Theme 1 in the low brass, big buildup!	Transition

RECAPITULATION   MARCH

3:05	m. 123	**Theme 1**	Tutti, *ff*	
3:15	m. 131		Theme 1 inverted, *ff*	

CODA   CODA

3:30	m. 140	Driving, fanfare-ish chords announce the arrival at the scaffold, *ff*	
4:05	m. 164	*Idée fixe*	One last thought of the beloved before the blade falls, in the clarinet, *pp*
4:10	m. 169	The beloved melody is brutally cut off by a dramatic drumroll, *ff* . . .	
4:30	m. 178	The blade falls! *ff*	

Franz Liszt, *Totentanz* for piano and orchestra (Chapter 16)

Quasi theme and variations form*

THEME

00:00		*Dies irae*	Phrases **a** and **b** of the *Dies irae* (see the second page of this Listening Chart) played by the trombones and tuba

Cadenza 1

00:25			Piano cuts in, amid cries of protest from the orchestra.
00:55	2	*Dies irae*	Phrases **a**, **b**, and **c** in the orchestra
01:20	4	*Dies irae*	Phrases **a** and **b** in the piano
Variation 1 01:50	5	|: a b :||: c :|	*Dies irae* in the basses, pizzicato, against a melody in the bassoon, *f*

Variation 2 02:40	8	|: a b :||: c :|	Dramatic glissando in the piano, ***mf***
Variation 3 03:20	10	|: a b :||: c :|	Short, rhythmic version of the *Dies irae* in the piano, ***ff***

(Internal form of each variation becomes freer and freer.)

Variation 4 03:50	12		Slow, expressive canon for piano alone, *p*
Variation 5 05:30			Flowing, love-theme-like variation for piano and clarinet, marked *dolce, pp*
07:00			Violent, rhythmic piano interlude breaks the quiet mood and hurls the music into . . .
Variation 6 07:15	14		Fast, rhythmic fugue for piano only, *f*
Variation 7 07:45	15		Fast, playful, highly elaborated *Dies irae* in piano and orchestra
08:15			Loud, majestic piano interlude, ***ff***
Variation 8 08:25	17		Fast, developmental variation for piano and orchestra. Variation ends with the first four notes of the *Dies irae* in the French horn and bassoon.
Variation 9 09:25	21		Polka-like piano (***pp***) alternates with orchestra (***ff***). Variation builds up to a climax on phrase **c** of the *Dies irae*.

---

*Rehearsal box numbers are used instead of measure numbers.

Cadenza 2
10:00

New Theme 22
11:15

The new theme resembles the *Dies irae* but is noticeably different. Interspersed throughout are dramatic horn calls, *f.*

Variation 1 23
11:40

Light, bell-like variation for piano, pizzicato strings, and flute, *pp*

Variation 2 24
12:00

Faster, more elaborate variation. Note the urgent violin motives, *pp.*

Variation 3 25
12:21

Quieter, faster variation features incredibly light piano elaboration, *pp.*

Variation 4 26
12:35

Theme in *col legno* strings; piano plays dramatic accompaniment, *ff*

Variation 5
12:55

Elaborate, virtuosi variation for piano alone, *f*

Variation 6 27
13:15

Fast, dramatic variation for piano and orchestra, *ff*

Cadenza 3
13:45

The *Dies irae* returns in the bass of the piano, against long, dramatic arpeggios in the top.

Variation 10 28
(*Dies irae*)
and Conclusion
14:25

Rousing, exciting variation features piano *glissando*; builds to a monumental final statement of the *Dies irae* in the brass and a cataclysmic descent in the strings, *ff.*

Richard Wagner, Prelude to *Tristan and Isolde* (Chapter 17; 5th ed.)

(Note: **d/c** stands for deceptive cadence.)

MAIN THEMATIC GROUP (a d/c B): dynamics *pp*, surge to *f*, back to *p*

0:00	**a** in threefold sequence	With fermatas (long gaps)
1:33	**d/c**	Deceptive cadence, *f*: French horn
1:37	**B**	B followed by extension: cellos
2:23	**C**	Descending sequence
2:41		Somber trombone motive

B WITH NEW EXTENSIONS

3:06	**B**	B followed by extension: woodwinds
3:29		Quieter material; strings answered by strings and woodwinds
4:10	**d/c**	
4:16	**C**	Descending sequence: woodwinds, horn
4:27		Trombone motive, louder now
4:38		Big surge begins
5:09	**B**	

RETRANSITION PASSAGE (bass is more static)

5:54		New, yearning string music
6:09	*y*, 4 times	(y is first heard in the oboe)
6:45	**d/c - B** overlaps	Louder and louder: *ff*
7:17	*x*, played twice ⟶	Climactic horn calls, in preparation for:

ENTIRE THEMATIC GROUP   Dynamics *ff*, then down to *p* and *pp*

7:26	**a** in threefold sequence	Varied, and with the gaps filled in
8:38	**d/c**	Deceptive cadence, as at first, but *p*
8:42	**B** fragments	Varied; minor-mode coloration. Drumroll
9:24	**a** in twofold sequence	Varied (English horn) ⟶ curtain goes up

Bedřich Smetana, "Vlatava" ("The Moldau"), from *Ma Vlast* (Chapter 18)

Symphonic poem

THE RIVER IS BORN

00:00	**First source of the Vlatava**	Swirling, perpetual-motion flutes and pizzicato strings create a watery impression. Compound duple meter, *p*
00:25	**Second source of the Vlatava**	Swirling clarinets join the flutes.
01:00		Strings and triangle enter as the tributary streams become wider and deeper.
	River theme	Lush, Bohemian-flavored tune, *p*
01:05	|: a :|	
01:35	|: b a′ :|	

A HUNT IN THE FOREST

03:05		Hunting horns and blaring trumpets announce the hunt, *f.*
		Swirling strings represent the river as it flows past the hunt.
03:50		The sounds of the hunt recede.
04:05		The meter shifts to duple; decrescendo to *ppp*

VILLAGE WEDDING

04:15	|: a :|	Simple, rustic dance tune, *mf*

04:40	a′	Tutti; note triangle.
04:55	a	
05:05	b	
05:20	b′	The wedding dance fades into the background as the river flows on; decrescendo to *ppp*

MOON, DANCE OF THE WATER NYMPHS

05:45		Sustained winds create nocturnal mood, *pp*
06:10	a	Quiet, ethereal tune in swirling strings, flutes, clarinets, and harp, *p*

07:25	a′	Brass enters quietly.
08:20	b	Modulation; crescendo to *f*

THE RIVER

08:40		Swirling flutes and clarinets from beginning return.
	River theme	
08:50	**a**	
09:00	**b**	
09:30	**a′**	

THE RAPIDS OF SAINT JOHN

09:40	The music begins to swirl violently, *ff*
	Crescendo . . .
10:50	Climactic *fff,* followed by a long descent and decrescendo to *pp*

VLATAVA, POWERFUL STREAM

11:00	A grand, forceful version of the river theme, played by the entire orchestra, *ff*

THE CASTLE OF VYSEHRAD

11:30	The wide river flows past the castle, which itself is the subject of an entire movement of *Ma Vlast, ff.*

FINAL SECTION

11:45		Vigorous, grandiose closing section, *fff*
12:20	**The river flows from view**	Decrescendo to *pp*
12:50		Closing chords, *ff*

Bedřich Smetana, Overture to *The Bartered Bride* (Chapter 18; 4th ed.)

Modified sonata form

EXPOSITION

0:00	**Theme 1**	Fanfare version of theme 1

0:11		Fugal version, rustling strings: violin 1

	0:25	violin 2
	0:41	viola
	0:58	cellos and basses
1:19	**Bridge**	Starts with one phrase of the polka (new key)
1:45	**Modulation—buildup**	
1:55	**Theme 2**	The complete polka

2:10	**Cadence theme**	
2:17	**Fanfare**	The fanfare makes the final cadence

BRIEF CENTRAL EPISODE (Development)

2:30		The rustling comes to a near ⬚stop⬚
2:34	**New tune**	Modulating: oboe
2:51		A new phrase in the tune: strings

RECAPITULATION

3:00	**Theme 1**	The fanfare breaks in suddenly
3:09		Fugal version—this time modulating, with winds
3:41		Polka fragments
4:00	**Theme 2**	Polka, longer than before
4:18	**Cadence theme**	(Much longer than before)
4:47	**Fanfare**	The cadence is suddenly evaded: abrupt modulation

CODA

4:58		Another ⬚stop.⬚ Quiet, slower, dreamlike polka fragments: oboes
5:22		Original tempo: timpani roll
5:44		Polka fragment
6:00		Fanfare, new cadential material
6:15		Ends with just the first eight notes of the fanfare

Nicolai Rimsky-Korsakov, *Russian Easter* Overture (Chapter 18)

Concert overture

INTRODUCTION—LENTO MISTICO

00:00	m. 1	"Let God Arise"	Prayerful, chantlike winds intone the morning hymn, *p*.

00:15	m. 4		Strings play the hymn.
00:30	m. 7		Violin solo
00:50	m. 10	"An Angel Wailed"	Beautiful, lyric hymn in solo cello, *p*

01:05	m. 15		Flute solo
01:25	m. 20	"Let God Arise"	In trombones, played responsorially
01:50	m. 26		Played by the winds
02:10	m. 29		Flute solo
02:30	m. 32	"An Angel Wailed"	In solo clarinet, *p*
02:45	m. 37		Violin solo
03:05	m. 42	"Let God Arise"	In the tuba and bassoon, meant to "depict the holy sepulcher"
03:25	m. 55		Cello solo
03:40	m. 60	"Let God Arise"	Accelerando . . .

ALLEGRO AGITATO

04:15	m. 82	"Let Them Also That Hate Him Flee before Him" alternates with "Let God Arise"	Agitated, *mf*

05:15	m. 157		Powerful, bridgelike sequence played in tutti; chords alternate with fast string and wind melody, *ff*.
05:50	m. 202	"Christ Is Arisen"	Lyric, singing tune in upper strings, *p*

06:15	m. 221		Initially quiet, pizzicato passage builds to a rousing fanfare in the trumpets.
07:20	m. 270	"Christ Is Arisen"	In winds, with string accompaniment
07:45	m. 291	"Let God Arise"	Striking, prayerful solo trombone intones a new version of the hymn.
08:41	m. 302		Violin solo
08:50	m. 304		Powerful, bridgelike sequence returns, at first *p*, crescendoing to *f*.

09:40	m. 370	"Let God Arise"	Spirited, developmental version of hymn, heard responsorially between brass and winds
10:10	m. 409		Vigorous, syncopated tune, *f*
10:30	m. 433		Powerful, bridgelike sequence returns, *ff*. Decrescendo to *p*
11:05	m. 479	"Christ Is Arisen"	In violins
11:35	m. 502		Violin solo
11:45	m. 505		Initially quiet pizzicato passage builds to a rousing fanfare in the trumpets.
12:20	m. 541		Bell-like version of previous pizzicato passage, *f*
12:25	m. 547	"Christ Is Arisen"	Grandly played by trombones and tubas
13:10	m. 604		Quiet, transitional passage
13:25	m. 626		Powerful, bridgelike sequence played by tutti; chords alternate with fast string and wind melody, *ff*.
13:55	m. 661	"Christ Is Arisen"	Ringing, *maestoso* version of hymn in low brass. Note the celebratory bells.
14:14	m. 675		Grandiose, tutti ending, *fff*

Johannes Brahms, Symphony No. 4, IV (Chapter 18)

Passacaglia form

0:00	**Theme**	Full orchestra, with the brass prominent		Theme
0:18	**Variation A 1**	Syncopated version of theme: pizzicato strings, muffled drumrolls		
0:33	**Variations A 2–3**	Moving mostly in quarter notes		Variation A 3
1:04	**Variation A 4**	Dotted quarter notes and eighths	GRADUAL RHYTHMIC BUILDUP	
1:21	**Variations A 5–6**	Eighth notes: romantic string melody		
1:50	**Variations A 7–9**	Shorter notes; builds to a climax, but dies down		
2:36	**Variations A 10–11**	Quieter, a little slower: sighing figures		
		Leads to a contrasting **B** section; the **B** variations go twice as slowly		Variation B 1
3:18	**Variation B 1**	Expressive flute solo, *p*		
4:04	**Variation B 2**	Major mode: clarinet and oboe		
4:40	**Variations B 3–4**	Major mode: quiet trombones, winds. Fermata (⌢)		
6:06	**Variation A′ 1**	Sense of recapitulation: begins like the theme, *f*		
6:19	**Variations A′ 2–6**	Another gradual rhythmic buildup, analogous to **A 2–9. A′ 6** is climactic: trombone punctuation		
7:17	**Variation A′ 7**	Sudden "scherzo" quality		
7:29	**Variation A′ 8**	Theme is heard behind triplet figures; louder		
7:41	**Variation A′ 9**	A louder version of variation **A 1**	SENSE OF RECAPITU- LATION	
7:53	**Variation A′ 10**	A louder version of variation **A 2**		Variation A′ 12
8:06	**Variation A′ 11**	Recalls variation **A 3**		
8:19	**Variations A′ 12–14**	Quieter, waltzlike		
8:56	**Variation A′ 15**	Picks up energy to prepare for the coda. Ritardando		
9:17	**Coda**	Faster; begins with the theme and ends with up-the-scale cadential figures		

Claude Debussy, *Festivals (Fêtes)*, from Three Nocturnes (Chapter 20)

Three-part form

0:00	**The Music Begins**	A pulsation begins in the high instruments.
		The music is in duple meter, with two regularly alternating beats: one strong beat, one weak.
0:04		A short, fast melody is heard, running up and down, played by woodwinds.
0:17		Same melody, repeated
		With a new **tone color** (played by different woodwind instruments)
0:23		Buildup: repetitions of a fragment of the original melody
		A small musical figure is called a **motive.**
0:35		Slowdown: loud trumpet fanfare, drumroll
		The speed, or **tempo,** of the music changes momentarily.
0:46	**A Second Beginning**	Another kind of pulsation, then the fast melody again
		Music that is heard again and again in a piece is called its **theme,** or one of its themes. The theme now has a new ending, or **cadence.**
1:03		French horn figure
		The meter changes to **triple meter**—one strong beat and two weak beats.
1:22		New melody, oboe
1:40		New, lilting melody, strings
2:18		Buildup
		An increase in music's **dynamics** (volume) is called a **crescendo.**
2:35	**Stop**	
2:36	**A Distant March**	A steady pulsation—a little slower
2:51		March melody, distant trumpets: first time
		The march is played with chords—a **homophonic texture.**
3:04		(Second part of the march)
		The march consists of two similar segments, or **phrases.**
3:18		March: second time, louder
3:42		March, third time, louder yet, with the original fast theme played simultaneously
		A texture with two or more melodies sounding simultaneously is called **polyphonic.**
4:04		Climax—new figure in brass
4:10	**Return to the Original Music**—approximately	
		The satisfaction of recognizing that we have returned to something familiar is one consequence of the musical **form** of *Festivals.*
4:23		New, passionate theme in the strings
4:33		A rapid flash of the march music (trumpets)
4:38	**Return to the "Second Beginning"**—almost literally	
5:10	**The Music Runs Down**	"Rumbling" effect
5:35		Slowdown: new motive (oboe)
5:59		The original tempo is resumed; the rumbling, again
6:13		Quiet cymbal clash

Claude Debussy, "La Cathédrale engloutie," from Preludes, Book 1 (Chapter 20)

SUNRISE—EARLY MORNING

0:00   m. 1   **Organum Harmonies**   Profoundly calm parallel chords invoke both a predawn mood and medieval organum, *pp*.

0:40   m. 7   **Plainchant**   A quiet, chantlike tune emerges as the priests intone their dawn-time prayers.

1:25   m. 16   **The Mists Part**   Rippling arpeggios punctuated by bell-like chords signal the sunrise and the lifting mists. Crescendo . . .

2:00   m. 22   **The Cathedral Arisen**   The risen cathedral gleams in the morning sun; clangorous fragments of the plainchant announce its appearance, *f*.

NOON

2:15   m. 28   **Bells**   A celebratory passage in which the bells of the cathedral ring out across the water. Note long pedal note underlying the entire section, *ff*.

3:05   m. 42   The bells slowly stop. Decrescendo to *pp*

AFTERNOON

3:30   m. 47   **Plainchant**   The plainchant returns, supported by new and mysterious harmonies. Note pedal that underlies the entire section. Crescendo to *ff*

4:20   m. 62   Falling parallel chords signal the slowly sinking sun. Decrescendo to *pp*

EVENING

4:55   m. 72   **Echo of the Bells**   The once-celebratory bells appear as an echo of the past, muffled by the water, as the cathedral sinks back into the sea. Note ostinato that underlies the entire section, *pp*.

5:30   m. 84   **Organum**   The cathedral has vanished; the religious, calm atmosphere of the opening returns, *pp*.

The timings on this Listening Chart are more approximate than those in the others. A performance of this prelude that literally follows the tempos indicated on the score will last about nine minutes. Debussy's own recording of this work treats the tempo very flexibly and takes but six minutes. The timings on this Listening Chart are based on Debussy's own rendition of this prelude.

Igor Stravinsky, *Pulcinella* Suite (Chapter 20 or 21)

Ballet suite

I. Sinfonia (Overture)	Wry, fanfare-like movement. Note: 1. Short, repetitive phrases 2. Harmony hardly moves from G major during entire movement 3. Subtle changes of meter
II. Serenata	Flowing, dotted rhythms. Note: 1. Pedals and ostinato throughout 2. Fantastic orchestral timbres
III. Scherzino	A series of three different pieces, juxtaposed without transitions or segues Part 1: Playful, fast tune in duple meter Part 2: Starts with "chirps" in flute and pizzicato strings; triple meter Part 3: Slow, lyric piece in duple meter
IV. Tarantella	Very fast, exciting Neapolitan dance in compound duple meter. Note pedal tones and ostinatos.
V. Toccata	Striking and sudden change to slower, duple meter. Note the sudden, unexpected accents.
VI. Gavotte (with variations)	Lovely aria-like tune, heard in oboe and flute. Duple meter Variation 1: Scored for oboes, bassoons, and French horns. Compound duple meter Variation 2: Scored for flutes, bassoons, and French horns. Duple meter
VII. Vivo	Brusque, playful, very Stravinskyan! Note: 1. Trombone glissando 2. Static harmony 3. Unexpected accentuation
VIII. Minuetto	Starts quietly and gradually becomes louder. Moves directly into . . .
IX. Finale	Joyful, *ff* finale for the entire orchestra. Note cross-rhythms in trumpet at end.

Béla Bartók, String Quartet No. 2, II (Chapter 20 or 21)

Hybrid sonata/minuet and trio form

0:00	**Introductory motives**	
0:07	**Theme 1**	Violin 1, accompanied by fast repeated notes in violin 2
		This repeated-note accompaniment always starts prior to theme.
0:33	**Continuation**	Cello and viola; then viola, *ff*
0:40		(The introductory motives interrupt briefly, *ff*.)
0:51	**Continuation**	Cello in the high range and viola, once again, *mf*
1:10		Transition
1:17	**Theme 2**	Theme 2 starts after a short glissando (slide); brief and repetitive. (This theme includes one of the introductory motives.)
1:34	**Cadential passage**	This passage includes three fermatas (brief slowdowns), followed by a motive:
1:49	**Theme 1**	In the three low instruments; like a rondo return
2:07	**Continuation**	New, exuberant continuation for theme 1, *ff*
2:33		Three very abrupt stops!
2:44	**Development**	Development of theme 2 and the introductory motives; much stopping and starting
3:03		Theme 2 developed with pizzicato background
3:19		Forceful descending chords, in sequence, prepare for the Trio.
3:29	**TRIO**	Introduction: short phrases of the coming melody, interrupted by stops and fragments of theme 1, gradually getting slower
3:46		A long graceful melody moving from instrument to instrument, with guitarlike accompaniment. Slower tempo, *p*
4:31		Development is resumed, at the original tempo.
4:53	**Cadential passage**	Fermatas again; more expansive treatment of the motive (with all instruments playing very high)
5:18		Speedup—using the same motive
5:26	**Theme 1**	A thematic transformation in fast **3/4** meter, starting in the cello
5:46		New continuation recalls theme 2.
5:59		The sequential chords that prepared for the Trio, now in rollicking 3/4 meter
6:18		Brief recollection of the Trio—two phrases only, medium tempo
6:27	**Coda**	Fast whirling passage, *p,* made up of tiny bits of theme 1
7:14		Ends with a clear motive from theme 1, repeated *ff*

Béla Bartók, Music for Strings, Percussion, and Celesta, complete work (Chapter 21; 3rd ed.)

FIRST MOVEMENT (**Andante tranquillo: fugue**) *starts pp, with mutes on all the string instruments*

			Countersubject
0:00	**Fugal exposition**	Viola ——⌇	
0:21		Vn 2 ——⌇	
0:40		Cello ——⌇	
1:01		Vn 1 ——⌇	
1:22		Bass ——	
1:44	**Episode 1**	Short	slow **crescendo**
2:09	**Stretto**	Vn 1 ——	
2:11		Cello ——	slow **crescendo**
2:44	**Episode 2**	Using fragments of the subject; *mutes off*; **cresc.** to *f*
4:01	(**Textural**	**First climax,** *ff*: percussion enter
4:17	**break**)	**Second climax,** *fff*: single high note, downward scoops
4:21		Fragments of *inverted subject* announced, *fff*, then *mf, p*: *mutes on again*
5:09	**Stretto**	*Inverted subject:* violin 2 (muted), then viola, then violin 1+cello
5:53	**Combination**	Celesta enters: subject (above) + *inverted subject (below)*
6:16		Fragments of subject and inverted subject; "converging" cadence

SECOND MOVEMENT (**Allegro: sonata form**)

0:00	**Exposition**
2:29	**Development**
5:09	**Recapitulation**
6:25	**Coda**

THIRD MOVEMENT (**Adagio: arch form**)

0:00	**A**	Introductory: xylophone and pedal timpani, viola and violin ruminations
1:57		(**Background cue: fugue subject: a**) *low strings*
2:26	**B**	More oscillations: celesta and solo violins. Background trills, *pp*
3:19		(**Background cue: fugue subject: a′**) *strings* (after a brief recollection of **A**)
	C	Further slow oscillations. Background glissandos. **Crescendo** ——→ *f*
4:18		Piano: new motive in 5/4 meter, *f*—faster, climactic
4:55		(**Background cue: fugue subject: b**) *strings*
5:05	**B**	B melody now in canon
5:55		(**Background cue: fugue subject: b′**) *celesta and piano*
6:04	**A**	Terminal: violin and viola ruminations, xylophone, pedal timpani

FOURTH MOVEMENT (**Allegro molto: rondo form**)

0:00	**A**	With a *pizzicato* "preface"
0:26	**B**	Timpani launch a repetitive theme: piano and *pizzicato* strings.
0:43	**A**	
0:52	**C**	
1:14	**A′**	Piano; theme is transformed
1:25	**D**	Timpani launches another folklike theme.
1:58	**A″**	Piano; extension of **A′**
2:22	**E**	
2:35	**B**	Piano
3:02		Transition
3:26	**Original**	Transformed; slower tempo ⎫ strings
4:42	**fugue subject**	Fragments in inversion ⎭ alone
5:11	**F**	Cello solo—reference to the third movement (the string solos in **A**)
5:27	**A‴**	In various transformations

Steve Reich, *Tehillim,* fourth section (Chapter 22; 5th ed.)

0:00		Transition from part 3—accelerates to a new steady beat
0:14	**Theme: a b c c′**	Two sporanos in harmony with irregularly placed chords accompanying the singing
0:43	**Variation 1**	Two-part canon **a b c c′**
1:11	**Variation 2**	Four-part canon—**a** repeated many times
1:54		After a brief punctuation, **b** (starts with voices alone)
2:19		After a brief punctuation, **c** (starts with voices alone)
2:54	**Variation 3**	Two voices with clarinets, drums
3:41	**Instrumental interlude**	Background chords continue
4:17	**Variation 4**	
5:12		Climactic high note
5:28	**Coda**	on the word "Hallelujah" only; electric organ, bells
6:41		Abrupt stop

George Gershwin, Piano Concerto in F, III (Chapter 23; 4th ed.)

Rondo form

0:00	**Rondo Theme** **A**	A fast theme built out of a syncopated motive is played first by the orchestra, next by the piano (in a new key).	
		A modulation is carried out by the piano.	
0:57	B	Syncopated, bluesy theme (piano and strings; in a new key)	
1:23	A	Sudden return to **A** in the piano	
1:41	C	Jaunty muted-trumpet phrase—slowdown—trumpet again	
2:14	A	An expanded, developmental version of **A**, blended with the **C** motive	
2:26		**A** in the xylophone	
2:46		**A** in the piano, very briefly	
2:49	D	A sentimental new tune in the strings; the piano answers with **C**.	
3:21		Brass instruments play a loud contrapuntal treatment of **C**.	
3:35	A	Another sudden appearance of **A** in the piano and xylophone	
3:57	E	A new, playful tune in the strings (with piano runs); the piano answers with **C**, once again.	
4:12		Brief piano solo	
4:33	A	The climactic *orchestral* presentation of **A**; big slowdown	
4:53	B	A gong stroke introduces a loud, slow, swinging version of **B** in the orchestra (the piano plays chords). This dies down for a moment.	
5:47	A	The climactic *piano* presentation of **A**, back in the original tempo; orchestral crescendo	
6:03	**Coda**	Nine powerful timpani strokes quote the first-movement theme. The piano winds the piece up.	

APPENDIX II

Texts and Translations

To facilitate photocopying and distribution, additional texts and translations are contained separately in this appendix. Some texts come from works for which Kerman and Tomlinson do not provide the complete text; others come from works suggested in Further Listening Examples for various chapters. "5th ed." indicates a performance on the recordings for *Listen,* Brief Fifth Edition; "4th ed.," a performance on the recordings for *Listen,* Brief Fourth Edition; and "3rd ed.," a performance on the recordings for *Listen,* Brief Third Edition. For suggested CD or video recordings, see Multimedia Resources for the chapter indicated in the heading for each chart below.

GREGORIAN HYMN "Ave maris stella" (Chapters 5 and 6)

Ave maris stella	Hail, star of the ocean,
Dei mater alma,	Kind Mother of God,
Atque semper virgo	And also still a virgin,
Felix coeli porta.	Our blessed port to heaven.

GREGORIAN INTROIT "Viri Galilaei" (Chapter 5; 4th ed.)

Introit	*Viri Galilaei,*	Men of Galilee,
	quid admiramini	what are you marveling at
	aspecientes in coelum?	as you look up at the sky?
	ALLELUIA	Hallelujah!
	Quemadmodum vidistis eum	Just as you have seen Him
	ascendentem in coelum,	ascending to heaven,
	ita veniet.	so He will return.
	ALLELUIA (3 times)	Hallelujah!
Recitation	*Omnes gentes, plaudite in minibus;*	All you nations, clap your hands;
(Psalm 47)	*Jubilate Deo in voce exsultationis.*	Acclaim our God with shouts of joy.
	Gloria Patri et filio,	Glory to the Father and to the Son,
	et Spiritui Sancto;	and to the Holy Ghost.
	Sicut erat in principio et nunc	As it was in the beginning, is now,
	et semper et in saecula saeculorum.	and ever shall be, world without end.
	Amen.	Amen.
Introit	*Viri Galilaei . . .*	

704

GREGORIAN INTROIT "Requiem aeternam" (Chapter 5)

R—*Requiem aeternam dona eis Domine:* Grant them eternal rest, Lord,
et lux perpetua luceat eis. and let perpetual light shine upon them.
V—*Te decet hymnus, Deus, in Sion,* A hymn becometh Thee, O God, in Zion,
et tibi reddetur votum in Jerusalem. and a vow shall be paid to Thee in Jerusalem.
Exaudi orationem meam, Hear my prayer:
ad te omnis caro veniet. to Thee all flesh shall come.
R—*Requiem aeternam dona eis Domine:* Grant them eternal rest, Lord,
et lux perpetua luceat eis. and let perpetual light shine upon them.

SEQUENCE "Dies irae" (Chapters 5 and 16)

Dies irae, dies illa, The day of wrath, that dreadful day,
Solvet saeculum in favilla, Shall the whole world in ashes lay,
Teste David cum Sibylla. As David and the Sibyl say.

Quantus tremor est futurus, Oh, what fear shall it engender,
Quando judex est venturus, When the Judge shall come in splendor,
Cuncta stricte discussurus. Strict to mark and just to render!

Tuba mirum spargens sonum The last loud trumpet's wondrous sound
Per sepulcra regionum, Shall through the rending tombs rebound,
Coget omnes ante thronum. And wake the nations under ground.

Mors stupebit et natura, All aghast then Death shall shiver,
Cum resurget creatura, And great Nature's frame shall quiver,
Judicanti responsura. When the graves their dead deliver.

Liber scriptus proferetur, Then shall, with universal dread,
In quo totum continetur, The sacred mystic Book be read,
Unde mundus judicetur. To try the living and the dead.

(fifteen more stanzas)

GREGORIAN HYMN "Pange lingua" (Chapters 5 and 6)

Pange lingua gloriosi Sing, O tongue, of the glorious
Corporis mysterium mystery of the body
Sanguinisque pretiosi and of the precious blood,
Quem in mundi pretium which, to redeem the world,
Fructus ventris generosi our King—fruit of a noble womb—
Rex effudit gentium. poured out for us.

LÉONIN Organum on the plainchant "Alleluia. Pascha nostrum" (Chapter 5)

Alleluia. Alleluia.
V—*Pascha nostrum immolatus est Christus.* V—Christ our Passover has been sacrificed for us.

PÉROTIN Organum quadruplum on the plainchant gradual "Viderunt omnes" (Chapter 5)

Viderunt omnes fines terrae All the ends of the earth
salutare Dei nostri: Have seen the victory of our God.
jubilate Deo omnis terra. Make a joyful noise to the Lord, all the earth.
V—*Notum fecit Dominus salutare suum:* The Lord has made known his victory;
ante conspectum gentium In the sight of the nations
revelavit justitiam suam. He has revealed his vindication.

—Psalm 98:2–4 (adapted from NRSV)

ANONYMOUS Qur'anic recitation, "Ya Sin" (Chapter 5)

Bismi Allahi alrrahmani alrraheemi

1. *Ya-seen*
2. *Waalqur-ani alhakeemi*
3. *Innaka lamina almursaleena*
4. *AAala siratin mustaqeemin*
5. *Tanzeela alΛΛazeezi alrraheemi*
6. *Litunthira qawman ma onthira abaohum fahum ghafiloona*
7. *Laqad haqqa alqawlu AAala aktharihim fahum la yu/minoona*
8. *Inna jaAAalna fee aAAnaqihim aghlalan fahiya ila al-athqani fahum muqmahoona*
9. *WajaAAalna min Bayni aydeehim saddan wamin khalfihim saddan faaghshaynahum fahum la yubsiroona*
10. *Wasaw a on AAalayhim aan th artahum am lam tun th irhum la yu/minoona*

Ya Sin.
By the wise Qur'an,
Lo! thou art of those sent
On a straight path,
A revelation of the Mighty, the Merciful,
That thou mayst warn a folk whose fathers
were not warned, so they are heedless.
Already hath the judgment (for their infidelity)
proved true of most of them, for they believe not.
Lo! We have put on their necks carcans
reaching unto the chins, so that they are
made stiff-necked.
And we have set a bar before them and a
bar behind them, and (thus) have covered
them so that they see not.
Whether thou warn them or thou warn them not,
it is alike for them, for they believe not.

HAWAI'IAN CHANT, *mele pule* (Chapter 5)

Mele oli
Aia no ke 'kua la I uka;
[Ke hoá la I ka papa a enaena,
A pulelo mai ka ohi'a o ka lua;
Maewa ke po'o, pu'u, newa I ka makani,
I ka hoonane ia e ka awaawa, e-e!]

The god is at work in the hills;
[She has fired the plain oven-hot;
The forest-fringe of the pit is aflame;—
Fire-tongues, fire-globes, that sway in the wind—
The fierce bitter breath of the Goddess!]

—Nathaniel B. Emerson, *Pele and Hiiaka—A Myth from Hawaii*

Mele Inoa Ali'i
'Ike ia Kaukini he lawai'a manu
He 'upena ku'u i ka noe ko Pokahi
Ke ho'opuni la i ka 'ohu
Ke ho'opuni la i ka 'ohu na kikepa
Ke na'i i ka luna o Ka'auana
'O ka 'uahi ke kapeku
E hei 'ai ka i'a manu o Puoali'i
'O ke ali'i wale no ka'u makemake
'O ka luhi o maua me 'ia nei
'O ka makou le'ale'a no 'ia

You will recognize Kaukini, the bird catcher
Spreading his nets like the mist of Pokahi
The mist stretches
Stretching the mist-like nets around
And over the uplands of Ka'auana
The dark smoke will drive
The bird Puoali'i into the net
I delight in serving the chief
Whom I and others care for
This is our joy

—Leilehua Yuen, *Hulu Manu: Featherwork of Hawai'i*

DUFAY "Veni Creator Spiritus" (Chapter 6)

Veni Creator Spiritus
Mentes tuorum visita:
Imple superna gratia
Quae tu creasti pectora.
Qui Paraclitus diceris,
Donum Dei Altissimi,
Fons vivus, ignis, caritas,
Et spiritalis unctio.

Come, Holy Spirit, our souls inspire
And lighten with celestial fire;
Thou the anointing spirit art
Who dost thy sevenfold gifts impart.
Thy blessed unction from above
Is comfort, life, and fire of love;
Enable with perpetual light
The dullness of our blinded sight.

(five more stanzas)

DUFAY "Hélas mon dueil" (Chapter 6)

Hélas mon dueil, a ce cop sui le mort,	Alas, my woe, at this blow I am dead,
Puisque Refus l'esragié si me mort.	Because insane Refusal kills me thus.
Certes, c'est fait de ma dolente vye;	Indeed, all is over with my sad life;
Tout le monde ne me sauveroit mye,	The whole world could never rescue me,
Puisque m'amour en a esté d'acort.	Because my love has let this happen.
Il ne fault ia que ie voise a la mer	No more need I go to the sea
N'a Saint Hubert pour moy faire garir;	Nor to Saint Hubert to make me well;
La morsure me donne tant d'amer	The biting wound gives me such grief
Que de ce mal il me fauldra morir.	That from this illness I must die.
Hélas mon dueil . . . (etc.)	Alas, my woe . . . (etc.)

JOSQUIN "Petite Camusette" (Chapter 6)

Petite camusette,	Little snub-nose,
A la mort m'avez mis.	You'll drive me to my death.
Robin et Marion	Robin Hood and Maid Marion
S'en vont au bois joly,	Have gone to the greenwood fair,
Ilz s'en vont bras à bras,	They have gone arm in arm,
Ilz se sont endormis.	They have dropped off to sleep.
Petite camusette,	Little snub-nose,
A la mort m'avez mis.	You'll drive me to my death.

JOSQUIN "Scaramella va alla guerra" (Chapter 6)

Scaramella va alla guerra	Scaramella goes off to war,
Colla lancia et la rotella,	With his lance and with his shield.
La zombero boro borombella,	With a rum tum tum,
La zombero boro borombo.	(Etc.)
Scaramella fa la gala	Scaramella plays the gallant
Colla scarpa et la stivala.	With his fine shoes and his boots.
La zombero . . . (etc.)	With a rum-tum-tum, (etc.)

JOSQUIN *Ave maris stella* Mass, Agnus Dei (Chapter 6)

Agnus Dei, qui tollis peccata mundi, miserere nobis.	Lamb of God, who takes away the sins of the world, have mercy upon us.
Agnus Dei, qui tollis peccata mundi, miserere nobis.	Lamb of God, who takes away the sins of the world, have mercy upon us.
Agnus Dei, qui tollis peccata mundi, dona nobis pacem.	Lamb of God, who takes away the sins of the world, grant us peace.

JOSQUIN "Absalon, fili mi" (Chapter 6)

Absalon, fili mi,	Absalom, my son,
Quis det ut moriar pro te,	Would I had died instead of you,
fili mi, Absalon?	my son, Absalom.
Non vivam ultra,	Let me live no longer,
sed descendam in infernum plorans.	but descend into hell weeping.

BYRD **"Sing joyfully unto God"** (Chapter 6)

Sing joyfully unto God our strength.
Sing loud unto the God of Jacob.
Take the song and bring forth the timbrel,
    the pleasant harp and the viol.
Blow the trumpet in the new moon,
    even in the time appointed and at our feast day.
For this is a statute for Israel,
    and a law of the God of Jacob.

ARCADELT **"Il bianco e dolce cigno"** (Chapter 6)

Il bianco e dolce cigno cantando more,	The white, sweet swan singing dies,
Ed io piangendo giung'al fin del viver mio.	and I, weeping, approach the end of my life.
Stran' e diversa sorte,	Strange and different fates,
Ch'ei more sconsolato,	that he dies disconsolate,
Ed io moro beato,	and I die happy,
Morte che nel morire	a death that, in dying,
M'empie di gioia tutto e di desire.	fills me with complete joy and desire.
Se nel morir' altro dolor non sento,	If in dying no other pain I feel,
Di mille morte il dì sarei contento.	a thousand deaths a day would make me content.

GESUALDO **"Moro, lasso"** (Chapter 6)

Moro, lasso, al mio duolo	I die, abandoned, in my grief
E chi mi può dar vita,	and she who could give me life,
Ahi, che m'ancide e non vuol darmi aita!	alas, she kills me and doesn't want to give me aid.
O dolorosa sorte,	O sorrowful fate,
Chi dar vita mi può, ahi, mi dà morte!	she who could give me life, alas, gives me death.

GIBBONS **"The silver Swanne"** (Chapter 6)

The silver Swanne, who living had no Note,
When death approacht unlockt her silent throat,
Leaning her breast against the reedie shore,
Thus sung her first and last, and sung no more,

Farewell all joyes, O death come close mine eyes,
More Geese than Swannes now live, more fooles than wise.

GABRIELI **"In ecclesiis"** (Chapter 7)

In ecclesiis benedicite Domino.	Praise the Lord in the congregation.
Alleluia!	Alleluia!
In omni loco dominationis benedicat	In every place of worship my soul
anima mea Dominum.	blesses the Lord.
Alleluia!	Alleluia!
[Interlude]	[Interlude]
In Deo salutari meo et gloria mea.	In God is my salvation and glory.
Deus auxilium meum et spes mea in Deo est.	God is my help, and my hope is in God.
Alleluia!	Alleluia!
Deus meus, te invocamus, te adoramus.	My God, we invoke thee, we worship thee.
Libera nos, salva nos, vivifica nos.	Deliver us, save us, revive us.
Alleluia!	Alleluia!
Deus adiutor noster in aeternum.	God is our help unto eternity.
Alleluia!	Alleluia!

MONTEVERDI "Lamento della Ninfa" (Chapter 7)

[Men]	*Non havea Febo ancora*	The sun had not yet
	Recato al mondo il dì,	Brought day to the world,
	Ch'una donzella fuora	When a maiden
	Del proprio albergo uscì.	Stepped forth from her lodging.
	Sul pallidetto volto	On her pale face
	Scorgeasi il suo dolor;	Was inscribed her sorrow,
	Spesso gli venia sciolto	And often from her grief
	Un gran sospir dal cor.	Issued a great sigh.
	Si calpestando fiori	Aimlessly over the flowers
	Errava hor qua, hor là,	She wandered here and there,
	I suoi perduti amori	Her lost love
	Così piangendo va:	Lamenting, in these words:
[Soprano]	*"Amor," dicea, il ciel*	"God of Love," she said,
[Men]	*Mirando, il piè fermò,*	Stopping and gazing up at the sky,
[Soprano]	*"Amor, dov'è la fè,*	"Love, where is that faith
	Che'l traditor giurò?	That the traitor swore to me?
	"Fa che ritorni il mio	"Make my love return
	Amor com'ei pur fu,	To me as he was,
	O tu m'ancidi ch'io	Or else kill me, so that I
	Non mi tormenti più."	No longer torment myself."
[Men]	*Miserella, ah, più, no, no—*	Unhappy girl, no more:
	Tanto gel soffrir no può.	She cannot suffer such scorn.
[Soprano]	*"Non vo' più ch'ei sospiri*	"I do not want him to sigh,
	Se non lontan da me,	Unless he is far from me,
	No, no che i martiri	No, nor to tell me
	Più non dirammi, affè."	Of his sorrows—no indeed!"
[Men]	*Miserella, etc.*	Unhappy girl, etc.
[Soprano]	*"Perchè di lui mi struggo,*	"Since I long for him,
	Tutt'orgoglioso sta,	He haughtily ignores me;
	Che sì, che sì se'l fuggo	But if I were to leave him,
	Ancor mi pregherà?"	Would he beg me again to stay?"
[Men]	*Miserella, etc.*	Unhappy girl, etc.
[Soprano]	*"Se ciglio ha più sereno*	"If my rival has
	Colei che'l mio non è,	A fairer face than mine,
	Già non rinchiude in seno	She does not have in her heart
	Amor si bella fè."	So true a devotion."
[Men]	*Miserella, etc.*	Unhappy girl, etc.
[Soprano]	*"Nè mai si dolci baci*	"Nor shall he ever from her lips
	Da quella bocca havrà,	Taste such sweet kisses,
	Nè più soave—ah taci,	Nor such exquisite—but enough:
	Taci che troppo il sa."	He knows this only too well."
[Men]	*Miserella, etc.*	Unhappy girl, etc.
[Men]	*Si tra sdegnosi pianti*	Thus with indignant complaints
	Spargea le voci al ciel,	Her voice rose to the heavens;
	Così ne' cori amanti	Thus in the hearts of lovers
	Mesce Amor fiamme e giel.	The God of Love mixes fire and ice.

MONTEVERDI *Orfeo*, selection from Act IV (Chapter 7)

[Chorus of Spirits]	*Pietade oggi e Amore*	Pity, today, and Love
	Trionfan nel' inferno.	Triumph in Hades.
Spirit:	*Ecco il gentil cantore*	Behold the gentle singer
	Che sua sposa conduce	Who leads his wife to
	al ciel superno.	the heavenly sky.

[*Orpheus enters playing his lyre; Eurydice follows him.*]

ARIA

Orpheus:

Qual onor di te sia degno,	What honor shall you deserve,
Mia cetra onnipotente,	My lyre omnipotent,
S'hai nel tartareo regno	Since in Hades' realm
Piegar potuto ogni indurata	You have been able to sway every hardened
mente?	spirit?
Luogo avrai fra le più belle	You shall have a place in the fairest
Imagini celesti,	Images of heaven,
Ond'al tuo suon le stelle	Where, to your sound, stars
Danzeranno in gir', hor tard',	Will dance in a ring, now slowly,
hor presti.	now fast.
Io per te felice a pieno	I, thanks to you all-happy,
Vedro l'amato volto	Shall see that beloved visage,
E nel candido seno	And in her white breast
De la mia donna oggi sarò raccolto.	My lady will today enfold me.

RECITATIVE

(1)	*Ma mentre io canto, ohime!*	But while I sing, ah me! who can
	chi m'assicura	assure me
	Ch'ella mi segua? ohime!	That she is following me? Ah me!
	chi me nasconde	who is it denies me
	De l'amate pupille il dolce lume?	The sweet light of those beloved eyes?
(2)	*Forse d'invidia punte*	Perhaps, stung by envy,
	le deità d'averno	The deities of Hades—
	Per ch'io non sià quaggiù felice appieno	Lest I become all-happy in this world—
	Mi toglono il mirarvi,	Are taking from me the vision of you,
	Luci beati e lieti,	Your bright eyes, blessed with light,
	Che sol col squardo altrui bear potete!	Which could bless others merely with a glance!
(3)	*Ma che temi, mio core?*	But what do you fear, my heart?
	Ciò che vieta Pluton, commanda	Pluto forbids, but Love commands! . . .
	Amore! . . .	

[*He turns and looks at Eurydice.*]

(4)	*O dolcissimi lumi, io pur vi veggio;*	O sweetest of eyes, now I see you;
	Io pur . . . ma qual eclissi,	Now . . . but what new eclipse,
	ohime! v'oscura?	alas! is hiding you?
Voice of a Spirit:	*Rotto hai la legge, e se' di*	You have broken the compact; you
	grazia indegno!	are unworthy of mercy.
Eurydice (*dying*):	*Ahi, vista troppo dolce e troppo amara:*	Ah, sight too sweet and too bitter:
	Così per troppo amor, dunque mi perdi?	Is this how you have lost me—by loving me too much?
	Ed io, misera, perdo	And I, wretched, am losing
	Il poter più godere	The power to enjoy henceforth
	E di luce e di vita, e perdo insieme	Both light and life; and at the same time I lose
	Te, d'ogni ben più caro, o mio consorte.	You, dearest of all, my husband.

SUDANESE MINSTREL SONG (Chapter 5; 5th ed.)

Doia, ben uli Kana	Kana, he comes!
Kaya ba cuzon nabore	Kaya desires her brown lover;
turi koleth Ebasel gnalek	she admired the knife on his shoulder.
bungur ley agamat ben	When he arrived at the house, he said:
ering-ei-yama kol mal.	"I need a large goat."

HANDEL *Rodelinda,* **recitative and aria "Tirannia"** (Chapter 10; 3rd ed.)

RECITATIVE (SECCO)

Unulfo:	*Massime così indegne*	Such shameful notions—
	consigli così rei tu progi, o duca,	can you give such evil counsel, O duke,
	a chi sostien la maestà reale?	To the upholder of royal majesty?
Garibaldo:	*Lascia che chi è tiranno opra da tale.*	Let him who is the ruler act like one,
Unulfo:	*Vorrai?*	You want . . . ?
Garibaldo:	*Sì, che spergiuro*	Yes, I want that perjurer
	tradisca la sua fè	to betray his word!
Unulfo:	*Vorrai?*	You want . . . ?
Garibaldo:	*Che impuro insidi l'onestà*	. . . that villain to subvert her virtue!
Unulfo:	*Vorrai?*	Can you really want . . .
Garibaldo:	*Che crudo con massime*	. . . that oaf, with his instincts
	Spietate, ingiuste ed empie. . .	for villainy, injustice, and evil . . .
Unulfo:	*. . . sparga il sangue reale?*	. . . to spill royal blood?
Garibaldo:	*Così d'usurpatore il nome adempie.*	That's how to earn the name of usurper!

ARIA

Garibaldo:	A	*Tirannia gli diede il regno;*	Tyranny brought him the kingdom;
		gliel conservi crudeltà.	He will retain it only by cruelty.
	B	*Del regnar base e sostegno*	Power's base and support
		è il rigor, non la pietà	is severity, not pity!
	A	*Tirannia . . .* etc.	Tyranny . . . etc.

HANDEL *Messiah* **versus BACH** *Christmas Oratorio* (Chapter 10)

The Angel's announcement to the shepherds, as presented—with additions—
in two Baroque oratorios:

Handel, from *Messiah*

RECITATIVE, **part I** (soprano) (Luke 2:8):
There were shepherds abiding in the field,
  keeping watch over their flocks by night.

RECITATIVE, **part II** (soprano) (Luke 2:9):
And lo, the angel of the Lord came upon them,
  and the glory of the Lord shone round about
  them: and they were sore afraid.

RECITATIVE, **part III** (soprano) (Luke 2:10–11):
And the angel said unto them, Fear not: for
  behold, I bring you good tidings of great joy,
  which shall be to all people. For unto you is
  born this day in the city of David a Saviour,
  which is Christ the Lord.

Bach, from *Christmas Oratorio*

RECITATIVE (tenor) (Luke 2:8–9):
There were shepherds . . . and they were
  sore afraid.

CHORALE: Break through, oh lovely
  light of morn,
And let the heavens dash!
You shepherd folk, be not afeared,
Because the angel tells you
That this weak babe
Shall be our comfort and joy . . .

RECITATIVE (tenor and soprano) (Luke 2:10–11):
And the angel said unto them: Fear not;
  behold, I bring you good tidings of great joy,
  which shall be to all people. For unto you
  today the Saviour is born, which is Christ,
  the Lord, in the City of David.

RECITATIVE (bass): The shepherds have been
  privileged to see God . . .

ARIA (tenor): Hasten, you glad shepherds, and
  Do not wait too long to see the beloved child! . . .

RECITATIVE (tenor) (Luke 2:12): And this shall
  be a sign: ye shall find the babe wrapped in
  swaddling clothes, lying in a manger.

CHORALE: Behold, there in the gloomy stable lies
He whose sovereignty encompasses all;
Where the oxen used to look for food
There rests now the Virgin's child.

RECITATIVE (bass): Go, shepherds, behold
The wonder, and sing to Him . . .

ARIA (contralto): Sleep, my darling, in peace;
Awake for the good of mankind . . .

RECITATIVE, **part IV** (soprano) (Luke 2:13):
And suddenly there was with the angel a
multitude of the heavenly host, praising
God, and saying:

RECITATIVE (tenor) (Luke 2:13):
And suddenly there was with the angel a
multitude of the heavenly host, praising
God, and saying:

CHORUS (Luke 2:14): Glory to God in the highest,
and peace on earth, good will toward men.

CHORUS (Luke 2:14): Glory to God in the highest,
and peace on earth, good will toward men.

ARIA (soprano) (Zechariah 9:9–10): Rejoice greatly,
O daughter of Zion; shout, O daughter of
Jerusalem: behold, the King cometh unto thee.
He is the righteous Saviour, and he shall speak peace
unto the heathen.

BACH Chorale Prelude, "Christ lag in Todesbanden" (Chapter 10)

Christ lag in Todes Banden
für unsre Sünd gegeben,
Er ist wieder erstanden
und hat uns bracht das Leben.
Des wir sollen fröhlich sein,
Gott loben und Ihm dankbar sein
und singen halleluja.
Halleluja.

Christ lay by death enshrouded,
from mortal sins to save us,
He is again arisen.
Eternal life He gave us.
So now let us joyful be
and magnify Him thankfully,
all singing Hallelujah.
Hallelujah!

—translation by Henry S. Drinker

BACH *Christmas Oratorio,* "Wie soll ich dich empfangen" (Chapter 10)

Wie soll ich dich empfangen,
Und wie begeg'n ich dir?
O aller Welt Verlangen,
O meine Seelen Zier!
O Jesu, Jesu! setze
Mir selbst die Fackel bei
Damit, was dich ergötze
Mir kund und wissend sei.

How should I receive Thee,
And how am I to encounter Thee?
O, you the desire of all the world,
O, you my soul's adornment!
O Jesu, Jesu, shine
Upon me Thy light,
So that whatever pleases Thee
May be shown and known to me.

BACH *Christmas Oratorio,* "Nun seid Ihr wohl gerochen" (Chapter 10)

Nun seid Ihr wohl gerochen
An eurer Feinde Schar,
Denn Christus hat zerbrochen
Was euch zuwider war.
Tod, Teufel, Sünd, und Hölle
Sind ganz und gar geschwacht,
Bei Gott hat seine Stelle
Das menschliche Geschlecht.

Now indeed you are avenged
On the multitude of your enemies,
For Christ has shattered
All that opposed you.
Death, the devil, sin, and hell
Are all disarmed utterly;
Close by to God shall mankind
Henceforth have its place.

BACH Chorale Prelude, "Herzlich tut mich Verlangen" (Chapter 10)

Herzlich tut mich Verlangen	My heart is ever yearning
nach einem sel'gen End,	for blessed death's release,
weil ich hie' bin umfangen	from ills that here surround me
mit Trübsal und Elend.	and woes that never cease.
Ich hab Lust abzuschneiden,	This cruel world to banish
von dieser argen Welt,	would be a blessed boon,
sehn' mich nach ew'gen Freuden,	I sigh for joys eternal,
o Jesu, komm nur bald.	O Jesus, Lord, come soon!

—translation by Henry S. Drinker

MOZART *Don Giovanni*, scene xv, from the Act II finale (Chapter 13)

[*As Leporello (Don Giovanni's manservant) hides, Don Giovanni opens the door and admits the statue.*]

Statue:	*Don Giovanni! A cenar teco*	Don Giovanni, you have invited me to
	M'invitasti e son venuto!	dinner, and I have come.
Don Giovanni:	*Non l'avrei giammai creduto*	I never would have believed it,
	Ma farò quel che potrò.	But I will do what I can.
	Leporello, un'altra cena	Leporello, see to it
	Fa che subito si porti!	That another dinner is served at once!
Leporello:	*Ah, padron! Siam tutti morti.*	Ah, master, we are lost.
Don Giovanni:	*Vanne, dico!*	Go, I said!
Statue:	*Ferma un po'!*	Wait a moment!
	Non si pasce di cibo mortale	He who dines on heavenly food
	Chi si pasce di cibo celeste!	Has not need for the food of mortals!
	Altre cure più gravi di queste	Other more serious considerations
	Altra brama quaggiu mi guido!	Have caused me to come here!
Leporello:	*La terzana d'avere mi sembra*	I feel as if I have a fever,
	E le membre fermar più non so.	For I cannot control my limbs.
Don Giovanni:	*Parla dunque! Che chiedi?*	Speak, then! What do you ask?
	Che vuoi?	What do you want?
Statue:	*Parlo; ascolta! Più tempo non ho!*	I will speak. Listen! My time is short!
Don Giovanni:	*Parla, parla, ascoltando ti sto.*	Speak, then, for I am listening.
Statue:	*Tu m'invitasti a cena,*	You invited me to dinner,
	Il tuo dover or sai	Now you know your duty.
	Rispondimi: verrai tu a cenar meco?	Answer me: will you come dine with me?
Leporello:	*Oibo; tempo non ha, scusate.*	Oh, my! Excuse him, but he has a prior engagement.
Don Giovanni:	*A torto di vitate*	No one will ever say of me
	Tacciato mai sarò.	That I have ever been afraid.
Statue:	*Risolvi!*	Make up your mind!
Don Giovanni:	*Ho già risolto.*	I have already.
Statue:	*Verrai?*	You will come?
Leporello:	*Dite di no!*	Tell him no!
Don Giovanni:	*Ho fermo il core in petto.*	My heart beats firmly.
	Non ho timor: verri!	I am not afraid: I'll come!
Statue:	*Dammi la mano in pegno!*	Give me your hand on it!
Don Giovanni:	*Eccola!*	Here it is!
[*He gives the statue his hand.*]		
	Ohimè!	Oh, my!
Statue:	*Cos'hai?*	What's wrong?
Don Giovanni:	*Che gelo è questo mai?*	What is this deadly chill?
Statue:	*Pentiti, cangia vita,*	Repent! Change your ways,
	È l'ultimo momento!	For this is your last hour!
Don Giovanni:	*No, no, ch'io non mi pento,*	No, no, I will not repent.
	Vanne lontan da me!	Leave me alone!

Statue:	*Pentiti, scellerato!*	Repent, scoundrel!
Don Giovanni:	*No, vecchio infatuato!*	No, you old fool!
Statue:	*Pentiti!*	Repent!
Don Giovanni:	*No!*	No!
Statue:	*Ah! Il tempo più non v'è!*	Ah, your time is up!

[*The statue disappears. Flames appear on all sides and the earth begins to tremble under Don Giovanni's feet. Don Giovanni is engulfed in flames and disappears.*]

SCHUBERT "Der Jüngling an der Quelle" (Chapter 13; 3rd ed.)

Leise, rieselnder Quell,	Gentle, rippling spring
Ihr wallenden, flispernden Pappeln:	With your tossing, whispering poplars:
Euer Schlummergeräusch	Your lullaby stirrings
Wecket die Liebe nur auf.	Speak of nothing but love.
Linderung sucht ich bei euch	Comfort I sought with you,
Und sie zu vergessen, die Spröde;	And to forget her, that coy one;
Ach, und Blätter und Bach	Ah, both the leaves and the brook
Seufzen, Luise, dir nach.	Are sighing, Louise, for you.

VERDI *Aida,* Act IV, scene ii—Judgment Scene (Chapter 17)

Amneris:	*Ohime! morir mi sento! Oh! chi lo salva?*	Alas! death overcomes me! Oh, who will save him?
	E in poter di costoro io stessa lo gettai! Ora, a te impreco, atroce gelosia, che la sua morte e il lutto eterno del mio cor segnasti!	And I have betrayed him into those hands, I, I myself! Curses on you, foul jealousy, which now prescribes his death and everlasting regret in my heart!
	Ecco i fatali, gl'inessorati ministri di morte:	Here are the inevitable, inexorable ministers of death:
	Oh! ch'io non vegga quelle bianche larve!	Ah! let me not see those white hoods!
Ramphis & Priests:	*Spirto del Nume sovra noi discendi! ne avviva al raggio dell'eterna luce; pel labbro nostro tua giustizia apprendi.*	Spirit of the gods, over us descending, kindle the rays of the eternal light; lend justice to our sentence.
Amneris:	*Numi, pietà del mio straziato core, Egli è innocente, lo salvate, o Numi! Disperato, tremendo è il mio dolore.*	Gods, have pity on my broken heart! He is innocent; save him, O gods! Desperate, overwhelming is my sorrow.
Ramphis & Priests:	*Spirto del Nume sovra noi discendi!*	Spirit of the gods, in our hearts descending!
Amneris:	*Oh! chi lo salva? Mi sento morir! ohimè! ohimè! mi sento morir!*	Oh, who will save him? Death overcomes me! Alas! alas! Death overcomes me!
Ramphis:	*Radamès! Radamès! Radamès!*	Radames! Radames! Radames!
	Tu rivelasti della patria i segreti allo straniero. Discolpati!	You revealed your country's secrets to the foreigner: Defend yourself!
Priests:	*Discolpati!*	Defend yourself!
Ramphis:	*Egli tace.*	He is silent.
Ramphis & Priests:	*Traditor!*	Traitor!
Amneris:	*Ah pietà! egli è innocente, Numi, pietà, Numi pietà!*	Ah, have pity! he is innocent, gods have pity, gods have pity!
Ramphis:	*Radamès! Radamès! Radamès!*	Radames! Radames! Radames!
	Tu disertasti dal campo il dì che precedea la pugna. Discolpati!	You deserted the encampment on the day preceding the battle. Defend yourself!
Priests:	*Discolpati!*	Defend yourself!
Ramphis:	*Egli tace.*	He is silent.
Ramphis & Priests:	*Traditor!*	Traitor!
Amneris:	*Ah pietà! ah! lo salvate, Numi, pietà, Numi pietà!*	Ah, have pity! save him, gods have pity, gods have pity!

Ramphis:	*Radamès! Radamès! Radamès!*	Radames! Radames! Radames!
	Tua fè violasti, alla patria spergiuro,	You broke faith, your country perjured,
	al Re, all'onor. Discolpati!	your King, your honor. Defend yourself!
Priests:	*Discolpati!*	Defend yourself!
Ramphis:	*Egli tace.*	He is silent.
Ramphis & Priests:	*Traditor!*	Traitor!
Amneris:	*Ah pietà! ah! lo salvate,*	Ah, have pity! save him,
	Numi, pietà, Numi pietà!	gods have pity, gods have pity!
Ramphis & Priests:	*Radamès, è deciso il tuo fato:*	Radames, your fate is decided.
	degli in fami la morte tu avrai;	A traitor's death will be yours:
	sotto l'ara del Nume sdegnato,	beneath the altar of the god whom you scorned
	a te vivo fia schiuso l'avel.	you shall be buried alive.
Amneris:	*A lui vivo la tomba—oh! gl'infami!*	Buried alive—oh, you wretches!
	nè di sangue son paghi giammai	ever bloodthirsty and blind,
	e si chia man ministri del ciel!	who serve heaven's shrine.
Ramphis & Priests:	*Traditor! Traditor! Traditor!*	Traitor! Traitor! Traitor!
Amneris:	*Sacerdoti, compiste un delitto!*	Priests, you are committing a crime!
	Tigri infami di sangue assetate,	Hateful tigers devoted to blood,
	voi la terra ed i Numi oltraggiate,	you outrage earth and heaven,
	voi punite, chi colpe no ha!	you are punishing an innocent man!
Ramphis & Priests:	*E traditor! morra!*	Traitor! he dies!
Amneris:	*Sacerdoti: quest'uomo che uccidi,*	Priests: this man you murder,
	tu lo sai da me un giorno fu amato:	whom you well know I once loved:
	L'annatema d'un core strazziato	May the curse of a heart whose hope has perished
	col suo sangue su te ricadrà!	fall on him who denies mercy!
Ramphis & Priests:	*E traditor! morra!*	Traitor! he dies!
Amneris:	*Voi la terra ed i Numi oltraggiate—*	You outrage the earth and the gods!
Ramphis & Priests:	*Morra!*	He dies!
Amneris:	*Voi punite chi colpe non ha.*	You punish one who is guiltless!
Ramphis & Priests:	[simultaneously with Amneris]	
	E traditor! morra! morra!	Traitor! he dies! he dies!
Amneris:	[simultaneously with Ramphis and the Priests]	
	Ah no, ah no, non è, non è,	Ah no, ah no, not he, not he,
	non è traditor, pietà! pietà!	he is no traitor, have pity! have pity!
Ramphis & Priests:	*Traditor! Traditor! Traditor!*	Traitor! Traitor! Traitor!
[*Exeunt Ramphis and Priests*]		
Amneris:	*Empia razza! anatema su voi!*	Evil hierarchy! a curse on you!
	la vendetta del ciel scenderà!	May the vengeance of heaven descend on you!
	anatema su voi!	A curse on you!
[*Exit wildly*]		

WAGNER *Tristan and Isolde,* "Philter" Scene, from Act I (Chapter 17; 5th ed.)

(Note: The English translation attempts to reproduce the "antique" quality of Wagner's poetry.)

BRANGAENE'S SONG

Brangaene:	*Wo lebte der Mann,*	Where lives a man
	Der dich nicht liebte? Der Isolden säh'	Who does not love you? Who sees you
	Und Isolden selig nicht ganz verging'?	And sinks not into bondage blest?
	Doch, der dich erkoren, wär' er so kalt,	And, if any bound to you were cold,
	Zög ihn von dir ein Zauber ab,	If any magic drew him from thee,
	Den Bösen wüsst' ich bald zu binden	I could soon draw the villain back
	Ihn bannte der Minne Macht.	And bind him in links of love.

DIALOGUE

		[*Secretly and confidentially*]
	Kennst du der Mutter Künste nicht?	Mind'st thou not thy mother's arts?
	Wähnst du, die alles klug erwägt,	Do you think that she, the all-wise,
	Ohne Rath in fremdes Land	Helpless in distant lands
	Hätt' sie mit dir mich entsandt?	Would she have sent me with you?

Isolde:	*Der Mutter Rath gemahnt mich recht;*	My mother's counsel I mind aright;
	Willkommen preis' ich ihre Kunst;	And highly her magic arts I hold:
	Rache für den Verrath,	Vengeance for treachery,
	Ruh' in der Noth dem Herzen!	Rest for the broken heart!
	Den Schrein dort bring' mir her!	Yon casket hither bear!

Brangaene:	*Er birgt was heil dir frommt,*	It holds a balm for thee:
		[*Brings out a golden medicine chest*]
	So reihte sie die Mutter,	Your mother filled it with
	Die mächt'gen Zaubertränke:	The most potent magic philters;
	Für Weh' und Wunden Balsam hier,	For pain and wounds there's salve,
	Für böse Gifte Gegengift;	For poisons, antidotes;
	Den hehrsten Trank, ich halt' ihn hier.	The noblest draught is this one—
		[*Takes out a flask*]

Isolde:	*Du irrst, ich kenn' ihn besser;*	Not so, you err: I know a better;
	Ein starkes Zeichen schnitt ich ihm ein.	I made a mark to know it again:
	Der Trank ist's, der mir taugt!	Here's the drink that will serve me!
		[*Seizes another flask*]

Brangaene:	*Der Todestrank!*	The death philter!

Sailors [*offstage*]:	*Ho, he, am Untermast!*	Ho, heave ho! Watch the lower mast!
	Die Segel ein! Ho, he!	The mainsail in! Heave ho!

Isolde:	*Das deute schnelle Fahrt.*	They tell of a swift journey;
	Weh' mir, Nahe das Land!	Woe's me! Near to the land!

KURVENAL'S SONG

[*Kurvenal enters, boisterous and insolent*]

Kurvenal:	*Auf, auf, ihr Frauen!*	Up, up, ye ladies!
	Frisch und froh! Rasch gerüstet!	Look lively, now! Bestir you!
	Fertig nun, hurtig und flink!	Be ready, and quick, prepare!
	Und Frau Isolden, sollt' ich sagen	Dame Isolde, I'm told to tell you,
	Von Held Tristan, meinem Herrn:	By Tristan our hero, my master:
	Vom Mast der Freude Flagge	The mast is flying the joyful flag;
	Sie wehe lustig ins Land;	It waveth landwards aloft;
	In Marke's Königschlosse	From King Mark's royal castle
	Mach' sie ihr Nahen bekannt.	It makes our approach be seen.
	Drum Frau Isolde bät' er eilen,	So, Dame Isolde, he bids you hasten
	Für's Land sich zu bereiten	For land to prepare you,
	Dass er sie könnt' geleiten.	So that he may there conduct you.

WAGNER *Tristan and Isolde*, "Liebestod" (Chapter 17)

Mild und leise wie er lächelt,	Mild and gently he is smiling;
wie das Auge hold er öffnet,	how softly he opens his eyes!
seht ihr's, Freunde? Seht ihr's nichts?	See, my friends? See you not
Immer lichtet, wie er leuchtet,	How he, bright and brighter gleaming
stern-umstrahlet hoch sich hebt?	in streaming starlight, rises high?
Seht ihr's nicht?	See you not
Wie das Herz ihm mutig schwillt,	How his heart with courage swells,
voll und hehr im Busen ihm quillt?	strong and pure within his breast it wells up?
Wie den Lippen, wonnig mild,	How, from his lips, delightfully mild,
süsser Atem sanft entweht:	sweet breath softly escapes:
Freunde! Seht! Fühlt und seht ihr's nicht?	Friends! See! Feel and see you not?
Höre ich nur diese Weise,	Hears no one else this tune,
die so wundervoll und leise,	that so soft and full of wonder,
Wonne klagend, alles sagend,	delight lamenting, all things telling,
mild versöhnend aus ihm tönend,	softly reconciling, from him sounding,
in mich dringet, auf sich schwinget,	penetrates into me, rises [vibrates] up,

hold erhallend um mich klinget?	sweetly echoing, around me sounds?
Heller schallend, mich umwallend,	Sounding clearer, flowing around me,
sind es Wellen sanfter Lüfte?	are they waves of softer air?
Sind es Wolken wonniger Düfte?	Are they clouds of more delightful perfume?
Wie sie schwellen, mich umrauschen,	How they rise, rushing around me.
soll ich atmen, soll ich lauschen?	Dare I breathe? dare I listen?
Soll ich schlürfen, untertauchen?	Shall I sip, and dive among them?
Süss in Düften mich verhauchen?	to sweetly in perfume breathe my last?
In dem wogenden Schwall, in dem	In their surging flood, in their
tönenden Schall,	resounding sound,
in des Welt-Atems wehendem All,	in the world-breath's blowing universe,
ertrinken, versinken	drowning, sinking down into
unbewusst höchste Lust!	unknowing highest pleasure!

WAGNER *The Valkyrie,* Act III, Wotan's Farewell (Chapter 17)

[*Wotan, overcome and deeply moved, turns eagerly to Brünnhilde, raises her from her knees, and gazes with emotion into her eyes. He sings:*]

Leb' wohl, du kühnes, herrliches Kind!	Farewell, thou valiant, glorious child!
Du meines Herzens heiligster Stolz!	Thou holiest pride of my heart,
Leb' wohl, leb' wohl, leb' wohl!	farewell, farewell, farewell!
Muss ich dich meiden, und darf nicht	If now I must leave thee and
minnig mein Gruss dich mehr grüssen,	nevermore greet thee,
sollst du nun nicht mehr neben mir reiten,	if never again mayst ride beside me,
noch Meth beim Mahl mir reichen,	nor bear me a cup of mead at banquet,
muss ich verlieren dich, die ich liebe,	if I must abandon the child I love,
du lachende Lust meines Auges—	thou laughing delight of my eyes
ein bräutliches Feuer soll dir nun brennen,	such a bridal fire for thee shall be kindled
wie nie einer Braut es gebrannt!	as ne'er yet burned for a bride!
Flammende Gluth umglühe den Fels;	Threatening flames shall flare round the fell;
mit zehrenden Schrecken Scheuch' es den	Let withering terrors daunt the
Zagen; der Feige fliehe Brünnhilde's Fels!	craven! Let cowards fly from Brünnhilde's rock!
Denn Einer nur freie die Braut,	For one alone shall win the bride,
der freier als ich, der Gott!	one freer than I, the god!

[*Brünnhilde sinks in ecstasy on Wotan's breast; he holds her in a long embrace as the orchestra plays. She throws her head back again and, still embracing Wotan, gazes with deep enthusiasm into his eyes. Wotan resumes:*]

Der Augen leuchtendes Paar,	The brightly glittering eyes
das oft ich lächelnd gekos't,	that, smiling, oft I caressed,
wenn Kampfeslust ein Kuss dir lohnte.	when valor won them a kiss as reward,
wenn kindisch lallend der Helden Lob	when childish lispings of heroes' praise
von holden Lippen dir floss;	from thy sweet lips flowed forth;
dieser Augen strahlendes Paar,	these gleaming, radiant eyes
das oft im Sturm mir gegläntzt,	that oft in storms on me shone
wenn Hoffnungssehnen das	when hopeless yearning
Herz mir sengte, nach Weltenwonne	my heart had wasted, when world's delight
mein Wunsch verlangte,	all my wishes wakened
aus wild webendem Bangen:	through wild sadness—
zum letzten Mal letz' ich mich heut'	For the last time, lured by their light,
mit des Lebewohles letztem Kuss!	my lips will give them love's farewell!
Dem glücklicher'n Manne glänze	On a more blessed mortal those eyes
sein Stern: dem unseligen Ew'gen	will open; but for me, Immortal,
muss es scheidend sich schliessen.	they close forever.
Denn so kehrt der Gott sich dir ab,	For thus I, the god, turn from thee;
so küsst er die Gottheit von dir!	thus I kiss thy godhead away!

[*He clasps her head in his hands. He kisses her long on the eyes. She sinks back unconscious in his arms. He gently bears her to a low mossy mound. He turns slowly away, then again turns round with a sorrowful look. Wotan strides with solemn decision to the middle of the stage and directs the point of his spear toward a large rock. He calls upon Loge, the god of fire:*]

Loge, hör'! Lausche hieher!	Loge, hear! attend!
wie zuerst ich dich fand,	When first I found you,
als feurige Gluth,	a flickering flame,
wie dann einst du mir schwandest,	you fled from me
als schweifende Lohe;	in a devious blaze.
wie ich dich band, bann' ich dich heut'!	I caught you then; I release you now!
Herauf, wabernde Lohe,	Appear, and wind thee
umlod're mir feurig den Fels!	in flames around the fell!
Loge! Loge! hieher!	Loge! Loge! attend!

[*A flash of flame issues from the rock, which swells to an ever-brightening fiery glow. Wotan stretches out his spear as if casting a spell.*]

Wer meines Speeres Spitze furchtet,	He who my spear point's sharpness feareth,
durchschreite das Feuer nie!	ne'er cross the flaming fire!

[*He looks sorrowfully back at Brünnhilde. He looks back again. He disappears through the fire.*]

PUCCINI *Madame Butterfly*, Act II aria, "Un bel dì" (Chapter 17 or 21)

Un bel dì vedremo	One day we shall see
Levarsi un fil di fumo	A tiny thread of smoke rise up
Sull'estremo confin del mare;	On the horizon, out at sea;
E poi la nave appare.	And then the ship will appear.
Poi la nave bianca	Now the white ship
Entra nel porto; romba il suo saluto.	Sails into port; cannons roar a welcome!
Vedi? è venuto!	You see? he has come!
Io non gli scendo incontro—io no;	I shan't run to meet him—not I;
Mio metto	I shall come
Là sul ciglio del colle e aspetto,	Up here on the hilltop, and wait,
E aspetto gran tempo,	And wait as long as I have to,
E non mi pesa la lunga attesa.	And not count the hours of waiting.
E uscito dalla folla cittadina	Then out of the crowd down in the city
Un uomo, un picciol punto,	A man—a little speck—
S'avvia per la collina.	Is starting up the hill.
Chi sarà, chi sarà? E come sarà giunto	Is it he? is it he? And when he's come
Che dirà, che dirà?	What will he say? what will he say?
Chiamerà: "Butterfly" dalla lontana . . .	He'll call out: "Butterfly!" from afar . . .
Io senza dar riposta	Without answering,
Me ne starò nascosta	I'll hide myself,
Un po' per celia, e un po'	Partly to tease him a bit, and partly
Per non morire al primo incontro!	So as not to die when we first meet!
Ed egli alquanto in pena chiamerà, chiamerà:	And then he'll be worried and call:
"Piccina mogliettina, olezzo di verbena"—	"Little child-wife! Verbena blossom!"—
I nomi che mi dava al suo venire.	The names he gave me when he was here before.
Tutto questo avverà, te lo prometto!	All this will happen, I promise you!
Tienti la tua paura;	Suppress your fears!
Io con sicura fede l'aspetto!	Full of faith I am waiting!

STRAUSS *Der Rosenkavalier*, Act II, Presentation of the Rose (Chapter 17 or 21; 3rd ed.)

[*Enter Octavian, bareheaded, dressed all in white and silver, carrying the Silver Rose in his hand. Behind him his servants in his colors, white and pale green. Octavian, taking the rose in his right hand, advances with high-born grace toward Sophie, but his youthful features bear traces of embarrassment, and he blushes. Sophie turns pale with excitement at this splendid appearance. They stand opposite each other, each disconcerted by the confusion and beauty of the other.*]

Octavian:	*Mir ist die Ehre widerfahren, dass ich der hoch-und wohlgeborenen Jungfer Braut, in meines Hern Vetters Namen, dessen zu Lerchenau Namen, die Rose seiner Liebe überreichen darf.*	The honor has fallen to me, most noble and high-born [*very formal*] lady and bride, on my kinsman's behalf, by name the Baron von Lerchenau, to present to you the rose of his love.
Sophie:	*Ich bin Euer Liebden sehr verbunden . . . ich bin Euer Liebden in aller Ewigkeit verbunden . . . Hat einen starken Geruch wie Rosen, wie lebendige!*	I am deeply indebted to your highness . . . I am forever eternally indebted to your highness . . . [embarrassed] Oh, it has a powerful fragrance, just like a real rose!
Octavian:	*Ja, ist ein Tropfen persichen Rosenols darein getan . . .*	[*Tries to make conversation*] Yes, a drop of Persian attar has been put on it . . .
Sophie:	*Wie himmlische, nicht irdische, wie Rosen vom hocheiligen Paradies. Ist Ihm nicht auch?*	It's like a heavenly rose, not an earthly one— like the roses of paradise. Do you think so too?
	Ist wie ein Gruss von Himmel . . . ist bereits zu stark als dass man's ertragen kann! Zieht einen nach, als lagen Stricke um das Herz . . .	It's like a message from heaven . . . it's so strong, I can scarcely bear it! It's like something pulling at my heart . . .
Sophie (with Octavian):	*(Wo war ich schon einmal und war so selig? Dahin muss ich züruck, dahin, und musst' ich vollig sterben Auf dem Weg. Allein ich sterb ja nicht. Das ist ja weit!*	[*To herself*] (Have I ever been here before? Was I ever so blissful? If I could recapture this moment, I'd be ready to die—but I'm not dying, not yet!
	Ist Zeit und Ewigkeit in einem sel'gen Augenblick, den will ich nie vergessen bis an meinen Tod.)	All time and eternity are in this moment, which I'll remember till the day I die.)
Octavian (with Sophie):	*(Wo war ich schon einmal und war so selig? Ich war ein Bub, da hab ich die, die noch nicht gekannt. Wer bin denn ich? Wie komm' denn ich zu ihr? Wie kommt denn sie zu mir?*	[*To himself*] (Have I ever been here before? Was I ever so blissful? Up to now I've been just a child, before I saw her. Who am I? What fate has brought me to her, brought her to me?
	War' ich kein Mann, die Sinne möchten mir vergehn; das ist ein sel'ger Augenblick, den will ich nie vergessenbis an meinen Tod.)	If I weren't a grown man, I'd go mad. This moment I'll remember till the day I die.)

SCHOENBERG *Pierrot lunaire* (Chapter 20; 4th ed.)

1. *Mondestrunken*	No. 1: Moondrunk
Der Wein, den man mit Augen trinkt,	The wine that only eyes may drink
Giesst Nachts der Mond in Wogen nieder,	Pours from the moon in waves at nightfall,
Und eine Springflut überschwemmt	And like a springflood overwhelms
Den stillen Horizont.	The still horizon rim.
Gelüste, schauerlich und süss,	Desires, shivering and sweet,
Durchschwimmen ohne Zahl die Fluten!	Are swimming without number through the flood waters!
Der Wein, den man mit Augen trinkt,	The wine that only eyes may drink
Giesst Nachts der Mond in Wogen nieder.	Pours from the moon in waves at nightfall.
Der Dichter, den die Andacht treibt,	The poet by his ardor driven,
Berauscht sich an dem heilgen Tranke,	Grown drunken from the Holy drink—
Den Himmel wendet er verzucht	To heaven he rapturously lifts
Das Haupt und taumelnd säugt und schlürft er	His head and, reeling, sips and swallows
Der Wein, den man mit Augen trinkt.	The wine that only eyes may drink.

19. *Serenade*

Mit groteskem Riesenbogen
Kratzt Pierrot auf seiner Bratsche,
Wie der Storch auf einem Beine,
Knipft er trüb ein Pizzicato.
Plötzlich naht Cassander—wütend
Ob des nächtgen Virtuosen—
Mit groteskem Riesenbogen
Kratzt Pierrot auf seiner Bratsche.
Von sich wirft er jetzt die Bratsche:
Mit der delikaten Linken
Fasst den Kahlkopf er am Kragen—
Träumend spielt er auf der Glatze
Mit groteskem Riesenbogen.

No. 19: Serenade

With a giant bow grotesquely
Scrapes Pierrot on his viola—
Like a stork on one leg,
Sadly plucks a pizzicato.
Suddenly here comes Cassander, fuming
At this nighttime virtuoso,
With a giant bow grotesquely
Scrapes Pierrot on his viola.
Now he throws aside the viola:
With his delicate left hand
Grasps the baldpate by the collar,
Dreamily plays upon his bald spot
With a giant bow grotesquely.

20. *Heimfahrt*

Der Mondstrahl ist das Ruder,
Seerose dient als Boot:
Drauf fährt Pierrot gen Süden
Mit gutem Reisewind.
Der Strom summt tiefe Skalen
Und wiegt den leichten Kahn.
Der Mondstrahl ist das Ruder,
Seerose dient als Boot:
Nach Bergamo, zur Heimat,
Kehrt nun Pierrot zurück;
Schwach dämmert schon im Osten
Der grüne Horizont.
—Der Mondstrahl ist das Ruder.

No. 20: Journey Home

A moonbeam is the oar,
A water-lily serves as a boat
On which Pierrot journeys southward
With a good wind for sailing.
The stream hums deep scales
and rocks the delicate boat.
A moonbeam is the oar,
A water-lily serves as a boat:
Toward Bergamo, homeward bound,
Pierrot turns back;
The green horizon begins to dim in the east.

—A moonbeam is the oar.

21. *O alter Duft*

O alter Duft aus Märchenzeit
Berauschest wieder meine Sinne!
Ein närrisch Heer von Schelmerein
Durchschwirrt die leichte Luft.
Ein glückhaft Wünschen macht mich froh
Nach Freuden, die ich lang verachtet:
  O alter Duft aus Märchenzeit,
  Berauschest wieder mich!
All meinen Unmut gab ich preis;
Aus meinen sonnumrahmten Fenster
Beschau ich frei die liebe Welt
Und träum hinaus in selge Weiten:
  O alter Duft . . . aus Märchenzeit!

No. 21: O Ancient Scent

O ancient scent from days of fairy lore,
Intoxicate again my senses!
A foolish swarm of idle thoughts
Pervades the gentle air.
A happy whim makes me aspire
To joys that I have long not known;
  O ancient scent from days of fairy lore,
  Intoxicate again my senses!
All my depression is cast off;
From my sun-encircled window
I gaze out freely on the lovely world
And dream far beyond the fair horizon:
  O ancient scent . . . from days of fairy lore!

REICH *Tehillim, fourth section* (Chapter 22; 5th ed.)

1 *Haleluhu betof umachol,*
  Haleluhu beminim ve-ugav;
2 *Haleluhu betzil-tzilay shamah,*
  Haleluhu betzil-tzilay teruah;
3 *Kol hanshamah tehalail Yah, Haleluyah.*
  Kol hanshamah tehalail Yah, Haleluyah.

a Praise the Lord with tambourines and dancing,
  praise him with flute and strings;
b praise him with the clash of cymbals,
  praise him with triumphant cymbals;
c let everything that has breath praise the Lord! Hallelujah.
c′ Let everything that has breath praise the Lord!
  Hallelujah.

APPENDIX III

Index of Terms and Musical Examples

Examples begin at the beginning unless otherwise indicated. [Square brackets indicate examples from the text that are not in the recordings.]

A cappella
Anonymous, preface, "Vere dignum"
Anonymous, antiphon, "In paradisum"
Pérotin, "Alleluia, Diffusa est gratia"
Qur'anic recitation, "Ya Sin"
Hawai'ian chant, *mele pule*
Dufay, "Ave maris stella"
Josquin, *Pange lingua* Mass, Kyrie and "Qui tollis"
Palestrina, *Pope Marcellus* Mass, "Qui tollis"
Weelkes, "As Vesta Was from Latmos Hill Descending"
Processional hymn from the Andes, "Hanaq pachap kusikuynin"
Pygmy polyphony, elephant-hunt song
Ligeti, *Lux aeterna*
Saariaho, *From the Grammar of Dreams*
Linda, "Anoku Gonda"

Accelerando (*see* **Tempo**—*Accelerando*)

Accent
Vivaldi, Violin Concerto in G, *La stravaganza*, I
Handel, *Julius Caesar,* "La giustizia"
Haydn, Symphony No. 95, I (track 22, 1:31–1:44; track 23, 0:00–0:20, 0:29–0:42; track 24, 0:09–0:25, 1:08–end), II (track 28, 0:12–0:42), III (track 30, 0:13–0:25, 1:20–end)
Beethoven, Symphony No. 5 in C Minor, I and IV
Beethoven, String Quartet in F, Op. 135, II (0:00–0:33)
R. Schumann, *Dichterliebe,* "Die alten, bösen Lieder"
R. Schumann, *Carnaval,* "Florestan"
Berlioz, *Fantastic* Symphony, V (track 4, 0:00–0:21; track 6, 0:00–0:23)
Tchaikovsky, *Romeo and Juliet* (track 22, 0:00–0:20)
Musorgsky, *Pictures at an Exhibition,* "Gnomus"
Stravinsky, *The Rite of Spring,* Part 1 (track 23; track 24, 0:00–0:37; track 25, 0:00–0:55)

Adams, *El Niño,* "Pues mi Dios ha nacido a penar"

Wallace, *"If You Ever Been Down" Blues*

Andante

Purcell, *Dido and Aeneas,* "When I am laid in earth" (at 0:58)

Haydn, Symphony No. 95, II

Mozart, *Don Giovanni,* "Là ci darem la mano"

Beethoven, Symphony No. 5 in C Minor, II

Tchaikovsky, *Romeo and Juliet* (tracks 19–21)

Copland, *Appalachian Spring,* Sections 1 and 6 (ending)

Tchaikovsky, "Dance of the Sugar-Plum Fairy," from *The Nutcracker* (DVD)

Andantino

Schubert, Moment Musical No. 2 in A-flat

Antiphon

Anonymous, antiphon, "In paradisum"

Arch form

Copland, *Appalachian Spring,* Section 1

Archlute (*see* **Lute**)

Aria

Monteverdi, *The Coronation of Poppea,* "Speranza, tu mi vai"

Purcell, *Dido and Aeneas,* "When I am laid in earth" (0:58–4:00)

Handel, *Julius Caesar,* "La giustizia"

Bach, Cantata No. 4, "Christ lag in Todesbanden," Stanza 3

Mozart, *Don Giovanni,* "Ho capito"

Arioso

Monteverdi, *The Coronation of Poppea,* "Io non posso da te" (track 16, 0:23–0:56)

Verdi, *Aida,* Tomb Scene, Act IV, scene ii (track 10, 0:00–track 11, 1:13)

Arpeggio

Vivaldi, Violin Concerto in G, *La stravaganza,* I

Handel, *Messiah,* "There were shepherds" (0:10–0:33)

Haydn, Symphony No. 95, II (track 26, 0:12–0:24), III (track 31), and IV (track 36, 0:04–0:12)

Mozart, Piano Concerto in A, K. 488, I (track 41, 1:44–1:59)

Schubert, "Erlkönig" (2:14–2:31)

R. Schumann, *Dichterliebe,* "Im wunderschönen Monat Mai"

Schubert, Moment Musical No. 2 in A-flat—B sections (1:20–2:23, 3:57–4:54)

Verdi, *Aida,* Tomb Scene, Act IV, scene ii (track 11, 0:26–0:40, 0:53–1:06)

Mahler, Symphony No. 1, III (track 9, 2:00–track 11, 0:00)

Ravel, Piano Concerto in G, I (track 37, 0:00–0:15; track 40, 1:15–2:04)

Beethoven, Piano Concerto No. 5, "Emperor," III (DVD—0:00–0:10, 1:06–1:21, 1:36–end)

Tchaikovsky, "Dance of the Sugar-Plum Fairy," from *The Nutcracker* (DVD—0:59–1:06)

Ars antiqua

Pérotin, "Alleluia. Diffusa est gratia"

Ars nova

Machaut, "Quant en moi"

Atonality

Schoenberg, *Pierrot lunaire*

Berg, *Wozzeck,* Act III

Webern, Five Orchestral Pieces, Op. 10, No. 4

Ligeti, *Lux aeterna*

Varèse, *Poème électronique*

Saariaho, *From the Grammar of Dreams*

Avant-garde
  Debussy, Three Nocturnes, *Clouds*
  Stravinsky, *The Rite of Spring,* Part 1
  Schoenberg, *Pierrot lunaire*
  Berg, *Wozzeck,* Act III
  Ives, "The Rockstrewn Hills"
  Ives, *The Unanswered Question*
  Webern, Five Orchestral Pieces, Op. 10, No. 4
  [Riley, *In C*]
  Ligeti, *Lux aeterna*
  Varèse, *Poème électronique*
  [Cage, 4'33"]
  Saariaho, *From the Grammar of Dreams*
  Davis, *Bitches Brew*
Ballet
  Stravinsky, *The Rite of Spring*
  Copland, *Appalachian Spring*
  Tchaikovsky, "Dance of the Sugar-Plum Fairy," from *The Nutcracker* (DVD)
Balletto
  Frescobaldi, Suite: Balletto
Bar form
  Bernart, "La dousa votz"
  Anonymous, "Kemp's Jig"
  Bach, Cantata No. 4, "Christ lag in Todesbanden," Stanza 7
  Bach, chorale prelude, "Christ lag in Todesbanden"
Baroque
  Gabrieli, "O magnum mysterium"
  Monteverdi, *The Coronation of Poppea*
  Purcell, *Dido and Aeneas*
  Frescobaldi, Suite
  Vivaldi, Violin Concerto in G, *La stravaganza*
  Bach, *Brandenburg* Concerto No. 5
  Bach, Contrapunctus 4, from *The Art of Fugue*
  Bach, Orchestral Suite No. 3 in D
  Handel, *Julius Caesar*
  Handel, *Messiah*
  Bach, Cantata No. 4, "Christ lag in Todesbanden"
  Bach, chorale prelude, "Christ lag in Todesbanden"
Baroque dance form (*see* **Dance form**)
Baroque orchestra (*see* **Orchestra**—*Baroque*)
Basic Baroque orchestra (*see* **Orchestra**—*Baroque*—*Basic Baroque orchestra*)
Bass (stringed instrument; *see also* **Electric bass**)
  Vivaldi, Violin Concerto in G, *La stravaganza,* II
  Bach, Orchestral Suite No. 3 in D, Air
  Mozart, Symphony No. 40, I (track 18, 0:16–0:44; track 19, 0:33–1:19)
  Beethoven, Symphony No. 5 in C Minor, III (track 16, 0:00–0:21; track 17, 0:00–1:03)
  Berlioz, *Fantastic* Symphony, V (track 2, 0:00–0:12; track 4, 1:00–1:19; track 5, 0:00–0:07, 0:46–0:54)
  Mahler, Symphony No. 1, III (track 7, 0:07–0:28)
  Debussy, Three Nocturnes, *Clouds* (track 20, 0:32–end)
  Stravinsky, *The Rite of Spring,* Part 1—Round Dances of Spring (track 26, 0:34–1:11)
  Ellington, "Conga Brava"
  Parker and Davis, "Out of Nowhere"
  Schubert, Symphony No. 8, "Unfinished," I (DVD—0:00–0:13)

Gershwin, "Who Cares?" (DVD)

Beethoven, Symphony No. 9, IV (DVD—0:00–1:34)

Britten, *The Young Person's Guide to the Orchestra* (DVD)—variation 8
(track 22, 2:52–3:48) and fugue (track 25, at 0:55)

Bass clarinet (*see* **Clarinet**—*Bass clarinet*)

Bass drum

Berlioz, *Fantastic* Symphony, V (track 4, 1:00–1:19; track 6, 0:00–0:23,
0:55–1:32; track 8)

Verdi, *Aida,* Tomb Scene, Act IV, scene ii (track 11, 1:23–1:33)

Musorgsky, *Pictures at an Exhibition,* "Gnomus" (0:46–1:33) and "The Great Gate
at Kiev" (0:42–1:01, 4:59–end)

Mahler, Symphony No. 1, III (track 8, 0:30–0:43; track 13, 0:23–0:41)

Stravinsky, *The Rite of Spring,* Part 1 (track 25; track 27, 0:54–1:33)

Ravel, Piano Concerto in G, I (track 41, 0:08–end)

Bartók, Music for Strings, Percussion, and Celesta, II (track 4, 0:14–0:49;
track 7, 0:24–0:30)

Britten, *The Young Person's Guide to the Orchestra* (DVD)—variation 13
(track 24, at 0:15) and fugue (track 25, at 1:44)

Bass flute (*see* **Flute**—*Bass or alto flute*)

Bass voice

Qur'anic recitation, "Ya Sin"—baritone

Navajo song, "K'adnikini'ya'"

Bach, Cantata No. 4, "Christ lag in Todesbanden," Stanzas 4 and 7

Mozart, *Don Giovanni,* "Ho capito" and "Là ci darem la mano"—baritone

Schubert, "Erlkönig"—baritone

Berg, *Wozzeck,* Act III, scenes iii and iv—Wozzeck (baritone) and Doctor (bass)

Adams, *El Niño,* "When Herod Heard"

Basso continuo

Gabrieli, "O magnum mysterium"

Monteverdi, *The Coronation of Poppea*

Purcell, *Dido and Aeneas*

Vivaldi, Violin Concerto in G, *La stravaganza*

Bach, *Brandenburg* Concerto No. 5

Bach, Orchestral Suite No. 3 in D

Handel, *Julius Caesar*

Handel, *Messiah*

Bach, Cantata No. 4, "Christ lag in Todesbanden"

Mozart, *Don Giovanni,* "Alfin siam liberati"

Bassoon

Haydn, Symphony No. 95, I (track 22, 1:02–1:14; track 23, 0:42–0:49;
track 24, 0:41–1:08) and IV (track 33, 0:21–0:29; track 34, 0:00–0:10;
track 35, 0:14–0:21)

Mozart, Piano Concerto in A, K. 488, I (track 37, 1:11–1:26)

Beethoven, Symphony No. 5 in C Minor, I (track 10, 0:53–0:56), II (track 14,
1:03–1:26), III (track 17, 1:37–2:54), and IV (track 18, 0:34–1:00)

Musorgsky, *Pictures at an Exhibition,* "Gnomus" (2:24–2:38), "Promenade [2]"
(0:09–0:17, 0:27–0:36), and "The Great Gate at Kiev" (1:01–1:37)

Mahler, Symphony No. 1, III (track 7, 0:28–0:48; track 14, 1:21–1:36)

Debussy, Three Nocturnes, *Clouds* (track 15, 0:00–0:15; track 20, at 0:54)

Stravinsky, *The Rite of Spring,* Part 1 (track 21, 0:00–0:50; track 22, 0:29–0:37;
track 24, at 0:00)

Ravel, Piano Concerto in G, I (track 38, 0:37–0:50)

Copland, *Appalachian Spring,* Section 1 (1:25–2:14) and Section 5—variation 1
(0:37–1:05)

Adams, *El Niño,* "When Herod Heard" (at 0:30 and 1:50)
Schubert, Symphony No. 8, "Unfinished," I (DVD—1:06–1:15, 2:48–2:57)
Beethoven, Symphony No. 9, IV (DVD—0:48–1:34)
Britten, *The Young Person's Guide to the Orchestra* (DVD)—Variation 4
 (track 21, 2:21–3:20) and Fugue (track 25, at 0:30)
Beat
 Bernart, "La dousa votz"
 Pérotin, "Alleluia. Diffusa est gratia" (0:37–2:36)
 Navajo song, "K'adnikini'ya'"
 Weelkes, "As Vesta Was from Latmos Hill Descending"
 Anonymous, galliard, "Daphne"
 Anonymous, "Kemp's Jig"
 Processional hymn from the Andes, "Hanaq pachap kusikuynin"
 Monteverdi, *The Coronation of Poppea* (track 16, 0:23–0:56; track 17)
 Purcell, *Dido and Aeneas* (track 18, 0:58–4:00)
 Frescobaldi, Suite (any movement)
 Vivaldi, Violin Concerto in G, *La stravaganza*
 Bach, *Brandenburg* Concerto No. 5
 Bach, Contrapunctus 4, from *The Art of Fugue*
 Bach, Orchestral Suite No. 3 in D
 Handel, *Julius Caesar,* "La giustizia"
 Handel, *Messiah,* "Glory to God" and Hallelujah Chorus
 Bach, Cantata No. 4, "Christ lag in Todesbanden," Stanzas 3, 4, and 7
 Bach, chorale prelude, "Christ lag in Todesbanden"
 Mozart, Symphony No. 40 in G Minor, K. 550, I
 Haydn, Symphony No. 95, I, II, III, and IV
 Mozart, Piano Concerto in A, K. 488, I
 Mozart, *Don Giovanni,* "Ho capito" and "Là ci darem la mano"
 I Lotring, *Bopong*
 Beethoven, Symphony No. 5 in C Minor, I, II, III, and IV
 Beethoven, String Quartet in F, Op. 135, II
 Schubert, "Erlkönig"
 R. Schumann, *Dichterliebe,* "Die alten, bösen Lieder"
 C. Schumann, "Der Mond kommt still gegangen"
 Chopin, Nocturne in F-sharp, Op. 15, No. 2
 Berlioz, *Fantastic* Symphony, V (track 3, 0:00–0:30; track 5, 0:00–0:27)
 Verdi, *Aida,* Tomb Scene, Act IV, scene ii (track 9, 2:41–3:16)
 Musorgsky, *Pictures at an Exhibition,* "Promenade" and
 "The Great Gate at Kiev"
 Brahms, Violin Concerto in D, Op. 77, III (track 6, 0:11–end)
 Mahler, Symphony No. 1, III (track 7, 0:00–0:07; track 8, 0:00–0:30)
 Beijing opera, *The Prince Who Changed into a Cat* (0:24–end)
 Debussy, Three Nocturnes, *Clouds* (track 17, 0:36–1:27)
 Stravinsky, *The Rite of Spring,* Part 1 (track 23, 0:00–0:24; track 23,
 0:36–track 24, 0:27)
 Schoenberg, *Pierrot lunaire,* "The Moonfleck"
 Berg, *Wozzeck,* Act III, scenes iii and iv (track 30, 0:26–0:44)
 Ives, "The Rockstrewn Hills" (track 36, 0:44–0:55)
 Ravel, Piano Concerto in G, I
 Bartók, Music for Strings, Percussion, and Celesta, II
 Copland, *Appalachian Spring,* Sections 2 and 5
 [Riley, *In C*]
 Wallace, *"If You Ever Been Down"* Blues
 Ellington, "Conga Brava"

Anonymous, galliard, "Daphne"

Anonymous, "Kemp's Jig"

Processional hymn from the Andes, "Hanaq pachap kusikuynin"

Gabrieli, "O magnum mysterium"

Purcell, *Dido and Aeneas* (track 18, 0:00–0:58)

Frescobaldi, Suite, especially Balletto, Corrente, and Passacaglia

Vivaldi, Violin Concerto in G, *La stravaganza*, I (1:17–1:33, 2:23–end) and II (1:22–1:44, 2:26–end)

Bach, *Brandenburg* Concerto No. 5, I—ritornello (track 1, 0:00–0:21)

Bach, Contrapunctus 4, from *The Art of Fugue* (1:08–1:17, 2:03–2:10, 2:25–2:33, 3:07–end)

Bach, Orchestral Suite No. 3 in D, Gavotte

Handel, *Julius Caesar*, "La giustizia" (0:00–0:16, 1:10–1:47)

Handel, *Messiah*, "There were shepherds," Hallelujah Chorus (0:00–0:16, 2:52–end)

Bach, Cantata No. 4, "Christ lag in Todesbanden," Stanza 7

Haydn, Symphony No. 95, I (track 22, 0:48–1:44), II (track 25), III (track 30, 0:00–0:09, 0:50–1:09), and IV (track 33)

Mozart, Piano Concerto in A, K. 488, I (track 37, 0:00–0:33, 0:56–1:27)

Mozart, *Don Giovanni*, "Ho capito" and "Là ci darem la mano"

Beethoven, Symphony No. 5 in C Minor, I and II

Beethoven, String Quartet in F, Op. 135, II (0:00–0:08)

Schubert, "Erlkönig"

R. Schumann, *Dichterliebe*, "Die alten, bösen Lieder"

C. Schumann, "Der Mond kommt still gegangen"

R. Schumann, *Carnaval*, "Eusebius"

Chopin, Nocturne in F-sharp, Op. 15, No. 2

Berlioz, *Fantastic* Symphony, V (track 8, 0:08–end)

Tchaikovsky, *Romeo and Juliet* (track 24, 0:58–2:00; track 30, 1:40–end)

Brahms, Violin Concerto in D, Op. 77, III (track 2, 0:36–0:46; track 4, 1:34–1:44; track 6, 1:07–end)

Mahler, Symphony No. 1, III (track 9, 0:48–1:19; track 14, 0:19–1:21)

Bartók, Music for Strings, Percussion, and Celesta, II (track 2, 0:47–0:54)

Copland, *Appalachian Spring*, sections 5 (0:00–0:37) and 6 (0:00–1:19)

Wallace, *"If You Ever Been Down" Blues* (0:10–0:44)

Ellington, "Conga Brava" (0:00–0:58)

Parker and Davis, "Out of Nowhere" (0:00–0:47)

Bernstein, *West Side Story*, Meeting Scene (0:00–0:47) and "Cool" (0:00–1:06, 3:58–end)

Linda, "Anoku Gonda" (1:26–end)

Schubert, Symphony No. 8, "Unfinished," I (DVD—0:53–1:06, 1:15–1:35)

Joplin, "Maple Leaf Rag" (DVD)

Gershwin, "Who Cares?" (DVD—1:39–1:52, 2:29–2:50)

Beethoven, Symphony No. 9, IV (DVD—0:00–0:48, 2:20–end)

Tchaikovsky, "Dance of the Sugar-Plum Fairy," from *The Nutcracker* (DVD—0:07–0:37)

Britten, *The Young Person's Guide to the Orchestra* (DVD)—theme (track 20, 0:00–0:04, –0:18)

Cadenza

Bach, *Brandenburg* Concerto No. 5, I—harpsichord (track 4)

Handel, *Julius Caesar*, "La giustizia" (3:17–3:35, 3:35–3:53)

Mozart, Piano Concerto in A, K. 488, I (track 39, 1:38–1:54; track 41, 1:08–2:30)

Beethoven, Symphony No. 5 in C Minor, I—oboe (track 10, 0:18–0:33)

Brahms, Violin Concerto in D, Op. 77, III (track 5, at 0:45; track 6, at 0:00)

Bernstein, *West Side Story,* "Cool" (2:56–3:39)

Schubert, Symphony No. 8, "Unfinished," I (DVD—2:20–2:46)

Rachmaninov, *Rhapsody on a Theme by Paganini* (DVD—0:11–0:21, 3:56–end)

Beethoven, Symphony No. 9, IV (DVD—2:20–end)

Beethoven, Piano Concerto No. 5, "Emperor," III (DVD—0:20–0:28, 0:55–1:03)

Britten, *The Young Person's Guide to the Orchestra* (DVD)—theme (track 20, 0:00–0:19, 1:36–1:55; track 25, 1:54–end) and variation 5 (track 22, 0:00–0:33)

Soft

Palestrina, *Pope Marcellus* Mass, "Qui tollis" (beginning)

Purcell, *Dido and Aeneas*

Bach, Orchestral Suite No. 3 in D, Air

Handel, *Messiah,* "There were shepherds"

Haydn, Symphony No. 95, II (track 25; track 29, 0:00–0:29), III—Trio (track 31), and IV (track 33, 0:00–0:15)

Mozart, Piano Concerto in A, K. 488, I (track 37, 0:56–1:27)

Beethoven, Symphony No. 5 in C Minor, III (track 16, 0:00–0:21; track 17, 1:37–2:54)

R. Schumann, *Dichterliebe,* "Im wunderschönen Monat Mai"

C. Schumann, "Der Mond kommt still gegangen"

Schubert, Moment Musical No. 2 in A-flat (0:00–0:53)

R. Schumann, *Carnaval,* "Eusebius"

Berlioz, *Fantastic* Symphony, V (track 2, 0:00–0:32)

Verdi, *Aida,* Tomb Scene, Act IV, scene ii (track 12, 4:17–end)

Tchaikovsky, *Romeo and Juliet* (track 19, 0:00–0:34; track 23, 0:00–0:25)

Musorgsky, *Pictures at an Exhibition,* "The Great Gate at Kiev" (1:01–1:37, 2:13–2:47)

Mahler, Symphony No. 1, III (track 7, 0:00–1:02)

Debussy, Three Nocturnes, *Clouds* (track 15, 0:00–0:34; track 20, 0:54–end)

Stravinsky, *The Rite of Spring,* Part 1 (track 21, 0:00–0:44; track 26, 0:00–0:34; track 27, 1:49–end)

Schoenberg, *Pierrot lunaire,* "Night" (0:00–1:01)

Berg, *Wozzeck,* Act III, scenes iii and iv (track 33)

Ives, "The Rockstrewn Hills" (track 36, 0:55–end)

Ravel, Piano Concerto in G, I (track 40, 0:00–0:38, 0:46–1:15)

Copland, *Appalachian Spring,* Sections 1 (0:00–0:44), 5 (0:00–0:37), and 6 (0:00–0:22, 2:12–end)

Prokofiev, *Alexander Nevsky,* "The Battle on Ice" (beginning)

Webern, Five Orchestral Pieces, Op. 10, No. 4

Adams, *El Niño,* "Pues mi Dios ha nacido a penar" (beginning)

Ellington, "Conga Brava" (0:00–0:23, 2:29–end)

Bernstein, *West Side Story,* Dance at Gym: Meeting Scene

Schubert, Symphony No. 8, "Unfinished," I (DVD—0:00–0:34, 3:10–end)

Rachmaninov, *Rhapsody on a Theme by Paganini* (DVD—0:52–1:46, 2:23–3:03)

Beethoven, Symphony No. 9, IV (DVD—0:00–0:48)

Tchaikovsky, "Dance of the Sugar-Plum Fairy," from *The Nutcracker* (DVD—0:00–0:37)

Britten, *The Young Person's Guide to the Orchestra* (DVD)—woodwind theme (track 20, 0:23–0:39), variation 1 (track 21, 0:00–0:15), and variation 6 (track 22, 0:33–1:53)

Loud and soft
  Handel, *Messiah,* "Glory to God" (1:19–end)
  Haydn, Symphony No. 95, I (track 22, 0:00–0:35; track 23, 0:00–0:29;
      track 24, 0:00–0:25), II (track 27), III (track 30, 0:00–0:25, 0:50–1:30),
      and IV (tracks 33–34; track 35, 1:05–track 36, 0:27)
  Mozart, Piano Concerto in A, K. 488, I (track 40, 0:00–0:37)
  Schubert, "Erlkönig"
  R. Schumann, *Dichterliebe,* "Die alten, bösen Lieder"
  R. Schumann, *Carnaval,* "Florestan"
  Berlioz, *Fantastic* Symphony, V (track 6, 0:00–0:23)
  Stravinsky, *The Rite of Spring,* Part 1 (track 23, 0:00–track 24, 0:53)
  Berg, *Wozzeck,* Act III, scenes iii and iv (track 30, 0:29–1:43)
  Ives, "The Rockstrewn Hills" (track 35, 0:00–0:48)
  Ravel, Piano Concerto in G, I (track 40, 0:00–1:15)
  Varèse, *Poème électronique* (0:00–0:45)
  Ellington, "Conga Brava" (0:00–0:58)
  Davis, *Bitches Brew* (0:00–1:04)
  Bernstein, *West Side Story,* "Cool" (0:00 1:06, 1:11–2:09)
  Schubert, Symphony No. 8, "Unfinished," I (DVD—1:54–2:57)
  Beethoven, Piano Concerto No. 5, "Emperor," III (DVD—0:20–1:03)
Crescendo
  Handel, *Messiah,* Hallelujah Chorus (1:16–1:34)
  I Lotring, *Bopong* (3:40–4:04)
  Beethoven, Symphony No. 5 in C Minor, I (track 5, 0:20–0:46), II
      (track 14, 1:03 1:41), III (track 16, 1:20–1:52), III (track 17, 2:54)
      to IV (track 18, 0:34), and IV (track 19, 3:44–end)
  Schubert, "Erlkönig" (3:27–3:41)
  R. Schumann, *Carnaval,* "Florestan" (0:38–end)
  Chopin, Nocturne in F-sharp, Op. 15, No. 2 (1:28–1:58)
  Berlioz, *Fantastic* Symphony, V (track 2, 0:33–0:57; track 4, 1:34–1:52;
      track 6, 0:55–1:42)
  Verdi, *Aida,* Tomb Scene, Act IV, scene ii (track 9, 2:04–2:43)
  Wagner, Prelude to *The Valkyrie* (1:24 2:10)
  Tchaikovsky, *Romeo and Juliet* (track 20, 1:50–2:24; track 21;
      track 27, 0:43–1:07; track 28, 0:49–1:21)
  Musorgsky, *Pictures at an Exhibition,* "The Great Gate at Kiev" (3:17–4:12,
      4:30–5:17)
  Debussy, Three Nocturnes, *Clouds* (track 17, 0:00–0:36)
  Stravinsky, *The Rite of Spring,* Part 1 (track 24, 1:50–2:23; track 27,
      0:54–1:33)
  Schoenberg, *Pierrot lunaire,* "Night" (1:02–1:29)
  Berg, *Wozzeck,* Act III, scenes iii and iv (track 30, 0:00–0:15, 0:15–0:26;
      track 31)
  Ives, "The Rockstrewn Hills" (track 35, 1:25–2:18)
  Ravel, Piano Concerto in G, I (track 40, 2:34–track 41, 0:28)
  Bartók, Music for Strings, Percussion, and Celesta, II (track 3, 0:20–1:08;
      track 5, 0:31–1:21)
  Copland, *Appalachian Spring,* Sections 2 (0:29–0:51, 1:45–2:07) and
      5 (1:42–1:50)
  Prokofiev, *Alexander Nevsky,* "The Battle on Ice"
  Davis, *Bitches Brew* (1:04–3:39)
  Gershwin, Prelude No. 1 (0:54–1:17)
  Bernstein, *West Side Story,* "Cool" (2:09–3:27)

"Emancipation of dissonance"
 Schoenberg, *Pierrot lunaire*
 Berg, *Wozzeck*
 Webern, Five Orchestral Pieces, Op. 10, IV
Embellishment
 Anonymous, galliard, "Daphne"
 Anonymous, "Kemp's Jig"
 Monteverdi, *The Coronation of Poppea* (track 16, 1:20–2:25)
 Vivaldi, Violin Concerto in G, *La stravaganza*, II
 Handel, *Julius Caesar,* "La giustizia" (2:22–end)
 Haydn, Symphony No. 95, II (track 26, 0:12–end; track 28, 0:12–end)
 Mozart, Piano Concerto in A, K. 488, I (track 38, 0:00–0:29)
 Japanese *gagaku* orchestra, *Etenraku*
 Beethoven, Symphony No. 5 in C Minor, II (track 14, 4:16–5:18)
 Chopin, Nocturne in F-sharp, Op. 15, No. 2 (0:00–0:58, 2:13–2:54)
 Berlioz, *Fantastic* Symphony, V (track 3, 0:00–0:30)
 Japanese *kabuki, Dojoji* (Parts 2, 3, and 5)
 Beijing opera, *The Prince Who Changed into a Cat* (0:24–end)
 Ravel, Piano Concerto in G, I (track 40, 1:15–2:04)
 Wallace, *"If You Ever Been Down"* Blues
 Parker and Davis, "Out of Nowhere" (0:00–0:47)
 Bernstein, *West Side Story,* "Cool"—fugue subject (1:11–1:34;
  embellished at 2:39–2:56)
Enemy Way ceremony
 Navajo song, "K'adnikini'ya'"
English horn
 Tchaikovsky, *Romeo and Juliet* (track 22, 1:57–2:12)
 Debussy, Three Nocturnes, *Clouds* (track 15, at 0:15; track 16, at 0:33;
  track 17, at 0:36; and track 20, at 0:00)
 Stravinsky, *The Rite of Spring,* Part 1 (track 21, 0:36–0:44, 0:49–1:03)
Ensemble (operatic)
 Mozart, *Don Giovanni,* "Là ci darem la mano"
 Verdi, *Aida,* Tomb Scene, Act IV, scene ii—"O terra, addio" (track 12)
 Berg, *Wozzeck,* Act III, scenes iii and iv
 Bernstein, *West Side Story,* "Cool"
Episodes (*see also* **Fugue; Rondo form**)
 Bach, Contrapunctus 4, from *The Art of Fugue*
 Haydn, Symphony No. 95, IV (track 34; track 35, 0:28–end)
 Schubert, Moment Musical No. 2 in A-flat (1:20–2:23, 3:57–4:54)
 Musorgsky, *Pictures at an Exhibition*, "The Great Gate at Kiev"
  (1:01–1:37, 2:13–3:50)
Erhu
 Beijing opera, *The Prince Who Changed into a Cat*
Exoticism
 Verdi, *Aida*
 Musorgsky, *Pictures at an Exhibition* (to Ravel, not Musorgsky)
Exposition—fugal
 Frescobaldi, Suite: Canzona
 Bach, Contrapunctus 4, from *The Art of Fugue* (0:00–0:27)
 Handel, *Messiah,* Hallelujah Chorus (0:49–1:16, 1:34–1:58)
 Bach, Cantata No. 4, "Christ lag in Todesbanden," Stanza 4 (0:00–0:12)
 Haydn, Symphony No. 95, IV (track 34, 0:00–0:15)
 Beethoven, Symphony No. 5 in C Minor, III—trio (track 17, 0:00–0:16)
 Berlioz, *Fantastic* Symphony, V (track 5, 0:00–0:27)

Bass or alto flute
   Stravinsky, *The Rite of Spring,* Part 1 (track 27, 1:49–end)
Form (*see* names of individual forms)
Fortepiano
   LeBrun, Sonata in F, II
Fragmentation
   Bach, Contrapunctus 4, from *The Art of Fugue* (0:27–0:39)
   Mozart, Symphony No. 40, I (track 18, 0:44–1:01)
   Haydn, Symphony No. 95, I (track 22, 0:16–0:27; track 23, 0:49–end)
   Beethoven, Symphony No. 5 in C Minor, I (track 9, 0:00–0:29)
   Berlioz, *Fantastic* Symphony, V (track 6, 0:40–0:55)
   Verdi, *Aida,* Tomb Scene, Act IV, scene ii (track 12, 3:44–4:17)
   Tchaikovsky, *Romeo and Juliet* (track 25; track 28, 0:00–0:25)
   Debussy, Three Nocturnes, *Clouds* (track 20, 0:54–end)
   Rachmaninov, *Rhapsody on a Theme by Paganini* (DVD—0:36–0:52)
Free Forms
   Anonymous, antiphon, "In paradisum"
   Pérotin, "Alleluia. Diffusa est gratia"
   Qur'anic recitation, "Ya Sin"
   Hawai'ian chant, *mele pule*
   R. Schumann, *Carnaval,* "Florestan"
   Berlioz, *Fantastic* Symphony, V
   Musorgsky, *Pictures at an Exhibition*, "Gnomus"
   Japanese *kabuki, Dojoji*
   Stravinsky, *The Rite of Spring,* Part 1
   Ives, "The Rockstrewn Hills"
   Ives, *The Unanswered Question*
   Copland, *Appalachian Spring*
   Webern, Five Orchestral Pieces, Op. 10, No. 4
   Ligeti, *Lux aeterna*
   Varèse, *Poème électronique*
   [Cage, *4'33"*]
   Saariaho, *From the Grammar of Dreams*
   Davis, *Bitches Brew*
French horn
   Haydn, Symphony No. 95, I (track 22, 0:48–1:14), II (track 29, 0:25–0:28),
      and IV (track 33, 0:21–0:29; track 35, 0:14–0:21)
   Beethoven, Symphony No. 5 in C Minor, I (track 6, 0:00–0:02), III (track 16,
      0:21–0:40), and IV (track 18, at 0:34)
   Tchaikovsky, *Romeo and Juliet* (track 24, 0:00–0:58; track 27, at 1:00)
   Musorgsky, *Pictures at an Exhibition*, "Promenade [2]" (0:00–0:09, 0:17–0:27)
   Brahms, Violin Concerto in D, Op. 77, III (track 5, 1:30–1:46)
   Debussy, Three Nocturnes, *Clouds* (track 16, at 0:33; track 20, at 0:00 and 1:21)
   Stravinsky, *The Rite of Spring,* Part 1 (track 23; track 24, 0:53–1:27;
      track 25, 0:00–0:55; track 27, 0:00–0:54)
   Ravel, Piano Concerto in G, I (track 40, 0:46–1:15)
   Schubert, Symphony No. 8, "Unfinished," I (DVD—0:34–1:15)
   Rachmaninov, *Rhapsody on a Theme by Paganini* (DVD—2:52–3:56)
   Beethoven, Piano Concerto No. 5, "Emperor," III (DVD—0:28–0:30)
   Britten, *The Young Person's Guide to the Orchestra* (DVD)—variation 10
      (track 23, 0:00–0:51) and fugue (track 25, at 1:24)
French overture
   [Bach, Orchestral Suite No. 3 in D, Overture]

Fusion
Davis, *Bitches Brew*
Gagaku
Japanese *gagaku* orchestra, *Etenraku*
Gakuso
Japanese *gagaku* orchestra, *Etenraku*
Galliard
Anonymous, "Daphne"
Gamelan
I Lotring, *Bopong*
Gamelan pelegongan
I Lotring, *Bopong*
Gangsa
I Lotring, *Bopong*
Gapped chorale
Bach, Cantata No. 4, "Christ lag in Todesbanden," Stanzas 3 and 4
Gavotte
Bach, Orchestral Suite No. 3 in D, Gavotte
Genre (*see* names of individual genres)
German Romantic opera
Wagner, *The Valkyrie*
Gesamtkunstwerk
Wagner, *The Valkyrie*
Gigue (*see* **Jig**)
Glissando
Japanese *gagaku* orchestra, *Etenraku*
Musorgsky, *Pictures at an Exhibition*, "Gnomus" (0:24–0:33, 1:45–2:22, 2:24–2:40) and "The Great Gate at Kiev" (3:25–3:28)
Ravel, Piano Concerto in G, I (track 37, 0:15–0:24, 1:17–1:24; track 40, 0:38–0:46)
Bartók, Music for Strings, Percussion, and Celesta, II (track 3, 1:18–1:28; track 7, 0:11–0:24, 0:28–0:44)
Varèse, *Poème électronique* (2:58–end)
Linda, "Anoku Gonda"
Rachmaninov, *Rhapsody on a Theme by Paganini* (DVD—1:58–2:06)
Britten, *The Young Person's Guide to the Orchestra* (DVD)—variation 9 (track 22, at 4:00 and 4:31)
Globalism
Davis, *Bitches Brew*
Linda, "Anoku Gonda"
Glockenspiel
Musorgsky, *Pictures at an Exhibition*, "The Great Gate at Kiev"— glockenspiel campane (2:47–3:50—especially 3:17–3:32—and 5:17–end)
Copland, *Appalachian Spring*, Sections 5 (1:03–1:42) and 6 (2:34–end)
Rachmaninov, *Rhapsody on a Theme by Paganini* (DVD—0:21–0:32)
Gong (Tam-tam)
I Lotring, *Bopong*
Musorgsky, *Pictures at an Exhibition*, "The Great Gate at Kiev" (5:17–end)
Mahler, Symphony No. 1, III (track 11, at 0:00; track 14, at 1:36)
Beijing opera, *The Prince Who Changed into a Cat*
Stravinsky, *The Rite of Spring*, Part 1 (track 27, 0:54–1:53)
Britten, *The Young Person's Guide to the Orchestra* (DVD)—variation 13 (track 24, at 1:06) and fugue (track 25, at 1:54)

Hichiriki
   Japanese *gagaku* orchestra, *Etenraku*
High Renaissance style
   Josquin, *Pange lingua* Mass
   Palestrina, *Pope Marcellus* Mass
   Weelkes, "As Vesta Was from Latmos Hill Descending"
   Processional hymn from the Andes, "Hanaq pachap kusikuynin"
Hocket
   Machaut, "Quant en moi"
   I Lotring, *Bopong*
Homophony
   Bernart, "La dousa votz"
   Dufay, "Ave maris stella" (even stanzas)
   Josquin, *Pange lingua* Mass, "Qui tollis" (0:21–0:34, 0:45–0:59)
   Palestrina, *Pope Marcellus* Mass, "Qui tollis"
   Weelkes, "As Vesta Was from Latmos Hill Descending" (1:21–1:33, 1:54–2:05)
   Anonymous, galliard, "Daphne" (0:00–1:35)
   Anonymous, "Kemp's Jig"
   Processional hymn from the Andes, "Hanaq pachap kusikuynin"
   Monteverdi, *The Coronation of Poppea*
   Purcell, *Dido and Aeneas,* "Thy hand, Belinda" and "When I am laid in earth"
   Frescobaldi, Suite: Balletto, Corrente, and Passacaglia
   Bach, *Brandenburg* Concerto No. 5, I—ritornello (track 1, 0:00–0:21)
   Bach, Orchestral Suite No. 3 in D, Gavotte (0:00–0:30)
   Handel, *Julius Caesar,* "La giustizia"
   Handel, *Messiah,* "There were shepherds," "Glory to God" (1:19–1:31, 1:41–1:53)
   Handel, *Messiah,* Hallelujah Chorus (0:00–0:25, 1:16–1:34)
   Bach, Cantata No. 4, "Christ lag in Todesbanden," Stanza 7
   Mozart, Symphony No. 40, I (track 16, 0:00–0:25)
   Haydn, Symphony No. 95, I, II, III, and IV (track 33)
   LeBrun, Sonata in F, II
   Mozart, Piano Concerto in A, K. 488, I (track 37)
   Mozart, *Don Giovanni,* "Ho capito," "Alfin siam liberati," and "Là ci darem
      la mano"
   Beethoven, Symphony No. 5 in C Minor, I, II (track 14, 0:00–0:21), III, and IV
   Beethoven, String Quartet in F, Op. 135, II
   Schubert, "Erlkönig"
   R. Schumann, *Dichterliebe,* "Im wunderschönen Monat Mai" and "Die alten,
      bosen Lieder"
   C. Schumann, "Der Mond kommt still gegangen"
   Schubert, Moment Musical No. 2 in A-flat
   R. Schumann, *Carnaval,* "Eusebius" and "Florestan"
   Chopin, Nocturne in F-sharp, Op. 15, No. 2 (0:00–0:58)
   Berlioz, *Fantastic* Symphony, V
   Verdi, *Aida,* Tomb Scene, Act IV, scene ii
   Wagner, Prelude to *The Valkyrie*
   Tchaikovsky, *Romeo and Juliet*
   Musorgsky, *Pictures at an Exhibition,* "Promenade" (0:08–0:17, 0:22–0:26,
      0:31–end), "Gnomus" and "The Great Gate at Kiev" (0:00–1:01, 1:01–1:37)
   Brahms, Violin Concerto in D, Op. 77, III
   Mahler, Symphony No. 1, III (track 8, 0:00–track 9, 0:49; track 9,
      2:00–track 11, 0:00)
   Berg, *Wozzeck,* Act III, scenes iii and iv (track 30, 0:29–2:29)
   Ives, "The Rockstrewn Hills" (track 35, 2:06–2:34)

Interlocking ostinatos
>   Pygmy polyphony, elephant-hunt song
>   Schoenberg, *Pierrot lunaire,* "Night"

Inversion
>   Bach, Contrapunctus 4, from *The Art of Fugue* (0:04–0:08)
>   Bach, Orchestral Suite in D, Gavotte (0:00–0:30, motive inverted at 0:30)
>   Brahms, Violin Concerto in D, Op. 77, III (tune at track 2, 0:00–0:21;
>   tune inverted at track 2, 0:21–0:36)

Irregular Meters (*see* **Meter**—*Changing or irregular*)

Isicathamiya
>   Linda, "Anoku Gonda"

Isorhythm
>   Machaut, "Quant en moi"

Italian opera
>   Monteverdi, *The Coronation of Poppea*
>   Handel, *Julius Caesar*
>   Mozart, *Don Giovanni*
>   Verdi, *Aida*

"Jamming" (*see* **Collective improvisation**)

Jazz (*see also* specific jazz styles)
>   Wallace, *"If You Ever Been Down" Blues*
>   Ellington, "Conga Brava"
>   Parker and Davis, "Out of Nowhere"
>   Davis, *Bitches Brew*
>   Gershwin, "Who Cares?" (DVD—0:50–end)

Jazz-rock (*see* **Fusion**)

Jig
>   Anonymous, "Kemp's Jig"
>   Parker and Davis, "Out of Nowhere" ("Kerry Dancers"—2:02–2:06)

Jing **role**
>   Beijing opera, *The Prince Who Changed into a Cat*

Jinghu
>   Beijing opera, *The Prince Who Changed into a Cat*

Jingju (*see* **Beijing opera**)

Kabuki
>   Japanese *kabuki, Dojoji*

Kakko
>   Japanese *gagaku* orchestra, *Etenraku*

Keyboard (*see* names of individual keyboard instruments)
>   Gabrieli, "O magnum mysterium"—organ
>   Monteverdi, *The Coronation of Poppea*—harpsichord
>   Frescobaldi, Suite—organ
>   Bach, *Brandenburg* Concerto No. 5 (track 4)—harpsichord
>   Handel, *Julius Caesar,* "La giustizia"—harpsichord
>   Handel, *Messiah,* "There were shepherds," "Glory to God," and Hallelujah
>   Chorus—harpsichord
>   Handel, *Messiah,* "Glory to God" and Hallelujah Chorus—organ
>   Bach, Cantata No. 4, "Christ lag in Todesbanden"—organ
>   Bach, chorale prelude, "Christ lag in Todesbanden"—organ
>   LeBrun, Sonata in F, II—fortepiano
>   Mozart, Piano Concerto in A, K. 488, I—piano
>   Mozart, *Don Giovanni,* "Alfin siam liberati"—harpsichord
>   Schubert, "Erlkönig"—piano

R. Schumann, *Dichterliebe,* "Im wunderschönen Monat Mai" and "Die alten, bösen Lieder"—piano

C. Schumann, "Der Mond kommt still gegangen"—piano

Schubert, Moment Musical No. 2 in A-flat—piano

R. Schumann, *Carnaval,* "Eusebius" and "Florestan"—piano

Chopin, Nocturne in F-sharp, Op. 15, No. 2—piano

Musorgsky, *Pictures at an Exhibition,* "Gnomus"—celesta (0:24–0:33)

Schoenberg, *Pierrot lunaire*—piano

Berg, *Wozzeck,* Act III, scenes iii and iv—piano (track 30, 0:29–2:29)

Ives, "The Rockstrewn Hills"—piano (track 35, 0:48–1:25; track 36, 0:55–end)

Ravel, Piano Concerto in G, I—piano

Bartók, Music for Strings, Percussion, and Celesta, II—celesta (track 3, 1:18–1:28)

Bartók, Music for Strings, Percussion, and Celesta, II—piano (throughout)

Copland, *Appalachian Spring*—piano, Section 5 (1:03–1:42, 2:30–end)

Webern, Five Orchestral Pieces, Op. 10, No. 4—celesta (at 0:16)

Varèse, *Poème électronique*—organ (at 2:30)

Adams, *El Niño,* "Woe unto Them That Call Evil Good"—piano

Ellington, "Conga Brava"—piano

Parker and Davis, "Out of Nowhere"—piano

Davis, *Bitches Brew*—electric piano

Gershwin, Prelude No. 1—piano

Joplin, "Maple Leaf Rag"—piano (DVD)

Rachmaninov, *Rhapsody on a Theme by Paganini*—piano (DVD)

Beethoven, Piano Concerto No. 5, "Emperor," III (DVD)

Tchaikovsky, "Dance of the Sugar-Plum Fairy," from *The Nutcracker*—celesta (DVD)

Kuchka

Musorgsky, *Pictures at an Exhibition*

Late Romantic opera

Verdi, *Aida*

Wagner, *The Valkyrie*

Learned fugue (*see also* **Fugal devices**)

Bach, Contrapunctus 4, from *The Art of Fugue*

Legato

Anonymous, antiphon, "In paradisum"

Hildegard, "Columba aspexit"

Pérotin, "Alleluia. Diffusa est gratia"

Dufay, "Ave maris stella"

Josquin, *Pange lingua* Mass

Palestrina, *Pope Marcellus* Mass, "Qui tollis"

Weelkes, "As Vesta Was from Latmos Hill Descending"

Anonymous, galliard, "Daphne"

Processional hymn from the Andes, "Hanaq pachap kusikuynin"

Gabrieli, "O magnum mysterium"

Purcell, *Dido and Aeneas*

Vivaldi, Violin Concerto in G, *La stravaganza,* II

Bach, Contrapunctus 4, from *The Art of Fugue*

Bach, Orchestral Suite No. 3 in D, Air

Mozart, Symphony No. 40, I (track 16, 0:00–0:18)

Haydn, Symphony No. 95, II (track 27, 0:00–0:12)

Mozart, Piano Concerto in A, K. 488, I (track 37, 0:00–0:33)

Mozart, *Don Giovanni,* "Là ci darem la mano"

Japanese *gagaku* orchestra, *Etenraku*

Beethoven, Symphony No. 5 in C Minor, I (track 6), II (track 14, 0:00–1:03), and IV (track 18, 0:34–1:00)

Bach, Orchestral Suite No. 3 in D
Handel, *Messiah,* "Glory to God," Hallelujah Chorus
Haydn, Symphony No. 95, I (track 22, 0:48–1:44; track 24, 0:41–end),
    II (tracks 25–26 and 28–29), III—trio (track 31), and IV
LeBrun, Sonata in F, II
Mozart, Piano Concerto in A, K. 488, I
Mozart, *Don Giovanni,* "Ho capito" and "Là ci darem la mano"
Beethoven, Symphony No. 5 in C Minor, I (track 6, 0:00–track 7, 0:09),
    II, III—trio (track 17, 0:00–1:03), and IV
Beethoven, String Quartet in F, Op. 135, II (0:00–0:33)
C. Schumann, "Der Mond kommt still gegangen"
Schubert, Moment Musical No. 2 in A-flat—**A** sections (0:00–1:20, 2:23–3:57,
    4:54–end)
R. Schumann, *Carnaval,* "Eusebius"
Chopin, Nocturne in F-sharp, Op. 15, No. 2
Berlioz, *Fantastic* Symphony, V (track 2, 1:40–track 3, 0:54; track 5, to
    end of movement)
Verdi, *Aida,* Tomb Scene, Act IV, scene ii (track 10, 0:00–track 11, 1:07;
    track 12)
Tchaikovsky, *Romeo and Juliet* (track 24, 0:00–0:58; track 27, 1:00–2:03;
    track 30)
Musorgsky, *Pictures at an Exhibition,* "Promenade" and "The Great Gate at Kiev"
Brahms, Violin Concerto in D, Op. 77, III
Mahler, Symphony No. 1, III—trio (track 9, 2:00–track 11, 0:00)
Beijing opera, *The Prince Who Changed into a Cat* (0:24–end)
Ives, *The Unanswered Question* (strings)
Ravel, Piano Concerto in G, I
Copland, *Appalachian Spring,* Sections 1, 2, 5, and 6
Prokofiev, *Alexander Nevsky,* "The Battle on Ice," second excerpt
[Riley, *In C*]
Reich, *Music for 18 Musicians*
Wallace, *"If You Ever Been Down"* Blues
Ellington, "Conga Brava" (0:51–2:28)
Parker and Davis, "Out of Nowhere"
Gershwin, Prelude No. 1
Bernstein, *West Side Story,* Meeting Scene (0:00–0:47)
Linda, "Anoku Gonda"
Schubert, Symphony No. 8, "Unfinished," I (DVD—1:15–1:54)
Joplin, "Maple Leaf Rag" (DVD)
Gershwin, "Who Cares?" (DVD)
Beethoven, Symphony No. 9, IV (DVD)
Beethoven, Piano Concerto No. 5, "Emperor," III (DVD)
Britten, *The Young Person's Guide to the Orchestra* (DVD)—woodwind
    theme (track 20, 0:23–0:39) and brass theme (track 20, 0:45–1:00)
Mandolin
Webern, Five Orchestral Pieces, Op. 10, No. 4 (0:00–0:03)
March
Beethoven, Symphony No. 5 in C Minor, IV (track 18, 0:00–0:34)
Brahms, Violin Concerto in D, Op. 77, III—Coda (track 6, 0:11–end)
Mahler, Symphony No. 1, III (track 7)
Ives, "The Rockstrewn Hills" (track 35, at 2:44)
March and trio form
Mahler, Symphony No. 1, III

Mass
  Anonymous, preface, "Vere dignum"
  Anonymous, antiphon, "In paradisum" (Requiem Mass)
  Josquin, *Pange lingua* Mass
  Palestrina, *Pope Marcellus* Mass, "Qui tollis"
"Master rhythm"
  Berg, *Wozzeck,* Act III, scene iii (track 30, 0:26–track 31, 1:12)
Medieval modes
  Anonymous, preface, "Vere dignum"—Dorian
  Anonymous, antiphon, "In paradisum"—Mixolydian
  Hildegard, "Columba aspexit"—Mixolydian
  Bernart, "La dousa votz"—Mixolydian
  Pérotin, "Alleluia. Diffusa est gratia"—Mixolydian
  Machaut, "Quant en moi"—Lydian
  Dufay, "Ave maris stella"—Dorian
  Josquin, "Mille regrets"—Phrygian
  Josquin, *Pange lingua* Mass—Phrygian
  Palestrina, *Pope Marcellus* Mass—Ionian (major)
  Bach, Cantata No. 4, "Christ lag in Todesbanden," Stanza 7—Dorian melody
Mele pule
  Hawai'ian chant, *mele pule*
Melisma
  Anonymous, antiphon, "In paradisum"
  Pérotin, "Alleluia. Diffusa est gratia"
  Dufay, "Ave maris stella"
  Josquin, *Pange lingua* Mass
  Monteverdi, *The Coronation of Poppea,* "Speranza, tu mi vai"
  Purcell, *Dido and Aeneas,* "When I am laid in earth" (0:58–4:00)
  Handel, *Julius Caesar,* "La giustizia"
  Bach, Cantata No. 4, "Christ lag in Todesbanden," Stanzas 1 and 4
  Ligeti, *Lux aeterna*
  Varèse, *Poème électronique*
  Saariaho, *From the Grammar of Dreams,* Song 3
Melody
  Anonymous, preface, "Vere dignum"
  Anonymous, antiphon, "In paradisum"
  Hildegard, "Columba aspexit"
  Bernart, "La dousa votz"
  Pérotin, "Alleluia. Diffusa est gratia"
  Machaut, "Quant en moi"
  Qur'anic recitation, "Ya Sin"
  Hawai'ian chant, *mele pule*
  Navajo song, "K'adnikini'ya'"
  Dufay, "Ave maris stella"
  Anonymous, galliard, "Daphne"
  Anonymous, "Kemp's Jig"
  Processional hymn from the Andes, "Hanaq pachap kusikuynin"
  Monteverdi, *The Coronation of Poppea*
  Purcell, *Dido and Aeneas* (track 18)
  Frescobaldi, Suite: Balletto and Corrente
  Bach, *Brandenburg* Concerto No. 5 (ritornello theme)
  Bach, Contrapunctus 4, from *The Art of Fugue* (0:00–0:27)
  Bach, Orchestral Suite No. 3 in D, Air and Gavotte

R. Schumann, *Dichterliebe,* "Im wunderschönen Monat Mai" and "Die alten, bösen Lieder"

C. Schumann, "Der Mond kommt still gegangen"

Schubert, Moment Musical No. 2 in A-flat

Chopin, Nocturne in F-sharp, Op. 15, No. 2

Berlioz, *Fantastic* Symphony, V

Verdi, *Aida,* Tomb Scene, Act IV, scene ii (tracks 10, 11, and 12)

Wagner, Prelude to *The Valkyrie*

Tchaikovsky, *Romeo and Juliet*

Musorgsky, *Pictures at an Exhibition,* "Promenade" and "The Great Gate at Kiev"

Brahms, Violin Concerto in D, Op. 77, III

Mahler, Symphony No. 1, III

Beijing opera, *The Prince Who Changed into a Cat* (0:24–end)

Stravinsky, *The Rite of Spring,* Part 1—Dance of the Adolescents (tracks 23–24)

Schoenberg, *Pierrot lunaire*

Berg, *Wozzeck,* Act III

Ives, "The Rockstrewn Hills"

Ravel, Piano Concerto in G, I

Bartók, Music for Strings, Percussion, and Celesta

Copland, *Appalachian Spring*

Prokofiev, *Alexander Nevsky,* "The Battle on Ice," second excerpt

[Riley, *In C*]

Webern, Five Orchestral Pieces, Op. 10, No. 4

Reich, *Music for 18 Musicians*

Adams, *El Niño,* "When Herod Heard" and "Woe unto Them That Call Evil Good"

Wallace, *"If You Ever Been Down"* Blues

Ellington, "Conga Brava"

Yoruba drumming, "Ako"

Parker and Davis, "Out of Nowhere"

Davis, *Bitches Brew*

Gershwin, Prelude No. 1

Bernstein, *West Side Story,* Meeting Scene (0:00–0:47) and "Cool"

Schubert, Symphony No. 8, "Unfinished," I (DVD)

Joplin, "Maple Leaf Rag" (DVD)

Rachmaninov, *Rhapsody on a Theme by Paganini* (DVD—0:00–0:52, 2:23–end)

Gershwin, "Who Cares?" (DVD)

Beethoven, Symphony No. 9, IV (DVD)

Stravinsky, *Symphony of Psalms,* II (DVD)

Beethoven, Piano Concerto No. 5, "Emperor," III (DVD)

Tchaikovsky, "Dance of the Sugar-Plum Fairy," from *The Nutcracker* (DVD)

Britten, *The Young Person's Guide to the Orchestra* (DVD)

Mezzo-soprano voice

Hawai'ian chant, *mele pule*

Monteverdi, *The Coronation of Poppea*—Nero

Handel, *Julius Caesar,* "La giustizia"—Sextus

Verdi, *Aida,* Tomb Scene, Act IV, scene ii—Amneris

Schoenberg, *Pierrot lunaire*

Berg, *Wozzeck,* Act III, scene iii—Margret

Adams, *El Niño,* "Pues mi Dios ha nacido a penar"

Gershwin, "Who cares?"—Ella Fitzgerald (DVD)

Middle Ages
 Anonymous, preface, "Vere dignum"
 Anonymous, antiphon, "In paradisum"
 Hildegard, "Columba aspexit"
 Bernart, "La dousa votz"
 Pérotin, "Alleluia. Diffusa est gratia"
 Machaut, "Quant en moi"
Miniature compositions
 Schubert, "Erlkönig"
 R. Schumann, *Dichterliebe,* "Im wunderschönen Monat Mai," "Die alten,
  bösen Lieder"
 C. Schumann, "Der Mond kommt still gegangen"
 Schubert, Moment Musical No. 2 in A-flat
 R. Schumann, *Carnaval,* "Eusebius" and "Florestan"
 Chopin, Nocturne in F-sharp, Op. 15, No. 2
 Musorgsky, *Pictures at an Exhibition* (in Musorgsky's original version for
  piano, at least)
 Schoenberg, *Pierrot lunaire*
 Webern, Five Orchestral Pieces, Op. 10, No. 4
 Saariaho, *From the Grammar of Dreams*
 Gershwin, Prelude No. 1
 Schubert, Moment Musical No. 3 in F Minor (DVD)
 Tchaikovsky, "Dance of the Sugar-Plum Fairy," from *The Nutcracker* (DVD)
Minimalism
 [Riley, *In* C]
 Reich, *Music for 18 Musicians*
Minor mode
 Anonymous, galliard, "Daphne"
 Processional hymn from the Andes, "Hanaq pachap kusikuynin"
 Purcell, *Dido and Aeneas,* "When I am laid in earth" (0:58) and
  "With drooping wings"
 Vivaldi, Violin Concerto in G, *La stravaganza,* II (1:44–2:26)
 Frescobaldi, Suite: Canzona and Passacaglia (2nd section, at 1:37)
 Bach, Contrapunctus 4, from *The Art of Fugue*
 Handel, *Julius Caesar,* "La giustizia"
 Bach, Cantata No. 4, "Christ lag in Todesbanden," Stanzas 3, 4, and 7
  (Dorian mode melody)
 Bach, chorale prelude, "Christ lag in Todesbanden" (Dorian mode melody)
 Mozart, Symphony No. 40, I
 Haydn, Symphony No. 95, I (track 22, 0:00–0:27; track 24, 0:00–0:41),
  II (track 27), III (tracks 30 and 32), and IV (track 35, 0:41–0:55)
 Mozart, Piano Concerto in A, K. 488, I (track 37, 1:27–1:57—alternates
  with major mode)
 Beethoven, Symphony No. 5 in C Minor, I, II (track 15, 0:00–0:21), and
  III (track 16; track 17, 1:37–2:54)
 Schubert, "Erlkönig"
 R. Schumann, *Dichterliebe,* "Die alten, bösen Lieder"
 Schubert, Moment Musical No. 2 in A-flat—**B** sections (1:20–2:23,
  3:57–4:54)
 R. Schumann, *Carnaval,* "Florestan"
 Verdi, *Aida,* Tomb Scene, Act IV, scene ii—recitative: parts 1 (track 9,
  0:00–2:04) and 3 (track 9, 2:41–3:32)
 Wagner, Prelude to *The Valkyrie*

Tchaikovsky, *Romeo and Juliet* (tracks 19–22; tracks 25–26; track 27, 0:00–0:22; track 28, 0:35–1:57; track 29)

Mahler, Symphony No. 1, III

Berg, *Wozzeck,* Act III, scenes iii and iv—concluding orchestral lament (track 34)

Prokofiev, *Alexander Nevsky,* "The Battle on Ice," first excerpt

Bernstein, *West Side Story,* "Cool"

Schubert, Symphony No. 8, "Unfinished," I (DVD—0:00–1:06)

Rachmaninov, *Rhapsody on a Theme by Paganini* (DVD)

Stravinsky, *Symphony of Psalms,* II (DVD)

Schubert, String Quartet in A Minor (DVD)

Beethoven, Piano Concerto No. 5, "Emperor," III (DVD—at 1:36)

Tchaikovsky, "Dance of the Sugar-Plum Fairy," from *The Nutcracker* (DVD)

Britten, *The Young Person's Guide to the Orchestra* (DVD)—theme (track 20, 0:00–0:19)

Minstrel

Bernart, "La dousa votz"

Minuet

Haydn, Symphony No. 95, III

Rachmaninov, *Rhapsody on a Theme by Paganini* (DVD—2:23–3:56)

Minuet form

Haydn, Symphony No. 95, III

Beethoven, Symphony No. 5 in C Minor, III (scherzo and trio form)

Beethoven, String Quartet in F, Op. 135, II (scherzo and trio form)

Mixolydian mode (*see* **Medieval modes**)

Mode (*see* **Major mode; Medieval modes; Minor mode**)

Moderato

Tchaikovsky, *Romeo and Juliet* (tracks 34 and 35)

Musorgsky, *Pictures at an Exhibition,* "Promenade [2]"

Copland, *Appalachian Spring,* Section 6 (0:00–1:19)

Rachmaninov, *Rhapsody on a Theme by Paganini* (DVD—0:52–2:23)

Modernism

Musorgsky, *Pictures at an Exhibition*

Debussy, Three Nocturnes, *Clouds*

Stravinsky, *The Rite of Spring,* Part 1

Schoenberg, *Pierrot lunaire*

Berg, *Wozzeck,* Act III

Ives, "The Rockstrewn Hills"

Ives, *The Unanswered Question*

Bartók, Music for Strings, Percussion, and Celesta

Webern, Five Orchestral Pieces, Op. 10, No. 4

[Riley, *In C*]

Ligeti, *Lux aeterna*

Varèse, *Poème électronique*

[Cage, 4'33"]

Saariaho, *From the Grammar of Dreams*

Davis, *Bitches Brew*

Stravinsky, *Symphony of Psalms,* II (DVD)

Modulation

Frescobaldi, Suite: Corrente (**a**) and Passacaglia (1:11–end)

Vivaldi, Violin Concerto in G, *La stravaganza,* I (1:17–1:33)

Bach, Contrapunctus 4, from *The Art of Fugue*

Bach, Orchestral Suite No. 3 in D, Air (0:00–0:55) and Gavotte (0:00–0:15)

Handel, *Julius Caesar,* "La giustizia" (0:00–0:50; 1:31–1:55)
Handel, *Messiah,* Hallelujah Chorus (0:00–0:25)
Mozart, Symphony No. 40, I (track 16, 0:00–track 17, 0:11)
Haydn, Symphony No. 95, I (track 22, 0:16–1:02; track 23, 0:00–0:29),
    III (track 30, 0:00–0:25, 0:50–1:04; track 31, 0:00–0:13)
Mozart, Piano Concerto in A, K. 488, I (track 38, 0:00–1:14; track 39, 0:36–1:18)
Beethoven, Symphony No. 5 in C Minor, I (track 5, 0:29–0:46),
    II (track 14, 1:03–1:41, 1:26–2:12), and IV (track 18, 0:00–1:11)
Beethoven, String Quartet in F, Op. 135, II (0:55–1:38)
Schubert, "Erlkönig" (0:55–1:34)
R. Schumann, *Dichterliebe,* "Im wunderschönen Monat Mai" (0:15–0:41),
    "Die alten, bösen Lieder" (0:23–0:41)
Schubert, Moment Musical No. 2 in A-flat (0:35–1:40)
Chopin, Nocturne in F-sharp, Op. 15, No. 2 (0:27–1:28)
Verdi, *Aida,* Tomb Scene, Act IV, scene ii—recitative (track 9)
Ravel, Piano Concerto in G, I (track 37, 0:24–0:41; track 39, 0:00–0:26)
Copland, *Appalachian Spring,* Section 5 (0:00–0:49; 1:42–2:02)
Gershwin, Prelude No. 1 (0:23–0:48)
Schubert, Symphony No. 8, "Unfinished," I (DVD—0:38–1:35)
Joplin, "Maple Leaf Rag" (DVD—1:28–2:11)
Stravinsky, *Symphony of Psalms,* II (DVD—0:00–0:50)
Beethoven, Piano Concerto No. 5, "Emperor," III (DVD—0:20–0:45,
    0:55–1:21)
Britten, *The Young Person's Guide to the Orchestra* (DVD)—theme
    (track 20, 0:00–0:39)

Moment musical
Schubert, Moment Musical No. 2 in A-flat

Monophony
Anonymous, preface, "Vere dignum"
Anonymous, antiphon, "In paradisum"
Hildegard, "Columba aspexit" (with drone)
Pérotin, "Alleluia. Diffusa est gratia" (0:00–0:37, 2:36–end)
Qur'anic recitation, "Ya Sin"
Hawai'ian Chant, *mele pule*
Navajo song, "K'adnikini'ya'"
Dufay, "Ave maris stella" (odd stanzas)
Handel, *Messiah,* "Glory to God"—And peace on earth (1:31–1:41, 1:53–2:01,
    2:30–2:38)
Handel, *Messiah,* Hallelujah Chorus—For the Lord God omnipotent reigneth
    (0:25–0:32, 0:37–0:44)
Handel, *Messiah,* Hallelujah Chorus—King of Kings (at 1:58, 2:04, 2:12, 2:18,
    2:26, 2:33, 2:52, and 2:56)
Haydn, Symphony No. 95, I (track 22, 0:00–0:04, 0:16–0:27)
I Lotring, *Bopong* (4:04–end)
Beethoven, Symphony No. 5 in C Minor, I (track 5, 0:00–0:08)
Musorgsky, *Pictures at an Exhibition,* "Promenade" (0:00–0:08, 0:17–0:22,
    0:26–0:31)
Gershwin, Prelude No. 1 (0:00–0:07)
Schubert, Symphony No. 8, "Unfinished," I (DVD—0:00–0:12)
Beethoven, Symphony No. 9, IV (DVD—0:00–0:48)

Motet
Machaut, "Quant en moi"
Gabrieli, "O magnum mysterium"

Motives
  Navajo song, "K'adnikini'ya'"
  Frescobaldi, Suite: Canzona
  Bach, Contrapunctus 4, from *The Art of Fugue*
  Bach, chorale prelude, "Christ lag in Todesbanden"
  Mozart, Symphony No. 40, I
  Haydn, Symphony No. 95, I, III, and IV
  Beethoven, Symphony No. 5 in C Minor, I (track 5, 0:00–0:08, 0:08–0:20;
     track 6, 0:00–0:02, 0:02–0:21; track 7, 0:00–0:08; track 8, 0:00–0:05,
     0:36–0:46; track 12, 0:15–0:20), II (track 14, 1:26–1:41), III (track 16,
     0:21–0:40), and IV (track 18, 1:00–1:27)
  Beethoven, String Quartet in F, Op. 135, II
  Schubert, "Erlkönig"
  R. Schumann, *Carnaval*, "Eusebius" and "Florestan"
  Berlioz, *Fantastic* Symphony, V (track 3, 0:51–0:54; track 4, 1:34–1:52;
     track 5, 0:00–0:27)
  Wagner, Prelude to *The Valkyrie*
  Tchaikovsky, *Romeo and Juliet* (track 19, 0:34–1:03; track 21, 0:26–0:55)
  Brahms, Violin Concerto in D, Op. 77, III (track 5, 1:02–1:46)
  Debussy, Three Nocturnes, *Clouds* (track 15, at 0:15; track 19, at 0:33;
     track 17, at 0:36; and track 20, at 0:00)
  Stravinsky, *The Rite of Spring*, Part 1 (various motives tracks 23–24)
  Schoenberg, *Pierrot lunaire*, "Night"
  Bartók, Music for Strings, Percussion, and Celesta, II
  [Riley, *In C*]
  Varèse, *Poème électronique*
  Saariaho, *From the Grammar of Dreams*, Song 3
  Yoruba drumming, "Ako"
  Parker and Davis, "Out of Nowhere" (2:02–2:06)
  Gershwin, Prelude No. 1
  Bernstein, *West Side Story*, Meeting Scene (0:10–0:26, 0:32–0:47, at 0:47)
     and "Cool" (0:00–1:06)
  Schubert, Symphony No. 8, "Unfinished," I (DVD—0:13–1:06, 2:13–2:33)
  Rachmaninov, *Rhapsody on a Theme by Paganini* (DVD—0:00–0:52, 3:56–end)
Motivic consistency
  Navajo song, "K'adnikini'ya'"
  Frescobaldi, Suite: Canzona
  Bach, Contrapunctus 4, from *The Art of Fugue*
  Bach, chorale prelude, "Christ lag in Todesbanden"
  Haydn, Symphony No. 95, III and IV
  Beethoven, Symphony No. 5 in C Minor, I
  Beethoven, String Quartet in F, Op. 135, II
  Schoenberg, *Pierrot lunaire*, "Night"
  Bartók, Music for Strings, Percussion, and Celesta
  Saariaho, *From the Grammar of Dreams*, Song 3
  Yoruba drumming, "Ako"
  Bernstein, *West Side Story*
  Rachmaninov, *Rhapsody on a Theme by Paganini* (DVD)
  Stravinsky, *Symphony of Psalms*, II (DVD)
  Beethoven, Piano Concerto No. 5, "Emperor," III (DVD)
  Britten, *The Young Person's Guide to the Orchestra* (DVD)
Movement
  Frescobaldi, Suite
  Vivaldi, Violin Concerto in G, *La stravaganza*

[Cage, 4'33"]

Saariaho, *From the Grammar of Dreams*

Nocturne

Chopin, Nocturne in F-sharp, Op. 15, No. 2

Debussy, Three Nocturnes, *Clouds*

Noise

Varèse, *Poème électronique*

[Cage, 4'33"]

Saariaho, *From the Grammar of Dreams*, Songs 1 and 4 (0:00–0:15)

Nonimitative polyphony (*see* **Polyphony**—*Nonimitative polyphony*)

Nonmetrical

Anonymous, preface, "Vere dignum"

Anonymous, antiphon, "In paradisum"

Hildegard, "Columba aspexit"

Pérotin, "Alleluia. Diffusa est gratia" (0:00–0:37, 2:36–end)

Qur'anic recitation, "Ya Sin"

Dufay, "Ave maris stella" (odd stanzas)

Monteverdi, *The Coronation of Poppea* (track 16, 0:00–0:23, 0:56–2:25)

Purcell, *Dido and Aeneas,* "Thy hand, Belinda" (0:00–0:58)

Handel, *Messiah,* "There were shepherds"

Mozart, *Don Giovanni,* "Alfin siam liberati"

Japanese *gagaku* orchestra, *Etenraku* (0:00–0:51)

R. Schumann, *Carnaval,* "Eusebius," "Florestan"—rubato

Verdi, *Aida,* Tomb Scene, Act IV, scene ii (track 9, 0:00–1:51)

Brahms, Violin Concerto in D, Op. 77, III—Short cadenza (track 6, 0:00–0:11)

Beijing opera, *The Prince Who Changed into a Cat* (0:00–0:24)

Debussy, Three Nocturnes, *Clouds* (track 20, 0:00–0:54)

Stravinsky, *The Rite of Spring,* Part 1—Introduction (track 21, 0:00–1:04)

Berg, *Wozzeck,* Act III, scenes iii and iv (tracks 32–33)

Ives, *The Unanswered Question*

Ligeti, *Lux aeterna*

Varèse, *Poème électronique*

[Cage, 4'33"]

Bernstein, *West Side Story,* Meeting scene (0:47–end)

Rachmaninov, *Rhapsody on a Theme by Paganini* (DVD—0:52–1:34)

Non-Western scales

Qur'anic recitation, "Ya Sin"

Navajo song, "K'adnikini'ya'"

Japanese *gagaku* orchestra, *Etenraku*

I Lotring, *Bopong*

Musorgsky, *Pictures at an Exhibition*, "Gnomus"

Japanese *kabuki, Dojoji*

Beijing opera, *The Prince Who Changed into a Cat*

Oboe

Bach, Orchestral Suite No. 3 in D, Gavotte

Haydn, Symphony No. 95, I (track 22, 1:38–1:44; track 24, 0:18–0:25, 0:41–1:08), III (track 30, 0:55–0:59), and IV (track 33, 0:29–0:36; track 35, 0:21–0:28, 1:05–1:08)

Japanese *gagaku* orchestra, *Etenraku—hichiriki*

Beethoven, Symphony No. 5 in C Minor, I (track 10, 0:18–0:33)

Musorgsky, *Pictures at an Exhibition*, "Gnomus" (0:16–0:24) and "Promenade [2]" (0:09–0:17, 0:36–0:47)

Beethoven, Symphony No. 9, IV (DVD—0:00–0:16, 0:48–1:04, 1:34–1:50, 2:20–2:35)

Tchaikovsky, "Dance of the Sugar-Plum Fairy," from *The Nutcracker* (DVD—0:00–0:37)

Paraphrase

Dufay, "Ave maris stella"

Parody

Berlioz, *Fantastic* Symphony, V (track 3, 0:00–0:30; track 4, 0:00–1:34)

Mahler, Symphony No. 1, III (track 7; track 8, 0:00–track 9, 1:19)

Rachmaninov, *Rhapsody on a Theme by Paganini* (DVD—0:00–0:52)

Passacaglia

Purcell, *Dido and Aeneas,* "When I am laid in earth" (0:58–4:00)

Frescobaldi, Suite: Passacaglia

Vivaldi, Violin Concerto in G, *La stravaganza,* II

Schoenberg, *Pierrot lunaire,* "Night"

Pentatonic scale

Navajo song, "K'adnikini'ya'"

I Lotring, *Bopong*

Musorgsky, *Pictures at an Exhibition,* "Promenade" (0:00–0:08)

Beijing opera, *The Prince Who Changed into a Cat*

Debussy, Three Nocturnes, *Clouds* (track 19, 0:00–0:27)

Percussion (*see also* specific percussion instruments)

Japanese *gagaku* orchestra, *Etenraku*

I Lotring, *Bopong*

Musorgsky, *Pictures at an Exhibition,* "Gnomus" and "The Great Gate at Kiev" (2:47–2:17, 5:17–end)

Japanese *kabuki, Dojoji*

Beijing opera, *The Prince Who Changed into a Cat*

Debussy, Three Nocturnes, *Clouds* (track 15, at 0:20; track 20, 0:32–end)

Stravinsky, *The Rite of Spring,* Part 1 (track 25; track 27, 0:54–1:33)

Berg, *Wozzeck,* Act III, scenes iii and iv (track 30, 0:00–0:26; track 32, 1:02–1:12)

Ives, "The Rockstrewn Hills" (track 36, 0:27–0:55)

Ravel, Piano Concerto in G, I (track 41, 0:05–end)

Bartók, Music for Strings, Percussion, and Celesta, II (track 4)

Varèse, *Poème électronique*

Adams, *El Niño,* "Woe unto Them That Call Evil Good"

Yoruba drumming, "Ako"

Davis, *Bitches Brew*

Bernstein, *West Side Story,* Cha-cha, Meeting Scene, and "Cool"

Rachmaninov, *Rhapsody on a Theme by Paganini* (DVD—0:11–0:21)

Britten, *The Young Person's Guide to the Orchestra* (DVD)—percussion theme (track 20, 1:19–1:36), variation 13 (track 24), and fugue (track 25, 1:44–end)

Phrase

Balanced phrases

Anonymous, "Kemp's Jig"

Frescobaldi, Suite: Passacaglia

Vivaldi, Violin Concerto in G, *La stravaganza,* II

Bach, Cantata No. 4, "Christ lag in Todesbanden," Stanza 7

Bach, chorale prelude, "Christ lag in Todesbanden"

Mozart, Symphony No. 40, I (track 17, 0:00–0:18)

Haydn, Symphony No. 95, I (track 22, 0:48–1:05), III (track 30, 0:00–0:09; track 31, 0:00–0:26), and IV (track 33, 0:00–0:24)

Mozart, Piano Concerto in A, K. 488, I (track 37, 0:00–0:15, 0:56–1:27)

Mozart, *Don Giovanni,* "Là ci darem la mano" (0:00–0:40)

R. Schumann, *Dichterliebe,* "Im wunderschönen Monat Mai," "Die alten, bösen Lieder"

C. Schumann, "Der Mond kommt still gegangen" (0:00–0:58)

R. Schumann, *Carnaval,* "Eusebius"

Chopin, Nocturne in F-sharp, Op. 15, No. 2

Verdi, *Aida,* Tomb Scene, Act IV, scene ii—arioso II (track 11, 0:00–1:07) and duet (track 12, 0:00–2:11)

Musorgsky, *Pictures at an Exhibition,* "Promenade" (0:00–0:34)

Mahler, Symphony No. 1, III (track 7, 0:07–0:28)

Copland, *Appalachian Spring,* Section 5

Wallace, *"If You Ever Been Down"* Blues

Parker and Davis, "Out of Nowhere"

Joplin, "Maple Leaf Rag" (DVD)

Rachmaninov, *Rhapsody on a Theme by Paganini* (DVD—3:56–end)

Beethoven, Symphony No. 9, IV (DVD)

Beethoven, Piano Concerto No. 5, "Emperor," III (DVD—0:00–0:25)

Tchaikovsky, "Dance of the Sugar-Plum Fairy," from *The Nutcracker* (DVD—0:07–0:37)

Unbalanced phrases

Anonymous, antiphon, "In paradisum"

Hildegard, "Columba aspexit"

Bernart, "La dousa votz"

Qur'anic recitation, "Ya Sin"

Navajo song, "K'adnikini'ya'"

Dufay, "Ave maris stella"

Anonymous, galliard, "Daphne"

Processional hymn from the Andes, "Hanaq pachap kusikuynin"

Monteverdi, *The Coronation of Poppea* (track 17)

Purcell, *Dido and Aeneas,* "When I am laid in earth" (0:58–4:00)

Frescobaldi, Suite: Balletto and Corrente

Bach, *Brandenburg* Concerto No. 5 (ritornello theme)

Bach, Orchestral Suite No. 3 in D, Air and Gavotte

Handel, *Julius Caesar,* "La giustizia"

Mozart, Symphony No. 40, I (track 16, 0:00–0:25)

Haydn, Symphony No. 95, I (track 22, 0:00–0:35), II (track 25), III (track 30, 0:09–0:25; track 31, 0:26–0:59), and IV (track 33, 0:15–0:35)

Mozart, Piano Concerto in A, K. 488, I (track 37, 0:00–0:33)

Mozart, *Don Giovanni,* "Là ci darem la mano" (0:40–1:01)

Beethoven, Symphony No. 5 in C Minor, I, II, III, and IV

Beethoven, String Quartet in F, Op. 135, II (0:08–0:32)

Schubert, "Erlkönig"

C. Schumann, "Der Mond kommt still gegangen" (0:58–end)

R. Schumann, *Carnaval,* "Florestan"

Berlioz, *Fantastic* Symphony, V

Verdi, *Aida,* Tomb Scene, Act IV, scene ii—recitative (track 9) and arioso I (track 10)

Tchaikovsky, *Romeo and Juliet* (track 24, 0:00–0:58)

Musorgsky, *Pictures at an Exhibition,* "Gnomus" and "The Great Gate at Kiev"

Brahms, Violin Concerto in D, Op. 77, III

Stravinsky, *The Rite of Spring,* Part 1

Schoenberg, *Pierrot lunaire*

Berg, *Wozzeck,* Act III, scenes iii and iv

Pizzicato

Haydn, Symphony No. 95, II (track 26, 0:12–0:29) and III—trio (track 31)

Beethoven, Symphony No. 5 in C Minor, II (track 15, 1:30–1:46) and III (track 17, 1:37–2:54)

Berlioz, *Fantastic* Symphony, V (track 2, 0:22–0:27; track 4, 0:31–0:37; track 6, 0:23–0:40)

Verdi, *Aida,* Tomb Scene, Act IV, scene ii—arioso I (track 10, 0:00–0:58)

Tchaikovsky, *Romeo and Juliet* (track 19, 1:58–track 20, 0:26)

Musorgsky, *Pictures at an Exhibition,* "Gnomus" (2:24–2:40)

Brahms, Violin Concerto in D, Op. 77, III (track 1, 1:05–1:13; track 4, 0:48–0:57)

Mahler, Symphony No. 1, III (track 8, 0:00–0:30)

Debussy, Three Nocturnes, *Clouds* (track 17, 0:36–1:27)

Stravinsky, *The Rite of Spring,* Part 1 (track 22, 0:58–1:04; track 23, 0:08–0:13, 0:23–0:36)

Ravel, Piano Concerto in G, I (track 37, 0:00–0:24)

Bartók, Music for Strings, Percussion, and Celesta, II (track 2, 0:00–0:03; track 4, 0:05–track 5, 0:31)

Ellington, "Conga Brava"—bass (0:58–1:38)

Parker and Davis, "Out of Nowhere"—bass (throughout)

Schubert, Symphony No. 8, "Unfinished," I (DVD—0:13–0:34)

Beethoven, Piano Concerto No. 5, "Emperor," III (DVD—0:00–0:10)

Tchaikovsky, "Dance of the Sugar-Plum Fairy," from *The Nutcracker* (DVD—0:00–0:37)

Bartók (slapped) pizzicato

Bartók, Music for Strings, Percussion, and Celesta, II (track 4, 0:14–0:49)

Plainchant

Anonymous, preface, "Vere dignum"

Anonymous, antiphon, "In paradisum"

Hildegard, "Columba aspexit"

Pérotin, "Alleluia. Diffusa est gratia" (0:00–0:37, 2:36–end)

Dufay, "Ave maris stella" (odd stanzas)

Berlioz, *Fantastic* Symphony, V—*Dies irae* quotation (track 4, 0:00–1:34)

Plucked stringed instruments (*see* individual instruments or **Stringed instruments**—*Plucked stringed instruments*)

Point of imitation

Josquin, *Pange lingua* Mass, Kyrie (at 0:08, 0:53, and 2:10)

Josquin, *Pange lingua* Mass, "Qui tollis" (at 0:00, 0:34, and 0:59)

Weelkes, "As Vesta Was from Latmos Hill Descending" (at 0:11, 0:53, and 2:05)

Purcell, *Dido and Aeneas,* "With drooping wings" (0:00–0:37)

Frescobaldi, Suite: Canzona

Bach, Contrapunctus 4, from *The Art of Fugue* (0:00–0:27, 0:39–1:02; 1:35–2:01)

Handel, *Messiah,* "Glory to God," (2:01–2:21, 2:38–3:02)

Handel, *Messiah,* Hallelujah Chorus (0:49–1:16, 1:34–1:58, 2:40–2:52)

Bach, Cantata No. 4, "Christ lag in Todesbanden," Stanza 4 (at 0:00, 0:37, 1:15, 1:33, and 1:51)

Haydn, Symphony No. 95, IV (track 34, 0:00–0:19)

Beethoven, Symphony No. 5 in C Minor, III (track 17, 0:00–0:16)

Berlioz, *Fantastic* Symphony, V (track 5, 0:00–0:27)

Mahler, Symphony No. 1, III (track 7)

Schoenberg, *Pierrot lunaire,* "Night" (0:00–1:01)

Bartók, Music for Strings, Percussion, and Celesta, II (track 5, 0:36–1:21)

Copland, *Appalachian Spring,* Section 5 (1:16–1:42)

Ligeti, *Lux aeterna*

Bernstein, *West Side Story,* "Cool" (1:11–2:25)

Stravinsky, *Symphony of Psalms,* II (DVD)

Britten, *The Young Person's Guide to the Orchestra* (DVD)—fugue (track 25, 0:00–0:41)

Polyphony

Imitative polyphony

Josquin, *Pange lingua* Mass, Kyrie (all), "Qui tollis" (0:00–0:21, 0:34–0:45, 0:59–end)

Weelkes, "As Vesta Was from Latmos Hill Descending" (0:04–0:31, 0:53–1:11, 2:05–end)

Purcell, *Dido and Aeneas,* "With drooping wings"

Frescobaldi, Suite: Canzona

Bach, *Brandenburg* Concerto No. 5 (solo passages)

Bach, Contrapunctus 4, from *The Art of Fugue*

Handel, *Julius Caesar,* "La giustizia" (at beginning of each stanza)

Handel, *Messiah,* "Glory to God," (2:01–2:21, 2:38–3:02)

Handel, *Messiah,* Hallelujah Chorus (0:49–1:16, 1:34–1:58, 2:40–2:52)

Bach, Cantata No. 4, "Christ lag in Todesbanden," Stanza 4

Haydn, Symphony No. 95, I (track 23, 0:00–0:20) and IV (track 34; track 35, 0:28–0:36)

Mozart, Piano Concerto in A, K. 488, I (track 39, 0:51–1:18)

Beethoven, Symphony No. 5 in C Minor, III—trio (track 17, 0:00–0:33)

Berlioz, *Fantastic* Symphony, V—Witches' Round Dance (track 5, 0:00–0:27, 0:46–1:01)

Tchaikovsky, *Romeo and Juliet* (track 19, 0:34–1:03; track 20, 0:26–0:55; track 22, 0:20–0:46)

Mahler, Symphony No. 1, III (track 7)

Schoenberg, *Pierrot lunaire,* "Night" and "The Moonfleck"

Berg, *Wozzeck,* Act III, scenes iii and iv (track 31)

Bartók, Music for Strings, Percussion, and Celesta, II (track 5, 0:36–1:21)

Copland, *Appalachian Spring,* Section 5 (1:16–1:42)

Ligeti, *Lux aeterna*

Saariaho, *From the Grammar of Dreams,* Song 3

Bernstein, *West Side Story,* "Cool" (1:11–2:25)

Schubert, Symphony No. 8, "Unfinished," I (DVD—2:48–3:07)

Stravinsky, *Symphony of Psalms,* II (DVD)

Schubert, String Quartet in A Minor (DVD)

Britten, *The Young Person's Guide to the Orchestra* (DVD)—fugue (track 25, 0:00–1:54)

Nonimitative polyphony

Pérotin, "Alleluia. Diffusa est gratia" (0:36–2:37)

Machaut, "Quant en moi"

Josquin, "Mille regrets"

Anonymous, galliard, "Daphne" (1:35–end)

Anonymous, "Kemp's Jig" (0:58–1:08)

Purcell, *Dido and Aeneas,* "When I am laid in earth" (0:58–4:00)

Pygmy polyphony, elephant-hunt song

Vivaldi, Violin Concerto in G, *La stravaganza,* II

Bach, Cantata No. 4, "Christ lag in Todesbanden," Stanza 3

Bach, chorale prelude, "Christ lag in Todesbanden"

Mozart, Symphony No. 40, I (track 18, 0:16–0:44; track 19, 0:22–1:19)

Haydn, Symphony No. 95, I (track 24, 0:09–0:25) and II (track 25, 0:26–0:46; track 26, 0:00–0:12, 0:24–0:41; track 28, 0:24–0:42)

I Lotring, *Bopong*

Bach, Cantata No. 4, "Christ lag in Todesbanden," Stanza 3

Mozart, Symphony No. 40, I

Haydn, Symphony No. 95, I—theme 1a (track 22, 0:00–0:27), I—recapitulation (track 24, at 0:09 or 0:25), III—a' (track 30, 0:59), III—c' (track 31, 0:39), III—trio (track 32), and IV—rondo theme (track 35, 0:00; track 36, 0:01)

Mozart, Piano Concerto in A, K. 488, I—theme 1 (track 37, 0:00–0:33; returns at track 38, 0:00, and track 40, 0:00)

Mozart, *Don Giovanni*, "Là ci darem la mano"—**A** (0:00–1:28)

Beethoven, Symphony No. 5 in C Minor, I—recapitulation (track 10), II—theme 2 (track 14, 3:06), III—c (track 17, 0:40), III—scherzo (track 17, 1:37), and IV—recapitulation (track 19, 0:32)

Beethoven, String Quartet in F, Op. 135, II (0:00–0:55; returns at 1:58)

Schubert, "Erlkönig"—"Mein Vater" (at 1:52, 2:31, and 3:12)

R. Schumann, *Dichterliebe,* "Die alten, bösen Lieder" (0:00–0:23; returns at 1:17–1:48)

Schubert, Moment Musical No. 2 in A-flat—**A** (0:00–1:20; returns at 2:23 and 4:54)

R. Schumann, *Carnaval,* "Eusebius"—a (0:00–0:11; returns at 0:38, 1:06, and 1:32) and "Florestan" (entire work)

Chopin, Nocturne in F-sharp, Op. 15, No. 2—a (0:00–0:27; returns at 2:13)

Berlioz, *Fantastic* Symphony, V—fugue subject (track 5, 0:00–0:27; returns at track 5, 0:46; track 6, 1:32; track 7, 0:00 and 0:31)

Tchaikovsky, *Romeo and Juliet*—recapitulation (track 27)

Musorgsky, *Pictures at an Exhibition,* "Promenade," "Gnomus" (0:00–0:16; returns at 0:33, 1:07, 1:33, 1:42, and 2:40), and "The Great Gate at Kiev" (0:00–1:01; returns at 1:37, 3:50, and 5:17)

Brahms, Violin Concerto in D, Op. 77, III—return of **a** (track 1, 0:00–0:46) and return of rondo theme (track 1, 0:00–0:46; returns at track 3, 0:00; at track 5, 0:20; and at track 6, 0:11)

Mahler, Symphony No. 1, III—march (track 7; returns at track 9, 1:19, and at track 12, 0:00)

Debussy, Three Nocturnes, *Clouds*—a (tracks 15–16; returns at track 18, 0:00), **A** (tracks 15–18; returns at track 20, 0:00), and **B** (track 19; returns at track 20, 1:13)

Stravinsky, *The Rite of Spring,* Part 1—bassoon "fanfare" (track 21, 0:00–1:04; returns at track 22, 0:29)

Ravel, Piano Concerto in G, I (track 37, 0:00–0:35; returns at track 39, 0:09, and at track 41, 0:00)

Bartók, Music for Strings, Percussion, and Celesta, II—recapitulation (tracks 41–42)

Copland, *Appalachian Spring,* Section 6 (hymnlike tune from Section 2 returns at 1:19; opening from Section 1 returns at 2:12)

Gershwin, Prelude No. 1 (all)

Bernstein, *West Side Story,* "Cool"—Riff's song (0:00–1:06; returns at 3:39)

Linda, "Anoku Gonda" (0:00–0:57)

Schubert, Symphony No. 8, "Unfinished," I (DVD)—theme 2 (1:15–1:54; returns at 2:48–3:07)

Joplin, "Maple Leaf Rag" (DVD—0:00–1:50)

Beethoven, Symphony No. 9, IV (DVD—0:00–0:32)

Schubert, Moment Musical No. 3 in F Minor (DVD—0:00–1:25)

Tchaikovsky, "Dance of the Sugar-Plum Fairy," from *The Nutcracker* (DVD)

Britten, *The Young Person's Guide to the Orchestra* (DVD)—theme
  (track 20, 0:00–0:19; returns at track 20, 1:36, and at track 25, 1:54)

Rhythm section
  Ellington, "Conga Brava"
  Parker and Davis, "Out of Nowhere"
  Davis, *Bitches Brew*
  Bernstein, *West Side Story,* "Cool"
  Gershwin, "Who Cares?" (DVD—0:50–end)

Rhythmic drive
  Vivaldi, Violin Concerto in G, *La stravaganza,* I and III
  Handel, *Julius Caesar,* "La giustizia"
  Haydn, Symphony No. 95, IV (track 34; track 35, 0:28–end; track 36,
    0:04–end)
  I Lotring, *Bopong* (4:04–end)
  Beethoven, Symphony No. 5 in C Minor
  Beethoven, String Quartet in F, Op. 135, II
  Schubert, "Erlkönig"
  Stravinsky, *The Rite of Spring,* Part 1 (track 23, 0:00–track 24, 0:37;
    tracks 25–26; track 26, 0:34–track 27, 0:54)
  Schoenberg, *Pierrot lunaire,* "The Moonfleck"
  Ravel, Piano Concerto in G, I
  Bartók, Music for Strings, Percussion, and Celesta, II
  Copland, *Appalachian Spring,* Section 2
  Davis, *Bitches Brew*
  Gershwin, Prelude No. 1
  Bernstein, *West Side Story,* "Cool"
  Beethoven, Piano Concerto No. 5, "Emperor," III (DVD)
  Britten, *The Young Person's Guide to the Orchestra* (DVD)—fugue (track 25)

Rhythmic motive
  Mozart, Symphony No. 40, I
  Haydn, Symphony No. 95, III (track 30)
  Beethoven, Symphony No. 5 in C Minor, I, II, III, and IV
  Berg, *Wozzeck,* Act III, scene iii (track 30, 0:26–track 31, 1:12)
  Copland, *Appalachian Spring,* Section 2
  Yoruba drumming, "Ako"
  Gershwin, Prelude No. 1
  Bernstein, *West Side Story,* Meeting Scene (0:00–0:47) and "Cool"
  Schubert, Symphony No. 8, "Unfinished," I (DVD—0:13–1:02)
  Beethoven, Piano Concerto No. 5, "Emperor," III (DVD—0:20–0:30,
    1:26–end)

Ritardando (*see* **Tempo**—*Decelerando*)
Ritornello
  Monteverdi, *The Coronation of Poppea,* "Speranza, tu mi vai" (0:00–0:25)
  Vivaldi, Violin Concerto in G, *La stravaganza,* I (0:00–0:26) and III (0:16–0:30)
  Bach, *Brandenburg* Concerto No. 5, I (track 1, 0:00–0:21)
  Handel, *Julius Caesar,* "La giustizia" (0:00–0:16)
  Bach, Cantata No. 4, "Christ lag in Todesbanden," Stanza 3 (0:00–0:10)

Ritornello form
  Vivaldi, Violin Concerto in G, *La stravaganza,* I and III
  Bach, *Brandenburg* Concerto No. 5, I

Romantic melody
  R. Schumann, *Dichterliebe*
  C. Schumann, "Der Mond kommt still gegangen"

Schubert, Moment Musical No. 2 in A-flat

R. Schumann, *Carnaval*

Chopin, Nocturne in F-sharp, Op. 15, No. 2

Verdi, *Aida*, Tomb Scene, Act IV, scene ii—duet (track 12, 0:00–2:11, 2:38–3:44)

Tchaikovsky, *Romeo and Juliet* (track 27, 0:56–2:03)

Mahler, Symphony No. 1, III (track 10)

Schubert, Symphony No. 8, "Unfinished," I (DVD—0:13–1:06, 1:15–1:54)

Romantic nostalgia

Mahler, Symphony No. 1

Romantic orchestra (*see* **Orchestra**—*Romantic*)

Romanticism

Schubert, "Erlkönig"

R. Schumann, *Dichterliebe*

C. Schumann, "Der Mond kommt still gegangen"

Schubert, Moment Musical No. 2 in A-flat

R. Schumann, *Carnaval*

Chopin, Nocturne in F-sharp, Op. 15, No. 2

Berlioz, *Fantastic* Symphony

Verdi, *Aida*

Wagner, *The Valkyrie*

Tchaikovsky, *Romeo and Juliet*

Musorgsky, *Pictures at an Exhibition*

Brahms, Violin Concerto in D, Op. 77, III

Mahler, Symphony No. 1, III

Schubert, Symphony No. 8, "Unfinished," I (DVD)

Rachmaninov, *Rhapsody on a Theme by Paganini* (DVD)

Tchaikovsky, "Dance of the Sugar-Plum Fairy," from *The Nutcracker* (DVD)

Rondo form

Haydn, Symphony No. 95, IV

LeBrun, Sonata in F, II

Schubert, Moment Musical No. 2 in A-flat

Musorgsky, *Pictures at an Exhibition*, "The Great Gate at Kiev"

Brahms, Violin Concerto in D, Op. 77, III

Beethoven, Piano Concerto No. 5, "Emperor," III (DVD)

Round

Mahler, Symphony No. 1, III (track 7)

Rubato

R. Schumann, *Dichterliebe*, "Im wunderschönen Monat Mai"

R. Schumann, *Dichterliebe*, "Die alten, bösen Lieder"—coda (2:35–end)

C. Schumann, "Der Mond kommt still gegangen"

R. Schumann, *Carnaval*, "Eusebius"

Chopin, Nocturne in F-sharp, Op. 15, No. 2

Verdi, *Aida*, Tomb Scene, Act IV, scene ii—duet (track 12)

Tchaikovsky, *Romeo and Juliet* (track 24, 0:00–0:58)

Brahms, Violin Concerto in D, Op. 77, III

Mahler, Symphony No. 1, III (track 9, 2:00–track 11, 0:00)

Ravel, Piano Concerto in G, I (track 38, 0:00–0:37)

Ryuteki

Japanese *gagaku* orchestra, *Etenraku*

Saxophone—alto, tenor, or baritone

Ellington, "Conga Brava" (especially at 0:58–1:38, 1:46–2:06, 2:22–2:28)

Parker and Davis, "Out of Nowhere" (0:00–0:47, 1:35–2:24, 2:48–end)

Bernstein, *West Side Story,* "Cool"

Gershwin, "Who Cares?" (DVD—throughout; alto solo at 1:52–2:09)

Scales (*see* **Chromatic scale; Major mode; Medieval modes; Minor mode; Non-Western scales; Octatonic scale; Pentatonic scale; Whole-tone scale**)

Scherzo

Beethoven, Symphony No. 5 in C Minor, III (track 16)

Beethoven, String Quartet in F, Op. 135, II (0:00–0:55)

Scherzo and trio form

Beethoven, Symphony No. 5 in C Minor, III

Beethoven, String Quartet in F, Op. 135, II

Secco recitative

Monteverdi, *The Coronation of Poppea,* Act I, "Tornerai?" (0:00–0:23, 0:56–2:25)

Purcell, *Dido and Aeneas,* "Thy hand, Belinda" (0:00–0:58)

Handel, *Messiah,* "There were shepherds" (0:00–0:10, 0:33–1:01)

Mozart, *Don Giovanni,* "Alfin siam liberati"

Second Viennese School

Schoenberg, *Pierrot lunaire*

Berg, *Wozzeck*

Webern, Five Orchestral Pieces, Op. 10

Semichoirs

Gabrieli, "O magnum mysterium"

Sequence (form)

Hildegard, "Columba aspexit"

Sequence (transposed repetition)

Anonymous, "Kemp's Jig"

Gabrieli, "O magnum mysterium" (0:00–0:30, 1:55–2:05, 2:26–2:37)

Bach, *Brandenburg* Concerto No. 5, I (track 2, 0:58–1:35)

Bach, Contrapunctus 4, from *The Art of Fugue* (0:27–0:33, 0:33–0:39, 1:08–1:17, 2:25–2:34)

Bach, Orchestral Suite No. 3 in D, Air (0:17–0:35, 2:51–3:12, 3:12–3:31)

Handel, *Messiah,* "Glory to God" (2:43–3:02) and Hallelujah Chorus (0:07–0:25, 1:58–2:40)

Bach, Cantata No. 4, "Christ lag in Todesbanden," Stanza 3 (0:00–0:10)

Mozart, Symphony No. 40, I

Haydn, Symphony No. 95, I (track 22, 0:27–0:35; track 23, 0:29–0:42, 0:49–0:59), II (track 25, 0:00–0:13), III (track 30, 0:50–0:59), and IV (track 34, 0:00–0:15, 0:48–0:55; track 35, 0:28–0:36)

Beethoven, Symphony No. 5 in C Minor, I (track 12, 0:30–0:56) and IV (track 18, 1:00–1:18)

Beethoven, String Quartet in F, Op. 135, II (1:03–1:10)

R. Schumann, *Carnaval,* "Eusebius" (0:00–0:11)

Chopin, Nocturne in F-sharp, Op. 15, No. 2 (0:58–1:14, 1:28–1:48)

Berlioz, *Fantastic* Symphony, V (track 6, 0:00–0:23)

Tchaikovsky, *Romeo and Juliet* (track 27, 1:16–1:44)

Debussy, Three Nocturnes, *Clouds* (track 17, 0:00–0:30)

Schoenberg, *Pierrot lunaire,* "Night" (1:29–end)

Ravel, Piano Concerto in G, I (track 38, 1:10–1:48)

Gershwin, Prelude No. 1 (0:23–0:48, 0:42–0:54)

Schubert, Symphony No. 8, "Unfinished," I (DVD—2:13–2:33)

Rachmaninov, *Rhapsody on a Theme by Paganini* (DVD—4:06–4:25)

Gershwin, "Who Cares?" (DVD—0:29–0:39, 1:26–1:39, 1:39–1:52)

Beethoven, Piano Concerto No. 5, "Emperor," III (DVD—0:00–0:10, 0:20–0:30)

Stringed instruments (*see also* specific stringed instruments)
   Bowed stringed instruments
      Machaut, "Quant en moi"
      Anonymous, galliard, "Daphne"
      Monteverdi, *The Coronation of Poppea,* "Speranza, tu mi vai"
      Purcell, *Dido and Aeneas,* "When I am laid in earth" (0:58–4:00)
      Vivaldi, Violin Concerto in G, *La stravaganza*
      Bach, *Brandenburg* Concerto No. 5, I
      Bach, Contrapunctus 4, from *The Art of Fugue*
      Bach, Orchestral Suite No. 3 in D, Air
      Handel, *Julius Caesar,* "La giustizia"
      Handel, *Messiah,* "Glory to God" and Hallelujah Chorus
      Bach, Cantata No. 4, "Christ lag in Todesbanden"
      Mozart, Symphony No. 40, I
      Haydn, Symphony No. 95, throughout, but especially in II (tracks 25–26),
         III—trio (track 31), and IV (track 33, 0:00–0:21)
      Mozart, Piano Concerto in A, K. 488, I (throughout, but good examples
         in track 37, 0:00–0:15 and 0:57–1:11)
      Mozart, *Don Giovanni,* "Ho capito" and "Là ci darem la mano"
      Beethoven, Symphony No. 5 in C Minor, I, II, III, and IV
      Beethoven, String Quartet in F, Op. 135, II
      Berlioz, *Fantastic* Symphony, V (track 2, 0:00–0:33; track 5, 0:00–0:27;
         track 6, 0:40–1:42; track 7, 0:28–0:42)
      Verdi, *Aida,* Tomb Scene, Act IV, scene ii (track 9, 0:00–2:09; track 11,
         0:00–1:07); string harmonics (track 12, 0:00–2:11); tremolo (track 12,
         2:38–3:44)
      Wagner, Prelude to *The Valkyrie*
      Tchaikovsky, *Romeo and Juliet* (track 19, 0:34–1:03; track 20, 0:26–0:55;
         track 23; track 27, 1:00–2:03)
      Musorgsky, *Pictures at an Exhibition,* "Promenade" (0:34–0:56),
         "Gnomus," and "The Great Gate at Kiev"
      Mahler, Symphony No. 1, III (track 10)
      Beijing opera, *The Prince Who Changed into a Cat* (0:24–end)
      Debussy, Three Nocturnes, *Clouds* (track 15, 0:34–track 16, 0:33;
         track 19, 0:27–0:44)
      Stravinsky, *The Rite of Spring,* Part 1 (track 23; track 25, 1:01–1:17;
         track 26, 0:34–track 27, 0:54)
      Schoenberg, *Pierrot lunaire,* "Night" and "The Moonfleck"
      Berg, *Wozzeck,* Act III, scenes iii and iv (track 34)
      Ives, "The Rockstrewn Hills" (track 35, 0:16–0:29)
      Ives, *The Unanswered Question*
      Ravel, Piano Concerto in G, I
      Bartók, Music for Strings, Percussion, and Celesta, II
      Copland, *Appalachian Spring,* Sections 1 (0:44–1:09), 2 (0:00–0:24),
         5 (1:50–2:14), and 6 (0:00–0:43)
      Prokofiev, *Alexander Nevsky,* "The Battle on Ice"
      Webern, Five Orchestral Pieces, Op. 10, No. 4
      Adams, *El Niño,* "Pues mi Dios ha nacido a penar"
      Bernstein, *West Side Story,* "Cool" (2:09–2:25)
      Schubert, Symphony No. 8, "Unfinished," I (DVD—0:00–0:22,
         1:15–1:54, 2:13–2:33, 2:48–2:57)
      Rachmaninov, *Rhapsody on a Theme by Paganini* (DVD—3:56–end)
      Gershwin, "Who Cares?" (DVD)
      Beethoven, Symphony No. 9, IV (DVD)

Beethoven, Symphony No. 5 in C Minor
Berlioz, *Fantastic* Symphony
Mahler, Symphony No. 1
Schubert, Symphony No. 8, "Unfinished," I (DVD)
Beethoven, Symphony No. 9, IV (DVD)
Stravinsky, *Symphony of Psalms,* II (DVD)

Symphony movement plan (*see* **Standard movement plan**)

Syncopation

Bach, Contrapunctus 4, from *The Art of Fugue* (2:42–2:56)
Haydn, Symphony No. 95, I (track 23, 0:00–0:20) and III (track 30, 0:50–0:59)
LeBrun, Sonata in F, II (2:45–end)
I Lotring, *Bopong* (4:04–end)
Beethoven, String Quartet in F, Op. 135, II (0:00–0:33)
Berlioz, *Fantastic* Symphony, V (track 5, 0:00–0:46; track 6, 1:24–1:32)
Verdi, *Aida,* Tomb Scene, Act IV, scene ii—arioso II (track 11, 0:00–1:07)
Tchaikovsky, *Romeo and Juliet* (track 22, 0:00–0:20; track 26, 0:35–0:51; track 30, 1:40–end)
Stravinsky, *The Rite of Spring,* Part 1 (track 23, 0:00–track 24, 0:37; track 26, 0:34–track 27, 0:54)
Berg, *Wozzeck,* Act III, scenes iii and iv (track 30, 0:26–0:44)
Ives, "The Rockstrewn Hills" (track 35, 0:48–1:25)
Ravel, Piano Concerto in G, I (track 37, 0:24–0:41)
Copland, *Appalachian Spring,* Section 2 (0:29–1:34, 1:45–2:07)
Adams, *El Niño,* "When Herod Heard"
Ellington, "Conga Brava"
Parker and Davis, "Out of Nowhere"
Davis, *Bitches Brew*
Gershwin, Prelude No. 1
Bernstein, *West Side Story,* Meeting Scene (0:00–0:47) and "Cool" (throughout, especially at 2:25)
Schubert, Symphony No. 8, "Unfinished," I (DVD—1:15–1:54)
Joplin, "Maple Leaf Rag" (DVD)
Rachmaninov, *Rhapsody on a Theme by Paganini* (DVD—0:00–0:21, 3:56–end)
Gershwin, "Who Cares?" (DVD—0:50–end)
Schubert, String Quartet in A Minor (DVD—1:27–1:39, 1:56–end)
Beethoven, Piano Concerto No. 5, "Emperor," III (DVD—0:00–0:10, 01:36–end)
Tchaikovsky, "Dance of the Sugar-Plum Fairy," from *The Nutcracker* (DVD—0:07–0:37, 0:37–0:59)
Britten, *The Young Person's Guide to the Orchestra* (DVD)—fugue (track 25)

Syncretism

Processional hymn from the Andes, "Hanaq pachap kusikuynin"
Frescobaldi, Suite: Passacaglia
Japanese *gagaku* orchestra, *Etenraku*
Musorgsky/Ravel, *Pictures at an Exhibition*
Brahms, Violin Concerto in D, Op. 77, III
Mahler, Symphony No. 1, III
Debussy, Three Nocturnes, *Clouds*
Stravinsky, *The Rite of Spring,* Part 1
Ives, "The Rockstrewn Hills"
Bartók, Music for Strings, Percussion, and Celesta, II
Copland, *Appalachian Spring,* Sections 1 and 6

Josquin, *Pange lingua* Mass, Kyrie

Weelkes, "As Vesta Was from Latmos Hill Descending"

Frescobaldi, Suite: Balletto

Pygmy polyphony, elephant-hunt song

Vivaldi, Violin Concerto in G, *La stravaganza,* I

Bach, Contrapunctus 4, from *The Art of Fugue*

Bach, Orchestral Suite No. 3 in D, Gavotte

Handel, *Messiah,* "Glory to God" and Hallelujah Chorus

Bach, Cantata No. 4, "Christ lag in Todesbanden," Stanza 7

Bach, chorale prelude, "Christ lag in Todesbanden"

Haydn, Symphony No. 95, I and III

LeBrun, Sonata in F, II

Mozart, Piano Concerto in A, K. 488, I

R. Schumann, *Dichterliebe,* "Die alten, bösen Lieder"

C. Schumann, "Der Mond kommt still gegangen"

Tchaikovsky, *Romeo and Juliet* (track 24, 0:00–0:58; track 27, 1:00–2:03)

Musorgsky, *Pictures at an Exhibition,* "Promenade," "Gnomus," and
  "The Great Gate at Kiev"

Mahler, Symphony No. 1, III

Stravinsky, *The Rite of Spring,* Part 1—Dance of the Adolescents
  (track 22, 0:58–track 25, 0:00)

Berg, *Wozzeck,* Act III, scenes iii and iv (track 31)

Copland, *Appalachian Spring,* Section 5

Saariaho, *From the Grammar of Dreams,* Song 1

Adams, *El Niño,* "When Herod Heard"

Ellington, "Conga Brava"

Parker and Davis, "Out of Nowhere"

Davis, *Bitches Brew*

Bernstein, *West Side Story,* Meeting Scene (0:00–0:47)

Linda, "Anoku Gonda" (0:57–end)

Schubert, Symphony No. 8, "Unfinished," I (DVD)

Joplin, "Maple Leaf Rag" (DVD)

Gershwin, "Who Cares?" (DVD—0:50–end)

Beethoven, Symphony No. 9, IV (DVD)

Schubert, String Quartet in A Minor (DVD)

Tchaikovsky, "Dance of the Sugar-Plum Fairy," from *The Nutcracker* (DVD)

Britten, *The Young Person's Guide to the Orchestra* (DVD)—theme
  (track 20) and variation 13 (track 24)

Fast tempo

Anonymous, "Kemp's Jig"

Gabrieli, "O magnum mysterium," *Alleluia* (1:55–2:05, 2:26–2:37)

Monteverdi, *The Coronation of Poppea,* "Io non posso da te" (track 14,
  0:23–0:56) and "Speranza, tu mi vai"

Frescobaldi, Suite: Canzona and Corrente

Vivaldi, Violin Concerto in G, *La stravaganza,* III

Bach, *Brandenburg* Concerto No. 5, I

Handel, *Julius Caesar,* "La giustizia"

Bach, Cantata No. 4, "Christ lag in Todesbanden," Stanzas 3 and 4

Mozart, Symphony No. 40, I

Haydn, Symphony No. 95, IV

Mozart, *Don Giovanni,* "Ho capito"

Beethoven, Symphony No. 5 in C Minor, I, III (especially the trio), and
  IV (especially track 19, 3:55–end)

Beethoven, String Quartet in F, Op. 135, II

Schubert, "Erlkönig"
R. Schumann, *Carnaval,* "Florestan"
Berlioz, *Fantastic* Symphony, V (track 2, 1:40 to end of movement)
Tchaikovsky, *Romeo and Juliet* (track 22, 0:20–track 28, 1:21)
Brahms, Violin Concerto in D, Op. 77, III
Stravinsky, *The Rite of Spring,* Part 1—Game of Abduction (track 25)
Schoenberg, *Pierrot lunaire,* "The Moonfleck"
Berg, *Wozzeck,* Act III, scenes iii and iv (track 30, 0:26)
Ives, "The Rockstrewn Hills"
Ravel, Piano Concerto in G, I
Bartók, Music for Strings, Percussion, and Celesta, II
Copland, *Appalachian Spring,* Section 2
Prokofiev, *Alexander Nevsky,* "The Battle on Ice," second excerpt
Saariaho, *From the Grammar of Dreams,* Song 4
Reich, *Music for 18 Musicians*
Yoruba drumming, "Ako"
Gershwin, Prelude No. 1
Bernstein, *West Side Story,* "Cool"
Rachmaninov, *Rhapsody on a Theme by Paganini* (DVD—3:56–end)
Beethoven, Piano Concerto No. 5, "Emperor," III (DVD)
Britten, *The Young Person's Guide to the Orchestra* (DVD)—
   variations 1 (track 21, 0:00–0:36), 5 (track 22, 0:00–0:33), and
   11 (track 23, 0:51–1:22); fugue (track 25)

Accelerando
Japanese *gagaku* orchestra, *Etenraku* (extremely gradual)
Beethoven, Symphony No. 5 in C Minor, IV—coda (track 19, 3:44–4:11)
R. Schumann, *Carnaval,* "Florestan" (0:45–end)
Chopin, Nocturne in F-sharp, Op. 15, No. 2 (1:28–1:55)
Berlioz, *Fantastic* Symphony, V (track 8)
Tchaikovsky, *Romeo and Juliet* (track 21)
Mahler, Symphony No. 1, III (track 14, 0:00–0:19)
Beijing opera, *The Prince Who Changed into a Cat* (0:00–0:20)

Decelerando (*or ritardando*)
Schubert, "Erlkönig" (3:41–3:49)
R. Schumann, *Dichterliebe,* "Die alten, bösen Lieder" (1:17–1:48)
R. Schumann, *Carnaval,* "Florestan" (0:00–0:11)
Chopin, Nocturne in F-sharp, Op. 15, No. 2 (1:47–2:13)
Berlioz, *Fantastic* Symphony, V (track 3, 0:39–1:12)
Tchaikovsky, *Romeo and Juliet* (track 22, 1:12–1:57)
Beijing opera, *The Prince Who Changed into a Cat* (0:20–0:24)
Stravinsky, *The Rite of Spring,* Part 1 (track 27, 1:15–1:33)
Ives, "The Rockstrewn Hills" (track 35, 1:55–2:44)
Bartók, Music for Strings, Percussion, and Celesta, II (track 5, 1:21–1:36)
Rachmaninov, *Rhapsody on a Theme by Paganini* (DVD—3:34–3:56)

Tenor voice
Bernart, "La dousa votz"
Machaut, "Quant en moi"
Gabrieli, "O magnum mysterium" (especially 0:38–1:55)
Pygmy polyphony, elephant-hunt song
Bach, Cantata No. 4, "Christ lag in Todesbanden," Stanzas 3, 4, and 7
R. Schumann, *Dichterliebe,* "Im wunderschönen Monat Mai," "Die alten,
   bösen Lieder"
Verdi, *Aida,* Tomb Scene, Act IV, scene ii—Radames
Wagner, *The Valkyrie,* Act I, scene i—Siegmund

Thematic unity

Navajo song, "K'adnikini'ya'"
Josquin, *Pange lingua* Mass
Bach, *The Art of Fugue*
Handel, *Julius Caesar,* "La giustizia"
Bach, Cantata No. 4, "Christ lag in Todesbanden"
Beethoven, Symphony No. 5 in C Minor
R. Schumann, *Carnaval*
Berlioz, *Fantastic* Symphony
Tchaikovsky, *Romeo and Juliet*
Musorgsky, *Pictures at an Exhibition*
Bartók, Music for Strings, Percussion, and Celesta
Copland, *Appalachian Spring*
Reich, *Tehillim*
Gershwin, Prelude No. 1
Bernstein, *West Side Story*
Linda, "Anoku Gonda"
Rachmaninov, *Rhapsody on a Theme by Paganini* (DVD)
Beethoven, Symphony No. 9 (DVD)
Stravinsky, *Symphony of Psalms,* II (DVD)
Britten, *The Young Person's Guide to the Orchestra* (DVD)

Theme

Frescobaldi, Suite: Canzona, Balletto, and Corrente
Vivaldi, Violin Concerto in G, *La stravaganza,* I (0:00–0:26), II (0:00–0:21),
    and III (0:16–0:30)
Bach, *Brandenburg* Concerto No. 5, I (track 1, 0:00–0:21)
Bach, Contrapunctus 4, from *The Art of Fugue* (0:00–0:27)
Bach, Orchestral Suite No. 3 in D, Gavotte (0:00–0:15)
Bach, Cantata No. 4, "Christ lag in Todesbanden"
Mozart, Symphony No. 40, I (track 16, 0:00–0:25)
Haydn, Symphony No. 95, I—theme 1 (track 22, 0:00–0:48), I—theme 2
    (track 22, 0:48–1:14), II (track 25), and IV (track 33)
Mozart, Piano Concerto in A, K. 488, I (track 37, 0:00–0:33, 0:57–1:27)
Mozart, *Don Giovanni,* "Là ci darem la mano" (0:00–0:40)
Beethoven, Symphony No. 5 in C Minor, I (track 5; track 6),
    II (track 14, 0:00–1:03, 1:03–2:12), III (track 16, 0:00–0:40), and
    IV (track 18, 0:00–0:34, 1:00–1:27)
Beethoven, String Quartet in F, Op. 135, II (0:00–0:08)
Schubert, Moment Musical No. 2 in A-flat (0:00–1:20 and 1:20–2:23)
R. Schumann, *Carnaval,* "Eusebius" and "Florestan"
Chopin, Nocturne in F-sharp, Op. 15, No. 2 (0:00–0:27)
Berlioz, *Fantastic* Symphony, V (track 3, 0:00–0:30; track 4, 0:00–0:37;
    track 5, 0:00–0:27)
Verdi, *Aida,* Tomb Scene, Act IV, scene ii—duet (track 12, 0:00–1:09)
Tchaikovsky, *Romeo and Juliet* (track 19, 0:00–0:34; track 22, 0:00–0:20;
    track 24, 0:00–0:58)
Musorgsky, *Pictures at an Exhibition,* "Promenade" (0:00–0:34) and
    "The Great Gate at Kiev" (0:00–1:01, 1:01–1:37)
Brahms, Violin Concerto in D, Op. 77, III (track 1, 0:00–0:46)
Mahler, Symphony No. 1, III (track 7, 0:00–0:38; track 8, 0:00–0:43; track 10)
Debussy, Three Nocturnes, *Clouds* (track 15, 0:00–0:15; track 19, 0:00–0:27)
Ives, *The Unanswered Question*
Ravel, Piano Concerto in G, I (track 37, 0:00–0:41, 0:44–1:39; track 38,
    0:00–0:56)

Bartók, Music for Strings, Percussion, and Celesta, II (track 2, at 0:00; track 3, at 0:00, 0:13, 0:36, and 1:08)

Copland, *Appalachian Spring*, Sections 1 (0:00–0:44), 2 (0:00–0:37), 5 (0:00–0:37), and 6 (0:00–0:22)

Wallace, *"If You Ever Been Down" Blues* (0:10–0:44)

Ellington, "Conga Brava" (0:00–0:58)

Parker and Davis, "Out of Nowhere" (0:00–0:47)

Gershwin, Prelude No. 1 (0:00–0:28)

Bernstein, *West Side Story*, "Cool" (0:00–1:06)

Schubert, Symphony No. 8, "Unfinished," I (DVD—0:15–1:07, 1:15–1:52)

Rachmaninov, *Rhapsody on a Theme by Paganini* (DVD—3:56–end)

Beethoven, Symphony No. 9, IV (DVD—0:00–0:48)

Stravinsky, *Symphony of Psalms*, II (DVD—0:00–0:25)

Beethoven, Piano Concerto No. 5, "Emperor," III (DVD—0:00–0:10)

Tchaikovsky, "Dance of the Sugar-Plum Fairy," from *The Nutcracker* (DVD—0:00–0:37)

Britten, *The Young Person's Guide to the Orchestra* (DVD)—theme (track 20, 0:00–0:19)

Theme and variations form

Haydn, Symphony No. 95, II

Beethoven, Symphony No. 5 in C Minor, II

Copland, *Appalachian Spring*, Section 5

Beethoven, Symphony No. 9, IV (DVD)

Britten, *The Young Person's Guide to the Orchestra* (DVD)

Third-period style

Beethoven, String Quartet in F, Op. 135, II

Through-composed song

Schubert, "Erlkönig"

R. Schumann, *Dichterliebe*, "Die alten, bösen Lieder"—modified

Saariaho, *From the Grammar of Dreams*, Songs 1, 3, and 4

Timpani

Bach, Orchestral Suite No. 3 in D, Gavotte

Handel, *Messiah*, "Glory to God" and Hallelujah Chorus

Haydn, Symphony No. 95, IV (track 36, 0:04–end)

Beethoven, Symphony No. 5 in C Minor, I (track 10, 0:00–0:08; track 12, 0:00–0:16; track 12, 0:30–track 13, 0:27), II (track 14, 1:26–1:44), III (track 17, 2:54–end), and IV (track 18, 0:00–0:34)

Wagner, Prelude to *The Valkyrie* (2:09–3:15)

Tchaikovsky, *Romeo and Juliet* (track 20, 1:50–2:24; track 28, 1:21–track 29, 0:38; track 30, 1:40–end)

Musorgsky, *Pictures at an Exhibition*, "Gnomus" (0:46–1:45) and "The Great Gate at Kiev" (roll—3:09–3:17; rolls and strokes—4:53–end)

Mahler, Symphony No. 1, III (track 7; track 9, 0:48–2:00; track 12, 0:00; and track 14, at 0:19)

Debussy, Three Nocturnes, *Clouds* (track 15, 0:20; track 20, 0:32)

Stravinsky, *The Rite of Spring*, Part 1 (track 24, 0:27–0:34; track 25; track 27, 0:54–1:33)

Berg, *Wozzeck*, Act III, scenes iii and iv (track 30, 0:00–0:26, at 0:42, and at 1:00; track 32, at 0:00 and 1:02)

Ravel, Piano Concerto in G, I (track 41, 0:13–end)

Bartók, Music for Strings, Percussion, and Celesta, II (track 2, 0:00–0:32; track 4, at 0:00; track 5, 0:27–1:04; track 5, 1:21–track 6, 0:18; track 8)

Copland, *Appalachian Spring*, Section 5 (2:30–end)

Trombone
Gabrieli, "O magnum mysterium"
Beethoven, Symphony No. 5 in C Minor, IV (track 19, 0:00–0:34; 3:55–end)
Berlioz, *Fantastic* Symphony, V (track 4, 0:21–0:31; track 6, 0:00–0:18;
    track 8, 0:22–end)
Musorgsky, *Pictures at an Exhibition*, "The Great Gate at Kiev" (1:37–1:52)
Ives, "The Rockstrewn Hills" (track 35, 2:44–3:00)
Ravel, Piano Concerto in G, I (track 38, at 1:21; track 40, at 0:38)
Copland, *Appalachian Spring*, Section 5 (1:03–1:42, 1:50–2:14)
Webern, Five Orchestral Pieces, Op. 10, No. 4 (0:11–0:15—muted)
Ellington, "Conga Brava"
Bernstein, *West Side Story*, "Cool"—muted (1:51–2:09)
Schubert, Symphony No. 8, "Unfinished," I (DVD—1:54–2:10, 2:27–2:46)
Gershwin, "Who Cares?" (DVD)
Britten, *The Young Person's Guide to the Orchestra* (DVD)—variation 12
    (track 23, 1:22–2:32) and fugue (track 25, 1:38–end)

Troubadours
Bernart, "La dousa votz"

Trumpet
Gabrieli, "O magnum mysterium"
Bach, Orchestral Suite No. 3 in D, Gavotte
Handel, *Messiah*, "Glory to God" and Hallelujah Chorus
Haydn, Symphony No. 95, I (track 24, 1:08–end) and IV (track 36, 0:04–end)
Beethoven, Symphony No. 5 in C Minor, II (track 14, 1:26–1:44) and
    IV (track 18, 0:00–0:34; track 19, 4:11–end)
Berlioz, *Fantastic* Symphony, V (track 7, 0:00–0:20)
Tchaikovsky, *Romeo and Juliet* (track 26, 0:23–0:36)
Musorgsky, *Pictures at an Exhibition*, "Promenade" (0:00–0:34) and
    "The Great Gate at Kiev" (0:00–1:01, 1:52–2:13, 3:17–3:32, 3:50–4:30,
    4:59–end)
Mahler, Symphony No. 1, III (track 8, 0:00–0:30; track 9, 0:00–0:31;
    track 13, 0:00–0:23; track 14, 0:00–0:19)
Stravinsky, *The Rite of Spring*, Part 1 (track 21, 1:27–1:42; track 24,
    2:04–track 25, 1:17)
Ives, "The Rockstrewn Hills" (track 35, 1:25–1:50; track 36, 0:00–0:24)
Ives, *The Unanswered Question*
Ravel, Piano Concerto in G, I (track 37, 0:00–0:41; track 38, 0:50–0:56;
    track 41, 0:00–end)
Copland, *Appalachian Spring*, Sections 1 (1:09–1:25—muted) and 5 (1:50–2:14,
    2:30–end)
Webern, Five Orchestral Pieces, Op. 10, No. 4 (0:06–0:11—muted)
Wallace, *"If You Ever Been Down" Blues* (0:10–0:44, 1:18–1:50, 1:50–2:24)
Ellington, "Conga Brava" (0:23–0:58, 1:38–2:28)
Parker and Davis, "Out of Nowhere" (0:47–1:35, 2:48–end)
Davis, *Bitches Brew* (1:04–end)
Bernstein, *West Side Story*, "Cool" (1:11–1:34, 2:39–3:39)
Schubert, Symphony No. 8, "Unfinished," I (DVD—2:27–2:46)
Gershwin, "Who Cares?" (DVD)
Beethoven, Symphony No. 9, IV (DVD—2:20–end)
Britten, *The Young Person's Guide to the Orchestra* (DVD)—variation 12
    (track 23, 0:51–1:22) and fugue (track 25, 1:29–end)

Tsuridaiko
Japanese *gagaku* orchestra, *Etenraku*

Tuba
  Gabrieli, "O magnum mysterium"
  Berlioz, *Fantastic* Symphony, V (track 4, 0:00–0:21; track 8, 0:00–0:08)
  Musorgsky, *Pictures at an Exhibition*, "The Great Gate at Kiev" (1:37–1:52, 2:47–3:42)
  Mahler, Symphony No. 1, III (track 7, 0:48–1:02)
  Britten, *The Young Person's Guide to the Orchestra* (DVD)—variation 12 (track 23, 1:37–2:13)
Tubular bells
  Berlioz, *Fantastic* Symphony, V (track 3, 1:12–track 4, 1:34)
  Musorgsky, *Pictures at an Exhibition*, "The Great Gate at Kiev" (5:17–end)
Tune
  Dufay, "Ave maris stella"
  Anonymous, galliard, "Daphne"
  Anonymous, "Kemp's Jig"
  Haydn, Symphony No. 95, IV
  Mozart, Piano Concerto in A, K. 488, I (track 37, 0:00–0:33, 0:57–1:27)
  Mozart, *Don Giovanni,* "Là ci darem la mano"
  Beethoven, String Quartet in F, Op. 135, II (0:00–0:08, 1:31–1:53)
  Chopin, Nocturne in F-sharp, Op. 15, No. 2 (0:00–0:27)
  Verdi, *Aida,* Tomb Scene, Act IV, scene ii—duet (track 12, 0:00–1:09)
  Musorgsky, *Pictures at an Exhibition*, "Promenade" (0:00–0:34) and "The Great Gate at Kiev" (0:00–1:01)
  Brahms, Violin Concerto in D, Op. 77, III (track 1, 0:00–0:46)
  Mahler, Symphony No. 1, III (track 7, 0:07–0:28)
  Ravel, Piano Concerto in G, I (track 37, 0:00–0:41)
  Copland, *Appalachian Spring,* Section 5
  Prokofiev, *Alexander Nevsky,* "The Battle on Ice," second excerpt
  Wallace, *"If You Ever Been Down" Blues* (0:00–0:44)
  Ellington, "Conga Brava" (0:00–0:58)
  Parker and Davis, "Out of Nowhere" (0:00–0:47)
  Gershwin, Prelude No. 1 (0:00–0:28)
  Bernstein, *West Side Story,* Meeting Scene (0:00–0:47) and "Cool" (0:00–1:06)
  Linda, "Anoku Gonda"
  Schubert, Symphony No. 8, "Unfinished," I (DVD—1:15–1:54)
  Joplin, "Maple Leaf Rag" (DVD—0:00–0:44, 2:34–end)
  Rachmaninov, *Rhapsody on a Theme by Paganini* (DVD—3:56–end)
  Beethoven, Symphony No. 9, IV (DVD—0:00–0:48)
  Gershwin, "Who Cares?" (DVD—0:50–end)
  Britten, *The Young Person's Guide to the Orchestra* (DVD)—theme (track 20, 0:00–0:19)
Twelve-bar blues
  Wallace, *"If You Ever Been Down" Blues*
Unpitched percussion instruments (*see* specific instruments or **Percussion**)
Variation form (*see also* **Ground bass; Passacaglia; Theme and variations form**)
  Frescobaldi, Suite: Passacaglia
  Purcell, *Dido and Aeneas,* "When I am laid in earth" (0:58–4:00)
  Vivaldi, Violin Concerto in G, *La stravaganza,* II
  Haydn, Symphony No. 95, II
  Beethoven, Symphony No. 5 in C Minor, II
  Schoenberg, *Pierrot lunaire,* "Night"
  Copland, *Appalachian Spring,* Section 5

Viol

Anonymous, "Kemp's Jig"

Monteverdi, *The Coronation of Poppea*

Purcell, *Dido and Aeneas*

Viola

Bach, Contrapunctus 4, from *The Art of Fugue* (1st entrance at 0:15)

Haydn, Symphony No. 95, IV—lowest voice, doubled by bassoon
    (track 33, 0:00–0:10)

Beethoven, Symphony No. 5 in C Minor, II (theme 1)

Beethoven, String Quartet in F, Op. 135, II

Debussy, Three Nocturnes, *Clouds* (track 18, 0:00–0:15)

Stravinsky, *The Rite of Spring,* Part 1 (track 27, 0:00–0:54)

Copland, *Appalachian Spring,* Section 5 (1:03–1:42—doubled by trombone)

Webern, Five Orchestral Pieces, Op. 10, No. 4 (at 0:04)

Beethoven, Symphony No. 9, IV (DVD—0:48–1:34)

Tchaikovsky, "Dance of the Sugar-Plum Fairy," from *The Nutcracker*
    (DVD—0:40–0:44, 0:47–0:51)

Britten, *The Young Person's Guide to the Orchestra* (DVD)—variation 6
    (track 22, 0:33–1:53) and fugue (track 25, at 0:41)

Violin

Anonymous, galliard, "Daphne"

Monteverdi, *The Coronation of Poppea,* "Speranza, tu mi vai"

Purcell, *Dido and Aeneas,* "When I am laid in earth" (0:58–4:00)

Vivaldi, Violin Concerto in G, *La stravaganza*

Bach, *Brandenburg* Concerto No. 5

Bach, Contrapunctus 4, from *The Art of Fugue*

Bach, Orchestral Suite No. 3 in D, Air

Handel, *Julius Caesar,* "La giustizia"

Handel, *Messiah,* "Glory to God" and Hallelujah Chorus

Bach, Cantata No. 4, "Christ lag in Todesbanden," Stanza 3

Mozart, Symphony No. 40, I

Haydn, Symphony No. 95, throughout, but especially in I (track 22, 0:00–0:35,
    0:48–1:31; track 23, 0:20–end; track 24, 0:25–1:02), II (entire movement),
    III (track 30, 0:00–0:25), and IV (track 33; track 34, 0:10–0:40; track 35,
    0:00–0:41; track 36); solo violin in I (track 24, 0:56–1:02)

Mozart, Piano Concerto in A, K. 488, I

Beethoven, Symphony No. 5 in C Minor, I (track 5; track 6, 0:02–track 7, 0:08),
    III (track 17, 0:00–1:03), and IV (track 18, 1:00–1:27)

Beethoven, String Quartet in F, Op. 135

Verdi, *Aida,* Tomb Scene, Act IV, scene ii (track 12, 4:21–end)

Musorgsky, *Pictures at an Exhibition*

Brahms, Violin Concerto in D, Op. 77, III

Debussy, Three Nocturnes, *Clouds* (track 19, 0:27–0:44)

Schoenberg, *Pierrot lunaire,* "The Moonfleck"

Copland, *Appalachian Spring,* Sections 1 (0:44–1:09) and 2 (0:00–0:37)

Webern, Five Orchestral Pieces, Op. 10, No. 4 (0:19–end)

Bernstein, *West Side Story,* Meeting Scene (0:47–end)

Schubert, Symphony No. 8, "Unfinished," I (DVD—1:35–1:54,
    2:13–2:33, 2:48–2:57)

Gershwin, "Who Cares?" (DVD)

Beethoven, Symphony No. 9, IV (DVD—1:34–2:20)

Britten, *The Young Person's Guide to the Orchestra* (DVD)—variation 5
    (track 22, 0:00–0:33) and fugue (track 25, at 0:41 and 1:54)

Stravinsky, *The Rite of Spring*, Part 1 (track 21, 0:00–track 22, 0:37; track 26, 0:00–0:34)

Schoenberg, *Pierrot lunaire*, "Night" and "The Moonfleck"

Ives, "The Rockstrewn Hills" (track 35, 0:29–0:48)

Ives, *The Unanswered Question*

Ravel, Piano Concerto in G, I (track 40, 0:38–1:15)

Copland, *Appalachian Spring*, Sections 1 (0:00–0:44, 1:25–end), 5 (0:00–1:03, 1:42–1:50, 2:14–2:30), and 6 (0:43–0:56)

Prokofiev, *Alexander Nevsky*, "The Battle on Ice," second excerpt (0:29–0:38, 1:46–1:59)

Adams, *El Niño*, "Pues mi Dios ha nacido a penar" (0:59–1:39)

Ellington, "Conga Brava" (0:58–1:38; 1:46–2:06)

Parker and Davis, "Out of Nowhere"

Schubert, Symphony No. 8, "Unfinished," I (DVD—0:22–1:02, 2:48–3:07)

Rachmaninov, *Rhapsody on a Theme by Paganini* (DVD—0:05–0:11, 1:34–1:58)

Gershwin, "Who Cares?" (DVD)

Beethoven, Symphony No. 9, IV (DVD—2:20–end)

Stravinsky, *Symphony of Psalms*, II (DVD)

Tchaikovsky, "Dance of the Sugar-Plum Fairy," from *The Nutcracker* (DVD—0:14–0:37, 1:06–end)

Britten, *The Young Person's Guide to the Orchestra* (DVD)—woodwind theme (track 20, 0:23–0:39), variations 1–4 (track 21), and fugue (track 25, 0:00–0:41)

Word painting

Weelkes, "As Vesta Was from Latmos Hill Descending"

Gabrieli, "O magnum mysterium"

Monteverdi, *The Coronation of Poppea*, "Speranza, tu mi vai"

Purcell, *Dido and Aeneas*, "With drooping wings"

Handel, *Messiah*, "Glory to God"

Bach, Cantata No. 4, "Christ lag in Todesbanden," Stanzas 3 and 4

Schubert, "Erlkönig"

Saariaho, *From the Grammar of Dreams*, Songs 1 and 4

Xylophone

Musorgsky, *Pictures at an Exhibition*, "Gnomus" (2:24–2:38)

Bartók, Music for Strings, Percussion, and Celesta, II (track 4, 0:30–0:40; track 7, 0:44–0:52)

Copland, *Appalachian Spring*, Section 2 (at 0:00, at 0:18, 0:45–0:50, 1:25–1:35)

Bernstein, *West Side Story*, "Cool" (4:03–end)

Britten, *The Young Person's Guide to the Orchestra* (DVD)—theme (track 20, 0:00–0:19) and variation 13 (track 24, at 0:48)

Yueqin

Beijing opera, *The Prince Who Changed into a Cat*

APPENDIX IV

Computer Technology in the Music Classroom

This appendix contains practical suggestions for the use of computer and Internet technologies in music appreciation courses. These suggestions can help both beginning and intermediate computer users who want to develop computer resources and incorporate technology into the curriculum.

The Changing Face of Education

Today's personal computers, online networks, and a host of digital gadgets offer possibilities unheard of even ten years ago. Computers were once the sole domain of trained professionals, and beginners had to learn complex computer languages. Today's computers offer intuitive graphic user interfaces, and most software must be as user-friendly as possible to survive in a competitive market. As a result, even novices can learn to create impressive multimedia documents in minutes—and learn they must! In colleges and universities nationwide, the pressure is on to incorporate technology. Faculty offices are generally equipped with computers hard-wired to the Internet, "smart" classrooms are increasingly available for teachers who use *PowerPoint* or the Web, and online course management tools such as *Blackboard* are rapidly ubiquitous in academia. Of course, our students now come in *expecting* to use technology. More and more institutions encourage students to apply online, register for courses online, use library resources online, do research online, check their grades online . . . and even take entire courses online!

Just as the call for "student-centered" learning questioned the effectiveness of the lecture approach, these technological changes pose serious challenges to traditional learning models. Of course, technology used for its own sake does no one any good. For all its wonders, technology is a tool—no more, no less. The trick is to find ways to use technology to support your pedagogical strategies, but how? In 1996, Ehrmann and Chickering[1] offered the brilliantly simple notion of using seven educational principles advanced by Chickering and

---

[1]Arthur W. Chickering and Stephen C. Ehrmann, "Implementing the Seven Principles: Technology as Lever," *AAHE Bulletin* 49.2 (Oct. 1996): 3–6 (available at http://aahebulletin.com/public/archive/sevenprinciples.asp).

Gamson (1987)[2] as starting points for the use of technology. These seven principles include such practices as encouragement of "contact between students and faculty," "active learning," development of "cooperation among students," and giving "prompt feedback." If, as these principles suggest, good teaching hinges on effective communication between teacher and student, then why not examine all possible points of contact and think about the ways technology can help in each case? David B. Williams (Illinois State University) and Peter Webster (Northwestern University) pose the problem and the opportunities with a simple chart that juxtaposes different time and place possibilities.[3]

	T I M E	
	Same	**Different**
Same	Same Time Same Place	Different Time Same Place
Different	Same Time Different Place	Different Time Different Place

(P L A C E)

Same Time/Same Place—This model, familiar to anyone with any educational experience, describes the traditional classroom, where teacher and students meet together at a specific time and place. Here technology can support multimedia presentations or online demonstrations of all kinds; if the place is a computer lab, students can try multimedia activities for themselves with direct teacher supervision.

Same Time/Different Place—This model points to *distance* learning opportunities that occur synchronously, at a specific meeting time. Possibilities include videoconferencing with experts, cable television broadcast of lectures, online class meetings, class "chat rooms," instant messaging, or "distance learning" courses held in classrooms linked through video and telephone connections.

Different Time/Same Place—Professors have used this model for years in traditional college courses, sending their students to labs, libraries, archives, and so on—locations where students could find course materials, software tools, recordings, and assignments for use outside of class. In the online world the possibilities increase exponentially. New resources include online databases and library catalogs, Web pages, downloadable *PowerPoint* presentations and software tools, streaming audio or video, discussion boards, or even course management environments. These online locations contain lectures, materials, tools, and assignments that students can access at any time.

Different Time/Different Place—Several models have emerged from this nexus. The asynchronous communication model points to contacts between teacher and students at different locations. Voicemail, e-mail, listservs, and discussion boards all permit students to ask questions, share ideas, or collaborate on assignments—at any time of day or night. A second model makes use of portable "course-paks," or CDs containing course materials that students can use anywhere, anytime.

---

[2]Arthur W. Chickering and Zelda F. Gamson, "Seven Principles for Good Practice in Undergraduate Education," *AAHE Bulletin* 39.7 (Mar. 1987): 3–7 (available at http://aahebulletin.com/public/archive/sevenprinciples1987.asp).

[3]Adapted from David B. Williams and Peter R. Webster, *Experiencing Music Technology*, 2d ed. New York: Schirmer Books, 1999, p. 64.

The last three models pose direct challenges to traditional, face-to-face classroom instruction, yet they need not play an adversarial role. In fact, all three can supplement a same time/same place course in wonderful ways. Some colleges and universities, most notoriously the University of Phoenix, have developed a large body of online courses. The jury is still out on the question of the quality of an education "delivered" purely online. Although many institutions are frankly uncomfortable with the thought of giving up face-to-face encounters between students and faculty, these same schools are busy developing a large repertory of blended courses—courses that mix same time/same place and online components in varying proportions. Such hybrid courses range between two extremes: One course might meet three times a week throughout the term with syllabus, assignments, discussion board, and practice quizzes available online; another might meet for a week both at the beginning and at the end of the term, with everything else done entirely online.

A few brave souls now offer music appreciation courses entirely online. These courses are new enough that instructors enjoy heavy support from their IT support staff. Most of us, however, can count on a more traditional same time/same place course environment, but that should not prevent our borrowing from the other time/place models whenever and wherever appropriate. Many colleges and universities have worked hard to provide an array of technological resources that support traditional courses. If you are fortunate enough to teach at such an institution, you will have no trouble finding mentors and support staff to introduce you to this technology. If not, see the section below titled "Learning More about Technology." This appendix is not intended as an exhaustive list of multimedia techniques, but I hope it will suggest some possibilities. Before you read on, consider these basic principles:

1. *It's not as hard as it looks!* Well-designed software packages such as PowerPoint or Dreamweaver make it easy to create multimedia documents and presentations, and authoring programs such as Director can give you control over various media and even animation.

2. *It's not how much you have but how well you use it!* Instructors who can spend only $200 a year on software have nonetheless found ingenious ways to use that software to meet student needs. On the flip side, some gizmos look really cool, but when you finally buy one you discover you don't know what on earth you'll do with it.

3. *Use your imagination!* What would really help your students most? Once you define your needs, you can more easily find various hardware and software solutions. Remember, even inexpensive sequencing programs can be used in a thousand different ways if you approach them creatively.

Putting Technology to Work

♪ Networking and the Internet

The Internet is the one pivotal resource that is doing more to revolutionize education than any other single factor. Multimedia presentations are a fascinating outgrowth of current technology, but the Internet is education's future. Three of Williams and Webster's four time/place models rely on the Internet, but even same time/same place multimedia presentations now rely more and more on the Internet, as the new *Listen* Web site demonstrates vividly (further information below). Many other online sites have built incredible libraries of multimedia resources—digital movies, photographs, graphics, sound files, public-domain books, and so on—that instructors can download in class as needed. With the appropriate hardware and software, you can even confer with guest experts through Web-based videoconferencing.

What Can I Do?

Internet technology is advancing so rapidly that anything I write here may be out-dated by the time you read it. Nonetheless, here are a few current possibilities.

Listen *Web Site*—Before you walk into class at the beginning of the term, you must visit this site: **bedfordstmartins.com/listen**. It includes several extra-ordinary teaching tools. First, every numbered Listening Chart in the textbook can be found here in an interactive format, providing users with point-and-click access to any excerpt from these works. Second, annotated Web links for each chapter provide quick access to information on all major composers and Global Perspectives topics in the book, as well as general music and ethnomusicology sites. Third, study tools include listening and reading quizzes, vocabulary flash-cards, a hyperlinked glossary of important terms, and other helpful resources. Finally, the instruments of the orchestra feature descriptions of each instru-ment and provide full-color illustrations with point-and-click access to the real (not synthesized) sounds of each instrument.

Course Management Tools and Course Web Sites—Once upon a time you had to create your own course Web site. You can still do this, of course, and soft-ware such as *Dreamweaver* makes it easier than ever, but why go to all the trouble when powerful new course management tools are available? The best known of these, *Blackboard,* makes it easy to mount course materials or entire courses on a course Web site. These tools accept most standard file formats, including the documents you create with your word processor, so you can create and mount your course syllabus, your schedule, and all of your assignments without learning a stitch of HTML code. And *Listen* makes it easier yet, provid-ing ready-to-go content for course management systems! Such course manage-ment tools also offer a discussion board, an online gradebook, a digital drop box for easy exchange of documents, and even online tests—automatically graded and entered into the gradebook! Tools such as these force the instructor to consider an entirely new range of educational experiences, no longer limited to the classroom or the library.

Course Web Pages—You can also create your own Web pages for use in the classroom. Any texts, images, sounds, or video clips you choose to incorporate become instantly available during class. If you mount your pages on the campus server (perhaps on your *Blackboard* site), your students can revisit pages later on to guide their study.

Web Exploration—Take your class online! Your students spend lots of time there already. The appendix in the *Listen* textbook includes a guide to relevant sites, including Web pages on composers, Western music genres, and various non-Western musics (find the same links and more on the *Listen* Web site—at **bedfordstmartins.com/listen**). Try them! In addition, try commercial and gov-ernment sites, libraries, databases, blogs, wikis, or even personal Web pages; any site that provides information, pictures, and audio or video files can be valuable. When you cover popular and world musics, try sites that allow visitors to sample sound or video clips. To supplement Global Perspectives coverage, visit government tourism pages for foreign countries. Of course, many online sites contain reference or multimedia materials that you can use in class for lectures or demonstrations.

A quick tip: If you have used the Web, you know how long you must wait for pages to download at busy times of day—and some sites are so busy that you can't gain access at all. Save valuable class time by visiting these sites "off-line" instead. Visit potentially busy sites before class and save the pages you need to your hard drive (most newer browsers now automatically save the .gif, .jpg, and other files that accompany Web pages). During class, open up your Web browser, go to the appropriate menu, and choose "Open Page" or "Open File" instead of "Open Location." Since it's all on the computer already, you won't waste time connecting and transferring data over the Internet. (To avoid copyright infringement, make sure you trash all copyrighted files when class is over.)

Student Assignments—Once you have modeled Internet strategies for your students in the classroom, give them assignments that require going online. Ask them to get information from online libraries or museums, to bring back a response to an email inquiry, to download files, to participate in a blog, or to bring back the address of a particularly interesting Web site.

Other assignments can take students online without going so far from home. You can use Web-based discussion board programs (built into *Blackboard* and *WebCT*) to set up an online forum for your class on the campus network. Students can access your class's discussion page from any computer with Web access. Ask students to collaborate on assignments online, or give informal writing assignments on a given topic. Enter a set of questions into the discussion page for your class and assign students to log on and respond—whoever logs on first writes a paragraph. The Web board posts responses so that subsequent visitors can see both your question and previously posted student answers. As each student logs on, he or she must read what earlier writers said, agree or disagree, and add his or her own ideas. The relative anonymity of the medium encourages shy or unassertive students to participate fully in online discussions; students who never say "boo" in class can be the most valuable contributors in this new medium. At the next class meeting, you can call up the discussion page and review the class's accumulated wisdom. If you have access to a lab, you can use it to generate online discussions in class as well.

Email—Don't overlook email as a powerful tool for communication with students, for electronic submission of assignments, or for instructor responses. *Blackboard* offers communications modules that make it easy to send email to the entire class or any subgroup.

♩ Multimedia Presentations

What Can I Do?

Audio/visual once referred to any teaching supplements that added sights and sounds to lectures. These included filmstrips, movies, videotapes, and sound recordings. *Multimedia* also refers to teaching supplements that add sights and sounds to lectures, but these supplements are now controlled by a personal computer. *Multimedia presentations* are lectures that rely on a computer as they incorporate digital audio, video, graphics, and/or text files. You can expand the power and variety of your presentation by adding peripheral devices such as MIDI keyboards, CD–ROM, and DVD drives.

These multimedia resources make marvelous teaching tools. Once you complete a presentation, you can store it on a disk and use it forever. Multimedia presentations in the music classroom can take several forms. All of the following assume that you can use a multimedia projector to display the contents of your computer screen on a movie screen.

Electronic Blackboard—Anything you write on the board can be presented just as easily at the computer. If you have the facility and you like to work things out "on the fly," try inputting your ideas directly into *PowerPoint* or a word-processing or paint program right there in class. If that sounds too tricky, prepare materials in advance. Many faculty members use *PowerPoint* these days, and although you can get fancier yet with *Director* or *Flash*, even a nicely formatted word-processing document works just fine. Use your imagination! Timelines, outlines, diagrams, graphs, charts, and discussion aids all work better than just plain text. (You'll want to prepare these ahead of time.) For example, the following simple timeline juxtaposes Wagner's operas (given here in their German titles) and their dates against the various places he lived and worked.

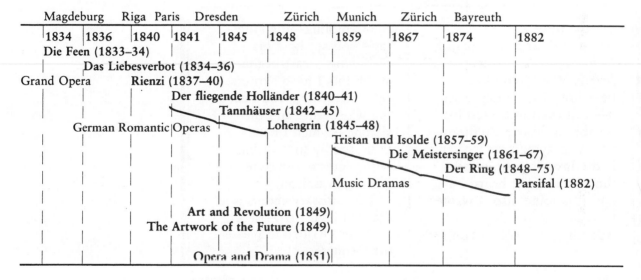

Lecture Outlines—Many instructors like to work from an outline. Try putting the outline on-screen, where it will help students as well as the instructor. *PowerPoint* is ideal for this purpose.

Slide Shows—Imagine a series of images—photographs, color pictures, charts, graphs, and so on—that you can display one after another on-screen. Such slide shows can be created easily with many software programs, ranging from high-end multimedia authoring programs (*Director*) to presentation software (*PowerPoint*) down to inexpensive integrated software packages (*AppleWorks* or the *Microsoft* suite—available for both Windows and Macintosh). You can assemble digital photographs, scanned images, clip art, or other visual images for your presentation.

Video Presentations—Movies are always a hit with students. The advent of DVD players is proving to be a boon for teachers, offering the same ability to jump around that made CDs so useful in class. No more fast forward or rewind! If you are adventurous, digital movie cameras and editing software make it easy to create your own video resources and burn them onto CD or DVD.

Interactive Listening Tools—The *Listen* Web site **bedfordstmartins.com/listen** provides interactive Listening Charts; with one click of the mouse you can hear any passage in the piece. It looks complicated, but anyone can create this kind of interactive tool. With the right tools, anything you put on-screen can be wired for sound. It could be an arch map for Debussy's Nocturnes.

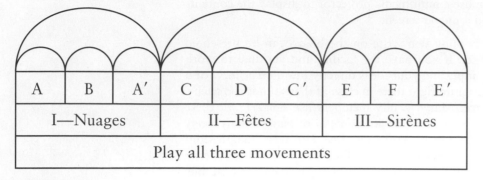

A	B	A′	C	D	C′	E	F	E′
I—Nuages			II—Fêtes			III—Sirènes		
Play all three movements								

Or it could be the text of a Mozart letter.

Let me now turn to Belmonte's aria in A major, *O wie ängstlich, o wie feurig*. Would you like to hear how I have expressed it—and even indicated his throbbing heart? By the two violins playing octaves. This is the favorite aria of all those who have heard it, and it is mine also. I wrote it expressly to suit Adamberger's voice. You feel the trembling—the faltering—you see how his throbbing breast begins to swell; this I have expressed by a crescendo. You hear the whispering and the sighing—which I have indicated by first violins with mutes and a flute playing in unison.

The Janissary chorus is all that can be desired—short, lively and written to please the Viennese.

Or it could be the program for Berlioz's *Fantastic* Symphony, Wagner leit-motivs in music notation, or text with translation for a Schumann lied.

What makes these images so powerful is point-and-click access to the sounds of these pieces. Just click on the arch-map buttons to hear sections of Debussy's Nocturnes—in any order. Or click on the words from Mozart's letter to hear the "throbbing heart," the "whispering and sighing," or the Janissary chorus. Where do the sounds come from? *Option 1*—They can come from digital sound files that you record or extract from audio CDs using *iTunes* or other utilities, and it's never been easier to burn these files onto your own CD. *Option 2*—You can use MIDI sound files—*QuickTime,* for instance, allows you to convert any standard MIDI file into a soundtrack-only QuickTime movie available for playback in a Web page, *PowerPoint* presentation, or any other multimedia application. *Option 3*—They can come from any commercially available CD that you insert into your CD-ROM drive. Some programs give the user control over the CD-ROM drive, including *PowerPoint* (yes, *PowerPoint*) and *TimeSketch Editor.*

Many of you will find the Listening Charts on the *Listen* Web site sufficient for classroom use. Still, some of you will have good reason to create your own interactive listening materials, especially if you want to supplement the *Listen* site charts with interactive images, charts, arch maps, and the like, or if you want to explore works not included in the *Listen* package.

Commercial CD-ROM Packages—Many current CD-ROM packages can find good uses in music appreciation classes. Depending on which packages you buy, you can, without any effort on your part, use ready-made Listening Charts (as described above), play a musical work while verbal descriptions of musical events flash by on the screen, display musical instruments and listen to the sounds they make, or look at famous paintings from great museums.

♪ MIDI-Based Tools

In one of the most miraculous events of the early 1980s, a group of synthesizer manufacturers established an industry standard for the interface between computers and electronic instruments—the MIDI protocol (Musical Instrument Digital Interface). The interface allows MIDI instruments to send information to the computer (note on, note off, attack velocity, and so on), and computers in turn can control the functioning of various aspects of the MIDI instrument. Many currently available music software programs rely on the MIDI protocol, including sequencing and notation software. Notation and sequencing programs produce documents in a proprietary format devised by their publishers, but they all permit you to save scores and sequences as standard MIDI files— files that can be read and edited in any other MIDI-based program. These MIDI files offer one significant advantage over digital audio files: their incredibly small size.

What Can I Do?

Although MIDI files can never replace the sound recordings that accompany the *Listen* textbook, they can nonetheless serve many valuable functions in the classroom. Take the example of the Frescobaldi Canzona. Its dense texture and full organ timbre can make it hard to follow the various polyphonic voices. But when you open up a MIDI file for this canzona in your notation or sequencing program, the playback controls allow you to start from any measure, slow down the tempo, play only one or two voices at a time, and so on. Students can really hear how the music works—one voice at a time, if necessary. Best of all, for many works in the standard repertory, you don't even have to make your own MIDI file—you can quickly download one from any of several Web sites.

Sequencing Software—If you know your way around a sequencing program, try creating alternative performances of musical works discussed in the *Listen* text, to demonstrate the effect of changes in mode, tone color, ornamentation, melodic shapes, rhythms, and so on. Students always seem to benefit from comparisons. Sequencing software is a boon for instructors with limited keyboard skills; you can record your performance at a painfully slow tempo, select "Quantize notes" to clean up the rhythms, and speed up the tempo for playback.

Educator William Smith adopted a hands-on approach to music appreciation: He took his students into a lab equipped with sequencing software and MIDI keyboards. Of course, sequencing software requires no knowledge of music notation; it simply records MIDI events in time and plays them back just as the user entered them. Students in Smith's class learned about musical elements by experimenting and manipulating those elements for themselves. In this exciting class, students moved beyond listening to actually creating musical sounds. If you have a lab large enough to accommodate your class, try this approach.

Notation Software—Most high-end notation programs offer a real-time note entry option—you play the music on a MIDI input device and the computer simultaneously turns your notes into notation. (Ask your students what Mozart might have done with such tools!) You can use this feature to provide visual reinforcement when you demonstrate melodic motion and contour or beat and meter. You can use the copy-and-paste feature to demonstrate imitative polyphony or repetition and return.

❦ Software and Hardware

The materials above describe many possibilities for the use of technology in music appreciation courses. This section lists the software and hardware you will need to make it happen.

Software—What Do I Need?

Software comes before hardware for a reason. When you go to the supermarket, you read the labels to find out how much fat or fiber per serving; when you go to the computer store, you read the System Requirements label on each software package to find out how much computer it needs. Once you know what the software requires, you can choose an appropriate computer system. It would be tragic to buy a mid-range computer only to discover that you need a high-end machine to run a video editing program. On the other hand, it makes little sense to buy the fastest, most expensive computer if you just want to do some word processing and routine music sequencing.

The following describes several categories of software programs you can use to create multimedia presentations. They range from sophisticated authoring programs that require you to build your presentation from the ground up to commercial CD-ROM packages that do everything for you, whether you like the content or not.

Authoring programs—Short of learning to write your own computer programs, authoring programs give you the most power and flexibility in creating a multimedia presentation. Most "authorware" allows you to integrate digital movies, photographs, graphics, and sounds. Programs such as *Director* or *Flash* (Macintosh and Windows) can create any of the possibilities listed above. In general, the more powerful the program, the more time you will spend learning it. Software packages that automatically create listening charts based on the audio clips you define include *TimeSketch Editor* (Macintosh and Windows) and AABACA's *Clip Creator*.

Web Authoring Software—For simple classroom presentations, Web pages can provide a useful display tool that combines text, images, video, and sounds. Many of the ideas listed above under Multimedia Presentations: What Can I Do?—electronic blackboard, lecture outlines, slides, video, and so on—can be done on a Web page. In addition, a course syllabus, schedule, and other course management materials can be mounted on a Web site.

Web pages have become such a staple item in the world of technology that you may already use a software package capable of creating a Web page—and not even know it! These programs include recent versions of most standard word-processing programs, including Microsoft *Word* and *AppleWorks,* and even presentation packages such as *PowerPoint.* Easiest of these are the word-processing programs. No knowledge of HTML (HyperText Markup Language) is required; just choose Save As . . . and select HTML as the document format; the computer does the rest. You may not get exactly the look you want, but for quick, "down and dirty" pages, this can be a godsend. Finally, there are many commercial applications geared specifically toward Web page creation. Some packages have you working directly with HTML code (*BBEdit,* for instance), but most of them, including Adobe's *GoLive* and Macromedia's *Dreamweaver,* permit control over virtually every detail of Web page construction. Although they all permit the user to edit HTML code directly, none of them require it. *Dreamweaver* is probably the smartest, most robust Web authoring tool. The instructional technology staff at your school can help get you started.

Online Course Management and Discussion Software—*Blackboard* and other course management programs allow you to mount virtually any digital document, be it sound, text, image, or video. Through these digital "front ends," your course Web site can become a digital reserve shelf containing syllabus, assignments, readings, listening selections, Web links to the campus library or any other site on the Web, gradebook, and various communication tools. These communication tools include email lists, a "virtual" classroom, and a discussion board. Email lists make it simple to communicate with all or just a few of your students. The "virtual" classroom permits real-time communication between the teacher and one or more students, offering the ability to post digital documents for all to see, type in text, or point out and highlight any feature of the document. The discussion board is geared toward asynchronous communication, class discussion, group discussion, and the like—a forum in which all class members can participate. These front-end programs must be installed on a server on your campus network; check with the network administrator to find out which programs are available on your campus. If your campus is still deciding which way to go, *Blackboard* allows you to create and offer one course, mounted on its Web site, on a trial basis. Try it!

Presentation Software—Presentation packages such as *PowerPoint* are incredibly easy to learn, but you sacrifice the flexibility that authorware offers. *PowerPoint* can create most of the possibilities listed above. All movies, photographs, graphics, and sounds must be stored in digital format on your computer. As a result, a single multimedia presentation can easily take up ten megabytes (or much more) of hard-drive space, but now that many of you can burn your own CDs, this no longer seems to matter. MP3 file formats also help to save space. Recent versions of *PowerPoint* also permit limited control over audio CD playback, but test it out first; this can be buggy. These software packages come with ready-made full-color templates that make it easy and fast to create presentations that look great. Now you can also save these documents in HTML format and mount them on the Web!

Integrated and Word-Processing Software—Less expensive than authorware or presentation software, integrated software packages such as the Microsoft suite or *ClarisWorks* combine features of word-processing, database, spreadsheet, painting, drawing, and presentation programs. You can use these various modules to quickly create charts, graphs, tables, outlines, or color graphics for your presentations. Many of the ideas listed above under Multimedia Presentations: What Can I Do?—electronic blackboard, lecture outlines, slide shows, and so on—can be done easily. These packages also allow you to import digital movies and clip art, aid in the creation of many useful graphics, and allow the inclusion of MIDI or digital audio files. The individual components of the Microsoft suite, a cluster of programs including *Word, PowerPoint, Excel,* and *Outlook Express,* clearly offer more power than any single module in Apple's integrated package, but they also cost more.

Commercial DVD and CD-ROM Packages—All of the software categories above allow the user to create customized multimedia presentations. With commercial DVD or CD-ROM packages, what you see is what you get; either you can use it easily or you can't. Several types of packages can help in music appreciation courses. In the mid-1990s, an entirely new genre developed for the presentation of famous musical works—a body of CD-ROM packages devoted to single, significant musical works. The now-defunct Voyager Company invented this genre with packages devoted to *The Rite of Spring* and Beethoven's Ninth Symphony.

A lot of exciting CD-ROMs were produced in the 1990s, but with the demise of HyperCard they are no longer usable (unless you are running Mac's older System 9). Right now it takes serious programming to produce a CD-ROM comparable to the old Voyager products, and we must wait patiently for the release of new material. At this writing, ECS Media's *TimeSketch* series is one of the best options, with nearly twenty titles available (including many works from the *Listen* recordings), and enhanced CDs have also filled at least part of the void, though their quality varies from disc to disc. With their enormous storage capacity, DVDs are gradually taking the place of the older CD-ROM packages (*Listen* itself now comes with a DVD rather than a CD-ROM).

These CD-ROM and DVD packages are lots of fun to play with, but since they were designed for individual, interactive exploration, they don't always work well for class presentation. If you want a canned lecture, you won't find it here. Nonetheless, these packages make wonderful resources for student assignments outside of class, and some features work very well in the classroom. For instance, the listening charts make it easy to skip around within a movement for demonstration purposes, and the "Listen to the Music" sections flash verbal descriptions of musical events on the screen while the music plays (much the same as the interactive Listening Charts on the *Listen* Web site).

MIDI Software—For multimedia presentations you may not even need a MIDI instrument! Programs such as *iTunes* permit easy conversion of MIDI files to many standard sound-file formats, such as MP3. Once converted, your MIDI file can be played back in any program that recognizes standard sound files, including *Netscape, Internet Explorer, Flash,* and *PowerPoint.* Hardware note: The multimedia-ready Macintosh computer needs no further equipment to take advantage of the features described above; Windows users must have a sound card installed. Check with your dealer or IT staff to determine which is appropriate for your needs.

This paragraph identifies some of the most frequently used notation and sequencing software. These packages are often expensive, but remember that many of these are available in "lite" versions that cost far less. For notation, MakeMusic!'s *Finale* has long been the industry standard, but *Sibelius* has mounted a serious challenge, especially given its built-in OCR capabilities (optical character recognition—for music!) and its ability to export documents in HTML format—as a Web page. Both are available for Windows or Macintosh. Among sequencing programs, GVOX's *Master Tracks Pro* is probably the best program available that works both on Windows and Macintosh; Apple's *Logic* series and Mark of the Unicorn's *Digital Performer* are good choices on the Macintosh platform.

Hardware—What Do I Need?

What you need depends on the software and media you plan to use. All multimedia presentations require a computer and a projection unit. Beyond that, you can customize your classroom workstation according to your needs.

Computer—The computers most commonly used for multimedia work in colleges across the United States are "Windows" and Macintosh computers. For beginners, I would still recommend Macintosh. Macs are easier to assemble and use, and the Macintosh "plug-and-play" philosophy makes it especially easy to handle multimedia. In addition, the new *iLife* suite can integrate various media with impressive results. For experienced users, it hardly matters anymore; music and multimedia programs are readily available for either platform.

In the Windows world, plan to use a Pentium 4 (or later) machine for multimedia; in the Macintosh world, seek out a Mac G5 or the equivalent (eMacs and iMacs are worth looking at). Whether you choose IBM or Macintosh, you need at least 1 gigabyte of RAM (random-access memory) and as large a hard drive as possible. For serious multimedia development, buy as much extra RAM as you can afford. Since digital movies and sound files gobble up hard drive space fast, don't forget to acquire the means to store these large files—CD or DVD burners, iPods, or "flash keys" can serve you well. As mentioned above, let your software decisions guide your hardware decisions.

Finally, you can't do multimedia presentations for your students without a computer in the classroom. Some colleges and universities have designated multimedia classrooms with computers and supporting hardware already plugged in—all you need to do is install your software and go. Others provide projectors and jacks so that you can plug in your laptop and display your materials. Although the situation is improving dramatically at many colleges and universities, some of you must still fend for yourselves, and even designated multimedia classrooms often lack sound reproduction equipment adequate for the needs of a music classroom. A simple solution: Put the additional equipment you need on a small cart that you can wheel into your music classroom. A small set of powered computer speakers can do wonders in smaller classrooms.

Multimedia Projectors—These projection units are now much more common than they were just a few years ago. They were once prohibitively expensive, but prices are dropping dramatically as you read this. Ceiling-mounted projectors offer several advantages: You don't have to move them around, they don't block anyone's view, and they are difficult to steal. Portable models can be extremely useful if you must teach in classrooms that are not already equipped with projectors. Serviceable portable projectors can be found for less than $3,000; ceiling-mounted units cost somewhat more. Check around your campus before you buy—your instructional media office may have units available for checkout.

CD-ROM—These are now so ubiquitous as to hardly bear mentioning. You can't operate newer computers without one!

DVD drive—This new technology is the future. As with CD technology, some DVD drives employ a read-only format (DVD-ROM), while others can both read and "burn" DVDs (DVD-R). Look for one that lets you "mark" locations you would like to jump to in your classroom presentation—this can save a lot of time.

MIDI Instruments—MIDI instruments are musical instruments with MIDI capability (Musical Instrument Digital Interface). If you choose not to use the MIDI software synthesizer options described above, you will need such an instrument for multimedia presentations that incorporate MIDI sounds. The most common MIDI setups include a General MIDI keyboard or sound module (a MIDI synthesizer without the keyboard). Prices start at a few hundred dollars (many vendors offer package deals that include hardware and software for a low price). Note: Any external MIDI device you attach to your computer must go through a MIDI interface. The interface is often built into newer instruments; older instruments require an external MIDI interface and MIDI cables.

Many MIDI instruments are currently available. In addition to the synthesizers and sound modules mentioned above, you can find drum machines, MIDI wind instruments, MIDI guitar synthesizers, and samplers. Samplers allow the user to record short digital "samples" of any sound that can be recorded with a microphone. Once recorded, these sounds can be played back at different pitches on an electronic keyboard and subjected to various sound editing and manipulation techniques. Samplers are especially useful for demonstrations in acoustics or *musique concrète*.

Speakers and Amplification—The sound that once came out of your computer's speaker was laughably inadequate for classroom needs. Although built-in computer speakers have improved, they still fail to provide a realistic listening experience. Your students deserve better. If you are using digital sound files, CD-ROM playback, DVDs with stereo soundtracks, or even MIDI instruments, you will want decent quality sound reproduction. If your classroom is equipped with a good sound system, connect your computer and any external drives or MIDI instruments directly to the stereo amplifier. If not, you can purchase small, portable powered speakers designed for multimedia presentations. Visit your local computer store to find a pair that sounds good to you.

Other Tools for Multimedia Development

In addition to the software and hardware required as part of any multimedia presentation (described above), there are other tools that help enormously in the preparation of presentations.

iPods and other MP3 players—First and foremost, these are external hard drives with anywhere from a 20 to 80 gigabyte capacity in a case you can hold in your hand. Anything you store on your computer can be put on your iPod, whether it's a Word document, software, or digital photos—and you can easily move things from computer to iPod and back again. The iPod is also a music player. *iTunes* (Mac and Windows) makes it simple to "rip" sound files from your audio CDs and convert them to MP3 (or another standard sound file) format. You can then copy these compressed files to your iPod and play them to your heart's content (but you cannot copy them from iPod back to *iTunes*; Apple wants to avoid file-sharing lawsuits). The iPod has changed my life. I can put everything I need for a lecture on the iPod—*PowerPoint* documents, digital video, musical examples, and so on. I carry it into the classroom, and plug it into the computer, and everything I need is there in one place.

CD-R/CD-RW/DVD-R drives—If you get serious about multimedia presentations, consider "burning" your own CDs or DVDs. You can put everything you need for a presentation—your software documents, sound files, image files, video files, and so on—onto a single disc that can be used on any computer with a CD-ROM or DVD-ROM drive. Once prohibitively expensive, these drives are now eminently affordable; in fact, many students may already own them. Once burned, these discs provide a permanent, portable storage medium for your presentations, allowing you to use and reuse your presentations from one year to the next. Simply carry the disc to class, pop it in the drive, and you're up and running.

Scanners—A scanner is a photocopy machine that saves the scanned image as a digital picture on your computer (instead of transferring it to a sheet of paper). Color scanners can accommodate color or black-and-white images, and even lower-quality scanners can produce very nice graphics for multimedia programs. Most scanned images can be imported with equal ease into authoring, presentation, Web page creation, and integrated software programs. You can also import a scanned image into an image editing program (e.g., PhotoShop) to crop and edit the image before using it in class.

Digital cameras—Both "still" cameras and video cameras are available. Prices are dropping, and quality gets better every year. Buy as many megapixels as you can afford. These images and videos provide another excellent resource for your presentations and Web pages.

Connections to the Internet—What Do I Need?

The sophistication of networks and Internet access can vary widely from campus to campus, so it is difficult to generalize about what you might need in a given situation. Talk to the IT staff at your institution. They can tell you if you have network access in your classroom and how to use it. (Some classrooms are probably already networked on your campus.) They can also show you how to get online, set up email accounts, establish online forums for your students, and so on.

In the best of possible worlds, your campus is hard-wired to the Internet and you have full access to the multimedia resources of the World Wide Web. Under these circumstances, your support staff already has and can help you install the software needed to "surf the Web." You once needed many small programs to deal with the Internet, but now *Netscape Communicator* and *Internet Explorer* provide all the tools you need to explore the Web, handle your email, deal with newsgroups, and so on. Of these older programs, the most useful are the file-transfer programs like *Fetch* (Mac) and *WS_FTP* (Windows), especially useful for uploading Web pages.

For less-sophisticated campus networks, check with your institution's computer support staff to find out exactly what is required to go online. In dire cases, it may prove easiest to circumnavigate the campus system completely. Online services such as America Online or CompuServe are only a phone call away, and they all offer access to the Internet. Many metropolitan areas offer an even less expensive alternative: For a small monthly fee, local Internet service providers can connect you to the Internet. All you need is a modem attached to a phone line (high-speed data lines work best). No matter where in the world you roam online, your phone call is still a local call to the service provider. The newest option, especially popular due to the speed of its connection, is the cable modem. Consult with your local cable-TV provider to find out how this works.

7 Starting a Lab

Building a lab from scratch can be an exciting and harrowing task. Labs can be constructed to meet so many different purposes that it would be impossible to cover all possible situations in this short space. What follows is a series of questions that must be answered in order to create a well-designed computer lab.

What needs will your lab meet? Labs can vary in size—they can serve many users or only one user at a time. Labs can serve many different functions— some labs are reserved for a single activity, whereas others accommodate many different activities. What tasks will this lab make possible? Should the lab be networked internally, connected to campus network and/or Internet, or not networked at all?

These questions directly affect budget decisions and hardware or software acquisitions. The size of the lab depends on the number of anticipated users. The function of the lab depends on the needs you want to meet. Whether you buy DVD-ROM drives, scanners, printers, an Ethernet hub, and/or MIDI keyboards, everything you purchase should meet the lab's mission—as you define it. In their excellent book *Experiencing Music Technology,* David B. Williams and Peter Webster encourage multipurpose labs for several important reasons. It costs more to develop separate workstations for music, graphics, multimedia, and/or computer-assisted instruction activities, and the lack of uniformity can be detrimental when the lab is used as a classroom. In either situation, such labs become a common resource for students and teachers alike, a place where ideas are exchanged in a cooperative learning environment. Further, the multifunction lab promotes open access to technology and, surprisingly, proves easier to manage because there are more users.

Make sure you seek annual funding for lab maintenance. In addition to ongoing expenditures for new hardware and software, labs require regular upgrades to existing hardware and software as well as routine repairs, maintenance, and replacement of stolen or damaged equipment.

Who should have access to the lab? Is it important for the lab to be supervised? These questions raise the issues of security and technical support. You must take appropriate measures to protect the investment in your lab without unduly restricting access to the intended users—your students. Lab supervision can serve several functions: In addition to protecting against theft, lab aides can assist inexperienced students and make sure that students sign in and sign out. The sign-in can help instructors monitor whether students are doing lab assignments or not. Unsupervised labs require more security precautions, and access must be restricted to users experienced enough to work without direct supervision.

Will the lab be used for class meetings? If so, you will need a well-equipped teaching station with projection unit, multimedia software, and appropriate peripheral devices. Further, consider the arrangement of workstations in the lab; all users should be able to see their own computer monitors and the instructor's screen with equal ease. Finally, try to make the lab as comfortable and inviting as possible; too many labs look sterile and uninviting.

❡ Purchasing Computer Equipment

If you want to secure funds from your institution for hardware or software acquisitions, you can do several things to help.

Learn about the budget process—How does the budget approval process work for your department? Which budget lines cover computer hardware, software, and supplies? Who oversees budget requests for your department? Who ultimately approves your department's budget requests? Once you know how the process works and who the players are, you can implement a plan of attack.

Define and justify your needs—Explain why technology is important to you and your students in light of your department's (and your institution's) educational mission. Develop a long-range strategic plan that places your computer needs in this larger educational context. Include reasonable, manageable suggested goals for gradual growth over, say, a five-year period. Make your proposal as strong as possible and write it in terms that anyone can understand. Don't take anything for granted. Nonmusicians who control the purse strings often need to be educated first about the importance of music in the curriculum and only later about your department's need for computer technology.

Build support in your department—Proposals that come with the support of an entire department carry much more weight than individual requests. If need be, educate your colleagues about the exciting educational possibilities inherent in recent technology.

Be a squeaky wheel—Don't just mail your proposal to the powers that be; take time to talk with them, get to know them, acquaint them with your needs and your proposals, and do so regularly. Once you begin to implement technology in your curriculum, update them on your progress and results. Make them feel good about their wise decisions.

Exercise good stewardship—When budgeted funds come your way, spend them wisely. First, make sure your spending conforms to your strategic plan. Clarify your priorities and stick to them. Educate yourself about the pros and cons of competing software packages or hardware items, and look for bargains and academic prices. For example, Macromedia and MakeMusic! offer academic prices on packages such as *Director* and *Finale* that can save you hundreds of dollars on the purchase of a single unit. Some software companies offer site licenses that can save you money in the long run.

Whatever you buy . . . use it!—Nothing infuriates budget administrators more than expensive allocations for equipment or software that sits in the box untouched. Don't ask for more than you have time to learn and use, and find effective uses for your purchases. Once you establish a good track record for the implementation of technology, you don't have to work quite as hard to justify your requests.

Get to know the technical support staff—These folks can provide all kinds of help and advice to you and your students if you treat them well. They also know from daily experience who uses computer resources regularly and who doesn't—and they talk with the powers that be who control the purse strings. These are good people to get along with if at all possible.

Be prepared to consult with colleagues outside your department—When exciting things start "happening" in your department, instructors from other departments will beat a path to your door. Don't hesitate to help them, within reason, since they will likely return the favor someday. We all have many of the same goals, and a little cooperation goes a long way toward achieving both personal and institutional goals.

❼ Learning More about Technology

Once you get started with technology, you will find there is always more to learn. Fortunately, many resources are available for continuing education in computer technology, both formal and informal.

People

People will probably be your most important sources of information and encouragement as you seek to learn more about computer technology. These people can be technical support staff, reference librarians, or faculty colleagues on your campus; faculty members with similar interests at other area colleges or universities; knowledgeable technical support staff from computer vendors with whom you do business; or other computer users in your community.

Educational Opportunities

You don't have to look far for courses in all aspects of computer technology—your institution or another nearby college or university can usually meet your needs. Private groups such as MacAcademy provide another source of training; geared toward the corporate world, these peripatetic institutions provide short-term, intense, expert instruction on specific software programs or multimedia tasks. Many educational institutions also offer summer courses, workshops, or seminars on technology and music instruction.

Organizations

Let me single out two organizations that stand out by virtue of the breadth of their academic interests and their overriding concern for teaching. Other organizations may do more to further specific scholarly or disciplinary interests, but you cannot afford a narrow focus in a music appreciation class. Your students come from too many different disciplines, and their backgrounds are too diverse. If you cannot meet them at their various levels, you will fight an uphill battle.

College Music Society—This organization does far more than publish a job-vacancy list. Theorists, performers, musicologists, conductors, ethnomusicologists, and music educators of all types gather regularly to discuss common problems, share current ideas from their disciplines, and consider the future of music education. National meetings take place each fall, and regional chapters meet in the spring. Since the mid-1990s, the society has sponsored an annual workshop series titled Centers for Professional Development. Several centers focus on topics relevant to music appreciation, especially workshops such as World Music or Women, Music and Gender. Most significant for technology is the Center for Professional Development in Music Technology. This center, located at Illinois State University in Normal, Illinois, serves as the location for a five-day June workshop that covers Internet basics, MIDI applications, and pedagogical issues. Contact Professor David B. Williams at Illinois State for further information.

Association for Technology in Music Instruction—A congenial, collaborative group of teachers committed to the use and exploration of technology in music education. ATMI holds its annual meetings in conjunction with the College Music Society, an arrangement that benefits both organizations. The meetings, demonstrations, and presentations offer a terrific way to keep up with the latest uses of technology in education. An annual highlight is a workshop series on a current topic presented by David B. Williams and Peter Webster. Much of their focus has been on the Internet in recent years. Membership in ATMI allows you to participate in the ATMI listserv, a forum that permits you to "pick the brains" of other members. Members also have access to the ATMI Technology Directory. The directory is a comprehensive annotated online catalogue of current music hardware and software with additional information about useful books, online sites, organizations, magazines, and so on.

Magazines

There are no current magazines devoted solely to the use of technology in music education, but it's not hard to find magazines that can keep you abreast of current developments in computer, music, and Internet technologies. The magazines listed below offer a sample of what's available, and many of them can be found online.

Computer Music. Not to be confused with *Computer Music Journal,* this is a magazine for those who use computers to create, record, and perform music. Accompanying CD includes sample files, demo versions of software, shareware, and other goodies.

Electronic Musician. Magazine for users of electronic musical instruments and personal computers.

Keyboard. Magazine for keyboard players, with extensive information on MIDI keyboard instruments and software.

MacADDICT. Magazine for die-hard Mac users includes a CD full of software (demo versions, shareware, and so on) and Web links. Provides articles and reviews of Macintosh-related hardware and software.

MacWorld. Magazine provides thorough coverage of hardware and software for Macintosh users. Many articles on multimedia products.

PC Magazine. Magazine provides thorough coverage of hardware and software for IBM users. Many articles on multimedia products.

PC World. Magazine provides thorough coverage of hardware and software for IBM users. Many articles on multimedia products.

Wired. The "magazine for the digital revolution" stays on top of recent developments in electronic technology of all kinds.

Books

These books provide further information on topics discussed in this appendix.

Altman, Rebecca Bridges. *Microsoft Office PowerPoint 2003 for Windows and Macintosh: A Visual Quickstart Guide.* Berkeley: Peachpit Press, 2003. Handy guide provides illustrations and clear step-by-step instructions. Excellent for a quick introduction to this easy-to-use multimedia presentation program.

Chambers, Mark L. *CD and DVD Recording for Dummies.* New York: Wiley Publishing, 2004. Equally useful for Macintosh or Windows users, this book provides step-by-step instructions for those who are new to burning CDs or DVDs.

Counts, Edward L., Jr. *Multimedia Design and Production: Projects for Students and Teachers.* New York: Allyn & Bacon, 2003. Written with teachers in mind, this book can help you explore a variety of strategies for incorporating multimedia into your teaching.

Finkelstein, Ellen. *How to Do Everything with PowerPoint 2007.* New York: McGraw Hill Osborne Media, 2006. User-friendly guide is appropriate for beginning and intermediate-level users. Filled with practical suggestions.

Persidsky, Andre, and Mark Schaeffer. *Director MX 2004 for Macintosh and Windows: A Visual Quickstart Guide.* Berkeley: Peachpit Press, 2004. Easy-to-use book provides illustrations and clear step-by-step instructions. Excellent for a quick introduction to this industry-standard multimedia program, especially if you need hand holding.

Rathbone, Andy. *MP3 for Dummies*. Second edition. New York: Wiley Publishing, 2001. Part of the "for Dummies" series, this book provides practical ideas and step-by-step instructions for use of a recorded music format that has revolutionized the World Wide Web.

Rothstein, Joseph. *MIDI: A Comprehensive Introduction*. Second edition. Madison, Wis.: A-R Editions, 1995. Clearly written, thorough coverage of MIDI principles with many practical suggestions for building a MIDI studio; selecting instruments, software, and other equipment; and using what you have.

Smith, Bud, and Arthur Bebak. *Creating Web Pages for Dummies*. Eighth edition. New York: Wiley Publishing, 2006. Part of the "for Dummies" series, this book provides practical ideas and step-by-step instructions for making your own Web pages. Accompanying CD contains sample pages, demo software, and other goodies.

Stern, Judith, and Robert Lettieri. *QuickTime 6 for Macintosh and Windows: A Visual Quickstart Guide*. Berkeley: Peachpit Press, 2002. Easy-to-use book provides illustrations and clear step-by-step instructions. Excellent introduction to these simple video-editing and playback tools. The digital video equivalent of a Swiss Army knife, *QuickTime* makes it easy to combine and edit digital video, audio, and MIDI files; extract excerpts from audio CDs; add subtitles (for example, translations) to video clips; and so on.

Towers, J. Tarin. *Dreamweaver MX 2004 for Windows and Macintosh: A Visual Quickstart Guide*. Berkeley: Peachpit Press, 2004. Easy-to-use book provides illustrations and clear step-by-step instructions. Excellent for a quick introduction to this state-of-the-art program for creating Web pages.

White, Paul. *MIDI for the Technophobe*. Sanctuary Press, 2004. Written for the complete beginner, this book provides a good introduction to MIDI protocols and the instruments, hardware, and software needed in a MIDI recording studio.

Williams, David B., and Peter R. Webster. *Experiencing Music Technology: Software, Data, and Hardware*. Third edition. New York: Schirmer Books, 2005. A wonderful textbook for anyone who wants to explore music and technology. A modular approach helps the user find needed information quickly. Equally useful for Windows and Macintosh users, the book includes fascinating historical time lines, thorough coverage of current hardware and software options, and a visionary yet practical guide to networking and the Internet. The book's strengths include its practical, problem-solving approach and its emphasis on people. Each chapter addresses a specific problem encountered by various computer users in Williams and Webster's fictitious rogue's gallery. In addition, the authors provide interviews with real musicians of all types who use technology every day.

Hardware and Software Publishers

The following list provides contact information for some of the most important publishers mentioned in this appendix. Products that are not labeled "Mac only" or "Windows only" can be acquired for either platform.

Apple Computers. 1 Infinite Loop, Cupertino, CA 95014

Phone—408-996-1010   URL—www.apple.com

Products—Macintosh computers, *GarageBand, iLife, iPod, iTunes, Logic, QuickTime*

Blackboard, Inc. 1899 L Street NW, 5th Floor, Washington, D.C. 20036
   Phone—952-424-9299   URL—www.blackboard.com
   Products—*Blackboard*

Electronic Courseware Systems. 1713 South State, Champaign, IL 61820
   Phone—800-832-4965   URL—www.ecsmedia.com
   Products—*TimeSketch Editor*

GVOX. Box 2755, Westfield, NJ 07091-2755
   Phone—unavailable   URL—www.gvox.com
   Products—*Master Tracks Pro, Encore, Music Time Deluxe*

Macromedia. 600 Townsend St., San Francisco, CA 94103
   Phone—415-252-2000   URL—www.macromedia.com
   Products—*Director, Dreamweaver, Flash*

MakeMusic! (Coda Music Technologies). 6210 Bury Dr., Eden Prairie, MN 55346-1718
   Phone—952-937-9611   URL—www.makemusic.com
   Products—*Finale*

Microsoft. 1 Microsoft Way, Redmond, WA 98073
   Phone—425-882-8080   URL—www.microsoft.com
   Products—*Windows, Internet Explorer, Word, PowerPoint, Excel, Outlook Express*

Netscape. P.O. Box 7050, Mountain View, CA 94039-7050
   Phone—650-254-1900   URL—www.netscape.com
   Products—*Netscape Communicator*

Sibelius Software. P.O. Box 702628, Dallas, TX 75370
   Phone—888-474-2354   URL—www.sibelius.com
   Products—*Sibelius*

APPENDIX V

Printed Resources

This appendix is designed for any teacher who wants to "bone up" on a given subject before walking into the classroom. First-time teachers or teachers who are new to music appreciation courses may benefit most from this annotated bibliography, but all are welcome to browse for ideas and sources.

For a "face-to-face" encounter with the composers in *Listen,* turn to the final section in this appendix, Primary Sources. The books in that section allow composers to speak for themselves through letters, interviews, and other documents that help us understand more fully their thought, their music, and their lives.

General Sources

♪ Dictionaries and Research Tools

Duckles, Vincent H., and Michael A. Keller. *Music Reference and Research Materials.* Fourth edition. New York: Schirmer Books, 1994. This standard guide to music research inventories dictionaries, encyclopedias, yearbooks, handbooks, bibliographies, music library and instrument collection catalogues, guides to historical and systematic musicology, and so on.

Hitchcock, H. Wiley, and Stanley Sadie, eds. *The New Grove Dictionary of American Music.* 4 volumes. London: Macmillan, 1986. This reference source makes up for many deficiencies in the original *New Grove.* Contains much more detailed coverage of American composers, musicians, and musical institutions, yet it retains the advantages of the *New Grove* format. Highly recommended research tool.

Randel, Don. *The New Harvard Dictionary of Music.* Cambridge, Mass.: Belknap Press, 1986. Handy, often-recommended single-volume desktop reference. The new version also includes information on composers.

Sadie, Stanley, ed. *The New Grove Dictionary of Music and Musicians.* Second edition. 29 volumes. London: Macmillan, 2001. The most comprehensive music reference source in the English language. Excellent place to go when you begin a research project. Not only is the information reasonably up-to-date, but every article includes a selected bibliography of sources for further research. *New Grove* is also an excellent source if you need information on Global Perspectives materials. If your school is at all serious about music, you can also access *New Grove* online at www.grovemusic.com. Best of all, the online version is constantly updated to ensure the most current information.

Sadie, Stanley, ed. *The Norton/Grove Concise Encyclopedia of Music*. Revised edition. New York: Macmillan, 1994. Single-volume desktop reference, similar to the *New Harvard Dictionary*.

Slonimsky, Nicolas. *Baker's Biographical Dictionary of Musicians*. Eighth edition. New York: Schirmer Books, 1991. I'd probably go to *New Grove* instead, but this is a handy single-volume source for information on composers and other musicians.

Stone, Ruth M., ed. *Garland Encyclopedia of World Music*. New York: Garland Publishing, Inc., 1998. The "*New Grove* for world music," this excellent new encyclopedia focuses on ethnomusicological studies of world music. The set includes ten volumes: Vol. 1, *Africa*; Vol. 2, *South America, Mexico, Central America, and the Caribbean*; Vol. 3, *The United States and Canada*; Vol. 4, *Southeast Asia*; Vol. 5, *South Asia: The Indian Subcontinent*; Vol. 6, *The Middle East*; Vol. 7, *East Asia: China, Japan, and Korea*; Vol. 8, *Europe*; Vol. 9, *Australia and the Pacific Islands*; and Vol. 10, *The World's Music: General Perspectives and Reference Tools*. Highly recommended.

⁊ General Histories

Bonds, Mark Evan. *A History of Music in Western Culture*. Second edition. Upper Saddle River, N.J.: Prentice-Hall, 2006. One of several excellent music history textbooks on the market today. Perhaps its best feature is its emphasis on primary source readings. Accompanying score anthologies and recordings.

Burkholder, J. Peter, Donald J. Grout, and Claude V. Palisca. *A History of Western Music*. Seventh edition. New York: Norton, 2006. The seventh time is the charm. Grout's was for decades *the* standard music history textbook, and Burkholder's complete rewrite corrects most of its predecessors' problems— this is the best edition ever! Beautifully illustrated with a wealth of study aids, including maps, charts, time lines, and chapter summaries. Highly recommended. Accompanying score anthologies and recordings.

Crocker, Richard. *A History of Musical Style*. New York: Dover, 1986. Dover reprint of this handy guide to changing musical styles over the centuries, from the Middle Ages to the twentieth century.

Stolba, K Marie. *The Development of Western Music: A History*. Third edition. Boston: McGraw-Hill, 1998. This book once gave Grout's *History* a real run for its money. Still an excellent book, though it hasn't been revised for a while; the publisher is seeking a new author following Stolba's recent death. Accompanying score anthologies and recordings.

Wright, Craig, and Bryan Simms. *Music in Western Civilization*. Belmont, Calif.: Schirmer, 2005. The best feature of this fine textbook? It places Western music history in its cultural contexts. Wright, a highly respected medievalist, has produced a lucid, well-written book. Accompanying score anthologies and recordings.

⁊ Other General Sources

Brown, Howard Mayer, and Stanley Sadie, eds. *Performance Practice*, Vol. 1: *Music before 1600* and Vol. 2: *Music after 1600*. New York: Norton, 1989. Recent essays on performance practice provide insight into the "educated guesswork" undertaken by performers of early music.

Haywood, John. *Atlas of World History.* New York: Barnes & Noble Books, 1997. This "visual history" of the world is nicely done. The 121 maps depict all corners of the earth from ancient times up to the modern day; detailed annotations help tell the stories. Like many works of its genre, it favors Europe and the Middle East, but this one provides surprisingly good coverage of Asia, Africa, and the Americas as well. Useful reference.

Kerman, Joseph. *Write All These Down.* Berkeley: University of California Press, 1994. Collection of writings that cover the range of Dr. Kerman's scholarly interests over the years. Most useful as supplements to the *Listen* text are articles on Beethoven, Mozart, Wagner, and Verdi.

Raynor, Henry. *Music and Society since 1815.* New York: Schocken Books, 1976. This volume continues the work Raynor began with the book immediately below.

Raynor, Henry. *A Social History of Music: From the Middle Ages to Beethoven.* New York: Schocken Books, 1972. Raynor was one of the first scholars to write about music in relation to the social institutions that support it. You can use these fascinating articles to help your students understand the role of music in society at different times and places in history.

Period Histories

❦ Middle Ages

Hoppin, Richard. *Medieval Music.* New York: Norton, 1978. From Norton's series of period histories. Excellent, comprehensive source by an important scholar. Accompanying score anthology.

Knighton, Tess, and David Fallows, eds. *Companion to Medieval and Renaissance Music.* Berkeley: University of California Press, 1997. Good collection of articles on important issues in early music scholarship.

MacKinnon, James, ed. *Ancient and Medieval Music. Music and Society* Series, edited by Stanley Sadie. Englewood Cliffs, N.J.: Prentice-Hall, 1990. These articles on the cultural history of music can help you bring the Middle Ages to life for your students.

Wilson, David Fenwick. *Music of the Middle Ages: Style and Structure.* New York: Schirmer Books, 1990. Interesting study of medieval music, distinguished by its accompanying score anthology, with superb recordings by the Hilliard Ensemble and Western Wind; directed by Paul Hillier.

Yudkin, Jeremy. *Music in Medieval Europe.* Englewood Cliffs, N.J.: Prentice-Hall, 1989. From Prentice-Hall's period-history series. Like the other volumes in the series, this one is concise, readable, and authoritative. Recommended for a quick, thorough overview. Accompanying recordings.

❦ Renaissance

Atlas, Allan W. *Renaissance Music. Norton Introduction to Music History* Series. New York: Norton, 1998. Survey of European music of the fifteenth and sixteenth centuries. Accompanying score anthology includes 102 works.

Brown, Howard Mayer, and Louise K. Stein. *Music in the Renaissance*. Second edition. Upper Saddle River, N.J.: Prentice-Hall, 1999. From Prentice-Hall's period-history series. Like the other volumes in the series, this one is concise, readable, and authoritative. Recommended for a quick, thorough overview.

Fenlon, Iain. *The Renaissance. Music and Society* Series, edited by Stanley Sadie. Englewood Cliffs, N.J.: Prentice-Hall, 1990. These articles on the cultural history of music can help you bring the Renaissance to life for your students.

Perkins, Leeman L. *Music in the Age of the Renaissance*. New York: Norton, 1999. From Norton's series of period histories. Excellent, comprehensive source by an important scholar.

Reese, Gustave. *Music in the Renaissance*. Revised edition. New York: Norton, 1959. An excellent, thorough reference source, in spite of its age. Not recommended for a quick overview.

℘ Baroque

Anderson, Nicholas. *Baroque Music: From Monteverdi to Handel*. London: Thames and Hudson, 1994. Recommended by Nikolaus Harnoncourt. An intelligent study of Baroque music, informed by recent research.

Buelow, George. *A History of Baroque Music*. Bloomington: Indiana University Press, 2004. Long-awaited survey of Baroque music by this respected Baroque scholar.

Bukofzer, Manfred. *Music in the Baroque Era*. New York: Norton, 1947. One of the first major studies of the Baroque era. Still valuable, but I would recommend other sources for a general overview.

Hill, John Walter. *Baroque Music: Music in Western Europe: 1580–1750. Norton Introduction to Music History* Series. New York: Norton, 2005. Very fine new survey of Baroque music. Accompanying score anthology includes 130 works.

Palisca, Claude V. *Baroque Music*. Third edition. Englewood Cliffs, N.J.: Prentice-Hall, 1991. From Prentice-Hall's period-history series. Like the other volumes in the series, this one is concise, readable, and authoritative. Recommended for a quick, thorough overview.

Price, Curtis A., ed. *The Early Baroque Era: From the Late 16th Century to the 1660s. Music and Society* Series, edited by Stanley Sadie. Englewood Cliffs, N.J.: Prentice-Hall, 1991. These articles on the cultural history of music can help you bring the early Baroque era to life for your students.

Sadie, Julie Anne, ed. *Companion to Baroque Music*. Berkeley: University of California Press, 1998. Unusual work begins with articles on various regions, coupled with an extensive biographical dictionary, and followed by chapters on Baroque voices, instruments, forms and genres, national styles, and ornamentation. Useful source.

℘ Classical

Downs, Philip G. *Classical Music: The Era of Haydn, Mozart, and Beethoven*. New York: Norton, 1992. From Norton's series of period histories. Excellent, comprehensive, engaging source by an important scholar. Accompanying score anthology. Highly recommended.

Heartz, Daniel. *Haydn, Mozart, and the Viennese School, 1740–1780*. New York: Norton, 1995. Useful look at the development of Classical style.

Landon, H. C. Robbins. *Mozart and Vienna*. New York: Schirmer Books, 1991. Especially valuable if you want to introduce your students to the Vienna of Haydn, Mozart, and Beethoven.

Pauly, Reinhard G. *Music in the Classic Period*. Third edition. Englewood Cliffs, N.J.: Prentice-Hall, 1988. From Prentice-Hall's period-history series. Like the other volumes in the series, this one is concise, readable, and authoritative. Recommended for a quick, thorough overview.

Rosen, Charles. *The Classical Style: Haydn, Mozart, Beethoven*. New York: Norton, 1972. Rosen's landmark work provides valuable insights into Classical style. Much analysis is more sophisticated than your students can handle, but your teaching will benefit nonetheless.

Zaslaw, Neil, ed. *The Classical Era: From the 1740's to the End of the 18th Century. Music and Society* Series, edited by Stanley Sadie. Englewood Cliffs, N.J.: Prentice-Hall, 1990. These articles on the cultural history of music can help you bring the Classical era to life for your students.

♪ Beethoven

Forbes, Elliott. *Beethoven: Symphony No. 5 in C Minor. Norton Critical Scores* edition. New York: Norton, 1971. Fascinating volume contains analytical notes by Forbes; the complete score; and commentary on Beethoven's Fifth by E. T. A. Hoffmann, Berlioz, Schenker, and others. See Scores below for a list of other scores in the *Norton Critical Scores* series.

Forbes, Elliott, ed. *Thayer's Life of Beethoven*. Princeton, N.J.: Princeton University Press, 1969. Model biography by an unusual nineteenth-century scholar made even better through Forbes's careful editing and enlightening commentary. Filled with references to primary sources. Highly recommended.

Kerman, Joseph. *The Beethoven Quartets*. New York: Norton, 1966. Landmark study of Beethoven's quartets. Stravinsky read this book late in his life while revisiting Beethoven's quartets; he called Kerman a "high-minded guide."

Solomon, Maynard. *Beethoven*. New York: Schirmer Books, 1977. A good, often moving modern biography of Beethoven; not as eccentric as his recent biography of Mozart. Until further documents come to light, it appears that Solomon has solved the riddle of the "Immortal Beloved." If you show your students scenes from *Immortal Beloved,* make sure you have this book handy when they ask how it really happened.

Solomon, Maynard. *Beethoven Essays*. Cambridge, Mass.: Harvard University Press, 1988. Further thoughts on Beethoven's life, creativity, and internal world by this leading scholar.

♪ Romantic

Dahlhaus, Carl. *Nineteenth-Century Music*. Translated by J. Bradford Robinson. Berkeley: University of California Press, 1989. Significant work on Romanticism.

Longyear, Rey M. *Nineteenth-Century Romanticism in Music*. Third edition. Englewood Cliffs, N.J.: Prentice-Hall, 1988. From Prentice-Hall's period-history series. Like the other volumes in the series, this one is concise, readable, and authoritative. Recommended for a quick, thorough overview.

Plantinga, Leon. *Romantic Music: A History of Musical Style in Nineteenth-Century Europe.* New York: Norton, 1984. From Norton's series of period histories. Excellent, comprehensive survey by an important scholar. Detailed coverage of Beethoven, Schubert, Schumann, Wagner, Italian opera, and nationalism. Accompanying score anthology.

Ringer, Alexander, ed. *The Early Romantic Era between Revolutions: 1789–1848. Music and Society* Series, edited by Stanley Sadie. Englewood Cliffs, N.J.: Prentice-Hall, 1990. These articles on the cultural history of music can help you bring early Romanticism to life for your students.

Rosen, Charles. *The Romantic Generation.* Cambridge, Mass.: Harvard University Press, 1995. The long-awaited follow-up to Rosen's *Classical Style,* based on his Harvard lecture series. Rosen does for early Romanticism what he did for Classical style, and this time he demonstrates his points with musical performances on an accompanying CD; all performances by Rosen himself.

Samson, Jim, ed. *The Late Romantic Era: From the Mid-19th Century to World War I. Music and Society* Series, edited by Stanley Sadie. Englewood Cliffs, N.J.: Prentice-Hall, 1991. These articles on the cultural history of music can help you bring late Romanticism to life for your students.

♪ Twentieth Century

Cope, David H. *New Directions in Music.* Fifth edition. Madison, Wis.: Brown and Benchmark, 1989. Fascinating survey of music since World War II. Recommended.

Griffiths, Paul. *Modern Music: A Concise History from Debussy to Boulez.* New York: Thames and Hudson, 1978. Quick, lucid guide to twentieth-century music up to the years after World War II.

Morgan, Robert P. *Twentieth-Century Music.* New York: Norton, 1991. From Norton's series of period histories. Excellent, comprehensive source by an important scholar. Accompanying score anthology.

Nyman, Michael. *Experimental Music: Cage and Beyond.* Second edition. Cambridge: Cambridge University Press, 1999. One of the best books written on the 1960s avant-garde, finally back in print! Recommended.

Prendergast, Mark. *The Ambient Century: From Mahler to Trance: The Evolution of Sound in the Electronic Age.* New York: Bloomsbury Press, 2001. Prendergast explores the roots of contemporary "house" music in twentieth-century classical, avant-garde, and popular traditions. Includes sections on Cage, Reich, Glass, and other important musicians. Fascinating in its sweep, but watch out for factual inaccuracies.

Salzman, Eric. *Twentieth-Century Music: An Introduction.* Third edition. Englewood Cliffs, N.J.: Prentice-Hall, 1988. From Prentice-Hall's period-history series. Like the other volumes in the series, this one is concise, readable, and authoritative. Recommended for a quick, thorough overview.

Samson, Jim, ed. *The Late Romantic Era: From the Mid-19th Century to World War I. Music and Society* Series, edited by Stanley Sadie. Englewood Cliffs, N.J.: Prentice-Hall, 1991. These articles on the cultural history of music can help you bring the early twentieth century to life for your students.

Schwartz, Elliott, and Daniel Godfrey. *Music since 1945: Issues, Materials, and Literature.* New York: Schirmer Books, 1993. Another lucid summary of music after World War II.

Watkins, Glenn. *Soundings: Music in the Twentieth Century.* New York: Schirmer Books, 1988. Good, basic text for an overview of twentieth-century music. Fairly good coverage of more recent music.

Music of the World

⁊ Ethnomusicology

Sources for Books, Recordings, and Videos

Multicultural Media. 56 Browns Mill Road, Montpelier, VT 05602; 1-802-223-1294 (www.multiculturalmedia.com or www.worldmusicstore.com). Good source for books, CDs, videos, and CD-ROM resources in world music. Very helpful staff.

Smithsonian Folkways Recordings. Dept. 0607, Washington, DC 20073-0607; 1-800-410-9815 (www.folkways.si.edu). Two catalogues are available. (1) The active Smithsonian Folkways catalogue was begun in 1988. It includes music from around the world and offers new releases on a regular basis. (2) The inactive World of Sound catalogue consists of the entire archive of 2168 Folkways LPs built up by Mo Asch during his lifetime. Asch was a man with wide-ranging tastes, and his treasure trove includes not only folk music from around the world but American avant-garde, electronic, and other musics as well. These recordings are all available again on CD or cassette, but on a custom-made basis—plan on waiting a couple of weeks.

World Music Institute. 49 W. 27th St., #930, New York, NY 10001; 1-212-545-7536 (www.HearTheWorld.org). Another good source. WMI's extensive catalogue includes world-music books, CDs, videos, and CD-ROM resources.

www.amazon.com. Of the major dot-com merchants, Amazon probably offers the best selection of world-music books, CDs, and DVDs. It tends to carry products with "commercial appeal," so you'll still need to go to Multicultural Media or the World Music Institute for obscure or "educational" recordings such as the JVC series. As much as I would prefer to support the world-music specialists above, if Amazon has it in stock, it usually sells for less.

About the Discipline

Bergeron, Katherine, and Philip V. Bohlman, eds. *Disciplining Music: Musicology and Its Canons.* Chicago: University of Chicago Press, 1992. Several scholars reflect on the "canon," that which we consider most worthy of study. Curiously, musicians in American higher education take a much more fixed view of the canon than do their colleagues in most other arts. Most relevant to *Listen* materials are articles by Gary Tomlinson ("Cultural Dialogics and Jazz"), Bruno Nettl ("Mozart and the Ethnomusicological Study of Western Culture"), and Katherine Bergeron ("A Lifetime of Chants").

Hood, Mantle. *The Ethnomusicologist.* New York: McGraw-Hill, 1971. A useful look at the concerns and methods of the ethnomusicologist. Includes chapters on literacy, transcription and notation, organology, and field methods and techniques.

Myers, Helen, ed. *Ethnomusicology: Historical and Regional Studies*. New York: Norton, 1993. This history of ethnomusicology outlines the significant contributions of scholars over the years, organized by continent, then by country. Good starting point for serious study; you can look up your country of interest and find a summary of important issues faced and approaches used by specialists in that area.

Myers, Helen, ed. *Ethnomusicology: An Introduction*. New York: Norton, 1993. Good introduction to the discipline. It includes articles on fieldwork, ethnography, transcription, analysis, iconography, organology, dance, and historical issues. The final two sections deal with ethical concerns, new directions, and reference aids.

Nettl, Bruno. *The Study of Ethnomusicology: Twenty-nine Issues and Concepts*. Urbana, Ill.: University of Illinois Press, 1983. Collection of creatively titled essays deal with comparative studies, cultural studies, and field studies. A useful, issues-based explanation of the discipline.

Stone, Ruth M., ed. *Garland Encyclopedia of World Music*. New York: Garland Publishing, Inc., 1998. Vol. 10, *The World's Music: General Perspectives and Reference Tools,* is highly recommended for an overview of the discipline of musicology.

General Studies

Hart, Mickey. *Drumming at the Edge of Magic: A Journey into the Spirit of Percussion*. San Francisco: Harper Collins Publishers, 1990. Percussionist with the Grateful Dead weaves an intriguing narrative that wanders from experiences with the band to experiences with traditional musicians from countries around the world, including India, Africa, and Native America. The reader readily senses Hart's more-than-superficial fascination with percussion music of other cultures.

Jackson, Irene V., ed. *More Than Drumming: Essays on African and Afro-Latin American Music and Musicians*. Westport, Conn.: Greenwood Press, 1985. Collection of articles by various scholars. Includes essays on the concept of preservation, women and music in Sudan, Yoruba religious songs, and so on.

Lomax, Alan. *Folk Song Style and Culture*. New Brunswick, N.J.: Transaction Books, 1968. The report on the findings of Lomax's Cantometrics Project, an extensive research effort to discover connections between cultural parameters and musical styles. His conclusions have never been widely accepted, but the book nonetheless includes interesting information on music from around the world.

Malm, William P. *Music Cultures of the Pacific, the Near East, and Asia*. Third edition. Upper Saddle River, N.J.: Prentice-Hall, 1996. Useful survey includes information on Indonesia, Muslim Africa, India, China, Japan, and other regions. Good introductory source.

May, Elizabeth, ed. *Musics of Many Cultures*. Berkeley: University of California Press, 1980. Collection of articles on music from countries around the world, including China, Japan, India, Bali, South Africa, and Native America.

Nettl, Bruno. *Folk and Traditional Music of the Western Continents*. Second edition. Englewood Cliffs, N.J.: Prentice-Hall, 1973. After setting out his basic principles and procedures, Nettl looks at folk traditions from eastern and western Europe, Africa, and the Americas. Nice overview.

Nettl, Bruno. *The Western Impact on World Music: Change, Adaptation, and Survival.* New York: Schirmer Books, 1985. Fascinating work picks up on many issues identified in *Listen*'s Global Perspectives segments: the impact of colonization, migration to urban centers, and so on. Also includes an article by Christopher Waterman on Nigeria *juju* music. Recommended.

Nettl, Bruno, et al. *Excursions in World Music.* Second edition. Upper Saddle River, N.J.: Prentice-Hall, 1997. Designed as a world music appreciation textbook, this survey provides nice introductions to the music of India, the Middle East, China, Japan, Indonesia, sub-Saharan Africa, Latin America, and Native America. Covers many of the same genres found in *Listen,* including Qur'anic recitation, Beijing opera, *kabuki nagauta, gagaku,* and Mbuti polyphony. Highly recommended for those with little or no background in world music.

⁊ Africa

African Music: Meeting in Yaoundé (Cameroon), 23–27 February 1970. Paris: La Revue Musicale, 1972. Transcripts of papers given at the 1970 UNESCO conference on African music south of the Sahara, possibly the first international conference devoted to this music. Given the nature of the conference, most papers take a general approach. Includes writings on West Africa and Sudan.

Agawu, Kofi. "The Invention of 'African Rhythm.'" *Journal of the American Musicological Society* (1995): 380–95. Agawu's recent contribution to the debate on African rhythm suggests that the very concept, whose roots lie deep in old, Eurocentric views of African music, needs a drastic overhaul. Recommended.

Barz, Gregory. *Music in East Africa. Experiencing Music, Expressing Culture* Series. New York: Oxford University Press, 2004. This useful, readable volume from this wonderful new global-music series is highly recommended for your study of African music. Comes with a CD.

DjeDje, Jacqueline Cogdell, ed. *African Musicology: Current Trends,* Vol. II. This *Festschrift* for J. H. Kwabena Nketia contains a variety of writings on African music, including articles on the blues scale, African American connections, and Yoruba music in the church.

Essays for a Humanist: An Offering to Klaus Wachsmann. New York: Town House Press, 1977. This *Festschrift* contains articles on many topics, but most of them deal with Africa. Of special interest are several articles on the music of the Yoruba, both in Africa and Haiti, and the Zulu peoples.

Merriam, Alan P. *African Music in Perspective.* New York: Garland Publishing, 1982. Retrospective anthology of Merriam's writings on African music. Some look at broad trends in African music; others look at specific cultures, instruments, and genres.

Nketia, Joseph H. Kwabena. *The Music of Africa.* New York: Norton, 1974. Introduction by one of the significant African musicologists.

Stone, Ruth M., ed. *Garland Encyclopedia of World Music.* New York: Garland Publishing, Inc., 1998. Vol. 1, *Africa,* is highly recommended for your study of African music.

Stone, Ruth M. *Music in West Africa. Experiencing Music, Expressing Culture* Series. New York: Oxford University Press, 2004. This useful, readable volume from this wonderful new global-music series is highly recommended for your study of African music. Comes with a CD.

Wachsmann, Klaus P., ed. *Essays on Music and History in Africa*. Evanston, Ill.: Northwestern University Press, 1971. Collection of writings on various African topics, including articles on Nguni and Yoruba peoples and their music.

Benin—The Yoruba

Agawu, V. Kofi. "'Gi Dunu,' 'Nyekpadudo,' and the Study of West African Rhythm." *Ethnomusicology* (winter 1996): 64–83. Western African rhythm has been a topic of contention in published articles over the past few decades. Agawu makes a contribution to the debate, this one based on detailed analysis and transcription of two pieces, one from Mali and the other from Benin.

Bascom, William. *The Yoruba of Southwestern Nigeria*. New York: Holt, Rinehart and Winston, 1969. Ethnographic study of the Yoruba peoples looks at their history, economics, government, social structure, life cycle, religious practices, and esthetics. Useful introduction to this culture.

Harper, Peggy. "Dance in Nigeria." *Ethnomusicology* (1969): 280–95. Takes religious dance of the Yoruba as its central focus, with information on Egungun rituals.

Central Africa—The Mbuti

Brandel, Rose. *The Music of Central Africa: An Ethnomusicological Study*. The Hague: Martinus Nijhoff, 1973. Detailed analytical and ethnological study includes fifty-two transcriptions of musical works from various peoples, including the Mbuti Pygmies covered in *Listen*.

Mungazi, Dickson A. *Gathering under the Mango Tree: Values in Traditional Culture in Africa*. New York: Peter Lang, 1996. Informative look at African culture, family, religious practices, medical practices, and art forms, with emphasis on the influence of Western culture. Chapter 7 deals specifically with the Masai and Mbuti peoples.

Sarno, Louis. *Song from the Forest: My Life among the Ba-Banjelle Pygmies*. New York: Penguin, 1993. The first half provides a fascinating, worthwhile look at the music of this pygmy tribe, but the almost embarrassing, "confessional" second half makes it clear that Sarno lacks the scholar's objectivity.

Turnbull, Colin M. *The Mbuti Pygmies: Change and Adaptation*. New York: CBS College Publishing, 1983. Covering the years from the colonial era to the present, this later work by Turnbull focuses on Mbuti adaptations to social and political changes in the world that surrounds them.

Turnbull, Colin M. *Wayward Servants: The Two Worlds of the African Pygmies*. Garden City, N.Y.: Natural History Press, 1965. The first and still one of the best major surveys of Mbuti music and culture, written by the scholar who recorded the elephant hunting song in the *Listen* anthology. Highly recommended.

The Gambia—Griot Traditions

Cherry, Eric. *Mande Music*. Chicago: University of Chicago Press, 2000. An excellent, detailed study of Mande music and traditions in West Africa. It describes both vocal and instrumental music, with descriptions of specific instruments and transcriptions of musical examples. Recommended.

Hale, Thomas. *Griots and Griottes.* Bloomington: Indiana University Press, 1998. Excellent source looks at the phenomenon of the "praise-singer" in West Africa, including its history, traditions, and music. Recommended.

South Africa and Isicathamiya

Andersson, Muff. *Music in the Mix: The Story of South African Popular Music.* Johannesburg: Ravan Press of South Africa, 1981. Useful study of twentieth-century popular music includes information on Solomon Linda.

Erlmann, Veit. *African Stars: Studies in Black South African Performance.* Chicago: University of Chicago Press, 1992. Excellent volume looks at the nineteenth- and twentieth-century roots of contemporary South African music. Especially valuable for its detailed study of the roots of *isicathamiya.*

Erlmann, Veit. "Migration and Performance: Zulu Migrant Workers' Isicathamiya Performance in South Africa, 1890–1950." *Ethnomusicology* 34 (spring–summer 1990): 199–220. One of the best sources available on the history of *isicathamiya.* Highly recommended.

Meintjes, Louise. "Paul Simon's Graceland, South Africa, and the Mediation of Musical Meaning." *Ethnomusicology* (winter 1990): 37–73. Thought-provoking article on the complex relations between two different musical cultures.

Rycroft, David. "Nguni Vocal Polyphony." *Journal of the International Folk Music Council* 19 (1967): 88–103. Useful study of the indigenous music of the Zulu, Xhosa, and Swazi peoples. Good background for understanding traditional features of *isicathamiya.*

⁊ Asia

Bali

Belo, Jane, ed. *Traditional Balinese Culture.* New York: Columbia University Press, 1970. Collection of articles by various scholars on Balinese culture, customs, and music. Good source for serious study.

Gold, Lisa. *Music in Bali. Experiencing Music, Expressing Culture* Series. New York: Oxford University Press, 2004. This useful, readable volume from this wonderful new global-music series is highly recommended for your study of Balinese music. Comes with a CD.

McPhee, Colin. "The Five-Tone Gamelan Music of Bali." *Musical Quarterly* (1949): 250–81. Early report on Balinese music by this leading scholar.

McPhee, Colin. *Music in Bali: A Study in Form and Instrumental Organization in Balinese Orchestral Music.* New Haven, Conn.: Yale University Press, 1966. Landmark work by the leading expert in Balinese music. Comprehensive study of various types of *gamelan* orchestras, including the *gamelan pelegongan* covered in *Listen.* Contains biographical information on I Lotring as well.

Schaareman, Danker, ed. *Balinese Music in Context: A Sixty-fifth Birthday Tribute to Hans Oesch—Forum Ethnomusicologicum* 4. Winterthur: Amadeus

Verlag, 1992. *Festschrift* offers articles by leading scholars on many aspects of *gamelan* music and the performing arts in Bali. Good resource once you know something about this music.

Stone, Ruth M., ed. *Garland Encyclopedia of World Music.* New York: Garland Publishing, Inc., 1998. Vol. 4, *Southeast Asia,* is highly recommended for your study of Balinese music.

Tenzer, Michael. *Gamelan Gong Kebyar: The Art of Twentieth-Century Balinese Music.* Chicago: University of Chicago Press, 2000. Comprehensive study of the popular, virtuosic *gamelan* style that emerged in the twentieth century. Includes several references to I Lotring.

China

Dolby, William. *A History of Chinese Drama.* London: Paul Elek, 1976. Fairly detailed history of Chinese theater. Especially appealing are translations of extended scenes that demonstrate the features of each significant historic genre.

Kuttner, Fritz A. "Prince Chu Tsai-Yü's Life and Work: A Re-evaluation of His Contribution to Equal Temperament Theory." *Ethnomusicology* (May 1975): 163–206. Intriguing, technical article looks at Chinese systems of temperament. We don't have all the facts yet, but Chinese musicians and thinkers may have developed systems of equal temperament before similar systems came into use in the West.

Mackerras, Colin P. *The Rise of the Peking Opera, 1770–1870: Social Aspects of the Theatre in Manchu China.* Oxford: Clarendon Press, 1972. Good history of Beijing opera. Begins with sixteenth century roots of *jingju,* but gives most emphasis to its golden age.

Mackerras, Colin, ed. *Chinese Theater from Its Origins to the Present Day.* Honolulu: University of Hawaii Press, 1983. Several scholars contributed chapters to this look at the history of Chinese theater. Good background on both early theatrical genres and contemporary theater in the People's Republic. Forty-three plates present black-and-white photographs of scenes from Chinese theater.

Northeast Drama Institute, ed. *Traditional Chinese Textile Designs in Full Color.* New York: Dover Publications, 1980. Full-color reproductions of costume designs from traditional Chinese opera. Striking images.

Scott, A. C. *The Classical Theatre of China.* London: George Allen & Unwin, Ltd., 1957. A short chapter on theatrical history is followed by detailed information on music, acting techniques, roles, plays, and theatrical facilities associated with Beijing opera.

Siu Wang-Ngai. *Chinese Opera: Images and Stories.* Vancouver: University of British Columbia Press, 1997. Wonderful color photographs throughout the book, along with some background material and stories.

Stone, Ruth M., ed. *Garland Encyclopedia of World Music.* New York: Garland Publishing, Inc., 1998. Vol. 7, *East Asia: China, Japan, and Korea,* is highly recommended for your study of Chinese music.

van Gulik, R. H. *The Lore of the Chinese Lute: An Essay in the Ideology of the Ch'in.* Tokyo: Sophia University, 1968. This excellent source on the *qin* describes its history, music, symbolism, and significance in Chinese culture.

India—General

Cooper, Robin. "Abstract Structure and the Indian Raga System." *Ethnomusicology* (January 1977): 1–32. Interesting article applies linguistic theories to the analysis of Indian *ragas*.

Deva, B. Chaitanya. *An Introduction to Indian Music.* New Delhi: Government of India Patiala House, 1973. Nice introduction to both Hindustani and Karnatak traditions in Indian music. Discusses melody, *raga, tala,* forms, instruments, and so on. Also contains brief biographies of significant Indian composers, including Tansen, Tyagaraja, and Rabindranath Tagore.

Gautam, M. R. *Evolution of Raga and Tala in Indian Music.* New Delhi: Munshiram Manoharlal Publishers, 1989. Technical guide to the history of raga and tala with a brief comparative look at Indian and Western esthetics.

Nijenhuis, Emmie te. *Indian Music: History and Structure.* Leiden: E. J. Brill, 1974. Nice introduction to both Hindustani and Karnatak traditions in Indian music. Four sections cover documentation, melody, rhythm, and composition. Describes important genres as well.

Ruckert, George E. *Music in North India. Experiencing Music, Expressing Culture* Series. New York: Oxford University Press, 2003. This useful, readable volume from this wonderful new global-music series is highly recommended for your study of North Indian music. Comes with a CD.

Stone, Ruth M., ed. *Garland Encyclopedia of World Music.* New York: Garland Publishing, Inc., 1998. Vol. 5, *South Asia: The Indian Subcontinent,* is highly recommended for your study of Indian music.

Viswanathan, T. and Matthew Harp Allen. *Music in South India. Experiencing Music, Expressing Culture* Series. New York: Oxford University Press, 2004. This excellent, readable volume from this wonderful new global-music series is highly recommended for your study of South Indian music. Comes with a CD.

India—Hindustani Music

Blum, Stephen, Philip V. Bohlman, and Daniel Neuman, eds. *Ethnomusicology and Modern Music History.* Urbana, Ill.: University of Illinois Press, 1993. This excellent collection contains many insightful articles. See especially Stephen Slawek's "Ravi Shankar as a Mediator between a Traditional Music and Modernity" on pp. 161–80.

Daniélou, Alain. *The Ragas of Northern Indian Music.* London: South Asia Books, 1981. Important book by this leading European scholar. Daniélou also recorded the Rag *Mauj-Khammaj* found on the *Listen* set.

Jairazbhoy, Nazir Ali. "Factors Underlying Important Notes in North Indian Music." *Ethnomusicology* 16 (1972): 63–81. Useful for a look at performance and theory in North Indian music.

Jairazbhoy, Nazir Ali. *The Rags of North Indian Music.* Revised edition. Bombay: South Asia Books, 1995. Important book by this contemporary Indian scholar.

Kaufmann, Walter. *The Ragas of North India.* New York: Da Capo Press, 1984. This comprehensive guide is arranged by family groups (*thata*), providing the basic tones and characteristic melodic figures for more than a hundred *ragas*. Introductory materials are also useful. Recommended.

Neuman, Daniel M. *The Life of Music in North India: The Organization of an Artistic Tradition.* Chicago: University of Chicago Press, 1995. Fascinating social and cultural study of the lives and training of musicians in North India.

India—Karnatak Music

Ayyangar, R. Rangaramanuja. *History of South Indian (Carnatic) Music: From Vedic Times to the Present.* Second Edition. Bombay: Vipanchi Cultural Trust, 1993. Detailed history dwells heavily on the history of Indian theory.

Jackson, William J. *Tyagaraja: Life and Lyrics.* New Delhi: Oxford University Press, 1996. Useful biography by a professor of religious studies at Purdue. Of special interest are Jackson's excellent translations of 160 of Tyagaraja's *kritis* and *kirtanas* and an extremely helpful analysis of Tyagaraja's poetic/musical structures, providing insight into the composer's deep spiritual roots.

Lakshmi, T. Seetharma. *A Study of the Compositions of Purandaradasa and Tyagaraja.* Bangalore: Veda Sruti Publications, 1994. Detailed, often technical comparison of these two Indian composers, including biographical sketches.

L'Armand, Kathleen, and Adrian L'Armand. "One Hundred Years of Music in Madras: A Case Study in Secondary Urbanization." *Ethnomusicology* (September 1983): 411–38. Interesting research takes a sociological approach to the study of performance practices from the 1880s to the 1970s. Useful for a look at the current state of classical music performance in South India.

Sambamoorthy, P. *South Indian Music,* Books I–VI. Seventh edition. Madras: Indian Music Publishing House, 1966. Classic multivolume work on the theory and practice of music in the Karnatak tradition of South India. Good source, but it takes some time to find your way around, especially since there are no indexes.

Japan—General

Harich-Schneider, Eta. *A History of Japanese Music.* London: Oxford University Press, 1973. Major, comprehensive work on Japanese music history. Good information on Japanese theater, but especially useful for its coverage of the *gagaku* tradition. Recommended.

Stone, Ruth M., ed. *Garland Encyclopedia of World Music.* New York: Garland Publishing, Inc., 1998. Vol. 7, *East Asia: China, Japan, and Korea,* is highly recommended for your study of Japanese music.

Wade, Bonnie C. *Music in Japan. Experiencing Music, Expressing Culture* Series. New York: Oxford University Press, 2004. This excellent, readable volume from this wonderful new global-music series is highly recommended for your study of Japanese music. Comes with a CD.

Japan—Gagaku

Bent, Ian, ed. *Source Materials and the Interpretation of Music: A Memorial Volume to Thurston Dart.* London: Stainer & Bell, 1981. This *Festschrift* includes Laurence Picken's article "'Tang Music' and Its Fate in Japan," an interesting study of the Chinese style that influenced the origins of *gagaku.*

Bugaku [Treasures from the Kasuga Shrine]. Nara: The Kasuga Shrine, 1989. The Kasuga Shrine is home to a *gagaku* performance tradition dating back to the days when Nara was Japan's first capital. This volume contains color photographs of live performances as well as gorgeous costumes, masks, and instruments from the shrine museum's collection. Several instruments from *Etenraku* are represented here, including the *sho, ryuteki, hichiriki, gakuso,* and *kakko.* Introductory materials include a brief but useful overview of *gagaku* genres and instrumentation.

Garfias, Robert. "Gradual Modifications in the Gagaku Tradition." *Ethnomusicology* 4 (1960): 16–19. Brief historical survey of changes in this genre.

Marett, Allan. "Togaku: Where Have the Tang Melodies Gone, and Where Have the New Melodies Come From?" *Ethnomusicology* (fall 1985): 409–31. *Gagaku* in Japan was originally a Chinese import from the T'ang dynasty's court. Noting that the main melodies in current *togaku* music no longer resemble T'ang melodies, the author traces the history of this *gagaku* genre to see what happened to the original Chinese tunes. Recommended.

Japan—Kabuki

Ernst, Earle. *The Kabuki Theatre.* Honolulu: University Press of Hawaii, 1974. Provides a brief history of *kabuki,* but its primary concern is the current practice of this genre, with a careful look at the physical layout of the theater, the audience, performance practices, current plays in the repertory, and so on.

Immoos, Thomas. *Japanese Theatre.* Translated by Hugh Young. New York: Rizzoli International Publications, 1977. Somewhat impressionistic look at *bugaku, noh, bunraku,* and *kabuki* traditions. Its strength is contained in the profuse, beautiful color and black-and-white photographs that fill this book.

Kamimura, Iwao. *Kabuki Today: The Art and Tradition.* Translated by Kirsten McIvor. New York: Kodansha International, 2001. An overview of current features and practices in *kabuki,* filled with beautiful glossy color photographs.

Malm, William P. "Four Seasons of the Old Mountain Woman: An Example of Japanese Nagauta Text Setting." *Journal of the American Musicological Society* (1978): 83–117. Thorough study of a single work from the *kabuki* tradition, with detailed transcriptions. Recommended.

Malm, William P. *Nagauta: The Heart of Kabuki Music.* Westport, Conn.: Greenwood Press, 1973. Detailed study of *nagauta* music as found both in *noh* and *kabuki* theater. Covers its history, theory, music, and instruments, and includes thorough analysis of two examples with extensive transcriptions.

Malm, William P. *Six Hidden Views of Japanese Music.* Berkeley: University of California Press, 1986. Fascinating work by a leading scholar. Even the structure of this book indicates his absorption of Japanese esthetics. Includes several studies of *nagauta* music and concludes with a comparison of Britten's *Curlew River* and the *noh* play that influenced it.

Scott, A. C. *The Kabuki Theatre of Japan.* New York: Collier Books, 1966. This useful guide to *kabuki* contains historical background, material on *noh* drama, and detailed discussion of *kabuki* music, dance, and acting. Playwrights are also given attention, and the book describes six representative *kabuki* plays in detail. Especially useful are the six pages discussing features, plot, and variants on the *Dojoji* play.

Yoshinobu Inoura and Toshio Kawatake. *The Traditional Theater of Japan.* New York: Weatherhill, 1981. Handy guide to the history of Japanese theater, covering ancient genres as well as *noh, bunraku,* and *kabuki* drama. Historical detail, charts, and black-and-white photographs make this a useful source.

❦ Latin America

Béhague, Gerard. *Music in Latin America: An Introduction.* Englewood Cliffs, N.J.: Prentice-Hall, 1979. A good survey of music from the "cultivated" tradition. For folk and traditional musics from this region, look elsewhere.

Schechter, John M., ed. *Music in Latin American Culture: Regional Traditions.* New York: Schirmer Books, 1999. A look at indigenous regional and community music-making traditions throughout the Latin Americas, from Mexico to Peru to Chile.

Stevenson, Robert Murrell. *Music in Aztec and Inca Territory.* Berkeley: University of California Press, 1968. Excellent source covers music from precontact times through the colonial era. Especially useful are seventy pages of European eyewitness accounts and transcriptions of Aztec and Incan music and culture.

Stone, Ruth M., ed. *Garland Encyclopedia of World Music.* New York: Garland Publishing, Inc., 1998. Vol. 2, *South America, Mexico, Central America, and the Caribbean,* is highly recommended for your study of Latin American music.

The Aztecs

Martens, Frederick H. "Music in the Life of the Aztecs." *Musical Quarterly* (1928): 413–37. Interesting if somewhat dated study of Aztec music, replete with gory details. Martens falls into the traps Tomlinson warns against below.

Tomlinson, Gary. "Ideologies of Aztec Song." *Journal of the American Musicological Society* (1995): 343–79. *Listen* coauthor's excellent article pleads for new approaches that recognize and move beyond deeply embedded Western thought patterns that hinder full appreciation of Aztec culture. Highly recommended.

Peru and the Inca

Cobo, Bernabé. *History of the Inca Empire: An Account of the Indians' Customs and Their Origin Together with a Treatise on Inca Legends, History, and Social Institutions.* Translated and edited by Roland Hamilton. Austin, Tex.: University of Texas Press, 1979. Modern translation of Father Cobo's book based on his experiences in Cuzco, 1609–1613. This is the conquest seen through Spanish eyes.

Romero, Raúl R. *Debating the Past: Music, Memory, and Identity in the Andes.* New York: Oxford University Press, 2001. This study looks at traditional elements and their role in contemporary musics of Peru.

Stevenson, Robert Murrell. *The Music of Peru: Aboriginal and Viceroyal Epochs.* Washington, D.C.: Pan American Union, 1960. Fascinating look at Peruvian music during the time "Hanaq pachap kusikuynin" was written. Pages 47–50 contain a facsimile reproduction of the four voice parts from the original publication along with a modern transcription in score.

Turino, Thomas. "The Coherence of Social Style and Musical Creation Among the Aymara in Southern Peru." *Ethnomusicology* 35, no. 1 (winter 1989): 1–30. Excellent article takes a careful look at performance practices, compositional methods, and song structures, comparing these with characteristic Aymara social behaviors. Recommended.

Wachtel, Nathan. *The Vision of the Vanquished: The Spanish Conquest of Peru through Indian Eyes, 1530–1570.* Translated by Ben and Siân Reynolds. New York: Barnes & Noble Books, 1977. Using primary sources and modern community festivals that reenact the fall of the Inca, Wachtel offers a fascinating antidote to the Spanish eyewitness accounts of Poma de Ayala, Cobo, and others.

❧ Middle East

Qur'anic Chant and Islam

Farmer, Henry George. *A History of Arabian Music to the XIIIth Century.* London: Luzac & Co., 1929. Despite its age, this work remains a classic. Especially useful for a summary of early Muslim attitudes toward music—especially those of Muhammad.

Lings, Martin. *Muhammad: His Life Based on the Earliest Sources.* Rochester, Vt.: Inner Traditions, 1983. Fascinating scholarly biography of the prophet Muhammad.

Nelson, Kristina. *The Art of Reciting the Qur'an.* Austin: University of Texas Press, 1985. Excellent study conveys the fullness of this revered tradition. Deals with the musical aspects of recitation as well as issues of training, vocal production, and interaction between reciter and audience. Recommended.

Nelson, Kristina. "Reciter and Listener: Some Factors Shaping the *Mujawwad* Style of Qur'anic Reciting." *Ethnomusicology* (January 1982): 41–47. A brief look at a modern virtuoso style of recitation. Useful if you can't find the Nelson book above.

Sells, Michael. *Approaching the Qur'an: The Early Revelations.* Ashland, Ore.: White Cloud Press, 1999. An excellent source for background information on the Qur'an and its significance.

Shiloah, Amnon. "The Arabic Concept of Mode." *Journal of the American Musicological Society* (1981): 19–42. Good explanation of the history and characteristics of Arabic modal scales (*maqamat*), including many concepts that influence the virtuoso style of modern Qur'anic recitation.

Smith, Jane I. *Islam in America.* New York: Columbia University Press, 1999. Excellent study looks at the impact of Islam on the United States.

Stone, Ruth M., ed. *Garland Encyclopedia of World Music.* New York: Garland Publishing, Inc., 1998. Vol. 6, *The Middle East,* is highly recommended for your study of Islamic chant.

❧ North America

Hawai'ian Chant

Kanahele, George S., ed. *Hawaiian Music and Musicians: An Illustrated History.* Honolulu: University Press of Hawaii, 1979. Useful one-volume encyclopedia focuses primarily on Hawaiian popular music but contains articles on chant and other traditional music and musicians. Includes extensive discography of Hawaiian music.

Stone, Ruth M., ed. *Garland Encyclopedia of World Music*. New York: Garland Publishing, Inc., 1998. Vol. 9, *Australia and the Pacific Islands,* is highly recommended for your study of Hawai'ian music.

Tatar, Elizabeth. *Nineteenth Century Hawaiian Chant*. Pacific Anthropological Records, No. 33. Honolulu: Bernice P. Bishop Museum, 1982. One of the most significant works available on traditional Hawai'ian chant authored by a leading expert in the field. Includes spectrogram analysis of early chant recordings. Recommended.

Tatar, Elizabeth. "Toward a Description of Precontact Music in Hawai'i." *Ethnomusicology* (September 1981): 481–92. Excellent overview of materials found in her subsequent book, cited above. Use this article if you can't find her book.

Native American Music

Frisbie, Charlotte J. "Vocables in Navajo Ceremonial Use." *Ethnomusicology* (September 1980): 347–92. Excellent article on the derivation and meanings of those elusive vocables. Highly recommended.

Hatton, O. Thomas. "Performance Practices of Northern Plains Pow-wow Singing Groups." *Yearbook for Inter-American Musical Research* 10 (1974): 123–37. Excellent article describes many aspects of performance practice, including song length, vocal qualities, placement of "hard beats," tempo changes, and singing off the beat. Recommended.

Hatton, Orin T. "In the Tradition: Grass Dance Musical Style and Female Pow-wow Singers." *Ethnomusicology* (spring–summer 1986): 197–222. Good history of the Grass Dance, with emphasis on women's roles.

Howard, James H. "Pan-Indianism in Native American Music and Dance." *Ethnomusicology* (January 1983): 71–82. A brief, anecdotal survey of the spread of pan-Indianism and the intertribal powwow in the past few decades.

Kurath, Gertrude P. "A Comparison of Plains and Pueblo Songs." *Ethnomusicology* (1969): 512–17. A brief look at song styles by this noted dance ethnologist.

Lassiter, Luke E. *The Power of Kiowa Song: A Collaborative Ethnography*. Tucson: University of Arizona Press, 1998. Recent study of the Kiowa people of the southern Plains. Part II gives significant attention to dances, songs, and powwows.

McAllester, David P. *Enemy Way Music: A Study of Social and Esthetic Values as Seen in Navaho Music*. Papers of the Peabody Museum of American Archaeology and Ethnology, Harvard University, vol. 41, no. 3. Cambridge, Mass.: Peabody Museum, 1954. Landmark study considers music of the Enemy Way Ceremony in its cultural context. Good background for an understanding of the Navajo song in the *Listen* anthology. Highly recommended.

Nettl, Bruno. *Blackfoot Musical Thought: Comparative Perspectives*. Kent, Ohio: Kent State University Press, 1989. Thoughtful, comprehensive study of music in the life and thought of this northern Plains tribe. Recommended.

Stone, Ruth M., ed. *Garland Encyclopedia of World Music*. New York: Garland Publishing, Inc., 1998. Vol. 3, *The United States and Canada,* is highly recommended for your study of Native American music.

American Music

❧ American Music History

Chase, Gilbert. *America's Music: From the Pilgrims to the Present*. Third edition. Urbana: University of Illinois Press, 1987. One of the first books on American music history. Still worth a read.

Crawford, Richard. *America's Musical Life: A History*. New York: Norton, 2001. Crawford's engaging new book offers an unabashedly comprehensive look at American music history, covering folk and popular genres often overlooked in scholarly volumes. Recommended.

Hamm, Charles. *Music in the New World*. New York: Norton, 1983. One of my favorite books on American music. Filled with fascinating quotations from primary sources, Hamm's work creates vivid portraits of the way it was. Good comprehensive survey.

Hitchcock, H. Wiley. *Music in the United States: A Historical Introduction*. Fourth edition. Upper Saddle River, N.J.: Prentice-Hall, 2000. Like the other volumes in Prentice-Hall's period-history series, this one is concise, readable, and authoritative. Recommended for a quick, thorough overview.

Southern, Eileen. *The Music of Black Americans*. Third edition. New York: Norton, 1997. The first comprehensive history of black American music. Starts with slave trading in the sixteenth century and ends with a look at twentieth-century black composers and performers of both classical and popular music, including rap. A companion volume contains a fascinating collection of primary source materials (see Primary Sources—American Music and Composers below).

❧ Film Music

Hickman, Roger. *Reel Music: Exploring 100 Years of Film Music*. Second edition. New York: Norton, 2005. Focuses on the history of film music. Representative examples are examined in detail.

Kassabian, Anahid. *Hearing Film: Tracking Identifications in Contemporary Hollywood Film Music*. New York, Routledge, 2001. This fine book takes us into the world of film criticism. It is a critical study of the ways music colors our perceptions of gender, race, and diversity in movies of the 1980s and 1990s.

Prendergast, Roy M. *Film Music: A Neglected Art*. Second edition. New York: Norton, 1992. Good source for a look at the history, esthetics, techniques, and tools of film music.

❧ Jazz

Gridley, Mark C. *Jazz Styles: History and Analysis*. Ninth edition. Upper Saddle River, N.J.: Prentice-Hall, 2006. One of the most detailed jazz textbooks available, within its self-imposed limits. Covers mostly instrumental jazz from New Orleans up to jazz-fusion styles—go elsewhere for jazz vocalists. Recommended for a lucid overview of the evolution of various jazz styles. Excellent accompanying CD.

Jasen, David A., and Trebor Jay Tichenor. *Rags and Ragtime: A Musical History*. New York: Dover, 1989. Study of ragtime.

Kernfeld, Barry, ed. *The New Grove Dictionary of Jazz*. 2 volumes. London: Macmillan, 1988. *New Grove* even does jazz—and does it well. Highly recommended research tool.

Kernfeld, Barry, ed. *The New Grove Dictionary of Jazz*. New York: St. Martin's, 1994. A more compact, less expensive softbound version of this wonderful resource.

Schuller, Gunther. *Early Jazz*. New York: Oxford University Press, 1968. Schuller is one of the finest jazz scholars working. He played with Miles on the *Birth of the Cool* sessions and went on to lead the New England Conservatory. Comprehensive landmark study of early jazz.

Schuller, Gunther. *The Swing Era: The Development of Jazz, 1930–1945*. New York: Oxford University Press, 1989. Schuller continues his study of jazz history with a look at the swing era. Another thorough landmark work.

Tanner, Paul O. W., David Megill, and Maurice Gerow. *Jazz*. Tenth edition. Boston: McGraw-Hill, 2004. A slick, glossy jazz textbook. It covers the full range of jazz in the twentieth century, but only superficially. Accompanying CDs.

Tirro, Frank. *Jazz: A History*. New York: Norton, 1993. Textbook and accompanying CD survey the history of jazz. Coverage of jazz roots and early jazz is especially good. Many useful appendices.

Williams, Martin, ed. *The Smithsonian Collection of Classic Jazz*. Revised edition. Washington, D.C.: The Smithsonian Collection of Recordings, 1987 (CD). The best single-volume comprehensive recorded anthology ever produced. If you don't have it, get it. Martin Williams's accompanying booklet provides detailed notes on each recording, but it also offers an explanation of the elements of jazz, a look at jazz history, and brief biographical sketches for each major jazz musician. Well-chosen examples document the history of jazz from Joplin to Coltrane.

♪ Musicals

Bordman, Gerald. *American Musical Theatre*. Expanded edition. New York: Oxford University Press, 1986. Fascinating volume goes year by year through the history of American musical theater, with a column or two on each major show from that year.

Gänzl, Kurt. *Encyclopedia of the Musical Theatre*. 2 volumes. New York: Schirmer Books, 1994. Good reference source.

Gänzl, Kurt, and Andrew Lamb. *Gänzl's Book of the Musical Theatre*. New York: Schirmer Books, 1989. Musical theater's equivalent to Kobbé's *Opera Guide*. Summaries of librettos and songs from more than three hundred shows from around the world.

Mates, Juliane. *America's Musical Stage: Two Hundred Years of Musical Theatre*. New York: Praeger, 1987. A history of American musical theater.

Norton, Richard C. *A Chronology of American Musical Theater*. New York: Oxford University Press, 2002. Designed as a companion to Bordman's book, this volume provides production information (cast, crew, songs, composer, lyricist, and so on—just the facts!) for more than three thousand shows presented on New York's main stages from 1850 to 2001. Unfortunately, off-Broadway productions are omitted, no matter how popular.

Smith, Cecil, and Glenn Litton. *Musical Comedy in America*. Second edition. New York: Routledge/Theatre Arts Books, 1991. Comprehensive history of American musical theater, from *The Black Crook* to *Sweeney Todd*.

♩ Popular and Vernacular Music

Berliner, Paul F. *Thinking in Jazz: The Infinite Art of Improvisation*. Chicago: University of Chicago Press, 1994. Fascinating study takes an ethnomusicological approach to the study of jazz improvisation. Recommended for insights into ethnomusicological methods as well as the world of the improvising musician.

Cantwell, Robert. *When We Were Good: The Folk Revival*. Cambridge, Mass.: Harvard University Press, 1996. Good source on the folk revival in the twentieth century.

Carlin, Richard. *English and American Folk Music*. New York: Facts on File Publications, 1987. Study of the relationship between English and American folk music.

Charlton, Katherine. *Rock Music Styles: A History*. Second edition. Madison, Wis.: Brown and Benchmark, 1994. Recent textbook does a nice job with the variety of rock styles from the 1950s on.

Cohn, Lawrence, ed. *Nothing but the Blues: The Music and the Musicians*. New York: Abbeville Press, 1993. Eleven chapters contributed by ten blues scholars cover the history and spread of the blues from the late 1800s to the present. More than three hundred illustrations provide a powerful sense of time and place.

DeCurtis, Anthony, and James Henke. *The Rolling Stone Illustrated History of Rock and Roll*. New York: Random House, 1992. Not a scholarly study and not arranged to provide continuous narrative, but it does provide many insightful, generously illustrated articles on major figures in popular music since the 1950s.

Floyd, Samuel A., Jr. *The Power of Black Music: Interpreting Its History from Africa to the United States*. New York: Oxford University Press, 1995. Excellent book by a leading scholar. Important look at interactions between African and European cultures in America.

Forcucci, Samuel L. *A Folk Song History of America: America Through Its Songs*. Englewood Cliffs, N.J.: Prentice-Hall, 1984. Interesting study looks at American history through the lens of its songs. Useful source if you want to take your class on a galloping tour of American music history.

Garofalo, Reebee. *Rockin' Out: Popular Music in the USA*. Upper Saddle River, N.J.: Prentice-Hall, 1997. Encyclopedic resource focuses on popular music as a social indicator, examining the complex interrelationships between music and culture.

Hamm, Charles. *Yesterdays: Popular Song in America*. New York: Norton, 1983. Excellent resource.

Herzhaft, Gérard. *Encyclopedia of the Blues*. Trans. Brigitte Debord. Fayetteville: University of Arkansas Press, 1997. Good source.

Kingsbury, Paul, ed. *The Encyclopedia of Country Music*. New York: Oxford University Press, 1998. Superb resource, compiled with the assistance of the staff at Nashville's Country Music Hall of Fame and Museum.

Malone, Bill C. *Country Music, USA*. Second revised edition. Austin: University of Texas Press, 2002. One of the finest scholarly works on country music. Includes a discography and extensive bibliographic essays.

Oliver, Paul. *The Story of the Blues*. Boston: Northeastern University Press, 1997. Good historical source.

Oliver, Paul, et al. *The New Grove Gospel, Blues, and Jazz*. New York: Norton, 1986. Useful collection of materials from the *New Grove* dictionaries.

Roberts, John Storm. *The Latin Tinge: The Impact of Latin American Music on the United States*. Second edition. New York: Oxford University Press, 1999. Interesting book looks at a "collision of cultures." Latin American music, itself the result of multicultural interactions, has influenced many varieties of American music.

Romanowski, Patricia, and Holly George-Warren, eds. *The Rolling Stone Encyclopedia of Rock and Roll*. Third edition. New York: Fireside, 2001. Excellent source of information on bands and musicians associated with rock'n'roll and its offshoots from the 1950s on.

Rose, Tricia. *Black Noise: Rap Music and Black Culture in Contemporary America*. Hanover, N.H.: Wesleyan University Press, 1994. Good source.

Sandberg, Larry, and Dick Weissman. *The Folk Music Sourcebook*. New York: Alfred A. Knopf, 1976. Provides short essays on a wealth of North American folk styles, including music of African Americans, Native Americans, Anglo Americans, and others. More valuable than the essays are the long lists of bibliographic and discographic resources.

Small, Christopher. *Music of the Common Tongue: Survival and Celebration in African and American Music*. Hanover, N.H.: Wesleyan University Press, 1998. Thoughtful look at connections between African and African American music and culture.

Stambler, Irwin, and Lyndon Stambler. *Folk and Blues: The Encyclopedia*. New York: St. Martin's Press, 2001. Good, comprehensive source of information on important "vernacular" musicians.

Starr, Larry, and Christopher Waterman. *American Popular Music: From Minstrelsy to MP3*. Second edition. New York: Oxford University Press, 2006. One of the best single-volume books I've seen on the subject. Blends a deep knowledge of the music with a wonderful sense of humor. Comes with two CDs. Highly recommended.

Stuessy, Joe, and Scott Lipscomb. *Rock and Roll: Its History and Stylistic Development*. Third edition. Upper Saddle River, N.J.: Prentice-Hall, 1999. Good, recent source provides what the title implies.

Szatmary, David. *Rockin' in Time: A Social History of Rock and Roll*. Second edition. Englewood Cliffs, N.J.: Prentice-Hall, 1991. Applies methods pioneered by Henry Raynor to the study of rock'n'roll. A useful text that looks at rock in its cultural context.

Women in Music

Bowers, Jane, and Judith Tick, eds. *Women Making Music: The Western Art Tradition, 1150–1950*. Urbana: University of Illinois Press, 1987. Excellent, thorough history of the role of women in music. Highly recommended.

Briscoe, James R., ed. *Contemporary Anthology of Music by Women*. Bloomington: Indiana University Press, 1997. Anthology of scores by twentieth-century women, including avant-garde and popular composers. Representative composers include Sofia Gubaidulina, Betsy Jolas, Joan La Barbara, Joni Mitchell, Dolly Parton, Shulamit Ran, Joan Tower, and Judith Lang Zaimont. Useful for instructors who want to cover more music by women in Chapters 22 and 23.

Briscoe, James R., ed. *Historical Anthology of Music by Women*. Bloomington: Indiana University Press, 1987. A score anthology provides many scores written by women over the centuries. Useful for instructors who want to cover more music by women. Accompanying recordings.

Drinker, Sophie. *Music and Women*. New York: Feminist Press, 1995. Published posthumously forty years after it was written, this book was one of the first to take a feminist approach to the study of music history.

Hixon, Don L., and Don A. Hennessee. *Women in Music: An Encyclopedic Biobibliography*. Second edition. Metuchen, N.J.: Scarecrow Press, 1993. Comprehensive index of biographical information on women in music. A useful reference source.

Jezic, Diane Peacock. *Women Composers: The Lost Tradition Found*. New York: Feminist Press, 1988. Short biography, summary of musical significance, and bibliography for many important composers—from Hildegard to the present. Concise, user-friendly guide for instructors in a hurry.

Neuls-Bates, Carol, ed. *Women in Music: An Anthology of Source Readings from the Middle Ages to the Present*. New York: Harper and Row, 1982. Fascinating resource includes letters by Hildegard of Bingen and by Clara Schumann.

Pendle, Karin, ed. *Women and Music: A History*. Bloomington: Indiana University Press, 1991. A good collection of recent articles on women in music.

Sadie, Julie Anne, and Rhian Samuel, eds. *The Norton/Grove Dictionary of Women Composers*. New York: Norton, 1995. Important reference book for the study of women in music.

Musical Genres

♪ Chamber Music

Griffiths, Paul. *The String Quartet*. New York: Thames and Hudson, 1983. Concise, lucid overview of the history of the string quartet. Unusually thorough coverage of twentieth-century quartets.

Ulrich, Homer. *Chamber Music*. New York: Columbia University Press, 1966. Good overview of the history of chamber music. Begins with early music and continues up to the twentieth century.

♩ Concerto

Hinson, Maurice. *Music for Piano and Orchestra: An Annotated Guide*. Enlarged edition. Bloomington: Indiana University Press, 1993. Covers many works for piano and orchestra, from the Classical piano concerto to significant twentieth-century works.

Layton, Robert, ed. *A Guide to the Concerto*. Oxford: Oxford University Press, 1996. This collection of articles covers the history of the concerto up to the present day.

Roeder, Michael Thomas. *A History of the Concerto*. Portland, Ore.: Amadeus Press, 1994. Handy, thorough history of the concerto.

♩ Dance Music

Arbeau, Thoinot. *Orchesography*. Translated by Mary Stewart Evans. New York: Dover, 1967. Reprint of Arbeau's Renaissance dance treatise. Arbeau includes tunes, dance steps, and diagrams throughout; it's not at all hard to read or teach yourself the steps. Most useful when you look at galliards and jigs in Chapter 6, though it gives some insights into dances described in Chapters 8 and 10.

Nettl, Paul. *The Story of Dance Music*. New York: Greenwood Press, 1969. Handy history of music associated with dance, especially from the eighteenth century on.

♩ Electronic Music

Chadabe, Joel. *Electronic Sound: The Past and Promise of Electronic Music*. Upper Saddle River, N.J.: Prentice-Hall, 1997. This engaging history of electronic music by the respected composer discusses many important figures, including Varèse, Cage, Boulez, Stockhausen, Subotnick, Reich, and Saariaho.

Deutsch, Herbert A. *Synthesis: An Introduction to the History, Theory, and Practice of Electronic Music*. Revised edition. Sherman Oaks, Calif.: Alfred Publishing Company, 1985. More emphasis on the theory and practice of sound synthesis than most other books below.

Ernst, David. *The Evolution of Electronic Music*. New York: Schirmer Books, 1977. A textbook on twentieth-century electronic music. Arranged by medium—tape alone, voice with tape, and so on.

Griffiths, Paul. *A Guide to Electronic Music*. New York: Thames and Hudson, 1979. Handy, lucid guide to the history of electronic music in the twentieth century.

Manning, Peter. *Electronic and Computer Music*. Revised edition. New York: Oxford University Press, 2004. My first choice for a concise, clear, well-organized history of electronic music.

Schwartz, Elliott. *Electronic Music: A Listener's Guide*. Revised edition. New York: Da Capo Press, 1989. Another guide to electronic music, but with more of an emphasis on listening.

❦ Opera and Oratorio

Grout, Donald Jay. *A Short History of Opera*. Third edition. New York: Columbia University Press, 1988. Short but thorough single-volume history of opera. Good source for a quick overview.

Kerman, Joseph. *Opera as Drama*. Revised edition. Berkeley: University of California Press, 1988. Short, readable book contains essays on opera and dramaturgy throughout opera's history. Most relevant for *Listen* are the chapters on Monteverdi, Purcell, *Don Giovanni, Tristan and Isolde,* and *Wozzeck.* Recommended for thoughtful, insightful background material.

Kobbé, Gustave. *The New Kobbé's Complete Opera Book*. Edited by the Earl of Harewood. New York: G. P. Putnam's Sons, 1976. If you need some background information and a quick summary of an opera's plot, this is a good place to go.

Pahlen, Kurt. *The World of Oratorio*. Translated by Judith Schaefer. Portland, Ore.: Amadeus Press, 1990. Survey of the oratorio from its roots in vocal works by Machaut and Ockeghem up to twentieth-century works by Ligeti and Penderecki. Good source for a quick overview.

Parker, Roger, ed. *The Oxford Illustrated History of Opera*. Oxford: Oxford University Press, 1994. Paul Griffiths's chapters on twentieth-century opera stand out. Profusely illustrated with color photographs.

Sadie, Stanley, ed. *History of Opera*. New York: Norton, 1989. Draws material from the *New Grove Dictionary of Opera* in a single-volume format.

Sadie, Stanley, ed. *The New Grove Book of Opera*. New York: St. Martin's Press, 1996. Good one-volume encyclopedia of opera.

Sadie, Stanley, ed. *The New Grove Dictionary of Opera*. 4 volumes. London: Macmillan, 1992. An excellent recent addition to the *New Grove* family. Highly recommended research tool.

Smither, Howard E. *A History of the Oratorio*. Chapel Hill: University of North Carolina Press, 1977. Multiple-volume comprehensive history of the oratorio begins in the early Baroque. Recommended for serious research.

❦ Songs

Gorrell, Lorraine. *The Nineteenth-Century German Lied*. Portland, Ore.: Amadeus Press, 1993. Covers male and female composers of this important Romantic genre.

Osborne, Charles. *The Concert Song Companion: A Guide to the Classical Repertoire*. New York: Da Capo Press, 1985. A guide to specific songs and song cycles.

Smeed, J. W. *German Song and Its Poetry: 1740–1900*. London: Croom Helm, 1987. Interesting look at the history of German poetry as well as German music between 1740 and 1900. Also studies the relationship between poetry and music in German lieder of this period. Useful if you want to make connections between music and other arts in Unit IV.

Stevens, Denis, ed. *A History of Song*. Revised edition. New York: Norton, 1960. Handy one-volume guide compiled by this noted scholar.

Whitton, Kenneth S. *Lieder: An Introduction to German Song.* London: J. McRae, 1984. A serviceable overview of German song literature from the eighteenth century on.

๚ Symphony

Cuyler, Louise. *The Symphony.* Second edition. Warren, Mich.: Harmonie Park Press, 1995. Quick guide to the history of the symphony.

Layton, Robert, ed. *A Guide to the Symphony.* New York: Oxford University Press, 1995. A guide to every major symphonist from Haydn to the present, including Beethoven, Tchaikovsky, and Mahler. Nicely put together, with articles by many scholars, including H. C. Robbins Landon.

Preston, Steadman. *The Symphony.* Second edition. Englewood Cliffs, N.J.: Prentice-Hall, 1992. A somewhat more comprehensive single-volume history of the symphony.

๚ Form and Analysis

Berry, Wallace. *Form in Music.* Second edition. Englewood Cliffs, N.J.: Prentice-Hall, 1986. Textbook on the analysis of musical form.

Diamond, Harold J. *Music Analyses: An Annotated Guide to the Literature.* New York: Schirmer Books, 1991. You can find it in the reference collection for any well-stocked library. When you don't have time to do your own analysis, this book can help you track down musical analyses of specific works.

Moore, Earl V., and Theodore E. Heger. *The Symphony and the Symphonic Poem.* Sixth revised edition. Ann Arbor, Mich.: Ulrich's Books, 1974. This book contains only analytical charts for major orchestral works by Haydn, Beethoven, Mozart, Schubert, Liszt, Tchaikovsky, and others. Useful if you need a quick analysis and don't have time to do your own.

Rosen, Charles. *Sonata Forms.* Revised edition. New York: Norton, 1988. Penetrating study of the variety of sonata forms and their salient features in the hands of Classical and early Romantic composers. A wonderful corrective to the "fill-in-the-blank" approach to musical form that some texts foster.

Spencer, Peter, and Peter M. Temko. *A Practical Approach to the Study of Form in Music.* Prospect Heights, Ill.: Waveland Press, 1994. Reprint edition of the 1988 Prentice-Hall publication. Avoids the obsessive morphology and rigid classification of forms found in many textbooks. Stays close to primary structural principles throughout. The book begins with chapters on structural phenomena, units, and functions. If you are not conversant with binary or ternary forms, fugues, variation forms, sonata-allegro forms, or rondo form, this provides an excellent starting point. Each chapter contains two or more complete works that you can play easily at the piano and ends with a list of relevant scores in standard anthologies by Wennerstrom, Burkhart, Turek, and Kamien (*Norton Scores*).

Tovey, Donald Francis. *Essays in Musical Analysis.* 6 volumes. London: Oxford University Press, 1943. Ready-to-go analyses of many standard-repertory tonal works from the seventeenth century to the early twentieth century. Tovey was a gifted analyst and writer, and his books offer much to ponder even today. Another useful source of musical analysis when you don't have time to do your own.

Musical Instruments and Orchestration

Baines, Anthony. *Brass Instruments: Their History and Development*. New York: Dover, 1993. The title tells the story.

Baines, Anthony. *The Oxford Companion to Musical Instruments*. Oxford: Oxford University Press, 1992. Comprehensive one-volume dictionary. Contains more than you ever want to know about Western instruments, and does a respectable if not complete job of presenting instruments from other cultures (e.g., includes *jinghu* but not *jangar*).

Baines, Anthony. *Woodwind Instruments and Their History*. New York: Dover, 1991. The title says it all.

Benade, Arthur H. *Horns, Strings, and Harmony*. New York: Dover, 1994. This book covers basic acoustics as it discusses the acoustic features of different types of instruments. Interesting, readable study of the science of musical instruments.

Blades, James. *Percussion Instruments and Their History*. New York: Frederick A. Praeger, 1970. The title says it all.

Carse, Adam. *The History of Orchestration*. New York: Dover, 1964. Not an orchestration text! This significant historical study describes how composers from Lully to Schoenberg used the orchestra. This book can help you teach about the orchestra from the time you distinguish between basic and festive Baroque orchestras up to the time you point out Debussy's unique use of tone color.

Diagram Group. *Musical Instruments of the World: An Illustrated Encyclopedia*. New York: Facts on File, 1976. Glossy picture book provides a good overview of instruments from around the world, organized according to the Hornbostel-Sachs classification system.

Kirby, F. E. *A Short History of Keyboard Music*. New York: Schirmer Books, 1966. Useful volume covers music for organ, harpsichord, clavichord, and piano from before the Baroque to the twentieth century. Also includes a description of the mechanical action of each instrument.

Marcuse, Sibyl. *Musical Instruments: A Comprehensive Dictionary*. New York: Norton, 1975. This single-volume dictionary can help answer many questions about specific musical instruments from around the world.

Montagu, Jeremy. *The World of Baroque and Classical Musical Instruments*. Woodstock, N.Y.: Overlook Press, 1979. Wonderful combination of scholarly understanding and illustration—a feast for the eye. Highly recommended.

Montagu, Jeremy. *The World of Medieval and Renaissance Musical Instruments*. Woodstock, N.Y.: Overlook Press, 1976. Wonderful combination of scholarly understanding and illustration—a feast for the eye. Highly recommended.

Montagu, Jeremy. *The World of Romantic and Modern Musical Instruments*. Woodstock, N.Y.: Overlook Press, 1981. Wonderful combination of scholarly understanding and illustration—a feast for the eye. Highly recommended.

Sadie, Stanley, ed. *The New Grove Dictionary of Musical Instruments*. 2 volumes. London: Macmillan, 1984. Another wonderful research tool from *New Grove*.

Stiller, Andrew. *Handbook of Instrumentation*. Berkeley: University of California Press, 1985. Not an orchestration text! Stiller describes how instruments work. Unlike most other such books, this one describes how to produce many unusual special effects on modern instruments, describes many early instruments, and describes many electronic instruments as well. Probably the most comprehensive discussion of instruments available to the modern musician. Highly recommended.

Acoustics and Cognition

Benade, Arthur H. *Fundamentals of Musical Acoustics*. New York: Dover, 1990. Concise, readable introduction to the science of sound.

Butler, David. *The Musician's Guide to Perception and Cognition*. New York: Schirmer Books, 1992. A concise introduction to the study of perception and cognition. Careful overview of acoustics and the physiological and sensory attributes of sounds lays the groundwork for a study of cognition—the awareness and understanding of musical elements. The book concludes with a look at developmental stages of cognitive awareness in music, and explains several current theories of cognitive and musical development. An interesting guide to problems and possibilities if you want to help your students listen better. Accompanying listening examples on CD.

Campbell, Murray, and Clive Greated. *The Musician's Guide to Acoustics*. New York: Schirmer Books, 1987. Comprehensive introduction to musical acoustics written from a musician's point of view. Covers the creation and transmission of musical sounds, the processes of hearing sounds, intonation, and sound production, with chapters on each instrument family, including voice and electronic instruments.

Helmholtz, Hermann. *On the Sensations of Tone*. New York: Dover, 1954. Classic nineteenth-century book on acoustics by an eminent scientist. Helmholtz reports on a lifetime of research, describing physical acoustical phenomena, the physiology of hearing, and many of his experiments as well. Fascinating study by a thorough, inquisitive mind.

Huron, David. *Sweet Anticipation: Music and the Psychology of Expectation*. Cambridge, Mass: MIT Press, 2006. Excellent new book on music cognition and perception gives a good sense of the current state of the discipline as well as new insights into how we listen to music.

Meyer, Leonard. *Emotion and Meaning in Music*. Chicago: University of Chicago Press, 1961. An early classic in the field of music cognition and perception, this book is still highly recommended.

Seashore, Carl E. *Psychology of Music*. New York: Dover, 1967. An early landmark study in acoustics, perception, and cognition by the man who developed the Seashore test.

Scores

❦ Dover Publications

Dover Publications, New York, N.Y. Dover has established a reputation for selling high-quality, low-cost softbound reprints of scores and books whose copyrights have expired. Dover offers a wide range of music from Palestrina and Monteverdi up to Debussy and early Stravinsky. Within that time frame, you can find Dover scores for most works in the *Listen* recordings, including Palestrina's *Pope Marcellus* Mass; Bach's *Brandenburg* Concertos, *Orgelbüchlein,* and Cantata No. 4; Handel's *Messiah*; Haydn's symphonies; Mozart's piano sonatas, concertos, and *Don Giovanni*; Beethoven's string quartets, symphonies, and piano sonatas; lieder by Schubert and Robert Schumann; Romantic piano works by Robert Schumann, Schubert, and Chopin; Berlioz's *Fantastic* Symphony; operas by Verdi and Wagner; Tchaikovsky's *Romeo and Juliet*; Brahms's concertos; Mahler's symphonies; Debussy's Three Nocturnes; Stravinsky's *Rite of Spring*; and Schoenberg's *Pierrot lunaire*. For scores for *Listen* works, the prices range from $11.95 for Chopin's Nocturnes to $36.95 for *Tristan and Isolde,* and the vast majority of Dover scores fall within that range. Better yet, if you buy more than a hundred dollars' worth of Dover scores at a time, you can often get 20 percent off; Dover sells its books to retailers at only 60 percent of list price compared with 80 percent for most other publishers.

❦ Norton Critical Scores

Norton Critical Scores Series. New York: Norton. These volumes contain authoritative editions of the scores themselves, but they also include analytical essays and a generous sampling of historical writings and commentary on each work by various composers and other writers. This series includes scores for many of the works discussed in *Listen*: Bach's Cantata No. 4, Beethoven's Symphony No. 5, Berlioz's *Fantastic* Symphony, Mozart's Symphony No. 40, Palestrina's *Pope Marcellus* Mass, Purcell's *Dido and Aeneas,* Schumann's *Dichterliebe,* and the Prelude and *Transfiguration* from Wagner's *Tristan and Isolde.*

❦ European Publishers

European branches of dot-com vendors such as Amazon make it easy to find books and CDs published in Europe, but scores can be another matter. If you can find online sources, great; if not, try this. Establish an account with a music retailer in London (or wherever in Europe you want to do business). Importers charge scandalously high rates for the music they import, and even with the cost of shipping overseas added in, you are better off ordering direct from music retailers in Europe. Do a little research, and when you find a nice little music shop in London, send them a check for $25.00 to open an account. You can save a bundle on European scores. N.B.: Avoid DVDs from foreign vendors! They are manufactured using a different format (PAL, not NTSC), and they require a different region code than U.S. discs.

Guides to Recordings

All Music Guide Series. San Francisco: Backbeat Books. This useful series provides a guide to recordings in any category you like, including rock, jazz, blues, electronica, soul, country, and hip-hop.

Gramophone: Classical Good CD, DVD & Download Guide: 2007. Emma Roach, ed. Middlesex, England: Gramophone Publications, 2006. Another fine guide to compact discs and DVDs, though not as comprehensive as the *Penguin Guide*.

The Penguin Guide to Compact Discs and DVDs: 2005/06 Edition, by Ivan March et al. London: Penguin Books, 2006. The most comprehensive, reliable guide available for classical recordings. Thousands of reviews help you find the best recordings available. This edition also includes many DVDs. Highly recommended.

The Penguin Guide to Jazz on CD. Eighth edition, by Richard Cook and Brian Morton. London: Penguin Books, 2006. Comprehensive guide to jazz recordings. Even great artists have their off nights, and this guide can help you find the best performances available. Contains reviews of thousands of recordings.

World Music: The Rough Guide. Third edition. Three volumes. Simon Broughton et al., eds. London: Rough Guides, 2006. Still in press, this useful guide provides background information and a discography for each country and region represented. Of course, the *Rough Guide* series includes guides to everything but the kitchen sink. You can find travel guides to many countries and major cities worldwide as well as guides to rock, music of Scandinavia, the Beatles, piano, trumpet, flute, electric guitar, Delta blues, techno, jazz, Elvis, Cuban music, reggae, opera, reading music and basic theory, Irish music, house music . . . even cult movies or English football!

Primary Sources

♩ General

Amis, John, and Michael Rose. *Words about Music: A Treasury of Writings.* New York: Marlowe & Company, 1995. Covers a broad span of Western music history. Lean on the twentieth century.

Burney, Charles. *Music, Men and Manners in France and Italy, 1770.* Ed. H. Edmund Poole. London: Eulenburg Books, 1969. An inveterate traveler with an appetite for good music, Burney kept fastidious journals of his experiences. He provides a fascinating look at music in Europe during the Classical era, often mentioning composers and important figures such as J. C. Bach, Corelli, Farinelli, Handel, Mozart, Palestrina, Vivaldi, and Voltaire.

Crofton, Ian, and Donald Fraser. *A Dictionary of Musical Quotations.* New York: Schirmer Books, 1985. Standard source covers most of Western music history. Lean on the twentieth century.

Dufallo. *Trackings: Composers Speak with Richard Dufallo.* New York: Oxford University Press, 1989. Interviews with significant contemporary composers. Composers discussed in *Listen* include Copland, Cage, Crumb, and Ligeti.

Fisk, Josiah, ed. *Composers on Music.* Second edition. Boston: Northeastern University Press, 1997. Excerpts from composers' writings from the Middle Ages to the present describing many facets of the musical art. Composers treated in *Listen* include Hildegard, Machaut, Palestrina, Monteverdi, Purcell, Haydn, Mozart, Beethoven, Schubert, Berlioz, Chopin, Robert Schumann, Wagner, Verdi, Brahms, Tchaikovsky, Mahler, Debussy, Schoenberg, Ives, Bartók, Stravinsky, Webern, Berg, Gershwin, Copland, and Ligeti.

Ford, Andrew. *Composer to Composer: Conversations about Contemporary Music.* St. Leonard's, Australia: Allen & Unwin, 1993. Collection of interviews with important composers, including Kaija Saariaho, Steve Reich, John Cage, and many others.

Lebrecht, Norman. *The Book of Musical Anecdotes.* New York: Free Press, 1985. Some fun stories from Western music history. Lean on the twentieth century.

Neuls-Bates, Carol, ed. *Women in Music: An Anthology of Source Readings from the Middle Ages to the Present.* New York: Harper and Row, 1982. Fascinating resource includes letters by Hildegard of Bingen and by Clara Schumann.

Schwartz, Elliott, and Barney Childs. *Contemporary Composers on Contemporary Music.* Expanded edition. New York: Da Capo Press, 1998. Interviews and writings from significant twentieth-century composers, including the following composers discussed in *Listen*: Debussy, Stravinsky, Berg, Bartók, Ives, Copland, Varèse, Cage, and Ligeti.

Strunk, Oliver, ed. *Source Readings in Music History.* Revised edition, ed. Leo Treitler. New York: Norton, 1998. One of the first single-volume anthologies of primary source materials, now even better in its revised edition. Contains writings by Monteverdi, Wagner, and many others. Also available in seven separate volumes that take a single era each, from the Greeks and the early Christians to the twentieth century.

Weiss, Piero, ed. *Letters of Composers through Six Centuries.* Philadelphia: Chilton Book Company, 1967. Letters to and from famous composers, including the following composers discussed in *Listen*: Machaut, Dufay, Palestrina, Monteverdi, Bach, Handel, Vivaldi, Haydn, Mozart, Beethoven, Schubert, Berlioz, Robert Schumann, Chopin, Verdi, Wagner, Brahms, Tchaikovsky, Mahler, Debussy, Bartók, Schoenberg, Berg, and Webern.

Weiss, Piero, ed. *Opera: A History in Documents.* New York: Oxford University Press, 2002. Valuable primary sources from most eras in the history of opera. Many *Listen* composers are represented.

Weiss, Piero, and Richard Taruskin, eds. *Music in the Western World: A History in Documents.* New York: Wadsworth, 2000. Valuable primary sources from most eras in the history of Western music. Many *Listen* composers are represented.

⁊ Global Perspectives

General

Harrison, Frank. *Time, Place, and Music: An Anthology of Ethnomusicological Observation c. 1550 to c. 1800.* Amsterdam: Frits Knuf, 1973. Fascinating collection of firsthand European accounts of music of Brazil, the Aztecs, Persia, Lapland, Congo, Japan, China, and other nations. Unfortunately, not many of them pertain directly to Global Perspectives material in the textbook.

Africa

Bascom, William. *Ifa Divination*. Bloomington: Indiana University Press, 1969. Translations of the verses of Ifa associated with divination ceremonies in the Yoruba religious tradition. Bascom's introduction provides a thorough study of Yoruba deities and religious practices.

Southern, Eileen, ed. *Readings in Black American Music*. Third edition. New York: Norton, 1997. Fascinating collection of letters, articles, reports, and so on. Includes reports by slave traders about the music of African tribes.

Asia

Cao Xueqin and Gao E. *The Story of the Stone, or The Dream of the Red Chamber*. Vol. 4, *The Debt of Tears*. Translated by John Minford. London: Penguin Books, 1982. Chinese novel of manners written c. 1760 follows a Chinese family and two engaging teenagers who fall in love. Of particular interest is Chapter 86 (pp. 151–57), in which Dai-yu is playing the *qin*. Bao-yu, realizing that he can't make much sense of the *qin* tablature, tries to pretend he knows more than he does—rather like Radar O'Reilly's "Ah, Bach" on the M*A*S*H television series. The passage provides some interesting insights into practices and cultural expectations surrounding the *qin*.

Fox Strangways, A. H. *The Music of Hindostan*. 1914; reprint, Oxford: Clarendon Press, 1914. Interesting early study of Indian music by an Englishman, with some of the Eurocentrism expected of his generation. Nonetheless, his respect for important figures such as Rabindranath Tagore is palpable.

Keene, Donald, ed. *Twenty Plays of the No Theatre*. New York: Columbia University Press, 1970. English translations of twenty dramas, including *Dojoji*, the *noh* drama that inspired the *kabuki* dance work described in the *Listen* textbook.

Legge, James, ed. and trans. *The Chinese Classics*. Vol. 1, *"Confucian Analects," "The Great Learning," and "The Doctrine of the Mean."* Hong Kong: Hong Kong University Press, 1970. Classic translations of significant works from the heart of the Confucian tradition.

Leiter, Samuel L., ed. and trans. *The Art of Kabuki: Famous Plays in Performance*. Berkeley: University of California Press, 1979. Translations of significant scenes from important *kabuki* dramas, with copious notes and photographs that provide a fuller sense of the theatrical experience.

Lo Kuan-Chung. *Romance of the Three Kingdoms*. Translated by C. H. Brewitt-Taylor. Rutland, Vt.: Charles E. Tuttle Co., 1959. Extremely popular historical novel provided material for many Beijing opera dramas of the nineteenth century.

Masakatsu Gunji. *Kabuki*. Translated by John Bester. Tokyo: Kodansha International Ltd., 1969. Marvelous picture book with helpful essays on the history and practice of *kabuki*. Several color and black-and-white plates depict recent and historical productions of *Dojoji*, providing examples of stage layout, colorful costumes and scenery, and the quick costume changes required. Excellent resource.

Murasaki Shikibu. *The Tale of Genji*. Translated by Edward G. Seidensticker. Perhaps the world's earliest true novel, this fascinating work from Japan's Middle Ages (eleventh century C.E.) was written by a lady of the Heian court. It includes frequent descriptions of musical activities at court, including the *gagaku* that was so popular with Heian nobles.

Piggott, Sir Francis. *The Music and Musical Instruments of Japan*. Second edition. Yokohama: Kelly & Walsh, 1909. Interesting turn-of-the-twentieth-century Western account of Japanese music and instruments by the chief justice of Hong Kong.

Shankar, Ravi. (See under Individual Composers below)

Wade, Bonnie C. *Imaging Sound: An Ethnomusicological Study of Music, Art, and Culture in Mughal India*. Chicago: University of Chicago Press, 1998. This beautiful book is filled with miniature paintings and other artwork from the Mughal period of Indian history. This fascinating study uses art as a primary source from which to glean insights into Indian music and culture.

The Americas

Black Elk and John G. Neihardt. *Black Elk Speaks: Being the Life Story of a Holy Man of the Oglala Sioux*. Lincoln: University of Nebraska Press, 1979. Fascinating introduction to Native American spirituality.

Martí, Samuel. *Music Before Columbus*. Second edition. Perugino, Mexico: Ediciones Euroamericanas Klaus Thiele, 1978. Short, annotated collection of black-and-white photographs depicting precontact instruments of the Americas. Some instruments are from Peru and North America, but the majority come from Aztec and Mayan traditions.

Stevenson, Robert. *Music in Aztec and Inca Territory*. Berkeley: University of California Press, 1968. Excellent source covers music from precontact times through the colonial era. Especially useful are seventy pages of European eyewitness accounts and transcriptions of Aztec and Peruvian music and culture.

The Middle East

Al-Hilali, Muhammad Taqi-ud Din. *Interpretation of the Meanings of the Noble Qur'an in the English Language*. Riyadh: Maktaba Dar-us-salam, 1993. Complete translation and interpretation of the Qur'an, the sacred scripture of Islam.

❡ American Music and Composers

Chase, Gilbert, ed. *The American Composer Speaks*. Baton Rouge, La.: Louisiana State University Press, 1966. Excerpts from the writings of significant American composers, including the following composers discussed in *Listen*: Ives, Gershwin, Copland, Varèse, and Cage.

Cowell, Henry, ed. *American Composers on American Music: A Symposium*. New York: F. Ungar, 1962. Excerpts from the writings of significant American composers, including the following composers discussed in *Listen*: Ives, Copland, Gershwin, and Varèse.

Duckworth, William. *Talking Music: Conversations with John Cage, Philip Glass, Laurie Anderson, and Five Generations of American Experimental Composers*. New York: Schirmer Books, 1995. Excerpts from the writings of significant American experimental composers, including the following composers discussed in *Listen*: Cage, Riley, and Reich.

Gottlieb, Robert, ed. *Reading Jazz: A Gathering of Autobiography, Reportage, and Criticism from 1919 to Now*. New York: Pantheon Books, 1996. Fascinating collection includes autobiographical materials by Armstrong, Ellington, Davis, and others.

McCutchan, Ann. *The Muse That Sings: Composers Speak about the Creative Process*. New York: Oxford University Press, 1999. Fine collection of twenty-five interviews with living composers, including John Adams and Steve Reich.

Morgan, Robert P., ed. *The Twentieth Century*. New York: Norton, 1998. Forty-five selections from the writings of composers, performers, writers, theorists, and critics, including Ives and Stravinsky.

Perlis, Vivian, and Libby Van Cleve. *Composers' Voices from Ives to Ellington: An Oral History of American Music*. New Haven: Yale University Press, 2005. Essentially Vivian Perlis's life's work, this is an excellent collection of oral histories from many important American composers. Comes with a CD.

Shapiro, Nat, and Nat Hentoff. *Hear Me Talkin' to Ya*. New York: Dover, 1966. A written-down oral history of jazz and jazz musicians told by many important jazz musicians themselves. Well worth exploring.

Smith, Geoff, and Nicola Walker Smith, eds. *New Voices: American Composers Talk About Their Music*. Portland, Ore.: Amadeus Press, 1995. Interviews with Adams, Anderson, Cage, Crumb, Glass, Harrison, Lentz, Monk, Oliveros, Reich, Riley, and others.

Southern, Eileen, ed. *Readings in Black American Music*. Third edition. New York: Norton, 1997. Fascinating collection of letters, articles, reports, and so on. Includes W. E. B. Du Bois's writings on the living conditions of African Americans in the late nineteenth century and William C. Handy's description of the birth of the blues.

Individual Composers and Performers

Adams, John

May, Thomas, ed. *The John Adams Reader: Essential Writings on an American Composer*. Pompton Plains, N.J.: Amadeus Press, 2006. Excellent new collection of writings on Adams by his critics, commentators, colleagues, and collaborators.

Armstrong, Louis

Armstrong, Louis. *Satchmo: My Life in New Orleans*. New York: Da Capo Press, 1986. Reminiscences by Armstrong on his formative years in what many regard as the "cradle of jazz."

Brothers, Thomas, ed. *Louis Armstrong: In His Own Words: Selected Writings*. New York: Oxford University Press, 2001. This reader provides excerpts from all phases of Armstrong's career. Recommended.

Gerlach, Horace, ed. *Swing That Music, by Louis Armstrong*. New York: Da Capo Press, 1993. Writings on swing by one of the first jazz masters.

Bach, Johann Sebastian

Cox, Howard H. *The Calov Bible of J. S. Bach*. Ann Arbor, Mich.: UMI Research Press, 1985. Contains reproductions of 286 pages from Bach's own copy of the Calov Bible (Wittenberg: C. Schrodten, 1681), with Bach's hand-penned comments as well as English translations of Bach's comments and the passages on which he comments.

David, Hans T., and Arthur Mendel, eds. *The New Bach Reader.* Revised and enlarged by Christoph Wolff. New York: Norton, 1998. Superb resource includes Bach letters, contracts, payment receipts, and so on.

Fischer, Hans Conrad. *Johann Sebastian Bach: His Life in Pictures and Documents.* Translated by Sylvia Lutz. Holzerlingen, Germany: Hänssler, 2000.

Bartók, Béla

Antokoletz, Elliott, and Guy A. Marco. *Bela Bartók: A Guide to Research.* Second edition. New York: Garland Publishing, 1997. As with the other volumes in this series, the most valuable part of this book is the annotated bibliography, but it also includes biographical materials, discography, and so on.

Bonis, Ferenc. *Bela Bartók: His Life in Pictures and Documents.* Second edition. Translated by Bertha Gaster and Lili Halay. White Plains, N.Y.: Pro/Am Music Resources, 1989.

Demeny, Janos, ed. *Bela Bartók: Letters.* Translated by Peter Balaban and Istvan Farkas. London: Faber and Faber, 1971.

Suchoff, Benjamin, ed. *Bela Bartók Essays.* Lincoln: University of Nebraska Press, 1993. Essays by Bartók on many musical subjects. Includes his own analyses of many works, including Music for Strings, Percussion, and Celesta.

Beethoven, Ludwig van

Albrecht, Theodore. *Ludwig van Beethoven: A Guide to Research.* New York: Garland Publishing, 1997. As with the other volumes in this series, the most valuable part of this book is the annotated bibliography, but it also includes biographical materials, discography, and so on.

Hamburger, Michael, ed. *Beethoven: Letters, Journals and Conversations.* New York: Thames and Hudson, 1992. Recent collection of primary sources on Beethoven.

Kalischer, A. C., ed. *Beethoven's Letters.* New York: Dover, 1972.

Krehbiel, F. Kerst, and H. Krehbiel, eds. *Beethoven: The Man and the Artist as Revealed in His Own Words.* New York: Dover, 1964. Beethoven's writings from many sources, including letters, articles, and conversation books.

Landon, H. C. Robbins, ed. *Beethoven: A Documentary Study.* Translated by Richard Wadleigh and Eugene Hartzell. New York: Macmillan, 1975. Beethoven studies based on primary sources.

Sonneck, O. G. *Beethoven: Impressions by His Contemporaries.* New York: Dover, 1954. Wonderful collection of writings describing Beethoven.

Berg, Alban

Brand, Juliane, Christopher Hailey, and Donald Harris, eds. *The Berg-Schoenberg Correspondence: Selected Letters.* New York: Norton, 1986. Letters between pupil and teacher, both committed to new artistic ideals.

Simms, Bryan R. *Alban Berg: A Guide to Research.* New York: Garland Publishing, 1996. As with the other volumes in this series, the most valuable part of this book is the annotated bibliography, but it also includes biographical materials, discography, and so on.

Berlioz, Hector

Barzun, Jacques, ed. *Evenings with the Orchestra*. Chicago: University of Chicago Press, 1999. My favorite book by Berlioz, finally reissued after being out of print. This modern-day *Canterbury Tales* finds orchestra members swapping stories in the opera pit during interminable passages of recitative. Some are fanciful fairy tales, some are tales of macabre revenge, and some are fantastical love stories, but taken together they provide a remarkable portrait of early nineteenth-century Paris and the Romantic temperament.

Barzun, Jacques, ed. *New Letters of Berlioz, 1830–1868*. Westport, Conn.: Greenwood Press, 1974. Recently discovered letters by Berlioz.

Langford, Jeffrey, and Jane Denker Graves. *Hector Berlioz: A Guide to Research*. New York: Garland Publishing, 1989. As with the other volumes in this series, the most valuable part of this book is the annotated bibliography, but it also includes biographical materials, discography, and so on.

MacDonald, Hugh, ed. *Selected Letters of Berlioz*. Translated by Roger Nichols. New York: Norton, 1997. Recent collection of Berlioz's letters.

Newman, Ernest, ed. *Memoirs of Hector Berlioz: From 1803 to 1865*. Translated by Rachel Holmes and Eleanor Holmes. New York: Dover, 1960. Not as imaginative as *Evenings with the Orchestra*, but Berlioz's writing boasts the same flamboyance as his music. Fun to read.

Searle, Humphrey, ed. *Hector Berlioz: A Selection from His Letters*. New York: Vienna House, 1973.

Bernart de Ventadorn

Bernart de Ventadorn. *A Bilingual Edition of the Love Songs of Bernart de Ventadorn in Occitan and English*. Lewiston, N.Y.: Edwin Mellen, 1999. Scholarly collection of Bernart's poetry provides many insights.

Bernstein, Leonard

Bernstein, Leonard. *Findings*. New York: Doubleday, 1993. Collection of writings by Leonard Bernstein from later in his career.

Bernstein, Leonard. *The Infinite Variety of Music*. New York: Plume Books, 1966. Many articles and broadcasts on a variety of composers. Includes a question-and-answer session at the University of Chicago where Bernstein describes his compositional process.

Bernstein, Leonard. *The Joy of Music*. New York: Simon and Schuster, 1959. Writings and transcripts of broadcasts on many composers and topics. Includes a section where Bernstein compares himself with Gershwin.

Laird, Paul R. *Leonard Bernstein: A Guide to Research*. New York: Garland Publishing, 2001. As with the other volumes in this series, the most valuable part of this book is the annotated bibliography, but it also includes biographical materials, discography, and so on.

Brahms, Johannes

Avins, Styra, ed. *Johannes Brahms: Life and Letters*. Translated by Josef Eisinger and Styra Avins. New York: Oxford University Press, 2001. At long last, a wide-ranging collection of more than five hundred Brahms letters. These writings provide a rounded portrait of the composer and his personality.

Barkan, Hans, ed. *Johannes Brahms and Theodor Billroth: Letters from a Musical Friendship*. Westport, Conn.: Greenwood Press, 1977.

Litzmann, Berthold, ed. *Letters of Clara Schumann and Johannes Brahms*. New York: Vienna House, 1971. Correspondence between Brahms and the woman he loved.

Musgrave, Michael. *A Brahms Reader*. New Haven, Conn.: Yale University Press, 2000. A compilation of documents that give us Brahms in his own words and those of friends and contemporaries.

Cage, John

Cage, John. *Silence*. Middletown, Conn.: Wesleyan University Press, 1961. Cage's first major book, and still the most informative. A mixture of articles, poems, stories, and other writings. Cage describes how the piano came to be prepared and how he used chance procedures in Music of Changes and prophesies about music's future in his Credo from the 1930s. Important resource for any study of Cage.

John Milton Cage: A Guide to Research. New York: Garland Publishing, 2001. As with the other volumes in this series, the most valuable part of this book is the annotated bibliography, but it also includes biographical materials, discography, and so on.

Kostelanetz, Richard, ed. *Conversing with Cage*. New York: Limelight Editions, 1988. Fascinating book of conversations with Cage.

Nattiez, Jean-Jacques, ed. *The Boulez-Cage Correspondence*. Translated by Robert Samuels. Cambridge: Cambridge University Press, 1993. Letters between Boulez and Cage from the 1950s, when they led the avant-garde in Europe and America, respectively.

Retallack, Joan, ed. *Musicage: Cage Muses on Words, Art, Music*. Hanover, N.H.: Wesleyan University Press, 1996. Extensive interviews with John Cage late in his life. Good source.

Chopin, Frédéric

Azoury, Pierre. *Chopin through His Contemporaries: Friends, Lovers, and Rivals*. Westport, Conn.: Greenwood Press, 1999. In a novel approach to biography, Azoury bases his conclusions on the quotations by Chopin contemporaries that riddle this book.

Hedley, Arthur, ed. *Selected Correspondence of Fryderyk Chopin*. New York: Da Capo Press, 1979.

Karasowski, Maurycy, ed. *Frederic Chopin: His Life and Letters*. Translated by Emily Hill. Westport, Conn.: Greenwood Press, 1970. Biography of Chopin woven around his letters.

Smialek, William. *Frédéric Chopin: A Guide to Research*. New York: Garland Publishing, 2000. As with the other volumes in this series, the most valuable part of this book is the annotated bibliography, but it also includes biographical materials, discography, and so on.

Copland, Aaron

Copland, Aaron, and Vivian Perlis. *Copland: 1900–1942*. New York: St. Martin's Press, 1987. The first installment of Copland's autobiography covers his training with Nadia Boulanger and his growing fame as a young modernist.

Copland, Aaron, and Vivian Perlis. *Copland: Since 1943*. New York: St. Martin's Press, 1990. The second installment of Copland's biography covers his life from World War II on.

Kostelanetz, Richard. *Aaron Copland: A Reader*. Routledge, 2003. New collection of writings by the quintessential American composer.

Robertson, Marta, and Robin Armstrong. *Aaron Copland: A Guide to Research*. New York: Garland Publishing, 2000. As with the other volumes in this series, the most valuable part of this book is the annotated bibliography, but it also includes biographical materials, discography, and so on.

Davis, Miles

Carner, Gary, ed. *The Miles Davis Companion: Four Decades of Commentary*. New York: Schirmer Books, 1996. Collection of writings by musicians, music critics, and authors that span Davis's career.

Davis, Miles, and Quincy Troupe. *Miles: The Autobiography*. New York: Simon and Schuster, 1990. Autobiography of one of the greatest, most enigmatic figures in jazz history.

Kirchner, Bill, ed. *A Miles Davis Reader*. Washington, D.C.: Smithsonian Institution Press, 1997. Excellent collection of articles on Davis, including one by Gary Tomlinson.

Debussy, Claude

Briscoe, James R. *Claude Debussy: A Guide to Research*. New York: Garland Publishing, 1990. As with the other volumes in this series, the most valuable part of this book is the annotated bibliography, but it also includes biographical materials, discography, and so on.

Cobb, Margaret G., ed. *The Poetic Debussy: A Collection of His Song Texts and Collected Letters*. Second revised edition. Translated by Richard Miller. Rochester, N.Y.: University of Rochester Press, 2002. Interesting collection of primary sources focuses on his fascination with poetry.

Smith, Richard Langham, ed. *Debussy on Music*. New York: Alfred A. Knopf, 1977. Collection of Debussy's writings, including many of those on *Monsieur Croche, Antidilettante*.

Dufay, Guillaume

Allsen, J. Michael. *Guillaume Du Fay: A Guide to Research*. New York: Garland Publishing, 2001. As with the other early music volumes in this series, the most valuable part of this book is the documentary biography. It also includes a comprehensive bibliography, discography, and so on.

Ellington, Duke

Ellington, Duke. *Music Is My Mistress*. New York: Da Capo Press, 1976. The Duke's autobiography.

Tucker, Mark, ed. *The Duke Ellington Reader*. New York: Oxford University Press, 1993. Excellent resource. Includes Ellington interviews and articles, concert reviews and other articles in the press, and many other documents that record the career of this great composer.

Vail, Mark. *Duke's Diary: The Life of Duke Ellington*. Two volumes. Metuchen, N.J.: Scarecrow Press, 2002. Mixes primary sources (news articles, rare photographs, posters, and so on) with Vail's diary-style entries.

Frescobaldi, Girolamo

Frescobaldi, Girolamo. *Il Secondo Libro di Toccate*. Florence: Studio per Edizioni Scelte, 1980. This facsimile edition of Frescobaldi's 1637 publication includes the score to the Canzona Prima included in the *Listen* set. Display pages from this score so your students can see the six- and eight-line staves Frescobaldi used.

Frescobaldi, Girolamo. *Partite et Toccate, Libro Primo*. Florence: Studio per Edizioni Scelte, 1980. A facsimile edition of the 1637 reprint of Frescobaldi's 1614–1616 publication. Its Aggiunta includes the scores to the balletto, corrente, and passacaglia included in the *Listen* set. Display pages from these scores so your students can see the six- and eight-line staves Frescobaldi used.

Hammond, Frederick. *Girolamo Frescobaldi*. Cambridge, Mass.: Harvard University Press, 1983. Not a primary source, but this biography is especially useful for its look at the music included in the *Listen* set: the Canzona Prima from *Il Secondo Libro di Toccate* (1637) and the dances and passacaglia from the Aggiunta to the 1637 reprint of *Partite et Toccate, Libro Primo*. Also includes notes on performance practice.

Hammond, Frederick. *Girolamo Frescobaldi: A Guide to Research*. New York: Garland Publishing, 1988. The most valuable part of this volume is the documentary biography, but it also includes a comprehensive bibliography and other useful information on Frescobaldi's surroundings, colleagues, and so on.

Silbiger, Alexander, ed. *Frescobaldi Studies*. Durham, N.C.: Duke University Press, 1987. This collection of presentations from the Frescobaldi Quadricentennial Conference contains several articles relevant to the suite presented in *Listen*.

Gershwin, George

Johnson, John Andrew, and Robert Wyatt, eds. *The George Gershwin Reader*. New York: Oxford University Press, 2004. Excellent, soon-to-be-released resource chock-full of writings by and about Gershwin. Highly recommended.

Kimball, Robert, and Alfred Simon. *The Gershwins*. New York: Bonanza Books, 1973. Lavishly illustrated with photographs of Gershwin, his friends, family, musicals, letters, programs, sketches, and other documents and memorabilia, this book also contains excerpts from writings by Gershwin and recollections by those who knew him. It even includes a look at "Who Cares?"—Balanchine's 1970 ballet set to Gershwin's music.

Handel, George Frideric

Deutsch, Otto Erich, ed. *Handel: A Documentary Biography*. New York: Da Capo Press, 1974. Full of primary source materials that help flesh out his life in eighteenth-century Europe and England.

Muller, Erich H., ed. *The Letters and Writing of George Frideric Handel*. Freeport, N.Y.: Books for Libraries Press, 1970.

Parker-Hale, Mary Ann. *G. F. Handel: A Guide to Research*. New York: Garland Publishing, 1988. As with the other volumes in this series, the most valuable part of this book is the annotated bibliography, but it also includes biographical materials, discography, and so on.

Haydn, Joseph

Grave, Floyd K., and Margaret G. Grave. *Joseph Haydn: A Guide to Research*. New York: Garland Publishing, 1990. As with the other volumes in this series, the most valuable part of this book is the annotated bibliography, but it also includes biographical materials, discography, and so on.

Landon, H. C. Robbins, ed. *Haydn: A Documentary Study*. London: Thames and Hudson, 1981. Tells the story of Haydn's life through documents and illustrations, including quotations from Haydn's first biographers.

Hildegard of Bingen

Bowie, Fiona, and Oliver Davies, eds. *Mystical Writings: Hildegard of Bingen*. Translated by Robert Carver. New York: Crossroad, 1990. If Hildegard had been only a composer, we would probably know very little about her. Fortunately, she also became a saint, and many of her writings on many subjects have been preserved. This volume provides Hildegard's careful record of many of her mystic visions.

Hildegard [of Bingen]. *The Letters of Hildegard of Bingen*. Translated by Joseph L. Baird and Radd K. Ehrman. New York: Oxford University Press, 1994. More writings by this fascinating twelfth-century mystic, composer, medicinal expert, and abbess.

Hildegard of Bingen. *Selected Writings*. Translated by Mark Atherton. New York: Penguin Books, 2001. Handy single-volume collection includes excerpts from Hildegard's visions, scientific treatises, songs, and letters.

Hildegard of Bingen. *Symphonia*. Translated by Barbara Newman. Ithaca, N.Y.: Cornell University Press, 1998. New translation of Hildegard's poetic texts, her *Symphony of the Harmony of Celestial Revelations*.

Ives, Charles

Block, Geoffrey. *Charles Ives: A Bio-Bibliography*. Westport, Conn.: Greenwood Press, 1988. Comprehensive review of primary and secondary sources in Ives research.

Boatwright, Howard, ed. *Essays Before a Sonata and Other Writings*. New York: Norton, 1962. Ives's words provide an intriguing counterpoint to his music. Highly recommended.

Kirkpatrick, John, ed. *Charles E. Ives: Memos*. New York: Norton, 1972. Fascinating collection of letters, memoirs, and other formal and informal writings by Ives.

Perlis, Vivian. *Charles Ives Remembered: An Oral History*. Champaign, Ill.: University of Illinois Press, 2002. Fascinating collection of reminiscences by many who knew Ives.

Josquin Desprez

Steele, Timothy. *Josquin Desprez: A Guide to Research*. Second edition. New York: Garland Publishing, 2003. This new edition was urgently needed owing to startling changes in the Josquin biography that have emerged from recent research. These changes affect the most valuable part of this book, its documentary biography. It also includes a comprehensive bibliography, discography, and so on.

Ligeti, György

Ligeti, György. *György Ligeti in Conversation with Peter Varnai, Josef Hausler, Claude Samuel and Himself*. New York: Da Capo Press, 1984.

Richart, Robert. *György Ligeti: A Bio-Bibliography*. Westport, Conn.: Greenwood Press, 1991. Comprehensive review of primary and secondary sources in Legeti research.

Machaut, Guillaume de

Earp, Lawrence Marshburn. *Guillaume de Machaut: A Guide to Research*. New York: Garland Publishing, 1995. As with the other early music volumes in this series, the most valuable part of this book is the documentary biography. It also includes a comprehensive bibliography, helpful background information on the manuscript sources, discography, and so on.

Palmer, R. Barton. *Guillaume de Machaut: The Complete Poetry, A Dual-Language Edition*. New York: Garland Publishing, 2001. An opportunity to sample Machaut's literary side in both the original language and an English translation. Remember that Machaut was equally famous as a poet!

Mahler, Gustav

Blaukopf, Kurt, ed. *Mahler: A Documentary Study*. Translated by Paul Baker. New York: Oxford University Press, 1976. Study of Mahler based on primary source materials.

Mahler, Alma, and Knud Martner, eds. *Selected Letters of Gustav Mahler*. Revised edition. Translated by Eithne Wilkins, Ernst Kaiser, and Bill Hopkins. New York: Farrar, Straus, Giroux, 1979. Letters selected by Mahler's wife.

Mahler-Werfel, Alma. *Diaries 1898–1902*. Ithaca, N.Y.: Cornell University Press, 1999. Fascinating look at Gustav Mahler through the eyes of his wife.

Monteverdi, Claudio

Adams, K. Gary, and Dyke Kiel. *Claudio Monteverdi: A Guide to Research*. New York: Garland Publishing, 1989. As with the other volumes in this series, the most valuable part of this book is the annotated bibliography, but it also includes biographical materials, discography, and so on.

Stevens, Denis, ed. *The Letters of Claudio Monteverdi*. Revised edition. New York: Oxford University Press, 1995. Fascinating insights into the thought of the man who helped create Baroque music.

Mozart, Wolfgang Amadeus

Anderson, Emily, ed. *The Letters of Mozart and His Family*. Revised edition. New York: Norton, 1985. Look for this translation. Anderson lets us see unexpurgated versions of Mozart's letters. Fascinating portrait of the composer, sometimes outrageously funny, sometimes poignant. Every musician should browse through these letters at least once in his or her life.

Angermüller, Rudolph. *Mozart's Operas.* New York: Rizzoli, 1988. This surprisingly valuable glossy picture book covers *every* Mozart opera, providing information on premiere performances (location, singers, and so on) as well as drawings and photographs of productions from Mozart's day to the present.

Deutsch, Otto Erich, ed. *Mozart: A Documentary Biography.* Translated by Eric Blom, Peter Branscombe, and Jeremy Noble. Stanford, Calif.: Stanford University Press, 1966. Incredible array of documents paint a remarkable portrait of Mozart and his life. Find out where the writer of *Amadeus* got his ideas.

Eisen, Cliff, ed. *New Mozart Documents: A Supplement to Otto Erich Deutsch's Documentary Biography.* Stanford, Calif.: Stanford University Press, 1991. A needed update to Deutsch's classic volume.

Hastings, Baird. *Wolfgang Amadeus Mozart: A Guide to Research.* New York: Garland Publishing, 1989. As with the other volumes in this series, the most valuable part of this book is the annotated bibliography, but it also includes biographical materials, discography, and so on.

Spaethling, Robert. *Mozart's Letters, Mozart's Life.* New York: Norton, 2000. Superb new translations of Mozart's letters capture the flavor of Mozart's writing like no others. Highly recommended.

Musorgsky, Modest

Leyda, Jay, and Sergei Bertensson, eds. and trans. *The Musorgsky Reader: A Life of Modeste Petrovich Musorgsky in Letters and Documents.* New York: Da Capo Press, 1970.

Parker, Charlie

Woideck, Karl, ed. *The Charlie Parker Companion: Six Decades of Commentary.* New York: Schirmer Books, 2000. Fascinating look at Parker's career and influence.

Pérotin

Wright, Craig. *Music and Ceremony at Notre Dame of Paris, 500–1550.* New York: Cambridge University Press, 1990. In this masterful work, Wright explains liturgical and performance practices based on his careful study of archival materials from the famed cathedral. Don't let the thousand-year span fool you—he provides as full a picture as we can hope to have of Léonin, Pérotin, and the Notre Dame School. Highly recommended.

Purcell, Henry

Zimmerman, Franklin B. *Henry Purcell: A Guide to Research.* New York: Garland Publishing, 1989. As with the other early music volumes in this series, the most valuable part of this book is the documentary biography, it also includes a comprehensive bibliography, discography, and so on.

Ravel, Maurice

Perlemuter, Vlado, and Hélène Jourdan-Morhange. *Ravel According to Ravel.* White Plains, N.Y.: Pro/Am Music Resources, 1988. Translated by Frances Tanner.

Zank, Stephen. *Maurice Ravel: A Guide to Research*. New York: Garland Publishing, 2001. As with the other volumes in this series, the most valuable part of this book is the annotated bibliography, but it also includes biographical materials, discography, and so on.

Reich, Steve

Hoek, D. J. *Steve Reich: A Bio-Bibliography*. Westport, Conn.: Greenwood Press, 2001. Comprehensive review of primary and secondary sources in Reich research.

Reich, Steve. *Writings on Music: 1965–2000*. New York: Oxford University Press, 2002. Edited by Paul Hillier. Excellent new resource provides fascinating insights into the music of this important composer. Includes an essay on and frequent references to *Tehillim*.

Schwarz, K. Robert. *Minimalists*. London: Phaidon Press, 1996. Liberally sprinkled with quotations from interviews, this books looks at the major figures of minimalism, placing special emphasis on Reich and Glass.

Saariaho, Kaija

Beyer, Anders. *The Voice of Music: Conversations with Composers of Our Time*. Burlington, Vt.: Ashgate Publishing, 2000. Edited and translated by Jean Christensen and Anders Beyer. This collection places special emphasis on too-often-neglected composers from Scandinavia and the former communist bloc. Many composers are represented, but the interview with Kaija Saariaho is of special interest.

Saariaho, Kaija. *Prisma*. Montaigne Naïve MO 782087. Packaged with the *Private Gardens* CD, this hybrid CD-ROM offers an excellent introduction to this Finnish composer's life, music, and career. Various modules offer performances of Saariaho's music, an interactive biography, a musicological analysis, information on her compositional methods and electronic techniques, and so on. This package was produced with Saariaho's cooperation and participation, so it provides a genuine encounter with this fascinating composer.

Schoenberg, Arnold

Auner, Joseph. *A Schoenberg Reader*. New Haven, Conn.: Yale University Press, 2003. This collection of Schoenberg's writings, letters, and other documents provides new insights into Schoenberg and his importance in the twentieth century.

Brand, Juliane, Christopher Hailey, and Donald Harris, eds. *The Berg-Schoenberg Correspondence: Selected Letters*. New York: Norton, 1986. Letters between pupil and teacher, both committed to new artistic ideals.

Stein, Leonard, ed. *Style and Idea: Selected Writings of Arnold Schoenberg*. Translated by Leo Black. Berkeley: University of California Press, 1975. Important collection of Schoenberg's writings on a wide variety of topics. Articles discuss various musical works, the development of the twelve-tone system, and other topics. Highly recommended.

Schubert, Franz

Deutsch, Otto Erich, ed. *Franz Schubert's Letters and Other Writings*. Translated by Venetia Savile. New York: Vienna House, 1974.

Deutsch, Otto Erich, ed. *Schubert: A Documentary Biography*. Translated by Eric Blom. New York: Da Capo Press, 1977. Comprehensive collection of Schubert documents. Important resource for any study of the composer.

Schumann, Clara

Litzmann, Berthold, ed. *Clara Schumann: An Artist's Life, Based on Material Found in Diaries and Letters*. Translated by Grace E. Hadow. New York: Da Capo Press, 1979.

Litzmann, Berthold, ed. *Letters of Clara Schumann and Johannes Brahms*. Westport, Conn.: Hyperion Press, 1979. Correspondence between Clara Schumann and the much younger Johannes Brahms. The record of a long-lasting friendship.

Neuhaus, Gerd, ed. *The Marriage Diaries of Robert and Clara Schumann*. Edited by Peter Ostwald. London: Robson Books, 1994. Fascinating new publication looks at the relationship between Robert and Clara in a new light. Poignant reflections on Clara's aspirations as a composer.

Schumann, Robert

Neuhaus, Gerd, ed. *The Marriage Diaries of Robert and Clara Schumann*. Edited by Peter Ostwald. London: Robson Books, 1994. See under Schumann, Clara, above.

Schumann, Clara, ed. *Early Letters of Robert Schumann*. Translated by May Herbert. St. Clair Shores, Mich.: Scholarly Press, 1970. Reprint of the 1888 edition in translation.

Storck, Karl, ed. *The Letters of Robert Schumann*. Translated by Hannah Bryant. New York: Arno Press, 1979.

Weissweiler, Eva. *The Complete Correspondence of Clara and Robert Schumann*. Two volumes (third on the way). Translated by Hildegard Fritsch and Ronald L. Crawford. New York: Peter Lang Publishing, 2002. Fascinating record of the lives and events of these two composer/pianists in the years before their wedding.

Wolff, Konrad, ed. *Robert Schumann: On Music and Musicians*. Translated by Paul Rosenfeld. New York: Norton, 1946. Excerpts from Schumann's reviews and articles as editor of *Neue Zeitschrift für Musik*. Introduce your students to Eusebius and Florestan—the Siskel and Ebert of nineteenth-century music.

Shankar, Ravi

Ravi Shankar in Portrait. BBC Opus Arte OA 0864 D (DVD, color, 190 minutes). A DVD to treasure! Disc one, "Ravi Shankar between Two Worlds," provides a video documentary of Shankar's life filled with interviews and archival footage going back to the 1930s. Disc two, "Ravi Shankar in Concert," features a 2002 live performance with daughter Anoushka, Bikram Ghosh, and Tanmoy Bose. Extras include Shankar's excellent twenty-minute introduction to the sitar and Indian music, and a video of Shankar working with a student. Highly recommended.

Shankar, Ravi. *My Life, My Music*. Second edition. London: South Asia Books, 1995. In addition to biographical information, Shankar provides valuable information on Indian music.

Shankar, Ravi. *Raga Mala: The Autobiography of Ravi Shankar,* ed. George Harrison. New York: Welcome Rain Publishers, 1997. Excellent source of information on Shankar's life, relationships, travels, and music. Highly recommended.

Stravinsky, Igor

Craft, Robert. *Chronicle of a Friendship.* Revised edition. Nashville: Vanderbilt University Press, 1994. Fascinating record of Craft's life in the Stravinsky household, with many excerpts from Craft's journal of activities.

Craft, Robert, ed. *Stravinsky: Selected Correspondence,* Volume 2. New York: Alfred A. Knopf, 1984. Stravinsky letters.

Stravinsky, Igor. *An Autobiography.* London: Calder and Boyars, 1975. Limited in use, since he wrote it in the 1930s, but it provides information about *The Rite of Spring.*

Stravinsky, Igor. *Poetics of Music.* Cambridge, Mass.: Harvard University Press, 1975. The six Norton Lectures Stravinsky delivered at Harvard University in the 1930s. Difficult reading, but a valuable portrait of Stravinsky's "anti-expressive" polemics of the 1920s and 1930s.

Stravinsky, Igor, and Robert Craft. *Conversations with Igor Stravinsky.* Berkeley: University of California Press, 1980. One of several fascinating books of conversations between Stravinsky and Robert Craft during the 1960s. Stravinsky's musical insights and biting humor make for fascinating reading.

Stravinsky, Igor, and Robert Craft. *Dialogues.* Berkeley: University of California Press, 1982. Another volume in the conversations series.

Stravinsky, Igor, and Robert Craft. *Expositions and Developments.* Berkeley: University of California Press, 1981. Another volume in the conversations series.

Stravinsky, Igor, and Robert Craft. *Memories and Commentaries.* New York: Faber and Faber, 2002. This new one-volume edition combines material from the five previously published books of conversations between Stravinsky and Robert Craft. Craft claims to have left out superfluous material, but many of my favorite passages have gone AWOL.

Stravinsky, Igor, and Robert Craft. *Memories and Commentaries.* Garden City, N.Y.: Doubleday, 1960. Another volume in the conversations series.

Stravinsky, Igor, and Robert Craft. *Retrospectives and Conclusions.* New York: Alfred A. Knopf, 1969. Another volume in the conversations series.

Stravinsky, Igor, and Robert Craft. *Stravinsky in Conversation with Robert Craft.* Harmondsworth: Penguin Books, 1962. Another volume in the conversations series.

Stravinsky, Igor, and Robert Craft. *Themes and Episodes.* New York: Alfred A. Knopf, 1967. Another volume in the conversations series.

Stravinsky, Vera, and Robert Craft. *Stravinsky in Pictures and Documents.* New York: Simon and Schuster, 1978. Visually rich portrait of Stravinsky. Photographs, scenes, and sets from early ballets, with many other images and Stravinsky writings arranged in chronological order.

Tchaikovsky, Pyotr Ilyich

Garden, Edward, and Nigel Gotteri. *"To My Best Friend": Correspondence between Tchaikovsky and Nadezhda von Meck, 1876–1878.* Translated by

Galina von Meck. Oxford: Clarendon Press, 1993. Letters document Tchaikovsky's curious relationship with his most celebrated patron.

Poznansky, Alexander, and Brett Langston, eds. *The Tchaikovsky Handbook: A Guide to the Man and His Music.* Two volumes. Bloomington: Indiana University Press, 2002. Excellent new resource provides a comprehensive guide to available Tchaikovsky primary source materials, including autobiography, photographs, and letters.

Poznansky, Alexander, and Malcolm H. Brown, eds. *Tchaikovsky through Others' Eyes.* Translated by Robert J. Bird. Bloomington: Indiana University Press, 1999. Fifty documents—journalism, interviews, diaries, letters, and memoirs—paint a fascinating portrait of the composer.

Tchaikovsky, Modeste, and Rosa Newmarch, eds. *Life and Letters of Tchaikovsky.* New York: Vienna House, 1973.

Varèse, Edgard

Parks, Anne F. *Edgard Varèse: A Guide to Research.* New York: Garland Publishing, 1993. As with the other volumes in this series, the most valuable part of this book is the annotated bibliography, but it also includes biographical materials, discography, and so on.

Verdi, Giuseppe

Harwood, Gregory. *Giuseppe Verdi: A Guide to Research.* New York: Garland Publishing, 1998. As with the other volumes in this series, the most valuable part of this book is the annotated bibliography, but it also includes biographical materials, discography, and so on.

Osborne, Charles, ed. *Letters of Giuseppe Verdi.* London: Gollancz, 1971.

Weaver, William, ed. *Verdi: A Documentary Study.* London: Thames and Hudson, 1977. Handsome collection of illustrations, Verdi writings, and documents paints a picture of the composer's life.

Werfel, Franz, and Paul Stefan, eds. *Verdi: The Man in His Letters.* Translated by Edward Downes. New York: Vienna House, 1973.

Vivaldi, Antonio

Kolneder, Walter, ed. *Antonio Vivaldi: Documents of His Life and Works.* Translated by Kurt Michaelis. New York: Heinrichshofen Edition, 1982. Collection of historical documents paints a portrait of the composer.

Talbot, Michael. *Antonio Vivaldi: A Guide to Research.* New York: Garland Publishing, 1988. As with the other volumes in this series, the most valuable part of this book is the annotated bibliography, but it also includes biographical materials, discography, and so on.

Wagner, Richard

Barth, Herbert, Dietrich Mack, and Egon Voss, eds. *Wagner: A Documentary Study.* New York: Oxford University Press, 1975. Paints a visually attractive portrait of Wagner with important documents and illustrations.

Bergfeld, Joachim, ed. *The Diary of Richard Wagner 1865–1882: The Brown Book.* Translated by George Bird. London: Cambridge University Press, 1980.

Burk, John N., ed. *Letters of Richard Wagner: The Burrell Collection.* New York: Macmillan, 1950.

Ellis, William Ashton, ed. *The Family Letters of Richard Wagner.* Ann Arbor, Mich.: University of Michigan Press, 1991.

Goldman, Albert, and Evert Sprinchorn, eds. *Wagner on Music and Drama.* Translated by H. Ashton Ellis. Lincoln: University of Nebraska Press, 1992. Collection offers highlights from Wagner's prose works. Highly recommended.

Hueffer, Francis, ed. *Correspondence of Wagner and Liszt.* Second edition. 2 volumes. New York: Vienna House, 1973. Fascinating record of the friendship between the renowned pianist and the struggling opera composer. Many letters in the second volume describe the genesis of *Tristan and Isolde.*

Saffle, Michael. *Richard Wagner: A Guide to Research.* New York: Garland Publishing, 2001. As with the other volumes in this series, the most valuable part of this book is the annotated bibliography, but it also includes biographical materials, discography, and so on.

Spencer, Stewart, and Barry Millington, eds. *Selected Letters of Richard Wagner.* New York: Norton, 1988.

Wagner, Richard. *The Authentic Librettos of the Wagner Operas . . . Complete with English and German Parallel Texts and Music of the Principal Airs.* New York: Crown Publishers, 1938. Wagner wrote his own librettos. Most are not great poetry, but they still provide profound insights into Wagner's thought.

Wagner, Richard. *My Life.* Translated by Andrew Gray. Edited by Mary Whittall. New York: Da Capo Press, 1992. Wagner's autobiography.

Wagner, Richard. *Richard Wagner's Prose Works.* Translated by William Ashton Ellis. London: K. Paul, Trench, Trübner, 1893–99. Wagner's major writings in English translation, reissued from time to time by various publishers in whole or in part. The eight volumes include Wagner's *Artwork of the Future, Opera and Drama, Religion and Art,* and other works.

Wallace, Sippie

Grossman, Roberta, and Michelle Paymar, producers and directors. *Sippie.* New York: Rhapsody Films, 1986 (VHS). This video presents a film biography of Beulah "Sippie" Wallace, including conversations with Wallace, concert footage, rare recordings, and photographs.